THE AMERICAN ECONOMY

Principles, Practices, and Policies

THE IRWIN SERIES IN ECONOMICS

Consulting Editor
Lloyd G. Reynolds
Yale University

AMES *Soviet Economic Processes*

ANDERSON, GITLOW, & DIAMOND (Editors) *General Economics: A Book of Readings* rev. ed.

BALASSA *The Theory of Economic Integration*

BEAL & WICKERSHAM *The Practice of Collective Bargaining* 3d ed.

BLAUG *Economic Theory in Retrospect* rev. ed.

BORNSTEIN (Editor) *Comparative Economic Systems: Models and Cases*

BORNSTEIN & FUSFELD (Editors) *The Soviet Economy: A Book of Readings* rev. ed.

BUCHANAN *The Public Finances* rev. ed.

CARTTER *Theory of Wages and Employment*

CARTTER & MARSHALL *Labor Economics: Wages, Employment, and Trade Unionism*

DAVIDSON, SMITH, & WILEY *Economics: An Analytical Approach* rev. ed.

DAVIS, HUGHES, & MCDOUGALL *American Economic History: The Development of a National Economy* rev. ed.

DOLL, RHODES, & WEST *Economics of Agricultural Production, Markets, and Policy*

DRUMMOND *The Canadian Economy: Organization and Development*

DUE *Government Finance: An Economic Analysis* 3d ed.

DUE & CLOWER *Intermediate Economic Analysis* 5th ed.

DUNLOP & HEALY *Collective Bargaining: Principles and Cases* rev. ed.

FELLNER *Probability and Profit: A Study of Economic Behavior along Bayesian Lines*

FERGUSON *Microeconomic Theory*

GAMBS & KOMISAR *Economics and Man* 3d ed.

GORDON *The Investment Financing and Valuation of the Corporation*

THE

AMERICAN

C. LOWELL HARRISS, Ph.D.

Professor of Economics
Columbia University

ECONOMY

PRINCIPLES, PRACTICES, AND POLICIES

SIXTH EDITION

1968
RICHARD D. IRWIN, INC., Homewood, Illinois
IRWIN-DORSEY LIMITED, Nobleton, Ontario

To my parents
ALICE and CLEMENT HARRISS
who, like untold millions of other
parents, have worked to build us a better world

PREFACE

Still more years of experience have prompted, and guided, this revision. My own continued teaching of the basic course in economics has been supplemented by suggestions from other teachers, and from no small number of students. Consequently, an accumulating experience has gone into this reworking of prior revisions, each of which drew heavily upon advice from teachers and students. The outcome, I believe, is an up-to-date volume carefully designed and balanced to meet the essential needs of the overwhelming majority of college courses in the principles and problems of economics.

Organization of topics has been modified somewhat. The Part dealing with government finance now follows price and distribution. The material on big business and concentration has been integrated with that on monopolistic pricing and antitrust policy. The discussion of problems of poverty appears, in much expanded form, after the treatment of the various types of income shares.

Three added chapters deal, in addition to the analysis of poverty, with *goals* of national income *policy* and the relations of government to business. Much that is new has been blended with material brought from various places in the earlier edition. Fortunately, I have been able to draw upon personal experiences and research, involving both business and governmental problems, in this country and several called "under-developed." Yet the basis for judging relevance, realism, and relative importance must rest heavily upon the help of other teachers of economics —and in selecting things to include and exclude I have tried to make constructive use of such help.

The present arrangement continues what seems to me a most attractive feature—a natural break at mid-point. The analysis of policies and problems for full employment and stability of the national economy is completed, and price theory begins, halfway through. Many teachers, I believe, will find this spacing ideal. One semester will end with the study of a topic of high interest toward which the early material has built, bit by bit. The next will start building again, this time microeconomics.

Yet a characteristic of earlier editions remains—a high degree of flexibility. The instructor has wide freedom to take up topics in the sequence which will best suit his own preferences. The *Teacher's Manual* suggests various possibilities for organizing the material for two-semester, three-quarter, two-quarter, one-semester, and one-quarter courses.

Rewriting has been undertaken wherever improvement warrants it. Numerous sections of chapters have been largely recast. My goal, as in prior revisions, has been to take reasonably full advantage of recent thought and experience.

Wherever possible, I have tried to clarify, to economize in the use of words, and to achieve a consistent and uniform level of analysis. The addition of new material, and the deletion of older, represents an effort to keep the contents abreast of the world in which the student will be learning and living. Illustrative material has been modernized where a useful educational purpose could be served.

In reviewing and revising the 400 or so end-of-chapter questions, I have sought variety and a range of difficulty that respects the spread of ability and interest found in the typical class—the question which will be thought-provoking or which will aid in some other way the understanding of material in the text and the world around. Hundreds of other questions, including extensive material for objective examinations, as well as suggestions for teaching and for supplementary reading, will appear in a new edition of the *Teacher's Manual*. An entirely new *Student's Workbook in Economics* will provide far more material, in much greater variety, to meet the increasingly broad needs of so many modern economics courses.

The factual material has, of course, been brought up to date. At more than a few points I have revised the discussion to take account of developments in thinking in the last few years. This revision reflects renewed efforts to present theory as simply as possible and to avoid resort to inappropriate levels of difficulty—without sacrificing essentials.

The following paragraphs, adapted from earlier editions, still express my general purposes.

This volume covers both the elements of economic *analysis* and a *description* of the structure and functioning of the American economy. Each is a substantial undertaking. Yet some knowledge of both is essential for a person who is to understand the world in which he or she will live. The elementary course can provide both, even to the student who has had no previous training in economics. I have tried to prepare a useful tool for this student and his teachers.

Our economy has such diverse problems—economics as a branch of social science, or as a discipline often studied with the rigorous tools of mathematics, contains such a growing number of varied elements—that no single "approach" can be best suited for all. Yet all aspects *are* related. This volume, without slighting price theory, contains an extensive analysis of aggregate problems. It also includes a generous amount of institutional material and description of the significant elements of the U.S. economy today.

Among other things this book pays considerable attention to business;

the developing world of business, and the interactions of business and broader economic change, justify the time of the student of economics even though he (or she) does not plan a career in business. Public *policy* issues and problems get frequent attention. I try to be realistic and to distinguish aspects which involve primarily value judgments from those of cause and effect in the more strictly scientific, objective sense.

The analysis of national income and its determinants appears relatively early. My colleagues and I, like so many other teachers, have found that this arrangement makes the course more interesting and meaningful to students than the earlier introduction of price theory. A textbook treatment of employment theory must not ignore the fact that professional analysis continues to change as we accumulate experience. I have tried to present the basic thinking simply and clearly. Yet I have taken care to avoid oversimplifying and (inadvertantly) glossing over the fact that, as has been evident in recent recessions (fortunately—now in February, 1968—not really so recent), and periods of price-level increase (all too recent), economists still do not have the final solutions.

My goal in developing price and distribution theory has been more than clarity and accuracy. I have also tried to point out the significance of the analysis. The insights we associate with "welfare economics" can help the student see the meaning of the adjustments of price and quantity as well as to understand the process. *Efficiency* is a concept students recognize and respect. When the traditional technical apparatus of price theory is shown to be a guide to efficiency, it takes on a new significance.

The selection of institutional, factual, and descriptive material presents a staggering task. My criterion has been to include substance bearing upon the most significant problems of today and tomorrow. Much material of this nature seems essential if we are to avoid the pitfall of oversimplification. This is not a simple world. Part of our responsibility as teachers of a vital social science is to help students understand the complexity of the economy and the society in which they live.

This text is focused on the American economy as it is developing today. Yet the materials on international economics, on development and growth of poor lands, and on Russia bring the student into contact with much that is vital beyond our borders.

The two closing chapters deal with some of the big problems ahead for this country. Some are problems of economic growth as we ordinarily think of it. Others, though having a large economic element, also touch politics, usually at many points.

The men and women studying in college today have an economic future which can be glorious indeed. Their actual achievement will depend to no small extent upon the way they deal with problems of *political economy*. And this book continues to emphasize economics as political economy. I have related the discussion of issues of governmental policy to the earlier analysis and description. In this way controversial aspects are handled, I trust, with a minimum of bias—a goal which is one of the major justifications for studying economics as a discipline.

So many people have helped that I hesitate to try to acknowledge any by name. A full list would be much too long to serve the real purpose of acknowledgment. Ignoring the uncounted dozens who have helped on one or a few chapters, I limit myself to thanking here by name only those who reviewed substantially the entire volume, in the preparation of this or earlier editions. Of course I, not the reviewers, must accept responsibility for the final result, including any errors. Yet my debt to the following is great indeed: Professors T. J. Anderson, New York University; Taulman A. Miller, Indiana University; Gerald Warren, Temple University; Royall Brandis, University of Illinois; R. L. Carey, Columbia University; M. M. Davisson, University of California; F. S. Doody, Boston University; Melvin Eggers, Syracuse University; Otto Ehrlich, New York University; J. M. Ford, The Ford Motor Co.; D. M. Holland, Massachusetts Institute of Technology; P. G. Hudson, University of Arizona; F. L. Kidner, University of California; R. J. McEwen, S. J., Boston College; G. M. Mellin, Tulane University; L. G. Reynolds, Yale University; E. S. Shaw, Stanford University; Carl W. McGuire, University of Colorado; L. L. Cantrell, Los Angeles City College; Elmer Pendell, Jacksonville State College; Charles F. Phillips, Jr., Washington and Lee University; S. N. Whitney, New York University; Don V. Plantz, Arizona State University; and R. H. Johnson, University of Virginia (now with the National Association of Mutual Savings Banks). Another expression of obligation is in order—to the untold numbers in government, universities, business, and research organizations who have given us the growing wealth of statistical and other information about our economy.

Finally, my gratitude to my wife for her help of many types is unbounded.

Columbia University   C. LOWELL HARRISS
February, 1968

TABLE OF CONTENTS

PART 1

INTRODUCTION

1

THE NATURE OF ECONOMICS, ECONOMIZING, AND PRODUCTION

The ideas of economists and political philosophers, both when they are right and when they are wrong, are more powerful than is commonly understood. Indeed, the world is ruled by little else. Practical men, who believe themselves to be quite exempt from any intellectual influences, are usually the slaves of some defunct economist. . . . Soon or late, it is ideas, not vested interests, which are dangerous for good or ill.

J. M. Keynes

A Modern Aladdin's Lamp—Economic Organization. A modern economic system is an amazing thing. To illustrate, let's think about a cup of coffee. It costs 10 cents, which the American worker earns in less than 3 minutes—not much longer than it took Aladdin to rub his lamp. To have this coffee available so easily is little short of an economic miracle. So much was needed to provide so little.

Huge plantations were started in distant lands many years ago to grow the coffee. Roads, railroads, and warehouses were built, often with materials and money from Europe, advanced by investors willing to take the risks of foreign ventures. Laborers, perhaps using machinery from America, cultivated and harvested the beans and packed them in bags of burlap from India. A Greek ship powered by fuel oil from Venezuela brought the beans to any one of several ports. Piers with highly ingenious equipment were ready for docking and unloading. Warehousing, grading, blending, roasting, and packing required many different types of skill and equipment, some the result of long study and planning. The can in which the coffee was packed used Malayan tin refined in England. The railroad that carried the coffee from the coast required the investment, during a

3

century, of $2 billion by thousands of thrifty families. A wholesaler stored the can until the restaurant manager ordered it, using a dial telephone that is the result of untold man-years of skilled engineering. Delivery was by trucks, rolling on rubber from the Far East over streets made possible by a complicated series of political and economic events, including tax payments.

The water for the coffee may come from wells close by, or perhaps from hundreds of miles away through great aqueducts. Natural gas piped hundreds of miles provides the heat. The sugar may be from a Hawaiian plantation, or a Michigan beet field; or the weight watcher may use a synthetic sweetener developed by modern chemistry. Highly bred cows, fed grain from Iowa, produced the cream, which was transported and prepared by expensive, automatically controlled equipment, inspected to meet hygienic standards. We used a paper napkin made out of wood from a Canadian forest. And so it goes. There is almost no end to the list of things that have in one way or another helped make possible this cup of coffee—every continent, every industry, every skill may have contributed. The total capital investment would stagger the imagination. Many governments, directly and indirectly, have helped. Finance, insurance, medicine, and law have played a part. The beginning? As far back in history as we want to go!

Somehow all these parts—science, nature, human effort—have been organized so the coffee is ready if we want it. Yet we are free to use, or ignore, it as we wish. This *organizing*, which helps put so much at our disposal, is an aspect of economics. Like modern technology, modern economic organization is little short of miraculous, though generally taken for granted.

Economic Disorganization—Plague and Challenge. The economic system, however, will not always let us take it for granted. Sometimes things go wrong. The price of the cup of coffee, for example, doubled in only a few years. Here is evidence of a vast, unsettling change; not merely coffee, but almost everything, seems more expensive than a few years ago. Let's look at other examples of economic disorganization.

In the 1930's, millions of men could find no jobs. Despite their skills and their desperate desire to work, they were helpless because the jobs did not exist. Only a few years later, however, employers were almost as desperately "beating the bushes" for workers and were resorting to seemingly childish inducements to get an effective day's work for a generous day's pay. Booms and depressions have engulfed mankind like giant waves. Smaller waves of adversity have brought unemployment in postwar recessions.

Can men cure the plague of economic disorganization as decisively as medicine has cured so many plagues? Hardly! But we can make improvements. For example, only a generation ago great numbers of Americans properly feared that their savings might be wiped out by bank failures, that joining a labor union might lead the boss to fire them, that their only chance to retire would depend upon their own savings, that their children could never hope to go to college. Today, with insurance of bank deposits, powerful labor unions, social security, and increased opportunities for college education, many old fears are largely unwarranted. Yet we have new worries, some resulting from the cures of the old plagues. Social security taxes cut our own paychecks and add to the costs which the employer tries to recover in prices. Inflation has been worse than bank failures ever were in wiping out the purchasing power of past savings. Entrenched labor unions can force our complex economy either to meet their demands for price-raising wage increases or suffer heavy losses in the disruption of production.

Some groups have benefited more than others: the corporation president's salary after taxes has probably gone down, while the domestic servant and the factory worker have, after taxes, more than tripled their prewar wages. After 25 years of unprecedented national prosperity, millions live in poverty. When a glorious boom turned in 1957 into a recession which reduced the rate of total production 5 percent—not a big percentage—unemployment doubled to over 5 million. Then, and again in 1961, some people lost their source of earnings, and many more worried about what might come to them. Most Americans, however, enjoyed rising incomes.

As individuals, we benefit or suffer not only when the whole economy swings but also when there are changes in *specific* parts, even those which we have absolutely no power to influence. A thriving movie industry was knocked groggy by TV. Untold thousands of families and businesses are forced to move as highway construction pushes into built-up areas. New Englanders lost jobs as textile manufacturing moved South—then got better ones as electronics and other industries based on new technology flourished in the Northeast. In 1963–64, when unemployment remained above 5 percent, many companies could not get the labor they needed.

The change which to one group seems a cursed dislocation will give others the promise of a better future. Here one meets a major fact: the lifeblood of progress is change. Change involves dislocation. Specific dislocations have features which, though good for the majority, are bad for some. Fearing change that will hurt, men are tempted to build protections. Sometimes it is hard to know when a protective breakwater can shut us off from the voyage of progress, a voyage whose waves may rock us, making some seasick but moving the whole group forward.

But is economic disorganization really so bad? "Money won't buy happiness." Do we not overestimate the importance of economic influences? Perhaps. Yet they pervade our lives so thoroughly that the difference between good and bad economic organization can mean the difference between happiness and misery.

Economics, the Study of How to Get the Most Benefit from Things That Are Scarce. The issues with which economists deal have many non-economic aspects, political, psychological, legal, sociological, technical. What, then, is the economic element? It exists when there is a "more or less," a scarcity, aspect—not necessarily scarcity in the sense of dearth so much as "not enough" or insufficient. Not everything wanted is available. We must choose among alternatives. One *choice* will lead to better results than will any other. In making the best, however, we must sacrifice other opportunities. Such decision involves economics. It requires selection when the means at hand (resources) are scarce—not plentiful enough to permit one to have everything desirable. Wise choice demands a comparison of quantities to get the "more" rather than the "less."

We have wants. We have productive capacity (resources)—time, materials, machinery—and technical ways of using them. The problem of economizing is **(1) to use available productive capacity (resources), which is limited, (2) in the best way the existing state of technical knowledge will permit (3) to satisfy wants.**

Sometimes, it is true, economic problems result from "surpluses" rather than scarcity. Any such surplus, however, consists of *particular* things, not of goods and services *in general.* Despite our alleged affluence, few Americans (any?) find all good things abundant. Any overproduction of this or that represents an error in economic judgment, a choice less good than might have been made.

FUNCTIONS OF AN ECONOMIC SYSTEM

Success in "economizing" requires that we make the best choices possible. Some uses of productive capacity are more efficient than others. How can we choose the best? The job of an economic system—any system, anywhere—is to help in making choices. The total job can be thought of as production, distribution, and consumption or, more helpfully, divided into six parts.

1. Showing What People Want. *What* goods and services are to be produced, and in what amounts? What do people want? A total of everything all of us desire would far exceed the output possible. The problem of choice is: What is the relative urgency of these wants, specific things? What tonnage of paper and lipstick, what gallonage of milk and gasoline, what medical and recreational facilities, will best satisfy our desires? *Production needs a guide.* As producers we cannot work efficiently unless we know what to produce.

Individual wants vary widely, and they change. *Groups* also have wants, and they too change: a better church or more destructive armaments. Consumers need an opportunity to express their wishes. Then the facts about these choices must be made known to producers. The more promptly and accurately this information gets from consumer to producer, the better the chances that the productive system will turn out the balance of goods and services which will provide greatest satisfaction.

Wants are not simply those of consumption as narrowly defined. (1) *Activity itself* can be pleasant or obnoxious. So much of life is spent at work that high among man's desires is one for a more, rather than a less, attractive job. "Blessed is he who has found his work; let him ask no other blessedness." An economic system that functions well gives opportunity to express preferences about work—to leave coal mining or domestic service or barren farms, to seek employers who offer good working conditions and jobs we like. (2) Up to some point, among the highest of our desires is that for "the mother of philosophy, the civilizer of man"—*leisure*. (3) *Economic progress*, growth in material well-being, is now a conscious goal, not only of ambitious individuals in societies long known for such achievement but also in civilizations for centuries tradition-bound and economically stagnant. (4) Other wants fall outside the common definition of "consumption": the desire for freedom, liberty, power, equality, equity, security. It is not clear how well an economic system can help reveal wants for such intangibles, even though it may efficiently show wants for more air conditioners and fewer office fans.

2. Balancing Production and Consumption. Consumption and production must be balanced in the short run—to restrict use or to push "surpluses" off the shelves. We cannot consume more than is available: seats on the 50-yard line, housing space, or fresh strawberries. Assume that a "shortage" appears. What adjustment will enable us to make the best of a bad situation? The solution requires (*a*) that what is available go to those most able and willing to sacrifice (pay) to get it and (*b*) that all consumers are induced to "go slow," to substitute other things, to economize in consumption of what is short. Some short-run changes, however, such as an especially large crop, lead to "surplus". Then we want a signal to consumers to step up consumption to get the benefit of the good fortune.

3. Indicating Which Method of Production is Best. Another job of the economic system is to help answer the question: *How* shall things be produced? We must choose among different possible ways of using manpower, time, machines, and other productive resources. What methods are most efficient? The state of technical knowledge may seem to give the answer. Not completely, though; the engineer alone cannot say which is the most efficient process until he has economic data; he must know the *costs* of the different methods. The best way to build a highway in India, where labor is cheap and capital equipment scarce, would not be best in Ohio. A bank mechanizes clerical operations when hourly wage rates rise to a point that the saving in labor cost justifies the expense of the machines. A new branch factory is built to serve the Pacific Coast market when transportation costs rise in relation to others.

Technology, invention, and engineering create the possible ways of doing a specific job. From these, economic knowledge (the prices of different inputs) helps select that possibility which will yield the most in relation to the alternatives sacrificed. Some productive capacity is scarcer than others. We want to know how to use the scarcer things, to *allocate* resources, to best advantage.

4. Dividing the Income Produced. *Who* gets what is produced? In what proportions? The money income produced must belong to someone. Who will receive it, and why? How will one or another basis of allocating income affect incentives and the resources available for production? The economic system answers, perhaps well, perhaps not so well. In doing so, it also influences both consumption and productive capacity.

5. Providing for Economic Progress. A fifth function is to provide for economic progress. What is possible? How can we prepare to get it? How much can and will we sacrifice now for the future, that is, give up in consumption to add to productive capacity? More and better housing and hospitals, for example, require saving and investment. New and better products require research and new skills. The economic system plays a part in showing how, and in creating ways, to progress economically: education, invention, construction of new equipment. Both opportunity and incentive to provide for the future make a difference in what develops. Economic signals guide the public in making choices—between the present and the future and between different possible ways of using the resources that become available for improving life.

6. Encouraging Full Use of Productive Capacity. The existence of productive capacity does not assure that it will serve its purpose. When human and material resources are not used "fully," some wants must go unsatisfied needlessly. Such waste of opportunity is a type of inefficiency in society's use of its potential for satisfying human desires. The economic process influences the total of its own operations.

These are things any economic system does. They must be done. But they are not necessarily done *well*, or as well as possible. How can we develop more efficient ways of performing each? For man *does* have power to modify the ways he handles his economic affairs. Better accomplishment is part of the goal of the study of economics.

WHY STUDY ECONOMICS

Like the retired florist turned artist who said he had never really *seen* flowers until he began to paint them, the modern man and woman cannot understand the world around without the vision developed and sensitized by a knowledge of economics. But why seek such understanding? Most of us have innate curiosity about matters of such sweeping and intimate importance. Some of us find this particular branch of learning, rather than biology or linguistics, especially fascinating. The chief reason for studying economics, however, is that the knowledge gained can be a positive instrument for improving welfare.

As generally studied, economics gives little attention to the management of family affairs. Nor does it say much about how to run a business. True, the *principles* we study and the *description* of the economic system, can help in solving personal and company problems. Businesses, in fact, try increasingly to foresee developments in the economy as a whole; to do so, managers need insight into the problems with which economists deal. One exciting and profitable new method of improving the efficiency of business operations makes heavy use of the principles of economizing developed by economic theorists. Nevertheless, economics deals primarily with the *broad sweep* of affairs and especially with *public policy*.

What are "economic" problems of public policy? They change, of course. Burning issues at one time become unimportant later. Fundamentally, the task is to find what choices exist and what the results of each are likely to be. But choices about what? In general, about things governments do, or may do, in such areas as banking, taxation, labor-management relations, business cycles, invention, monopoly, foreign trade, and a host of others. In addition, however, there are choices about less obvious matters: how business firms may be organized, the rules under which they may operate, the kind of jobs people may take. These are not trifling matters. Wise decisions can help toward more efficient solutions. Errors may be tragic. But by what standards, against what objectives, shall alternatives of public policy be judged? What are the economic goals of large groups—even of all mankind?

Economic Goals. Americans never have reached, and probably never will reach, full agreement on goals. An economy exists for, and is made up of, human beings—individuals and groups. How could we expect agreement among tens of millions of human beings and uncounted millions of groups, from small families to large religious denominations? Nevertheless, the vast majority would give high priority to such goals as:

1. Efficient and full use of available productive capacity to attain the best level of current consumption possible.
2. Economic growth in the form of a rising standard of living.
3. Expansion of opportunity for each of us to make full use of his or her life's potential.
4. Economic justice.
5. Economic security.
6. Stability of prices and output in the sense of avoiding inflation and business recession.

In deciding questions, including those of governmental policy, most of us would prefer solutions which move ourselves, and our children, toward these objectives. But can we define these goals with enough precision to enable them to serve as practical guides? The first two are reasonably clear. The third, rather broader than the more familiar expression "economic freedom," calls for further discussion. The fourth arouses so much disagreement that it can prove elusive, slippery, even divisive; yet it, too, remains a goal of high value.

The fifth and the sixth are more limited but receive widespread endorsement. To a large extent, they are not so much objectives in themselves as means of achieving one or more of the first four, as well as noneconomic, goals. As individuals and as small groups, of course, we have all sorts of economic goals; they are more specific and usually more important to us directly than the broader objectives of the whole society. But our chances of achieving them depend a lot upon what happens in the economy at large.

Actions to achieve one goal sometimes make the achievement of another more difficult. Fortunately, however, policies often support or reinforce one another, especially policies for the first two goals cited above. And success in moving toward these basic objectives will ease the task of progressing toward other goals, major and minor, social and personal.

Economic activity is a tool or servant of other aspects of life, a *means* to other *ends*. Material success will ordinarily help us achieve other objectives. Economics can be an ally, rather than a rival, of other values. Though "there is no wealth but life," material wealth can help us gain the intangibles. Churches can do their work better if they have economic resources. So can fraternities and charities, ball clubs and symphony orchestras. Generosity, beauty, humor, courtesy, and kindness are more likely to be achieved when men are free from the nagging pressure of economic need. The artist, the sportsman, the clergyman, and the scientist have an easier time when economic resources are available.

Buyer and seller, employer and employee, will generally find their human relations more satisfactory when free from great economic pressure. Life within the home or the nation moves more harmoniously with the reduction of economic frictions. Material success helps to better health, to aid our neighbors here and abroad; it gives us more assurance of defense against foreign enemies. The stingy, greedy, ignorant, disease-ridden man is not our ideal; and he is more likely to be the progeny of poverty than of economic comfort. Obviously, economic success does not solve all problems. The wellsprings of human discontent have deep origins. Rich people sometimes seek divorce. Yet, as a rule, the better we solve our economic problems, the greater our power to realize other aspirations. To a degree, everyone must be an economist, in his personal life and as a citizen.

HOW DO WE STUDY ECONOMICS?

How do economists study? By observing, and thinking. We use both the inductive and the deductive methods of reasoning. The economist looks for facts and tries to generalize from the particulars he discovers. He also reasons from given premises to the conclusions which follow, from the general to the particular. Economists will frame a hypothesis, then try to test it with evidence. They get hunches, insights, brilliant ideas; their emotions are aroused; they get furious and curious.

Getting Facts. We must *observe* to learn facts, to get evidence. This year's corn acreage, the wage rates of typists, the increase in population, the difference between the price of a new car and last year's model—these are observations of *facts* needed to answer some economic questions. To a varying degree, they are specific, dull, elusive, multitudinous—but essential.

For example, a case of *personal* economics, what kinds of facts would help in deciding on the type of job career to seek? Financial rewards are by no means all that count, but they do make a difference. How much will different jobs be likely to pay over a lifetime? How do vacations and other fringe benefits compare? What are the costs of training for different jobs, and how much might employers provide? What are the chances of earning much more or much less? What are the opportunities for advance? In an economy of change, which basic skills are likely to be best suited to jobs of new types? And so on—try to think of the kinds of facts you would like to have.

Or, for example, take an issue of *public* policy: one involving use of the power of government, that is, compulsion, to achieve the objective of reducing property and body damage from auto accidents. What facts would be desirable in compelling manufacturers to provide, and buyers to pay for, changes in auto design? Think of such things as: costs of specific possibilities, one by one, in relation to the probable effectiveness of each; the political and industrial questions of assigning authority to particular human beings to require, or not require, one or another change; alternative methods of trying to attain part of the goal—different design of streets and highways, lighting and policing, standards for renewing driver licenses, and tougher penalties for bad driving—national versus regional standards; effects on consumers and producers of nonmass-market autos; the incidence of the burden of increased cost (is it not much like a form of taxation?) on car buyers. And so on. Did Congress have such information? Not much of it.

Statistics—the systematic compilation of quantitative data—must play a big part in economics. Today, fortunately, the economist has access to far more statistical data than ever before.

The "facts" the economist needs include a large range of *nonstatistical information*—for example, the nature of money, the legal elements of a corporation, the availability of natural resources, the respect for agreements, the misery of long unemployment. Some involve "institutions"—customary ways of doing things; they may vary widely from region to region and from time to time, significantly affecting the economic system. Not all the facts we need will apply directly to features of today's economy. Some are history. The present is the child of the past. The more we know about the parents and grandparents, the better we can understand the offspring, our own economy. So we dip into economic history, but in most beginning studies rather little.

To do well, a painter must know colors, a surgeon anatomy, an engineer the strength of materials. An economist must know the facts of his economy, its **structure.** No one can decide wisely about big economic issues—inflation or unemployment—or smaller ones—local tax rates or increasing the appropriation for the state university—until he knows the facts.[1] Important, too, are personal, qualitative facts—the way people feel, their honesty, the vigor of their desire to take advantage of opportunity. Although powerfully important, such facts can never be known with measured precision.

Developing Theories. Thinking goes along with observation. Use of the grey cells helps one frame challenging questions and suggests what groups of facts to try to get. Common sense, what we have learned from other studies, and thoughtful consideration can rule out irrelevant data.

Then as we gather facts, thought helps tell us what we have. Words do not make a sentence until they are arranged, and the meaning depends upon the arrangement. The advance of knowledge depends upon the way we arrange and use our facts. Which movements on the surface of an economic ocean are minor ripples, which are big waves, and which are the powerful tides?

Can we support a *generalization,* verify (or upset) a *theory* of relationships? Perhaps we can find "laws," things that are invariable. Do some things—such as business losses and unemployment or higher taxes and attempts at tax evasion—always go together? Does an increase in the supply of money always precede a rise in the cost of living? Do we have basis for *prediction*—good prediction? When things are associated, may one be the *cause* of the other? If so, we may have freedom and power to exercise control over some future development by what we do now. But if the association does not exist, we have another kind of power or freedom; we can do one thing without necessarily getting the other.

Thinking, however, sometimes leads, not to higher ground but to pitfalls.

1. It is easy, but dangerous, to assume that when two things have something in common they are, therefore, alike in other respects. Two businesses may be similar in that they both make soap, but they may have widely

---

[1] But one could never hope to learn every fact that bears upon even a simple problem. The mass would be overwhelming. Fortunately, we can usually do well with a relatively small fraction of a whole mass if our fraction is a "representative sample." Statisticians have made brilliant progress in learning how to select a sample scientifically and then to judge how fully we can rely upon the facts obtained.

different labor policies. Two business cycles may differ greatly in some respects, little in others.

2. Another error (logicians call it "the fallacy of composition") is to conclude that what is true of a part is also true of a whole. One housewife may be helpless to influence the price of beef, but all housewives together exert a mighty power. An invention that hurts the makers of machines of traditional types may benefit greatly the mass of consumers. The individual finds that he can usually get a seat in a restaurant or airplane, a medical checkup or an apartment, when he wants one and is willing to pay; but if hundreds of people who had not been expressing such demands suddenly do so, they encounter results almost the opposite of those experienced by one or a few individuals—shortage and scarcity in contrast with comfortable availability.

3. Another error, one so easy to make (the *post hoc ergo propter hoc* fallacy), is to conclude that, because one thing *follows* another, the first *caused* the second. The second was certainly caused by something that went earlier. But we may not always know for certain *which* earlier thing caused a particular result.

4. What is best in one set of conditions is not necessarily best in others. The diabetic needs different treatment from the man with pneumonia. The prescription for the economic illness of poverty should not be the same when the cause is lack of jobs for people qualified and willing to work as when illness and illiteracy figure prominently.

Theorizing, which we have just been discussing, does not always inspire the respect it deserves. Men who consider themselves realists often think of "theory" as something unrealistic and impractical. Nothing could be farther from the truth. A correct theory—that a certain germ is always present in a certain disease or that an auto without gasoline will not run—is both realistic and of practical value. We have facts on some cases; they all agree. We see logic to account for the result. Therefore, we theorize, confidently predicting that the malaria germ will be present in malaria fever or that an empty gas tank will leave us stranded. Nothing can be more practical than a good theory.[2] Much of economics consists of the search for broad and accurate principles.

[2] The economist must *analyze*—break a problem into its parts and examine the units which make up the whole. In this way, the problem will be small enough to handle. He must study things one by one, not jumble a dozen together, even though all are related. He must also *synthesize*—combine the parts into a whole to find the essence, the generalities that mean so vastly much more than the particulars. But here we run a real danger: oversimplification. To get anywhere we must simplify—*abstract* the crucial from the trivial. Physicists, for example, simplify, in a sense unrealistically, when they assume the absence of friction. So economists must ignore some aspects of every problem. For example, they sometimes use symbols that can be examined with the accuracy of mathematics. But to get this precision, we may sacrifice truth of great value. The trick is to find what can be sacrificed without serious loss. By oversimplifying, the man in the street (and even the professional economist) may go far wrong in judging economic issues. On the other hand, since economics touches such a wide range of topics, we are tempted to include so much of politics, sociology, psychology, business management, technology, and other disciplines that nothing can be done well.

Experimentation. Can economists use that powerful tool of some disciplines, *the controlled experiment?* Are we able to try several things to see which works best? Can we "hold other things constant" and by making many tries, see how small changes in one element affect others? Seldom, unfortunately, and not with the precision of physics or chemistry. The economist cannot find people who are similar in every respect and then subject human beings to differences in one element as in a test tube. Even in the most nearly possible of such cases, he could not really be certain that the results were due to the one difference alone. So many other forces are always operating. Moreover, findings for the "control" group would not necessarily apply to others. A tax on fur coats in Georgia might have effects different from the same tax in New England. If we try different methods in dealing with the *big* problems which affect the whole economy—the laws governing labor unions—we obviously cannot *control* the experiments; important factors change constantly.

Economists use what may be called "mental experiments." We define a situation—"build a model"—and then think about what is likely to happen when some element changes. Sometimes the model rests on solid knowledge of relationships. The responses to an assumed change will then be clear. Even in the more common situation when information leaves much to be desired, this system of "trying things out" often serves well.

Is Economics a Science? It is, and it is not. If we know certain fact situations of economics, we can sometimes predict the results. Economics thus meets one test of a science, as contrasted with an art. Uniformity and system are great enough to permit good, even though not perfect, prediction. When a price goes up or down, some effects can be forecast closely enough to be very useful. Predicting the job outlook and the level of business cannot be done precisely. But with the facts and the theoretical underpinnings now available, economists can show very much indeed about the results which would follow one or another action of government or some other change, such as a big strike or a wave of consumer optimism.

Economists use some of the basic methods of science: the collection of data, the formulation of generalizations based on these data, the testing of the generalization by using other observations. Like natural sciences, economics does deal with *quantities* or amounts. Quantities can be compared: the distances of planets, the weights of gases, the incomes in different professions. Economists can measure, not always perfectly but often well enough to support confidence in the results. The better the measurement, the more dependable or "scientific" the conclusions.

Where economics differs so greatly from the natural sciences is that the facts do not stay put. The physicist, the astronomer, and the botanist work with more stable materials. The mathematician can build on unchanging assumptions. Economics, however, concerns people and society.

They change. The world around changes. No two sets of fact situations are likely to be identical. Men respond to a multitude of motives. All these factors combine to alter the assumptions from which we can begin reasoning.

Predictions may, or may not, go wrong. We may have learned, for example, that conditions A, B, and C will produce D; when A becomes Aa, however, and B turns into Bb, with C unchanging, we cannot be certain of the result. A tricky football play may lose its power as the opponents catch on; the reactions to depression and inflation will be different as the public gets experience. A man is not a machine, like an auto. Men make the cars and drive them. Men, likewise, have some freedom to guide their economy by what they learn. But in what directions? By action or inaction this query *must* be answered. In doing so, we find that the worthiness, the quality of different results—issues usually thought to lie outside the realm of science—become matters of concern in economic discussions.

"Intrusion" of Value Judgments into Economic Analysis.   Science claims such characteristics as impartiality, honesty, and lack of bias. Find the facts and let the chips fall where they may! The scientific study of ways to do things (the *means*) is not confused by whether or not the uses (the *ends*) are good or bad. Economic debate, however, suffers because feelings about the goodness or badness of the ends become confused with the merits of the means. Emotions get in the way. Since the problems are important, we *feel* about them. Personal and group interests can outweigh the concern for pure intellectual truth.

Interests often conflict. What is best for the individual may not be so for the group, and what helps one individual may hurt another. Wishful thinking, unconscious prejudice, and deliberate deception crop up in economics, more than in chemistry, biology, and other natural sciences. Certain words become fighting symbols; when they are used, tempers flare, making good analysis impossible. Use of such terms as "socialism," "capitalism," "justice," or "monopoly" can distort discussion.

The job of the economist as an objective scientist includes study of the economic effects of various policies. Will heavier taxes and a better municipal hospital raise or lower local property values? How much will higher prices paid to farmers hurt poor consumers? The economist can hardly escape critical examination of the merits of different effects. We cannot avoid judging policies; and no economic policy that is precise enough to be a guide for action can be accepted as finally best and beyond criticism. Even the most conscientious economist may "get off base." As an objective scientist, he studies the results which will follow from certain actions or conditions, such as U.S. limits on oil imports. He does so to help society do a better job. Having his own idea about which results will be best, he may argue for the policy to achieve them.

An economist's *advocacy* of policy may rest on a well-developed sense of justice, charity, or aesthetics; still, such advocacy is not impartial and scientific in the same sense as the objective analysis. In this, the "welfare" area of economics, the economist can speak with less definite assurance than in the more "scientific" areas. An engineer can tell how to make a car go faster, but not whether we are wise in trying to get to our destination more quickly. The ambulance driver speeding to an emergency and the student stretching out a "date" have different speed objectives.

We are likely to progress most rapidly if we distinguish between (1) how to accomplish something, and (2) whether we ought to try to do so, and why.[3] A factual, carefully reasoned analysis is a powerful thing. It helps by bringing out into the open the conscious and unconscious bias that appears so often in discussion of economic problems. We can best serve our feelings by first ignoring them.

Understanding the System as a Whole.   Economics is not a simple subject. The principles as well as the facts are numerous. We cannot learn them all at once. Everything relates to everything else. Each topic could be studied more profitably if it had been preceded by all the others—something obviously impossible. Learning economics is a bit like building a machine. The only feasible approach is to build the parts separately to fit a design plan. Then, gradually putting them together, we eventually get something that operates. Until a workman sees the whole, he may not fully understand the functions of some of the parts and their relation to others, though the designer did. The student of economics must lay a solid groundwork, just as the medical student who dissects a cadaver before operating on live patients.

Understanding is cumulative. The more we know, the easier we can see the significance of everything that went before. When reviewing for the final examination, therefore, you ought to find more in each chapter than you could appreciate without knowing what comes later. Economists (and various instructors using this book) differ about the best sequence for studying many elements of the subject, while agreeing that the elements belong to an interrelated whole.

PRODUCTION

Production—the source of income, of what we get to consume or add to our wealth—can be defined simply as creating utility, adding to usefulness, as *doing something someone wants*. It is the use of "inputs" to get "outputs," the **transformation** of one resource (or more) into something

---

[3] The cause-to-effect aspect, the purely factual and rational study of what exists, is called *positive economics*. We distinguish it from *normative economics*, which covers the "ought," the "should," the desirable and the undesirable, by some value standards.

more desirable. A person may produce for himself or the family—mother's cooking, the son's assembly of a hi-fi set. Or a person may produce by doing what others want. He may not have the slightest idea who those people are; the cotton farmer does not know who will wear the clothes made from the cotton he raises. The barber, however, knows precisely whom he serves. The "someones" for whom we produce, and who produce for us, are far more numerous than we can imagine. They are of all sizes and shapes, tastes and skill—saints and sinners. The "somethings" done are also myriad but fall into a few broad categories.

Change of Form. Changing the physical form of things—fabrication—can make them more useful: the processings of scrap iron until it can become part of a refrigerator; the conversion of trees into paper, bricks into a house, or leather into shoes. (Not every change of form is productive, only those which increase the desirability of the materials used.) The farm, the factory, and the construction gang are typical agencies that produce by changing forms.

Change of Place. Transportation can add to well-being. Tea in India, oil in Texas, and oranges in California are not useful to the New Yorker. Factories could not run without trains, trucks, and ships to bring raw materials and deliver the products. Transferring an item to a place where it is more wanted adds to its utility. The process of bringing things to us—or taking us to them—is productive activity.

Transfer through Time. Transfer through time is a little like transfer through space. Wheat harvested in July is used through many months. We are better off if we can consume it over the year, rather than if all had to be used at once. Storage is beneficial. Most manufacturing requires that raw materials be owned and processed over a considerable period. If the material cannot be stored—fresh tomatoes—canneries or other plants remain idle much of the year; someone must hold the productive capacity. If things are to be available in the retail store when consumers want them, someone must previously have held them, perhaps for a long time. This holding is useful. What if each of us had to pay for our year's wheat supply when it is harvested in the summer? An obvious nuisance! Most people are better off if someone else does the transferring through time.

Direct Services. Many other services are rendered to consumers more directly. Transfer of possession—getting things from one owner to another—presumably benefits both; the real estate broker, the clerk in the store, and the traveling salesman all render services of transfer. The services of doctors, lawyers, accountants, teachers, artists, musicians, government officials, athletes, newspaper reporters all satisfy wants more or less directly. Frequently, the service, like that of a waitress, is the final link in a long chain. Services seem less tangible than physical things and sometimes, therefore, of a lower order of usefulness. This attitude is misguided. The proper test is whether someone wants the service. If so, it is productive, no less than the work of fabrication, and to be valued at what it brings in free exchange.

Production in Major Industries.   The American economy produced net income of about $650 billion in 1967. Figure 1–1 shows the percentage

FIGURE 1–1.   Income of the People of the United States, by Industry of Production*

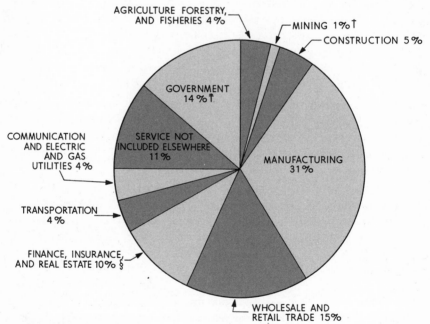

* The income concept used here is net national income, described in Chapter 9. *Net* income from abroad of less than 1 percent is excluded.
† Much extraction of petroleum, natural gas, and other minerals is done by companies whose major activities cause them to be classed under manufacturing.
‡ Does not include goods and services produced by other industries—cement, military equipment, schoolbooks—but purchased and used by governments. States and localities combined account for about 55 percent of the total.
§ Includes the net rental value of owner-occupied houses.
Source: Survey of Current Business, July, 1967. Data apply to 1966. The small percentage not accounted for originated outside the United States.

of the economy's total income produced by each of 10 broad industry groups in 1966. Manufacturing accounted for more than any other industry—about 31 percent. But note the size of the various service industries.

American Production—and That of Some Other Economies. American production in 1967 amounted to an average of about $3,600 of output for every man, woman, and child—a highly impressive achievement. (Nevertheless, perhaps 20 percent of all *families* had incomes under $3,600.) Comparison with the output per person of some other economies will show our production from another point of view. Such international comparisons have a large margin of possible error; yet the general magnitudes shown in Table 1–1 represent the state of affairs moderately well.

TABLE 1–1. Gross Production per Capita in Selected Countries, Estimated Annual Rates, 1965*

U.S. Dollars		U.S. Dollars	
United States	3,300	Italy	900
Canada	2,300	Japan	700
Sweden	2,200	Greece	600
Switzerland	2,000	Argentina, Chile, and Spain	500
Australia and New Zealand	1,800	Mexico, Jamaica, and Portugal	400
United Kingdom, France, Norway,		Brazil, China (Taiwan), Ghana,	
and West Germany	1,700	Tunisia and Turkey	200
Israel	1,200	India, Kenya, and Pakistan	80 to 100

* In dollars of 1962 purchasing power. In several cases the figures are at best rough approximations. Estimates are rounded to nearest hundred dollars except for last three countries.
Source: Agency for International Development.

Growth of Production. America also has an impressive record of economic growth. Total production has grown substantially from decade to decade. See Figure 1–2. Though measurement is difficult, the average annual rate for 55 years has been about 3.5 percent. Some periods have shown much better results than others. What might be done to get the

FIGURE 1–2. Average Annual Percentage Growth in Real Output of Private Domestic Economy

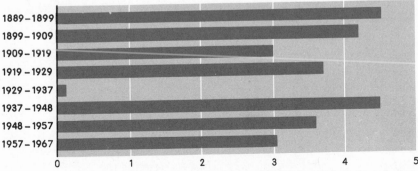

Source: J. W. Kendrick, *Productivity Trends in the United States* (New York: Nationa Bureau of Economic Research, 1961), p. 72; 1957–1967, partly estimated by the author.

best results, not occasionally but year in and year out? The hope of doing better gets strength from another demonstration that faster economic progress is possible. Some foreign economies have been growing more rapidly than ours. Why? Others, however, lag far behind. The contrasts are striking. What factors account for the differences? One part of the answer will be found in the amounts of total productive capacity and the rate of increase. But also highly significant is the effectiveness with which resources are used: *productivity*.

PRODUCTIVITY

Production is output while *productivity* is output in relation to input, the amount of production per unit of cost. The higher the productivity of a person, an industry, or a nation, the greater is the amount being produced per unit of input. America's productivity, as well as total production, has risen markedly. Per man-hour and per unit of tangible capital (buildings, machinery, etc.) output in 1967 was more than double that of 1929 and one fourth above the 1950 level. Any such estimates of amounts have imperfections. The nature of both outputs and inputs changes over time; measurement proves very difficult, especially when two dates are several years apart. The trend, however, is clear.

For the whole economy the annual productivity growth has averaged around 2 percent a year compounded. In many years, however, and for considerable periods in some industries, as shown in Figure 1–3, rates double this or even higher have been achieved.

Scientific advance accounts for much of the increase in productivity. Yet a significant role will be found in the functioning of the economic system as it works (or fails to work) toward the goal of efficient utilization of existing productive capacity. One of the central purposes of the study of economics is to learn what things encourage, and what obstruct, the growth of productivity. Some findings will appear almost self-evident, at least after they have been stated. Productivity growth is aided by conditions that facilitate the shift of workers from jobs with low output per man-hour to jobs with higher output, such as the movement from poor farms to factories. In contrast, average productivity suffers from conditions that discriminate against workers for reasons not related to ability and willingness to produce.

Some explanations for differences in achievements, however, are less clear—for example, the deeper causes of the reasons we see, such as differences in inventiveness or personal ambition.

WHAT ARE COSTS?

Economizing means producing (and consuming) efficiently or, to use a term often employed by economists, "maximizing." The challenge is to learn how to get *the more rather than the less* (at the same cost), or a

FIGURE 1–3. Man-Hour Output: Increase in Selected Industries, 1950–64*

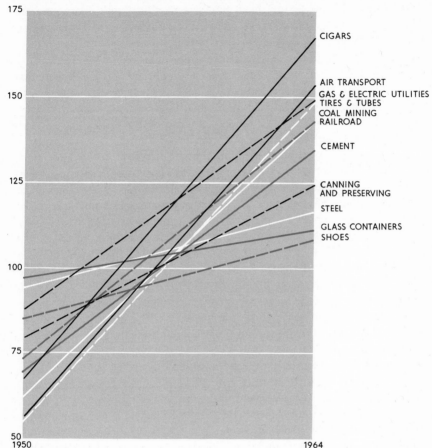

* Output is measured in physical units.
Source: Bureau of Labor Statistics, *Indexes of Output per Man-Hour for Selected Industries, 1939 and 1947–65.*

particular output at minimum cost. But what, precisely, are the costs to be minimized?

To most of us and to most businesses, it may seem foolish to ask: "What does one mean by cost?" Is it not obviously the money we must pay? Yes, but not exclusively. A "money veil" often conceals some of the underlying reality of cost. What we see and measure in our ordinary affairs may not tell us "the truth, the whole truth, and nothing but the truth." In a fundamental sense a cost is the best **alternative** or **opportunity** which must be **sacrificed** or given up (for whatever one gets).

To a person taking a job, the cost is the total of attractions of the best thing he gives up, including leisure and the joys of fishing, but chiefly the next best job. Some people have few sets of alternatives, others several. Always, however, an employer—and then consumers—must offer enough to compensate for the best opportunities which workers sacrifice. There is a cost for everything we do, wherever any choice is possible. The cost of going to a movie is what one could otherwise get with the time and money. A man taking care of his own garden should count as a cost the next best thing he could do with his time. If we use a piece of land or a machine, the cost of this use includes the yield that could be gained in the best alternative use.

The business world generally puts money prices on costs. Most things are valued in dollar terms. Money provides a highly convenient measure, one which permits us to compare widely varied things. Yet businesses and households face some choices where dollar measures are incomplete. The costs for which consumers must pay do not include the full worth of the alternatives sacrificed—the opportunity of the widow or deserted mother to care for her children when she leaves home to work for pay which is no different from that of the girl with no responsibilities for others. Money costs do not always cover important *social costs*. Air pollution provides the classic example: the factory does not include in its cost the extra work its smoke makes for housewives; the business world does not make us, as consumers of the factory's product, pay for what the housewife suffers on our account.[4]

Another case deserves notice. *If productive capacity would otherwise be idle, it can perhaps be used for production with no (significant) sacrifice of desirable alternatives.* In one sense there is no cost. When there is widespread unemployment, therefore, society has the opportunity of increasing the output of desirable goods and services at no true economic cost—by using labor and equipment that would otherwise be unwillingly idle. Money payments can give a misleading impression of cost under such conditions. (Even then, however, money costs have an important function: to indicate the best of different possible ways of using the capacity that would be idle.)

Economizing consists of choosing the best alternatives. Economic progress requires the creation of still better opportunities to choose from. The next chapter shows how the economic system guides the making of choices to help achieve production at least cost and to develop better alternatives from which to choose.

---

[4] Pollution of air, rivers, and lakes has emerged as an issue of increasing public concern. What and where are the problems? Why have they not been dealt with as have the improvement in TV sets or in stretch fabrics or in interstate highways? What is technically possible? What are the costs of alternative methods? Who shall bear what costs when the persons who will benefit are not directly related to the business processes which are the source of much pollution? And so on.

TERMS AND CONCEPTS

scarcity	resource allocation	output
wants	economic structure	goods and services
resources	economic model	productivity
leisure	positive (versus nor-	"maximizing"
consumption	mative) economics	opportunity cost
production	inputs	

QUESTIONS

1. Describe the functions of an economic system.
2. Explain why technical, engineering knowledge alone will not necessarily show which method of production is best.
3. What is the difference between predicting the results of an economic policy and judging their desirability?
4. What are major goals of economic policy? How would an individual's goals differ?
5. What is "cost"? Give examples of nonmoney costs.
6. Define "production" and describe different types.
7. "Rising production is good, but rising productivity is better." Discuss.
8. "It is a mistake to theorize before one has data." "Theories are all right for professors, but men who get things done look at the facts." Comment.
9. What goes into making available a college course? Why have others exerted the efforts needed to serve you? What kinds of "organization" have been necessary?
10. List *public* problems—local and national—which seem primarily economic. What kinds of facts would help in solving them? List public problems which seem primarily noneconomic and then indicate whether greater economic prosperity would help solve them and why or why not. Repeat for *personal* problems.
11. Might a public policy which was excellent under one set of conditions be unwise under others? Why? Does your answer indicate that there can be no "laws" of economics?
12. Why would each of the six functions of an economic system need to be performed in an economy with government ownership and direction of most productive activity, as in Russia?
13. "The men with the muck-rakes are often indispensable to the well-being of society; but only if they know when to stop raking the muck." (Theodore Roosevelt.) In what respects will criticism of an economic system aid progress?

2

SPECIALIZATION, EXCHANGE, THE MARKET ECONOMY

After all, the greatest meliorator of the world is selfish, huckstering trade.
Ralph Waldo Emerson

The economic world is a giant cooperative. Competition and rivalry exist, as on a football squad, but they are minor compared with the community of interest that every squad member has in trying to win over the opponent—poverty. As a society—and as individuals—we can accomplish far more working together than if we try to keep one another from succeeding. The cooperation of the economic world leads us to do things for each other in overcoming the limits of scarcity—yet for the most part without explicit, deliberate concern for the other fellow.

THE PROBLEM

A summary of mankind's economic problem might run as follows: Goods and services are needed to satisfy our wants. These wants, including the desire for opportunity and freedom, seem limitless. The goods and services available for meeting them, however, are limited. They are limited by our production: by the time, the skills and techniques, the machines, the whole of the productive capacity (including knowledge) at our disposal. Although the American economy has done well in making possible the highest standard of living in the world, our wants are by no means satisfied. So we seek to learn what makes our present production possible and what will enable us to satisfy more fully our unsatisfied, changing, and expanding wants.

How has our economy reached its preeminent position? What will

24

keep the trend not only good but as good as it can be? From Chapter 1 we can pick out three elements of the answers to such questions. (1) Much depends upon the effectiveness and efficiency with which *existing* resources are used—resource allocation, using labor and materials and machines where they will contribute most to the output that will satisfy wants. (2) Output growth also benefits from increase in the quantity and the quality of productive capacity. Workers with higher skills, aided by more and better mechanical equipment, produce more per hour of work. (3) Possibly first in importance stands technological advance, the "state of the arts," knowledge in every sense.

Past progress has come from a combination of these three. They have gone along together—and will in the future. Much of the process takes the form of increasing specialization.

THE DIVISION OF LABOR: SPECIALIZATION

Specialization is a time-tested device for making scarcity less oppressive. By looking at seven ways specialization yields benefits, we can learn much about why productivity has increased.

Developing Human Skills. "Practice makes perfect." By specializing we develop skills. Anyone can learn to do a job better when he can concentrate time and effort on a relatively small task and acquire the ability to do it expertly. The factory worker, mailcarrier, pastry chef, and machine designer all learn their work better by cultivating a small area.

Quicker Mastery. One needs less time to learn a small job well than a bigger one. To become either a good typist or a good bookkeeper proves less difficult than to become equally skilled at both. When a person can specialize, he can become proficient earlier than if he must spread his efforts over more kinds of work. An apprenticeship, not many decades ago, may have required several years; now each of several parts of many complicated processes can be learned in a few days. A radio tube is far more complex than a drinking glass. Yet women on the assembly line in a radio tube factory learn their jobs in only a tiny fraction of the time needed to learn glass blowing. A lifetime would not be long enough to become adept in half of the phases of law, chemistry, or medicine; but a few years of specialized effort will permit a person who has acquired the basic training to master a restricted but significant portion.

Concentrating Effort to Best Advantage. Some parts of many jobs call for more skill than do others. Specializing on aspects of the whole enables each person to spend his time where his natural capacities and developed skills permit him to contribute most. The manager of a business, drawing upon his experience, concentrates on key, strategic work, leaving to others the less crucial jobs: filing correspondence, hiring most of the staff, buying the insurance.

Serving More People by the Same Effort. Specialization can enable us to serve several people in a single effort. One factory, for example, will produce small electric motors of a type that goes into the appliances of dozens of products; it makes the design, gets the apparatus set, and then with the same basic equipment produces a large quantity. It has a long "production run"; the effort in getting set serves many users. The wholesaler who stocks large quantities provides in one storage center services for scores of retailers.

Reducing Cost of Moving from Job to Job. Concentration makes it possible to avoid loss of time in switching from one job, or part of a job, to another. Movement itself and the "warming up" take time. By sticking to a single thing, a worker increases his effective working day.

Use of Complex Equipment. Specialization permits us to use tools and machines most fully. As a result, utilization of advanced technology becomes possible more generally. Modern specialized equipment is often extremely expensive, as well as wonderfully productive. The individual worker cannot have a multitude of these costly machines to work with. Nor can he rotate, spending a few minutes a day with a wide variety of machines. If each person, however, spends his working time with one piece of equipment, each of these expensive, specialized machines can be used rather fully. Employers can afford them—the computers which calculate each customer's utility charges, the giant cranes on construction projects. Dividing a process into many parts often aids mechanization because specialized machines can be developed for each of separate elements of the whole.

Advantages of Geographical Specialization. By specializing we can take advantage of favorable conditions of nature or of the acquired characteristics of an area. Oranges grow better in Florida than in Michigan, but auto parts are produced more cheaply in the Michigan-Ohio area, nearer where nature left iron ore and coal. Auto workers, however, from company presidents to young men with their first good job, enjoy a vacation in Florida. There the hotel employees who serve them drive to work in cars made in Michigan. A different geographical specialization is illustrated by the concentration of finance in a few "streets" (areas)—Wall (New York), State (Boston), LaSalle (Chicago), Montgomery (San Francisco). As men with common interests are enabled to contact each other easily, they draw on one another's knowledge and interest promptly and with awareness of what all prefer in an ever fluid situation.

EXCHANGE

The Need for Exchange—and a Danger.   When people specialize, they must exchange. A person's needs in his own line of specialization are satisfied easily. If men spend their time doing a small job, but doing it many times, the work is valuable only if the things produced become available to others. Availability appears as an offer to sell. We exchange goods and services for money and then use the money to buy goods and services others produce. The person who works with a machine, and those who make and finance it, want what others make and do. The farmer, with a tractor made in the city, produces a good harvest; but for his sick child he desires an antibiotic and for his son in the armed forces the best of weapons systems. If exchange is possible, the myriad of specific activities which can be done well and cheaply as small units will combine to make up an impressive total of things that people want. Without exchange no one could make a house or a flashlight or even a cup of tea. But most American families are able to have them because we work for each other and exchange.

Thumbing through the classified section of a telephone directory will suggest the untold years of specialization anyone can tap by picking up the telephone—if he can pay. He must be able to give something in return. To do so, he needs a buyer for what he has; sometimes it is hard to find such a buyer.

Interdependence, then, can be not only a blessing but also a threat. It makes people vulnerable. It puts them at the mercy, not only of each other, but also of the forces that enable them to work together. My decision not to buy a new suit is a decision not to buy the labor of clothing makers. If steelworkers strike for a long time, auto factories close, railroads lay off workers, landlords cannot collect rent and pay taxes, and city treasuries find themselves short of funds as relief demands rise. A permanent shift in demand can also cause trouble. A drop in the use of coal plus mechanization of mining brought prolonged unemployment for some miners. Whole communities lost their major source of income. New jobs in the area were few. Fortunately, specialization also helps in adjustment to interdependence; the workers on tasks which have been simplified can often fit easily into new jobs, perhaps in different industries, when the demand for labor shifts.

Exchange Results from Different Estimates of Worth.   Why do people exchange? *Because they place different values on things.* The transfer from a point of lower to one of higher value is beneficial. It is something people want—one of the services we noted as "productive." Value does not inhere in a physical thing, or a service. It is not intrinsic. Value depends upon what someone feels, his estimate of the worth to him. This feeling results from complex factors. The nature of the product is only one of the things affecting our feelings about its value. The spinach farmer may never eat his product.

Exchange Requires Specialists in Exchange.   The process of helping people find out what others have to exchange also requires specialization. Skill and organization both need developing. The same man cannot be intimately familiar with New York City real estate, Oregon fruit, and used trucks. Best results generally come from thorough knowledge of a narrow field. But, although the trader's specialization serves us well, it sometimes gives him a large advantage over the buyer or seller who is not so well informed. Since we are so constantly dependent upon exchange, and since we cannot match the specialized skill of the middleman, we in some cases impose governmental regulations to "police" the process; for the most part, however, we lean heavily upon the competition of these specialists to give us the best terms possible.

The services of exchange are perhaps like the fuel for an engine. Without fuel, the motor could not operate; and without the services of exchange, the economic system would not work. Yet, as the fuel serves, it is used up. Similarly with the services of exchange. Nevertheless, the better these services are performed, the greater the possibilities of the rest of the economic system.

COSTS OF SPECIALIZATION

Effort Devoted to Exchange.   Specialization has costs. Maintenance of the exchange mechanism, although costly, is a paying proposition, like the cost of the gasoline in the auto. Yet who can be certain that he pays the best amount? The tendency to think of the services of exchange as unproductive, as lost effort, adds to a feeling that "distribution costs too much." Recurrently, men argue that if society could somehow put more effort into creating things and less into exchanging them, we could have more of the end results they really seek. Perhaps so. Thirteen million Americans employed in wholesale and retail trade alone does seem large. Possibly, however, even more effort in exchange might pay off. We might find welcome benefits if more middlemen competed for our business; beyond some point, however, the duplication of effort seems wasteful. Whatever the best balance among all types of activities, there is no blinking the fact that we must pay to enjoy specialization.

Making Robots out of Humans?   Specialization, it is said, leads people to "know more and more about less and less." We see the caricatures of routine assembly line jobs—years tightening bolt 729. Routine, uninteresting labor, jobs that seem to have little meaning, conditions of work that are unpleasant and, worse still, that restrict opportunity to put forth one's best efforts—all these plague society. They always have.

Today an incredibly large number of jobs challenge our highest capacities. Though specialized, they are not humdrum: designing the atomic power plant; planning the flow of hundreds of different parts to be assembled into a single end product; preparing a legal brief on a new issue of constitutional law; handling a $10 million machine that rolls steel coils at 80 miles an hour with thickness controlled to 0.0001 of an inch. The chief concern, however, is not whether we have improved on the past but whether we can do better in the future. We can and will, on and off the job, thanks partly to specialization. The automated factory and the electronic computer, and also simple machines, take over more and more of the truly routine, backbreaking work. Women no longer drag loaded carts in coal mines, and fewer each year keep the company's books by hand with pen and ink. Hope also lies outside work: the fruits of specialization include not only more education and material things but also more leisure to develop nonjob interests: symphonies or jazz.

In some plants, betterment now comes from a reduction of specialization. "Job enlargement," giving the worker a wider range of activities, proves successful; for in terms of productivity only, specialization had gone too far.

Losses from Imbalance. When men and businesses concentrate on smaller and smaller parts of a job, their decisions may not harmonize most effectively. There may be too much of one part (autos) relative to other elements (parking space) of the same interdependent process (providing transport). When things get out of balance, waste results. To reduce such losses may cost effort: the planning and expediting staffs of giant businesses, expensive stocks of inventories, special staffs to provide information, or, where government decides, the apparatus of an official agency. No one can know how much we lose because specialized parts of an interdependent economy are not coordinated ideally.

Lack of Sense of Common Interest. Specialization has another cost: a loss of the feeling of common interest. People doing a tiny part of a job may not see clearly the connection between what they do and what they get. In fact, there may be no apparent physical connection at all. The GE accountant may use Westinghouse light bulbs at home. A man may work all his life and never consume any of the physical things he produces.

Work seems to be, not for oneself but for the employer, and under conditions he controls. We may, therefore, have little reason or even opportunity to put forth our best effort. The vague sense of general social interest hardly provides incentives for the typical person to do the best that is in him. Sometimes, the way to benefit ourselves the most may seem to be to oppose, rather than to help, our employer or others with whom we deal. Impeding exchange, rather than producing, becomes profitable to the individual or group. Clearly, the economy must produce what it is to consume. Could anything be more obvious? Individually and as groups, however, we can sometimes hope to get more of what others produce by *demanding* more for what we do, rather than by *doing* more.

Like the medieval lord with his toll station on the river, the modern group in a strategic position may be powerful enough to stop trade unless its terms are met. Millions live at the partial mercy of such potentates. To enjoy the full benefits of specialization, we must protect ourselves against those who, whether solid blocs of voters, labor unions, professional groups, or businesses, try to throw up obstacles to our dealing with one another.

Human effort and material things must be organized for production and consumption. Cooperation, intricate division of labor, exchange— these things do not "just happen." They depend upon the functioning of the economic system.

ORGANIZING ECONOMIC LIFE

The state of technology gives us many ways to use the productive resources available at any time. Some ways are more desirable than others, considering what we have and what we want. The problem of economizing is to find the combination of choices which will serve best under the circumstances. The total of goods and services that become available to satisfy wants depends upon the way we organize economic life.

Three Types of Agencies for Making Economic Decisions.

Many kinds of units make the decisions that direct the use of economic resources. By looking at three types—households, governments, and businesses—we can see the major features. Within the country's 61 million *households*, the family decisions are made in many ways: dictation, altruism, nagging, persuasion, and careful reasoning all play a part. Such diverse forces as personal taste, parental love, insistent necessity, and religious devotion guide choice. The broad objective is to maximize the total benefit that can be obtained. The funds (resources) available must be *allocated* among many possible uses. The organizing of economic affairs *within* the household is a personal problem of its members—and the same applies to the 13 million or so individuals who are independent "spending units."

Governments direct much economic activity. Here, too, the decisions are made by people. For brevity, we often speak of government as some nonhuman thing with a life of its own. Nevertheless, "its" decisions are made, "its" actions are done, by human beings: voters, politicians, civil servants, the military, pressure groups. Humanitarian considerations, national survival, and the meanest greed affect these decisions. Some result from careful comparison of benefit and cost. Most are the outcome of decision making which is more "rough and ready" than refined, if only because there is little way to measure benefit or to forecast the bad effects of taxes. Sometimes there is broad consensus among the public, such as spending for fire protection; at other times a small minority holding the balance of power will force a decision.

When people act through government, they can *coerce* others, force even those who disapprove to "cooperate." Using the police and the courts, lawmakers and administrators can exercise overwhelming power. Much as we may dislike this or that spending or tax policy, as individuals and as groups we may have little choice. Mistakes, poor policies, may continue indefinitely. No guiding economic principle can be expected to explain government economic activity. Noneconomic factors are influential. Yet governments, like families, are by no means independent of the economic forces that more clearly guide the third type, "business."

The function of *business* is just this: organizing to economize. So we now sketch a broad picture. Two aspects of the businessman's job must be distinguished, though they cannot be separated clearly: (1) management in the sense of keeping things running along more or less as they have been going; (2) *entrepreneurship*. The latter involves the undertaking of new things: new products, new techniques of manufacture or raising capital funds, new personnel policies. When a businessman ventures into something new and uncertain, he acts as an entrepreneur. Risk of loss exists but more enticing is the hope of success that will bring higher than normal profit.

The business firm seeks to earn profit by (1) reducing costs and (2) selling to best advantage. Businesses "organize" resource use by selling and buying in markets. These markets give people more or less free opportunity to form and to express their wishes, individually and in groups. The business world, to a great extent, is a world of markets.

Market System Not a Machine. The operations of a market economy are intricate and interrelated, a little like those of the human body; widely varied parts function to serve one another without any conscious determination. Yet the market system is strikingly different from the human body. (1) No central directing system, like the brain, operates. (2) No single set of purposes, like our conscious personal desires, exists to be satisfied; each person (or each business) has his own life and set of purposes. Though the different units depend to varying degree on each other, they are separate entities. (3) These units change not only by replacing something of similar form, like cells of the body, but also by developing new forms. Is it hard to conceive of things operating without some conscious control? Functioning systems—airlines, factories, or ball teams—we may think of as the result of a plan made by human beings to achieve certain more or less specific purposes. The market system is an exception. It functions, but it is not the product of deliberate creation. Economic order results because (or despite the fact) the individual units are themselves independently acting agencies, conscious humans with purposes of their own. These individual units are not machines engineered and guided by the plan of some human director who set up the system.

The market system operates (1) by exchanges of goods (and services) for money, and (2) by the use of money to buy goods and services. Two circuits exist, one for money and one "real" (goods and services). Figure 2–1 illustrates. Members of households work for businesses, providing

FIGURE 2–1.   The Circular Flows Connecting Households and Businesses*

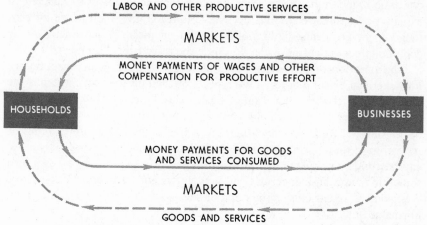

* The place of government is shown in the somewhat different type of diagram of Figure 9–2.

chiefly labor services. In return they receive money, their wages. Businesses use the services to produce things (or other services) which they sell to households for money. Things for money for things for money. " 'Round and 'round it goes," at least when all goes well.

The Meaning of "Market."   What is a "market"? A market may be thought of as a place (an area) in which things are bought and sold. This concept, however, is not broad enough. "The market" is a set of pressures exerted by actual or potential buyers and sellers for a total of *related* transactions. The transactions are related (1) in time, a few minutes in some cases, but a much longer period in others; (2) in area, from a tiny space to most of the world; and (3) in type of item. The variety is enormous. The local market for tickets to a particular sporting event differs from the world market for crude oil or copper. The market for scrap steel may not seem much like the market for waiters in college dining halls or an auction of fine cattle. Relations between transactions, even in identical goods, may be close or distant.

The size of a market depends upon many things. (1) *Transportation costs* are crucial. A reduction in transport costs broadens markets. At one set of freight rates, a factory in Chicago may be able to sell profitably over the entire country, while with much higher rates, its market may be restricted to a few states. Things that cannot be moved, such as real estate, have a circumscribed market. (2) *Communication* is important for much the same reason. The more and better we can learn what others want and what they offer, the larger the number with whom we can deal. Both the want-ad section of a newspaper and the long-distance telephone help people get information. The chances of exchanging goods and services increase as a result of all improvements in facilities for communication. (3) Some markets are larger than others because some products are more *storable*. Markets for fish were once narrowly local, especially in hot weather; refrigeration broadened the market, and quick-freezing widened it still more. (4) *Uniformity of product* affects the size of its market. Worldwide markets can exist in grains, metals, and other products that can be described precisely in technical terms. Dresses, on the other hand, vary so much that the customer usually wants to see the specific garment before buying.

Competition versus Cooperation. The forces in a market are pressures exerted by people with opposite interests. Persons with things to sell are rivals trying to get the best offers from buyers. Sellers, as a group, have interests opposed to those of buyers, as a group. Buyers, in turn, are rivals for the best terms sellers will offer. Here there are clashes, opposed interests, competition. They create a picture that seems different from the cooperation stressed earlier. There *is* a difference. Sometimes the conflict may overshadow the harmony. Opposition of interests, however, serves a constructive purpose. The pressure puts people "on their mettle," tending to force them to serve others better than if there were less pressure. These forces help direct effort and scarce resources to their best uses; such pressure induces us to do what others want most. In other words, in free markets the pressure from interests that oppose each other leads people to contribute more productively.

Impersonality. Cooperation is often enhanced by another feature of the market, its *impersonality*. Buyers and sellers consider chiefly material (economic) gain. Other personal considerations do not greatly modify the result as determined by the best economic judgment. Sentiment alone does not ordinarily lead one to buy at a store where the price is higher; considerations of humanity do not often lead to higher wage rates for widows with dependent children than for unmarried girls doing the same work; we do not choose our meat according to the way farmers vote. The human differences mean much to the people involved and impel most everyone to try harder for better bargains; and sentiment does sometimes guide our purchases and sales. Yet in general, the hard, cold, exacting, and unsentimental facts are final. One result is a simplification of exchange as compared with the embarrassing, time-consuming, and even frustrating problems of buying and selling which often appear in markets where personal factors are important—professional services, for example.

HOW THE MARKET FUNCTIONS

To describe the market process, we simplify, focus on general elements and neglect the multitude having only narrow significance. We learn how blood circulates without studying what goes on in each tiny blood vessel with each pump of the heart.

Consumer "Votes" with His Dollars.   Consumers deciding how to use their income have choices; a stupendous number and variety of things are offered. A walk down Main Street will bring one within a few yards of hundreds of different things for sale for, say, $10 or less. A Sears, Roebuck catalog offers a myriad of ways to spend $100. No household has enough money to buy everything, and it would not want everything. Each buyer must *select* from what is available and within the limits of what he can spend. The urgency of consumers' wants—or the folly of their tastes— leads to priorities. Milk comes before nylons, sometimes; and shoes have priority over cameras. The urgency of wants, however, is not the only consideration. *Price* is another.

The price of a thing measures the amount of other goods one must sacrifice to get it (the opportunity cost). We sacrifice dozens of movies to get a TV set but few new dresses for a sweater. Prices range gradually from item to item and shift constantly; one week apples are cheaper than oranges and later vice versa. If the price of beef seems high and the price of pork low, some consumers who in a sense prefer beef will take pork and have money left for ice cream or shoes. *The relation of prices to one another*, therefore, helps determine what consumers buy. Relative prices compete with relative urgency in determining the specific things on which we spend.

A consumer's buying will range from large amounts for some things (housing), to trivial amounts on others (white shoestrings), and to nothing at all in some years for many products (engagement rings). For each of hundreds of items a certain dollar expenditure results.

The number of dollar "votes" any item gets determines its relative popularity. Some things hardly run in the same "elections"—submarines versus hairdos; others are close rivals—gasoline from neighboring stations. The "elections" go on all the time. Day after day we vote with our money. Dollar votes thus help perform the first of the six functions of an economic system: they show what we want. They show it not vaguely and hesitantly but down to the last penny and as we spend it. With each paycheck we can vote in a new election. And we do. The candidates, goods for sale, must keep renewing their appeal.

The consumer is sovereign, the boss—within limits. His *spending power* limits his sovereignty. Moreover, the frequent change of models and designs (speeding the process by which the familiar item becomes obsolete), the efforts of advertisers, the highly persuasive pressure of sellers, hardly leave the consumer's independence unscathed. And restrictions of many kinds curb his freedom.[1] Yet from a great variety of opportunities we take what suits us best, not what a dictatorial producer has chosen to offer.

Retail Store Managers Transmit News of Consumers' Wants. The retail stores from which consumers buy must constantly replenish the $30 billion or so of inventory on hand at any one time. The stores that have been most successful in meeting consumer choices have the biggest orders to place to keep their shelves stocked. Managers may keep the long-distance telephone wires "hot" getting items in urgent demand, or they may fight off salesmen trying to push things consumers are not buying. The store manager will, himself, react to price. If his suppliers insist upon a higher price, he must judge how an increase will affect buying by his customers; if suppliers offer a price reduction on a slow-moving item, the retailer will buy more if he thinks consumers will be attracted by a lower price. Different suppliers make all sorts of offers—quality, variety, price.

If you were one of the country's 2 million retailers, you would face a host of uncertainties: future styles, the needs for the next Christmas season, your customers' income prospects, the degree to which consumers have stocked up, your rivals' policies. Present and past sales do not give an airtight guide. The consumer's freedom to "vote" in different ways would give you headaches, hope, and opportunity. Using your best judgment, you place orders.

Retailers order from many kinds of suppliers. Grocers, appliance dealers, florists, dress store managers, druggists—all have varied buying arrangements. Middlemen of many sorts provide retailers a rich assortment of services. However, let us assume that the retailer skips the stage served by 505,000 wholesalers, and orders from a manufacturer. (By no means all the 408,000 manufacturers sell directly to retailers.)[2]

Manufacturer's Reaction to the Retailer's Orders. Manufacturers react to retailers' decisions by adjusting outputs (or prices). Many changes are minor—shifting from blue to red finishes. Others are major. Production of some items may stop entirely, output of others may be boosted.

The judgment of what is wise for the manufacturer depends upon two

---

[1] The person in Boston has little choice of swimming pools in Miami Beach; the man who has contracted to buy, sell, or rent has limited his own freedom in some respects in order to enlarge his opportunities in other respects; few of us are free to buy opium or diseased meat.

[2] The rest of the country's 7.9 million nonfarm businesses consist of some 2.6 million service firms, about 900,000 in contract construction, and about 4.4 million "all other."

sets of prices: (1) the prices of what he buys (his costs), and (2) the prices he can get from retailers (his sales). Presumably, he should stop turning out, say, wool dresses if they cost more to produce than the price at which he can sell them. He will increase the output of, say, nylon dresses that promise to sell for more than they cost. His costs for each set of dresses depend upon (*a*) the *quantities* of inputs, materials and productive services he must buy, and (*b*) the *price* of each unit of these materials and services.

Costs, for the most part, are what a producer pays to others for labor, raw materials, machinery. Obviously, he must pay enough to attract them. Just as the consumer of finished products must pay the market price, the manufacturer, as a consumer of raw materials, will have to pay the market price. The employees of the manufacturer, and those who sell him raw materials, are generally free to accept the best offer available. Let us assume that they want as much as they can get. The manufacturer, on the other hand, will want to buy as inexpensively as possible. If some other producer can turn out as good a dress more cheaply, or if high dress prices generally lead women to use more of their money for other things, our manufacturer will suffer.

When the demand for the manufacturer's dresses is increasing, he will need more labor and materials. To attract additional labor, he must pay at least as much as, and probably a bit more than, the labor has been getting elsewhere. He judges what he can afford to pay to get more workers by the price he can get from retailers. If other firms do not meet his offer, and he succeeds in attracting labor and materials to his plant, we conclude that consumers prefer more of his product (dresses) and less of another's (perhaps suits). The shift of productive resources from making suits to making dresses, therefore, is from a point of lower to one of higher usefulness. The shift results (1) if movement is possible, and (2) if manufacturers are able to make their desires known—if there is *freedom* and a *mechanism* letting people know each other's wishes. Price is an important part of the mechanism, giving direction signals.

Choice of Production Methods. Enterprises in active competition are under constant pressure to make another type of adjustment. Each firm's costs depend not only upon what it must pay for material and labor but also upon *how* it uses them. If it can find more efficient ways to operate, it can increase its profit per unit or lower its selling price. Let's assume that it finds how to operate more efficiently and lowers its price. If retailers then cut their asking price, consumers will tend to buy more dresses. Even if retailers do not lower prices to stimulate sales, our manufacturer can benefit as some merchants shift orders to him, the more efficient supplier. Other firms must meet the competition, presumably by adopting the more efficient methods. This process leads to better use of productive resources.

The producer who fails to use the best methods will lose out in rivalry with others. Firms that do not keep up in the race to employ the best methods may be forced to close, as thousands do each year. Some producer adjustments are *technical*, such as the use of a new machine which requires less labor. Such a technical change will be wise only if the saving in labor cost (and possibly others) will pay for the added equipment. Differences in prices of materials also call for adjustment; an electric utility may alternatively shift from coal to oil and then to coal, depending upon the relative prices of the two fuels. The economic system is performing its function of helping show "how" to produce most efficiently. Competition through the market forces business to seek the least expensive methods. Prices help show what are cheapest.

Process of Economizing. This simple description of response to the signals transmitted by the market system illustrates a central problem of "economizing," guiding the use of productive resources toward what is best under the circumstances. (1) Consumer buying guides production by enabling some firms to bid resources away from those producing other things. The output of those things consumers want the most can be increased by sacrificing things they want less. (2) The firms that produce a given item most efficiently can set the pace. They tend to get the orders away from companies that use more resources per unit of output. (3) Within firms, the low-cost methods can be identified and used when prices signal the relative worths of different inputs; resources of highest value are put to the uses of greatest worth; and more plentiful types of productive capacity can be used less sparingly. Thus business firms seeking to maximize their earnings (that is, to make receipts from sales exceed costs by as much as possible) play a crucial part in allocating productive resources.

Nonhuman productive capacity is owned by people who can demand payment for its use. Some machines, buildings, or other property will produce more output than do others. The amount the owner of a piece of property can get for its use will depend upon the output attributable to it. If you are a businessman, the amount you can afford to pay will depend upon what you can get from consumers. If you can use property, say a building on a busy corner, more advantageously for consumers than some other businessman, you can afford to outbid him. Your higher price directs or allocates the property to a use that does more to satisfy consumers. To keep the use of the building, you must match the offers of any other bidder, and, of course, pay the owners what you promise. The hope of getting payments of this sort gives us inducements to use some of our income to acquire wealth which then brings income.

Business Costs as Income: Sharing the Product. Following the circuit, we find that what firms have paid out as production costs are receipts—the income—of those who provided the services that cooperated in production. The retailer's costs are income to his staff and to his suppliers. The manufacturer's costs are income to his employees, to the farmers and miners who supply raw materials, to other manufacturers who provide parts and machines, to governments, and to others. The profits remaining are income to owners.

Income from producing makes up the spending power the community can use as consumers. What each family gets will depend upon (1) the *amount* of productive capacity it sells and (2) the *price* of that productive capacity. The farmer with 100 bales of cotton collects more than one with 50 bales, and the personnel director gets more per month than the office boy. Market competition will drive up the prices of some productive services as consumers want the products of these services more urgently. High demand may also mean more hours of work, and higher income. The families which benefit because of a rise in either rates of pay or hours of work will be able to increase their consumption. As for owners, the more successful a business, the more they can buy out of the profits.

Jobs become more attractive with a rise in the incomes they yield. Newcomers are attracted. Workers are thus getting the signal of what they can do to serve consumers better. Where consumer demand falls, less labor is needed, there is less work, and people tend to shift to the employer who has jobs. In reducing its costs, the business cuts the incomes of employees and suppliers. By adjusting to a decline in consumer demand, however, the firm prevents the still larger drop in the incomes of its employees that would result if it had losses which put it out of business entirely.

The Market and Economic Growth.   So far we have seen how the market transmits news of consumer wants, how it helps indicate which methods of production are most economical, and how it distributes money income. Now we ask: "How does the market help guide decisions about economic expansion?"

Market forces determine the costs of producing new machines and other equipment. The market governs the prices of labor and materials, whether used for producing items for current consumption or for machines which are additions to productive capacity. These costs help the businessman in deciding where and how to expand. Far harder is the problem of estimating the price he can get in the future for what the machine will produce. Today's market cannot answer that puzzler, but it can help. Trends of consumer tastes can be detected and measured, at least roughly. Then business firms and families with income being saved rather than used for consumption can decide where the prospects of future gain seem to justify outlays for expansion.

Deeper forces also operate. Economic growth depends heavily upon the advance of science and of knowledge in all its aspects. The market creates powerful forces for introducing new products and for improving techniques. On the one hand, are rewards for cutting costs or developing something the public wants; on the other hand, the market holds out threats of loss from failure to match successful competitors. The market shows where costs are high, suggests where to concentrate inventive effort, and indicates the more promising lines for developing new products and services to satisfy consumers.

The process of invention and innovation can be made to pay, sometimes fabulously. Success provides a firm with funds to finance not only more research but also the building of new productive capacity. High business earnings signal to investors the places where growth funds should be placed—low earnings tell what to avoid. The amounts firms will pay provide an incentive to investors to make funds available for expansion. In such ways do market forces spur economic growth.

The Process of Adjustment, One of Relatively Small Changes. Most adjustments to changing economic conditions are small. Occasionally, there is a big and sudden change, a sort of economic hurricane. More often, however, changes needed to adjust to new economic forces are small. *A little bit more or a little bit less* will do the trick. A small difference in the size of a shoe or the placing of a forward pass has a large effect on the result. In the same way, a firm having trouble hiring labor will find that meeting competition requires not a drastic, but a modest, increase in wage rates. The constant flux of our economy representing forces of growth, freedom, and natural change, is accommodated in markets by uncounted millions of small movements of prices, materials, people, and property.

Unseen Order in Free Markets: The Invisible Hand. Each day markets relate billions of particular economic transactions. The result is a total which is predominantly orderly, not chaotic. There is system without conscious central direction. Households and enterprises do the reasoning and the planning. They act as seems best but, of course, in an environment beyond their direct control; yet in acting they help change the conditions of that environment. Selfishly we seek our own gain. The best chance of serving ourselves is by doing things for others, things for which they will pay most. Self-interest makes each person serve others. Then, as consumers, as employees, and as investors we insist on choosing the best offered us, thereby putting pressure on others.

Market forces work like an "invisible hand," to use Adam Smith's famous term. Market competition is not "dog eat dog," not governed by jungle law. Unobtrusively the market guides by harnessing and then directing a powerful force, the human motive of self-interest. The myriad of decisions are made by the persons familiar with the conditions involved. The system is not limited to guidance by a few people, a few whose capacities and information could never be great enough to under-

stand more than a tiny fraction of what the millions know. There is order
and direction; there is system and coordination; there is also freedom and
opportunity. Each household and business both limits and reinforces
others, affected to varying degree by restrictions of monopoly, ignorance,
government, lassitude, and some of man's less admirable propensities.
Despite the system's merits, which are far greater than most of us appreciate, neither it as an operating process, nor the results it yields, will meet
our ideals. There is room for improvement—one reason we study economics.

THE MIXED ECONOMY

One of the recurring problems of society involves the extent to which
the public will use government—political institutions—to guide, direct,
and control economic life. In communist lands, government officials make
a large proportion of the economic decisions, especially the big ones.
Elsewhere, the extent and the type of governmental action on economic
matters vary widely. In our country, we use the government more
extensively than in the past. Some of the results of this extension of
governmental activity have served the public interest well; mistakes have
also been made, and not all have been corrected; and in some cases we
have doubtless erred by not making greater use of government.

Economic issues of public policy center largely upon problems of the
"mix" of governmental and nongovernmental (business, household, and so
on) activities. As the economy becomes more complex, the difficulties of
intervening wisely and constructively by using government also increase,
if only because of the impossibility of foreseeing the full results of any
action. For example, ceilings on interest rates payable to the depositor by
savings and loan associations were designed to help them keep expenses
down. But in 1966, by reducing their ability to compete for new savings,
the ceilings aggravated a sudden and drastic drop in funds for mortgage
loans, then in new housing starts, then in work in factories producing
building materials, and so on.

Both private enterprise and government are institutions which exist to
serve us. We and our predecessors have created these institutions. We and
our children can change them. Many changes are proposed. Some would
serve the public interest. Some would not. Which are which? Views will
inevitably differ, but study should help make our answers more rational.
This book closes with some observations on the general problem of using
government to deal with economic problems. From the present point to
the end, we shall examine many specific cases.

Government Essential to the Free Market System.   The market system
could not function without government, as even the staunchest advocates
of free enterprise recognize. Our system mixes government and business.

Sometimes controversies about "government versus business" will mislead by focusing on rivalry. Yet serious issues do arise.

For generations Americans have done some things through the political process and some through markets—without agreement on the best dividing line. The things to be done cannot be separated as clearly as the functions of eyes and ears.

At a minimum, we use government to set certain general rules of law to secure order, the protection of person and property, internal peace, and the judicial settlement of disputes; to hold the power to use force so that private groups cannot coerce and thus threaten the life of efficient cooperation; to define weights and measures; to regulate the monetary system; and in general to fix a framework within which we can carry on our affairs. This function is like setting the rules of a football game and determining how to select and control the officials who are to enforce them; there can be no game until we have done so. The football rule making is a sort of government. A market system must also have rules. It cannot create the basic laws itself, any more than football teams can make the rules as they play. The fundamental laws must apply generally throughout the economy. Otherwise some maverick could abuse his freedom to escape from the regulations. Some coercion (enforced through courts) is essential.[3]

In using the political system to make and enforce these rules, we may do well or poorly, with profound effects on the way we work in markets. For example, if business is to operate efficiently, there must be good laws defining who owns what and how one person can sell what he owns— whether an hour's work, fruit from the orchard, or an office building. Bad laws or bad enforcement will add to the difficulties of exchange and cut the effectiveness with which we work and trade. Good rules—whether of music, traffic, or business dealings—aid mightily.

Extension of Government Activity. *Rule making is an inherent function of government* and one that has great bearing on our economic life. Today, however, Americans do far more through government and political decision making. From 1900 to the late 1960's, government employment (excluding military) rose from 4 to about 14 percent of the total. Governments carry on hundreds of different activities. The relatively new functions range from rule making (regulation of new details of financial markets) to activity that in the past was done by business (running a bus line), and some things once left to charity. The public now looks to government for the performance of some functions that are not inherently governmental.

---

[3] The existence of coercive power makes the open use of the power generally unnecessary. There is power to compel us to pay our bill in the restaurant. Knowing that we can be forced to pay, we do so without feeling coerced.

Judging the results is difficult, partly because the system *is* so thoroughly mixed (not "mixed up"). Petroleum refining seems generally efficient and progressive. It might be more so, and gasoline would certainly be cheaper, were it not for taxes. Yet without vast government spending on highways and streets, what would our oil industry be? Certainly not the giant it has become. When we try to do things through government, we find ourselves helped and hindered by what we do in business. Market forces, for example, may raise wage rates, which government must match, thus increasing what we must pay through taxes for armament or education. Market pressures to economize lead some firms to dismiss workers, creating need for government to provide relief; but the growth of new businesses not only provides more for consumers but also cuts down relief payments by government. The good economy, like a good cake, is a mixture. Perhaps we can get a good product with any of several mixes. So far the bakers—economists, businessmen, politicians—have not agreed on the recipe. Controversy rises and falls. People have different impressions of the efficiency of government. More basic, however, they disagree about the desirability of extending the use of coercion.

TERMS AND CONCEPTS

specialization	market economy	invention
exchange	competition	innovation
entrepreneurship	opportunity	mixed economy
	relative prices	

QUESTIONS

1. Does the businessman's search for profit serve the consumer? Why? The employee?
2. Assume that a retailer finds a cheaper method of operation. What would be the results if he alone could use the process? If all others could do so?
3. Why is it said that competition in a market economy serves as an "invisible hand" promoting the general welfare while each individual pursues his own interests?
4. "One man's gain must be someone else's loss." Discuss. Can both participants in an exchange be gainers? Why?
5. How does specialization increase productivity?
6. How does the function of price as a director of production resemble its function as a guide to economizing in consumption?
7. In an economy without central planning, what keeps the myriads of producing and consuming units working in general harmony?
8. "Although our economy is essentially one of cooperation, it depends upon individual rivalry and opposition of interest to produce the best adjustments." Discuss.

PART 2

RESOURCES AND

BUSINESS

ORGANIZATION OF THE

UNITED STATES

Resources, in the economic sense, are all the factors of production. Included are not only physical things—natural and man-made—but also human beings and the knowledge and institutions, including the mechanisms of government, they have accumulated. Not the least is the organization of business, the establishments that have been developed for production and distribution in the private economy.

3

NATURAL RESOURCES, CAPITAL FORMATION, AND POPULATION

That roundabout methods lead to greater results than direct methods is one of the most important and fundamental propositions in the whole theory of production . . . the kind of production which works in these wise and circuitous methods is nothing else than what economists call Capital Production. . . . And Capital is nothing but the complex of intermediate products which appear on the several stages of the roundabout journey.

Eugen von Bohm-Bawerk

The "resource base" obviously influences what an economy can produce and at what cost. The level of economic welfare attainable depends upon the productive resources available—the gifts of nature, the man-made instruments of production accumulated over the ages (or built last month), and the intangibles of skill and knowledge embodied in human beings.

Americans, today, are marvelously fortunate—the heirs of the ages. Our legacy includes wealth accumulated over untold millennia. Although "wealth" has varied meanings, economists often think of it as *material* or *real*, physical things, but not as a rule the human being. We value them in money terms, being careful not to count both the physical thing and the piece of paper representing its ownership. An individual would consider his bonds and stocks and cash as part of his personal wealth, but economists apply the broader term "property" to include such items and limit "wealth" to underlying material things. Some of the world's resources were *created by nature* alone: oil, copper, and oceans. Some were *made by people* using products of nature: highways, factories, and dentists' drills.

THE GIFTS OF NATURE: NATURAL RESOURCES

The Concept of Natural Resources. The term "natural resources" ordinarily applies to things created by nature and which will help human beings satisfy their wants. The same gift of nature may at one time be a nuisance and at another a "resource" because of changing tastes or technological advance.

By now, however, man has so mixed his efforts with those of nature that things predominantly gifts of nature may have significant elements of man's work. Many of nature's creations do not become "resources" in the sense of being useful to man until he has exerted effort. Thus, although in one vital sense the quantity of basic gifts of nature is fixed, men by their efforts can and do expand their effective command over natural resources. (1) *Exploration* and *discovery* disclose things we had not been using. The earth's surface is well known, but below there may be much of which we are still ignorant: elves or oil or the elixir of life. (2) *New ways of using* resources can increase their economic value. Man has made huge strides forward in learning how to use known resources to his advantage. The end is not in sight. (3) *Trade makes resources available far from where nature left them.* Cheap transportation and the extensive organization of exchange multiply the human usefulness of natural resources. Autos run far from oil wells. Some economic activity must of necessity be carried on where natural resources exist—such *extractive* work as mining, fishing, and farming. Generally, of course, the lower the cost of transport, the greater the economic benefit from gifts of nature. Man can also narrow his effective command over natural resources, for some, in a practical sense, *are exhaustible.* Depletion reduces the amount for future use. Ol' man river keeps rolling along, generation after generation; but the fuel oil that heats our house is gone when it has done its job. Between natural resources that are not exhausted in use (water falling from mountains endlessly) and those that disappear as they are used, like coal, there are others, like soil, whose preservation depends on *how* they are used.

Natural Resources of the United States. Nature has blessed this country. Here, natural resources in the combinations useful to man have been more plentiful *in relation to population* than in most of the world.

First, think how *climate* influences economic life. It shapes our wants—the things we try to buy or to produce. It also affects the capacity to produce. U.S. climate varies widely, but throughout most of the country it is good enough to permit and encourage life, and even vigorous activity. Fighting cold does require effort, yet frost kills insects and breaks the soil. Although at times and places the weather gets hot enough to impede best effort, we do have long hours of sunlight in the growing season. Even if moisture seems to fall at the wrong times—on picnic days or when crops are ripe for harvest—it is adequate to provide for crops and people over large areas. In still larger areas, however, *water* is inadequate for development of the fullest potential; modern industry needs water in prodigious quantities: on the average in all manufacturing, over 1.5 million gallons a year per employee. Industrial usage of water more than doubled in the 1950's and has risen even more rapidly in the 1960's. Some climates are either too hot or too cold, too wet or too dry, to permit or encourage human life in its most productive forms. On the whole, despite personal griping and Chamber of Commerce adulation, our climate is generally neither execrable nor ideal; it is good.[1]

The *cover of the earth's surface* is widely varied: farmland rich and loamy, soil too thin for anything but the most meager of output, barren rocky mountains, miles of sand and desert. Over an area equaling approximately 2 acres per capita, both the soil and the terrain are friendly. Crop farming is possible on a reasonably satisfactory basis. The land then grades off from "good" to a huge variety of types harder to use profitably. Scientific development yields new crops and animals adapted to areas whose earlier value had been far less. Largely unused land provided the basis for cattle production in Florida with development of new grass and cattle types. Vegetation grows in the few feet, or even inches, of *topsoil*, the product of ages of growth and decay. This priceless treasure can be lost by wind or water erosion. Its productive value can be destroyed by *leaching*, draining away of mineral elements by water, and by improper use. Increasingly, farmers are learning what can be done to preserve and enhance the value of the topsoil.[2]

Natural resources on the earth's surface both eased and hampered the development of this continent. Cutting the forests and breaking the sod to make land usable for growing cotton and grain were expensive in time and effort. Yet the lumber was useful for building and for heating. What would our development have been if the settlers had been forced to make brick to build their dwellings and to mine coal to heat them? Animals, birds, and fish were a source of food and clothing.

The *water features* of the earth's surface mold economic life. Rivers do more than take away excess water. With lakes and oceans they provide an

---

[1] One achievement of recent decades has been the partial mastery of climate. Success in inducing rain when we wish is far from complete, but scientists have developed new types of crops that tolerate formerly deadening climate. Air conditioning and building insulation help deal with problems of temperature.

[2] Throughout much of our history land use was often poor. Farmers disturbed the age-old rhythm of nature without improving on it. Great forests east of the Mississippi River were cut—erosion and depletion began. Farther west the long natural grasses were plowed under. Nature, with wind as well as water, began to undo her work of centuries in building useful soil. Tragic dust storms wreaked a terrible vengeance for man's shortsightedness in not protecting topsoil. Yet the picture has improved greatly. Men the world over have found how to make better use of soil, and how, with special fertilizers and crops, to build it to higher economic usefulness. For example, improved ways to use the soft, fast-growing pine of the South brought great promise to areas which were once of slight value.

avenue of communication. This country has been fortunate. Cheap transportation based on water played a large role in our economic development. Major settlements and huge surrounding areas have had at least moderately good water access to the chief economies of the world, notably Europe. A *long coast line* has many excellent harbors. Large eastern *rivers*, such as the Hudson and the St. Lawrence, and many smaller ones, flow directly into the Atlantic; the Mississippi-Ohio-Missouri network makes much of the rest of our economy accessible to the Atlantic community by water.[3] The transportation of iron ore, coal, grain, and some other bulky items relies heavily on the Great Lakes. The Middle West has become closer, economically, to the rest of the world because of the improvement of the St. Lawrence Waterway.

Another aspect of *water* is its *flow*. The tremendous *power of falling water* can be made our servant. The old water wheel has almost disappeared after powering the mills and factories that were our early industries, but the principle remains as rivers are harnessed to generate electricity for business and home. Although by 1967 hydroelectric capacity installed was four times that of 1940, important potentialities remain to be utilized; some in Canada are being developed for sale of power in the United States, aided by improvements in the long-distance transmission of electricity. Such projects are expensive to build, of course, and nature has localized them. Yet, once built, they offer a source of power almost as permanent as the sun's willingness to raise the water again. Sometime, too, winds and the moon's work in creating tides may be made to generate electricity in this country as is already done to some extent in Europe.

Below the earth's surface America has been blessed. The two standbys of industrial civilization—*coal and iron ore*—appear in several parts of the country. Soft coal exists in amounts that will last for centuries, but as the most accessible deposits are exhausted, the costs of mining will depend upon man's speed in improving techniques. Moreover, the *economic* "supply" depends upon *how* a resource is used; electric utilities now average more than three times as much electricity per ton of coal as in 1920, and new plants do much better than the average. High-quality, cheaply used iron ore will not last long. Lower qualities are plentiful, however, and new techniques make their use feasible; moreover, excellent iron ore can be imported. Though we have "picked the apples we can reach from the ground," the prospects are not discouraging.

For heating, for operating machines and autos and planes, for lighting, and for so many other purposes we rely on fuel (and water power). Figure 3–1 shows how per capita consumption rose in 46 years. Even

---

[3] In an economic sense, the Erie Canal cut distances from the West (then) to the Atlantic and to Europe to a tiny fraction of what they had been. The Mississippi system now carries far more river freight than in the romantic era of paddlewheelers.

FIGURE 3–1.   Consumption of Fuel and Water Power, 1920 and 1966

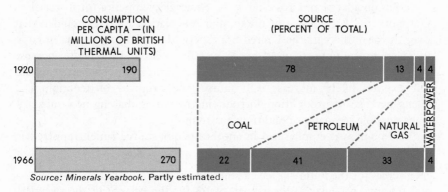

Source: Minerals Yearbook. Partly estimated.

more striking has been the change in sources. *Oil and natural gas* are indeed pillars of modern civilization. In some respects they are superior to coal—drawn from the earth more easily and humanely, often easier and cheaper to transport and handle, and convenient for powering moving vehicles. Several regions yield these fuels, and our use has been, and is, heavy. It is profligate? Are we exhausting limited resources recklessly, like the drunken sailor his bankroll? For at least another decade, oil and natural gas will be available to meet projected needs at about present costs.

Copper, essential for an age of electricity, and bauxite, the ore from which aluminum is made, exist in large quantities; sulfur, though reputedly one of Satan's standbys, is an angel of an industrial society; the United States has its own good supplies. Zinc, lead, uranium, silver, gold, several other metals, and elements for fertilizers are also mined here. The conditions of cost, the extent of unmined reserves, the possibilities of new discoveries vary considerably.

What about metals and other natural resources scarce or nonexistent in this country? Some are essential for alloys and processes that are highly valuable, even critical, for things we consider vital, including armaments. Tin, chromium, nickel, mercury, industrial diamonds, manganese, cobalt, mica, asbestos, quartz, and at least two dozen others fall in this class. A few, such as cobalt, we seem to use very little; but much of our life depends upon them. In a peaceful world, deficiencies within our borders would not worry us seriously. We could count upon offsetting them by trading something we can produce.[4] In case of war, however, such trade might become dangerous or impossible. Here again we are lucky because Canada and Mexico produce some important things we lack; federal stockpiles of storable items also give protection.

[4] The vigorous growth of Britain's economy before World War I did not rest primarily on her natural resources; she imported on a large scale. Nor does Switzerland's prosperity today rest on rich gifts of nature.

Our Changing Resource Position. The United States imports raw materials on a large and growing scale. America's "appetite for materials is Gargantuan." A 1960 National Planning Association study concluded that over the next 20 years the United States would require large or very large increases in the imports of 14 major raw materials and moderate increase in 7. Only for three products (coal, molybdenum, and phosphates) would our exports likely increase. Of course, the progress of technology—changing costs of production, introducing new uses, making new substitutions possible—can alter conditions profoundly.

This point was emphasized in another major study, which reported in 1963:

[Resources for the Future's] recent study of the adequacy of natural resources and resource products in the United States for the balance of the twentieth century suggests small likelihood of any widespread, continuing scarcities. This generally optimistic conclusion . . . , however, is based on three large assumptions: (1) a reasonably free flow of world trade, (2) improvements in social and political arrangements to keep pace with changing situations, and (3) continuing gains in technology of resource production and use. The last of these vital provisos—technological advance—pervades the whole system of forty-year projections of demand and estimates of supply, and the details of working it through are as elusive as they are important.[5]

A changing resource need that bears directly on the quality of life is the growing demand for outdoor recreation areas. An expanding population with rising income wants space in great variety to enjoy increasing leisure and mobility: parks for the annual vacation, open beaches for summer weekends, playgrounds around the corner for after school. Postwar years have witnessed huge increases in use of state parks and national forests and even larger growth in the recreational use of natural and artificial bodies of water. Congress and some states have provided funds for enlarging the areas to be available in the future. The Wilderness Act of 1964 set aside millions of acres of public lands to remain in their natural state and, along with other laws, provided for purchase and development of other land for recreation—to a total addition of some 54 million acres.

Tradition of Using Natural Resources. Despite gaps, our heritage of natural resources has been generous. Yet the American Indians "had" the same resources. The contrast between their economy and ours should demonstrate that much depends upon how resources are used. Use is a complex of people, scientific techniques, and organization.

By and large, Americans have preferred to use natural resources rather than save them for the future. The speed of our economic development has rested partly on this willingness to use—to "use up"—the heritage of nature. The public, through the federal government, which once owned

[5] Resources for the Future, *Annual Report . . . 1963* (Washington, D.C., 1963), p. 13.

most of our country, sold or gave away the land and with it the mineral, timber, and water rights.[6] Thus came private ownership and with it generally unrestricted free use. The owners focused chief interest on prompt development. Freedom was joined with the opportunity created by an expanding market. Americans used natural resources freely.

Were they shortsighted, neglecting the interests of future generations? Sometimes yes. But they built railroads, factories, cities, and farms, *using* natural resources. Individual freedom doubtless resulted in both stupid and brilliant decisions, crass waste and canny foresight. It is easy to look back and see cases in which more conservation would have been wise, at least for us today. The "invisible hand" led to destinations which now seem dead ends. The "hand" guiding owners of timberland to cut rapidly did not require them to include in their costs the damage resulting from floods hundreds of miles away, floods that might not have come if the trees had stood to hold the rains. Yet, judging whether, on balance, the job was done well requires knowledge of "might have beens" that we do not have. This we do know: Private and widely dispersed ownership encouraged rapid use, whether we call it "development" or "exploitation."

Gradually, public and private action have evidenced more concern for conservation: government payments to farmers to preserve their land, stricter rules to reduce the "uglification" caused by strip mining, restrictions by Texas on the amount of oil that may be shipped out of the state (proration), business concern to preserve its sources of supply, use of scrap, and other economizing measures. Meanwhile, pollution of rivers by some private businesses and communities creates new problems for downstream users—business or consumer. Pollution can be prevented but at a cost which those responsible for the evil are not always willing to undertake. Governmental regulations, financial aids, and active participation to deal with pollution are getting under way.

How can we learn what is best? The consumer of the year 2068 cannot express his preferences in the market of 1968. Even the most conscientious and foresighted—teachers, government officials, business leaders, scientists—have little basis for comparing present costs and benefits with the values of a distant future. Clearly, however, anything to cut costs and raise efficiency today will help make limited resources serve longer.

MAN-MADE PRODUCTIVE CAPACITY: CAPITAL FORMATION

Our economic inheritance includes "capital goods," man-made productive capacity. "Capital," like "wealth," is a term of varied meanings. In this section we shall use it to mean physical productive capacity made by man

---

[6] Some legal systems provide that minerals (including oil) under the surface belong to the government, not to the owner of the land. Relatively late, our federal government began to reserve certain mineral rights; it still owns a huge public domain, including mineral rights, whose value is unknown but large enough to cause many a "developer" to seek permission to explore and extract.

(using natural resources, of course) and not, as is common in the business world, as dollars and financial accounts. Machines and other such equipment obviously account for much of the difference between our use of natural resources and that of the American Indians. Machines multiply fabulously man's power over nature. In looking now at some of the economic problems of this part of our inheritance, we do not seek to inventory what exists but to look at the economic processes of building and using man-made productive capacity, to sketch advantages and to examine the obstacles that must be overcome, and some of the problems.

Machines and "Roundabout" Production. Today's consumption depends upon production yesterday—and for untold thousands of yesterdays. Some of what man produces today he consumes at once, some in the near future, and some in far distant years. A part may not be consumed at all. What is created and not consumed is added to the stock of wealth.

Primitive men had tools which helped them get more from nature. Gradually, the tools were improved, new ones developed. Houses, ships, and then simple machines were built. Productive capacity grew. More time could then be spared from meeting the insistent demands of daily living, and some people were willing to forego producing for current needs to build tools with which to produce more later. The process fed itself; the more and better the tools, the easier it was to produce a living and the greater the time that could be spent in adding to and improving productive equipment. "Taking thought for the morrow" brought bigger and bigger "payoffs." The process of *indirect* or *roundabout* production began to create the cumulative results that were eventually to give the ordinary worker power over nature that hundreds of Pharoah's slaves could not have matched. The best way to catch fish may be roundabout, to build a net; the best way to move food, in the long run, may be to build steel mills that make railroads possible. The fishnet, the steel mill, the railroad are capital equipment. It is easier to have Kansas wheat for our breakfast toast shipped by railroad than to walk to Kansas for it; to get shoes which are stitched by automatic machinery than to stitch them ourselves. Obvious, but not inevitable. Tools do not just happen.

Men must learn what can be done and then do it. Scientific knowledge is not easily mastered and expanded, a conclusion which is not news to college students. Moreover, formidable economic obstacles cannot be wished or voted away. Even Aladdin's lamp had to be rubbed.

Saving Necessary for Capital Formation. The material equipment that science proves to be technically possible becomes available as people build it. The building process is like planting an orchard to bear fruit for many years. The effort creates something not available for consumption now. Yet the laborers must consume every day; hence part of what the economy produces now must be made available to the men building for the future. The men who built about $800 billion of housing and other construction from 1946 to 1968 did not eat the buildings, nor did they starve. To add to its capital equipment, the economy must produce more than it consumes. Think of the difference between what it produces and what the economy consumes as *saving*. The process of adding to productive capacity is *capital formation;* the thing created is real *capital.*

One aspect of economic specialization is that the men who build the equipment, or those who buy to use it later, are not necessarily those who do the saving. The farmer who digs his own drainage ditches and the man who builds his own garage invest their own effort. They save as they work to produce something they do not consume currently. As a rule, however, people save and then invest indirectly. We get money income, spend somewhat less, and either buy capital equipment ourselves (a house) or hand over our savings, the money, to someone who will buy a new building or machine. Like other features of the division of labor, this process sometimes gets out of gear; but without it the advance of capital formation would be much slower.

The process of capital formation requires not only saving but also confidence in "property rights." Security against theft and wanton destruction is basic. Without it, accumulation will lag.[7] In addition, the owner, whether an individual, a group, or a government, must have confidence in the benefits of possession. True, the rights of an individual in his property are not absolute; and some are more important than others. For example, it is less vital that I be able to count upon continuing to use my house than that I know that if it is taken from me (perhaps for a new highway) I shall be compensated. The bundle of property rights which attach to a thing—a factory or a bank or a pair of shoes—will vary from time to time and place to place. The size and the nature of that bundle must influence the sacrifices which men will make to create such property and make it available for use by others, in housing, factories, school buildings, or electric power systems.

How much of its output can an economy devote to adding to its productive facilities? No single fraction can apply generally. No country can use more steel than it produces or can import. Nor can it devote all its current production to provision for later years; just to live "on the scale to which we have become accustomed" takes most of what we produce. The poorer the economy, of course, the less of its production it can spare for the future. In India and other lands where income per person is under $100 a year, the average family is not *able* to save enough to add much to its productive equipment. Moreover, people must be not only able, but

---

[7] The city riots of 1967 and earlier years gave a sampling of tragic and utterly wasteful destruction of property. One of the basic elements of modern life, one we have generally been able to take for granted, was shown to be more vulnerable than we had assumed—confidence in protection against wanton violence. At the very least, it seems, we must now incur greater cost as a precaution against recurrence.

also *willing*, to sacrifice and work for the future. The more they choose to consume now, the less they can add to their capacity for future increases in consumption.

Selecting the Capital Goods to Add. Money saved and hoarded in an old mattress does not help build machines so that mattresses can be made more easily. Putting the savings to use is itself a job. Machines, houses, and other productive capacity are obviously not all the same. Some are more valuable than others, and the "economizing" job is to select the best. New buggy factories are hardly needed today. A new railroad between cities already connected by railroads which have unused capacity might be wasted. Such possibilities present no real problems of choice. Others are tougher. Should we try to meet housing needs by concentrating on single-family dwellings or apartments? Is a more efficient rayon mill as desirable as a new power plant? Would a computer pay?

How can such questions be answered? Engineers, builders, and other technicians can tell what is possible physically, showing how one possibility compares with another in physical accomplishment. The market tells the prices of these different things. Businessmen can compare the alternatives in dollar terms and select those that seem most promising. But the benefits will appear in the future. Present prices are not a trustworthy guide to the years ahead. You probably do not know what you will be doing 5 years from now; yet you will then need capital equipment (directly and indirectly) which must be started now. Both business and governmental predictions of human behavior can go far wrong. New Jersey Turnpike traffic estimates were made carefully; yet in 1952, a few months after the highway was opened, traffic had reached the estimate for 1957. The second largest auto company spent around $250 million to introduce a new car in 1957 only to find few buyers. Clearly, the selection of how best to use savings to build for the future must be a puzzle.

In purchasing $550 billion of new equipment and buildings for business use in the 10 years through 1967, American businessmen made decisions of all qualities. Yet even if there were many errors, the gross total—over $10,000 per nonfarm, nongovernment worker—more than made up for wearing out; productive capacity grew tremendously.

Capital Equipment Must Be Preserved. Man-made productive capacity, including housing, is not immortal or even self-maintaining. Like natural resources, usefulness for further production may disappear. Unless the economy is to retrogress economically, we must preserve this wealth. Machines wear out, like a pair of shoes. For years there may be no perceptible change, then parts go wrong, and eventually the whole thing gets to be too expensive to use; some deteriorate beyond redemption. This loss of value, wearing out, is depreciation. For the country as a whole, excluding government property, the 1968 total will rise above $80 billion.

Some things have long productive lives—apartments and well-built dams; others wear out much more quickly—trucks. Obviously, however, one can delay the wearing out by care in use and repair. Such maintenance takes effort and resources. A society that does not provide this maintenance will be like an individual who uses a little of what he has saved in the past to help pay his current expenses. He then has less property to bring him income. For a while the change in his income may seem small. But gradually, and then with increasing speed, the deterioration of his position will become apparent. Temporarily, during a war or a depression, an economy may actually consume more than it produces, drawing on capital by failing to maintain it fully. Every month of such capital consumption reduces the powers of recuperation. Even the best maintenance will not keep things working in good order forever (though a solid building may serve for centuries). Replacement becomes necessary.

Growth of Knowledge Increases Productive Capacity.   An important aspect of man-made productive power is knowledge. In one respect productive capacity, natural or man-made, is something like a developing mind. The physical elements may change constantly without expanding; yet the usefulness may grow and grow. As our knowledge expands, improvements in capital equipment become possible. A relatively small investment in equipment for Centralized Traffic Control permitted some railroads to get almost as much use out of a single track as others got from two. New techniques for producing aluminum save more electricity each year than used in Connecticut or Iowa. New controls on an automatic machine increase its output (and incidentally enlarge the output from a given building and land). Things that wear out are replaced by better ones that require about the same labor and materials. The constant change of the world of capital equipment is not "machine-for-the-same-machine" but "machine-for-a-better-machine."

Technological change, as noted earlier, also influences the use of natural resources, sometimes by improving, modifying, and extending techniques already in use, sometimes by radically new departures. Science creates new needs for some things and makes old ones disappear. The demand for uranium zoomed when the atomic bomb proved successful. Plastics replace some metals; synthetic fibers replace cotton, silk, and wool in many uses. No one can be certain about the relative values of different natural resources a decade or a generation from now. Fortunately, a flexible economy can adjust, replacing one thing with another in the production process.

If copper becomes more expensive, other things are substituted for some of its uses. Perhaps science will find vast new uses for plentiful natural resources: for the ocean, the repository of untold, but heretofore relatively unusable, wealth; for silicon, the substance which makes up most of the earth's surface but which we use relatively little as a raw material (for bricks, some other building materials, and glass); for air, whose oxygen and nitrogen we already use commercially and whose movement, as wind, has much unused power; for sunlight, whose heat and power may have vast unused potentialities. Yet we must not act on a romantic belief that science will find ways to save us from all troubles; we do better to conserve, not penuriously but cautiously.

One of our most valuable heritages is the emphasis on improvement, plus the facilities for directing and controlling such progress. More than ever before, we have machines for making machines. Inventors are less restricted than in the past by the physical limitations of what the community can do with their ideas. Today's scientist knows that if he devises something very complicated and delicate, industry can probably make it. The opportunity to use new knowledge profitably adds stimulus to research. The process builds on itself cumulatively. The tremendous productivity of invention has impressed itself so dramatically that we spend huge sums to increase the creativeness of capital and natural resources.

The fruits of discovery come more quickly and more broadly because business accepts change. Competition requires the businessman to take advantage of improvements which technical advance makes economically possible. As a result, however, skills, methods, and equipment are anything but permanent, always in danger of becoming obsolete. Thus a major source of benefit to the public as a whole is a source of risk to some who have sunk money in investment goods and time in developing skills.

How Much Man-Made Productive Capacity Have We?   Items of man-made equipment cannot be listed in a meaningful way, nor can we measure them by any fully satisfactory means. Think of trying to add sorority houses, bridges, oil refineries, telephone exchanges, and the myriad of other things in physical terms—pounds or length or cubic contents—to get a total. The significant thing about capital equipment is not some common physical characteristic. The vital aspect is "worth," a "value" feature—the measure of how much something helps men get what they want. This feature, however, varies according to what the thing can do, what else is available, and what people want. A house in a deserted mining town may have no value. A smooth-running machine may be worth little if a much better one is available. Relatively new factories for making sulfa drugs became worth little as penicillin appeared in quantity. Worth itself is hard to measure, especially for things seldom bought or sold, such as a chemical plant built to minute specifications a few years ago. Fortunately, dollar estimates can be suggested. The American people own wealth (including land but not subsurface resources) worth around $2.5 trillion, as follows:[8]

[8] Detailed estimates for 1958 by Dr. R. W. Goldsmith appear in the *Statistical Abstract*. The figures in the text above are *Finance Magazine's* extensions to 1966 of Dr. Goldsmith's estimates. The range of possible error is large; hopefully, the

Houses, factories, and other structures, including government	$1,220 billion
Producer's durable goods (machines, tools, railroads, etc.)	285
Consumer durable goods (autos, furniture, etc.)	290
Nonfarm land	300
Inventories (goods in process and waiting to be sold)	180
Farmland and forests	110
Gold and silver	14
Foreign investment, net	50

Looking beyond the dollars to the real things which count, we would see, if our vision would permit, a huge and varied total of productive capacity. Some of it represents the very best that man has ever produced, unbelievably productive facilities. Some, one would think, should have been junked long ago—the slums of many cities. In between lies much which is excellent and also much which falls far short of the best. American industry has not replaced older with newer equipment as rapidly and as thoroughly as some of us probably assume. For example, the average age of business plant (buildings) in 1967 was nearly 24 years; equipment averaged almost 10 years in age. Around one fifth of all machinery and other equipment was over 15 years old, while nearly 45 percent of all plant was over 20 years old.

About 15 percent of the total gross production of our economy is capital equipment, including housing and additions to inventory—around $120 billion in 1968. The net addition in 1966 was approximately $54 billion, $270 per capita or somewhat over $700 per person in the labor force. The rest was replacement.

Another approach is to figure how much, on the average, we have to work with in the form of physical productive capacity. There is a range from almost nothing (the paper delivery boy who does not have a bicycle) to vastly more than most people can save in a lifetime. Figure 3–2 shows a few averages; the amounts include financial assets as well as physical wealth. In large manufacturing firms, recent expansions have generally cost over $20,000 per job, often very much more.

One measure, physical rather than financial, is the *power at our command*. As our bodies burn food, they release energy we can use to work (or play). Yet the energy released by the burning in our body is not all we can command. The burning of coal, oil, or other fuel, the work of sun, wind, and moving water create energy which can be made to work for us. Machines permit us to harness power so burning oil or falling water can

---

generalizations of magnitude are "in the right ball park." Military and naval supplies are not included. See Wealth Inventory Planning Study, The George Washington University, *Measuring the Nation's Wealth . . . Joint Economic Committee* (New York: Distributed by Columbia University Press for National Bureau of Economic Research, 1964).

not only relieve our muscles but vastly add to their strength and speed. The greater the nonhuman power at our command, the greater, generally, our control over nature. From the Asian peasant today, to a worker in a modern factory or the American housewife, the gap between the power available is tremendous. Few southern plantation owners ever had slaves

FIGURE 3–2.   Assets per Employee, Selected Industries*

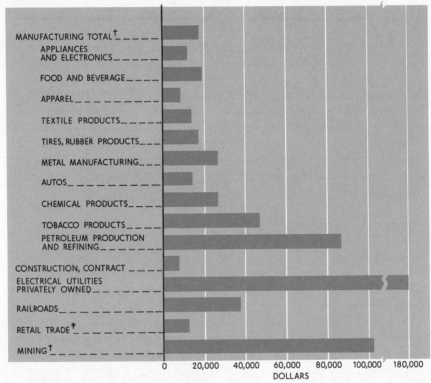

* Incorporated firms. Estimates, for 1966, indicate orders of magnitude only and have varying margins of error.
† Medians of firms among the 500 largest.
‡ If unincorporated firms were included, the total would be around $10,000.
Sources: Statistics of Income, Statistical Abstract, and Fortune.

whose combined power could equal that aiding the average American worker—tens of thousands of horsepower-hours from electricity alone each year. The development of *electricity* has been revolutionary, not only in the *amount* of power we get from it but also in the *kind* or quality. It is flexible, movable, without bulk, easy to control, for most purposes vastly superior to mechanical power relying on rigid shafts, gears, and moving belts. Commercial and industrial use of electricity per employee grew fivefold from 1940 to 1967. Figure 3–3 shows the growth of our per capita use of electricity over 47 years.

FIGURE 3–3.   Electricity Produced in the United States per Capita, 1920–67, Selected Years* (In Kilowatt-Hours)

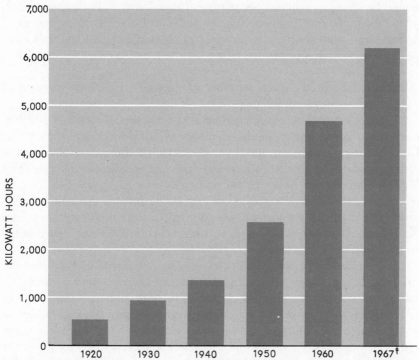

* Includes power generated by industrial establishments for their own use. From 1940 to 1967 residential use rose from 16 to around 30 percent of the total, but industrial and commercial usage increased eightfold.
‡ Partly estimated.
Source: Edison Electric Institute, *Statistical Yearbook of the Electric Utility Industry* and *Survey of Current Business.*

POPULATION: QUANTITY AND "QUALITY"

Economic activity is by and for *people*. We are concerned with natural resources, capital equipment, and all other issues because they are problems of human beings—those who live, love, hope, and fear, and those who are as yet unborn.

Why Economics Considers Population.   When studying America's resources, you may have thought: "But my parents and their friends are not rich. Who owns this treasure? How many people must share these resources?" Or "How is population related to income, wealth, and material progress?" Obviously, average well-being must depend upon the number of people who must share the heritage.

In the best sense possible, people are "resources." What they are and what they can do productively have a decisive influence on the way they can live and develop. Though people are *the end*, they are also *a means*. "Ill fares the land where wealth accumulates and men decay." Even truer would be "Wealth will not accumulate if men decay." The achievements of an economy rest upon the *quality* and *number* of its members. Economics deals with people but not quite as religion, psychology, medicine, or other such studies of man.

Significance of the Total Number of People.   The sheer *number* of people vitally affects their living.

1. There can be *so few* in a group that little specialization is possible. Each must do so many kinds of things that few develop high skills. Consequently, trade, to draw on the specialization, is difficult; the "jacks-of-all-trades" will produce little that appeals greatly outside. The United States is not likely to suffer in this way. In many localities, of course, some skills of great value cannot be developed. A small community may be able to support no specialist in endocrinology or patent law. Knowledgeable advice, however, will often be available not many hours travel away.

2. There can be *so many* bodies to be housed, fed, and clothed that the productive and living resources available are spread thinner than the butter on a roadhouse sandwich. A family with four children can get fewer things per person from the father's earnings than a family with one child. And a half-billion fathers sharing existing natural and man-made resources cannot have as much per father as if there were only a quarter billion. Space per person, not only in large cities, shrinks as population grows; this process tends to make living less satisfactory.

3. No one knows what population total would permit the optimum or highest average level of material satisfaction. Do such considerations seem unworthy? They certainly affect humanitarian achievements. The needs of the orphanage and old-people's home depend upon the number of orphaned children or aged. However one evaluates spiritual issues, mankind has few economic problems greater than those presented by population growth.

The Malthusian Doctrine.   The famous Malthusian doctrine provides a starting point.[9] Its essence is that the impulses driving people to have children are much more powerful than the ability of the earth to support increased population. The number of humans will tend to grow, but (assuming that other things, especially technology, are the same) the added hands will find less productive land (resources) to use to create income. Average income will fall remorselessly. There is, however, a level below which income cannot fall and remain: the level that will maintain

---

[9] T. R. Malthus was an English clergyman deeply impressed by the poverty of mankind. His *Essay on the Principle of Population* (1798) remains a classic.

life. If population increases until average output is below subsistence, misery will deepen into tragedy; starvation and illness will relentlessly kill until population numbers are down to a level the economy will support.

Malthus was more specific. He said that there is a *tendency* for population to grow by *geometric* progression 2, 4, 8, 16, and so on. A husband and wife, say, have not two children, just replacing themselves, but four; these four will not merely replace themselves but will have eight children. So it will go, if unchecked. In about a century, then, each human would have only one sixteenth as much of the earth's surface to farm as his ancestors. Malthus then suggested that food production would increase at an arithmetic progression 2, 4, 6, 8, and so on, a much slower rate. Why the gap? Because of the "law of diminishing returns." Briefly, the "law" is that (with the existing state of production techniques) as more and more of one productive resource (here labor) is used with a fixed quantity of another productive resource (here land), the extra additions to output will eventually get smaller and smaller. Table 3–1 and Figure 3–4 illustrate

TABLE 3–1. Diminishing Returns*

Units of Land	Units of Labor	Units of Output	Output per Unit of Labor (Average)	Output Added by Extra Unit of Labor
1	1	10	10	10
1	2	24	12	14†
1	3	36	12	12
1	4	44	11	8
1	5	50	10	6
1	6	54	9	4
1	7	56	8	2

* Assuming given techniques and no change in capital equipment.
† At this stage returns are increasing. Diminishing returns begin with the addition of the third unit of labor.

the principle. Added workers have less with which to work. For each new mouth there will be two more hands but no more land. No matter how much effort we may put into the cultivation of a flowerpot, we cannot produce the world's food supply in it.

Malthus himself pointed out that war, pestilence, famine, and disease operate as positive checks to keep population from increasing at the geometric rate at which he said it tended to grow. Yet his figures bring out boldly the central thesis: Mankind following its natural instincts will tend to increase in numbers much more rapidly than it can raise production (in the absence of increased resources or improved techniques). The number competing for work increases, and eventually they cannot get more in food, housing, and other necessities than the minimum that will support life—not because of the greed of employers, but because there simply would not be sufficient production. Living standards and wage levels, therefore, will hover at the margin of subsistence.

Admittedly, mankind could limit the growth of population. Young people could delay marriage, and after marriage they might exercise "moral restraint." Moreover, abortion and infanticide, horrible "solutions," are possible. (Modern methods of controlling conception were, of course, unknown.) Malthus remained gloomily pessimistic—and economics was tagged the "dismal science."[10]

FIGURE 3–4.   Diminishing Returns

As more employees are used, the output per worker rises for a time; then it begins to fall and eventually becomes negative. Nonlabor factors of production are assumed to be fixed. An improvement in technology permits an upward shift in the whole curve.

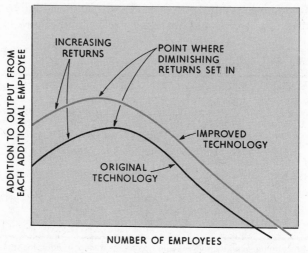

For over a century after 1800, the population of Europe and America, and then Asia and Africa, grew tremendously. The great increase in world population—from about 840 million in 1800 to 3.4 billion in 1968—has depended heavily upon a drop in death rates. Over large areas, birth rates actually declined. The average person lives longer. Allowing for differences in the ages of our population, U.S. death rates have fallen to less than half the rate in 1900. Medicine has taught men how to reduce the killing power of many diseases; improved economic welfare has helped us finance better medical treatment. Cleanliness and relatively inexpensive medicines work wonders. The reduction in infant and child death rates has been astounding. Half a century ago the death rate of U.S.

[10] Karl Marx's theories of the doom of capitalism rest partly on the Malthusian population predictions. Yet socialist and communist writings have proposed no generally uniform method of dealing with a tendency of population to grow more rapidly than productive capacity.

children under a year old was over 5 times that today; for children from one to four the rate was 14 times as high.

Most of mankind faces a population pressure much like that Malthus predicted. Hundreds of millions live at the margin of subsistence. Mouths increase more rapidly than food production, bodies faster than housing; and meager incomes provide little surplus for saving for capital formation. Death rates are falling. In the 20-year period ending in 1954, crude death rates fell by the following percentages:

Pacific Islands	60	Mexico	40
Greece	57	India	39
Japan	48	Egypt	31
Chile	43		

Yet, with few exceptions, deaths rates throughout the world remain much above those where incomes are highest. And modern medicine is spreading, working its miracles. For example, in Ceylon and Formosa, death rates from Malaria dropped over 95 percent in 4 years. One billion more humans are now alive than when Hitler marched into Poland in 1939.

Although one part of Malthus' prophecy was fulfilled in Europe and America, the other proved wrong. The number of mouths multiplied many times, but living standards rose. Where was Malthus wrong? In his underestimate of the potentialities for increasing production! Rich new lands remained to enlarge food output. Improvements in transportation enabled people in densely settled areas to eat food grown far away; science helped increase the yield from older areas. In the expansion of industry, man continually added to his ability to produce. Diminishing returns did not operate so terribly; *man-made productive resources expanded continually;* and the knowledge of technology and organization grew far beyond the dreams of Malthus.

For more than two decades population in the Western world expanded very rapidly, not so much because of a decline of *death* rates as a startling rise of the *birth* rate after 1940—the "population explosion." Why? Economic prosperity helps explain why a bigger percentage of young people are married. Prosperity may also help explain why families feel they can afford more children, and why they can provide better medical care. Yet the number of births depends upon many things other than economics: religion, medicine, custom, intimately personal feelings. Late in the 1950's, the birth rate began to drop and (adjusting for ages of women) in 1967 was one fourth below that of 1957 but still above the 1940 level. The stupendous growth in population will create economic conditions inconceivable 30 years ago. The increase in U.S. population from 1947 to 1967 exceeded the 50 million in all of Italy. Our annual growth of 3 million is nearly one sixth of all Canadian population. For the whole world, Professor H. H. Villard points out, continuation of the present rate of increase would, in a period equal to that since the first permanent settlement in this country, lead to a total population of about 300 billion—a 110-fold increase. Try to imagine the problems, not of 250 years but of 50, if, as now seems indicated, world population has more than doubled.

Prospect. Millions of families must expect difficult strain as the economic cost of raising and educating children appears in fuller force. As a whole, this country must provide much more housing, food, school facili-

FIGURE 3–5.   Population Growth since 1900: Projections to 1985

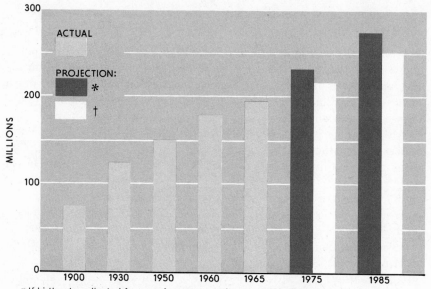

* If birth rate, adjusted for age of women, continues at 1962–65 level.
† If birth rate, adjusted for age of women, falls by about one fifth.
Source: U.S. Bureau of the Census. Estimates for July 1.

ties, and other items of consumption or see the average level of living decline. By 1985 our population will probably exceed 265 million, a growth in 20 years half as large as the total population at the end of the war (Fig. 3–5). Census projections for the year 2000 range from 283 to 358 million. We must produce more just to stay where we have been, on the average, not only for consumption but also for production. In the 10 years through 1975, the *labor force* (the number of people working or seeking work) will increase about 1.6 million a year. New workers will need tools and raw materials—huge amounts—merely to produce as much as the average person today. Such demands will weigh heavily.

Other economic problems will result from *changes in age distribution.* The needs and wants of infants differ from those of older people. The surge of births of the late 1940's created a big demand for diapers, comics, schools, summer camps, and colleges. The demand for higher education, autos, wedding rings, apartments, and furniture is now with us but far from its culmination. The diaper round is again on the way, but how big will it be? School boards and businesses alike face a perplexing job of prediction.

The pressure on public schools will relax as numbers in primary grades actually fall in most communities and the growth in high school ends in many places and slows down elsewhere. College crowding, however, will keep on because the wave of that age group moves ahead. A new baby

FIGURE 3–6.   Growth in Population, U.S. and Key European Countries (Indexes, 1965 = 100)

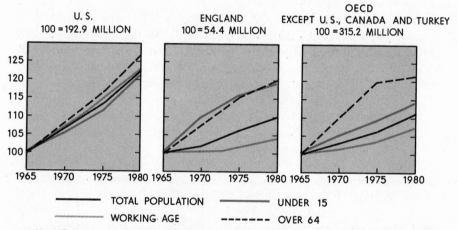

Note: Projections by Organization for Economic Cooperation and Development. The OECD consists of all countries of Western Europe except Finland but including Greece and Turkey; Canada; Japan; and the United States. Population excludes migration. Data as of January 1 of years shown.
Source: OECD.

boom must lie before the country as the number in the 18 to 34 age group zooms upward. Household formation in the 1970's will greatly exceed that of the 1960's; young families are heavy spenders and for rather different kinds of "product mix" than the things purchased later in life. Labor markets will feel the influx of people in their twenties. But how many of the women will work and for how many years?

Figure 3–6 compares the relative changes in population by age group to 1980 for this country, England, and others in the Organization for Economic Cooperation and Development. All three sets of curves show that the proportion over age 64 will rise more rapidly than the total but strikingly faster in the other countries. Our working-age population will rise at a rate just slightly above that of the total, but in the others the growth in the proportion of potential producers will lag. Our group under age 15 will go up less than in proportion to the total population; in England the increase of children will be very much, and in the others somewhat, faster than the total; and children, remember, are consumers but not producers.

Businesses, governments, and all of us now have current population figures which can be used to prepare for the future on the basis of what has happened up to now. No one knows how many children you will have in the next decade, but we can estimate how many of your generation, your parents', and your grandparents' will be alive over the coming decades. The probable growth in the numbers at the middle and the upper end of the age scale is not hard to predict because only the death rate is involved. Clearly, *many more older people*—5 million more over age 65 in about 15 years—must be supported.

Yet numbers are only part of the problem—all football teams have 11 men. What will be the health, vigor, and desires of the aging population? How many will need wheelchairs in sunny climates, and how many will want to keep producing in their jobs? Medical science may make as profound a change in our concept of age as it has in infant death rates. Older people, it is said, consume but do not produce. True, but who is "older"? Will the nonproductive group be those over 65 or 70 or 75? In terms of the burden on the rest of the economy, the difference between 65 and 70 would be momentous. The potential working force also depends upon the proportion of women, as well as men, of all ages who seek jobs. The percentage of women working outside the home has risen for many decades. This increase has just about offset a drop in the percentage of men wanting jobs—a drop due largely to longer periods of schooling and earlier retirement. Consequently, the "labor force participation rate"—the portion of the population over 14 desiring to work outside the home—has remained relatively stable at just under 60 percent.

Occupations of American Workers in 1967. The industries that produce our income, as shown in Figure 1–1, are of course the industries where we work. (However, the relation of number employed to income produced in different industries varies.) What about occupations? Table 3–2 presents data on employment grouped in 11 occupational classes, plus the unemployed. While the groupings and their designations are too broad to give a reliable indication of such important factors as differing degrees of skill, there is no doubt that much of the working force is in occupations which require, and make use of, extensive training and skill. Changes in the percentages since 1950 reveal significant shifts among groups—such as the drop in the percentage working on farms and the increases in professional, managerial, and clerical jobs.

TABLE 3–2.   Occupations of Members of U.S. Labor Force, 1967*

Major Occupational Group	Estimated Number (In Millions)	Percentage of Total	Change in Percentage of Total, 1950–67
Professional, technical, and kindred	9.9	12.9	4.7
Farmers and farm managers	1.9	2.5	−4.6
Proprietors, managers, and officials, except farm	7.3	9.5	0.8
Clerical and kindred workers	12.0	15.6	3.6
Sales workers	4.5	5.9	−0.9
Craftsmen, foremen, and kindred workers	9.6	12.5	1.6
Operatives and kindred workers	13.6	17.7	−2.0
Private household workers	1.9	2.5	−0.1
Service workers, except private household	7.5	9.8	2.4
Farm laborers and foremen	1.3	1.7	−2.3
Laborers, except farm and mine	3.1	4.0	−2.3
Unemployed	2.9	3.8	−1.1
Total	75.5	100.0	

* Excludes about 2.5 million in the armed forces. Because of rounding, details will not necessarily add to totals. Partly estimated.
    Source: Bureau of the Census Population Series. Publications of the Census present a wealth of information. The occupations of people employed in 1960 are tabulated in much detail. For example, the Census found 27,000 boilermakers, 272,000 female hairdressers, 701,000 auto mechanics and repairmen, and 179,000 college professors and instructors.

Migration and Immigration. From the time migrations began with the expulsion from Eden, men and their women have moved over the earth, seeking new and better homes. Within nations and across frontiers, such movements have played a decisive and creative role in the lives not only of individuals but of whole nations. Since 1820, for example, 40 million immigrants have come to live in this country; few left. Emigration—from Ireland, for example—has for the most part tended to check the growth of population rather than to reduce it.

Why do people move? Economic opportunity is a dominant attraction, but one often reinforced by religious and political aspirations and the desire to live in a more congenial social order. In fact, considering the large differences in living conditions, we might better ask, "Why do not more people move?" One answer is obvious—some governments will not let people enter, some will not let them leave. Governments restrict adjustment that would appeal (to many) on economic grounds. Until World War I, however, governments imposed few restrictions on immigration and emigration. This was a period of great movement from Europe to the United States. Yet poverty (it costs to move, even by the poorest of means), ignorance, tradition, and inertia checked movement which on economic grounds would have been beneficial to many who stayed behind. International movement of people remains small in relation to growth of population and differences in social, economic, and political attractions. Government prohibitions, cost, and social pressures have kept the totals from rising to what might have been expected.

Partly because of labor union influence stemming from desire to restrict the supply of workers, Congress in 1921 put numerical limits on immigration. For 40 years, to 1965, the ceiling was around 155,000 for quota immigrants with allowance for numerous nonquota exceptions. The total was apportioned on the basis of U.S. population by national origin in 1890. The present law permits 170,000 a year from outside, and up to 120,000 from within, the Western Hemisphere. The national origins basis has been abolished. Selection now rests on a first-come, first-served basis but with preferences for family reunification and persons with skills and talents needed here. (Some countries complain of a "brain drain" as we attract their doctors, scientists, and others with advanced training.) Drastic reduction in admission of temporary agricultural workers (*braceros*) from Mexico represented a defeat for U.S. farm employers.

Why, in view of our already large and rapidly growing population, do we still admit 2 million immigrants each decade? Humanitarian feelings—for example, to permit families to reunite or to provide haven for refugees—provide one reason. Employers see need for persons with special skills. Moreover, we can always expect a stimulus from the presence of people with new and different ideas, viewpoints, trainings.

Movement of people within nations is important. The migration of pioneers westward is familiar to all moviegoers, but it is only one of the many stories of our internal flux of population. Less spectacular has been a shift, decade after decade, from farm to city. Each year since World War II the number changing residence has equaled almost one fifth of the total population. Over 5 million a year move to another state. Since 1940, for example, California has gained as many people as live in all six New England states. Two thirds of the country's population increase since 1940 has been in and around cities of over 50,000. Florida's increase of 110 percent from 1950 to 1966 compared with New York's 24 percent. A few states have actually lost population.

The number of people to work, to go to school, or to consume in any area depends partly upon such shifting. For specific economic problems—and practical issues do involve something specific, such as the labor supply for a factory here, the need for a new hospital there, or whether to build suburban houses or city apartments—population shifts inside a country may be more significant than changes in the total. It is no surprise that, when the Census Bureau publishes new population figures, alert businesses put staffs to work analyzing the long, dull-looking tables.

Quality of Population. People differ—a set of examination answers or track tryouts will vividly demonstrate that human talents are not distributed equally. Our political and religious traditions lead us to emphasize vital similarities of human beings. Yet in some respects important for economics, people are not equal. Human differences exist, and for lack of a better term we shall call them differences in *quality*.

Individual Ability to Produce.   A feature of human quality that is obviously important in economic life is what people can and will do for others, contribute to the total of cooperation in production. As producers some people create more than others. The economic well-being of a group—family, city, nation, or world—depends upon the capacities, some inherited, some developed, of its individual members.

Strong backs, keen eyes, sensitive nerves, their opposites, and other characteristics are hereditary. Nature blesses some of us and limits others. But working with nature's physical endowment, mankind can work great change. For example, health, in the broadest sense of the term, plays a vast part in determining how much, and how well, we produce. People in good physical and mental health produce more than those who are sickly; health, in turn, depends partly upon economic conditions.

Poverty leads to undernourishment and disease, which check the ability and willingness to produce; life proceeds in a vicious circle—poverty, illness, low production, poverty, and so on. But the circle can be broken. Science has made it possible for even very poor communities to free themselves from age-old curses; a start upward can be made, one improvement helps another (unless, as Malthus feared, the number of people grows to absorb the gain). Outside help, whether private charity for individual families or broad international programs, can also help break the circle.

The productive capacity of a land consists to large degree of the *training*, defined broadly, of a population. A million good-hearted but ignorant peasants can produce only a fraction as much as a million highly skilled mechanics. Almost every kind of work, every new type of machine and process, requires special training. The work whose results we value most highly often requires years of education, practice, and other preparation. Occasionally, of course, nature produces talents which are highly valuable without much training. As a rule, however, time, effort, and direction are needed to develop native capacity. Whatever the natural endowment, training can enhance its value. Opportunities grow as mankind learns how to become more effective in developing potential human abilities—knowledge which itself is a priceless resource.

In listing wealth, we do not ordinarily include our bodies or skills. Yet as individuals and as groups we have some economic choice about how much to "invest" in people. Raising a child and providing it a good education, say through college, is expensive, as many fathers know only too well. Yet a full-grown man can accomplish more than an infant; the better his training, the more he can produce. Development and training absorb large effort before they produce much. Better training, like improving health, makes for a *cumulative improvement*. Each gain facilitates the next. The man who develops greater capacity can earn more and thereby offer his children better training opportunities. Much the same is true for the economy as a whole. As the average quality of human training rises, the community finds it easier to bear the costs of developing still higher skills. Young people can then be supported through more of the years of training in which they produce little.[11] The larger the number of children in lower income families, however, the greater the difficulty of raising the average training which each is offered.

The productive value of schooling is suggested by Figure 3–7. The

FIGURE 3–7.   Lifetime Earnings Related to Education

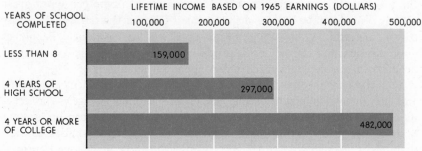

LIFETIME INCOME BASED ON 1965 EARNINGS (DOLLARS)

YEARS OF SCHOOL COMPLETED

LESS THAN 8 — 159,000

4 YEARS OF HIGH SCHOOL — 297,000

4 YEARS OR MORE OF COLLEGE — 482,000

Source: Data from U.S. Department of Commerce, Current Population Survey, *Statistical Abstract, 1967.*

United States has a long tradition of emphasizing *schooling* and other more or less formal training. The results are not always gratifying to the teacher reading the final exam or the employer seeking good-quality work. Dissatisfaction with the quality of our schools has been widespread. We still debate about the kind of training most fruitful in developing human capacity. Nevertheless, the mass of Americans undoubtedly get more and better schooling than their grandfathers. Only about 7 percent of persons of high school age were in secondary schools in 1890; today's figure is over 93 percent. The number graduating from high school was 44,000 in 1890 and will exceed 2.5 million in 1968.

In fact, what was, and in most parts of the world still is, a rare privilege—a college education—is now commonplace here; college enrollment has gone above 6.5 million, 3 percent of our total population compared with 0.7 percent in Western Europe. In 1870 there was one engineer for each 2,000 persons in the labor force; by 1964 there was one for every 130. Some 80,000 chemists today compare with 800 in 1870, except that each can do vastly more. The number of lawyers has about kept pace

[11] Often the major cost of going to school is neither the instruction (whether paid for out of taxes or tuition fees) nor the expense of living. Rather it is the loss of what the student could earn in a job. Even where free public instruction is available and the extra earnings from more training are recognizable, a poor family may not let children continue in school. Their earnings are needed at once.

with the growth of population, while the proportion of ministers declined. The number of nurses per capita increased 2½ times from 1920 to 1965, while medical technicians and social workers grew from negligible numbers to about 120,000 and 110,000, respectively. Another educational development of great economic importance is the growth of systematic job training provided by business. Millions of workers get practical training furnished by employers. Many of the tens of millions of people taking one or another adult education course are trying to prepare themselves for better jobs, or new ones as changing technology abolishes some jobs and creates need for new skills.

But are we getting as much top-quality education as we should? How can we combine instruction for huge numbers with the need for excellence? Is our democratic goal consistent with getting the best possible from the minority who have highest potentialities? These are just a few of the questions that must receive serious thought and appropriate action.

"Moral" Qualities. "Moral" qualities are crucial. Honesty, integrity, a sense of justice and honor, and other qualities we associate with "morality" in its broadest sense are not only desirable in themselves. They also enhance economic productivity. In fact, the division of labor, specialization, and the interdependence and cooperation of our economy rest on broad moral agreement. Exceptions exist. Trickery and dishonesty sometimes bring economic benefit to the perpetrator. Yet if you had a choice between dealing with an honest or a dishonest firm, or hiring two people of equal technical competence but one of whom was trustworthy and the other a cheat, would you ignore the difference? You may deal with people you cannot trust, but if so, you will try to protect yourself—by detailed formal contracts, by using more supervisors if you are an employer, by inspecting more rigidly. Such protection adds to cost.[12] How immeasurably cheaper, more efficient, to deal by word of mouth, by mutual trust!

Good credit and reputation are valuable assets; the system of trust they signify is a priceless community resource. We do well to encourage probity, for it is an asset of incalculable economic productivity.

The ethical system of Western Europe was generally favorable to commerce and exchange when economic development began to surge ahead. (General freedom of markets offers ethical conduct a chance to prove itself, become appreciated, and thus valuable. "Honesty is the best policy.") The ethics that men actually lived by were by no means perfect, but beliefs that God-fearing men held profoundly did help in the kind of economic growth that has proved very productive. One drag that hinders the economic progress of some areas, and of some individuals everywhere, is a sense of right and wrong (as actually lived) that obstructs the achievement of economic efficiency. The costs of doing business are higher when a man's word cannot be trusted.

---

[12] Think how much it would cost to inspect carefully every glass of milk, or other purchase, instead of relying upon the seller.

Another quality relates to capital formation: *thriftiness*. Thrift and the willingness to abstain from consuming all one's income are human qualities that rank high in some systems of values. The doctrines of Calvin emphasized the positive religious merit of sobriety, conservation, and provision for the future; hard *work* and a life lived sparingly please God. Success, for the Calvinist, could be measured by capital accumulation; moreover, duty required him to use his wealth constructively, not hoard it. Human values believed to be right were also eminently useful for economic advance. Such religious convictions help explain not only why people saved but also why they planned rational investment.

Human Factors as Intangible Resources Influencing Economic Development.   Human factors, the way people think and do things, create intangibles that sometimes exert a dominating influence on economic life. Some are in a sense "resources." We often take them for granted, like health or drinking water, unless they disappear.

The idea of *progress*—something relatively new in world tradition—permeates our economic thinking. Americans expect change. They believe that change can be for the better and that an increase in real income is an improvement. Man, not doomed to his ancestors' way of living, has some power over his fate; he should, we believe, work hard to rise and to give his children more than he had. Striving for economic advance is part of our heritage, not merely wishing, nor relying upon someone else for the effort, but exerting oneself.

Our *social system* has been free and relaxed, relative to the systems of Europe and the Orient. Custom and tradition have imposed fewer restraints than in most parts of the world. Diversity of all sorts has provided stimulus, variety, scope for many kinds of talents. People have been able to move from one place, job, or profession to another. True, social impediments to "careers open to talent" have existed, especially for Negroes. Yet, on the whole, this country has been blessed with freedom from social barriers to change. Class lines have not erected confining restrictions. Progress as a goal had valid meaning throughout society; (white) people "on the rise" had little fear of being confined by a class ceiling. Movement in the social structure, change, opportunity, innovation, pioneering, and personal advance have been more than pie-in-the-sky dreams; despite heartbreaking disappointments, they have been realities for millions. The dreams of penniless, illiterate immigrants—dreams fantasied in slums, sweatshops, and mines—have sometimes become realities as the dreamers built model factories, led labor unions, endowed hospitals, headed great businesses.

In some societies, strongly organized religious organizations have discouraged change and supported patterns of action that hinder the kind of economic growth prized in this country. The American religious heritage, however, has contained much variety and dissent, much questioning, change, innovation. Generations of Americans have been stimulated by religious enthusiasm, inspiration, and aspiration, which seem also to encourage economic growth.

Our *legal system* has been generally stable. Such stability aids development which requires long-term commitment of property. Yet the law has adapted to meet new conditions, not perfectly, but without intolerable delay. On the whole, it has favored enterprise. The judges, lawyers, and legislators who developed British and American law had in mind the needs of commerce and industry. They built a legal system that helped make the process of carrying on business transactions simple and cheap. The law took care to help protect property, thus reducing the risk of investment. Restraints on the free use of land and other wealth were removed so "the dead hand of the past" would not obstruct new venture. Laws became generous in permitting the use of forms of business organization that seemed desirable to businessmen. Despite exceptions, which have perhaps increased during the last generation, we still have a legal system affecting business that favors the division of labor, exchange, and economic growth.

Our *common language* eases exchange. It is also the same as that of Britain, another leading participant in economic development. Unlike Oriental languages, ours uses few symbols: 26 letters and 10 numerical digits. Printing, typing, and other mechanical communication are far cheaper than in, say, Chinese.

Until recently, the peacetime influence of military personnel and defense considerations (with their huge economic burdens) have been small. *Government* was run by people who, with exceptions, generally sympathized with business. In some countries, on the other hand, the dominant political groups have disdained business; government threw its weight in favor of agriculture or old and not very progressive business; then as labor and socialist groups gained more power, they used government against business. *Bureaucracy* has been less powerful here than in Europe; on balance it favors stability rather than dynamism and enterprise. Finally, in spite of local loyalties, our *feeling as a nation* has been strong enough so that, with powerful support from the "commerce clause" of the Constitution, we did not (like Europe) throttle ourselves by internal tariffs or similar trade barriers. Specialization within a large and varied area was not impeded greatly by man-made obstacles.

We return to some of these issues later.

TERMS AND CONCEPTS

wealth	saving	law of diminishing
natural resources	capital formation	returns
federal stockpiles	depreciation	brain drain
capital goods	Malthusian doctrine	teaching
depletion	resource base	roundabout
natural origins	emigration	production

QUESTIONS

1. "An economy cannot expect to raise its living standards by much unless its members will produce more than they consume." Discuss.

2. Was Malthus wrong? Why?

3. "The truly effective richness of a country's natural endowment depends to a great degree upon what men have learned about how to use the gifts of nature." Discuss.

4. If you were an employer, what kinds of personal qualities would you prefer in persons you were hiring? Why?

5. How would discovery of a cheap way to use sand as a motor fuel affect the natural wealth of, say, Florida? The relative position of oil-producing areas?

6. Does the principle of diminishing returns apply to the stock of capital equipment as well as to land? Why?

7. Can men in effect increase the economic usefulness of irreplaceable natural resources? Explain.

8. Examine from the point of view of a local government official, a manager in each of three different types of businesses, and a farm leader, economic problems posed by the population changes now in prospect for the United States.

4

THE ORGANIZATION OF BUSINESS: CORPORATION CONTROL AND MANAGEMENT

Good management consists in showing average people how to do the work of superior people.

John D. Rockefeller

Nearly 82 percent of all income originates in business, including farms and independent professional service. Clearly, business is our main agency for organizing resources to produce. Around 4.8 million nonfarm businesses, plus about 3 million farms and an equal number of small service establishments, operated in 1967. The term "firm" applies to a business owned and controlled as a unit. A few are huge, more tiny; some are new, others old; some operate over much of the world, others in a "hole in the wall." "Business," therefore, is a concept which includes tremendous variety. Yet most businesses have important features in common.

BUSINESS AND PROFIT MAKING

A typical business gets productive resources, uses them to produce what it believes someone else wants, and sells the product. The resources may be a farmer's own labor and his land; they may be tens of thousands of items on the purchasing list of a giant company. These inputs are combined in endless ways by the people who *are* the business. Whether huge or tiny, *every business is run by people;* decisions are human decisions.

The chief goal is to make the *net* money return to the owners as large as possible (over the long run). How? By getting more dollars from the sale of what it offers than it must pay out as the costs of what it buys. Of course. there are other goals. Neither the business manager nor the owner, any more than the teacher, politician, or labor leader, will be motivated solely by the desire for his own economic gain. Businessmen wish to serve, to satisfy the public, to help in national defense, to do work because it is pleasant. Such nonprofit goals, although found everywhere and at times influential, do not explain what makes business really "tick." More nearly correct is the generalization that a business operates to earn money. What a company earns we generally call "profit." Since businesses do most of the buying, selling, and employing in our economy, and since businesses focus on earning "profit"—our whole economic system is often said to rest primarily on the profit motive. In a sense it does, even though profits are only a small fraction of wages. Profit seems dominating, and it *is* important, because of its part in guiding business and hence much of economic life.

Since business organizes so much of production, we need to know more about how businesses themselves are organized. Our legal system permits three general types of organization: the individual proprietorship, the partnership, and the corporation.

SOLE PROPRIETORSHIP

Legal Simplicity.   Most American businesses are owned by one person. Legally, they are single or sole proprietorships. Some are small and fleeting. Some grow to modest size but never reach the status of big business. A proprietorship cannot survive the owner because each one *is*, in a sense, the economic life of the owner and dies with him; in fact, however, the essentials may be carried on by a successor, who legally creates a new firm. To form a proprietorship is easy; the legal requirements are simple when there are any at all. Generally all that is needed is to start operating.

A single owner gets all of any profits, suffers any losses, and assumes all legal responsibilities. This form permits great *flexibility;* it gives the rugged individualist an important freedom. Yet he may not have the economic power to use his legal freedom. The boy who sees an opportunity when the heat soars and nearby workmen long for lemonade cannot use the freedom the law gives him to start a business unless he has resources to make his product.

Poorly Adapted for Getting Capital.   Assume that you own a business as a proprietor. You would find the form, itself, a source of some frustration. It may *hinder getting capital from others*—the money to hire labor and buy other resources. If a business is static and the owner has no wish to grow, he needs no more capital. Any success, however, suggests that growth is desirable. As an owner, for example, you have evidence that you can do something the public wants, evidence in the profit the public has paid you. You work hard yourself—but see greater opportunity. You need things to work with: more employees, inventory and raw materials, machinery, space. If you have funds yourself, perhaps an inheritance, savings from past efforts, or the gain from a successful speculation, you may be able to finance expansion. Most proprietors, however, find such sources distressingly inadequate.

If you are typical, you "plow back" some of the earnings, to grow by keeping profits in the business; perhaps you buy a truck instead of the sedan your family wants. As an individual proprietor, however, you find that tax collectors consider the business earnings as yours and apply the personal income tax to the business profits. You would not need to be remarkably successful to have taxes take over a fourth of the profits. Living expenses must come out of the rest. Taxes absorb much of what might be plowed back, a problem your father could almost have ignored had he started at your age and your grandfather may not have heard of.

If you do well, a natural thing is to try to *borrow* to get capital from others; after all, many people and financial institutions want to lend money. Here, however, the position as a single proprietor can be a disadvantage. If you have real estate or securities which can be pledged to protect the lender if you fail to repay, there will probably be no difficulty. More likely, you will not have enough such assets. Can you borrow on your general reputation? Since the firm is so much *you*, lenders will be at the mercy not only of general business trends but also of *your* judgment, industry, luck, honesty, and mortality. The last risk may be covered, at a cost, by taking out life insurance; some important risks, however, cannot be eliminated by insurance. If things go badly for you, lenders can try to get their money back by selling not only your business assets but also your home and almost everything else you own (except furniture, clothing, life insurance, some government bonds, property you may have in certain kinds of trusts, and occasionally other assets); if you have other wealth, therefore, lenders have protection—unless you use up the assets (or give them to your family) before the debt falls due. Perhaps after a short time you build a reputation for integrity—and also for skill and success. To achieve this happy state, however, may require many years.

In applying for a loan, you may show the need for money to buy raw materials and pay labor that will produce something to show for the spending—perhaps dozens of dresses you think will be popular. But will they be salable for the amount due, and without a lot of trouble? You might make fine yellow wool dresses when women want blue nylon. If the lender relies upon the sale of your assets plus your success, he must, in self-protection, keep close contact with your affairs and have frequent chances to intervene if he wishes. So he will tend to limit loans to short terms, say for a few months. He can then keep in touch with how you are doing; but for you the possible nuisance of his interference and the dread of uncertainty about loan renewal, detract from the desirability of such financing. Money obtained from temporary loans cannot be used for more permanent, even vitally important, purposes. After the lender turns over his money for a loan of perhaps 3 years, he may feel largely at your mercy. He cannot then control your decisions or, as a rule, intervene to prevent what he believes would be an error. This possibility will deter him. So you will likely find it hard and expensive to borrow as much as you feel you could use to advantage.

Poorly Adapted for Getting Skilled Assistants.   Modern business calls for many types of human skill, more, ordinarily, than one person can claim. Rarely can the "one-man show" be large enough to yield much total profit. To operate on even a moderate scale, the businessman must get and hold assistants—good ones if he is to succeed. One attraction of the proprietorship is the opportunity it gives a person to work long, hard, and skillfully and get the benefits for himself. Incentive operates directly, but as a rule for the owner alone. A disadvantage, for you as a proprietor, is that others will not ordinarily have the same chance to exert themselves for their own benefit. If you go crazy, get killed by a car, or are impoverished by a mistake of judgment, a person working with you can find himself "out in the cold." Permanence and opportunity are more than you can promise securely. Yet you are greatly dependent upon assistants; their mistakes can cost you not only some of this year's business profit but personal wealth as well. Giving others serious responsibility is risky; if you do not, however, the business is confined to what you, one person, can oversee.

The single proprietor, in short, finds it almost impossible to make the kind of binding, stimulating, long-term employment contracts that are necessary to get and to hold the best assistants. Except for a very small firm, this limit can be a serious hindrance, because no one person can be highly competent in many things: buying, selling, hiring, product development, taxes, finance, invention.

Wide Use.   The individual proprietorship, in short, has two major limitations: *limited life* and *unlimited liability*. Yet it is still the most common form of business. Most farmers use it; 73 percent of nonfarm businesses and about 88 percent of service firms are proprietorships. (Doctors, lawyers, and others who practice as individuals may be said to work as proprietors.) Businesses that are just getting started, especially if they are small, are as a rule sole proprietorships. One element of a "free enterprise" system is that it does not erect serious *legal* obstacles to starting new businesses.

PARTNERSHIP

Legal Features.   Another relatively informal type of organization is possible: the partnership. Two or more people agree to own and operate a business. Forming the partnership can be easy—a verbal agreement may do, but written "articles of partnership" provide safeguards against misunderstanding. In any case, government consent is not needed. The association (simple or complex) is one of persons, and the partnership as an entity does not own things or make economic commitments—one or more of the partners do that. The relative interests can be equal or vary widely, but each partner can commit the others. Each (with occasional exceptions) has *unlimited liability*. The total wealth of all partners (with the exceptions noted in discussing the proprietorship) can be drawn upon to meet the obligations of the firm. If one partner dies or withdraws, the firm dissolves; but the survivors may create another.

Advantages: Financing and Personnel.   If you were to form a partnership, you would find some distinct advantages over the proprietorship—if you could get good partners. You could pool the capital of other people with yours so the business could have more resources to work with. The partnership form can also help in building personnel strength, equally vital to a business. You may use a partnership interest to attract the men (or women) you want, and to offer such promising persons a direct, personal incentive to do the best they can. You can give an employee an interest in the firm by making him a partner, even though he has no capital—granting him, perhaps, a one-twentieth interest. You may join up with people whose special competence differs from yours, to build a better all-around team. Or you can give others a share when they put up capital without doing any work. The possible variation is large.

Disadvantages.   When a person becomes a partner, he assumes not only unlimited liability: he is also committed to the extent that he cannot end his liability or get his money out of the business without a technical dissolution requiring the consent of the other partners. Personal relations count for a lot. A man's fortunes are bound up with the actions of his partners. If they are stupid, foolish, or dishonest, he may lose his wealth and prospects. As problems and opportunities arise to require decisions, getting agreement among several partners can be difficult, with the least qualified sometimes in a position to prevent the others from acting. Even partners' wives can draw upon the firm's potential resources as they spend money a partner might use for the business. Or the women may prove a big help. Clearly, a partnership can involve complex personal affairs.

Though the partnership as such is not subject to income taxes, each partner's share is taxable (along with his other income) whether or not he withdraws it from the business.[1] Taxes impose a barrier to expanding the business by reinvesting earnings. Moreover, since a partnership ends when any member dies, this form is not well suited to businesses requiring long-term commitments.

---

[1] Special provisions of the tax law now offer both partnerships and small corporations the choice of being taxed on either partnership or the corporation basis—subject to numerous technical conditions.

Extent of Use. About 10 percent of nonfarm businesses are partnerships. This form is used by some retail and other small businesses and in professions—lawyers, accountants, and architects—where personality, reputation, and skill, rather than large amounts of capital, are most important. Furthermore, partnerships are common among investment bankers and brokers; the potential backing of the personal wealth of all partners supplements the reputation for integrity in giving the public reason for confidence. For most economic activity, however, the partnership does not loom important. There is something better—the corporation. Figure 4–1 suggests the relative importance of the three types.

FIGURE 4–1.   Corporations, Partnerships, and Sole Proprietorships

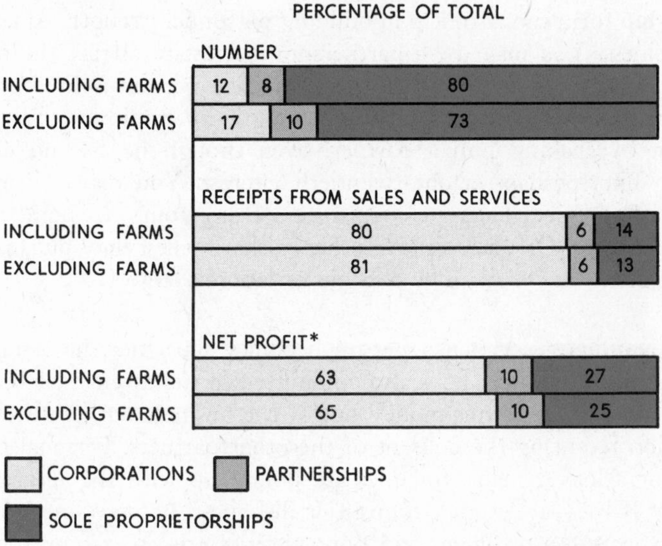

PERCENTAGE OF TOTAL

NUMBER

INCLUDING FARMS	12	8	80
EXCLUDING FARMS	17	10	73

RECEIPTS FROM SALES AND SERVICES

INCLUDING FARMS	80	6	14
EXCLUDING FARMS	81	6	13

NET PROFIT*

INCLUDING FARMS	63	10	27
EXCLUDING FARMS	65	10	25

☐ CORPORATIONS   ▨ PARTNERSHIPS
■ SOLE PROPRIETORSHIPS

* After corporation income taxes but before taxes on owners of partnerships or sole proprietorships or on dividends received by stockholders.
Source: Statistics of Income, U.S. Business Tax Returns, 1963–1964.

THE CORPORATION

"A corporation," in the words of Chief Justice Marshall,

. . . is an artificial being, invisible, intangible, and existing only in contemplation of law. Being the mere creature of law, it possesses only those properties which the charter of its creation confers upon it, either expressly or as incidental to its very existence. . . . Among the most important are immortality, and, if the expression may be allowed, individuality; properties by which a perpetual succession of many persons are considered as the same, and may act as a single individual.

The corporation, as a device for doing business, is one of those highly developed elements of life which are often taken for granted. Yet, if legislatures, by accident or deliberate intent, had created another body of laws dealing with corporations, our economy today might be considerably different. The corporation offers people a mechanism for working together, but without the limits on human capacity which face any individual or small group and without impediments of human mortality. Americans do most of their business with and through corporations. Though these artificial "persons" do not eat or breathe or think, the law treats them as entities which act; it assumes that they have a life distinct from that of the individuals who own, run, or work for them. By acting as a corporation, thousands of people become an "it," collectively a person.

Legal Features.   The legal creation of a corporation rests upon an act of government. For several centuries each chartered company, joint-stock company, and corporation resulted from a special chartering act of the king or legislature. The provisions varied from case to case. Getting a charter was likely to be expensive, time consuming, and a result of political maneuvering that was better left concealed. During the 19th century, however, governments, including those of American states, passed laws permitting one and all to form corporations under general terms, without special acts of the legislature.[2]

Advantages of the Corporate Form.   A corporate charter grants existence as an entity with legal permission to do a wide variety of things. Not all states offer the same powers, but, because of the U.S. Constitution, each state must respect the corporations of other states. Consequently, a group wishing to incorporate can usually "shop around" and get its charter in the state that will grant the most generous terms; few, if any, states are more generous than Delaware.[3]

As far as the law goes, corporations, in practice, can be **immortal.** This fact permits long-term commitments, such as building a factory to operate for decades. Without such near permanence, how could a highly industrialized economy develop? (Imagine trying to finance a railroad if the business, as such, must end when its guiding spirit dies. Or even if it had to end at an arbitrary date dictated by charter terms.) The corporate form has proved to have another advantage: so organized, a business, even one of great size, can be run with **central, unified direction.**

Another feature is **limited liability.** The owners can lose no more than

[2] State law usually requires three or five original stockholders. The cost of a corporate charter will include a tax (fee) to the state government, but even with the necessary legal fees, total costs will usually not exceed $200 or so.

[3] The efforts of most states to tighten laws of incorporation to prevent abuses can be effectively frustrated by sister states. The "offenders" presumably wish to get organization fees and tax revenue and to create work for local attorneys and banks.

they have put into the business. (The price of the stock can go no lower than zero.) If things go bad, the people to whom the corporation owes money cannot draw upon the private resources of the owners. If you give credit to a corporation in any way, therefore, be careful to see that the corporation, not its owners, is able to pay; they may be rich as Croesus, but if the money is not in the corporation, no debtor can get at it. Will not limited liability, then, hurt a business's credit? Perhaps. Yet, limited liability generally eases the task of getting capital. Owners of a corporation can rest assured that they cannot lose more than they invest; they are effectively insulated from danger that their personal estates will be assessed for debts of the firm. Investors can put money into businesses which they cannot watch closely; they may venture their capital in many diverse firms, knowing that they can lose no more than they put in willingly.

If you were trying to get money and other assets for a corporation, limited liability would not be the only advantage over a partnership. You would be permitted to issue different types of securities (considered later) to suit different groups of investors. These securities could be lumped into large amounts or divided into small units—useful flexibility. The buyer of corporation securities can count upon being able to transfer them easily (if he can find a buyer) without the consent of other owners or of the corporation. The easier it is to get out of an investment, the greater the willingness of some investors to get in. The life and operation of the firm can remain unaffected by shifts of ownership. This *transferability*, of course, means that a manager cannot, as in a partnership, count upon the personal advice and help of a fellow owner; the latter may sell out to a fool or rival. No one should think for a minute, however, that in forming a corporation one can surely get others to put their money into the business. By no means!

Abuses of the Corporate Form.   The corporate form has made possible abuses which are peculiar to it. (1) A group planning to use shady business practices, or to do things for which as individuals they do not want to be held responsible, can act through a corporation. This abuse is largely a problem of small and often temporary corporations. (2) Innumerable investors have lost untold sums in the purchase of securities of corporations that were outright frauds. Glib promoters have issued worthless, or nearly worthless, corporation stock to sell to the gullible and greedy. Fortunately, higher standards of business ethics, the forces of competition, and government regulation have reduced—not eliminated— the practical seriousness of such abuses.

COOPERATIVES

People who want to *buy* the same sort of things—groceries, electricity, or gasoline—or *sell* similar products—oranges or milk—or provide a service—cotton ginning, storage, or insurance—sometimes form a cooperative. Such a business is owned by its customers or suppliers. They ordinarily receive a fixed payment for the funds they advance to buy "shares." Any distribution of profits will be in proportion to the purchases from (or sales to) the firm. In fact, such "patronage refunds" are delayed price reductions (or supplements). Shareholders, usually with one vote each, elect directors who choose a manager. Success among over 6,000 retail, 7,000 farm marketing, and thousands of farm purchasing and service co-ops has varied widely. A few are large and firmly established in agricultural areas; farmers may in fact have little freedom to carry on some types of marketing and buying except through the co-op; local control is at times small compared with that from a central office.

Sometimes owner loyalty is strong enough to create a distinct advantage in building business volume. Almost always the quality of management is determining. If it is poor, the venture will likely prove a disappointment. One opportunity of the cooperative movement is to discover and utilize managerial ability that would otherwise go to waste, as in minority groups and rural areas. Often, however, the management is not notably good, the capital available is inadequate, and the co-op does well to survive the competition of private business. Freedom to form cooperatives may provide a way to test the efficiency of profit-seeking business. However, tax favors and sometimes, as in the case of rural electrification and telephone cooperatives, government aid in financing, make impossible the valid comparison of the achievements of co-ops with those of ordinary businesses.

CORPORATION CONTROL AND MANAGEMENT

Corporations run so much of our economy that we need to know something about how they function. Though hemmed in by market forces that limit its freedom to act, every business does have some power. The decisions of the human beings who manage companies do influence our lives. Legally, a corporation is a soulless person; in fact, it is a group of "human beings acting." The ways of operating vary greatly. No sketch can be both clear and accurate.

Business methods change. The full significance of new trends will be clear only after many years. Managements serve different masters: owners, consumers, employees, the rest of the public. Sometimes interests conflict; the management that would suit employees best (at least in the short run) might sacrifice owners or consumers. Yet the diverse elements of the economy have high mutual interest in the quality of corporation management. Everyone benefits when business runs well.

Need for Competence and Good Human Values. Competence in business management looms as a social need of the utmost importance—competence in many fields: personnel, engineering, innovation, finance, to name a few. Most important, perhaps is *competence to select and run a* *team of widely varied skills.* Native ability and training of high degree are needed, as well as many personal traits which are by no means plentiful. Only a minute fraction of a population can qualify as superior, can excel—and we need excellence. One challenge of an economic system is to devise ways to get people who are most competent for key jobs into those spots. An even greater challenge is to develop more such people, a task colleges and universities are helping to perform.

It is not enough, however, that leaders be competent for their particular jobs. We want a world in which men with power are men of goodwill, as well as of skill. Happily, evidence of concern for broad public interest is increasingly recognized as a necessary quality in management. But what *is* the public interest? Is it other than what will yield the largest profit in the long run? If so, to what extent, and for what, should management incur avoidable costs? Or sell for less than the most profitable price? The business world seeks answers to such questions. Leaders of business, in themselves serving in community affairs, in assigning some corporation earnings for colleges and artistic organizations, and in other ways, now do more than ever before to put into practice those aspirations of economic statesmanship which extend beyond strictly defined monetary norms.

Human Limitations and the Size of the Job.   A constant threat to good management is the growth of the job, beyond limits of human capacity. Even the ablest person working under the best of conditions can do a thorough job on only a few big problems a year. If he must spread his efforts thin, or if working conditions hinder him, then he cannot give the high-quality results of which he is potentially capable. The "system" can frustrate a genius. But systems can be changed to enhance (or reduce) the effective capacity of managers. So "system" is a subject of concern.

Formulation of Overall Policy: Board of Directors.   The actual management of a small corporation need not be very different from that of a partnership. In large corporations, however, features of management peculiar to the corporation appear. Owners delegate the responsibility to a board of directors. These are elected, usually each year, by the common stockholders, with one vote for each share of stock. The directors then select the president and chief officers, who actually run the business. The directors meet, perhaps monthly or quarterly, to decide on major matters of policy: building a new plant, introducing a new product, revising the advertising plan, and voting dividends.

For small and medium-sized corporations, most directors are likely to be officers, family members, and others closely associated with the firm. They participate actively and have enough specific knowledge about the business to be able to make informed judgments about many detailed problems. A close tie to the firm, unfortunately, may create an outlook so limited that a director cannot judge broader trends well or learn of new things that would be useful.

Few directors of big corporations have day-to-day contact with the business. (No stock ownership is required, and only recently has payment to directors become common.) A corporation may get its directors from the richest cream of the economy. They may be selected for a variety of reasons: proved success in their own lines; legal knowledge or ability; useful contacts with banks, suppliers, customers, the scientific world, or government officials (local, state, national, or foreign); relations with large owners; prestige in the community. Some bring valuable experience and devote enough attention to specific problems to make wise and informed judgments. Others give little more than passing attention.

How well does this system operate to get highly competent, top-level direction of business, compared with possible alternative systems? No one can be sure. A director relying upon intuition and hasty review of summary reports is not likely to give the best possible answers to the policy questions that are his responsibility. Other arrangements are used. Payment of fees of good size and careful briefing on problem issues help get more serious attention from directors. A small number of men of wide and tested experience, sometimes called "professional directors," serve on several boards, making this almost a full-time job. The directors of one of the country's most successful corporations, Standard Oil of New Jersey, spend full time on the job and have had long and intimate contact with the firm.

Loss of Owner Control. Owners of large corporations seldom control their property.[4] Directorates tend to be self-perpetuating. Stockholders do not generally have the practical power to change directors. If you were a stockholder, you would get a notice of the annual meeting, together with a report on operations for the past year. Also, you would likely get a request to sign and return a *proxy*—your authorization for some designated officials to vote your shares if you cannot attend in person.[5] You would receive information about the salaries, pension rights, and stockholdings of officers and directors and their families, together with any items of business to be presented and perhaps statements of views of opponents.

---

[4] This condition applies even more clearly to government enterprises.

[5] Managements try to encourage stockholder attendance. Special transportation, some free lunches, a trip through one of the plants, a semiholiday good time, coupled with serious business and sometimes searching questions of management policies have led to greater attendance. A few men and women "specialize" in asking management about certain points. Some corporations shift the annual meeting from one city to another to bring opportunities of attendance to more stockholders over a period of years. Or follow-up meetings for explanation and discussion may be held in various parts of the country.

What you cannot be given is an objective appraisal of the competence of the directors and of possible alternatives. How, then, can you make an intelligent choice? The "in group" will control votes of stock it and its associates own; other stockholders can be counted on automatically to mail in their proxies for management. Men in control need fear no adverse vote on the many proxy forms which end in the stockholder's wastebasket. So if you want to elect someone else, or just defeat one of the nominees of the present group, you will have great difficulty.[6] The bigger the corporation and the wider its ownership, the harder to substitute men you believe to be better than those in control.[7]

Moreover, few owners can know enough about the caliber of the directors and of possible substitutes to make a persuasive case. To judge their competence, one should know nearly as much as the directors themselves about the company's problems and operations. Few stockholders, however, would want to be troubled with the complex affairs of a giant corporation, even if they had the ability and the power to do so practically.[8]

Our tradition has held to the following belief: *Property will be managed best when managed by its owners.* The marriage of ownership and control will, it is said, bring forth the use of property which is most fruitful for the owner and for society. Today, obviously, the property of big corporations is not managed by owners. Does the weakening of the basis for the original faith create a source of inefficiency for the economy? Reasons cited for fearing trouble are not as a rule well documented. We do not always rely on our own judgment in medical matters, even though no one else can be expected to have an equal interest in our own health. When skill is needed, we rely on experts, seeking protection in the legal system and in professional ethics. Perhaps the same principle applies to property management.

[6] In some cases, voting is cumulative. For example, if there are 15 directors and you own one share of stock, you may cast one vote for each, 15 votes for one, or split some other way. In such cases, a unified minority may elect one or two directors.

[7] The giant mutual life insurance companies also have self-perpetuating directorates. Policyholders own the company and elect directors. To upset management would require the agreement of hundreds of thousands of people scattered all through the country.

[8] Tendencies in the other direction may appear. (*a*) Millions of Americans own mutual funds (investment trusts), corporations which buy stocks and bonds of other corporations. Though these organizations have not as a rule tried to participate in management, they have potential power. Perhaps they will tend to give at least reasonably competent outside scrutiny to the management of large corporations from the owners' point of view. (*b*) Banks as trustees for widows, orphans, pension funds, and other investors now own large and growing amounts of common stock. Eventually, banks may exert informed influence on big corporations. (*c*) Pension funds owned around $35 billion of stock in 1967. In some cases, large amounts are placed in the stock of the employing corporation; within a decade or so such pension funds may gain so much voting power, and such interest as owners, that their concentrated ownership may sway management.

Yet, when conflicts arise, how ought directors to decide? There may be conflict over compensation; owners may feel that officers are paying themselves too much. Moreover, there may be conflict of interest over the distribution of earnings. No matter how profitable the corporation, the owners do not share directly in the earnings unless the directors vote a dividend. Who can decide, wisely, whether it is better to retain earnings or let the owners have them to use (after taxes) for living or for investment in other businesses? If corporations are "persons," they are fictitious persons, while their owners are flesh and blood people who will not live indefinitely.

The numbskull and the wastrel may, as stockholders, be served by the country's keenest and most provident men. Our system permits (but does not assure) the concentration of management functions in people who are competent, even though they own none of the property. Managers of great businesses do not need to be men of great wealth, any more than do the engineers, lawyers, or other employees of high skill. To add to incentives for best effort, however, and to take advantage of special features of the income tax, corporations under strict limits offer key officials the opportunity to buy stocks at discounts from the market price or provide the means of making employees also stockholders. The men with major responsibility thus get a significant interest as owners; no one man's holdings may be a big fraction of the whole, but it may be a large portion of *his* wealth.

Pyramiding: The Holding Company. Control of 51 percent of a corporation's voting stock will assure control (as long as the company pays its bills). In fact, if you have control, you can probably keep it with a much smaller percentage—widely diffused majority ownership may have little effective power. The wealth controlled by management includes, in addition to the total value of the voting stock, all that the corporation has borrowed, plus preferred stock. One dollar can easily control five—at times many more. Extreme cases sometimes arise when corporations can and do "hold" stock in other corporations. X controls B, which controls C, which controls D, and so on. Extreme pyramiding can develop but is not characteristic of large holding companies such as AT&T, U.S. Steel, Bordens, or Allied Stores. Corporations often organize the parts of the business as separate corporate entities.[9] The joining of corporations to form larger businesses may involve the use of a holding company.

Managerial Organization. How are corporations organized below the board of directors? What any group accomplishes depends partly upon

---

[9] There are many reasons. (*a*) Where the units will have incomes under $25,000, dividing the total earnings can produce income tax savings. (*b*) Each unit can be free from the liability of others. (*c*) Separate corporations may help in meeting state or local legal requirements (*d*) and may provide a device for giving managers of individual units (stores in a chain) an ownership interest.

how it arranges its work. People can be busy getting in each other's way, or they can cooperate to help each other. Organizational efficiency ranks in importance with engineering efficiency. The variety of ways firms arrange their internal organization is large.

Between the president at the top and the humblest employee at the bottom, there will ordinarily be several levels; 10 is a high number, 5 common. The higher the level, the fewer people on it. Like a tree, the number of branches increases the farther from the main trunk, yet each branch gets its sap (orders) through one source only. The person on each level is responsible to someone at the next higher level, just as privates take orders from corporals who take orders from sergeants, and so on, up to generals. Such hierarchical system is essential if the group is to work together; some persons give, and many more take, orders. Corporations always have elements of this, the *line*, type of organization. It fixes authority and responsibility clearly. Orders go from the president, for example, to a general manager, to a plant superintendent, to a foreman, and finally to the man at the machine.

Staff officers are specialists in certain functions that involve more than one part of the business. A legal department, for example, may assist officials all up and down the line. A personnel department may hire, train, and fire people at all levels; or it may advise and help the line officials. Staff departments provide special skill in performing functions common to several departments. They make many kinds of competence more broadly available. They give the top officers assistance on specific problems and may also help carry out directions or check to see that line officers do so. One difficulty of staff participation in the execution of policy is that responsibility may become confused. If a poor worker is not discharged, for example, the foreman may blame rules of the personnel department, while personnel blames the foreman. If a product sells poorly, the sales division may blame advertising or engineering or the credit manager.

The balance between line and staff in organization varies tremendously.[10] Unusual parts, such as the division handling foreign sales, may be pretty much separate. One common modification is the use of *committees*. If the president does not have time to take the recommendations of all departments and weld them into a coordinated plan, he may rely on a committee. In deciding on a new product, for example, he will perhaps have top men from engineering, factory management, sales, and finance thresh out the problems. Committee work keeps key men informed of what is going on, helps them challenge and teach each other, and forces coordination. Apparently, too, committees prove useful in developing a long range point of view among individuals who would otherwise focus

---

[10] An *organization chart* is a diagram showing the formal units of the business and how they are related.

on operating duties of day-to-day urgency. A committee may be formed to carry out plans after they have been adopted. The effectiveness of any group depends partly upon the people involved, their personalities, and intangibles that are hard to pinpoint—including the danger that in a committee several people can drag their heels.

Sometimes much influence is exerted by *informal groups* for which there is no provision in the formal organization. The golf foursome, wives, old college ties, or jealousies and rivalries—such things affect the way a business actually operates. Wise managers try to make such groupings constructive aids to efficiency.

Big firms usually engage in several distinct activities: a steel company may mine coal and iron ore, manufacture cement, build ships, erect bridges, operate several types of transportation facilities, make thousands of different products, and finance buyers who do not wish to pay cash. The units engaged in different activities may be organized differently, or one pattern may be imposed with less than adequate recognition of varying needs.

Businesses exist to do many different things. What would be the best management organization for one would be poor for another. Fortunately, each business has almost complete legal freedom to try the organization plan that seems best. No central authority imposes a uniform system for, say, furniture manufacturers, retail food stores, and hotels. The flexibility and the adaptability are elements of strength for our economy.

Decentralization of decision making as an aid to efficiency gained increasing favor after World War II. The person on the spot knows the facts and may need to act quickly; decentralization gives executives below the top more stimulation to develop responsibility, while freeing those higher up for the most vital problems; costs of coordination are reduced. On the other hand, different units may adopt inconsistent policies; specialized personnel and equipment at headquarters may not be used effectively in serving dispersed branches; some companies do not have enough competent executives for many centers of independent authority.

Business (like government) is still feeling its way in studying the conditions that lend themselves to decentralization and the most effective techniques. Computers and electronic data processing have already altered ("revolutionized" is still too strong a term) the balance between centralization and decentralization. New devices enable the central office to coordinate dispersed activities with efficiency undreamed of a few years ago; for some types of problems headquarters can now make better decisions than the man on the spot. Figures on orders, shipments, prices, and other details pour into a central computer within microseconds of being recorded at dozens of distant locations; then calculations of complex interrelationships, involving perhaps the whole company, are performed at once; answers and directions go to all concerned—the best plant or warehouse from which to ship is indicated; the shipping order goes out with routing and the customer's bill; inventory records are adjusted and with them production schedules and purchase orders; marketing analyses are revised. The local manager, as a result, may have less responsibility for decisions on inventory or production runs; but he must still handle personnel relations, deal with local traffic, analyze critically elements regarding his part of the company which go into the calculations ("programs") of the computer, and cope with other problems. Many college students have already utilized the centralized nationwide (or worldwide) reservations systems of airlines and hotel chains but without seeing how management, on its side, uses the same computer information.

Many corporations have units doing about the same thing in several areas and face the age-old problem of the conflicting needs of freedom and authority. Some centralize to a high degree. Others give the individual units great autonomy, perhaps designating them as "profit centers" and judging and compensating the managers of each on the basis of identifiable performance. Parts of the business may be encouraged to compete with one another. The manager of the Buick Division of General Motors, for example, faces competition from Oldsmobile and Chevrolet; he is expected to buy parts, say spark plugs, where he can get best value even though this may not be the General Motors division which makes spark plugs.

Efforts to Improve Organization.   Increasingly, businessmen are making a deliberate point of trying to study and improve organization. Business leaders realize that the man at the top of a big firm cannot possibly keep track of everything. Even if he could, he would not be sure of getting the best results. He may have biases or special interests which lead to poor balance in his judgments; he may favor product design to the detriment of selling, or concentrate on manufacturing methods and subordinate foreign development, tax planning, or public relations. The need for skill and intelligence in tackling internal organization has become more and more evident—and so have the possibilities of profit from good organization.

Businesses, trade associations, universities, and specialists in organization have advanced our awareness of the problems and the different possibilities of solution. Objectives are defined. Jobs are analyzed. Specialized staffs are added. Relationships are clarified. Methods of developing executives for the future are devised. The identification of obstacles to cooperation will aid in removing them. Waste of many kinds may be found and cut—including an excess of men near the top. Good organization adapts to changing conditions.

Some businesses tackle the problem themselves. They can draw upon a wealth of guidance from the publications of the American Management Association, the National Industrial Conference Board, trade associations, and other organizations. Companies often bring in outsiders.[11] Time and again, studies reveal ways to improve significantly. Outsiders, of course, make mistakes: they may fail to recognize that Joe is a prima donna who needs unusual conditions to exercise his talents or that this firm must have a special kind of personnel department because of the union with which it must deal. Organization is art as well as science. Nevertheless, results leave no doubt that disciplined, rational analysis has helped many a business find more effective ways of improving its internal organization. This progress owes no small amount to the development of mechanical facilities, not only computers, which have multiplied the information management can obtain and disseminate. Important, too, has been improvement in methods for the selection, training, and assignment of people.

The picture is not all rosy. Businesses age. Leaders get set in their ways. A form of organization becomes fixed and thereby multiplies the difficulties of making any major change. Traditions within the firm give the engineering, sales, or legal department a position which is hard to alter to meet new needs. Union contracts may prevent desired modernization of something like the authority of foremen; tax laws make certain actions costly. Subtle forces molding the "organization man" endanger creativity. The established organization may be well adapted for some things, but badly for others. Businesses become bureaucracies inside. Routine dulls imagination and initiative. Internal rivalries and conflicts distort operations. Always there will be uncertainty about what is best.

BIG BUSINESS

A few hundred businesses account for a large fraction of total output. We may look at 200 or 500 large companies, but wherever we draw our line, we find giants at the top, dwarfing the majority. Some serve us every day and serve us well. Yet their dominance may make us uneasy. This section presents some of the facts and issues. The analysis resumes later as we study the cost advantages and disadvantages of large-scale operations, the price-output possibilities of firms with monopolistic power, and the efforts of government to deal with monopoly, business concentration, and restraints on trade.

Difference between "Firm" and "Plant." To begin, we distinguish the "firm" or "company" from the "plant." The firm is the business

---

[11] Firms of business consultants, industrial engineers, management counselors, or men using other titles have been growing rapidly and becoming ever more specialized. Such help may be called upon to plan a new system of purchasing, reorganize the flow of parts to an assembly line, set up a pension plan, study locations for expansion, advise on the economic merits of different types of equipment or pricing, or recruit executives. Operations research and linear programming represent modern developments for dealing with business problems by applying scientific methods. They use, among other things, the economic concept of maximizing, or rational search for the optimum solution.

organization, the corporation—Ford or Swift—legally a unit. (It is also part of a larger group—the industry—engaged in essentially similar activity.) A plant is a physical unit—a single factory, grocery store, mine, warehouse, and so on. A plant is not self-contained. It relies upon outside sources for supplies. Yet it has a cohesion and unity of its own. It is a tangible thing, one that can be identified as distinct from other physical units.

One firm may own and operate many plants—big corporations usually do. General Motors, for example, has about 127 plants in 70 U.S. localities. Plants may be generally similar to each other (A&P supermarkets) or very different (Bethlehem Steel's ship lines, rolling mills, and coal mines). A huge firm may consist mostly of relatively small plants, Woolworth's for example. A single plant may serve several firms: an office building used by dozens of businesses or the parking lot of a shopping center.

Statistics on Big Business.   There is no better way to start discussing bigness than with the facts. What are they? Or, better, what are the most significant facts? Answering such questions baffles the experts. In sheer size, some businesses are huge. Whether we measure by their balance sheet totals of assets, by sales, by employment, by number of stockholders, by number of separate stores or factories, we see bigness.

A few business corporations employ more people, own more property, and handle more money than several state or large city governments combined. General Motors' 1966 sales equaled almost three fifths of *all* state tax collections, while General Electric has almost twice as many employees as the state of California. When you look for a job, the chances are great that you will try one of the business giants. Or if you invest in stock, you will likely buy their shares. One out of every 70 persons—men, women, and children—in the country is a direct owner of stock in AT&T. One firm can produce more steel than Britain or France. The industrial and merchandising corporations with sales of over $1 billion each in 1966 sold a total of about $190 billion and had around 7 million employees.

Measuring size in terms of assets (Table 4–1), we find that six of the

TABLE 4–1. Corporations with Assets over $12 Billion Each, 1966 (In Billions)

American Telephone and Telegraph	$35.2
Prudential Insurance	23.6
Metropolitan Life	23.5
Bank of America	18.2
Chase Manhattan Bank	15.8
First National City Bank	15.1
Standard Oil, New Jersey	13.9
General Motors	12.9
Equitable Life Assurance	12.6

TABLE 4–2. Large American Corporations: Selected Data, 1966*

Name	Assets, Billions	Sales, Billions	Employees, Thousands	Assets per Employee, Thousands†	Profit† as Percent of Owners' Investment (Net Worth)
Manufacturing					
General Motors	$12.9	$20.2	745	$ 17	20.6
Standard Oil, N.J.	13.9	12.2	149	93	12.2
Ford Motor	8.1	12.2	388	21	13.0
U.S. Steel	5.8	4.4	206	27	7.8
General Electric	4.9	7.2	350	14	15.3
Swift & Co.	.7	3.0	50	14	1.2
Mobil Oil	5.5	5.3	81	64	9.7
Gulf Oil	5.9	3.8	56	105	12.3
International Business Machines	4.7	4.2	198	24	15.8
DuPont	3.0	3.2	115	26	16.8
Douglas Aircraft	.9	1.0	80	116	Loss 15.8
Borden	.9	1.5	40	23	10.0
Avon Products§	.2	.4	14	18	37.0
Coastal States Gas‖	.3	.2	1	312	20.8
Merchandising					
Great Atlantic and Pacific	$ .8	$5.5	140	$ 6	9.2
Sears, Roebuck	5.3	6.8	300	18	14.6
Safeway	.6	3.4	75	9	15.7
Woolworth	1.0	1.6	90	11	10.3
J.C. Penney	.8	2.5	105	8	16.7
Transportation and Utilities					
Pennsylvania RR	$ 3.8	$ 1.1	66	$ 58	4.9
New York Central RR	2.5	.8	42	60	5.0
Southern Pacific RR	2.8	1.0	50	55	5.9
United Airlines	1.2	.9	41	29	9.1
Greyhound Bus	.4	.5	34	13	19.9
American Telephone and Telegraph	35.2	12.1	650	54	9.5
Pacific Gas and Electric	3.5	.9	22	158	10.0
Consolidated Edison	3.5	.9	24	145	7.0
Commonwealth Edison	2.3	.7	13	172	13.0

* Many corporations not included are larger in one or more respects than are some listed here. Treatment of foreign operations and assets varies.
† Rounded.
‡ Profit is after payment of taxes. The year 1966 was one of peak profits; the figures here, therefore, are above the average.
§ Included because of high rate of profit.
‖ Included because of high investment (assets) per employee.
Sources: Fortune, summer 1967 issues. Moody's financial services.

nine with assets over $12 billion each are insurance companies and banks. In a sense they are intermediaries—getting their size because of the property they hold for others. Thus they have features that distinguish them from, say, a manufacturing or commercial business. Their assets, and especially their liabilities (large amounts being subject to call on short notice), differ substantially from those of other businesses. They operate under the supervision of government. So does another, AT&T.

Table 4–2 presents figures on size of a few of the largest nonfinancial corporations, especially manufacturing companies. One oversimplifies, of course, in calling many of these "manufacturing" firms. Most engage in other activities, such as transportation (oil companies with their own pipelines and tankers), mining (steel firms with their own ore and coal mines), finance, selling at retail, and other. This small sample indicates a little of the great variety in the relations between a few of the many factors: assets, sales, number of employees, and profit rates.

Concentration in Industry.   Bigness itself presents problems. Other problems are associated more with bigness *relative* to something else. For example, the size of a firm in relation to the size of the industry or the market in which it functions seem important. What is big in one case may be small in another. The Green Bay Packers may be big business in the sports world; but they handle much less money than, say, Commercial Solvents, which is small in the chemical industry. Life insurance, an industry with around $175 billion assets (1968), can accommodate more billion-dollar firms than a much smaller industry without running up against the problems of domination by a few units. Recognizing this element of the problem, statisticians have tried to measure *concentration*—not the absolute size of firms, but the proportion of total industry assets, of value added in production, of employment, or of sales of a few firms.

Unfortunately, this measuring also turns out to be surprisingly difficult. The facts are incomplete. Moreover, even defining "industry" proves baffling. The general definition is that an *industry* consists of all the plants producing a single product or a closely related group of products. One can define a *product* broadly or narrowly: clothing, men's clothing, shirts, white shirts, white shirts selling for less than $4. Where should we draw lines?[12]

---

[12] The *Standard Industrial Classification Manual* of the U.S. government classifies all activities (profit and nonprofit) into 10 broad divisions. These include 99 "major groups" (2-digit numbers). For example, "manufacturing" is one of the 10 divisions, with numbers from 19 through 39. "Furniture and fixtures" is a major group under manufacturing with number 25. "Food and kindred products," another major industry group in manufacturing has number 20. Major industry groups are subdivided into "industry groups" (3-digit) which are then subdivided into "industries" (4-digit);

Even if we define product or industry broadly—chemicals, meat, steel—the corporations in which we must become interested produce other things. Allied Chemical produces textile fibers; Armour, a meat packer, produces drugs; and Wilson, another packer, is a leading maker of sporting goods; soap companies manufacture shortening, a food, and toothpaste. The typical large business produces many types of things and services, and thus claims a position in different industries. Eastman Kodak is a leading producer of plastics; General Motors is the largest producer of railroad locomotives. Though we do as well as humans can in drawing a line to define a product and decide which firms are in the industry, some smart fellow can point to something relevant that does not fit in neatly. His point is not a quibble but has deep significance; *where product frontiers are vague, invasion is always a threat.* With this reservation about the fuzziness of the industry classifications, revealing facts are presented (Table 4–3).

Clearly, in the manufacture of telephone equipment, steam engines, TV tubes, and numerous other things not listed here, the four largest firms—not plants—account for the lion's share of output. Note that in some cases concentration increased in the period. In others, however, it fell. If we were to present data on industries supplied predominantly by the largest eight firms, there would be many more with high concentration by this measure.

In sharp contrast is the lack of concentration in clothing. In between the extremes of high and low concentration are areas of the economy where the eight largest firms account for a big fraction, sometimes over half, of output. If products were defined more narrowly, the figures of concentration would be larger.

In local markets concentration is often high. The significance depends heavily upon costs of transportation and communication. For example, in the United States as a whole, the four largest producers of ready-mixed concrete accounted for only 4 percent of shipments in 1963. This product, however, cannot be transported economically over long distances; what counts, then, will be concentration locally. An earlier study found

---

these are then subdivided by "product class" (5-digit) and "product" (7-digit) groupings, for example:

Standard Industrial Classification Code	Designation	Name
20	Major industry group	Food and kindred products.
201	Industry group	Meat products.
2011	Industry	Meat packing.
20111	Product class	Fresh beef.
20111–12	Product	Whole carcass beef.

TABLE 4–3. Concentration in Selected Manufacturing Industries, 1950, 1958, and 1963

Industry	Percentage of Output* Accounted for by Four Largest Firms		Percentage of Employ- ment Accounted for by Four Largest Firms	
	1958	1963	1950	1963
High-Concentration Industries†				
Tires and inner tubes	74	70	78	72
Gypsum products	88	84	89	84
Telephone and telegraph apparatus	92	92	90	89
Steam engines and turbines	87	93	87	90
Soap and glycerine	90	72	69	55
Cigarets	79	80	81	74
Rubber footwear	65	62	n.a.	54
Motor vehicles and parts	75	79	59	67
Vacuum cleaners	70	81	53	83
Cathode-ray picture tubes	n.a.	91	n.a.	85
Aircraft engines and parts	56	56	54	51
Computing machines	n.a.	67	70	65
Low-Concentration Industries‡				
Metal-cutting machine tools	21	20	25	22
Weaving mills, cotton	25	30	14	26
Folding paperboard boxes	n.a.	21	12	16
Men's and boys' suits and coats	11	14	13	12
Commercial printing	10	13	9	12
Wood furniture, not upholstered	9	11	6	9
Sawmills and planing mills	8	11	4	9
Women's suits, coats, and skirts	3	8	n.a.	4

* Measured by shipments in most cases, by value added in others. Industry definitions are not entirely uniform for the periods compared.
† Four largest firms account for over 50 percent of total.
‡ Four largest firms account for less than 50 percent of total.
n.a. = Not available.
Source: Bureau of the Census, Concentration Ratios in Manufacturing Industry, 1963.

that in the District of Columbia the four largest suppliers shipped 100 percent, in the small state of Delaware, 87 percent, effectively high concentration; for large states, such as California, the figure of 21 percent reveals rather little about local concentration. Confectionery products showed national concentration of 15 percent (the four largest suppliers); for Virginia the figure of 95 percent does not necessarily prove high concentration because supplies can come from other states. The degree of intercommunity competition or substitution tends to be relatively low—and local concentration is often high—in service industries.

Facts on concentration deal with the *structure* of industry. They do not tell us about *performance*. In general, however, we can reasonably conclude that industries with many firms—low concentration—are likely to be competitive. The higher the degree of concentration, the greater the public needs to be aware of monopolistic practices, obstacles to the broad and vigorous competition which is the powerhouse of economic progress.

Big Business: Types of Organization.
Each big firm differs from others. Yet general patterns throw light on important issues. Some big businesses consist largely of many units that do about the same thing. They are organized *horizontally*. Chain stores offer an example; by adding more and more stores, each much like the others, the firm can build to large size. Such expansion is growth in *breadth*, with most units on the same level of the economic process. A firm can be large, of course, with relatively few units—the big cigaret producers.

Contrasting is *vertical* organization, also known as *integration*. The firm has units which perform two, several, or all of many different functions; successive stages in the productive process are integrated into a whole. Oil companies explore, drill, transport, refine, market; they also carry on research, manufacture numerous products, help their retailers in a variety of ways. From raw material in one place to finished product in another, the integrated firm may, itself, perform most of the important functions. In a sense, it grows in *depth*.

Large companies almost always have elements of both horizontal and vertical organization. Other internal characteristics help to account for organization of vast activities. A common *raw material*, such as cattle or oil, may lead a business into many different fields, to a great variety of end products. Or one general type of *processing* may lead a firm to do things—producing diverse chemicals—which require widely varied materials and appeal to entirely different markets. Success in research and pressures to produce for the military sometimes account for a surprising medley of activities.

The combination, in one firm, of plants making a large variety of food products may be explained partly by hopes that *selling effort* can be more effective; once a salesman gets into the purchasing agent's office, he needs little more time to canvass for several products than for one or two, and so also with delivery. The ability to offer a *full line* may be an advantage, leading a firm into some branches of business it might not otherwise enter—the Fuller Brush Company's selling of cosmetics and toothpaste.

Some firms diversify to even out *seasonal* variations, some to avoid the danger of having "all their eggs in one basket" in case of a general or regional recession, change of taste, rise of new competition, or other development. Some companies are such groupings of apparently unrelated activities that one looks in vain for any real coherence. The term *conglomerate* (or "circular") is applied to such firms, and they seem to be growing in their relative importance in the world of big business. When companies merge because of their major operations, the secondary aspects of each firm can be utterly unrelated. Today the paths of growth are frequently determined by the discoveries of the research staff, and such discoveries can involve things quite different from anything deliberately sought.

In a few industries, two or more separate corporations sometimes form joint subsidiaries. For example, three large steel companies acquired 25 subsidiaries jointly, often sharing ownership with one or more additional corporations. Large steel firms also own subsidiaries jointly with chemical and other corporations. Rather little is known publicly about how these joint ownership arrangements function in running the various subsidiaries. Yet if firms act *jointly* in one activity, may they not in doing so find ways to reduce the vigor of competition in other aspects of business?

Advantages of Large Size. Why have a few firms become so big in relation to the total market—not in corn farming but in making cigarets; in manufacturing, not low-priced dresses but autos? Some reasons apply more to plants, others to firms. Some *productive* advantages reflect real efficiency—fewer inputs of labor and materials per unit of output. Or the nature of the product or service, or its quality, requires "large-scale" instead of "small-scale" production.

Some advantages of large size in a business are those of *bargaining*, however; big size enables the company to get some inputs at lower prices, or sell some outputs at higher prices, than if it were smaller. The benefits of the corporation's size to it are offset by monetary disadvantages to others in the economy. We shall wait until Part 4 to examine more fully the cost aspects of large-scale operations.

How Did Firms Become Big? No single or simple fact explains the growth of today's great corporations. Some have developed more or less in step with the whole economy. They have expanded to supply rising demand, and the growth of firms has been essentially that of the industry. Highly important has been the *reinvestment of earnings*. Ford is a striking example, but growth from retaining profit has played some part in all cases. From 1946 to 1966, General Motors grew about $5.4 billion through undistributed earnings. In nature, only the redwoods may grow endlessly; but, in business, any profitable firm can expand indefinitely. Orders for military equipment have played a decisive role in the growth of some companies, not only the giants.

Growth has also come from the *combining* or *merger* of firms. Small or medium-sized or even big firms join to make a bigger one. Different legal forms may be used. A *holding company* may be formed to acquire voting control of existing corporations, some of which keep their corporate identities. Or one corporation in exchange for its own shares may acquire another and dissolve it as a separate entity; this form, *merger,* is today the most widely used. Another device is to form a new corporation to buy the stock of others, which are then dissolved.[13] There was a wave of industrial combinations around 1900 (combinations of separate small railroads into larger systems had begun much earlier), another in the 1920's, and some in the late 1930's. Since World War II, there has been a more or less continuous flow of mergers.

In the combination movement around the turn of the century, and again in the 1920's, two motives were more influential than were admitted publicly: (1) to restrict competition and (2) to make profit for the promoters, who hoped to get a generous fee for joining companies. The two reasons were related because some of the promoters' profit was what the buyers of stock would pay (at once) to receive the additional long-run earnings expected from the reduction of competition.

Were the combinations designed to bring greater operating efficiency? Evidence is by no means complete. The railroad consolidations were often designed, at least in part, to improve operations. Rockefeller, in forming Standard Oil, was motivated by a desire to reduce what he thought were wastes of competition. Another factor played a part: the desire of leaders to build industrial empires, to gain power and prestige by controlling larger organizations. Generally, the dominating reason does not seem to have been a prospect of lowering production costs. The combinations were not the inevitable result of drives for technical efficiency.

The numerous and widespread mergers of recent years—many of local or regional scope only—spring from highly complex facts. Reasons (in addition to those for cost reduction, "empire building," and softening competition) include the desire to (*a*) diversify the product line, (*b*) get a foothold in an industry with a high growth potential, (*c*) enter new regions, (*d*) acquire management, physical facilities, or research organization, (*e*) assure sources of supplies or marketing organization, (*f*) get a business with better growth possibilities than one's own for the use of retained profits, (*g*) "take over" a corporation whose stock, perhaps because of lethargic management and poor earnings, can be acquired for appreciably less than the underlying assets are worth, and (*h*) meet one or another tax problem.

For various reasons—shortage of capital for modernization, lack of younger managers to carry on, tax considerations, intensity of competition—the owner of a smaller business may actively seek to sell out to one much larger. The antitrust laws give the government power to prevent mergers that will "substantially" lessen competition "in any line of commerce in any section of the country"; the law has unquestionably prevented many mergers, but the rate since 1960 seems to have averaged

---

[13] At one time, men who wanted to combine companies would give a trustee enough stock of each to assure voting control. He then had legal control and could operate the different corporations as a unit. This early use of the *trust* device has left its name in our language of big business.

appreciably above that a decade earlier.[14] Chapter 21 deals with governmental policy toward big business.

TERMS AND CONCEPTS

sole proprietorship	cooperative	conglomerate
limited life	board of directors	merger
unlimited liability	pyramiding	productive advantage
limited liability part-	holding company	bargaining advantage
nership	decentralization	integration (vertical
corporation	concentration	and horizontal)
transferability	consolidation	firm

QUESTIONS

1. What is the economic significance of the legal features that are peculiar to the corporation?

2. "If a single proprietorship involves personal financial risks for the owner, a partner in a business firm runs still greater risks." Under what conditions, if any, is this statement true? Untrue? Why do businessmen choose to form partnerships?

3. Distinguish between the *productive* advantages and the *bargaining* advantages of large size in (a) the firm and (b) the plant. The disadvantages.

4. "The permanence of the corporation virtually assures that efficient firms will eventually become large." Comment.

5. Why are most U.S. businesses sole proprietorships, even though the bulk of business assets is owned by corporations?

6. Could a large business operate efficiently if decisions were made democratically by employees? By stockholders? Why?

7. What are the major features of cooperatives?

8. "The corporation as a form of organization permits not only great flexibility but also continuing development." Comment.

9. In what sense is a business manager limited by market forces? What power does he have?

10. What would you judge to be nonprofit goals of businesses?

11. "The public interest requires that business leaders be trained not only in the skills needed for financial efficiency but also in ethics." Discuss. Would the same apply to leaders of other groups? Why? How could such needs be met?

---

[14] The increase in the business population would lead one to expect more mergers because more companies exist to join together. The Federal Trade Commission identified 1,008 mergers in 1965, compared with 673 in 1956. Figures cover only larger firms and do not include many smaller companies. The effectiveness of the law cannot be suggested by any available figures because no one knows how many mergers which might have taken place were not attempted because of the existence of the law.

5

THE FINANCING OF BUSINESS:
SECURITY MARKETS

To double the standard of living in a quarter-century, with all that that means in the final abolition of want and squalor, is not a fantasy. It is a practical possibility—but only with the aid of a massive, unobstructed, and enterprising investment of capital, not in the places where it will "do most social good," but in the places where it will be most productive.
                                    The Economist (*London*), Oct. 16, 1954

Businesses, like college students, often find the job of getting resources more involved than merely wishing. The acquisition of buildings, machines, materials, and labor requires money.

Every business has some *equity* capital unless losses have eaten it away. Equity ("net worth" or "proprietorship") is what the owners have put in—money, earnings retained in the company, effort, real estate, inventions—for which they have received only a general claim on the firm. Before discussing equity, however, let us look at another way businesses get resources: by going into *debt*—or getting *credit*.

DEBT

"Open Account" and "Trade Credit" Debt. The most common debt is on "open account." Businesses go into debt to employees who work a week or two before payday and to suppliers who send goods before receiving payment. The debt incurred in this way provides financing but, to a large degree, the amounts cancel out from one firm to another. Though for the individual firm open account debt is a source of borrowing, the amount thus obtained may be offset by short-term advances made to its own customers, who ordinarily get 10 days or so to pay.

101

For all nonfinancial corporations in 1967, accounts receivable (loans to others) were over $220 billion; accounts payable (debts to others), except taxes, were about $190 billion. On balance, "open account" debt is less a net source of funds than an immensely valuable convenience, one which provides a means of flexible adjustment to small and temporary changes. The ability to grant, or to get, "trade credit" can be important in competition. The order may go to one supplier rather than another because of differences in the time allowed for payment. During periods when companies find that loans are difficult to get, as in 1966, some big firms with access to funds do much, more or less informally, to finance customers and suppliers.

Formal Short-Run Financing.   More formal borrowing will also provide funds. An individual proprietor, partner, or manager of a corporation trying to borrow may want the money for only a few months. A bank is the logical place to turn, but other, more specialized and often more expensive, sources of short-term loans are available for many businesses. Short-term loans rise and fall, providing a convenient way to adapt to changing conditions. Yet, if you were a businessman, you might dislike being dependent upon an outside source for even temporary financial needs. Who can then be the master of his own affairs?

Long-Term Debt: Bonds.   To pay for more permanent facilities, or to be free from the uncertainty of your banker's decisions, you may borrow for a period of many years. Any business with real estate can try to get funds by *mortgaging* it. A corporation may also sell *bonds*. In return for dollars received now, the corporation promises to pay a specific amount (interest) periodically, say every 6 months; it also promises to return a fixed number of dollars at the end of a period, perhaps 15 or 50 years. Bonds may be *negotiable* or *registered*.

1. A negotiable bond can change ownership as easily as a $5 bill, and the corporation may have no idea who owns it. One side of the bond will look somewhat like a sheet of big postage stamps; each "stamp" is a *coupon* with a date, one coupon for each interest payment due. As the interest date rolls around, the owner of the bond can cut off ("clip") the coupon and give it to his bank; the bank will give him the amount shown if it knows that the corporation has made funds available to its "paying agent," usually a big-city bank. Or the bondholder may send the coupon directly to the paying agent.
2. If the bond is registered, the owner is listed with the corporation's agent, and interest checks are mailed; changes of ownership must be recorded.

If all of a bond issue matures (falls due for repayment) at the same time, the corporation may be hard-pressed for enough cash. Therefore, *serial* bonds are now common; a small fraction of the total falls due on each of a series of specific dates. Or the corportation may reserve the right to *call* some or all of the issue for repayment (redemption) when it wishes, perhaps paying a little extra for requiring the lender to find another use of his funds.

But what if a corporation cannot or will not live up to the terms? The lender in turning over good money for long periods faces some hazards, and ordinarily he will try to protect himself. One safeguard can be essentially a mortgage—a claim on specific physical assets, perhaps those to be bought with the loan funds; some of the property may be generally salable. Often, however, machines, buildings, and land are so built around each other that it is not practical to sell a fraction only; taking advantage of a mortgage provision in a bond may be clumsy and expensive. For this reason, the chief concern in arranging for the issue of long-term bonds is usually the total net value of the business, especially the prospects for earning income. A *debenture bond* gives a general pledge on the property and earnings of the business. An *income bond* offers less protection, for the interest will have to be paid only when earned. A corporation issuing bonds may give other assurances, such as promising to keep the lenders informed, or agreeing not to go further into debt without their consent, or not to pay out profits to owners unless there is ample money for bondholders. Otherwise, however, the *bondholder has neither the right nor the responsibility to take part in running the business.*

Another type of corporation debt, the *convertible bond,* has gained popularity. The owner of the bond gets the right to convert it into common stock on certain specified terms. Thus Bethlehem Steel sold debenture bonds which, for each $1,000, could be converted into 40 shares of common stock at $36.25 each. Such debt gives the bondholder an opportunity to share in any substantial rise in the worth of the corporation—in this case if the company's stock went, for example, to $40. Meanwhile, the bondholder is assured of the fixed income of debt and the eventual return of at least the face amount of the bond.

The amount any firm can borrow, and the cost of borrowing, depend significantly upon the amount of equity capital. The more a company's equity capital, the less the risk to lenders. The proportion of debt to equity varies greatly, but as a rule each added dollar of equity will support more than one dollar of added debt.

Leases. Instead of buying land, buildings, or even equipment, a business may contract to pay a rental and get the use of the property for a few years or many decades. The typical chain-store organization does not, ordinarily, own the buildings in which it has stores. Chains (and other businesses, too) lease, perhaps for many years, on terms which often give the owner a fixed minimum rental plus a percentage of sales.[1] Equipment

---

[1] Colleges, insurance companies, and even some small investors welcome an opportunity to finance such leases. Long-term real estate leases are often on a "net" basis; the occupant agrees to pay real estate taxes, maintenance, and operating costs; the

leasing grows for several reasons; some producers of machines have better access to financing than smaller companies which use the equipment; servicing, repair, replacement, and tax factors are sometimes arranged more smoothly when machines are leased rather than sold.

EQUITY: PROPRIETORSHIP

Equity capital comes as a result of both formal transfer of property by owners to the business, and the "plowing back" of earnings. Equity represents what exists for the proprietors. It is the difference between the value of what the firm owns and what it owes others. The equity in a corporation is represented by shares of stock.

Preferred Stock.   Preferred stock, though varying widely in details, is a share in ownership. Though there are several types, some features are customary. This stock is a little like a bond in that it ordinarily provides for a fixed payment (a dividend) each year, $5 a share perhaps. Unlike a bond, however, preferred stock does not fall due and thus have to be redeemed on a set schedule. If the corporation ceases to exist, and after its debts are paid, the owner of preferred stock has a claim of a fixed amount on any assets that remain, $100 a share for example, before the owners of other stock get anything. Usually, preferred stock gives the owner no right to vote for directors or otherwise to determine the firm's policies, unless the dividends have not been paid for 2 years or so. As a rule, dividends are *cumulative;* any amount unpaid in the past must be paid before common stockholders get anything. The failure to pay preferred dividends will not send the corporation into bankruptcy, as will failure to pay interest on debt. Sometimes preferred stock may be *convertible* into common stock on specified terms, perhaps two shares of common for one of preferred. Occasionally, preferred stock is *participating;* in addition to the fixed dividend, it shares in extra earnings after the common stock has gotten some specified amount.

Common Stock.   Common stock represents the "residual" ownership. Those who own the shares usually have all the power to vote for directors, and also the right to all the earnings (after prior claims have been met). If the corporation is liquidated, the common stock gets what is left after the debtors and preferred stockholders have been satisfied. Operating losses, therefore, reduce whatever will be available for owners. Obviously, the owner of common stock risks more than the owner of preferred stock or bonds. For the owner of common stock nothing is fixed. Not only is there much more doubt about dividends—the amount

---

owner of the property is free of both expense and management responsibility. The yields can be attractive. Businesses would rather use their funds for inventory and other operating purposes than tie them up in real estate. The U.S. government leases almost all post-office buildings.

of profit earned and the fraction paid out—but also more doubt about what the owner can get if he wants to sell. Why? Because the amount people will pay for any property, in this case shares of stock, depends upon their estimates of what it will earn and pay in dividends in the future; these estimates vary more when nothing is fixed.[2]

Internal Financing for Expansion. Earnings reinvested rather than distributed to the owners make up an important source of funds for expansion. In recent years, AT&T, in relying almost exclusively, and other utilities less completely, on the sale of new stock and bonds for additional capital, are exceptions.[3] Many businesses grow for years while depending predominantly on reinvested profit. From 1950 to 1966, corporations retained, for internal investment, some $200 billion out of a little over $390 billion after-tax earnings. Profits retained by corporations have for several years ranged from one fourth to one third of net savings for the whole economy. Internal financing frees the company from the need to pay interest later, an expense associated with borrowing,[4] and has the advantages of equity financing without the cost of selling new securities.

Table 5–1 shows the sources and uses of corporate funds in 1966, i.e., dollars available for financing expansion and replacement and the major types of outlays on which funds were used. The very large amounts consisting of depreciation can be used to pay for new equipment and properly belong in "cash flow"; over the years, however, these dollars do not pay for more than replacement and so do not finance expansion.

Relative Advantages of Debt and Equity Financing. In choosing among financing devices, what would be the relative merits of each? The obvious advantage of short-term debt financing is that it provides flexibility; the needs of peak periods—financing Christmas business—can be met without tying up funds during the rest of the year. Some stockholders

[2] A corporation may "split" its stock, issuing, say, 2 or 10 new shares for each old one. Or it may pay a dividend in stock, perhaps 1 new share for each 20 held. Though in each case the stockholders really own no more of the business than before, they may feel happier with more shares; marketability of each share is somewhat greater when price is, say, $30 than $60.

[3] In the spring of 1964, AT&T sold $1.2 billion of new stock, much more than all new issues of corporate stock in 1963.

[4] Financing in this way *does* have an economic cost—the value of sacrificed alternative. It may be expressed in terms of the interest which the owner could obtain if he used the earnings to buy bonds. During the early postwar period, a special fact or often added an important reason against sale of new common stock. Shares already outstanding frequently sold below the per share amount which had been put into the corporation previously (book value). To sell new stock at the current market price would "dilute the equity." For example, when J. I. Case, Inc., wanted to raise additional funds in 1958, the common stock with book value of $37 a share was selling for about $20. If new shares were sold for $20, the new stockholders would in a sense be "given" some of the property of the former stockholders. Rising stock prices have eliminated many such cases.

TABLE 5–1. Sources and Uses of Corporate Funds, 1966 (In Billions)

Uses	
Plant and equipment outlays	$62.3
Inventory change, book value	10.9
Customer net receivables, change	12.0
Cash and other assets	7.6
Total	$92.8
Sources	
Internal	
Retained profits*	$21.2
Depreciation†	37.5
External	
Change in bank and mortgage loans, net	$19.5
Stocks, net new issues	1.2
Bonds, net new issues	10.2
Other‡	6.4
Total	$96.0
Statistical discrepancy§	3.2

* Includes depletion.
† Includes amortization.
‡ Includes change in federal income tax accrued but not yet paid.
§ Total sources are known to be greater than the amounts which can be accounted for in the separate categories; since it is not possible to decide which of the categories is shown incorrectly, a balancing item, "statistical discrepancy," appears.
Source: U.S. Department of Commerce, Office of Business Economics.

prefer to have the corporation go into debt rather than issue more stock, because debt does not require owners to share the key responsibilities or threaten their control as long as things go well or require sharing the fruits of especially successful growth. Otherwise, the chief *advantage of debt* is that it provides new funds at less cost than does equity financing by the sale of new stock.

1. The fixed and prior claim on earnings, and the priority if the business is liquidated, give the owner of debt some or complete *protection against loss.*[5] Laws require life insurance companies, savings banks, and some other institutions to put most of their funds into such fixed-claim securities. Other investors are willing to sacrifice a chance for higher yield to get safety and

[5] The market price of debt obligations of a corporation can fall much below par ($1,000 for a $1,000 bond) in spite of the existence of property which is apparently worth more than the obligations of the business. Why? One reason is that investors recognize that past management, which is presumably experienced, could not earn enough to cover costs. Will future earning power be better? Unless there is special basis for optimism, the practical possibilities of benefiting from ownership of the debt do not justify paying the face amount of the bond or mortgage. The economic strength of the business as such counts for more than the claim on its fixed assets. Changes in the general level of interest rates, as we shall see, can also reduce the market prices of bonds issued in the past.

stability. Moreover, they need not assume the worries of management. A corporation may be able to borrow for 5 percent when it would have to offer half again as much on preferred stock.

2. For the firm, an advantage of debt over equity is lower taxes, as illustrated in Table 5–2.

A *disadvantage of* (*long-term*) *debt* to the borrower, and perhaps to the economy, is its *inflexibility*. When business is poor, interest and debt falling due cannot always be paid. Bankruptcies and forced sales result, disrupting, distorting, and aggravating the decline of business out of proportion to the seriousness of the original drop. Even when business is good, the inflexibility of debt can have bad results; earnings of the equity are exaggerated, leading some businessmen and investors to make unwise decisions.[6] Moreover, debt must be repaid; as the due date approaches, operations may have to be curtailed—or expansion restrained—as cash is accumulated and then paid out to retire debt. A defect of the debt to the lender appears during inflation, i.e., when the general level of prices goes up. The owner of the debt has a claim expressed in a fixed number of dollars, but these become worth less in purchasing power. If the price level falls, of course, the positions of borrower and lender are reversed.

Common stock has more risk for the buyer; therefore, the corporation must offer the prospect of benefits greater than the rate of interest. The prospective benefit can include sharing in the growth of the company, a consideration which has been rated highly since World War II. A disadvantage in small- and medium-sized firms is that *complications over control* may develop. Some investors will not want to turn over money for a general, nonfixed claim without some control of the business.[7] Common stock financing, however, minimizes the exaggeration of the effects on a firm of fluctuations in business generally, with the contrasting dangers of bankruptcy and overoptimistic expansion. Preferred stock falls between common stock and debt in most of these respects and is not widely used.

In choosing between debt and equity, taxation strongly *favors debt* (*and leasing*). The interest (or rental) cost of debt (or a lease) is deductible in figuring the corporation's taxable income. But the amounts available

---

[6] This is a result of "leverage." Assume a corporation with $1,000,000 capital, $900,000 debt with an average interest of 5 percent, requiring $45,000 a year. If the firm earns 5 percent after tax on its total capital, common stockholders get $5,000, that is, 5 percent of what they have put in. If overall earnings go up to 7 percent, a rise of $20,000 (40 percent) the $70,000 will leave $25,000 for the common stock; this is five times as much as before.

[7] In small corporations, the owner-officers may vote themselves salaries which absorb most of the earnings: The corporation can save income tax by such action because the profit subject to tax is the amount after salaries. If, instead of the extra salary, officers had chosen to show more profit and distribute it as dividends, the corporation's tax would have been greater. Other stockholders may find themselves in a rather hopeless situation if owner-officers decide to take "large" salaries which are not unreasonable in the eyes of the law.

to owners of stock are taxed to the corporation and then again (with minor exceptions) to the stockholders if paid out in dividends. This extra burden on equity financing is considerable because the corporation income tax rate is 48 percent of all earnings over $25,000. For example, assume a corporation has $12 million capital on which it earns an average of slightly over 8 percent, $1 million a year. If it has only common and preferred stock, it must pay tax on the whole earnings, leaving about $480,000. If it has borrowed $8 million at 6 percent, it must pay $480,000 interest each year—*but* it can deduct this annual cost from the $1 million in figuring the amount on which it must pay tax. The tax on $520,000 would be about $249,000 (Table 5–2). Assuming that the same persons

TABLE 5–2.   Tax Advantages of Debt Financing for a Corporation: Illustration*

All Equity Financing		$8 Million Debt Financing	
Income	$1,000,000	Income	$1,000,000
Taxes	480,000	Interest	480,000
		Taxable income	520,000
Net for suppliers of capital	$ 520,000	Taxes	249,000
		Net for common stock	$ 271,000
		Net for suppliers of capital	
		($480,000 plus $271,000)	751,000
		Tax reduction	$ 231,000

* Personal income tax and minor adjustments not considered.

supply the total $12 million, they can usually keep much more of the annual earnings by choosing to take debt rather than equity securities.

Let us look at the alternatives in another way, assuming a combined federal-state tax on corporation earnings of 50 percent. If suppliers of risk capital insist upon 7 percent, the new productive facilities must produce 14 percent net before tax to leave stockholders with 7 percent.[8] No project which fails to give high prospect of such yield will be undertaken. But debt-financed projects producing only 7 percent (or even less) can be acceptable.

Figure 5–1 shows the relative importance of debt and other financing in recent years. New issues of common stock have been averaging around $3 billion a year. This amount is small in relation to the demands of pension funds, various kinds of trusts, and other institutions for shares which go into portfolios more or less permanently. Much stock, it seems,

[8] Most industrial countries which tax both corporations and individuals allow the stockholder some credit for tax paid by the corporation—Canada 20 percent and other lands sometimes more. The United States made essentially similar allowance of around 4 percent until the mid-1930's and from 1954 to 1964. President Kennedy convinced Congress that the revenue loss from this partial offset to "double taxation" benefited large stockholders unduly and cost the Treasury too much; the law was changed to give all stockholders exemption from personal income tax of $100 of dividends but nothing more.

FIGURE 5–1. New Financing and Reinvested Earnings of Nonfinancial Corporations, 1960–67*

Figures are *net* change in amounts outstanding and do not represent gross sales of new securities.

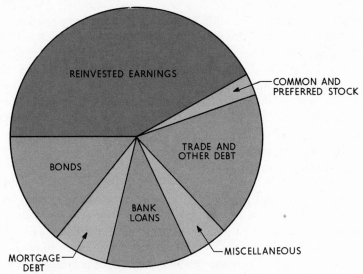

* Partly estimated. Data for 1967 for first 6 months only.
Source: Securities and Exchange Commission.

thus flows out of the source of potential supply available for future buyers in the market.

SELLING NEWLY ISSUED SECURITIES

Investment Banking. What organization brings together savers with funds to place and businesses or governments who want money to pay for new capital equipment? Special firms provide the machinery for selling newly issued securities. These firms also arrange the sale of shares which have been owned by a few people who decide that the corporation should "go public."

If you owned a business which could profitably use more capital, you would probably discuss the problem with your banker. From the facts you could present readily, he could suggest the approximate terms you would need to offer. You might then try to shop around to see if better terms were probable, asking "Should I try to sell long-term bonds, short-term notes, preferred stock, or common stock? Or get a mortgage? Or deal directly with an insurance company or other financial firm?" If you decided to go ahead and sell new securities—stocks or bonds—you would probably find the mechanics distressingly complex. For one thing, there would be a formidable job of getting together data.

More important would be negotiating with investment banks. But what are they? Until the 1930's, some were rather like other banks in that, among other things, they handled deposits. This is no longer permitted.

They now act as middlemen who specialize in marketing new securities.[9] After negotiating with two or three to get their tentative offers, you would select one and make a contract with it.

Preparing to Sell. The staff of the investment firm, working with yours, would then proceed with the costly and tedious job of assembling and checking data. (The work is simpler for security offerings by a state-local or foreign government, those restricted to residents of the state in which the issuing company is organized, banks, charitable institutions, and carriers subject to Interstate Commerce Commission regulations. Issues for less than $300,000 and those for private sale are exempt from the more strict of federal rules.) Securities and Exchange Commission rules, and the banker's own reputation, require that the figures be complete and accurate; the investment banker is subject to heavy penalties for material error (even jail, if the mistake is willful). The data must go beyond purely financial problems—for example, into the general history and prospects of the firm, its competitive position, the way it plans to use the money. Sometimes the banker engages his own engineers and appraisers to examine and value the property, his own auditors to review the accounts, and so on. When the job is done, the data are filed with the SEC, which makes a brief check for accuracy. Compliance with state regulations also requires attention.

The investment bank may feel able to sell the securities to its own customers, but commonly it needs a bigger market. So it gets in touch with other investment firms and invites them to participate in selling the issue. Arrangements, often called *syndicates*, vary from issue to issue; sometimes the firms contract to buy parts of the total and assume the risk of sale; other times they "underwrite" the issue, agreeing to buy any unsold amount at a specified price; sometimes they merely pledge to try to sell certain amounts.

Selling Procedures. While the SEC is checking the registration—to assure "truth in securities"—the major data are printed in a *prospectus*, a document of many pages which *must* be distributed to buyers of the issue. It discloses the major facts about the corporation, its business, and such details as just how much of the money which the investor pays will go to the corporation and how much to the bankers. Advertisements appear, and salesmen get in touch with potential purchasers. If the SEC finds no

---

[9] Investment banking firms often carry on stock brokerage operations as well. Securities sold by investment bankers are not necessarily to raise new money; they may be *refunding* issues, to get money to repay bonds falling due, or to replace existing securities with ones that seem more attractive. A few leading investment banking firms are Halsey Stuart & Co.; Kuhn Loeb & Co.; First Boston Corp.; White, Weld & Co.; Kidder, Peabody & Co.; Blyth & Co., Inc.; Goldman, Sachs, & Co.

errors, actual sale begins at the price fixed in advance. Sellers may canvass hundreds of small investors or find enough buyers in trusts, insurance companies, and other large investors.

The results depend partly upon the vigor of the selling effort and partly upon the price. If the bankers judged well on price and work energetically, the entire issue may be sold within a few hours. But what if market prices generally have fallen so that investors will not pay the price which has been set? The bankers must cut the offering price, wiping out some or all of their compensation. If market prices in general have risen, however, purchasers enjoy a quick gain. The process has risks that result partly from the volatility of prices on the stock exchange. New securities must always compete for investors' funds with a huge supply of seasoned, outstanding issues.

Judging the System. Asking: "How well does this system work?" you find the following ideas running through your mind:

1. Perhaps most impressive, you realize that you have money, probably from hundreds of investors scattered throughout the country.[10]

2. The cost may seem high. If your firm was not well known, 23 percent (or more) of the amount the buyers paid may have gone in costs of issue and sale. Even one of the country's industrial giants would probably pay over 5 percent to sell common stock.

3. Yet the investment firm did pay out some of its own money in acquiring data and arranging the sale (a good staff requires good pay), and it assumed risks.

4. You might feel that more competition could reduce the cost. You may take comfort in the fact that competition among investment bankers is greater than in the past. Yet no firm can undertake the expensive study needed to make firm bids unless it is certain to get the business. Each deal is tailor-made, and tailors cannot afford to cut and sew suits to individual measurements if they know that only one out of a half dozen tailors can make a sale.

5. In studying your affairs, the investment company may have suggested or insisted upon changes in your ways of doing things, perhaps demanding representation on your board of directors. At times investment bankers have exercised great control over even large corporations—the power of the purse—giving rise to the term *finance capitalism*. Such banker participation in business direction has been widely condemned. Wasteful, monopolizing results have perhaps been more than rare exceptions. Yet there have been constructive results: (*a*) banker directors may pass good judgments; and (*b*) by keeping in touch with the corporation, bankers can help protect the people who trusted them in buying securities.

[10] When U.S. Steel sold $300 million of bonds through a Morgan-Stanley Syndicate, there were 9,228 transactions in 48 states; half were for less than $20,000; over 35 percent, involving $110 million, were bank purchases, often for their clients. Life insurance companies and pension funds bought $109 million.

In the 1920's, investment firms with good reputations sponsored securities that had little merit and were grossly overpriced. The full facts were not disclosed to the public, and markets were manipulated deceptively to stimulate sales. One of many results was a public discrediting of the financial community. Gradually, however, confidence was rebuilt, and at times in the 1960's the public seemed almost avid for new common stock.

Improved financing facilities are needed for small- and medium-sized businesses. High taxes now make it difficult for many such firms, by re-investing their own earnings, to grow as rapidly as their business prospects would seem to justify. Inevitably, raising capital for small firms through security issues encounters obstacles. The amounts involved in individual cases are too small to justify the cost of much effort in investigating and selling. The outside investor, especially if he buys common stock, is at the mercy of management, an element of risk which cannot be evaluated readily. And the market for such securities will be unreliable.

Other Methods of Financing.   Well-known businesses or governments use *direct placement*. They negotiate with a buyer (such as a life insurance company), selling the entire issue directly and saving the investment firm's charges. In other cases, banks and insurance companies have combined to make long-term loans, the banks providing funds for the early years and the insurance company for the later period. Some businesses occasionally help finance others for long terms and, as noted earlier, provide tens of billions of short-term "trade credit" (waiting to be paid). The federal government through the Small Business Administration and a variety of other agencies has provided some private businesses with capital funds directly. Federal guarantees to banks and other private lenders encourage them to advance their own money to a business (such as a real estate developer); the funds are then secure against serious loss. Such guarantees usually apply to loans of a few years (longer for real estate), not permanent equity financing.

A few wealthy individuals or groups seek small (and risky) ventures for investment. The tax law now favors Small Business Investment Companies which, under SBA regulation, raise funds to provide equity capital and long-term loans to small businesses, especially those with good growth prospects. Many state and local governments also sponsor agencies to aid industrial development.

Valuable experience about financing new enterprise is being acquired—at the cost of tiring effort. Most applicants do not justify an investment, even by someone who is willing to assume heavy risks. Which new products will in the next decade develop as did nylon, and transistors? Testing the technical qualities of a proposal and comparing it with possible competitors requires costly engineering effort; production and marketing problems need analysis. The financing of existing small firms that are doing poorly raises other difficult problems: the quality of management, the outlook for competition, the reasons for current difficulties. We now look at the market for securities issued in the past.

SECURITY MARKETS

Between the sports section and the want ads of the daily paper, we find a list of leading American corporations with rather dull figures. A few readers will examine the list eagerly; others will ignore it on the way to the funnies. It summarizes an important feature of our economy: stock exchange transactions.

New York Stock Exchange. The New York Stock Exchange is the center of a large market, the spot where transactions are concluded.[11] The things exchanged are the evidence of ownership and of debt of a big part of our economy (and some foreign firms). Factories, railroad tracks, and oil tankers may be difficult to buy or sell (especially in small parts). Yet the pieces of paper which prove ownership in such things can be bought or sold in a matter of minutes. In some respects the large securities exchanges provide about as good an example as one can find of highly organized, smoothly functioning markets; unfortunately, they have not always operated ideally.

The NYSE has 1,366 members, some of whom live far from New York. To get a membership (seat), one must pay the prevailing price (around $400,000 in 1967); one must also prove acceptable financially and by one's reputation for integrity and knowledge. Membership permits one to buy and sell with other members on the "floor," a room larger than four basketball courts. Members are guided and regulated by an elaborate set of rules made by the exchange and by government. Most members are brokers who arrange transactions for the public.

Buying Stock. Assume that you wish to buy some stock. You may know a broker, or your banker may suggest one. You introduce yourself and perhaps meet a polite request for evidence of your financial responsibility. Then, when you want to place an order, you write, phone, or go directly to the broker's office. He, or a "registered representative" on his staff, who will also have met certain standards of competence, will take your order. If you do not know specifically what you want to buy, he may make suggestions and will gladly provide data about any one of hundreds of securities.

Assume that you decide to buy 100 shares of Ford common stock. The broker's "board" and ticker (a running sort of telegram which records

[11] Other exchanges include the American Stock Exchange, also in New York; the Midwest Stock Exchange in Chicago; and the Boston and Pacific Coast (San Francisco) Exchanges. In 1966 the 2.2 billion shares traded on the NYSE accounted for 80 percent of total volume on all exchanges. For figures and discussion of a wide range of topics, see the annual *Fact Book* published by the NYSE.

every deal on the exchange) shows that it sold a few minutes earlier for $50 per share. The broker phones your order to his firm's member on the NYSE floor, who then goes to the "post" on the floor where Ford stock is traded. For each stock, there is a specialist who handles all transactions and who *must* buy or sell upon demand. He knows all recorded bids (what someone will pay) and offers (the price at which someone will sell); he must tell your broker the highest bid or lowest offer which are then in effect. If they are not close, some room for bargaining exists. If you give your broker an order to buy "at the market" regardless of price, he will then buy at the lowest price offered, say $50¼. If you specified a top price that you will pay, say $50, he will buy only if your terms can be met. If not executed, your order will be left with the specialist; it will be "touched off" when someone is willing to meet it (by selling at $50). If the deal is made at once, the broker will get the word back to you before you have finished a cursory discussion of the weather. What you pay goes not to the corporation but to the previous owner of the shares.

The seller's broker will send the old stock certificate to the corporation's transfer agent (a New York bank) who will cancel it and issue a new one in your name. You then become a shareholder of record, and the corporation will send your dividend checks or regular payment dates. The broker's commission averages around 1 percent but ranges up to 6 percent on small orders. Sometimes the market is very active, with 10 million (or more) shares bought a day. When the market is active, sales in blocks of hundreds of shares of a stock can be made at prices often near those of very recent sales. But when markets are "thin," the sparsity of bids and offers may leave relatively large gaps.

Listing.   Only about 1,700 of the hundreds of thousands of corporation stock issues can be bought on the NYSE, but they represent about 1,300 corporations that do most U.S. business. Before being listed, securities are generally "seasoned" by years of trading elsewhere and by fairly wide ownership. Listing of its securities on the NYSE is a privilege for which corporations must pay a fee; more important, they must meet such conditions as publicly reporting income each quarter, disclosing other data, and having outside audits. Listing also subjects a firm to tighter SEC regulation.

Margin Purchases and Short Selling.   Buying stock on margin resembles buying a house on a mortgage. The buyer puts up only part of the money and borrows the rest, in this case from the broker. Before the crash of 1929, one could buy on very small margins, 10 percent or so.[12]

---

[12] There are two reasons for buying on margin. One reason, less feasible in the mid-1960's than a decade earlier, is income. Assume that you can borrow on margin for 6 percent. If you have $5,000 and can borrow half of the purchase price, you can buy $10,000 worth of stock or bonds. If they yield 10 percent, you will get $1,000 a

Both the NYSE and the Federal Reserve now impose high cash requirements, 70 percent in 1967.

Short selling needs to be mentioned. If you believe that a stock is selling for too much and is likely to go down, you can sell short. You tell your broker to sell some for you even though you do not own it; you give him cash or pledge other securities to cover his risk. He makes the sale. But where does he get stock to deliver to the buyer? He borrows it just as you might borrow money. A month, or years, later you "cover," buy the stock, and the broker returns the number of shares he borrowed. To illustrate: You believe that X stock is too high at $50 a share and so sell 100 shares short; the broker credits your account $5,000 and debits you the shares (minus the cash you put up). You are right, and the stock falls; at $40 a share you buy, for $4,000, the 100 shares which will repay what you owe; you close the transaction, ending with a gain of $1,000 ($10 a share) minus broker's commission and taxes. If the stock rises, you are out of luck. You must pay, say, $6,000 ($60 per share) to get stock to close out your debt.

Facilities for short selling permit more judgments to be expressed in the market, the judgments of people who do not own a stock but who believe the present price is too high. If these additional judgments are more good than bad, they add an element of market stability. Price rises tend to be curtailed by short sales, and stock price declines are cushioned as the "shorts" buy to "cover."

Economic Function of Stock Exchanges.   A security exchange provides a spot where buyers and sellers may deal with each other but never meet. A place where shoes are sold is obviously useful. What about a place where the parts of the ownership of shoe factories are sold? The essentials are similar—shoes would not be made unless the maker could expect to sell them; plants to make shoes would not be built, or not so extensively, unless the builders could expect to sell their interests if they wished. The process of sale itself, whether of shoes or parts of ownership of shoe factories, costs something; the cheaper the process of selling the better. (1) *Because stock exchanges provide a more efficient mechanism for selling securities than if individuals had to seek out and negotiate with possible buyers, the exchanges reduce the cost of the process of financial investment.* (2) *Exchanges provide liquidity for individual owners of securities.*

---

year; after paying the broker $300, the 6 percent on $5,000 you borrowed, you will have $700, that is, 14 percent on your own $5,000. The most common reason for buying on margin, however, has been the hope of capital profit. If you believe a stock will rise and buy $10,000 worth, putting up cash for only half and borrow the rest on margin, and if the stock does rise by one tenth, you have a $1,000 profit. This is one fifth of your $5,000. If the stock goes down, your loss is also larger in relation to your commitment than if you had paid cash in full.

Investors will accept a lower yield when they can count upon selling easily. In essence, the cost to business of getting capital funds is reduced, although indirectly. Corporations do not get money to build plants by selling shares through the exchange. But the original marketing of such stock is easier when buyers know that they can sell later if they wish. Of course, stockholders will not know what price they can get in the future, but they can be certain of this: The stock exchange gives assurance that a sale be made quickly. For stockholders these facilities are a convenience, for business an economy.

By reflecting the consensus of judgment, prices on the stock exchange give an opinion about the future course of business. They do more. They also help to shape the future. Prices indicate community valuation of business prospects, the quality of management of different corporations, and the firms and industries which seem to warrant more investment. Different parts of the financial investment market are tied together by an organization which records mercilessly, impersonally, and publicly the views of a host of investors.

Many views are crude, poorly informed, and erroneous. From hour to hour and day to day prices can be determined by shifting attitudes of relatively few buyers and sellers. When the market is thin, price fluctuations may result from relatively few transactions prompted more by hunch, a tip, an income tax consideration, or other irrelevant and often highly personal reasons. Moreover, the mass judgments, the true tide of opinion, can be wrong. As a guide for new investment, stock market prices are by no means a satisfactory substitute for intensive analysis. They have often been wrong.

No one knows just how much effect security market valuations have on new investment. In general, however, the higher the prices of outstanding stocks and bonds, the easier businesses can sell new issues on favorable terms. In 1961, for example, the public eagerly bought shares of little-known corporations when newly offered for sale. One reason for the boom in demand was a feeling that the prices of stock of older and bigger companies were high in relation to earnings prospects. Perhaps, then, best opportunities were to be found in newer firms. Three years later many prices were much lower, a few higher.

The investor today has better information than in the past, though access to inside "dope" on a firm's business or a government's plans can sometimes bring exceptional gains which the ordinary person cannot expect. Perhaps the greatest danger to the investor today is that he will not take time, and is not qualified, to study the available facts. By acting on hunches, by yielding to greed, people make avoidable mistakes.[13] Many investment firms make available, at little or no charge, facts, advice, and

---

[13] There is a saying that in Wall Street "bears" (people who believe prices will go down, and sell short) can make money, "bulls" (people who expect prices to rise) can make money, but pigs never can.

service which, while not perfect, are of good quality. Leading financial services—Moody's, Standard and Poor's, Value Line—and most brokers have high standards of integrity in providing data. But there are more than a few advisory services whose data are superficial, whose recommendations are overpriced, and whose overall records are poor.

Over-the-Counter Market. What about the thousands of issues of stocks and bonds which are not listed on an exchange? These include, in addition to *all* new issues, almost all government bonds and stocks of banks, mutual investment funds, and insurance companies, as well as the stocks and bonds of the vast majority of corporations. For some issues, notably the stock of small firms and bonds of small localities, there is no organized market; each sale must be arranged individually. For other securities, there is an excellent over-the-counter market. Physically it is a complex of dealers in constant touch by telephone. Except for dealings in U.S. Government bonds, conditions are not so standardized as on the exchanges; commission charges tend to be higher, and more effort must be exerted to get the best price possible. Information available is generally less complete, the markets are "thinner." Quotations on about 7,750 securities are assembled daily by the National Quotation Bureau. During a year, however, the 4,000 or so firms dealing in unlisted securities quote prices more or less regularly on perhaps 50,000 issues.

GOVERNMENT REGULATION OF SECURITY DEALINGS

In the past, at least, "insiders" could sometimes control situations and benefit thereby. Manipulation, deception, even fraud, played a part. Such practices may still be used, but the reforms imposed by governments, competition, and the financial community itself have largely eliminated the more notorious abuses. Having lost a lot of horses, Americans closed the barn door, tightly enough, at least, to give much protection against old-style thefts.

State Regulations. After years of being cheated and deluded by promoters selling stock backed by not much more than the blue sky above, Americans began to seek protection in state regulation. The resulting "blue sky" laws, generally established by 1920, are not uniform; but many offer helpful protection to buyers of newly issued securities. Some states require a license or other specific consent of state officials for a security issue; others give officials power to intervene if they suspect fraud or sharp dealing. Information about the corporation and the promoters must be supplied, sometimes in great detail, unless there is indication, such as listing on a stock exchange, that comparable requirements have been met. Other state laws and their administration have many weaknesses, especially the opportunity for swindlers to escape control by working from outside the state.

Federal Regulation. The stock market crash of 1929 and the revelations of what had gone on in the 1920's convinced the public that state regulation had been inadequate. The first New Deal Congress, using the constitutional powers over interstate commerce, the mails, and money, imposed regulations which have since been elaborated, most recently in response to an extensive study in the 1960's. Two general approaches are used: (1) By law, specific things are either prohibited or required. (2) An administrative agency, the Securities and Exchange Commission, is empowered to make and to police general rules.

A wealth of information must be supplied the public—*truthful information*. Buyers can still be fooled, but at least they now have available an elaborate dossier of facts in the registration statement and prospectus.[14] Regulation goes farther. It requires that all companies whose securities are traded on stock exchanges must supply continuing information to the SEC and the public not only about the affairs of the business but also about the dealings of officers and large stockholders in the comany's stocks.

The law also prohibits (1) certain trading practices which formerly gave unscrupulous insiders a way to fleece the public, and (2) the issuing of false and misleading statements about securities. In addition, the SEC has wide power to regulate the trading on stock exchanges to eliminate manipulation. Brokers who deal in the over-the-counter market also come under SEC supervision, and unethical action can result in withdrawal of the right to continue. As of 1967, however, the SEC was asking Congress for authority to make controls somewhat tighter. It was also trying to get the brokerage community voluntarily to alter commission charges (allow quantity discounts), reduce some of the charges made by mutual funds, and modify practices which seemed to restrict the freedom of competition.

BANKRUPTCY

Another slant on the problems of business finance is raised by the question, "What if things go bad and my business cannot pay its bills?" The answer: "You can go through bankruptcy, or receivership, legally different but much the same economically. Though this development would be tragic, you should be thankful for what the law permits—you can clear yourself and start afresh, free from the burden of past error and misfortune."

For centuries, people who could not pay their debts were thrown into jail, a procedure not only cruel but also foolish. How can a man in jail

---

[14] A comparison of the record of prices of new securities from 1 to 5 years after purchase in the pre-SEC period (1923–28) with a comparable record of new issues under the SEC (1949–55) revealed that buyers of new issues did little if any better in the years of regulation. G. J. Stigler, "Public Regulation of the Securities Markets," *Journal of Business of the University of Chicago*, April, 1964, pp. 117–42.

earn anything to repay his creditors? The purpose was to make people terriby afraid of incurring debt they could not pay. Yet it became clear that misfortune sometimes results, not from individual rascality, but because business in general is poor. Moreover, anyone facing the prospect of spending long years in jail if a venture turns out badly will not feel encouraged to undertake economic pioneering in a world loaded with risk. So the laws were changed.

Under specific provision of the Constitution, Congress makes the bankruptcy laws for the entire country. Bankruptcy is permitted when (business or personal) assets are not great enough to pay debts. A court takes charge, but the creditors usually participate actively.[15] The assets are generally sold; and certain preferred debts, chiefly wages due, are paid in full, if possible. The remaining funds are distributed among other debtors, respecting priorities if any, or in equal proportion. The bankrupt individual is free to start his economic life again.

If the bankrupt is a corporation, operations may stop, the property may be sold, and creditors paid whatever is possible. The managers and owners, are free of liability unless guilty of criminal acts. For large firms, however, the court and a committee representing creditors will probably select new managers; and business will continue (without obligation to meet the terms of old debt). Groups of creditors then negotiate for what remains.

Typically, the plan is to set up a new corporation with less debt and lower fixed charges. Bondholders may get a smaller amount of bonds of the new corporation and, say, some preferred stock and new common shares. Owners of the old preferred may get some of the new common stock, but owners of the old common shares are likely to get nothing. Individuals suffer losses, but the business can go on.

TERMS AND CONCEPTS

equity	internal financing	current assets
open account debt	investment bank	fixed assets
trade credit	finance capitalism	owners' equity
negotiable bonds	stock exchange	surplus plus undivided profit
registered bonds	"sell short"	
debenture bond	over-the-counter market	bankruptcy
revenue bond		reserve
convertible bond	double-entry account	inventory
lease	balance sheet	depreciation
preferred stock	profit and loss statement	margin
common stock		

---

[15] Many settlements are made out of court to get quicker and cheaper action. The National Association of Credit Men has pioneered in working out friendly adjustments.

QUESTIONS

1. Why might a growing corporation prefer to get new funds by issuing bonds rather than selling additional stock? How does leasing differ from borrowing?

2. What needs of (*a*) business and (*b*) investors does each type of security serve?

3. Assume that government were to force corporations to distribute at least 90 percent of net income to stockholders as dividends. What would be the probable results?

4. Explain the economic functions of stock exchanges.

5. Explain the difference between a balance sheet and a statement of profit and loss. How are the two related?

6. Why does government exercise more control over the sale of new stock than over, say, new typewriters or old houses?

7. How does reinvestment of profit also aid in borrowing?

8. What productive service does the investment banker perform? The stock-broker?

9. "Modern bankruptcy procedures spare the businessman who fails to pay his debts the necessity of languishing in jail." What are other features of the modern procedures?

10. "The inflexibility of debt is an evil whose disadvantages appear too late for remedy." Discuss, explaining the nature of the inflexibility of debt.

11. What problems of judgment arise in preparing a balance sheet?

12. Why might a person sell stock short? Buy on margin?

13. Compute and compare the yields on common stocks of leading and less well-known corporations.

14. What makes a balance sheet balance?

15. Why might an inventor prefer to exchange the patent he is turning over to a corporation for common stock rather than for a bond?

16. Study a prospectus of a recent issue of new corporation stock. How, if at all, do you think it might be improved as an aid to prospective investors?

17. Find the requirements for becoming a Certified Public Accountant in your state.

18. "In a thin market speculative dealings for securities may predominate, making market prices a poor guide for new investment." Explain. Under what circumstances would market prices be a good guide for capital formation?

APPENDIX
Business Accounting

The modern economic world requires accounting. Business operations, and the results of these operations, are guided and measured by figures. Governments, households, and other organizations also rely upon the use of numbers. Accounting provides a logical, systematic tool for organizing some of the most vital money figures. The organization of rational and dispassionate accounts enables us to assess business failure or success. This ability to "account" is indispensable for efficiency and growth. The principles and methods of accounting can take a lifetime of study. We touch upon major points that can be understood by the beginning economist.

Accounting Deals with Financial Amounts. A business keeps "a count" of many things other than dollar figures: the number of employees, the square feet of floor space, the quantity of each item in the inventory. There is no end to the quantities that we measure and keep track of by accounts. Without records that permit us to know these amounts, the organization that makes modern life possible could never have developed. Many of these records are not tied in closely with financial accounts; what we generally think of as accounting is the organization of financial records.

Businesses' financial accounts deal first with two different, though related, sets of facts: (1) The *balance sheet* shows the condition at a given date. (2) The *statement of profit and loss* (or the *income and expense* account) summarizes what happened during some period. The elements which make up the income and expense accounts include the *cost accounts*, which we shall not discuss; they show the expense of producing particular goods or services. The accounting methods and the terms businesses use vary in detail. On most points, however, the general presentation is fundamentally uniform. Nevertheless, difficult problems of measurement and classification create challenges for thoughtful accountants. Leaders of the accounting profession point to "generally accepted accounting standards" but have not yet reached agreement on some issues growing out of complexities of modern business and taxation.

Double Entry. Modern accounting leans heavily on an old device, double-entry bookkeeping. It in turn rests upon a truism: *the value of a thing that is owned (an asset) equals the value the owner possesses.* Similarly, each separate business *transaction* has contrasting sides: what the firm gives up and what it gets. Double-entry bookkeeping is the device used to record the dual parts of each fact of ownership or each transaction. Everything affecting the firm in one way (what it owns or has gotten) is recorded on one side of the accounts, and everything affecting it in other ways (what it owes or has given up) is recorded on the other side. Within the two broad categories there will be many subdivisions; in fact double-entry bookkeeping permits endless flexibility and variation. Yet the system makes it easy to combine parts into a whole where the two major sections can be compared.

The Balance Sheet. The name itself gives a clue to the nature of the balance sheet: it shows a balance. It is two different ways of looking at one set of values. The basic equation is simply:

Value of assets = Value of claims to those assets

However, because there are different kinds of claims, the balance sheet consists of three, not two, major parts: (1) what the business itself owns, its assets; (2) the debts it owes, its liabilities; (3) what is left for the owners, the net worth, the proprietorship, the amount the owners have put in. The value of the assets must equal the value of the liabilities plus the value of the net worth (though the latter may be negative). By convention the three parts are arranged to show this equality, with assets on the left-hand side and liabilities and net worth together on the right-hand side:

Value of assets = Value of liabilities (what is owned) plus net worth (what is left for the owners)

One fundamental assumption is almost always made: *When acquired, an asset is worth just what it cost.* Let us look at a simple balance sheet. The numbers of the items are for convenience in the discussion below and would not appear on an actual balance sheet (see Table 5–3).

Current Assets. It is customary to list first what are called "current assets," those which are most liquid. By "liquid" we mean readily convertible into dollars of a known amount. The standard practice is to include as current those assets which can be converted into money within a year without danger of loss of value from forced sale. (1) First, we find cash—currency in the cash register and deposits in the bank. (2) Many businesses own U.S. government securities; these can usually be sold at a moment's notice at an easily determined price; they may be thought of as cash which brings a little interest income. (3) Accounts receivable—what is due within a few months from buyers—can be counted on to bring in funds. Since there may be some "deadbeats," the firm cannot be sure of collecting everything; so to be safe, it deducts an allowance, called a "reserve." Here the first serious problem of judgment appears. How much should be allowed for uncollectible accounts? Experience provides a guide, but it may be off a good deal if business takes an unexpected turn. (4) Raw materials, supplies, work in various stages of completion, and goods ready for sale present a more difficult problem. (*a*) It is not always easy to learn just what physical units the firm has. The job is more difficult than going to the pantry shelves and counting or measuring everything there. Sometimes it is possible to "take inventory," perhaps closing down for a day or so; individual units are counted either entirely or by sample checks. (*b*) But even a perfect physical count is not enough. Each item must also be valued. The complexities of this valuation are tremendous—we say more about them later. The common practice is to value "conservatively,"

TABLE 5–3.   Balance Sheet of XYZ Company as of December 31, 1967

Assets

A. Current assets:
   (1) Cash $220,000
   (2) U.S. Government securities   30,000
   (3) Accounts receivable $ 82,000
      Less reserve for uncollectible items   2,000   80,000
   (4) Inventories on hand   200,000
B. Fixed assets:
   (5) Equipment $200,000
      Less reserve for depreciation   40,000   160,000
   (6) Land and building $160,000
      Less reserve for depreciation   20,000   140,000
   (7) Patents and goodwill   10,000
       Total $840,000

Liabilities and Net Worth (Owners' Equity)

Liabilities

C. Current liabilities:
   (8) Accounts payable $150,000
   (9) Bank note   80,000
   (10) Accrued taxes   60,000
D. Long-term liabilities:
   (11) Bonds (or mortgage)   100,000

Net Worth (Owners' Equity or Proprietorship)

E. Capital:
   (12) Preferred stock, 1,000 shares at $100   100,000
   (13) Common stock, 5,000 shares at $30   150,000
F. Surplus:
   (14) Capital surplus   75,000
   (15) Earned surplus   125,000
       Total $840,000

tending toward the lower of available choices.[1] "Error" can be large, especially when prices are fluctuating. Sometimes there is a special deduction of a "reserve" for possible declines in the value of inventory.

Fixed Assets.   Fixed assets are property that will not as a rule be converted into money in a year. (5) Machinery, equipment, (6) land and buildings may be lumped together or separated. In our simple balance sheet, fixed assets have been put into the above two groups. They also present the dual problems: What exists physically? and, What are the items worth? It may or may not be hard to find what the firm owns in a broad physical sense—to list the trucks, typewriters, and factory buildings. Determination of the *physical condition* of each item can be very difficult.

---

[1] For example, the "lower of cost or market" is common; if the firm has cotton for which it paid 28 cents a pound and the current price is 30 cents, the valuation will be at cost, 28 cents; if the market price is 26 cents, however, this value will be used.

It is customary, therefore, to apply "rules of thumb" in valuing these longer lived assets—rules that make rough allowance for changes in physical condition. The XYZ company's accounts show deductions from original cost as *depreciation*. In other words, there is a judgment which combines the estimate of (*a*) physical condition and (*b*) value. Valuation of real estate and equipment will often be difficult, and competent opinions differ. The usual practice is to start from the assumption that when acquired, an asset is worth just what it cost. Thereafter, the value is this original cost (including outlays for improvements) minus arbitrary deductions for losses of value due to use. This method may yield generally accurate results; if the price level rises or falls, however, the use of historical cost figures may give a very misleading impression of the present market value of assets the firm owns.

(7) Finally, there are intangibles: patent rights and goodwill. Goodwill is the reputation of the firm, its hold on clientele, its established position, the value of being a "going concern." *Copyrights and franchises* might also appear. What is the best way to treat such intangible items? Perhaps some have cost a great deal and have large earning power. Others may have cost much but have no earning power, such as a costly patent on a product that cannot compete with what another firm now produces. Occasionally, intangibles with good earning power cost little—a lucrative patent that was developed cheaply. Intangibles may appear safe and stable or likely to vanish overnight. At one time, some businesses put unreasonably high values on intangibles. How easy to impress the public, and to further financial manipulations, by increasing the asset total by merely entering a larger figure as the value of goodwill! Abuses brought a reaction, and intangibles were often "written off," the swing being to unrealistically low amounts. Valuations at $1 often grossly understate the worth of intangibles.[2]

Current Liabilities.   The liabilities due within a year appear first. (8) *Accounts payable*—wages to employees, interest to creditors, bills for goods bought from suppliers, and amounts due the U.S. Treasury for taxes withheld from employees—head the list and are valued at the full amount due. (9) Debts due within a year—notes to banks or the maturing parts of longer-term debts—are shown next. They present no valuation problem because contracts fix the amounts. (10) Taxes payable are commonly listed separately.

Long-Term Liabilities.   (11) Debts due in more than one year are grouped together as long term; the net amount remaining is shown at face value.

The Net Worth (Owners' Equity, Proprietorship) Section.   The difference between the total value of the assets and the total liabilities—termed variously net worth, owners' equity, or proprietorship—is what remains for the owners. The term "owners' investment," preferred by some accountants, may seem to be more accurate; the accounts show what owners have put in far more often

---

[2] U.S. Steel, for example, reports a value of $1 for its intangibles. General Motors carries a value of only $63 million for patents and goodwill, Chrysler nothing. When a company has purchased a patent on some right, the balance sheet may show an amount equal to the purchase price.

than they reveal what the equity would now sell for. (Asset values, we recall, rest on historical prices.) (12) *Preferred stock* appears first.[3] The number of shares is easily determined from the company records. The value shown is the total number of shares multiplied by the *par value* per share (often $100), the total of the claims of preferred stockholders against the company's assets. The par value is presumably the amount the corporation received when it issued the stock and may be far indeed from the price at which the stock now sells in the market.

(13) For the *common* stock there will be a par or stated value, but it need have no relation at all to the amount originally paid into the corporation. Large corporations generally use an artificially low book figure for the common stock. This practice should deceive no one; the common stockholder is the residual claimant, owing all that remains after the claims of creditors (those to whom the firm owes debts) and preferred stockholders.

The residual equity (after provision for common stock at stated value) is *surplus plus undivided profit* and contains the true "balancing" item, the buffer for absorbing all errors (plus and minus). Two major distinctions must be made. (14) A *capital surplus* is a sum that was paid in by owners, usually when the corporation was formed.[4] (15) The *earned* surplus (undivided profit, retained earnings) consists of the total of net earnings, over the years, which have not been distributed as dividends to stockholders. This is the item which, in effect, is increased or lowered to make the total of liabilities-plus-other-net-worth items equal the total of assets.

Why list some of the values of the owners (stockholders) as a *surplus* rather than as "common stock"? State laws restrict what can be done with capital (the value shown for stock) but leave great freedom for use of surplus. If things turn bad, or if owners wish to take property out of the corporation, surplus can be drawn upon simply, whereas reducing capital may be complicated at best. Owners gain flexibility by calling part of what they own "surplus" rather than "capital." This amount may be surplus in no sense other than legal terminology; it may have been put in deliberately and directly by the owners, as well as through reinvested earnings; the surplus may represent value absolutely essential for the operation of the firm. Surplus is not an asset. It consists of no particular asset, such as cash; there may, or there may not, be assets of equal value which the firm can give up without impairing operations.

The total owned by the common stockholders, then, consists of everything in the net worth except the preferred stock. To figure the *net worth per share of common stock*, we add the values shown for the common stock and surplus (and undivided profit) items and divide by the number of common shares. In the XYZ Co., it is $70 per share.

These classifications are reasonably typical. In details, however, the terms used by businesses vary considerably. Major types of businesses—public utilities, retail stores, banks—have different needs; even firms in the same industry use

---

[3] Accounts for a proprietorship or partnership would have no entries for "stock" and would probably lump together all net worth, equity, or proprietorship items.

[4] Assume that the corporation issues and sells common stock for $100 cash and records a book value of $50; the other $50 is shown as a capital surplus.

different classifications. Government and nonprofit organizations often have substantially different kinds of accounts. Certain general points, however, should be emphasized. (1) Though the totals balance precisely and thus conform to the fundamental equation *Value of assets = Value of liabilities plus net worth,* this is so because of the inclusion of a "balancing item," whose job is to balance. There is no magic, nothing mysterious, simply an item which *is* the amount left after everything else is "taken care of." (2) Despite the appearance of precision, *there is likely to be considerable doubt about the valuation of some assets.* The doubt may affect the asset totals more than a little, and it may influence the net worth, ownership, total appreciably. A 10 percent total error in the valuation of assets may easily mean a 50 percent error in the valuation of what remains for owners of common stock. (3) *No asset item matches any specific item on the other side of the balance sheet.* The totals are equal. Yet there is no necessary connection between other items.[5]

Statement of Income and Expense (Profit and Loss, Earnings). The other major account, that of *income and expense*—often called the *profit and loss statement*—shows the net financial results of the operations over a period. This report is usually prepared at least every three months and certainly every year.[6] A simple income statement for the same hypothetical business appears in Table 5-4, with numbers to help in identification.

(1) The major item of income, receipt, or revenue is the proceeds of sales. These are valued at net selling price; discounts from quoted prices and estimated reserves for amounts uncollectible are subtracted. (2)–(8) The costs of producing and selling the goods are then deducted. The amount of detail shown varies widely; labor costs, raw material, general administrative and overhead expenses, power and heat, depreciation, maintenance and repair of buildings and equipment, and some taxes may all be itemized. Some amounts present no problems except accurate record keeping. Yet a few are both difficult and important.

Valuing Inventory. One problem is that some of the expenditure for labor and materials during the period will not have gone into the items sold. The company may have spent money to make things due for sale next year— December's production, for example. Or during the year, prices and wages may have risen so the amount spent per unit on things made was different from the amount spent on the same things made earlier but sold in this period; December, 1966, production which sold in January, 1967, cost less

---

[5] One of many relations deserves mention, that between current assets and current liabilities. The difference is significant in determining what the business can do in the coming months. The excess of current assets over current liabilities ($530,000 − $290,000 = $240,000) is "net working capital." To relate this amount to the current affairs of the business, the working capital ratio is computed by dividing current assets by current liabilities; here the ratio is $530,000 ÷ $290,000, or 1.8 to 1.

[6] Many businesses, like governments, keep books on a *fiscal year,* that is, a 12-month period which may not coincide with the calendar year. The fiscal year may start on the anniversary of the day the business originated years ago. Or it may be geared to the rhythm of business; retailers, for example, often close their fiscal year on January 31, after the sales to clean out Christmas inventory.

TABLE 5–4. Income and Expense (Profit and Loss, Earnings) Statement of XYZ Company for the Year Ending December 31, 1967

(1) Sales net		$1,000,000
(2) Manufacturing and selling cost of goods sold:		
(3) Materials	$400,000	
(4) Labor	300,000	
(5) Depreciation	30,000	
(6) Maintenance and repairs	20,000	
(7) Administrative and selling costs	90,000	
(8) Taxes, other than income taxes	60,000	
		900,000
(9) Net profit from operations		$ 100,000
(10) Interest receivable		1,000
(11) Interest payable		11,000
(12) Net income before income taxes		$ 90,000
(13) Income taxes		42,000
(14) Net income		$ 48,000
(15) Allocation of net income:		
(16) Dividends on preferred stock		6,000
(17) Dividends on common stock		30,000
(18) Increase in earned surplus		12,000

than what was made in December, 1967, to sell in 1968. When the rate of operations is steady and when prices and wage rates do not change, no serious problem arises. Otherwise, one asks: Which costs of labor and materials were spent on the goods or services sold during the year? It is often too expensive to try to trace the specific inputs—which wool went into which cloth.

Shortcuts are used. Errors introduced by attributing costs to the output of the wrong year will often cancel out over a period of years; too much expense charged against one year's income will mean too little charged against that of another year. Yet errors can sometimes be substantial in relation to a single year's net earnings. Should the cost figure be the price paid for the material actually used (if the items can be traced), the price when the material was taken from inventory for fabrication, the price of the last material put into the inventory, or something else? Dispute is more than academic hairsplitting. Roughly half of whatever is shown as corporation "income" usually goes in federal and state income taxes. Uncle Sam once ruled, in effect, that since "what goes up must come down," any error in exaggerating profit when material prices rise will be reversed when prices fall. During World War II, however, prices rose so much with little prospect that they would fall by an equal amount, and tax rates became so high, that Congress approved a new method. Many businesses, for tax purposes, may now figure the costs of raw materials on approximately the market price at the time they were *used*, rather than the price when they were purchased.[7]

Depreciation. The problem of depreciation is unending. How much does the wearing out of machinery and buildings add to the cost during any

---

[7] The older method "first-in, first-out" is called "Fifo"; the latter, "last-in, first-out," is called "Lifo." Perhaps we shall eventually permit "Nifo"—"next-in, first-out"—to keep taxes down in a period of upward price trends.

period? Some things, such as truck tires, may clearly have worn out during the year. The mass of equipment, however, will serve for many years or decades if kept in good repair; the change from year to year may be imperceptible. Yet such things do lose their value because they (*a*) wear out physically (depreciate) or (*b*) are supplanted by something better (become obsolete). This loss of value is a cost which ought to be charged as we go along. Yet until the end of the story, the length of the *economic* life is inherently unknowable.[8] Even *physical* life can be hard to judge; only time will tell.

The effect of different rates of use on the physical life may depend upon the care of users and the quality of maintenance, as well as upon the characteristics of the thing itself. The general practice is to charge as a cost each year an arbitrary percentage of the original price until that has been completely "written off" (except for any salvage value) and then to make no more charges. In other words, the business presumably recovers from the purchasers of its products enough money to buy a replacement by the time an item has worn out. Different companies may have widely divergent views about how much to charge to depreciation each year. Tax regulations exert great influence because companies are reluctant to keep accounts on two or more bases ("two sets of books"). The depreciation used for computing tax will usually be used for pricing and other purposes. For tax purposes the law permits relatively large "write off" (deduction) when an asset is new and relatively less later. New "guidelines" issued by the Treasury in 1962, give business more freedom in deciding on the "time pattern" of depreciation deductions for tax purposes. Some companies use a "service-unit" basis; after estimating the number of units of service a machine will provide over its lifetime, the depreciation cost per unit can be used to compute a total for each period.

If a firm sells natural resources from its own properties—oil, coal, timber—it will charge *depletion* as a cost; the estimates of such values used up are subject to much uncertainty. Tax laws permit deductions which can be more than the company has put into property.

(8) Real estate and other state and local taxes and social security taxes are costs which can generally be determined without much error. It is customary to separate them from the tax on income (item 13). The result to this point is shown as operating profit (9).

(10) The interest receivable is that on the government bonds which the company owns, while (11) interest payable is due on the mortgage and bank note. If the firm had to make rental payments, they would also be costs. Any of a wide variety of other costs may be listed separately. There may also be other receipts: dividends or rentals from investments in subsidiaries, associated firms, or other property.

---

[8] In an economy with much emphasis on invention, *obsolescence* can be a major factor. Busses made streetcar tracks obsolete. A fine apartment building may lose value because the neighborhood deteriorates. After World War II, one large railroad whose past experience showed that individual steam locomotives would serve 50 years or more, added some of the best ever designed. Yet within a few years it was scrapping them, not because they would not run well but because diesel locomotives were more economical.

The difference between the income and expense items (14) is *net income* (*profit or loss*). Dividends paid are then shown. The remainder, appearing in earned surplus (undivided profit), is the change in net worth resulting from operations. *This change ties in the statement of income and expense with the balance sheet.*

The business has done well. On the net worth of $450,000 it has earned $48,000, after taxes, or almost 11 percent of the owners' equity (5 percent on sales). The preferred stockholders get their share, $6,000, leaving $42,000 for the common stockholders. On their investment of $350,000, this is a return of 12 percent.

Relation of Profit and Loss to Balance Sheet.

What will have happened to the balance sheet? The net worth will have risen by the $12,000 addition to earned surplus. Depreciation has cut the net asset value of the property owned at the beginning of the year. Beyond this we cannot say from the profit and loss statement what happened to the balance sheet or to any items on it. We do not know how the receipts were used or what may have been done "on capital account." For example, the corporation might have raised new funds by selling bonds (increasing its liabilities), and added to the plant (increasing assets). It might have used the retained earnings and cash to reduce accounts payable so that, despite the increase in net worth, there was an actual fall in assets. The firm might also have used cash to add to inventories so the end of the year found it with a fine earnings record, an increase in net worth and in total assets, but low on cash.

Reserves.

The term "reserve," which appears frequently, can be confusing: (*a*) Like the term "surplus," it may give the impression of cash held aside. Some reserves *are* held in cash, but this is exceptional. (*b*) Reserves appear on both sides of balance sheets. For example, accountants may want to show that a liability exists but may not know the exact amount; they then enter an estimate: "Reserve for taxes," "Reserve for damage claims," and so on. This accounting entry does not mean that a cash or other asset is available or set aside. It does, however, make everyone aware that net worth is less than would otherwise appear. There may also be net worth or surplus reserves. Their function is, in a sense, to establish some priority in the use of net worth. Reserves on the asset side are different. They may be assets earmarked or set aside for a special purpose. Cash or bonds, for example, may be labeled "reserve" so that they will not be touched for other purposes. Perhaps they are held for payment of taxes, to buy a new machine, or for pensions. Or a sinking fund of cash or securities (assets) may be created to pay off a debt. The term "reserve" is used in another way on the asset side, as a *deduction* from the value of an asset to warn that the asset is worth less than might be expected (items 3, 5, and 6 might use the term).

Reliability of Business Accounts.

Are accounts reasonably satisfactory? Yes and no. Accounts *must* deal with many matters of judgment. Numerous values are partly *estimates*. It is no fault of accountants that life is uncertain and that they cannot know the unknowable future which they would need to know to eliminate all estimating. Despite the precision with which amounts are shown, down to the last dollar of billion-dollar accounts, the underlying figures are subject to error. The fault in misinterpreting the accountant's work is our own—but not entirely. The public's disadvantage is that published accounts rarely give adequate information about the major uncertainties, how the decisions have been made, and the range of reasonable error.

What about "manipulation" of accounts? The term is hard to define. Looking back, we can spot practices that were deceptive. *Stock watering* was notorious. Certain assets would be valued at far more than they were worth or than had been paid for them. Then, maintaining the equality of the balance sheet, extra stock would be issued or the value of existing stock raised. If you had a house for which you had just paid $15,000 and you said it was worth $20,000, you might "write up" the value of your personal net worth by $5,000, but you would hardly fool a buyer. If you controlled a big corporation, however, you might be able to deceive people to whom you wished to sell stock. You might, for example, merely raise the figures at which you valued the assets by $10 million, issue yourself and friends 500,000 more shares of common stock with a value on your books of $20 a share. Then you could offer to sell the shares to the public at an apparent bargain of $18 a share. If you succeeded, you would be ahead $9 million. Or, if your business were a public utility, by inflating the value of your assets, with corresponding "water" in the net worth accounts, you might be able to get a higher value on which to base the rates you charged customers.

A related problem arose when corporations joined together and reduced competition. As monopolies or near monopolies they could earn more as one business than when competing. Should the new and higher value to the owners be recognized on the balance sheet? A juicy figure could be entered for goodwill, as an asset, then balanced with an equally inflated addition to net worth. The promoters could then pocket, or sell, new stock.

Obligations such as payments due under long-term leases or pension agreements can be understated. Assets may be valued and revalued by directors in ways that are marvelous to behold, if they can be seen. What is much harder now than in the past, however, is to conceal what is done, especially if securities are sold publicly. Today, the public also has another source of protection: auditing.

Though accounts are generally kept by the firm's own staff, publicly owned businesses have their books *audited* by outside Certified Public Accountants. The latter must have passed tests of competence and proved their reputation for integrity. Becoming a CPA is not easy, and accountants, like doctors and lawyers, try to maintain and raise their professional standards. The public has much protection. The audit checks on the honesty and also on the skill and judgment of the firm's own accountants. Stockholders, lenders, regulatory agencies, and tax officials get an objective review. In fact, for many firms the audit provides useful guidance on specialized problems of management (inventory control, dealings with branches and subsidiaries, insurance, pensions, leases, foreign operations), finance, law, taxation, and so on.

Accounts are designed to help solve certain kinds of problems. For other problems, however, customary accounts may serve poorly. Thus accounting has developed with heavy emphasis on the protection of stockholders and persons to whom the company is in debt. For other problems, such as product pricing and the determination of how much of each product to turn out, the accounts may serve inadequately. Accounts have a backward-looking feature; they rest on values of a past rather than of the present or future. Therefore, especially when the general price level has changed, accounts provide inadequate, even misleading, guidance in deciding how best to utilize existing equipment or in acquiring new facilities.

The leaders of the accounting profession recognize the need for development and refinement of concepts. Challenges arise in trying to measure more accurately for more kinds of purposes—internal management in its many aspects, demands of regulatory authorities, the needs of owners, and the interest of the general public. Communication, too, presents problems which seem to demand ever more in clarity, precision, and elaboration by accountants. Perplexing, demanding, and exciting issues arise more rapidly, it seems, than older ones are resolved.[9]

[9] For analysis of the environment and topics of contemporary concern, see Herman Bevis, *Corporate Financial Reporting in a Competitive Economy* (New York: Macmillan Co., 1965).

PART 3

MONEY, BANKING,

PRICE LEVELS, AND THE

VOLUME OF ECONOMIC

ACTIVITY

The four topics in the title of this part are closely related. Each is important in itself, but the first two take on unusual significance because of their bearing on the third and fourth—the great issues of inflation, the scarcity or plenty of jobs, business cycles.

6

NATURE AND SUPPLY OF MONEY: BANK LENDING

Rags make paper; paper makes money; money makes banks; banks make loans; loans make poverty; poverty makes rags.

Jacob Coxey

Money creeps into our consciousness early. A seven-year-old has a fair idea of what his weekly allowance will buy. By the time we get to college, we likely feel that we know a good deal more about money than about other economic topics. Most of us may even feel qualified to make one expert judgment—there is not enough money. Yet, when we stop to think about money, rather than about how to get and use it, we may find it mysterious. Just what is money? What brings it into being? Does all our money have the same legal and economic power? How does money affect prices and employment?

Questions like these lead one into some of the more fascinating areas of economics. To understand the major economic problems of the day, one must certainly have some knowledge of money.[1] And to learn about today's money, one must learn about banking. So this and the next chapter discuss two closely related subjects: money and banking.

THE NATURE OF MONEY

The love of money may or may not be the root of all evil; but most economic problems seem to involve money. Churches, households, even

[1] Money has been a favorite topic of "crackpots and cranks," people with unconventional ideas for improving the economy. Sometimes such notions have more than a trifle of merit. At best, however, they are usually oversimplified, like plans to build a new auto by devising a new carburetor. One purpose of systematic study of economics is to be able to see through such plausible but inadequate proposals.

135

colleges, center major concerns around money. Money is one of man's most serviceable inventions. It gives us untold freedom. Only a few dollars will enable us to buy any of thousands of things, a few of the things we can choose coming from the ends of the earth. Yet money itself, as well as our getting it, is a source of many problems. "Money" is easier to define than "gracious lady" or "fairness," but more difficult to define than "gold" or "grass." Different specialists have different ideas about what is "money." Yet for our purposes here the differences can be ignored.

Money Is Important for What It Will Buy. Money is not like food, dignity, or excitement—desirable in itself. We value money for what it will get us. The struggle to get money and to hold on to it may easily deceive us into feeling that money has intrinsic worth: the "money illusion." But is it not obvious that what is important, what we want, are the things we can get with money? The income and the wealth that really count are not money but the *real* things, goods and services, money will buy. Nevertheless, money does perform functions whose value can scarcely be conceived.

Functions and Uses of Money. We employ money because it is marvelously useful. The division of labor depends upon the use of money. The alternative is barter, the direct exchange of things for things. It would be impossibly complex except at a primitive level of living. Imagine trying to exchange the services or things you or your parents produce for the specific things you want to consume! The mechanics themselves stagger the imagination. If money and the ability to replace it were taken from us, the industrial system would collapse—not physically but as a functioning organization.

Man needs a common feature for the varied things he exchanges. He must have something to **measure** and **express the relative values of different things**—a week's labor, a glass of milk, or a textbook. At one time $1 will buy a pound of steak or 2 dozen eggs. This ratio, 1 to 2, may change, perhaps to 1½ to 2, or 1 to 3; the steak and eggs may be the same physically, but their relative values change. Just as there are units to measure distance, weight, time, and other quantities, there must be a unit to measure economic quantities (values). This measuring device or **unit of account** is money (used ordinarily in statements expressing price).

Society could, it is true, have a measure which did not exist in tangible form; for example, we measure distance and time without seeing or handling yards or minutes. Did anyone ever feel an ounce, see a decibel, or pocket a calorie? No, but we use them to measure weight, sound, and food value. Society could use "dollars" to measure economic value, without having physical things called dollars which are handled back and forth.

Money and prices relate things that are widely dispersed in space, as well as infinitely varied in physical features. We can compare the worth of lumber in Chicago with the value of beef in San Diego or gasoline in Dallas. Such comparisons help us learn which exchanges promise the greatest benefit.

Money also serves as a **medium of exchange.** No one can transfer time by exchanging hours, or space by exchanging miles. But the use of money permits us to exchange economic values. To make such exchanges, Americans use dollars (which bear the same name as the unit we use to compare and measure values). This exchange function of money is indispensable— but not always done well. Human blood systems are indispensable but do not always work well, as the obituary columns prove. Defects in a monetary system can disrupt the mechanism of exchange and the production of *real* things.

Money relates things through time. It ties together the past, present, and future. Money can serve as a **store of value.** Instead of holding magazines, milk, or real estate to meet future needs, we can hold dollars and decide later just what to select to satisfy our demands as they have developed. Money, by making such choice possible, thereby increases our range of opportunities. And money relates future to present in another way: debts to be paid or received in the future are expressed in dollars. The dollar thus serves as a common denominator, relating values today to those in years to come. **Money serves as a standard for determining the magnitude of future (or postponed) payments.** The wisdom of any economic decision involving the future will be determined (*a*) by expressing the prospects in terms of money and (*b*) relating them to present sacrifices, which are also expressed in terms of money.

Contracts are often made in dollars: you give dollars to your savings bank, and it promises to return dollars in the future, or you borrow dollars to buy a house and promise to pay back a certain number of dollars in the future. Frequently, of course, men must plan and make commitments for the future without binding agreements in terms of dollars and covering all aspects: a farmer may buy land even though he cannot be certain what production costs and prices will be in 5 years; an engineer may spend 2 extra years getting special training though he cannot be positive how much people will pay 20 years hence for the improvement in his skill. Despite gaps in knowledge, everyone *must* make calculations for the future; money, the dollar, as a measure serves in relating the past (experience) to the present and both to the future. The better our money system, the smaller the difficulties of preparing for the future. If the dollar itself changes in some way—or if we think it will—it provides an uncertain bridge to the years ahead.

Obviously, the functions money serves differ. What we use for one of the functions may not serve for another. In postwar Europe, for example, cigarets often served as a unit of account and a medium of exchange, but not for any long-run store of value or standard of (distant) future payment.

Definition of "Money." A definition of "money" should perhaps cover all functions. Yet such a definition would be unduly complex. So we define in the customary way: **money is anything generally used as a medium of exchange** or, in other words, **money is anything generally accepted in payment of debts.** (Most debts are incurred and settled day-to-day or month-to-month in current transactions.) The crucial word is *accepted.* Whether a thing is serving as money can be decided only by seeing how people act. There is a sort of contagion; we accept something as money because we believe others will accept it from us.

Early Types of Money. Many things have served as money: cattle, furs, tobacco, iron, wampum, slaves, beer, cotton cloth, and huge rocks (under the ocean). As money, each had usefulness but also defects. Most had some worth other than as a medium of exchange. They themselves, that is, served a useful purpose and were wanted for that reason (in contrast with, say, today's paper money which, as printed paper, has little use—for heating, papering a wall, or other purpose).

Yet these physical money-things also had defects. A slave was hard to divide for use in a small transaction. The quality of cattle or furs varied, making difficult the comparison of different units. Iron was so bulky that not much value could be readily transported. Some things might deteriorate so that, as they were held, they lost value. Some were hard to identify. Beer, according to reports, tended to be "issued to excess and difficult to store." Most had one fatal defect; they were not limited in supply. The variation in quantity of tobacco, for example, could be great enough from year to year to upset all money transactions and accounting.

Coins came into use. As techniques developed, coins of uniform weight were minted so that it was no longer necessary to appraise each individual coin whenever used. The royal seal impressed on the metal at the mint testified to the contents, though the prevalence of "clipping" and other ingenious methods for debasing the coinage justified the prudent man's desire to examine all coins which were not obviously fresh from a trust-worthy mint. People learned that the royal mint might put in a little less of the valuable metal than it promised.

Precious Metals: The Gold Standard. Gradually, most of the world settled on two precious metals: silver and gold. Their rareness made it certain that amounts small enough to be carried easily would be worth a good deal in terms of other things: transportation and storage were simplified. In their pure forms, silver and gold were not hard to identify; and they were readily divisible and coined. They had and have some nonmonetary uses. They are durable so that annual additions to the amount above ground are small relative to the existing stock; consequently, their value cannot be changed sharply by annual fluctuations in their quantity. Of course, silver and gold had defects as money, but the defects were fewer than those of other materials. Eventually, one country after another went on to the gold standard.

When countries adopted the gold standard, they defined the monetary unit—dollar, franc, pound, or other unit—as a certain physical amount of gold. The *unit of account*—the unit in which men measure economic relations—was thus fixed by law in terms of the metal gold. Such a legal fixing may have little meaning, no more perhaps than a law prescribing Sunday conduct. Something more is needed to put significance into the statute. The "enforcement" of the gold standard was government willingness to buy or to sell gold at the price fixed by law. In this way the medium of exchange was also tied to gold. Anyone with dollars could use them to buy gold, without limit, at the fixed price. On the other hand, anyone with gold could exchange it for dollars at the fixed price.

Did this complete *convertibility* require that the government have a dollar of gold for each dollar of currency, or dollar of bank deposit which might be exchanged for gold? No, merely "enough." For ordinary transactions, people would generally prefer forms of money other than gold. Some fraction would do. How big? No one could say for sure. Sometimes a small fraction would be adequate. At other times, much more would be needed.

Convertibility of the medium of exchange imposes a discipline on governments. If monetary authorities pursue policies which seem likely to reduce the purchasing power of a unit of money (inflation), some people (at home and abroad) will demand gold for other forms of medium of exchange. Such a gold drain reduces the monetary base. We shall touch upon the significance of latter later. Today's advocates of the gold standard emphasize its value as a preventive of inflation; if the quantity of money is tied closely to gold, increases large enough to cause appreciable inflation are almost impossible.

In World War I, most countries suspended convertibility of currency into gold. Then, between the two World Wars, governments modified their systems, retaining some of the features of the traditional gold standard but altering others.[2] During the Great Depression of the 1930's, the ties of currency to gold were weakened materially. Even the United States made fundamental changes, going to a modified gold standard, at a new gold-to-dollar ratio. The dollar was still defined in terms of gold, but equaled only 59 percent as much gold as previously. (In other words, the dollar price of gold went up, from $20.69 to $35 an ounce.) Moreover, the public could no longer buy or sell gold except for purposes of foreign

[2] Many governments (not ours) cut their own holdings of gold. They considered, as part of their gold reserve, the deposits their banks had in British, U.S. or other banks where money could be converted into gold freely. Countries following this plan were said to be on the *gold exchange standard*. Several governments became "choosey" about selling gold; they kept to a fixed price, but limited sales in various ways. For example, they would sell only when gold was desired for certain uses, such as to pay for (approved) imports. See Chapter 35.

trade and for artistic, industrial, and similar nonmonetary uses. The Treasury took a monopoly on gold transactions. It also received the $2 billion profit which resulted from the upward valuation of gold that had previously belonged to private individuals, banks, and the Federal Reserve.

SUPPLY OF MONEY IN THE UNITED STATES

Unit of Account. Our unit of account, the dollar, is defined by law as the equivalent of a certain amount of gold ($\frac{1}{35}$ of an ounce). The law, however, forbids us to use gold as a medium of exchange or for ordinary payments. Obviously, however, we do accept other things called, or treated as, dollars. Some of these things are more *generally* accepted than others, acceptability being a matter of degree like heat and value.

Coins. Coins, of course, meet the test of being generally accepted. They have a certain convenience. They serve well for small transactions and odd amounts. They are durable. (What would happen to a paper cent?) Differences in color and size help us to see or feel quickly what we have, so that small deals can be concluded readily. Automatic vending machines can take coins and thus serve us.

Government manufactures coins at government-owned mints and determines the metallic content. At times the market value of the metal in coins has equaled the face amount of the coin: the metal in a $5 gold piece would sell for $5. Today, however, the metal in coins is worth less than the coins themselves. The difference is a profit to the government (seigniorage); in three years to 1968, when the silver content of coins was reduced, the Treasury got a largely "one-shot" windfall of over $2 billion. We accept this "token money" not because of the value of the metal but because we know the coins will be accepted at face value. The chief thing determining the issue of U.S. coins is not the Treasury's profit but the needs of the public and the capacity of the mints.

Paper Currency. Paper money is more convenient than coins for hand-to-hand payments of more than a dollar or two. At one time or another, this country has had hundreds of different issues of such currency. Today, however, one type predominates.

Only a few silver certificates remain. Rising industrial demand for silver in the 1960's raised its price. To try to prevent the price from rising above $1.29 an ounce, the Treasury sold silver, a policy welcomed by the industrial users of the metal; silver certificates had to be withdrawn from circulation as the "backing" was disposed of. *Federal Reserve notes* now constitute most of our currency.

These bills, ranging from $1 to $10,000, are liabilities of, and issued by, the 12 Federal Reserve banks (though printed and guaranteed by the U.S. Treasury). Each dollar of such notes must be matched by a dollar of asset held by the Federal Reserve. At least 25 percent must be gold certificates, issued by the U.S. Treasury in return for gold, dollar for dollar. The remainder may consist of gold certificates, notes or other eligible debts of business firms, or U.S. government obligations.[3] This requirement does not mean that you can get any of the "backing" for your currency if you try to turn it in; all you can get is other currency or a deposit at a bank. Before 1933, in contrast, some currency was legally redeemable, dollar for dollar, in gold; you could take a $20 gold certificate to the bank and get $20 worth of gold. In January, 1968, President Johnson recommended removal of the 25 percent requirement. It was no longer needed to enable government to control the ability of the Federal Reserve to create currency. Our paper money is valuable to us, not so much because of some "backing" in a vault but because of our confidence that others will accept it.

Paper and ink, even the good quality used in our currency, cost very little per bill. Once the plates are engraved, they can be used abundantly. It costs no more to print a $100 than a $1 bill. Printing affords government a cheap way to get money which it can use to pay its expenses. This way is easy and so tempting that it has been used much too often, in more than one country, bringing inflation and even economic disaster.

Suppose, however, that the paper money were convertible to some desirable physical thing. Then if you were to present paper money at the Treasury, the official would be required to turn over to you the physical thing which was being used to back the money—gold or wheat. Under these conditions, the amount of paper money the government would issue would be restricted by the amount of whatever commodity was used as the base or "backing." In this sense, gold still serves to some extent as a base for the dollar. Although one cannot take currency to the Treasury and get gold by merely demanding it, if one wants the gold for industrial uses it is available at a price fixed by law; the central banks of other countries can also use dollars to buy gold at $35 an ounce.

Legal Tender. All our currency, coins and paper, is now *legal tender.* If you offer (tender) them to someone, including the U.S. government, to whom you owe a debt expressed in dollars, your payment discharges your legal obligation dollar for dollar. The courts must recognize your offer.[4]

---

[3] Newly printed paper money enters circulation, chiefly, in exchange for old torn and dirty bills. Public demand for more or less paper currency will be satisfied, with offsetting changes in amounts on deposit in banks.

[4] The power to decide what is legal tender is one of the far-reaching powers of government. Today's complex division of labor and the use of capital lean heavily upon contracts. These contracts usually employ the common denominator of money. The effectiveness of contracts depends crucially upon belief that the courts will bring the power of government to enforce them, to compel the parties to observe the terms, including those expressed in money. National government also defines the unit of money. It can say that the dollar equals a certain physical thing; a piece of paper engraved in a particular way, or so much gold or tea. Thus, while requiring us to observe faithfully the *dollar* terms of our contracts, it can change the economic significance of contracts by redefining the legal-tender dollar. Once the legal-tender

Legal-tender status does not determine the value—the purchasing power—of the monetary unit but does tend to make the money more acceptable. I value peanuts or dollars more highly if I know that I can use them to discharge my legal obligations. But legal-tender status is only one of the factors that determine what the money will buy. For example, in the 35 years that Federal Reserve notes have been legal tender, their buying power has fallen by more than half.

Bank Deposits (Accounts).   Most of what we give and accept in payment of debts is not currency but checks. So we call a third type of money "checkbook money" or "bank money"—*bank deposits upon which we can draw on demand by check.* A balance of $300 in your checking account at the First National Bank is money. You can write checks to pay your bills. A check is not a promise to pay but an order you give to the bank. You can convert the deposit into paper money or coin if you wish. The deposit will exchange *dollar for dollar* with currency (coin or paper). The dollars in checking accounts can be used not only to pay debts but also to compare and "store" values. We never worry about the "price" of these dollars. Such deposits have the essential qualities of money.

The use of bank accounts and checks has *advantages* over the use of currency. We can pay odd amounts ($23.82) and make large payments ($8,764.91—or 10 times this amount) more easily than with currency. We can mail payments conveniently, safely, and anywhere in the country. The canceled check is a record and receipt with the endorsement of the person who received the payment. Checks can be prepared by machine and, especially when in the form of punched cards, can be used as part of mechanical accounting systems that save large amounts of labor. Robbery and loss are less of a danger if our money is kept in the bank than if currency is held at home or in our wallet, or sent in the mails. The temptation to walk away with some of the employer's money is reduced if one handles only checks. If a check is lost, we can "stop payment."

Checks have *disadvantages*, of course. They take time and effort to write out, to endorse, and to process through banks. They are sometimes less acceptable than cash because the credit standing of the writer is not known; checks do not pass as freely as currency. Through dishonesty, the amount written on the check may be "raised," causing someone a loss and others a lot of trouble. Occasionally, the record that the check provides may be unwelcome—to the man engaged in illegal activities or to a person anxious to "forget" some income at tax time.

Checks are used more widely than in the past and more extensively in this country than in other parts of the world. Over 90 percent of all dollar

---

dollar has been defined—as equal to a quart of milk, a ton of coal, or a day's tax liability—men can adjust and make their contracts accordingly. In itself, however, a change in the definition of the legal-tender dollar can be disrupting, especially to anyone with long-term contracts.

payments are made by check. Today's 70 million checking accounts compare with 35 million in 1939. Some of the rise resulted from special efforts to devise types of checking accounts to appeal to the person with a modest income. Banks have developed highly mechanized procedures for smooth and quick processing of checks.

What about other deposits, those in savings banks and savings and loan institutions and time and saving deposits in commercial banks? They are not quite the same as checking accounts. If you have such a deposit, you cannot use it *directly* to pay a bill; you must first convert your claim into cash (coins or paper) or a deposit in a checking account. No one else can get or use *your* deposit except as you convert it into currency or a checking account. Leading commercial banks now issue negotiable *time certificates of deposit*, "CD's." These bear a fixed rate of interest and mature in 90 days, one year, or on some specified date. The owner ("depositor") may sell a CD to get cash, but the bank will not redeem it before the maturity date.

A time or savings deposit is not acceptable for payment of a debt. Here is the point on the scale of acceptability where economists sometimes disagree in drawing the line between money and a very close substitute. The most general practice excludes from the stock of money time and savings deposits against which one cannot write a check. These deposits, however, do serve one important function of money: They provide a store of value in highly liquid form. With little or no delay, they can be converted into cash, dollar for dollar. Thus, time and savings deposits have important qualities of money and may be treated by their owners as equivalent to checking accounts. They are "near money," so near that some economists prefer to treat them as money.

Government securities redeemable on demand at a fixed price closely resemble a savings account. Not much different are short-term government securities, a fixed amount payable in a few days or weeks. They have almost as much "moneyness" as currency or a checking account. Yet the pieces of paper are seldom handed over to pay a debt; and they may not *always* be convertible, dollar for dollar, into cash. If you have $1,000 in a checking account, you can be sure of getting $1,000 today; if you have a $1,000 Treasury security due in 6 months, you may be certain of getting $1,000 in 6 months but perhaps only $990 now; the market prices of government debt rise and fall as other security prices change. In planning personal and business affairs, we properly think of such assets as very nearly the equivalent of money.[5]

[5] The following assets have high, though varying, degrees of acceptability and may serve some or most of the functions of money: credit balances, with a broker or a firm with which we do business, that are payable on demand; long-term U.S. Treasury debt even without a fixed redemption value before maturity; travelers' checks, postage stamps, money orders, cashier's checks, and so on; the cash surrender value of life insurance; and readily marketable bonds and stocks, ranging from high-quality bonds, which one can count upon selling without any appreciable doubt about the price, to common stocks which, while easily sold, fluctuate widely in price.

TABLE 6–1.   Money Stock, September, 1967 (In Billions)

Total money supply*	$179.4
Currency component	
Federal Reserve notes	35.3
Silver certificates and other paper	.5
Coins	3.9
Demand deposit component	139.7
Time deposits adjusted*	$179.1

*Averages of daily figures. Money supply consists of (1) demand deposits at all commercial banks other than those due to domestic commercial banks and the U.S. government, less cash items in the process of collection; (2) foreign demand balances at Federal Reserve banks; and (3) currency outside the Treasury, Federal Reserve banks, and vaults of all commercial banks. Time deposits adjusted are time deposits at commercial banks and mutual savings banks, except those due to domestic commercial banks and the U.S. government.
Source: Federal Reserve Bulletin. Partly estimated.

Table 6–1 summarizes the stock of money (and also time and savings deposits) in 1967. Figure 6–1 shows the growth from 1933 to 1967. One striking revelation is the increase from 1940 to 1947. How did it come about? In discussing coins and paper currency, we noted briefly how they come into existence. Now we shall learn how checking deposits are created.

FIGURE 6–1.   Growth in Supply of Money, 1933–67

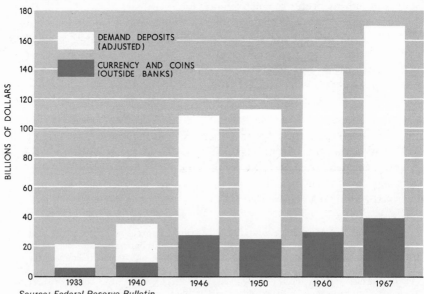

Source: Federal Reserve Bulletin.

CREATION OF BANK DEPOSITS

Introduction. The modest effort needed to understand the creation of bank deposits will pay big dividends in understanding modern economic life. Obviously, one can take paper money to a bank, deposit it, and have a larger checking account. Yet, as shown in Table 6–2, checking accounts total many times as much as the currency held by banks. So most of the deposits must have come into existence some other way. They have. This is the process we now describe. The best beginning is a bit indirect—a look at the nature of banks.

Central banks—in this country the Federal Reserve—are "bankers'

TABLE 6–2. Principal Assets and Liabilities of All Commercial Banks, 1967 (In Billions)

Assets		Liabilities	
Cash and deposits in other banks, including Federal Reserve banks	$ 61.7	Demand deposits, including interbank and U.S. Government deposits	$183.5
Notes and other obligations received from borrowers to whom loans have been made	226.9	Time deposits	180.1
		Total deposits	$363.6
U.S. government securities	60.2	Borrowings and other liabilities	
Other securities and miscellaneous assets	71.2	*Capital*	22.3
		Common and preferred stock, surplus, and other capital	33.1
Total assets	$419.0	Total deposits, capital, and miscellaneous liabilities	$419.0

Source: Federal Reserve Bulletin. Data are for September.

banks" with which the public has little or no direct contact. Commercial banks (in no sense limited to commerce in the sense of retailing and wholesaling) are the kind in which we keep checking accounts. They are business institutions operated to yield an income to their owners by providing certain services to the public. They furnish safe facilities for holding money. They handle the millions of checks used each day to pay obligations; in the sorting and accounting for these checks, and in transferring funds from one place to another, banks act as one of our more important *service industries.*

Yet commercial banks do something that sets them more clearly apart from other businesses, even from other lenders. Commercial banks earn money (in part) by creating it—not counterfeiting but nevertheless "printing" it (when an accounting machine prints figures on card records) and by charging the customer (borrower) for the use of what they have created. Although other types of business earn income by lending, only commercial banks create a part of what they lend: additions to checking accounts which we consider money.[6] Most of a bank's lending in any week or other period will in effect consist of the relending of funds which have been received from earlier borrowers as they have repaid what was due. Our concern lies with net additions to, that is, the growth of, demand deposits.

The balance sheet for all commercial banks combined, Table 6–2, differs somewhat from the balance sheet used to illustrate a typical business (p. 123). The general principles of accounting apply even when the items shown are not the same. The balance sheet presents a statement of condition as of a specific date.

The total assets must equal the total of liabilities plus net worth (capital is the designation used by banks). Any change which affects the total on one side will have its counterpart in one or more changes on the other side so that the totals remain equal.

The deposits are obligations of the banks. To be able to meet its obligations, a bank has assets. Some, as we shall see, are reserves required by law. Most assets, however, are either claims which the bank has acquired from borrowers or debt securities of government. A glance back in history to learn about reserves and a description of modern handling of checks will help in understanding the relation between bank lending and the creation of deposits.

Fractional Reserves. Centuries ago people with precious metals often left them with goldsmiths who had safekeeping facilities, getting receipts for the metal deposited. Gradually, the smiths learned that they could lend some of the gold or silver on deposit and earn interest. Not all depositors would demand all their property back at the same time; new deposits and repayments of loans could be expected to offset withdrawals, at least roughly. Something else developed. Depositors began to pay their own debts by handing over to creditors the receipts for the gold and silver rather than the metal itself. These notes or IOU's of the smiths, or bankers as they became, began to pass almost like money. Meanwhile, the bankers learned that they could often give borrowers, not gold itself but IOU's redeemable in precious metal. The promise that IOUs' would be exchanged for gold or silver made them generally acceptable. Moreover, these notes could be issued for total amounts greater than the value of the gold on hand, because many notes would circulate without being presented for redemption.

Bankers thus learned how to operate with "fractional reserves." The system rested on precious metals, but they were only a fraction of the receipts or notes outstanding. The system worked as long as the people who had deposited gold or silver did not suddenly withdraw it, and as

[6] Banks formerly created money in the form of currency. Until the 1860's, the typical bank issued its own bank notes.

long as bad loans were relatively small. Much of the success of such a system depends upon the banker. What fraction should he try to hold— half, one tenth, or less? How can he judge whether a loan is good or bad? Of course, he does not control broad economic developments and the general forces affecting his borrowers. But he approves each loan and has power to adjust his assortment of loans to spread his risks. If he uses good judgment, he can keep losses within tolerable limits and, year after year, operate successfully with only a small fraction of his assets in precious metal or other reserve.

When smiths or bankers were first experimenting with operating banks on fractional reserves, they encountered problems which need not arise today. Much experience has been accumulated—at the cost of untold loss. The modern banker has a bigger assortment of assets to acquire. Spreading of risk is easy. By borrowing from the central bank or by other steps, a bank today can replenish reserves when they are low. A modern bank, however, operates under a set of laws and government regulations far more exacting than those of the past.

Clearing and Collection of Checks. Suppose that you write a check on your account in Bank *A* to a store which deposits it in Bank *B*. How does *B* get its money from *A?* Long ago banks developed an economical way to solve such problems: *clearing.* In a city with several banks, each bank will ordinarily have claims against all the others. At the end of the day each bank might try to settle with each of the others, *A* with *B, C, D,* and so on. A bank would find itself owing funds to some and having net claims against others. It might try to have a separate settlement transaction with each bank, even though, overall, these might balance completely. Messengers would be running crisscross over each others' paths.

Not much acumen is needed to realize that a central pooling of checks can save much work. Banks in large cities set up clearinghouses. Every day each bank sends the checks which it has received and which are drawn on other banks, to the clearinghouse. These are its claims. The clearinghouse then figures how much of this total it will receive from each of the other banks. When this has been done for each bank's claims, the net totals are computed. It is a simple matter then for the banks to pay, or to be paid by, the clearinghouse. Its staff arranges final sorting and transmission of checks. Annual clearings in New York City exceed a trillion dollars.

What if a bank has claims against out-of-town banks? The 12 Federal Reserve banks perform the same service. In simple terms, Bank *A* can deposit in its Federal Reserve account the checks which it has on banks in other cities. On the other hand, the Federal Reserve charges *A's* account with the checks that other banks have presented against it. The process operates smoothly and rapidly. Federal Reserve banks clear with each other and make payments through a special account, the Inter-District Settlement Fund at Washington.[7] The costs are paid out of the earnings of the Federal Reserve; the New Yorker pays no specific charge for the services in helping him make a payment in Dallas or Denver.

Expansion of Deposits: An Example.[8] Let us start the study of how banks create deposits (money) with the pleasant assumption that your rich aunt takes $1,000 in cash (currency) out of a safe at home and gives it to you. You do not have a safe, and so you take the cash to a bank. The bank agrees to establish a checking account in your name with $1,000 on deposit. We call this a *primary* deposit. It is not at the expense of another bank. If your aunt had given you a check for $1,000, her account at whatever bank she uses would have gone down by as much as your deposit rose. The total of deposits in all banks would not change as it does when a primary deposit is created by something from outside the existing total of bank deposits.

The bank's balance sheet shows the following changes:[9]

Bank A
First Step

Assets		Liabilities	
Cash increases (Excess reserves $850)	$1,000	Deposits increase	$1,000

Your deposit, though an asset to you, is an obligation or liability of the bank, which must pay when you demand. Any time you wish, you may write a check and draw out some or all of the money.

The cash in the bank's vault earns it nothing. And, we shall assume, as is now roughly the fact, that law and custom require the bank to keep as reserves only 15 cents for each dollar of deposits (15 percent). (Today, U.S. banking laws require a large portion of all banks, including virtually all of the larger ones, to maintain their legal reserves in the form of vault

[7] "Float" is a term used for the difference between the dollar value of checks for which banks have received credit and the amount which has actually been deducted from accounts on which the checks have been drawn.

[8] It is common to speak of such deposits as "bank credit." Unfortunately, the term "credit" has varied meanings. On the accountant's records, for example, a "credit" is a very different thing from what it is when I say that my "credit is good" at the grocer. Often "getting credit" means obtaining a loan, perhaps but not necessarily from a bank.

[9] The description here of balance sheet changes follows the general form of what is often called "T account" presentation; the vertical line separating assets from liabilities joins with the horizontal at the top to make a "T." A bank's actual account records, however, would not use terms such as 'increase." Textbooks use them, or pluses and minuses, to help understand what has changed and in which direction.

cash or a deposit at a Federal Reserve bank.) The bank must have a dollar of assets for each dollar of deposit (liability), but only 15 cents must be in legal reserves. Certain other kinds of assets can make up the other 85 cents. For simplicity we shall say "cash and legal reserves" rather than "cash and deposits at the Federal Reserve." The $1,000 cash you deposited is 15 percent of $6,667; it will therefore provide the reserves for $6,667 of deposits, your $1,000 and $5,667 more. As far as reserves are concerned, the bank's deposit liabilities could be $5,667 larger.

The banker wants to increase the bank's income; and soon after you leave, an auto dealer comes in asking for a loan. He needs the money to stock up on spare parts for new models. Your banker knows that if he were to make a loan for $5,667 the bank might earn interest on it for a few days but that the dealer would then write a check to the auto manufacturer in Detroit. The manufacturer would deposit the check for, say, $5,667 in his bank in Detroit, (*B*) which would demand payment from your bank. The latter would have to pay out 5.7 times as much as you paid in, an impossible condition. Your banker, however, can be reasonably sure that you will not withdraw all your deposit at once. Therefore, he can, for a time at least, make a loan for most of the $850 difference between your $1,000 deposit and the $150 reserve he must keep for that deposit. Perhaps he agrees to a loan of the full $850, which is added to the account of the auto dealer. The accounts of the bank then stand, as a result of the transactions we are studying, as follows:

Bank A
Second Step

Assets		Liabilities	
Cash: legal reserve	$1,000	Your deposit	$1,000
Auto dealer's note	850	Auto dealer's newly created	
	$1,850	deposit	850
			$1,850

The dealer then writes and mails a check for $850 to Detroit. Your bank, in effect, sends $850 to the Detroit bank (*B*) by transferring that amount of its reserve deposit at the Federal Reserve. Your bank is safe—at least as long as you keep your deposit. Assume you do.

The bank's assets, then, are $150 cash (reserve) and the auto dealer's note for $850. The note brings it some interest. You still have your $1,000 deposit, but the auto dealer has none (from his loan). In Detroit, a bank (*B*) has $850 more reserves; and the auto manufacturer has increased his deposits by $850. The two banks together (*A* and *B*) have total deposits $850 larger than before. For the $1,850 of deposit liabilities (to you and the auto manufacturer), they hold $1,000 of legal reserve and the dealer's $850 note.

Detroit Bank *B*
First Step

Assets		Liabilities	
Cash: legal reserve in- increases (Excess reserve $722)	$850	Auto manufacturer's de- posit increases	$850

The Detroit bank does not need a legal reserve of $850 for the $850 deposit; 15 percent, $128, is enough. Therefore, it has $722 more than its minimum needs. Jones, who was just graduated from dental school, needs some money for equipment and asks the Detroit bank for a loan. He gives his note and gets $722, which he immediately sends to the manufacturer in New York. Bank *B's* assets are now $128 cash (reserve) and the $722 note. The deposits of its customers have risen $850, net. The following two steps lead to this result.

Second Step

Cash: legal reserve (Required reserve $128)	$ 850	Auto manufacturer's de- posit	$ 850
Dentist's note received	722	Dentist's deposit increases	722
	$1,572		$1,572

Then the dentist writes a check for $722, leaving the following:

Third Step

Cash: legal reserve drops to	$ 128	Auto manufacturer's de- posit	$ 850
Dentist's note	722	Dentist's deposit declines by $722 to	0
	$ 850		$ 850

The New York bank (*C*), with increases of $722 in both cash (reserve) and deposits, must keep at least $108 in legal reserve but can lend the remaining $614, which it does to a fruit dealer who pays a grower in Florida. Three steps involving Bank *C* can be illustrated as follows:

New York Bank *C*
First Step

Assets		Liabilities	
Cash: legal reserve in- creases (Excess reserve $614)	$722	Dental manufacturer's de- posit increases	$722

Second Step

Cash: legal reserve	$ 722	Dental manufacturer's de-	
(required reserve $108)		posit	$ 722
Fruit dealer's note	614	Fruit dealer's deposit in-	
	$1,336	creases to	614
			$1,336

Then the fruit dealer writes check for $614, leaving the following:

Third Step

Cash: legal reserve	$ 108	Dental manufacturer's de-	
Fruit dealer's note	614	posit	$ 722
	$ 722	Fruit dealer's deposit de-	
		clines $614 to	0
			$ 722

The accounts for three banks (the fourth bank, in Florida, is not included) then stand as follows:

Total Changes in Banks *A, B,* and *C*

Assets		*Liabilities*	
A Cash: legal reserve	$ 150	Your deposit	$1,000
Auto dealer's note	850		
B Cash: legal reserve	128	Auto manufacturer's	
Dentist's note	722	deposit	850
C Cash: legal reserve	108	Dental manufacturer's	
Fruit dealer's note	614	deposit	722
	$2,572		$2,572

These three banks hold $386 cash or legal reserve. What has happened to the remaining $614? It has gone to a bank in Florida. So the process can continue. Cash—the legal reserve—moves from bank to bank but does not grow. There **is** an increase in notes on the asset side **and** an increase in *deposits* on the liabilities side. *It is this increase in deposits that we set out to describe.*

Borrowers' notes become the "backing" of deposits just as cash did originally. If the public wants to borrow, and if the banks are willing to lend, deposits grow. Together, the banks and the public create deposits. *These deposits are liabilities—debts—of the banks; they are assets of depositors.* Offsetting the new deposits are debts of the public, notes in our example, which are assets of the banks. The typical loan process consists of exchanging (*a*) private promises to pay which are not money for (*b*) bank promises to pay (demand deposits) which are money.

How far can this process go? At each step the maximum loan possible was smaller than at the earlier steps. Each time 15 percent of the amount of the total deposit had to stay as legal reserve. As the series gets smaller, the items become so slight that no banker in his right mind would go to the expense of handling them. Yet for all banks combined there is a "theoretical" top. It is an expansion to 6.7 times the amount of the original cash deposit, or that deposit plus 5.7 times its size. The $1,000 could conceivably grow to $6,667, as shown in Table 6–3 and Figure 6–2.

Each banker can make a loan equal to only a portion, but a large one, of the cash (reserve) that he has received. A deposit is created when the cash

TABLE 6–3. Expansion of Deposits in a Banking System, Assuming a Reserve Ratio of 15 Percent*

	New Deposits	New Loans (or Investments)	Reserve Retained
Original bank	$1,000	$ 850	$ 150
2d-stage bank	850	722	128
3d-stage bank	722	614	108
4th-stage bank	614	522	92
5th-stage bank	522	444	78
6th-stage bank	444	377	67
7th-stage bank	377	320	57
8th-stage bank	320	272	48
9th-stage bank	272	231	41
10th-stage bank	231	197	34
Total of first 10-stage banks	$5,357	$4,559	$ 803
Total of remaining banks	1,315	1,118	197
Total for entire banking system	$6,667	$5,667	$1,000

* Figures are rounded to nearest dollar with minor adjustments.

comes into the bank. That *original* deposit is not decreased when someone who borrows later (giving his IOU, a note) writes a check; this check permits still another person to draw out cash or, through the clearing mechanism, get a deposit at his bank. This bank thereby obtains part of the deposit (legal reserve) at the Federal Reserve. For the whole system the "trick" is that, in a sense, some of the reserve can be deposited over and over again, the amount getting smaller each time. In the process, of course, the banks acquire other assets which have a more attractive feature than cash. These assets earn income for the bank. Even though no bank lends out more than the cash (reserve) it receives, the banks in series do "manufacture" deposits as they acquire other assets (notes). The public gets more deposits on which it can write checks.

The process takes time and does not work so smoothly as pictured here. Our illustrations of deposit expansion have assumed implicitly that the income obtainable will be greater than the cost to the bank of handling the added deposits. Under some conditions such may not be the case. Deposit expansion depends upon borrower as well as bank action; businesses or individuals whom the banks consider good risks may not want to borrow all that banks can lend. If banks have excess reserves, however, an expansion of deposits is possible—a bank with excess lending capacity can, by the simple use of ink and paper, create a deposit.

FIGURE 6–2.   Cumulative Expansion in Deposits on Basis of $1,000 of New Reserves and Reserve Requirement of 15 Percent

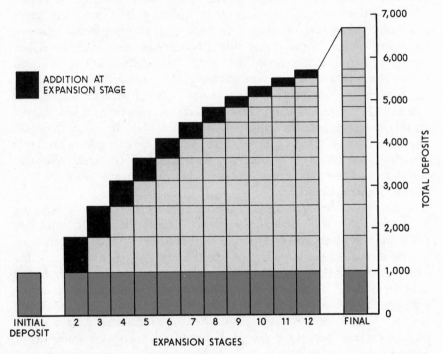

Source: Federal Reserve Bank of Chicago.

Suppose, however, that instead of leaving that original $1,000 on deposit, you decided to spend some of it. If you write a check for $100 to pay a bill in Boston, your bank is in a tight spot, as it loses $100 of the $150 legal reserve it had retained. The bank must cut its deposit liabilities by $567 more than the decrease in your deposit—to $333 (the $50 reserve remaining is 15 percent of $333). But the Boston bank can then expand. What one bank loses, the other gains.

The individual bank is at the mercy of its depositors. Each banker may thus feel narrowly limited in his power to create deposits by expanding loans. But all banks together have entirely different power. The group can do vastly more than the total of what each one acting separately can do. The bank that expands more rapidly than the others must watch its step. If its own depositors do business with one another and shift their deposits from one account in the bank to another, the bank need not worry—it is like a whole nation's banking system. But such self-contained banks do not exist. People in one town buy from, and sell to, people in hundreds of other places. Each bank constantly loses deposits to other banks and in turn gets deposits from others. If the two flows are even, the expansion process can continue smoothly.

Moreover, borrowers, as a rule, do not withdraw all the proceeds of a loan at once but leave some in the bank for days, weeks, or months. To this extent the loan expansion does not immediately draw down the bank's cash (reserve) by the full amount of the loan, as assumed in our example. However, except to the extent that a bank insists that some of a loan remain on deposit, it cannot be certain. Its liabilities are payable on demand, and people can act unpredictably. Of course, if there were only one bank in the economy, it could at once expand deposits to the limit when the $1,000 cash first appears (assuming no prospect that new money would leave the economy through foreign trade). If, as in England, Canada, or many other countries, only a dozen or so banks with many branches serve the entire economy, each can feel confident that any withdrawals from the branch making a loan will partly come back to some of its other branches.

If the reserve requirement is 15 percent, the total expansion (including the first $1,000) will not actually reach 6.7 times the original injection. (1) Some borrowers will take part of their loan in currency, and some of the employees or the suppliers to whom they give checks will ask for currency. And if the general level of business activity is rising, people will need more money in their pockets to finance the transactions they handle with cash. (2) Banks may not use all their lending power, perhaps because they wish to be able to meet anticipated or unexpected loan demand, perhaps because there is not enough demand from borrowers whose credit is good.

As banks expand deposits, they also expand their assets. We assumed that notes, IOU's (such as the auto dealer or the dentist gave), constituted the increase in the bank's assets. Other kinds of assets, government securities, for example, might have been acquired. Treasury obligations, especially those within a few months of maturity, can be purchased in the open market by a bank with excess reserves. The seller then has a deposit (money) instead of Treasury debt.

Deposits and Debt.   Modern money is debt. Money exists only if someone—individual, business, or government—is willing to assume an obligation. The growth or contraction of the supply of money depends upon changes in debt. Some obligations are those which a government assumes when it issues currency; a $10 bill is a promise to pay of government (or an agency having authority of government). "Checkbook money" also rests on debt because the assets which banks get as they create demand deposits are the formal debt obligations of business, government, and individuals. Does it seem odd that our money supply rests upon someone's willingness to be in debt? Whether or not odd, such is the fact. Another fact follows: the quality of debts accepted by banks will influence the country's monetary experience.

Deposit Contraction. Paying off debts which are owed to commercial banks reduces the quantity of money. One example of deposit contraction will illustrate. Suppose that you write a check for $850 to the auto dealer as you buy one of his used cars. He uses the check to repay his note at the bank. The bank's accounts show the following:

Starting Condition: Step 1

Assets		Liabilities	
Cash: legal reserve	$ 150	Your deposit	$1,000
Auto dealer's note	850		
	$1,000		$1,000

Then you write a check of $850 to the auto dealer:

Step 2

Cash: legal reserve	$ 150	Your deposit drops to	$ 150
Auto dealer's note of	$ 850	Auto dealer's deposit rises	850
	$1,000		$1,000

Auto dealer then writes a check for $850 to pay off his note, and the result is:

Step 3

Cash: legal reserve	$ 150	Your deposit	$ 150
(Excess reserve $122.50)			

You have the auto, and the dealer is out of debt to the bank. The bank may later make another loan; but until it does, its total deposits have fallen from $1,000 to $150. (What happened to the other $850 of assets? Remember, they went first to the Detroit bank and then in decreasing portions on to other banks.)

Indirect Effects. The expansion and the contraction of bank deposits in our example were obviously important to the people involved. In making the loans, the banks obtained a source of income: interest-bearing notes. Borrowers received the advantage of having money to help them carry on their affairs; presumably the benefit was at least equal to, and probably was expected to be more than, the interest paid. Each loan affected a borrower's actions. The auto dealer got spare parts, the dentist his equipment, and so forth.

Banks and borrowers, however, are not the only people affected by deposit creation. Others—for example, workers making auto parts—feel the influence. The creation and destruction of bank deposits have effects which spread out from the persons directly concerned. The results influence the world of business. What are these effects? How are they diffused through the economy? Answers depend partly upon the loans banks make—the next topic.

COMMERCIAL BANK LENDING

Lending Influenced by Need for Both Income and Liquidity. Banks make loans of many kinds, but for one dominant reason: *to earn income.* The more they can lend and earn, the better for their owners. The profit incentive provides a constant inducement for banks to lend as much as possible as long as the interest obtainable exceeds the full costs of handling larger deposits. This condition, however, creates a continuing problem for society. Bank lending is guided by the desire to earn income; but the lending process changes the money supply and thereby affects the rest of the economy, indirectly, but at times profoundly. The bank's desire for income may not always coincide with the public's interest in a change in the stock of money. Moreover, the search for income tempts a bank to grant loans where the interest yield is attractive but risk is more than minor—loans whose quality leaves too much to be desired.

Commercial bank lending is also shaped by the bank's need for liquidity, its ability to get cash easily. This need arises from the nature of a bank's liabilities to depositors. *Deposits in checking accounts are payable on demand.* The depositor, not the bank, has control. With liabilities payable upon the demand of depositors, banks must be able to produce currency or deposits in other banks—"cash" in ordinary terminology— without advance warning. If the bank cannot meet this obligation, it must close. Therefore, commercial banks must have assets which are highly liquid, that is, assets which the banker can readily convert to cash, or, perhaps better still, assets that convert themselves into cash. In making loans, therefore, banks try to get assets (debts of others) which can be transformed to cash readily, "just in case." Yet borrowers are in the opposite situation; they are willing to pay for the privilege of borrowing because they are short of cash.

The Self-Liquidating, Short-Term Loan. A happy compromise seems (or used to seem) available: Loans that increase demand deposits can be self-liquidating loans for business or agriculture. The clear, simple type was the loan to a retailer to finance the purchase of goods for sale, or to a manufacturer to buy material for fabrication. A good example would be to loan to a dealer in household appliances who is receiving a shipment of new models. He must pay on delivery, say, $50,000. He has only $15,000 of his own money available, so he goes to the bank. He should be able to sell the new style refrigerators and other products in 90 days or less; they are a tangible asset which the bank could seize and sell if he did not pay his loan; his business is profitable and well established, as he proves by showing his accounts. He can make more sales if he has the appliances on hand to show and deliver at once, than if he must sell from a catalog. The bank agrees and lends $35,000 on the dealer's note (perhaps taking a lien or chattel mortgage on the products).

The note may be payable in 90 days or, perhaps, on demand; in the latter case, there is likely to be mutual understanding that the bank will not demand payment before the end of 90 days. The dealer gradually sells the appliances and accumulates funds which he then uses to pay off his debt. The loan is self-liquidating. The borrower wanted it because he had a specific transaction in mind and one that was productive. The loan made the deal possible. The funds to repay the loan came naturally as the business proceeded. The borrower benefited because he could do business more advantageously with the added money. The bank was not committed for long and could expect to get dollars back through the normal working of the business system.

By staggering loans of this type, the bank would receive repayments of some loans every day or so. If its needs for cash rose, the bank would have the dollars; but, if not, some new loan could be made to bring income. The ability to borrow provided the business with financial flexibility, notably for financing peak-period needs.

The banks making loans of this type, it is said, would react to the "needs of trade," accommodating "legitimate" business in accordance with fluctuating needs for funds. Are not loans such as these ideal? They help "productive" business. They provide banks with assets which more or less automatically become cash.[10] These short-term, self-liquidating, "commercial" loans give the bank a chance to reconsider each case frequently. If things begin to go wrong with the borrower's business, the banker is in a position to spot the trouble within a few weeks and adjust his lending.

Our economy, we often hear, does not have adequate facilities for providing the small, but growing, business with all the funds it can use

---

[10] Although each individual loan of this sort may be liquid, a mass of such loans will not be readily converted into cash on short notice. Shifting of assets and deposits may provide funds for repaying any one specific loan; but shuffling of a small amount of cash cannot provide the total cash needed to repay a huge percentage of loans at any one time.

profitably. Commercial loans of the type described do provide some funds at myriads of strategic points in the business world. The energetic young man with ideas and good character may get a chance he would not have otherwise. The banker who knows the man (and his chances of success in the community) can create deposits to give him help. The banker's shrewdness in judging ability and character, plus his freedom in granting loans, has helped many a worthy business to get started and to keep expanding. The growth of such loans has also provided some of the increase in the stock of money needed by an expanding economy.

These loans may have disadvantages for business other than the interest cost. The 90-day due dates roll around frequently. The banker may say no to a request for a new loan and thereby disrupt a company's operations. The business may find the banker imposing his judgment and vetoing projects that seem profitable. Businessmen have often concluded, therefore, that it is wise to get free from bank influence. Many seem to prefer to borrow on a long-run basis, sell stock, or reinvest earnings to get dollars to finance operations. By 1940 not a few leading businesses seemed to have freed themselves from need to borrow from banks. Since World War II, however, businesses large and small have made extensive use of short-term borrowing from banks.

Term Loans.   Another development gains ground. Banks frankly and systematically lend to business for terms of years. In the past, a businessman could not count upon getting a loan renewed at the end of 90 days, though time and again he might have no trouble doing so. Such an insecure source of funds could not safely be used for buying equipment which would require several years to pay for itself. Term loans have been developed to help provide for just such needs. Banks lend for 1 to 8 years or more. The borrower repays (amortizes) the principal in installments.

Discounts.   In published bank statements, you will see the term "discounts" linked with "loans." Essentially, the discount is a loan on which the interest has been deducted in advance. For example, if you were to ask your banker what he would charge for a loan, he might say "6 percent discount." He means that if you borrow $100 for a year, he will deduct the 6 percent at once, giving you only $94; you repay him $100 at the end of the year. The $6 is the "interest," though there is no specific statement of an interest charge. The purpose of doing things this way is simple: the bank receives $6 for lending $94 rather than $100, an interest rate of 6.4 percent.

Credit "Rationing."   The total a bank will lend to any borrower often depends upon the banker's judgment. A kind of rationing results. Some borrowers will find that they cannot borrow as much as they would like at the interest rate the bank is charging. A fringe of unsatisfied borrowers will be wanting more loans (credit) than the bank will grant. Shifts in the attitudes of bankers can enlarge or reduce this margin when legal reserves permit.

Personal and Consumer Loans.   Commercial bank *consumer* loans were more than $32 billion in early 1968. A person with a job can borrow to buy an auto or other durable consumer good or to pay medical bills, taxes, or any such personal need, repaying regularly over a year or more. Some of us borrow directly from a bank. Others deal with the seller, who may then transfer the loan to a bank. Today, consumer installment loans account for a considerable part of the income of some banks. Although the bank cannot liquidate such loans easily if some emergency creates need for cash, the banker can make fewer new loans and hold on to what is received from loans which are maturing. Interest charges tend to be higher than on other bank loans, and despite the relatively high handling cost (because of record keeping and occasional collection difficulties) banks find personal loans profitable.

Loans on Real Estate and Securities.   Real estate mortgage loans above small totals have not ordinarily been considered appropriate for commercial banks. Such loans will very often bring higher interest yields than would be available from additional loans to businesses. Yet real estate loans cannot generally be converted to cash easily, quickly, and at an assured price. Hence, they have seemed inappropriate for an institution whose debts are payable on demand. Some justification for real estate lending by commercial banks derives from the fact that the law does not require that time and saving deposits be paid on demand (and on balance they grow). Real estate loans by commercial banks have increased to 5 times the level of 1947, making up about one sixth of current total loans and investments. Part of the expansion is related to a large increase in time and saving deposits (from $34 billion in 1947 to $180 billion in 1967). Moreover, as we shall see in the next chapter, new types of mortgages with less risk have become available.

Commercial banks lend to brokers whose customers wish to purchase stocks and bonds on margin. Banks also make security loans, to help finance sale of new issues of stocks and bonds. Security loans in 1967 were only about 3 percent of the total of loans and investments.

Bank Purchase of Securities.   U.S. government obligations bulk large among commercial bank assets. Ownership of state and local government debt trends upward partly because the interest received is exempt from income tax. Bank purchase of government debt may not appear as bank lending, since what the bank in fact does is to buy a security, not negotiate a loan. Yet such purchases are essentially lending. Over the years this government debt has been paid for primarily by the same process of deposit creation we described earlier. In 1940 banks held $17 billion government diet; 5 years later, $84 billion. The total fell to $54 billion in 1957, but rose to $61 billion by 1964 and was about the same in 1967.

Some of the government debt held by banks is for very short periods. A bank can arrange its holdings so that some mature every month or two; therefore, it can get funds from the Treasury, if necessary, either to meet the demands of depositors or to make a more attractive loan. Another fact assures a high degree of liquidity. U.S. government debt can always be sold. These assets are easily *shifted* to other banks. If a bank is pinched for cash, or sees a better loan prospect, it can sell the debt for cash. On the other hand, if a bank has excess reserves, purchase of government securities can be especially attractive. There is no appreciable trouble or expense in handling these assets. The risk varies from negligible to appreciable. Short-term debt of good quality fluctuates insignificantly in price; the owner can always hold it a few days or weeks more and receive the face value at maturity. In contrast, the market prices of bonds which will not fall due for several years often rise and fall by as much as one or two years' interest. Though always salable, long-term government bonds are not always salable without loss. Banks must often fact this question: Shall we buy short-term debt which is highly liquid but yielding low income, or debt which is more lucrative but less assuredly convertible into cash without loss? Answers vary with changing conditions and individual judgments.

This chapter started with general comments on money. It ends with a discussion of lending by the institutions which create most of our money. In between we covered a variety of important topics. Now we go on to other parts of the same broad subject: banking and its control.

TERMS AND CONCEPTS

"money illusion"	legal tender	deposit creation
unit of account	demand deposit	commercial loans
medium of exchange	time or savings deposit	term loans
store of value	fractional reserves	discounts
gold standard	primary deposit	

QUESTIONS

1. "It is misleading to speak of different functions of money, for all are intimately related." To what extent is this statement true? Why?

2. Suppose that 100 students each withdraw $100 in currency from the bank to pay for new typewriters, and the merchants put the money aside in store safes. Trace the effects on the total of bank deposits, assuming no excess reserves.

3. What are the major assets and liabilities of commercial banks?

4. Even cautious bankers feel safe in keeping on hand an amount of cash (legal reserve) that is only a fraction of their total liabilities to depositors. Why?

5. "Five dollars payable to the bearer on demand," is inscribed on some of our money. But the payment will be made only with other paper "promises to pay" (or token coins). Why then do people accept this money, which is nothing but a promise to pay more promises?

6. "Banks can create money only if the public wants more money badly enough to pay the cost." Comment.

7. "No country can have really good money unless the currency is freely convertible into gold." Discuss.

8. What is a self-liquidating commercial loan? A term loan?

9. Assume that a few banks were to try to go against the trend of the banking system in (*a*) expanding and (*b*) contracting deposits. Discuss the probable results.

10. What would be the effect of removing legal-tender status from our currency? Why?

11. For which, if any, of the uses of money should savings deposits be included in the money supply?

12. In what sense are banks "dealers in debt"?

7

THE U.S. BANKING SYSTEM, MONETARY CONTROL, AND FINANCIAL INSTITUTIONS

Monetary policy is directly concerned with the provision of money, defined to include currency and demand deposits at commercial banks. In the United States, monetary policy is essentially Federal Reserve policy. . . .
Commission on Money and Credit

The last chapter showed how banks create deposits. Now we examine the banking system more closely. The focus will be on controls over deposit creation—chiefly controls set by law or resulting from discretionary action of the Federal Reserve.

Briefly, our banking system is one of two layers: nearly 14,300 commercial and savings banks with which the public does business and 12 Federal Reserve banks which deal with banks, the U.S. Treasury, and central banks of other countries.[1] Our tradition has been for each town to have one or more of its own banks free from nonresident domination. Obviously, then, most banks have been "small." Our system has its own history, one loaded with stories of optimistic wishful thinking and unnecessary tragedy. For example, 50 years ago Americans (half of the 1968 total) had almost twice as many banks as today. In the time it takes to go from first grade through high school, from 1921 to 1933, about half the banks in the United States failed (mostly small ones). The history of

---

[1] Most states permit a bank to have branches. Today, some 2,800 banks have about 17,000 branches or separate units. California's Bank of America has the largest number of branches, over 800. Recent mergers of banks have been designed in part to build larger branch organizations. A big bank with a central headquarters and many separate offices can provide wider diversification, greater stability, and more specialization at top levels than can a multitude of small institutions.

banking trouble did not begin in 1921, however, but goes back about as long as we have had a history.

HIGHLIGHTS IN THE DEVELOPMENT OF U.S. BANKING

The Tradition of Separate Local Banks. In relation to population or income, why does this country have many times as many banks as Canada or Western Europe? Part of the explanation is that banking has sometimes been a highly lucrative business and more often has seemed to be one. Think of the profit that appeared possible. Bankers investing $10,000 capital, in cash, and attracting some deposits from outside could dream of making loans at 8 percent up to a total of several times their capital. The interest income on loans of $100,000 would be $8,000 a year, or 80 percent on the capital put in. Banking offered bright prospects.

Men influential in state and national legislatures did not want to see an end to the opportunities for setting up new banks. "Free" banking became the standard; anyone who had the cash to put up as capital could generally get a bank charter. Businessmen and farmers wanted more banks, for they needed money. (America was chronically "short" of capital.) Moreover, they wanted independent local banks and dreaded the thought of a money monopoly controlled outside which could hurt local borrowing opportunities.

Establishing the National Banking System. When war came in 1861, the South issued its own money and set up its own banks. It issued more and more currency and suffered an inflation which by 1865 wiped out the value of Confederate money. The North, too, printed paper money—greenbacks—and suffered inflation which cut the purchasing power of its dollar almost in half by 1865. In the meantime, however, Congress established the National Banking System, but respected the traditions of local control and "free" banking. The new law fixed minimum capital requirements for banks obtaining charters from the federal government. It also provided that these banks maintain minimum reserves against deposit liabilities and restricted their power to make loans. National banks were to be examined from time to time by the Comptroller of the Currency. These requirements were higher than those of most states.

Why, then, try to obtain a national charter? For one thing, Congress soon imposed a clearly prohibitive tax of 10 percent a year on the currency of state banks. At that time the "money" which the banks created and loaned—the transactions producing most of their income—consisted primarily of bank notes rather than checking deposits. The new tax, therefore, seemed to be a death blow to nonnational banks. National banks, however, were authorized to issue currency with federal government bonds as backing. The bank received interest on the bonds, and in addition, it could charge interest on the loans which it made with the notes. Congress sought (1) to encourage the sale of bonds to pay for the war and (2) to improve the country's currency and also its banking system.

After fighting ended in 1865, "Northern" currency had to supply the whole country—a country whose economy continued to expand. Yet the volume of this currency soon began to contract; the national government was redeeming greenbacks because tax collections were greater than its expenses. Later on, the Treasury retired much of the debt that was the backing of national bank notes, forcing reduction in the quantity of these notes—from over $300 million in the early 1870's to a low of $124 million in 1891. An expanding economy with a contracting currency will likely have trouble—ours did in the depressions of the 1870's, 1880's, and early 1890's. Discontent with the money system was widespread.

True, the currency was safe from the pre-Civil War troubles; in effect the country got a uniform national currency. Yet the system seemed inelastic, not appropriately responsive to changing needs. The "saving grace" in providing money for the growing economy was the increased use of checking accounts for making payments. Banks with state charters found that they could operate profitably without issuing bank notes. From 1864 to 1900, demand deposits increased at least tenfold.

Generous Lending, Bank Failures, Financial Strain.   Local bankers, tempted by prospects of growing profit, faced a persistent demand from their neighbors for loans. Such lending was a favor to the community, or so it seemed. Popular pressure for "easy" lending was common.

Lending power rested in the hands of a man who knew his neighbors and could judge their character and prospects. The system also put banking in the hands of unskilled and often incompetent, shortsighted, and ignorant part-time bankers. Some were principally promoters. Avoidable mistakes were made. Individual banks were tied in so intimately with local conditions that a crop failure on the nearby farms or a slump at the local factory could bring default on loans and force the bank to close, sending trouble elsewhere. Adequate diversification and the spreading of risks were generally impossible.

Barns and factories were built, but banks failed, depositors lost their deposits, and borrowers lost their properties to the banks' receivers. Then business, locally at least, suffered seriously. Trouble in one community often spread to others. Deposits in a closed bank could not be used to pay debts or buy new things. A bank failure in one town would often cause uneasiness in the next so that depositors would begin a "run" on their bank, demanding cash it did not have and forcing it to close. Less dramatically, a bank failure in one town might scare the neighboring banker into tighter lending.

The banking system had another defect. Though seasonal needs for money were known to rise and fall in patterns which varied from one region to another, temporary strains often caused distress in one area when funds elsewhere were not so tight. The country clearly needed facilities for more widespread pooling of liquid financial resources.

National, and often state, banks were permitted to hold much of their legal reserves in the form of *demand deposits* in large city banks, especially New York. If many banks throughout the country began to draw upon their checking accounts with these "correspondent" banks in New York, the latter might not have cash to pay. Or if a New York bank got into trouble and shut down, the banks having their reserve on deposit with that bank might be forced to close. In 1907 there was a serious panic as one big bank failure in New York touched off a chain reaction of distress. Congress then undertook an extensive study, and in 1913 created the Federal Reserve System.

THE FEDERAL RESERVE SYSTEM: STRUCTURE AND MAJOR FUNCTIONS

Organization and Structure. Opinion was torn between a central bank on European patterns and regional bankers' banks. One central bank could be impregnable; it could pool money and distribute risks over the entire country; a money shortage in one region could be alleviated by funds from another. Regionalism had its chief appeal in that no single power would gain a monopoly; "Wall Street" (or Washington) would have less chance to throttle Main Street; regional banks, moreover, could adapt their operations to the differing needs of various areas. The upshot was a compromise. Twelve regional banks were established, but they were made part of a national system with headquarters in Washington. Each of these 12 banks was to be, within its region, a "central bank" for the commercial banks which joined the System.

Which banks should join? Congress decided that national banks must join. State-chartered banks were given the option of becoming members, by meeting the requirements, or of staying out. Over half of the commercial banks in the country are not members of the Federal Reserve System. Outside the System they have somewhat greater freedom and better earning possibilities. Yet today nonmembers have considerable access to the System's facilities, through correspondent banks which are members, and directly for some miscellaneous service functions. Around 80 percent of the country's demand deposits are in member banks.

The capital stock of each of the 12 Federal Reserve banks is owned by the member banks in its region. Like other corporations, the banks have boards of directors, a majority being elected by the stockholding banks to represent industry, commerce, and agriculture as well as banks. Above them is the Board of Governors, seven members appointed by the President of the United States to serve staggered 14-year terms. The law does not require any proof of competence, but it does specify that the selection must give "due regard" to different industrial and geographical interests. This Board's influence has grown over the years so that the major policy decisions are made in its handsome Washington headquarters. Gradually, we have acquired a system which is much like a central bank for major issues. Yet the 12 banks and their 24 branches still have some discretion on specific regional matters.[2]

Member Bank Reserves.   What does the System do? One major function is to *hold the legal reserves* of the member banks. Our banking system still operates on the basis of fractional reserves. *Today the legal reserves of member banks,* in addition to the currency in bank vaults, are *deposits at the Federal Reserve bank.* For every dollar of its liabilities to its depositors, a member bank must have a certain percentage in vault cash or on deposit at its Federal Reserve bank ("Fed" for short). A bank may have *excess reserves,* that is, reserves above those needed to meet its legal requirements.

The Board has limited power to alter the reserve requirements. Table 7–1 summarizes both the basic law and the situation in early 1968.

TABLE 7–1. Member Bank Reserve Requirements (Percent of Deposits)

	Demand Deposits		Time Deposits
	Reserve City Banks	Country Banks	
Legal minimum	10	7	3
Legal maximum	22	14	10
In effect January, 1968	17	12½	3 and 6*

* The higher rate applies to the portion of time deposits over $5 million of any one bank.

How does a bank make a deposit in its Federal Reserve bank? It does this in about the same manner as you would make a deposit in your bank. The bank has a checking account in which it makes deposits at the "Fed." It sends currency or coins; it also sends checks on other banks. To honor such checks, the bank on which they are drawn must send either cash or draw down its own deposits at the Reserve bank. When your bank has a deposit (reserve) at the Federal Reserve, it can then create deposits in making loans (or in buying securities, such as those of the U.S. Treasury).

The reserve itself earns the member bank nothing. Published bank

[2] Opportunities for initiative and difference of view are also greater with 12 than only 1 bank. Among the offices and staffs of the 12 banks one does find public disagreement occasionally, and within the System, debate must be livelier and research more imaginative. The Board appoints three of the nine directors of each of the 12 banks, approves appointments of their presidents, and may remove their officials. Its operating income comes from the 12 banks. To assure that the Board of Governors knows the views of the banking world, there is a Federal Advisory Council, made up of 12 commercial bankers, one selected by each of the Federal Reserve banks. The Council has only advisory functions.

statements include it under "cash due from banks." Obviously, member banks must keep a significant fraction of their assets "unproductive" at the "Fed."

The Federal Reserve bank itself can, like a commercial bank, create deposits. It can acquire assets that earn income. Table 7–2 shows the assets, liabilities, and capital of the System late in 1967.

Functioning of the Federal Reserve System. The Reserve bank's job as *holder* of member bank reserves is less important for the economy than another part of the job—its *control over the amount of reserves.* The

TABLE 7–2. Consolidated Balance Sheet of the Twelve Federal Reserve Banks, 1967 (In Billions)

Assets		Liabilities	
Gold certificates	$10.7	Federal Reserve notes	$39.7
Redemption fund for Federal Re-		Deposits:	
serve notes	1.8	Member bank reserves	19.8
Other cash	0.3	U.S. Treasury	1.1
Discounts and advances	0.1	Foreign and other	0.6
U.S. Government securities	46.7		
Uncollected cash items*	6.5	Deferred availability cash items†	4.8
		Other	0.3
		Total	$66.1
Bank premises and other assets	1.5		
Total	67.5		
		Capital	
		Capital paid in	$ 0.6
		Surplus and other	0.7
		Total liabilities and capital	$67.5

Figures are rounded and will not necessarily add to totals.
* Amount of checks that have been deposited in one Federal Reserve bank but for which the funds have not been finally transferred from the other Federal Reserve banks.
† Amount of checks which member banks have deposited for collection but which have not yet been credited to the reserve accounts of banks. Member banks are credited with checks they deposit according to an arbitrary scale.
Source: *Federal Reserve Bulletin,* October 1967.

amount member banks can lend, and the amount of the deposits they can owe, depend upon legal reserves. These reserves, therefore, influence the total of deposits in checking accounts, deposits which are part of the money supply. Changes in the stock of money affect the way the economy functions—hence our interest in the "control" aspects. So we ask again: "How does a bank get reserves (deposits) at the Reserve bank? Can the Reserve authorities exercise effective control?"

One bank can get a deposit (reserve) at the Fed by depositing a check drawn on another member bank; the latter, of course, loses a deposit of equal size. So we ask, "How, then, do banks as a group get reserves at the Federal Reserve?" Depositing currency can account for only a little, if any, growth. When member bank deposits at the Fed were almost $20 billion (late 1967), the 12 Reserve banks held only about $350 million in currency and coins (other than unissued bank notes). In what other ways do the deposits originate? Two are most important. (1) Reserve banks (*a*) lend to member banks and (*b*) purchase assets, such as government bonds, from member banks or others; the Fed pays by adding to the accounts of member banks. (2) If the U.S. Treasury deposits "gold certificates," the totals in the reserve accounts of member banks will rise.

Gold Certificates.   Let us look at the latter first. If banks or private individuals receive gold from a foreign country or from new mining, they must sell it to the Treasury. The latter pays with a check on its account at the Federal Reserve. The seller of the gold deposits the Treasury's check in his bank, which will then get a larger deposit balance at the Federal Reserve. In other words, some of what had been the Treasury's deposit is transferred to the account of the member bank. To rebuild its own checking account, the Treasury then issues a gold certificate and deposits it in the Reserve bank; the gold itself goes into the Treasury's vaults. At the end, the Treasury's checking account (deposit) at the Reserve bank is back where it was originally. The member bank's deposit is larger by the amount of gold; the Reserve Bank has an increase in assets—gold certificates—of equal amount.

The economic significance of the Treasury's part in this process is ordinarily small. Ignoring it, therefore, an addition of $1,000 of gold would have the following effects—all being increases:

Federal Reserve Bank		Member Bank	
Assets	Liabilities	Assets	Liabilities
Gold certificates $1,000	Member bank deposit $1,000	Deposit at Federal Reserve $1,000 (Reserve required for deposit of seller of gold, $150; excess reserve, $850.)	Deposit of seller of gold $1,000

Over the years, to 1968, deposits of gold certificates at the Federal Reserve exceeded withdrawals by over $10 billion. Congress for many years made these gold certificates a basic reserve of the System. For every dollar of its own liabilities to depositors, each Reserve bank had to hold a minimum percentage, for several years, of 25 percent, in gold certificates. Removal of the requirement came in 1965 as a result of the export of gold to other countries. In a sense the gold certificates were the tip of our (inverted) banking and monetary pyramid (Figure 7–1). As a rule, the Reserve authorities have almost no control over this part of their total assets; mining and international trade are dominant. When the 25 percent rule applied, one dollar of new gold (from mines or abroad) which

FIGURE 7-1.   The Pyramid of Money* (In Billions)

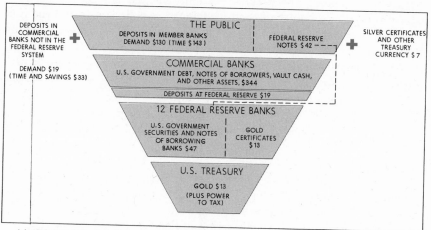

* Interbank deposits, U.S. government deposits, and deposits in mutual savings banks excluded. Summer, 1967.

entered the monetary system could support about $24 expansion in commercial bank deposits; the Federal Reserve could expand member bank reserves (deposits) on a 4 to 1 basis. Then the member banks could expand about 6 to 1. Loss of gold could have the opposite effect. However, such multiple response was not inevitable, because other forces also operated.

Discounting and Advances.   Now we turn to the other way deposits come into existence at the Fed. The Reserve banks create deposits in about the same way commercial banks do for their depositors. The Reserve bank makes a loan to member banks, in return for an IOU. If a bank wants to borrow, it exchanges its own debt and receives a deposit, just as the auto dealer turned over his debt (a note) and received a deposit at his bank, for example:

Federal Reserve		Member Bank	
Assets	Liabilities	Assets	Liabilities
Note of member bank $1,000 (Secured by an eligible asset)	Deposit of member bank $1,000	Deposit at Federal Reserve $1,000	Note to Federal Reserve $1,000
		(No change in required reserve)	

The mechanics of the process may involve (*re*)*discounting*, the method originally intended to be the major means for member banks to borrow from the Reserve bank. A member bank wishing to increase its deposits at the Fed can take certain kinds of short-term notes it has received from its borrowers and turn them over to the Reserve bank in return for a deposit. This process is roughly like taking a bond or share of stock you own to your bank and pledging it as collateral for a loan. The law, however, requires the Reserve to be rather "choosey" about the kind of "paper" it will accept.

The Reserve bank charges for the service of lending to banks. It may quote the charge as a rate of discount. This "price" is often called the *(re)discount rate*, the whole process, *(re)discounting*. (Today, the "re" does not ordinarily apply.[3]) What happens? The Reserve bank's assets increase by the amount of the asset discounted; its liabilities grow by the amount of the deposit created for the bank. The Reserve bank can increase its loans to member banks as long as they and it wish.

More commonly, member banks that are short of reserves and seek the Fed's help will borrow directly. Collateral, usually government securities, will support the bank's promise to pay. In making such *advances*, the System has a wide range of discretion in deciding what collateral it will accept. The rate charged is the same as for (re)discounting. The basic economics are similar, the mechanics simpler.

Why would a bank be willing to pay a price for such borrowing? (1) The bank may wish to take advantage of its own customers' demand for loans. A member bank is able to create deposits for its customers when its own reserve (deposit) at the Federal Reserve increases. There is an obvious advantage in paying, say, 4 percent rediscount on $1 and lending at least as much at 6 percent. If a member bank could increase its loans to 5 or more times its reserves, the profits could be handsome. Banks as a group *are* able to expand in such multiple fashion, but no individual bank can do so. The Federal Reserve objects to the use of its lending facilities for the primary purpose of increasing a member bank's earnings.

(2) Member banks borrow to help adjust to special needs of the type which had much to do with the creation of the System. In certain seasons of the year, or in periods when business conditions were unusual, individual banks in the pre-Federal Reserve era could not always meet the "legitimate" requests of customers for loans. Bank reserves were too small. Sometimes banks could not even meet the demands of depositors for currency. The old system lacked elasticity. When banks had to disappoint their clients or depositors, business in general suffered. Sometimes financial stringency spread out broadly. Temporary help in the form of larger reserves, however, permits the bank to tide its borrowers over periods of short-run difficulty. In doing so, the assistance, it is argued, helps prevent trouble from cumulating. The facilities for member bank borrowing were designed to add elasticity, flexibility, and adaptability. A business needing money (credit) temporarily for a "sound" purpose has a better chance of

---

[3] A commercial bank in lending to a customer may discount his note (page 158). If the bank then uses this note in borrowing from the Fed, the latter will also discount—hence the "re."

getting it when the member bank can itself get accommodation at the Federal Reserve.

Yet meeting all requests for apparently good loans may lead to an unwholesome increase in the total of demand deposits, money. Some control seems desirable. Congress gave the Federal Reserve an instrument of control in the form of power to adjust the (re)discount rate. If conditions seem to call for discouraging the expansion of bank loans, the Fed can raise the cost of member bank borrowing. When easier credit for business seems desirable, the rate can be reduced. Variations in the (re)discount rate can thus have some influence on member bank lending to business.

Banks use the borrowing privilege sparingly. Its existence, however, assures a member bank of ability to make up temporarily a deficiency in legal reserves. *Banks can count upon access to liquidity.* They can, in effect, turn over assets of low liquidity and receive deposits at the Federal Reserve which are perfectly liquid.

Open-Market Operations. The Federal Reserve's chief method of controlling member bank reserves is known as open-market operations. It consists of purchase and sale of securities, primarily federal debt. The amounts involved can be large. Moreover, in using this method *the Reserve banks can take the initiative.* They need not wait upon member banks to seek accommodation. In acquiring government debt, or other securities, the Reserve bank creates its own liabilities to pay the seller. These liabilities are deposits of member banks. The System does not ordinarily buy government debt directly from the Treasury. Purchases and sales are made in the open market where government securities are constantly traded.

When the System buys $1,000 bonds, increases result:

Federal Reserve		Member Bank	
Assets	Liabilities	Assets	Liabilities
Government bond $1,000	Deposit of member bank $1,000	Deposit at Federal Reserve $1,000	Deposit of seller of bond $1,000
(Fed. check for $1,000 goes to seller of bond who)		(Required reserve, $150; excess reserve, $850.)	(Deposits check in his checking account)
	(Check canceled and member bank account increased by $1,000)	(Bank returns check to Federal Reserve)	

The Reserve bank receives the bonds. Its assets rise by $1,000; but its liabilities, the amount due the seller, increase by the same amount. With what does the Fed pay? It writes a check on itself. If the seller wants currency, he can get it by cashing the check. More likely, he will deposit the check in his bank, increasing his deposit there; the bank will then deposit the check in its account at the Federal Reserve. (If the seller was a bank, it would deposit at once.) The net result as far as the Reserve bank is concerned is an increase of $1,000 in both assets and liabilities. The new liabilities of the Fed are assets of the member banks—an exceptionally valuable type: legal reserves. So the member banks may increase their lending, their source of income.

Federal Reserve officials meeting every 3 weeks in Washington determine the general policies.[4] Actual operations center in New York.

The System sometimes buys, sometimes sells. (1) It owns large amounts of government debt from which it can make sales if it wishes. (2) When it buys, it can pay with deposits it creates; this ability to enlarge its deposit liabilities is in a sense an inventory of purchasing power for securities. Such buying and selling not only alter bank reserves. They also affect, perhaps by only minute fractions, the prices of securities and interest yields.

To *reduce* the reserves of member banks, the System can sell securities.[5] The buyer may be an insurance company, bank, trust fund, state or local government, or corporation. It receives the security and pays the Reserve bank with a check on its deposit at a commercial bank. The Reserve bank deducts this amount from the member bank's account.[6] The Reserve has (1) lost an asset, the security, and (2) reduced its liability to the member bank. The liability of the Federal Reserve, of course, was a deposit due the member bank. This amount is "wiped out"—in essence an obligation that has been paid with the government security.

The member bank whose depositor bought the security from the Fed had to give up something very valuable. The deposit it lost was not an "ordinary" asset. It lost part of its legal reserve, something on which it, and other banks as a group, could base loans of several times as much as the deposit. If you were a banker forced to give up legal reserves, you would by no means rejoice. The bank's income will go down. Yet there is nothing much you can do to prevent this forced contraction. If one of your customers wants to use some of his deposit with you to buy a Treasury bill, you must pay the Fed when the depositor's check is presented to you for payment. You may sigh, moan, or berate the bureaucrats in Washington for forcing you to give up legal reserves. But the

---

[4] The final authority is the Open Market Committee, consisting of the seven members of the Board of Governors and five representatives of the 12 Reserve banks. These 12 banks must buy, hold, and sell securities as the Committee directs. Purchases and sales are ordinarily restricted to short-term securities, Treasury bills for the most part.

[5] Actual net sale is uncommon. Slowing the growth in bank lending capacity, or stopping it for a time, will in fact have restrictive effect in an expanding economy.

[6] New York's highly organized money market offers banks facilities for buying and selling deposits at the Federal Reserve (called "Federal funds"), as well as short-term securities of many types.

initiative is not in your hands. If your reserves fall below the legal requirement, you may cover the deficiency temporarily by borrowing from the Fed or by purchasing the excess reserves of some other bank.[7]

To *increase* member bank reserves, the System can buy government debt. It must offer a price which will compete with the offers of other potential buyers. If it offers a good price, its orders will be filled. The Reserve pays by check which the seller of the bond—an insurance company or trust fund, for example—deposits in its own bank. If you were managing a bank receiving such a check, you would, of course, send it to the Fed for credit to your account there. The increase in your account does not bring any more income directly. Yet it is unusually welcome because it is a reserve on which you can base more loans (or buy securities). The System has taken the initiative, putting banks in a better position. You may sit tight, breathing more easily with the more comfortable reserve position; or you may actively take advantage of it by lending more, perhaps aggressively seeking borrowers, or buying securities.

Let us see the contrast between two types of bank reactions. Assume, for example, that as a banker your reserves (deposits) at the Federal Reserve were $1 million and that you were "fully loaned up," having demand deposit liabilities of $6.7 million. Then the System goes into the open market and sells securities. Your depositors write checks for $150,000 on their accounts for the securities they buy. The Federal Reserve, as the seller, receives these payments and deducts them from your account there, reducing it to $850,000. The largest possible volume of checking accounts you can now hold for your depositors is about $5.7 million. You *must* contract or take some other action.

The System, by sales in the open market, can force bankers to reduce loans (or to sell securities). It can wipe out reserves to the point where, in order to stay within the law, banks must somehow reduce their liabilities. In other words, banks must then force a reduction in the total of checking accounts owed to depositors. Borrowers will be required to use deposits to repay loans due banks.

The Federal Reserve cannot, on the other hand, force banks to make loans; it may buy securities in the open market and thus provide banks with more reserves. Yet it cannot compel banks to expand loans. Nor can banks force customers to borrow. Assume that you are a banker and that the System buys in the open market. Your depositors put $150,000 (which they receive for the securities sold) in their checking accounts at your bank. For this deposit increase, the required reserve, is $22,500; your excess reserve of $122,500 would support a deposit rise of about $850,000 throughout the system. Nothing compels you to expand at all, to get the chain of deposit expansion started. You may hold on to excess reserves without using them, remaining free always to expand if you wish. Gen-

---

[7] If the check is drawn on a nonmember bank, the latter can arrange payment through a member bank.

erally, however, banks do take advantage of reserves and keep fully loaned up. It is not common for expected costs of handling added deposits to exceed the interest obtainable.

Net Free and Net Borrowed Reserves.   At any one time some banks will have excess reserves, and some will be borrowing from the Federal Reserve. When for all member banks excess reserves are greater than borrowings, the banks have *net free reserves*. The banking system is then in a position to increase lending or add to holdings of securities. On the other hand, when borrowings exceed the total of excess reserves, the banking system is under pressure to restrain growth of lending. If business

FIGURE 7–2.   Member Bank Excess Reserves, Borrowings from the Federal Reserve, Net Free Reserves, and Net Borrowed Reserves, 1956–67

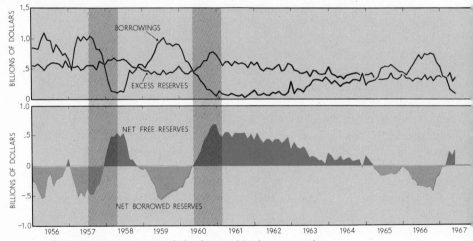

Shaded areas represent periods of general business recession.
Source: Federal Reserve Bulletin.

generally is poor, the Fed tries to assure that member banks have net free reserves. To force banks to curtail credit expansion when inflation threatens, the Federal Reserve can reduce reserves by selling in the open market. But under such conditions, member bank borrowings may rise to satisfy growing loan demand. Figure 7–2 shows some of the changes in the net reserve position of banks in recent years.

Limits on Federal Reserve Expansion.   In describing deposit creation by commercial banks, we emphasized that each individual banker might feel that he could lend only as much as his bank had received above the 15 percent legal requirement. Otherwise, as his borrowers wrote checks on their enlarged accounts, the bank would find its deposit at the Fed falling below the legal requirement. Is each Federal Reserve bank limited in the same way? No. For one thing, the Reserve bank is more nearly self-contained in its area than any one commercial bank. As member banks receive the larger deposits at the Reserve bank and write checks against them, a substantial fraction of these checks will go to banks in the same Federal Reserve district. To the extent that this happens, the ownership of deposits at the Reserve bank will shift from bank *A* to *B*, and so on, but there will be no net decline that forces the Reserve bank to lose assets. Moreover, there is pooling of resources of all 12 Reserve banks; if one is pressed, it can draw on others. No longer does a legal requirement for gold certificates impose restrictions.

Changing Member Bank Reserve Requirements. The Federal Reserve holds member bank reserves, a task far less important than the job we have been examining—*controlling the amount* of reserves, through lending to member banks and by open-market operations. The amount of reserves determines bank lending capacity and to large extent the quantity of money, but not entirely. Congress has given another power over bank lending. The Board of Governors has authority to change reserve requirements, the percentage of deposits which member banks must hold as legal reserves. Table 7–1 shows the ranges of this power. An increase in reserve requirements reduces the power of member banks to lend. For example, if reserve requirements were raised from 15 to 20 percent, the amount of deposit liabilities a member bank could have for each $1 of reserve would fall from roughly $6.7 to $5.

How effective is this tool? The answer depends upon conditions. (1) If you were running a bank that was fully "loaned up," having about all the deposit liabilities your reserves would support, and the Federal Reserve increased the requirements, you would have to do something. You would probably try to find some way to get more reserves; borrowing from the Fed is one possibility. Yet you might have to induce your customers to cut deposits by using them to repay loans, for your reserves are not adequate for the new requirements. As loans to your borrowers came due, you would probably say: "The bank cannot renew the full amount." Applicants for new loans would be refused. By raising your interest charge, you could offset some of the loss of income and discourage borrowers.

(2) But a bank holding excess reserves at the time the Reserve raised the percentage requirements might be able to absorb the shock without any appreciable difficulty. This is largely what happened when the requirements were raised in 1936.

Now let us look at the other side. Suppose the Reserve reduced requirements. (3) You would not be compelled to do anything. You might "sit tight" with reserves that have become excess, not because the amount has grown but because the rate required was reduced. (4) On the other hand, you might see the chance to increase the bank's income by making more loans or by buying securities. You could start the process of expanding the bank's assets and liabilities. Banks have the initiative—*the Reserve cannot force expansion.*

From the mid-1930's till the early 1950's, the reserve requirements were nearer the top than the bottom of the range. The Board had little room to move in a restrictive direction. But if it wished to move toward lower requirements, it was free to go a long way. It started such a trip in 1953. It has cut requirements several times when an expansion of bank lending

FIGURE 7–3.   Bank Reserve Changes in Relation to Changes in the Stock of Money

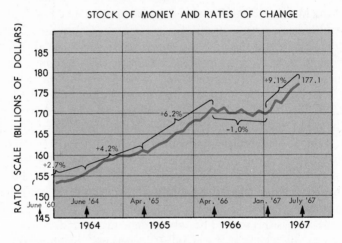

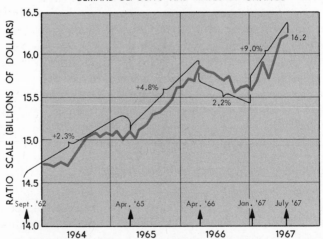

Monthly averages of daily figures seasonally adjusted.
Percentages are annual rates of change between periods indicated.
They are presented to aid in comparing most recent developments with past "trends," and may not be relevant for other purposes.
Source: Federal Reserve Bank of St. Louis.

seemed desirable. A change of 0.5 percentage point on demand deposits, though seemingly small, increases the lending potential of banks by over $3 billion. Banks welcome any such reduction, for their earning power grows. In 1966 and 1967, both increases and decreases were made in reserve rates required for time and savings deposits. (See Figure 7–3.)

Much tighter control could be exercised by abolishing the fractional reserve basis, replacing it with *100 percent reserve requirements*. The Fed's open-market purchases would then determine (with some adjustments for time deposits and other special factors), dollar for dollar, the total of demand deposits. Proponents of this system in the 1930's believed that it would eliminate the ups and downs in the stock of money which aggravated business cycles.

Selective Controls. The Federal Reserve has other powers, less directly affecting the supply of money. It can fix the *margins* which brokers (or banks) must require their customers to pay at once when they borrow to buy on the stock exchange.[8]

The Board of Governors can also fix the maximum rates of interest which member banks may pay on time and savings deposits. For a quarter of a century to 1957, the ceiling in most cases was 2½ percent. Other thrift institutions came to pay more, however. Member banks, therefore, had difficulty competing for such deposits, but wanted them to permit the expansion of mortgage and other relatively long-term loans on which the interest rates obtainable had gone up appreciably. So the Federal Reserve over a period of years changed its Regulation Q, thus lifting the permitted ceilings. (If any state-imposed ceiling is lower, however, it applies to member banks in the state.) In 1965 an increase in some ceilings to 5½ percent made news; banks then became tougher competitors for time deposits and drew funds from other thrift institutions. Other controls have been used. Two major examples can be given:

During and after World War II, Congress gave the Federal Reserve authority to fix limits to terms of *installment loans* (*credit*). It could say, for example, that anyone buying an auto with installment credit must make a down payment of at least one third of the purchase price in cash or trade-in value and pay the full cost within not more than 15 months. The specific terms that the System set varied according to the price and type of article. New rules were imposed after fighting began in Korea, but in 1952 Congress eliminated this power. Tightening and relaxing controls such as these can have some influence on the total use of money in the country, especially if the terms imposed are strict. The main effect, however, may be on the demand for individual products or groups of products. For example, the demand for autos might be reduced significantly by strict terms set for the use of installment credit, with consumers shifting their expenditures to goods and

[8] In the late 1920's, no such power existed; if it had, the authorities might have prevented wild excesses in margin buying of securities. For many years, however, borrowing to buy securities has not fluctuated enough, or been large enough, for this power to be important in the arsenal of monetary controls.

services which do not ordinarily require payment to be spread over 2 years or so. The businesses dealing in products subject to controls, and the labor unions, naturally press for relaxation.

Temporary control over terms of *financing real estate* purchases was given to the Federal Reserve after the outbreak of fighting in Korea. The System fixed the amount of cash down payment to be required of any purchaser and also the number of years for paying off the loan. On a $10,000 house, for example, a buyer had to pay cash of at least 15 percent; and he had not over 25 years to pay the balance. Reserve officials were guided by two considerations: the rest of the monetary situation and the availability of resources for building houses.

Moral Suasion. The Federal Reserve authorities can exercise some influence by what is known as "moral suasion," "direct pressure," or "jawbone control." By exhortation, pleading, appeals to patriotism, and carefully reasoned logical argument, Reserve officials, from the chairman of the Board of Governors to the operating officers of the 12 Federal Reserve banks, can try to persuade bankers to do what the authorities think wise. For example, there is a firm tradition of urging banks not to make loans for "speculation"; verbal pressure will likely be directed to the officials of a bank that seems to be making such loans. Occasionally, one or more banks may be tending toward policies which the board may have power to prohibit; it dislikes the use of compulsion, however, and so will try moral suasion. Or it may lack power to do something that it thinks is highly desirable, such as to increase the lending of member banks when business is poor. By persuasion, however, it may be able to exert some influence. On the whole, moral suasion seems a crude tool and one which is not generally effective, except as it is the velvet glove over an iron fist of power that can give force to suggestions or requests that are not followed.[9] For some months late in 1966 the Fed restricted use of the "discount window" by banks wishing to get borrowed reserves. The authorities said, in effect, "We will grant accommodation only when the member bank will restrict its new lending to types which are consistent with System policies to help prevent inflation."

Federal Reserve Bank Earnings. When the Federal Reserve banks own government bonds or when they charge for lending to member banks, they receive interest income. What do they do with their earnings? The first claim is for operating expenses—bank officers and staff. Member banks then receive 6 percent on their investment in the Federal Reserve

[9] The Federal Reserve is also authorized to remove bank officers, withdraw membership, and exert other controls. Under certain conditions it may, but never does, make loans to businesses directly. Its day-to-day operations include a tremendous volume of important, but more routine, functions: issuing Federal Reserve notes, clearing checks within and among the 12 districts, and acting as agent for the Treasury, in handling the great mass of "paper work" involved in managing the government debt.

bank stock; most of the excess goes to the Treasury, estimated at over $2 billion for 1967.

TREASURY-FEDERAL RESERVE RELATIONS

An inescapable fact today is that Federal Reserve monetary policies must take account of U.S. Treasury problems.[10] The Treasury is a big borrower, not so much because the national debt is increasing as because much of the debt is short term. As it falls due, new borrowings are needed to repay the old. The Treasury, therefore, wants to be able to count on orderly financial markets in which it can borrow without undue complications. Moreover, the $13 billion annual interest on the debt is a significant expense item. The Treasury, aware of the taxpayer's concerns, will prefer lower rather than higher levels of interest rates. Unfortunately, there is no necessary reason why policies which the Federal Reserve believes are desirable for the economy as a whole will be the policies which Treasury officials prefer. Modern history has more than a few examples of conflicts between (a) governmental agencies which want to get money easily by turning to the banking system as the money creator and (b) the central bank seeking to prevent price-level increases (inflation) as newly created money flows into the economy.

During World War II, the Federal Reserve acquired U.S. securities— essentially open-market purchases—creating deposits for the Treasury. As the government used this new money to pay for munitions, the recipients deposited the checks in their own accounts at commercial banks. The banks, therefore, got larger reserves as their deposits at the Fed grew by the amount by which the Treasury's declined. The banks, in turn, could then acquire more government debt. They paid the Treasury by increasing the deposits in its accounts. This lending cost the banks little in terms of sacrificed alternatives since they had ample reserves. So the Treasury could borrow at very low interest rates. The money stock grew easily. (Recall Figure 7–1.) When the war ended, the Treasury insisted on continuation of low interest rates, "easy money." The Federal Reserve, therefore, could not impose the monetary restraint which was needed to help prevent inflation. "Adequately tight" money would have meant

---

[10] The Treasury can keep its funds as deposits in either commercial or Federal Reserve banks. By shifting deposits from commercial banks to the Fed and vice versa, it can influence the total reserves of commercial banks. It can produce a smaller result by shifting deposits from commercial banks that must keep, say, a 12 percent reserve to those needing 16½ percent. Thus, the Treasury, in its ordinary affairs, influences the banking system. In fact, the Treasury keeps deposits of tax money at the commercial banks in special "tax and loan" accounts and withdraws them upon "call," after advance notice. If the Treasury desires to ease or tighten the money market, it has limited power in its ability to decide where it will place its deposits. (The term "money market" applies to the market for very short-term loans and securities.) Similarly, by changing its total deposit holdings, it can influence the money market. Federal Reserve open-market action can offset or reinforce any such Treasury action.

higher interest rates. Year after year the price level rose. The Fed, in effect, agreed to buy outstanding long-term government debt (from banks or other owners) at $1,000 for a bond yielding $25 a year. Such a bond price was artificial, higher than would have prevailed in a free market.

Finally, in 1951, an "accord" between the Federal Reserve and the Treasury ended the unfortunate arrangements. Since then the two agencies have recognized that while the Federal Reserve can try in its day-to-day operations to create "orderly" conditions which take account of Treasury borrowing needs, basic monetary policy should not be dominated by Treasury desire to borrow at "low" interest rates. Yet, as we shall see in Chapter 11, an underlying problem remains. If the public, Congress, or the Treasury objects to the annual interest cost, the Federal Reserve may be pressed to create money, or permit the commercial banks to do so—money for the Treasury to borrow cheaply.

A fundamental question has not been decided. If the White House and Treasury disagree with the Federal Reserve, who should have the final word? A President elected by the people cannot count upon carrying out the policies which he believes are best, because the monetary authorities have power to "drag their heels" or actually, and even actively, work against White House policies. Strong support exists for giving the President more power to influence the Federal Reserve, but opposition seems stronger, resting upon fears that elected officials will tend to be unduly inclined toward "easy" money. Deliberate efforts to assure mutual understanding and efficient coordination have been fruitful. When the men at the top lunch together at least once a week, and when the research and operating staffs discuss major and minor matters every day, potential disagreements and misunderstandings will be averted. As a rule, purposes will be melded into cooperative policy. Not for certain, however. The Fed, for example, feels a responsibility to its creator, Congress, where powerful voices often differ from those of the Executive Branch.

PREVENTING BANK FAILURES

Bank failures, like smallpox, seem to be a plague we have almost conquered. It would be hard to find a college student today who had personally witnessed the tragedy of a bank failure. Yet, as late as the early 1930's, such failures were one of the country's major economic evils. What has been done? Action has been taken to remedy the two types of bank failures—insolvency and lack of liquidity. *Insolvency* exists when the value of the bank's assets falls below the total of its liabilities. A bank is *illiquid* when it cannot get currency and deposits at other banks to meet the immediate demands being made on it for cash (even though it may be manifestly solvent).

Fractional Reserves Continue.   Our banking system remains one in which the bank's perfectly liquid assets are only a fraction of the liabilities it may be called upon to honor in cash upon demand. Always there is a potential threat: liquidity may be inadequate. Moreover, though a bank's assets are the contracts of someone to pay it fixed amounts of money, the bank cannot always get the full number of dollars at once; liquidation may have to be at sacrifice prices. Solvency is not assured.

A system built on fractional reserves (even of highly liquid assets) will be somewhat precarious. Yet the size of the fraction has a bearing on the adequacy of reserves. What fraction of its assets will a bank need to keep in currency and deposits at the Fed and other banks? What portion need it hold in such "secondary reserves" as short-term government debt? Assuming that neither government nor custom has imposed standards, the following is as specific as any rule: In good times, reserves of only a few percent of deposits will be adequate; in really bad times, almost no fraction may be large enough. Our history records a few such crises, the worst being the long-drawn-out trouble from 1929 to 1933.

Real danger arises if depositors lose faith in the bank and try to convert their deposits into cash just to be safe. A "run" on the bank results. The system that operated beautifully as long as few depositors exercised their right to demand cash at about the same time can break down completely when they "gang up." Not enough currency or its equivalent is available.

If only one bank is in trouble, it can perhaps sell bonds and shift business loans to other banks for cash (at a cost). Yet panics have a way of spreading as depositors lose faith. If many banks are under pressure, they are likely to aggravate each others' troubles. The officers of bank *A* may want to help bank *B* but may themselves be in trouble, or fearing it. An asset that on one day could have been easily shifted (sold) to any of a dozen other banks can become "frozen."

What about loans which borrowers have pledged to pay on demand? Some borrowers may have cash, but most probably never really expected that it would be necessary to pay on short notice. They had assumed that if the lending bank were to demand repayment, they could sell securities or borrow from other banks as in good times. In a crisis, however, other banks will not lend; and there may be few cash buyers for securities. In the past, almost literally, banks that seemed in good shape with customary reserves on one day were forced to close before the end of the week. The disease of distrust spread like a plague.

A system built on fractional reserves carries some risk of a liquidity crisis. Moreover, fractional reserves present a paradox. The higher the reserve requirements, the more reserve the bank must keep—yet the sooner it may fall below the mark in a time of stress. If the legal requirement is 25 percent, a fall in the reserve holdings to 24 percent may force the bank to close; if the legal requirement were 20 percent, however, the bank could continue serenely with the 24 percent reserve. The merit of a "high" requirement is this: *Multiple expansion and contraction are reduced.* The significance of this point will appear in the discussion of business fluctuations.

Reasons for Believing that Banks Are Safer than in the Past. Fortunately, there are convincing reasons for believing that our banks are stronger than before the 1930's:

1. *Banks' deposits are now insured.* The Federal Deposit Insurance Corporation, formed in 1935, has established a record which properly inspires confidence. Banks that are members of the Federal Reserve must be insured, and others may be insured if they meet FDIC standards. About 96 percent of all banks, holding 98 percent of all checking and saving deposits, are covered by FDIC insurance. They pay a gross annual insurance premium of $\frac{1}{12}$ of 1 percent of their deposits subject to check. In return, the first $15,000 of each account is insured, guaranteed against loss. In fact, however, deposits over $15,000 are generally covered. How? *The FDIC tries to keep the bank from closing.*

When FDIC aid is required, one practice is to have another bank take over the operations of the bank in trouble, continuing large as well as small deposits.[11] The FDIC pays the losses on the assets that have "gone sour." The FDIC has accumulated over $2 billion to cover losses. It can also, if necessary, get additional funds from the Treasury or sell its assets to the Federal Reserve. Deposit insurance provides a bulwark because of its economic strength—the assets that are accumulated—and also because of its psychological effect. It gives depositors confidence. They are less likely to run in panic when they hear that their bank may be in trouble and thus, in demanding cash, force it to close.

2. Federal and state *laws and regulations impose standards* which limit the kinds of assets banks may hold. *Diversification* of loans is required, assuring that a few misfortunes will not overwhelm the bank. Presumably loans and investments must be of good quality. Most assets will not fall in value greatly, even if business takes a turn for the worse. Bankers are probably better trained and informed than in the past. The establishment of new banks is permitted only when the chances of survival seem good.

3. Once or twice a year *government examiners check on a bank's operations.* These examinations are likely to reveal any straying from the "straight and narrow" of prescribed banking practice, so the bank can be set right before things get hopeless. The certainty of such examinations undoubtedly reinforces the caution of bankers. Bank examiners are better trained than in the past, and changes in technical requirements enable examination to be more effective in preventing bank failures when the economy goes into recession. For example, examiners are less arbitrary in forcing banks to revalue downward loans and investments that are not up to expectations but which have promise of ultimately proving sound.

4. *Bank holdings of government debt* and of other high-quality secondary reserves are a substantial fraction of assets. The assets are easily sold for cash if banks need liquid funds. The relative stability of value of such assets under normal conditions helps preserve bank solvency. The Treasury and the Federal Reserve have the power to prevent a collapse in the prices of

---

[11] Bank troubles occasionally result from the attractions of horseracing or other nonbanking, but costly, activities that lead bank staffs to help themselves to bank assets. Ordinarily, banks insure against loss by dishonest employees.

government debt, and only a real collapse would seriously endanger most banks. Nevertheless, the prices of even high-quality long-term debt can fluctuate enough to influence bank management decisions.

5. Some bank *assets*, as well as deposits, *are insured*. Real estate mortgages, especially, have taken on a different aspect. Federal Housing Administration insurance of mortgages not only keeps them from falling greatly in price but also makes them much more easily salable than before 1940.

6. *The Federal Reserve has more emergency powers than in the early 1930's.* When member banks require cash to meet crisis needs, they can borrow from the Reserve.

INVESTMENT INSTITUTIONS

Safe, efficiently operating commercial banks and adequate control of the quantity of money will not meet all our needs for financial institutions. Another important need is for financial *intermediaries* between people who save money and those who want money to buy capital equipment. We now look at financial institutions, other than commercial banks, which act as middlemen between savers and the users of savings.

Life Insurance Companies. By 1968 life insurance companies had assets of $180 billion, compared with $110 billion 10 years earlier. Among our institutions, life insurance is a leader. The prominence is due partly to the fact that its members are more than insurance companies. The typical life insurance policy provides for building up a fund of savings for the insured; consequently, the companies (under regulation by state government) have become major recipients of savings and lenders or buyers of financial assets. The industry consists of a few giants, which do most of the business, and numerous smaller firms. Most insurance is with mutual companies: the policyholders are owners with no stockholders.

Assets have grown largely because of the savings element in life insurance. The companies guarantee a minimum rate of interest to policyholders, to owners of annuity contracts, or to beneficiaries who have left proceeds of death claims with the companies to earn income. Actual interest payments often exceed the guarantee.

The constant inflow of premium receipts and income from earning assets—$39 billion in 1967—plus funds received in repayment of loans made in the past all eliminate the need for cash to meet other than immediate requirements for liquidity. The companies seek new assets to earn income. State laws and common prudence force reliance upon assets that will pay the specific dollars called for; the obligations of the companies are in dollars.

Life insurance companies keep their large and growing wealth in bonds of governments, utilities, industrial firms; mortgages; preferred and a little common stock. The companies seek yields as high as will be consistent with safety. Their opportunities are restricted to assets with little risk; but within the limits permitted, companies adjust in the light of expected yields. Competition in selling new policies is keen, and the higher a company's income from its assets, the better the offers it can make. Insurance companies in lending over the whole nation make savings mobile geographically. Large sums are made available to business—from 1957 to 1967, around $30 billion in buying bonds and some stock, plus large amounts in mortgage loans. The firms receiving the funds, of course, will generally be well established, less often the struggling pioneers.

A few companies have begun to follow the example of a company set up for college professors—to sell variable annuities. Premium receipts are used to buy common stock. The size of the amount received during retirement will vary with stock prices. One objective is to participate in general economic growth, another to hedge against inflation.

The net rate of interest earned on assets is around 4.7 percent before income taxes.

Savings Banks and Savings and Loan Associations.   Savings banks and mutual savings banks vary in type from one state to another. Generally, their appeal is to the person of modest income who makes savings of a few dollars at a time and wants a convenient and safe depository. He seeks interest, although he will accept a low rate; and he wants to be able to get his money readily in case of emergency. A 30 to 60 days' notice can be required before a depositor must receive his money; most banks, however, do not insist on this advance notice. The kinds of assets savings banks may hold are limited by state law, ordinarily to types of greatest security: government or other high-quality bonds and conservative real estate mortgages. The early 1968 asset total, $60 billion, reflected a 10-year growth of four fifths.

Savings and Loan Associations, whose assets grew from about $9 billion in 1945 to around $140 billion in 1968, accept funds in apparently much the same way as savings banks (actually, the saver "buys" a share). These associations for many years offered appreciably higher yields than commercial and savings banks and in seeking new accounts emphasized the attractive yields. Recently, however, their competitive advantage dropped greatly.[12] They use the dollars received to acquire mortgages, especially on local residential property. Some of the 6,200 institutions are under state, some under federal, regulation. The Federal Home Loan banks offer member associations privileges of rediscounting; to obtain cash

---

[12] Savings and loan associations hold as assets large totals of long-term mortgage loans which were made at interest rates significantly lower than those of the mid-1960's. The market value of the loans fell appreciably below face value. The holder of the account ("deposit") had the right to shift to another thrift institution offering higher rates. Such shifts took place in 1966. To hold on to deposits, and to continue to attract a flow of new funds, the savings and loan institutions were under pressure to raise the interest rates they paid. Yet they could not also raise the rates they were getting on older mortgages. A very difficult situation developed for some associations, not only as regards earnings but also for cash to meet net outflows of funds; for the future, they saw, more provision would need to be made for liquidity.

to meet demands of shareholders, for example, an association can, within some limits, borrow by pledging mortgages it holds as security. Most, but not all, savings and loan associations now offer deposit insurance of $15,000 per account provided by a federal government agency but paid for by the associations.

Trust Functions. The trustee functions of financial institutions play a growing role in our economic life. There are trust companies (essentially banks with state charters) which carry on ordinary commercial banking but, in addition, like most large commercial banks, have departments that concentrate on trustee functions. The major job is to hold and manage property for others: widows and orphans, the idle rich and the industrious aspirant to wealth, and millions whose employers have pension funds.

A trust may be simple or highly complex, lasting a few years or decades; state laws set broad limits but offer wide freedom. A person who "trusts" his wealth to a trust company can generally count upon careful, conservative, impartial, and sometimes highly competent management. He and his heirs are freed from the trouble of handling the property and making investment decisions. They can reasonably assume that specialists will decide on which assets to buy and sell; there is comfort in knowing that any loss through malfeasance by a trust company must be made up out of its own assets. State laws restrict the kinds of assets trustees may purchase with money entrusted to them (often those a "prudent man" would buy), unless the person setting up the trust authorizes more liberal investment. The practice of giving trustees broad investment discretion is now common. Personal trusts managed by banks probably had assets worth around $120 billion in early 1968; common stocks made up 60 percent or more of the total. In addition, much of the $9 billion net annual growth in pension funds flows into trust institutions.

Pressures on These Institutions. All these groups of institutions, and others such as the pension funds of local, state, and national governments for their employees, are alike in one important respect: they must handle the wealth entrusted to them conservatively. Law, custom, and fiduciary responsibility, combine to force careful and relatively riskless employment of property. The funds received by these institutions must flow generally into high-quality assets—government bonds, debt of firmly established businesses, well-secured mortgages, real estate leased to tenants of excellent credit, and, for trustees, top-quality preferred and common stock. The dollars do not necessarily become available for use where their productive value would be greatest. Rather, the funds must go to what seems best among a limited range of conservative opportunities. Geographically, however, the range is more nearly nationwide than in the past.

Even when these institutions may buy common stock—and, increasingly, laws permit them to do so—the choice is likely to be stock of well-established, large firms, not by any means small pioneers. (The sellers of the shares, of course, receive funds which they may choose to reinvest in property of somewhat greater risk.) Conceivably, an appreciable discrepancy might develop between the yields of property eligible for acquisition by these institutions and other assets. Within such limits, however, the rational approach of fiduciary institutions will tend to make for careful selection and hence good allocation of funds.

All feel pressure to "keep their money working." Some have contractual obligations to pay investors at least a steady minimum income. A company that has sold life insurance or an annuity promising to pay at least 4 percent cannot tolerate a big fraction of its assets being held idle as cash. Moreover, these institutions want to grow. To do so, they must meet competition. The higher their earnings, the more attractive the offers that can be made to get new business. The need to keep funds invested, and at good rates of interest, has led institutions to direct financing of such things as housing, toll roads, and business facilities.[13]

An important aspect of these institutions, except trusts, is that their liabilities are largely payable on demand. Even holders of life insurance policies have rights to borrow which create highly liquid claims. Assets, however, are not so liquid as the claims on these institutions. Of course, any single company encountering demands for money can sell assets to other institutions and receive cash. For the group as a whole, any widescale demand can be satisfied only by action of central monetary authorities. What are the implications of this liquidity for the economy? Economists are not sure. A "squeeze" developed in the autumn of 1966. For a few days, fears of a credit crisis had some foundation—except that confidence in the ability of the financial system to cope with emergencies proved justified.

The extent of governmental regulation varies considerably. The weight of taxation is also uneven.

Mutual Funds.   Mutual funds (investment trusts) hold stocks and bonds as assets and sell their own shares (stock). If you save a few dollars and do not know how to invest them but want a larger, albeit less certain, income than a savings bank will pay—or if you seek a chance to benefit from growth of business—you can go to a broker, bank, or other investment firm and buy shares of a mutual fund. You would then be part owner of a company with investments in dozens of leading businesses; you would own small parts of many eggs in many different baskets. You

---

[13] Union Carbide and Carbon Corp., for example, once borrowed $300 million from two life insurance companies on 100-year promissory notes to finance expansion. Perhaps $62 billion of bonds held by life insurance companies in 1967 had been acquired by direct placements with businesses.

get diversification, probably good management, and freedom from worries of handling your property. To withdraw your money, the shares may be sold at approximately the market price of the underlying assets. The price for the services of the fund often exceed 7 percent when you buy; but a few "no-load" funds make no such charge. Operating costs are deducted before earnings are distributed.

Growth of mutual funds is 2 to 3 billion dollars a year. Like other institutional investors, they are under pressure to keep their $38 billion or more of assets yielding income. As a group, they use most of their funds to buy stock of well-established corporations. Rarely will they finance business growth directly. Different funds emphasize somewhat different goals—current income, long-term capital gain, growth—and in several cases specialize in one or a few industries—chemicals and utilities, for example.

INSURED AND GUARANTEED MORTGAGES

The insured mortgage for financing the construction and improvement of residential property began to become a major feature of the investment scene in the 1930's. Home mortgages play a large role in American economic life—for the millions of homeowners, for lenders, and for builders. In the not-so-olden (or golden) days, mortgages were generally expensive and short term, the market was largely local, and provisions for regular repayment were unusual.

Today the FHA (Federal Housing Administration) insured mortgage is common. If a building meets FHA construction standards (not always high but superior to what might sometimes pass as "construction"), a buyer with a satisfactory credit rating can get a mortgage insured by the FHA. The mortgage will cover most of the cost of the property, so the down payment in cash is small. The buyer pays an insurance premium of 0.5 percent a year which goes into a fund that protects the lender against loss. The borrower must repay the principal in monthly installments over 15 to 30 years (sometimes longer) or 3 to 5 years for improvement loans. Because of the insurance feature, mortgages become a liquid (shiftable) investment. Lenders in New York, for example, may, and do, feel confident in buying the mortgages of homeowners in cities and towns scattered all over the country. Conservative institutions now put funds into mortgages backed by little equity but with slight chance of loss. In short, the market for mortgages has broadened widely. Much the same applies to loans guaranteed by the Veterans Administration. By reducing risk, both programs have also cut the cost of funds for home finance. Insured and guaranteed loans were about $80 billion early in 1968. The regular repayment feature also reduces the lender's risk, because each month he gets some of the money back.

Governmental ceilings on the interest rate on such loans are sometimes too low to satisfy lenders. Borrowers may then be required to take conventional type mortgages (paying higher interest rates and making larger down payments) or resort to subterfuges.[14]

OTHER AGENCIES

This country has many other kinds of financial agencies. Over 23,000 Credit Unions (cooperatives) accept deposits from, and make loans to, their 18 million members. Commercial factors and dealers in short-term business loans serve giant firms, and smaller ones too, at the lowest of competitive rates. Consumer loan companies, sometimes called industrial banks, make small loans to be repaid on a weekly or monthly basis. Pawnshops lend to the little man at high interest rates.

The Small Business Administration helps in the financing of small firms. The SBA tries to work with local banks (and give nonfinancial aid, too). The Small Business Investment Corporations which it has helped to get established are intended to finance new risky ventures. The results have fallen much short of hopes. Both SBA and SBIC find that small and new companies and their project proposals are difficult to evaluate. Keeping abreast of their affairs to prevent loss also proves troublesome. Need is greatest for equity capital; as a rule, however, the cost tends to be inherently high because of risk and often the need to undertake some management activity to forestall serious loss.

Government agencies supervised by the Farm Credit Administration exist to help farmers, individually or in groups, to obtain financing.

In total, the many types of special lenders have a broad, pervasive role in our economy. Nevertheless, unlike commercial banks, their lending does not directly affect the supply of money.

TERMS AND CONCEPTS		
national bank	excess reserves	net free reserves
Federal Reserve System	gold certificates	net borrowed reserves
commercial bank	discounting	mutual funds
legal reserves	open-market operations	conventional mortgage
FHA	credit union	gage
solvency	liquidity	FDIC
moral suasion	selective controls	"accord" of 1951

QUESTIONS

1. What methods does the Federal Reserve System have to influence the volume of bank deposits? How does each affect bank lending? Can deposits grow without an increase in (*a*) bank lending or (*b*) legal reserves? Explain.

[14] Conventional mortgages, those with no governmental guarantee or insurance, finance about twice as much housing as FHA plus VA combined and around 10 times as much mortgage debt for office, industrial, and other nonhousing purposes.

2. How does creation of deposits by the Federal Reserve resemble commercial bank deposit creation?

3. How do Federal Reserve purchases and sales of government debt affect the quantity of member bank reserves?

4. "The Federal Reserve can see to it that banks have enough reserves to make money available at low rates; but it cannot make the people borrow or spend." Discuss.

5. "In rediscount policy, the Federal Reserve has an essentially passive tool. Open-market policy, on the other hand, provides a tool that is not only powerful but which also permits the System to take the initiative." Explain.

6. What would happen if reserve requirements were raised to 30 percent? Lowered to 5 percent?

7. What factors influence a commercial bank's loan policy? Can the bank's desire for profit conflict with the public interest? Explain.

8. Why do you suppose 7,500 commercial banks have not joined the Federal Reserve? If there is such a bank in your community, you might get the banker's own reasons for remaining outside the System.

9. What is the economic function of reserve requirements?

10. How can change in ownership of government debt affect the quantity of money?

11. How can the Federal Reserve help the Treasury borrow "cheaply"?

12. What would happen if geese began to lay golden eggs?

13. What are the reasons for believing that banks are safer than in the 1920's? Is the improvement in solvency, in liquidity, or both?

14. Discuss (*a*) selective controls and (*b*) moral suasion.

15. Who bears the cost of deposit insurance?

16. Compare the operations of (*a*) savings banks, (*b*) savings and loan associations, and (*c*) life insurance companies, with those of commercial banks.

8

THE VALUE AND SIGNIFICANCE OF MONEY

Thus money, which is a source of so many blessings to mankind, becomes also, unless we can control it, a source of peril and confusion.
Sir Dennis H. Robertson

The purchasing power of money, and the effect of monetary change on the economy, are related topics which we now begin to examine.

Key Facts about Money. The preceding chapters have shown some key facts about money:

1. Though our Constitution gives Congress the power to coin money and regulate its value, much of this power has, in fact, been transferred to commercial banks and the public. As a result, the major part of our supply of money—bank deposits subject to check—does not depend solely upon what government does. Congress has fixed general rules (bank reserve requirements, the kind of loans banks may make, and so on) but left us free to operate within their limits.

2. Part of our money supply depends (*a*) upon the changing demand of business and consumers for borrowed funds, and (*b*) upon the ability and the willingness of bankers to make loans.

3. Federal Reserve officials have considerable discretionary power to alter the ability of banks to lend to business and consumers.

Two other facts have no small economic significance:

4. We have varying amounts of freedom as to whether we shall spend money or hold it.

5. Though a dollar is always a dollar, its worth is not always the same.

VALUE OF MONEY: PRICE LEVELS

The worth of a dollar is what it will buy: real goods and services. When economists speak of the "value of money," they mean the purchasing power or worth of the dollar. This is the opposite (inverse) of prices. At any moment a dollar will buy so much bread, clothing, or inumerable other things. We discover its value by looking at prices. Sometimes it will get us more than at other times. In some places it will buy more than in others. If prices are going up, the value or purchasing power of the dollar is going down. If we bought only one thing, its price would indicate the value of money. But when there are so many prices, we must find some way to take account of all of them if we are to measure the value of money, not just its worth for some of the items it will buy. The goal is to measure the level of prices in general.

A fundamental difficulty appears at once. The value of the dollar for buying different goods and services—the price of each different thing— does not change uniformly. If the price of everything doubled, we could easily measure for the change in the worth of money. But if some prices rise a great deal, others only a little, and still others fall, the problem becomes very much more difficult indeed. Fortunately, statisticians have developed measures of the *average* change in prices—index numbers of prices. These enable one to compare the prices of groups of things (the contents of the housewife's "market basket," for example) under different conditions such as from one year to another. Yet the measures are not perfect, especially for studying *price levels*—the value of money—in general. No single price index can meet all needs. A good index of consumer prices, for example, will not measure so well the changes in the value of the dollar for purchasing dynamos or guided missiles. Some price indexes rest upon very complicated statistics and theory, but the basic principle is shown simply in the appendix to this chapter.

MONEY, AN ACTIVATING FORCE

"The important thing is not money, itself, but what money will buy." Statements like this are more true than false. Yet, in a complex, interdependent economy, money is more than an essential, but passive, lubricant.

Money is what men use to measure prices, and prices relate the myriad parts of our economy to each other and the present to the future. If money, our measuring rod, itself changes, our measurements and standards are disrupted. Economizing becomes more difficult. Changes in the value of money, therefore, actively influence the rest of our economy. *Money and our monetary system play an active part in determining* (1) *how much is produced and consumed in total, and* (2) *who gets it.* Money, of course, is lifeless. People act, not money. Therefore, it would be more accurate, but unduly clumsy, to say that as we do things to, and with, our money, we change the rest of the economy.

The economic developments that result from monetary change are due to one, or both, of two kinds of action: (1) an increase or decrease in the **quantity** of money, and (2) changes in our **ways of using** money. If you had *more* money, would you act any differently as a result? You would probably spend more. In doing so, you would stimulate business to produce more, if it could. If you had *less* money—perhaps if your wallet were to fall into a fire—you would probably spend less. Some business would suffer a little. Our use of money can affect the economy in another way. Without getting any more money, a family, a company, or a unit of government can still give business a temporary lift by using cash "reserves" to buy more today. On the other hand, if we decide not to spend the money we receive—just hold on to it—we hurt those who plan to sell to us.

THE EQUATION OF EXCHANGE

Two Ways of Looking at the Same Thing.   To see certain key relationships, we look at the equation of exchange. It starts with a simple fact: *The total amount that the people in an economy spend as buyers is the total amount they receive as sellers.* Money is exchanged for goods and services (the two circuits of Chapter 2 and having much in common with the principle of double entry in accounting). In other words the amount of money spent to pay for things is the amount for which those things are sold. The dollar value of what we buy is the price of each unit (the number of dollars per unit) multiplied by the number of units. You buy three pairs of stockings at $1 a pair; the dollar value of your purchase is $3, the amount you pay. Physical things exchange for your $3. The money and the things are opposite parts of a two-way transaction.

If we add together all transactions in a week, month, or year, the *price* of everything bought, multiplied by the *quantity* of everything we buy, must equal *the total amount we spend.* Spending is the use of money (for payments). Such spending is *our demand for the employment* of others. The actual use of money in any period depends upon the *amount* of money we have and the *speed or velocity* with which we spend it. In a study of how money affects the economy as a whole—the objective of this chapter—the "we" includes everyone in the economy. So, also, the money, the velocity, and the transactions are those for the whole country.

The Equation Stated.   The general relationship is shown in a simple expression of equality—the equation of exchange: $MV = PT$. The amount of *money* multiplied by the *velocity*, or rate of turnover of money, equals the *prices* paid for things (and services) multiplied by the *number of units of goods and services exchanged.*

The Quantity of Money.   We know generally what makes up M, the total stock of the quantity of money: coins, paper currency, and checking accounts in banks. Each of these magnitudes is fairly clear-cut; good data are available to measure them, and changes in the quantity of money can be discovered easily. However, near monies—such as deposits in savings accounts and short-term debt of government—are common. Changes in their totals can make a difference in the quantity of things doing some of the "work" of money. Economists cannot yet measure the significance of alterations in the use of near monies. The changes, however, are probably not large enough to disturb other relationships in the short run.

Velocity of Circulation. Velocity of circulation, V, is the average number of times, during a period (we almost always think of a year), that a dollar of the stock (quantity) of money (M in the equation) changes hands to make a payment. Some money has high velocity—some 10-cent pieces may change hands several times a day; some money has low velocity—$10,000 bills may lie idle in safety deposit boxes year after year. We look at the *average*. The two uses of a $1,000 bill for transactions totaling $2,000 counts the same as 200 uses of a $10 bill or four complete turnovers of $500 in a checking account.

Velocity of circulation depends upon the way we act as individuals, as businesses, and as governments.[1] For many of us, a big part of the money we receive moves along all too quickly, in a few days; we hold on to some, however, until our next payday, and some we keep still longer. Businesses and governments have widely varied patterns of holding money. Velocity is not an automatic, inflexible thing. It results from human decisions. It requires a closer look, but after we lay more foundation.

The Price Level. The P, prices, in the equation is the price level, in the broadest sense. *The price of everything exchanged for money in the year must be included:* Fords and footballs, common stocks and bobby socks, appendectomies and tuition at law schools, services of labor and land. Prices at the farm and factory are included as well as prices to the final consumer. The variety is endless. Each type of item must be weighted according to its relative importance. No price index can apply accurately to such a broad conglomeration.[2] We are not hopelessly lost, however, because major indexes cover, directly or indirectly, items which make up a substantial percentage of transactions.

The concept of an all-inclusive measure of prices, though useful, does lack precision. And it can mislead. For example, some prices rise while

---

[1] Another way of looking at this velocity is to think of it as the opposite of the average length of time (as a fraction of a year) we hold money. If, on the average, we hold money 2 weeks, then there is complete turnover every 2 weeks, or 26 times a year. Velocity is thus 26. For many households, this figure may be about right; as we shall see later, however, the economy as a whole averages nearly twice as much.

[2] The use of an index number of prices requires that the other elements of the equation be expressed in index numbers.

others fall: a given quantity of penicillin fell from $20 to 2 cents, while consumer prices generally almost doubled; in the 6 years after the end of World War II, the wholesale price of lumber rose over 120 percent, while chemicals rose about 50 percent. From 1955 to 1961, plywood prices dropped 12 percent while the prices of construction machinery rose 30 percent. From 1960 to 1963, the price of silk rose over 40 percent while the price of cattle went down more than 10 percent. Figure 8–1 shows

FIGURE 8–1. Prices of Selected Items, Spring, 1967, Compared with 1957–59 (Average)

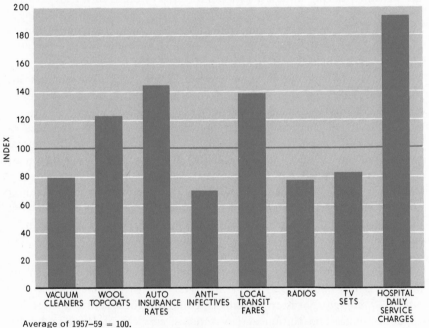

Average of 1957–59 = 100.
Source: U.S. Department of Labor, Bureau of Labor Statistics.

some contrasts. P hides such differences. Moreover, some prices at the beginning of the year are not the same as they are at the end. Many prices in Maine will differ from those in California, though some may be identical (postage stamps, for example). Despite such weaknesses, the concept of an average of all prices will prove helpful in understanding broad issues.

Transactions. The T, transaction or trade, represents the items exchanged. It includes every physical article or service for which people spend money during the period; each thing is counted every time it is exchanged for money. Does this seem like another hopeless conglomeration—shoes and ships and sealing wax, cabbages and (the services of) kings (or other government officials)? Real estate and oranges, the services of musicians and coal miners, wheat and rubber, everything is included. Yet all these *are* a part of our economic life; all are related to *employment* and to both the creation and the use of income.[3] Like *P*, the concept *T* is useful, even though there are bound to be transactions that are never reflected in statistics. (Index numbers of physical transactions are less complete than index numbers of prices.)

So much for the meaning of the symbols. Both their vagueness and the difficulty in obtaining the facts are disturbing. Yet the difficulties arise because we are studying broad aggregates of a huge and richly varied economy. In dealing with problems of national scope, ought not our conception-aggregates be as inclusive as the economy?[4]

USES OF THE EQUATION OF EXCHANGE

The Major Lessons the Equation Can Teach. Let us see what the equation can tell. If one item changes, one, two, or all of the other three must change. If two are fixed and one of the others changes, the fourth cannot remain the same. If three are fixed, so is the fourth—an impossible condition in our economy with its ceaseless change. Now for a few "experiments."

If the stock of money (*M*) *increases, what will happen?* If velocity, (*V*), peoples' spending habits, remains about the same, then *P* or *T*, or both, must increase. If the economy is operating at full capacity, *T* cannot go up; and *P*, prices on the average, must increase. Assume that the index number for each of the four elements is 100 in the base period. Then $MV = PT = 10,000$. Now assume that *M* goes up to 105: *V* remains at 100; *T*, we assume, cannot go up and will not go down. Then $MV = 10,500 = 100$ (*i.e.*, *T*) × *P*. And in this case *P* can be only 105.

Can we conceive of an economy operating at absolutely full capacity so that *T* cannot rise? Perhaps not really. Physical limits do exist, of course. Only during war, it may seem, do industrial economies press to the absolute limits of capacity. More often, however, economies reach the

[3] Transactions, *T*, are not employment; nor are they necessarily related in any fixed way to the total man-hours of work. For example, transactions in existing assets—securities or real estate—will require much use of money and little labor. Overall, however, one will seldom be far wrong in assuming that employment and transactions, *T*, are closely associated. The tantalizing problem is that we cannot be certain of this relationship. Consequently, prediction cannot confidently rest on a relation—*T* to employment—that may change somewhat.

[4] A form of the equation of exchange which is vastly superior for actual statistical study relates to measures of national income described in the next chapter. This alternative version uses (*a*) total final product or national income rather than *T*, the total transactions, (*b*) the price of final output, and (*c*) *income velocity*. The last is the average number of times money "turns over" during a year to create a dollar of income. Today, as shown in Figure 9–3, it is about 4, compared with *V*, which seems to be around 56. The income version, however, comprehends fewer of the total uses of money than does the transactions version.

point where virtually no room for increasing output remains. The working force, on the average, may be unwilling to work more hours per week at anything like wage rates then prevailing. Such is the situation we have in mind when we say that T almost cannot expand. Then if V remains the same, an increase in the quantity of money, M must lead to a rise in P, the general price level. This is the phenomenon we call *inflation*. More money but nothing more to buy will mean higher prices (V remaining the same). Prices, P, will rise by even more if the increase in M is also accompanied by an increase in V, but depending always upon the ability of the economy to turn out more goods and services (T). Now assume that in the illustration, V also goes up, to 103, so that $MV = 10,815$. Then P becomes just a shade over 108.

On the other hand, *if the quantity of money falls* to 90 with no change in V, $MV = 9,000$. Either P or T, or both will go down. A drop in T, unlike a rise, can always occur because even in the worst of depressions, further drop in physical production is never impossible. Conceivably, a decline in the total of MV might result in a fall of prices to 90 with no decline in T. Experience indicates, however, that P and T move together downward, not necessarily by the same percentage but in the same direction. In this illustration, one might become 96 and the other a little under 94. In any case, *a decline in the stock of money, unless counterbalanced by an increase in V, will lead to a decline in the general price level and also in the volume of transactions.* These transactions involve goods and services, and therefore *employment*. Here, indeed, is a point worth knowing. It helps explain why employment dropped so much after 1929. M fell nearly one third by 1933.

If an economy is operating with substantial unemployment of men and machines, the physical volume of output, the basis for T, *can* increase considerably. Suppose that when T is 100, the potential upper limit is around 130. If spending increases because M grows (or V goes up, or both), there is no inherent compulsion for the price level, P, to rise—more goods and services can be produced. In other words, the effects can work out through increasing T.[5] If M rises to 105 making $MV = 10,500$, then T may also go up to 105, with no change in P.

Inflation need not result. The expansion in spending (MV) can stimulate more production and employment. Conditions not only permit but favor a rise in real income. However, if all the rise in buying is directed toward things which already exist (conceivably, securities and existing real estate) or those whose output cannot increase, two cases both highly improbable, prices will rise without appreciably boosting output (em-

---

[5] Assume that people are begging for jobs, that firms are competing for orders, and that new spending appears from somewhere. A few companies then try to raise prices. Other firms, however, have plenty of excess capacity. Are they not likely try to get some of the business by offering goods at prices that rise less or not at all? Or, if some prices do rise, consumers will shift part of their consumption to things offered at more attractive prices.

ployment). Far more likely, the increased spending will tend to raise both prices and production. In what proportions? No one can say for certain.

In general, the greater the unemployment of men and machines, the higher the probability that employment and production will rise relatively more than prices. The nearer the economy is to full employment, the greater the prospect that an increase in spending (MV) will raise prices relatively more than output. Increases in prices will tend to absorb the effects of the increase in M. Price increases may in fact choke off rising employment before output gets close to the potential maximum. Suppose, for example, that in the case above, the upper limit for T were not around 130 but nearer 110. MV goes up to 10,500 and prices rise so that P becomes 103. Then T (and, let us assume, employment also) will increase, not by 5 percent but to a bit under 102.

In brief, more money and spending will be at least a little inflationary when the economy is near full employment. When there is much unemployment, on the other hand, an increase in money can stimulate production without necessarily leading to much of a rise in the level of prices. An increase in production, which permits an increase in T, will tend to forestall a rise in prices. In other words, the public can spend more dollars to get more things rather than devote the greater total outlay to the same quantity of goods and services.

Can the price level rise even though there is no increase in the quantity of money? Yes. An increase in V can bring about an increase in prices without any increase in the stock of money—if output does not grow. If V is stable while T drops (or if V goes down but T falls relatively more), the price level will rise without an increase in M. Even though output may expand tremendously, as during World War II, the price level may also rise. Why? In the war M increased—it more than doubled. (V fell.)

In a growing economy, T rises. There is more physical output to be paid for. If the quantity of money does not rise along with T, there is likely to be a fall in P. Of course, V may rise; we cannot be certain. Yet if velocity is stable, or if it declines, an expanding economy must expect a generally falling price level unless the stock of money rises. And a declining price level will probably keep the expansion of real output below its potential, discouraging business, at least a little. (Some of the economic troubles of the period 1865–1900 can be attributed to the failure of M to grow with the country's production potential.) Over the years the economy will grow more easily if the stock of money expands at more or less the same rate as the capacity for growth of real output.[6]

The equation shows that (1) the amount of money and (2) the speed with which we spend it must affect the level of prices, the volume of

[6] One feature of the gold standard can be noted: When the quantity of money is tied to the quantity of gold, there is no assurance that the output of newly mined gold will increase in harmony with the potential expansion of total output of the economy.

production, or both. One fact will now be clear. *There is no simple connection between the quantity of money and any of the other elements in the equation.* The equation is not an all-powerful tool of analysis. We do not know for certain how the different elements influence each other. In fact, all probably work on each other and in different ways at different times. A knowledge of what a new drug will do offers no solution of all the questions that face the doctor. But it can be helpful. Similarly, the equation is useful for studying important relationships, i.e., some of the variables which are related closely (1) to output and employment (*T*), and (2) to the value of money (*P*).

Less money—fewer jobs; more money—more jobs, this formula of monetary cranks is all too simple, yet it has an element of truth. *More money—inflation:* this warning is sometimes, but not always, well founded.

The Quantity Theory of Money.   Does the value of the dollar depend upon the quantity of dollars in existence? We answer: "Yes, but not entirely." When there is more wheat (other things being the same), each bushel is worth less. When there is more money, each dollar is worth less (other things the same). Some observers at times have gone farther, accepting a strict version of the *quantity theory of money.* The change in money's value, they concluded, is in direct proportion to a change in quantity, that doubling the number of dollars in circulation will cut the purchasing power of each dollar in half. The equation of exchange, however, shows that other things (*V* and *T*) also affect the result. If a change in the quantity of money is to be followed by a directly proportionate change in its purchasing power, two other magnitudes (*a*) must remain unchanged, a most unlikely result, or (*b*) move in opposite directions to counterbalance each other, even more unlikely.

The simple quantity theory—that the purchasing power of a dollar depends only upon the quantity of money in circulation—is too simple. How, then, have intelligent men gotten "off base"? They oversimplified. They tacitly assumed conditions under which *V* and *T* did not change much (except perhaps temporarily). Are these assumptions realistic? Obviously not. *T* certainly varies. The great depression of the 1930's showed that production can fall drastically and remain for long much below the normal level. At that time, clearly, an increase in *M* could have been matched by a rise in *T*, rather than in *P*. We discuss *V* in a moment.

The "Value" of Fiat Money.   The equation helps answer a sometimes puzzling question. How can money without any "backing" have value? Most of the world gets along with *fiat* money, paper and bank deposit money, that is not convertible into gold or silver. What keeps the money from becoming as worthless as the paper on which it is printed? We now have a reasonable answer. The value of such money depends upon the quantity in relation to the other elements of the equation. If the government and the banks pour more and more money into an economy, each unit will likely become worth less and less. If the quantity of money does not increase, however, its purchasing power will remain stable (V and T the same). The purchasing power of money will also remain stable if M and T rise together (V unchanged). Success in running a fiat money system depends upon restraint in creating money. Such restraint is not always easy, especially for governments hard-pressed for funds, but it is by no means impossible.

THE VELOCITY OF CIRCULATION OF MONEY

The equation of exchange tells us that *velocity* plays a significant role in the total spending that fixes the price level and the amount of employment. So we ask: "What forces determine the speed with which people pass their money on to someone else? Are the practices firmly fixed in habit or in necessity?" If they are fixed, so that V is stable, we can then predict with confidence how much a change in M will change PT. For example, if V is always 40 per year, then a fall of $1 billion in M will lead to a fall of $40 billion a year in PT. The more that V is subject to change, however, the harder the job of predicting the relation between changes in M and the level of prices or the volume of employment.

The best way to study velocity is a bit indirect—to see why people hold on to money. Holding money is the opposite of spending it. Therefore, if one sees why people *hold* money and why they may try to hold more or less, one also knows a great deal about what governs the velocity or speed with which the public *spends* money.

Reasons for Holding Money. The chief reasons why households, businesses, governments, and other economic groups hold money fall into a few broad classes:

1. *Transactions Motive.* People hold money to be able to transact their affairs. The common, ordinary needs of life, and the giant affairs of business and government, call for money. We need coins for making small payments, and checking accounts for large ones. Convenience, and sometimes gain, will depend upon our being able to make payments at a strategic moment. Since our incomes do not come precisely and assuredly on the same schedule as our obligations and desires to make payments, we need some cash on hand.

A parent facing a tuition bill, or a business its taxes, due on a fixed date, may not be able to count upon receiving an equal payment on that date; the thing to do is to accumulate some money beforehand. Investment as well as consumption transactions require funds. When we save, we often find it convenient to hold cash until we get enough for the specific purchase we have in mind. The amount needed for transactions depends upon such things as (a) the frequency with which we receive income and with which we must make payments, (b) the ease with which we can borrow for short periods (charge accounts or bank borrowing), (c) the size of our affairs, (d) the level of prices, and (*e*) a variety of factors involving the mechanics of payment and the availability of close substitutes for cash. The greater the *quantity of business* a firm (or an economy) carries on, the more money it needs on hand, just as you need more if you buy a big lunch instead of a snack. The *height of prices* affects needs for money—a firm must have more money to meet the payroll when wages average $2 an hour than when they averaged $1. As either *P* or *T* rise, therefore, the need for money rises.[7]

2. **Precautionary Motive.** Sometimes misfortunes hit, and cash can help mightily in coping with them: a "date" who wants an expensive dinner, a sudden illness, a machine breakdown. If we can pay at once, we may prevent things from becoming worse. A good cash position improves a company's credit rating because others know that funds will be available to pay bills if, for any reason, money does not come in as planned. How much should we keep for precautionary reasons? Enough—depending upon estimates of need. If conditions seem secure, if one feels little danger of serious risk from unusual developments, if one is confident of being able to borrow, to sell securities with no danger of loss, or to draw on a savings account, then less money will be held for precautionary reasons than if there is insecurity and great uncertainty.

3. **Speculative Motive.** At times people hold money because they expect a fall in the price of something they want to buy. In a sense, then, they keep money as a speculation. If we think the price of a suit or dress, bond, stock, machine, inventory, or piece of real estate will fall, we may delay purchase, holding on to our dollars. But when a price rise seems probable, we may use money we are holding for other purposes and buy the asset sooner than normally. The speculative motive can account for much of any volatility in total holdings of money. Transactions and precautionary needs are not likely to change much from month to month. But expectations about the future can change quickly. Such changes will affect our views about the wisdom of holding money instead of other assets. If attitudes change, for good or foolish reasons, men may decide suddenly to hold more or less money. The store manager who thinks prices will rise hurries to buy inventory. The stockholder who turns pessimistic sells shares to get money to hold.

Can We Predict Velocity Accurately?   Is *V* stable enough to provide a firm foundation for predicting the effects of changes in *M* on *PT?* Clearly, there are strong underlying reasons to expect stability: the established rhythm of payments, the regularity of paychecks, monthly bills, quarterly tax payments. The income that flows in flows out again as we spend; for most of us the two rates are roughly equal. Accurate measurement of velocity of circulation of money is impossible, but figures of the annual turnover of demand deposits, the major part of the money supply,

---

[7] What would you expect if the price level were rising by several percentage points a week, or a day, as happened during hyperinflations in Germany and Eastern Europe after World War I and in some lands after World War II? People rush to spend their money the day or hour they get it, before it can fall in purchasing power. Velocity rises to unbelievable heights.

FIGURE 8–2.   Annual Turnover of Demand Deposits

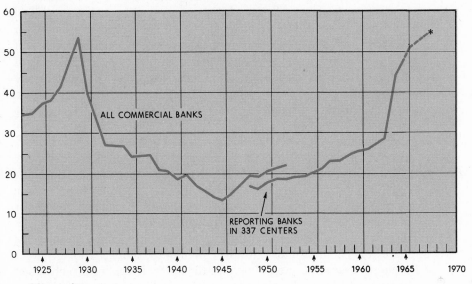

* New series.
Source: Federal Reserve Bulletin.

give a fairly good indication (Fig. 8–2). Until 1926 the data tended to confirm the belief that V is stable. Then V rose briefly, only to fall sharply for a time, then slowly for almost 15 years. A considerable rise followed World War II. In the 2 years 1966 and 1967 V went up from about 52 to more than 56. Clearly, velocity changes can be great enough to make predictions of MV and PT uncertain. Why?

Cost of Holding Money, Interest, and Velocity.   Any rational decision about how much money to hold will consider the cost, the value of the best alternative sacrificed. One close substitute for money is an interest-yielding asset of high quality and near maturity. The higher the yield from such assets, the greater the cost of holding dollars idle.

Most money is held by businesses, not families. Business firms will often have enough at stake to make worthwhile the effort to get interest instead of letting unused money remain in checking accounts. In recent years velocity has risen as interest rates have shifted upward. Other factors also operate, of course, especially over the longer run; but evidence confirms what theory leads one to expect: rising interest rates have been associated with an increase in V.

The Effects of a Change in the Desire to Hold Money (Hoard).   A household, a business, or a government treasury has some freedom in deciding how much money to hold. For the public as a whole, however, things are different. *If the public on balance decides to try to hold more money, it can do so only if there* is *more money.* After all, every bit of money is always owned. If you decide to keep more money on hand, for any reason, you can succeed only (1) if someone else holds less, or (2) if the stock of money rises. If most of us try to build up our holdings of money and there are no more dollars, what happens? We hold money longer between payments or cut our spending. In doing either, however, we reduce the flow of dollars into someone else's hands. If he is to maintain his holdings of money, or to build them as we are trying to do, he must then cut his payments. The next fellow gets less. And so on.

Although as a nation we cannot hold more money unless there *is* more, we can, on the average, hold each dollar longer between transactions. Velocity, *V*, falls and so does spending, *PT*. The efforts to hold more money, to *hoard*, will tend to drag down the national income in dollar terms and, in all probability, both employment and prices. On the other hand, if we try to reduce our holdings of money, we shall produce the opposite results: more rapid turnover of money, more spending, larger *PT*—higher prices and greater output, the latter depending largely upon the amount of idle productive capacity.

Decisions to try to hold *more* money (reducing velocity), or to try to hold *less* (increasing velocity), rest with millions of us. This choice is inherent in economic freedom. Individual decisions may offset each other, or they may combine in waves. In the latter case, the results may be highly undesirable, or "just what the doctor ordered." When such a broad change does occur, can it be offset or reinforced by changes in *M*, the quantity of money? To some extent it can, but at a risk—the risk of going too far.

THE NATURE OF INFLATION

Throughout the broad sweep of history, there appear to be no exceptions to this generalization: Over centuries, money has always lost purchasing power. Inflation has come to one country after another. Some of America's most challenging economic problems today, as we shall see in Chapter 13, are aggravated by the threat, or existence, of inflation. Consequently, we need to know more about the nature of inflation, for this is a topic about which "the years teach much which the days never know."

Inflation is a general, overall increase in prices—in the price level (*P*). Not every price may rise. Certainly not all will go up in the same proportion. But the average rises.

Inflation, like a submarine, cannot always be spotted. It is a phenomenon of many degrees. The term is applied to illnesses ranging from a mild cold to a massive cancer. Some inflations are astronomical—the German inflation after World War I (prices rose by about 400 billion times).

Others are disruptive, revolutionary, overwhelming, yet not great enough to make the currency worthless; in Italy and France after World War II, for example, money depreciated to one fiftieth or thereabouts of its prewar value. Then there are inflations like ours since 1940 in which prices have somewhat more than doubled. For 15 years or so our inflation has been described as "creeping." Figure 8–3 shows two measures of prices in this country. Figure 8–4 gives for selected countries the 10-year

FIGURE 8–3. Inflation in the United States, 1939–1967: Consumer and Wholesale Price Rises

INDEX 1957–1959=100

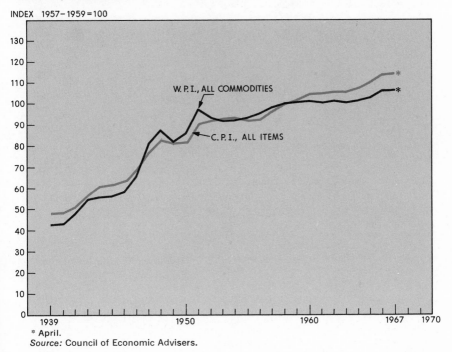

* April.
Source: Council of Economic Advisers.

change in the purchasing power of money, that is, the other side of inflation.

Chapters 12 and 13 deal with causes and effects of changes in the price level and what may be done about them.

CONCLUSION

The purchasing power of the dollar, and also the amount of business and employment, are influenced by the amount of money in the economy and the speed with which we spend it. Yet knowing this important fact is not enough. We want to know much more about Hows and Whys and

FIGURE 8–4.   Decline in Purchasing Power of Money, 1956–66, in 22 Countries

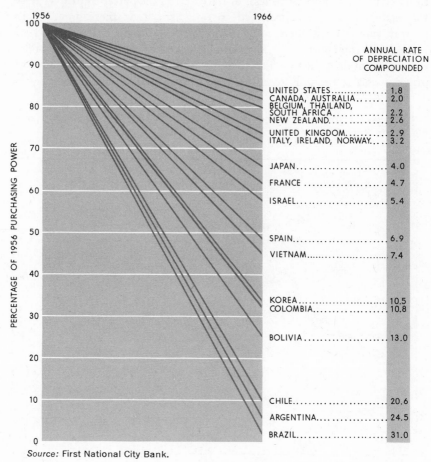

ANNUAL RATE
OF DEPRECIATION
COMPOUNDED

UNITED STATES	1.8
CANADA, AUSTRALIA	2.0
BELGIUM, THAILAND, SOUTH AFRICA	2.2
NEW ZEALAND	2.6
UNITED KINGDOM	2.9
ITALY, IRELAND, NORWAY	3.2
JAPAN	4.0
FRANCE	4.7
ISRAEL	5.4
SPAIN	6.9
VIETNAM	7.4
KOREA	10.5
COLOMBIA	10.8
BOLIVIA	13.0
CHILE	20.6
ARGENTINA	24.5
BRAZIL	31.0

Source: First National City Bank.

Wheres. Most of all, we want to know what can be done to get the best results possible. In predicting the economic outlook, and in recommending governmental policy, some economists attach much importance to changes in the stock of money. As a tool for guiding national policy, however, the equation of exchange, even in more refined forms not presented here, does not seem adequate. It helps. Figure 8–5 shows that over a long period, rates of changes in money stock have been closely associated with income and prices. But we need more help. So we try to get it. During the 1930's the need was urgent. Economists had to have better tools, especially to analyze the problem uppermost then: unemployment. One set of tools was for measuring, and these we study in the next chapter.

FIGURE 8–5.   Rates of Change in Money Stock, Real Income, and Implicit Prices, 1890–1961

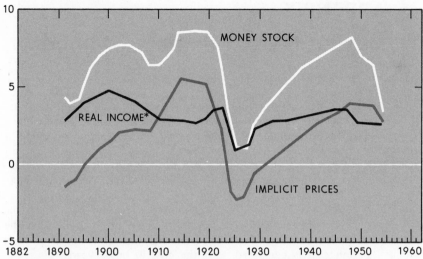

* Real income represents "normal income," not shown, and implicit prices.
Source: M. Friedman and A. J. Schwartz in National Bureau of Economic Research, *Anticipating the Nation's Needs for Economic Knowledge* (New York: 1966), p. 49.

TERMS AND CONCEPTS

equation of exchange	transactions equation of exchange	speculative motive
velocity	income equation of exchange	hoarding
"near-money"		inflation
stock of money	fiat money	consumer price index
general level of prices	transactions motive	wholesale price index
	precautionary motive	implicit price deflator

QUESTIONS

1. Under what conditions will an increase in the quantity of money (*a*) certainly, (*b*) probably, and (*c*) improbably be followed by a rise in the level of prices? Why?

2. What is an index number of prices?

3. In what respects is it correct to say that money is an activating force?

4. "A growing economy cannot avoid trouble unless the supply of money also grows." Comment.

5. Explain the meaning of each symbol used in the equation of exchange.

6. Describe the uses and limitations of the equation of exchange. How is it related to the quantity theory of money?

7. What would you expect to happen if *V* were to change suddenly to the turnover rate of demand deposits of 1929? Of 1945? Why?

8. Explain the reasons for including checking account deposits in *M* in the equation of exchange.

APPENDIX
Making Index Numbers of Prices

Index numbers are used for comparing aggregates of many quantities other than prices. Our concern, however, is with the making of price indexes.
The Consumer Price Index. The most familiar measure for adjusting for changes in price levels is the Consumer Price Index for Urban Wage Earners and Clerical Workers—CPI—compiled by the U.S. Bureau of Labor Statistics.[1] The first step in computing this index is to select a "market basket" composed of the *quantities* of goods and services purchased by consumers in some *base period*, say 1957–59. The second step is to find how much the contents of this market basket cost at the prices in the base period; third, the cost of the contents at prices in one or more other years is determined. Then the base-period cost is compared with the cost in other years. The ratio between the cost of the basket in, say, 1968, and in the base period gives a measure of the change in prices between the two periods. If, for example, the market basket consisted of only three goods bought in the following quantities:

Market Basket	
Steak	5 lbs.
Shoes	1 pair
Gasoline	20 gallons

then base-period (1957–59) cost and given-year (1968) cost might be as follows:

1957–59		1968	
Steak, 4 lbs. at $1.25 per lb.	$ 5.00	Steak, 4 lbs. at $1.50 per lb.	$ 6.00
Shoes, 1 pair at $12.00 per pair	12.00	Shoes, 1 pair at $14.00 per pair	14.00
Gasoline, 20 gal. at 30 cents per gal.	6.00	Gasoline, 20 gal. at 32 cents per gal.	6.40
Total: base-period cost	$23.00	Total: 1968 cost	$26.40

Base-period cost is $23.00, while 1968 cost is $26.40, or about one-tenth more. The ratio between them is 1.10. For easier use, we multiply the ratio by 100.

[1] The CPI is *not* a cost-of-living index. The amount a family spends on living depends not only upon prices but also upon the types and quantities of things consumed. In the United States the pattern of consumption, the constituents of the actual "market basket," have changed markedly. We want and get more things of better quality. Consequently, a portion of the increase in the cost of living results from our efforts to *better* our standard of living. Only a part of the total increase in what we spend results from higher prices of the same kinds of things.

206

In this case, then, the index number for 1968 is 110, the base-period index being always 100. Similarly, index numbers for a series of months or years can be computed, each expressing the ratio (times 100) of the cost of the market basket at a given time to the cost in the base year.

The CPI measures the price changes that affect much of the public as consumers. It figures prominently in discussions about public policy. It also influences private business decisions. The wages of perhaps 3 million workers are geared to changes in the index by escalation provisions in wage agreements and company policies. Long-term real estate lease rentals are sometimes tied to the rental element of the CPI.

Construction of the Index. 1. *Weighting.* Common sense tells us that if we are going to gage the movement in all consumer prices by changes in a single index number, we must allow for changes in many prices: movie admissions in Detroit, shoes, candy bars, 1964 Ford sedans in Atlanta, Philadelphia surgeons' fees, and many more. It is also obvious that not all items are equally important in consumer spending. Bus fares loom much more important than prices of merry-go-round rides, beef more than shoestrings, coffee more than roses. Though lipstick may be important in our lives, a 10 per cent rise in its price would be less significant than a 10 per cent rise in the price of fuel. Our goal must be to measure the significance of many different prices as parts of the total of what consumers buy.

How, then, can we allow for differences in the relative importance of particular goods and services? The solution is to weight the price of each item in the index in proportion to its importance in total consumer spending. Notice in the illustration for 1957–59 and 1968, that the price of each item is not the price of a unit quantity of the item, but the *total cost of the quantity* purchased in some period by a "typical consumer." In effect, each unit price is counted a number of times, the number being the quantity of units purchased in the base period. The selection of the quantities in the market basket, then, weights each price according to its importance in consumer spending (Table 8–1).

2. *Expenditure Information.* Who is the typical consumer? He, or she, is something of a statistical, rather than a real-life, person or family. (Until 1964 only families were covered.) In fact, the sampling does not include important groups—for example, retired persons, residents of farms and small communities, the unemployed, professional and management personnel, and proprietors. To define its market basket, the Bureau of Labor Statistics has collected information about the expenditures of people with moderate incomes, leaving out those with very high or low incomes; a different market basket is constructed for each of 50 cities. Each of these bundles of goods and services represents the purchases of a "typical consumer," family or single person. The separate baskets are combined into a national composite, with the weighting this time by population.

Gathering information about consumer expenditures is a big job. Obviously not all consumers in the cities chosen could be interviewed. Just as sample cities are picked, so sample consumers are chosen. A survey in 1960–61 provided the basis for modernizing the index in 1964, the first since the early 1950's. If the index is to reflect accurately the changes in the prices that are

TABLE 8–1.   Relative Importance of Selected Items in the Consumer Price Index, All Cities

Item	Relative Importance: Expenditure on Item as a Percentage of Total Expenditure on the "Market Basket"	Item	Relative Importance: Expenditure on Item as a Percentage of Total Expenditure on the "Market Basket"
White bread	0.63	Mortgage interest	3.09
Hamburger	0.60	Real estate taxes	1.83
Fresh milk, delivered	0.68	Electricity	1.32
Frying chickens	0.48	Telephone	1.26
Oranges	0.17	Rugs	0.32
Eggs	0.68	Men's haircuts	0.55
Cigarets	1.83	Automobiles, new	2.41
Baby sitter	0.29	Gasoline	3.08
Restaurant meals	3.90	Medical care	5.97
Men's suits, year-round	0.39	College tuition	0.25
Women's street shoes	0.27	Bank service charges	0.12
Rent	5.34	Recreation	4.13

important—in the proportions that they are important—the market basket must be kept up to date. The BLS tries to adjust for quality change and for consumer shift of buying to new items. But experts are by no means agreed whether the adjustments leave a residue of under- or overstatement. The base period remains the 3 years 1957–59, the cost of the 1960–61 market basket in the base period being 100.

3. *Representative Price Movements.*   American families buy thousands of different kinds of articles and services. To trace the monthly price movements of all these in each city would be far too expensive. What the BLS does is to price some 400 items whose price movements seem representative, collecting prices on the most important items monthly; in 5 cities all prices are obtained monthly, while in 45 cities the less important items are priced quarterly.

A good index of prices of the main things consumers buy provides a useful measure for correcting, or "deflating," dollar figures. The index shows roughly what we can get as consumers from the money income we receive, compared with what the dollars would have brought in the base period. Since most income is, in fact, spent on consumption, a well prepared and comprehensive index number will apply without great errror to the use of most of our income. The index is far less applicable to purchases of things not in the consumer's basket. Some are things—brain surgery, divorces, or fraternity pins—bought by nontypical consumers. Other goods and services omitted are investment items such as turbines, pipelines, factory buildings, and engineering fees; changes in their prices may eventually get into the consumer price index as a part of the cost of consumer goods. Still other omissions are things governments buy: teachers' services, traffic lights, military equipment.

Wholesale Price Index.   Another important index is that of wholesale prices. It, too, figures, in making many economic decisions. Just as some wage contracts tie wage rates to the consumer price index, a wide variety of business contracts provide that specific prices will vary with the level of wholesale prices.

The WPI covers some 2,200 items and applies to "large quantity" sales rather than strictly sales at wholesale. Some of the items have prices quoted on organized exchanges. But for most the figures are obtained by mail from businesses (seller not buyer) and are subject to an unknown reporting error. The base period is 1957–59. Weighting has changed, of course. Two big groups, farm products and processed foods, accounted for 53 percent of the total in 1918, only 25 percent now. Meanwhile, industrial products have risen from 47 to 75 percent. They are weighted, for the most part, on transactions as reported in the *Census of Manufactures,* supplemented and modernized from time to time. Iron and steel are weighted 5.5, livestock 3.5, natural rubber 0.1, toys 0.5, and machine tools 0.8. Part of the index is computed daily. Weekly figures are based on sample data, and the reporting errors may be numerous but largely corrected as the months pass.

The WPI is much too comprehensive to represent any segment of the economy—an industry or group of products. Many subgroupings, however, are representative; most business uses involve one or another subgroup. Goods and services at the consumer level are not covered. Whereas the WPI as a whole was relatively stable for several years, subgroups have changed through a considerable range.

Implicit Price Deflator for Gross National Product.   An index applying to the entire economy is computed each year—the implicit price deflator (index) for gross national product, with 1958 now used as the base. We can illustrate the procedure. The 1966 GNP was $743 billion in 1966 dollars. To get values expressed in 1958 (base-year) dollars, each category of products is deflated by the index appropriate to it. Consumer services were valued at $188 billion in 1966, but when these services are expressed in 1958 dollars, the total is $159 billion. This process is followed for all elements of GNP (though for some, such as government services, there are in fact no good figures for adjusting prices). The result is a total of $653 billion in 1958 dollars. When this amount is related to the actual total, the result is a figure—113.9—which corresponds to an index for the entire GNP. For groups of products and services, of course, the figures differed greatly. For consumer services the average was 118.3; for new nonresidential construction, 110.2; for purchases of state-local governments, 129.0; for durable consumer goods, 98.6.

9

NATIONAL INCOME MEASUREMENT

Measure what is measurable and make measurable what is not measurable.
Galleleo Galilei

Success in trying to understand and to deal with economic problems hinges upon ability to measure. To act wisely, the individual, the business, or the national government must know the magnitudes involved, the sizes of the whole, and of those parts relevant to the problem. One must be able to measure *changes* and their *relations* to each other. To help meet such needs, measures of the entire economy have been developed. Moreover, excellent presentations subdivide the totals in ways that reveal much about the structure of the economy, about how various parts are interrelated, and about all sorts of changes. This chapter discusses, first, the accounts or measurements of national income as a whole, and then looks briefly at some of the subdivisions.

Two Ways of Measuring National Totals. Economic transactions usually consist of an exchange of money for a thing or a service. We can look at the transaction from either side, or both. Similarly, if we want to look at national totals, two approaches are possible. Each corresponds to one of the circuits of Figure 2–1. (1) One measures national income as the total of the **income earned by owners of productive capacity**—as wages and salaries, as interest from loans and rents and dividends from capital, and as the net earnings of business. (2) The other looks at products, **the final goods and services produced.**

The two approaches deal with different aspects of the same thing. They must give identical totals in terms of values (except as the statistics

210

vary in accuracy or the methods seek somewhat different objectives). Both have one thing in common: the use of production as the criterion of what is to be covered. The definition generally used limits "production" to economic activity reflected in *purchase and sales transactions in the market*. Exceptions appear, however, and as we examine them and measurement problems, we shall get two different insights: one into what the figures can and cannot tell; the other into economic issues of importance in themselves.

THE INCOME (FACTOR PAYMENTS) APPROACH

Income Received in 1967. The *income approach* adds the income obtained by everyone, as shown in Table 9–1. The groupings, those of the

TABLE 9–1. National Income: Amounts Earned by Factors of Production, 1960 and 1967*

	1960			1967		
		Billion	*Percentage of Total*		*Billion*	*Percentage of Total*
Wages, salaries, and other compensation of employees		$294	71		$463	72
Income of unincorporated enterprises and professional service		36	9		43	7
Income of farm proprietors		12	3		14	2
Rental income of persons		12	3		20	3
Corporation profits before tax†		45	11		79	12
Dividends	$14		3	$23		3
Undistributed profits	9		2	24		4
Income taxes	22		5	33		5
Net interest		18	4		22	3
Total national income		$417	100		$642	100

* Data for 1967 are annual rate in second quarter. Because of rounding, details will not necessarily add to totals.
† Between 1960 and 1967 the Department of Commerce changed the concept of corporation profit. Included now are amounts which mutual savings banks, life insurance companies, and savings and loan associations distribute as dividends. These amounts, it seems, are in fact interest. They are not treated as profit for tax purposes.Hence the total of income tax shown is below the 50 percent rate which applies to corporate profit as ordinarily defined.
Source: Survey of Current Business.

U.S. Department of Commerce, are somewhat the same as those that economists have long used to describe payments for the "factors of production": labor, capital, natural resources, entrepreneurship. Hence, the income approach is sometimes termed the "factor payments" approach. In general, to decide what to include we apply a simple test: Is a payment received in return for the services of a factor of production.

Labor Income. Most productive services for which payments are received are for services of labor: wages, salaries, commissions, bonuses, and tips. What employers pay, however, will be more than appears in the employee's income, as he thinks of it. Employers must pay social security taxes (equal, but in addition to, what the employee pays), which build up employee rights to future benefits; many companies contribute to pension funds for their employees and pay for medical and life insurance. Such items, called "supplements to wages and salaries" and totaling $44 billion in 1967, are logically treated as payments for services; Table 9–1 includes them as "other compensation of employees."

A departure from the basic rule now appears. We find included as labor income something that does not exchange as a purchase or sale. Some of us get "income in kind" for our services—the meals a student receives for waiting on tables, for example. The Department of Commerce tries to include payments-in-kind, chiefly meals and lodging, where they are significant and can be identified. It "imputes" to them a money value equal to the employer's cost.

Much of the world's work is done by *housewives in the home*. Should their efforts be reflected in national accounts? If a man hired a housekeeper and paid her a salary, the payment would be considered part of her income; if he were to marry her and pay the same amounts for her living expenses, the payments would not ordinarily be thought of as compensation for her services. Valuable as is the housework of wives, the national income figures include nothing for such services. (As wives go to work outside the home—in a sense serving each other in commercial laundries, bakeries, canneries, and clothing factories that produce what was once done at home—the national income figures rise because payments are then made for the services.) Men, too, work a lot around the house—gardening, painting the kitchen, keeping the accounts—intrigued or compelled to join the "do-it-yourself" movement. The worth of what they accomplish, however, escapes the figures. How could statisticians measure the value of services which are not paid for with money? Moreover, the fact that no money payment is made, *does* put such activity in a special class in a predominantly money economy.

Property Incomes.   The incomes received as payment for the service of property—rent, interest, dividends, and parts of business income—present some statistical difficulties. Some property provides services for which no payment is made; there is then no exchange. The person who lives in a house he owns gets services from his property directly, without payment of rent. Applying the payment-for-productive-services test, we would not treat as income the rental value of a house occupied by its owner because he makes no payment. But if two owners were to move into each other's houses and pay rent, both rental payments would be considered income. To keep from omitting a total which is far from minor, the estimators "impute" money amounts. The 38 million families that live in houses they own are assumed to receive payments equal to the net rental value of the property, around $11 billion a year.

Property income includes something else that does not get into the owner's bank account. Corporations commonly retain some of the income received from the public in payment for what business produces. Total national income therefore includes the *undistributed earnings (profits) of corporations.*

Mixed Labor and Property Incomes. Farms and many other businesses present another problem. Often there is no way to learn what part of the income is payment for a service of the owner (labor), and what part is payment for the use of his property. So for unincorporated firms the two are lumped together. The same is done for professional persons—such as doctors, lawyers, accountants—who work independently rather than as the employees of someone else; most of their earnings are for their services. The figures include the value of food and fuel produced and consumed on farms; in producing such consumption items (a form of real income), the farmer and the property perform services not exchanged in the market.

Corporation Income. Table 9–1 divides the corporation income that is included in national income into three parts: the amount owners received as dividends, the profits left in the business, and the amount taken by governments in income taxes.

Deducting the Costs of Getting Income. For businesses, certainly, the income figure which is significant is a "net" amount, after the costs of production have been deducted. Yet it is not always clear *what* costs ought to be subtracted. And there is often doubt about how to *measure* a cost like depreciation which we agree should be deducted. Especially troublesome are those business costs on the borderline of personal expense—the expense of the station wagon which sometimes takes the family to the movies. The wage earner, too, has costs of getting income. Present practice deducts the businessman's truck and the doctor's auto expense, but not the wage earner's cost of getting to work. An individual's expenses are generally deemed to be personal *uses* of income rather than costs of getting it. Otherwise, where could we stop? Food, clothing, shelter, and education are all necessary to earn income. If we counted them as costs, national income figures would dive to a meaninglessly low level. No allowance is made for nonmoney costs of earning income—"toil and trouble," time spent commuting and ulcer-creating worry.[1]

---

[1] Ignoring these nonmoney costs is the only treatment possible. As a result, however, comparisons of income today with those many years ago, or among cultures, may omit significant differences.

Transfer Payments. Many of us get money in what are called *transfer payments*. If we sell an asset—a house or last year's sweater—the funds received are ordinarily a return of capital, a transfer, and not income. Another type of transfer is what the wife gets from her husband's paycheck to buy groceries. Government *forces* us to make other transfers, such as payments of relief to the poor. The recipient of welfare aid may consider what he gets to be income, as the college man considers his allowance income. Yet both are one-way affairs. No productive service is rendered in exchange. A waiter's tip is treated as income since he has given a service for it, but a gift is not income because there is no service. The rule: *If no productive service is provided (by a person or by something he owns), the payment is a transfer and is not treated as part of national income.* This distinction makes sense. It rules out payments for which nothing was created; and one reason we are interested in national income figures is that they serve as a measure of what has been created, not merely shifted around.

The interest paid for the use of capital is considered as payment for a productive service—except the interest on government debt. Interest on state and local government debt is not treated as part of the national income, even though most of the borrowed funds were spent to build such capital facilities as schools, sewers, and streets which yield valuable services. Inconsistently, we include as income interest on railroad bonds (private debt) but exclude as a transfer the interest on highway bonds (government debt). Why exclude interest on federal debt? The reason is that the debt was incurred chiefly to fight a war and not for the creation of income-producing items of wealth. Interest paid now for money to help defeat Hitler hardly seems payment for a current productive service. The person who receives the interest, of course, thinks of it as income.

Leisure. Over the last 60 years or so, Americans have freely chosen to utilize *one third* or more of their potential increase in production to work fewer hours per year. Longer work schedules would undoubtedly bring far more material things than we have now. But shorter workweeks, more holidays and vacations, and earlier retirement have seemed more attractive. Nevertheless, leisure is not included as part of national income. Consequently, in tracing national income changes over time, or in making income comparisons from one country to another, differences in desired leisure ought to be considered. But necessary data are not available.

Labor Income Much the Largest Part of National Income. National income figures show that most income and, of course, most of the cost of production is payment for labor. The wage and salary portion has trended upward to 72 percent of total national income. Most, although of course not all, of the income of professional persons, farmers, and owners of unincorporated businesses results from their labor rather than the capital used. On the whole, therefore, four fifths or so of total national income is received from (paid for) work. About one fifth will then remain for payment for the use of factory, utility, housing, and other nonhuman productive capacity.

Corporation earnings, the outstanding type of property income, vary widely from year to year. In two years in the 1930's they were negative. Almost half of today's profits go for taxes. The $22 billion dividends that owners received were about 3 percent of the national income. Employee compensation in 1967 was about $215 billion above that 10 years earlier; profits after tax had risen around $20 billion.

PRODUCTS APPROACH

Products Approach Must Rest upon Money Values. The second approach to measuring what the whole economy accomplishes seeks to compute the total of goods and services produced. Immediately, we find that there is no way, except in money terms, to compare and measure these goods and services. How could one possibly get a meaningful total by adding myriads of different physical things and intangible services? Tons of coal, gallons of milk, miles of transport, hours at the movies, new houses—there is no way to combine such outputs into a total that can be measured in physical terms. The things are different. To add them, or their economic significance, we must utilize some feature which is common to all. In a money economy, most things produced have prices. Although no one can add chairs and concerts or magazines and gardenias, we can add the money values which the public puts on them. So in computing national output as the total of goods and services produced, their money values are used.

Elimination of Double Counting. *Gross national product* (GNP) is the total of goods and services produced by the whole economy during a period. But what things? Do we merely add the market value of shirts, shoes, bus rides, cotton, steel mills, and everything else which has become available in the year? No. We must first answer the question: "When is a thing 'produced'?" *The solution must avoid counting the same thing twice but must be sure to count everything once.* Difficulty arises because most things pass through several intermediate stages in the production process before final sale to the consumer. Cotton that the farmer grows is made into yarn, then into cloth, then into the shirt we buy, passing through many other steps on the way. If we count the value of the cotton at the farm, then the full value of the yarn, then the full value of the cloth, then the shirt, we include the cotton itself four times. The objective, however, is to count it once, and only once. How can we disentangle the cotton element from all but one stage?

One way is to consider the product of each business, or of each stage in the production process, as the "value added" in that stage. Table 9–2 gives

TABLE 9–2.   Value Added in Producing a Shirt (Illustrative)

Stage of Production of a Cotton Shirt	Number of Cents		
	Sales Price	Cost of Materials Purchased	Value Added
Suppliers to the farm (seed, fertilizer, etc.)	10	0	10
On the farm	80	10	70
Spinning yarn	100	80	20
Weaving cloth	130	100	30
Manufacturing the shirt	200	130	70
Retail	300	200	100
Total			300

a simple illustration. The farmer sells the cotton for 80 cents, having paid others 10 cents for materials to grow it. His *value added* was 70 cents, and so on through the rest of the stages. The manufacturer paid $1.30 for the cloth and other material, and he sold the shirt for $2; the value added by manufacture was 70 cents. What we count for each stage is the amount it adds to the value of the product, measured by (1) finding what the firm receives from consumers or other businesses and then (2) subtracting what the firm has paid to other companies for goods and services.

Such information is generally available from business records. Let us look at a specific case. In 1966 companies in the steel industry:

Received from customers	$18.1 billion
(This is the market price of sales)	
Paid to suppliers	8.0 billion
Difference	$ 10.1 billion

The difference, $10.1 billion, seems to be the value added by the industry; ($6.8 billion was paid for labor services).[2]

The other method of avoiding double counting is to include only the value of final products—shirts, steel, and so on. One difficulty appears at once: we cannot always say for certain, "This is a final product, that is not." If we included only shirts, for example, we might miss thread and cloth that were final products—those sold to the housewife for a garment to be made at home. The fuel oil or light bulb or payment for postal service used by a household is a *final* product, but the same thing used by a business is an *intermediate* product. Many borderline cases appear.

In Practice We Use the Value of Final Product.   In practice, the Department of Commerce does try to summate final products rather than to

---

[2] Two major items must be deducted to measure net product, depreciation of $1.2 billion and taxes of $1 billion. The net value added by the industry, its product, was then about $7.9 billion.

compute and total values added. Commerce assumes that a product is final when it is purchased not for resale. I buy a shirt to wear. It is a *final* product. Things purchased for resale, however, are treated as *intermediate* products. If I am a retailer of shirts, I buy shirts for resale; they are intermediate products. They become final products, with my value added, when I sell them to a customer. But how can anyone distinguish cloth for shirt factories (intermediate products) from cloth (final products) for garments to be made at home? In effect, we say, "Perfection is not a thing of this earth. Broad groupings of types of buyers and kinds of goods will serve reasonably well."

The national product is (1) identified and (2) measured by expenditure, that is, by purchases or buying. It is identified as that which is bought not for resale. It is measured by the prices buyers pay.

Consumption, Investment, Government Purchases.   Three types of spending (buying) are generally assumed to be for final products. They are purchases of:

1. *Consumption goods and services,* those things bought by individuals, households, and nonprofit institutions; we also add those income-in-kind items which are to be included (food produced on the farm and the rental value of an owner-occupied dwelling). However, the purchase of a new house is treated not as a consumption transaction but as one belonging in the next category. (Purchase of an old house is a transfer expenditure rather than one made for something newly produced.)

2. *Investment goods,* including machinery, factory buildings, new houses, and changes in inventory. Foreign investment presents problems noted later.

3. *Government services* "purchased" by taxpayers (from policemen, librarians, mail carriers, etc.) and *goods* bought by government (ornaments, fire-fighting equipment, asphalt for streets, etc.).

The total of these three groups of final products is gross national product. Figure 9–1 shows some detail for 1967; Table 9–3 gives a longer view.

Depreciation.   We saw that customers pay the steel industry more for the steel it sells than the companies paid for the raw materials (intermediate products) purchased. One reason for the difference is that the 520,000 employees had worked to make the materials more useful. Another reason is that the corporation's machines and other facilities also helped make the materials more desirable for consumers. Its factories and machinery added value. Much of the equipment was there when the year started and when it ended. The company did not pay suppliers for this machinery during the year. Over time, however, machinery wears out. During the year it was partly used up; some of its value became part of the value of the company's output in the year. In other words, *a portion of the value of the goods (final and intermediate products) shipped from factories in 1966 was, in an economic sense, created* (and counted in GNP) *in earlier*

FIGURE 9–1.   Elements of Gross National Product, 1967*

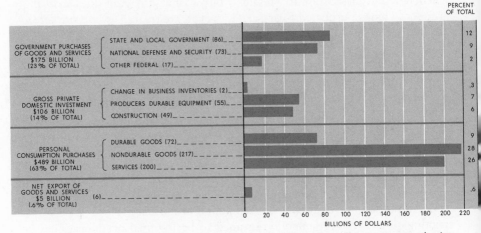

* Because of rounding, details will not necessarily add to totals. Figures are annual rates in the second quarter, seasonally adjusted.
Source: Survey of Current Business.

years. It was not this year's accomplishment. The GNP, then, includes double counting: economic values produced this year along with some produced, and counted, in earlier years. The latter is this year's depreciation.

For periods of a few years, such as during a war, our major concern may properly be our potential gross production. For a time the equipment produced earlier can be used without replacement. Clearly, however, such ignoring of depreciation cannot go on indefinitely. We would be stupid to plan for a very long period on the basis of *gross* product; some of that product must be devoted to replacing the facilities which wear out in creating it. A net figure is more significant.

TABLE 9–3.   Consumption, Investment,* Government Shares of Gross National Product, Selected Years, 1929–67 (Billions)

	1929	1933	1939	1946	1955	1963	1967†
Consumption	$ 77	$46	$67	$143	$254	$375	$489
Private domestic investment, gross	16	1	9	31	67	87	106
Excess of exports over imports	1	‡	1	7	2	6	5
Government purchases of goods and services	8	8	13	27	74	122	175
Gross national product	$103	$56	$90	$209	$398	$591	$775

* As used here, the term "investment" refers to the creation (purchase) of new capital goods, not the purchase of a share of stock or a bond. See Chapter 10.
† Annual rate, second quarter.
‡ Less than $500 million.
Source: Survey of Current Business.

Net National Product. To measure the net value of this year's accomplishment, we must deduct depreciation, the value of what was used up from the output of earlier years. Yet how much? No one can know the precise amount. Statisticians generally use the estimates businesses make for their own purposes, estimates made in different ways and of varying accuracy.

Depletion is even harder to judge. Parts of what we pay for oil, copper, and the fruits of the good earth go to the owners of the natural resource. Such receipts are logically treated as a return of investment or capital, not as income. Yet, because of difficulties in measuring such values, no deduction for depletion is made in computing net national product.

When depreciation has been deducted from GNP, net national product—NNP—remains. It is generally about 8 percent less than GNP. Although NNP seems a better measure than GNP for most purposes, it is used rarely. One reason is the unsatisfactory nature of the estimate of depreciation. Another reason is that both the services of government and the taxes to pay for them are handled crudely. Anyone wanting a true net measure must look farther.

The Product of Government: Taxes in the Value of Final Product. In measuring what the people in an economy produce, how should we treat what they do through government? Many things accomplished by government are final products, services we want in themselves, such as the work of schoolteachers. Such outputs in themselves are unquestionably part of the product of the economy. But what about other things done by government employees, such as services of the military, police, tax collecting staff, or judiciary? Are they final products, things we want in themselves? Or are they more properly classed as "intermediate," activities that make possible, and whose fruits are embodied in, other things? If the latter, we should perhaps treat them as we do the services of freight trains.

Some government services are mixtures of final and intermediate products. Highways, for example, serve as final products for consumers, providing a source of pleasure; they also help us get to work, as do commuting railroads. In addition, highways provide what are clearly intermediate products—as surfaces on which trucks travel in helping create values which businesses will include in the prices they get for things sold to the consumer. What about military services? Are they final output or intermediate products? The answer: "Opinions differ." *

Government activity presents still another problem. How should it be valued? Some government output may not be worth its cost, and some more.

The Department of Commerce treats all government services as final products and values them at cost. One result is some double counting, such as fire and police protection for business. The things governments buy for their own use—electricity, schoolbooks, cement—are treated as output of government where they provide final services. A military airplane, the fuel it burns, and the pilot's services are all treated as the product of government.

When we buy steel, cigarets, gasoline, light bulbs, anything in fact, part of what we pay is tax; over 5 percent of what the steel industry customers paid in 1966 went for taxes, not counting social security taxes. In other words, some of the money business collects from us is not for the product of businesses. They must pass the tax dollars on to government. If business sells a package of cigarets for 40 cents, of which 8 cents is federal tax used to pay for airplanes, we would be counting the 8 cents twice if we valued the cigarets at 40 cents and the airplane at its market price. The 8 cents can be payment to a factor of production only once, at the airplane, not the cigaret, factory.

When products are valued at their market price (including taxes) as in computing both GNP and NNP, there is double counting of the tax element. How can it be eliminated? The accepted method is to *deduct indirect taxes*—commodity, real estate, and other nonincome taxes imposed on or collected through businesses. When these are deducted from NNP, we have a figure of the value of goods and services produced which equals the national income figure (the income of the factors of production). By subtracting these indirect taxes from NNP, we reach (at least approximately) the total net value of things produced. This value—a dollar figure—equals the money received for producing these things. The latter dollar amount is the net income obtained as wages, business profit before income tax, interest, and other receipts for the use of factors of production.

National income and national product estimates are in fact computed from quite different types of data. If the source data were perfect, the dollar totals of income and product would be identical. They are two ways of looking at the same thing. The amount people all over the country pay for what is produced equals the amount people as a whole get for their produce.

International Transactions.   Not everything produced in the United States is consumed by those of us who live here, but we all spend part of our income for things produced abroad. And some of us get income from other lands. How can we avoid over- or underestimating the production of our own economy?

National product figures are measured by total expenditures, including those we make for imports. If we import more than we export, then as an economy we have bought more than we have produced—by the amount of the excess of imports over exports. An accurate figure of *our* total production cannot be computed until the excess is deducted. If we were to export more than we import, however, *our* total expenditures would understate the total production of our economy.

Exports are treated as part of our product, for we create (but not consume) them. Imports are considered as someone else's product, even though we consume them. If we send more abroad than we receive in return, we are assumed to have made *net foreign investment;* part of the product created here has been used to acquire property abroad. In figuring the national income as the payments we earn in producing, the U.S. total includes the incomes of everyone permanently resident in the United States, and of U.S. citizens temporarily outside of the country if they are working for a U.S. employer (including the armed forces). U.S. gifts to foreigners, such as military aid, are in effect treated as part of the U.S. income and product.

OTHER RELATED CONCEPTS

Personal Income. A figure for the whole economy, however, does not give the details needed for some purposes. A businessman, for example, trying to forecast what he can sell to consumers would want to know what they will have to spend, for they do not lay their hands on all of the national income. (1) Corporations retain some profits and decide on how these dollars will be spent. (2) Taxes on corporation earnings are treated in the national accounts as income rather than as a payment for the services of government to business. Households do not get a chance to spend this money. (3) All businesses pay social security taxes. The dollars come from the public in the form of higher prices or lower income; in either case they are not available for consumer (or business) buying.

To find how much comes to consumers, therefore, we deduct corporation profits taxes, retained profit, and business social security taxes. On the other hand, some people get dollars which are not payments for productive services included in the national product. Two such items are: (1) social security and various welfare payments by government, and (2) interest on government debt. When these two items are added to national income and the three earlier items deducted, total Personal Income remains.

Disposable Personal Income. Yet Personal Income is not the income we can spend at our own discretion. Tax collectors get there first with claims too large to be ignored. What individuals have to dispose of as they choose, therefore, is Personal Income *minus* personal taxes: Disposable Income. The taxes deducted are federal and state personal income taxes, social security taxes, and taxes on real estate for personal uses.

Figure 9–2 shows how the concepts are related. Figure 9–3 relates the concepts to the circular process of product and income creation; this

FIGURE 9–2.   The National Income and Product Accounts, 1967* (Relation of the Four Major Measures of Production and Income Flows)

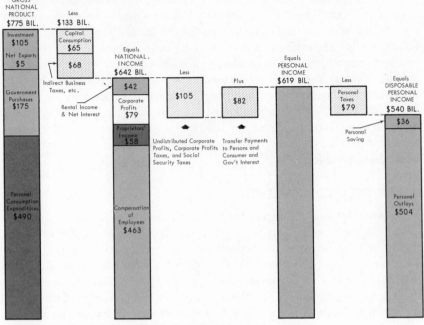

* Annual rate, second quarter. Partly estimated.

figure warrants careful study.[3] Note that we do not include wealth concepts. Although we saw some estimates in Chapter 3, the figures are less satisfactory than those for national income and product. The total

[3] The "raw data" used in making national income estimates, though far from perfect, seem generally satisfactory. Tax returns, business reports of many kinds, carefully conducted inquiries of scientifically selected samples of business firms, families, and state and local governments, and other sources combine to provide figures which, after cross-checking and adjustments to get consistency, make the basis for generally reliable estimates of the national aggregates. Yet the range of doubt is large in relation to *changes* from month to month and even from year to year. Occasionally the Department of Commerce changes some of its concepts; in 1965, for example, it announced several revisions with adaptation of figures for earlier years.

Other approaches to the study of the economy as a whole and the relations between the parts are also developing. One traces the *flow of funds*, learning how and where money goes from one sector to another; these studies reveal, tracing changes as they are transmitted by money, the action of movement of parts of the system in relation to other parts. *Input-output* analysis examines each industry to find what inputs it buys from every other industry and how much of its output it sells to every other industry. The results reveal detailed relations among industries that show the economy's structure far more intimately than national income figures. *Econometrics* seeks to measure significant economic relationships, such as the way the purchase of new autos has varied with income, the stock of old autos, the price of food, the price of autos, or other variables; when the past has shown close relationships, we may be able to assume similar connections in the future. We can then predict with confidence the developments to expect from changes that seem probable or certain.

FIGURE 9–3.   National Income Measures: Flow of Income and Expenditures

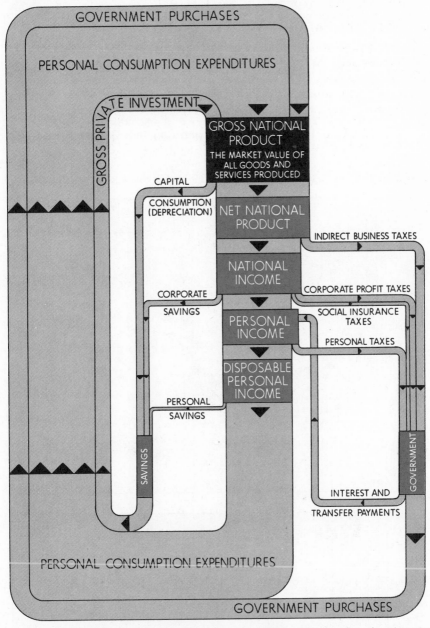

As we shall see in Chapter 10, the funds saved by individuals and corporations do not necessarily go into investment as directly as shown here.
Source: Twentieth Century Fund, *America's Needs and Resources, A New Survey,* p. 15.

wealth of the economy grows as some of each year's production is added to the accumulations of the past. See Table 9–5.

CHANGES IN NATIONAL INCOME

Changes in national product and income over periods can be measured reasonably well, to determine trends and deviations from trends, at least for the years back to 1929. To determine changes in real income, however, we must adjust for price-level changes. For this our data are less satisfactory, better for 5 than 10 or 20 years ago.

Gross National Product in Current and Constant Dollars since 1929. Figure 9–3 shows GNP for 1929–67 in the dollars in which it was valued

FIGURE 9–4.   Gross National Product, 1929–67, and the Money Supply

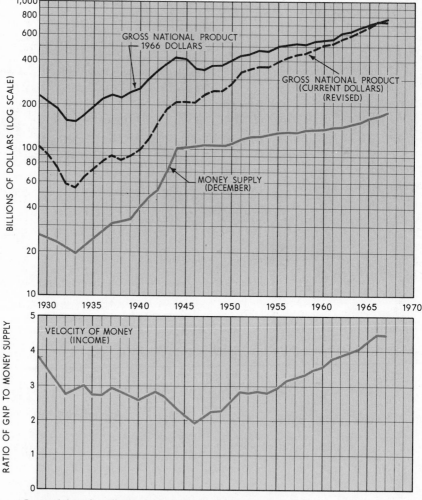

* Demand deposits adjusted and currency outside banks.
Note: 1967 data are second quarter figures.
Sources: Department of Commerce and Federal Reserve Board.

when produced—"current" dollars—and in dollars in 1966 purchasing power. This graph also includes changes in money supply and in velocity, thus bringing in two of the elements of the equation of exchange.[4] The velocity measure is not the V analyzed in Chapter 8 but the version mentioned there in footnote 4. The gross output of our economy, adjusting for price changes, has more than tripled since 1946.

Per Capita Income in Constant Dollars since 1929. The average person's real income has not increased to the same degree as national product. Population has grown so that the total must be shared by more and more people. Figure 9–5 shows for selected years per capita Disposable In-

FIGURE 9–5. Per Capita Disposable Income, 1929–67, Dollars of 1966 Purchasing Power

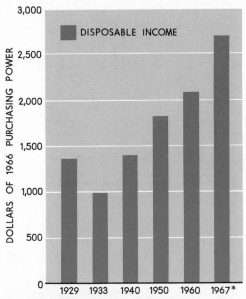

* Annual rate during second quarter.
Source: Economic Report of the President and Survey of Current Business.

come—in dollars of 1966 purchasing power. We find a rise of 40 percent since 1950.

INDUSTRIAL ORIGIN OF U.S. NATIONAL INCOME

National income data can also help us answer a question of key importance to understanding the structure of our economy: How much of our

---

[4] Note that the GNP and money supply are graphed on a ratio or logarithmic scale. This basis of presentation shows not only the absolute amounts but also enables the reader to compare relative amounts and rates of change of different sets of data.

income originates in (is produced by) different industries? Figure 1–1 showed the percentages of the total by the large producing divisions of the economy. The detailed accounts present 60 major industrial groups. Table 9–4 shows 16 industries. This small sampling suggests the differences in the dimensions of a few industries.

TABLE 9–4.   National Income Originating in 16 Industries, 1966

	Percentage of National Total
Metal mining	0.2
Manufacturing	
Food	2.6
Apparel	1.2
Chemicals	2.2
Electrical machinery	2.8
Automobiles and parts	2.4
Primary metals (steel, copper, aluminum, etc.)	2.6
Railroads	1.2
Banking	1.6
Retailing	9.3
Real estate (excluding construction)*	7.5
Telephone and telegraph	1.8
Services	
Private household	2.7
Medical and health	2.8
Amusements and recreation, except motion pictures	0.4
State and local government, except enterprise activities	7.1

* Chiefly net rental value of owner-occupied housing.
Source: Survey of Current Business.

TYPES OF INVESTMENT: SOURCES OF SAVING: DEBT STRUCTURE

One of the chief uses of national product and income figures is to study the general business outlook and the problems of economic fluctuations. In doing so, one needs to focus on strategic elements, those things of key importance. These, as the next chapter will emphasize, include saving and the spendings on newly created investment goods. Table 9–5 shows the major figures, enough to give an idea of the orders of magnitude with which we shall be dealing. That part of GNP which consists of investment goods is mostly (1) plant and equipment for nonfarm businesses and (2) housing. Businesses also provide a large part of gross saving, especially of gross saving which includes depreciation funds.

In building the economy and in fighting wars, Americans have gone into debt on a large scale (almost all being owed to other Americans). Table 9–6 shows the chief items. Comparing these with National Income,

TABLE 9–5.   Types of Investment and Sources of Savings, 1966 (Billions)

Investment, Gross (Excludes Government)	1966	Saving	1966
Residential construction (non-farm)	$ 24	Undistributed corporate profit plus business depreciation capital outlay charged to current expense	$60
Commercial, industrial, utility, and all other construction	28		
Producers' durable equipment	52	Personal saving: changes	
Increase in business inventory	13	Demand, time, and saving deposits, and currency	9
	$118	Savings and loan accounts	4
Consumer purchases of durable goods	$ 70	Private insurance and pensions	12
		Securities purchased	16
		Ownership of housing and other tangible assets	42
		Borrowing in excess of debt repayment (subtraction)	−51
		Total personal saving, net	$32
		Government insurance and pension, including Social Security	5

Sources: *Survey of Current Business* and *Statistical Abstract*. Because of rounding and of statistical discrepancies details will not necessarily add to totals.

we see total debt at more than twice one year's income. Dollar income in 1967, however, exceeded that of 1950 nearly half as much as debt grew in the entire 17-year period. Incidentally, private debt increased $5 for each $1 of expansion of federal-state-local debt.

GEOGRAPHICAL ORIGIN (RECEIPT) OF NATIONAL INCOME

Economic activity crosses and crisscrosses geographical lines, and it does not always leave its trail well marked. As we try to find the income (or the value of the product) of a particular region, we run into a

TABLE 9–6.   Debt, Private and Government, 1950 and 1967* (Billions)

	1950	1967
Gross debt		
Corporate	$167	$ 595
Individual and noncorporate:		
Mortgage	65	302
Nonmortgage	43	166
State and local government	24	106
Federal government†	266	370
Total	$566	$1,539
Net debt		
Total	$490	$1,346

* As of beginning of year.
† Includes amounts not subject to debt ceiling.
Source: Statistical Abstract.

FIGURE 9–6.   Per Capita Personal Disposable Income, 1966

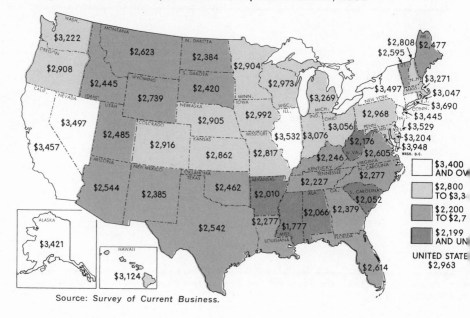

Source: *Survey of Current Business.*

quagmire of obstacles. For nations, the political boundaries are so important that domestic and foreign transactions are fairly well distinguished.
Therefore, we expect better figures for distinguishing German and Dutch
than Michigan and Illinois incomes. Yet estimates by states are now
available. Figure 9–6 shows per capita Personal Disposable Income by state
for 1966. Although differences are still substantial, they have declined
markedly, as indicated in Table 9–7.

Of course, the relative importance of industries varies considerably
from one region to another. Around the Great Lakes, manufacturing

TABLE 9–7.   Increase in Per Capita
Personal Income, by Regions, 1950–66

	Percentage Increase
United States	105
New England	100
Middle Atlantic	89
East North Central	92
West North Central	97
South Atlantic	110
East South Central	127
West South Central	96
Mountain	86
Pacific	87

Source: *Statistical Abstract.*

accounts for three times the percentage of total income that it does in the Rocky Mountain area. In 1966 transportation as a source of income was over twice as important in the Plains states as in New England. Transfer payment receipts—including social insurance, farm benefits, and interest on government debt—are 7½ percent for the whole country. In Mississippi, with lowest per capita income, transfer payments were twice the percentage in Delaware where incomes average highest. Federal government disbursements as a proportion were much below the national average around the Great Lakes; at 16 percent in the Southeast they were much above the average.

One conclusion is clear: Ours is an economy of great variety.

If we were to present data for other countries, contrasts would be more striking than for parts of the United States. United Nations efforts have done much to get the same methods used widely. The quality of underlying data is good for some economies, worse than poor in some. Even when they are generally good, the results must be used with much caution in international comparisons. Broad outlines will be shown with enough accuracy to be highly useful for some purposes, but only if used with discrimination.

TERMS AND CONCEPTS

factors of production	value-added	personal income
imputed income	net national product	disposable income
undistributed earnings	intermediate goods	input-output
transfer payments	and services	analysis
gross national product	national income	final product

QUESTIONS

1. Explain the difference between product and income measures. Why do both use money figures? Does either include leisure?
2. What is a "transfer payment"?
3. How is double counting avoided in computing national income and product?
4. What are the differences between GNP and disposable personal income?
5. Compare the size of consumer spending and private investment.
6. "Businessmen as well as government officials can operate more effectively if they have good national income (and product) figures." Discuss.
7. Why do you believe the per capita income in your state differs from that in other states in the same region? Why do regions differ?
8. Approximately what portion of national income is paid for the services of human beings?
9. How would you account for the fact that private debt grew more rapidly during the years of prosperity after World War II than government debt?

10

DETERMINATION OF THE LEVEL OF NATIONAL INCOME AND EMPLOYMENT

It is hardly too much to say that the understanding of the Keynesian model constitutes the difference between an almost total failure to comprehend the phenomena of mass unemployment and a reasonable understanding of its essential nature.

Kenneth E. Boulding

Men and women of college age today have been spared the terror of economic depression—long, deep, haunting, hopeless depression. Their grandparents and parents knew it only too well. It was *the* economic problem of the 1930's, the long decade of economic collapse, that brought not only tragic and needless poverty but probably war and incalculable loss to mankind. Unemployment at times reached 30 percent at the labor force. Why were there not more jobs? Why was national income so low? And for so long? More recently, why, apparently, did our economy remain significantly below its potential, month in, month out, after the late 1950's?

Income and product—for the individual and the nation—come from the *use* of resources, not merely from their existence. (The dollar size of national income will, of course, depend not only upon the amount produced but also upon prices, but for the moment we ignore price aspects.) Clearly, the individual, and the public as a whole, will be better off the more "fully" that resources are used. The individual, however, does not always find opportunities to work, or to use his other resources as fully as he would like. And many of us under such conditions are not able to create better opportunities for ourselves. Does the same apparent helplessness apply to the economy as a whole? No, fortunately. So we now study the forces that produce one level of national income rather than some other.

ELEMENTS OF EMPLOYMENT THEORY

Development. Ups and downs of the "business cycle" have troubled the world for a long time. Yet the economics textbooks used 40 years ago contained little discussion of what determines the **level of employment,** or national income, except the temporary "lapses" of cyclical depression. The 1930's, however, changed all this; we increasingly came to fear that the worst part of the cycle, depression unemployment, might persist like chronic tuberculosis rather than pass as a severe, but temporary, cold.

The Western world had not experienced a period of prolonged depression for over half a century. Economists had not been challenged to analyze clearly the problem that became so crucial in the 1930's. But Great Depression demand for more careful and realistic analysis created supply. After heavy unemployment had lasted for several years, economists armed with the "new economics" had better theories to guide the fight for recovery, just as we have better weapons after a war has been going for a time than at the beginning.[1] Like Monday morning quarterbacks, many economists felt that they knew generally what might have been done in the early 1930's. Many were confident that they could prescribe what might be done to insure continuing full employment. This chapter deals with the theory of employment, the determination of the level of national income, much as Keynes developed it but embracing additions and modifications made since he wrote.

We must distinguish two elements: (1) the tools of analysis, and (2) the specific findings or conclusions which some users of the tools reach. Any set of tools—surgeons', plumbers', or economists'—can be used for different purposes. The better our tools, the easier and better we can do our work; however, good tools are not necessarily used well. Nor is the man who invents a tool always the most skillful user. So it is with employment theory. Economists generally find this theory a helpful tool,

---

[1] The most prominent work was that of John Maynard Keynes. His book *The General Theory of Employment, Interest, and Money* (New York: Harcourt Brace & World, Inc.) appeared in 1936 and stimulated much other study. Unfortunately, his name became widely associated with proposals for governmental action that many people do not like. One result is some popular (and often poorly informed) antagonism to anything Keynes proposed. This attitude can be needlessly wasteful, for it may lead to the discard of good, as well as the not-so-good, ideas. The sweeping, emotionally determined attitude also adds an element of controversy which diverts energies, thus inducing men to oppose or to defend Keynes rather than to analyze and to improve the facts and the logic of his argument. Keynes had a brilliant and varied career. He taught economics at Cambridge University in England, and achieved notable success in the practical world of finance. In addition, he was a patron of the arts, a distinguished essayist, and a respected advisor of British Prime Ministers. Winston Churchill, Britain's Conservative leader, had Keynes made a baron for his work in World War II.

but not adequate. Using it as best we know how, for example, we cannot be certain what level of employment will prevail next year if certain business and government policies are followed. Still, it is sharper and more refined than the tools the man in the street will use to build ideas about what determines the number of jobs available in the entire country.

The theory centers around the economy's total spending or buying, which creates (or is) total demand for goods and services and hence for the labor to produce them. The businessman knows that employment in his firm declines when demand for the product drops. Similarly, a fall in demand throughout the economy can be expected to reduce total employment.

Spending (Buying), Employment, and National Income. Our concern is with this total spending in the economy: spending which buys the GNP, which creates demand for labor. To avoid monotony, the two terms "spending" and "buying" will be used to mean the same thing.

If I buy a pair of shoes, I thereby create a demand for employment of those who supply shoes. Their income results from buying like mine. One man's income, then, depends upon the demand for his labor and for the services of property he owns; such demand is reflected in the spending of others. If buying is large, the demand for labor is large, and vice versa. (The number of man-hours associated with any dollar total of buying will depend, of course, upon wage rates per hour.) The amount of spending in the country as a whole determines, generally, the level of employment at a given level of prices and wage rates. Such buying makes up the demand which calls forth and thereby creates national income.

National income is the total of all our incomes—what is received for efforts spent in creating the national product. These incomes provide most of the funds we spend. We buy to get what we want—books, belts, or bacon—not because of a desire to create jobs or to provide sales for business. Yet our buying does provide the markets for businesses and the demand for employment.

But who is "we"? Three sets of buyers are ordinarily distinguished because the motives for their actions, and the analyses needed to understand what they do, are different: (1) households and other private consumers, (2) business firms, and (3) governments. (Complications are reduced by assuming a "closed economy" and ignoring foreign transactions until Part 7.)

Household buying for consumption, plus business purchase of materials and equipment to be used in providing goods and services for consumers, constitute most of the demand for labor. What, then, determines the amount we spend for consumption? Consumer buying depends primarily upon the amount of income received. The size of the national income, therefore, plays the major role in determining how much consumers will buy, and thus how much income will be created in the weeks and months ahead.

Some of what we spend for consumption is essential for life, while part is desired but not essential. In either case, the choices are personal. Business and government buying, however, depend upon rather different kinds of considerations. Although these are related to the income the business or the government agency is receiving, other forces exert substantial influence.

The fact that national income *does* change shows that buying in one period (day, week, or year) is not fixed absolutely by the income received for efforts in the previous period. Households may spend more or less than the income they get, and so may businesses and governments. Therefore, the demand for labor—the buying—in one period can be different from the income being received at the time or that flowed in last month or last year.

Saving and Investment as Sources of Changes in Spending.   Changes in total spending can stem from changes in saving or in investment. We save when our spending for consumption is less than our income. If my income, after taxes, is $6,000 and I spend $5,500, my saving is $500. Others have spent $6,000 (plus my taxes) for my services. If I spend only $5,500, however, my demand for the services of others is less than the demand which led to my income. Whether the total dollar value of employment will fall depends upon what happens to the $500 I saved. I may hold this $500 idle—hoard it. Thus it is not spent. The spending stream gets smaller—national income falls—by $500 unless some other change occurs.

The change may be **investment** of $500. The word "investment" has various meanings; troublesome confusion arises from the differences in meanings. Ordinarily, we say that we invest when we buy shares of stock, a bond, or a piece of real estate. For the economy as a whole, however, such a purchase is a transfer; what the buyer "invests," the seller "disinvests." The concept in this sense is financial. The total stock of wealth or investment goods does not change. To the economist dealing with employment theory, however, "investment" applies to real things. **Investment means the increase in real wealth or capital goods**—machinery, factories, houses, inventory[2]—generally physical things. Or as noun, verb, or adjective, a form of the word "invest" relates to **the spending to create** physical things for future production. The term "capital formation" can also be used to mean such real investment.

Is there any true significance to the difference between the real and the financial concepts of investment? There most certainly is. Assume that Jones has saved $15,000 to buy a house. If he uses the money to buy an old house, his spending creates no jobs for builders. He makes a financial

---

[2] Parts for the assembly line, raw materials in storage, goods on the retailers' shelves—these and other forms of inventory—are essential elements in the process of production. Like plant and equipment, they are acquired and held for what they contribute to the creation of "value added." Until purchased by the final consumer, they are not to be classified as consumption.

outlay that does not add to the economy's stock of real wealth. But if he spends the money to have a new house built, his action will create jobs; capital formation, a growth in real wealth, will result. It is possible to save dollars and to use them to buy existing things—securities or physical property—or merely hold the money as cash; neither of these two actions involves any spending for new capital formation. Neither is "investment" as we now use that term.

If I spend my $500 on a new item of capital equipment, or if I let a business have the $500 to spend on new machinery, my saving—my "not spending for consumption"—is matched by spending for investment. When the two actions are considered together, no change in either total income or demand for labor results.

The nation is made up of tens of millions of individuals and groups. Assume that they receive a combined after-tax income of $60 billion in July. As they plan their affairs, they decide to spend $55 billion on consumption in August. Spending of this amount will not, of itself, create demand for as much employment in August as there was in July. There is a gap of $5 billion. If spending on capital formation (investment) is $5 billion, however, total spending will be $60 billion. August income will equal July's in dollar terms. If investment spending is $3 billion, however, August income will be $58 billion. But assume that investment spending is $6 billion, as $1 billion is borrowed from banks or taken from funds held idle ("hoarded"). Then August income will be $61 billion. The essential relationship for the economy is:

INCOME = CONSUMPTION SPENDING + INVESTMENT SPENDING

Symbols commonly used are Y for income, C for consumption, and I for investment. Measurement is in dollars. The equation, then, can be put into the briefer form $Y = C + I$. The job of analysis is to learn what we can about the forces that influence the size of C and I and the level of employment.

Since buying for consumption accounts for most of the demand for labor, the better one can predict consumption spending, the better one can predict national income. If we know how consumption spending will rise or fall as a result of any other change, we can tell the effect of that change on national income. Income in the past, last month for example, will be known (at least generally); changes from the prior month can be spotted. Can we, then, use what we know, past income, to predict consumption spending and most of the demand for labor in the month ahead?

The Propensity to Consume (or to Save).   Each of us has his, or her, own buying habits, but certain general features are common. Statistics confirm one commonsense principle: not only the absolute amount, but also the *proportion*, of a household's income used for consumption varies with the amount of income. People with very low incomes generally spend all of it on consumption. They must do so to live. People with larger incomes do not as a rule spend everything for consumption; they save something. The higher up in the income scale, the smaller the percentage of income spent on consumption and, of course, the more that it saved.

Family expenditure figures, when shown graphically as in Figure 10–1, give a curve which indicates how much, on the average, families at different income levels spent on consumption. The relation between the

FIGURE 10–1. Spending and Saving by Urban Families and Single Consumers

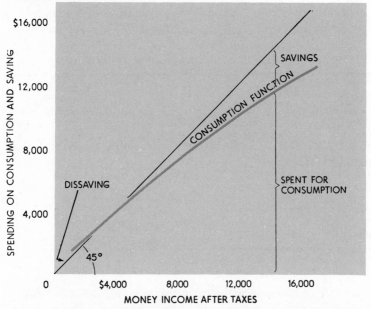

Source: Bureau of Labor Statistics. Data are for 1960-61. The figure for each income level is an average; some actual cases will differ considerably in one direction, some in the other. The study puts individuals who live alone and families with several children in the same group because they have equal after-tax incomes.

amount spent on consumption and income is the "propensity to consume," or the "consumption function." The propensity to consume may also be expressed as the proportion (fraction, percentage) of income used for consumption.

As a standard for comparison we use a line showing what would be spent if the family used all its income for consumption, saving nothing. On Figure 10–1 this line has a 45-degree angle. Every point on this line is the same distance from both the income and the spending axis when the scales are the same. If the average family with $9,000 income spends $9,000, the point showing the relationship will be on the 45-degree line, since the two amounts are equal. By comparing the point for the actual consumption buying from any income with the point on the 45-degree line for the same income, we can see at a glance if consumption spending at any income level equals, exceeds, or falls short of income.

Can consumption buying be more than income? Certainly. Families may (*a*) go into debt or (*b*) draw on past savings and spend more than their income in a certain period. People living on pensions often consume out of accumulated savings. Others may borrow in one year to buy furniture or an auto. Even a whole economy may consume more than it produces, in severe depression or war.

Marginal Propensity to Consume (or to Save). The knowledge of how consumption relates to income provides a useful tool for understanding the forces that influence employment. There is a sharper tool, however.

TABLE 10–1.   Marginal Propensity to Consume, an Illustration

| Disposable Income (after Taxes) | Spending on Consumption | | Increase in Income | Increase in Spending | Percentage of Increase in Income Spent for Consumption | Marginal Propensity to Consume |
	Amount	Percentage of Income				
$5,000	$4,800	96				
			$1,000	$900	90	0.9
6,000	5,700	95				
			1,000	800	80	0.8
7,000	6,500	93				
			1,000	700	70	0.7
8,000	7,200	90				

As in so much of economics, the thing that is most helpful for study is the *margin*, the sensitive aspect. It is the change from one point to another, or the extra amount. Even though small, it is the push or slight change that may mean so much, the increment which makes a difference that counts—a little extra speed in a halfback, a little better quality on an examination. Things which are apparently small can exert great influence. To understand what happens, we look at the *differences*. What is the effect of a *rise* or *fall* in my income on my demand for goods and services—that is, for the labor of others?

The *marginal propensity to consume* is the ratio of the change in spending for consumption to a change in income. We compute it as follows, using assumed figures of personal income after taxes: at $5,000, a person spends $4,800 or 90 percent of his income (Table 10–1). At $6,000, an increase of $1,000, he spends $5,700. Only $900 of the *increase* is spent. Of the additional dollars he receives, he spends 90 percent. This is the marginal propensity to consume. On the average, over all his $6,000 income, he spends 95 percent; of the increase in income, however, he spends only 90 percent. Instead of using percentages, it is now customary to use a number expressed in tenths; 90 percent becomes 0.9. In a graph such as Figure 10-1 the amount of the marginal propensity to consume at each income level is shown by the slope of the spending curve at that income. Where the curve rises steeply, people spend on consumption a big part of *increases* in income. Where the curve rises gradually (has little slope), people spend little from the dollars of added income.

People differ greatly, of course, in their spending patterns, but on the average, the marginal propensity to consume is high at low incomes; the urgency of additional consumption needs presses insistently. Moreover, throughout most of the income range, individuals and families raise their whole scale of living after income has remained at a higher level; the family whose income goes from $7,000 to $8,000 may for a time spend about as before, but before long the pattern will be that of the higher level.

What is not spent on consumption is saved. If we think of the dollar of added income as 1.0 and subtract the part spent on consumption, the remainder is the part saved. The *marginal propensity to save* is thus 1.0, representing the whole change in income, minus the marginal propensity to consume. If either marginal propensity is 0.8, the other will be 0.2; they always add to 1.0. What we spent for consumption is demand for the services and products of others. *What we save becomes demand for labor and other factors of production only if the money saved (or its equivalent) is spent to buy some item of new investment.*

National Figures.   The job for which we started to develop these conceptual tools is to study employment and income on a national scale. The immediate goal is to be able to predict—and accurately. For example, can the economist tell the businessman or government official with certainty how much of a national income of, say, $700 billion will be used to buy consumption goods and thus create demand for labor? Or can we say how much of any *change* in national income, such as a rise of $10 billion, will be saved?

If we knew the number of families at each income level and the relation between family income and spending, we could, for a national income of any size, compute the total amount that households would spend on consumption. At every level of national income, C will be different from the C at every other level. Data for the country as a whole show that as national income has risen, consumption buying has risen in about the same proportion (except for wartime disturbances). Figure 10-2 graphs the national figures of spending and saving out of each dollar of disposable income, for the years 1929–66.

The data fall into a moderately clear pattern, but not one that is as definite as a law of physics. The aggregate consumption function—the amount of consumption buying out of any total disposable income for the country as a whole—seems generally stable, but not completely so. Spending has averaged around 93 percent of disposable income for almost 15 years.[3]

When income rises, net personal savings will probably, but not necessarily, rise as in the past. Corporation savings, a form of earnings that do not enter personal income, rise and fall with national income but in no close relation to personal savings. Undistributed corporation profits generally total almost as much as net personal savings; early in 1961, however, they were only one sixth as large, a year later nearly one third, indicating

FIGURE 10–2. Spending and Personal Saving: Part of Each Dollar of Disposable Income Spent or Saved, 1929–67*

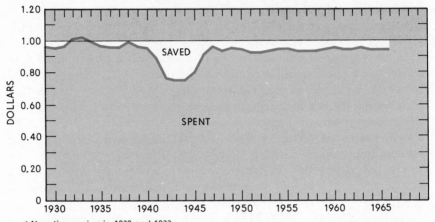

* Negative saving in 1932 and 1933.
Source: Survey of Current Business.

considerable short-run variability. Much greater in total is a form of gross saving which is important for studying the determination of national income in the short run: business depreciation charges. They were around $66 billion in 1967, compared with about $37 billion net personal savings.

Whether gross or net, large or small, personal or business, the part of national income that is saved must be spent on new investment goods to create demand for labor and thus generate new income. *Will* the savings be used to pay for capital formation?

Decisions to Save and to Invest. Much saving is done by people who have no power to guide investment. Much investment, on the other hand, rests upon decisions by men who had nothing to do with the saving required. The underlying reasons for the two kinds of actions differ.

[3] At any given time, individual and family saving, as shown in Figure 10–1, go up more than proportionately with a rise in after-tax income. For the economy as a whole, however, the propensity to consume has risen from year to year. Thus, disposable income of 1966 was 74 percent over that of 1956, but the saving percentage was almost the same.

Consequently, decisions to save and decisions to invest do not of necessity fit together neatly and smoothly.

Some saving, of course, is made to get funds to buy specific new items of investment goods. Business managers typically plan to retain in the business (save) some of the earnings to buy new machines, inventory, or something else that will increase earning power. In such cases, the two decisions, to save and to invest, are made by the same people—the firms' managers. Here, saving and investing (capital formation) move together as parts of the same process. The amount saved depends (at least partially) upon the possibilities of profitably using more physical capital.

Individually and in groups, we save in other ways. Why? Our motives are varied. We put something aside for emergencies, old age, or to send the children to college. Deep-seated emotional forces may lead us to save for reasons of which we are only dimly aware. Our club wants to build a new clubhouse and saves some of our dues. Businesses retain some earnings without any specific investment project in mind. Corporations may increase (or decrease) their savings because profits are unexpectedly high (or low), and no change in dividends seems wise at the moment. Unions pressing for larger pension funds do so for security later, not to get money to buy more capital equipment (or make jobs) today. All such saving can be distinct from investment in the *real* sense of the creation of new productive capacity. We can hold money.

To repeat for emphasis: Because we receive income in the form of money we can, if we wish, hold as cash the wealth we save. Or institutions to which we entrust the dollars may hold them in the form of money (or buy securities whose sellers then hold cash, perhaps for the speculative motive described in Chapter 8). Moreover, individuals and businesses may use dollars saved to repay old debts, and no new borrowers may spend equal amounts to buy newly produced investment goods. Repayment of loans at commercial banks can reduce the quantity of money. In short, the **money flow can contract because of the way we use our savings.**

Capital formation—real investment in new things—depends largely upon *business* decisions. Individuals and families, of course, make some of the decisions for personal reasons—those to build or improve a house. Governments and nonbusiness groups, such as churches, also make some decisions about investment (capital formation); but heavy responsibility rests with business. *And one of the chief facts of business life is that capital formation can vary tremendously from year to year.* In whatever way we measure, we find investment spending unstable. From late 1966 into early 1967, not a recession, the annual rate of gross private domestic investment fell by $11 billion in 6 months. A rise of over 11 percent occurred during 1963.[4] Obviously, businesses whose sales depend upon orders of other businesses for capital goods (and inventory) face fluctuating demand.

[4] Figures are seasonally adjusted. Tables 9–3 and 11–3 present other evidence of the variability of investment.

Businesses choose to invest in new equipment or inventory because they think it will be profitable. Their desire to change their productive capacity—whether a new plant to be used for many years or inventory to sell next month—depends upon the vision of an opportunity to benefit by expanding capacity, reducing production costs, or some combination. What creates such opportunity? Development, change of innumerable kinds: new techniques, larger population, discovery of new ideas, invention, higher national income, a shift in demand, a new tax law or safety requirement, a new territory or natural resource, change in a foreign country, competition that forces the use of new and more efficient equipment, war. Most such forces are largely unpredictable. Many originate, at least partly, "outside" of the economic system. Laboratories and legislatures, accident and farsighted preparation, bankruptcy and high profit, animal spirits and cold rationality, skillful selling and a changing "social conscience," exploration and art, the fear of war and the hope for peace—these and many more factors play a part. They can be volatile, uncertain, capricious. They may bunch up quite by accident, or distribute themselves fairly regularly. We cannot be sure what lies ahead.

This is beyond dispute, however: **Economic forces do not create and control *all* of the important forces that determine investment opportunities.** Moreover, the specifically economic forces do not operate regularly. The prospects for new investment that attract business can swing widely. The amounts that businessmen want to spend to buy new capital equipment and to stock their shelves with inventory can depend upon very different visions from those that make you and me decide not to spend on consumption.

Plans and Realizations. In business, as in our personal lives, plans do not always succeed fully. Sometimes accomplishments during a period (a month or a year) are better than we had planned for, sometimes worse. Almost always they will be somewhat different. The amount we *plan* to save during a period can differ considerably from the amount we *do* save. Similarly, the amounts that businesses actually spend on investment goods during a year can depart from plans made at the beginning.[5] Change in income is one of the most important factors making both investment and saving as actually realized differ from what has been planned. And as we shall see, changes in national income result from the lack of balance between planned saving and planned investment.

Investment and the Level of Employment. How does spending on new investment goods affect income and employment? Table 10–2 and Figure 10–3 show the basic relationships. Assume that plans for investment have

---

[5] Economists use the term *ex ante* to apply to plans and *ex post* to what is actually realized. *Ex ante* saving (or investment), for example, is the amount we plan to make in some period. *Ex post* is the amount actually done in a period.

been fixed for the time being. Temporarily, the total of business (and other) spending on capital formation will not depend upon the amount of business done.

In Table 10–2 we assume certain levels of gross national income and the amount that the public, as a whole, will spend on consumption from each of these incomes. The difference is the amount the public (including business firms) will save. The total spent on buying new investment goods is assumed to be fixed at $80 billion. If we ignore government and make other simplifying assumptions, the national income in any period is the amount paid out by business as wages, interest, dividends, and so on. The amount businesses receive back in the next period, B (column 6), is not necessarily what they have paid out in period A (columns 1 and 5), but is the total spending, on consumption and investment (column 2 plus column

TABLE 10–2.   Determination of National Income: Investment Spending Assumed Fixed, Taxes and Government Spending Excluded (Annual Rates in Billions of Dollars)

Gross National Income in Immediately Preceding Period, A (1)	Consumption Spending (2)	Planned Saving (3)	Investment Spending (4)	Paid Out by Businesses in Immediately Preceding Period, A (5)	Received Back by Businesses in Current Period, B (6)	Movement of National Income (7)
800	700	100	80	800	780	Down
780	690	90	80	780	770	Down
760	680	80	80	760	760	No change: Equilibrium
740	670	70	80	740	750	Up
720	665	55	80	720	745	Up
700	650	50	80	700	730	Up

4), in period B. When national income has just been $800 billion, businesses then, we assume, receive back less than they have paid out; saving ("not spending") is greater than the amount spent buying new investment goods. Income falls. Businesses then pay out less. As income drops, so does saving. When national income is $760 billion, however, the amounts balance; the dollars businesses pay out equal those they receive back. This is an equilibrium—the situation in which the various forces are balanced. No further alteration will occur until at least one of the underlying conditions changes.

Now let us look down in Table 10–2. When businesses have just paid out $700 billion, consumption spending is $650 billion; investment is $80 billion. Businesses then receive back $730 billion. Income is more than in the previous period. The total spending on consumption and investment has been greater than the income received earlier. The rise will continue until the $760 billion level is reached.

Let us now go over the same ground using Figure 10–3. Investment spending at $80 billion appears as a line at a fixed level.[6] Saving, of course (column 3, Table 10–2), depends upon the amount of the national in-

FIGURE 10–3.   Equilibrium Level of National Income* (Ignoring Government)

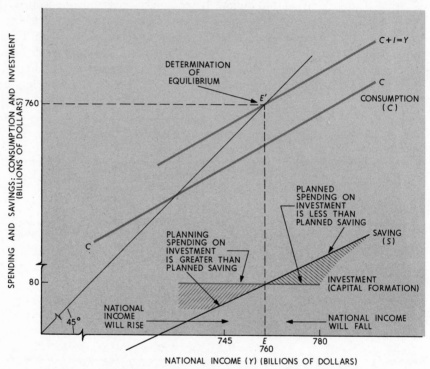

* At equilibrium, *E*, (1) *planned savings* equal amount spent to buy investment goods, *S* = *I*. And (2) *total spending*, *C* + *I* (consumption plus investment), equals the total income received, *Y*. On balance, then, consumers and business exert no pressure for change.

To permit clearer presentation, the Savings-Investment portion is shown as larger relative to the totals than the figures in the text indicate.

come, rising as income rises. However, we assume that for the moment investment plans are fixed and do not depend upon the size of national income. When graphs of the two schedules, *S* and *I*, are placed on the same

---

[6] The *CC* curve is shown as a straight line rather than, as in Figure 10–1, a curve which is convex when viewed from above. The two curves apply to different bodies of data. The earlier graph dealt with families at different income levels. Here we deal with the whole body of consumers at different levels of national income. Perhaps *CC* should bend; that is, the larger the national income, the smaller the percentage used for consumption, other things the same. As indicated above, in footnote 3, historical evidence is not clear enough to substantiate any specific curvature. This and later diagrams use straight lines because they are simpler.

chart, they intersect. (Remember, the investment spending creates jobs and income; the saving, or "not spending," may be thought of as a decision not to demand productive services currently.) An important relationship appears. The amount of national income at which the two lines intersect is an equilibrium. It is the level of national income toward which the economy will move, assuming no change in the underlying conditions (consumption-saving propensities and investment plans). Any other national income will be temporary and tend to shift toward this. Let us see how.

1. Assume that national income were higher, say, $780 billion. This income, when we look at it from the other side, is what is paid for the services of production, that is, it is the total expense of business. Out of an income this large, people would try to save, say, $90 billion; this amount is more than the $80 billion the community wants to invest under the conditions. Total spending for consumption plus investment would then be $10 billion less than the total cost of the national production in the prior period. Business has paid out as costs $10 billion more than it receives back as demand for its products. Businessmen would then be disappointed; the logical thing for them is to cut their output, their spending. Employment and income fall, and so does saving. After a while, national income will have dropped to a point where (a) the amount people and businesses wish to save out of income is equal to (b) the amount they want to spend on new investment goods. No more decline would be expected under these conditions.

2. Let us take the other case, starting with a lower national income, say, $740 billion. Out of an income of this size, the community plans to save $70 billion; this amount is less than the $80 billion which will be spent on investment in the present period. (a) Total spending (dollar purchases) on consumption plus investment would be more than (b) what was spent in the prior period. Business would find advantage in expanding output. Consequently, employment and income go up. The rise would tend to stop at the equilibrium point where the amount the community as a whole wanted to save was equal to what it wanted to spend on capital formation.

If our habits of consumption and saving are stable, then, the size of the national income will depend upon the amount of investment, ignoring government. If we know (1) how much of a national income of any size we shall spend on consumption, and (2) investment plans, we can predict the level of income. The volume of employment can also be predicted if we know the average price of labor, that is, the number of man-hours each billion dollars of expenditure will purchase.

Another approach will bring us to the same objective by another route. Let us look not only at saving and investment but also at consumption. Excluding government outlays, the $C + I$ line shows total spending (consumption and investment) in relation to national income: the money costs of national output. The equilibrium point, where things are in balance, is the point where total spending to *buy* output equals all costs incurred to *create* the output. This point must be on the 45-degree line—income equals total spending; the distances from the two axes measuring the amounts are equal.

The 45-degree line (which indicates, at any point, equal distances along the vertical and horizontal axes) really plots income against income—the two different sides of the same thing. But the line is more illuminating. At any point, it indicates the amount which business units in the aggregate must expect to *receive* (as a result of total outlays through the whole economy for consumption and investment) to induce them to produce an amount of output which is associated with a given level of what they as businesses must *pay* (income payments) to the factors of production. The income payments equal the money value of output.[7]

We also plot total demand—the spending that the community would plan to make at different levels of total output. It consists of (1) consumption spending, which depends chiefly on income (the functional relationship being shown in line *CC*), and (2) spendings for investment goods, assumed here to be at a given level. Curve *C + I* is above *C* by the amount of investment, *I*, at all levels of income.

We, therefore, plot (1) planned spendings—total demand, *C + I*—and (2) expected (or required) receipts—what the business world requires to supply different quantities of national product. The equilibrium income is determined by the intersection of the two schedules; it is the point where the two sets of plans or forces are in balance. At any other point, total buying (*C + I* in dollar terms) is either larger or smaller than the dollar payments for supplying that output (the money income generated in producing it). Change will result. Where the two dollar totals are equal, businesses are getting back from sales just what they are paying out in costs; these costs include the amount of profit which is needed to induce businesses to undertake the risks involved. Businesses are investing as much as they wish under prevailing conditions. No force such as declining consumer demand induces them to curtail activity. No factor such as increasing demand creates inducement to expand.

"But," you ask, "as spending and income move to the equilibrium, where does the money go, or come from?" New money can come into the system as banks create deposits. Existing money can be destroyed as bank loans are repaid, and existing money can be used more or fewer times each period—*V* (velocity) changes.

People can interrupt the circular flow of national income by saving. They then pay back to business for consumer goods and services less than they receive as wages, interest, dividends, and other forms of income. The

---

[7] Equity capital supplied by owners is one of the factors of production. Profits are one type of income payment.

difference in itself is nothing unexpected. Business devoted some of its efforts to producing investment goods which it never expected to sell to the ordinary consuming public. If business plans are to succeed, sales to consumers need equal only what business pays out to produce consumer goods. In a sense, business expected consumers to use the rest of their income for saving. *This amount can be drawn off from the consumer spending stream without causing business to contract, but only if total investment demand is at least as large.* If the financial mechanism is working well, the money which consumers save will probably—but not certainly—flow back to business to finance business spending on investment.

Investment spending can pump new money into the income stream, money that comes from bank borrowings or out of previous savings that have been held as idle dollars in a checking account. Such injection of new money (or higher velocity) leads the income stream to swell, unless saving (not spending) grows by the same amount. Whether national income and employment rise or fall depends (in part) upon the balance between saving and investment. Yet we took pains earlier to show that the two are, to a great degree, made by different people for different reasons. Precise matching of plans to save and to invest would be a miracle. Large differences are possible. When a difference exists, it is likely to set in motion forces which for a time will grow, feeding upon themselves.

The Multiplier. To portray this process of magnification, economists use another concept: the multiplier. It is a number showing how great an increase (or decrease) in national income may result from each increase (or decrease) in investment. Changes in consumption propensities, or in net government spending, will also start a process of multiplied income change. If an increase of investment of $5 billion leads eventually to an increase in income of $20 billion, the multiplier is 4; if the total increase is $15 billion, the multiplier would be 3. The number is closely related to the marginal propensity to consume.

Assume, for example, that a contractor hires unemployed men to build drainage ditches for a new housing development. He pays them $1,000, an increase in his investment in the project; for them it is an increase of $1,000 in income, most of which they will spend. Assume that their marginal propensity to consume is ⅔ (the other ⅓ perhaps going to pay past debts or into a savings account).[8] Their spending is $667 larger than it would have been otherwise. The people who sell to them then have incomes which are larger by $667; if, in turn, their marginal propensity to consume is also ⅔, they will increase their spending by $445. The process continues. Each new set of spending we assume to be ⅔ of the previous

---

[8] Actually, one fifth or so will be drawn off by taxes, but we are not yet ready to bring government into the discussion.

spending figure. The wave can go on and on, but it continues to dwindle. The added increments eventually become too small to warrant concern. Yet we can figure out what all the additions might eventually total. The *additional* spending will be two times the original. The additional and the original together will be three times the original. The multiplier in this case is 3. The $1,000 increase in investment leads to a total growth of income of $3,000. If the marginal propensity to consume were much

FIGURE 10–4.   Illustration of the Multiplier

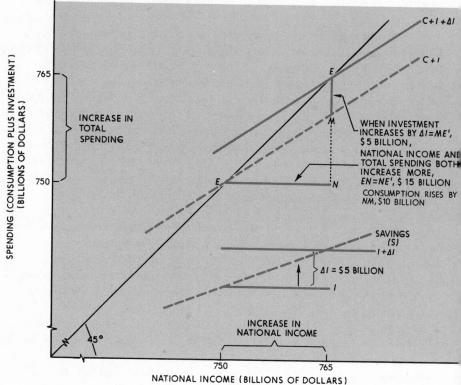

NATIONAL INCOME (BILLIONS OF DOLLARS)

An increase in investment leads to a larger increase in national income.

larger, say $\%_{10}$, the multiplier would be larger, 10, indicating that people spend on consumption almost all of what they receive, thus boosting demand and stimulating business.

Since the public saves what it does not spend, we can obtain our answer by working through the propensity to save—a process that may be a bit easier. Think of the amount saved as "leakage" or "evaporation" from the buying stream. Figure 10–5 illustrates. More disappears as the flow moves on. The amount "lost" is the amount shown by the marginal propensity to save. Remember, the marginal propensity to save measures the amount of an additional unit of income that will not be spent on consumption. The multiplier is the obverse, the reciprocal, the upside down of this marginal propensity to save. To find the multiple effects of an increase in spending, reverse the fraction of what is not spent (at the margin), that is, of what is saved (at the margin). If ⅓ is not spent on consumption, but is saved, the multiplier is 3; if ½, the multiplier is 2.

FIGURE 10–5. The Income-Multiplying Process: "Leakages"

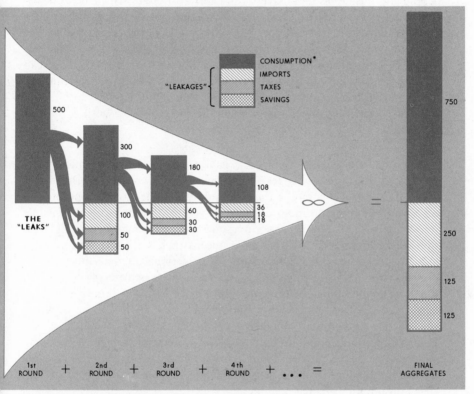

* Domestic consumption out of each round of income increase.
Source: Adapted from S. C. Yang, "The Multiplier Process," *Finance and Development,* June, 1967, p. 96.

During a depression, a businessman, making an investment outlay for his own benefit, will likely help others more. His purchases of investment goods create employment and income which is then spent, although not fully, on consumer goods.

Can we show the effects of the multiplier on graphs like those used earlier? Certainly. If we raise the rate of investment shown in Figure 10–4 by $5 billion, *ME'*, when the marginal propensity to save is ⅓ (and the marginal propensity to consume is ⅔), the national income will rise by

$15 billion, *EN* and *NE'*. This is the additional income which will bring out $5 billion saving to produce an equilibrium.[9]

The multiplication of income does not happen overnight. In our economy, the first two or three rounds or steps, which are most important, probably work themselves out within a year or so. The remainder dwindle along indefinitely but will have no significant effect after the second year. Nor is the process smooth and simple. A great deal indeed depends upon monetary conditions, which may stifle or spur the process. Different people and businesses may have significantly different marginal propensities to save, even at the same time. Variations in marginal propensities from year to year can be more than negligible. However, if we assume that the average for the country as a whole is fairly stable and that we know its size—probably around 2 after allowing for taxes—then we can predict roughly how much the national income will change when investment rises or falls by any specific amount. But note the "probably." Even for past periods it is impossible to compute the multiplier with comfortable accuracy.

Induced Investment. So far we have assumed that investment plans were fixed temporarily. Yet real-world plans change constantly. One major cause of change is the state of the economy itself. The more prosperous the economy, the more businesses want to invest. So the investment schedule slopes upward. In Figure 10–6, investment, *II*, is shown as varying with the size of income. The rising slope means that the higher the national income, the greater the investment; when national income increases, so does investment. Economists call the increase in investment resulting from the increase in national income *induced investment*. It differs from *autonomous investment*, that which results from a new invention, or anything that shifts the investment schedule.

Two important points follow: (1) The amount of induced investment depends upon *expectations*. Some anticipations, certainly, will be personal and unpredictable. Investment is subject to greater percentage variation than consumption. As national income rises, businesses and individuals will likely revise their investment plans upward—on the basis of what they expect. Yet who knows how expectations will change? Perhaps the line correctly graphing investment will slope slightly, perhaps a great deal.

---

[9] The symbol for the multiplier is commonly *K*. The following relationships hold: $K = \Delta Y / \Delta I$, where the symbol Δ stands for "very small change."

Substituting $\Delta Y - \Delta C$ for ΔI in the first equation, $K = \Delta Y / (\Delta Y - \Delta C)$.

Dividing both numerator and denominator by ΔY, we find that $K = 1 / [1 - (\Delta C / \Delta Y)]$.

If consumption, *C*, rises $3 when income, *Y*, rises $4, the denominator, $1 - \frac{3}{4}$, is $\frac{1}{4}$ which "goes into" the numerator 4 times. *K*, then, is 4. A large literature on the multiplier reveals many complications. Another relationship, the acceleration principle described in the next chapter, also helps explain magnified changes in national income when either investment or consumption buying rises or falls.

Real-world investment schedules also shift in their entirety over the business cycle. Prediction of the level of employment, then, becomes more difficult and less certain than suggested by our earlier use of the assumption of a given amount of planned investment.

(2) If the economy is in the doldrums with considerable unemployment, an increase in consumption buying will stimulate demand for the

FIGURE 10–6.   Equilibrium at Less Than Full Employment: Spending Gap

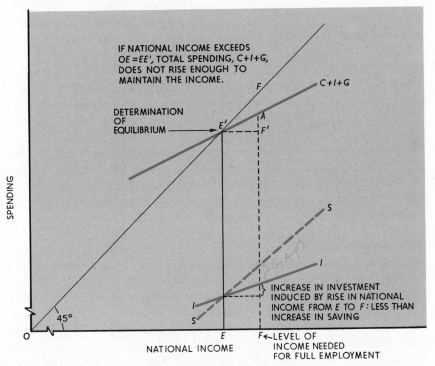

OE = EE' indicates the equilibrium national income at existing prices. (Government buying can be included.) The full employment level of national income would be OF = FF. If income reaches OF = FF, however, there will be a gap. Income will then drop. The spending of that income, C + I + G, does not create enough demand to maintain the income. E'F', the gap, is FA, times the multiplier. The upward slope of line II shows how the amount that businesses want to invest will depend partly upon the size of national income. A rise in income from OE to OF would induce an increase in investment, but not so much as the rise in savings.

products of business. Then there is more employment, a larger national income, and probably more induced investment. Larger consumption and more investment then support each other. They do not compete for limited resources because the community has idle productive capacity which, when getting to work, increases the volume of both consumption and investment.

Let us look at a less happy possibility, the *paradox of thrift*. If, in a depression, some of us prudently decide to consume less and save more, we may do our compatriots a bad turn. Thrift, then, adds to the wealth of those individuals who save, but it makes us poorer as a group. Suppose that I have been hiring you to type for me, but I begin to worry about sending my children to college, so I discharge you and do my typing myself in the evenings; I put the cash I would have paid you in my safety deposit box. I may be better off, but you are not. Other jobs are hard to find, and you lose earnings. You cut your buying, a process that hurts others, reducing their income. For the moment, my increased saving has led to a drop in the national income. As I save (and hoard), I force loss of income on others. However, if, instead of hoarding the money which I do not spend for your typing, I use it to pay for a new typewriter, someone else gets work and income equal to what you lost.

The results depend, of course, upon what happens to the money that is saved. Dollars that remain idle do not provide a market for business. During a depression our efforts to save more, though seemingly wise for us individually, can hurt business and the economy as a whole. As consumption buying falls, businesses have less *incentive* to buy more capital equipment, and they *need* less plant and inventory for the smaller volume of sales. Postwar recessions, however, have shown that a decline in business and poor profits, even losses, actually reinforce one incentive to invest: the desire to increase efficiency. New equipment may offer an opportunity to reduce costs per unit when such betterment is urgently needed.

The equilibrium level of national income as conceived by Keynes is not necessarily the most desirable. It is a level which, ignoring government, results from the existing propensity to consume and from investment plans. The level may be one of substantial unemployment or one reached only after an inflationary price rise. Assume that the objective is a national income involving (*a*) full employment (*b*) at stable prices. The difference between this income level and any other will depend upon the balance between plans to save and plans to invest—*gaps* amplified by the multiplier. Two kinds of gaps may develop, one leading to unemployment, the other to inflation.

Spending Gap: Failure to Sustain Full Employment.   The gap leading to unemployment, sometimes called the "deflationary gap," but perhaps better termed the "spending gap," is illustrated in Figure 10–6. (Government spending is now included.) At full employment, *OF*, there is a gap between total saving (where *SS* crosses *FF*) and the amount the public wishes to invest (where *II* crosses *FF*). National income drops by *EF*. This amount is greater than the difference between *II* and *SS* at *FF*— because the multiplier operates.

Will such a level persist until there is some important change in underlying conditions? Or will forces within the economy work toward a *better* level? If so can we expect to get the *best* level, and with reasonable promptness? These questions arouse debate. On one matter, however, there is no debate: we cannot be confident that funds saved will be spent to buy new investment goods. Dispute arises over the question: Will a discrepancy lead to more than temporary maladjustment? Before Keynes, most economists would have said that forces within the economic system would tend to bring a desirable adjustment, pushing toward full employment. (1) People without jobs and businesses with idle plants would be willing to offer their services at lower prices and wage rates; some income is certainly better than none at all. At some lower level of wage rates, existing dollar demand would provide full employment. (2) Savers would find that demand from businesses seeking funds to invest would be low. The price that savers could get for the use of their savings—the rate of interest—would fall.[10] (3) The lower rate of interest would discourage saving; consumer buying would rise a little. Business would tend to improve. (4) The lower rate of interest by reducing the cost of borrowing would encourage businesses to invest more. (5) Lower costs of investment goods would stimulate capital formation; an apartment house that would not seem profitable to build at a cost of $200,000 might be worth risking at $180,000. Consumers would also buy more things (and the labor to produce them) at the lower prices; on the average, the dollars being spent would buy more man-hours. (6) The fall in the price level would reduce the amount of cash balances needed for ordinary purchases of goods and services, so that (7) some money no longer needed for transactions would seek borrowers. Gradually, unemployed resources would come into use.

Keynes disagreed. He pointed out reasons why the self-adjusting or self-correcting features might not be sufficient. Some of his stagnationist followers were even more emphatic. They argued as follows:

1. Wage rates are not in fact flexible downward.
2. Even with considerable unemployment, national income would be high enough to lead to substantial saving, regardless of a very low rate of interest.
3. A low rate of interest would induce hoarding; some persons with new savings or wealth acquired in the past would prefer liquidity to the low return. For a small interest yield, they would not risk turning their savings over to business to put into a new plant.[11]

---

[10] Chapter 26 discusses interest. The rate of interest plays an important part in Keynes' analysis; the simplification in the text here is essentially accurate.

[11] The risk would be greater than we might expect. A low interest rate has little room to fall more, but it may rise. If a person buys a bond bringing a fixed return when interest rates are low, he loses the chance at a higher rate. Moreover, he runs the risk of a capital loss because bond prices will fall. Low interest rates, then, involve a risk which makes the holding of funds in idle cash or bank accounts more attractive than when interest rates are high. This is in addition to the fact that, as shown in Chapter 8, when the interest rate is low, one sacrifices little annual income in holding savings idle. Changes in perferences for holding assets in the form of cash can, in the Keynesian theory, lead to changes in total spending, unless the quantity of money adjusts appropriately.

4. Business, however, would perhaps not be *able* to pay a higher rate if savers tried to get it: the prospects of profitable investment would not be great enough. In Keynes' language, the *marginal efficiency of capital*—the net yield the businessman expects—is not high enough to induce businessmen to spend as many dollars on capital formation as would be saved from a full employment national income. The most attractive opportunities for using capital equipment would already have been developed. The investment possibilities remaining would be lower down the scale of diminishing productivity. Relatively few would have enough promise to justify the costs. (Funds set aside for depreciation would buy replacements, thus incorporating technical improvements.) Yet, if the rate of interest could somehow be reduced, the buying of new capital goods would increase; planned investment might rise from, say, $70 billion to $75 billion.

5. Price reductions would not, on balance, have great effect in stimulating consumption, investment, and employment. Falling prices and labor costs, in fact, could be a disadvantage: they reduce money income of groups, make some people gloomy, and for a time even reduce demand as postponable buying is delayed in hope of still lower prices.

At this point, we can see a divergence between tools and the results we

FIGURE 10–7.   Inflationary Gap

When productive capacity is fully employed and national income has reached *OF*, there is a gap, *EF'*. The amount which people now want to spend, C + I + G, is greater than the amount needed to buy the full output at prevailing prices. The spending will raise prices and money income until the new equilibrium, E_i, is reached. National income rises by $EA = AE_i$; this amount is the gap, *EF'*, times the multiplier.

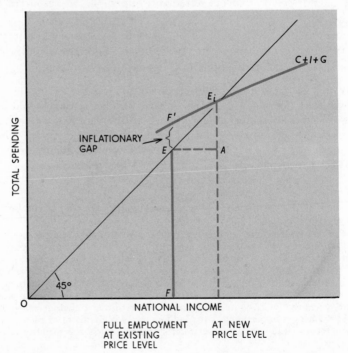

get when we use them on or with different materials (assumptions). A critic might explode: "Keynes is wrong. Investment opportunities are fabulously promising." Then he might proceed to use the Keynesian tools to predict widely different results—perhaps an inflationary gap.

Inflationary Gap. If, at a full employment level of national income, the public as a whole having decided on a total of consumption and government spending, tries to invest more than its members want to save, total spending—$C + I + G$—will rise (Fig. 10–7). There is an "inflationary gap." People have received income of $OF = FE$, but they want to spend FF'. As they do so, national income rises. Since output cannot increase—productive capacity, we have assumed, is fully employed—the rise in money income will take the form of higher prices. Increasing money income will, in turn, lead to larger savings, so a new equilibrium for these conditions will be reached. The difference between this equilibrium level, with inflation, and the full employment level without inflation will be larger than the gap itself, depending upon the multiplier. Will this new price level persist? That depends. If people again try to invest more than they want to save, inflation will get another boost.

THE ROLE OF GOVERNMENT FINANCES

The economy's total buying includes what we buy collectively through government, buying which also brings employment. Taxes, however, reduce the ability of families and businesses to buy for consumption and investment. The government is on both sides, then; its spending creates income and jobs, its taxing curtails them. The two sides are not necessarily equal. From any given position either or both—taxes or spending—may change.

Any net change in government spending will produce larger effects, as the multiplier operates. If government employees get more income, they spend more. On the other hand, if taxpayers must pay more to the Treasury, but government does not increase its spending, the net effect is lower spending by taxpayers and less business (fewer jobs) for others. Government spending increases by ΔG without any change in taxes. The level of national income rises by more because of the multiplier.

Now let us examine the effect of a tax increase which is not matched by a reduction in G (plans for I remaining fixed). The public will reduce C. How much? Perhaps for each dollar increase in taxes, consumption buying will drop by 90 cents—perhaps more, perhaps less. Some taxes will reduce consumption more per dollar of revenue than will others.

Government is an agency through which society can act more or less deliberately and consciously as a unit that includes everyone. Individuals and businesses act on their own account; the total of their separate economic actions does not always lead to the best possible level of income, employment, and prices. If not, government may be able to add an influence operating in the right direction. The deficiencies in our individual (personal and business) actions may be offset by what we do through government.

If people are trying to save more than they wish to spend on investment goods so that income and employment are falling—or if planned saving and investment balance, but total spending is not enough to produce full employment—government finance seems to offer a remedy. If government *maintains its spending* but *cuts taxes*, private spending will

FIGURE 10–8. Increase in Income Following a Rise in Government Spending Not Offset by an Increase in Taxes

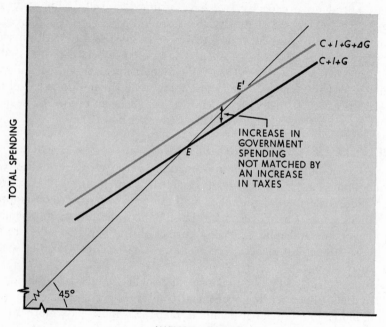

rise as households and businesses are left with more income after taxes. Government, on the other hand, can counteract tendencies toward inflation by raising taxes or reducing expenditures, or some combination. Chapter 13 deals with these possibilities.

HOW ADEQUATE IS THE THEORY?

When Keynesian theory appeared in 1936, it inspired high hopes in at least most of those economists who understood it. Society was shown a means by which to achieve and to maintain essentially full employment. This is the picture: If spending and saving habits are generally stable, careful study of the past and the present will reveal our marginal propensities, which also tell us the multiplier. We use this and other knowledge to build a "model" of our economy. Special procedures can be established to estimate foreign trade and to learn how much the business world is planning to spend on investment goods. Government financial plans can be forecast. Then we put the figures for the future into the formula developed from the model and find what the national income will be; if it is less than is needed for full employment, or more than is consistent with the avoidance of inflation, government can change its own financial plans to get the desired level of jobs.

The highest hopes were not justified. We indicate here some reasons for disappointment.

Predicting the Tie between Consumption Spending and Income. The relationship between national income in one period and consumption in the next is fairly close but not rigorously tight. What once seemed to provide a reasonably firm foundation for prediction is not fully reliable. Common sense puts us on guard for some things which influence the propensity to consume—the disruption of war, depression, or large inflation. Other, less sweeping, conditions and changes affect aggregate consumption.

The distribution of a total income of any particular size among groups in the economy will influence the percentage used for consumption. Consumer spending seems to vary with expectations, with holdings of liquid assets, with wealth, and with other factors that change. The size and the condition of stocks of durable consumer goods may be highly important; from an income of any given size, we are likely to spend more if our stock of durables is worn out and suffers from obvious gaps than if it is new and apparently complete. And the amount spent for consumption out of any income depends upon a family's notion of *its* living standards. From one year to the next, some families may stick to their habitual pattern of expenditure, even though their income rises and falls; they do not, for a while, spend in a pattern like others with the same income, but rather as they did with an earlier income. Their living standard does not change promptly. Over time, however, it does change. From decade to decade there is an upward shift in the propensity-to-consume schedule. The puzzler is that we cannot be certain *how much* change to expect in the months or year ahead—the period for which we are so very anxious to plan our affairs.

From the first to the third quarters of 1961, the percentage of personal disposable income saved rose from 6.9 to 8.0, almost one sixth. From the third quarter of 1965 to the third of 1966, the percentage fell from 6.1 to 4.8. (These figures are all seasonally adjusted.) Predictions of the amount of investment needed to balance changes in saving in the short run cannot rest on the assumption that changes in the consumption function are insignificant. A small percentage of change in consumption makes a big percentage change in saving.

The Balance between Plans for Saving and Plans for Investment.
Economists agree that balance between plans for saving and plans for capital formation is both highly important and far from assured. A discrepancy will disturb the economy—to some multiple. The theory, therefore, aids us in spotting strategic elements that need watching and perhaps action—the factors influencing decisions to invest, the functioning of the financial system to help bring savers and potential investors together, and the reasons for different quantities of overall saving, to mention only three. To know what to seek is no small gain.

Decisions which determine investment are subject to many influences. Keynes was well aware of the importance of the role of the "job creator," the man who makes or fails to make decisions involving risk, and of the conditions which influence attitudes toward investment. A boom in total demand will bring out all sorts of vigorous effort by businessmen. Other conditions, however, are also important. In policies regarding taxation, monopoly, business regulation, and other matters, government can do much to help or hinder the achievement of the kind and level of investment which will best serve the general welfare.

Effects of Changes in Total Spending on Prices.
Keynesian analysis proves inadequate, just as does the equation of exchange, in *failing to tell how much of the effect of changes in aggregate spending will be felt on prices and how much on employment*, especially when an economy is below full employment. When the economy is at full employment, increased spending will bring higher prices.[12] In the conditions of unemployment for which the theory was developed, there is room for both prices and employment to change. Keynesians originally tended to assume that as long as appreciable unemployment exists, increased spending will be felt mostly in more output (jobs); any undesirable effects of price rises would be more than offset by the good effects of more employment and output. But when nearly, but not quite, all productive capacity is in use, the problem is tougher, very much so. Doubt about how an increase in spending will be divided between (a) higher prices and (b) more work magnifies the difficulties of prediction and of policy decision. Action to boost employment might do more harm by stimulating inflationary price rises. Or, if prices are rising, government restraint to check inflation might create unemployment. Keynesian models do not yield solutions to these difficult problems.

---

[12] An increase in imports from abroad is also possible and probable. Troublesome aspects of policies to stimulate employment can arise from effects on international trade and finance.

A total demand of $800 billion will buy more labor if the average wage rate is $3.50 an hour than if it is $4. A rise in prices or wage rates will reduce the quantity of real goods and services which can be bought with any given dollar amount of purchasing power. The theory, however, gives no indication of when, or how much, price and wage change may affect the quantity of real output (and labor) demanded.

Finally, the theory, was designed to throw light on the forces determining the general level of employment. It does not deal with another problem—business fluctuations.

TERMS AND CONCEPTS

level of employment	marginal propensity to	induced investment
investment	consume (save)	autonomous invest-
consumption	ex ante savings (invest-	ment
national income	ment)	deflationary gap
propensity to consume	ex post savings (in-	inflationary gap
propensity to save	vestment)	
consumption function	multiplier	

QUESTIONS

1. In what sense are decisions to save and decisions to invest made by different people for different reasons? What is the significance for the level of employment and national income?

2. Why may investment vary from year to year? Consumption?

3. Show why (a) if the people of the country try to save more than businessmen are willing to spend for investment, national income will fall, and (b) if business spends more on investment than people plan to save, national income will rise.

4. "Keynesian analysis does not tell us how much of any change in total spending will be felt in prices and how much in employment." Is this criticism true? If so, is it significant?

5. Explain the multiplier. How is it related to the average and to the marginal propensity to consume? What is "leakage"?

6. What knowledge is needed to use the Keynesian tools to guide government policy?

7. Why is it useful to separate government spending from other spending in studying the forces that create employment? What is the role of taxes in the analysis?

8. In what sense can there be a general shortage of demand in the economy?

9. Does the Keynesian analysis necessarily lead, as sometimes charged, to the conclusion that thrift should be discouraged? Why?

10. In what sense do expectations play a key role in the Keynesian system?

11. What is an "inflationary gap"?

11

BUSINESS FLUCTUATIONS (CYCLES)

Every boom represents a distortion . . . [which] consists essentially of an unmaintainable rate of capital formation.

Alvin H. Hansen

Our economy does not sail along on an even keel. Investment schedules and the propensity to consume are not stable. Figure 11–1, covering a long sweep of history, shows how business has fluctuated. Ups and downs seem to be more normal than stability. This is unfortunate because fluctuations involve much that is disruptive and wasteful. Change, itself, though necessary for progress, creates uncertainties that hamper economic decision making. Depression brings human distress and misery; lives are wasted in brooding idleness. Booms, too, have bad features, such as mistaken uses of labor and materials and increased living costs.

Can fluctuations be prevented or controlled? How do the problems of fluctuations tie in with the forces which determine the general level of employment? We search to encourage the change that is *progress* without the ill effects of fluctuations. But can government really take deliberate action to neutralize forces creating fluctuations without causing other troubles?

As a result of vast statistical analysis and penetrating theoretical study, economists know a great deal about past business movements and the principal features—or causes—of fluctuations. This knowledge can help in forming plans for future action, but, as you might guess, agreement among economists is not unanimous. Nor is any cure-all in sight. Nevertheless, we do have solid basis for believing that business fluctuations can be kept within narrower limits than in the past. First, however, a warning must be underscored: Cycles, as this country has known them, should not be thought of as the depression of the 1930's. Of course, it was a reality, but it was uniquely bad, both in length and in severity.

SEASONAL AND SECULAR CHANGE

Seasonal Fluctuation. Some economic changes occur with more than accidental regularity. *Seasonal* changes present a clear example. Some, such as the Christmas and Easter increase in retail sales, the autumn buying of back-to-school clothes, and quarterly income tax payments, result from *human habits* that might be different. Others, such as the harvesting of crops or the use of heating fuels, result from *changes in nature*. Electricity for lighting follows the sun but also changes with the adoption of, and then departure from, daylight saving time. Construction, as suggested by Figure 11–2, varies with the seasons.

Businesses can predict such seasonal fluctuations, and can arrange to meet them. Ups and down are certain. We are confident of a cycle, but we cannot always be sure of the *timing*. Consumers may concentrate Christmas purchases in a few days or spread them out over weeks. The peak of the changes that are due to climate will depend upon just *when* the hot, cold, wet, or dry periods come. Moreover, though seasonal rhythms are certain, their *amounts* vary. The pressures on railroads for late summer and fall movement of grain vary with the harvest. In some winters the sales of overcoats or skis are higher than in others, simply because of the weather. For these and other reasons, seasonal variations are not absolutely predictable. Yet there is enough regularity for us to prepare to meet them. Travel to Europe reaches its peak early in the summer, return travel at the end of the summer. In the winter, some of the ships can be used for cruises to sunny waters. By varying their prices and publicity, Miami hotels have been highly successful in drawing vacationers and "conventioners" in what used to be seasons so dull many hotels closed entirely. Airlines schedule group and special flights at bargain off-season rates. New techniques now make construction possible during more of the year than in the past. "Seasonals" occur in different parts of the economy at different times so that to varying degree they cancel out or offset each other; they do not set up forces which feed on one another.

Secular Trend. Another kind of change, *secular trend*, consists of a movement in the same general direction over a period of many years. Its patterns, if there are any, are not so clear and certain as those of seasonal change. Secular trends are changes that require years, decades, or generations to work out their effects. Population increases. Knowledge of science grows. Habits of work and saving change. Eating and other consump-

FIGURE 11–1.   American Business Activity since 1860

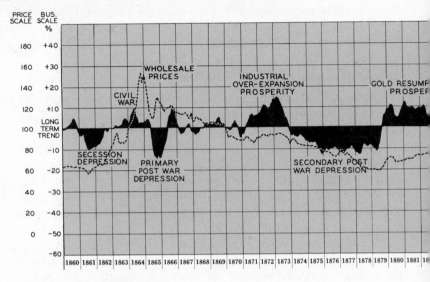

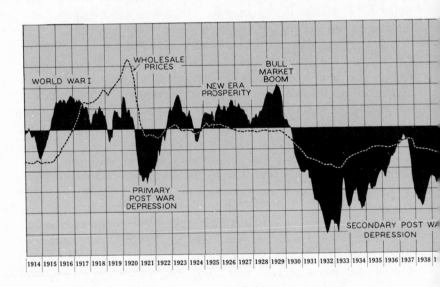

tion habits change.[1] People move to cities, then to suburbs. Government grows. Such changes cross others, reinforcing some, offsetting some. The effects are often hard to disentangle from those of more temporary

[1] In the 50 years after 1910, per capita consumption of potatoes fell from 198 to about 103 pounds, while ice-cream consumption increased tenfold. From 1940 to 1966, sales of coal for home heating fell 70 percent while sales of natural gas rose sevenfold.

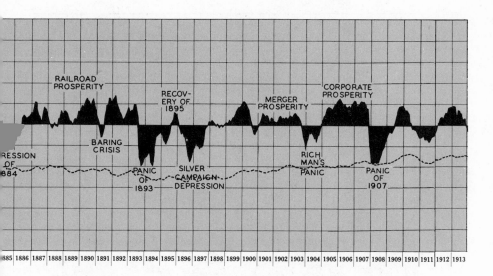

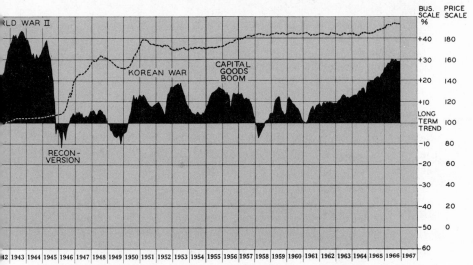

conditions.[2] Though often disruptive, they are part and parcel of the development that brings improvement in living standards.

[2] Statisticians have methods of adjusting the figures to separate the influences of these trends from the short-term fluctuations. Yet doubt will remain after using even the best methods. They measure results and do not isolate causal factors. The

FIGURE 11–2.   Seasonal Fluctuations in Construction

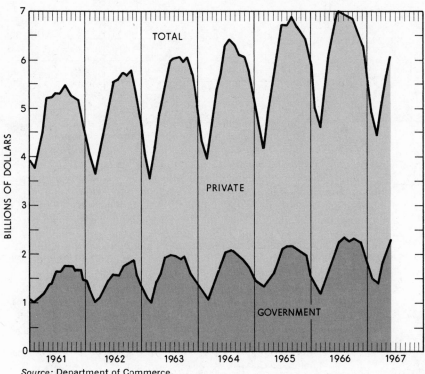

Source: Department of Commerce.

Secular changes result from many factors which alter the structure of the economy, for example, the decline in the relative size of agriculture or the rise in education. Some trends are not easily foreseen, especially before they really get under way. Yet, we do know that such long-run changes, some large, some small, are inevitable.

BUSINESS CYCLES

Our economy experiences still another kind of fluctuation, generally termed the *business cycle*. There are ups and downs that do not coincide with seasonal changes and which are clearly different from long-term trends. Records going back many generations show sizable swings in

---

measured result is produced by many interrelated forces of varying strength. No one can know that the trend observed will extend into the future. Trend measures are historical. They must not be projected into the future unless the causal forces can be measured, analyzed, and judged to be likely to continue. Extension of a trend can be hazardous even in those short-run situations where our interest is greatest. For the long run, too, prediction can be tricky. For example, it was once pointed out that if New York City and New York State each continued to grow at the rate observed then, the city would become larger than the state.

important economic quantities every few years: prices, production, and employment.

Definition. Two specialists define a business cycle as follows:

Business cycles are a type of fluctuation found in the aggregate economic activity of nations that organize their work mainly in business enterprises: a cycle consists of expansions occurring at about the same time in many economic activities, followed by similarly general recessions, contractions, and revivals which merge into the expansion phase of the next cycle; this sequence of change is recurrent but not periodic; in duration, business cycles vary from more than one year to ten or twelve years; they are not divisible into shorter cycles of similar character with amplitudes approximately their own.[3]

Several terms appearing in discussions of fluctuations might be examined, except that difference in usage gets in the way of clear definition. In general, one group applies to the *direction* in which business is moving: "recession," "contraction," "expansion," "recovery," "revival." Other terms, however, apply to the *level of production* or activity at any given time as compared with the level at some other time: "depression," "boom," "prosperity." Usage remains imprecise. Confusion arises when the same term is used to apply to both phenomena, a direction of movement and a level. Additional confusion may result from the use of other terms, such as "rolling readjustment," which may help picture a specific process or condition, perhaps in a somewhat slanted way, without indicating whether there is movement up or down or whether business is higher or lower than at some other time.

Successive cycles have much in common, and yet they vary tremendously. They belong to the same family but are not twins. In fact, the term "cycle" may give a misleading impression of symmetry and regularity; movements of business are not like those of a pendulum, of the tides, or of day and night. In the United States, for example, *duration*, the length of time between the low points of two cycles has varied from 28 months to 99 months—a range of 350 percent. Moreover, some peaks are higher, and troughs lower, than others. The *turning points* vary, sometimes being smooth and gradual, at other times marked by some sharp, dramatic event. The internal features differ. At any moment, there are many crosscurrents in the economic stream. Cycles differ, as do concerts or summers.

Yet cycles have enough common features to permit generalized study. The most striking thing is that our economy contains forces making for **cumulation**. Once the economy is moving either up or down, internal forces tend to reinforce each other, to accentuate the movement; they

---

[3] A. F. Burns and W. C. Mitchell, *Measuring Business Cycles* (New York: National Bureau of Economic Research, 1946), p. 3.

make an internal force feed upon itself, pushing it farther on the way that it has started to go. These forces are partly financial and monetary. They are partly physical and psychological. To some extent, they are inherent in economic life in an industrial society. Nevertheless, they are, at least partially, subject to "control."

A good way to begin is to take a "trip around the cycle." We can see the forces that operate and the ways they are related to each other. Since no two cycles are identical, our "trip" will not correspond precisely with any of those of the past. Two features call for repeated attention: (1) the *cumulation* of economic activity, and (2) *turning points*.

Revival and Cumulative Expansion.   Let us begin when business is expanding after substantial unemployment of men and machines. Perhaps because of a price reduction, a better product, more sales effort, as well as generally "better business," factories receive more orders. To fill them, they hire more employees and operate 41 instead of 38 hours a week. As employees get more pay, they will spend more, increasing the demand for consumers' goods. The marginal propensity to consume tends to be relatively high after income has been below the normal to which a family has gotten accustomed. During a period of low incomes, consumers will, of necessity, have let their autos, refrigerators, sheets, shoes, and so on, wear down or out; obsolescence and rising maintenance costs make old equipment unsatisfactory; the longer the depression, the more will such stocks need replenishing. The pressure to spend almost all of the increases in income will be high.

A store or factory that begins to make more sales will need a larger physical quantity of inventory to satisfy customers and to prevent costly interruptions of production. It *must* increase this form of investment. Other firms must therefore produce more, paying out wages. The expanded business spending on investment in inventory (goods in process) is not matched by an equal increase in intended saving by those who get the payments for production. Especially in manufacturing and construction do wage payments go up before added output is ready for sale. The spending of these wages will lift demand at the retail level, add to the orders of businesses, and stimulate employment.[4] Here is one important force making for a *cumulative* movement, one that feeds on itself. Not all of the increase in output is consumed; there is a net addition to inventory. One result: the income earned in producing the added inventory is not offset by purchasing and consuming it. Table 11–1 illustrates; it assumes that for each unit of final product which the factory turns out in a week, it tries to keep raw materials in the storage bins and on the assembly lines equal to twice the amount sold.

---

[4] How would this be shown on figures in the preceding chapter? The investment schedule would shift upward and also slope upward. In other terms, MV rises.

As the expansion gathers momentum, the firm's earnings rise, perhaps sharply. During the preceding period of depression, management has found ways to cut costs; these efforts now "pay off." Though wage rates per hour, taxes, and some other costs per unit tend to increase, there is usually a lag. Overhead costs do not grow in proportion to the rise in volume; therefore, total cost per unit may fall. Selling prices, thanks to rising demand, frequently rise before the bulk of costs. Profits expand encouragingly.

We immediately ask: "Where does the business get the money to pay for more man-hours of work and inventory? How is expansion financed?" When expansion began, some businesses had been holding bank balances that were larger than were being used to finance the depression volume of business. Companies now use funds that had been idle (increasing the velocity of circulation). Financing of some of the rise in PT comes from an increase in V.

TABLE 11–1. Inventory Purchase Fluctuations: Desired Inventory Is Twice Sales

Sales	Inventory	Purchases*
100	200	100
100	200	100
150	300	250
200	400	300
200	400	200

* Amount to replenish sales and provide the change in inventory.

Many firms, however, will need more money. Some will get capital by *sale of securities*, as business expansion makes the public more willing to exchange idle bank deposits for stocks and bonds. A more important source of funds for increased business, however, is the banking system. Banks will have lending capacity (excess reserves); interest rates will be low, and bankers will welcome good loans. Such loans create new deposits. The stock of money, M, grows and businesses then spend these funds. The expansion of physical production thus leads to growth in the amount of money. The spending of this new money adds to demand for goods, induces more production and more deposit creation, and keeps the spiral rising.

Another factor begins to exert an upward pressure. Economists call it the **acceleration principle.** It helps account for the induced investment noted in the last chapter. As we look back at Table 11–1, we see that an increase in sales from 100 to 150 units—one half—led to an increase in purchases from 100 to 250, three times the increase in sales. Greater business also begins to require more productive equipment. More factory or store space, machines, trucks, and electric generators are needed. The need may be *physical*—the old trucks, for example, do not have enough capacity to handle the bigger volume—or *economic*—newer capacity can do a job at lower cost. Whatever the cause, a growth in the demand for consumers' goods may bring a much greater percentage increase in demand for capital goods. To illustrate, we assume that consumers are

TABLE 11-2.   Example of the Acceleration Principle *

Period	Ships in Use	Change in Demand for Shipping (Percent)	Sales of Ships			Change in Spending on Ships (Percent)
			Replace-ment	Addi-tions	Value	
1	1,000	0	50		$250,000,000	0
2	1,050	+5	50	50	$500,000,000	+100
3	1,080	+3	50	30	$400,000,000	− 20
4	1,000	−7	0	0	0	−100

* For simplicity, we neglect the replacement spendings on shipyard facilities.

buying coffee, oil, and other freight requiring 1,000 ships. We also assume that shipyards have considerable excess capacity. Each ship costs $5 million and has a life of 20 years, and the age of ships is evenly distributed over time so that 50 per year come due for replacement. Line 1 in Table 11-2 shows the usual condition under these assumptions: shipyards supplying the annual replacement demand for ships needed to satisfy consumer demand for shipping.

Then economic activity rises and consumers need more shipping. Assume an increase of 5 percent. The data in the line for period 2 summarize the results of such a change. An additional 50 ships will be needed. The annual output of ships will increase 100 percent. So will the amount of spending on new ships. An increase in the need for shipping of 5 percent has led to a 100 percent increase in the output of the goods (ships) meeting this need.

Now suppose that there continues to be an increase in the need for shipping, but at a slackening rate, say a little under 3 percent. Line 3 summarizes the results. The sales of ships will be *lower* than in period 2—only 80 will be sold, 50 for replacement needs (none of the 50 added in period 2 needing to be replaced) and 30 for the new demand. Therefore, a slackening in the *rate of growth* of the demand for the service (shipping) will lead to an absolute fall in the sales of the thing supplying this service. Spendings on ships will fall to $400 million. Though demand for shipping went up by 3 percent, outlays on ships fell 20 percent. Then demand for shipping drops to the original level. No ships at all need to be built because the 80 which were added in periods 2 and 3 are above the replacement need. A drop of about 7 percent in demand for shipping wiped out one year's demand for ships.

Let us now assume that the shipyards were being used about as fully as possible in the first period. To make the additional 50 ships, more shipyards will be needed; assume that spending on this score increases by $250 million. The net result is spectacular. Before consumers increased their demand for shipping, $250 million was being spent annually on ships with no spending on new shipyards. (Actually, there was some shipyard replacement spending, but we neglect it for simplicity.) Now, with shipping needs increased by 5 percent, expenditures on shipping and shipyards have each increased $250 million, so that the total becomes $750 million. Here is impressive magnification or multiplication of spending.

What happens now when the increase in demand for shipping services slides from 5 to 3 percent? Let us assume that the number of shipyards available will be sufficient to provide these 80 ships. So no new spending will be made for shipyard facilities. Total spendings on ships and shipbuilding facilities will fall from $750 million to $400 million (80 ships at $5 million).

This illustration, though exaggerated, helps us see one major factor in business fluctuations. However, its influence is hard to judge. Several limiting forces operate. For example, businesses ordinarily have flexibility in the form of excess or standby capacity, as we first assumed regarding shipyards; considerable output change can often be accommodated. Moreover, the ratio of productive plant to output is subject to variation, such as by a change in the number of hours used per week. Businesses would not make major capital investments (building shipyards and even ships in our illustration) on the basis of immediate demand, but rather on the basis of long-term expectations. Finally, a sharp rise in demand can be met by price increases which reduce the quantity sold and raise profits.

Whether or not the acceleration principle provides the best explanation, outlays on *construction*—new houses, office buildings, and factories—do swing upward. For many months the rise in construction is slow. Typically a builder must go through time-consuming steps to make plans, arrange financing, get his land and labor and materials—all after he has weighed the prospects and decided to take the risk. Eventually, however, spending on construction increases.

Consumers may borrow and buy. As earnings rise, some families for a time spend even more than their incomes. The auto, washer, or rug may be worn out, or out of style; a growing household will need more furniture. A family "itching" to buy durable goods may find that out of its larger income it can spare $10 a month, and spend $200 at once, borrowing to repay in installments. Or it may make extensive repairs on the house or buy a new one for which it arranges to pay over 20 years. Clearly, then, the *growth in demand for durable consumers goods and housing is not limited to the increase in immediate income;* such spending can rise by whatever multiple the increase in monthly income can pay for over a period. The multiple depends upon financing arrangements. During the 1964–65 business expansion, consumers borrowed net (above repayments) about $600 million a month to finance installment purchases. About half was an injection into the economic stream of new money—more *M*—created by banks. Here, clearly, is another cumulative force.

As business improves, *psychological forces* can give another boost. Profits in real estate make construction projects attractive. As earnings increase, businesses become more willing to invest in new equipment and new ventures. The added earnings themselves provide some of the funds for business expansion. They also justify firms in borrowing and in using funds that may have been idle. Bankers are not immune to the germ of optimism. They become more willing to lend; borrowers are more prosperous, and bankers may become less cautious. Optimism that feeds upon success justifies risk taking and the creation of new bank credit which provides expansionary financing and adds to a spirit of euphoria. Government officials and voters feel better and decide to repave the rutty street or add a school gym.

Psychology enters in another way. We saw earlier how the upswing enlarged the demand for inventory. Speculation can add more demand. Prices rise in a business expansion. Business and consumers, seeing the trend, realize that if they can buy now to meet future needs, they can likely avoid having to pay still higher prices later. The reaction may be cautiously realistic or distinctly speculative, but it adds to current spending. And as prices rise, banks may feel well justified in expanding credit to finance business purchases for future needs. Such finance in itself helps push the boom higher.

Why Does Expansion End?   So goes the expansion, permeating the economy; of course, it is more complex and varied than we have indicated. Things not examined here—stock prices, international trade, political change, government finance—can be highly significant. Eventually, though, expansion ends. What stops it? Are the forces that end the expansion of a type that make business *contraction* inevitable? Or could the economy perhaps continue to operate more or less steadily at about the peak level?

One thing can certainly stop expansion: physical limits on productive capacity. The economy cannot rise beyond the limits of its resources. Bottlenecks here and there may choke off particular expansions. Physical barriers, however, have hardly been a major explanation of the end of expansions.

The creation of bank deposits, which plays such a large role in the expansion, may stop even before the economy reaches capacity output. Remembering past difficulties, or seeing trouble as it appears here and there in the economy, some bankers become cautious and curtail expansion of demand deposits. Perhaps such cessation of expansion is forced on banks by action of monetary authorities in checking the growth of legal reserves. Rising interest rates make some long-term projects unattractive.

Rising costs play a part. As businesses expand, of course, they get the advantage of the new cost-reducing capital equipment they have been installing. Other forces, however, operate to increase costs. Labor receives higher wage rates (and extra payments for overtime). Workers who are less productive must be hired as the economy scrapes the bottom of the manpower barrel. There may be a decline in the willingness of some employees to work as efficiently as formerly (perhaps because jobs seem secure). Near the limit of a plant's productive capacity, added volume does not give much advantage in reducing overhead costs per unit.[5] Rising raw material, interest, transport, and tax costs appear. Inefficient plant may have to be used. Strikes or bottleneck interruptions create costly idleness. After the cream has been skimmed off the market, more selling expense may be needed to get orders.

A relatively small percentage increase in costs will cut profit margins greatly. Assume, for example, that the pretax profit margin has been 10 percent of sales. Then costs per unit rise only one nineteenth, from 90 to 95 cents per dollar of sales. The profit margin has fallen 50 percent, from 10 to 5 cents per dollar.

Firms become less anxious to *increase* the scope of their operations as earnings from added output fall. The number of companies with improving profits starts to decline long before business begins to drop; more and more firms encounter adverse movements in earnings (and hence disappointed expectations). Some business plans and commitments made under the stimulus of boomtime optimism prove sadly wrong. Banks, seeing declines in net profits, will be less willing to renew, and unwilling to expand, loans. Consumers may "balk" at price increases so that firms cannot pass on their higher costs; some companies are bound by custom, contract, or government regulation that keeps their prices from rising "adequately." Higher costs will likely affect, somewhat subtly and immeasurably, psychological factors which influence decisions to expand.

Unemployment appears here and there as work on construction projects turns to the finishing touches before occupancy. Businessmen may come to feel that demand is "saturated." Some needs are certainly met, and the buying they prompted disappears. It is not replaced. During the upswing, for example, enough new office buildings and stores are built to satisfy most present needs at prices that will cover costs. Many of the families who want, and are able, to buy new autos or furniture at present prices have done so. Part of the purchases during the upswing were to meet needs carried over from the depression, some to satisfy normal current demand, and others to meet needs which, if it were not for fears of price rises or for easy installment financing, would have appeared in the market later. Purchases will fall off as the demand gap of the past, present, and future is filled.

Housing presents somewhat the same problem—the eager buyers are

---

[5] Assume fixed overhead costs of $1 million a year. When volume increases by 100,000 units from 100,000 to 200,000, overhead per unit falls from $10 to $5; when volume increases by 100,000 units from 1 million to 1.1 million, overhead costs per unit fall from $1 to 91 cents, a much less spectacular decline.

satisfied; then their part of the expansion demand disappears. Moreover, after inventories reach a certain level, no significant increase is needed to handle even a larger volume of business. Investment spending for *additions* to inventory declines, while that for plant and equipment drops with the completion of facilities to take advantage of the best of the new processes.

Does either "overproduction" or "underconsumption" account for the end of the business expansion? As producers offer more goods on the market, selling at "satisfactory" prices becomes harder. Large output is not unsalable; there is no general lack of people willing to consume. Production generates enough income to buy the goods; the cost of the products is income. The trouble is that buyers will not pay "enough." People are not willing to spend all of their income. Why?

Today, business and personal income tax, and some commodity and sales tax, payments increase more than proportionately with income. As a result, consumer buying, as a percentage of income, *must* fall, and government spending may not rise as much. *Savings*, too, go up. The marginal propensity to consume is less than 1.0. More and more families, and businesses, find that they must use part of their income to repay installment and other debts. (Interest and amortization of nonmortgage installment debt now average nearly one seventh of disposable income.) Buyers who had been purchasing more than they were paying for out of income must now pay for more than they are getting. If there had not been a bulge in consumption and investment spending earlier, there would need be no overall decline now, since buyers somewhere would be purchasing as much as others are repaying.

Rising prices also help bring the expansion to a halt. Some articles are "priced out of the market." Foreigners stop adding to their buying here as they find prices lower elsewhere. Higher prices here, however, invite foreigners to send us goods; as we pay for them, some of our bank balances are transferred to foreigners. If they choose to withdraw gold, pressures on the banking system grow as the reserve base contracts. Domestic consumers also balk at higher prices, creating at least temporary lulls here and there. Higher prices of new buildings and other capital equipment discourage capital formation. Business and family needs for funds to handle normal transactions go up as prices rise; building up larger bank accounts reduces V and constitutes a form of saving which is not matched by capital formation.

Recession and Cumulative Contraction. Thus there are at least moderately clear reasons why an expansion may stop, though the balance of forces will vary from one cycle to another, from one industry or region to another. But can the rise stop without turning into a decline? Will a decline, once started, feed upon itself and cumulate as did the expansion? Part of the expansion, we saw, consisted of *providing capacity for* *expansion.* If expansion stops, its contribution to the upswing disappears. A gap, a vacuum, then appears. Thus if half of the output of the machine tool industry is to provide *more* capacity for manufacturing, and if manufacturing companies stop adding capacity and decide to stay at the size they have reached, there will be a 50 percent decline in output of machine tools. When one part of the economy *stops expanding*, therefore, the businesses that have been supplying it with materials for growth must *decline*, unless, as seems most improbable, something new appears to fill the gap. Enough of our economy is devoted to providing growth that if expansion falls off, decline is almost inevitable.[6] The acceleration principle and the multiplier can both operate downward.

Once a decline has started, powerful forces operate to induce cumulation, like a snowball rolling down hill. Some workers will be laid off, and more will be put on part time. As their earnings decline or disappear, they must cut their own purchasing (though unemployment insurance benefits and welfare payments now assure supports not present in cycles before the New Deal). Businesses find orders falling and reduce employment; orders drop further. Induced investment declines.

New depressants appear. As volume falls, businesses find, not only that they can stop adding to existing facilities but also that they can put maintenance outlays below the long-run normal level. Firms need less office space; vacancies appear and discourage construction. Families get along with the housing they have had and sometimes double up; the demand for new residential construction falls. The employees laid off by these capital goods industries reduce their own buying.

As sales fall, businesses need less inventory. For a time they can meet much demand out of current stocks (without those amounts becoming so low as to disturb normal customer accommodation). Therefore, though current sales may not decline greatly, production may fall much more. A 5 per cent drop in sales at the consumer level may, for a time, result in a 20 per cent (or larger) drop at some earlier levels for several weeks. New orders melt away like butter on a hot griddle. What seemed a good inventory at the factory or wholesale warehouse becomes top heavy. From early 1960 to early 1961, inventory buying fell from an annual rate involving an *addition* of over $11 billion to a *reduction* of nearly $4 billion. In the fourth quarter of 1966, nonfarm business inventories rose at a seasonally adjusted annual rate of $19 billion; in the second quarter of 1967, the rate was $2 billion.

Prices fall. Stores, wholesalers, factories, farmers, and others restlessly feel that it is better to sell early than late to beat the other fellow. Here is speculation again, but now in reverse. As one firm shades prices, others must meet the competition or lose out. The manager rightly fears that if

---

[6] The more that investment for growth is *bunched* in a few years, the greater the chance that growth in several lines will end about the same time rather than being spread out more or less evenly over the years.

he waits to reduce his prices, the best of the market demand will likely be met by a competitor; and other troubles may then become worse for the company which is laggard in cutting prices. Though price reductions are welcome for the consumer and may help speed readjustment, they accentuate one contractive influence. As prices of inventory drop, the backing for some bank loans also falls.[7] Banks press the borrower to repay before conditions get worse. Businesses are thus forced to sell inventory and contract more rapidly than they would otherwise. Prices are forced lower. The overall effects on the economy do not cancel out, with buyers' gains equaling sellers' losses. Money that firms collect from consumers is paid to the banks and then "destroyed" as the borrowing firms' loans and their deposits are canceled. Here again is saving not matched by increased spending on new investment goods. M falls. The stream of potential purchasing power narrows. In the past, bank failures operated to wipe out purchasing power.[8]

Bank deposits and purchasing power also decline as installment and other loans are repaid. During a recession, banks and other lenders will watch requests for installment loans with special care; moreover, consumers will make fewer justified requests for such loans. But the loans that were made during the expansion will continue to be repaid, taking money from consumers without matching it by equal amounts of new funds loaned to consumers. The net repayment of loans (a rise in saving) thus results in wiping out deposits (or keeping them idle in the accounts of finance companies).

If, as we have just seen, falling prices bring one sort of trouble, stable prices create another type of difficulty. Some firms with monopolistic power will try to retain the old price.[9] To the extent that they succeed, the adjustment to bad times must be in the quantity, or the physical volume, of their sales. To illustrate, assume that families decide to cut their spending on gasoline for pleasure driving from an annual rate of $100 to $75. If the price of gasoline stays at 30 cents a gallon, they must cut purchases from 333 to 250 gallons; but if the price were to drop to 22½ cents, they could continue to buy 333 gallons a year. In short, when prices do *not* fall, the quantities sold must decline to absorb all the shock. Employment and use of materials and equipment drop more than would

[7] Assume that a bank had loaned 70 percent of the market value of a wool inventory when wool was selling at about $4 a pound (some months after fighting began in Korea). If the price of wool falls to $3, as it did (on the way down to well under $2), the banker may get uneasy and press for sale at once; he knows that if the price falls below $2.80, he will not be able to get his money back from sale of the wool.

[8] Even if the stock of money were not to decline, its failure to grow with expansion in the labor supply and potential capacity for production would act as a depressant, as we noted in Chapter 8.

[9] Public utility rates regulated by government agencies are notably stable. So also are many of the tax elements in price—property taxes and excise taxes, such as 10 cents or more per gallon of gasoline.

otherwise be "necessary"; the men who thus lose work, which they would have had, obviously suffer loss of purchasing power. Inflexibility of prices thus drags down business, some kinds more than others. One of the most important groups of prices, the price of labor (wage rates), is generally inflexible downward. If workers refuse to lower their wage rates when demand is dropping, unemployment will probably rise more than if wage rates were reduced.[10]

Business earnings fall. Losses appear. Managers have less money to enlarge capacity and certainly less incentive to do so. Skimping on spending may be the best way to adjust to losses and in some cases to a squeeze for liquid funds. Poor business reduces the price of existing capital assets: machinery, real estate, and securities. As a result, people wanting to buy either capital goods or securities will tend to buy what already exists because the prices are favorable. Why build a new house if an older one is cheaper, as it will be unless production costs fall by more than is probable?

Gloom and pessimism will add their intangible, sometimes irrational, depressing effects. Doubt and uncertainty make us decide against going ahead with new purchases or investment. Unwarranted fears can lead to bad judgments. Yet, for many businesses, the fear is justified. The result of a bad move may be the loss of much more than is involved in the particular action. A little push may send the firm over the edge into bankruptcy, leading to the forced sale of assets at sacrifice prices and wiping out other values. Mortgage foreclosures, as well as bankruptcies, force sales that depress prices abnormally, and both cause and justify extreme caution.

Why Does Contraction Stop? The fall does not continue forever. What makes it stop? The reasons are not always the same. Some forces within the economic system itself tend to check the drop; others can come from outside—a "lift" from foreign orders. A good crop requires more labor and equipment for handling. Population grows. Eventually, families and businesses with financial resources face needs which they do not want to postpone any longer. Durable and semidurable consumer goods, machinery and other productive facilities, wear out or become outdated. New

---

[10] Warning! This is a controversial issue. Economists agree that individual firms have a better chance of maintaining employment if they can cut wage rates, costs, and selling prices when demand falls. Economists disagree about the effects on the whole economy if many businesses were to reduce wage rates. In the past, wage rates did not fall significantly until a substantial number of months after business and employment began to decline. More recently, the growth of union power has added obstacles to wage rate reductions. In each postwar contraction, many unions have even received increases. A year after recession began in 1957, and again in 1961, most of the more than 60 industries for which the Bureau of Labor Statistics collects data each month were paying higher hourly wage rates. The result appeared even in several industries suffering serious unemployment. Wage rate reductions have been rare in postwar recessions.

models or new products have appeal. Purchases increase. Pressure to reduce costs induces some businesses to install better equipment. Payment is made with money that has been held idle in bank accounts or by borrowing which creates new deposits, money added to the income stream. Advertising, energetic selling, and intense efforts to design new articles stimulate buying. So does the availability of easy financing.

Innovations of a bigger kind may help bring the turn. Invention and discovery go on during the contraction, slower in some cases but faster in others. Some new possibilities have unquestioned merit; others seem good risks. Existing firms, and even new ones, select promising developments and begin spending money for materials, plant, and labor to get the new product under way. The adoption and the financing of innovations are unpredictable and subject to many hazards and queer chances; yet they help offset contractions and even start an upswing.

As some costs of production fall, their decline can help stop the general contraction of business. Workers may produce more per hour for fear of losing their jobs otherwise; employers will try to weed out the poorer employees and hold on to the most efficient. Raw materials get cheaper; suppliers quote lower prices; managements try harder to operate more efficiently.

As the dollar buys more, money comes out of hiding. At the lower price level, less money need be held to finance transactions. Purchases and output increase. The flood of truly distress sales passes, as inventory is "worked off" and weakly held debt wiped out or refinanced. Forced liquidation gets smaller. The easing relieves some of the downward pressure, real and psychological.

Banks become more willing to lend. As they accumulate excess reserves, bankers are *able* to make new loans; they compete harder; interest rates fall. Borrowers find not only that costs of borrowing decline but also that loans are more readily available. The stream of purchasing power grows—for capital equipment as well as for consumer goods.

By open-market purchases that pump excess reserves into the banking system, the monetary authorities can play a part in reversing the "destruction" of bank deposits and in offsetting the growth of hoarding (a fall in V or a rise of savings not spent for new investment goods). Government itself can inject purchasing power into the economy. It can enter as a purchaser of capital goods, largely construction, and by transfer payments which enable families to buy more consumer goods. Moreover, important tax liabilities—on businesses and on families—fall more, percentagewise, than does income. In fact, the business which suffers losses will generally get a refund of taxes paid in prior profit years.

Conclusion.   Our trip around the cycle has been shorter and more direct than one around any real cycle. Actual events are more complex. We have failed to *measure:* (1) the amounts by which elements lead or lag,

(2) the amounts by which they fluctuate, or (3) the amount by which one part of the cycle depends upon what has happened in earlier phases. Having made the trip, however, we are better able to view the whole landscape, and especially the interrelations of varied parts.

The trip will save us from one pitfall: reliance upon a *simple* theory of cycles or fluctuations. Simple theories exist. They give useful insights. At best, however, simple explanations are partial.

FORCES GIVING RISE TO FLUCTUATIONS

Now let us stand off a bit and look at elements of the economic system which seem to account for fluctuations. Such a look, of course, must be at past experience, and we know that the economy changes. In the last 15 years or so, there have been large structural changes in the tax system, in financing business and consumers, in business management, in international trade. As a result, analysis of historical data will be less than perfectly applicable to the future.

1. *Elements within the economic system contribute to fluctuation.*[11] Forces that can *initiate* changes may come from outside: the weather and international affairs. Other initiating forces have origins that are at least partly noneconomic. Changes in total population, in the number of marriages or new households formed, or even in age distribution may create elements of instability. Wars, technical discovery, and changes in government budgets modify the movements in the cycle. Clearly, our economic system contains elements that create successive ups and downs. Equally clear is the fact that forces outside this interrelated system operate on these elements. Exceptional, perhaps random, forces—dominant leaders, striking events, for example—may act as forces initiating change or acting as exceptional offsets to developments taking place.

2. *Fluctuations result partly from our freedom.* When we are able to change our minds on what to consume, or on where and how and when to invest, we are able to affect the lives of others.

3. *The large role of durable goods in our consumption raises our susceptibility to fluctuations.* If we existed, poorly, on things that are short-lived, we could vary our spending less than today. Now we can either buy such things as household equipment in anticipation of needs, or wait months or years until needs press imperatively. Spending, production, and employment in durable consumer goods fluctuate more than in nondurables. Examine the evidence graphed in Figure 11–3. A small rise in income may bring a much larger proportionate increase in the demands for the services of a durable good. Or a rise in demand for the services of a durable, such as garbage disposal units, may lead to a large rise in purchases of the units until a considerable stock is obtained, a stock that will provide the services for several years with little more expenditure.

---

[11] The term *endogenous* is often applied to those forces within the system. Forces from outside are *exogenous*.

FIGURE 11–3.   Consumer Buying of Autos and Food, 1957–64 *

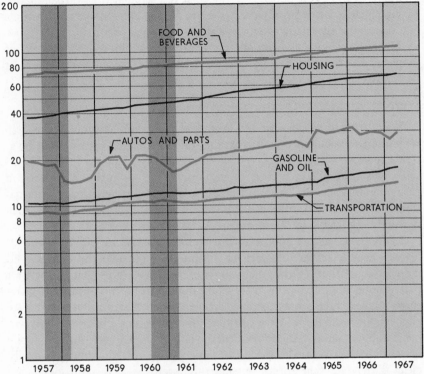

* By quarters, seasonally adjusted annual rates.
† Does not include alcoholic beverages.
Source: Survey of Current Business.

The acceleration principle is in evidence. The spending to buy the goods may spurt and then fall back, even though income does not decline. The condition of durable equipment which provides services will affect the short-run outlook of business. Longevity, greater for houses than auto tires, will affect postponability. Swings in inventory can be relatively large.

Changes in manufacturers' inventory investment have been particularly significant during business cycles, especially in contractions. During the recessions of 1948–49, 1953–54, and 1957–58, they accounted for 79, 56, and 25 per cent of the change in gross national product from the peak to the trough business cycle quarters. . . . During expansions change in investment tends to reach a maximum during the first half of the expansion. . . .[12]

4. *Economic growth is likely to subject an economy to fluctuations.* Spending on capital goods, the things that typify growth, will fluctuate more widely than consumer spending. Capital goods output (including housing) constitutes less than one eighth of GNP. Yet this output is

[12] T. M. Stanback, Jr., *Postwar Cycles in Manufacturers' Inventories* (New York: National Bureau of Economic Research, 1962), p. 12.

subject to such alterations of good and ill fortune that this segment of the economy accounts for a large fraction of the total fluctuations in output. Figure 11–4 shows how total gross private domestic investment and inventory change have fluctuated since World War II in relation to GNP. Capital formation produces a much larger percentage of the fluctuation in total production than its percentage of GNP, which averages around 15 percent. Inventory change can be especially unsettling. Invention, discovery, entrepreneurial initiative, and forecasts of profitability do not come in a smooth, even flow. Fluctuations are a price we pay for innovation and progress. Surges and slumps in investment, magnified by the forces of the

FIGURE 11–4.   Changes in GNP, Gross Private Domestic Investment, and Business Inventories (By Quarters, 1952–66)

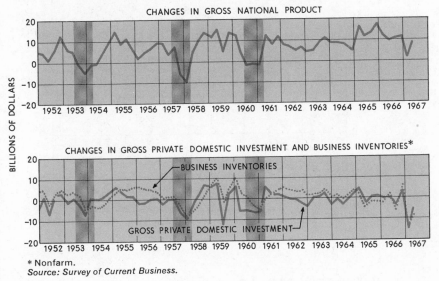

* Nonfarm.
Source: Survey of Current Business.

multiplier, seem certain. The possibility of getting capital formation when it appears best to the people making the decisions may result in unevenness in economic growth. Economically healthy growth, however, does not require big surges and then steep declines. Figure 11–5 shows that unemployment is closely, but inversely, related to changes in business capital spending on fixed investment.

5. *Moods, emotions, psychological attitudes affect decisions.* One man's optimism is sometimes matched by another's pessimism. On balance, however, there seems to be a tendency in economic affairs for us to share each others' feelings. A dominant mood rolls and grows like a snowball. A dramatic event or decisive leadership may tip a balance. For a time the mood actually helps create conditions which justify it: general optimism stimulates business, pessimism depresses. An important molder of business psychology is the state of profit. And profits fluctuate relatively more

than other important elements of our economy. (Unlike most economic magnitudes, profits can and do become negative.) The business spending that is most amenable to wide swings—spending on capital goods and inventory—tends to depend upon attitudes which themselves result in part from changes in the volatile element of profit. Attitudes, of course,

FIGURE 11–5. Business Fixed Investment and Unemployment Relation of Changes, 1948–65

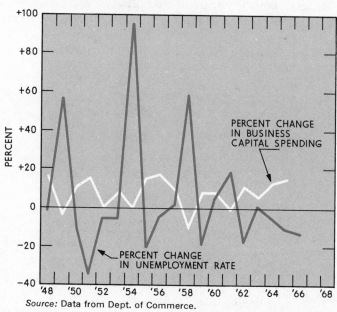

Source: Data from Dept. of Commerce.

are the fruit of many subtle forces; wide-scale concern over instability and increased knowledge about the economy have led to greater caution in investment by leading businesses. Perhaps the conditions of boom may not in the future, as in the past, lead to so many examples of poor business judgment and actions that can cause only trouble when the painful, but inevitable, correction occurs.

6. *International trade* is less important in business cycles in our economy than in many other countries, such as Australia or Belgium. Changes in the level of business activity in one country flow to other parts of the world. Cyclical developments in one land are to some extent the result of what happens in many near and remote spots. Impacts vary widely, of course. Canada is affected more by changes in the United States than Brazil is affected by what happens in Finland. The relative size and internal diversification of economies is one factor accounting for such differences; distances and the composition of trade are others. In the past,

movements of gold had special significance; by changing monetary reserves, a shift of gold could lead to a multiplied change in the amount of
money, including, of course, deposits in commercial banks.

In much of the world, the United States included, buffers now reduce
the influence of impacts from foreign trade. Some countries have deliberately tried to set up shields that insulate them against influences from
foreign economies, but complete insulation is neither possible nor desirable.

When one economy is expanding more rapidly than the rest of the
world, its consumers, individual and business, will increase their consumption of imports. This rise reduces the dollars spent on home products, that
is, the purchasing power at home, and increases it abroad, transferring the
forces of expansion. In a contraction, on the other hand, consumers
reduce imports, cutting both the outflow of funds and demands in other
countries, depressing business there. The extent to which an economy will
be pulled up or down by fluctuations in outside countries will depend
upon the relative weight of foreign trade. To some extent, our cycles are
the product of expansion and contraction abroad. A boom in Europe
helped cushion the 1960–61 business decline in America.

7. Parts of our economy are more *flexible* than others. We can adjust
to some change in small doses and without great disturbance. If income
declines, it is easier to shift food spending to cheaper items than to reduce
the interest on the mortgage. If business drops off, an employer may find
it impossible to reduce the hourly pay rate of his employees but fairly
easy to reduce the hours worked per week. Things that are inflexible
cannot adjust. More of the shock must then be absorbed by parts that *are*
free to move. If, as is not the case, wage rates and other prices were to
adjust easily to changing conditions, the *quantities* (of employment and
physical production) would fluctuate less than if wage rates and prices are
more rigid; many prices and wage rates, we know, respond only a little,
and then slowly, as demand and supply conditions change. The change
compels some sort of response, and quantity feels the brunt. It may seem a
bit odd to assert that business, union, or government actions to stabilize
particular prices and wage rates will in fact aggravate *overall* instability.
Nevertheless, such is probably the case. Adjustment to the inevitable
changes of economic life is easier as a myriad of small moves than fewer
large ones; inflexibilities in some cases require larger changes than in others
from any given amount of disturbance.

8. *Inflexibility also arises out of debt.* When businesses have fixed
debts, the "leverage" causes profits to rise more rapidly than business
volume after some point; unwarranted optimism may than result, leading
to unwise risk.[13] On the downswing the results are more marked. The fall

---

[13] Assume two businesses, each with $1 million physical equipment. One has debts
(bonds and mortgages) of $600,000 on which it must pay 5 percent ($30,000). The
other has no debts. Both earn 6 percent on capital, $60,000. The first has $30,000 left

in profits may seem more dismal than the underlying facts justify, leading to exaggerated pessimism. Worse still, individuals and firms which cannot meet their debt obligations during a contraction may be thrown into bankruptcy. This not only brings loss to the owners but also disrupts the business. Moreover, forced liquidation of inventory and capital assets will get other firms into trouble. The mere possibility of bankruptcy induces some managements to follow especially cautious policies; they "play things safer." In general, therefore, the more that business relies upon debt in obtaining funds to pay for investment goods, the more will booms and depressions tend to feed upon themselves. The need to repay debt requires debtors to save fixed amounts; those whose incomes go down will be forced to reduce their buying more than if the debt did not compel so much saving.

9. A chief feature of the cyclical process is the *expansion and contraction of bank deposits*.[14] Here, certainly, is one reason for cumulation. If banks were to operate differently, business fluctuations would be different. In this respect, business cycles depend upon the functioning of institutions which not only can and do change but which are subject to deliberate official control. Velocity of circulation of money also changes and can contribute to instability, but it is not controllable by monetary officials.

The discussion so far has said little about *government*. Yet it operates on a huge scale. Its actions result from human decisions which may be conscious and carefully considered or haphazard, fickle, and ignorant. Three different types of government activity should be distinguished: (*a*) the formation of general institutions, affecting the structure of the economy—the banking system, the planning of land use, the tax treatment of new investment; (*b*) dealing with specific situations, either according to some prearranged system or as developments arise; (*c*) the sheer magnitude of government activity, vast and subject to many noneconomic considerations, such as changes in defense spending.

FORECASTING

Fluctuations in national income and employment result in part from conditions such as freedom and the opportunity for economic progress that are essential for the good life. Some of the causes, however, are not

---

for owners (before taxes), the second $60,000. Now assume business improves so that they earn 8 percent (one third more): profit for the first company rises from $30,000 to $50,000 ($20,000), two thirds for the owners (before taxes); while for the second firm the rise from $60,000 to $80,000 is one third for the owners (before taxes). Earnings then drop to 3 percent on capital, $30,000. Owners of the first company have no profit at all since everything goes to pay interest. Owners of the second have $30,000.

[14] Some economists believe that uneven, jerky growth in the stock of money creates instability in the economy even in the absence of any actual contraction of the quantity of money.

unquestionably good in themselves: swings of mass psychology, uneven and at times perverse fluctuations in the stock of money, inflexible prices. Can we get more stability without disadvantages which outweigh the benefits? Yes. Success, however, requires accurate forecasting.

How will economic activity develop in the next few months and over a longer period under existing policies? What changes within the power of authorities would lead to what kinds of results? In what amounts? Expert appraisals disagree about the reliability of various forecasting techniques. Organizations selling forecasting services have incentive to direct attention to successes, ignore the failures. Unquestionably, however, various approaches now in use contribute to improved understanding of what lies ahead.

The scholarly research of the (private) National Bureau of Economic Research has laid the foundation for one approach to forecasting. Exhaustive analysis of the past has revealed about 90 "series" of economic data which have generally been trustworthy indicators of cyclical movements. Thirty-six leading series in nine separate areas of economic activity— marginal employment adjustments (5), formation of business enterprises (2), new investment commitments (8), inventory investment and purchasing (7), sensitive commodity prices (1), stock prices (1), profits and profit margins (4), flows of money and credit (6), and credit difficulties (2)—move ahead of the economy as a whole. Another 25 series usually *coincide* with the general trend of business during the cycle. A third group of 11 series *lag* behind. A fourth group, comprised mostly of series on the federal government, also help to indicate economic change.[15] The Bureau has also prepared statistical measures of the *diffusion* of changes through the economy, their breadth and depth.

Business Cycle Developments, a Department of Commerce monthly, presents figures on these series of data and others arranged in categories which research has shown to be important; electronic computers now perform the complex calculations so quickly that businessmen and government officials have the significant facts weeks or months earlier than used to be the case. Hopefully, these revelations of the recent past will also indicate approaching events, especially a turning point. Unfortunately, the best inference must still be uncertain. Each group or type of average experience—such as that industrial stock prices for nearly a century have turned down on the average from 3 to 4 months before business in general—covers wide diversity. Any movement, however, may turn out to be only a temporary "jiggle," not a true change in direction. The signals are often mixed and inconclusive. Therefore, clear indication of a turning point does not necessarily precede by many weeks the actual event.

[15] G. H. Moore and J. Shiskin, *Indicators of Business Expansions and Contractions* (New York: Columbia University Press, 1967).

Most forecasters rely heavily upon methods which seek to predict total demand. For each category of GNP—C plus *I* plus *G* plus net foreign demand—forecasters study the major subgroups, i.e., the various elements of investment, such as types of construction, plant and equipment expenditure (industry by industry), and other subgroups of investment. An estimate of the total of *C* + *I* + *G* for the coming quarter or entire year will emerge. But how can one add parts when elements depend upon each other as well as upon other developments?

Different approaches are used to answer this question, each requiring extensive information about what the economy is doing and about plans for the future. Governmental agencies and many private organizations collect and publish data on what has occurred, last month or yesterday. Then crude or more elaborate methods utilize this information to suggest what lies ahead. For example, *econometric* study of past relationships between measurable economic quantities—interest and marriage rates as related to housing demand, disposable income and holdings of cash as related to consumer expenditure—will provide formulas which, it is hoped, will enable us to use current data to learn what lies ahead.

Economic forecasting is complicated by *feedback*. Just as facts registering on a thermostat set up reactions which change conditions, economic predictions themselves will cause some revision of private plans and perhaps lead to government action—monetary, fiscal, or other—which alters the conditions assumed in making the forecast. The economy, however, does not react so mechanically as a heating system. The results of the feedback from the thermostat are known, but not those from the economic forecast.[16]

Our knowledge of *V* for the next month or year, or of the multiplier or the force of acceleration, remains highly uncertain. A forecast error or a change in conditions can upset carefully prepared plans. Changes in the net foreign balance can be significant in relation to *changes* in national income; consequently, surprises developing abroad can have more than insignificant effect. The continuing force of longer run trends will accentuate some cyclical changes, offset others; experience may provide little basis for estimating the amount of such modification.

Predictions are often less helpful than they appear; for example, the only serious likelihood may be that within the next year GNP will vary up or down 3 percent—about $24 billion one way or the other (a total of $48 billion), with either extreme improbable. A forecasting error of $15

---

[16] "One of the basic difficulties in making quantitative predictions of the effects of public-policy changes on the course of economic events is the uncertainty concerning the impact of the inauguration of a new program on the expectations of individuals. . . . it is even conceivable that a sufficiently authoritative and credible announcement that steps will be taken to stabilize the economy may so change expectations that stabilization is achieved without any concrete steps actually having to be taken." (W. S. Vickrey, *Metastatics and Macroeconomics* [New York: Harcourt, Brace & World, Inc., 1964], pp. 270–71.)

billion would be less than 2 percent of GNP. This hardly seems large. Yet it is over one third of the largest probable change. More significant, it is perhaps half of any likely change, and an error of 50 percent can lead to costly mistakes.

In forecasting government finances, forecasters have not made a record which inspires high confidence. The actual 1958 federal budget deficit was seven times the official estimate made 7 months before the end of the

FIGURE 11–6. Certainty of Forecasts of Cyclical Peaks and Troughs, 1948–61

The line up from zero marks the peak or trough of business cycles in the postwar period. The upper curve shows that eight analysts making forecasts were accurate in predicting 3 months in advance in only about 40 percent of the cases. Even 3 months after the trough had passed, only about 80 percent of the estimates had yet identified it. The record regarding peaks was even less satisfactory.

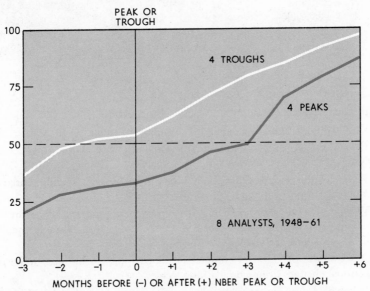

Source: National Bureau of Economic Research, *Contributions to Economic Knowledge Through Research* (New York, 1967), p. 32. Based on work of V. Zarnowitz and R. Fels in analyzing the work of leading forecasters.

fiscal year; for 1963 one concept of the deficit, as estimated when the year was half over, was almost "on the nose" while another was twice as large as the actual and a third one fourth too low. Which deserves greatest respect? Views will differ. Look carefully at Figure 11–6.

The economy is complex and varied. One region or industry goes in one direction, while others move in varied ways.[17] Whatever actions

[17] Commercial construction rose during the 1957–58 recession while auto production dropped about 30 percent. During the 1962–63 economic expansion, per capita personal income in the Dakotas dropped while that in Delaware rose by almost twice the national average. From early 1966 to early 1967, business investment in machinery and equipment went up one tenth while outlays on new housing dropped one fifth (seasonally adjusted annual sales).

government takes to alter the course of the cycle—interest rate changes, spending, and taxing—will apply in fact to *particular* persons, regions, and industries. Consequently, forecasts of broad trends need to be supplemented by predictions for particular segments of the economy. Such forecasting requires special data and skills. The results may be excellent or, as businessmen with good staffs have sometimes found, distressingly misleading.

Techniques of prediction are being elaborated and refined. Data are improving. But no assuredly satisfactory methods can appear "where wealth and freedom reign."

TERMS AND CONCEPTS

seasonal change	depression	endogenous
secular trend	prosperity	exogenous
business cycle	turning point	econometrics
expansion	cumulation	forecasting
contraction	acceleration principle	

QUESTIONS

1. In what respects are business cycles "self-generating"?
2. Would fluctuations be smaller if the supply of money were stable? Why?
3. Which causes of economic fluctuations originate within the economic system and which are noneconomic?
4. Why do you suppose that fluctuations in investment spending attract so much attention from students of business cycles?
5. Why may companies pursuing their own best interests adopt inventory policies that tend to make business as a whole more unstable than businessmen would prefer?
6. Describe the process of "cumulative contraction" in business activity. Do seasonal changes bring cumulation? Why?
7. What part does the acceleration principle play in expansion? Why might a businessman expand his plant by more than (or less than) needed to meet the increased demand for his products over the next year?
8. "Wage rate and price maladjustments growing out of a business boom accentuate the difficulties of the contraction." Discuss.
9. Discuss forces which may account for the turning points in business cycles.
10. "Although no one wants a depression, business contractions result partly from the fact that we have great freedom to do what we want." Discuss.
11. It is sometimes said that to make full use of our productive capacity we must always be adding to it. Discuss.
12. Discuss economic forecasting.
13. Can a business expansion end because of physical limits on productive capacity? Why? Does the opposite apply to a contraction?

12

EMPLOYMENT, PRICES, AND OTHER GOALS

The Congress hereby declares that it is the continuing policy and responsibility of the Federal Government to use all practicable means consistent with its needs and obligations and other essential considerations of national policy, with the assistance and co-operation of industry, agriculture, labor, and State and local governments, to co-ordinate and utilize all its plans, functions, and resources for the purpose of creating and maintaining, in a manner calculated to foster and promote free competitive enterprise and the general welfare, conditions under which there will be afforded useful employment opportunities, including self employment, to those able, willing and seeking to work, and to promote maximum employment, production and purchasing power.

The sentence above, from the Employment Act of 1946, commits our national government. But to what? Not specifically to either full employment or the prevention of inflation, two objectives frequently associated with broad stabilization policy. The act's words, you can see, deal with both goals and means and yet with neither fully or concretely. As statesmen, professors, and others have worked during a 22-year period to make the act a success, a continuing quesiton has been, "What do we want?" Much of the answer seems obviously easy. But not all. This chapter deals with the "what" and "why" of objectives. The next discusses the "how."

OBJECTIVES AS FINAL ENDS AND AS MEANS TO OTHER ENDS

Objectives—of individuals and of groups—are of many types. Some are life's "ultimates," as nearly as a mortal can express them. A sample list could include health and vigor, freedom, affection, opportunity, peace, beauty, personal and national security, excitement, progress, hope, humor, variety, and justice. Other things which we sometimes call ends or objec-

285

tives are more truly instruments or means. They are intermediate, to be judged on the basis of their effectiveness in serving the more basic goals. Discussions of economic policy may deal so extensively with instruments as to seem to elevate means to the high status of ends. If they are desirable, the reasons must be found in whatever they help achieve. For example, at one time or another low interest rates, budget balance, and retaining gold have seemed to be objectives of public policy. None, however, in itself is inherently important. Focus of attention on such goals can misguide policy. Much the same applies to reducing cyclical instability.

The term "economic stabilization" does not convey the full sense of the relevant goals. We also want progress. And stability and progress as goals will sometimes conflict, especially in the short run. Development, growth, advance—all inevitably mean doing things differently. Freedom, opportunity, and hope itself all require an opportunity to change. Yet change can become a positive hindrance. Even stimulation can degenerate into disruption. Instability has often become a costly evil. A large measure of economic stability is essential for progressive change—not stability as a straightjacket but something which replaces the severe parts of business cycles.

Neither this country nor any other, except to some extent in time of war, will have an explicit, clearly articulated, formulation of collective objectives. For all its merits, the Employment Act of 1946 does not formulate a *set* of goals. The statement of purposes and of priorities among them is certainly not complete enough to serve as a basis for practical action. No consensus emerges, nothing clear enough to indicate how to resolve hard questions. Nevertheless, decisions must be made.

FULL EMPLOYMENT

"Full," "maximum," or "high" employment—"low" or "minimum" unemployement—will appear generally as an objective of prime and fundamental importance. To some extent it is almost a final end. But it is also more. As a *means*, too, full employment has such value as to command high priority in any ranking of the things federal policy seeks to achieve.

Human Value of Jobs.   Undesired idleness of men and women, and of their nonhuman possessions, means loss of attainable income. Any avoidable deprivation of material well-being is bad in itself. In a poor world or country—and ours will not soon be one of plenty—such losses are so obviously evil that further condemnation should need no underlining. The resolution of racial conflict, the myriad problems of cities and farms, of youth and the aged, will be less difficult when employment is high.

More, however, remains to be said. For many people, certainly, idleness brings loss of human dignity and of personal satisfaction. These qualities, though falling in a different scale from money equivalent, are very much part of the whole which should command attention in any discussion of human affairs. The value of meaningful activity must rank high, most of all to each individual but also to others in society. Social discontent with the tragic results it can bring will not be ended by full employment. But unemployment certainly makes such things worse.

Nevertheless, despite the desirability of full employment, some commentary is in order.

What Is Full Employment?   Most national income is compensation for human services. Factories and other nonhuman capacity are, of course, decidedly important; the fullness with which they are utilized directly affects human welfare. Yet our concern centers on the employment of human productive capacity. For, in general, the more fully the labor force is employed, the more completely will we be utilizing machinery, railroads, power lines, and other such instruments of production.[1]

One thing is clear: full employment does not mean everyone working all the time. The aged, children, the infirm, and some other groups will be excluded. But at what age or other condition should the line be drawn? What about housewives whose time is not fully absorbed by work at home? Undoubtedly, many Americans not now "in the labor force," people not actively seeking jobs, would welcome at least part-time work if the conditions were favorable. Around many margins, it is hard to determine whether a particular group is fully employed.

No one, of course, wants to work 24 hours a day, 7 days a week, 52 weeks a year. Some of us, however, want to work more than others. A college student may want only a 15-hour-a-week job. One man may feel fully employed when he works 35 hours a week, while another thinks 48 hours appropriate, and still others hope to work more. "Full employment," therefore, means more than having a job. A man with a job but limited against his wishes to part time is not fully employed. In contrast, a person required to work long hours of overtime, or to sacrifice his vacation, may be overfully employed. To date, we have no agreement on the average number of hours in a standard workyear.

Another unsolved problem involves rate of pay. If there is a job available at a lower rate of pay than I want to accept, I may remain unemployed. The reason, however, is not the absence of a chance to work. Should government policy undertake to provide me a job at the rate of pay I want? Some unemployment—but no one knows how much—arises and continues because men and women insist upon higher wage rates than employers and customers will pay.

The ceaseless change of economic life creates, and requires some unem-

---

[1] See Chapter 15 for an illustration of the difficulty of defining "capacity" use of physical equipment.

ployment. The movements of the seasons, the cycles of graduation from school and college, the ups and downs of specific businesses, changeovers to new models—these and other such factors inevitably mean that some people wanting work will not have it, even in times of boom. Illness, from the common cold to serious heart disease, produces unemployment. The search for better jobs, sometimes involving a move to another community, creates its own special kind of unemployment. One big construction job will not always follow another in the same locality. Employers discharging the square pegs which have gotten into round holes give rise to unemployment of a type essential for efficiency. Strikes create some unemployment, not only for the strikers but also for workers whose markets decline or whose necessary supplies no longer arrive.

To operate efficiently an economy needs flexibility. Growing businesses can expand more easily if the right kind of labor can be hired without drawing workers away from other employers. Unemployment provides one form of flexibility, but no one knows how much will give the best results. If the average person loses a week's work a year (except for vacations), employment averages about 2 percent. Job shifts alone will often require more than one week, while choosing a new job if a large number are open can occupy several weeks if a person can afford to wait. And is it not better to be able to take time to look for the best rather than be forced to accept something quickly?

Types of Unemployment. Neither "full" nor "maximum" as applied to employment leads to a clear concept. How large is "the labor force?" We have no unambiguous measure. Unemployment has many causes. Three major types, other than seasonal, can be distinguished, but not precisely: (1) frictional—people changing jobs and new entrants to the labor force; (2) cyclical—the men and the women who are out of work or on part time because the general level of business activity has dropped, presumably because of inadequate total demand; those people may or may not still have jobs; (3) structural—the people unemployed because they lack the skills desired by employers, or have some physical or mental disability, or have been displaced by machines, or because of a decline in the industry or region with which they have been (or might be) identified, or for other reasons which involve the "structure" of the economy.

These three groups cannot be demarcated clearly. They present different kinds of problems. They require different remedies. How much joblessness does result from a shortage of total demand? Experts disagree. No dispute arises on two points, however: The stimulation of total demand (1) will reduce all types of unemployment but (2) will not eliminate unemployment before labor shortages and price-level increases appear.

Causes of unemployment sometimes seem clear and obvious. When unemployment reaches low levels, however, when unfilled job openings rise from a few hundred thousand to a million or more, the reasons for the unemployment which remains are probably complex. Discussions of causes of unemployment often omit one element of no small significance—the wage rate. "Labor"—in the aggregate and in particular occupations, industries, and companies—can price itself out of work; $800 billion of demand (for the constituents of GNP) will buy fewer man-hours at an average rate of $3.80 than at one of $3.50. It was no accident that rates of unemployment among young people with little training have gone up when the legal minimum wage has been increased and coverage broadened. What is the relation of wage rates to cost-push inflation, to general and specific unemployment, to creeping inflation—and to public policy generally? At issue lies one of the most difficult problems of economic policy, one to which we shall return later.

Measurement. U.S. government agencies estimate unemployment by sample surveys which ask, in effect, whether a person has a job or is seeking one. All those answering "Yes" to either question are considered members of the civilian *labor force*. When this method is used, an average of 4 percent of the labor force unemployed seems to be near the reasonable minimum.[2] Under such conditions employers will ordinarily have many unfilled jobs for which they are seeking satisfactory workers—but about which we have no reliable data.

The 4 percent figure does seem high. It is an average, however, and includes groups which tend to show considerable unemployment even in times of high prosperity. Some young people with little experience frequently report themselves seeking a job quite a time before they begin work.

Figures now give more detail about the numbers of jobseekers by age, sex, and color and for different parts of the country than used to be the case. The improvement in information will provide help in analysis and guidance of policy. Unhappily, our data on job openings and vacancies are much less complete.

Indifference as an Obstacle. Does the public *really* want the labor force to be about as fully employed as possible? Perhaps not. Experience of the last dozen years suggests a distressing thought: A public almost "fully" employed—95 percent or so—may have little enthusiasm for acting to raise employment (or reduce unemployment) by one percent-

---

[2] It would be far from an acceptable goal, of course, if many persons with jobs were working "short time." The measurement of the total labor force and of the number employed presents difficulties which still arouse much debate. Our measure of the labor force includes many housewives, young people (especially students), and older persons who are not "firmly attached" to the labor force. Some do not want jobs strongly; some are interested in seasonal work only; and some have special requirements, such as part-time employment of special types. For a more extensive discussion of this and related topics of this chapter see C. Lowell Harriss, *Money and Banking* (2d ed.; Boston: Allyn and Bacon, 1965), Part Five.

age point. That single point and the billions of GNP it represents may seem rather important to an economist, and highly so to the million or so young people (and their family members) most directly affected. To the vast majority of the public, however, the problem will appear remote and of rather low urgency. Many more people, in fact, may encounter annoying results of worker shortages than of joblessness.

Full employment in itself has "costs," to individuals, groups, and to the whole economy. Here, there, and perhaps through most of the economy, labor shortages create difficulties for those who cannot readily (for example, by paying more) get what they want as promptly as otherwise—whether a taxi, nursing service, repairs, or the more popular manufactured products. Although total output at 96 percent employment exceeds that at 94 percent, some disadvantages result. One hesitates to suggest that business recession and avoidable unemployment are anything but evil. However, experience suggests ("proves" may be too strong a term) that periods of economic slack do help prepare conditions for higher employment later while avoiding inflation.

AVOIDANCE OF INFLATION

Employment has human value. Price-level stability in and of itself cannot claim comparable merit. Yet both price-level stability and employment are means to ends beyond themselves. Price-level changes affect (1) the total of real output and (2) the way it is shared. Each is of true significance.

Inflation means a rise in the general level of prices—a decline in the purchasing power of the dollar. Measurement will perhaps always be difficult, for reasons cited in Chapter 8. Sometimes, however, there can be no doubt that inflation has occurred. We now look at causes, then effects.

Causes of Inflation: Demand-Pull.

Prices rise when buyers are both able and willing to pay more. What causes such an increase in willingness and ability? The main reason is that people have more to spend. Where do they get the money? Some may be dollars that the public has been holding idle. Others may be newly created as a result of consumer borrowing from banks.

Another source, one more generally apparent, will be rising income. Additional dollars come from employers. They get the additional funds by borrowing from banks or by selling to consumers or governments who borrow from banks.

The initial origin (if there is one) of this chain reaction is not our concern here, but rather, the fact that businesses and individuals will go into debt to banks because the probable benefits seem greater than the costs. Good business prospects certainly make borrowing attractive. Optimism tends to induce an expansion in the stock of money, which in turn encourages buying. Rising prices themselves increase the need for dollars for transactions.

Governments issue currency or borrow when their spending exceeds revenue. A government will borrow from banks when unwilling to pay the higher interest rates demanded by other potential lenders (Banks lend, of course, only if they have the necessary reserves. Clearly, one link in the chain of causation of inflation is the fixing of the size of bank reserves.) National governments increase the stock of money on a large scale chiefly because of war. Yet war is not the only reason. Of the countries shown on Figure 8–4, those with worst inflation in the 1950's were not involved in war. Ambitious plans for economic development and other forces can stimulate government spending and discourage tax increases; budget deficits result, to be financed by money creation.

National income depends in part upon the considerations which lead people to save and to invest (Chapter 10). Inflation itself may reduce voluntary saving while boosting the desire to acquire investment goods—leading to more reliance upon banks as a source of dollars. Inflation will also create the expectation that prices are to rise further. In consequence, a rational person will try to hold more goods and less money, to spend dollars more quickly, thus *raising velocity*. Demand gets another pull.

Rising Output. Cannot output rise to offset the price-raising effects of more spending? When there is idle productive capacity, the added spending can, in effect, lead to an increase in output (at perhaps about the same cost per unit as formerly). When the economy is operating at essentially full capacity, however, not much more can be produced; injection of added purchasing power will not meet up with a matching increase in goods and services. More money for the same output means higher prices. The massive productive capacity of America's economy does help provide a safeguard against rapid inflation in peacetime. The production potential, however, will not assuredly prevent creeping inflation.

The Cost-Push. Peacetime pressures *raising costs* have for many years given prices many an upward *push*, as contrasted with the pulls of demand. If production costs rise, goods will be offered (on a sustained basis) only at higher prices. Does the "cost-push" cause inflation? What raises costs? Or, what makes the biggest cost, wages, go up more than labor productivity?

Powerful labor unions succeed in getting wage-rate increases that exceed productivity growth. Moreover, some wage contracts have escalator clauses which provide that, regardless of efficiency, wage rates *must* go up if the consumer price index rises. Once inflation starts, then, higher wage costs encouraging still more inflation seem inevitable. The increased wage bills lead to more spending (in dollar terms), which requires more borrowing by employers and perhaps their customers, including government. In addition, some companies charge for the services of management and capital by imposing a percentage of other costs; if the standard markup is 40 percent, an increase in cost from $1 to $1.10 will raise the markup from 40 to 44 cents and a final price of $1.54 instead of $1.40.

The inflation-creating power of these practices is easily exaggerated. There must be buyers *able* and *willing* to pay more—in the latter case, 14 cents. Union success in raising wage rates depends upon consumer demand, but perhaps indirectly. Over the long run, employers must think they can afford to pay labor more, or they would not boost wage rates. If consumers are not willing and able to shoulder the higher prices, the larger wage costs cannot be recovered by employers. Wages rise throughout the economy when the community will pay more.

Are there buyers whose "demand" is not greatly affected by price and who will pay the higher costs? One such buyer is government, especially during time of war. And by borrowing from banks, national government can get new money to inject into the economy. Even in peacetime, government is now a large buyer. When it faces higher prices or wage demands, it may grant them more readily than would buyers or employers operating in a more competitive market. Some consumers and businesses, if they can borrow easily, may show little resistance to a price increase which is based on higher costs; loans for new housing offer an example.

While the cost-push is not so independently powerful as sometimes alleged, it does supplement other forces which raise the price level.

Other Considerations.   Restriction of crop production and price-raising farm policies can add inflationary forces, though numerous cross-currents confuse the picture. High tax rates (not necessarily collections) may also create some inducements for inflation: higher prices of taxed products, waste in business spending (lavish expense accounts), and preference for leisure over work. Some groups may feel themselves moderately well insulated for the immediate evils of inflation; they consequently have little reason to oppose it.[3] In some countries inflationary pressure can originate in rising demand for abroad.

Creeping Inflation.   Dramatic inflation in this country is most unlikely, barring war. Creeping price rises, however, seem probable—not much in any one year but perhaps 8 to 15 percent a decade. (1) Powerful groups

---

[3] Some may favor inflation. They "never had it so good." Why should a union with an escalator clause which raises wages with prices oppose inflation if anti-inflationary policy might for a time bring its members some unemployment? Those farmers who have assurance of a high price floor may not favor policies to control price increases. A businessman may endorse short-term economic stimulants which will keep order books full even though adding to the forces of inflation. The apparent willingness of Congress to increase social security retirement benefits every 2 years may have reduced the tendency of people in retirement to oppose inflation actively.

can exert almost irresistible pressures to raise the prices, including wage rates, they charge the community. (2) Prices and wage rates rise more easily than they fall. Strong demand in some sectors of the economy, such as construction, will increase some prices and wage rates. Where business is less buoyant, unions may insist upon equally large wage boosts. In other sectors where demand lags badly, wage rates may not go down at all. Unemployment appears. (3) Rather than permit large amounts of resources to remain idle for any extended period, national government is likely to inject new money into the economic system.

Workers naturally seek more income. The union leader wants to keep his job, and he sympathizes with the aspirations of members. One thing he can try to deliver for the membership is higher earnings—and from higher wage rates rather than from more work. Rivalry among unions can make it hard for one leader to settle for much less than someone else, even if conditions are widely different. Someone is always behind someone else. The process is like leapfrog. Union officials must press for increases, and if employers do not concede, strikes will result. If the employer does grant higher wage rates, the prices of his products will tend to rise. When business is good throughout the economy or in certain industries or areas only, management is inclined to grant wage increases rather than risk a strike or the drift of the best workers to more generous employers.

Some unions may combine with employers to create monopolistic conditions and restrict potential competitors. The union leader can see the limits to what one employer in a competitive world can pay. But perhaps the union can help employers "cooperate" and by establishing a single policy for the industry for the industry, such as construction in an area, make higher prices stick. Not only will prices then rise, but at least short-run unemployment will tend to grow. The labor thus unemployed will compete for jobs elsewhere. Will other wage rates then go down? "Unlikely!" Resistances to wage-rate cuts are powerful; unemployed are not easily absorbed by declines in wage rates. However, governments (here and abroad) are pledged to maintain full employment. To do so, they will provide financial (inflationary) stimulation.

Without serious threat of unemployment among 94 percent of the labor force, the argument continues, restraint on wage demands will be weak, not firm. Unions press for more and more. If government assures adequate total demand, businesses need have no great fear that price increases to absorb a few percentage points of wage boosts will price products out of the market. When employment is high but still not "full," some parts of the economy will be suffering from shortage of labor— especially of really good workers. Employers seeking to fill the job rolls will bid up wage rates. Expanding industries offer higher wages to recruit workers. Even if no labor unions existed, wage rates would rise when and where the demand for labor is high. When demand is weak, however, wage rates go down little, or not at all.

Unquestionably, there has been a tendency here and abroad for wage rates to rise more than productivity. Figure 12–1 summarizes experience in a few industries. Price increases have in general been related closely to the *excess* of wage rate increases over gains in productivity. If wages throughout much of the economy rise more than productivity, price levels can be expected to go up. The old "correctives"—a serious shakeout, price reductions, unemployment, lower wage rates, lower prices—seem less probable in the future. In the past, too, depression would wipe out some of the money supply. Today there is not much chance of appreciable contraction in the stock of money.

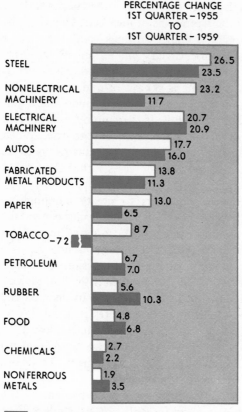

FIGURE 12–1.   Price Increases in Relation to the Excess of Wage Rate Increases over Productivity Gains

PERCENTAGE CHANGE
1ST QUARTER – 1955
TO
1ST QUARTER – 1959

STEEL   26.5 / 23.5
NONELECTRICAL MACHINERY   23.2 / 11.7
ELECTRICAL MACHINERY   20.7 / 20.9
AUTOS   17.7 / 16.0
FABRICATED METAL PRODUCTS   13.8 / 11.3
PAPER   13.0 / 6.5
TOBACCO –7.2   8.7
PETROLEUM   6.7 / 7.0
RUBBER   5.6 / 10.3
FOOD   4.8 / 6.8
CHEMICALS   2.7 / 2.2
NONFERROUS METALS   1.9 / 3.5

☐ PRICE INCREASES
■ EXCESS OF INCREASES IN WAGE RATES OVER PRODUCTIVITY GAINS

Source: J. M. Clark, *The Wage-Price Problem* (American Bankers Association, 1960), p. 41.

The prediction of creeping inflation rests in part upon a political prediction—that government will not tolerate large unemployment. "Modern politics," it has been said, "has an inflationary bias." Perhaps so. There is no "perhaps" about another assertion, "The problems of creeping inflation create some of the greatest worries of the officials who try to use the modern tools of monetary control and public finance to maintain prosperity."

Effects of Inflation. Inflation—of even apparently modest amounts—is bad. Like the glamorous siren, it may lure us with tempting visions, but the rocks below can shatter the ship. A listing of effects, not all of equal importance, will help us see why price-level stability deserves high priority as a goal of public policy.[4]

[4] Adapted from C. Lowell Harriss, "Inflation's Hidden Effects," Tax Foundation, Inc., *Tax Review*, July, 1967.

1. Inflation operates cruelly. It alters real purchasing power (*a*) of newly received income and (*b*) of wealth and debts accumulated in the past. Some people benefit, some suffer, without regard to their contribution to current production. People who have put their savings into forms that give them claims in dollars—life insurance, pensions, savings accounts, bonds—find that their money buys less and less, money which had been saved for a period when they will be unable to provide for themselves: illness or retirement. Only slightly less distressing are the cases of people whose incomes, at best, increase less rapidly than the cost of living. The occupations involved will not always be the same, but some will always lag.

Effects of inflation other than the redistribution of income and wealth are less familiar. Yet their combined influence can be substantial. Over the long run, the accumulated results of inflation on growth, efficiency, and general well-being will be more adverse, and in more ways, than is generally recognized.

2. When broad economic forces produce changes in the general *level* of prices, the myriads of *particular* prices do not all change in the same direction and amount. A few prices are fixed for longish periods; many more are "sticky." The pressures resulting from the sources of inflation differ in *magnitude* as they apply to one or another product or service—meat, new buildings, postal rates. *Timing* also varies. As a result, *relations* among prices change for reasons other than the working of the *real* forces of demand and supply. Particular prices, therefore, and the price system, cannot do their proper job of indicating relative scarcity and plenty. Prices as guides to production and consumption fail to reflect underlying economic reality as well as otherwise.

To some extent, therefore, the conduct of business, and of all economic affairs, rests upon inflation-caused changes in relations among prices as well as upon basic demand and supply. Yet buyers and sellers cannot know how their actions are being affected by forces which at best are visible only obscurely and incompletely. Rational calculation in the comparison of alternatives suffers. Actions which reflect the best possible evaluations of alternatives as indicated by comparisons of current prices will in some cases prove later to have been less desirable than if inflation had not distorted price relations. Errors which would otherwise have been avoided impair resource allocation over the long run.

Price-level stability does not, of course, assure that the relations of prices at any moment are close to ideal. But changes in the price level, by altering relations, will create distortions which serve no useful purpose. Many occur even if there is no consciousness of inflation, no attempt to make special allowance for it. *Expectations* that the price level is going to change will alter actions; the responses must inevitably rest upon less good evidence than if knowledge were more accurate.

3. Among the most important of price relations are those relating the present to the future. In deciding for the future, some uncertainty is inevitable. It is greater if it includes the possibility of price-level change. The *longer-lived* a commitment, the greater will be the chance of error arising from changes in the level of prices. Calculations can go further awry if the gap between decision and end result is 15, than if it is 5, years.

When the value of the monetary unit is felt to be uncertain, some

undertakings which would benefit the community will be foregone or curtailed. There will be others which are made to seem wise in dollar terms
because of expected price-level changes. These undertakings will get relatively more resources than are desirable in light of the real alternatives.
Today's best judgments, in other words, will be made wrong by price-level
changes which have no basis in underlying resource availability, technological reality, consumer taste, and other real elements of economic life.

4. Uncertainty about the price level will *discourage the use of debt
contracts, leases, and other such commitments which extend for other than
short periods.* No one will freely assume the cost of uncertainty and make
agreements extending through time—except for compensation. In debt contracts the characteristic device for reflecting such costs is in the interest
charge—a "premium" above some riskless rate. When the time period of a
debt is a few months, the effect on *interest rates* of uncertainty about the
price level will be of no great consequence. For intervals of 5 years, however,
the magnitude can be significant and for periods of 20 to 40 years very great
indeed. If Americans expected inflation on more than minor scale, would
not interest rates go up?

What interest rate *level* would be consistent with degrees of uncertainty
that lie within the range which recent experience suggests as possibly
realistic? Let us imagine, for example, an expectation that the price level will
probably rise by at least 1½ percent in most years but with a considerable
possibility that in some years the rise will be 2 to 3 percent; moreover, we
assume virtually no expectation that the price level will decline by as much as
1 percent in any year. What terms would either borrowers or lenders be
willing to agree to for a loan for a period about equal to the life of a new
house? Or even for 15 years? The interest rate would certainly be higher than
we have come to expect as normal. Assume, for example, that under stable
conditions the interest rate for good mortgages would be 6 percent. If the
price level is expected to rise 2 percent a year, the interest rate will tend to
become 8 percent. If prices later stop rising, the interest on existing debt
becomes a truly onerous burden. But who can know the rate of future
inflation, if any? Here is a source of risk that adds to the costs of investment.

The *structure* of interest rates would also be affected—on 30-year loans
relative to 10- and 5- and 2-year debts. Would not long-term rates tend to
become much higher than short? The flow of new capital, and the structure
of economic arrangements, would be altered.

The use of debt instruments, leases, and other contracts expressed in money
terms would be impaired. Our economy has benefited from the financing of
housing and other capital facilities by fixed-money commitments, notably
mortgage loans. Expectation of price-level uncertainty would impede, rather
than help, the use of debts for durations more or less in line with the life of
housing and other productive capacity.

5. The economy's accumulation of capital facilities would probably be
slower in dollar amount and in technological quality as a result of inflation.
Admittedly, the factors relevant to this subject are complex. Not all point
unequivocally in the one direction. But the stock of productive facilities and
new housing will probably grow less rapidly in quantity and quality in an
environment of inflation as compared with one of price-level stability.

Both the (*a*) *fact* of price level change, given our tax laws and accounting practices, and (*b*) *uncertainty* about the purchasing power of money seem likely to retard capital accumulation.

The saving which is essential for capital growth results from many causes whose relations to inflation are uncertain. For example, the saving which must be done to pay back mortgage and other debt incurred in the past will not respond in the same way as saving which depends upon new decisions taken from week to week. A feeling that the dollar will lose purchasing power will make some people less willing to sacrifice the present for the future, i.e., save. Yet the expectation of inflation might stimulate some saving by adding to the attraction of owning equities (the vision of capital gains in the stock market and real estate) and by enlarging the need for retirement dollars.

When depreciation calculations by business rest upon historical cost, the economy with inflation will experience unintended capital consumption in a real as contrasted with a dollar sense. Some dollars which are really return of capital will be treated as income for tax purposes, converted to tax, and spent by government. Tax laws and business accounting methods might possibly be devised to allow enough deduction for depreciation to keep capital consumption allowances from being labeled "income."

6. A rising level of prices in one country alters the position of its economy relative to the economies of the rest of the world. Its balance of international payments will be influenced. If it has a deficit, as we do, domestic inflation will make it larger than otherwise. Imports will tend to be greater and exports smaller. Whatever is required to get the international accounts in order will have to be done on larger scale, overcoming even greater obstacles.

7. Inflation (except perhaps when small and gradual) has bad social effects. It adds a source of discontent and internal dissension. Group can be pitted against group on the basis of inequality in sharing inflation's burdens. Social cohesion is reduced. Rancor, bitterness, loss of scruple are likely, and growth of crime has been noted where inflations are large; corruption and efforts to benefit by evading regulations thrive. If money seems easy to come by and jobs assured, the determination to put forth the best day's work possible may weaken. Careless, slovenly results are to be expected during the time when inflation stimulates a boom which reduces the threat of unemployment, weakens employer discipline, and deprives customers of good service and value. Stresses and strains of many types develop. As prices and some money incomes go up, there can, for a time, be a spirit of euphoria as many people are misled by the gap between reality and appearances, the money illusion. Soon, however, social and economic life become more difficult at many points.

8. Anticipation of inflation tends to create conditions which cause either unemployment or more inflation. Why? There are parts of the economy in which wage rates can go up by more than the average and by more than man-hour productivity, where labor unions are strong, where demand for the industry's output seems likely to be high (government construction projects), and where particular skills are in short supply. A pattern of wage settlements then extends beyond. And it then prices some man-hours into idleness more or less quickly, others as time passes. The process can be gradual, indirect, and utterly impossible to identify.

Downward flexibility of other wage rates will not provide offsetting accommodation to eliminate the inflation-caused unemployment. The "remedy" will be money creation to "validate" the higher wage rate, thus providing support for a bit more inflation.

The belief that a little inflation is a low price to pay for fuller employment has wide acceptance among economists. But this alternative does not reflect the real choice. An additional element must be considered: the unwelcome fact that actual price-level increases, and the expectation of more, will lead to wage-rate rises which in turn will cause unemployment.

9. The unpleasantnesses of a rising price level will eventually lead to demands for some sort of preventive action. One apparent possibility will be direct controls. At first the "guideposts" approach of a "voluntary" nature may get support. Such restraints will (initially) seem innocuous, their scope narrow—and their results unsatisfactory. A direct control will not do the job intended unless it *does force* people to act against what they believe to be to their advantage. European "income policies" of noncompulsory restraints on wage rates and prices have failed time and again.

No controls (other than monetary and fiscal) are likely to affect the price level by very much. They operate on symptoms, not causes. Yet various controls backed by law and sanctions can significantly influence parts of the economic structure—public utility rates, interest ceilings paid by thrift institutions, rents, the flows of new capital, for example. Over any substantial period specific controls can damage the productive system (and the social fabric). The resource allocation mechanism cannot work with full effectiveness. Distortions develop.

Unless the underlying forces making for inflation are themselves moderated, the realities of inflation will appear at different places and in different forms. Many effects of direct controls will be concealed and beyond measurement. Repression of some effects pushes the causal forces elsewhere.

10. What if the public really insists upon ending a protracted inflation? Economists can tell how the job can be done—but not painlessly. The rate of creation of new money can be slowed until the price level stops rising.

Unfortunately, ending an upward trend in the price level will in itself involve strains and losses. Each case has unique characteristics. The problems of such extremes as have appeared in Brazil and Chile are not the kind we need to think about. Our own experience of the late 1950's, however, proved costly in terms of employment, income, and growth. Economists know of no policies which will put an end to inflation and do nothing undesirable.

Benefits, Actual or Alleged, of Inflation.   Good effects are sometimes attributed to inflation. An extreme example is the endorsement of inflation as a way to expropriate some of the property of the middle and upper wealth groups. Such bloodless revolution can destroy segments of a society and shift power and income to a new group. For example, when the Communists took over Hungary after World War II, inflation seems to have been produced deliberately. Less extreme is the argument that some inflation is good because it cuts the burden of debt; when the purchasing power of money drops, less sacrifice is involved in paying a given number of dollars of interest and principal—on government debt, for example; the owners of the debt, of course, suffer a loss equal to the gains of others. Inflation has been defended under some conditions as producing desirable shifts of resources. Assume that an economy is up against a severe strain, such as war. Perhaps, then, changes in relative prices within a given price level (and direct allocations of labor and materials) cannot transfer resources quickly enough to maximize military output. Price and wage increases for some industries and occupations can speed the shift of labor and other productive capacity. Reducing wage rates and incomes in industry producing "civilian" output may be a slow process, but boosting them in military industries can be easy and quick. Higher prices will also reduce consumption to release resources for military production.

Finally, a modest price rise may act as a business stimulant in the short run. For some businesses, inflation boosts profits, at least in money terms. Profits tend to encourage economic expansion, not only by providing stimulus and buoying optimism but also by producing funds to pay for new and modern equipment. Whatever the merits of this argument, they disappear if we cannot assume that inflation will be restricted to relatively unexpected, and certainly small, amounts. The presumed benefits would disappear as businessmen and investors came to realize what was happening.

Deflation. The avoidance of price-level declines seems desirable as an objective even though, in principle, some benefits of rising productivity might well be taken in lower prices. Deflation, too, disrupts economic life. Downward pressure on the price level will lead to unemployment, the more so the greater the rigidity of prices and wage rates. Relative positions of different groups are altered, creditors benefiting and debtors suffering. Investment plans are distorted. Reluctance to incur debt because of the prospect of being required to repay in dollars of greater purchasing power will not necessarily be offset by a decline in market rates of interest.

To repeat, in an economy with rigidities and inflexibilities, the forces which lead to a general decline in the price level will also lead to decline in the utilization of labor and other productive capacity. Many wage rates and other prices are inflexible downward, at least for many months and even years. If money demand declines, the quality of man-hours purchased will drop unless wage rates per hour go down. Moreover, a decline in prices may create expectations of further declines. As a result, some purchases will be postponed, temporarily reducing total demand, perhaps for inventory for the next few weeks, perhaps for new construction over a much longer period.

OTHER GOALS

Two other goals get attention even though the Employment Act of 1946 mentions neither. One grows out of the desire to keep our economy in a favorable position relative to the rest of the world. Concern for this goal tends to focus attention on the "gold situation" or the balance of international payments. The true importance, however, attaches more to the underlying forces which influence imports, exports, and movements of capital. The goal does involve matters of high value, but we must postpone the anaysis until Part 7. For present purposes we can note that monetary actions which affect interest rates in this country thereby influence the international flow of capital. Funds move from one world financial center to another in response to changes in relations among interest rates. Moreover, any fiscal or monetary action which raises or lowers domestic income or prices will affect both imports and exports and in this way influence the balance of international payments.

Economic growth in the sense of longer run expansion of the economy receives wide support as an objective of governmental policy; it, too, we discuss later. Its relations to fiscal and monetary policy are complex. Unquestionably, the specific features of the tax structure, and the specific patterns of governmental spending, will make a difference in the rate of economic growth. These aspects of fiscal policy, however, must generally be analyzed on their own merit and largely separate from considerations of employment and prices in the next year or so. The rate of economic growth depends heavily upon capital formation, which in turn depends somewhat on monetary and fiscal policy.

The Employment Act does refer specifically to the fostering and promoting of "free competitive enterprise and the general welfare." The latter is too broad to be of much help as a guide to decision making. The former has received some attention in discussions of policy, but more in relation to antitrust policy as a means of helping achieve other goals.

TERMS AND CONCEPTS

Employment Act of 1946	frictional unemployment	price-level stability
economic stabilization	cyclical unemployment	inflation
full employment	structural unemployment	demand-pull
labor force		"creeping" inflation
		cost-push
		deflation

QUESTIONS

1. In what sense is a goal of full employment an end as distinguished from a means? Does the same apply to price-level stability? Why?

2. Discuss problems of defining "full" employment and of measuring actual unemployment.

3. Why do hundreds of thousands of job openings go unfilled when two or three times as many people are unemployed?

4. Write in your own words the quotation (at the beginning of the chapter) from the Employment Act of 1946. Try to explain or define the major terms included.

5. Describe the effects of inflation.

6. What are likely to be the long-run effects of inflation on capital accumulation? On the use of debt contracts?

7. "Labor unions cannot themselves cause a rise in the general level of prices. But union actions do create conditions which lead to greater increase in the stock of money than would otherwise be the case." Discuss.

8. Can increases in wage rates cause unemployment? Why?

9. Describe the probable effects of deflation assuming the existence of considerable rigidity in wage rates.

13

MONETARY AND FISCAL POLICY FOR STABLE PROSPERITY

The checkrein of taxes on private spending and productive incentives must be loosened if our economy is to perform at maximum efficiency. . . . It is now clear that the restraining effects of the tax system on the economy [have not been] adequately recognized. . . . The issue must be faced squarely. Our present [1963] choice is not between a tax cut and a balanced budget. The choice, rather, is between chronic deficits arising out of a slow rate of economic growth, and temporary deficits from a tax program to promote fuller use of our resources and more rapid economic growth.
President Kennedy's 1963 budget statement

Employment and national income result from forces which earlier chapters have examined from the three somewhat different, but related, approaches: the quantity of money and velocity, savings and investment, and cyclical forces of cumulative change and reversal. Economists disagree about the relative usefulness of these approaches for making public policy more constructively effective. Experience will continue to reveal many unexpected realities and change our conclusions about the directions of highest promise. And "promise" it is. For we deal with modern man's hopes for using government to supplement the market economy by offsetting the forces which tend to create instability in national income.

STABILIZATION AS NATIONAL POLICY

Place of Government in Stabilizing a Predominantly Private Enterprise Economy. Yet why turn to government to try to achieve broad economic goals in a predominantly private enterprise economy? The answer is not that economic stabilization requires political domination. The essential is action on a broad scale. Total income and employment *do* involve the economy as a whole. Changing the workings of the entire economy cannot be the responsibility of private groups—of even the biggest and finest. National government, however, is an agency through which (*a*) the public (*b*) can act (*c*) more or less deliberately (*d*) as a unit (*e*) on a broad scale.

The modern world leaves no choice—government economic action will be large no matter who wins elections. Our hope, of course, is to make the action excellent. By no means does great size assure excellence. Big actions may be less good than smaller ones, and, if bad, produce greater harm. Because government acts on a large scale, we have compelling reasons to see that what it does is as good as possible.

Automatic, self-correcting actions in the world of business have not been adequate to assure stable full employment. The process of business expansion and contraction described in the "trip around the cycle" was largely self-generating. Yet our economic system is not mechanical; nor is it foredoomed. Small fluctuations are inevitable. Large ones are not.

Although disagreement still challenges, economists' studies have enlarged impressively man's knowledge of the factors influencing national income. The founders of the Federal Reserve System, or government officials and businessmen in the 1930's (or even in the 1950's), could not have had today's understanding. Success in reducing economic instability requires at a minimum that government's own operations do not create large instability. More than such a minimum is envisaged, however, in policies to which this country is now committed.

MONETARY AND BANKING POLICY

Total buying, viewed as PT or $C + I + G$, is related to the quantity of money, M. Similarly, the process of *cumulation*, the self-generation of economic change, depends upon the monetary system. Governments, we know, have in effect turned over to commercial banks and their borrowers much of the control over *changes* in the amount of M. Consequently, M rises and falls as a result of personal and business decisions which do not necessarily serve the public interest in the broadest sense. That interest, the welfare of 200 million Americans, can be served by deliberate action by a few men.

Monetary Control as a Function of Government. People who object strongly to government direction of economic activity may still favor monetary control by an official agency. Money is an essential responsibility of government. Legislatures frame the laws under which banks must operate. Congress, presumably reflecting views of the public, accepts the principle of Federal Reserve and other government intervention, acting with a considerable range of discretion.

Monetary action operates indirectly. A central group largely insulated from politics but operating according to rules (fixed by Congress) makes a decision. The rest of the economy adjusts, a little bit here, a little bit there, and privately, in business and the home. Specific changes are widely dispersed. The personal aspects are those between borrower and lender. The adjustment is made without direct government dictation of the details of private economic decisions. Broad, indirect controls may seem inefficient, striking the "just and unjust" alike; but they relieve the authorities of the job of deciding who is "just."

Official monetary action can be prompt, responsive to changing conditions, without the delay necessary to get Congress to legislate for specific conditions. (Note that we speak of the *action*, not the full results. These may be anything but prompt.) Each of the three parts of total spending—*C*, *I*, and *G*—can be influenced. The parts of *C* and *G* which monetary action affects directly are those financed by borrowing—installment purchase of consumer durables and state-local construction and thus much like *I*. The initial effect of action by monetary authorities falls chiefly on investment, but after a while all types of spending respond.

Tools of Monetary Policy.   Earlier chapters discussed the Federal Reserve's three major tools of monetary policy: (1) the (re)discount or borrowing rate, (2) open-market operations, and (3) the changing of reserve requirements.[1] These three affect (*a*) the cost and (*b*) the availability of loans from commercial banks. The cost is the bank's interest charge. Availability refers to the ease or difficulty which the borrower encounters in getting loans at the interest rates prevailing. Differences in accessibility to bank credit are not in fact reflected fully in the rate of interest. The loan volume which some borrowers get depends not only upon the rate of interest they are willing to pay but also upon the amount the bank will lend under prevailing conditions.

Controls through the Quantity of Money.   How effective are the powers of the U.S. monetary authorities? Before answering, let us note a fact often overlooked: The vast bulk of the supply of funds for lending come from new saving. The Federal Reserve's control over the supply of *credit* covers only a small percentage, under 10 percent, of the total. At the margin, of course, $2 or $3 billion more or less in relation to a total of around $80 billion, can have significance on interest rates.

1. Officials have considerable power (*a*) to determine the rate of increase in *M*, (*b*) to prevent any rise in *M*, and even (*c*) to force a decline. Monetary restraint can keep investment and total spending lower than otherwise. The investment which is repressed directly is that which would be paid for by borrowing from commercial banks, as distinguished

---

[1] Congress has additional power to alter the structure of the financial system. The insurance of bank deposits and other changes to eliminate the danger of widespread bank failures were structural modifications.

from investment that the public will finance by saving out of its income. Authorities certainly have power to prevent the monetary exuberance of booms which, financed by bank loans, will lead to mistakes that can aggravate recession later.

Yet no one can be absolutely certain of the amount, the timing, or the "location" (by area or industry) of the effects of policies that do restrain *M*. Those same policies will not necessarily restrain *V*. Or, using the Keynesian approach, the public by trying to reduce (enlarge) its holdings of cash balances will alter the balance between attempted savings and planned investment. The use of money rests upon individual decisions and is not subject to central control. Man's ingenuity finds escapes from what may appear as limits to *V*.

2. How much can monetary policy do to stimulate business? Federal Reserve action can increase the ability of banks to lend and thus do something to ease credit, raise the quantity of money, and reduce interest rates. But will lower interest rates and easier availability of money induce banks to lend, and customers to borrow, more? For several years many economists tended to answer this question with the skeptical statement, based on experience in the mid-1930's, "You cannot push on a string." But money is not a string. Year after year we have seen that an increase in the lending capacity of banks will lead to the creation of more money. Lags may be short or extended into months because only a small portion of the full potential of expansion occurs in the first month or two.

Except possibly for truly crisis conditions, there will always be bank willingness to lend (or to buy securities) which coincides with someone's desire to borrow (or sell securities). Borrowed money will be used for spending. Bank purchases of securities increase the liquidity of sellers. The seller of securities to a bank will probably use the dollars received to finance new investment rather than hold them idle for long. Nevertheless, the response to expansionary monetary policy does have elements of uncertainty, not about direction but about amount and timing.

3. What is the practical power of monetary authorities to keep a boom from getting out of hand? One obstacle will be widespread pressure to enable banks to meet demand for loans. Under such conditions, however, increased lending capacity for banks—"easier" money—will stimulate what ought not to be stimulated: investment financed by newly created money. Tightening money, of course, will check a boom. Unfortunately, it may do more—bring on contraction. Here is a risk: if monetary authorities do restrict too much, they cannot be confident that a later reversal will undo the harm and revive business, except after delay, months during which real human distress makes the error exceedingly unfortunate.

To summarize: Authorities unquestionably have the power to prevent monetary stringency which in the past has aggravated recessions needlessly. It is difficult today to imagine officials tightening money after a business contraction has gotten started, as happened in the early 1930's, to the country's great misfortune. Positive, expansionary action can stimulate business. No one can be certain, however, of the amount by which any Federal Reserve action will alter national income. The "when" is also open to doubt. A change in monetary policy will have some immediate effects. Short-term interest rates, and bond prices, will react at once. Some investment may then change within a few weeks. The major results

FIGURE 13–1.   Money Stock and Time Deposits,* Changes 1959–67

Percentages are annual rates of change between periods indicated. They are presented to aid in comparing most recent developments with past "trends."

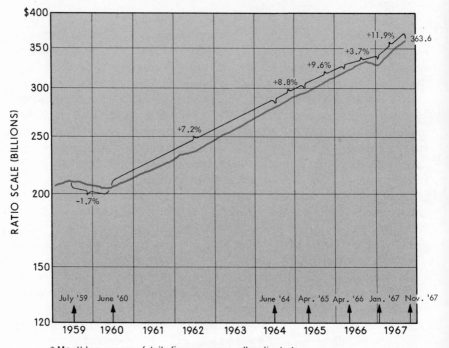

* Monthly averages of daily figures, seasonally adjusted.
Source: Federal Reserve Bank of St. Louis, *Review,* December, 1967.

develop only gradually; the full reaction takes many months.

Unfortunately, we cannot be confident of getting the best official action. The Federal Reserve remains under pressure, to which it some-times bows, to expand the stock of money to meet demands for credit and thus feed expansion when the economy is exuberant. As shown in Figure 13–1, the stock of money was permitted to grow very rapidly in 1965 and again in 1967. After such liberal policy has been in effect for a while, inflationary forces can gather so much strength—1959 and 1966—that abrupt reversal of policy disrupts the economy. At other times, when loan demand has been sluggish, the authorities have not provided banks with as much new lending capacity as needed for appropriate growth in the stock of money. Such was probably true most of the time from mid-1960 to mid-1964. The 2.7 percent note shown in Figure 13-1 was in itself scarcely high enough, but very rapid increase in time and savings deposits may have made up, or more than made up, any inadequacy in growth of demand deposits.

Actual Federal Reserve policy, in short, does not always conform to the needs for stabilization plus potential economic growth. The Board, it seems, respects the commercial loan theory of banking (p. 157) which is cycle-aggravating. So much attention of the Fed centers on the rate of interest and the demand for *credit* that the stock of *money* gets secondary place in decision making. According to some economists, however, changes in the quantity of money are of such importance as to justify top billing. On balance, over the years, the argument runs, the economy would be better off if the monetary authorities were to center their actions on a steady expansion in the quantity of money and give up attempts to adjust to changing conditions in the short run. Economists who do not go so far will argue that the Federal Reserve uses it own experience as a basis for bettering policy actions.

Every economy which uses money must have policies regarding its creation. Experience leaves no doubt that the policies will exert powerful influence. To make them as constructive as possible requires more exploration. New unknowns and unanswered questions, several of which are discussed in the appendix to this chapter, appear as the economy becomes more complex.

Monetary Policy for Long-Run Growth. Although tomorrow may seem more pressing than dates 5 and 10 years ahead, we hope for monetary action which considers the needs of the longer run. One such need is clear: A gradual increase in the stock of money—not rapid then slow increase, not spurts followed by retreats, not "no net increase," but expansion as productive capacity grows—3 to 4 percent a year. Business and the public generally will not necessarily wish to expand their bank borrowings in close harmony with the economy's needs for growth in M. What supplementation or restraint are possible? The banking system could be permitted, induced, even compelled, to increase or decrease its holding of securities "appropriately."

Conclusion. Critics of determined use of monetary policy to minimize fluctuations base their objection on belief that one result will be less than reasonably full employment on the average. Restrictive monetary policy can be effective. On the other hand, it is said, monetary ease cannot assure a desired amount of expansion with the right timing. Delicate control of national income by monetary policy must not be expected, but the public can properly hope for continuing improvement. Here economists are in agreement. Disagreement arises over the adequacy of monetary policy as it can operate in the real world and the relative potential of fiscal policy.

FISCAL POLICY: GOVERNMENT FINANCE AS A STABILIZER

Fiscal action includes government taxing, spending, borrowing, and debt management. Although state and local, as well as national, finances are involved, discussions that concern stabilization policy deal chiefly with the activities of the national "fisc," federal government finances.

What Governments Can Do: General Principles. When national governments spend as much as a fourth of the whole national income, any appreciable change in such spending can have a pronounced effect on the level of business. Hundreds of thousands of business managements and millions of families cannot get together to act as a unit to raise or lower their spending. Yet a relatively few people at the top of a government can form a program and swing the mighty power of public finance.

If total spending by families and businesses (their part of MV) is increasing when resources are fully employed, inflation (a rise in P) threatens. To prevent it, total buying must be reduced. Families and businesses following their *individual* interests cannot be counted upon to do what is in their *total* interest. Their government, however, might serve them by (1) reducing its spending (not cutting taxes), thus making more of the community's resources available for private purchase, or (2) raising taxes (but not its spending) so that families and businesses can spend less.

Just the opposite can counterbalance a drop in private buying (C and I): increase in government spending or a cut in taxes. The government spending involved in any of these changes may be either purchases of goods and services or such transfer payments as welfare aid.

By such shifts a government can tip the balance and keep the economy from going too far in either direction—and certainly keep expansion or contraction from cumulating dangerously. The principle when stated so broadly may seem to say no more than that the way to win baseball games is to make runs or that the way to have a high income is to get a good job. Fortunately, we can be more specific.

Importance of Source of Funds. First, we distinguish between two points: (1) the *amount* of government spending and (2) the *source* of the funds. If the government cuts or increases its spending while private spenders make equal, but opposite, changes, there will be no net alteration in aggregate demand. The items bought will be different, but not the dollar totals. Equal runs keep the score tied when we want victory, in this case a change in *total* spending.

If *inflation* threatens, how can fiscal action cut overall spending? The government can take more money (in taxes) from private spenders than it spends itself. By reducing disposable income in this way, it cuts business and family buying. Treasury officials can use the surplus to retire securities held by commercial banks.[2] The total volume of M will fall. Or the Treasury, by merely holding the surplus as idle bank deposits can give them a V of zero. No restraint on inflation can be expected, however, if a cut in taxes matches the reduction of government spending.

If *recession* seems in the offing, government can lower taxes to leave families and businesses with more disposable income. Government can also increase total demand by itself spending more without taking more from the public. Where can it get the money to make up the difference? By increasing M. How? It can borrow from commercial banks. (If it has been holding deposits idle, it can use them, raising the V from zero; currency issue is also possible.) The stream of purchasing power grows.

The effective force changing national income (in the short run) comes *not* from the amount of government spending, nor even solely from changes in such spending. What counts more will be the way the changes are financed. *Without altering appreciably the total volume of its spending, a national government by raising or lowering taxes can do much to determine the level of employment and prices.* (This fact was not widely recognized in the early 1930's.) Government can use its own financial activities to *supplement*, or to *counterbalance*, the activities of families and businesses. It can compensate for undesirable changes in private spending. So we speak of *compensatory fiscal policy*. Some economists question the effectiveness of monetary policy in a recession because businesses cannot be counted upon to react promptly to "easy" money by borrowing and spending enough more to give full employment. By fiscal action, however, government can do "enough"—by creating purchasing power and injecting it into the stream of national income, directly and quickly.

Compensatory Fiscal Policy Possible without an Increase in the Amount of Government Activity. Does not such fiscal policy almost assure an expansion of the scope of government? Possibly, but not inevitably. Let us look at an extreme case. Assume a depression, and a party in power which favors an excess of government spending over tax receipts. Yet it also opposes expansion of government activity. How can it meet its goals? By slashing taxes. Private spending can then rise. The government may even cut its own spending; for the same stimulation, however, the tax reduction must be correspondingly larger. (Checking inflation, on the other hand, does not require a reduction, or even preclude an expansion, in government spending; taxes must increase, however.) In fact, a rise in government spending does not necessarily mean an expansion in the scope

[2] The effect will be greater if debt changes are those of the Federal Reserve banks or if currency is retired. The monetary authorities must, of course, prevent increases in bank loans to business that offset declines in government debt. Note the imperative necessity of the coordination of monetary with fiscal policy.

of its activity. Government may merely speed things it would do in any case—building highways or post offices today rather than next year. Or it may do some part of its job better—equipping the national parks. Or outlays for a well-established function may increase, perhaps as a result of the recession—grants for aid to the poor—without enlarging the scope.

The Unbalanced Budget: Change in the Public Debt. Compensatory fiscal policy as ordinarily envisaged requires that government budgets sometimes be "unbalanced." Here we think in terms of the cash budget concept—total actual receipts and payments—with perhaps modifications to make figures conform more closely to national income concepts.[3] The Treasury must in some years take in more than it pays out, in some years less. A means of balancing the total *national* economy consists of a change in the government debt, depression calling for a rise, inflation for a reduction. So we ask, "What does the public get in return for an increase in the national debt? What do we give up if we reduce the debt?"

A depression increase in federal debt may be matched by an increase in real assets, or improvement in "human capital," resulting from the spending. Resources that would otherwise be wasted produce benefits of more than passing value. In addition, income rises elsewhere as the multiplier operates. Such a bargain seems good indeed. Still, a budget that involves spending of more than the government receives in taxes stands to some as a symbol of waste and extravagance—it may be. To others it stands as a symbol of more inflation—it may be.[4] Yet in neither case must it be.

Perhaps over a business cycle the budget can be balanced while contributing most effectively to balancing the national economy. There is no assurance, however, that the amount of surplus most desirable at one time will equal the deficit which is appropriate during slumps.

Problems of Discretionary Fiscal Policy. What practical problems must be solved to make a stabilizing fiscal policy succeed? In examining them, we must make the following distinction: (1) *discretionary* policy operates when government deliberately alters its taxing and spending as conditions change; (2) *automatic* stabilizers are features built into the economy that force government finances to exert a stabilizing effect without deliberate action to change (*a*) direction or (*b*) amount.

Its mammoth size prevents the federal government from shifting poli-

---

[3] For purposes of analysis, some economists prefer to use another concept, the "full-employment budget." It attempts to show what deficit or surplus would exist if the economy were operating at full employment with existing tax and spending policies.

[4] A government deficit is not necessarily inflationary even during full employment. If the Treasury gets the money by sale of bonds to persons or institutions who have saved, instead of by sale to the banking system, no inflationary impetus need result. With appropriate monetary policy, a government can finance deficits year after year without adding any inflationary—or stimulating—effect.

cies easily and promptly. So does great complexity—and the existence of many interest groups and centers of power. The President in January, 1963, urged prompt tax reduction to spur business. Although unemployment remained sadly above any reasonable minimum, Congressional action took 13 months. Conscious changes of direction in federal policy are less like those of an agile boxer than of a lumbering elephant or a stubborn donkey. Officials have differences of opinions and disagree. Even when there is a dominant consensus, change is not always easy.

Economists may speak glibly of government "spending," the Keynesian G, as a big, broad aggregate. Yet in practice we must "disaggregate." Every Treasury check must have a name after "Pay to the order of. . . ." Deciding just whose name will get these welcome spots must present tantalizing perplexities. Most government spending, for example, results because specific programs seem important. For each there is a purpose— national defense or paying a postal deficit—which is not economic stabilization. The urgency of the need may not vary with the business cycle.

Another problem: Expansion of government spending is easier than contraction, especially if economic efficiency in spending is not an overwhelming consideration. Even expansion, however, may require many months. If an increase of $5 billion is the goal, there may be interminable wrangling over who shall get the business, where, on what terms, and when. And to spend money without waste calls for well-developed organization. Major construction projects require plans and bids and "getting going." Spending on complex military equipment can be highly unpredictable, as well as slow in starting. Some expenditure when once started cannot be turned off without apparent breach of faith and perhaps great loss—an established plan of helping veterans or a dam half built. The budgetary process takes time; it has been developed to help prevent waste, and relaxing the precautions to serve short-run stabilization purposes risks waste in the "not so long run." The goal—the thing to be stabilized— might soon become continued reelection of the party in power or pet projects of a few special interest groups, *spending* rather than *spending to get good value.*

Increases in federal expenditures can unquestionably help fill the gap from a big deficiency in private buying. Moreover, any budget as large as that of our federal government includes outlays whose timing can be adjusted. Some programs agreed upon by Congress in its normal procedures can be speeded up or slowed down. The amount of such spending might be large enough *at the margin* to make an appreciable difference in the amount of change in national income. As a precaution against bigger swings, we can *prepare in advance.* What spending might be cut if inflation impends? Where? Why? What outlays could best be increased if the economy were to suffer a serious decline? A "shelf of blueprints" for public works or other spending can be kept up to date; progress has been made since the 1930's in advance planning of federal public works for emergency needs; but no "turning on the tap" will quickly boost total activity, and no easy reversal has been developed.

Demand involves "specifics," and changes in the national total must each be for some specific product or service. The national government is not equipped to buy many of the things for which private demand may drop: dancing lessons, facials, inventories for the local hardware store, tricycles. Uncle Sam could, it is true, buy some such things and perhaps even pay for services for individual families. The practical difficulties, however, would be overwhelming, especially if even moderate precautions were taken to prevent undue favoritism and sheer waste. Of course, an increase in transfer payments, especially for "public assistance" (welfare aid), will lead to a diffusion of buying throughout the economy; but the amounts then flowing into the most distressed sectors may be small. The products of industries suffering depression may not be subject to a special tax that could be removed to stimulate purchases.

Peacetime threat of inflation may occur when government is buying little or none of the output of the booming sectors. In such circumstances reduction of federal buying to serve stabilization needs may not be compatible with other responsibilities.

Even with categories as broad as "construction," the things governments normally build—highways, hospitals, airfields, school buildings—do not require the same kinds and combinations of skilled labor, materials, and equipment as do the houses, apartments, factories, and office buildings that make up most private construction. A dollar increase in government spending on its normal kinds of construction may not compensate for a dollar of decline in private spending on construction (Fig. 13–2).

FIGURE 13–2.   Public Works and Private Housing: Ratios of Requirements for Selected Materials and Skills

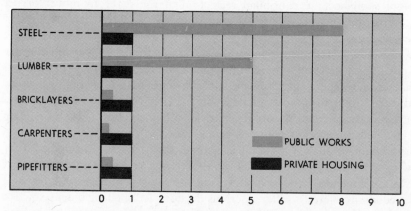

Source: S. J. Maisel, "Varying Public Construction and Housing to Promote Economic Stability," Joint Economic Committee, *Federal Expenditure Policy for Economic Growth and Stability* (Washington, D.C., 1957), pp. 391–92.

When unemployment exists everywhere, government can boost outlays where it is competent to spend—getting better post offices and other good things. Other sectors will be aided as the multiplier operates. Yet our hope is to prevent unemployment from becoming so very general, to check cumulation before it gets serious. If government, acting before conditions become really bad, tries to compensate directly for declines here and there in the private economy, it may have to participate in sectors where it does not, in the normal course of events, operate directly. On short notice, it can hardly build the necessary organization to do new, detailed jobs, or to do them well. Moreover, governments are subject to political and social pressures which magnify the inevitable difficulties of functioning in specific localities, with these industries but not those, for one occupational or age group but not another. Still another complication appears. Some expenditures may promise greater multiplier or accelerator influence than others. If the case seems clear—but it may not—then officials do wisely to emphasize the "high-powered" spending. Public understanding may not, however, support such distinctions.

Taxes are not easily changed. Congress has many other claims on its time. Whenever a tax bill is considered, dozens of legitimate but conflicting interests clamor for consideration. Many groups want to share a reduction or avoid an increase. Can Congress meet its full obligations and also act quickly? Probably not, but Congress might vote in advance to give the President, or a group including some of its own key members, authority to raise or lower certain tax rates under specified conditions. President Kennedy requested such authority, but Congress refuses to give up the "power of the purse," even to the extent of granting administrative discretion under specified conditions.

Should not reasonable men be able to agree on some workable method? One would think so. Realists point out, however, that the record of recommendations by leaders in the White House and on Capitol Hill shows that no one's judgment has yet been good enough to warrant freeing him from the need to face questioning. Another fundamental objection arises from the fact that so long as the monetary authorities are independent and have the great power they do, any arrangement which will really meet needs must involve the Federal Reserve. Therefore, the task of devising a plan is bigger, even, than it has seemed. Federal Reserve officials are more than merely reluctant to commit themselves to any one specific course of future action. They refuse to do so.

Compensatory Policy and Desirable Readjustment. One tough question is this: Will anticyclical government actions encourage or discourage desirable readjustments of underlying conditions? Unemployment—not massive, but "too much"—will result from prices and costs higher than consumers or investors want to pay—not all prices but some that are important. Flexible prices and high resource mobility would "correct" such maladjustments rather promptly. But where there is much wage rate and price rigidity and also (at least in the short run) immobility of productive capacity, the unemployment may persist because specific prices remain too high. For example, there would likely be great unemployment in the rug industry if rug prices went well above what many potential buyers thought the rugs were worth. To repeat, unemployment on a wide scale does not result from maladjustments of individual wage rates and prices; not every price can be too high relative to others. Yet employment changes are specific, more here than there; and particular jobs do count.

Let us illustrate a possibly widespread problem with an imaginary example. Suppose that government has adopted a policy of assuring full employment. The high price—or unappealing style—of furniture has cut sales and employment. In the economy generally, however, business is good. Government steps in to meet the problem where it exists by buying large amounts of furniture with money created for the purpose. It could do so at the prices demanded by the manufacturers or retailers. (Conceivably, as an alternative, it might cut taxes on anyone buying furniture.) Employment in the industry would rise. Aggregate spending would increase. Business would then improve even where employment had been essentially full. Prices would edge upward. Perhaps full employment, including furniture workers, appears quickly. Government officials, heaving a sigh of relief, could cut the buying of furniture, or reimpose the taxes, to prevent a tendency toward inflation. Furniture prices, however, would still be "out of line." Normal private demand would not be enough for full employment at the price desired by the furniture producers. So we again get unemployment. And if the government's commitment for full employment holds, furniture producers have little reason to lower prices because they can expect help again from Washington—at their price.

This imagining illustrates a disturbing problem. Change "furniture" to "bricklaying" or "primary metals" or "beef"; the principle remains the same. Any group can price, and more than one can style, itself out of some sales or employment. Can public policy meet this problem? Not very well.

Assume that government spends more in the aggregate (or by tax reduction encourages private families or businesses to spend more). Some of the spending increase will flow where prices have been "right," employment high, and where in the short run not many more workers or much more equipment can be used. Or perhaps part of the government spending is directed deliberately to sectors where unemployment exists due to the fact that prices are relatively too high. In the first case, prices increase and not much inroad is made on unemployment. The second bolsters a bad price situation; the spending may do little long-run good. The stimulation may actually harm the economy in three ways; (a) by encouraging poor allocation of resources; (b) by making maladjustments a little greater so that any eventual correction will cause, not mild, but serious distress; and (c) by adding an inflationary force. Minor imbalances which might be corrected by gradual and relatively small changes in prices and quantities may get larger and more firmly entrenched so that only major action can do the job.

If government adopts a policy of intervening directly to stimulate business, it is likely to involve action where unemployment appears—no point bolstering the strong spots. The results, unfortunately, will include not only an increase in national income and employment but also the perpetuation of maladjustments which helped cause trouble. In the 1930's, this problem did not seem important. Unemployment was so huge that almost any expansionary policy would have been sensible.

Directionary fiscal action, by adding stimulation and checking tendencies for a contraction to cumulate, may ease the smooth adjustment and contribute to healthy change in the private sector. Such action, however, can also encourage a poor allocation of resources. For example, assume that a monopoly (union or business) or a farm bloc were to succeed in pricing its product above what the public wanted to pay so that idleness resulted. If the government then steps in to buy to boost employment, the public would be paying a price higher than it would freely wish. Resources are used where they will not serve consumers best. Yet, when one alternative is no product at all, anything obtained costs little indeed; if the alternative, however, includes the strengthening of forces which will add to future unemployment, the cost can be high.

Anti-inflationary governmental repression at *specific* points—wages in auto manufacturing, construction costs, fresh fruit prices—would encounter serious political opposition even if Congress were to grant some officials the authority.[5] Any success would probably be temporary at best, a "holding action"; the secondary effects would likely include other maladjustments. A broader question to which we return later: Can we have prosperity and stabilization without subjecting ourselves to the "hijacking" of monopolistic groups?[6] Effective stabilization policies may

---

[5] A few officials have power which can be influential under some circumstances. President Kennedy used "persuasion" to get steel companies to cancel a price increase in 1962 which might, or might not, have been effective; he failed to get labor unions to accept "guidelines" he proposed to govern wage-rate increases.

[6] The question of incentive should not be ignored. The serious problem is not really that suggested by questions such as: "If Uncle Sam will take care of us, why not let him? Why work (and pay taxes)?" Loafers and wasters do not deserve aid, but stabilizing fiscal policy by no means involves handouts. Jobs, not relief, will be the preferred method of an increase in spending. There *is* a real incentive problem, however. It involves "price." No foreseeable price may be too high to prevent a deep depression or a feverish inflation. Unfortunately, the costs of some actions to counter smaller swings can be more than slight. Policies may impair materially private incentives to change. The social costs take the form of strengthening rigidities, discouraging readjustment, aggravating forces which will worsen the next phase of the cycle.

Some of those who are unemployed are jobless because they will not make the effort, in training or at the job, which employers (and consumers) demand for the wage. For how many such nonworkers shall government try directly and indirectly to provide jobs?

accentuate the tendency of monopolistic prices and wage rates to be flexible upward and inflexible downward. The long-run results will then be creeping inflation.

Automatic Stabilizers.   Fortunately, our hopes do not have to rest entirely on discretionary fiscal action. A national government can arrange its affairs so that when private spending moves in one direction, government finance will automatically set up forces working the other way. Our goal for "normal" would be reasonably good fiscal balance at full employment and stable prices. Then we try to "build in" tax and spending features which will make deviation self-correcting.

If families and businesses begin to spend more out of funds borrowed from banks (raising M) or money they have been holding idle (higher V), national income in dollar terms will rise. But if the tax systems siphons off a big chunk of the increase—$4 or so of each $10 rise in national income—then the growth of private spending will be slowed. Government use of the added revenue to retire debt held by banks can also act to reduce the rate of expansion.

If, on the other hand, the initial change is a decline in private spending, national income will start down. Tax collections, however, will also fall. Out of an income drop of $10, taxes may absorb $4. As a result families and businesses will not need to cut their buying as much as otherwise. Government runs a deficit; to pay its bills, it can borrow from banks, increasing M.

One automatic stabilizer is a tax system whose revenues fluctuate much more widely, percentagewise, than national income.

Government spending will also exert an automatically stabilizing influence if it rises when national income falls and falls as private incomes rise.

Both expenditure and revenue systems can be designed so that fiscal changes counterbalance changes in the private economy—with no need for discretionary action, with no problems of forecasting, timing, or of swinging a government into action. Somewhat by accident the United States has acquired powerful automatic stabilizers.

Personal and business income and social security payroll *taxes* are imposed on a mass basis and at substantial rates. Major taxes are collected at just about the time the income is received. As income rises, tax collections go up more than proportionately. A boom can hardly get going before government takes away more and more of the purchasing power that would feed an increase. When national income falls, tax collections drop substantially. In fact, refunds often appear. Within a year after it begins to suffer losses, a business can generally get a refund of taxes it paid in the last year of profit; money thus becomes available to help maintain the enterprise. Individuals also get refunds of overwithholdings.

Although most government *spending* does not fluctuate anticyclically, unemployment benefits certainly move against the business cycle. Checks begin to reach a family within 2 or 3 weeks after a person is laid off. The money adds to overall purchasing power because the dollars paid out have not been taken to appreciable extent from the consuming-investing funds of others. For 6 months or so while the unemployment benefits continue, there is a floor below which spending need not fall. Furthermore, a moderately comprehensive system of welfare benefits for persons in special need will assure at least a poverty level of buying—more in some localities than others.

Automatic built-in fiscal responses have much greater stabilizing effect than before World War II.[7] Cumulation has less chance to grow. But as Figure 13–3 shows, the timing of deficits and surpluses has been far from ideal. If the changes were some months earlier, the net stabilizing effect would be greater.

Nevertheless, as national income has declined in recent recessions, the offsetting effect of automatic stabilizers have been at least 40 percent of the drop in national income. The same forces, however, are also charged with retarding recovery before full employment is achieved. Federal taxes siphon off more and more income during recovery and thus, it is said, act as a "fiscal drag." Such restraining force helped account for the incompleteness of business recovery in 1959–60 and after 1961. A big income tax cut in 1964 and large reductions in commodity and service taxes did not allay economists' fears of "drag" in the sense of rapid increase in revenues before the economy reaches full employment.

Automatic stabilizers do not pinpoint stimulants for the sore spots in the economy—the critical areas in which unemployment strikes hardest. Responsibility for such situations remains with market forces, sustained by at least moderate adequacy of purchasing power. Changes in relative prices must guide the shifting of resources. Of course, adjustment will be pleasanter for persons working in businesses which consumers want to expand than for workers in firms whose output consumers wish to contract. Where prices are rigid and resources immobile, maladjustment may persist. Government will not, however, give special direct support which tends to perpetuate maladjustments.

Experience: to the Mid-1960's.   President Kennedy took office at the low point of a minor recession. Although unemployment was around 7 percent, he opposed tax cuts to stimulate total demand. His alternative tax plan (April, 1961) rested on belief that for some years the economy had suffered from a sluggishness in the rate of business modernization and

---

[7] The tremendous growth of government spending in relation to GNP—30 percent today compared with 10 percent in 1929 and 19 percent in 1939—in one sense constitutes a stabilizer. The market forces of cumulation get less foothold to swing the rest of the economy than before the war. In another sense, however, changes in governmental spending have been a source of instability.

expansion. To speed recovery in the short run, and to accelerate longer-run economic growth, he advocated an investment tax credit. In Keynesian terms, he proposed to raise the marginal efficiency of capital—shifting upward the $I\ I$ curve of Figure 10–6 by a tax credit which would offset part of the cost of capital goods.

FIGURE 13–3.   Federal Surplus and Deficit in Business Expansion and Contraction* (Seasonally Adjusted Quarterly Totals)

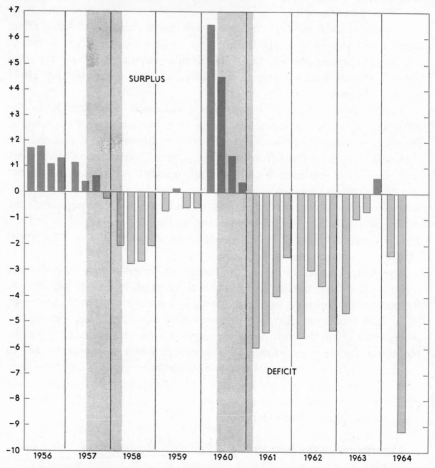

* Shaded areas show periods of economic contraction. The concept of surplus and deficit is that used by the Department of Commerce in estimating national income.
Source: Department of Commerce.

This change in the tax structure would enhance the attractiveness of installing new machinery and equipment because businesses would be permitted to reduce their income tax by part of the purchase price. To offset the resulting revenue loss, Mr. Kennedy advocated numerous changes which would raise tax burdens. The proposals raised many questions, and not until autumn of 1962 did the complex tax law take final form.

A few months earlier, after years of study, the Treasury changed the tax structure in another major reform by relaxing restrictions on depreciation deductions. Use of new guidelines, by reducing the demands on business for cash to pay taxes, would make more dollars available for spending on new plant, equipment, and inventory. Thus, within a few months—and without large stimulation of total demand by tax reduction—two actions on the tax front favored business expansion. One, in effect, reduced the cost of a considerable range of new equipment by permitting income tax otherwise payable to be credited against part of the purchase price. Both actions, by reducing the immediate outflow of cash for taxes, eased the financing of expansion. Other tax changes, however, were not welcomed as aids to business.

But unemployment remained excessive, and late in 1962 the White House began to mobilize support for a policy which, though "old stuff" to advocates of the "new economics," seemed to much of the public novel and perhaps even irresponsible. The President, in effect, was telling Americans to depart from economic traditions and to cut tax rates when the federal budget was in deficit, when the economy was prospering, and when increases in federal spending were on the way.

In January, 1963, Mr. Kennedy urged Congress to reduce tax rates in three stages in 1963, 1964, and 1965. The relief, to total well over $10 billion at an annual rate by 1965, was to benefit all income groups. The typical family, it was predicted, would use around 92 percent of the resulting increase in its disposable income to buy consumer goods and services. This addition to consumer buying would lead in turn to greater demand for capital goods. Furthermore, reductions of the highest tax rates, and other changes in the tax structure, would lower tax barriers, encourage risk taking, promote efficiency, and improve incentives.

Congress was unwilling to meet the President's request for speed even though the administration repeatedly told the public that each month of delay deprived the country of clearly desirable economic stimulation. A serious obstacle appeared in the form of widespread public skepticism about the propriety of cutting taxes when government spending was going up and the budget was in a deficit.

When he became President, Mr. Johnson continued to press for speedy action. The bill, which became law in February, 1964, concentrated reductions in that year. Because personal income and corporation profits were rising, total tax collections changed rather little. In 1965 President Johnson supported a tax program which eliminated or reduced commodity and service taxes to provide the economy with another stimulation of general buying power (estimated at $4.6 billion a year) and to bring numerous other benefits from structural tax reform. Budget deficits continued.

The 1961–65 tax actions have been widely hailed as highly successful. Beyond question, developments have been consistent with two major hypotheses: (1) Structural tax changes, such as the investment tax credit, can have a large effect on certain portions of the economy. Investment in new productive facilities soared, with dramatic increases in the purchase of those capital goods qualifying for the investment tax credit. (2) General, aggregative, tax reduction will stimulate business as a whole. Both C and I rose substantially as the prospects of tax reduction improved in 1963 and even more as the actuality appeared in 1964 and 1965. The rise in GNP in those two years was nearly $90 billion—compared with about $60 billion in the prior two years.

How much of the result was due to fiscal policy?

In a complex economy many forces combine to produce any set of results. During much of the period of economic expansion, Federal Reserve action also made monetary policy expansionary. For most of the 4-year period, bank reserves grew at an historically high rate. The Treasury, although not relying directly on new borrowing from commercial banks, was able to finance budget deficits in an environment in which bank leading expanded rapidly.

Demand deposits plus currency rose over the 3-year period from mid-1962 to mid-1965 at an annual rate of 3.9 percent, nearly double the 2.1 percent average for the entire postwar period. (The percentages in Figure 13–1 apply to somewhat different stretches of time.) In the 1958–60 period when the economy performed poorly, money supply grew only 1.1 percent a year and actually declined in 1960. From April, 1965, to April, 1966, the money supply rose at an annual rate of 6.2 percent. Economists will disagree about attributing independent casual influence to monetary developments. Nevertheless, a high rate of increase sustained for four years to mid-1966 must have contributed significantly to the economic expansion. Even a cautious appraisal, however, will also conclude that tax reduction can play a big part in helping the economy make fuller use of its productive capacity.

But what about predictions that a cut in taxes when the budget was already in deficit would lead to inflation? The record confirms the fear that expansionary fiscal and monetary policies are likely to bring price-level increases even before full utilization of capacity. During Mr. Kennedy's Presidency, the economy did not press on the limits of productive capacity. The Wholesale Price Index scarcely budged. The increases shown in the Consumer Price Index—1.2 percent or so a year—were frequently alleged to be spurious because of defects in the index, a conclusion which remains in doubt. From the summer of 1965, however, both the CPI and the WPI rose sharply at annual rates of 3.5 and 3.8 percent, respectively. Clearly, the experience is consistent with the conclusion that the nearer the economy comes to full utilization of productive capacity, the greater the likelihood that additions to demand will bid up prices.

1966–67. Early in 1966, forecasters were not by any means in agreement. The President did not recommend a tax increase with his budget message of January, which envisaged another large deficit. As months passed, the price level rose, and the economy pressed toward the limits of capacity in many areas. To dampen investment, the President in the autumn got Congress to remove temporarily the investment tax credit. A few months later (spring, 1967) when conditions seemed "easier" and pressures on capacity in the investment goods industries were less, the investment credit was restored.

Large budget deficits loomed, however, and by mid-1967 the President was led to recommend a temporary 10 percent surcharge on income taxes. The purpose was to restrain the economy by reducing purchasing power. Another stated objective was to keep interest rates from rising as high as they otherwise would. If the Treasury's demands for borrowing were reduced, the argument went, other borrowers could be satisfied more fully. The Federal Reserve would be able to follow a somewhat easier monetary policy.

Social security payroll taxes were raised, but benefit spending also went up. Leading members of Congress insisted that the growth of federal nondefense spending be slowed. Until the rise in expenditures seemed to be "under control," tax increases, it was argued, would soon be offset by more spending. Another argument against tax rate boosts was that the apparent cause of price increases was the wave of wage rate increases in excess of productivity. Would tax increases really be effective in such cases? Not directly and at once, the economist might reply; but indirectly a tax rise which slowed the growth in the stock of money would help check the all-too-rapid rise in prices. Still Congress held back.

Jobs or Price Stability: The Continuing Dilemma. The whole industrial world has now experienced a problem which no country has yet solved: Sustained high employment brings price-level increases too great to be ignored. Unquestionably, fiscal and monetary policies of the type we used in the mid-1960's can raise the general level of GNP in money terms. There is also no question that even with large budget deficits, monetary policy can prevent inflation. But the policies which will clearly prevent inflation are likely to create avoidable unemployment. Expansionary policies, on the other hand, are likely to lead to some inflation before full employment is achieved.

Figure 13–4 and 13–5 illustrate the dilemma: How much of the employment goal should we be willing to "trade off" for how much of a price-stability goal? Study of a long sweep of history by a British economist, A. W. Phillips, led him to conclude that some more or less stable relationship might exist between the rate of unemployment and the rate of price change. If so, we might be able to predict how much of one objective, say price-level stability, must be sacrificed in cutting unemploy-

FIGURE 13–4.

The band *FE* indicates the range of physical output when the economy is "fully employed"; the amount cannot be measured precisely. As output rises from *OA* to *OB*, the general price level does not go up. The output rise of *BC* which is the same in physical amount leads to some increase in prices even though full employment has not been achieved. Further increases in physical output are possible, but prices go up markedly before the absolute limits on production appear.

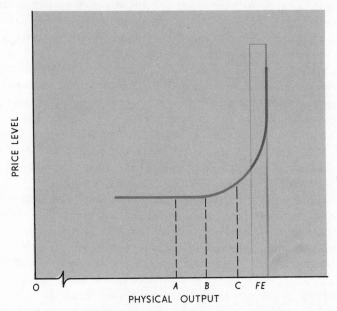

PHYSICAL OUTPUT

ment by one percentage point. American experience casts doubt upon the existence of any fixed and precise relation. For example, Figure 13–5 shows that in the 1954–60 period, the relations were different from those of the 1961–65 period. In the latter years the economy was less "inflation prone" than earlier. By mid-1967, however, conditions seem to have shifted back toward those of the 1950's as regards the tendency for prices to go up. Although we cannot use experience to predict with certainty just how much the forces which bring about a drop in unemployment will affect price levels, the record leaves no doubt that rising employment has been associated with price-level increases even when unemployment seems clearly large enough to mean that appreciable productive capacity is idle.

Developments lag behind their causes. Monetary and fiscal policies operating today will not exert their full influences tomorrow but over several months. We cannot, therefore, be sure that today's responses to what went on months ago will be repeated when today's policies bear their fruit. Such terms as "overheating," though lacking in precision, are suggestive. As business prospers, distortions in the price structure and stresses and strains of other types may be building up—but not be recognized.

FIGURE 13–5. "Trade Off": Unemployment and Inflation: "Phillips Curve (Industrial Wholesale Prices and Rate of Unemployment, Quarterly, 1954–65)

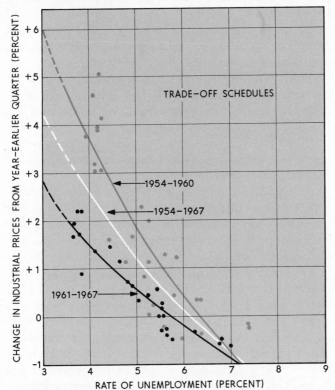

RATE OF UNEMPLOYMENT (PERCENT)

Source: U.S. Department of Labor, Bureau of Labor Statistics and Federal Reserve Bank of Cleveland. Federal Reserve Bank of Cleveland, *Economic Review,* April, 1966.

Part of the difficulty arises from the nature of present unemployment. Many unfilled jobs seek workers even though unemployment runs in the millions. How much unemployment results from inadequate total demand, that is, not enough buying power to purchase the full output of industry at current prices? How much unemployment results because people are not sufficiently skilled for the jobs available ("structural unemployment")?

GUIDEPOSTS FOR WAGES AND PRICES: PRODUCTIVITY AS A GUIDE.

One approach to relief from the dilemma seeks for effective but voluntary restraint on the upward pressure of wage rates and prices. Levels of income can go up as a result of rising productivity. But can income improvement be confined within such limits and thus avoid the exploitation of monopolistic bargaining power? Perhaps. But who then is to get the fruits of growing productivity? Suppose that net output is $800 of which the wage portion is $600, that of capital $200. Then real output goes up 3 percent a year. The added total to be shared consists of goods and services (product) worth $24 and also dollar income of $24. Wages can rise $18 (3 percent), leaving $6 (also 3 percent) for owners of capital. Prices will be stable because the increases in spending and output are equal. Such a result would probably be the outcome in a purely competitive economy with monetary stability.

Our economy, however, has elements that are not fully competitive. For dealing with them, President Kennedy and his Council of Economic Advisers in 1962 published "guideposts for noninflationary wage and price behavior." Labor and industry were urged to observe these guideposts on a voluntary basis. Where parties have "considerable room for exercise of private power" in wage bargains and price decisions, there is "parallel need for the assumption of private responsibility."

The general guide called for wage rates to rise as much as average man-hour productivity in the economy as a whole. On the average, no cost increase would result; returns to capital, specifically profits, could rise by perhaps about the same percentage (as in the example above). For the economy as a whole the Council, though recognizing some uncertainties due to measurement problems, suggested an average productivity and wage rate increase of around 3.2 percent a year.

The Council made very clear that although in its belief such a rule could properly apply in general, many exceptions were required for equity and for efficiency in resource allocation. For example, a bigger wage-rate increase will sometimes be required if a firm or industry is to attract labor to meet growth demands or to take account of past lags in wage increases. Less may be needed where earlier wage adjustments were higher. Competition must be recognized as a powerful force which companies and their workers must be free to meet. And so on.

The economic fundamentals underlying the guideposts came in for some serious questioning by economists; also, and quite properly, many aspects received sympathetic endorsement. Just possibly unions and businesses with monopolistic power would exercise self-restraint. Fatal weaknesses appeared, however. The exceptions and refinements of the basic rule which made the system defensible on economic grounds also destroyed the hopes of making it "operational" in the sense of workable. Any union or employer wanting a result different from that indicated by the general rule seemed able to find something in one of the many special cases for which exception would be allowed. Who could not argue that one or another of the special provisions applied to his case and thus warranted more for him?

When demand was generally strong, why not get more if possible? Perhaps profits were high (inviting the union to try for more) or low (so that the company would take advantage of opportunity to raise prices).

Big, highly visible unions and corporations were for a time under some pressure of public opinion. No one knows how much influence the White House exerted behind the scenes. Officials felt they achieved some successes. But generally throughout the economy, the guideposts carried far less weight than did economic self-interest. And when a few well-publicized strikes were settled with official "endorsement" of terms significantly above 3.2 percent, the claim of public support lost force. The power of booming aggregate demand proved strong.

We shall never learn how many wage negotiations were significantly affected by the existence of the guideposts or how many prices were kept more or less voluntarily lower than they might have been. Pressures of demand and shortages of labor grew stronger. By 1965 many wage settlements were enough above the basic guidelines to permit those managements which were sensitive to official approval and wanted to avoid appearing to neglect the national interest to explain, "We cannot settle with the union, or get the labor quality we need, without going above the guideposts." Or "Wage costs have risen more than productivity so that prices must also rise."

Several European countries have tried "income policies" relying on voluntary compliance. At best, the results were spotty but with some initial successes. Eventually, all the attempts proved to be failures if aggregate demand was strong and sustained. When one or the other, or both, parties in negotiations had an interest in a settlement on terms different from those of the guideposts, the influence of unofficial, voluntary suggestions proved weak. The failures must be considered as not unexpected, but discouraging. (See Figure 13–6.)

Job Training, Antitrust, and Other Approaches. Some hope does lie in other possibilities. The goal, we recall, is to find means for making more complete use of the potentials of expansionary fiscal and monetary policy to get really full use of productive capacity without inflation. Extensive training efforts have gotten under way. By 1963, it was clear that many of the men, women, and especially young people remaining unemployed after years of the upswing were not potentially very productive. They lacked skills, attitudes, and other things needed for employment in modern society. So a variety of programs, governmental and private, have been instituted. Costs sometimes prove high, but worker capacities do improve. Success brings experience on which to make future efforts more effective.

Another approach is to try to make the economy more competitive, to weaken the monopolistic elements which boost prices. Antitrust policy may help somewhat. Reduction of barriers to international trade can enhance competition and weaken the power of domestic sellers to raise prices unduly. Improved information on the availability of both jobs and workers also helps break down barriers to full employment when aggregate demand is adequate.

Coordination of Monetary and Fiscal Policy. The effects of any fiscal policy must work out in an environment which depends significantly

FIGURE 13–6. Wage Rate and Price Trends, Germany and Sweden, 1960–67

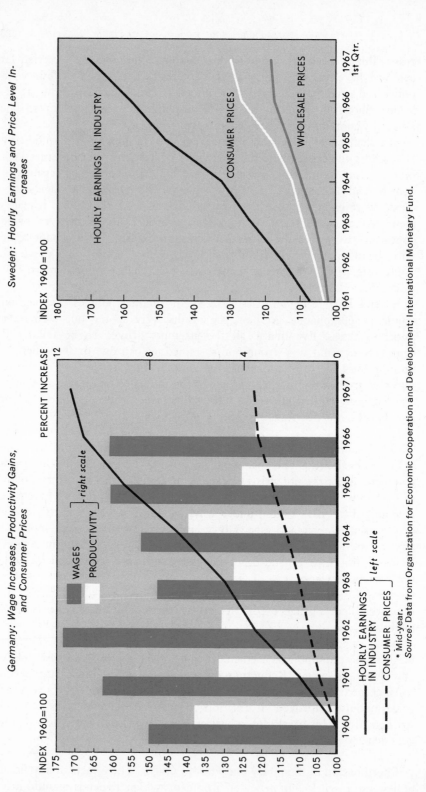

Germany: Wage Increases, Productivity Gains, and Consumer Prices

Sweden: Hourly Earnings and Price Level Increases

HOURLY EARNINGS
IN INDUSTRY } left scale

CONSUMER PRICES } left scale

* Mid-year.
Source: Data from Organization for Economic Cooperation and Development; International Monetary Fund.

upon monetary policy. The two major tools for economic stabilization—monetary and fiscal policy—must be thought of as allies. They work toward the same goals but are by no means perfect substitutes for each other. They are not fully interchangeable. Each can do much, either to reinforce or nullify the other, depending upon how they are used. In the mid-1960's, two unsolved issues were receiving more attention.

1. Success requires skillful coordination of policies, but as noted earlier, we cannot be certain of getting such harmony. The Executive Branch and Congress will not necessarily work together smoothly and promptly. And the Federal Reserve has much independence. As the members of the Federal Reserve Board see their responsibility, they may not agree with the fiscal policy being followed. Regular informal meetings now assure full understanding of Treasury and Federal Reserve attitudes. Is this enough, however? Not really. The alternative of reducing the independence of the Fed would meet with great opposition. There is considerable belief that a central bank needs to be free from political control to be able to resist pressures for inflation.

2. How much reliance can best be placed on monetary policy and how much on fiscal policy? No general rules can be set out in advance. As particular cases arise, each must be evaluated according to the specific elements of the time.

"Fiscal Drag?"   In the 1930's, many economists concluded that our economy had a tendency to *stagnate*, that is, to fail by a significant margin to use its resources fully. The major remedies proposed were that the government use: (1) its monetary powers to keep interest rates generally low and liquidity high, and (2) its fiscal powers to produce stimulating deficits most or all of the time. Inflation did not then loom as a problem.

In the early 1960's, a different version worried many leaders. The rate of the economy's growth was discouraging and unemployment excessive. Again, America's problem seemed to involve more than the recession phase of the business cycle. Some of the policies recommended by economists were about the same—budget deficits, for example. Much emphasis was placed on stimulating investment to speed economic growth. The investment tax credit was such a device. Tax rate reduction, it was hoped, would help liberate the capacities of "job creators" and ease their accumulation of capital. Easy money seemed desirable except for one reason which overruled others in the views of many: low interest rates would encourage the outflow of capital to other countries.

A new concern has arisen. The existing federal tax structure has a powerful, a very powerful, upward revenue potential. Rising national income automatically brings larger revenue increases. The exact relations between GNP and Treasury receipts have not been quite so easy to measure as had been expected, but the reality is simple: Most increases in personal income are received by persons already paying tax so that almost none is offset by unused personal exemption. Added income is taxed: the lowest individual tax rate is 14 percent (plus about 9 percent in total social security tax), but for most people the rate is higher, with 20 percent being on the low side. Here then is "big take"—but not compared with the burden on corporations. The great bulk of increases in corporation earnings are taxed at 48 percent. Over a few years, total corporation net income will go up appreciably. The Treasury is almost a fifty-fifty partner.

As a reasonable planning assumption, therefore, it seems that one can expect total federal revenue in 3 years or so, without any change in tax rates or tax structure, to be $20 to $25 billion greater than today. Depending upon the course of outlays for Vietnam and nondefense programs, the budget may become restrictive, or lose much of a stimulating element, before we sense the fact. Perhaps a "drag" on the economy will result. No such necessity will exist, but some danger of being overtaken by surprise may exist.[8]

TERMS AND CONCEPTS

commercial loan theory	debt management	discretionary fiscal
monetary policy	fiscal policy	policy
wage price guideposts	compensatory fiscal	automatic stabilizers
stagnation theory	policy	Phillips Curve
selective control	"income policy"	fiscal drag

QUESTIONS

1. "The problem of fiscal policy is not the lack of goodwill, or good intentions, or adequate power but the knowledge of what to do, when, where, and for whom." Comment. Do the same arguments apply to monetary policy? Why?

2. What method of financing a budget deficit will be most effective in eliminating unemployment? Preventing inflation?

3. Does the Federal Reserve have greater power to curtail an expansion in the quantity of money than to bring about an expansion? Why? How do monetary and fiscal policy supplement each other?

4. Why is it easier to formulate policies to stimulate employment than policies which will do so while not bringing inflation?

5. Explain the meaning of "automatic stabilizer." Do we have any now? In what respect may taxes act as a "drag" on expansion?

6. Explain why it is easier to prescribe generally what to do when inflation is strong, or when depression is deep, than when departures from the desired goal are not large but nevertheless deserving of remedy.

7. What fiscal policy would help adjust to a big cut in defense spending?

8. What are the risks of a tight-money policy?

[8] Tax rate reductions offer one possibility. Others include higher federal spending on revenue sharing with states. See Chapter 32.

APPENDIX
Topics in Monetary and Fiscal Policy

The study of monetary and fiscal policy includes several topics whose importance makes some discussion desirable but which for one reason or another are not near enough the mainstream of discussion today to include in the main text. A few occupied almost the center of attention in much of the postwar period, and may do so again.

Selective Monetary Controls. Might we develop monetary controls which apply selectively to lending for specific purposes rather than generally to the whole economy? Some parts of the economy will be moving differently from others. Why not adjust policy to the conditions in different sectors? Idle capacity in the housing construction industry, for example, may appear when other major sectors are going along nicely. Can easier lending terms for the one particular sector, housing, bolster it but not those which need no stimulus?

The possibilities, even with changes in the law, are not encouraging. Immediate results, it is true, might be gratifying. Yet spending in any one part of the economy will "spill over" into others. Easier credit for housing may increase the employment and income of carpenters who would otherwise be idle. Their enlarged spending, however, would go largely for products of industries operating about at capacity. In other words, the effects of *special* monetary aids cannot be confined. Financial markets will not for long sustain easy money in one place and tight in another.

Trouble in one sector is likely to be either temporary or the result of more basic changes in demand or supply. (1) If the first, temporary, a change in lending policy may work constructively—or not. A change may not be effective soon enough to help appreciably. Later it may do more harm than good by stimulating excessive activity that boosts costs and prices and "steals" business from the future; selective restrictive action, on the other hand, may dampen activity just when normal forces would be operating in the same direction.

(2) If the trouble results from more fundamental conditions—such as monopolistic prices and wage rates—monetary stimulants to counteract the basic forces today can add to trouble in the future by aggravating whatever is wrong. Either unusual distress or high boom in a particular industry signals the public to alter resource allocation and prices. A signal in the opposite direction from the monetary authorities will tend to delay correction and make future conditions worse.

Selective controls help and hurt particular groups. Naturally, they will try to exert influence for their own benefit—lower interest rates on new construction to make possible higher wages, prices of materials, or land. Restrictive policies here but not there invite evasion.

Still, there is some prospect of limited success in checking the growth of lending for specific purposes, such as for installment buying. Borrowing to buy on installments can accentuate business cycles; the problem of general public policy is not with credit buying per se but with fluctuations in the amount of credit outstanding. Selective controls might stabilize slightly the creation of money for such purposes.[1]

Selective control exists in the power to alter the terms of government insurance and guarantee of loans, especially for housing. By relaxing or tightening the terms of loans which qualify for insurance or guarantee, government without any current outlay of funds can influence investment. More than once, however, this power has been used to offset, instead of strengthen, Federal Reserve policy.

Limitations on Monetary Policy. From the 1930's until the late 1950's many economists had little confidence in monetary policy because they believed that little can be accomplished. The prevailing view today assigns much greater effect to monetary policy but many object to its vigorous use. Several points, varying in nature and significance, are made.

1. Some sectors of the economy are affected much more by interest rates and the availability of borrowings than are others. Some businesses, especially large ones, rarely use short-term bank lending. Ability to finance internally gives some companies immunity from pressure from the monetary authorities. Other firms can be certain of bank accommodation even when money is tightest. Therefore, only part of the business world, most likely small and growing firms, will be influenced directly by monetary actions—more often, it is alleged, hurt by restrictive policy than helped by easier conditions.

2. The economic activity most affected by interest rates is that associated with investment, especially construction. Some economists argue that we are unwise to concentrate pressure for economic restraint during boom periods cn investment rather than on consumption. Investment provides the basis for economic growth. If there is vigorous demand for credit, does it not seem sensible to create money to satisfy it if investment is encouraged as a result?

---

[1] The Federal Reserve now exercises selective restrictions on interest rates payable on time and savings deposits. Changes can, as in 1966, alter the position of banks in relation to other thrift institutions. The short-run effects in 1966 included a marked decline in the availability of loan funds for housing. The Federal Reserve also controls margin requirements for bank and broker loans for purchase of stock. A person wanting to get around the limits can go to nonbank lenders.

Because of the importance of inventory fluctuations in cyclical movements, would it not be helpful if controls were devised to stabilize spending for inventory, or at least to prevent extremes of borrowing to finance inventory accumulation? Yes—perhaps. The practical problems would be complicated, to say the least, because controlling the use of borrowed funds requires far more detailed intervention in business than our banks or monetary authorities can exercise. Would such restrictions on borrowing for inventory building (or some other purpose) violate an essential freedom of business? Hardly. Business can claim no basic right to have the community create money to enable a company to finance operations in its own interest. There seems little prospect, however, of developing workable policy to pinpoint monetary restraint on inventory buying.

(Not necessarily.) "Tight money" comes in for additional criticism on the grounds that it raises the cost of school construction and other state-local capital projects. Inflation, however, would raise all costs of local government, not just borrowing; higher interest rates are not an unreasonable price to pay to keep the general price level from rising.

3. The development of a wide variety of nonbank lenders and other financial intermediaries has reduced the relative importance of commercial banks. Businesses, individuals, and governments can often turn to institutions other than commercial banks for financing. These institutions do not create or destroy money. But they affect its use. Any given quantity of M can do more or less "work"—V changes, depending upon the use made of financial institutions which are not significantly affected by existing monetary controls. The growth and expanded use of near monies and money substitutes, it is said, has weakened traditional Federal Reserve controls.

4. National government receipts and spending are not affected appreciably by monetary policy. Debt management, however, is much influenced. Treasury borrowing to refinance maturing short-term debt creates at least some pressure for monetary ease at some time. Monetary authorities are not free to ignore Treasury needs.

5. Changes in interest rates and the prices of bonds bring windfall gains and losses to individuals in ways which, it is said, bear no rational relation to the proper sharing of the costs of stabilization of the economy as a whole.

6. Because a profitable business can deduct interest in computing taxable income, *changes* in interest rates may have little net effect on business expense. Though the conclusion is perhaps true in some cases, this argument is misleading—all expenses are deductible just as all the receipts they make possible are taken into account in figuring taxes.

7. Loan contracts have developed in ways which reduce the importance of interest as a cost and especially the significance of short-run changes in rates. For example, the period for repaying loans can be extended or shortened, so that at any of several interest rates the size of the periodic payment meets the borrowers' needs.

Experience indicates that changes in the quantity of money influence the economy even when the purely interest-rate effects as such may be of secondary significance.

Debt Management as an Instrument for Influencing National Income. Budget surpluses and deficits, changing the amount of the federal debt, will result from stabilizing fiscal policies, discretionary or automatic. Yet the existing debt, without any change in its size, can be used as a stabilizing force. The outstanding debt must be managed. As old issues fall due, nev securities must be sold—several billions of dollars a month on the average. A debt management policy which helps stabilize the economy as a whole will tighten money when inflation threatens and ease it when business slackens. As business booms, the Treasury would shift some debt from banks to private savers. How? Pay the price needed—offer interest rates that will appeal to savers.

Yet critics complain, and not only about the rise in interest cost to the taxpayer. They will also say that drawing savings away from private uses will discourage business. No Treasury Secretary welcomes such criticism. When depression threatens, just the opposite policy is appropriate. The Treasury would shift debt from savers to banks. This latter shift tends to reduce interest costs. But critics say that not much can really be done for the economy and that banks will try to sell the debt when loan demand increases, thus creating problems later. To date, debt management has not been an important stabilizer.

Defense Spending.   Does high national income require vast military spending? Some parts of the economy are entirely, and some largely, military. A decline in such spending would depress them but also permit a cut in taxes so that the public could spend more on other things. We could shift, not cut, our buying. Congress could say "You no longer need to spend so much on weapons, so we reduce your taxes and let you do what you want with the money." Personal spending would rise. Businesses could spend more on modernization and expansion. Most emphatically, we do not need great armament spending for prosperity. Aggregate dollar demand could be maintained by cutting taxes.

More difficult would be the transition from military to other production by persons with the specialized skills needed for today's intricate weapons production. No one knows how long a time and what kinds of retraining would be required, nor how much new capital equipment would be needed. Overall, however, the shift would be, not only possible but would also permit a significant rise in levels of living.

PART 4

PRICES, OUTPUT, AND

THE ALLOCATION OF

RESOURCES

Now we turn from the forces that determine the general level of national income and prices—the broad aggregates of *macroeconomics*—to the processes of business. The whole of national output consists of a huge variety of goods and services. Millions of economic units using the community's varied resources create this output. We have alternatives and must choose among them. The analysis of how these choices are made—*microeconomics*—looks at the smaller elements, as under a microscope, to see how they function as parts of the whole. The basic concern is with the organization of the parts of the economy—organization to serve us *efficiently*. By this term economists ordinarily mean: *allocating resources to best advantage.*

14

DEMAND

On a general understanding of the fundamental laws of price relations, and on their thoughtful application in measures of public policy, rests all hope for prosperity under democratic institutions, all hope for efficiency in industry. . . .

Frank H. Knight

Even if we were assured of a full employment level of national income without inflation, economic problems of the utmost importance would remain. What goods and services would make up this total? Who would get how much income? Why? It is such questions that we now begin to answer. The first step is to examine the "job" that prices do.

ROLE OF PRICE

In the broadest sense, **prices induce production** and **restrict consumption.**[1] Yet we can say more, especially about the role of the relationship among prices. **Relative prices** guide choices. They direct the process of economizing. Relationships among prices signal producers to increase the output of one thing and cut the output of another. A change in the price of one thing compared with the price of another will lead us to boost consumption of one, reduce that of another. The businessman selects a particular production method as best only after comparing the relative prices of inputs. The wage rates in different jobs influence our choice of

---

[1] Underlying prices are estimates of value—of worthiness. Economists often use the term *value theory* for what we call *price theory*. The term "value" is somewhat more personal, more philosophical, more likely to imply a sense of inherent goodness than the term "price." If a person pays dearly for something we think foolish, we may question his sense of values but not the economic importance it carries.

335

where we shall work. Relative prices of both inputs and outputs indicate where research is more needed to reduce costs and which of several possible new methods promises to be best.

Each price is a sort of guidepost or signal directing the way resources are used. A price change indicates that there has been a change in preferences (among consumers, producers, or both). A rise in the price of an item discourages its consumption but also provides incentive to enlarge production and furnishes the wherewithal in the form of greater revenue. A price reduction does the opposite. It tells us that we can now get more satisfaction from our limited income by substituting more of the cheaper item for something whose price has not dropped.

Let us restate. Prices not only induce production—so much of this, so much of that. They also indicate the relative economic desirability of different possible methods of production. Similarly, prices not only restrict consumption. They indicate which things need to be economized most and which we can consume more plentifully. The relations among prices, therefore, influence the pattern of consumption and help us get more rather than less satisfaction out of our limited income.

Each price reflects the effect of forces of supply and of demand. We start with demand.

DEMANDS OF INDIVIDUALS

The consumer must choose. A family with $150 a week to spend, $7,800 a year, has a myriad of possibilities of choice. Some combinations are better than others. As a consumer tries to shift from a poorer to a better combination of choices, his demands for particular goods and services change.

Individual and Aggregate Demand. The term "demand" applies to that of either an individual—a child's demand for popsicles—or of all persons in the market. Total market demand for a product—books or pencils—is the sum of all the demands of families, governments, businesses, clubs, and other associations. Our concern will ordinarily be with market demand. We start, however, with the demands of individuals, including households or families.

The Wants Underlying Demand. The demand for goods and services results from our wants and from the usefulness of various things in satisfying those desires.

Wants seem limitless—in quantity, variety, quality, and in the way they change. In this respect, wants present a striking contrast to man's productive capacity, which clearly is limited. Wants are not only greater in total than our ability to satisfy them, but specific wants differ in intensity. So we face a *problem of choice:* Which "want" should we try to satisfy? Decision is often hard because of another feature of wants—they are *states of mind*, or feelings.

Sometimes there seems little doubt which, among the multitude of wants, are most important. In other cases, however, individuals find their own wants difficult to compare at any one time: desire for physical comfort in a pair of shoes compared with the admiration we expect from a style which pinches. It is even more difficult to compare our wants from one time to another, a fact that complicates planning for the future. Many desires, except for those chiefly biological (for liquid, food of some sort, sleep, warmth), are molded by social pressures and our "unconscious" in ways of which we are not aware. Some of us want to "keep ahead of the Joneses"; others prefer to be liked rather than envied and are reluctant to buy some things because of the fear of disapproval.[2] It is difficult, indeed, for us to know, consciously, just what we want most and why.

Judging how and why the "other fellow" makes his decisions proves endlessly difficult—but challenging. And because of the personal, intangible, sensory nature of wants and of satisfactions, comparison among individuals appears impossible. *Economics provides no ideal criterion by which to compare what people do, or to say what would be better.* The engineer cannot judge how efficiently a machine works until he has a standard of efficiency. Nor can anyone, including economists, judge how efficiently people use their income to satisfy their own personal wants. We have no standard with which to compare what does happen with that which would best serve the consumer.[3]

Economists, for the most part, proceed somewhat as follows. (1) We accept the fact that the underlying basis of wants and demand is psychological and (2) assume (*a*) that wants are "given" for most of the analysis, (*b*) that people know what they want—so much food, so much worship, so much art—and (*c*) what will help satisfy those wants. We then assume that (3) consumers try to make choices that will give them a better, rather than a poorer, net result—more rather than less want satisfaction; in other words, we assume that the consumer tries to *maximize* the satisfaction he achieves.

Wants Expressed as Demands Are Specific. The first step is this: Demands as they are expressed in the market are not for "things in

[2] An airline survey found that many travelers had a sense of guilt about using first class, partly on account of social censure for ostentation. Advertising was shifted to the theme that first-class travel enabled one to do more work en route and to arrive more relaxed and readier to work effectively. Part of a large rise in first-class travel within a few months was attributed to new attitudes resulting from the advertising.

[3] The liberal tradition holds that, in general, adults are better judges of their own concerns than of the concerns of others. Yet who does not have values, based on religious or other convictions, which indicate, for example, that spending on milk for the children is generally better than on gin for adults? Should the individual's liberty be curbed? Where? By whom? Such questions remain unsolved. Most of us will agree that individual preference may wisely be limited when "neighborhood" or "spillover" effects are extensive. When the actions of the individual impose significant costs on others, or bring apppreciable benefits not charged for or compensated, individual choice cannot lead to best results. Will intervention by "outsiders" through government produce better results? Economists can point to theoretical possibilities, but practice presents many difficulties.

general" but for specific things. Who ever placed an order for "food"? We ask for a ham sandwich on rye, potato chips, or strawberry ice cream. No one says, "Sell me $20 worth of clothing"; actual orders are more likely to be for "an inexpensive sport dress, size 10, navy or maroon" or "a white shirt, size 15–33, with button-down collar." We do not order "outdoor entertainment" this fall but a pair of seats near the 50-yard line for the big game. Government does not order "armaments" but a weapons system which will do certain things. We even demand "brand X" instead of "toothpaste," the *Times* instead of "a newspaper." In short, desires as expressed in the market are for things or services defined in limited terms. The productive system is geared to provide specific things—in unbelievable variety.

Diminishing Utility.   Though one cannot conceive of wants in general ever being satisfied, the desire for a specific product or service can be met fully (under a given set of conditions at a given time). The more units of a thing a consumer has, the less he wants another of the same thing. Exceptions there are, within limits, but they *are* limited; and many apparent exceptions involve subtle shifts of assumptions.[4] If a man does not have a belt, one may be worth a lot; a second may also be worth a great deal, though not so much as the first; if he has 10 belts, still another, though somewhat useful, will add much less to his satisfactions than the first.

Dinner-table illustrations are perhaps even clearer—the last bite of a huge steak is appreciated less than the first. Conceivably, a man who begins a meal with ravenous hunger will leave some food uneaten. Durable goods (furnaces, typewriters, lawn mowers) or their services, and such services as tonsilectomies, present even sharper examples. *At any given time, successive, additional units of any one product or service have less want-satisfying power.* Economists call this want-satisfying power "utility." We cannot measure differences in utility from one unit to another. Nor can we compare changes from person to person. Yet the fact that additional units of a thing have diminishing utility is a principle indicated by common sense, and one that helps in the analysis of economic problems.

Of course, when we have more, rather than less, of something, the larger quantity will give us more *total utility*. What diminishes is not the total utility; I am not worse off with six than with two belts. What diminishes is the utility of the increments, one after another. Each incre-

---

[4] Possible typical cases are goods and services with snob appeal and things whose quality we tend to judge by price, perhaps unconsciously—the perfume or professional service we prefer more highly the greater its price. Some tastes develop so that, within limits, the more one gets, the more one will want—classical music, for example. Yet under given conditions—in a single evening—the satisfaction from repeated hearings of a Bach fugue may be very different from the utility of the same number of hearings in a month.

ment is a *marginal* unit from the one preceding or following. The utility of marginal units diminishes in the sense that each gives less satisfaction than the earlier one—the *n*th unit has more want-satisfying power than unit *n* + 1 but less than *n* − 1. (Remember, we are talking about the utility of a single product under given conditions, *not* about (*a*) the utility of *total* income or (*b*) the utility of a product as it appears over time, during which tastes can change.) Figure 14–1 shows the utility from 1 belt as around 10; from a second, about 7; from a sixth, scarcely 1. The total utility for the six is perhaps three times that from one. The *marginal utility* of a unit is the amount it adds to the total util-ity from all the goods or services of that particular type.

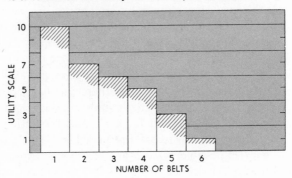

FIGURE 14–1. Diminishing Utility

The larger the number of belts owned, the smaller the utility of an additional belt (other things the same). Shading is to remind us that utility cannot really be measured.

What are the units in which utility is measured? Hardly money or "states of mind." There is no way, in fact, to measure utility well; and the cruder our measurement, the harder it is to make rational choices. In fact we cannot always answer the question: "What is the more or the less?"

Does Usefulness Determine Value? What role does the usefulness of a good—its want-satisfying power—play in determining demand? People, of course, will not sacrifice to get something unless they think it has value (utility) for them. Yet things with apparently high utility sell for less than others with apparently little usefulness. Air is of tremendous utility, but free. Diamonds sell for more per pound than bread, champagne for more than milk; electricity costs, but sunlight is free.

Such seemingly topsy-turvy relationships can be explained simply. The amount we are willing to pay for a unit of a good depends upon our estimate of the value of that unit to us. This estimate depends upon how easily one can get substitutes. The more we have of this or that, the less we will sacrifice to get another unit of the same thing. If a person has "enough" of something of great usefulness, he will not acquire more, even for very little sacrifice. If we have enough air, why pay to get more? In fact, we will not pay for any specific part of our total air if other air is available free. We can substitute what is free for those portions for which someone might try to charge us.

Scarcity. Therefore, if a good is to command a price it must be scarce. Yet rareness, or scarcity in the sense of small quantity, will not make us willing to pay for something that has no utility. Tickets to last year's football game may be scarce but not very desirable. It is when things have utility and are also scarce (not plentiful) that one must pay to get them. Unless we do pay, others will not give them up. Diamonds for ornament have utility for some people: the thrill of an engagement ring. Diamonds are rare enough so that people who want even a small one must get it from someone who also wants it (for sale if not for use). Air is useful; but to get the part we need to satisfy our wants, we do not have to take it from someone who also wants it. Something more than utility, therefore, enters into the determination of price. This other element is "supply."

Necessity of Choice. No one can satisfy all his wants. Purchasing power, what can be given to others, sets hard, practical limits. (Even the person with boundless funds finds another rigid limit: time.) A family having $9,000 to spend faces obvious restrictions. Since it cannot have everything, it must select. But on what basis? It would be clearly absurd, in fact impossible, to use all our money (and time) for one type of product, red dresses or chocolate malts. We must have many different things. How then to balance? Obviously, we cannot get a sensible balance by selecting 2 or 2 dozen of the myriad possibilities and dividing our total spending equally among them. Wisdom calls for dividing the total among many things, but with rational discrimination. The goal is to *maximize* by allocating as well as knowledge of utility will permit, that which is scarce (spending power) among different possible uses to receive the best total result. As we increase the consumption of any one thing, the utility of an additional unit declines. It would be foolish to buy units if they forced us to sacrifice something else which would give more satisfaction—to spend $4 on another necktie if a book would give more satisfaction.

Consumer Equilibrium. The ideal adjustment is made (1) when the benefit gained from what one receives from spending the last penny on each of all the things one buys is equal, and (2) when this benefit is also greater than the benefit that could be obtained from spending a penny on anything else.[5] Of course, no one can hit this point exactly except by accident (or by defining "what I want" as "what I get"). No one is likely

---

[5] The ratios of the marginal utility of each good or service to its price must be equal.

$$\frac{MU \text{ or product } A}{\text{Price of product } A} = \frac{MU \text{ of product } B}{\text{Price of product } B} = \frac{MU \text{ of product } C}{\text{Price of product } C}, \text{etc.}$$

If one ratio turned out to be higher than another, could the consumer make a better adjustment? Yes. Some shift of spending would permit him to gain. By cutting the purchase of one thing (that with smaller utility at the margin in relation to price), he would get funds with which he could buy a thing of greater utility (at the margin).

to have precisely the best diet each day. Perfection in life is rare, yet people can do better or worse. They can come closer to the ideal in allocating their spending on consumption, just as they can eat better diets if they understand nutrition or build more efficient machines as knowledge of science grows. Most families cannot afford much waste. They are under pressure to make better rather than worse adjustments in buying, to balance choices rationally, albeit most often unconsciously, according to personal preferences.

Only Meaningful Choices Have Economic Significance. Demand, in the economic sense, is more than desire for something. It is the desire or wish backed by money (or something else of value to the seller). The exhausted housewife may have an intense desire for a full-time maid, but she has no economic demand if she is not able to offer payment. The term *effective demand* is often used to emphasize the difference between wish, want, or desire, and "economic demand." There will be no demand in the economic sense unless there is an underlying desire, plus *ability and willingness to pay*.

Choices depend upon the consumer's estimate of what one more unit would be worth to him in relation to the worth of anything else he could get instead. Can you think of anything specific that you absolutely must have? Air, light, and possibly a few others; but liquids and most food elements are obtainable in many forms, and so are clothing, shelter, admiration, excitement, and on and on. Although desire for something may be intense, one does not act rationally in buying it if the purchase means giving up other things of still more utility.

Yet how can one compare such possibilities? Do we know our preferences well enough to decide wisely? How do we estimate subjective benefits, especially of units or even types of products which we are not consuming? In one sense, each person must answer these questions for himself. Often, of course, no estimate is needed because there is no problem of choice. A poor family will not be concerned about choosing between spending another few cents on milk or buying a new electric stove; a prosperous family would hardly feel any problem of choice in spending a few cents more for postage or food (it can afford both). Sometimes there is no problem of selection because the difference between a good and a bad choice is too slight to be a matter of concern.[6] In many cases, however, and not only when women buy dresses, the uncertainty may be harrowing.

---

[6] One thing some of us want is to be free of pressure to make choices. Habit becomes a powerful tool for increasing our total of want satisfaction. It saves us the annoyance of much decision making. Sometimes we bargain carefully. At other times, we take little pains. Perhaps the amounts are too small to justify our concern, perhaps we are on vacation and do not want to worry or are sick and in no mood to bargain with doctor or hospital.

Guidance of Price. In choosing among alternative expenditure opportunities, we get help from the market. Most things have one element in common, other than utility: prices expressed in the same monetary unit. Different things can therefore be related. The consumer has a measure of how much of other things he must give up to obtain each particular thing. He still has the problem of comparing values, to him, of the different physical possibilities that cost the same number of dollars—more cake and less bread, a new pair of shoes and the symphony series. We make mistakes, but prices give at least some basis for choosing with intelligence. Prices show quickly and accurately how much of one thing each consumer must sacrifice to get any of several other things. The optimum is the condition in which no shift of his money expenditures can permit him to buy something more desirable than what he would need to sacrifice.

As each buyer reacts to prices, he also helps to change prices. No one person will have perceptible influence, but thousands and millions exert considerable pressure. Consumers vote with their dollars. These votes change relative prices. In doing so, they guide both production and consumption and play a role in a self-adjusting mechanism of great effectiveness.

DIAGRAMMING DEMAND

The Demand Curve. A diagram will portray the general principle that the more one must sacrifice to get a unit of a given product, the fewer units he will take. We cannot, of course, show the hundreds of possible alternative purchases which a person must sacrifice to get, say, a new suit. Such a complicated picture is unnecessary. Sacrifice can be measured in one thing: money.

TABLE 14–1.   Demand of an Individual Consumer for a Single Product

Price per Unit	Number of Units That Will Be Purchased at Price
$5	2
4	4
3	8
2	10
1	15

Custom has fixed certain usages. Price is measured from the origin up, as north is represented by "up" on a map; the lowest price is farthest down, the highest price is farthest up. To the right, we measure the number of units of the particular commodity that a buyer will take. At, and above, some price the family would take none. At a slightly lower price, it might take 1 unit per month; at a slightly lower price, 2 units; at a still lower, 3, and so on. Illustrative figures are given in Table 14–1.

We assume "other things" to remain "the same," the most important being tastes, income, and the prices of other products. The lower the price, the larger the number of units that will be purchased. For each such combination, there is a point. A line connecting the points will slope

downward to the right (Fig. 14–2). Two related forces bring this result:
(1) diminishing utility, and (2) the fact that the higher the price, the
more of other useful things we must sacrifice to get a unit.

Possibilities of sub-
stitution help explain
the downward slope.
The higher the price
of any one thing, the
greater the induce-
ment to substitute
other goods or serv-
ices which will give
more satisfaction per
dollar. When the
price of something
falls, we tend to sub-
stitute more of it for
things whose prices
have not dropped.
And, of course, with
limited income, we
are able to buy fewer
units at higher than at lower prices.

FIGURE 14–2. Diagram of Demand Shown in Table 14–1

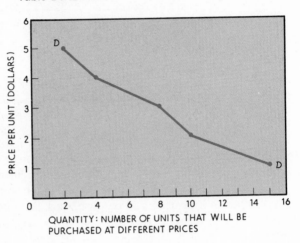

The line on the diagram, a *demand curve*, shows the *relation between
quantity demanded and price.* The number of units that will be purchased
depends upon the amount the buyer must sacrifice for each unit; a
demand curve summarizes this relationship. (Curves based on actual facts
would have many shapes; for simplicity we use straight lines.) Under the
conditions assumed, the number of units that will be bought will vary
from 2 to 15, depending upon price.[7] Warning! This meaning of "demand" differs from popular usage. Most of us tend to think of demand as
quantity, or the number of units. Economists, however, mean more. For
us, demand is a schedule. *Price and quantity must be dealt with together.*
Be careful, therefore, to use the term "demand" only when referring to a
price-quantity relation. When you mean quantity, the number of units,
say so. **Demand is the schedule of the quantities of a product (or
service) buyers will purchase at a series of prices in a given period of
time.**

Total Market Demand. Each consuming unit—individual, household,
business—has a set of preferences for using its income, a pattern of
demand. Some patterns are essentially alike; others are very different.

---

[7] Demand is a functional relation: Quantity = f (Price). The demand for anything
depends upon many considerations so that quantity will be influenced by changes in
factors other than price.

TABLE 14–2.   Demands of Individual Consumers Combine to Make Up Market Demand (Assuming Only Four Individuals in the Market)

| Price per Unit | Number of Units Each of Four Individual Consumers Will Purchase at Price | | | | Market Demand: Total of Individual Demands |
	A	B	C	D	
$5	3	2	1	0	6
4	4	5	2	1	12
3	4	10	5	4	23
2	5	13	7	6	31
1	6	17	12	10	45

Added together, however, their total is the total for the market. Table 14–2 illustrates how demands of several consuming units combine to make a total for the market. This total, the market demand, when charted, will, of course, slope downward to the right. The lower the price, the greater the number of units that will be purchased. Although markets as a whole are not alive in the sense that they can experience diminishing utility, each market consists of people. Since their demand curves all slope downward, so must the total. Moreover, differences in income and taste will lead to a market demand schedule that has a slope of this sort.

The "law of demand" says that, other things the same, the higher the price the smaller the quantity that will be purchased. Economists and businessmen would like to know much more: where the curve lies and how much it slopes. (The slope and position of the curve on a diagram will depend upon the scales used on the axes.) Generally, however, knowledge is limited to that part of the curve which is approximately at the current price-quantity point. Most consumers have no way of knowing how they would act if the price were much higher, or much lower, with other conditions unchanged. We may know how many pairs of shoes of the same quality we buy a year when they are priced around $12 but have little idea about how many we would buy if the price were $50 or $2.

With extensive data and skilled statistical analysis, it is occasionally possible to get a fairly good idea of some range of the curve. Unfortunately, we rarely have data for making good estimates. As students, we can blissfully extend curves beyond the areas for which facts might be available. The businessman as a seller, however, in estimating the demand for his products, will know the present price-quantity relation, and those of the past—but little or nothing about the quantity he could sell under present conditions at much higher or lower prices.

Changes in Demand.   What is a change in demand? It is *not* what the man in the street may think: a change in the quantity bought. Demand to the economist is a quantity-price relation. A change in demand is a shift of the schedule or curve, not a movement along any one curve. *Demand increases when more units will be bought at a given price or series of prices;* the demand curve, or part of it, moves to the right (or upward) on our graph. Or, as a general rule, an increase in demand has occurred if a price rise does not reduce the quantities sold. A *fall in demand* is the opposite: fewer units are sold at the same price, or the same number of units can be sold only at a lower price; the demand curve moves to the left (downward); its slope and shape may also change (Fig. 14–3). If the number of units sold increases when the price falls, demand has not necessarily increased. Buyers may merely be purchasing what they would previously have bought if the price had been lower. When the quantity

FIGURE 14–3. Changes in Demand

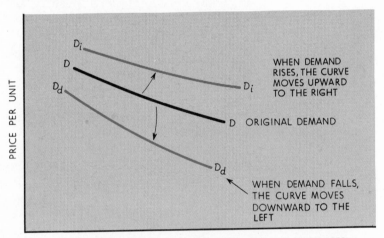

QUANTITY: NUMBER OF UNITS THAT WILL BE PURCHASED AT DIFFERENT PRICES UNDER THREE SETS OF CONDITIONS

sold rises only as the result of a decline in price, there has been movement along the schedule, not a change in demand.

Of course, demands do change, and for several reasons. 1. *Buyers' incomes rise and fall.* What we buy depends upon the amount of money we have to spend, chiefly from current income. If people get larger incomes, they will spend more, raising their demands for many things. A survey showed, for example, that families whose incomes rose by 5 percent or more in one year bought durable goods—"high-ticket" items—more often than families whose incomes were stable or dropping. But demands for specific things will not all rise proportionately or at the same time. If my salary were to rise, there might be no appreciable change in my demand for pepper but a big shift in my demand for books, steak, or new furniture. If incomes fall, demands will decline, but not uniformly and not necessarily following the pattern in which they rose. From 1929 to 1933, for example, spending on durable consumer goods fell 65 percent, while spending on nondurable goods fell 35 percent. From 1948 to 1950, spending on durable goods rose over 30 percent, while spending on nondurable goods rose less than 2 percent. In a later 2-year period, spending on durables rose only imperceptibly while spending on services rose 15 percent. In the 1960–61 recession, spending on durables dropped over 10 percent while that on services was rising 5 percent (annual rates).

The change of income that is important for a specific demand may be a change in national income or in the income of some regional or occupational or other group. The demand for fertilizer, for example, may respond quickly to changes in farmers' income and not at all to changes in the income of policemen. A change in the *distribution of income* will

TABLE 14–3.　Ownership of Autos and Planned Purchases of Autos, Houses, and Major Household Appliances, by Size of Income

| | Percent Planning to Buy Within Six Months | | | |
Money Income before Taxes	House	New Auto	Used Auto	Major Household Durable Goods
Under $1,000	2.2	0.7	2.7	9.5
1,000–1,999	4.8	2.2	4.5	11.4
2,000–2,999	6.7	3.8	5.3	13.6
7,500–9,999	7.9	6.0	5.2	18.7
$10,000 and over	7.7	11.0	4.7	19.2

Source: *Federal Reserve Bulletin.* Data apply to 1961.

change some demands; more equal distribution will probably reduce the demand for butlers and increase the demand for washing machines. We also vary our spending according to the *amount of liquid assets* we hold, *our ability to borrow* to finance payment (especially for such durables as new autos), and what we *expect* our income to be in the future. Table 14–3 shows how the planned purchases of houses, autos, and major household appliances can vary with income.

2. Demands change because *tastes change*—for many reasons. People may acquire a taste for hi-fi or foreign autos, or they may lose their liking for hoop skirts. Tastes shift: the availability of synthetic detergents cut demand for soap, nylon replaced silk for hosiery, guided missiles are replacing bombing planes. In 1929 Americans spent about the same dollar amount on shoes as they spent on tobacco products; in 1963 we spent almost 80 percent more on tobacco products than on shoes. When radio came in, the demand for victrola records fell markedly; then, after a few

years, it began a rise to new heights. Nature changes some of our wants. An especially cold winter will boost the demand for fuel, while rain on July 5th will cut the demand for hot dogs on the beach. Some taste changes result from deliberate effort, such as advertising. Subtly or blatantly, people around us change our wants, or try to. Actions of potential enemies influence our demand for military equipment. Changes in customs may have important effects on the tastes which sellers try to satisfy; growth of paid vacations increased demand for camp sites. New *techniques* alter demands; finding how to fabricate magnesium increased demand for the metal. Age influences demands. For example, a bigger proportion of families in the 25 to 34 age group buy durable goods more frequently than those either younger or older; establishing homes and raising children create real pressure for household equipment. Families over 65, even allowing for their generally lower incomes, buy durables less frequently than the average for all age groups.

3. A change in the number of buyers in the market will alter market demand. A tariff change abroad may enlarge or reduce the number of customers for some product of another country. A rise or fall in transportation costs will affect the range of the market for any specific product.

4. Demand for one product may change because of changes in the availability or demand for other things. The extension of electricity into rural areas helped boost sales of appliances. If golf courses are sold for housing projects, the demand for golf balls will drop. A growth in demand for college education will increase demand for dormitory rooms. Demands so related are *complementary*.

Somewhat similar are demands that are *derived* from other demands.[8] The demand for steel is derived from the demand for a multitude of steel products. The demand for corn is derived largely from the demand for meat. In general, the demand for the ingredients that go into the making of final products are derived demands. Some demands also *compete*. We gave examples in discussing changes in taste. There are innumerable others; for example, football games compete with the thirst for knowledge. In fact, all things, in a sense, compete for consumers' favor. But some compete very directly with each other because they are close substitutes.

5. *The demand for one product will vary with the price of competing (and also complementary) items*. Table 14–4 shows how the demand for pork might vary, depending upon beef prices. The easier it is to substitute one product or service for another—whether as an input in a business or as an item of final consumption—the more the price of one affects the demand for the other. The individual's best adjustment, we know, will

---

[8] How should we classify the case of the movie theater owner who found triple features profitable, even though they reduced admission receipts? Sales of candy and popcorn zoomed as customers became hungry while sitting through three thrillers. The soft-drink machines would also do a good business during these sitting marathons— better, if the water fountain were "out of order."

have been reached when he has balanced his spending so that no shift will permit him to sacrifice a lesser to obtain a greater value. A change in prices will obviously upset any such balance. If dance orchestras become more expensive, the demand for jukeboxes may rise. Rising prices of haircuts must be partly responsible for an increase in sales of clippers for home use.

An almost stable price of aluminum, from 1939 to 1954, helped it capture some of the markets of competing metals whose prices doubled. For the individual business, this feature of demand may seem the most important. Whatever is happening to personal income, consumer tastes, or the economy as a whole, the demand for the output of one company can always be reduced or increased by price actions of competitors. On the other hand, the firm can hope to capture more of the demand for its type of product by offering better terms than do competitors. Price changes for

TABLE 14–4.   Demand for Pork When Beef Sells at Two Substantially Different Prices (Hypothetical)

Price of Pork per Pound. Cents	Quantity of Pork Purchased per Week	
	When Beef Is $1 per Pound	When Beef Is 60 Cents per Pound
90	1,000	100
80	2,000	500
70	4,000	1,000
60	8,000	2,000
50	14,000	3,000

one set of products keep the demands for others changing, not jumping around recklessly, but on the move.

Forecasting Demand.   Some businesses put great effort into trying to forecast demand. Market research is an expanding aspect of business management. Firms have their own staffs, or engage outside agencies to estimate "sales potential" (demand) and the conditions that will raise or lower it. If you had such a job, how could you go about it?

You might ask customers, but except for special situations, such as with some industrial equipment, this method will seldom be reliable; and it may be very expensive to do well. You might search your past experience to see if sales have followed national income or the Federal Reserve's index of industrial production in some pattern. If so, you may base your estimate on someone else's estimate of what will happen to the bigger aggregate. You might conduct a study of various competing products to see which of their markets could perhaps be invaded successfully. Experiment with different prices, packaging, or sales appeal in various cities, or areas, sometimes proves useful. Sample surveys can yield valuable indications. The trade association may have data. Your product may be one for which the Survey Research Center gathers facts on consumer spending intentions. Yet you would probably be amazed at how poorly the data— from masses collected by the U.S. government to your wife's observations—will foretell the future. This should be no surprise. How many of us know what we shall buy and how much we shall spend next summer? Since "variety's the very spice of life, that gives it all its flavor," rising incomes lead us to seek *different* things.

If the job is to estimate for an entirely new product, you face a real challenge. And when you are almost ready to give the boss your answer, your clerk may tell you his girl friend is working on the same kind of job for a competitor who is planning to bring out a similar product. In a dynamic world, accurate forecasting of demand proves difficult, but challenging. A glance at books on marketing can prove immensely interesting.

DEMANDS OF BUSINESS AND GOVERNMENT

Most demands in markets today are not the demands of final consumers. Most buying is done by businesses in the process of producing and marketing merchandise for the consumer. This fact is more important than we may think at first. Businesses go about their buying in widely different ways; but, in general, they have some advantages over most final consumers. Without disparaging the housewife, we are probably correct in saying that a large firm can be more systematic and rational in its purchasing than can most housewives. Businesses often use scientific tests to compare competing products. Businesses can afford to study opportunities, to bargain carefully, to take account of future prospects. Sentiment need not interfere with judgment. The purchasing agents of big companies are often specialized, well-equipped people whose job is to buy efficiently.

The humble consumer benefits in at least two ways: (1) Economies which a business makes in its buying will be passed on to the final consumer through the force of competition. More efficient purchasing by GE or A&P will tend to reduce the prices they charge. (2) Prices and products will generally be kept closely aligned with underlying economic conditions. Penney, Sears, and other firms buying to sell to consumers, search systematically and rationally for good values; in doing so, they do a better technical job than we could hope to do; they keep manufacturers on their toes; and they help set producer standards which tend to determine what becomes available to smaller firms. In some cases the common man and the giant corporation buy the same things—gasoline, for example.

In some ways the big buyers help the small—by keeping the seller under pressure, by shifting purchases to take advantage of better opportunities, and by pressing for improvement in quality and service. The household can largely ignore the possibility of serious and persisting maladjustments; if apparent discrepancies exist, more skillful and powerful buyers than the ordinary consumer have apparently not been able to correct them.

Governments today account for no small fraction of the total market demand for some things: cement, gasoline, medicines, fire engines, telephone service, and, of course, defense equipment. Government is a final consumer for most of what it buys; its demands, however, are fixed in ways different from those which households and businesses use. Large units of government can, and many do, make systematic effort to buy wisely. In doing so, they add to the pressure on producers to operate efficiently. But all too many cases of governmental procurement are hampered by the small size of local units, inexperience of officials, restrictive laws, and favoritism.

PRICE ELASTICITY OF DEMAND

Meaning of "Elasticity." Whether a demand schedule is highly stable or moving constantly, it represents a set of relations between the price of an item and the quantity of that item which buyers will purchase. These relations are different for different things. I shall likely buy more pounds of beef than salt at 80 cents a pound. And from one product to another there is wide difference in the effects of a change in price on the number of units purchased. A 20 percent increase in the price of table salt will have no effect on the quantity purchased by most families, while a 20 percent increase in the price of beef may cut the purchases noticeably. The differences in these reactions are important to businessmen and to consumers.

In studying such differences, economists use the term "elasticity of demand." *It is the ratio of the percentage change in the quantity purchased to a small percentage change in price.* Elasticity is a measure of the responsiveness of purchases to changes in price.[9] Some rubber bands are more elastic than others; a pull of certain force will hardly budge one, while the same force doubles or triples the length of another rubber band. Similarly, a certain pull of price change will affect the quantity (number of units) purchased more for some products than for others.

[9] Though there are technicalities of definition and differences in usage, the essentials are simple and generally accepted. The symbolic statement is

$$\frac{\frac{\Delta Q}{Q}}{\frac{\Delta P}{P}} = \frac{\Delta Q}{Q} \times \frac{P}{\Delta P} = \frac{\Delta Q}{\Delta P} \times \frac{P}{Q}.$$

It is customary to ignore the negative sign needed to indicate a drop in price.

Here we discuss price elasticity. Quantities purchased will also vary with changes in income (price remaining the same). **Income elasticity** is the responsiveness of quantity bought to small changes in income.

There are five general degrees of elasticity of demand. Two are extreme, limiting cases. (2) Demand is *perfectly elastic* when an infinitesimal increase in price will cause an infinitely large decline in the quantity purchased, in other words, reduce sales to zero. If the price of wheat is $2 a bushel in the market, and a farmer says, "My price now goes up to $2.01," he will sell none. The demand for *his* wheat is perfectly elastic. This is the elasticity of a horizontal demand curve. (2) A *perfectly inelastic* demand, on the other hand, is one in which a rise or fall in price has no effect at all on the quantity purchased. For a considerable range of prices, this is true of many items of military equipment. The demand curve is vertical. (3) Between these extremes are many gradations, with a midpoint where demand has *unit elasticity*. Here the proportionate changes are equal but in opposite directions; the total dollar amount spent remains the same.[10] (4) A *relatively elastic* demand is one in which the response of quantity is greater, proportionately, than the change in price;

FIGURE 14–4. Demand Curves with Different Elasticities

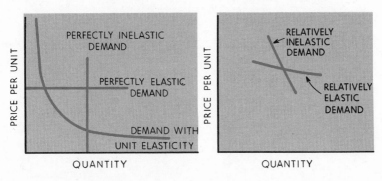

a 3 percent increase in price, for example, leads to a 5 percent decline in the number of units purchased. (5) Demand is *relatively inelastic* when quantity responds proportionately less than price; a 3 percent increase in price leads to only a 1 percent decline in the number of units bought. For simplicity, we shall leave out the word "relatively" when we speak of elastic and inelastic demand.

Figure 14–4 illustrates, but a warning is important: Judging elasticity by looking at demand curves is usually far harder than it may seem. The slope of the curve does not measure elasticity. The elasticity will vary at different parts of the curve except for two extreme cases—perfectly elastic or inelastic demand—or the one in the middle, unit elasticity throughout the whole curve.

Another way to look at elasticity is to see what happens to the *total amount spent* on a product when the price changes. If the price falls and I

[10] Geometrically, this curve is a rectangular hyperbola. For small changes, it is approximately correct to say that the percentages are equal and opposite, a 1 percent increase leading to a 1 percent decline in quantity.

then spend more on the product, my quantity response has been larger, proportionately, than the price change. What is this? My demand is *elastic*. But if as the price falls I continue to spend the same amount as before, my quantity response has been the same, proportionately, as the change in price but in the opposite direction—price down, quantity up in the same proportions. My demand here has *unit elasticity*. If, when the price falls, my total spending on the product also falls, my demand was *inelastic*; if price rises and my total spending on the product increases, my demand is inelastic.

Ordinarily, demands, like rubber bands, have some "give." The force of lower prices will stretch the quantity bought (sold). When the number of units purchased would be higher if price were lower, this fact does not

TABLE 14–5.   Elasticity Indicated by Changes in Total Amount Spent on a Product at Different Prices.*

Price per Unit (1)	Quantity Bought (Number of Units) (2)	Total Amount Spent (1 × 2)	Elasticity Condition
$6	100	$ 600	
			Elastic
5	200	1,000	
			Elastic
4	300	1,200	
			Unit elasticity
3	400	1,200	
			Inelastic
2	500	1,000	
			Inelastic
1	600	600	

* This illustration is defective in that the price and quantity changes are "large."

necessarily mean that demand is elastic. Demand is elastic only if the increase in quantity purchased is large enough to more than offset the effect of the lower price—the total dollar amount spent must increase. If the total spending on a product moves in the same direction as the price, demand is inelastic; if total spending changes in the opposite direction from the change in price, demand is elastic. Table 14–5 assumes a given demand schedule. The quantity bought goes up with each reduction in price; in fact, the increase in the number of units purchased is the same, 100 for each reduction in price of $1. Yet the total amount spent does not always increase. At first, it rises, showing that demand is elastic. Then, when the price falls from $4 to $3, the amount spent remains the same— unit elasticity. Below $3, demand is inelastic; the number of units sold increases as price falls, but the total amount spent declines.

Why Elasticities of Demand Differ. The elasticity of aggregate market demand depends upon: (1) the reaction of former buyers to a change in price, and (2) the entry of new buyers when price falls, the exit when price goes up. If price rises, some buyers may not reduce their purchases at all, others may cut somewhat and some may stop buying entirely. If price goes down some of the old buyers may not change their purchases, others will buy more units and new buyers may appear.

Why are some demands more elastic than others?

1. Differences in the *intensity of desire* provide part of the answer. The more urgent the want, the more inelastic the demand. Water for drinking compared with water for the lawn is a standard example. Demand for things that we feel are necessary (salt or light bulbs) tends to be inelastic.

2. Demand *tends to be inelastic for things on which one spends little:* hairpins, matches, pocket combs are probably examples. Small changes in price are insignificant for most budgets.

3. When demands are *joint or complementary*, in buying one we also buy another which we need with it: a textbook for a college course, laces for shoes, the auto license. In such cases, especially if the cost of one of the two is much less than for the other, the demand for the minor one will probably be inelastic; our decision to buy depends not upon the price of the minor thing but upon our choice of the more important.

4. The *more durable* an item and the *more it can be repaired*, the greater the tendency of the demand to be elastic. If the price of new items rises, old ones can be used longer or fixed up: autos, factory equipment, and shoes are examples.

5. The *more uses* an item has, the greater the likelihood that its total demand will be elastic. Some uses will be more sensitive to price than others. There are several uses of nylon, few for cigars. A rise in the price of nylon may reduce some of its uses. Except for smoking, however, cigars have no other uses which could be reduced.

6. When the buyers of a product include the *mass of consumers*, many low-income purchasers will of necessity be sensitive to price changes. This factor tends to make demand more elastic than it would otherwise be.

7. Demand elasticity depends heavily upon the *availability of substitutes*. If there are close substitutes for a product, one can expect its demand to be very elastic. If the price of the item rises, buyers will shift to substitutes; if price falls, users of substitutes will shift to it. Not all buyers may react, but many can and will shift if the substitute is readily available. For the specific demands which characterize practical business—a particular recording, slightly used or new cars, poultry or meat—this competition is perhaps the most important factor making for elastic demands.

Significance of Elasticity. Understanding the principle of demand elasticity helps us see why the public insists upon controlling prices of things desired so urgently as electricity and telephone service. Because demand is inelastic, at least in some ranges, the seller could charge a very high price. We try to protect ourselves from our own intensity of desire. But when good substitutes appear, as the auto and plane are substitutes for rail passenger transport, our demand for train travel becomes much more elastic and price regulation less important.

Though the businessman may never have heard of the term "elasticity," the principle plays a big part in his calculations. (People who never saw gravity use it.) Where the businessman has some control over the price he charges, he faces the question: "What will happen to my sales if I raise or lower my price?" He thinks in terms of demand elasticity, even if he does not use the term. In advertising and trying to build loyalty to its particular breakfast cereal or toothpaste, a business is, in part, trying to make the demand for its product more inelastic. The labor union leader in deciding how much to settle for a wage bargain, may take account of the possible effect that a higher or lower wage will have on the amount of employment. What opportunities are available to the employer to economize on labor? Will he raise prices to consumers when wages go up, reducing sales and his demand for labor?

Can price elasticity of demand be measured with the facts available? The best results are not fully satisfactory. After all, ours is a changing world. The Department of Agriculture has devoted extensive effort to analyzing the records of consumption of farm products. The estimates of demand elasticity vary widely in reliability and in ranges of doubt. The demand for fluid milk appears to have rather low elasticity—0.3 to 0.4—while that for American cheese seems to be from 0.75 to 0.90.

Studies of the demand for new autos have yielded elasticity estimates ranging from 0.8 to 1.5, for different periods; the latter is probably close to the facts of market conditions in the 1960's.[11] Some years ago the estimates in Table 14–6 were prepared for items then subject to special federal taxes. Legislatures in fixing commodity or service taxes should, of course, take account of elasticity. Other things the same, the more inelastic the demand, the greater the revenue potential. Reductions in plane fares, along with greater speeds of the jets, helped account for a 50 percent rise in payments for both domestic and international travel in the 4 years through 1967.

Consumer Surplus. Look back at Figure 14–1. Assume that one can buy belts at a price equal to the utility of the fifth belt. This price

[11] Income elasticity is markedly higher. The estimates range from 1.7 to 3.0. For each 1 percent of increase in income, the public probably increases its outlays on new autos by more than 2 percent. Income elasticities of dairy products also tend to be higher than price elasticities.

14: Demand 355

TABLE 14–6. Elasticity of Demand for Selected Products *

Jewelry	2.6	Business machines	0.50
Furs	2.3	Motion-picture attendance	0.43
Phonographs and records	1.5	Transportation of property	0.38
Refrigerators, washing machines, and sewing machines	1.1	Cooking and heating apparatus	0.26
Photographic supplies	1.5	Cabarets	0.26
Sporting goods	1.0	Electric light bulbs	0.33
Local telephone	0.83	Club dues	0.29
Luggage		Safe deposit box leases	0.0
		Matches	0.0

* Negative signs omitted. *Revenue Revision of 1950*, (*Hearings before the Committee on Ways and Means*, House of Representatives, 81st Cong., 2d sess. [Washington, D.C.: U.S. Government Printing Office, 1950]), Vol. I, pp. 980–82. Estimates of elasticity apply to price ranges approximating those of then current experience. The figures indicate, for example, that a 1 percent increase in the price of jewelry would reduce the number of units purchased by 2.6 percent.

measures the sacrifice of alternatives needed to get each belt. In buying five belts during some period of time, the consumer pays five times the *marginal* utility, that is, five times the price. Yet he gets a total utility which equals the utility of the first, plus that of the second, and so on. Figure 14–5 illustrates. The consumer seems to get something for which he need not pay, the area in the triangle *NaM*.

The great English economist Alfred Marshall called this "extra" *consumer surplus*. Intuitively, we find this concept meaningful. The modern

FIGURE 14–5. Consumer Surplus

The market price is *ON = Aa*. The consumer buys *OA* units. His total payments are *OAaN*. The line *MU* indicates the marginal utility (not the buyer's demand curve). The area *OAaM* measures the total utility obtained from *OA* units; this area is greater by the triangular area *NaM* than the area which represents the payments made. *NaM* represents a *consumer surplus.*

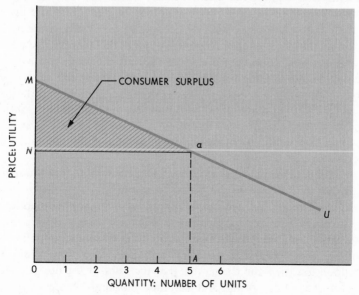

economy provides much for which we would be willing, if compelled, to pay more than is required. How much more? Who could possibly say? If conditions were to change to force us to pay appreciably greater prices to get the "first" (highest utility) items which now yield a consumer surplus, the whole pattern of consumption would change. The area of consumer surplus will be relatively greater for some things than for others.

Sometime, conceivably, methods of measurement, rough and crude but more accurate than misleading, will be devised. Perhaps, then, men of great wisdom could devise a system of subsidies to stimulate the use of things with large potential for exploiting unrealized consumer surplus, to be paid for by taxes on things yielding little such surplus. The dream of such "planning" has intrigued not a few persons who hope to improve human welfare. But try to imagine the practical problems of doing really the right thing—even if one had the power of a dictator, to say nothing of the problems of implementation in a free society.

TIME AND DEMAND

The passage of time affects the demand for a product. Tastes, income, population, and innumerable things of greater or smaller importance change as the months and years pass. Therefore, the longer the period one is considering, the greater the probability that new conditions will affect demand. Business success often depends heavily upon skill in foreseeing, controlling, and adjusting to both temporary and longer run changes in the demand for a firm's products.

The longer the time period, the greater the opportunity for quantity to adjust to price, assuming that other conditions, including tastes, do not change. For example, consumers often need time to make the other adjustments that will permit them to take advantage of a reduction in price. If the price of natural gas goes down (in relation to the prices of other fuels), new furnaces will be needed to take full advantage of a reduction in the price of gas. Even if the price of oil were to rise, some users will not shift to gas until present oil burners wear out. Merely to learn about a price change (in the sense of what one gets for the money) takes time, especially when the change is in quality. Sometimes the adjustment involved is so large that for most consumers prompt action is impossible. If the price of small houses were to go up markedly, not many families would shift to apartments at once because of the cost and trouble required to move.

Time affects demand in another way. Buyers will take account of the prices which they *expect* in the future. If we believe that the price of an item will go down, we tend to hold off buying—with exceptions, of course, such as electricity for lighting or gas for cooking. Businessmen do not ordinarily announce price reductions long in advance—sales would drop off in the interim. Yet some seasonal sales are well established, and buyers doubtless plan for them: the January sales of "white goods," the July "clearances" of spring and summer clothing. Prospectives price increases, of course, will induce consumers to stock up. When the tax on a product is about to rise, a spurt of buying is to be expected; talk of cutting commodity taxes will cause a sag in purchasing.

The longer the time period, the greater the change in the "mix" of what consumers demand.[12] From 1929 to mid-1960's, spending on medical and other health services increased tenfold while outlays for movie admissions did not even double.

Much demand today is for the services of durable things: houses, stoves, boats. The demand for the services is far more stable than the outlay on the durables to provide the services. The amount we spend in any one month, year, or longer period will depend, among other things, on the size, durability, and condition of existing stocks of durables. The more recently we have built up stocks, the smaller will be new purchases to provide for any given level of services.

TERMS AND CONCEPTS

price	scarcity	income elasticity
relative price	ceteris paribus	inelasticity
demand	complementary goods	relatively elastic
wants	substitutes	unit elasticity
utility	price elasticity	

QUESTIONS

1. Describe the diagrams economists use to summarize the conditions of demand. What is the difference between "change in demand" and "change in quantity demanded"? Why will the demand curve as diagrammed slope downward?

2. Do you believe that it is generally correct to assume that the individual is a better judge of his own wants than he is of the preferences of others? Why? What, if any, exceptions would you make? Why?

3. What are the "functions of price"? What is equilibrium?

4. Why may a student spend more for one week's cigarets than for a year's supply of fresh air? How does usefulness enter into the explanation? Scarcity?

5. Define "elasticity of demand." What influences the elasticity of your demand for shoe laces, typewriter ribbons, textbooks, long-distance telephone calls, housing? Try to list products for which your demand is (*a*) elastic and (*b*) inelastic.

6. Assume the following demand conditions:

Price Cents	Quantity Purchased	Price Cents	Quantity Purchased
26	750	22	970
25	820	21	990
24	890	20	1,000
23	930		

[12] Hence it is difficult to compare consumption in different periods. Our money measures, and the price indexes we use to "deflate" them, do not necessarily reveal all we need to know to compare consumption today with that 5 or 15 years ago.

What is the approximate elasticity of demand between 20 and 21 cents? Between 25 and 26 cents? In what price range does demand have approximately unit elasticity? (Ignore negative signs.)

7. Why do you not spend all of your income on milk, black shoes, or room rent? How does your answer illustrate the principle of diminishing marginal utility? The necessity of choice?

8. What may cause a total market demand for a product to shift? What may cause the elasticity to change? Explain why short-run changes may be different from long-run changes.

9. How do the purchasing staffs of business organizations help the individual consumer get good value for his money?

10. A large railroad reduced the fare on its crack passenger run by 23 percent. Two years later it asked permission to abandon the run because travel had dropped 25 percent. What, apparently, were the demand conditions?

11. What are some *specific* items of personal and of governmental expenditure for which there are no close substitutes? Some for which substitutes are close?

12. What factors influence the quantity of postage stamps, hoisery, and transportation you buy this week? This year? Is price a factor?

13. If price is no measure of true value, should we let prices guide our consumption spending?

14. Was the Eskimo who used his first welfare check to buy 22 alarm clocks irrational? Why?

15

*. . . Many of the poorer classes who are suffering from the recent rise in the
price of meat . . . have held numerous meetings . . . at which the high price
of meat has been ascribed to the interference of monopolists and to the high
profits of cattle-dealers . . . a practical course has been recommended at
several meetings by way of remedy which would not lessen the evil, but would
aggravate it. This remedy is a systematic reduction of consumption. . . .
But how the persons who abstain are to be benefited by so doing is not very
clear. If they succeed in reducing the price of animal food by not eating it,
they will only reduce it so long as they do not eat it. . . . And not only would
this remedy be ineffectual, it would be pernicious, for it would prolong the
duration of the evil. The scarcity which causes the dearness of food is an evil,
but when food is scarce it is desirable that it should be dear. A high price is
a natural remedy which is efficacious in two ways. It naturally limits consumption. . . . Moreover, a high price is the only sure source of an augmented
supply. . . . While the price is high, the breeder and the grazier will get much
for that which they bring to market: they will endeavour to augment the supply
as much as they can and as fast as they can.*

The Economist (London), July 7, 1860
(reprinted July 9, 1960)

Price-quantity, demand-supply relations are at the heart of economic
analysis and of economic life. Study of the "law" of supply and demand
gets us nearer an understanding of how prices are formed, of the making
of economic decisions and the allocation and reallocation of resources.
Prices guide. Businessmen and consumers, all of us in all aspects of life, act
under the guidance of price. In making decisions, we take some prices as
fixed. Yet as we act, we create forces which often make for different
prices and different relations among prices. Then some new adjustment, a
new allocation of resources, reflecting new conditions, becomes necessary

for economic efficiency. The new prices, however, tend to induce new change, a different resource allocation.

SUPPLY

What Is "Supply"? "Supply" is a word with different shades of meaning. The economist's usage differs from some popular meanings. At times, for example, a person may speak of supply as the stock of things on hand—the water in the reservoirs or housing in the city. Sometimes we think of supply as a source, or as the more or less regular offerings, of a good or a service for sale—the fresh fruit which comes to the city each morning. The economist's concept is more precise; it relates the *quantities* offered (supplied) to the *price*. Just as demand is a schedule of the number of units of a good or service that will be bought at different prices, *supply is a schedule of the number of units that will be offered at different prices.* We assume that other conditions are "given" or fixed, such things as the prices of other goods and the incomes of sellers and purchasers and the state of technology.

For any product, there will be several possible combinations of price and the number of units that will be offered. But one general relationship is clear: The quantity supplied will increase as the price offered rises. Things can be available for sale only if they exist or can be produced. And production involves costs. Firms will pay the costs and make the effort only if the price they can expect to get is sufficiently attractive. The higher the price, the greater the inducement to produce. This "law of supply" corresponds to the "law of demand." Our willingness to inconvenience ourselves, and to sacrifice other things, in order to produce more of a product will increase as the price offered to us rises.

Diagramming Supply. We can illustrate the relationship between quantity supplied and price on the same type of diagram that we used to show the relation of quantity demanded and price. Table 15–1 assumes the supply conditions of four firms. Figure 15–1 shows the *supply curves* for two of these firms and the aggregate or market supply, assuming only four firms in the market.

The graph in each case is a line rising to the right. Each line shows how

TABLE 15–1. Supply Schedules, Four Firms and the Market

Price per Unit	Firm A	Firm B	Firm C	Firm D	Market (Aggregate) Supply
$1			100	100	200
2	100	100	300	200	700
3	200	300	350	400	1,250
4	300	400	400	500	1,600
5	400	450	450	600	1,900

Number of Units That Will Be Supplied per Week

FIGURE 15–1. Firm and Market Supply Curves

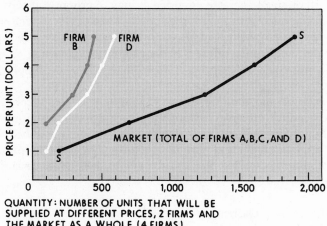

QUANTITY: NUMBER OF UNITS THAT WILL BE
SUPPLIED AT DIFFERENT PRICES, 2 FIRMS AND
THE MARKET AS A WHOLE (4 FIRMS)

many units would be supplied per week at each of the different prices, assuming that other conditions remain unchanged. As with demand, a shift from one point to another on a curve is not a change of supply but a change in the *quantity* supplied. *A change in supply is a shift of the curve* (Fig. 15–2). Why does the higher curve mean a lower supply? The higher position or upward shift of the curve says this: "To have the same quantity offered as before, you must pay a higher price," or, "At any given price, sellers will offer fewer units."

Elasticity of Supply. Supply, like demand, has elasticity. When price pulls, quantity "stretches," more so in some cases than in others. *The*

FIGURE 15–2. Changes in Supply

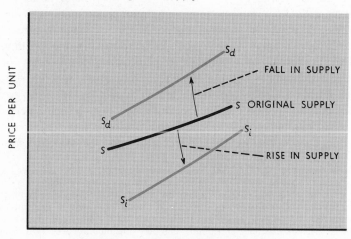

QUANTITY: NUMBER OF UNITS THAT WILL BE
SUPPLIED AT DIFFERENT PRICES

degree of responsiveness of quantity supplied to change in price is the elasticity. If a small increase in price brings a proportionately greater increase in the quantity offered, the supply is relatively *elastic.* Supply is relatively *inelastic* if a small increase in price has a smaller effect proportionately on the quantity offered. If the proportionate change in quantity supplied is just equal to the proportionate change in price, supply has *unit elasticity.*

Two extreme and limiting cases exist. Supply is completely *inelastic* when the quantity offered does not vary with price: the supply curve is vertical. Supply is completely *elastic* when any quantity will be offered at a certain price or higher and nothing at a lower price: the supply curve is horizontal (Fig. 15–3). The slope of the curves does not necessarily show elasticity.[1]

FIGURE 15–3.   Elasticity of Supply

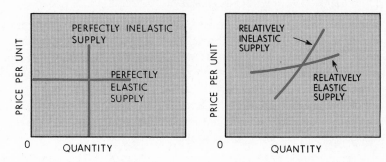

What factors account for differences in elasticity of supply? We must delay an answer until we consider costs, except to point out that supply, like demand, is related to *some period.* In a very short period, which economists call the "instantaneous" or "market period," the quantity offered for sale may not respond appreciably to a change in price: if so, supply is highly inelastic. Ripe fruit brought to market one morning will be sold at the best price available; the quantity offered is fixed for that day. At an auction in which the seller sets no reservation price, supply is inelastic. Within a week, no matter what we would be willing to pay, we could not get much in new apartment buildings. But, in such a period, we might easily get a big increase in the output of doughnuts.

The longer the period, the greater the opportunities for adjusting

---

[1] One may think of "flattish" supply curves as generally elastic and steep supply curves as inelastic; while such a generalization is by no means reliable—the scales of the axes in themselves make considerable difference in the "look" of curves—the beginning student will probably find this rule of thumb more helpful than misleading. When one tries to compute elasticity, the data are rarely adequate. The goal will usually be to measure elasticity at a point. The best possible, however, will ordinarily involve two points somewhat apart. They set off an arc. The measurement will be for the arc or range, a single figure representing an average.

output in response to changing prices or costs. Hence, *the longer the period for adjustment, the greater, generally, is the elasticity of supply.* A period that is long for some production is short for others. A few weeks may be adequate to change substantially the output of men's suits or chickens. For complex military equipment, however, years are needed to expand capacity to increase supply, but thereafter, up to some limit, quantities produced can change considerably on short notice.

For most goods (but not services) the time period has some variability. Typically, articles in stock, or inventory, provide a buffer. At different stages in the production process, businesses have some choice about how much to offer at today's prices. Generally, short-term fluctuations in quantities produced or sold can be met by changes in inventory. For crops like wheat or cotton, storage plays a big part. Day-to-day offerings may respond markedly to price changes, though the output for any 6-month period may have little elasticity. A few things, of course, are limited to the stock on hand—genuine paintings by artists now dead.

PRICE AND OUTPUT DETERMINATION

The Law of Supply and Demand. What is "the law of supply and demand"? Let us try to explain rather than to define it in a single sentence. We have seen that both (1) the *quantity* of a thing that will be *demanded*, and (2) the *quantity* that will be *supplied* depend upon price. Ordinarily there will be one, and only one, price at which the quantities demanded and supplied will be exactly equal. This is the *equilibrium price*, the point where things are in balance, where no net forces make for change. Think of it as the condition of best adjustment. No one who wants to alter the result has power to do so, while those with power to make a change have no desire to do so. This is the only price that can last—the price from which there is no tendency for the market to shift—as long as basic conditions are unchanged.

How does such a price—and balance of quantities—come into existence? Certainly, there is no supremely wise dictator to set equilibrium prices. But we do have buyers and sellers seeking to do as well as possible for themselves. Each wants what the other has: money or goods. As they try to exchange, they deal in terms of prices. To see how they would operate, let us look at what would happen if the market price were not at the equilibrium. Our approach is a little like that of the medical student who goes to the hospital to study sick people and how they become well. We can learn about economic health by looking at economic sickness and its cure.

At any price other than the equilibrium, there will be forces making for change. This is the key to the process of adjustment. Some buyers and sellers can benefit from doing something differently (assuming that they are free to do so). As they seek their self-interest, they will force the price toward equilibrium.

Let us illustrate, assuming the underlying conditions of Table 15–2, when "something new has been added," and when there are enough buyers and sellers so that no single one can exert appreciable influence on the whole.[2] Perhaps a product like silk is coming back on the market after a long wartime absence. As a starter, a government official sets a market price and then leaves buyers and sellers free to use their own judgments. The official begins by announcing a price of $5; suppliers offer a flood of 3,800 items, but there is distressingly little consumer interest. The public wants silk, but not much at this high price. Only 1,000 units will be bought. Goods pile up in hands of would-be sellers. This is not a situation of economic health.

TABLE 15–2.   Demand and Supply

Price per Unit	No. of Units Supplied per Week	No. of Units Demanded per Week
$5	3,800	1,000
4	3,000	3,000
3	2,500	5,000

The first prescription for a cure is obvious. Sellers have goods they cannot sell. The thing to do is to cut the price. Perhaps one or two suppliers become a little panicky as they see the size of the earlier error. They decide to move their product by reducing the price to $3. Buyers can then benefit themselves—improve their position—by buying more. They surge forward, for at this price they want to buy at a rate five times as high as before: 5,000 per week. Suppliers, however, change their tune almost as emphatically, but in the other direction. Some of them know that $3 will not cover the costs of labor, materials, and transportation; others prefer to eliminate some of their high cost output. They can do better for themselves by reducing their offerings, which in total fall about one third to 2,500 units a week. The medicine was again too strong. Once more the price has failed to balance quantities on the buying and the selling sides.

Buyers now want twice as much as sellers will offer at the price. "Enough" items are not to be had, but some people who have not been able to buy the product want it and are willing to pay more than $3. They can benefit themselves by offering to pay more than $3. They do, and suppliers respond. The next step is a price between $5 and $3. Whatever it is, it will not bring out such differences between the quantities demanded and the quantities supplied as either of the earlier extremes. And there is one price, $4, which will "equilibrate," which will produce an exact

[2] For realism we can also assume that no one has experience about current market forces.

balance of the quantities on the two sides. Perhaps buyers and sellers will be successful quickly and hit upon the $4 price next week. Perhaps the precise figure will appear only after many trials (Fig. 15–4, study carefully). But when the equilibrium—$4—price is reached, no buyer or seller (under the conditions given) can benefit by trying something else— except, perhaps, to learn the "wisdom of the market." The seller who tries to improve his position by charging a little more than $4 finds that no one will buy from him because buyers' needs can be met from other suppliers. On the other hand, the buyer who refuses to pay $4, hoping for a lower price does not get what he hopes for; he loses the advantage of buying at $4 what is worth that much to him. The equilibrium is not necessarily ideal in the sense that it is heaven, but it *is* the best possible adjustment under the conditions.

FIGURE 15–4.   Quantities Demanded and Supplied at Three Prices

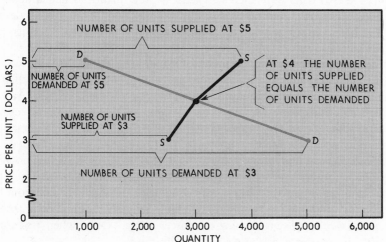

The forces of supply and demand have been operating. The market has been "cleared." We can see the law being enforced by the police of the market, buyers and sellers. If they have enough time and if these "police" are free, market *prices* and *quantities* change until the price which represents a balancing of quantities is reached—the equilibrium price. The better organized a market, the sooner the price will reach equilibrium. On the New York Stock Exchange only a few minutes may be needed to restore equilibrium when demand, supply, or both change.

Since people sometimes speak derisively, and more often inaccurately, of the law of supply and demand, we need to understand what it really means. As long as the market price is not at equilibrium, there *must* be change (in free markets). Ordinarily, both quantity and price will move. If one of the two is not free, however, all the adjustment must be in the other—or the community must make some coercive nonmarket adjustment. Until the equilibrium price is reached, some people who could be satisfied are not. Improvement is possible. We also learn what kind of maladjustments to expect. This law gives us a basis for prediction, somewhat like laws of physics which, though they do not tell us how engineers will build a bridge, let us know what to expect if the bridge is too weak. The equilibrium price does not necessarily make everyone happy; as a group, people just cannot do better at any other price. The process of moving to the equilibrium will be painful to some. The suppliers who were lucky enough to sell at $5, or the buyers who got the product at $3, undoubtedly deplored the move toward $4.

The general principles can now be summarized: (1) When, at the prevailing price, the quantity demanded exceeds the quantity supplied, price tends to rise. (2) A rising price tends to reduce the quantity purchased and increase the quantity supplied. The opposites of these two points are also true. (3) Price will settle where quantities demanded and supplied are equal. The forces that lead to these results are human desires backed by economic power. Demand and supply are people acting.

Changes in Supply and Demand. Of course, if the underlying conditions of demand and supply change, the equilibrium price will change. What was the best possible adjustment becomes less than the best. Any of many conditions can alter the equilibrium, all those which affect the demand schedule or the supply schedule. Let us illustrate, assuming that the supply schedule remains unchanged. Figure 15–5 shows the demand for pork before and after a big fall in the price of beef: when beef becomes cheaper, the demand for pork drops, shown by a shift of the demand curve downward to the left. The price of pork will fall from the level at E, perhaps fluctuating in seeking its new level. The quantity bought also goes down despite the lower price.[3] Only when price and quantity balance at E_d is there a new equilibrium.

Which is more important in determining price, supply or demand? This is as hard to answer as the question: "Which blade of the scissors does the cutting?" Both contribute to the result, which would not be reached if only one were working. Yet, only one blade may move. Sometimes one economic force may seem relatively more important than the other. For example, the newspaper may report that wheat or security prices fell, not because of pressure of sellers, but absence of buyers. Or differences in elasticities may make one element appear more important; for example, if the pork supply schedule were much more elastic in this price range (the demand schedules remaining as shown in Figure 15–5), the drop in quantity would have been larger; the supply blade might then seem relatively more important.

[3] Try to find what would happen to the quantity of pork bought if its price, for some reason, remained at the level of E.

FIGURE 15–5. Adjustment of Price and Quantity to a Fall in Demand (Assuming No Change in Supply)

When demand falls from *DD* to D_dD_d, equilibrium shifts from *E* to E_d, a point of lower price and smaller quantity than *E*. Some of the adjustment to the lower demand is in price, some in quantity.

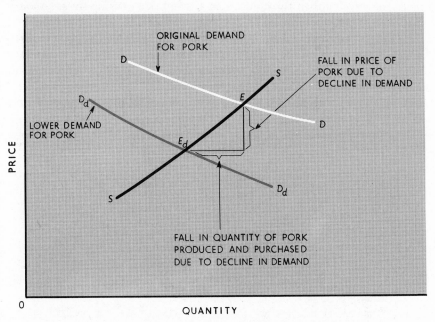

Costs of production generally determine supply because it is cost that hinders or discourages people from producing. Let us assume that there is no change in the demand for pork, but that supply increases; cheaper corn, perhaps, makes farmers willing to offer more hogs at each of the different prices shown. What happens? Price falls; the quantity bought increases, the relative amounts depending upon elasticities (Fig. 15–6).

Shifting of a Commodity Tax. Another way to illustrate a change in supply is to assume that a tax has been added or removed. Let us imagine that Congress has increased the taxes on jewelry (elastic demand) and on electric light bulbs (inelastic demand). For each unit sold, the seller must turn over to the Treasury the amount of the tax. Producers want to recover the tax. But how can a higher price be made effective? "By reducing output." (The process will probably be indirect, starting with quotations of higher prices.)

Figure 15–7 shows the two cases (hypothetical, of course, and with supply curves of the same shape). The effect of the tax is to shift the supply curve *SS* to S_tS_t. This shift means that with tax a higher price from the consumer is needed to have any given quantity produced and delivered. The new equilibrium price will obviously be higher, yet in neither case will price be above the old price by as much as the tax. Why? Sellers may wish that they could continue to supply as much as they had been producing, and mark up their prices by an amount equal to the tax. But, at the higher price, buyers will reduce their purchases, relatively more for jewelry than for light bulbs. If the price goes up by an amount equal to the tax, the quantity of jewelry sold will fall considerably. Sellers, therefore, rather than lose out so strikingly on sales will offer at a price somewhat lower than the old price plus tax. They must also cut production. Suppliers of light bulbs can pass more of the tax—almost all, in

FIGURE 15–6.   Adjustment of Price and Quantity to an Increase in Supply (Assuming No Change in Demand)

When supply increases from SS to S_iS_i, equilibrium shifts from E to E_i, a point of lower price and larger quantity. Some of the adjustment to the change in supply is in price; some is in quantity.

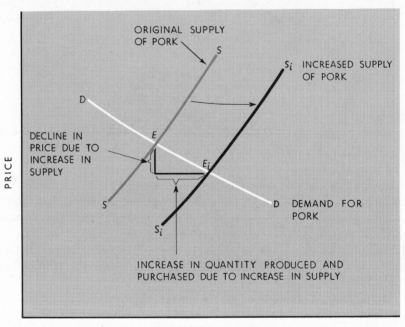

fact—to consumers; but these sellers, too, find the higher price reducing the quantity sold, a little. Some of the adjustment in each case is in quantity, some in price, the relative amounts depending upon elasticities.

Relations between Different Markets: The Law of Equal Price.   In a purely competitive market, price will be the same everywhere, except for differences in cost of transportation. If prices of wheat in Chicago and

FIGURE 15–7.   Adjustment of Price and Quantity to an Increase in Tax

The increase in tax per unit is shown by the shift of the supply curve from SS to S_tS_t. The equilibrium point shifts from E to E_t. In Case A, demand is elastic; price rises but by much less than the tax, while the quantity produced and purchased falls substantially. In Case B, demand is inelastic; price rises by nearly as much as the tax, while quantity declines much less than in Case A.

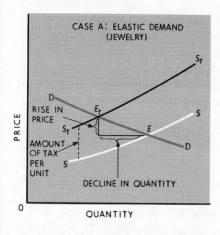
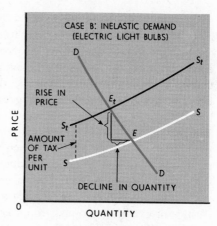

Omaha diverge by more than the cost of transportation, someone can make a quick profit. If it costs 20 cents a bushel to ship wheat from Omaha to Chicago, this is the maximum difference in price that will prevail. If wheat is $2.30 in Chicago and $2.05 in Omaha, a person can buy wheat in Omaha and ship it to Chicago, incurring a total cost of $2.25. He sells the wheat for 5 cents profit. There are people who make a business of doing something similar when they see a chance. Their actions tend to keep prices in different markets closely in line. Ordinarily, not much shift in quantity will be needed to eliminate a difference. Other buyers and sellers, as a result, gain freedom from risk of loss (or gain) by chance divergences of demand and supply. One source of inefficiency in the allocation of resources grows weaker.

Adjustment the Result of Many Small Changes.   A remarkable self-adjusting process works, as a rule, by small changes. The final adjustment ordinarily depends upon the "little more, little less" of both supply and demand, of quantity and price. A huge amount of total adjustment results from many changes at the margin, each individually small. Some buyers and sellers do not respond to price changes within the range of possible variation. Others alter somewhat the amount they purchase or sell. For still others, the question of whether or not they buy or sell at all depends upon price within the range. It is the purchases (actual or potential) subject to doubt which determine the final adjustment. In a sense, these amounts exert their influence within a framework which is largely fixed; but they determine the final size and shape of the framework—the extra few per cent—of quantity and price. They are what make the curves elastic or inelastic. The range or area in which they appear is the "margin." The marginal purchases and sales, as a rule, are most likely to get careful consideration.

Storage and Future Markets. How do forces of demand and supply mesh when different time periods are involved? Wheat, cotton, and other agricultural staples, we know, are harvested a few months of the year, but consumed more or less regularly over the whole year (unlike fresh sweet corn). Though the prices fluctuate, they do not fall deeply as the harvest flows to market and then rise to great heights when there is no production. Why, then, are fluctuations so small relative to changes in output? The answer is twofold: storage is possible, and the broad fluctuations are predictable. Someone can buy when the crops come to market and when price would be low, keep the product in storage, and sell later when there is no new output and when price would otherwise be high. Speculators will do so if the difference in price between the two seasons, autumn and spring for example, promises to exceed the cost of storage.

The process itself tends to reduce price fluctuations. Buying when output is high tends to raise a price that would be lower; selling when there is no output keeps prices lower than otherwise. (Consumers presumably benefit from a steadier price and a more even flow of the product.) The closer the prices of the different seasons come together, however, the smaller the chances of sure profit from speculation. In September, there may be no certainty that prices will go up enough by March to cover storage costs. Perhaps consumption demand will fall, or the prospects of the next new crop will become good enough to discourage March buying. Special market arrangements help persons with different interests and judgments about the future to deal with each other.

Dealings in *futures* are possible. To illustrate: August buyers for speculation (or producers who choose to hold on to their output) know they must sell in the future. On the other hand, users, such as bakers, know in August that they must have wheat or flour in the future to meet their production needs. Instead of waiting for the future, they may agree in August on the price at which they will buy in March. If so, the speculator and the baker can make a futures transaction. Each then knows definitely the terms on which the deal will be closed later. The business using the product, the bakery, need not speculate on the price it will pay in the future. The price of "futures" today may be either higher or lower than the present price plus storage.[4] A higher price signals shorter supplies or

[4] In September, 1967, wheat, corn, rye, cotton, wool, potatoes, sugar, flaxseed, cocoa, silver, and orange juice concentrate for March, 1968, delivery were selling for more than "spot" prices, that is, for immediate delivery. Hog, soybean meal, cattle, barley, copper, and frozen pork belly futures were selling for less than current delivery.

higher demand, or both, and warns users to economize more—a lower price does the opposite.

Some 30 different agricultural and mineral products have markets organized for dealings in "futures." The Chicago Board of Trade is the leading center, a place for registering the composite judgment of a large number and variety of interested persons. Some are amateurs whose buying and selling (perhaps on small margins) rest on uninformed rumor. Others are speculators who make this their business. Their actions, aided by extensive data on crop prospects provided by government, and data from industry on output and consumption, can perform a useful stabilizing function.

Can We "Repeal" or Modify the Law of Supply and Demand? No! Yet people may seem to depart from what the "law" would indicate as best: we make mistakes. Just as we may not eat the diet that would most nearly provide equilibrium in our health, we may not make the economic decisions that are best. Ordinarily, neither error is fatal, but both cause us loss of something. Buyers and sellers in the market, of course, need time to correct errors and bring about equilibrium. Meanwhile, constant change alters underlying conditions; before equilibrium is reached, therefore, a new one may become the goal.

In some cases prices are influenced or fixed by government to get a result above or below equilibrium. If so, one may ask: "In speaking of the law of supply and demand, do we mean something man is powerless to change or control, some immutable fact of existence like a law of nature?" The answer is: "Yes, in somewhat the same way that the law of gravity is immutable in a world of airplanes." Forces of demand and supply determine price-quantity relationships as definitely as the forces of physics produce their results. We are not helpless, however, any more than we are helpless against the law of gravity if we want to fly. Conditions of demand and supply can be changed just as man can control some of the many conditions of the physical universe. Man can use one force or law to counter or modify the effects of another. If we do not "obey" the "law," we can predict the results—as we can if we overload an airplane or fail to put fuel in the tank.

If an apparently equilibrium price-quantity adjustment seems unwelcome, we may be able to use other forces (our resources) to change the conditions of demand and supply. In this way, the results that would otherwise be obtained can be modified—at a cost. No one may ever label such actions as ways to bring a new price-quantity equilibrium, any more than one speaks of the use of engines to keep planes in the air as a method of altering the operation of physical laws. Yet when businesses use resources in advertising to try to change demand, they are trying to change the equilibrium. So, in a different way, an invention that lowers costs of production increases supply.

Price Control. The world has had many chances to learn what may happen when someone arbitrarily determines price. What shall we expect if the control price is not at the equilibrium? Quantity gets "out of kilter." In World War II, ceilings were set to keep the prices of a vast number of items from rising. Let us see what may happen, chiefly in situations with many buyers and sellers.

The beginning is something like this. The price of butter has been about 60 cents a pound, at, or very close to, equilibrium. A government agency fixes this as a legal ceiling price. Anyone who pays, or accepts, more than 60 cents is disobeying the law and (as part of the "cost" of the transaction to him) runs the risk of a fine and perhaps even a jail sentence. As the war progresses, people receive more income, and the total demand for butter rises. The cost of producing butter also rises, reducing the willingness of producers to supply it. The schedules shift as shown in Figure 15–8.

If the price cannot change, what happens? Buyers want more than producers will freely make available. Someone must be disappointed. Quantity is too small. Something "has to give." Any of several adjustments, or more probably a mixture, can appear. First-come, first-served at

FIGURE 15–8.   Lack of Balance between Quantities Supplied and Demanded under Price Control

The price fixed at 60 cents per pound was at the equilibrium, *E*, before the war. As war raises incomes, consumer demand rises to D_wD_w; rising costs shift supply to S_wS_w. The new equilibrium would be E_w. With price fixed at 60 cents, however, there is a large gap between the quantities that will be supplied and the quantities demanded.

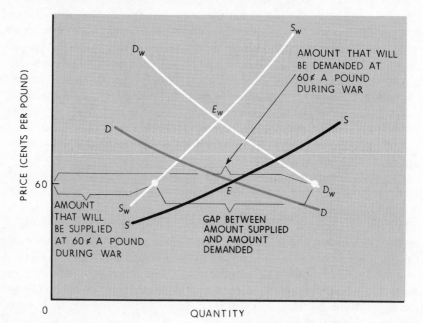

the store is a possibility. The housewife who puts her order in late is out of luck—no butter is left. It will not take her many days to catch on—she must try to get to the store early; but others do the same, frustrating each other. Perhaps they are forced to line up before things go on sale. This is a nuisance and a drain on time. Those who are near the end of the queue may find the butter all sold; some never had any chance at all—those who do not even get into the line, the mother who cannot leave her baby or the woman who has a job.

Dealers may try to spread what they have available by limiting the amount any one customer may buy. Yet, by going to enough trouble, some housewives may then be able to get all they want by shopping at several stores. Or grocers may reserve the butter at its fixed "bargain" price for favored customers—those placing the large orders or flashing the pleasantest smile. Dealers may require tie-in purchases, saying, "Butter goes only to those who buy something which sells slowly" (and probably has a good profit margin). Whatever the result, some consumers must do without butter that they would like to buy at the fixed price. Adjustment *must* be made somehow—perhaps by chance or by unofficial allocation; nonmonetary costs (the loss of time when standing in line) are added and reduce demand; or, as with the tie-in sale, concealed price increases may appear. Quality may be reduced, not so easy with butter as with meat or clothing, which some wartime sellers found ingenious ways to cheapen. Services normally provided by the dealer, such as free delivery, may be charged for or withdrawn. The minimum results include an addition of nuisances and concealed costs. (These may be less onerous than the advantages of keeping prices down.) The "law" of supply and demand has not been repealed; it has worked, forcing quantity adjustments, as we expect.

If the controlled price is much below the equilibrium that would exist in free markets, black (illegal) markets will likely develop. The risks of legal penalties may be worth running, and consciences eased somewhat by extenuating circumstances. Sellers know their costs are rising, perhaps because of government action. Buyers may know their time is worth more to the war effort working at the job than standing in line. There are so many gradations of fact, conscience, patriotism. Enforcement becomes expensive and exhausting. During war, however, patriotism aids enforcement powerfully; consumers and producers, in a sense, change the attitudes that underlie supply and demand.

Price, we know, performs a dual function: it guides both production and consumption. One result of a price not at equilibrium is that it does not do either job as well as price should. The 60-cent price of butter in our illustration will not deter consumption as much as wartime conditions require. People who can buy butter at that price—those who are lucky or make the right connections—can go ahead consuming as much as before at that price (or perhaps more). Yet the total market situation indicates that the community must gage consumption to a price around 90 cents. The 60-cent price makes it unnecessary for some to adjust; others must then adjust excessively (and unfairly?).

A more formal and systematic arrangement is possible: *rationing*. In a sense, a new form of "money" can be introduced—perhaps points or coupons. Butter now has two prices: a money price plus a coupon price. The quantity demanded can be reduced by raising the coupon price while keeping the money price below equilibrium. In effect, the government changes the conditions of demand and supply by cutting effective demand. If the issuing agency can gage accurately the amount of butter that will be available, it can issue just enough ration coupons to "buy" the amount supplied at the money price fixed. In practice, authorities cannot hit the mark on dead center; but they may reasonably expect to get closer than if there were no coupons. Rationing itself adds costs, if only red tape and nuisance; but during war such costs may seem a reasonable price for keeping money prices down.

Rationing of supplies to producers may be called *allocation* or *priorities*. The goal is to divide the available output of, say, aluminum forgings, among various uses on the basis of estimates of importance to the war effort. Price may then become almost insignificant as a guide.

Another type of special adjustment can be opened through supply. The price that has been set below equilibrium will discourage production. Some dealers may stop handling butter because it causes so much trouble—record keeping and consumer annoyance. Dairy companies may shift production to cheese, ice cream—items with more attractive price ceilings or those not subject to control. Farmers may shift to production of cattle for meat purposes, or to feeding hogs, or to factory work. Can as much or more butter be kept coming to market as before price control?

One possibility is to force people to do what they would not do otherwise. Men are forced into the army. Why not *make* farmers (their cows) and the dairy industry produce butter? Easy to say, but perhaps hard to do. What if dairy farmers cannot afford to pay for the feed needed? What happens to cheese or fluid milk production? The problem grows larger than appeared at first. But perhaps butter producers can be helped to reduce their costs. If so, there can possibly be equilibrium at the fixed price. But how? A subsidy may do the job. Figure 15–9 illustrates. The low control price assures serious discrepancy between quantities demanded and quantities supplied. Government then steps in with a subsidy to producers and enables them to offer more at any price on the schedule.

Notice that the *price is lower* and the *quantity is larger* than they would be under equilibrium (without subsidy). With the price lower consumers buy more than they would if the market were free; price is not

FIGURE 15–9. Effect of Subsidy in Balancing Quantities Supplied and Demanded under Price Control

At the control price, the quantity that would be supplied is substantially less than the quantity demanded. A subsidy, in effect shifting the supply curve from SS to S_sS_s, will lead to a substantial increase in quantity supplied. E_s, the new equilibrium with the subsidy, is at a point of larger output and consumption and lower price than E, the equilibrium without subsidy and price control.

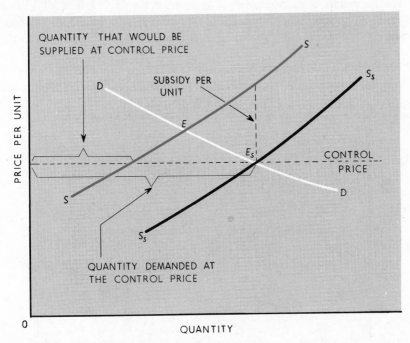

"fully" serving its function of economizing consumption. How much difference would there be if curves were much more, or much less, elastic? The source of the money for the subsidy makes some difference. If the source is new taxes, they will tend to shift the demand schedule downward as the disposable income of families falls. If funds come from newly created money, however, the increase in money income in later periods will tend to raise demand.

Prices Controlled above Equilibrium. Controlled prices may be above the equilibrium. Figure 15–10 illustrates. It might apply to a public utility rate. The price may have been set at about the equilibrium. Then demand falls—perhaps consumers find some other service preferable. If the law said, "This is the price, no one may pay less," then sellers would be offering more than buyers would take. If prices were free to fall, no discrepancy would persist. But if the price must remain and if the law forbids a reduction in productive capacity (supply), the disequilibrium may last until bankruptcy reduces supply. Price is higher and consumption smaller than if the market were free. Railroads believe that they have been forced to maintain some rates of this sort.[5]

Government Guarantees of Price. If a government undertakes to guarantee sellers a minimum price, as under some U.S. agricultural price support programs, what happens? If the guarantee is at the equilibrium point or below, the officials have no problem. Market forces will do the

FIGURE 15–10.   Price Control above Equilibrium

Price is fixed at *E*, equilibrium under the original conditions. Then demand falls from *DD* to *D$_d$D$_d$*. If price is free to fall, the new equilibrium will be at *E$_f$*. If price is not free to fall, however, the quantity that will be demanded will be smaller than the quantity that will be supplied (or that would be supplied if producers could find buyers at the price).

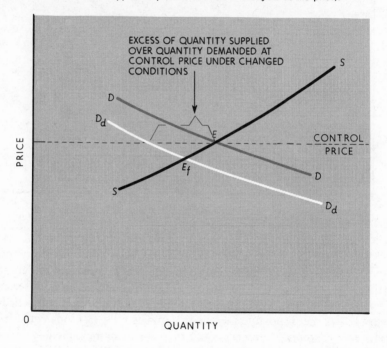

job. But if the guarantee is above the equilibrium, something more than the market must be set to work or the goal cannot be achieved. Figure 15–11 illustrates. Two things are possible. (1) Farmers may be compelled to restrict output so that all they do produce will be bought by consumers at the "high" price. (2) Government may buy or compensate farmers for storing or destroying whatever output buyers do not purchase voluntarily. Any use eventually made of government acquisitions should be a use that does not substitute for market demand. Otherwise the disposition, by

[5] Labor unions generally seek wage rates which are "controlled" above the free market equilibrium.

FIGURE 15–11.   Guaranteed Price: Adjustment of Quantity when Price Guaranteed Is above Equilibrium

In Case A, with inelastic supply and demand, the quantity the government would have to buy (or induce producers not to supply) is much smaller than in Case B, with elastic demand and supply. Shaded areas show cost to government if there is no reduction of output.

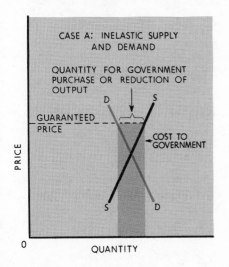
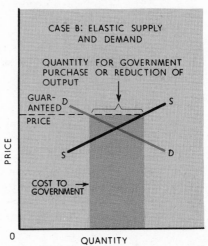

replacing private demand, would offset the effect of the government's purchases.

TERMS AND CONCEPTS

supply	law of supply and	elastic (inelastic) de-
supply elasticity	demand	mand
unit elasticity	equilibrium price	price control
inelastic (elastic)	futures market	rationing
supply	black market	price subsity

QUESTIONS

1. What is "supply"? What influences elasticity of supply? Diagram a decline in supply. When is an increase in quantity purchased not a result of a rise in supply?

2. Why does the seller benefit when a price above equilibrium goes down? If price is below equilibrium, will buyers benefit from a rise? Why?

3. Under what conditions of supply will most of a commodity tax be shifted to consumers?

4. In what sense are demand and supply "people acting," or trying to act?

5. Assume a price not at equilibrium. Trace the process of adjustment. What forces bring about the new results?

6. Can demand be greater than supply? Explain.

7. Under what conditions of demand or supply would the adjustment to a new equilibrium involve a change in price alone? Quantity alone? Why?

8. "Speculators buying and selling in the produce markets perform a valuable service for businesses which do not want to speculate." Discuss.

9. "Shortage" is another way of saying "price is too low," while "surplus" tells us simply that price is too high. Discuss. Would this apply to housing? Labor?

10. "A hefty price rise may be unpopular but it will induce economizing." Discuss.

11. When the price of a product is raised by government action, what is likely to happen? Would the results be the same for postage as for wheat? Why?

12. "Economic laws are neither moral nor immoral; they are inexorable. To accept them as such is the first business of one who would serve his fellow men." Would you agree as applied to the "law of supply and demand"? Why?

13. Discuss the problems of government action to keep the price of butter substantially above the free-market equilibrium. How might the problems be affected by (a) a rise in the price of margarine; (b) a substantial decline in the demand for cheese, fluid milk, or ice cream; (c) a drought in dairy areas; (d) a fall in price of feed?

16

COST AND SUPPLY: PLANT (FIRM)
AND INDUSTRY

Which of you, intending to build a tower, sitteth not down first, and counteth the cost. . .

St. Luke 14:28

Demand and supply in the market as a whole are the end result of the operation of forces in many smaller situations. Chapter 14 showed how total market demands reflect decisions of households, businesses, and governments. We now look more closely at supply, examining the forces that determine the amount each producer will supply and the number of producers. Briefly, we study *costs:* (1) certain major types of cost, (2) the difference that time makes, and (3) the way in which costs affect (*a*) the quantity of goods or services a business will offer and (*b*) on what terms. To simplify, we assume that each firm has only one plant.

A company produces to earn profit. The people who make business decisions have mixed motives, of course, just as we all do. Yet it is basically correct to assume that *supply results from hopes of gain* (or fear of loss).

TYPES OF COST

A firm must "put in" something to "get out" something else. The inputs are its costs.

Inputs: Costs as Physical Things and as Money. The *real* inputs of labor, materials, and other productive capacity are costs. The use of real inputs in one way keeps them from alternative uses. The businessman's prime interest will be in money costs; they depend upon (1) the *quantities* of real goods and services he must buy, and (2) the *price* per unit of these

379

inputs. Therefore, he must be concerned with inputs in the physical sense. What labor, materials, and so on, must he buy? Technology creates the conditions that are possible, that is, the production opportunities. Research, for example, showed how to use air, water, petroleum gases, and specialized equipment to produce nylon. What technology permits in using physical inputs to produce physical outputs can be called the range of *production possibilities*.[1] Ordinarily, there will be different ways in which inputs can be combined to produce essentially the same physical output. The real inputs, the real costs of a given physical output, can vary.[2] One material can be substituted for another—rayon in rugs when the price of wool soars—or machines replacing human brawn.

The physical costs, the real things sacrificed to create supply, make up only part of the story, like paragraphs and sentences with no organization—a mystery, perhaps, but not a story. What gives meaningful organization to the different production possibilities is *price*. The business needs a measure of the relative scarcity of different combinations of inputs. Otherwise, how can it tell which is most economical? The obvious solution is to use the money measure. For the firm, money costs become the expenses that are important.

Fixed Costs.   Some costs are fixed for the time being—overhead—and do not change with the amount of business done. In planning for a period of a few months, or perhaps a year, what should a business consider its fixed costs? These will differ from one case to another, of course, depending upon the kind of business. Generally, however, there will be (1) salaries of the key officials and staff members—people so important they must be retained if the company expects to survive; (2) costs of the major capital investment including the worth of alternatives sacrificed by the owners in providing equity capital (an implicit cost discussed later), interest on debt, fixed rental payments, insurance, and depreciation and maintenance (other than that attributable to wear and tear) are costs that often cannot be changed—if the firm is planning to stay in business over the long run, on the same scale; (3) real estate taxes.

Whether output is a few units or millions in the period, total fixed costs are the same. *The longer the period for which decisions are being made, however, the fewer the costs that are fixed.*[3] Calculations of truly fixed

[1] Our standards of what is right and, of course, what the law will permit also limit production possibilities. One evidence of progress is public reluctance to tolerate working conditions once deemed acceptable.

[2] The relationship between output in physical terms and various inputs, using a given set of techniques, is the *production function* for that method of production. It tells how much output one gets from using so much labor, power, capital, raw materials, and so on, with a particular set of techniques.

[3] Not all fixed costs must be paid out in cash—depreciation, for example. On the other hand, the firm may have obligations to make fixed cash payments which are not chargeable to that year's operations—debt retirement and taxes on last year's income are examples.

cost can be characterized as "backward looking." As such, they can give misleading guidance about the future.

Variable Costs. Far more costs are fixed for a 6-month than for a 6-year or 6-decade period. Some outlays rise and fall with the amount of business done in the period, assuming prices and techniques to remain unchanged: payments in wages and salaries to people who will not be hired if the plant is idle, raw materials, electric power, some maintenance, heat, some taxes, advertising. The total amount of these *variable costs* in any period will depend upon the firm's decisions on how much to supply to the market.

No sharp line divides variable from fixed costs. Much hinges upon the nature of the business and the length of the time of the planning period.[4] But the difference between these two types of expense has high significance for efficient management.

Cost per Unit of Output. Decisions on how many units to supply rest upon (1) costs per unit, which will vary according to the number of units produced, and (2) selling price per unit.

A firm's fixed costs do not change in total as output from the existing capacity rises or falls. Yet *fixed costs per unit* vary with the number of units; the bigger the output, the smaller the fixed cost per unit (Table 16–1). Fixed cost per unit drops sharply when small output expands, but the decline per unit becomes less and less as volume increases.

The total of variable costs, however, does depend upon the physical quantity of output. No output, no variable costs. Large output brings large variable costs in the aggregate—more labor, raw material, and other resources—obvious, but not very revealing. The important question is: "How do variable costs *per unit* of output change as production expands?"

TABLE 16–1.   Fixed Costs: The Relation of Fixed Cost per Unit to Number of Units Produced

Fixed Cost	No. of Units Produced	Fixed Cost per Unit (Average Fixed Cost)
$100,000	1	$100,000
100,000	2	50,000
100,000	1,000	100
100,000	10,000	10
100,000	100,000	1
100,000	1,000,000	0.10

For outputs that are small in relation to the size of the plant, variable costs *per unit* are likely to be high. The minimum staff needed to produce a tiny output will not be able to work fully or to specialize to best advantage. A store must have one clerk; but with a small volume of sales,

[4] One firm, for example, may lease retail store locations at a fixed dollar amount for a period of years; another may pay the landlord a percentage of receipts.

she may be idle much of the time. A movie theater needs at least one projectionist, and a train needs a minimum crew. Moreover, with any operation at all, some heating, advertising, purchasing, and any of several other costs will become necessary; they are a little like fixed costs in that, for small differences in output, their total will change only slightly. As production increases, these lumpy variable costs spread over a bigger quantity, so that *per unit* they fall. Eventually, however, quantity becomes large enough so that these costs are averaged over many units and change little on the average. Meanwhile, the firm takes advantage of specialization. Laborers, instead of shifting from one kind of work to another, can each concentrate on one job; equipment can be used more effectively to give larger output. Quantity discounts on materials, electric power, fuel, and advertising may permit savings; rates on carload freight shipments are less per ton than "l.c.l." (less than carload) rates. Thus, for a range of output, variable costs per unit decline—inputs are used in better proportions.

After a time, however, a main feature of variable costs per unit appears. Average variable costs remain fairly steady throughout a large range, for two main reasons: (1) With the machines and other installed productive facilities, there is little opportunity to alter the amount of physical resources used per unit of output. Workers' efforts yield about the same amount per man-hour. The firm must buy one motor per sweeper, or one wrapper per loaf of bread, whether production is x or $10x$ units. (2) Beyond a point, prices of raw materials and power, for example, do not become either cheaper or more expensive as purchases expand. The business pays a going market price, and its changing orders are not large enough to alter prices appreciably. Empirical studies of cost suggest that typically there is a wide range of fairly stable variable costs per unit.

The *law of diminishing returns* (Chapter 3), that is, *diminishing productivity*, however, warns us to expect a change. The problem involves a certain fixed capacity—a plant with equipment, a farm, a store—to which variable factors are added. If the firm uses more and more of one productive resource—labor—with others that are fixed—machines—the additions to output (in physical terms) eventually increase less than in proportion to the increased input (in physical terms). Ultimately, each successive input adds less output than the unit before. In other words, variable costs (physical inputs) per unit of output begin to rise as the additional inputs produce, on the average, smaller and smaller additions to output.

What factors in practice lead to rising variable costs? Less well trained or less industrious labor must be used; a given management cannot operate as efficiently when volume exceeds some point. The plant or working space becomes crowded, as in the mailing room or behind a store counter; poorer service to customers loses goodwill; more transportation is required to reach bigger markets, and more effort is needed to sell. Extra pressure on machines leads to inadequate maintenance or to such full use that, because there are no standbys, labor must be idle when a machine is being repaired. In addition to the inexorable working of the law of diminishing productivity—a technical, physical thing—*changes in financial costs* work in the same direction. The chief reason, probably, is the necessity of paying higher wage rates for overtime, night, weekend, and holiday work.

Sometimes the rise in variable expense per unit of output is slight, at other times sharp and substantial. In any case, however, because part of the productive capacity is fixed (for the period) the expansion of the volume of production beyond some point will inevitably lead to rising variable costs per unit.

Table 16–2 shows how variable costs are related to output, where

TABLE 16–2.   Variable Costs: Relation of Variable Cost to Amount Produced.*

	Physical Measures of Output				Money Costs of Variable Inputs	
Variable Input, Number of Units (Physical) (1)	Total Units of Output (2)	Increase in Output Resulting from Added Unit of Input† (3)	Average Units of Output per Unit of Input (4) Col. (2) ÷ Col. (1)		Total (5) Col. (1) × $10	Average Variable Cost per Unit of Output (6) Col. (5) ÷ Col. (2)
1	5	5	5		$10	$2.00
2	14	9	7		20	1.43
3	27	13	9		30	1.11
4	40	13	10		40	1.00
5	50	10	10		50	1.00
6	60	10	10		60	1.00
7	63	3	9		70	1.11
8	64	1	8		80	1.25

* This hypothetical schedule shows the possibilities for any given period of time, such as a day. Inputs are assumed to cost $10 each.
† This is the marginal product. It is the addition to total product, for example, when four rather than three, or seven rather than six, units of input are used.

different quantities of inputs are used with a given fixed plant. The larger the amount of variable inputs, the larger the total variable costs; in this case, total cost rises in direct proportion to the number of inputs. However, output does not increase uniformly (column 3). So, when variable costs of different total inputs are averaged over the outputs which they yield, variable cost *per unit* changes (column 6).

Total Cost.   Fixed and variable costs combine into total expenses. These depend upon (1) the quantities of fixed and variable inputs used to produce different outputs and (2) the money prices of these inputs.

Though obviously important, total expense does not provide the measure of cost which is best for deciding the most profitable output.

Graphs of Costs. Economists use graphs to show how costs vary with output. Like simple pictures, they portray essential relationships far more easily than words. *Costs per unit* are of especial interest to anyone who must decide how many units to produce. Figure 16–1 shows how costs per unit vary with output. The average total cost—the total cost per unit—

FIGURE 16–1. . Fixed, Variable, and Total Costs per Unit of Output

The three curves show average costs at different quantities of output.

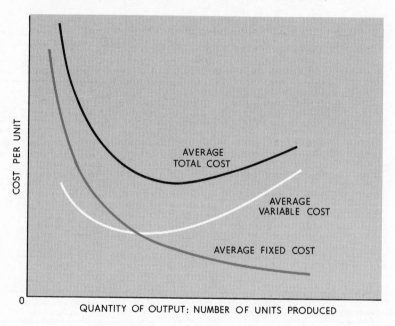

AVERAGE TOTAL COST

AVERAGE VARIABLE COST

AVERAGE FIXED COST

COST PER UNIT

0

QUANTITY OF OUTPUT: NUMBER OF UNITS PRODUCED

when graphed will have something of a U shape. Average total cost will fall rapidly as output increases from a few units; fixed costs are being spread over more units, and average variable costs are also falling. Then there will be a range where variable costs per unit do not change greatly and the additional spreading of overhead costs exerts little influence. At some point, however, the variable costs per unit begin to rise; eventually this rise will offset the additional decline in average fixed costs. The average total cost will then begin to rise.

Costs, we find, can be shown on the same kind of diagram used to show demand and supply. The money amount is measured on the vertical axis, up and down. The physical quantity, whether production or purchases, is shown on the horizontal axis.

Minimum Unit Cost of Production. The lowest point on the average total cost curve is where the fewest total resources (measured in dollars) are needed per unit of production. This is the *point of lowest or minimum unit cost*—thought of as the point of greatest technical efficiency. Output comes from the "best" use of resources. The lowest unit cost, and the size of output at which it is reached, depend upon both (1) technical conditions and (2) the prices of inputs. Other things the same, the public will benefit if output comes from plants operating at least cost per unit, where the fewest resources—value of inputs—are used to provide a unit of output. At greater output, though fixed plant would be used more intensively, the advantages of "spreading" fixed costs would be more than offset by the disadvantages of larger variable costs per unit.

Implicit Cost. The dollar figures in which businesses keep their accounts understate full economic cost to the company.[5] The figures reveal such expenses as wages, bills for raw materials, rent—*explicit* costs. In addition, however, businesses have *implicit* costs.

In unincorporated firms, including farms, the owner-manager does not ordinarily pay himself a salary. Whether a sole proprietor or one of several partners, he puts in effort and sacrifices a chance to work somewhere else. Although he does not charge the business with the cost of his time working for it rather than somewhere else, there is a sacrificed alternative which is part of the cost of the firm's output.

Giant corporations as well as tiny proprietorships incur another type of implicit cost—the cost of the equity capital which the owners have put in. By placing it here, the owners sacrifice other alternatives; they are willing to make the capital available only because they expect a gain large enough to compensate for giving up the best alternative. A part of the essential cost of production is "normal profit," what is needed (net, after taxes) to attract capital. The cost is implicit; the owners do not make explicit agreements about how much they will pay themselves (except preferred stockholders).

Throughout our business economy, cost as shown on a profit and loss statement (or in most cost accounts) understates full economic cost by ignoring implicit costs. **The cost curves in this book will include implicit costs—for all businesses a "normal profit," conceived as the net return required to maintain the equity capital in the business, plus for owner-**

---

[5] Financial accounts do not ordinarily show "opportunity" costs for use *within* the company. An integrated textile firm weaving its own gray goods may find the money costs 20 cents a yard; in figuring the cost of such material for making finished cloth, however, the firm should take account of what it could get for the unfinished cloth by selling in the market—the best opportunity sacrificed. If it could get 21 cents a yard from public sale of gray goods, such a figure is the cost it should use for planning its production decisions. Some businesses do use, where possible, the price obtainable in the market as the cost of its own products used within the company. Also ignored are "third-party" or "neighborhood" costs and benefits.

managers a salary equal to what could be earned in the best job sacrificed.

Relation of Costs to the Period of Time.   Costs, the value of the alternatives sacrificed, depend upon the period of time over which change can take place. A firm has more alternatives in a decade than in a year, and more in a year than in a day. One important feature of costs, in fact, is that the amount over which the company has control depends upon the period for which decisions (plans) are being made.

Some costs are more easily controlled within any period for which the firm is planning than are others. For a period of a month, some expenses are completely fixed; others are subject to control. The best start is to heed this guide: "Distinguish the things you can do something about from those which are beyond your power." Worrying over spilt milk is more than a waste of energy—it is likely to result in more spilling.

Time can be graded into any number of periods, but three will reveal the essential economic points.

1. A period can be so short that no adjustment is possible. This is the *instantaneous or market period*. Everything has been committed, *so all costs are fixed*. A scheduled showing of a movie or a passenger plane beginning a flight would be examples—or the morning's fish catch in a summer market without refrigeration. The supply is fixed, the production decisions made; and, for the moment, no change of price, cost, or demand will affect output. The suppliers' only problem is how to get the best price possible.

2. The other extreme is the *long run*.[6] This is a period long enough to permit all adjustments: for complete construction of a new plant, the training of a staff, establishing market position, the development of external economies (efficiencies in supplying industries). When contraction is involved, the period is long enough to permit complete liquidation of the investment. *No costs are fixed*. The time needed will depend upon the conditions of the particular firm and industry. For the lemonade stand the long run is rather shorter than for a railroad.

3. In between lies the *short run*, perhaps better called the *intermediate period*. Generally, it is a period which is too short to permit changes in plant, equipment, or specialized personnel, but long enough to permit changes in the use of present capacity. Short-run adjustments are those made to existing capacity of fixed facilities.

In the short run, with some factors fixed, the best or optimum input-output adjustment will likely be different from that of a longer period. In planning for the long run, the firm can choose what size and type of plant to have, not merely how to adapt to plants in existence as a result of past decisions. Ordinarily, a business will be making long- and short-run deci-

---

[6] Think of this "long" as a "planning" or "decision" period during which all elements of the firm's productive capacity can be altered.

sions at the same time. They are inevitably related. Always, however, the costs which a business can do something about, in contrast with those that are uncontrollable, depend upon the time period involved. The shorter the period, the greater the proportion of costs that are fixed.

Cost per Unit in Relation to Size. The minimum point on the average total cost curve, we saw earlier, identifies the rate of output at which a certain amount of fixed equipment (a given plant) is used most

FIGURE 16–2.   Average Total Cost of Production in Four Plants of Different Size

In deciding what size of plant to build for the long run, the businessman will try to select the most efficient size. In the case shown below, Plant C, when operating at its optimum point, will have lower costs than either the smaller plants, A and B, or the larger one, D.

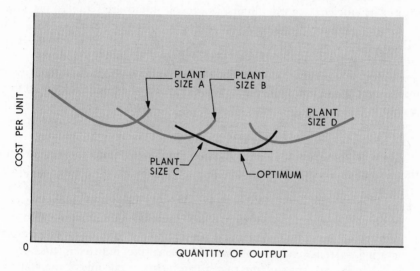

efficiently.[7] At this point, the fewest inputs in a value sense are needed per unit of output.

In long-run planning, however, a new element enters into the determination of least-cost production. The manager must then ask: "What is the most efficient plant size? What, if any, economies, can we expect from larger size? Are there economies of [large] scale?" Yes, often, up to a point. Let us look at factors affecting costs, trying to distinguish between those associated with (1) the plant, the physical producing unit, and (2) the firm, the business organization. Some differences are "real" or "productive" in the sense of inputs of labor, materials, or capital per unit of output. Others reflect differences in "bargaining" power, the effect of the

---

[7] This is not necessarily the point at which the firm will make the largest profit, as we shall see later when we take account of the price received for the output.

company's actions on the prices it pays for various types of input. Most of these we shall leave for consideration in Chapter 19.

Advantages of "Large" Size. Productive advantages result from operation on a large scale if the bigger plant can do a given job with fewer inputs of labor and materials per unit of output. But why? Some things can be done only with a "large" plant. A reasonably satisfactory steel mill, flat-glass factory, or paper mill must be large. The plant big enough to operate efficiently will produce a "great deal" in relation to total demand.

Complicated, expensive machines do some things that cannot be done any other way, and they do many things more effectively than simple machines or unaided hand labor—modern computers in banks or delicate controls in manufacturing wonder drugs. Specialization can be carried to more detail when the task is larger. Economists speak of the **internal** "economies of scale"; the larger the size or scale of a single plant, the greater its efficiency, within limits, i.e., fewer inputs are required per unit of output. Moreover, **external** economies are often achieved as an entire industry expands, perhaps by establishing more plants of essentially the same size and efficiency. Producers supplying a growing industry can themselves specialize, expand, and achieve greater economies in their own plants. As the motion picture industry expanded, the businesses supplying it with film could operate on a larger scale and themselves achieve internal economies. Growth of the chemical industry enabled railroads to provide tank cars engineered for different chemicals.

Even an economy as large as that of the United States cannot absorb the output of hundreds, or sometimes even dozens, of plants equipped with the intricate, miraculous machines that modern technology has developed. The $300 million or so of special tools, dies, and related equipment an auto company needs to produce really new models will supply a large part of the whole American market. A factory or hydroelectric generating system, embodying the best scientific improvements, often requires an investment so large that it can justify itself only if the volume of business is large. If the machines can operate more or less at capacity, they yield great economies over simpler methods.

An irresistible technological basis of bigness in plants exists in some industries, but not in all. For example, a large plant in a single location may produce complex medicines more cheaply than a tiny one; yet the "plants" to decide on which patients need how much (doctors' offices), must be both small and widely dispersed. Large and expensive equipment can produce auto fenders far more cheaply than the local garage; but when my car and another collide, the local garage, not a giant assembly line in Detroit will put on a new fender. In the steel industry, highly successful Inland Steel is small; yet its basic plant is hundreds of times as large as the typical plant of the giant of food distribution, A&P. Note this, however: The *technological* marvels that require, and make possible, mass production are found largely in *plants* rather than as part of the business organization, the *firm*. To get the fullest possible advantage of the best techniques for producing steel girders or retailing groceries, there is little need for a firm larger than one steel mill or supermarket.[8]

Savings in buying and selling may come as a business gets bigger. (Here the size of firm is likely to be more significant than the size of plant.) Sometimes the large firm gets lower prices because it has gained great bargaining power. This "bargaining" gain is someone else's loss, something much less desirable for the public than the savings a plant may, as it expands, make by using fewer inputs per unit of output. The large business, however, by dealing in large transactions to save paper work on each dollar involved, by searching out the best possibilities, and by offering sizable long-term contracts on which others may plan firmly, can sometimes create *real* savings. Less labor and material are needed per unit purchased.

When business is done on a large scale, little things, the bits and pieces that would otherwise be wasted can often be used advantageously—for example, the use of *by-products*. For decades college students have been told, correctly, that the meat-packing companies use everything from the hog but the squeal. Salvage of scrap becomes profitable when operations expand beyond some point. Such economies are largely real (not money saving from sharper bargaining). They depend chiefly upon the size of the plant rather than the firm. Yet operations need not be huge to get such advantages. Scrap collecting by outside firms is itself a highly developed activity which serves small as well as big plants.

Machines and other physical equipment are not the only things that can be more effective when specialized. *Legal problems, advertising, public relations, planning the use of computers, plant design and location, personnel relations, scientific research* of many kinds, and a host of things needed by modern business call for *skills* which are much more productive when highly developed than when amateurish. Larger size permits economies of greater skill which can be substantial to both the plant and the firm. The banking giant, for example, can afford many kinds of specialists (on products, industries, areas, financing devices) to help itself and its customers. The big resort hotel will present star entertainers.

The small firm may not be able to hire the experts that will show how to make a good contract with the union, or what "twist" in the design of its product will appeal most to the public, or how to take advantage of details of today's complex tax laws. The large firm can afford skillful programs to improve its public relations. It can develop or hire the specialized knowledge needed to find the best markets for buying and selling. A small company can rarely afford the costs of developing export markets, some of which yield attractive profits.

---

[8] Suppliers to the plants may be large but need not be under the same ownership. In fact, they can often operate more efficiently if serving end users under several different managements.

The building of specializations *within* the firm is not always essential to utilizing them. The American economy has extensive facilities for making many kinds of specialized skills available to business on an hourly or weekly basis. They are available *outside* the company. The firm doing $5,000 business a week may be reluctant to hire experts at $200 a day, but a firm far below the status of giant can draw upon all sorts of specializations. For example, to get help in marketing, it may engage a "manufacturer's representative" who will serve for a pecentage of sales or, for exports, it may deal through agents with established connections abroad. The efficiencies that rest upon the ability to use highly developed human skills, though real and often large, are not exclusively the possession of huge businesses. Dealership arrangements, for example, permit relatively small firms to draw upon specialized ability developed by giants. Auto dealers seldom rank as big businesses; yet they are part of a system which offers to each the technical guidance that has grown out of large-scale operations. Data processing firms serve companies too small to have their own computers. Nevertheless, small businesses are in general less able than large to make extensive use of the potential advantages of specialized skills.

In some cases, the *quality* of a product or service can benefit distinctively from operations on a large scale. In real estate development, for example, a project planned on a big scale can bring substantially different, and often incomparably better, results than a larger number of projects involving the same total investment. Whether business or residential construction is involved, the big development can offer facilities, including amenities, which smaller units are unable to match.[9] A big hospital, bank, law firm, advertising agency, or bookstore can provide elements of service unattainable by the small unit. The larger a newspaper or magazine's circulation, the broader and richer the coverage and features it can offer.

Disadvantages of Large Size to the Company Itself. Beyond some point, larger size brings disadvantages to a business. (The public interest, as we shall see, also suffers.) Looking first at the physical unit, the plant, we find that eventually the important technical economies are fully realized. No more advantages from the division of labor, or from the addition of more complicated equipment, are possible in the existing state of technical knowledge. Any larger size would require using more of the same kind of equipment rather than permitting the use of more efficient machinery. Moreover, the growth of a plant may require the use of inferior labor as the best of the area's workers already have jobs.

The larger a plant, the broader must be its market to buy and to sell; *transportation costs* per unit rise. For bricks or steel, this factor becomes crucial, although not for medicine or spice. Where service is important, from shining shoes to repairing household equipment, the advantages of

---

[9] Building and rebuilding cities, one of the outstanding problems of the modern world, can be done successfully only if operations on a relatively large scale are possible.

larger size are decisively limited by the extent of the market. So, too, in retailing. Imagine Safeway trying to use one location for selling $3 billion of groceries.

As a firm grows beyond some point, increasing difficulties arise in managing efficiently. Rules must be established to organize operations, but rules create inflexibility; they cost something to enforce, and they dull and hamper initiative. The man who has done his stint in the armed forces need not be told how exasperating can be the administration of a big organization. Communication becomes difficult. Men down the line may not understand fully the intentions of those at the top, while the latter lose close touch with much of the actual functioning. Head officials, even with the best assistance, must spread their efforts or concentrate on a few parts of the business to the neglect of others. Red tape and the stagnating effects of bureaucracy pose an unending threat. A large plant has its problems on this score. A still larger firm has more. Is top management, then, a "fixed factor"—not expandable within the firm beyond some point? To a degree, management may be so limited. Yet experience shows that much indeed depends upon both the quality of the men at the top and the type of organization.

The seniority that offers security in a huge firm can deaden initiative. The peace and relaxing comfort of established position can sap the energies and stimulation that feed advancement. Except at the very top, the individual, no matter how great his skill and energy, cannot be truly free to use his judgment in a big company. Scope for development and use of the talents so carefully recruited is limited, at times frustrated, by the size of giant firms.

Big businesses, more than occasionally, have been targets of attack. The political vulnerability of large size may be a disadvantage. The defense of their firms can drain management effort. A "goldfish bowl" existence may not aid efficiency. Officials of giant corporations must take account of the effects of their decisions upon public opinion, the union, and others; pursuit of the more traditional goals of profit making must be modified—in ways smaller firms need not consider.

Graphic Summary. If big plants produce more cheaply than small ones, then, over the long run, small plants cannot expect to survive the competition of large ones. Where small plants have lower costs per unit, big plants will not last. As new productive capacity appears, it will be in the more efficient forms. In some cases, the most efficient plant will be so large that a few, perhaps only one, can supply all the demand at prices covering cost.

Will all plants operating at any one time have about the same cost curves? No. A graph of total costs of different plants might show something like that in Figure 16–2. The lowest unit cost is different for each of the four plants, and least for the third. The largest plant is not the most efficient; neither is the smallest. Therefore, over the long run, when all have had time to adjust capacity as well as possible, the third of these sizes will prevail. This size permits production at minimum unit cost.

Marginal Cost. Now we come to a most important economic concept: *marginal cost*. For analysis, it is a little like the cutting edge of the knife, the sensitive part that does the job; everything else is necessary, but this is the most critical.

In Table 16–2, we started with *inputs* and saw that in physical terms the quantity of output per unit of input varied. Variable costs per unit of

TABLE 16–3.   Cost Schedules of an Individual Producer *

Units of Output (1)	Fixed Cost (2)	Total Variable Cost (3)	Total Cost (4) Col. 2 + Col. 3	Marginal Cost† (5)	Average Total Cost (6) Col. 4 ÷ Col. 1	Average Variable Cost (7) Col. 3 ÷ Col. 1
0	$200	0	$200	0		
1	200	$ 50	250	$50	$250.00	$50.00
2	200	80	280	30	140.00	40.00
3	200	105	305	25	101.67	35.00
4	200	127	327	22	81.75	31.75
5	200	148	348	21	69.60	29.60
6	200	168	368	20	61.33	28.00
7	200	188	388	20	55.43	26.86
8	200	210	410	22	51.25	26.25
9	200	240	440	30	48.89	26.66
10	200	285	485	45	48.50	28.50
11	200	350	550	65	50.00	31.82
12	200	440	640	90	53.33	36.67

* Schedules of costs like these apply to output during a specific period, a day, month, or year, for example. The period is that in which the fixed costs assumed do not change.
† Marginal cost might be shown as lying between the two units, 3 and 4 for example, to emphasize that the *shift* from one output to another accounts for this particular part of cost.

output were higher at both low and high volumes than in between. Now let us start with *output* and examine the way variable costs change. Column 5 in Table 16–3 shows marginal costs and how they are related to total and variable costs. *The marginal cost of any unit of output is the amount it adds to total costs.* Or, the other way around, marginal cost is the amount that could be saved by not producing that unit. This is the cost which is most immediately under control.

In deciding on output, the manager can expect best results by focusing on the costs over which he has most direct control. What are these costs? They are the variable costs of the units he is free to produce or not to produce. The marginal cost of each successive unit is the amount which that unit adds to total variable costs: the labor, materials, and so on. If the choice seems to be between producing three or four units, a glance at the marginal cost schedule shows that adding the fourth unit to the production schedule would add $22 to costs. If the choice is whether to produce 9 or 10 units, the manager should see that the 10th unit will add $45 to costs. At each point in Table 16–3, except the move from five to six and from six to seven units of output, marginal cost is different from the marginal cost before and later.

The relation of marginal costs to average total costs deserves careful study. At small outputs, average total cost is higher than marginal cost. For two units, average total cost is $140, yet the second unit added only $30 to total cost; by not producing the second unit, then, the firm would

FIGURE 16–3. Marginal and Average Cost

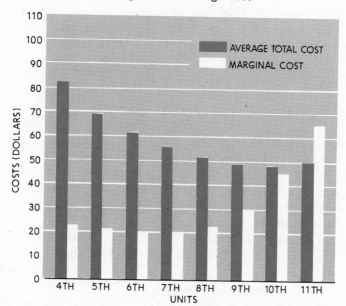

save not $140 but only $30. At seven units, average total cost is $55.43, but the seventh unit added only $20 to costs (Fig. 16–3). By producing seven rather than six units, the firm *adds* to costs the $20, the marginal cost of the seventh unit, not the $55.43 of average cost. At 11 units, however, average cost is $50, but marginal cost is $65. By deciding not to produce the 11th unit, the manager would not save $50, average total cost, but $65.

Average variable cost, similarly, diverges from marginal cost, remaining closer until the tenth unit, after which it (average variable cost) stays farther below marginal cost than does average total cost. Yet neither average can tell what marginal cost tells at a glance: the cost of one more unit. Decisions on the number of units to produce are decisions of more or less, and marginal cost is the measure (on the cost side) of the significance of a little bit more or a little bit less.

The shape of the marginal cost curve is related to the shape of the average variable cost curve. Marginal costs and average variable costs start at the same point; that is, for the first unit of output, the addition to total cost and the variable cost per unit are the same. But as average variable costs fall, marginal costs must diverge. For any output of more than one unit, the average variable cost is an average covering all units. The marginal cost, on the other hand, consists of the additional cost of the latest unit alone. Each point on the variable cost curve is an average; each unit that went before offsets some of the effect of the next unit in the average. Each point on the marginal cost curve, however, applies to a single unit. It, alone, tells its own story.

Marginal cost will be below average variable cost as long as the latter is falling; yet, while average variable cost is still falling, marginal costs will begin to rise. As output increases, the firm reaches the point at which successive units begin to cost more. Marginal cost rises. But the cost of the added unit cannot cause the average of all the units so far (average variable costs) to increase as long as the marginal cost, itself, is below the average. The marginal cost of the eighth unit is $22, a bit higher than for the seventh unit, but below the average of over $26 for all variable costs. (Compare the two for the ninth unit.) As marginal cost rises, and as average variable cost continues to decline, the two will come closer together. Finally they meet. This meeting must occur at the lowest point on the average variable cost curve. For larger outputs, marginal cost will be above average variable cost. Successive additions which lie above the average must, of course, raise it.

Average variable costs can never be greater than average total cost—since fixed costs *do* exist. Marginal cost, however, can be greater than average total cost. Your best grade in a college course can be higher than your average. The same relationship that holds between average variable cost and marginal cost holds between average total cost and marginal cost. As long as marginal costs are less than average total cost—through the tenth but not the eleventh unit in Table 16–3—each additional unit of output adds less to total cost than the average of those that have gone before; the average continues to fall.

The average total cost and the marginal cost will be the same at some point—the lowest point on the average total cost curve. After that what? Marginal cost is above average total cost, and so each additional unit pulls up the average. As marginal cost rises, so does average total cost. The geometry is simple but not terribly important (except for helping pass examinations). The economic relationship which the geometry summarizes *is* important. Figure 16–4 shows the general relationship. The marginal cost cure crosses the other two at their lowest points.

Does what we have covered so far tell what would be the best output? No, because the discussion of costs tells nothing about how much the firm can obtain for each unit of output; and the firm's decision about output

FIGURE 16–4.   Relation of Marginal Cost Curve to Curves of Average Total Cost and Average Variable Cost

The marginal cost curve intersects both the average variable cost and the average total cost curves at their lowest points. Curve of average fixed cost is not shown.

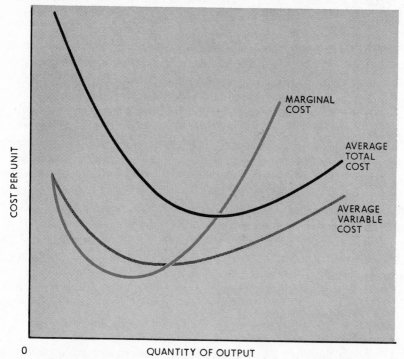

should rest upon costs in relation to selling price. The diagram shows the minimum cost output. The firm's interest, however, is not chiefly in minimizing costs but in maximizing the difference between total cost and total receipts (revenue).

Two things will alter a firm's cost schedules: changes (1) in the techniques, including methods of management, and (2) in the prices of inputs.

COST AND SUPPLY SCHEDULES

Difference between Long-Run and Short-Run Planning.   In the long run, all costs are variable. Therefore, in making long-run plans, the business has a choice about whether or not to build a plant, buy a machine, or undertake long-range research. The calculations that guide such decisions should include *all* costs, including those that will be fixed costs *if* they are undertaken. In emphasizing that price-output decisions should rest on marginal costs and that in the short run this rule leaves fixed costs out of account, the economist does not take a ridiculous position. He does not say that the costs of fixed plans should be ignored. When deciding whether or not to incur those costs, the businessman must allow for them most carefully. It is after the costs *are* fixed that they should be ignored for most profitable results. To maximize profit, management must be *forward-looking*. Future costs, the costs that the firm can still control, are what matter for current and future decisions.

Short-Run Supply. *The Plant (Firm).* What is the relation between cost and supply for the firm in the short run? Each firm will profitably offer to supply units that cost no more to produce than the price they will bring. The unit cost at which the firm should look is the *marginal cost—* the cost the firm would save by not producing the unit in question. Therefore, *the firm's marginal cost curve is the best supply schedule it can have.* In practice, marginal costs, even in the short run, may be nearly constant through a large range, stretching out the condition between the fifth and sixth and seventh units in Table 16–3. Above some output, however, marginal costs rise. So we draw short-run supply schedules for the plant that become inelastic. The fact that the plant is fixed insures that diminishing returns (productivity) will set in beyond some point.

The Industry. The industry is the total of all plants (firms). Their costs determine the industry supply schedule, which is the total of the supply schedules of all producers. The marginal cost schedules of different firms will not all be the same, but they likely will fall into much the same general pattern. In any case, since total capacity is fixed, the industry's short-run supply will be inelastic behond a certain point.

Long-Run Supply. *The Plant (Firm).* As the manager plans for the long run, deciding whether to retain or expand the fixed plant, he has more choices. What is best? In principle, the answer is illustrated in Figure 16–2. The plant with the lowest average total cost offers the best prospects. The quantity each producing unit will supply will depend upon the capacity of the plant of most efficient size. A firm can hardly hope to do better than to supply from plants with lowest costs. What about the industry?

The Industry. An industry may expand or contract by entry or exit of plants (or firms) of the most efficient size. They utilize the most efficient technology available. Large or small outputs can then be supplied at the same price, given time for adjustment (assuming no change in basic technology). This result is possible only if changes in the size of the industry do not appreciably alter the prices of inputs. This situation is one of *constant long-run supply price*. After there has been time for full adjustment of capacity, the supply price will be the same for a large output as it had been for a small output. For a significant range, therefore, the long-run industry supply curve is flat (Fig. 16–5). At any given time, the short-run supply schedule will be one of increasing cost because diminishing productivity appears—variable resources "operate" with some capacity fixed. The long-run schedule for the industry, however, may be one of constant supply price: with time for full adjustment, small, medium, or large outputs can be supplied at the same price.

Is constant cost in this sense realistic? Where industries are small, especially in manufacturing and commerce, constant cost (long-run supply price) is likely, assuming time enough to adjust fully. The industry in expanding or contracting will not have enough effect on the demand for

FIGURE 16–5.   Constant Long-Run Industry Supply Price

At any time, the industry supply schedule reflects the rising marginal costs of existing plants. Yet, if there is time to build new plant like the best existing, the new capacity of the industry will be able to supply very much larger quantities at the same unit price.

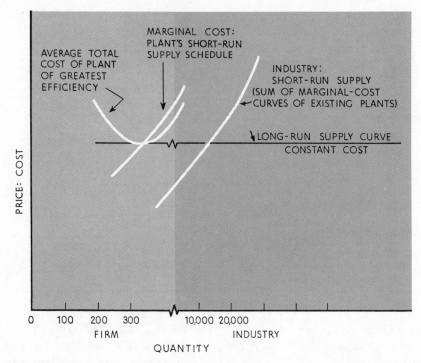

inputs to influence their prices appreciably. Nor does the size of the industry affect the efficiency with which individual plants operate. Of course, the total productive capacity of the whole economy is limited; society cannot escape diminishing returns as it pushes against the limits of capacity fixed by existing resources. Many industries, however, may be so small relative to the whole that no probable change in their size will influence input prices. New plants can enter and produce at the same minimum cost.

What about two other possibilities? Long-run supply price may either rise or fall as the industry grows (still assuming no changes in the knowledge of production techniques). As an industry adjusts to rising demands, the most efficient plants may have higher costs per unit than when the industry was smaller, a condition of **increasing long-run supply price.** Why? (1) The law of diminishing returns may explain reductions in physical output per unit of input: the new productive capacity may not be as efficient as older capacity; for example, inferior grades of natural resources may have to be used, or congestion or distance may add to transport costs. (2) Higher demand for inputs may raise their price. Either condition means that the long-run industry supply curve will slope upward like a marginal cost curve; in fact, the long-run supply schedule is the schedule of long-run marginal cost.

Under given conditions of technology, we should expect increasing

FIGURE 16–6.   Supply Curves of an   **FIGURE 16–7.**   Supply Curves of a
Increasing-Cost Industry   Decreasing-Cost Industry

In Case A, the short-run supply is the sum of the marginal cost schedules of existing firms. If more capacity is added, the supply price will follow the long-run curve. At any large fixed capacity, such as B, however, the short-run supply curve again rises more steeply than the long-run curve. In Case C, with relatively small capacity, the short-run supply curve rises because marginal cost with existing capacity rises. As the industry expands, however, costs per unit fall. In Case D, again, the short-run supply price curve slopes upward; but with still greater capacity the industry would supply larger quantities at a lower price because costs per unit would drop.

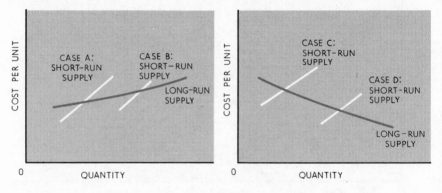

cost conditions in agriculture, in mining, and in an industry that is large in relation to the rest of the economy—local, national, or world, as the case may be (Fig. 16–6).[10] The amount of dependence upon specialized productive capacity is important; if high skills or other specialties are needed, expansion is more likely to involve rising costs than if more general productive capacity will do.

The final possibility is **decreasing long-run supply price.** (1) As the industry expands, other industries supplying it may be able to take advan-

[10] To grow, a large industry must make an appreciable drain on resources which will have uses in other industries. The shift of consumer demand to the product of the growing industry will release resources from other industries; but unless the freed resources are precisely those needed by the expanding industry, the latter must bid more for some resources. Moreover, the labor or other resources available for shifting may be relatively less suitable to the expanding industry than either the resources it already uses (a difference reflected in physical productivity) or in the other industry (a difference in the worth of alternatives for which the expanding industry must pay).

tage of techniques for larger scale and more efficient production. Facilities for building specialized equipment, training specialized labor, providing information, or marketing may develop. These economies *external* to the industry itself permit it to produce and supply at lower cost. (2) As plant size increases, costs within the plant may go down, i.e., expense per unit drops as expansion continues. If growing size of plant continues to bring economies, then one plant will tend to become the whole industry. By becoming larger, it gets an advantage over others. By growing still more, it can force the others out of business because it becomes able to supply the market at a lower price than two or more producers. Here are the makings of "natural monopoly," for example, public utilities.

Long-run supply curves (as economists define the long run) are predominantly either constant or increasing cost. When they do slope upward, they are flatter, less steep, than those of the short run. Long-run supply is more elastic than short-run. Of course, actual costs and supply over a period of years are likely to differ from those expected when decisions for the long run are made. Production techniques improve over time, reducing real costs. Then, too, forces outside the industry may alter the prices of inputs, raising or lowering costs. The uncertainties that exist in a dynamic world make it difficult to predict whether long-run costs will actually rise, fall, or remain essentially constant.

Two Questions. *What Is Capacity?* Measuring the capacity of a plant often proves very difficult.[11] Physical limits to production may differ sharply from the economic limits. The *economic limits* depend upon the physical limits, of course, but also upon the cost of inputs and the prices of outputs. The *physical limits* depend upon the resources available, both fixed and variable. At any time the economy would ordinarily be able to expand greatly the output of most factories, stores, railroads, and many other fixed physical productive plants; they could operate "around the clock." But would great expansion for a large fraction of the country's plants really be possible, physically? The answer depends upon the availability of variable resources: labor, raw materials, power. Measurement of overall physical capacity, therefore, is harder than adding the potentials of individual plants; the economy, certainly, does not have enough variable resources to use all fixed plant at the top limit.

Can Cost Guide Price Fixing when Prices Are Regulated? Well, which costs—short-run, long-run, marginal, average, or total? Another query: "At what volume of output?" A price that will just cover total costs at one output will be above or below those costs for other outputs. Further costs can be determined only if there is a reliable basis for

[11] Companies use different methods of estimating the capacity of plants. Ordinarily, the maximum possible rate of output will exceed the "preferred rate"; some relatively inefficient facilities are kept to meet peaks or to use when the better machines are being repaired.

predicting output. Moreover, a price that covers total cost will not necessarily lead to the *best allocation* of resources because this price probably ignores the relationships at the margin. Thus it is a poorer economizing device than a price that equals marginal cost, as we discuss in the next chapter.

TERMS AND CONCEPTS

input	implicit cost	internal economies
production function	market (instantane-	marginal cost
fixed cost	ous) period	constant cost
variable cost	long run	increasing supply price
diminishing returns	short run	decreasing cost indus-
total cost	external economies	try
minimum unit cost	economies of scale	capacity

QUESTIONS

1. What is the difference between fixed and variable cost? What is the significance of the length of the time period? Give examples of costs which are fixed in the short run but variable over a longer period.

2. In what respect is profit a cost? Depreciation?

3. What kinds of conditions tend to make mass production more efficient than smaller scale operation?

4. Why does the average total cost curve have a general U shape? Is the upward slope of the variable cost curve an example of the law of diminishing returns?

5. Why is the long-run supply curve likely to be more elastic than the short-run supply curve? Would you expect the costs of new types of products to fall in the long run? Why?

6. Explain the economics involved in the fact that the marginal cost curve intersects both the average variable, and average total, cost curves at their lowest points.

7. Under what conditions would the long-run supply curve for an industry be horizontal? Slope upward? Slope downward?

8. Why is the marginal cost schedule the firm's best supply schedule?

9. What is the relation between the costs of individual firms and the industry supply schedule? Illustrate.

10. If a company plans on the basis of total, rather than marginal, cost, how are its decisions likely to suffer?

11. "Our guide in setting prices will be costs of production." What problems would arise if a business or a government used "cost" as a guide in setting price?

12. In deciding whether to accept a repeat order, should a businessman consider all the costs, fixed and variable, or only the variable costs? Why?

13. Would it possibly be wise for a company to continue to operate at a loss for several years without closing down? Why?

14. What are the full costs of getting your college education? How do such costs affect the supply of college-trained personnel?

17

PRICE-OUTPUT ADJUSTMENT UNDER PURE COMPETITION: FIRM AND INDUSTRY

The battle of competition is fought by cheapening of commodities.
Karl Marx

A knowledge of costs does not give answers to such questions as: What will the price be? How much will be produced? Is price or output likely to change? Are resources being used to serve our welfare as well as possible? This chapter begins the answering; it describes the adjustments when an industry is purely competitive.

The Meaning of "Pure Competition." A market is purely competitive[1] if (1) there are so many sellers and buyers of (2) an essentially identical product that no one can have an appreciable influence on price by varying the amount which he offers to sell or buy, and if (3) firms can enter and leave freely in response to economic forces (without restraint by government, industry or union restriction, or other obstacle).[2] Most markets do not meet these requirements fully, and economists disagree about the extent of competition within industries which almost meet the three conditions. Farming is the most common example of production under purely competitive conditions—no single farm produces enough to make a dent in the total wheat, cotton, corn, or orange crop; the number of

---

[1] Economists sometimes distinguish "pure" from "perfect" competition. They then reserve the latter for the conceptual, limiting, case in which all participants in a purely competitive market also have complete knowledge of all elements, including substitute products, inputs, and technologies.

[2] We might also specify that there be no collusion between buyers and sellers.

buyers is great; producers can enter and leave.[3] Throughout some other big sectors of the economy, too, conditions are near enough to those of pure competition for the analysis of its forces to explain much of the process by which prices and output are determined.

In pure competition economic rivalry focuses on price. Advertising, distinctive features of the product of a firm, and many other devices businesses use to attract customers (or suppliers) have no place in pure competition. Hence the notion of pure competition is narrower and more precise than the concept used in everyday life, which includes a wide variety of nonprice inducements. The precision of our concept serves as a simplifying device to help understand the central, basic forces. Later we consider forms of rivalry which businessmen and consumers recognize as types of competition, but which do not exist in purely competitive markets.

The seller in a purely competitive market can assume that his actions will not affect the price he receives per unit. Whether he produces a larger or smaller quantity makes no significant difference for the industry. The manager of a firm in a purely competitive industry responds to price changes, but he does not have enough power to worry about influencing them. For him, the price is a fact that he cannot change. Like a drop in a bucket, his output is too small to have any appreciable effect on the level. He can focus on the problem of adjusting his firm's output to take fullest advantage of the price in the market. What, then, is the best adjustment?

THE PROCESS OF ADJUSTMENT

Output and Price in the Short Run. The best adjustment for the firm will depend upon both costs and price, and graphs provide the easiest way to see the relations. The last chapter showed how to graph costs of the plant (firm). How do we graph price? The price in a purely competitive market depends upon all producers and buyers, not upon the output of a firm. Price, therefore, is the same for both a large or small output of a firm, a condition represented by a horizontal straight line, as in Figure 17–1.

The firm's demand curve is a horizontal line at the market price. What is it? A perfectly elastic demand curve. At the market price the firm can sell all it can produce. If it tries to sell at a higher price, buyers will find another seller; on the other hand, there is no advantage in selling for less.

How much, then, should the company produce? In Chapter 16 we saw that the best place to study economic adjustment is at the margin. The firm's supply schedule is its marginal cost curve. To what do we look on the revenue (receipts) side that corresponds with marginal cost on the

---

[3] This is less true for agricultural specialties, such as garlic (which is grown by few farmers), and for products that are quickly perishable. Some farms produce a big enough fraction of the tomatoes (or other perishables) sold in the local market to have considerable effect on price. Obviously, too, government controls and others imposed by groups of farmers now restrict the freedom of individual producers to adjust as they judge best.

FIGURE 17–1.   Demand for the Product of an Individual Firm in a Purely
Competitive Industry

Demand and supply in the market as a whole determine the price, in this case $2 a unit.
The individual firm can then sell all its output at this price but nothing at a higher price.
Whether or not it produces a few hundred units more or less has no appreciable effect on the
quantity in the market as a whole, where dealings involve millions of units.

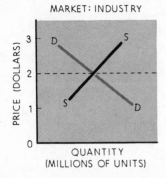
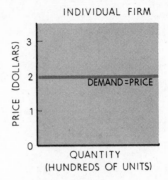

outlay side? We look at *marginal revenue*. It is the amount which sale of
the last or marginal unit adds to the firm's receipts (revenue). Since, in
this case, price is the same no matter how many units are sold, the last or
marginal unit adds the same amount to revenue as do all other units: the
price. For the firm in a purely competitive industry, threfore, price and
marginal revenue are equal.

**The best output is that where (1) marginal cost equals (2) marginal
revenue (which, under pure competition, is price).** The purely competitive firm adjusts best by carrying output to the point where price equals
marginal cost.[4] The reason is simple: The firm receives the price for each
unit of output, including the last; the marginal cost is what the firm must
pay for inputs to produce each successive unit of output.

If the price is above marginal cost, the firm can receive more from the
sale of additional units (marginal revenue) than it would spend to produce them (Fig. 17–2). If it produces more, each unit of output (for a
time) will bring more in revenue than the cost of additional inputs needed
to produce it. On the other hand, if the price (marginal revenue) is less
than marginal cost, some units are adding more to total cost than they
bring in revenue—better eliminate these. The best adjustment in both
cases is indicated by a general principle—obvious when stated. "Carry
output to the point where the additional cost of the last unit (marginal
cost) equals the revenue which that unit will add to the firm's receipts
(marginal revenue)."[5] Until the firm reaches this point, it is not at equilibrium; it has an incentive to change.

---

[4] Marginal cost must be rising at this stage. If it is falling, the thing to do is to set
output at the larger volume, where marginal cost is rising.

[5] Cost, as the term is used in this book, includes the implicit cost of a normal profit
on the equity capital provided by the owners.

FIGURE 17–2.   Determination of Best Output for Firm in Purely Competitive
Industry

If the firm produces less than the quantity OB, such as OA, units not produced would add
less to cost than the price they would bring. If output were greater than OB, such as OC, the
additional units would add more to cost than they would yield in receipts (price) since marginal cost is above price. The best adjustment is to carry output to the point where marginal
cost equals price.

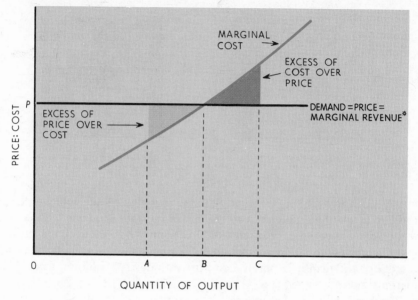

Now let us look at different "best adjustments" and what they can
show about economizing, the start being "abnormalities." Assume that
price has been equal to costs at the point of minimum total unit cost. For
some reason, consumers come to want this product more intensely. Will
there be more of it? At what price? With what effect on producers?
Demand in the market increases, raising price from $2 to $2.50 (Fig.
17–3). The firm can now earn more, even with no change in output. Yet
the firm can earn *most* by enlarging output. By how much? Highest profit
will result when output is increased to the point where marginal cost
equals the new price. Expanded output from one plant will not affect the
market price. However, as hundreds of producers enlarge output to take
advantage of the higher price, the total result will be an increase in the
aggregate quantity supplied. The total increase will be enough to influence market price. (This is not an increase in supply in the sense of an
upward shift of the supply schedule; the quantity offered from a given set
of supply conditions rises.) The expanding output keeps price from rising
(or remaining) above $2.50.

The price will settle above average total cost (including "normal"
return on equity capital) because the consumer is willing to pay. What
can we expect of a price above average total cost? If price is higher than

FIGURE 17–3.   Adjustment of Firm in Purely Competitive Industry to Rise in Market Price

As market demand rises from *DD* to *D$_i$D$_i$*, lifting price from $2 to $2.50, the individual firm can make the largest profit under the new conditions by expanding output from *OB* to *OC* units. If it did not expand to this point, it would sacrifice the opportunity to produce and sell units which add less to its costs, as shown by the marginal cost curve, than the price they bring. The expansion of output of firms adds up to the movement along or up the *SS* curve for the industry as a whole. Query: What would the new price be if firms did not increase output, that is, if the industry supply curve were vertical?

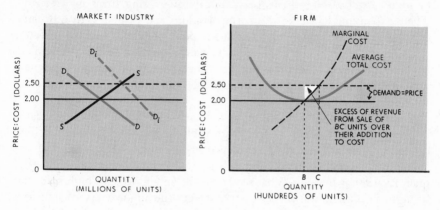

the lowest point on the average total cost curve, and if the company carries output to the point where marginal cost equals price,[6] the firm will (1) make more than a normal profit, and (2) produce more than if it operated at the point of minimum cost. In the short run, of course, fixed capacity cannot increase—by definition. The increased output must come from existing capacity. By expanding output in search of larger profit, firms serve consumers, not only in making more goods available, but also by keeping prices from rising as much as they would otherwise.

Output and Price in the Long Run: The Adjustment Process.   Chapter 16 showed what would be to the firm's long-run advantage: adjust to the most efficient size if it were not already there. Now we shift attention to the whole industry. The earnings (above normal) of existing firms will attract new productive capacity. (A shift of productive resources can serve the consumer; inputs can be transferred from producing things of less value under the new conditions of demand.) Investors will put more resources into the industry.

[6] Do we need to state not only that price must be above the lowest point on the average total cost curve but also that output will be carried to the point where marginal cost has risen to the level of price? Yes. A firm might extend production to the point where price equaled average total cost and earn no extra profit. Obviously, the company would be sacrificing a chance at higher earnings because the extra revenue to be gained by producing more units would be less than the extra cost. By sacrificing profit and producing more units, would it be serving the public better? No. The extra output requires resources worth more than the value of the added production.

Two conditions must prevail: (1) Businessmen need to know about the good profits. (2) No nonmarket restrictions, such as those of government, must impede entry of new productive capacity.

Good earnings can hardly be kept a secret if there are many firms. The second condition, however, is less certain. As a condition of a purely competitive industry, then, we have explicitly assumed *freedom of entry of new capacity*. New firms may appear, or existing firms may expand. Their expansion will take the form of additional plants. Why? Because existing plant is being operated at a point beyond that of greatest efficiency (marginal cost is above lowest average total cost). A new plant to produce some of the output at lower cost is attractive. The new capacity is a shift in the supply schedule—an increase, of course (Fig. 15–2).

Though no single unit of new capacity may make any appreciable impression on the total, a little from each of many will make a telling difference, just as more drops can eventually cause a bucket to overflow. Increased output begins to force a price reduction. Otherwise the larger quantity cannot be sold. What seemed to be an abnormally high price has brought into operation forces that "correct" the abnormality of long-run disequilibrium. As larger production causes price to fall, what happens? Reverse the adjustment process shown in Figure 17–3, assuming that price falls from $2.50 to $2. Consumers doubtless heave a sigh of relief. Smart, but probably unhappy, managers reduce output.[7] Why? Because the lower price does not pay for the costs of some units of output. At the old quantity, marginal cost was above the lower price that now prevails. By reducing output, the manager can get marginal cost again equal to price.

Why is it wise to look at marginal cost instead of average cost? The price may still be above average cost when the time to reduce output appears, that is, when a firm can cut costs more than revenue by reducing output. In other words, the business stops producing units that add more to cost than they do to receipts. This would be the case in Figure 17–3 if price fell from $2.50 to $2.20. If the businessman looks at the average cost, which combines high and low cost outputs, he might say: "We are still making a nice profit on all of these units, so why eliminate any?" If he focuses on the marginal cost, however, he will see that *some* output adds more to cost than the amount it brings in revenue. The marginal cost, in a sense, is the measure which shows the expense of producing the output over which the businessman has easiest control—the little more, little less.

Change takes place at innumerable margins. Since there are many

---

[7] The reduction in output from existing plants tends to offset some of the effect of increased output from the new plants. "Marginal firms" enter and leave the industry; firms with losses may be forced out, and superior firms whose managers see extraordinary profit opportunities elsewhere may shift to producing other things. Adjustment may also take the form of shifting the use of capacity from one product to another.

producers, not all will have seen what must come for the group as each expands in his own sphere. Overexpansion may result. If so, another disequilibrium, "excess" capacity, appears. People will buy the larger output only at a price below the cost of producing not only the additional output but also (on the average) all units that are sold. Price falls below the average total cost. Losses result. Resources are not serving the economy as effectively, on the average, in this industry as elsewhere.

What is wisest for the firm when price is below average cost? The best adjustment is to carry output to the point where price equals marginal cost (Fig. 17–4). At either larger or smaller output, the losses would be increased. In "cutting the losses," plants reduce output (moving down on the total supply curve).

FIGURE 17–4. Adjustment of Firm in Purely Competitive Industry to a Decline in Market Price

After supply has risen from SS (Figure 17–3) to S_iS_i, yielding the equilibrium price of $2, demand falls back to DD. Market price falls to $1.50. With its present capacity, the best adjustment for the firm is to reduce output from OB to OA, cutting out the units whose marginal cost is greater than the new and lower price. The firm will then lose money, but less than at any other output. If it produced less than OA, the saving in cost would be less than the price that could be obtained from the output sacrificed. The new equilibrium is one of the short run that may be part of the process of reaching long-run equilibrium. The firm, of course, should produce nothing if price is below average variable cost.

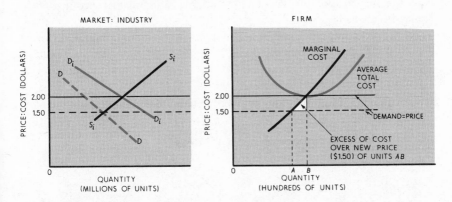

Why Operate at a Loss? Is it ever wise to produce at a loss? Of course —if the firm would lose more by not producing. If it can get a price above variable cost, then it should operate. It can get some revenue to "contribute toward overhead." How much should the company produce under such conditions? The answer is the same as ever: carry production to the point where marginal cost equals marginal revenue (price under pure competition). Such output gives least loss.[8]

If losses continue, the firm will go out of business—perhaps quickly, perhaps only after many years. In the process, it can cause trouble not

---

[8] Continued operation is wise if the costs of closing down and reopening would be greater than the temporary loss from failing to cover variable costs.

only for its owners but also for competitors. For a time consumers may benefit.

Exceptionally difficult problems arise when fixed costs are large. Then the difference between total and variable costs can be wide, especially in the short run. Then to operate at minimum loss, a company may still produce "substantial" quantities. As businesses compete aggressively for a share of total demand which is too small to give all firms a "fair living," the victims may call such competition "cutthroat." Since existing facilities do not earn a "normal" profit, new capital will not enter the industry; present owners will shift capital to other lines; for example, cash accumulated to cover depreciation will be invested elsewhere. The industry's capacity will decline. The supply schedule shifts to the left (upward on the vertical, price, axis). For the short run a decline in price induces a reduction in the output of existing plants; over the long run the number of producers will decline.

Long-Run Equilibrium for the Industry. The process of adjusting to changing demands—or to a change in the price of inputs or in methods of production—would end when there would no longer be any inducement to increase or to decrease capacity. What would be the conditions of this equilibrium? Productive capacity would earn a normal profit on the equity investment.

For every firm, price would equal average total cost of production at the most efficient, lowest-cost point (Fig. 17–5). This situation would be an ideal allocation of resources for the economy under the circum-

FIGURE 17–5.   Long-Run Equilibrium of Firm in Purely Competitive Industry

Output is carried to the point where marginal cost equals price. This is also the point of lowest average total cost of production—greatest efficiency. The cost curves include implicit costs, a normal return on invested capital and the value of owners' services.

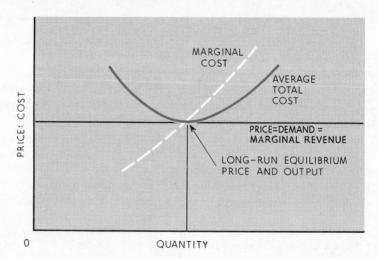

stances. (1) The total (and the marginal) cost per unit just equal the price which consumers are willing to pay. (2) The plant is being operated at its best efficiency—fewest inputs per unit of output, not only in the short run but also for the long run because the plants involve the best scale of production. Plants either larger or smaller would have higher average costs. Therefore, assuming no changes in techniques, the only plant that can survive in long-run pure competition is one whose lowest cost per unit just equals price.

This long run is one of tendencies, one in which economic forces tend to work out as described. Of course, new conditions develop constantly. They create new forces, some opposing, some reinforcing, and many redirecting the forces already operating. No set of long-run tendencies can ever proceed unmodified to an ultimate realization.

EVALUATION OF THE PURELY COMPETITIVE ADJUSTMENT

Let us look beyond the graphs to see more clearly what they mean. When the industry has reached equilibrium, each firm has done as well as possible for itself. How do the results appear for the community?

Efficiency in Use of Resources. When the purely competitive equilibrium has been realized, output and the use of resources are carried to the point where the value of the sacrifices (costs, inputs) matches the value, to consumers, of what is produced. The worth of the alternatives sacrificed at the margin—marginal cost—just equals the worth of what the inputs product. No switch of resources could add to consumers' satisfactions. Any shift would destroy the equality. An increase in production of item X would require inputs which the market values more highly than it would value a little more output of X. On the other hand, a slightly smaller output would save resources which are worth less than the output that would be lost. The allocation of resources seems beyond improvement as long as underlying conditions remain the same.[9]

How does this excellent result come about? By men seeking to do the public good? Not directly. The driving or organizing force is that of businesses seeking the best adjustment for themselves, the largest profit or least loss. A company hires resources, buys inputs—labor, material, and plant—as long as they cost less than consumers are willing to pay for the additional outputs. The prices (costs) of inputs reflect the sellers' estimate of the best alternatives sacrificed. Consumers offer prices that take account of all other alternative ways of using their spending power.

---

[9] Owners, of course, would prefer a situation bringing larger profit. Consumers would prefer lower prices regardless of losses to producers. The best balance of all interests, however, is the one of equilibrium. A change in tastes, in the prices of other products, in the techniques of production, or in any of many other things will require a new allocation of resources.

Resources are shifted from plants and industries where they produce things wanted less urgently (at the margin) to plants and industries where they are wanted more urgently (at the margin).

In this ideal situation, labor and other productive resources are fully employed. Rather than remain idle involuntarily, people will offer to work at wage rates that permit prices low enough to "clear the market" when full-employment quantities are produced.[10] The sellers of inputs, and the buyers of outputs, are all served to best mutual advantage. Though everyone would like to get more, each is restrained by others. Consumers and sellers of productive services play their part, all trying to do as well as possible for themselves. But the most active organizing force or agent is the businessman seeking profit.

The opportunity for larger profit lies in a change of conditions. In pure competition, what conditions does the firm have power to change? It can try to improve its methods of production, bettering its techniques (for example, relations with employees), using fewer inputs per unit of output. Sometimes, too, it can modify its product, hoping to appeal more effectively to consumers. It may have some scope for introducing new products or services, benefiting briefly until copied.[11]

The effectiveness of pure competition in stimulating and guiding economic growth, especially technical progress, is subject to dispute. The best adjustment to existing techniques, the things we know about, will not necessarily mean the best adjustment to the unknown, the things beyond the frontiers of existing knowledge. Perhaps the economy at purely competitive equilibrium would not be allocating the ideal amount of resources, in the best places, to improve science and the arts of life. The small firms of pure competition may not have the specialized labor and laboratories needed for pioneering research. Yet when numbers are large, there are many units free to seek improvement—and also many under pressure to do so. Greater efficiency in production offers hope of larger profit. The modern businessman knows that discovery of cost-reducing techniques may give him a competitive advantage. Some of his rivals will always be seeking such improvement. Successful survival, then, may depend upon the manager's skill in keeping up with the leaders, including potential rivals from outside, and trying to get ahead sometimes. Many small improvements can add to large totals throughout the economy.

Economists who praise the competitive adjustment do not claim that it is paradise but that it is the best possible attainment under a given set of conditions. In the short run, the equality of marginal cost and price may not be at the output of least average total cost. In the long run, however, output will be produced where efficiency is highest, underlying conditions remaining unchanged.

---

[10] This aspect of the purely competitive adjustment requires monetary stability.

[11] The meaning of "essentially identical product," an accepted condition of pure competition, is not always clear. Some latitude for temporary gain from product or service variation does seem consistent with the general concept of pure competition.

The Requirements of Competition. The claims made for competition as a device for getting efficient resource allocation are indeed impressive. Therefore, we should note carefully the conditions needed to realize these results.

(1) The firm in buying inputs must be able to deal with a large number of sellers. (2) No buyer or seller can have significant power to affect the market by his own refusal to buy or to sell. (3) The opportunities available must be known. Sellers need to have information on how much others are willing to pay; buyers must know *who* has *what* to sell, *where*, for *what price.* (4) Opportunities for taking advantage of potentialities must exist, as contrasted with legal restrictions, custom, and economic inability to move which impede adjustment.

The merits of the purely competitive adjustment will not be attained unless the judgments expressed in the market are accurate. In buying outputs, are consumers good judges of their own interest? In selling inputs, can we make good valuations of the relative desirability of opportunities to sell what we can offer? It is easy to doubt the quality of human valuations. By and large, however, there is good reason to expect better judgments in purely competitive markets than in markets with restrictions on freedom and opportunity.

The economist's rosy view of pure competition is not always shared by the businesses involved. Adaptation to change may be painful. Resources cannot always shift easily. Three other facts cast doubt upon the merits of the competitive adjustment.[12] (1) Not all benefits and costs are reflected in the market. Therefore, the allocation of resources which gives the most efficient results for the costs that the firm must economize, does not assuredly give the best results for total costs, as viewed broadly for the whole economy. Moreover, not all positive results are salable; the rewards offered by the market may be less than the full value to the public of what businesses accomplish. (2) The income distribution that gives consumers their "voting" power may not conform to our ideals. Most of us may feel that by some standards the market allows some sellers of inputs too much, others too little; our value judgments lead us beyond economic considerations alone. (3) Technological progress of some types requires operation on a scale far larger than is possible when production comes from many firms.

Purely competitive industries have small units, and entry is easy. Chronic overcapacity may result. Though small retail stores, restaurants, and other such businesses fail constantly, the long-run equilibrium adjustment is not reached; new entrants add to capacity. Each year, for example, around 160,000 retail establishments are discontinued and 170,000 new ones formed; about 275,000 transfer to new management. Why so much shifting?

The answer is partly that one of the essentials for equilibrium does not

---

[12] These criticisms also apply to less than purely competitive markets.

exist: full knowledge. New entrants do not know the market facts (or the conditions of future business) and their own capacities. Overoptimism leads them to error. Desire for independence and for an opportunity to work for themselves accentuates errors of overoptimism. Resources are wasted as a result, not only the capital and labor of the new entrants who fail, but those of others who suffer because the excess capacity keeps prices below the level yielding normal profit. Consumers may gain, but such benefit is not the mutual benefit from free exchange that we see as advantageous all around. How might the waste be reduced without arbitrary infringement on freedom of entry? The provision of fuller, more accurate information seems part of the answer. Another part is maintaining prosperity, to reduce one source of business loss and to ease adjustment.

TERMS AND CONCEPTS

pure competition	short-run equilibrium	labor-
perfect competition	long-run equilibrium	or land-
free entry		or market-oriented

QUESTIONS

1. Assume a purely competitive industry in equilibrium. Use diagrams to show both (*i*) the short-run and (*ii*) the long-run *market* and the *firm* adjustment to (*a*) a rise in market demand and (*b*) an increase in the price of labor.

2. Show why a firm under highly competitive conditions must operate at the point of lowest average cost after long-run adjustments have been completed, and why it may *not* operate at this point before the long-run adjustment is completed.

3. What are the forces in a purely competitive market which tend to drive market price down, or up, to unit cost at the output where such costs are at a minimum?

4. Why may a firm wisely carry output beyond the point where average costs are at a minimum?

5. If firms in a competitive industry are losing money, what is the process that leads to equilibrium?

6. Why does the demand curve for the output of a firm in pure competition have a different slope from that of the industry demand?

7. What conditions must exist if the economy is to get the general advantages of pure competition? Why does "overcrowding" appear in some competitive industries?

8. "Under purely competitive conditions, the economy gets the benefit of good use of resources." Explain, giving special attention to the forces which bring about the results.

9. Study the reasons which account for the chief economic activities in the area where you live.

APPENDIX

The Location of Economic Activity[1]

Much deliberate thought now goes into the location of economic activity. Increasing mobility gives more choice about where to do things than in the days before autos, trucks, planes, efficient transmission of electricity, etc. Tremendous expansion has forced business to think about where to build new facilities. National defense has raised its own problems of location. Broad patterns of location are determined more by our decisions as producers than as consumers. Consequently, the considerations that guide business in locating provide major insight into how we come to work and to live where we do.

Physical possibilities always guide decisions about economic location. The availability of natural resources obviously explains the location of some business—*land-oriented activity*. Mining, argiculture, fishing, and resorts, for example, are to a varying degree located where nature gives advantages. Favorable natural conditions act as a magnet; the more favorable the location, the stronger the pull. In general, early stages in production are most oriented toward materials. The attraction of favorable natural conditions, however, extends from *primary* to *secondary* activity. Sugar beet processing is near the fields; turpentine and rosin production are near pine forests; fruits and vegetables must be canned where they are grown.

Beyond the limits of what is possible, as determined by nature, business faces a sort of **dual pull**: *to raise revenues* and *to reduce costs*. Ordinarily there must be compromise. The spot with the best revenue-yielding (market or selling) possibilities will not be the one with the lowest production costs. Dresses may sell best in the centers of large cities, but the great dressmaking industry of New York City sends materials after cutting (from Paris designs) to dozens of little factories in other localities to be sewed. Theaters, retailing, personal services, and other *market-oriented* activities, those which seek out customers, will be located where people have settled largely for other reasons—in most cases because they can earn a living. (Within any community, however, the particular locations will depend upon more specific considerations.) The greater the sales or revenue potential of a location, the greater its appeal.

The other pull, keeping costs down, dominates many decisions. In most industries labor is the biggest cost. Managers will be especially attracted by favorable *labor conditions*, even to points distant from markets. The level of education, developed skills, social standards of intensity of effort, and variety of specialization make up one general set of conditions. The quantity of labor

---

[1] The process of competitive adjustment includes those bearing on location. They, of course, involve many elements; and this appendix might almost as appropriately be studied at other points in the course.

not fully employed and prevailing wage rates are others. People and businesses both move with wage rates and labor costs in mind—labor toward higher rates, employers toward lower costs. Differentials may persist, however. The cheaper, easier, and pleasanter the living conditions—the better the schools, churches, and cultural and recreational facilities—the lower wage and salary rates people will freely accept and the more will *labor-oriented* production be drawn to the area. Where population growth is high relative to emigration; and where exodus from a depressed area is slow, labor costs will tend to be low for the kind of work the people can do. The past flow of immigrants, some well skilled and many more willing to work long and carefully, helps explain the growth of the garment trades in New York. They will remain there only if adaptation to new conditions remains favorable. The climate of California has helped attract and hold workers by the millions; demand for labor, to some extent due directly to the same factors of climate, has also risen so that wage rates have not been depressed relative to the rest of the country.

Another major factor is *transportation cost* (money or time) (1) of materials purchased and (2) products to be sold. For some firms, of course, such costs are relatively unimportant. For others, notably those using large quantities of raw materials, transportation costs are highly significant. The pattern is complex, however, because the materials used must come from, and things produced must go to, varied points. Manufacturing of a product that requires large quantities of coal or other weight-losing material will tend to be near the source of the material to save weight to be shipped to consumers. Yet transportation rates per pound differ greatly, and each case has its own elements.

Costs of *electric power* and *natural gas* and the *availability of water* all influence location. Differences in state or local *taxes* may swing some decisions—the taxes on the firms themselves and the burdens put on more highly paid, key officers, scientists, and specialists of all types. Useful *auxiliary services* develop when several firms in an industry cluster in the same region: style information for fashion products, specialized financing or legal facilities, supplies of parts and facilities for machine repair. Many activities are tied to others; for example, locating near the furnaces those steel processes that require the metal to be hot can save the cost of reheating. Since 1940, the decisions of *military* officials and those in charge of *nuclear* projects and the *space* program have influenced much location—from military camps and ship repair bases to subcontracting of intricate subassemblies where truly skilled labor is available.

Technological changes have diverse effects on location. The improvement of transport is an example. The railroad made long hauls over land economically feasible for even bulky products; the auto and truck have added unbelievable flexibility and dispersion within broad areas; the airplane added speed. In general, as the development of technology changes transformation (production) possibilities, industry gets new location opportunities or requirements.

Basic economic forces determine general locations. Within the broad areas, however, firms may be able to do about as well one place as another. Accident or personal preference of a decision maker then explains some specific location. Moreover, one firm's location may preclude another's at the same spot. Two or more huge department stores may locate next to each other, but not on the identical space. And when a location is used for one purpose—a factory or warehouse—that use limits other uses. Growth must take place where there is room for growth. Hence in an expanding economy, the new activity will not generally be located exactly where the old was. The new may push uptown or seek suburbs or replace slums or locate in the country.

18

PRICE-OUTPUT ADJUSTMENT UNDER MONOPOLY, OLIGOPOLY, AND MONOPOLISTIC COMPETITION

Every piece of business strategy . . . must be seen in its role in the perennial gale of creative destruction; it cannot be understood . . . on the hypothesis that there is a perpetual lull.

Joseph A. Schumpeter

At the other extreme from the purely competitive world lies monopoly. In between there are many gradations of market structure—and most of our economic life. How are prices and output determined in markets that do not have the characteristics of competition described so far? This chapter develops the theory. The next describes the forces that create monopolistic tendencies and weaken or modify competition.

Monopoly in its pure form is rare. Yet a study of monopoly price-output adjustments is useful. It directs attention to the salient aspects of all market situations that differ significantly from the purely competitive— situations where individual sellers (or buyers) loom so large relative to the industry that they can affect market price through variations in their output (purchases).

MONOPOLY

Definition. Monopoly—what is it? Monopoly exists (1) if there is a single seller of a product or service (2) which is sufficiently unique to remove the possibility of significant rivalry from substitutes. If there is a *single supplier* in the market, he is a monopolist; the magnitude of his monopoly power depends largely on the closeness of substitutes. So, in practice, we reserve the term "monopoly" for situations in which substitutes are too poor to offer appreciable threat (within a considerable price

416

range). The single bank, newspaper, hospital, or other supplier in a locality may be a monopoly, as economists use the term, but not a big business, nor even a highly profitable one.

Monopolist's Demand Curve. If there is a single supplier, the demand for its output is the entire market demand for the product. Market demand curves slope downward; the amount that will be purchased varies with the price. Perhaps the quantity salable is only slightly responsive to changes in price (within the range of price that is of practical importance); demand, then, is highly inelastic. Or it may be relatively elastic. Whatever the elasticity, however, the seller must take account of the effects of his own output on the price it will fetch. The more he produces, the lower the price he can get per unit. In planning how much to produce, therefore, a monopoly seeking the best adjustment needs a more refined measure than the price at which different outputs can be sold.

Marginal Revenue. In setting his price (or in fixing his output which, with demand given, will determine price), a monopolist should look at *marginal revenue*. It is related to receipts or revenue in the same way that marginal cost is related to total cost. Marginal revenue shows the effect on total receipts of each unit sold. Under pure competition, marginal revenue as seen by any one seller is the same as price. Not so, however, for monopoly (Table 18–1).

TABLE 18–1. Relation of Price to Marginal Revenue for Monopoly

Number of Units Sold (1)	Price (Average Revenue) (2)	Total Revenue (3) (1) × (2)	Marginal Revenue (Net Addition to Total Revenue from Sale of Quantity Larger by One Unit)* (4)
2	$9	$18	$6
3	8	24	4
4	7	28	2
5	6	30	0
6	5	30	−2
7	4	28	

* Values are shown as falling between the number of units shown in column 1 to emphasize that the marginal revenue is the amount resulting from the *change* from one quantity to the next.

When the demand curve slopes downward, each unit sold brings in something: its price. Yet to sell a quantity which is larger by one unit, the price of all units must be reduced. Two units will bring $9 each, a total of $18; to sell three, the firm must lower its price to $8 each, so that total revenue is $24, only $6 more than when two units were sold.[1] The net benefit from the third, then, is $6. This amount is the **marginal revenue.** The *net* proceeds from the sale of the "one more item" will be, not its price but price *minus* the reduction in the price of the other items: the $8 price minus $1 each on the two units that otherwise would have sold for $9 each. Even when price is positive, marginal revenue can be negative; in the example in Table 18–1, an increase in sales from six to seven units leaves the firm with $2 *less* revenue.

The price per unit is the *average revenue:* total receipts divided by the number of units sold. Marginal revenue is a more sensitive, more delicate, measure or indicator than is average revenue (price). Marginal revenue is the measure of the significance of the little more, or the little less—those units most directly involved in decisions to expand or reduce output. The curve of marginal revenue lies below that of price (average revenue); it is steeper, falling more rapidly. Think of marginal revenue as what pulls down the average (Fig. 18–1). Marginal revenue is easily computed if the demand schedule is known—in practice, a mighty big "if." (At each point, quantity multiplied by price gives total revenue. Subtract this amount from the corresponding figure when the quantity sold is smaller by one unit. The difference is the marginal revenue.) The monopolist *must* make estimates of the prices at which different outputs can be sold. The problem, although difficult, is inescapable. His adjustments will be better if he guides them, not by price but by the more refined measure, marginal revenue, judging it as well as possible.

Best Price-Output Adjustment for a Monopoly.
What is the monopolist's best adjustment? It is to carry output to the point where marginal cost just equals marginal revenue—*MC = MR.* This statement is perhaps little more than refining the common sense advice: "Do not produce units that cost more than the revenue they bring in; do not fail to produce units that will bring more revenue than they add to total cost." Easier said that done. Rarely can a business hit the precise point, but it is more likely to come close if it knows what to look for than if it does not.

The firm operating under purely competitive conditions should seek the same goal: output carried to the point where marginal revenue equals marginal cost. For it, however, the price (set by broad market forces) is the marginal revenue. What distinguishes the monopoly's position is this: Its marginal revenue schedule is different from its demand (price) schedule. It can get a higher price by restricting output and selling less, charging more per unit for a small quantity. The monopolist has two ways to gain from the higher-price-smaller-output adjustment: (1) he saves the variable cost of units not produced (as would any producer),

---

[1] These are *alternative* possibilities. The firm may sell two, three, or four units at the price shown; but if it sells three units at $8 each, it cannot sell a fourth at $7.

FIGURE 18–1.   Monopoly: Equilibrium Price-Output Adjustment

The intersection of the marginal revenue and marginal cost curves determines the most profitable output, *OB*. The average total cost of producing a unit of output is then *OM* = *Bm*. The price at which this quantity of output can be sold, however, is *OP* = *Bp*. Price per unit, therefore, exceeds cost by *MP* = *mp*. Production is not carried to the point where plant is used most efficiently, *OA*, because beyond *OB* additional units add more to cost than to revenue.

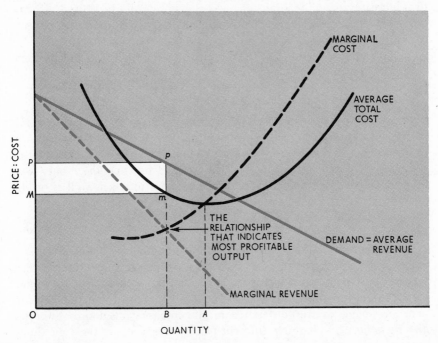

and (2) in addition he gets a higher price for the units sold. Figure 18–1 shows his best adjustment (for the period to which the conditions apply).

On a graph, the monopolist's marginal revenue curve must be below and to the left of the demand (average revenue) curve. This position tells a story which has economic significance. Being to the left is being on the side of *smaller output*. Therefore, the marginal cost curve must intersect the marginal revenue curve at an output which is less than that at which the marginal cost curve intersects the demand curve. The difference may be slight, or large. Firms may, or may not, attempt to take full advantage of the difference. Yet it exists if there is a monopoly. **The most profitable policy for the monopolist is to price higher and produce less than a firm operating under pure competition,** assuming similar cost conditions. More generally, even if a monopoly has lower costs (real inputs per unit of output) than would the more numerous producers of pure competition, the monopolist's most profitable output is one in which resources are used less fully than economic conditions justify.[2]

---

[2] There is no assurance that in the short run a monopoly will operate profitably.

Possible Gain as a Buyer (Monopsony). To this point we have looked at the benefits the monopolist has as a seller. If he buys his inputs in purely competitive markets, his own purchases have no effect on the prices he must pay per unit of input. However, in buying one or more types of input a monopoly may also be a monopsony: the only buyer. If so, as the firm increases its use of inputs, it raises their price and hence this element of cost.[3] Whether the increase is little or great depends upon the elasticity of supply.

In any case, the monopolist who is also a monopsonist has an additional reason for not pushing output to the quantity which a purely competitive industry would produce. To this point we have generally assumed that variable costs per unit (and hence marginal costs) rise because of diminishing returns—that is, physical productivity, output in relation to input, declines as more of (*a*) one type of input is used with (*b*) fixed quantities of others. Yet the monopsonist must also expect variable costs per unit to rise with increasing output because the *price* of one or more inputs rises. So if he restricts output, he saves on the price of inputs as well as on the quantity he uses. The sellers of inputs lose on both counts, lower prices and smaller volume.

Price Discrimination. The monopoly has another potential advantage. Some parts of the total demand for a product are more intense than others. Consumers, individually and as a whole, are willing and able to pay higher prices for some units than for others. A monopolist may be able to take advantage of this difference in the intensity of desires by *price discrimination*, by charging different prices for essentially the same thing. There may be a high price where demand presses strongly, a lower price where demand is "easier." The result is a larger total profit than if a single price were to prevail. Even when products differ, there may be discrimination.[4]

Though the term "price discrimination" may smack of unfairness, we accept the practice every day; and, if we stop to think, we hardly associate it with monopoly. Nor should we—always. It is hard to know when the difference in prices is due to differences in marginal costs (not true discrimination) and when it is due to discrimination, taking advantage of (1) differences in the intensity of demand coupled with (2) the seller's freedom from competitors who might undercut in the more profitable parts of the market. Wholesalers receive lower prices from manufacturers than do retailers. The suit for a large man will have more

---

[3] An exception would exist if the supplier of the input were operating under conditions of decreasing cost.

[4] We can say that price discrimination occurs when prices of somewhat different products are not proportional to marginal costs. Seats in different parts of the stadium are not identical, but prices vary more than do marginal costs. Some price differences are designed to take advantage of snob appeal and consumer impatience.

material than one for the small man, but we accept the "rightness" of a single price. The trade-in value of a used car may vary from dealer to dealer. Medical charges are often set with the patient's financial position in mind. Charges for the use of patents and the rentals of movie films commonly vary according to the economic position of the user. Children get lower prices for movies, women (sometimes) for ball games. Stores run *sales*. Discrimination on the basis of *use* is the rule in pricing electricity, postal, telephone, and railroad rates. Milk for drinking brings a higher price than milk from the same cow used to make cheese.

Geographical discrimination in pricing is common; we receive different services but pay the same to send a letter across the continent as to send it next door. Some sellers absorb (pay) delivery costs which are much greater for distant than for nearby customers. *Quantity discounts* in excess of any cost savings are another example of discrimination, but federal law limits the possibilities. (Chapter 20.)

Price discrimination raises highly complex issues for the business world and for public policy. The seller who discriminates will enjoy higher profit than if he charged a uniform price (other things the same). To make discrimination effective, a monopolist must separate his markets to keep the product from moving from the low- to the high-price areas.[5] Another problem is to keep "competitors," suppliers of substitutes, from supplying the more profitable parts of the market. Finally, of course, for the seller to profit, the cost of keeping his market (or parts) separate must not exceed the gains.

Discrimination on the buying side (as a monopsonist) presents opportunities and problems which are somewhat comparable in nature but less apparent in practice.

Long-Run Adjustment. Under pure competition, the short- and long-run adjustments may differ. What about monopoly? If the techniques, prices of inputs, and demand do not change, the best adjustment for the monopolist is the same price-output situation in the short run as in the long run. Yet when techniques, input prices, and demand do differ according to length of the planning period, the monopoly will obviously need time to adjust its fixed capacity.

Efficiency of the Monopoly Adjustment for the Whole Economy. For the economy as a whole, we found that pure competition is highly efficient in allocating resources; generally, the best adjustment for the firm is best for everyone else under the conditions given. In the case of monopoly, however, this will seldom be true. The best allocation of

---

[5] The Aluminum Company of America once sold aluminum wire (to compete with copper wire) for less than the aluminum ingots out of which the wire was made; the sale contract provided that the wire not be melted to make ingots. The surgeon who charges different fees need not worry about patients transferring his services.

resources for the community as a whole is to carry production to the point where marginal cost equals price. Here the value of the last unit of inputs just equals the value of the last unit of output. At any other output the values of marginal inputs and outputs are not equal. The most profitable adjustment for the monopolist, however, is one at which the price consumers pay for output is greater than the value of the inputs (including normal profit). The difference is the "extra" profit of the monopolist. The extra levy on consumers should be enough of an indictment of monopoly. The high price does more, however: it allocates resources inefficiently. Monopoly will employ fewer resources than economic conditions would justify. As long as price exceeds marginal cost, use of additional resources would add more to the value of output than would their former use.

For society as a whole, the use of monopoly power will keep output from being maximized. The plant may be highly efficient; even when operating at less than optimum capacity, it may have lower costs than the smaller plants of pure competition. Yet the public does not get the full potential advantages of the economies of large scale; prices are higher, and the labor and other resources used are fewer, than consistent with going valuations. Some productive resources must find employment under less favorable conditions than if the monopoly power were not exercised.

Sometimes, however, use of the power of monopoly might save the economy from wastes found in competitive industries. The latter in fact are often more than a little removed from equilibrium. Several firms must commit capital without full knowledge of what others are doing. Each, then, constitutes a factor which complicates the planning of others on projects which absorb resources in commitments for long periods. In competitive industries duplicative advertising and crosshauling are common. A monopoly would have no need for the kind of advertising which seeks to attract business to one supplier instead of others. A monopoly would presumably ship from the plant nearest (in terms of transportation cost); where there are several producers, however, they will often incur delivery costs to customers at considerable distance who might be supplied by a monopoly from a plant closer at hand and at smaller use of real inputs.

What if the monopoly keeps its prices below "what the traffic will bear?" Ordinarily, such action would seem to be in the public interest, but not always. Assume that an industry chooses, perhaps for patriotic reasons, or is compelled by government, to keep prices below those which would prevail in freer markets. We ask: "What will such a policy do to guide the allocation of resources?" If prices are set below marginal costs, the variable resources used to produce the marginal units of output are worth more than the value consumers are required to pay for the products. The company will not be doing one of its basic jobs: guiding the allocation of resources for best utilization. The producer uses up resources of greater value than those which consumers must sacrifice in exchange.

Economists are of two minds about the effectiveness of monopoly in stimulating economic progress. The higher earnings may aid the financing of research. Moreover, monopoly power may serve as a sort of "umbrella" protecting against risks which would otherwise make unattractive some ventures that turn out to benefit the public immensely. Insulation from intense rivalry, however, deadens creativity.

Pure monopoly, the type just discussed, is less common than two other kinds of market structure that are not purely competitive.

OLIGOPOLY

Definition. Oligopoly exists when there are so few sellers in an industry that each must take account of the effects of its own output and price decisions on those of its competitors. Bethlehem Steel, in setting its prices, must take into account the effect these will have on U.S. Steel's sales and the response of 8 or 10 steel companies. The products may be (1) virtually identical—cement of a standard type produced in the same area—or (2) somewhat differentiated but close substitutes—four brands of golf clubs all made with shafts from the same supplier, two nearby office buildings, Fords and Plymouths. Sellers may be about the same size, or one may dominate the market as a whole. Each supplier has close rivals, unlike a monopolist, but not many. A firm can be an oligopolist for one or a few of the things it produces, but not for others.

Price-Output Adjustment in an Industry with Oligopoly. The oligopolist can have a price policy in the sense that he can set prices (in contrast with the seller in pure competition who faces prices set by broad market forces). He can try for a price high enough to bring profit much above the normal of competition. He has opportunity to devise a *price-output* policy that will yield the largest income—not, as under pure competition, merely an output policy. The oligopolist will decide on a price, perhaps using methods discussed in the next chapter. He expects to adjust the quantity he will sell to meet buyers' orders at this price. Obviously, however, he must guide his policy by what others do and must meet their rivalry. His job, however, is more complex; for in making decisions, he must also consider how others will respond to his actions.

The demand schedule for the output of one seller will be flatter, more elastic, than that for the industry. Therefore, price reduction by one firm (others not following), might lead to a large increase in its sales (units and dollar amounts) even though industry sales expand little. A firm with unused capacity will be tempted to try to capture some of the other fellows' business by cutting price. But a smart manager must ask himself, "How will other sellers react?" If some have unused capacity, they are likely to follow his example. As they reduce prices, receipts may fail to increase as much as costs. Industry profits will go down, or losses increase. As one manager with unused capacity thinks about lowering price, he may rightly fear that one of the others will meet the challenge by reducing price a little more. In making decisions, therefore, each manager may recall such slogans as: "Live and let live." "Don't spoil the market." The smart businessman, however, may also think: "Some of the others will reduce prices, secretly, before they do so openly. I'd better start making some special offers in self-protection—quietly." Perhaps early "yielding to the inevitable" may be wise.

In an oligopolistic industry there may be few changes—in price, quality of product, or output—because all prefer to live a friendly life that is not unduly trying. Much will depend upon the confidence managers have in each other's reactions. If an oligopolist wants to raise price, he may not be able to count upon the others "going along." If some have unused capacity, they, by not raising price, are in position to supply some of his customers. So initiative taken by one firm to raise its price may be risky.[6] There may, however, be many price or quality changes, some large and sudden, others made more or less continuously without big shifts.

Problems of Oligopoly Pricing. For oligopolists *as a group*, the most profitable adjustment is generally a price-output combination that gives the same total result as would exist under monopoly. In this situation the total profit is largest, producing the biggest pie to cut—one that may be substantially larger than under pure competition. Market demand is more inelastic (the marginal revenue curve falls more steeply) than the demand of any single firm. There is advantage to be had by fixing price and output to exploit this inelasticity.

However, to achieve the price-output that would yield the largest total profit for the industry as a whole, firms would need to act as a unit. Joint action of this sort is far from easy for large firms in this country. Antitrust laws make explicit collusion—clear, definite agreement—generally impossible. Even tacit collusion in the form of an understanding, defined clearly enough to serve as a practical guide, is reached only with great difficulty and tends to be unstable. Since costs will likely differ from firm to firm, the relations of marginal cost and marginal revenue for the industry will be far more complex than for a monopolist. Firms do not know their demand and cost schedules as precisely as our analysis may suggest. When products or services of oligopolists are not identical, both costs and demand differ enough to hamper parallel action. Managers may have different ideas of the future; common action becomes harder if the actors do not agree on what is to their best interest.

---

[6] Industry-wide bargaining on wage rates may help firms act in unison not only on a major cost item but also on prices.

In the absence of tight legal controls, someone in the group may try to wiggle into a little better position and "upset the apple cart." Without shading price, a seller may seek to get ahead by various methods of rivalry. The firm's concern will likely be for *its* profit, not that of the industry as a whole. Price discrimination of the monopolist's variety, for example, becomes a tempting device for trying to get a little of the other fellow's better market. The antagonism among the interests of members of the group may be so fundamental that any peace is uneasy even though its persistence would maximize group profits. Antagonism may lead to nearly chaotic instability. On the other hand, perhaps no change may occur even if the group could benefit, because of disagreement about how to share benefits. For a time, price leadership—the prices and price changes of one firm set a pattern which other firms follow regularly—or some of the other practices described in the next chapter may serve to keep the group working—pricing and governing output—as a unit, or nearly so. The inducement, higher profit, is powerful; the opportunities exist even though they are far from perfect. The results depend upon the decisions of only a few men, each of whom can be expected to sense the situation and know enough to try to seize the opportunities.

The likely outcome will be prices above the lowest level consistent with normal profit, but below the monopoly level. Output and the use of resources are lower than community valuations would justify. Yet one maverick can keep the whole group on the run by refusing to settle down at some comfortable pace. The auto manufacturing industry would seem to offer good opportunities for oligopoly price-output adjustments. There is an impression, however, that, in its formative years, the personality of Henry Ford I kept rivalry active (but not so active that profits fell below a generous level). The number of sellers will affect the result. In general, the fewer the suppliers, the easier they will find "cooperative" pricing.

But markets are two-sided. What about buyers? Their strength and reaction influence the result. Some industries that meet the definition of oligopoly—steel, aluminum, rayon, cement—sell to buyers who are powerful, well informed, and generally equipped to bargain effectively. They can learn whether prices are yielding extraordinary profits or where unused capacity may make a seller sensitive to offers for special deals. Buyers want to get prices down. Their economic strength will enable them to play one seller against the other, to search for best bargains, in short, to prevent suppliers from charging anything like the prices they might (1) if they could legally act as a unit, or (2) if they faced a multitude of small buyers. Oligopolies in producers' goods, or those selling to big buyers (chain stores), therefore, will tend to be less successful in maintaining prices which yield much above a level of normal profit than will oligopolies selling to consumers. Uncle Sam as a buyer tries diligently to ferret out and break up oligopolistic bidding.

If the industry succeeds in getting profits that are above normal, it must expect another "upsetting" factor: new producers. Someone may begin to chip away at fringes of the market—someone from outside the area (or country), or a firm producing something rather similar, or a new entrant. Giant buyers, like chain store systems, can produce for themselves or finance new firms—and do. An interloper is likely to be more unsettling to an oligopoly group than to a single monopolist, because one or two oligopolists will probably be more directly and intimately affected by the newcomer than will other firms. Those most exposed may be inclined to meet the threat at the expense of any implicit group accord. An oligopoly that succeeds in remaining effective, therefore, probably has another feature: entry into the industry is difficult.

Conclusion. Neither theory nor factual studies have revealed a clear picture of the price-output adjustment to be expected where oligopoly prevails. Within limits, business executives *are* free to set prices and to keep them stable or change them, quite unlike the businessman in pure competition. Costs, of course, set limits, and so do many other things, such as fear of the entry of new producers, the reaction of rivals, the power of buyers. There is the opportunity of profit (price) above that of pure competition if sellers act together by clear agreement, informal cooperation, or commonsense recognition on the part of each that price reduction will be matched and therefore reduce profit all around.

Rivalry may cut profits to the level that would prevail under pure competition. Strong forces, however, offset tendencies of businessmen to depress each others' earnings to this level: their own incentives and market power. People who have no idea what the term "oligopoly" means, may clearly see that they can earn more by avoiding vigorous price competition—the two morticians in town, the country's two dominant producers of eyeglasses, or a city's sellers of office supplies. There are many situations with elements of oligopoly, especially at the local level; sellers are so few that agreement in practice may be reached.

MONOPOLISTIC COMPETITION

Definition. In the space on a scale between oligopoly and pure competition, Figure 18–2, there are industries (1) with numerous suppliers, (2) whose products, as a rule, are somewhat similar but not identical. The differences may be in such things as quality, color, packaging, location, service, or the dealer's reputation and methods of doing business. Although there are not a host of suppliers (of about the same product), there are many, at least more than for an oligopoly and too many to make joint action feasible. Thus there is a reason for expecting elements of competition. Yet the fact that products differ means that, in a sense, each seller has a market of his own; he is a little monopolist. (Businessmen deny that the term "monopolistic" can be used sensibly in such situations.)

Only one company makes Crest toothpaste, Gillette blades, and any of

FIGURE 18–2.   Competition and Monopoly: Factors Determining the Extent of Each

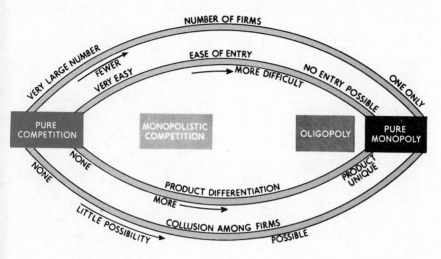

a vast number of other things, each of which is somewhat different from anything else (or buyers can be made to believe it is). There is only one gasoline station on a given location; but there may be many within a few miles, none identical but several offering essentially the same products. Numerous breakfast cereals are individually different, yet many are close substitutes. The seller of such a differentiated product can govern his own output. He can "set" a price, and he can influence demand by his own selling effort, product design, service, or other action which sellers in pure competition cannot do. The demand for his product, therefore, is a market demand; the amount he sells varies according to the price—the demand curve for his output slopes downward.

Price-Output Adjustment under Monopolist Competition.   As a starter, we can transfer bodily the general analysis of pricing under monopoly. The firm's best adjustment is to carry output to the point where marginal revenue equals marginal cost. This is a point of smaller output and higher price than if demand were as competitive as for corn; the difference in the competitiveness of the demand for corn and for Corn Flakes may be negligible or moderately large. If the difference is more than negligible, the seller (under monopolistic competition) may make a profit above normal (Case A of Fig. 18–3). Such profits attract new suppliers.

Now we see a key difference between monopolistic competition (new producers can enter the industry) and monopoly (where close competitors are excluded) and oligopoly (which can persist with above-normal profit only if newcomers can be kept out of the industry). Since the product has some distinguishing feature, even if merely a name, a new

FIGURE 18–3.   Monopolistic Competition: Nonequilibrium Conditions

In Case A, the seller can set a price which yields profit above the normal in the economy. New producers will be attracted. In Case B, however, no price will cover average total cost; producers will therefore tend to leave the industry.

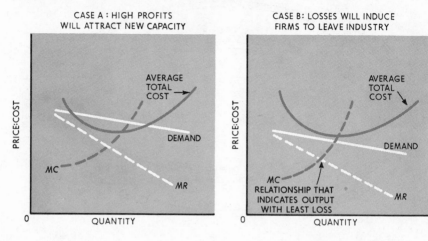

CASE A : HIGH PROFITS WILL ATTRACT NEW CAPACITY

CASE B: LOSSES WILL INDUCE FIRMS TO LEAVE INDUSTRY

producer will not turn out exactly the same thing. But he can try for a close enough substitute to satisfy some of the demand. The original seller will then find that his sales fall off and his profit declines, perhaps till there are losses. Losses, of course, will force out some producers while some "stick things out."

What will be the equilibrium at the end of this adjustment? It is the point where profits are normal, giving owners the rate of earnings that prevails generally in the market. So far so good—just like the equilibrium under pure competition. But there is a difference between the end of this adjustment process (Fig. 18–4) and that under pure competition. The normal-profit equilibrium is a point where price equals average total cost. (The demand curve is tangent to the average total cost curve.) This point in purely competitive markets will be the lowest point on the average total cost curve. Under the conditions of monopolistic competition we have been examining, however, the firm's demand curve has some slope. The demand curve will then be tangent, not at the point of lowest cost but somewhat higher and to the left, indicating smaller output and higher cost and price.

Significance of Monopolistic Competition.   What does this analysis tell? Except temporarily, producers in the situations we have been discussing cannot hope to earn more than normal profit. We may welcome a result which suggests that the consumer is not over-charged. The unfortunate feature is this: *The only time the seller can earn even a normal profit is when he keeps his output smaller than the amount that could be produced most efficiently.* As compared with pure competition—

FIGURE 18–4. Monopolistic Competition: Long-Run Equilibrium

Price just equals average total cost, the demand curve being tangent to the average total cost curve; the firm, therefore, earns a normal profit, one which neither attracts new production nor induces existing capacity to leave the industry. Output of *OA*, however, is not large enough to permit the plant to be used most efficiently, *OB*. Cost and price are higher, *OP*, than they would be, *OM*, if production were at the most efficient point. In a sense, compared with pure competition, the economy loses the production *AB* and pays a price higher by *MP* for the output it receives. Yet if output were increased, the price obtainable, as shown by the demand curve, would not cover average total cost.

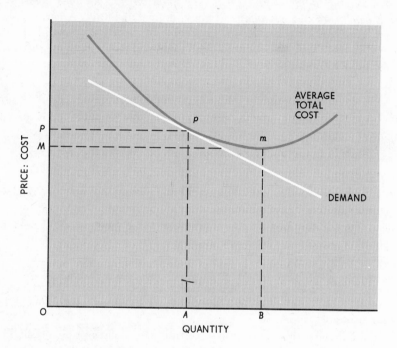

assuming similar techniques of production—prices are higher, at the expense of the consumer. Costs are also higher. Productive capacity is used less fully than under pure competition.

The firm's equilibrium is at a point where it is operating at decreasing average total cost. With a larger volume, it could produce more efficiently, but it would lose more than the benefit of the cost saving because of the price reductions needed to sell the larger output. Here is a partial explanation of why some companies do not seem to use fixed equipment fully and why more variable inputs are not hired.[7] To sell the additional output, the firm would need to cut its price below average total cost. The logic of the analysis survives criticism. Economists differ, however, about the significance. Actual results may, in fact, be close to those of pure competition.

The analysis teaches more. The producer has two general ways to try to increase his profit. One is to reduce costs, as under pure competition.

---

[7] Other reasons are the need for extra capacity to meet demands of peak periods and the desire to prepare for expected growth of demand.

The other is to try to increase demand. Since he has a product which can be distinguished from that of others, unlike the single wheat farmer, he has a chance to persuade the public to take more of *his* product. By product development, better service, advertising, and other selling effort he can hope to raise the demand for his product. Costs rise, of course, but receipts may go up even more. There is this chance: *A modest increase in cost may shift demand enough to pay handsomely, but no reduction in price can bring net advantage.* Today, as we all know, American businesses concentrate great effort on trying to increase demand. Before analyzing the issues, however, we shall examine other aspects of the broad problem of "monopoly."

TERMS AND CONCEPTS

monopoly	monopsony	monopolistic competi-
marginal revenue	price discrimination	tion
average revenue	oligopoly	

QUESTIONS

1. Define "monopoly" and "oligopoly." Give examples in your community. Do the same for "monopsony."
2. What is the best price-output adjustment for a monopolist? Would this point be harder to determine than the best output for a firm under competition?
3. Compare the long-run equilibrium adjustment under monopolistic competition with those under perfect competition and monopoly. What are the monopolistic, and what are the competitive, elements of monopolistic competition?
4. How does elasticity of demand affect the monopolist's profit possibilities?
5. How would frequent and large changes in demand affect the ability of oligopolists to achieve results that would bring them the largest profit?
6. Explain in your own words why output where marginal revenue equals marginal cost is the most profitable. Compare the results when demand is highly inelastic with those when it is highly elastic.
7. Show why a firm with substantial monopolistic powers will not serve its own best interest (*a*) by charging the highest price consumers will pay; (*b*) by producing the volume at which average cost is least.
8. Assume the following conditions of demand. Compute marginal revenue:

Price per Unit	Number of Units Purchased per Day
$10.00	2
9.50	3
9.00	4
8.50	5
8.00	6
7.50	7
7.00	8

19

**SOURCES OF MONOPOLISTIC
TENDENCIES: NONPRICE
COMPETITION**

*. . . Where more than adequate capacity exists for all the products you make,
prices in general tend to go down . . . the price is really dictated by the hungriest competitor. . . . The posture we are striving for is that [by reducing
costs of production] we shall be a bit ahead in our profit margin as compared
with our hungriest competitor.*
        President of a large corporation in an oligopolistic industry (1961)

Competition as economists think of pure competition—(1) a large number of firms producing (2) a uniform product or service (3) in an industry in which entry of new capacity is easy—is not what businessmen mean by competition. To them rivalry between, say, RCA and GE, is competition even though products differ, only two firms are involved, and entry of equal rivals is impossible. Perhaps it is fruitless to try to distinguish between competition and rivalry. Yet it is not fruitless to distinguish between competition (rivalry) on the basis of price and that which takes other forms.

Economists tend to prefer competition on the basis of price to at least many common forms of nonprice competition. Why such a preference? The basic reason is a belief that the public as consumers will get better value—that resources will be used to greater total advantage—from price competition than from many other forms of business rivalry. In the business world, however, one will often find the view that price competition is less desirable than other forms; the analysis of the Chapter 18 helps account for this attitude. The chance of profit above "normal," the only chance of large profit, depends upon securing a position that differs from that of pure competition. Price competition will keep profit from remaining for long above the rather unexciting "normal" of long-run equilibrium. But with rivalry of other forms, businesses may earn substantially more than purely competitive profits, and do so year after year. We now discuss the conditions which make this possible.

SOURCES OF MONOPOLY (OLIGOPOLY AND MONOPOLISTIC COMPETITION)

Restrictions on the number of sellers (or buyers) may be due to several causes. They give rise to what we shall call "monopoly" or "monopolistic tendencies" because a more accurate term ("monopoly, oligopoly, monopsony, oligopsony, monopolistic competition, and monopsonistic competition") would be much too cumbersome. A warning, however: The businesses having such powers may stoutly and sincerely deny that they are monopolistic. "Monopoly" is unpopular in America, and the natural reaction is to deny that one has any such power. Yet such power can be a source of high profit, and for this reason businesses desire it in substance, if not in name. Moreover, the requirements of modern technology so limit the number of producers in some industries that established firms will have monopolistic power in at least some of their many operations.

Legal Monopolies. Governments are the source of substantial monopoly power. Businesses we call *public utilities* are generally monopolies. Government—local, state, or national—gives them an exclusive right to provide certain services in an area. In return, the utility must ordinarily agree to meet standards of service and submit to regulation. A federal agency assigns the limited number of radio and TV channels. Governments sometimes operate monopolies, such as the post office, and prohibit competition.

State and local governments commonly *license* activities. These are seldom complete monopolies, but license requirements may restrict entry to a relatively small group and prevent high earnings from attracting more capacity. The New York City "medallion" that permits one to operate a taxi sells for thousands of dollars, indicating a scarcity value. Government regulations, such as building codes, restrict innovation.

Patents and copyrights give the owner a legal right to exclusive use for a period. They play an important part in establishing monopoly and sometimes even in maintaining it indefinitely. An outstanding example used to be the United Shoe Machinery Company; when founded, it acquired all the important patents in the field. It then leased, rather than sold, its machines; it continued to develop improvements on which it could get new patents. Shoe manufacturers who wanted equipment with new improvements were forced to use *only* the machines of United Shoe Machinery. As long as it had some good patents, then, these tying-clause leases, in effect, gave the company a monopolistic power over use of its other machines.

Control of Raw Materials.[1] Some resources are localized by nature. A single firm or group may be able to control the mines, for example, and thereby dominate not only mining but also activities which depend upon the resources made available. The Aluminum Company of America once had tight control of bauxite, the essential raw material. Today, diamonds and a few metals, notably nickel, are tightly controlled (outside this country) in their raw material stages; control has not been extended effectively through the later stages of fabrication and use. The U.S. government no longer exercises monopoly over helium.

Large Size as a Barrier to New Entrants. Economies of large-scale operations, some of which were sketched in Chapter 16, can be so great that small plants have no chance of survival in competition with large ones ("small" and "large" relative to the size of the market). Generally, the bigger the firm, the greater the likelihood that it has some monopoly power, for it will have fewer competitors. Any profits it gets from such relief from competition result partly from taking advantage of consumers (or suppliers) rather than from serving them. The company's benefit does not necessarily coincide with that of the public. A firm need not be a giant to exercise such power. This condition often exists when the market is local, more so than when markets cover the whole country or world.

The clearest cases are those of true decreasing-cost industries and so-called "natural monopolies," such as public utilities. Almost as clear a case, however, occurs when such a very big investment is needed that newcomers have formidable obstacles against them. Establishing a network of dealers to sell and service a product (notably autos and complicated household durables) may require a large total investment, not only of capital but also of management effort. Thus to get the full economies of mass *production*, there must also be a big total commitment in facilities for mass *marketing* and product *servicing*.

Let us look at more conditions which favor big firms and therefore reduce the opportunity for the competition which will be assured by the existence of many companies.

A small firm cannot have specialists to train staff or help suppliers to operate more efficiently. It cannot use some skills as fully as the giant. It cannot afford top scientists to work on all the problems of its operations, nor can it have enough highly prized patents to give it equal bargaining position with the giant in trading use of patents. The small producer cannot assure buyers that competent servicing facilities and stocks of spare parts will be available over the whole country.

At some size a firm may become big enough to set up its own productive capacity; its potential ability to supply itself give it a bargaining

---

[1] Ownership of favorable location is not ordinarily treated as a source of monopolistic power, although the economic results may be essentially like those of monopoly. The landowner will eventually get the benefit attributable to the location as such.

advantage. An auto parts firm cannot start making Chevrolets when they are highly profitable, but General Motors can and does make parts, as well as buy them from small independent suppliers. Where buying and selling loom large in total activities (retailing food rather than building dynamos), the large firm's advantages may lead to a nice extra profit. The big buyer may get a lower quoted price, a choice of quality, special packaging, more liberal credit, or selling and technical help. When business is disrupted, perhaps by shortages from war or a long strike, or when one or another item is in short supply, the big buyers may get preferential treatment.

Large businesses have an advantage in getting *capital*. Directors have wide freedom in deciding on the reinvestment of earnings. Big firms find that their names are known to investors, managers of large pension funds, and the man in the street. Businesses that are large (in the nation or the town) provide banks with profitable accounts and get an "inside track." Big firms can tap the main money markets, take advantage of the competition there, and use the facilities of specialized investment bankers. The firm trying to raise a few hundred thousand dollars of equity capital finds costs per dollar very much higher than would a giant. The more important that capital is as a cost, the greater this advantage of the large over the small company. After a firm reaches a size well below the billion-dollar mark, however, financing costs do not seem to vary greatly. Shell Oil Company's bonds sell on almost the same terms as those of Standard Oil of New Jersey, which is far larger. Moreover, leasing—a complex computer for a few hours, or space in the city's finest office building for 20 years—is often available to firms of modest size.

In *hiring labor*, large firms can afford to scour the country for top executives, send men to search for the cream of college graduates, and offer prospects of security, opportunities to buy stock on favorable terms, and soundly financed pension plans which small and poorly known businesses cannot match. Nothing is scarcer, or more determining of success, than really good human talent. Many people of unusual ability prefer to start their working careers with large corporations. The one-store retailer cannot match the big chains in offering prospects for long-run development of special capacity and eventual executive status. Such a bias may give large firms a considerable, and perhaps for the country an unwholesome, advantage as the years pass. Here again, the big company may do about as well as the giant; masses of small firms probably face the most serious disadvantages.

In an increasingly important aspect of American economic life, *research and the development of new methods and products*, the tiny firm suffers a heavy handicap. Du Pont spent $80 million on dacron before sales yielded any significant revenues. Minimum research costs, especially of anything like a balanced program, can run into large amounts. Moreover, in exchanging knowledge and the right to use technical developments, the big firm will tend to have greater bargaining power. In patent disputes, it can afford costly legal battles. Yet we should again recall that a company need not be a giant to research profitably. Excellent laboratories and scientific staffs exist in moderate-sized firms. By no means all the profitable inventions have been the fruit of even big business. In fact, the record shows encouraging fertility of real invention outside giant corporations.

The research department is not the only place where size helps those who want to plunge ahead. Financing a new project, like other financing, is easier for a large and well-established firm. It can pool its risks, trying new things with the knowledge that its entire future does not depend upon the result. Developing a new product or a new market may require so much money that a small company cannot take the risk, even if it has the funds; if the thing proves a failure, the business itself will die. The great corporation, however, can feel secure that a risk of the same size cannot be fatal. Moreover, any loss can be offset against profits in figuring taxes. Assume, for example, that corporation income taxes are 48 percent of earnings. A relatively small corporation with no other income goes into a new venture and loses $1 million. It may get little or no tax offset for the loss. A big corporation with income from other sources, Westinghouse or RCA, however, can deduct the $1 million loss and "save" 48 percent, $480,000, in taxes.

Advertising and Demand Creation. The cost of establishing a market position sometimes effectively limits the number of firms. Some sellers acquire a solid market standing by successful advertising. They exert efforts to make their products stand out so strongly, and to build such buyer attachment, that a newcomer would have great difficulty getting much of a market.[2] The small firm cannot afford advertising in the great national magazines or on the radio and television networks where cost per person reached may be low. A full-page, four-color ad in one issue of *Reader's Digest* costs around $60,000; an hour of prime TV network time costs over $200,000. Large buyers of advertising have another competitive advantage; they get discounts for which smaller users of the same media cannot qualify.

In selling, a large firm may "pressure" customers to handle its full line to get some highly desired item, effectively squeezing out rivals. It may use its power as a buyer to induce its suppliers, in turn, to buy from it (reciprocal buying). In the battle for space on the retailer's shelves, the big firm may have an advantage, especially in the introduction of a new product. The costs of supervising, serving, and perhaps financing an

---

[2] A manufacturer of a branded breakfast cereal was once asked how much it would cost to get into the business. He estimated that the cost of developing a market would be 10 times as much as the cost of factories to produce the cereal. The manufacturer's entire receipts from the first year's sales of a new cosmetic will probably be spent on advertising.

extensive group of dealers will be beyond the capacity of a small firm. The big department store or mail-order house can offer a richer variety of styles, colors, sizes, and price ranges than the small store. Large shippers persuade railroads to furnish specialized types of freight cars to accommodate certain products more efficiently. The list could be extended—longer each year.

Other Factors.   The *human element* may be decisive. Brilliance and skill may bring market dominance. Ruthless actions may drive out competitors or so intimidate them that they will not cause trouble. Really great human capacity is rare, and entrepreneurship is no exception. Even moderate managerial competence will be scarcer than is mediocrity.

Mergers and consolidations may reduce competition. In lines where repair and sales of replacement parts are important—perhaps for keeping a dealer organization prosperous—the firm whose products have already been widely sold has a solid advantage over a newcomer; as one result, most of the opportunities of growing markets in an expanding economy become the province of established firms. A company which buys large amounts may press its suppliers to buy from it in turn where possible—*reciprocal buying*—creating obstacles for others trying to market similar products or services.

The small company cannot keep hotel suites, lobbyists with lush expense accounts, and representatives in Washington and state capitals to swing legislation, to cut the red tape of getting government orders, to keep the head office informed of developments, or to get some of the many favors (or to avoid penalties) of government today. Today, established firms often gain a head start over newcomers from circumstances relatively new in importance to our economy, such as the momentum provided by the existence of a research staff, a good record in meeting the complex needs of military or space exploration projects, and well-developed sales organizations abroad.

Once a firm has gotten big, its established position may discourage new rivals; its size may give it shelter from serious threats of small rivals and assure respect from large. The mere fact that a marketing giant or a local mortician or newspaper is well established will deter potential suppliers of the same product or services.

METHODS TO REDUCE COMPETITION

Men have devised many ways to reduce the rigors of competition.

Private Agreements and Arrangements.   *Loose combinations* sometimes provide firms that are legally separate with a way to act in concert. The same men may be directors of different firms which sell about the same product or which buy and sell to each other or which have other relations that reflect opposing interests; such *interlocking directorates* may lead businesses to avoid hard bargaining, to substitute "understanding" for rivalry; the extent in actual practice cannot be documented, and such things as antitrust laws, the legal and ethical obligations of other members of the corporate directorates, and competition all exert corrective forces.

More or less *informal price agreements* are possible, though often illegal. Sellers, especially those in local areas, may get together and decide what they will charge or how they will share the business. Perhaps the meeting place is a golf course or a friendly dinner, perhaps the mayor's office or a lodge hall. Laundry, dry cleaning, barber, and other service charges for an area are frequently set by such agreements. Labor unions may participate, for example, in setting the charges on plumbing and electrical services. Such informal agreements, however, are often not enforceable. In such cases they are not likely to survive if the profitability of evasion is great. Under-the-counter price cutting to get business away from someone else will be tempting when there is not enough demand at the price agreed upon to keep everyone operating profitably. In Europe (and in the past in this country) the price agreements may be supplemented by more formal pools; each firm may be assigned a certain territory, a quota of sales, or even a share of the total earnings.

Existing firms may band together to keep out would-be newcomers. By making it impossible for a new firm to get transportation, labor, or financing, the existing group may secure its position. Such agreements are generally illegal (with perhaps some local exceptions); but in the past, at least, they have been powerful. *Exclusive dealerships* are common. A Ford dealer may now be fairly certain that another Ford agency will not be set up nearby, though Chevrolet and Plymouth dealers on the same block clearly reduce his protection from competition. The growing system of *franchising* also utilizes the principle of restricting the number of Howard Johnson, Holiday Inn, or other units in an area.[3]

Price Leadership. Firms may follow a uniform policy without any formal understanding. *Price leadership* provides an example. One firm may announce its prices for a wide range of products or services. Other companies then follow suit, always or most of the time. Do the small firms "know what is good for them," perhaps instinctively, and realize that "causing trouble" for the leaders would be suicide (*via* economic murder by the leader)? Who can say whether there is any prior agreement? The effect, however, can be about the same as if a formal arrangement had

---

[3] Restrictions necessary to make franchises effective were held not to be in violation of the antitrust laws in *Susser* v. *Carvel Corp.*, 381 U.S. 125 (1965). To get permission to use the Carvel name and to get the secret-formula ice cream mix, the franchised dealers were required to buy other supplies from Carvel. The Supreme Court refused to endorse the Federal Trade Commission's action to force abandonment of the agreement.

been made to eliminate price competition. If the leader observes that his prices are followed, he can feel freer to raise them, knowing that the "boys will come along." Nevertheless, even if he settles upon about the same price as would a monopolist, the results will likely be different unless the entry of productive capacity can be prevented.

Local builders are not the only businesses that use the *method of quoting prices* as a way to reduce competition.[4] The *basing point* system, now partially prohibited, served to modify competition (and to drive some resources into wasteful channels, like extra shipping costs). Prices were quoted as a certain amount at a basing point, such as Pittsburgh, plus freight from that point regardless of where the items were made. A dealer buying cement and hauling it from the plant down the road in his own trucks might have to pay freight from a basing point a hundred or more miles away. This system produced complicated results; but they included virtual elimination of open price competition, especially when a price leader set the pattern for the industry.[5] As with other cases of price leadership, the practical effectiveness declined when sagging business brought considerable excess capacity and incentive to enlarge sales.

Government Controls. Some government regulations restrict competition. Insurance and banking operate under state and federal rules that limit some forms of competition, notably in price.[6] New entrants may be denied charters on the ground that present facilities are adequate. Tariffs, quotas, and other restrictions on imports reduce the effectiveness of foreign competition. Although there is exaggeration in the old saying, "the tariff is the mother of trusts (monopolies)," the tariff and import quotas can act as a powerful big brother to keep foreigners away. Ships and airlines owned abroad are not allowed to transport freight or passengers between U.S. localities. "Buy American" rules permit U.S. firms to charge more for military and foreign aid products than would foreign suppliers and in some states put barriers against suppliers of materials and equipment for state-local projects.

Trade Associations. Some 13,000 business and professional associations provide a means by which firms can cooperate. (One company reported belonging to 500.) These associations permit their members to try to

---

[4] The bidding practices of the construction industry are complex, but in many communities they assure that numerous cost elements will be essentially the same.

[5] The devices cited here are forms of price discrimination; but, unlike those discussed in Chapter 18, the purpose is less to tap different parts of the market in ways to get most profit than it is to check competition. Twelve cement companies, with plants in Missouri, Kansas, Colorado, Texas, and Oklahoma, once bid identical prices, down to the sixth decimal point ($3.286854 per barrel), for cement to be delivered in New Mexico.

[6] An insurance salesman convicted of "rebating," turning back some of his commission to the insured, will probably lose this source of livelihood with the cancellation of his license.

advance common interests. They provide a wide range of services: joint research and advertising to develop and sell the product, lobbying, public relations, arbitration, negotiating about tax rulings or labor contracts, setting and maintaining standards of quality or ethics, providing credit information and mutual insurance, arranging trade shows, standardizing products and services, publishing a trade journal, operating an employment service, and developing accounting. Many activities are of distinct public service as aids to economy, efficiency, convenience, and higher standards. Yet, in 1776, Adam Smith wrote: "People of the same trade seldom meet together, even for merriment and diversion, but the conversation ends in a conspiracy against the public, or in some contrivance to raise prices." Today, trade associations sometimes provide welcome merriment (the annual meeting, paid for out of an expense account). Even though no conspiracy in the legal sense may result, some competition-restricting effects not good for the public can develop.

The associations may try to get members to pursue policies that weaken competition. Members are urged not to "overproduce." They are instructed in the use of accounting principles that include fixed costs (even with only partial use of capacity) and urged to use these "full costs" in setting prices. Information on inventories, costs, orders, and plans are gathered and circulated, providing one of the essentials of effective competition—knowledge—yet also a tool of collusive action, even if only implicit. The association may require members to provide data on price changes, thus giving others in the group a chance to try to change the decision. Members may be urged to avoid hurting another member by competing vigorously or by testifying against him in court. Professional associations, especially the American Medical Association, influence members; the county medical groups largely control the doctor's ability to treat patients in a hospital.

Cartels. The term "cartel" applies generally to a group organized to control the sale of a product. Cartels have been common in Europe (with government aid), covering a variety of products of agriculture, manufacturing, and mining. Different firms make a formal binding agreement to have a central agency sell their products or fix major conditions of sale. Ordinarily, there is some understanding on how the market is to be shared and about prices. The objective is to get a higher price, typically under the guise of "stabilizing" price and presumably the industry.[7] A recurrent

---

[7] Tungsten-carbide sold for about $50 a pound in the 1930's; then came a cartel, the price rose to $453; it dropped to about $225 as depression reduced demand; then, when antitrust proceedings were started, it fell to under $45. One plastic controlled by a cartel sold for 85 cents a pound for some uses, but $45 a pound for dental use. Sears, Roebuck's former president is quoted as saying that this firm liked to find what seemed to be cartel-like arrangements, for in such cases there was a mass market awaiting the seller who would go after it with lower prices and better product quality.

difficulty is the control of production. If the cartel succeeds in keeping prices high, new firms will be attracted; old ones may want to expand, to get a bigger quota.

To solve the key problem of controlling output, a cartel may exercise powerful influence over patents; then, by refusing to license their use, except upon its terms, may effectively restrain output and even bar newcomers. The cartel may be able to harass firms that will not cooperate, making life so miserable that they agree to play the game. Absolute limits on national territories have been provided, with one firm agreeing to stay out of another's bailiwick. Yet, if a recalcitrant is strong, or has solid backing, its invasion attempts may succeed.

In this country, cartels are generally illegal, except as applied to products of agriculture (where they may be called "marketing co-operatives"),[8] oil extraction in some states, and exports by groups qualifying under the Webb-Pomerene Act. Shipping firms belong to "conferences" which, with government sanction, fix some rates.

NONPRICE COMPETITION

Both the ivory tower economist and the child begging its mother to buy the cereal with the box top needed for the supersonic magic code ring know that businesses compete in ways other than price. Rivalry of many types grows increasingly important.

Variations in Terms of Sale. Most of us are familiar with discounts. Among businesses, small discounts for cash payments are common; and when competition increases, regular discounts are increased (uniformly or for special customers). Differences in credit terms and in charges for installment purchases, and financial aid of other forms, provide ways of adjusting the buyer's net cost a little. Closely related to discounts are variations in the allowance for "trade-ins." Manufacturers compete for dealers' favors by varying such things as the portion of the cost of local advertising assumed and charges for containers, thus altering the net charge. "Extras" of various types may be "thrown in"; a retailer may be given premiums, samples, or containers to distribute to his customers. The seller may provide demonstrators (the beautiful girl showing how to use the marvelous new cosmetic) or counter displays to save the retailer selling expense. Airlines give discounts for wives and children, offer package tours, and allow stopovers and inclusion of extra cities in foreign travel.

Some manufacturers will guarantee the retailer against loss from their

---

[8] Government compulsion supports, for example, sugar and milk cartels; in the 1930's, coal marketing at the mines was strictly regulated under federal law. The National Recovery Administration in the early New Deal days established NRA codes which had the elements of cartels. If the Supreme Court had not declared the law unconstitutional, might our economy have become saddled with pervasive restrictive agreements buttressed by law?

price reductions or give generous allowance for return of merchandise. The services provided with the article can vary widely. Is the guarantee for three months or three years? Who pays for installation? What are the terms for reconditioning? Who pays for delivery?

Other adjustments include such things as entertainment, gifts to a special charity, splitting of commissions and fees, reversing the telephone bill, settling old debts on favored terms, letting a buyer out of an onerous contract, or sending more or a better quality than had been agreed upon. The variety is huge. What suits one case will not apply in another—the seller of a new house who adds in some landscaping, the store that accepts returns without question, the chain of gasoline stations whose rest rooms are always clean, and the apartment owner who gives a "concession" of a month's rent.

These "price" variations may work both ways, of course, sometimes to the benefit of the buyer, sometimes the seller. During World War II, when prices were "fixed," businesses found many ways to adjust their effective charges upward.

Product Improvement. Product differentiation is at the base of monopolistic competition and may be important in oligopoly. The seller tries to distinguish his product from that of others. Having something that belongs to him alone, he can profitably spend effort on making it better. Rather than cutting price to sell more of the item in its present form, he may prepare to increase sales by improving the quality. Perhaps he feels certain that if he cuts his price, others will follow. But if he can develop an improvement, patent it, and get a head start in manufacturing and selling, he may benefit, at least for a time. If he does not make such product innovations, he will suffer as someone else gets ahead. One result is a powerful impetus to research and experimentation of all kinds.

Outside of specifically technical areas, there are also improvements. Life insurance companies develop new forms of policies. Banks improve their small-loan services. Advertising agencies offer more market research; railroads organize freight trains to give faster delivery; supermarkets increase the range of items for sale. Magazines try for more appealing articles and illustrations, colleges for better faculties.

Product Variation. Variations of product or service offer another dimension of nonprice competition. The seller may give better or poorer service, depending on what he thinks buyers want. "Cash and carry" permits price reductions for those who will take the less expensive service. Changing the size of a candy bar, or the years between redecorating an apartment, or the quality of a suit in a particular "price line" offers a form of competition—to get ahead of rivals, or to take advantage of the consumer. A company may alter its services by enlarging or narrowing its offerings—for example, the number of choices in a restaurant.

Sometimes the variations increase the net benefit to the public, even allowing for the extra costs that may be involved. Other product differences may do little more than use up skilled design talent, require scrapping of still good productive equipment, and add to the consumer's problem of choice, perhaps deceiving him and diverting his attention from features that he might consider more important. As products change from time to time, comparison and learning from experience become more difficult; product maintenance, especially getting replacement parts, tends to grow more costly.

Selling Effort. If a product is in some way distinctive, the producer can try to create a demand. Selling effort may then pay. The firm uses resources to try to raise the demand schedule for its product. Such action, notably advertising expense, may be largely a gamble. Does it not differ significantly from the use of resources to lower production costs? The gamble in devoting funds to selling effort results from two uncertainties, (1) consumer response and (2) the reaction of rivals.

Will competitors meekly let one firm take away customers by advertising and other more aggressive selling? More likely other firms will follow suit. Selling expense then becomes like competitive armaments. Protection demands as much as the "enemy" has. The whole process has a self-defeating aspect. Yet as rivals boost advertising expense to keep from losing out to each other, they may increase the demand for the whole industry. The huge increase in outlays by individual companies for advertising their own cosmetics must help explain a doubling of sales of all cosmetics in the 1950's (when total consumer buying rose by half). Hotels explain their individual merits while extolling the charms of the resort.

Selling takes many forms. Advertising itself uses many media: newspapers, magazines, billboards, radio, TV, premiums, and direct mail. The firm may use more salesmen, or pay its present salesmen more. It may allow greater discounts to dealers, or provide them with selling aids such as one sees in profusion in a drugstore. Packaging, delivery, or other selling services may be made more appealing. Staying open at night may add customers: husbands snared to "OK" buying of expensive items or lug home big grocery purchases. A larger parking lot or a playground appeals to some buyers. Free engineering service helps sell industrial equipment. Hotels finance conventions. Each industry has its own special devices for stimulating sales, and some of America's most fertile brains concentrate on adding to what is already a long list of ways to sell.

CONCLUSION: THE PROBLEM OF MONOPOLY

Words may mislead. *Monopoly, oligopoly,* and *monopolistic competition* are examples. What the economist means by monopoly, for example, is not necessarily what the man in the street means. Both monopoly and competition are matters of degree.

Pure competition is more a theoretical model than a fact of economic life. So is pure monopoly. Most buying and selling take place in markets somewhat removed from the extremes. Businesses generally are able to set prices as well as to adjust output. Sometimes their range of freedom to act is great enough to approach monopoly. More often they belong to a small group which could benefit by joint action, but which face serious problems of getting the oligopoly gain. In other cases sellers individually have some room for independent maneuver but find the competitive elements of their situation more powerful than the monopolistic.

Economists see the disadvantages of monopoly and its kin as more varied and less obvious than will the public: poorer resource allocation than under pure competition, less than optimum use of resources, encouragement of capacity that may be idle much of the time, good rewards for less than the best of service to others, prices higher than necessitated by economic conditions, the diversion of competitive efforts into relatively sterile forms of trivial product variation and wasteful selling, the distortion of prices, sluggishness in seizing opportunities for improvement. Profits may or may not be high; and the most serious effects of monopoly can exist where profits are low (and capacity excessive).

The possession and the use of (great or limited) monopoly power may be by people of good human qualities seeking an easier way to get a living—not repulsive men on a grisly mission of bloodsucking. The lusty buccaneering of the age when "the public be damned" attitude characterized many monopolists has been replaced by slick—and sincere—efforts to build good public relations. The civic-minded leaders of service clubs and professional associations, hoping to raise standards, may support policies the economist sees as monopolistic.

The search for freedom from the full force of competition is a normal, human striving. Success is welcome to those who realize it. Some such success, however, is at the expense of others, not the reward for serving them better. The possessor of monopoly power—whether the city's only eye surgeon or the free world's dominant producer of nickel—will do many admirable things and do them well. The goodness of the monopolist's service may be an obstacle to public policies designed to induce the highest quality at the lowest of cost with the best rate of progress.

The rivalry for the consumer's dollar is intense—even the open price competition of economic analysis. Some of the appearance of monopoly and price fixing is deceptive because we fail to recognize the intensity of competition of substitutes. Other competition, even when of dubious value to consumers, is also prevalent, effective, and often bitter. To businessmen, certainly, rivalry rather than the ease of monopoly seems the dominant fact. Photography is probably the most realistic of the arts. Yet two pictures of the same person may vary from grotesque ugliness to ethereal beauty, depending upon lighting and the photographer's skill and intent. So it is in trying to give a picture about the balance of monopoly-oligopoly and competition in our economy. Different observers reach different conclusions from about the same set of facts. Most will agree, however, that (1) the attraction of profits from monopolistic practices combined with (2) the technological factors limiting the number of sellers (or buyers) create forces limiting competition. These forces must be checked somehow if the public is not to suffer.

TERMS AND CONCEPTS

price competition	consolidation	average-markup pric-
nonprice competition	interlocking directo-	ing
monopolistic competi-	rates	penetration price
tion	price leadership	skimming price
oligopoly	cartel	administered prices
legal monopoly	full-cost pricing	share-of-the-market
natural monopoly	break-even pricing	pricing
merger		profit-target pricing

QUESTIONS

1. What barriers restrict the entry of new firms into certain industries? Give examples.

2. Give examples of nonprice competition. Which seem to you likely to benefit the consumer? Which, if any, represent the forces of "creative destruction" that lead to technological progress?

3. What do sellers have to gain from restricting competition? What methods do they sometimes use?

4. How do real economies of large size act as barriers to new producers? Give examples.

5. "Purely 'bargaining' advantages of big companies create monopolistic exclusions of competition." Explain and give examples.

6. "It is foolish to think of monopoly as a problem of national markets. Most of our buying is in local markets, and it is here that monopoly is likely to be most serious." Discuss.

7. Assume that a firm wants to set prices on the basis of long-run rather than short-run costs. How much different would be the results if it tried to use average rather than marginal cost?

8. Is the existence of advertising evidence that an industry is not purely competitive?

9. What problem does a firm face in pricing a new product?

10. What part do national, state, and local governments play in reducing competition?

11. Assuming that it were possible to do so, what might be the consequences of making the auto manufacturing industry purely competitive? The postal service? Of creating local monopolies in auto selling?

APPENDIX

Topics in Business Pricing Practices

"Theory" versus Practice. The relation between the type of price theory we have developed and the pricing practices of business is a topic for debate. The discussion here has emphasized that the theory deals with what will be to the firm's best advantage. Although we have identified "best advantage" with profit—long run or short run, a possible conflict of some significance—we did note that money earnings are not the exclusive goal of businessmen. To the extent that other goals influence decisions, our theory will be incomplete.

The business world, of course, is highly complex, while our model is simple. Relatively few business managers have looked to the economist's price theory. In seeking guidance, perhaps they are overlooking something of practical value. Let us, at least, note three points.

First, market forecasting and the study of demand do utilize economic theory. It helps indicate the kinds of information to seek. The second point is that a study of a group of corporations selected as being "best managed" and generally profitable found considerable use of marginal concepts. A third point is this: Whether or not businessmen do act as the theory would indicate to be to their best advantage, the results the firm achieves are determined by the elements treated in the models of the economist.

We now examine briefly some of the practical problems and methods of pricing.

Price-Output Adjustment Where There Is More than One Product. Earlier chapters presented a simplified analysis (1) of the output that is to the best advantage of the producer and (2) of the way prices come into being and change. This analysis, however, fails to take account of a fact that must be obvious. Producers, from small farms and stores to industrial giants, normally turn out more than one kind of product. Consequently, the practical problems businesses face in measuring the costs of production are more obstreperous than our discussion suggests. To get one thing, it is often necessary to produce several others; to get ham, one must grow the whole pig. In such cases, some inputs are used to help produce more than one final product; these costs are "common" or "joint."

There will be both fixed (overhead) and variable costs which are common to more than one product. For example, the same store building (fixed cost) and the same salesman's wages (a variable cost) serve the selling of several different things. In such cases no one can be certain what it costs to produce any specific item; some expenses are inextricably mixed up with the costs of producing other kinds of things. What can a businessman do in such cases? He must use arbitrary methods of saying how much of the common costs should be assigned to each of the different products. As a rule, any such

445

arbitrary method will be subject to dispute; different, but reasonably defensible, methods of allocating common costs may produce more than minor variations in the expenses assigned to specific products. This, however, is a topic for advanced economics and accounting.

Nevertheless, our analysis of the best adjustment holds. Even when *most* costs are so mingled that price-output determination of individual products cannot proceed along the lines we outlined for simpler situations, there will be *some* costs of any product and service that *are* separable from the others. The costs that are separable stand as the marginal costs, and they set a minimum which price must cover if production is to pay. They thus serve to help indicate the volume of output which will be best. By careful accounting and variation in output, perhaps with a change in the "product mix," the firm can measure these separable costs. It asks: "How would costs be different if we were to produce a little more or a little less of this particular product"? The answer gives a rock-bottom cost figure; if marginal revenue does not come up to it, then that particular output should be discontinued. For larger elements—groups of products, departments, or individual plants—the firm can find most of the costs which are properly attributable.

Full-Cost Pricing.   Accountants, in computing costs of particular products, often include overhead or fixed costs ("burden"). These "full," "standard," or average total unit cost figures play a part in business decisions on pricing and output. Yet, as we have seen, fixed costs are already sunk; they are no longer under control and cannot be "economized." If fixed costs are included in the expenses that determine output, the resulting estimates will indicate poorer points of adjustment than if fixed costs are ignored—with one exception, where the average total cost equals marginal cost.[1]

Break-even Points.   Businesssmen often refer to the "break-even point." While they do not always mean exactly the same thing, the basic idea is similar. With any set of prices obtainable, costs will just be covered at some volume of output. Smaller outputs mean losses, larger outputs will bring profits. The point at which the firm will "break even," of course, depends upon its costs and the prices it charges. With any given set of costs, the break-even volume will depend upon price. With any given price, the break-even point will depend upon costs. If important costs are fixed, profits may tend to rise rapidly after volume exceeds the break-even point, until variable costs turn up. (Figure 19–1.) While use of break-even point analysis may serve some purposes well, it is not, as a rule, an efficient tool for optimum price-output determination.

Average Markup Method of Pricing.   A pricing method which businesses use widely is the average markup. A retailer, for example, pays the wholesaler

---

[1] One crudity of average-cost pricing is that fixed costs per unit depend upon the number of units. The accountant may say: "The full average cost of manufacturing widget A is $5. Labor and other out-of-pocket costs average $3, while overhead is $2." Yet there can be only one quantity of output at which overhead cost will average precisely $2. We refer only to expenses that *are* fixed. In deciding whether or not to incur costs that will afterward be fixed, the firm would treat them as variable and take them into account in its planning.

FIGURE 19–1. Break-even Chart

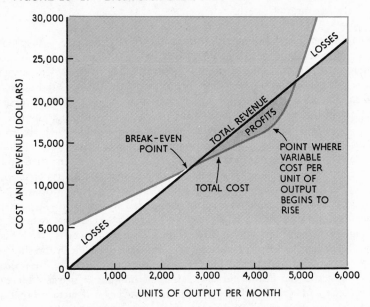

UNITS OF OUTPUT PER MONTH

$10 an item and then adds an arbitrary percentage, perhaps 50 percent, and sets his price at $15. How does he learn what percentage will be most profitable? Methods used vary from the crudest guesses to some fairly careful estimates based on trial and error. On one group of items the markup may be 100 percent (jewelry), on another 20 percent (unused textbooks), or even less (cigarets). Having thus fixed a price, the retailer observes the responses of the buyers. These, and the actions of competitors, suggest whether the markup rate could be raised, or whether it should be cut to boost sales and yield larger profit. There is a current trend to try to fix markups with closer attention to differences in the costs of handling different products.

"Share of the Market" and "Profit Target" Goals. Two guides to the price-output decisions of large businesses may or may not be consistent with the desire for maximum profit in the long run. But these guides do seem influential in some cases. Over a period of years a firm may have had a certain share of the market, perhaps 20 percent. It may be determined to maintain or expand this share, or perhaps to recapture it after having fallen below (or to avoid rising above if the government might activate proceedings under laws against monopoly). Price and output may then be set with this goal in mind. To the outsider, such actions may seem to sacrifice earnings for some less rational objective.

A study of the pricing policies of a few giant corporations concluded that investment, pricing, and output decisions are directed toward earning, say, 10 or 15 percent after taxes, on the investment. The firm will estimate unit costs of major products when operating at perhaps 70 or 80 percent of capacity. Then it will set prices which will bring the target profit if the assumed output is sold. The managers may believe that this method leads to "just prices" or "fair rates of return."

"Penetration" or "Skimming" Prices for New Products. A producer introducing something new will hope to have considerable monopoly power as regards that product—for a time. He may be able to get prices anywhere within a considerable range. One problem is to balance short-run and long-run objectives. Two major alternatives may appear. In both cases, of course, the extent of available productive capacity will influence the decision.

He may set a price well below the one that would bring the largest immediate profit. By doing so, he can enlarge his head start over copiers and other newcomers. The more extensively he can *penetrate* the market, and the more firmly he can establish his item as the product of this type, the more strongly his position becomes entrenched for the long run. Moreover, consumer (and dealer) acceptance may be stimulated by such pricing.

He may, on the other hand, set a *skimming* price, one which takes advantage of demand inelasticity often found when a product is novel. Such a price will enable the firm to realize a very high rate of profit in the short run. A high price may permit the innovator to recapture quickly the costs of development and the heavy initial expenses of building a market. Here is a chance to benefit quickly. The high price, however, will attract other producers and also retard the development of a broad market.

Price Rigidity: Administered Prices. In highly competitive markets, such as the securities or grain exchanges, prices fluctuate, perhaps from minute to minute. Similarly, where a seller has control over price, and if conditions of cost or demand change, we might reasonably expect fluctuations (except in some oligopoly situations where the response of others is uncertain or likely to be unfavorable). The most profitable price is one at the output where marginal cost equals marginal revenue. If variable costs or demand change—and both do change in the real-world economy—the best price-output adjustment for the seller would not remain stable. As we look at the real world, however, we find businesses that have power to set—administer—their own prices and whose quoted prices have remained the same for considerable periods.

How do we account for such rigidities? They certainly do not seem consistent with a desire to maximize profit. The price of steel rails was unchanged for 10 years; the prices of nickel and sulphur did not change from June, 1929, to May, 1937. When business declines, prices of some things do not fall with declining demand and marginal revenue; and when business booms, prices do not rise as much as changing demand and cost conditions would indicate to be in the firm's best interest.

Economists are not certain about the explanation. We know that things are not always what they seem. Businesses can and do sell for prices different from those they list publicly. During periods of business recession, the prices quoted on published price lists are often "shaded." "Only dopes and governments buy at list price" may have been an exaggeration as applied in the Great Depression, but it contained a measure of truth. Extensive, but unsystematic, undercover price cutting was common. In fact, therefore, price rigidities are less common than published figures indicate. Yet price fluctuations also seem to be fewer and rarer than our analysis would indicate to be in the best interest of the seller—a seller who can set his own prices. Why?

1. Probably the major reason for rigid prices in the downswing is a belief that demand is inelastic, that the number of units sold will not increase enough to make price reduction pay. Users of industrial equipment, for example, do not need much new equipment when business is deeply depressed; idle capacity is painfully evident. Lower prices would hardly stimulate sales to businesses that had more equipment than they were using. Any sales of more machines this month as a result of price cutting would be "stolen from the future"; better wait and get a higher price later. Therefore, although not maximizing profit in the short run, the firm may have acted to maximize over the longer period. Similarly, a business may believe that demand for durable consumers goods is influenced so dominantly by income and other nonprice considerations that price reduction would have little effect in stimulating sales. Here again, a durable item, such as a refrigerator, sold today may mean one not sold next year, perhaps at a higher price.[2] A seller may also feel that cutting a price will suggest that more price cutting is likely and induce buyers actually to hold off rather than to increase purchases. Such reasoning would apply less to bread or appendectomies than to autos and houses.

2. Costs do not seem to drop and thus obviously justify a price reduction. Important variable costs per unit may change little, especially where there is a long-term labor contract. As the volume of output falls, fixed costs per unit rise. A manager who looks at his total costs, therefore, will perhaps see the average actually rising. Can he sensibly reduce his prices? Unless he is well educated in the principle of always looking forward, not backward (to the commitments of the past over which he now has no control), he will possibly overlook the chance to make the best adjustment, one focusing on variable costs. Just the opposite may happen when prices are rising.

3. The possibility of intense (cutthroat) competition can discourage price reduction. If fixed costs are large, total and variable costs differ considerably. The firm that cuts price will expect its rivals to follow suit. They will take much of the possible benefit of increased buying that results from the reduction; everyone has lower earnings, and some perhaps face bankruptcy that would not have come otherwise. Rigid prices seem stable, a source of highly prized security. Stable prices, of course, do *not* assure stability of anything but the price; although they may appear as a symbol of stability during depression or inflation, *the price rigidity increases the instability of physical quantities.*

4. Change itself may be a nuisance—costs of new price lists, advertising, allowance to dealers, and such things add a small reason for "staying put."

5. Maintaining quoted prices of new output when demand falls may seem to help support prices of existing goods, such as used autos. A person who still owes a great deal for the car he bought on installments may be unwilling to keep on paying if the price of a new one falls openly.

6. Finally, businessmen may not want the higher profits that might come

---

[2] Prices of durable consumers goods did fluctuate. For example, the Detroit price of the least expensive new Plymouth fell from $655 in 1929 to $445 in 1933; dealers, of course, made all sorts of adjustments.

with changing prices. Especially if business is booming and earnings are already good, higher profits might antagonize consumers, increase pressure for government regulation, invite union demands for higher wages, and disappear largely (half or so) in taxes.

Rigid prices are "administered," but not all prices appropriately called "administered" are rigid. Typical retailers, manufacturers, builders, bankers—most businessmen in fact—do set prices. The price, then, does result from a kind of administrative decision which differs from the process of purely competitive markets. The significant factor, however, is the power of the businessman to make the price stick and to achieve optimum results thereby. What really counts for the public as a whole, in other words, is the extent and the nature of the forces pressing businessmen to "readminister" prices—the amount of competition. Considerable difference exists between a barber protected by a community-wide agreement and the druggist next door subject to competition of many others willing to "administer" prices down. In general, the concept of "price administration" is less useful for analyzing economic problems than was once expected by some economists. The factors of basic importance are the existence, or absence, of competitive pressures.

20

ANTITRUST POLICIES

Whatever economic justification particular price-fixing agreements may be thought to have, the law does not permit an inquiry into their reasonableness. They are all banned because of their actual or potential threat to the central nervous system of the economy.
Supreme Court in U.S. v. Socony-Vacuum Oil Co.

The making of some of the basic rules by which all of us must live is a function of government. Many rules apply to business and the market-place. Although we all agree that rule making is a job of government, we often disagree about the nature of the rules to adopt. In fact, many laws applying to business seek to put into effect policies which conflict with each other. Moreover, after reaching a general consensus on specific rules, we find ourselves with rather different notions about how vigorously the laws are to be enforced in practice.

Americans have a long history of using government to deal with problems of monopoly and competition. (This history in many respects differs markedly from that of other countries.) The record shows both settled lines of policy and conflicting objectives and methods. It is a record of both success and failure with many issues very much alive today.

Governmental policies toward business fall into four major groups: (1) Some policies are designed to maintain competition, to prevent monopoly. (2) Others seek to moderate and modify, at times to restrict and even discourage, competition and business rivalry. (3) Regulation, chiefly of public utilities, constitutes the third group of policies. (4) Finally, governmental units own and operate some businesses. This chapter deals

451

primarily with the first, and the appendix with the third. The next chapter takes up the second group, deals with various related topics, and draws general conclusions. An appendix to it examines policies for aiding one particular industry, agriculture.

REASONS FOR MAINTAINING COMPETITION (PREVENTING MONOPOLY)

Congress first enacted antitrust legislation in 1890;[1] about it a special Presidential committee reported in 1955, "The basic philosophy . . . today remains above partisan controversy as a 'charter of freedom.' " Yet why, really, try to curb monopoly? Why use government to encourage competition? At least seven reasons are given. They stem from the dangers of "monopoly"—not so much monopoly as strictly defined in Chapter 18 as monopoly and oligopoly in the sense of concentrated market power.

1. Competition offers the members of society more economic opportunity than does monopoly. "Monopoly" curtails individual opportunity, especially for those who would seek their economic fortunes in an industry, profession, or region where entry is impeded by monopolistic restrictions. New entrants to an industry may have greater difficulty gaining a secure foothold if they must face the rivalry of entrenched giants than if existing companies are smaller. (But not necessarily so, because big companies are at times less flexible and imaginative than smaller firms.)

2. Much antagonism to "monopoly" has resulted from fear of high prices on what monopolies sell or low prices paid for what they buy. Economists see, in addition, the flourishing of nonprice competition which tends to raise rather than reduce costs and prices.

3. Another reason follows from higher prices. "Monopolies" acting in their own interest will use resources less fully than the basic forces of demand and supply warrant. The poorer allocation of resources is a source of overall social inefficiency, a loss of real income. Even if the resources indirectly excluded from a monopolistic industry find use elsewhere, they produce less of what the community wants than they could produce in the industry monopolized.

4. "Monopoly" reduces the pressure to operate most efficiently and most progressively. It may slow technological progress; a monopoly may fail to adopt the best of new methods. With its invested capital and established position, it may prefer to keep what it has. New products and better methods may not be profitable for a firm that can exclude them. Or the entrenched business (or union) may not be alert enough to see what is in its own long-run interest. Human talent is wasted. Routines, inertia, and seniority thwart creative, pioneering urges of the majority who must be below top

---

[1] Why the term "antitrust"? One legal device used to form monopolies and combinations in the 1880's was the trust. Congressional action did not initiate legal moves to deal with monopoly. The common law had long provided certain basic prohibitions and regulations of business practices. State legislation had in some cases supplemented the common law before Congress acted.

positions. The everlasting threat of competition does not *force* the use of the most efficient methods. If the industry functions as a cartel, or a more or less deliberate oligopoly, the influence of the weaker members may foster stagnation. The inertia of standpatters can hold back more progressive firms and perhaps prevent the entry of innovators. Where a whole industry functions as a more or less conscious unit, unions can effectively protest against the adoption of methods that seem to displace labor while raising productivity, in contrast with a more competitive industry where a firm that fails to keep up with the best is bound to suffer. Monopolistic industries, of course, are not necessarily unprogressive. Often, in fact, such large resources are needed for innovation of new products or methods that only big firms can succeed.

5. Business (and unions) with large market power tend to hold prices (and wage rates) more *rigid* than would be the case if the power were shared by more units. Inflexible prices and wage rates tend to accentuate swings of the business cycle by, among other things, forcing more of the adjustment process on quantity of output.

6. Great *concentrations* of power are dangerous—socially, politically, and economically. This point merges with the problem of *bigness*. The two are by no means identical, but often analysis of the evidence cannot distinguish clearly between the existence and results of monopoly and those of bigness. When organizations are big, their top officials have great responsibility and power. The limitations of human capacity make it impossible for one or a few men to keep sufficiently familiar with the multitude of problems, and the facts involved, to make the best of informed and considered judgments. Even when the men at the top of businesses, unions, and other organizations are men of great ability and supreme goodwill—and such is not always the case—some things are likely to be done poorly, with the unfortunate results spreading widely through the economy. Bigness inevitably creates the danger that huge power and responsibility will rest on men who do not have ability on a corresponding scale (and whose day has only 24 hours).

Big business creates the demand for big labor and big government. The private affairs of a huge firm, just because it is so very large, become matters of public concern. When government intervention follows, the results often diverge far from those intended and desirable. Bigness, by inviting enlargement of the regulatory intervention of government, indirectly threatens freedoms which are valuable not only for economic progress but also for "the good society" as we in the Western world have dreamed of it.

7. Monopolies (business and labor) are likely to convert full employment into inflation. Hopes for sustained high prosperity without persistent rise in the price level rest upon passable solution of the problem of massed power in the market place.

Competition would not need to be superior on many of these counts, to say nothing of all seven, to give us strong reason for preferring it. Competition, however, is not always constructive. For one thing, there are rascals in the business world who fleece the consumer and who hurt other firms. Real-life rivalry in business is sometimes wasteful, even predatory. Society needs protection against destructive business methods.

The public, therefore, is concerned with the *ways* in which businesses compete. Government *does* have a job to do in regulating competition—not so much the pure (price) competition of theory as the rivalry, especially in nonprice forms, that develops in some markets. However, worse than confusing inconsistencies may result from efforts both to encourage competition (limit monopoly) and to control it. The inconsistencies occasionally leave us uncertain and, sometimes worse, unable to withstand pressures to convert policies designed to "police" competition into devices that create some of the conditions of monopoly.

ANTITRUST POLICY

The Laws. The Sherman Act (1890) provides: (1) "every contract, combination . . . or conspiracy in restraint of interstate and foreign trade or commerce is illegal" and (2) "every person who shall monopolize or attempt to monopolize . . . any part of the trade or commerce among the States, or with foreign nations, shall be deemed guilty of a misdemeanor."[2] The language is strong. The scope is broad. This is still the law of our land. Another major law, the Clayton Act (1914), specifically exempted labor unions from many features of the antitrust program; in addition, it prohibited exclusive sales contracts, price discriminations, rebates, interlocking directorates and stockholdings (in certain situations), and the acquisition by one corporation of stock in another—all "where the effect will be substantially to lessen competition or tend to create a monopoly." The same Congress created the Federal Trade Commission to help enforce the antitrust laws and enacted provisions declaring "unfair methods of competition" unlawful (subject to qualifications).

Congress has since made some changes in the Clayton Act. One (discussed later) deals with price discrimination, one with mergers.[3] The chief developments have involved enforcement and interpretation—by executive officials responsible for administering the law and by the courts. The history is too long and complex to summarize here. We cannot attempt even a reasonably complete summary of the present state of affairs. But we can look at some highlights involving the meaning of the laws as the courts interpret them, enforcement, and unsettled problems.

---

[2] Restraints of trade are not prohibited, only restraints brought about by one or more of the three devices (contract, combination, conspiracy). Section (1) applies even if there is no issue of monopoly. More than one person must be involved. The section dealing with monopoly, however, can be violated by one person or firm—and even if the person or business does not succeed in monopolizing.

[3] The provision of the Clayton Act designed to prevent corporations from joining together to limit competition applied only to the purchase of stock. There was no restriction on a corporation's buying the *assets* of another. Mergers were commonly effected by the surrender of stock of one corporation in return for stock of the other; acquisition of stock in this way to acquire assets was legal. In 1950, therefore, Congress, by the Celler-Kefauver Act, brought acquisition of assets within the scope of the law and modified wording in ways which greatly extend the scope of the provisions restricting mergers.

What the Laws Mean. Although around the margins there are trouble-some doubts about the meaning of the laws, many features of importance are reasonably clear. "Interstate" and "commerce," among other terms, are interpreted broadly. The laws, for example, have been held to apply to the activities of a local group of doctors, to building contractors in a particular community, to professional boxing and football, to fire insur-ance companies.[4] The laws cover much activity which the layman would perhaps consider local[5] or outside "trade and commerce."

The courts, however, have decided that "every" does not really mean "every" as the common man might think. Only "undue" restraints are prohibited. A "rule of reason" must be applied. The interpretation of "reasonable" may be wide or narrow. Provisions of the Clayton Act apply only "where the effect may be to substantially lessen competition, or to tend to create a monopoly." An area of uncertainty, and of flexibility, remains.

In important cases, however, no doubt, or virtually none, remains. Some things are illegal **per se,** in and of themselves. The landmarks erected by the Court indicate that certain actions violate the law. Agreements among businesses to fix prices, to exclude competitors from the market, to restrict output or purchases, to divide markets, to use tying contracts or other devices to eliminate the opportunity of others, and to use boycotts or other coercive devices to restrain trade—all these are illegal *per se.* The particular circumstances are irrelevant; there is no scope for the "rule of reason"—or so it seemed until the courts indicated that the facts of individual cases may outweigh a *per se* rule. As with so much in antitrust law, complexity compounds uncertainty.

The actions prohibited certainly include *horizontal* agreements—those made by firms on essentially the same level of economic activity—which businesses might employ to restrict competition. In general, the laws as interpreted, offer the public sweeping protection against arrangements by "competitors" to fix prices and otherwise restrain competition. Of course, borderline cases arise frequently. Businessmen and their lawyers are well aware of unsettled problems—for example, the permissible activities of trade associations. Yet the list of clearly prohibited practices is impressive.

In cases alleging monopolization, including mergers, the laws as inter-

---

[4] Groups getting varying amounts of exemption from antimonopoly laws are railroads, farm organizations, labor unions, insurance, air carriers, professional sport, and some exporters.

[5] "If it is interstate commerce that feels the pinch, it does not matter how local the operation which applies the squeeze." *U.S.* v. *Women's Sportswear Manufacturers Association* (1949). An indirect and remote effect on interstate commerce would give Congress power to act; for example, when a farmer planted 23, instead of a federally authorized 11, acres of wheat, produced 239 bushels extra, and used it at home, his actions were held to have a substantial effect in defeating or obstructing the purposes of Congress—*Wickard* v. *Filburn* (1942).

preted give less than clear guidance.[6] What distinguishes "substantial" from "insubstantial"? Each case will be decided on its own facts.

Postwar decisions have given weight to the analysis of economic evidence. Shares of the market receive serious attention, but no single line has been set to separate the permissible from the prohibited. The relation of the seller(s) to the size of the market is vital. What is "the" product? What are the economic bounds of "the" market? Bethlehem and Youngstown Steel were not permitted to merge into a company that would supply about 20 percent of the national market but a much larger part of more limited markets.

The courts ask, "What is the relevant market?" If the market and the product are defined broadly, the decision will be different from that if one or both are defined narrowly. For example, oversimplifying somewhat, in a case against Du Pont, the government claimed that there was a distinct market for "cellophane" while the court decided that the relevant market was for "flexible packaging materials." While Du Pont may well have had a virtual monopoly of cellophane, its share of the market for flexible packaging materials was not large enough to constitute monopolization within the meaning of the law. Substitutability of products and cross elasticity of demand become of substantial relevance.[7]

The Court has applied the law to *vertical* arrangements, under a rule of reason. The purchase (or ownership) by one company of the stock of another to which it sells or, presumably, from which it buys, is illegal if there is a reasonable likelihood of "substantial" restraint of commerce or monopoly. Du Pont's stock ownership was found to have given it an advantage in selling auto finishes and fabrics to General Motors, which made up a substantial part of the total market; more than a third of a century after acquiring the stock, Du Pont had to get rid of it (by distribution to its own stockholders). The Brown Shoe Company, manufacturing 4 percent of the nation's shoes and also retailing, was prohibited from acquiring a retail chain which would have made it the owner of 2.5 percent of total retail outlets. The Aluminum Company of America, with 27 percent of the market in aluminum cable, was held in violation of the Clayton Act in acquiring a company which fabricated 1.7 per cent of similar cable.

A series of decisions continuing into 1967 showed the majority of the

---

[6] Legal bans on various "loose" agreements and methods of reducing competition have encouraged mergers which more effectively cut down the number of potential competitors.

[7] Cross elasticity of demand is the relation between the change in the price of one commodity and the quantity of purchases of close substitutes. How can the parties in an antitrust controversy solve the practical problems of measuring cross elasticity of demand, for example, learning how prices and quantities of sales of substitutes in fact change? One merger was held illegal on a narrow definition of "the product," aluminum conductor rather than conductors of both aluminum and copper; another merger was prohibited by defining the product to include both metal and glass containers.

Supreme Court determined to take a firm stand against mergers. Congress, fearing a "rising tide of economic concentration," moved by the "desirability of retaining 'local control' over industry and the protection of small business," had voted in 1950 to tighten antimerger provisions. The Court would interpret the law to encourage "the economic way of life sought to be preserved by Congress."[8] Since Congress used the word "may," the Court would look to probable effects in the future, limiting itself to neither the record of the past nor certainties ahead. Even mergers consummated years in the past and mergers approved by other federal agencies have been declared illegal.

The only mergers that can confidently hope to survive a suit—*if* the government brings one—are those where: (1) one party is in danger of failure, or (2) the businesses of the acquired and acquiring companies are totally unrelated and noncompetitive (the so-called conglomerate merger), or (3) both parties are insignificant in both size and share of the market. Neither the second nor the third exception can be counted upon.

Problems of Enforcement. Enforcement of the antitrust laws is divided between the Antitrust Division of the Department of Justice and the Federal Trade Commission. Since World War II, enforcement has been more vigorous than before. Congress has voted more money. Heavy emphasis has been placed on prohibiting mergers which seem likely to reduce competition in important industries. The staffs, however, have not been able to pursue thoroughly more than a modest fraction of the complaints filed or to investigate mergers which the courts might hold illegal.

Proving violation can be difficult. One kind of case (merger or patent) requires elaborate study of markets. In other cases the vital issues arise over actions or policies that are not out in the open, not things that can be spotted easily and clearly. The violation of law alleged may involve conspiracy, intent, and jointness of action according to some agreement on parallel action. Did the firms plan or somehow get together to follow policies that would restrict competition? Intent is always hard to prove. Conspiracy (a combination for illegal action) is a serious charge, and good evidence is needed for conviction. Firms that may be guilty are alerted to destroy, or fail to create, evidence that will stand up in court. Other businesses that may have been hurt by unfair practices may be reluctant to testify, especially in public; their future success may depend upon continuing to do business with a company alleged to be guilty.

If the accused firm agrees voluntarily, or if a grand jury uses powers of subpoena, government agents can ransack a company's files for scraps of written evidence. In a big firm, however, such a search in itself is a huge

[8] Quotations are from *Brown Shoe Co.* v. *U.S.*, 370 U.S. 295 (1962).

job. Then sifting and analyzing the evidence found, and preparing a case, can require many man-months of careful, skilled effort. Is this interoffice memo an accurate expression of the firm's policy? What does this terse note about a telephone discussion really mean? Informal hearings and examination of the other side's evidence can stretch into months. Then a court trial may be lengthy and, of course, expensive.

Against mergers, however, the pendulum has swung so far that the government's problem of proof has been eased greatly. Nevertheless, if the firms seeking to merge insist upon trying to go ahead after the government indicates opposition, evidence required can take long months of preparation by both sides.

To economize, government officials and the firms charged with violation often agree to *consent decrees*. The businesses do not necessarily admit that they have been guilty; but they agree not to engage in certain specific practices in the future. There is no proof or disproof of the charges. Previous actions incur no penalty, but later violations of the decree can be punished as contempt of court. The Department of Justice, however, presumably because of shortage of staff, has devoted only trifling effort to "policing" existing decrees.

If the judge agrees, defendants may plead *nolo contendere*. They do not admit guilt, but decline to litigate, placing themselves at the mercy of the court.

Penalties. What happens when a person or a corporation signs a consent decree, pleads *nolo contendere*, or is found guilty of violating antitrust laws? Total penalties may be inconsequential, but they can add to severe punishment.

In 1961 jail sentences were imposed on officials of leading producers of heavy electrical equipment; dozens of men from some 27 companies had been guilty of conspiring to fix prices and share markets. The jailing of prominent businessmen, even for a month, had no small shock effect in the business world. Both the Executive (it was the Republican administration which developed and prosecuted the case) and the courts were shown to be clearly determined to impose penalties. Moreover, the risk of belonging to a conspiracy must have risen, for one or more members of any conspiracy might, as did some in the electrical equipment case, volunteer evidence in return for clemency.

The odium of conviction in a civil case is something of a penalty. Fines up to a maximum of $50,000 per offense can be heavy for individuals and potentially for some businesses. Of greater importance—if only because they affect future actions—are provisions in consent decrees or judicial directions to the guilty firm (1) to *stop doing* the illegal things with penalties for contempt of court for disobedience, or (2) to *do* certain things, such as (*a*) separate into more units, (*b*) sell where it does not want to sell, (*c*) license where it does not want to license, (*d*) refrain from entering lines of business it would like to undertake.

Businesses which have suffered from the illegal practices of others may sue for, and upon proof receive, *treble damages* from the guilty firm.[9] After the electrical conspiracy case (1961), the Department of Justice tried to get the companies to agree not to sell at "unreasonably low" prices. The leading firm balked, in part because the government would not define what it meant by such an unprecise term.

The Department of Justice appears reluctant to seek, and courts reluctant to grant, orders to big companies to split into two or more units. Yet, occasional application shows that this remedy is available. Motion-picture companies were forced to get rid of chains of theaters. A large maker of cans agreed to sell its glass bottle plants because courts held that cans and bottles are close substitutes. Perhaps the public interest would be well served by more division of giant firms, at least those having many plants. The plants, presumably, are the units of technology; if so, any loss of real productive efficiency would probably be slight. This complex subject, however, calls for analysis of a question we now raise, one whose answer has significance for antitrust but ought not to be decisive.

What Is the Best Size of Business? One goal of antitrust policy ought to be the encouragement of efficiency in production, conceived most broadly. As we have seen, much production takes place in plants so large that only a few will supply the whole market. The conditions of pure competition cannot be met. When does a plant or firm reach the most efficient or optimum size?

The best size will depend upon a host of factors, many constantly changing.[10] A new chemical that eliminates safety hazards reduced the optimum size of dry-cleaning plants; they can now be small enough to provide convenient, on-the-spot service without the need for trucking to a single, large plant.[11] A revision in a building code or an increase in elevator speed can alter the most profitable size of apartment houses or office buildings. Changes in management methods affect the ability of

[9] The companies convicted in the electrical equipment conspiracy case paid heavily in treble damages (plus legal fees); the total cost will exceed $200 million and perhaps reach $400 million when all settlements are made and legal fees are paid.

[10] The president of Du Pont used the following illustration in pointing out that business health requires giving up some types of activity: "A business is like a barrel that is set to catch rain water. When it [your research effort] rains new developments, the level of the barrel rises. But you must have a drain at the bottom to remove the things which have grown marginal. Only then will its contents remain fresh and healthy. The freshness . . . is really what counts for us." (*Better Living*, 1961.)

[11] A giant corporation developed the chemical. One result is increased opportunity for hundreds or thousands of small, local dry cleaners. They are no longer dependent upon use of a central dry cleaning plant or the transportation to and from it.

firms to cope with problems of size. A new tax or freight rate will alter decisions about the best size of many businesses. Cases differ; the same firm may set up plants of different size.

Study of selected manufacturing industries yielded the data in Table 20–1. From these and other facts Professor Bain concluded that, in all respects, the variation from one industry to another was significant. In some cases there is no doubt that each plant of optimum or most efficient size would be large enough to supply a significant fraction of the industry; not many such plants could find enough buyers to survive. In some

TABLE 20–1. Economies of Size in 10 Manufacturing Industries: Investment Needed for Plant of Optimum Size

Industry	Percentage of National Industry Capacity Contained in One PLANT of Optimum Size	Estimated Extent of Multiplant Economies as a Percentage of Total Cost	Percentage of National Industry Capacity Contained in One FIRM of Optimum Size	Total Capital Required for One Efficient Plant (Millions of Dollars)
Shoes	0.14 to 0.5	2 to 4	0.5 to 2.5	$0.5 to 2
Canned fruits and vegetables	0.25 to 0.5	none		2.5 to 3.0
Cement	0.8 to 1.0	2 to 3	2 to 10	20 to 25
Petroleum refining	1.75	none	1.75	193 without transport
Steel	1.0 to 2.5	2 to 5	2 to 10	265 to 665
Rayon	4.0 to 6.0	no estimate		50 to 75
Cigarets	5.0 to 6.0	slight	15 to 20	125 to 150
Gypsum products	2.5 to 3.0	small	27 to 33	5 to 6
Autos	5.0 to 10.0	no estimate	5 to 10	250 to 500
Tractors	10.0 to 15.0	no estimate	10 to 15	125

Source: J. S. Bain, "Economies of Scale, Concentration, and Entry," *American Economic Review*, March, 1954, pp. 15–39. Dr. J. M. Blair, in a comparison of trends in plant as contrasted with company concentration, concluded: "This evidence would tend to support the hypothesis that technology has reversed its long-term trend and is now making for optimal efficiency in smaller sizes of plants." See *Economic Concentration* (Hearings . . . Subcommittee on Antitrust and Monopoly . . . Senate . . . Part 4, "Concentration and Efficiency" [Washington, D.C.: U.S. Government Printing Office, 1965]), p. 1550.

cases, capital requirements for establishing a new plant would be large enough to constitute a serious obstacle to new entrants. Many times, however, the findings were substantially different: efficiency does not require plants that (1) are large in relation to the national market or (2) need great amounts of capital. The economies of having several plants in the same firm were nonexistent or small in all but a few of the industries for which estimates were obtained. Limiting factors tend to be much more significant for regional than for national markets, and, in some cases, markets *must* be regional because of high transport costs.

Are big companies generally more efficient than small? Figure 20–1 compares rates of return on investment, averaged for 5 years in each case, for the 10 largest corporations in 30 industries. For these companies there was absolutely no relationship between size and profitability. Generally, economists point out, profit figures are too complex for unequivocal conclusions—even if we could agree upon definitions of "big" and "small." Businesses keep their accounts in different ways and have differ-

FIGURE 20–1. Average Rates of Return, 1959–63 for 290 Manufacturing Corporations in 30 Industries (Arrayed by 1963 Asset Rank in Own Industry)

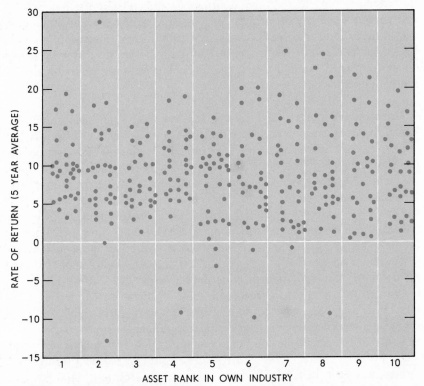

Source: Economic Concentration (Hearings . . . Subcommittee on Antitrust and Monopoly . . . Senate . . . Part 4, "Concentration and Efficiency" [Washington, D.C.: U.S. Government Printing Office, 1965]), p. 1552.

ent kinds of financial structures that make comparison of earnings difficult. Problems and opportunities vary. Moreover, even if big firms do show higher profits than small ones per dollar of capital or sales—and this is by no means uniformly true—lower cost per unit of output is not necessarily the reason. Some of the gain from great size may be the result of monopolistic power which benefits the owners at the expense of the public, with no saving of inputs per unit of output. To the businessman and stockholder, productive and bargaining advantages are of essentially equal worth; for the economy as a whole, however, bargaining advantages which do not also represent some real productive saving somewhere are of little or no net benefit.

In most industries, medium-sized and small businesses survive despite the presence of giants. Firms not more than one tenth the size of the largest survive and prosper, presumably giving at least as good a product as the biggest companies at no higher price. The giants freely choose to buy from, and sell to, much smaller firms rather than make, or distribute, many things themselves. If large size were clearly a source of great efficiency, would not the biggest firms become still more self-sufficient? The answer is not certain. We are probably right, however, in concluding that in many industries small units successfully meet competition from the giants. In such industries, therefore, antitrust policy need not be determined by fear that action against bigness will necessarily be action against productive efficiency.

Unsolved Problems.   *Objectives* are less clear than they might be. What do Americans really seek in antitrust policy? Can we formulate our objectives so they can serve more effectively as guides? For example, no real agreement is near on an issue related closely to that just discussed, "bigness." Present laws do not attempt to deal with problems of great size as such. Today (1967) one of the chief issues is that of mergers of companies in different lines of business. What, for example, will be the long-run results if large firms acquire smaller ones in other lines of business—conglomerate mergers? Are owners of small companies to be denied the opportunity to sell out to larger ones? What should be the policy when a merger will provide needed capital to a weak company, strengthen management, increase efficiency in marketing or research, facilitate exports, or serve other purposes which seem in the public interest? Bigness, however, is not a matter of slight significance.

Some members of the business community ask for greater *certainty*. They want a clearer idea of what is permitted and what prohibited. Others, however, believe that the law and administration should be more flexible. Movement toward one goal often means movement away from the other.

A serious attempt to lay down principles which the Department of Justice and Federal Trade Commission will follow in merger cases ran into great difficulty. Conditions differ in every conceivable respect. One specific result, however, was announced in 1967. In the food distribution industry, immediate attention, that is, potential challenge, would be given to any proposed acquisition by a food chain with sales over $500 million a year. Market-extension mergers by food chains with sales under $500 million would probably not be deemed to "pose a serious threat to competition."

Present policy considers seriously the challenge of any proposed merger acquisition by one of the three or four largest companies in an industry, dairy and cement, for example. But there has been no challenge for an apparently large number of acquisitions by firms which, though perhaps big by many standards, are not among the very top rank in the industry. The result will be fewer firms in the industry but enough, it is hoped, to prevent monopolization and to keep competition active. The importance of companies of "medium-rank" size will grow relative to that of the top three or four.

A little-recognized problem grows out of the way by which antitrust law actually comes into being. Much of the content of the law consists of the interpretations of the courts. Judges have the final say, at least until Congress by a new statute overrules the judiciary. Not all issues, however, get presented to courts for clear decision. And those that are litigated do not always, or even usually, force full analysis of the economic issues. The lawyers on both sides in our type of adversary proceeding try to win; their job is not to lead the courts to decisions which are best for the public as a whole. The wordings of the judges will guide businessmen and government officials; but there is no systematic procedure for assuring that the evidence and argument presented will represent the best of economics.

Other problems arise from doubt about the best way to serve the public interest where there are issues of exclusive dealerships, or restrictive agreements with subsidiaries, or operations abroad, or labor unions, or patents. Another puzzler is how to deal with oligopoly. In markets where a small number of sellers predominate, there may be no agreed-upon "parallelism of action" (that can be proved), perhaps not even a conscious policy. But the results may be a restriction of the economizing type of competition, with prices higher, and output less, than basic economic conditions justify.

One approach is to emphasize *structure* of an industry, especially the number of sellers, the opportunity for new entrants, and the absence of collusion. If there are "many" rather than "few" firms, or if entry of new productive capacity is easy, serious restrictions on competition are unlikely to last for long. Yet we ask, "Isn't big size needed to get economies of scale?" Once again we face the fact that a market may be too small for many big sellers and ask, "How big is best?" A football team averaging 200 pounds may be superior to one averaging 150 pounds and also superior to one averaging 250 pounds. Agility as well as weight is desirable; beyond some point, size is less beneficial than other qualities. (Perhaps giant firms and labor unions should have the burden of proving that their size is positively in the public interest.) The economist cannot specify industry structural characteristics that will be an adequate guide in all cases.

Perhaps, then, we can judge from *performance*, industry by industry, whether there is enough competition to be "workable." Are results in terms of price, wages, profits, technical progress, and other criteria apparently satisfactory? Unfortunately, we do not have clear standards by which performance in specific cases can be judged. And what if dominance results at least partly from success in free, open competition without the use of any methods that are predatory, morally reprehensible, or in violation of law?

Sometimes, a commonsense, pragmatic approach can lead to satisfactory judgments even though there is no formula or clear principle. As some economists argue, however, a performance test is not adequate because it does not show what was responsible for the result. Is there not great difference in the case in which the pressures of economic forces bring the result from that in which the suffrance of one or two powerful companies permitted the outcome?

Additional comments and evaluations are made in the next chapter.

TERMS AND CONCEPTS

Sherman Act	consent decree	natural monopoly
"charter of freedom"	Clayton Act	obligation to serve
conspiracy	*nolo contendere*	rate base
restraint of trade	treble damage	rate of return
interlocking directorate	market-extension	rate structure
per se rule	merger	value of service
horizontal agreement	conscious parallelism	peak-load problem
cross elasticity of demand	structure of an industry	certificate of convenience and necessity
vertical agreement	common carrier	yardstick
"relevant market"	eminent domain	exclusive dealership

QUESTIONS

1. What does the Sherman Act prohibit? The Clayton Act?
2. What are the functions of the Federal Trade Commission?
3. What broad interests of the public call for antimonopoly policy? How do they differ from, and resemble, the objectives of policies to eliminate unfair methods of competition?
4. What attitude do our laws as interpreted by the Supreme Court take toward mergers?
5. How can the existence of monopoly lead to unemployment?
6. How do concerns about the best size of business influence the formulation of wise government policy toward monopoly?
7. How do industry structure and performance differ as guides for antitrust policy?
8. Why do regulatory commissions permit rate discrimination in utility charges?

APPENDIX

Public Utilities and Their Regulation

The price-output policies of public utilities created some of the most burning economic problems of our grandfathers' day. Government regulation resulted—and continues. It offers one way to deal with monopoly. Perhaps it will enable us to get most of the best features of private management while we utilize government to prevent the social losses that might arise from monopoly. Yet, despite two thirds of a century of experience with regulation, there is still much uncertainty about (a) the best methods and (b) the extent to which we can wisely apply public utility treatment where competition seems inadequate. It is indeed sobering to note that the industry with the longest history of governmental regulation (banking excepted)—railroads—has been neither prosperous nor markedly progressive.

Today, industries commonly considered to be utilities originate about 7 percent of national income and employ 5 percent of the labor force. Our chief concern with such industries is not so much their size in the economy as our desire to get good, and constantly improving, services as economically as possible.

What Is a Public Utility? Certain features are generally common to public utilities, privately owned businesses "affected with a public interest," such as railroad, pipeline, electricity, gas, water, local transit, telephone, and telegraph companies.[1]

1. The business is a *common carrier*. It will serve anyone who will pay the price. The facilities exist for the entire public. The owner may not deny the use of the transportation, power, communication, or other facilities to anyone who will pay the price and meet other conditions.

2. To provide the service, a public utility must extend its physical plant through areas owned by others. Therefore, it must have special legal powers to compel property owners to sell, or to permit it to intrude on, their property, for fair compensation. Governments possess this power of *eminent domain* and may give it to others in the public interest.

3. Utilities are often *natural monopolies*. A single supplier in an area can provide better and cheaper service than two or more. It is worse than a nuisance to have two or more telephone systems in a city. When more than one set of gas mains or electric lines serve the same area, wasteful duplication

---

[1] The dividing line between utilities and nonutilities is not always drawn clearly. Generally, we exclude (a) economic organizations owned by governments and (b) such regulated businesses as banks and insurance companies. Borderline cases include airlines, trucking companies, radio and TV broadcasting, taxicabs, grain elevators, and milk distribution.

of facilities results. Through a big range, production is carried on under conditions of decreasing cost per unit. A public utility, therefore, is generally a business whose best size (the optimum scale) is very large, relative to the size of the market. Often it is the only supplier.

4. An *exclusive franchise* from government often seals the monopoly powers of a public utility; government will prevent anyone else from supplying the same service.

5. The services supplied have a high degree of essentiality, at least to some users and for some purposes. *Demand is inelastic* through a considerable range. Service of good quality is important to the public. If we have no choice, we would often be willing to pay more than the full long-run costs of providing the service.

Regulation: Agencies and Major Concerns.   Although local governments do some utility regulation, most is state and federal. Because of the Supreme Court's broad interpretation of "interstate commerce," federal authority may extend widely. Nevertheless, states regulate a large and important range of activities. The Interstate Commerce Commission (1887) regulates railroads and some buses, trucks, and pipelines. Interstate sales of electricity and natural gas are regulated by the Federal Power Commission; the Federal Communications Commission has varying authority over radio, telephone, telegraph, and television companies; the Civil Aeronautics Board provides economic and safety regulation of the air transport industry.

Usually the top officials of a commission are appointed, but in some states they are elected. Commissions are quasi-administrative and quasi-judicial; although their decisions may be taken to court for review, the cost of such appeal is usually prohibitive. Commissions and their staffs are of highly uneven quality. Regulatory agencies often develop attitudes favorable to the industries they regulate. Close contact leads to familiarity and sympathy, and the industry may work successfully to get appointments for its friends. Commission procedures are often slow, clumsy, and expensive. The Federal Power Commission estimated in 1960 that 13 years would be needed to dispose of cases on hand; new ones would accumulate meanwhile; if its staff were tripled, it could become current by 2043 A.D. New methods, however, have enabled it to expedite operations.

What aspects of a utility's affairs may a commission regulate? Ordinarily regulation covers the broad outlines of the services to be provided. They must be reasonably adequate and offered impartially, without undue or personal discrimination. It is this *obligation to serve* which explains, for example, why a railroad maintains a line that has not paid its costs for years, or why city buses regularly make some runs that seldom pay. Prohibition of unreasonable discrimination rests on the fact that people do not have a good alternative; if the members of the community give a monopoly, they want equal chances at the service. (But does the public have an obligation to help pay the expenses?) Of course, the utility's financial position may not permit it to provide as *much* service at a loss as the public wants. Moreover, we often want higher *quality* service than utilities provide—more frequent and less crowded buses. Generally, however, the rates utilities charge get most attention, and government regulation seems to center around rates. (Yet the FCC, which assigns radio and TV channels for exclusive use, has no authority over the rates charged advertisers.)

Elements of Regulation: A Summary. A formula can summarize the chief elements of regulation as it operates (quality of service excepted).

$$R = O + r(V - D)$$

R is total revenue, the amounts received from customers. O is operating expense; r is rate of return. $V - D$ is the rate base. It is made up of V, the original cost (or value as determined in some other way) of the property, minus D, the accumulated depreciation of the property.

Rate Base. In *Smyth* v. *Ames* (1898), the Supreme Court held that rates must allow "fair return on a fair value." The total earnings were to be measured by the amount of capital put into the business. The more dollars invested, the more dollars to be earned. This investment is the *rate base*.

But what investment? How can a commission find the investment in a railroad or telephone business? For many decades these questions aroused intense debate. Utility managements tried hard to get a rate base above anything like a reasonably prudent price for the productive facilities used, but most of the old problems have now receded to the background. Company records of purchases minus disposals and depreciation are now widely used and tolerably satisfactory.

If there has been price inflation, however, this method cannot encourage the best utilization of resources. Utility service rates will get out of line with current costs of providing the capacity. An out-of-date rate base leads to underpricing of utility services; we shall not economize enough. If further rises in the price level seem probable, investors will hardly provide new capital if the utility's future earnings are to be controlled without regard to changes in the value of money.

In the *Hope Natural Gas* case (1944), the Supreme Court held, among other things, that earnings must be high enough to permit the utility to attract capital on reasonable terms as needed to serve the public. The "end result" of the regulation becomes the significant criterion.

Rate of Return. Another part of the job is to fix the percentage the utility may try to earn on the rate base. Should it be 8 percent or 4? Utilities these days receive over half of their funds for 5½ percent (less on some old borrowings)—in bonds. Half of the over $55 billion invested in privately owned electric utilities is debt. The common stock equity funds, however, will require the prospect of a higher return if the utility seeks them in the market. But what rate? How much should be allowed on equity already invested?

The rate should be high enough to maintain a credit that will enable the utility to get new capital, on terms fair to the old stockholders, if the public needs more facilities. But debt or equity capital? In what proportions? We can, of course look at yields of other property, but what is truly comparable? Utilities seldom offer the investor a chance for large gain, but their monopoly position may give them great security. Some utilities, however, have no strong monopoly position, as many a railroad manager knows. A drop in consumer demand can hit any monopoly. Expansion to meet boom demands may make utilities vulnerable during a recession.

Commission rulings allow rates which, after income tax, generally fall within the wide range of 6 to 8 percent on the rate base as a whole (even though debts and preferred stock may cost less).[2] Franchises may occasionally specify the rate of return, and in some states a statute or court decision sets the figure. In 1967 the FCC decided that 7 to 7.5 percent was enough for AT&T; the company had pressed vigorously for at least 8 percent, emphasizing its continuing need to raise large amounts of capital.

Rate Structure. If the rate base is $10 million and the rate 6 percent, the authorized earnings each year would be $600,000. The next thing is to set rates which will collect $600,000, plus costs of operations, from users. Perhaps no possible set of rates will meet the goal. Demand may simply be inadequate. More probably, any of many combinations of rates would do the job.

Some utilities may have few charges—the city bus line or a gas or water company in a small town. A railroad, however, may have hundreds of thousands of separate rates; electric and telephone companies may have hundreds. Often there is elaborate price (rate) discrimination. It seeks to take advantage of differences in "value of the service."[3] Why not vary rates according to costs? Usually, costs are an inadequate guide. No one can know the exact cost of any specific service. Fixed costs are generally large, especially in the short run. Each service is a joint product. Most fixed capacity produces many services simultaneously. How, then, shall the joint costs be divided? It is impossible (1) to make rates as a whole cover costs as a whole (including fair return) and (2) to make individual rates equate with specific costs.

Spokesmen for particular groups of users are likely to argue, in effect: "The other fellows should pay the overhead." The 59 million residential customers of electric utilities, buying less than one fourth of total current, may want the 310,000 large industrial users, who buy nearly half the total output, to pay over half the overhead costs, and vice versa. In practice, political and social pressures are likely to play a part in decisions on how different groups of users shall share fixed costs. Schoolchildren may get lower transit fares; hospitals or government agencies may receive favored treatment, not because of any differences in cost. Farmers, export industries, or almost any group may try for favors. Differences in the strength of competitive pressures must be considered.

Demands for different services have different elasticity. Where the quantity purchased may not vary much with the charge—perhaps gas for cooking—the rate, without seeming exorbitant, can be set to bring a handsome profit. However, where the quantity of the service bought is sensitive to price—rail versus truck transport of perishables—perhaps the highest rate

---

[2] If the rate is 6 percent on all the investment, and half is obtained on debt that was incurred in the past and which costs only 4 percent, the amount for owners of common stock is 8 percent of their investment. Railroad earnings seldom reach even 4 percent on total investment.

[3] Trucks have been able to avoid some of the unprofitable business that has plagued the railroads by putting trucking rates on such service too high, by never undertaking to provide the service in the product or to the community, and, in many cases, by remaining private, rather than common, carriers. A diet confined to the cream is more nourishing than one with a large mixture of the skim milk.

possible may yield little above variable costs. Any effort to make such services contribute as much, relatively, toward overhead costs as in gas for cooking will drive away business. For some services, no possible rate may cover even variable costs. If such a service is to continue, someone must subsidize users who do not pay their own way.

It would help if commissions (and managements) knew more about elasticity of demand. Without doubt, some price discrimination is necessary to obtain best use of resources. Consumer A may find it difficult to see why charging B a lower rate helps keep A's rate down; yet if B bought substantially less because of a higher rate, A would have to pay more of the overhead. Railroad charges of less for a long haul, say Chicago to New York, than for a short haul along the same line may seem unfair. Yet the differences may be eminently wise. Retention of the long-haul business helps meet some of the common costs. Users who pay high rates may actually benefit from the sales to others more cheaply—unless the two are in direct competition. The same principle applies to the low price of electric power to business users who can set up their own generating plants.

More extensive discrimination might lead to better resource allocation. The same rate for all times will not help adjust consumption to different production conditions. To meet the 5 P.M., December 21, or hot sultry summer day peak-demand for electricity, producers need capacity that may be idle all spring and fall. Figure 20–2 illustrates the broad problem of uneven demand when fixed facilities loom large in total productive capacity. We could obtain a better use of resources by rates which forced more economy in consumption at the peak, and then stimulated consumption when productive capacity would otherwise be idle. Electric rates are adjusted somewhat to favor off-peak use (especially for industrial users). Telephone rates encourage evening use of long-distance lines.

Rate structures which yield about the same total net income can vary widely. In general, the problem is so complex, and the data needed for refined answers are so scanty, that the results have a big element of hit-or-miss. The structure is usually that proposed by the utilities themselves except as modified because of the efforts of particular user groups.[4]

Expenses. Can utilities spend whatever they want on operating expenses and make the public pay? What are the incentives to economy? These questions raise difficult, but unsolved, problems. Utilities must compete for capital, labor, and materials; so they must pay at least going prices. They may pay more if they wish or are careless. What about the quantities they use? If the consumer can be forced to pay any set of costs and if the income available to owners is fixed regardless of the quality of management, the normal competitive drives for efficiency lose their punch. Laxity in cost control will not, as a rule, be shown up by a competitor.

Staffs may be wastefully large. Yet when sleet and wind stop electric or telephone service, we are glad that the utility had crews for the emergency.

---

[4] Rates taking fuller account of marginal cost, rather than total cost, could lead to more productive resource allocation. Economists have had little success, however, in persuading utilities or regulatory authorities of the practical value of such guides for rate making.

FIGURE 20–2.   Peak-Load Problem

This hypothetical case illustrates the peak-load cost problem. To meet the demands of late afternoon, the company must have fixed capacity adequate for *OM*. Most of the facilities represented by *NM* will be idle all the rest of the time. Even the capacity to produce *QN* will be idle most of the time. Clearly, the producer has reason to develop discriminatory pricing policies to reduce demand around 6 PM and raise it most of the rest of the day.

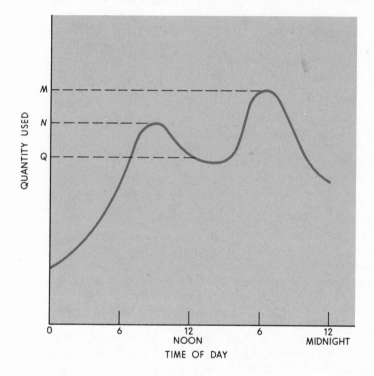

Buildings may seem unnecessarily nice, but expensive equipment may warrant careful housing. Orders may be given to friends or associated firms, but some highly intricate equipment must be made to order. Capacity may be excessive, yet it may represent careful economic preparation for later growth. Advertising is needed to inform customers and to plead the utility's case; yet some may be waste. Proper charges for depreciation (and obsolescence) present an unending problem for these "capital intensive" businesses (using exceptionally large amounts of capital per employee or per unit of service). How much should utility A in an eastern city pay to utility B in Texas for natural gas?

Generally, regulatory authorities intervene little in internal utility management. Yet government controls on utility operating costs exist. Expansions and new investments, to varying degrees, require "certificates of convenience and necessity"; companies must justify their plans. In the 1920's, some electric companies paid outrageously for services received from unregulated units of the same utility system; but holding company structures have been reformed. Some regulatory authorities have power to pass upon the type of security to be sold and to require competitive bidding on security issues.

Commissions do not, however, participate in decisions on wage rates or working rules. Decades of government regulation of railroads did nothing to eliminate the waste of featherbedding. Utilities themselves show widely different records of initiative in efforts to reduce costs and improve service.

If you were seeking a way to induce efficiency, you would hardly devise our system of utility rate regulation. Why, then, have many utilities made such progress in operating efficiency, in more output per unit of input?

FIGURE 20–3. Electric Rates and Usage, 1926–66

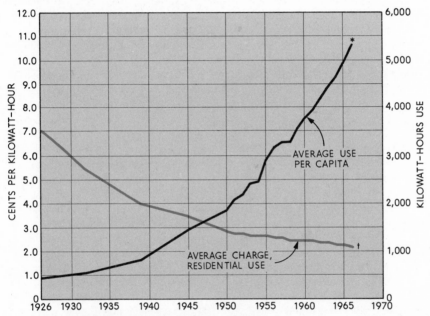

* Kilowatt hours per capita. Does not include electricity used by the producer. In 1966 such use was about 9 percent as large as all sales of electricity.

† Cents per hour. Residential rates are higher than those for commercial and industrial use. During the period 1926–66 the charge for small commercial and industrial use went from 4.5 to 2.1 cents per kilowatt hour; for large users the rate went from 1.5 to 0.9 cents.

Source: Edison Electric Institute.

Figure 20–3 shows electric rates and consumption over 40 years. While wages, materials, and taxes more than doubled in price, after 1940, telephone rates went up less than 40 percent. Railroad wage rates averaging about $3.20 an hour in 1966 were over four times the 1940 average, but the average charge for carrying a ton of freight a mile was only a little higher than in 1940. There are probably many explanations. In some cases general increases in demand brought fuller use of fixed plant. The desire of managements to do a good job, the "instinct of workmanship," is important. So, of course, has been the general progress of technology. Some gains are the result of initiative on the part of suppliers in improving equipment.

The pressure of competition explains part of the progress. Some utilities, such as railroads, have been up against intensive competition: trucks, buses, pipelines, airplanes, waterways, and industry relocation. Many other utilities have enough competition to make lethargy dangerous. Cheap air mail, for example, hurt the telegraph company. Privately owned electric power companies have been worried about government projects. Natural gas adds competition for electricity. Large users of electricity may set up their own generating capacity; in fact, private industrial plants, for their own use, generate almost as much electric power as all federal government facilities. Other products and services are always rivals.

Utility earnings have frequently been below the amounts authorized by commissions. Thus, management success in raising profits would not need to be given over to customers. Operating costs and taxes have risen, but the regulatory agencies have typically been slow in permitting utilities to pass cost increases on to users. Managements are pressed for efficiency. Yet some students of utilities criticize the inertia and poor quality of some managements, their lack of effort to produce technical advance, and the spirit of "using" regulation to consolidate a position of unprogressive monopoly.

By what standards should regulation be judged? Surprisingly little attention seems to have been given to the problem of evaluating the effectiveness of regulation, or the need.[5]

Keeping Regulation Up to Date. In a progressive economy, it seems difficult to keep regulation up to date. Conditions change more rapidly than the practices of regulatory authorities and the policies of legislatures and courts.

This lag has been markedly true in the case of the utility which has been regulated longest, railroads. Developing a rational transportation policy has been impeded by failure to keep regulation of railroads, trucks, and other carriers in line with real-world developments, to encourage each to concentrate on the type of service for which it is best suited. Railroads are still regarded almost as if they had their pre-World War I monopoly power. Only in 1958 did Congress begin to allow them a bit more freedom to compete more effectively with new types of carriers which have taken away more and more of the profitable traffic. Railroads in some cases, but not always, have been denied permission to reduce rates to use their capacity more fully. Meanwhile, a basic industry, transportation, has been somewhat distorted. New vested interests have developed and threaten the modernization of regulatory policy. Will other regulated industries be hampered by lags in public policy? The danger cannot be denied.

Government Operation versus Regulation. A good way to start an argument, in many groups, is to suggest that government should shift from

---

[5] One study undertaken "to investigate the feasibility of measuring the effects of regulation" reported an "inability to find any significant effects of the regulation of electrical utilities. . . ." G. J. Stigler and C. Friedland, "What Can Regulators Regulate? The Case of Electricity," *Journal of Law and Economics,* October, 1962, pp. 1–16. The authors have concluded that the "ineffectiveness of regulation" lies in the fact that individual utility systems do not have any great amount of long-run monopoly power and that regulatory bodies cannot in fact control any specified combination of output, price, and cost. The major point, however, is that we need greater analysis of purposes and results of regulation.

regulating utilities to actually owning and operating them. It is surprisingly difficult to stop such arguments. In fact, of course, there is today much government ownership and operation: the postal system, most water supply systems, about one sixth of all electric generating capacity, buses and subways. What do the facts show? What does theory suggest? Can we obtain service at lower cost, get better progress, or achieve other goals, by government operation rather than regulation?

One thing is clear. A community can make an initial saving by "municipalizing" its utilities. Federal and state taxes disappear as costs. In addition, agencies of state and local governments, because interest on their bonds is tax exempt, can borrow more cheaply than private utilities. Such savings, of course, are at the expense of the general body of federal taxpayers. Yet the fact that such advantages can be gained does create a reason for local and even state governments to "socialize" utilities. If municipal management is just the same as private management, tax savings can make municipal ownership advantageous to local consumers.

Beyond such "phony" economies, it is difficult to make valid comparison between private operation under regulation and government ownership and operation.[6] The localized nature of utilities hinders comparison of one with another. Nor can we compare *quality of service* satisfactorily.

The largest government-owned enterprise-type operation, the postal system, differs from private utilities in various respects. The freedom of private management to seek capital and to adopt economizing methods, independent of legislative appropriations, has proved an advantage. Yet some municipal utilities, perhaps in part because they possess considerable autonomy, have done well.

Since the mid-1930's, government ownership and operation of electric utilities has increased from 9 to 24 percent of the country's generating capacity (including what industries have for their own use). Just over half is owned by the federal government. Yet privately owned companies have expanded so greatly that their *growth* alone since 1955 has been twice as large as the total 1966 capacity of all governmentally owned plants, including the great hydro-electric installations such as Bonneville and Grand Coulee. Government expansion has obviously not killed the private industry. One signifi-

---

[6] If one does not know how a thing can be operated best, a logical procedure is to set up a controlled experiment. Government operation of utilities has been urged for just this purpose—to provide a "yardstick." What are the most efficient operating costs and practices? What patterns of rates give what results? Unbiased, imaginative, unhampered experimentation might help answer some big questions. On the whole, however, the results have been inconclusive. Where the federal government is a big supplier of electric power on a wholesale basis to both municipally owned and privately owned companies, the existence of two different kinds of organizations for retailing electricity may give some check. Yet tax exemption of municipally owned utilities, and below-cost provision of service to local government agencies, have created differences for which it proves difficult to adjust satisfactorily. Regional variations; special features of individual localities; the combination of different activities (in such multiple-purpose projects as TVA); the disruption of war; the lack of experimentation with rate structures; and budgetary and other restrictions on the "yardstick" managements—all these have made it difficult to help test and guide the regulation of private utilities, or to judge where government ownership appears better.

cant development, in fact, has been the growth of cooperation between private and government agencies. Federal aid for rural electrification has filled a gap private utilities had left.

Current Issues of Regulation and Utility Policy. This country faces important problems of utility economics. How shall the nation's transportation system develop? The question involves railroads, airlines, the merchant marine, trucks, pipelines, highways, local transit facilities, autos, and waterways. A few receive direct government subsidy. More get indirect help in the form of tax exemption or provision of such facilities as airports or city streets at less than full cost—or in the case of waterways (except the St. Lawrence) free. Others, especially railroads, are taxed heavily for general public purposes. Some are regulated strictly, while others, such as firms providing their own truck or barge facilities, are exempt from regulation. What policies will encourage a more efficient transportation structure—from the level that touches us immediately (local transit and parking) to the expenditure of fabulous sums on vast highway expansion? Freer competition, especially extensive decontrol of railroads, is part of the answer. Consolidations and abandonment of some facilities will reduce expenses. More equal tax treatment would also help get more rational use of resources. There are even good arguments for subsidy in some cases. Developing the best transport system requires planning on a large scale. Nevertheless, the interests involved, from small truckers to giant railroads or from the national public as a whole to the smallest village—such interests are so varied that comprehensive treatment is difficult. How shall the federal program for urban mass transit adopted in 1964 be developed to bring the public the best of value?

A second problem raises quite different issues. Taxpayers have spent large amounts for space, atomic, and military research. The potential peaceful uses will be many and varied. There is no prospect that government activities will, or even could, expand to bring us all the benefits. As private firms begin to use this new knowledge, however, we face contrasting issues. We want to assure ourselves that we shall not be charged by private producers for the results of research we have already paid for as taxpayers. Yet we can obtain full benefits only if incentives offered are large enough to offset the risks remaining.

Another issue results from the expansion of use of natural gas. The Supreme Court has ruled that the FPC may regulate not only the transmission of gas but also the terms of sale where it comes from the ground. Gas producers, however, wish to free such sale from federal regulation. They press Congress for a law to remove this power from the FPC. On the other hand, mayors and other representatives of consumers want regulation which they believe will keep rates to users "reasonable," not only for transmission but also for the gas as it leaves the earth.

Why does government give away valuable radio and TV channel monopolies? Why not auction them to the highest bidder? What will happen if more large businesses set up their own microwave radio long-distance telephone systems, depriving the common carrier of important parts of the market? How can we best deal with air and water pollution? Rent control, establishment of subscription TV, "public" housing, public versus private provision of additional power in the TVA area, and expansion of water-supply facilities are only a few of the other issues of public policy which touch upon economic problems of the kind we have discussed. Informed and unbiased use of economic principles can help toward good solutions.

Finally, covering the whole field, is a set of questions involving leadership—of men and of principles. Can we get and keep more really top-quality commission personnel? Will utilities attract, and give scope to, an appropriate quantity of managerial talent and scientific skill? Can better, more truly progressive, guides for regulation be devised and made effective? Can the responsibilities of regulation be reduced by an expansion of competition? or of government operation? Might the offer of higher profit for better effort induce better quality, or less expensive, service?

21

OTHER GOVERNMENT POLICIES
TOWARD BUSINESS

Decentralization of economic power has long been considered desirable for social and political reasons, as well as for its contribution to an efficient economy. Absence of active competition tends to result in higher prices and lower output, and thus in a less efficient allocation of resources. Noncompetitive industries may also lack the spur to innovation and change, as sellers find it easier as well as more profitable to use obsolete facilities or produce familiar products. They may be less concerned with keeping their costs under control if they have no difficulty in passing higher costs along to their customers.

Council of Economic Advisers (1965)

Consumers and businesses both need protection against some types of competition. Otherwise, abuses of free markets would lead to wastes which would be costly to society as well as to individuals.

PREVENTING UNFAIR COMPETITION

Misrepresentation of many types can deceive consumers. Without present "policing" there would be much more. The record of past actions demonstrates clearly that some firms will use deceit of many kinds. Not all consumers can protect themselves.

Businesses, too, suffer from disreputable actions of others. Coercion, bribery, malicious price discrimination, deliberate misrepresentation, cutting off of sources of supply, bribing employees of customers and competitors, spying, disparaging the products of competitors, sabotage, and raiding key employees of competitors are some of the practices whose use has been proved in court.

The Federal Trade Commission is the active agency for "policing" business practices (in interstate commerce). The Commission is a bipartisan body of five men appointed by the President. It has a staff of investigators, accountants, attorneys, and statisticians. In addition to its work enforcing the antitrust laws, it tries to prevent unfair competition, to nip bad practices in the bud before they crowd out other more desirable growth. Most of its energies go to investigating complaints of businesses about actions of competitors. On its own, however, the FTC can take the initiative and analyze practices it considers of questionable fairness, especially those involving the consumer. If businesses request, the Commission can study and render an opinion about the legality of a specific business practice.

The FTC's job is chiefly preventive. As an administrative agency that both prosecutes and judges (within limits), it can provide prompter, cheaper, simpler, and more expert action than court procedure. It can also be arbitrary, biased, legalistic, slow, and wrong. (Any "policeman doing his job" will be accused on one or more of these unattractive attitudes.) The staff, around 1,200 including clerical and stenographic, is too small for thorough discharge of varied responsibilities. The 1968 appropriation was $65 million.

The Commission receives about 7,000 complaints a year. Its staff will study those that seem most important—perhaps 2,000—hold hearings, and try to work out mutually satisfactory settlements. Apparent infringements of law will be discussed with the firm involved. A "stipulation," preventing repetition, may be agreed upon; about 9,500 are on the record. In fact, it does much semiarbitration of disputes between competitors. The Commissioners themselves pass on cases that are not settled by the staff. Decisions may produce "cease and desist orders" which, in case of violation, are subject to court injunction; around 7,000 are in effect. However, if a business wishes—and can afford the expense—it may contest a Commission decision in court.

The FTC helps business groups (trade associations) work out standards of competition. About 170 formal trade conference rules are in force. Such activity can play a constructive part in regularizing business practice, but it can also become a method of restricting types of competition that serve the public interest. Here is a knotty problem: defining and establishing conditions for rivalry. These conditions must induce efficiency and progress, for which order is essential; but we do not want them to lead businesses to insulate themselves from competitive stresses.

Competition is not always pleasant for competitors. The FTC thereby faces a dilemma. Part of its job is to protect competitors from unfair competition, while another part of its job is to help preserve competition. The puzzler here is one which runs through the whole range of governmental policies toward business. If competition is vigorous and effective, if it is ingenious, imaginative, and stimulating, it will also hurt the less successful competitors, who may feel aggrieved. What then is "unfair"? Is it unfair to be smarter or more industrious or more efficient than the other fellow? He may think so. Pressures to protect competitors may in fact be requests for the easing of competition, for "soft" instead of "hard" competition, for shielding the company whose performance cannot on its merits match that of others.[1]

In trying to protect consumers (and businesses which observe acceptable standards), the FTC conducts active campaigns against "deceptive practices." It checks on the validity of claims by advertisers of patent medicines, wool and fur products, textiles, and recently a much broader range of items and practices. Intensified struggle for business has brought an upsurge in deceptive advertising, phony "bargains," and misleading business practices, all of which increase the need for the FTC—and its enforcement job.

HAVE POLICIES SUCCEEDED?

Not many years ago a random survey of opinion of economists would probably have revealed extensive discouragement about the effectiveness of policies to check monopoly and encourage competition. Today, however, one would probably find more optimism.

Is Concentration Increasing?   Is American business becoming more concentrated? Are the big firms becoming *relatively* more powerful than in the past? Shortly after the war the general opinion was that concentration was increasing. Certainly the 200 or so largest corporations were growing, mergers continued, and orders for defense poured predominantly into a few giant firms.

---

[1] An actual case will illustrate. Its outcome was happier for competition than are some. The FTC "alleged that National Dairy's Kraft Foods Division sold a marshmallow cream topping . . . to its outlets in the Philadelphia, Pennsylvania, and Boston, Massachusetts, trading areas and in other New England States at prices lower than those at which it sold Marshmallow Cream in other trade areas. . . . The theory of the complaint . . . is that these price differentials 'have been or may be substantially to lessen competition. . . .' Everything was nice, sleepy and cozy until Kraft decided to get into the marshmallow cream topping business and sell in the areas sold by Durkee, Tweet and Cremo. In New England, Durkee had 92% of the market. Naturally, this strength provided no incentive for it to become competitive. [Evidence is cited.] This complacency in the marshmallow cream topping market suggests that it was ripe for a jolt and that it needed a little progressive competition. . . . Unquestionably, it got that jolt when Kraft entered the business, but the jolt was not harmful. It was, on the contrary, beneficial in several respects. . . . Certainly, the introduction of a new product, even by an old company, is a legitimate commercial objective. If losses are incurred in that venture . . . the mere fact that they are incurred is not a demonstration of predatory intent to justify a conclusion that the conduct was of a nature tending to lessen competition, create a monopoly or to injure, destroy or prevent competition in any market. . . . Only a company like Kraft seemed to have been willing to use the risk capital to make the entry. It did. Its successful entry, at the cost incurred by it, creating competition where none had existed effectively before, should not be cause for saying that it violated Section 2(a) of the Clayton Act, as amended." From the *Initial Decision* by the FTC Hearing Examiner *In the Matter of National Dairy Products . . .* Docket No. 8548 (1964). The examiner had not supported the allegations of the FTC.

Though statistics are not complete enough to give a clear measure, no *large* growth of concentration appears to have developed. True, from 1947 to 1963 the 200 largest companies in manufacturing increased their share of value added by manufacturing from 30 to 37 percent (and 4 more percentage points by 1963). More refined analysis, however, leads to the conclusion that variation from industry to industry is so great that a global figure signifies little. For 375 manufacturing industries the percentage of employment by the four largest firms in each industry rose, but not much—from 34.6 to 35.3. "The analysis demonstrates that, taken alone, the movement in average concentration has little significance. What seems to be more important is the suggestion that the turnover among industries, and this is pronounced in a modern large industrial system, operates to limit the growth of concentration levels."[2] Analysis of 213 industries showed that from 1947 to 1963 concentration among the largest four firms dropped 3 percentage points or more in 86 cases. In 81 cases there was a rise of 3 percentage points or more. Declines were much greater than rises in producer goods industries. In consumer goods industries, however, concentration rose more often than it fell; the advantage of large size lies, not so much in economies of scale in production as in advertising, promotion, and distribution.

Smaller firms have grown, maintaining their relative position in many industries. New businesses have become established. Today's leaders include firms unknown half a century ago and do not include some that were prominent then.[3] Firms, large and small, in one industry enter others. Imports introduce competition from abroad. The industrial giants subcontract and buy parts and supplies from thousands of smaller firms, as they have always done. A study of the 100 largest nonfinancial corporations found that 51 percent of the dollars received from customers was used to buy parts, materials, and services from others, small and large.[4]

Regardless of trends in concentration, we must certainly face the problem of existing size and concentration. In some industries, the control of the vast bulk of capacity is unquestionably concentrated in few firms.

---

[2] R. L. Nelson, *Concentration in the Manufacturing Industries of the United States* (New Haven, Conn.: Yale University Press, 1963). The summary, from which the quotation is taken, begins on page 9. New data suggest that manufacturing was more concentrated in 1963 than 1958, but initial impressions can be misleading. Changes from one industry to another go in different directions. For discussion of the dangers of superficial interpretation see the discussion, as well as most recent figures, in *Concentration Ratios in the Manufacturing Industry, 1963*, . . (Hearings . . . Committee on the Judiciary, U.S. Senate . . . *Part 1* . . . [Washington, D.C.: U.S. Government Printing Office, 1966]).

[3] The magazine *Fortune* makes an annual survey of the largest corporations. The list of the 500 largest manufacturers (according to sales) in 1966 did not include 17 listed in 1965 (plus 5 that disappeared because of merger). The 1966 group included 14 firms which had never been among the 500 highest and 8 which had appeared before but had lost out.

[4] A TV set sold by the largest company in the industry may have parts purchased from relatively small firms which in turn have bought materials from the giants of other industries.

Is there opportunity to improve the vigor and expand the freedom of our economy by reducing concentration and bigness? This question deserves unending attention. That concentration can be cut has been shown by the experience with breaking up public utility holding company systems. Between 1936 and 1952, roughly $16 billion of property was involved. The plants, large operating systems, were separated from holding company control, without evident decline in operating efficiency.

Bigness. Although it is by no means certain that monopoly is more of a problem than in the past, big firms are growing bigger. A few big businesses have been broken up; meanwhile, some have grown by merger and many more by plowing back profit. The great unknown is how much different the expansion would have been if there had been no antitrust program. The law has undoubtedly deterred the growth of large firms by consolidation. In some cases, however, mergers seem to have resulted because looser forms of acting in concert were illegal. The recent decisions of the Supreme Court, however, reduce greatly the possibilities of growth of largest firms by merger—horizontal, vertical, and even conglomerate. The biggest companies will continue to expand by reinvestment of earnings and by raising capital from outside. The companies below the ranks of largest in an industry can still grow by merger. Bigness will increase. How will our life be affected?

Business Practices. What about the effects on business practices. The language of the statutes is strong. Business officials would be foolish to invite trouble. Although they have often sought and used loopholes, they would probably have made greater use of methods now prohibited if the law had not been so positive. Monopolistic actions hold out profit opportunities that are tempting. Business will try to use monopolistic methods—if they are legal. Over the years, the FTC has induced or forced businesses to give up types of competitive action which were bad as well as to forego monopolistic practices. We have little way of evaluating the gains. Results are not limited to the cases in which government has taken action. Decisions set precedents that sometimes affect many times as many businesses as were involved directly. Moreover, the knowledge that there is a policeman may keep some people from wandering from the straight and narrow; and even if there is a willingness to engage in conduct of doubtful legality, the fear of detection helps prevent excesses.[5]

Though we cannot measure the results, one fact is clear: U.S. law makes it generally illegal for businesses in interstate commerce to work

---

[5] A businessman gets an idea about a new way to increase profit. When he checks with his lawyers, however, they warn him that someone else tried much the same thing and had the government on his neck. The plan is abandoned. Our statistics never record the abandonment as a result of antitrust action.

together to set prices (except wage rates), regulate output, share markets, or restrict entry of new suppliers.

Conclusion. Unquestionably, many more mergers would have been consummated if the law had not stood as an obstacle. An element of the "conventional wisdom" that antitrust is dead could not be more in error. Never has antitrust been a more vigorous instrument of economic policy. It has been "institutionalized," embedded in the regular operations of government. No longer is antitrust a temporary crusade. No longer is it a sort of weapon in reserve to use in dealing with an exceptional problem, the infrequent merger of giants or the coming to a head of a long-festering sore in some type of business practice. Today, antitrust is a part of the regular operations of government. All the greater, then, is the need to seek ways to make it as constructive as possible.

There is evidence that action to encourage competition is not futile. Such action cannot do the whole job of keeping the economy healthy any more than vitamins can do the whole job of keeping the body healthy. But it is just as essential. Unfortunately, we do not know the dosages; and the medicine will be distasteful and costly to some of the patients.

States might do more to enforce antimonopoly laws on their statute books, or enact and enforce such laws. Apparently, however, only a few states have significantly effective enforcement of state laws to check monopolistic practices. The potentialities of localized (intrastate) restrictions on trade are great enough to create real opportunity for constructive state action. For several years the Department of Justice has been trying to build more effective arrangements for federal-state cooperation in enforcing antitrust laws.

One undying need, certainly, is a clear understanding of the real merit of rivalry and competition, of the fact that exceptions spawn more exceptions, and of the value of an economic structure that makes monopolistic action difficult.

The problem, as we have said before, is not so much "bigness" as "how much bigness." What is good in one place may be wrong in another, as suggested in the following quotation:

> If I may use a homely illustration, I will take the common house cat, whose diminutive size makes her a safe inmate of our household in spite of her playful disposition and her liking for animal food. If, without the slightest change of character or disposition, she were suddenly enlarged to the dimensions of a tiger, we should at least want her to be muzzled and to have her claws trimmed, whereas if she were to assume the dimensions of a mastodon, I doubt if any of us would want to live in the same house with her. And it would be useless to argue that her nature had not changed, that she was just as amiable as ever, and no more carnivorous than she always had been. Nor would it convince us to be told that her productivity had greatly increased and that she could now catch more mice in a minute than she formerly could

in a week. We should be afraid lest, in a playful mood, she might set a paw upon us, to the detriment of our epidermis, or that in her large-scale mouse-catching she might not always discriminate between us and mice.[6]

STIMULATING COMPETITION: AIDS TO SMALL BUSINESS

The prevention of monopoly and unfair business practices does not exhaust the opportunities for encouraging competition. Perhaps there is more we could do through government. Since the war, about 1,000 businesses have folded up each day, and 1,150 new ones have started. Perhaps this record could be improved.

Sympathy for the "little man" is not the only reason for wanting to encourage small business. Efficiency and progress, opportunity for the individual and for exceptional creative talent, can benefit from—they may even require—the existence of small firms. Smallness in itself, however, creates no persuasively valid claim for favor. "Even casual observation discredits the myth that small business is innately more competitive than large."[7] Every individual is small in relation to groups that serve us daily. Part of the problem of business size which the public faces is to learn the appropriate range for different kinds of activities.

Smallness is "natural" in many fields, especially service activities; no obvious case for governmental concern will be expected. In such cases the small firm will survive because it is close to the optimum scale. Some giant firms are themselves dependent upon dispersed sources of supply or distribution agencies; these tend to be run most efficiently by firms which are small and which identify the operator's interest with his efforts.[8] Many businesses, of course, operate essentially on their own, not as part of an economic process intimately tied to giants. The retailer, clothing manufacturer, builder, independent trucker, manufacturer, motel operator, or other businessman may be in direct competition with a big firm; or he may face a variety of indirect competition. As a rule he will be at a distinct disadvantage in at least some parts of his activities—perhaps in research, hiring skilled labor, getting credit, advertising, dealing with unions, adapting his operations to changing conditions. Sometimes the chief disadvantages could be offset by organizations equipped to provide special needs at reasonable prices. Such organizations—commercial labora-

---

[6] Thomas N. Carver, *Essays in Social Justice* (Cambridge, Mass.: Harvard University Press, 1915), p. 332. Quoted with permission of the Harvard University Press.

[7] W. M. Hoad, "Is Government Doing Enough for Small Business?" *Michigan Business Review*, May, 1966, p. 12. The author is Professor of Small Business at the University of Michigan.

[8] No single fruit producer is vital to a great food chain, no one tool and die maker to Ford. No sales outlet is very important to, say, Gulf Oil. Yet the orchards, small highly skilled tool-making shops, and service stations as a group—small businesses —are essential links in the chain on which the big companies depend. The large corporation in its own interest will often try to give training, financial, techincal, advertising, and other aid to the hundreds or thousands with whom it is associated. Many small firms, then, can expect support from giants.

tories and management consultants, for example—exist and expand. Various arrangements for pooling facilities to serve many small independent firms have grown up. More will. Men who have retired from successful business careers volunteer to help small companies needing specialized, experienced guidance.

To some extent, government encouragement for small business is appropriate. Yet there is a danger that government action will be perverted. Some businesses remain small and, what is worse, unsuccessful because they are not efficient. They fail to adapt to changing conditions. Their managers are not competent, vigorous. Their employees may resist progress. If owners and workers use political power to get conditions that make such firms profitable, then the public will suffer. It is one thing for government to fill gaps in economic arrangements so that small firms can do a better job. Quite another thing is government action to help small firms get a tolerable living from poor service. Aiding small businesses may be wise. (It can also be wasteful and burdensome to existing companies which serve the public well.) The Small Business Administration helps some small firms get financing, and there is clear evidence that gaps in the credit market can be narrowed. But small companies cannot be given what they often really want, the equivalent of *equity* capital at the cost of high-quality *credit*, except as someone provides a subsidy.

The SBA also provides such management aids as hundreds of publications on business and technical problems, management counseling, and help in getting orders for federal purchases and research contracts. It keeps a watch on proposed laws and regulations and makes recommendations to protect what it believes to be the interest of small business. The Department of Commerce offers an important array of information and guidance to businesses of all sizes.

Various federal, many state, and some local government programs provide one or another form of aid or subsidy. Some are parts of bigger programs—aid to Appalachia, urban renewal, disaster relief, anti-poverty, aid to colored minority groups, transportation, local industrial development. A reasonably full list would be long, but most of the items apply to relatively few potential cases. Accomplishments grow but remain small (and often still experimental) in relation to the size of our economy.

Other possibilities include (1) tax reduction to all business or merely to small companies, (2) protection against restrictive labor union practices, (3) favoritism in placing military orders, (4) better information and guidance through the maze of government, (5) easing access to patents, (6) faster and more complete aid in adjusting to dislocation forced by urban renewal, highway, and other projects, and (7) encouragement of firms to provide the specialized services which many businesses need but which large firms provide themselves. Each of these proposals has merits and drawbacks. The danger of pouring out resources, or restricting the efficient, to help "weak sisters" must never be far from the front of attention.

Policies which help some small and new firms may stimulate competition more than other small businesses welcome.

Though not every small business is *new*, almost every new business starts small. Frequently the problems of *getting started* are in themselves distressingly difficult. The public will at times have an interest in helping the aspiring businessman solve such problems, not because the firm is small but because it is new. However, some industries where monopolistic conditions appear to be most probable are not industries which small and new firms are likely to enter. Most new firms would probably tend to enter industries in which competition is already active. In not a few cases, the market will not support more than one, two, or three units of reasonably efficient size—and may have them already—in most localities. In other cases, the new firm or plant must be so large to enter that newcomers really have no chance. Protection of the public interest must then rest largely on the competition of substitutes, of products from other areas (including foreign lands), of potential suppliers, and on enforcement or laws against restraint of trade.

The millions of small businesses play a tremendous role in our economy—a role that is more pervasive, more powerful, and often more profitable than implied in public expressions of concern for small business. The growth of discount houses after the war offers an example of businesses starting with almost nothing but then making a real impression on the economy. *Franchising* has also grown in significance. A company with an established name and proved method of successful operation grants operating rights to independent companies which agree to follow established practices. Successes have been numerous.

Yet many a hard problem faces small and new businesses. And when millions are operating, there will be more than a few examples to illustrate any type of hardship. These examples may be cited in trying to elicit public favor, which is not really needed by the overwhelming majority. The giants, too, have problems—many created by the myriads of smaller firms competing in all sorts of ways. The manager of a small business is often a man of anything but small ability. The existence of many small companies gives opportunity for big men, men of large capacities and energy, to get ahead by serving the public. This is one of the basic strengths of the American economy.

GOVERNMENT LIMITATIONS ON COMPETITION

A policy of preventing unfair methods of competition can blend into one for preventing competition which, though fair, some firms find unwelcome. Such is the situation today. Government supports some practices which reduce competition, and there is no slackening of efforts of economic groups to use government to make life easier for them—at the expense of the consumer and to the detriment of other businesses.

Where formal regulation exists—transportation, communications, banking and insurance, and others—insulation from competition can work against the public interest. The aura surrounding official participation can give a misleading impression. Subtle, and not so subtle, forces operate to reduce the pressures for progress.

Resale Price Maintenance and "Fair Trade."   Half the battle for public support may be won by latching on to a term with favorable connotations. Some business groups did just that in fixing the term "fair trade" to policies that limit competition. In the 1930's, state after state passed resale price maintenance laws; Congress finally gave its sanction where interstate commerce was concerned. These laws permitted a manufacturer to make a contract with a retailer that would set the minimum price at which a product—a Sunbeam toaster or an Arrow shirt—was to be sold. This price would then bind *all* retailers in the state.

This curious twist of government policy resulted partly from the pressures of some manufacturers, who argued that retail price reductions—a well-advertised product was excellent as a "loss leader"—destroyed public respect for their product and weakened other retailers. Most support came from retailers, especially druggists, who pleaded that such laws were necessary to prevent destructive competition.

There can be some truth in these contentions—competition was severe in the 1930's, and reasonable men might seek help in measures which over the longer run would be against the public interest. Resale price maintenance results in higher prices to consumers. It tolerates, even encourages, waste in retailing and so may not appreciably benefit retailers in the long run. Manufacturers may suffer, too, as higher average prices reduce the volume of sales. Where demand for a product is relatively inelastic so that retailers do gain by higher prices, the profit increase in retailing will attract more capacity and reduce average rates of net return. Extra overhead "eats up" the expected advantage unless, as in some countries, the industry can find ways to exclude new sellers.

The laws were moderately effective. In one way or another, however, firms that really wanted to compete found ways to do so, notably by developing their own brands. Then, in 1951, the Supreme Court ruled the federal law ineffective. Congress responded by passing a new one. While it was being upheld in court, however, most state laws were declared unconstitutional as applied to nonsigners, or weakened substantially.

If the law is effective, a more efficient retailer cannot compete on the basis of lower price. The consumer is deprived of the benefits of competition in reducing the costs of distribution, costs which are a big slice of the dollar he pays.[7] Actual results, however, depend upon such things as the

---

[7] What if a single retailer tried to control manufacturers' prices without regard to differences in costs? Or what if a single butcher tried to control the price of all cattle sold by farmers? Some advocates of price maintenance defended their position on the

prices manufacturers set and the efforts retailers make to escape. Enforcement depends upon legal action by private parties, not by government agencies. Stores that respected the rules complained that manufacturers winked at violation by small dealers and "discount houses." Most manufacturers have given up attempts at enforcement. Some rely on other, less sweeping, legal methods of controlling retail prices.[8]

Prohibitions on Price Discrimination: Robinson-Patman Act. The Clayton Act prohibition on price discrimination among customers turned out to be loose and largely ineffective. Chain stores and other large buyers got price advantages which favored them (unduly). The Robinson-Patman Act (1936) seeks to end such discriminations. Yet, to 1965 the meaning of this complex law remains far from clear. The act prohibits persons dealing in interstate commerce from giving or receiving, directly or indirectly, any discriminations, whether in price or service, that substantially lessen competition or injure competitors—unless the seller can show that the price (1) is justified by differences in cost or (2) is necessary to meet equally low prices of competitors. Both defenses are difficult to establish satisfactorily. The courts have not set clear and definite criteria. If goods differ in quality, selling or shipping costs, or in delivery, an appropriate price difference is permissible if made available to all on "proportionally equal" terms. Determining what is "proportionally equal," however, can lead to endless frustration.

The act gives FTC authority to set the discounts that can be allowed for size of shipment. If there is a reasonable possibility that a quantity discount given one buyer will hurt a competitor, it can be granted only upon proof that it is justified by savings in cost. Such proof, or whatever will establish that price differences reflect effort to meet competition, can be very difficult. This law represents another example of efforts to shelter competitors rather than to encourage competition.

State Restraints on Competition. State legislatures have been fertile fields for groups seeking relief from competition, especially price competition. Congress may be hard to move, but a trip to the state capitol may not require missing even one luncheon meeting to extol free competition; and the trip may succeed in getting your representatives to vote for a law giving you some freedom *from* competition. Many such laws exist. How do these rules get on the statute books? By pressure from the interests

---

ground that price-reducing competition should operate chiefly at manufacturing, not at retail, levels. The "loss leader" problem, which at times is real, might be met by specific prohibitions, but a serious effort to get such a law through Congress aroused no great support from "fair traders." The retail drug industry now presses Congress for a stronger law, designated "quality stabilization," to restrict price competition.

[8] A manufacturer may legally announce in advance the conditions under which he will sell to a retailer, conditions which include the price at which the product is to be sold. Courts have narrowed this power, however.

who hope to benefit and who, incidentally, often get control of enforcement.

Many states prohibit the sale of an article for less than it cost plus the expense of handling, often determined by a fixed percentage (6 to 12 percent).[9] Grocers have been prominent in supporting such laws. Commissions and licensing boards sometimes fix prices and enforce rules by threatening to revoke the license of any transgressor. Generally, the fixing is done by people more friendly to the profession or industry than to consumers. The kinds of groups involved are numerous: auto dealers, commercial photographers, morticians, doctors, and plumbers, to cite a few. In several states, marketing boards control the supply of various products; California has over 30. They can limit supply (destroy products) to keep prices at a level agreed upon. Who makes the agreements? Usually producers.

Something else will bear watching: the endorsement, and occasional enactment, of laws that make responsibility for enforcing price fixing a state function. Such laws relieve business of an onerous burden, and put government law enforcement agencies behind the private groups working to limit competition. States have also erected barriers to interstate commerce, some of which have survived tests of constitutionality. Local governments, too, restrict competition in some direct ways and indirectly by tolerating or supporting private groups in restrictive practices.

PATENTS; COPYRIGHTS; TRADEMARKS

The Purposes and Provisions of Our Patent System.
To get his 17-year patent, an inventor must disclose the details of what he has invented or discovered. If he can prove that he has done something truly original, he, in effect, gets exclusive right to use it for the life of the patent. Or if he wishes, he may sell the patent or license someone else to use it. The patent system has two dominant justifications: (1) Public disclosure, by letting others know what has been accomplished, will facilitate further progress, the cumulation of knowledge, to the benefit of the general public. (2) The temporary monopoly offers inventors an opportunity for gain. It thus provides an incentive for what is sometimes a highly valuable activity for the community and yet risky for the inventor.

The government does not certify that the patentee is the true inventor; nor will it come to his assistance if someone sues. The patent confers a claim which he can use in suit against another who allegedly infringes. Decision rests with the courts, and legal testing is highly expensive.

Stimulating the public disclosure of new knowledge seems of obvious general worth. (Incidentally, the federal government finances much research and makes many, but not all, of the results available without charge.) The granting of monopoly, however, does arouse debate. The

---

[9] Exceptions are made for special cases, such as perishables, damaged goods, and clearance sales.

public may be forced to pay "too much." But what is "too much"? The benefits of discovery and invention as a whole are incalculable. Is the patent system, however, an efficient method, in general, for stimulating technical progress? Can it be improved, not only in detail but also in its broader outlines?

The chances seem overwhelming that society will get more invention the more attractive the rewards its researchers (of all types) expect. The risking of skill, time, and money will depend upon the inducements, including prospect of economic gain for doing what appeals to the public. True, a vast amount of research would unquestionably be done without the prospect of patent protection. Getting there first with something new and keeping discoveries secret would in themselves constitute substitutes to some extent for patents, especially in big companies. Yet there is basis for belief that the offer of a chance for great profit is probably an inexpensive way to induce individuals or corporations to make more effort.

Patents, however, are instruments of restriction. The owner may deny use to others or make permission contingent upon a promise to restrict use according to place, time, price, quantity, or perhaps other condition. Many a patent is only one link in a long chain. The individual inventor may find that his patent is worth little, except when used with others which he does not control. The makers of other parts of an auto, for example, might be able to take or absorb much of the worth of a better transmission, which has no value without the other elements of the vehicle.

Problems of Governmental Policy. How can an owner of a patent work with others, especially if some are competitors? Pooling is one answer. Yet it may then seem natural to use the pool as a device for "cooperative" (oligopolistic) action. When AT&T and RCA each own thousands of patents, their massive power could be a positive *obstacle to invention;* the person making an improvement in any of several lines of communications or electronics could not hope to use it without the cooperation of patents owned by the giant, who could set its terms to absorb virtually all of the benefit. (These companies have agreed to license their patents for others to use on terms which a court must approve.) The inventor without much capital must know that he can benefit from his creation only with the cooperation of productive facilities whose owners in turn may be dependent upon the giant for use of patents. A firm with a mass of patents may try to license their use only on a "package" basis and thereby in effect demand a share of the other fellow's creation.

Perhaps, as sometimes said, the patent system is more the bulwark of invention and innovation in medium- and small-sized business than among the giants. The latter can depend relatively more upon large numbers, secrecy, and sheer momentum to keep exclusive use for a period approaching that of the economic worth of uniqueness. But our evidence, to say the least, is incomplete.

Do businesses abuse the power given by patents? How can one know?[10] Vast numbers of patents are never used. In some cases, there may be deliberate suppression of something good. Mostly, however, the patents have no economic value. The processes or products they control are not better, or not enough so, to warrant the cost of putting them into use; a still better improvement may have developed; or other necessary links in the chain have not been invented; or the owner does not have capital.

Government has a central part to play in preventing the misuse of patents. The Supreme Court has given the clue in distinguishing between a patent as a monopoly (permitted) and a monopoly of patents (illegal). It has ruled, for example (1) that patent pooling among "competitors" is illegal unless the terms assure that competition is not restrained and that the rates charged are reasonable, and (2) that a patent may not be used to fix the price of an unpatented product.

Invention, scientific and literary creation, and research play such a strategic role in progress that we should exert ourselves to encourage them. Patents and copyrights are "prices" we pay for these services; but, like other human institutions, they are not perfect. What would be practical improvements?[11] (1) An unused patent might expire long before the end of the 17-year period; suppression of something useful would then be less profitable. (2) The owner of a patent might be compelled to license its use to anyone. But at what charge? Who would decide? On what basis? How quickly? More holders of masses of patents might be required to license them to prevent a "monopoly of patents." (3) If licensing remains voluntary, our economy would probably benefit from some compulsion or inducement to broaden license terms to prevent control of one firm's policies by another or a group. (4) The effective life of a patent might in fact be limited to 17 years; today, by stretching out legal proceedings in the application, a patent can be protected for more than 17 years. (5) Conviction of illegal use or other abuse of a patent might carry as a penalty the requirement that other firms be granted royalty-free use.

The rapid internationalization of business has multiplied manyfold the

---

[10] The auto industry pools patents but makes them available to the public virtually without charge. Proof of shocking abuse of patents in bottle making and other cases has led the Supreme Court to limit greatly the use of patents to enforce price-fixing agreements or, through licensing or tying contracts, to monopolize an industry.

[11] "That the patent system is greatly in need of overhauling is a truth acknowledged by most students of the problem except, unhappily, the most influential, i.e., patent attorneys and congressmen." Donald Dewey, *Monopoly in Economics and Law* (Skokie, Ill.: Rand McNally & Co., 1959), p. 177. Few if any aspects of law and its practice are more complex. Setting clearer and higher standards for distinguishing justifiably patentable from other developments and speeding the operations of the Patent Office are being sought within the framework of the present system. Staggeringly difficult are the practical problems of storing highly technical and unique information so that it can be identified and recovered upon demand, for example, when a new patent application is filed. Modern electrical data processing equipment is being developed to meet some of the needs. A shortage of skilled patent examiners impedes progress.

inventor's problems in getting patent protection. At least a dozen, usually many more, different lands will have producers potentially able to duplicate a new product, often quickly. Heavy costs in time, money, and massive paperwork in different languages must be incurred merely to start the long process of seeking foreign patents. U.S. officials are leading in the difficult job of trying to improve international cooperation. The task is complicated by the fact that domestic patent systems differ and also by the fact that in not a few countries powerful interests will prefer easy and cheap access to the technology developed elsewhere.

Copyrights. A copyright, designed to yield much the same ends as a patent, runs for 28 years and may be renewed for another 28. The system presents somewhat similar, but not entirely parallel, problems as those which arise over patents. Broadcasting and other mechanical reproduction of music, and easy copying of printed materials, have sparked new interest by composers, authors, artists, publishers, and others. They seek better protection. Congress has been considering new legislation. Opposition has been powerful, however, and the outcome remains (1967) uncertain.

Trademarks. The first effective federal trademark law was enacted in 1946, but much of the present system goes back more than half a century. By entering words or symbols on a Principal Register at the Patent Office, a person or group can get prima facie evidence of ownership for 20 years. The aspect of public interest is to aid identification and to certify the origin of a product or service. One can get some idea of what a product with the name Polaroid or Chanel or Dacron will be on a repeat buy. Obviously, however, the exclusive use of a name buttressed by advertising departs from pure competition. Sometimes the result verges on undue restraint under the law or crosses over the line. The law is complex and not always clear. And as U.S. firms go more into foreign lands, they find difficulties in protecting the position of a trademark name.

TERMS AND CONCEPTS

Federal Trade Commission	trademark	parity price
concentration	intermediate services	crop restriction
merger	migrant worker	soil bank
fair trade	sharecropper	marketing quota
patent	indigent farmer	futures market
copyright	resale price maintenance	

QUESTIONS

1. "Major results of antitrust actions are rarely clear." Discuss.
2. Does patent policy conflict with antitrust policy? Discuss.
3. What are the economic issues of resale price maintenance policies? Why is excess capacity likely to result if the policy is effective?

4. Why do some business and occupational groups seek government intervention to restrict competition?

5. "Fairness in competition is often a matter of the point of view." What would seem to you (*a*) fair and (*b*) unfair methods of competition in the sale or provision of the following: (*i*) new houses, (*ii*) magazines and encyclopedias, (*iii*) pies, (*iv*) used autos, (*v*) TV programs, (*vi*) candidates for political office, (*vii*) surgery, (*viii*) movies, (*ix*) typewriters, (*x*) home maintenance services, and (*xi*) flower seeds?

6. What might be gained and lost by making the postal service a privately operated public utility? By relying on competition alone to regulate railroad rates?

7. "Bigness in and of itself presents problems which, though not necessarily the same as those of monopoly, deserve serious attention." Discuss.

8. Discuss reasons for, and problems of, governmental action to aid (*a*) small and (*b*) new businesses.

9. What are the major features of the Robinson-Patman Act?

10. "There is not a farm problem, for there are many different problems." What are some "farm problems"? Which resemble those in other parts of the economy?

11. "America's only real farm surplus is farmers." Discuss.

12. In what sense do governmental farm policies make the price system "work against" reforms needed for permanent balance of production and consumption?

13. How does the inelasticity of total demand for farm products affect the problem of stabilizing farm income in the short run?

14. How would you account for the great increase in land prices?

15. Why have farmers, although a rather small minority, been able to get so much aid from the rest of the country, and aid for the more prosperous farmers?

16. What will be the probable effectiveness of acreage (planting) restrictions as a method of controlling output?

17. What is the difference between flexible and fixed price supports?

18. How, if at all, will fixed supports at high levels and output controls restrict the opportunity of farmers?

19. Does the concept of fairness, which underlies the principle of "party," require adjustment for changes in the inputs needed to produce a given agricultural output?

20. "Today [1967] many of the distortions in agriculture are the result of government policy. Though drastic changes are needed to reduce the colossal waste, taxpayers should help pay for constructive readjustments." Discuss.

21. "The growth of large firms proves that size brings efficiency and that successful efforts to curb bigness are bound to slow the improvement of technology." "The survival of firms only a small fraction of the size of the giants of the industry proves that great size does not necessarily bring significant economies." Discuss these two statements.

APPENDIX
Government Farm Policy

For 35 years a major effort of government has been to alter the distribution of national income to favor farmers. Yet after expenditure of 60 billion of tax dollars in only about a dozen years (precise figures are open to difference of view, for example, how much is better assigned to foreign aid?), conditions remain unsatisfactory. Militancy among farmers, "strikes," and attempts to combine to shut off supplies to raise price testify (1967) to the continuation, even accentuation in some areas, of distress. This appendix discusses the problems and policies. Here we see the application of economic theory to practical problems. Moreover, we shall also learn something of the way political factors affect economic actions through government.

FARMING IN AMERICA TODAY

Agriculture Widely Varied. What are we talking about when we speak of "farming"? Certainly no one thing. The Texas cattle range and the New Jersey tomato farm or the Iowa corn farm; the wheat ranches of Kansas and the orchards of Oregon; the great cotton farms of California or Mississippi, the peanut or tobacco farms of North Carolina; the Wisconsin dairy farm, the Southern cotton patch, the orange groves of Florida, and the duck farm of Long Island—such contrasts illustrate a central point. Agriculture is made up of widely diverse units. Their problems are varied. So are the incomes they yield, the capital they require, their future in our economy. Some are rivals. The corn farmer likes high grain prices rather more than does the dairy farmer who must buy corn. In speaking of "agriculture," then, we often gloss over many differences.

The 1964 census defined "farm" as any place of more than 10 acres from which $50 or more of farm products were sold or places of less than 10 acres from which farm products of $250 or more were sold. There were then 3.1 million such farms. The 2 million "commercial" farms, each selling $2,500 or more produce a year, account for over 90 percent of all output.

The one-family farm is still an efficient operating unit throughout large sections of agriculture. Technological forces, however, induce farmers to try to increase the size of farms, with average acreage of commercial farms over 500 in 1964, compared with 421 in 1954. Nevertheless, there are so many farm units producing most crops that no one farmer in planning production will assume that his output can affect the market price.

The relative importance of different products is shown in Table 21–1 on the following page.

Economic Function of Farming. The broad economic function of farming is to supply the community with materials for eating, drinking, smoking, wearing, and industrial and other uses. Farming like manufacturing or trade

492

TABLE 21–1. Agricultural Products, Cash Receipts from Marketings, and Value of Amounts Consumed on Farm, 1966

Product	Value (Billions)	Product	Value (Billions)
Cattle and calves	$10.4	Tobacco	$ 1.2
Dairy products	5.6	Oil-bearing crops, chiefly soybeans	2.8
Hogs	4.0	Sheep, lambs, wool	0.5
Cotton, including cottonseed	1.6	Sugar crops	0.4
Feed crops, chiefly corn*	2.4	Other†	1.7
Food grains, chiefly wheat	4.0	Total	$42.9‡
Vegetables	2.6	Products consumed directly in farm	
Poultry and eggs	4.0	households	1.0
Fruits and tree nuts	1.7	Gross rental value of farm dwellings	2.4

* A considerable amount of grain is not marketed for cash but fed on the farm. Its value appears in the figures above as cattle, hogs, dairy products, etc.

† Includes horses, rabbits, fur animals, honey, forest and nursery products, popcorn, hemp and flax, etc.

‡ Farmers also received $3.3 billion of government aid not included in the figures above. Major expenses were feed, $6.5 billion; wages, $2.8 billion; taxes and interest, $3.3 billion; depreciation, repairs, and other costs of capital items, $9.4 billion; fertilizer, $1.9 billion; purchased livestock, $3.5 billion; net rent to nonfarm landlords, $1.4 billion; all other, $4.3 billion.

Source: The Farm Income Situation.

is primarily a means to other ends. To the farmer, the major purpose of farming is the income it brings him. The farmer's point of view, then, differs from that of the community as a whole. At least it *may*. The public's interest in abundant, cheap food and clothing may not always harmonize with the farmer's interest in high income. Obviously, the products of farms are essential to all of us. So are many other things: transportation, the services of factories, commerce, and government. In an interdependent economy it is dangerous to assume, and to base public policy on the belief, that one part, even the growing of wheat, is uniquely essential. The crucial issue is "how much" of each thing is needed to get equal utilities at the margin.

Decline in Relative Size of Farming in the U.S. Economy: Rising Productivity. In a look at agriculture's role in our economy two related facts stand out. (1) The proportion of the U.S. labor force engaged in farming has declined steadily. (2) Output per acre and per man-hour has increased. In the early 19th century, nearly 3 out of 4 people with jobs worked on farms, today 1 out of 17. Americans spend more per capita on food than in the past.[1] In 1966, for example, it would have required about $300 to buy what $156 cost in 1929. Yet on the average we spent nearly $500. The rise has not matched that of the rest of the economy. The income elasticity of demand for food is relatively low. Agriculture seems to lag—and does—in the rise in income per resident.

[1] Does the capacity of the human stomach limit narrowly the amount of food we can consume? Not in terms of either the satisfactions of eating or the demands on our farms, for diets vary tremendously. Meat, fresh fruits and vegetables, eggs and milk products, and alcohol, for example, require far more productive effort than the same calories and basic food values when obtained directly from cereals, potatoes, and other cheaper foods. In a pound of meat, we eat the equivalent of 6 to 10 pounds of grain. Increasingly, more of our food spending goes for intermediate services, as discussed later in the chapter.

Records for nearly 40 years show that food outlays as a percentage of disposable personal income dropped by one tenth.

People have left farms because opportunities looked better elsewhere. The average farmer (and his machines) can now produce vastly more than his father (Fig. 21–1). Since 1930 physical output of farms has more than doubled despite a 12 percent net reduction in acreage and a 75 percent drop in man-hour input.

FIGURE 21–1. Agricultural Output per Man-Hour and per Acre, Selected Years, 1940–66 (Index Numbers, 1957–59 = 100)

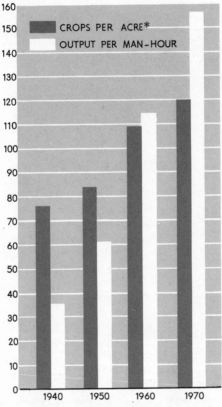

CROPS PER ACRE*

OUTPUT PER MAN-HOUR

*Excludes livestock. The index of production of livestock per breeding unit rose from 75 in 1940 to 114 in 1966.
Source: U.S. Department of Agriculture.

Science has helped immensely by developing better seed, plants, animals, fertilizers, and insecticides. Scientific farming and college-trained farmers have become more common. Many agencies participate in spreading knowledge about how to use improvements—4-H clubs and county agents, for example. Farmers have been able to benefit from many advances in knowledge without using much additional capital. Some improvement has been the result of normal development in fencing, barns, roads, orchards, houses, and drainage. Greater changes, however, have resulted from invention. The truck, tractor, corn picker, combine, milking machine—all have cut tremendously the labor needed to do the job. But they require large amounts of new capital. Many years of good farm income after 1940 helped provide it. Gasoline and electricity now supply power that used to come from horse and mule and man himself. At home and abroad synthetic materials have to some extent replaced cotton, wool, and leather.

Finally, we note the attractions of town and city. The appeal of the farm does not always equal the excitement and variety of the city. And a boy seeking to be a lawyer or an engineer—or a girl hoping to be a secretary, department store buyer, or hospital technician—has little chance for such a career on Dad's farm.

Total Farm Income. Farms produce less than 4 percent of GNP. Net farm income in the mid-1960's was about $15 billion a year from farming. For their efforts in agriculture and for the use of their land and capital (and including government aid), farmers get nearly 3 percent of the nation's disposable income. Farmers on the average have improved their net incomes; Figure 21–2 shows farm income in dollars of constant purchasing power for a quarter of a century. A rising total income has been shared by fewer and fewer farmers. An important source of improvement, especially for farmers with small plots, is the availability of part-time jobs off the farm. The waste of idleness in slack seasons is falling as nearly half of farm residents work at

FIGURE 21–2. Farm Production and Income, 1940–65, in Dollars of Constant Purchasing Power

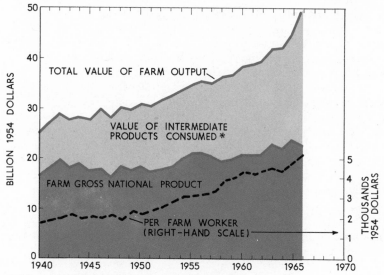

* Does not include depreciation, interest, and taxes.
Source: U.S. Department of Commerce, Office of Business Economics.

nonfarm jobs at least part of the year. Income of farm families from nonfarm sources must now be well above the $7 billion of 1960.

Nevertheless, agricultural incomes averaging around $5,100 per farm-operator family are less than 60 percent the average for nonfarm families. The proportion of farm families who are poor by any reasonable standard exceeds the proportion of nonfarm families. (The median farm income in 1965 was $3,800.)

Inelasticity of Both Total Demand and Total Supply. The demand for farm products *as a whole* is generally inelastic.[2] The total quantity purchased varies less, proportionately, than price. A small increase in quantity offered on the

---

[2] We do *not* say completely inelastic, not by any means. The quantity consumed *will* rise when price drops. Use of the term "surplus" is misleading, especially when there is no explicit discussion of the associated price and why it is not a free market price.

market brings a decidedly larger fall in prices, and vice versa. Note that we are talking about *total* output, not particular crops. The demand for particular products is much more elastic than the demand for output as a whole. For example, the total consumption of food responds rather little to price changes. But our choice of beef, oranges, or eggs will vary significantly with their prices in relation to prices of other foods.

Another aspect of the demand for food becomes increasingly important: the spread or margin between what the consumer pays and what the farmer gets. About 60 percent of our food spending goes for intermediate services, compared with 53 percent in 1950: the trucker for transport; the baker for making a cake; the frozen-food processor for selecting, cleaning, freezing, and packaging; the restaurateur for cooking and serving a meal. Intermediate costs tend to be inflexible. Consequently, price changes at the consumer level are passed in large part to the farmer. Assume that 60 cents of the consumer's food dollar goes to pay for intermediate services and 40 cents to the farmer. Then prices at the consumer level rise by 10 percent. The costs of intermediate services, being inflexible, remain at 60 cents; the farmer will now have 50 cents—a 25 percent increase. On the other hand, if the consumer price falls by 10 percent, the farmer gets only 30 cents, a drop of 25 percent.

Total supply, too, is inelastic in the short run. From year to year, and within wide limits, total output depends little upon the price farmers expect to get. This condition results from the large number of farms; the individual farmer cannot affect price by raising or lowering his output. Moreover, the nature of farm costs tends to make total supply inelastic. A large part of the farmer's expenses are fixed: the farm itself, property taxes, mortgage interest, depreciation, and especially his own time. He cannot cut these important costs by curtailing output. Some of these, and increasingly more of his variable costs—gasoline, electricity, commercial fertilizers, feeds and seeds, machine parts—must be paid in cash. (Note in Figure 21–2 the rise in "Value of Intermediate Products Consumed.") Moreover, farm families grow less self-sufficient; like others, they use food and clothing from stores. They need cash. Farm cost structures, plus the need for cash, create strong pressures to maintain production even when prices fall. Again, note that we talk of totals, not the output of individual crops. Farmers *do* shift from one crop to another—oats to corn—to take advantage of relative prices.[3]

With both total supply and total demand inelastic, price fluctuates through a relatively wide range when either demand or supply shifts only a little. Net farm income, as a result, can—and does—fluctuate much more than production and consumption.

BACKGROUND OF GOVERNMENT AID TO AGRICULTURE

Government gives (some) farmers special help. Why?

Uncertainties of Farming. Farming is a business with uncertainties. *Nature creates hazards,* more for some farmers than others; bad weather or an insect plague can cut a crop disastrously. (Bad weather, of course, can hurt

---

[3] One occasionally sees the statement that farm supply is perversely elastic, i.e., lower prices induce greater output. Neither logic nor evidence will bear out this assertion.

lots of businesses—ask a resort concessionaire.) Fortunately, science and capital are reducing this risk.[4]

The inflexibility of some farm production prevents farmers from adjusting promptly to changing conditions. The cotton, wheat, or fruit farmer, and many others, commit themselves for a year or more in advance. Thereafter, they have little freedom to adjust. If production costs or prices go up (or down), the farmer must go ahead pretty much as his earlier plans, and nature, prescribe. Moreover, like most businessmen he must sometimes make basic plans more than a year, or even 5 years, in advance. His predictions of the future may be very wrong.

Farm product prices fluctuate widely in free markets. Fluctuations result not only from the overall inelasticities just discussed. Prices of individual products rise and fall because of particular (as well as general) demand and supply conditions. The farmer finds his net income affected decisively by things over which he has no control and which he often cannot foresee in time to adjust his output.

Excess Capacity.   Is there in American agriculture excess capacity which depresses farm earnings? Yes. More people are now trying to earn their incomes as farmers than are needed to supply consumers at prices which will yield the producer a "satisfactory" income. And more land is used than is needed. The use of this land also involves farmers in the use of machinery which, from the point of view of the whole economy, does not produce output worth its cost.

Farming as a Low-Income Industry.   If we lump all farm incomes together and compute an average, we find that average gross income per farm was about $16,300 in 1966, but only $5,000 after allowing for all costs including those of the capital investment (but not including nonfarm income). But variation is wide. A million or more truly poor, nontypical farms depress the average. One fifth of commercial farms have net income over $10,000, but a larger number of farms will net under $2,500.

Farmers have pointed out that their incomes have not risen at the same rate as those of most of the public. Since the mid-1950's such has been the case. However, comparison of 1910 incomes with those in 1966 suggests—the data are imperfect—that people on the farms got about the same relative increases in income as those elsewhere. The net "proprietors' equities" of farmers rose from $148 billion to $228 billion between 1955 and 1967. Still, net incomes on commercial farms yield less for the farmer's hourly effort and his capital than received by workers and investors in most of the rest of the economy. Fundamentally, American agriculture has productive capacity which farmers acting freely will use to produce more than consumers will buy at prices that will yield "satisfactory" incomes to most commercial farmers.

A generation ago, the desire to reduce poverty was one reason for starting large-scale farm aid. Only a minor amount, however, has gone to the poor. Who are they?

[4] Drought-resistant seed strains, diversification, better ways of fighting insect plagues, irrigation, and improved buildings and machinery are a few of the things that help free farmers from the tyranny of nature.

1. One large group are hired farm laborers: the migratory workers who move with the crops, cultivating, picking, and packing; the person from town who gets work on the farm during the busy season. Many work only part of the year. Moreover, the rate of pay is low. Much work requires little skill and can be done by women, children, and men without much training. When minimum wage laws were applied to such workers, unemployment and the speed of mechanization rose.

2. Another group of farm poor are sharecroppers, often Negro. Of course, not all sharecroppers have low incomes, but many do. They farm land which someone else owns, often using his tools. He advances them credit for seed and food. After harvest the tenant repays with a share of the crop. Much of the land may be run down and little fertilizer used. A sharecropper without capital, knowledge, and incentive is not likely to get ahead or give his children much of a boost. More capital, education, trained management, personal incentive, and land rehabilitation at times pay off handsomely. As jobs open up elsewhere, sharecroppers leave by the tens of thousands.

3. Indigent farmers are found in the southern mountain country. Though they may own their land, it is poor and badly maintained. They have had little schooling, own little equipment, and simply cannot produce much, even if they have the health and incentive.

4. Even in generally prosperous areas there are farms where productivity is low—because of the soil itself or the distance from markets, or because capital is seriously inadequate.

5. The farmer, unlike most workers, must be a businessman and manager as well as a laborer; some, however, are not able to manage well. Poor management can lead to low income.

6. Most farms with gross sales under $2,500 are operated by persons (*a*) over 65 or (*b*) who are engaged primarily in nonfarm work. The little plot may fall within the definition of a "farm." It produces something for the market, perhaps, and something for the owner, supplementing a pension, wages, or other receipts.

7. Farmers just getting started may earn little, net, after paying rent and capital costs.

8. Some farmers begin or end operations during the year. Reported incomes cover only part of a year.

Development of Crisis.   Just before World War I, farmers were doing fairly well, by the standards of the time. That war brought an economic upheaval. Crop prices soared, the area under cultivation increased, and farm income skyrocketed. Farmers then borrowed money to buy land at high prices. But grain and cotton—and land—prices fell. The heavy debts were terribly oppressive.

Both demand and supply conditions developed adversely in the 1920's. (1) Foreign markets declined; the development of synthetic fibers cut demand for cotton and wool. (2) The shift to mechanical power released about 60 million acres from producing animal foods. (3) Better farming methods increased output. The industry was "overexpanded." The exodus of labor and capital was slow—and painful. (4) These forces combined to hit the industry when it was financially weak. Foreclosure of mortgages and a breakdown of credit facilities focused attention on financial problems. The chief tragedy, however, seemed to be low prices—5-cent cotton and 30-cent corn in the worst days of the 1930's.

Political Influence and Other Reasons for Aid to Farmers.   Farmers are able to get aid which costs taxpayers heavily. Why? For one thing, farmers have had much public sympathy. They also have political influence far out of proportion to their numbers. Each state has two votes in the U.S. Senate. Even states in which most people live in cities have enough farmers for their votes to be a concern to senators. Farmers, well organized in groups that cut across party lines, have failed to arouse much organized opposition—no "protect-the-eater" bloc. The low proportion of farmers in our population even helps them. If 185 million consumers and taxpayers give a little each to 2 million farm families, the burden may not seem oppressive.

Other groups, farmers point out, get government aid, some at the expense of farmers—the tariff. Does not fairness call for some counterbalance?[4] A powerful argument goes back a long time; farmers, it is said, have little market power compared with middlemen and monopolists on both the buying and selling side. "Purchasing power" provided an argument. "If farmers have more income, they will buy more and help stimulate business." (Where would the added money come from? In this case, the answer which should be obvious would generally be correct: "from the mass of consumers." Purchasing power would be transferred, not increased.) Other arguments are: (1) stabilizing one sector of the economy will help bring general stability; (2) our future food supply is so important that we do well to see that soil is conserved; (3) ample food supplies are essential for military security; (4) having started to give help, we must continue; (5) higher income will permit the farmer to give his children a better start; as they go to the cities later, the whole country will benefit.

FEDERAL AID TO FARMERS

Many federal aids to farmers had accumulated by 1930—in financing, research and education, land reclamation, inspection and regulatory services, and for cooperatives. Chief interest today, however, centers on policies dating from the 1930's.

Early New Deal.   The main efforts of the New Deal were directed toward raising the prices of farm products and giving farmers direct benefit payments. Leaders had learned one principle from an earlier effort: to make a price-raising policy effective, output must be curtailed. The New Deal, therefore, limited its payment of direct benefits to farmers who would reduce their crop acreage (or cut production in other ways). Pigs were killed (not many), cotton was plowed under, land was taken from cultivation of the special crops. This seemed wrong—consumers paying producers not to produce in a world wracked by poverty. Moreover, acreage restriction proved to

---

[4] At best, the argument is crude. Prosperity does not come from burdening others. The few who benefit from tariffs are not the ones who pay the bulk of the cost of farm benefits.

be a weak control. A farmer who cut his corn acreage might cultivate the smaller area more intensively, perhaps using his benefit check to buy more fertilizer. Instead of letting land stay idle, he would plant something else, increasing *its* output. Enforcement at the grass roots was difficult. Reduction of acreage was concentrated on poorest land. Weather changes inevitably upset output predictions.

Price Parity.   To understand federal policy, one must understand the concept of price "parity" as Congress has developed it. There is a parity price for each of several dozen farm products. (1) The original system was based on 1909–14 prices. In those years, the prices the farmers got seem to have been fairly well balanced with the prices they paid for what they bought. The parity system was designed to maintain this relation. If the price of a product is at parity, a unit such as a bushel of wheat will buy for the farmer as much today as it did on the average in the base period. (2) "Modernized" parity for any year, say 1966, rests on a formula which uses prices over the previous 10 years and also takes account of the cost of hired farm labor. This is the basis now used in most cases.

Economists point to many a defect in the "parity" concept.[5] One defect is that a fixed parity standard reduces the effectiveness of the economic system in adjusting to changes in consumer demands. Relative prices—bread in relation to meat, cotton in relation to nylon—help guide the use of productive capacity. Higher prices call out more of what we want and force us to economize in consumption; lower prices do just the opposite. If relative prices are not free to move, they cannot do these jobs. The 1909–14 base became grossly obsolete long before it was replaced. The use, in 1968, of prices of the 10 years immediately preceding is a lagging improvement. Perhaps the most serious defect is the failure of parity to take adequate account of costs of production *per unit of output;* productivity has grown marvelously in agriculture so that farmers can produce a unit of output with fewer *total* inputs. Figure 21–3 compares official parity for cotton with an estimate of what parity would be if allowance were made for increased efficiency in production.

"Parity" of price remains a goal. Government does not guarantee it to farmers, nor protect consumers if a price goes above parity.

Methods of Raising Prices.   Most of the billions Congress spends to help farmers go to raise some farm prices toward parity. The arrangements are varied and complex. There are no programs for products that make up about half of all marketings: in most years producers of cattle, hogs, chickens, and most fruits and vegetables get no help.

Chief emphasis has been on reducing supply. *Crop restriction* is one

---

[5] The actual statistical computations of parity raise problems. The nearly 500 items in the index weight living-cost items 40 percent, production-cost elements, excluding wages, 51 percent; taxes and interest are 3 percent and wages 7 percent. A few items are work shoes, canned corn, nylon hose, Buick Specials, dinner plates, house paint, 20-tube grain drills, hoes, 4–12–4 (fertilizer), and cowpea seeds. The same index is used for the entire country even though farmers buy rather different combinations of things.

method of cutting supply; Figure 21–4 shows how restriction may raise price to the farmer's benefit.

1. *Soil Conservation and Land Retirement.* Farmers are paid to restrict production, but indirectly and in the form of payments for soil conservation. Land used or developed in certain ways—and thus not producing some crops—brings the owner a government payment. The soil conservation work has yielded much positive accomplishment.[6] Improving land, however, will eventually increase output. Another method of taking land out of production, the "soil bank," was tried in the late 1950's. The government paid about the net amount the farmer could earn if he cultivated the acreage. Results were disappointing, partly because land withdrawn was inferior or was used to grow other crops. Payments to corn and sorghum farmers to reduce 1961 plantings by 30 percent, cost taxpayers, in effect, $1.80 per bushel of grain *not* produced, compared with support prices averaging somewhat over $1.10 per bushel. Output dropped only 11 percent.

2. *Marketing Quotas.* Production may be restricted in another way. For some crops marketing quotas may be established. These can be very stringent indeed. The Department of Agriculture estimates how many acres need to be planted to provide current consumption and export needs and to assure an "Ever-Normal Granary." If it seems that plantings may be greater, the total acreage needed is subdivided into allotments

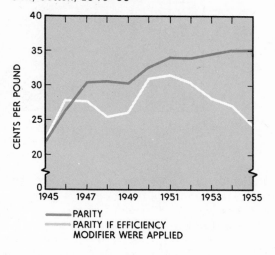

FIGURE 21–3. Parity Price with and without Allowance for Change in Efficiency of Production, Cotton, 1945–55

for states and counties. These allotment proposals are submitted to referendum of the farmers; if two thirds vote in favor, everyone is bound. If acreage reduction does actually reduce output, it will help raise price, presumably enough to benefit the farmers. Wheat acreage in 1964 was about 25 percent below the average of 1946–50; production was 5 percent greater. A farmer exceeding his quota is subject to a penalty tax on any output marketed from the acreage

---

[6] Is it not a bit foolish for the public to pay a farm owner for the improvement of his own land? The benefits do belong to the landowner, but good soil may help future consumers. Shortage of funds may prevent many farmers from doing what is in their own and the general interest. Individual farmers cannot always know what is best for conservation; some of the engineering, for example, is more complicated than the farmer can ordinarily know. Moreover, there are social costs of bad land use—the premature silting of power dams and navigable waterways from rapid erosion—that do not fall on the individual landowner; the general public may be wise to pay something to prevent them.

FIGURE 21–4.　Rise in Farm Income from Acreage Reduction

Taking land out of cultivation reduces supply. If demand is inelastic, the total revenue received will increase, that is, G (gain) is greater than L (revenue lost). The farmer also saves the costs of producing output AB.

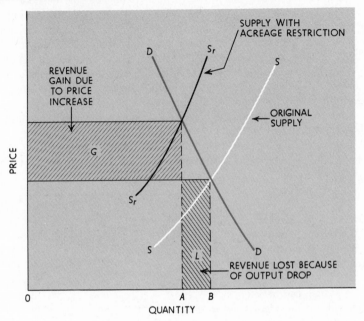

allotment. For some years, however, corn producers have been free to exceed allotments in return for lower price supports.[7]

For wheat and cotton, Congress in 1964 established new programs. For wheat the basic price support was cut from around $2 a bushel to $1.30. In addition, however, the farmer gets marketing certificates worth 70 cents a bushel on 45 percent of the normal yield from his allotted acreage and an equal number of certificates worth 25 cents. The farmer in addition gets cash of 20 percent of the basic support price on normal acreage output. The miller using wheat for domestic purposes buys at the market price; in addition he must buy marketing certificates at 70 cents a bushel; exporters must buy certificates for 25 cents. The net result, therefore, is that farmers get at least $2 for some of their output—the consumer rather than the government paying 70 cents of subsidy. The price of wheat exported will be less than that consumed at home.

For cotton the support price was lowered from 32½ cents to 30 cents a pound. But both domestic and foreign users of cotton are to be permitted to acquire it at 23½ cents a pound. In effect a subsidy of 6½ cents a pound was paid to farmers who produce within acreage limits. Then in 1966 the price was dropped to 21 cents, and direct payments of 9½ cents a pound were

---

[7] Corn fed to livestock on the farm and sold in the form of meat brings no penalty.

provided for cotton used domestically from farms whose operators agree to cut acreage by one third. Numerous complex details apply.

Acreage restrictions have two great defects (1) farmers may concentrate and produce more per acre on the smaller plot, and (2) they may use the freed land to produce something else.

For milk and dairy products and numerous vegetables, fruits, and nuts, producers decide among themselves how much to market. If the Secretary of Agriculture approves, the agreement (exempt from the antitrust laws) binds all producers. The enforcement of restrictive arrangements requires considerable local investigation, more or less arbitrary decision, and a large staff.

Two other programs seek to support prices by restricting the quantities supplied to the open market. Figure 15–11 illustrates what is involved.

3. *Purchase by Government.* Federal agencies purchase certain perishable and semiperishable products outright. Those not readily storable may be destroyed, sold ("dumped") abroad at sacrifice prices, given or sold cheaply for school lunches or relief,[8] or put into durable form (such as dried eggs).

4. *Loans on Crops Put in Storage.* Government withdraws some output from the market by means other than outright purchase. For a variety of storable products, the government will lend, up to some percentage of parity, even though the market prices is lower.[9] Wheat, for example, goes into storage. The farmer gets his loan. If the market price of wheat rises above the loan price, the farmer may sell the grain, pay off the loan, and keep the difference. If the market price stays below the loan price, the farmer turns the wheat over to Uncle Sam; the loan is canceled. In 1967 the Commodity Credit Corporation had around $3 billion of loans and crops, about half the total of earlier years. By 1967 cotton and tobacco accounted for almost all the holdings, food having largely disappeared.

The taxpayer stands any loss—while assuring the farmer a chance to benefit if the price rises. The loan-storage plan was originally designed to help make marketing more *orderly*, evening out fluctuations. Then it became a device to *raise* prices by withholding supplies from the market permanently. Large amounts have been sold abroad under Public Law 480 at prices well below cost to the government. Payment is received in the form of foreign currencies restricted for use in the land of purchase. By 1967 the equivalent of nearly $4 billion from such sales had been accumulated, above amounts used.

Level of Price Supports Fixed versus Variable Supports. Having set "parity" as an implicit standard, Congress faced the question of how fast to move toward it. In 1938 price support goals of 52 to 75 percent of parity were set. Then came World War II. The world's need for American food soared.

---

[8] In many communities a food stamp plan permits the distribution of surplus food through normal retail channels. Families qualifying for welfare aid receive stamps which they use as "currency" for purchase of designated foods at grocery stores.

[9] Import quotas *must* be imposed when certain price-support policies are in operation. Otherwise, we might find ourselves supporting prices for farmers in other countries.

Remembering the post-World War I collapse of prices, farm leaders argued that it was dangerous for farmers to expand output. Therefore, to reduce risk and thus to assure incentive, Congress agreed to support prices at a minimum of 90 percent of parity until 2 years after the end of hostilities.

Right after the war, market demand was high enough so that support at 90 percent of parity was not seriously burdensome. Net farm income and food prices were both high. Later, the inflation from the fighting in Korea made price-support operations generally unnecessary. The boom passed, however. Before long, storage facilities would not hold the growing tonnages farmers wanted to pledge for loans.

Discussion continued around two issues: the general *level* of supports and whether they should be "fixed" or "flexible." The higher the level, the greater the problem of restricting output and stimulating consumption, and the greater the probable cost to taxpayer and consumer.

Fixed supports mean that Congress sets a mandatory level below which price must not be permitted to fall regardless of output or consumer demand. Flexible support gives someone (the Secretary of Agriculture) the responsibility of adjusting support levels according to estimated conditions of demand and supply. Flexible supports permit adaptation to changing conditions. The larger quantities of bountiful years offset the lower support prices in determining farmers' incomes, which, of course, depend upon quantity as well as price. For specific products consumption has responded markedly to price changes.

In 1954 Congress voted flexible parities but within the relatively small and high range of 75 to 90 percent for corn, wheat, cotton, peanuts, and rice.[10] Yet dissatisfaction grew—and for good reason. *High* supports induce output, while discouraging consumption. *Fixed* supports reduce the possibilities of using price to help adjust output to existing supplies and foreseeable demand.

Farmers using modern methods can often make a good income when prices are well below parity. A price near 90 percent of parity will induce farmers to produce far more of some products than consumers will buy at those prices. Some prices in an old pattern, as provided by the parity system, will get out of line with others. Rigid supports, then, are bound to create trouble spots. Controls to deal with them would necessitate still more controls as land cut from one use was planted to something else, increasing the supply of the latter and probably requiring support.[11] Many farmers might actually lose income because of output restrictions. The whole straitjacketing of production would be far worse than a nuisance.

The leaders of the two largest farm organizations oppose high fixed price supports.[12] More than once farmers by large majorities have voted against high-price–tight-control proposals (termed "supply management" by the Kennedy administration).

[10] Farm prices averaged about 80 percent of parity through most of 1966. In the spring, however, grapefruit and oranges were above parity; rice, peanuts, soybeans, and calves, among others, sold from 80 to 85 percent of parity.

[11] From 1953 to 1957, cotton, wheat, and corn acreage dropped by 43 million while barley, soybean, and sorghum acreage rose by 25 million.

[12] The two biggest organizations are the American Farm Bureau Federation and the National Grange. The Farmers Union favors supports at 100 percent of parity.

Evaluation of Present System. The present program—in fact, much more varied and complex than described above—centers around price. Yet it does so in ways that prevent prices from doing their ordinary economic job.

A policy that raises prices hurts consumers. Since food is relatively most important in the budgets of low-income families, the price-raising policies bear most heavily upon those who will be hurt the most—somewhat like a hidden sales tax on food. The higher prices cut consumption. They discourage the feeding of animals to supply the meat that a growing and prospering public would consume. The high-price approach creates difficult regulation problems. Nothing short of detailed controls, planned with great intelligence and enforced by a vast, competent, incorruptible staff can succeed if basic economic forces are much out of line.

"Well," you may say, "the poor farmer at least gets help." Does he? Try to outline a system that would *not* help the poor farmer much; one like ours might well be the result. Though much of the justification for aid to agriculture is the poverty in farm areas, high prices give relatively little aid to most poor farmers. Farmers who sell little get slight benefit from high prices. The poorest farmers tend to be those who produce little. The big farmers benefit the most. Moreover, producers of about half of all farm products have no chance to benefit because there is no program for their product. As land diverted from one crop is used to produce nonrestricted crops, other farmers suffer.

Does the system offset the bad effects of weather? The farmer with a bad crop gets slight help, while the one where the weather is good gets larger benefits. The present system creates a pattern of prices of farm products built upon the pattern of the prior decade. Such relations are almost certain to be wrong in view of today's tastes and costs of production. An improving diet means different kinds of food—more fruit and dairy products and less cereal, for example. The more we freeze the past into our price system, the poorer will be the use we can make of our resources to suit our tastes today. The failure of parity to take account of full production costs (per unit of output) makes us ignore the effects of relative changes in the costs of producing different farm products. Controls deprive the farmer of opportunity to use his judgment to operate as seems most efficient with his land and capital. Restrictions raise costs per unit of output; some productive capacity is idled, and some is used in less than the best ways possible. Moreover, the system encourages production of low-quality output; the farmer can often get as large a loan for poor as for good quality product. Shortages of high-quality types of cotton and wheat have required imports (of types which could have been produced in this country) when our own warehouses were overflowing with cotton and wheat of mediocre and poor quality.

The system is in some respects an impediment to improving our international economic relations. Because high prices invite imports, farmers press for import restrictions, which antagonize foreign countries and give them arguments for putting restrictions on entry of our products. Our efforts to dispose of surpluses abroad often antagonize foreign farmers.

To benefit, a person must stay on the land, even when there is a relative oversupply of farm labor. Thus, instead of aiding, it obstructs a fundamentally desirable shift of resources.

Finally, over the long run, the present system will do farm operators far less good than the costs would lead one to expect. In studying rent (Chapter 26), we shall learn a basic principle: If an agent of production is in inelastic supply, an increase in the price of the product will raise the value of the agent. If you were a young man attracted to farming, you would obviously need a farm. Land is essential. Shopping around, you find that others—including landowners and other young men—know about the facts that attract you. The result is an upward pressure on land prices (or the owner's share when land is rented). To get land, you must bid a price which takes account of the expected benefits of government aid. The original landowner, then, can get the lion's share of the permanent benefit. If you rent or buy, the terms on which you acquire the fixed resource will take from you the value of the special government aid. In fact, 1967 farm land prices averaged about three times the 1947 figure. The right to grow tobacco—the allotment—sells for around $1,000 an acre.

Other Aids to Farmers. Farmers get other kinds of government help. Federal and state research provide a real basis for better farm output at lower cost. Special farm credit agencies give somewhat favored treatment. County agents and various educational aids help keep farmers informed and alert to better methods. Sugar growers benefit from a complicated set of controls which establish quotas to limit imports. Tariffs and import regulations give some favors; and in our programs of aid to other countries, farm exports have gotten distinct benefits.

Federal and state law protect and even encourage numerous arrangements which enable producers of certain farm products to restrict production and sales to raise price. The federal government continues to spend money on irrigation and reclamation projects. These make more land available for production at a cost to the farmer which does not cover the full expense to the taxpayer.

The Rural Electrification Administration was set up in the 1930's to bring electricity and telephones to farms. It lends $350 million or so a year to finance the construction of power lines and the purchase of equipment. Some subsidy is involved, chiefly in the form of an interest charge well below market rates. The Farmers' Home Administration lends around $450 million a year for the purchase and operation of farms and for farm housing. It seeks to help poor farmers directly. It aids in planning farm rehabilitation and resettlement; it provides capital for equipment, fertilizer, seed, and construction; it offers guidance on farm management. In general, it has tried to adapt aid to the needs of individual families. In the poorer areas of the South, for example, some accomplishments have been substantial among both white and Negro families.

A BETTER PUBLIC POLICY FOR AGRICULTURE

Finding defects in our farm program is easy. Getting agreement on changes is rather more difficult. Wide disagreement within the one-time unified farm bloc also complicates problems of getting Congress to reform policies. Leaders now see that there is no single problem. An efficient program, therefore, will consist of different parts to meet different needs.

The Outlook: Rising Demand.   Although prediction is hazardous, there seems no doubt that domestic demand for food will rise. Population growth means that more millions must be fed as the years pass. And as income rises, we spend more dollars on food, especially meat and the more expensive fruits and vegetables. Foreigners will want more food than they will be able to pay for. Heavy buying of grain by Russia and China have recently done much to alter the immediate picture in the free world. For our output foreign demand will probably rise. The demand for cotton and other natural textile fibers will probably rise as well, though synthetics provide serious competition.

The Outlook: Rising Supply.   Supply will also rise. One force, it is true, tends to reduce supply by taking labor and land out of agriculture—the exodus of farmers attracted by jobs off the farm and the expansions of cities, highways, airports, shopping centers, and other land-using elements of civilization, which remove from cultivation as much as 2 million acres a year. Yet the trend of rising productivity shows no signs of slackening.

Goals.   In planning future programs of governmental aid, the public can wisely keep certain objectives in mind.

1. *An Efficient Agriculture Serving Consumers Efficiently.*   With only minor exceptions, our food will continue to come from commercial farms. Clearly, there is general public interest in having them produce as efficiently as possible to satisfy consumers. (The more efficient our agriculture, the greater its ability to compete in foreign markets.) The farmer, as any businessman, stands to benefit over the long run from operating with maximum output per unit of input. Efficiency in a broad social sense requires remuneration which rewards resource owners at rates equal to those earned in the best alternatives. Such rewards would yield farmers net incomes on the average above those of recent years. One source of inefficiency today is the incentive given to use resources in producing output which is worth less than the inputs. Reduction of total inputs offers one way to raise net farm income by cutting costs.

2. *Elimination of Farm Poverty.*   One goal of public policy should be to speed the reduction of economic misery on farms.

3. *Minimum Burden on the Taxpayer and the Consumer.*   The cost of farm aid is a tragic drain on the taxpayer. Compared with other needs for government spending—and tax reduction—a grossly disproportionate amount has been going to farmers.

4. *Other Goals.*   Agriculture is related to many aspects of national life which must be taken into account in making farm policy. For example, we should seek farm programs that re-enforce, rather than conflict with, a constructive foreign policy. Defense needs must be considered. Costs of farm aid should be open rather than concealed.

Land Retirement to Reduce Total Output.   Farmers, if free, will cultivate more land than will be in their combined, and the general public's, interest. Except when weather is exceptionally bad, they will overproduce. What, then, is an efficient way to restrain output? (Restraining output is far more economical than producing and then destroying the product.) A land retirement program offers some promise—a program that will *really* take land from cultivation, not merely shift it from one crop to another.

Portions of many farms might be leased to remain idle; administering such a program is difficult, however. And there is a still greater disadvantage: a farmer's productive efficiency tends to drop when his operations are thus restricted. Productive efficiency calls more often for expansion than for contraction in the scale of the individual farmer's cultivation. A preferable approach might be to lease entire farms and remove them from cultivation for a period of years, a sort of "homesteads in reverse." The Cropland Adjustment Program getting started in 1966 will shift 40 million acres from crop uses under 10-year contracts. Costs are likely to be high, especially if the price paid the landowner is based upon assumed prices of output which themselves reflect unrealistic price supports. Sellers of fertilizers and farm equipment, truckers, and other suppliers oppose land retirement.

Nevertheless, farmers wishing to retire or take city jobs would often welcome a chance to get an income from the land while not farming it. For the public this would be less expensive than the present system which, in buying or subsidizing farm output, pays the costs not only of land but of labor and all other inputs. The purpose of land retirement would not be to raise the income of individual farmers (though leaving them as well off as they would otherwise be) but to reduce the total output of farm products.

Reduction of government spending to bring new land under cultivation—by irrigation, for example—seems obviously desirable.

Problems of Specific Crops.　Land retirement would help the total situation. But the producers of at least some products would still face problems. Perhaps improvement in the futures markets would enable the farmer to get rid of some of the risk of uncertainty of wide price flexibility. Considerable improvement could come from heavier reliance upon flexible price supports at lower levels but with no compulsion on the farmer to plant or not to plant any specific crop. The farmer could get protection from the *extremes* of price fluctuations. Moreover, the farmer would not be shackled in his production. The gambling element in farming would decline; at least one assumes that central authorities, who would be responsible for setting each year's support level, can predict more accurately than individual farmers.

There is another possibility—free prices with "production payments." Figure 21-5 illustrates. If they fell below some support level, however, the Treasury would give the farmer the difference between the support level and the market price. Consumers would benefit in the form of prices lower than under the present system. Farmers would get checks from the Treasury. Farm organizations have generally opposed the proposal but the system operates for wool. Farmers object to Treasury handouts—on practical grounds. Would Congress appropriate enough dollars? Might not very tight controls be imposed? It looks better, and seems politically safer, to collect in the form of higher prices charged to consumers rather than from tax funds. The proposal would cut food bills and raise taxes. It would correct the poor allocation aspects of the present system on the consumption side. It would eliminate the costs of storing surpluses. The system would not, however, economize on the use of resources to produce output of slight value.

FIGURE 21–5.   Production Payment with Prices Free (Brannan Plan*)

If the market were free, price would be *OP* and output *OA*. Government, however, promises farmers a subsidy which when added to price will yield farmers *OQ* per unit. At this price farmers will produce *QC = OB*. This quantity can be sold only at price *OR*. Farmers receive *OBCQ*, of which *OBFR* comes from consumers and *RFCQ* from government (taxpayers). By restricting output, of course, government could reduce the need for a production payment.

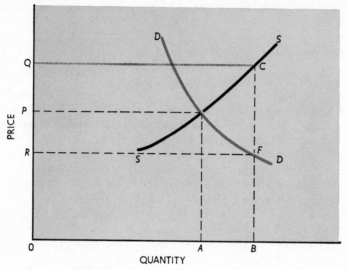

* So named after a former Secretary of Agriculture.

Improvements in marketing may enable the farmer to get more of the consumer's dollar. New industrial uses may stimulate demand for a few farm products.

"Dumping" abroad, sometimes supported, is to be condemned as a costly and inefficient way to help U.S. farmers. For many years disposal abroad for currencies of little apparent use to us did not seem wasteful. What else would be done with surpluses? But success in working off huge warehouse holdings and curtailing output now means that real costs of foreign aid are substantial.

Weather: Crop Insurance.   The weather seems likely to remain beyond control. Yet still more can be done to liberate farmers from the dictates of weather: crop diversification, crop strains that resist bad weather, irrigation, better methods of controlling pests, cheaper methods of fighting frost. If these and other ways of using science and capital can eliminate one third or more of the losses, the rest will be more easily tolerated. The risks that remain should be reflected largely in land values and thus, over a period of years, not burden the farmer as an operator.

Crop insurance, too, offers hope. A federal agency now provides insurance coverage in over one third of the nation's counties. The cost depends upon risk as judged from local experience. The farmer can get protection only against losing his investment in the crop, not for his possible profit. Around half a million farmers have some crop insurance; premiums average 6 percent. Losses have been a little less than premiums collected. Continued progress may induce private companies to offer crop insurance at a price that is adequate but not excessive. Perhaps a broader public program could be developed to provide something comparable to unemployment insurance for support of incomes in periods of unusual misfortune.

Reducing Poverty in Agriculture. Reasonable success in meeting the problems of commercial farmers would reduce—but by no means eliminate— poverty in agriculture.

The least expensive, and most effective, way of dealing with farm poverty in the *short run* is to provide funds to the rural poor directly on the basis of need. One advantage of this approach is that benefits would not get so identified with land that they could become capitalized in the price of the land and hence of slight benefit to future farmers. Even a modest fraction of the government aid now going to farmers with incomes above average could make a significant difference in the lives of very poor farm families.

For the longer run, the attack must be on fundamentals. Training and aid for those who wish to leave farms is desirable. Prosperity in nonfarm sectors of the economy will, as in the past, aid powerfully but unobtrusively in migration from submarginal farms. Fortunately, the number of human beings still on farms with inherently poor prospects is only a tiny fraction of our total population. The long-run solution must be not to hold them where the outlook is hopeless—as relief may do—but to raise their productivity, on or off the farm.

Improving Productivity. The true hope of farmers, as for all of us, lies in producing more per hour of effort and in cutting the hours of undesired unemployment. Farmers must hardly like the prospect of remaining, even indirectly, wards of government, losing the independence, self-reliance, and *opportunity* that have traditionally characterized the American farmer. Wise policy will stimulate, rather than discourage, rising productivity. New methods of vertical integration, and contract systems which link farmer and processor, reduce risk and raise efficiency. Here is a development in the free market which holds promise for both producer and consumer.

Research, much of it financed by government, shows no signs of reaching its limits. Society can confidently count upon better scientific techniques in agriculture. Moreover, farmers can learn to manage more efficiently. If the majority today managed as well as the best, man-hour output would rise appreciably. Desirable consolidation of small plots into larger and more efficient farms, however, is often difficult.

Many farmers need more training in management—and more capital. Some provide for their own needs. Much of what farmers saved out of the high incomes of war and postwar years went into equipment and livestock. Local financial institutions will ordinarily be able to meet justified needs for short-term capital and help arrange longer term financing. Sometimes, however, government help, perhaps subsidy, may be warranted. For example, where large loss from erosion or other damage would be irreparable, prompt action with government-financed aid may be in order if the landowner cannot get funds. The new generation of farmers will not always have the $50,000 to $75,000 or more often needed to buy and equip a modern farm;

carefully devised rental contracts and financing facilities are needed. (Tenancy is often criticized as substantially less desirable than owner operation. Some disadvantages can be eliminated by rental arrangements that assure a renter-operator that his efforts, including those for soil preservation, will benefit *him.*) Government lending agencies can sometimes serve. They can give local institutions the spur of competition that may help the farmer borrow at lower cost. In addition, they can transmit new ideas and expert knowledge.

The best farm policy, it has been said, is a good nonfarm (high-prosperity) policy. It will ease the outmigration of labor and keep demand high. Though an oversimplification, this point of view does have more than a germ of truth.

The fundamental political problem of getting consensus has grown more difficult. Farmers seem to be caught in a system with many obsolete elements (some never wise at their very best) but a system which proves exceedingly difficult to reform because, among other things, the many interested groups cannot agree.

PART 5

DISTRIBUTION OF

INCOME

Who gets what? How Much? Why? Questions such as these go to the heart of our personal economic problems. They also involve lively issues of public policy—the role of labor unions, for example—and two central problems of business (1) costs and (2) the purchasing power of buyers. This range of problems makes up that important segment of economics known as *distribution*. We mean "distribution" not in the sense of marketing or the physical movement of goods but as the sharing of national income. The issues are controversial. Fortunately, however, economics can help make the debates give light as well as heat. How? By providing a body of factual information and by showing how to analyze the problems.

22

INCOME DISTRIBUTION BY SIZE, POVERTY, AND INEQUALITY

Even in these highly prosperous times a relatively small yet significant number of American families have . . . incomes that are much too low. We must try to extend the magnificent performance of our economy. . . . The causes of low incomes are many. Special measures—both private and governmental— are needed to cope with some of them. . . . But the basic cause of low incomes has always been low productivity, irregular employment, or both.
President Dwight D. Eisenhower in his 1956
Economic Report

Americans today enjoy the highest standard of living in the history of mankind. But for nearly a fifth of our fellow citizens, this is a hollow achievement. They often live without hope, below minimum standards of decency. . . . There are two major prongs to our specific attack on poverty in America: First, to enable every individual to build his earning power to full capacity [and] second, to assure all citizens of decent living standards regardless of economic reverses or the vicissitudes of human life and health.
President Lyndon B. Johnson in his 1964
Economic Report

An outstanding event of 1964 was legislation to conduct a "war on poverty." Only a few years earlier we had heard about prevailing "affluence" in American society. In the meantime income—real income per capita—had risen year after year. Even though application of the term "affluence" to the economy had perhaps been inappropriate, some families certainly thrived. Unfortunately, poverty remained, and still does. Experience since 1964, which we shall examine in Chapter 29, shows that we do not know exactly what policies offer greatest promise of progress in reducing poverty. One essential for wise decisions is to learn what we can about the facts and about the forces which produce results, desirable and undesirable.

The receipt of income is tied in with production as part of the process of allocation. The analysis of this process involves price-quantity relationships. In essence, they are much like those studied earlier. We shall now look at the forces which determine the amount of income that will be paid for the use of each factor of production—labor, entrepreneurship and risk taking, capital, and natural resources. First, however, we examine the way the total is divided into shares of different sizes.

IMPORTANCE OF THE SIZE DISTRIBUTION OF INCOME

Dual Problems of Poverty and Inequality. Poverty and poverty alongside extravagant luxury present different problems. Inequality of income and poverty are not the same. Yet they are often confused. For some Americans, and for most of the world, pressing physical wants—grinding, unending poverty—are ruling facts of life. Others of us, who are by no means poor, sense eternally that with even a little more income we could have more fun or less worry.

Some of us are galled by the fact that our rivals are more prosperous. Some of what we want is more than, say, the pleasure of a luscious steak or the convivial emotional satisfaction of an evening at a first-class dance. Our emphasis instead may be the ego stresses of impressing a rival; for the dance, we want as attractive a "formal" as a rival. Some of us dread not being able to appear as prosperous as our neighbors. Thus, inequality of economic position can hurt us personally, not because we ourselves are starved or cold but because a gnawing envy can sap our lives. And are not we all worried, perhaps with an unspoken sense of guilt, at the poverty still existing?

Such personal reaction to inequality, however much it may affect individual comfort and motivation, is not the only reason for concern. Public policies are affected. Sensitive men and irresponsible radicals, bitterly condemning extreme inequality, have pressed for policies, governmental and private, to reduce inequality. Even if the poor were not so poor, the great difference between their economic position and that of the few at the top disturbs many critics, and even some strong supporters, of our economic system. Although the facts are too complex and the issues too subtle for us to distinguish always between the two issues—poverty and inequality—we learn about both by studying the evidence.

Interest of Business and Government. *Businesses* have an interest in the pattern of income distribution. For example, markets for the individual company are not the total national income but the incomes of different buyers. The company preparing to sell $20-a-pair shoes or $20,000 houses can do better if it knows the number of potential purchasers. A firm deciding where to try to develop a market or to locate a branch can plan more wisely if it knows the details about income in different areas. Controversies over wages and prices, utility rates, and other issues often involve questions of differences in income. Even when concealed and vague, these concerns can be influential.

Problems of government policy—especially taxation and spending— frequently touch both issues, poverty, and inequality. Progressive income and death taxes stem from the fact of inequality. Wide differences in tax rates to some degree result from the deliberate desire to make society more equal. Some government spending is designed to change the income distribution—welfare aid, for example. Some government expenditure to alter income distribution finds justification at least in part in a belief that, even after allowing for the necessary taxes, income growth will benefit.

Still more broadly, knowledge about income distribution can help in dealing with problems of the utmost importance. By comparing the types of people whose incomes are high with those of others whose incomes are low, we ought to get more insight into the *causes of differences.* Such knowledge will help us to see better how to solve some problems. Individuals, for example, may choose careers more wisely. The public will seek answers to the question. "How can people at the bottom of the scale raise their incomes and the level of their material well-being?" As a society we also want to avoid policies that deprive us—individually and nationally—of the benefits derived from the forces which produce high incomes.

Scholarly study of the size distribution of income is relatively new, partly because facts necessary for objective analysis were not available before. Today we have much more and better evidence, but it tells us less than we would like to know.

FACTS ABOUT THE DISTRIBUTION OF INCOME

Total Production. Data of total national production or other national aggregates give some help in seeing how income is distributed. Over 5 million new dwelling units and 36 million new autos produced in about 4 years give powerful evidence of widespread enjoyment of income far above the poverty level. In not much longer than it takes to get through high school, one new car was sold for every second family in the country. When nearly 99 percent of households have electric or gas refrigerators, 95 percent TV sets, 72 percent electric washers—then well-being is widely diffused. On the other hand, the fact that around 7 million people received public relief or old-age assistance during 1967, when national income was at an all-time high, leaves no doubt that poverty remains.

We can use broad totals in another way; the per capita national income available for consumption, saving, and taxpaying was almost $3,000 in 1967. This figure tells nothing about inequality, but it does show that equality would not make "every man a king." The average disposable income, $2,600 per capita, was about $500 (in dollars of the same purchasing power) more than in 1955, the growth representing a substantial achievement but not bringing the average family to affluence.

Size Distributions.   We need a sharper tool than overall national figures. We have something in a "size distribution"; it shows the number of families (or other income-receiving units) with incomes of different amounts. Table 22–1 presents a tabulation for 1956 and 1966. The size distribution gives us, at a glance, a general impression of how many consuming units are at the high and low end of the scale, how many are at or above an income level which seems reasonably satisfactory, and so on.

TABLE 22–1.   Income* of Families, 1956 and 1966

Money Income before Tax	Number of Families (Percent)	
	1966	1956
Under $2000	7.7	15.4
2,000 to 2,999	6.6	10.2
3,000–3,999	6.8	12.5
4,000–4,999	7.1	14.9
5,000–5,999	8.4	13.7
6,000–6,999	9.4	9.8
7,000–7,999	9.3	}15.6
8,000–9,999	15.1	
10,000–14,999	20.4	5.9
$15,000 and over	9.2	2.0

* Includes social insurance and other transfer payments received.
Source: Bureau of the Census, *Consumer Income,* Series P-60, No. 52, Aug. 1967. For detailed data on wealth see D. S. Projector and G. S. Weiss, *Survey of Financial Characteristics of Consumers* (Washington, D.C.: Federal Reserve Board, 1966).

From 1956 to 1966 there had clearly been a large and welcome upward movement of income. In the earlier year, for example, 12.5 percent of families had incomes from $3,000 to $3,999; ten years later the percentage was only half as large. And 38 percent had less than $4,000 in 1956—21 percent in 1966. The $10,000 to $14,999 group had come to include over one fifth of all families, contrasted with 5.9 percent in 1956. Some size distributions show how much of the total goes to the various groups. The data may be classified by age or occupation or residence, or some other basis.

Inequality.   A common device for showing inequality graphically is a Lorenz curve. We show on the bottom horizontal axis the percentage of consumer units (from 1 to 100); on the vertical axis, we show the percentage of total personal income (from 1 to 100). Then we plot the points. If income were distributed equally with 10 percent of the people having 10 percent of the income, 20 percent having 20 percent, and so on, the line would run straight from the lower left corner to the upper right corner. If the bottom 10 percent of the population has 1 percent of the income, the lowest 20 percent has 4 percent, and so on, the curve lies below the line of equality. The farther it lies below, the less equal are the incomes. (This form of presentation must not be interpreted as meaning

FIGURE 22–1. Distribution of Personal Income, after Taxes, 1962 Consumer Units, Lorenz Curve (Percentage of Total, Cumulative)

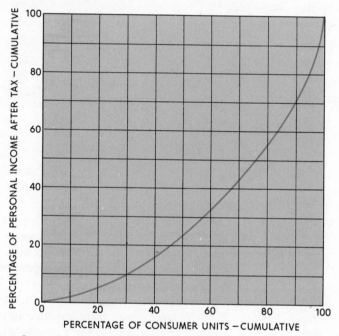

PERCENTAGE OF CONSUMER UNITS – CUMULATIVE

Source: *Survey of Current Business*, April, 1964.

that the line of equality sets a norm or goal of some ideal; issues raised by inequality are discussed later.) Figure 22–1 shows a Lorenz curve for U.S. income. Data on money income before taxes are graphed differently in Figure 22–2.

Poverty. The figures show a distressing number of persons with incomes far below what is necessary for healthful, happy, productive living. Human beings vary so much, and they live in such different conditions, that no single measure can give a reliable idea of what is needed for a minimum or a good standard of living. A sick person needs more than one who is well, a family with many children more than a single individual.

FIGURE 22–2.   Money Income before Taxes in 1965: Percentage of Total Received by Each Tenth of Spending Units and Lowest Income in Each Tenth

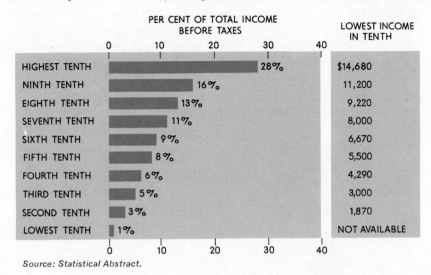

	PER CENT OF TOTAL INCOME BEFORE TAXES	LOWEST INCOME IN TENTH
HIGHEST TENTH	28%	$14,680
NINTH TENTH	16%	11,200
EIGHTH TENTH	13%	9,220
SEVENTH TENTH	11%	8,000
SIXTH TENTH	9%	6,670
FIFTH TENTH	8%	5,500
FOURTH TENTH	6%	4,290
THIRD TENTH	5%	3,000
SECOND TENTH	3%	1,870
LOWEST TENTH	1%	NOT AVAILABLE

Source: Statistical Abstract.

One concept of poverty looks primarily at some "minimum-decency" standard of living. Another focuses on the share or proportion of national income going to the lowest income groups and thus the amounts available to persons whose relative position is poorest. No sharp distinction will ordinarily be made. In a progressive economy, both concepts involve a rising or upward revision of the standard required to put a person above the poverty line. For example, "minimum-comfort" budgets computed for New York City put the per capita requirement in 1903–5 at $527 (in dollars of 1954 purchasing power); by 1959 the level had risen to $1,022 (1954 dollars). Recent (1967) federal government practice is to use as dividing lines $3,200 for a family of four, $2,030 for a couple, and $1,570 for a single individual. By this measure, 29.7 million Americans—more than one seventh—were poor in 1966. Fortunately, many rise above the poverty line (allowing for changes in the value of the dollar) each year; from 1965 to 1966 some 2.2 million moved above the arbitrarily drawn lines.

PROBLEMS OF LEARNING HOW INCOME IS DISTRIBUTED[1]

Are these, however, really *the* facts? Is the picture they give accurate? A closer look will reveal difficult problems of measurement.

Difficulties of Defining "Income."   What is income? This question is surprisingly hard to answer. On the *receipt* side, one doubt involves

---

[1] Actual collection of good figures from interviews, tax records, and other sources presents difficult problems not discussed here.

nonmoney income. The figures needed to add such amounts to money income are rarely available. Yet the amounts are far from trivial—the use of one's own house saves rent; homegrown food cuts grocery bills, and many services may be done within some families but not others. *Government* also provides services of value which we seldom include in estimates of personal income: education, protection, parks, highways, medical services. Though nonmoney income is received at all economic levels, it is likely to be most important percentagewise at the lowest.[2] The usual failure to take account of such income exaggerates the seriousness of the problem of low incomes. Farmers and retired persons tend to have disproportionately low money incomes, but they also often own a house or receive housing for which little or no rent is required.

At the lower end of the income scale, charity provides a welcome addition to the other receipts of some families. Many other problems arise in figuring what receipts are income: expense accounts, capital gains, gifts, meals on the job, travel allowance, or discounts allowed employees on purchases. Moreover, if we seek real, rather than money, income, differences in cost of living from one community to another must be considered. Low incomes are relatively most frequent where cost of living is below average—in rural areas, in small towns, and in the South.

Family or Individual as the Income Unit.   What is the unit whose income is to be tabulated: a family, a household, an income recipient, a person? Such considerations as the following are properly important: millions may have no money income but live well—small children, for example. Some families may enjoy luxuries, though no member has a large money income—when a young husband and wife both have good jobs.

For most purposes, the family (or household) figure is more useful than an individual income figure. However, the problem of deciding what individuals are to be grouped together can never be solved neatly; conditions vary widely, and statistics are inadequate. Yet, clearly, a household income of $9,000 may seem very different from two individual incomes of $4,500. The figures often used (compiled annually by the Census Bureau) apply to the *consumer unit*. This consisted (1967) of 49 million families "of two or more persons related by blood, marriage, or adoption, and residing together," and 12.4 million unattached individuals, "persons not living in institutions or with relatives." One-person units tend to have, and to need, smaller incomes than the ordinary family. Including them in the tabulations, therefore, gives an exaggerated impression of the low-income groups who are really poor. On a full-year basis unattached individuals had median 1966 incomes before tax of about $5,000 while the family average was $8,700 (per capita $2,200).

---

[2] If public education adds $500 of nonmoney value to the typical family's income, the value is 10 percent of the $5,000 income and 3 percent of the $15,000 income.

Adjusting for Taxes. How should we allow for taxes? Some taxes, such as those on business property or income, are included in prices or are so indirect that for studying income distribution they present no practical problem; in this respect they are rather like government services. Personal income taxes, however, obviously differentiate on the basis of income, just the thing we are studying. It is misleading to ignore them in any study designed to learn how much income such families are free to use. In 1965 the top 5 percent of consumer units paid 38 percent of the total of personal income taxes. Their tax was 21 percent of their total gross incomes. For the lowest fifth, tax was less than 1 percent of income; for those few, 130,000, with gross incomes of $50,000 or more, tax was 34 percent of gross income. (These figures do not include state income taxes.) When we want to know what the economy does on the income-generating, as contrasted with the consumption, side, we need to know what people *receive* (not what they are able to consume or to give away); income *before* income taxes is relevant.

Changes in Wealth. How should we deal with changes in wealth? At the upper levels, capital gains (and sometimes losses) are often large, not only in total but also in relation to salaries and other such income. Corporation profit not paid out in dividends does not enter personal income. It does, however, make stockholders better off—and upper income groups own most stock per family. Yet wealth changes are more than a high-income-level problem.

Assume a man has retired with $300 a month lifetime pension (not counting social security), of which $200 consists of the return of his own saving and the rest from interest on the accumulated capital fund. Should he be classed as having an income of $100 a month or $300? For his regular living expenses, he receives $300 a month which will continue as long as he lives. Yet two thirds of it is money he had saved in earlier years. Is the consumption of such prior savings income? Or think of a widow who gets $200 a month from her deceased husband's life insurance— nothing more. This is certainly not income in the common sense of payment for a service; yet it is regular and certain; it is available for her expenses. To exclude it and show her with zero income would give an entirely misleading notion of her ability to support herself, of her need, or of her claims on the production of others. In contrast, many of us receive increases in our wealth every month as our employer pays into a retirement fund for us. As a rule, we do not count such amounts as part of our earnings, even though they are payments by the employer. He must treat them as part of his cost of employing us, and frequently they are fully vested property of the employee—even though he cannot touch a dollar until retirement.

In general, figures on income distribution take little or no account of capital gains and losses but do include pension and insurance receipts. On almost every point, however, practice varies considerably.

Period Covered. Income is an amount received during a period of time. In terms of personal welfare, lifetime income may be more significant than that for shorter periods. Yet most data on income distribution apply to a year only. Since income often comes unevenly over life, millions of persons in any one year will be either well above or much below their lifetime average. Hence, figures ranking the total population by income in a given year will show much more inequality than would figures of lifetime incomes for the same persons or families. Moreover, people entering or leaving jobs during the year will have only part-year incomes and thus appear lower in the scale than their true annual rate.

Costs of Getting Income. What expenses, if any, should be deducted from receipts in figuring income? Some costs of getting income are not very important: the painter's brush or the babysitter's dry cleaning. But, for many earners, the matter of job-related expense is not insignificant: the farmer's trucking expense, the commuter's travel cost, the stenographer's clothing and lunches, the doctor's instruments, union dues. Some things are paid for by the employer, while some must be provided by the employee. What management or operating costs should be deducted for the man who owns a business, a farm, or a building as an investment? Again, the best we can say about actual practice is that it varies.

Transfer Payments. Should unemployment benefits, aid to veterans, social insurance, and welfare receipts—$45 billion or so in 1967—be included as income? If our goal is to learn what the production system in itself does in distributing income, these transfer receipts should probably be ignored. If the purpose is to learn what families have to live on, transfer payments should certainly be included. Such receipts often do appear in the figures widely used.

Conclusion. No single statement can summarize all the varied qualifications one should keep in mind in using data on the distribution of income from low to high. Figures collected in different ways and on bases about equally acceptable—even data collected by various federal government agencies—show results which diverge. For the income ranges that include most of the public, the differences in treatment do not influence relative showings appreciably. It is at the upper and lower ends ("tails") of the income distribution that the results are affected most. The published figures probably exaggerate both inequality and poverty as we ordinarily think of them.

WHO ARE THE POOR?

Who are the poor? In answering, we can learn much about the *causes* of poverty. The following seven reasons overlap.

1. *Death or desertion* by the major earner results in considerable poverty. A substantial fraction of the people living in poverty conditions are in families headed by women—widows and deserted mothers, many never having been married. They may not be able to get jobs that pay well, or they may not be in a position to spend much time working outside the home. This type of poverty tends to be especially deplorable since it seems to persist, perpetuating itself because many of the children carry the bad effects through life. The increase in life insurance and social security coverage, happily, supports the prediction that poverty due to death of the earner (but not desertion) will become less serious.

2. *Sickness and accidents* account for some low incomes. Poor health reduces productivity of a working person, and it forces idleness. A person may lose weeks of work because of ill health or be permanently disabled (such as the mentally ill). Sometimes the same family suffers year after year. Fortunately, however, many families in this group one year are spared in others. Moreover, hospital and medical insurance has done much to reduce the tragic financial burden of illness.

3 and 4. Two other groups make up a big fraction of the population at the low end of the income sale—the *young* and the *old*. Nearly half of the families with incomes under about $3,000 in 1967 were headed by a person under 25 or over 65 years old. If working, they may freely choose to work less than full time. Sometimes the productivity is low. A person beginning his working life will seldom be able to do as much of what others want as he will later after he develops more skill and shoulders responsibility. Then, still later, when he retires, he lives off of what remains from his production earlier, not much. The property he saved brings him or his widow only a small amount. About one third of the poor are retired. The young and old are often single. Approximately half of the spending units in the lowest fifth consist of unattached persons (unmarried, widowed, separated, or divorced persons without children).

5. Some of those whose incomes are low have jobs that do not pay well. *By and large, they are people whose efforts are not worth much to others.* Why? (*a*) The major explanation must be found in the analysis of what makes for personal productivity—education, training, natural aptitude, health, motivation, and attitude. Poverty incomes among working groups are highly concentrated in families whose head has no more than 8 years of schooling. (*b*) Yet special reasons will help explain the results, directly or indirectly. *Negroes and other nonwhites* tend to have a harder time, partly in getting jobs that make fullest use of their capacities, but even more in getting opportunities to develop their abilities. They make up twice as big a proportion of the under $3,000 group as they do of the

population as a whole. (*c*) Geography plays a part; education and job opportunities are better in some areas than in others. About 40 percent of all farm families—and three out of four nonwhite farm families—have less than $3,000 a year income. A southerner's chances of having less than $3,000 a year for a family ($1,500 for an individual) are twice as great as the chances of a person living elsewhere in the country. (*d*) Plain *bad luck* does its bit. (*e*) The shortage of the things one needs to work with—capital, natural resources, and leadership—helps account for much poverty. Some rural areas still contain families whose poverty results from a combination of poor land, inadequate capital, poor education, and low motivation. Billions of dollars of federal farm aid each year have done virtually nothing for these poor because the benefits go chiefly to farmers with higher incomes.

6. *The amount of work some people do is too small* to yield more than a small income. (*a*) They may be hard, steady workers, but the wage they can earn per hour is so low that in a "normal" workweek they will not earn enough to pay for a comfortable living.[3] However, except when expenses are extraordinarily high—for medical needs or college tuition—almost anyone working steadily can support one person on the earnings from any job in the country. But the income from full-time employment on many jobs will not support a family in "minimum comfort." (*b*) *Unemployment* part of the time keeps annual earnings from reaching their potential. In fact a significant fraction of poverty as measured above—not all by any means but a considerable amount—would disappear with the achievement of sustained full employment. (*c*) *Part-year work* is common. College graduates start their jobs in the summer. People retire at all times during the year. Though their monthly rate of earnings may be good, their total in the year is low. Entry and exit from jobs within the year account for some incomes that appear low in the tables but are not low in a meaningful sense. (*d*) Some people are *shiftless*, simply not willing to go to the trouble of working when the opportunity exists. They may have what others would consider a personality defect, or their tastes may differ from those of the more typical American.

[3] Perhaps they prefer leisure to larger money income, but many would work more if they had a chance. Assume two men working side by side on identical jobs with the same hourly rate of pay; one has no dependents, while the other is married with two children. The former might be well satisfied with the pay for 40 hours work a week, while the latter would welcome a chance to work 10 or 20 percent more. Opportunities for supplementary work "moonlighting,"—serving at banquets, off-hour work at a filling station or as a salesman, odd jobs for a farmer or homeowner, typing—vary greatly. The shortening of the standard workweek has probably tended to increase the search for second jobs. Such earnings, incidentally, often escape published income figures.

The reduction of the normal workweek has altered ideas of what is reasonable. The routines of business create inflexibilities, reinforced by requirements for higher rates of pay for overtime and by spread-the-work rules. Perhaps there has also been a tendency to downgrade the importance of working more as the appropriate means of getting more income.

7. *Fluctuation of income* accounts for some low incomes. A man on commission, a speculator, some professional people, artists, or similar persons may have an occasional bad year. When they do, they will be low in the scale even though their long-run average is good. Business owners are especially likely to get in a low bracket occasionally. Some cases may seem statistical freaks; a family with a normally large income and high consumption may occasionally fall "below zero" because the business lost money.

Comment. These groups are highly diverse. The human problems range from the most serious and tragic to some that are hardly cause for public concern. Moreover, some of those in a very low group one year are higher the next and much higher in 5 years. A hard core of serious poverty persists. Fortunately, however, it is not so large as an uninformed look as the figures suggests. It gets smaller. In dollars of 1966 purchasing power, more than 1 out of 4 families had money incomes under $3,000 around 1950; by 1966 the percentage had dropped to 1 out of 14.

The most serious cases develop when a family head has several of the characteristics frequently associated with poverty: ". . . a family headed by a young woman who is nonwhite and has less than an eighth grade education is poor in 94 out of 100 cases."[4] Although the factors associated with poverty throw light on its causes, we know too little about the relative importance of different causes. The forces are interdependent. Some tend to produce or aggravate others. Even the best experts are not sure about what really "causes the causes." Why do some people starting in essentially the same circumstances, as far as can be identified, accomplish much more than do others? Why do some people starting under relatively favorable conditions turn out poorly while others who achieve comfort and even wealth come from the most unpromising origins?

WHO ARE HIGH IN THE INCOME SCALE?

In dollars of 1966 purchasing power, 5 percent of families had total money incomes over about $10,000 in 1950; in 1966 almost 30 percent were at this level. In 1956 less than 250,000 families had before-tax incomes over $25,000; 10 years later, in 1966, the number was over three times as great. To some extent, these higher incomes result from the opposite of those factors accounting for low incomes.

Something depends upon living in an area which is growing. Working in an industry which is thriving also helps. And while some occupations are stable, a few will be enjoying a booming demand. Great energy, a willingness to prepare and to work hard, good health and education, and use of rare skills can be expected to bring rewards—and good ones.

Family incomes are boosted when a second or third person works at

[4] *Economic Report of the President . . . 1964*, p. 57.

paid employment. As the years pass, dividend and interest income from prior savings will in some cases add significant amounts. On a per capita basis, of course, income depends upon the number of persons in a family; the $15,000 which seems hardly large when four children must be supported will provide a high living standard for the parents after the children are on their own.

The very largest incomes are predominantly from property. Inheritance, a lucky oil strike, years of building a business—these can account for large holdings of wealth, even in days of high taxes. A few fortunes yield princely incomes (before taxes), but they are a minuscule fraction of the nation's total. Ownership of property can lead to large growth in wealth if capital values rise—and in the last quarter of a century common stock and real estate prices have, in most cases, gone up substantially.

Below the absolute top, but still in the upper 2 or 3 percent, most income (including a few individual incomes that are very large) will be from salaries and business and professional earnings. Men in the prime of life are receiving the salaries and fees for which they have been preparing for years. A business finally yields a good income. An occasional inventor, salesman, entertainer, athlete, artist, or author gets really big earnings, but for only a few years.

As at the bottom of the income scale, the group at the top contains transients due to fluctuations of receipts. A bountiful crop boosts a farmer one year; an especially successful investment or business deal will occasionally put a man whose normal income is modest far above his average. A general writes his war memoirs, a salesman closes a big deal, or someone composes a "hit" tune.

IS INEQUALITY NARROWING?

Use of the old saying "the rich get rich, and the poor get poorer" brands one as ignorant. The poor have not gotten poorer, and the number of the poor has dropped markedly. About the rich, it is not possible to speak with confidence—certainly not to assert that they are richer. Evidence about income distribution in the past is so sketchy that comparison of today with 1940 or 1920 must be unsatisfactory in some respects while generally reliable in others.

For studying problems which involve the masses of the public, some facts are generally clear. Incomes have risen substantially. The upward movement has been general and broadly based. Inequality has narrowed, but not greatly for the two thirds in the middle. For 30 years or so for which data are available, the lowest fifth has had from 4.1 to around 4.6 percent of all income (see Table 22–2). The share of the top fifth of families dropped from 43 to 41 percent in 18 years to 1965; for unrelated individuals the drop was from 59 to 52 percent, with more going to persons in the third or fourth fifth. For the top 5 percent the relative decline has been much larger. In the 20 years after the outbreak of World War II, average incomes (in dollars of 1950 purchasing power) rose 59 percent; for the bottom fifth, the rise was 79 percent and for the next fifth 84 percent; but for the top twentieth it was 30 percent.

Much of the explanation of the general rise is no mystery. An increasing portion of the public gets more and better preparation for producing—from public education to on-the-job training. As people acquire higher skills, they command higher earnings. The truly significant development has been the upward move in productive capacity of the great masses of workers.

Government finance exerts powerful forces on income distribution—generally as an equalizer. Income taxes take the lion's share of large incomes. The equalizing force is tremendous and sustained. Heavy taxes on inheritance and estates also reduce large fortunes. The "normal" forces

TABLE 22–2.   Family Personal Income Received by Each Fifth and Top 5 Percent of Families and Unattached Individuals

| Rank by Size of Income | Percent of Income | | Average Income | | Percent of 1965 Income of Group | |
	1935–36	1962	1935–36	1962	Families	Unrelated Individual
Lowest fifth	4.1	4.6	$ 337	$ 1,662	5	3
Second fifth	9.2	10.9	749	3,966	12	7
Third fifth	14.1	16.3	1,146	5,938	18	13
Fourth fifth	20.9	22.7	1,708	8,241	24	25
Highest fifth	51.7	45.5	4,216	16,505	41	52
Top 5 percent	26.5	19.6	8,654	28,482	15	20

Source: Statistical Abstract.

of the market, of inheritance, and of wealth accumulation have been altered.[5] Inequality cannot grow by building on itself as would otherwise be the case.

Some government spending supplements poverty incomes. Expenditure programs almost nonexistent a generation ago now give millions of the poor both money and services that boost their real incomes appreciably. Publicly supported schools reduce inequality of opportunity.

The gap between the *ways of life* of the top 5 percent and the masses—the 60 to 70 percent—has narrowed. Today the typical family

[5] Years of high tax rates have undoubtedly led to an increase in the absolute amount of "income" which escapes tax as taxpayers take advantage of loopholes. However, the growth of fringe benefits has also occurred on a large scale through all but the very lowest income ranges. The importance of tax shelters relative to taxable income is doubtless greater at upper income levels. The absolute amounts, however, are probably less than the totals of, say, employer payments into pension funds on which employees pay no income tax (till the pension is received and often not even then).

has much more labor-saving equipment, and the high-income family far fewer servants, than a generation ago. The rich give up their great estates and big houses while millions—tens of millions perhaps—live in larger and certainly more congenial housing than their parents. The masses as a matter of course get medicines that are incomparably better than the wealthy ever had in 1940 (to say nothing of the Gilded Age) and as good as they buy today. Much of what we choose to do with what is really our *own*, the use of our leisure, is about the same for the rich and the masses—spectator sports and TV programs, for example. Even boating has become a popular sport; trips abroad are within the reasonable aspiration of millions. Until the postwar period, the paid vacation time of the corporation president and the plant worker differed immensely; now for persons of equal years of service, vacation periods are often about the same.

With a few exceptions, such as personal service, the rich doubtless have a better standard than in the past, though the point might be difficult to prove or disprove. The really important fact, to repeat, is the *improvement* in levels of living of the masses of families. The reduction of inequality that must count most for the good society is not what pulls down the thousands near the very top but what raises the tens of millions of the masses.

ISSUES IN THE STUDY OF INCOME INEQUALITY

Do the reasons which have led Western ideals to endorse legal equality, then religious equality, then political equality also support the case for economic equality? Emotion and loose thinking, as well as the inability to measure the things being compared, have made discussions of inequality more exciting than illuminating.

Equality of *opportunity* has long been prominent as a goal in this country (by no means fully realized, of course). There has also been advocacy of more equality (or less inequality) in income, the *results* of what a person gets for his efforts and the yield of his property. These two ideals are different. Opportunity and accomplishment are *not* the same.

The discussion which follows will be in terms of large inequality of income. No clear line divides "large" from either "huge" or "small," and our meaning must be vague. The difference between incomes of $100,000 and $1,000 is certainly "large"; but for some of the issues discussed here, a $6,000 to $12,000 range (200 percent) is not "large." We are *not* talking about the inequality that results because at any time the population consists of persons of widely different ages and in all the varied stages of normal economic life. Persons in their prime will normally earn distinctly more than those younger and older.

Arguments against Large Inequality of Income.   A feeling that the great good fortune of some is the *cause* of the poverty of others leads to some of the condemnation of inequality: the wealthy landowner bleeding his tenants, the usurious moneylender fattening on the necessity of the debtor, the factory owner sweating women and children. Men have also hated large inequality because they felt it unjust, unfair, inequitable. Differences in income often seem to bear no reasonable likeness to human deservedness. We may resent the success of our neighbor, even when we have no grounds for questioning the "rightness" of the way he got ahead. A critic may easily arouse us against inequality (of those who are better off) by playing on this very human sensitivity.

Writings of economists include criticism of large inequality on the ground that it brings waste in consumption. Can the frivolous, extravagant consumption of the few really bring them much utility? Their satisfaction must be small compared with the satisfaction the same resources could have yielded to persons facing true deprivation.[6] Certainly there is waste in consuming to "keep up with the Joneses." Some persons who inherit property may "take life easy" and fail to exert themselves. The driving spur of economic necessity, initiative, and enterprise matching opportunity are missing.

Economic inequality tends to be cumulative, to feed upon itself. Human beings die, ending the individual's ability to amass power and dominate others. Inheritance, however, makes it possible for property to pass from one generation to another, growing constantly. Lucky heirs get economic power that far transcends anything they have contributed, power that puts them much more ahead of others than would their own ability and effort. Children born into prosperous families have above-average chances of educational opportunities which help open the doors to the most remunerative jobs.

Finally, we note a point raised in the 1930's but not cited now—large incomes lead to savings which can be large enough to depress business if the demand for funds to buy new investment goods is inadequate.

Arguments for Large Inequality of Income.   What are the arguments in favor of large inequality of income?

One point is just the opposite of the last above—*inequality makes possible capital accumulation.* In a relatively poor society, total income is so low that if it were distributed equally few people would save, or save enough, to provide resources for adding to the community's capital. Inequality does not assure capital accumulation—the few with large incomes may fritter them away on consumption or hoard savings in jewels or other uncreative forms. Without inequality, however, there may be

---

[6] Economists have used a more refined argument. The marginal utility of income is assumed to fall as the amount of income rises; each additional dollar will satisfy a less urgent want. Therefore, the marginal dollars in the hands of people with very large incomes provide less utility than if those dollars were used by people with much lower incomes. Because we have no firm basis for comparing utilities from one person to another, this argument is too "fuzzy" to serve as a guide to action in public policy.

little saving. Table 22–3 shows that, on the average, only persons with incomes well above the poverty line make net personal savings. On the average, persons with low incomes "saved" a negative percent of their incomes.

Considerable *inequality is helpful,* if not necessary, *to permit new businesses to grow.* A chief source of capital for business growth is reinvested earnings. The small, new, one- or two-family enterprise must rely on owners for growth capital. Therefore, the owners must have well-above-average income to be able to finance much expansion.

True *excellence* owes much to inequality. Some of the highest points of culture, the masterpieces of civilization, the challenging standards that inspire untold generations, could not have developed without large inequality. Not every rich noble has financed art. Not every great artist, author, or scientist has benefited from the patronage of the wealthy. Yet some of the superlative achievements of mankind, the world's artistic treasure, would not have developed in a society with substantially equal incomes. Education, too, owes much to the gifts and the encouragement of the wealthy. Artistic, literary, scientific creation; exploration, experiment, and the search for the unknown—all generally require leisure and freedom from many of the worries and humdrum annoyances of life.[7]

TABLE 22–3.   Personal Saving by Income Group

Income after Taxes	Percent of Income Saved
Under $1,000	−91
$ 1,000–1,999	−14
2,000–2,999	− 7
3,000–3,999	− 7
4,000–4,999	− 1
5,000–5,999	0
6,000–7,499	2
7,500–9,999	4
10,000–14,999	6
$15,000 and over	17

* The figures are for 1960–61 and are based on interviews. Changes in assets and abilitiies as reported by the person interviewed were used to estimate net saving. There is reason to believe that net savings are understated (or negative saving overstated), but figures for adjusting are not available. *Source:* Bureau of Labor Statistics.

Inequality of income can create such opportunities. What would happen to our communities without the efforts of civic leaders, men and women, who can give their time only because they have incomes which permit it? The list of America's most prominent political leaders includes some of top wealth; George Washington was not the first, and the Kennedys and Rockefellers will not be the last.

Moreover, *good leadership*—in government, the military, religion, business, and the professions—calls for years more training than even the

[7] What will help make efficient use of that scarcest of resources, the time of people with great responsibilities? Equality may be served if everyone must wash dishes or grow his own potatoes. Yet we know that efficiency is served by specialization, and specialization means that we serve each other. The persons who serve many of us in important ways—from entertainment through invention and business direction to statecraft—must, in return, have many of us serve them if they are to concentrate. A large income for them to use in paying us is then necessary. The "one-class" society is a sure-fire weapon for inefficient use of rare capacity.

richest economy can give the masses. The existence of some large incomes has made it possible for a few people to get training for leadership, though there is no assurance that the good opportunities fall to the most promising persons. Great athletic accomplishment requires more than a coolie's bowl of rice. High achievement in activities of crucial importance to society needs exceptional training, leisure, opportunity, privilege—if not "large" inequality, at least considerable inequality. Inequality in earnings results, to an unknown extent, from inequalities in nature's distribution of skill, intelligence, and energy.

Large incomes have a constructive *incentive* function.[8] A few large prizes may be strategically effective in getting people to do things the community wants. Economic progress owes something indeed to the existence of chances for great fortune. Less extreme inequalities also provide incentives—to develop skill, work harder, or take more responsibility.

Private ownership of property leads to economic inequality. Some people will acquire more property, and income from it, than do others. The benefits of private ownership—the accumulation, conservation, and efficiently directed use of nonhuman means of production—defy measurement. Control of property gives the owner power; he can get things and exert his influence over others. He may use power well or ill, but he has a degree of independence. Perhaps a politician finds it easier to be a statesman if he knows that he has property to fall back upon if necessary. With so much power now concentrated in government, the military, giant businesses, and labor unions, the existence of additional private centers of power can serve as a counterweight. They offer some small insurance against the oppression of great concentration. Private wealth provides a diffusion of power, but with enough concentration in some cases to be meaningful. Property gives freedom, a chance to strike out against obstacles set by other holders of power, independence from forces which limit most people.

Difficulty of Balancing the Arguments.   How do these arguments, pro and con, balance? On each side there are points of great weight. Another, perhaps less obvious, point is that the force of some of these arguments depends upon the sister problem, poverty. If the economy is generally prosperous and poverty slight, our evaluation of inequality will not be the same as if poverty is massive.

Conclusions will also vary with answers to the question "When is inequality inequitable?" As we gain understanding of the causes of ine-

---

[8] The testing ground for new things, the stimulation of demand for new products, has often been the luxury market. The spending of the rich, who can afford to pay high for some new gadget, permits business to develop it. Research and testing begin, economies of production are found; eventually the masses get a chance to buy an improved product for less than the wealthy paid earlier. The auto is an example. If many incomes are high, no large inequality may be needed to yield this result.

quality, we get some idea of whether the results seem fair and equitable. We even progress as we become sensitive to the difference between *equality* and *equity*. They are different terms, not synonyms. If one worker produces five times as much as another, equal compensations seem hardly fair. Is it equitable to give both football teams equal scores? Or everyone in the class the same grade?

Another query suggests a problem of balancing the arguments. "How important is equality compared with other values?" Even though we may agree that large inequality of income has undesirable features, we may disagree on what is better or worse. How much of some other value— such as growth of new businesses—might we wisely (or foolishly) sacrifice to get more equality? The practical problems require comparisons of specific alternatives; they usually involve facts and choices that are hard to balance.

What are the ultimate objectives? Is the pressure for more economic equality an outgrowth of a feeling (perhaps not fully recognized) that political decisions ought to gain greater influence over those of the market place? If so, would the distribution of political power, as exercised, become more or less unequal? And economic power? Was Justice Holmes at least partially correct in writing, "I have no respect for the passion for equality, which seems to me merely idealizing envy . . ."? Or would a more egalitarian economy be one of more brotherhood?

Chapter 29 will resume the analysis of problems of poverty and of policies for dealing with them.

TERMS AND CONCEPTS

distribution of income	Lorenz curve	equality
income size distribu-	poverty	equity
tion	inequality	consumer unit
transfer payment	moonlighting	inheritance

QUESTIONS

1. In what respects do the problems of inequality differ from those of poverty? Are there similarities?
2. How do the types of poverty seem to differ in seriousness?
3. What, if any, benefits does society get from income inequality? Disadvantages?
4. What factors account for large incomes?
5. What government policies tend to reduce inequality?
6. Why is it difficult to measure the distribution of income by size?
7. Would you favor equalization of income on a worldwide basis? Why?
8. When governmental aid to low income groups comes to billions of dollars a year, as it does in this country, why does poverty continue?

23

PRODUCTIVITY AND THE DEMAND
FOR PRODUCTIVE SERVICES

It is totally false to ascribe to a single factor of production what is in fact produced by joint activity; and it is completely unjust for one factor to arrogate to itself what is produced, ignoring what has been contributed by other factors.

Pope Pius IX

The distribution of income in any society results from the interaction of myriad forces: economic, political, sociological, legal, philanthropic. How do they work? What is the process by which wages and other shares are determined?

INTRODUCTION

Everything will be owned by someone. No more exists to be shared. The part of the total money income each person receives depends upon (1) the amount of productive services he sells (from his labor and his property) and (2) the price of each service. The man who works 2,000 hours at $3 per hour will receive a pretax income from his labor services of $6,000. Price and quantity both play a part.

The next few chapters deal with the pricing of productive services. The basic point: The price of a productive service is determined by the forces of supply and demand. The essentials of the previous analysis apply. Yet on both sides, demand and supply, special considerations call for attention. This chapter deals with certain broad features of the demand for productive services. The appendix discusses one special aspect of supply.

"Essentiality" as a Test of the Worth of a Productive Service. First, however, let us dispose of one point that can be confusing. Sometimes it is said that someone ought to be paid more because without him (or property he owns) a whole process might fail. Does not labor deserve the whole product of the economy, since obviously labor's efforts are essential? Yet the machines, railroads, telephones, turbines, libraries, and office buildings are also essential; without them hard labor would yield little. Could a theory resting on "essentiality" get us far?

Think again of the economic system as a giant cooperative. Many things combine to produce each result. In this mutual effort, it is ordinarily impossible to say which of the several different things that depend upon each other is more important in some basic sense. A minute catalyst has a vital effect on a whole chemical reaction, and yet it may be unimportant without the other elements. An auto will not run without gasoline, spark plugs, and many other parts. Each is vital, though many, like a cigaret lighter, are hardly necessary. Should the price we pay for each "essential" part then be equal to the total value of the auto? Obviously not!

Demand for a Productive Service as a Derived Demand. The demand for a productive service—of labor, machines, natural resources— differs from most of the demands discussed in Chapter 14. Generally it is a *derived demand*. The buyer is usually a business.[1] The service is demanded not for itself but because it will create something which can be sold. The demand for the thing that can be sold, therefore, is what makes the business want the labor or other productive service. The demand for printers, for example, derives partly from the demand for books; the demand for borrowed funds to buy freight engines is derived from the demand for transportation, which in turn comes from the demand for fruit, coal, and innumerable other things.

The businessman, in buying labor and other productive services, will pay, not according to the satisfactions he expects to get directly but according to (1) the amount and kind of things the services produce and (2) what these things will sell for. Two different considerations enter: production in a *physical* and in a *value* sense.

Production is basic. To study its connection with distribution, economists have a simple analytical tool that is like other simplifying aids to study, such as the concept of a frictionless machine. It points out the extreme or limiting possibility. Perhaps it is not so useful to the businessman as it is simple to the economist, but it reveals a central economic reality, reality in the sense of the adjustment that can bring the greatest

---

[1] Among exceptions are government, the housewife hiring a laundress, the "student" a tutor, the church a minister.

efficiency (largest net benefit). The principle is this: **The price paid for use of a factor of production shall equal its marginal productivity.** We now explain this concept.

DEMAND FOR A FACTOR OF PRODUCTION IN THE SIMPLEST CASE: ONE FACTOR ONLY[2]

We assume a business operating in purely competitive markets; at the moment, it is buying only one type of input or factor of production: labor. It uses other factors, of course, but for the time period they are fixed and do not enter the calculations. Labor inputs working with the fixed factors produce outputs. The more labor used, the larger the output. Yet the forces of diminishing returns enter—diminishing productivity is a better term. The variations in output are not uniform with changes in the amount of labor used. Table 23–1 shows the kind of relationship that

TABLE 23–1.   Firm in Pure Competition

Number of Units of Input: Labor (1)	Output: Total Product per Day (2)	Marginal Physical Product* (3)	Price (Marginal Revenue) (4)	Total Revenue Col. (2) × Col. (4) (5)	Marginal Revenue Product† (6)
9	100		$1.50	$150	
		12			$18
10	112		1.50	168	
		10			15
11	122		1.50	183	
		8			12
12	130		1.50	195	
		6			9
13	136		1.50	204	

* Values of marginal amounts are shown to fall between the values of the first two columns to emphasize that the marginal values are associated with the changes or differences.
† This is the value of the marginal physical product.

might be expected. Total product rises as more inputs are used, but successive inputs do not add equal amounts to output. To spot the differences, we look at the *marginal physical product,* which we can define in this case as the addition to total physical product resulting from the employment of one more unit of labor.

The businessman, of course, is interested in the physical product for what it will bring him in dollars. His decisions about buying productive services will depend upon such dollar calculations. Under pure competition the price of the product will not vary with the output of the firm. We can thus compute the *marginal revenue product* or, in other words, marginal productivity in each case; **this is the increment of total revenue resulting from the use of an additional unit of input** (labor). In pure competition it is price (marginal revenue) multipled by marginal physical product.

[2] This analysis is closely related to the dicussion of cost and output for the firm.

Now we have a key to help answer the question "How much can the employer afford to pay for labor?" Clearly, he cannot afford to pay more than the value of what is produced. But since there is a wide range of value of what is produced, there is a wide range of possible wage rates. In our illustration, there are conditions under which the employer might pay $15 a day, or $9. The *amount* of labor he would hire would vary, however, according to the different rates he must pay. If he can get labor for $9, he will wisely hire 13 units; but if he must pay $15, he will hire only 11. Thus there is a *demand schedule*—a series of quantities that will be purchased at different prices. **The schedule of the marginal revenue product is the employer's demand schedule for labor.**

If the going wage rate is $12 a day in the community, the employer will profitably hire 12 men. His labor cost will be $144 a day. The value of his total product will be $195 (130 units of output multiplied by the price, $1.50). He will then have $195 minus $144, or $51, to cover his other costs. The twelfth man, in a sense, just pays his way when the wage is $12 a day. If the going wage rate is below the marginal revenue product, the employer can increase profit by hiring more labor. But if the wage rate is above the marginal revenue product, he will enlarge his profit by cutting employment.

The employer's demand schedule for labor depends upon the productivity of labor. The demand schedule is the schedule of the marginal revenue product because the latter is the amount which each successive laborer adds to the firm's revenue. The quantity of labor that will be hired is that at which the wage rate, the price of labor, equals the marginal revenue product. See Figure 23–1; study the explanation carefully.

But why *marginal* rather than *average* product, which is higher (when the firm is operating under conditions of diminishing productivity)? If the employer were to add labor until the wage rate equaled the value of the average product, he would, by paying some laborers more than the value of what they added to the firm's revenue, lose money. A clearer reason, however, explains why average product cannot be used as a guide to the demand for any one factor. The average product results from the cooperation of *all* factors. If we divide the total product by the number of units of one factor, say, labor, to get the average and pay wage rates equal to that average, nothing would be left to pay other factors.

The market demand schedule for the service will be the total of demand schedules of all firms. Each business makes up part of the total, but in a purely competitive market it is too small a part to influence price (of the factor) appreciably. Yet as firms use more or less of the input in adjusting output for best results, the price (of the factor) tends to change until it reaches equilibrium. At that point the quantities demanded equal the quantities supplied in the market.

How is the demand schedule for each of the other inputs (factors of production) determined? In the same way. Marginal productivity is the

FIGURE 23–1.   Marginal Revenue Product as Demand for an Input

E represents equilibrium, output OA being optimum. If output were OB, the employer could benefit by hiring additional man-hours BA, for man-hours add more to revenue than they cost by the triangle Ebb'. But if he employed more men, say a total of OC, he would pay more for the man-hours AC than the worth of what the man-hours add to revenue by the triangular area Ecc'. If labor productivity rises, or if the selling price of the product goes up, and marginal revenue product rises as indicated, then at the prevailing wage rate, the number of man-hours hired which is optimum will be OD.

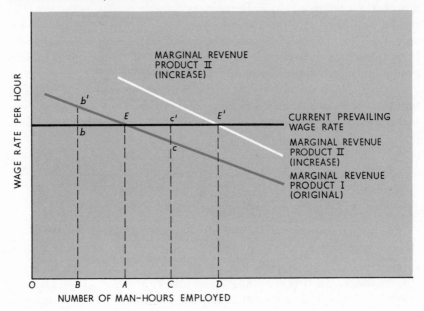

key. The demand will depend upon what different quantities of the factor will add to the firm's revenues, assuming other factors remain fixed. In other words, each factor will produce under conditions of diminishing productivity. Two things play a part in determining a firm's demand: (1) the factor's physical productivity when working with other factors and (2) the price of the firm's product. The quantity of the factor the firm will use depends upon the firm's demand for the factor and the price prevailing in the rest of the market for the factor.

DEMAND FOR FACTORS OF PRODUCTION: MORE THAN ONE FACTOR

Chapter 16 showed how a film will try to find the best production possibility, the least-cost combination. Two general sets of factors govern: physical productivity and the prices of inputs. The physical aspects are essentially an engineering or technical problem. The state of technology makes it possible to do a specific production job, such as making chairs, in different ways. Some methods use relatively large amounts of labor of cabinetmakers and few machines; other methods use highly complicated equipment, some skilled machinists, and relatively unskilled machine operators. The physical combinations that are feasible will vary according to the rate of output. How will a firm judge what is the least-cost combination for any given scale of output?

In deciding upon which combination of factors to use, the firm should look at the schedules of the marginal physical products of each factor. (Unfortunately the best figures that can be obtained may have a considerable range of possible error.) These products are comparable because they are units of the same physical thing, such as chairs. The inputs, however, are physically different: labor, machines, and so on. Yet they have one thing in common—price. So these varying inputs can be compared in a meaningful way. Consequently, it is possible to find which pattern of expenditure on inputs will be most profitable—and adjust accordingly.

Let us illustrate: assume three kinds of inputs, A, B, and C. At the margin, 1 unit of A produces 12 units of output, 1 unit of B yields 8 of output, and 1 unit of C produces 2 units of output. Input A costs \$4 per unit, B costs \$2, and C costs \$1. Then three ratios or proportions can be computed:

$$\frac{\text{Marginal physical product of } A}{\text{Price of } A} = \$3$$

$$\frac{\text{Marginal physical product of } B}{\text{Price of } B} = \$4$$

$$\frac{\text{Marginal physical product of } C}{\text{Price of } C} = \$2$$

This firm has not yet done best for itself. A dollar spent on B brings twice as much as a dollar spent on C and a third more than a dollar spent on A. Clearly, it is desirable to shift some spending from C to B. As the business does so, the use of more B reduces the marginal physical product of B—the law of diminishing productivity is operating. (When two factors change at the same time, with the third remaining fixed, the effect of diminishing productivity is likely to be somewhat different from the effect when only one changes.) Just the opposite happens with C: reduction in use will eliminate inputs which had been applied where diminishing productivity was greatest. As less C is used, the marginal product of what remains rises. Perhaps a few shifts will reduce the marginal physical product of B to six and raise that of C to three. Then the ratios for all three types of inputs are equal. Probably, however, there will be a more complex change. More or less of A may be used before all three proportions are equal.

If many factors of production are used, many different ratios must be considered. When the ratios are the same, there can be no benefit from any change. The least-cost combination of factors has been achieved. In total amounts, physical or dollar, the differences may be huge. It is *at the margin* that equality is achieved. At this point—the equilibrium—there is no shift from one type of resource to another which can give more revenue at the margin for a dollar spent on any input. So much for *proportions*.

What about the amounts of each input used? The firm's demand for all inputs, and hence for *A*, *B*, and *C*, depends upon the price of the final product. The firm will earn most (or lose least) by carrying total output to the point where the price of the final product (marginal revenue under pure competition) equals marginal cost. It will buy enough of each factor to produce this output.

Another equality must be noted. The discussion earlier in this chapter led to an important conclusion: The firm's optimum position is that where **the marginal revenue product of a type of input equals the price of that input.** This applies not only when a firm uses one factor but also when it uses several. For each, price and marginal revenue product must be the same if the firm is to minimize cost (maximize profit). The marginal revenue products of *A*, *B*, and *C* will not be equal to each other, but each will equal its price.

Do businesses really act this way? Very few businessmen would describe what they do in the terms we have used. Yet we seldom describe our dinner as calories, minerals, vitamins, and the other terms of the dietician. Things can be done by people who do not know the technical terms to describe them. We have used technical terms to explain conditions of least cost as they affect the demand for inputs. The more nearly a firm discovers these conditions, the lower its costs and the better its competitive position. Success and survival depend, in part, upon how well a company does in approximating the least-cost combination not whether the manager can pass an economics quiz. It will be a miracle if a firm makes absolutely the best adjustment, but it will be no less a miracle if a business survives in strong competition while remaining far from the least-cost combination.

Changes in the Firm's Demand for Inputs.   Now, we can see two ways in which equilibrium can be upset so that a firm's demand for inputs will change (assuming no shift in the demand for its product). (1) A change in the *price* of a factor of production will change its ratio. If one kind of input becomes more expensive, for example, the thing to do is to use a smaller amount of it and more of the less costly factors. This essential of economizing is called the *principle of substitution:* As the price of one input rises relative to the prices of others, the firm, to minimize its costs, must reduce the amount of the input with the rising price and substitute other inputs. Just as demand for beef depends partly upon the price of pork, the firm's demand for a productive service depends partly upon the price of other productive services which can be substituted. When a union forces up the price of labor, the union's action increases the demand for labor-saving machinery. (2) A change in the *physical output* will change the ratios. If one type of labor, for example, begins to turn out more product per hour, this labor becomes less expensive per unit of output. The economical thing for the firm to do is to substitute such labor for other factors whose physical productivity has not risen. Thus, if textile workers, after their wage increase, work harder and better, no rise in demand for machinery may result.

Influence of the Demand for the Firm's Product. The demand for a factor of production is derived from the demand for the firm's product. Under pure competition, any one company's actions have little influence on the market. The firm reacts to market conditions—the costs of inputs and the price of outputs. The quantity a producer sells, however, depends upon the price of the product and also upon costs. If demand falls or if costs rise—because the price of one or more factors increases or the physical productivity falls—the firm will find that the best thing to do is to reduce output. It should cut out the production whose marginal cost now exceeds the marginal revenue. With output smaller, a company will use less of some, perhaps all, factors of production. The total market demand for the inputs tends to drop.

MONOPOLY AND MONOPSONY

Two kinds of departures from pure competition influence the demand for inputs: monopoly and monopsony.

Monopoly. Under pure competition any single firm's actions have little influence on the market as a whole. The firm reacts to market conditions—to the costs of inputs and the price of outputs. Changes in its output will not affect price of inputs or outputs appreciably.

But what if the firm is a monopoly, a single seller? We assume that it buys inputs in competitive markets so the price it pays per unit for inputs does not depend upon the quantity it buys. Its sales, however, present a very different situation. Since it supplies the whole market for its output, the quantity it sells will depend upon the price it sets. If it wishes to sell more units, it must lower the price. This reduction applies not only to the additional units but also to the units that would otherwise have been sold. For the monopolist, we recall, marginal revenue is below price. The net addition to its receipts from the sale of one more unit—the marginal revenue—may be small, certainly less than the selling price of that unit. Therefore, to make the best adjustment of output, the firm must look not at the price of the marginal unit produced but at the effect of the sale of this unit on the price of all units. In Table 23–2, for example, the marginal revenue product (Col. 6) falls relatively more than does the marginal physical product (Col. 3). To sell the larger output, the firm must lower the price on all outputs. This firm's demand for the input, therefore,

TABLE 23–2.   Firm in Monopolistic Position

Number of Units of Input (1)	Output: Total Product per Day (2)	Marginal Physical Product (3)	Price per Unit (4)	Total Revenue Col. 2 × Col. 4 (5)	Marginal Revenue (6)
9	100		$1.50	$150	
10	112	12	1.48	166	$16
11	122	10	1.45	177	11
12	130	8	1.41	183	6
13	136	6	1.35	184	1

differs from that of a business in pure competition. Recall that one of the indictments of monopoly stems from this condition.

Monopsony. Occasionally a firm will find that the price of a factor of production—local labor, for example—will depend upon the company's own demands. *Monopsonistic* situations like this are, on the buying side, like degrees of monopoly on the selling side.[3] Suppose a businessman sees that the supply of one of the productive factors he buys is not perfectly elastic. The more he buys, then, the higher the price; so, for him, the significant point to watch becomes not the price of a kind of input but its marginal cost. The firm as it adds more of this factor must count as the cost of an additional unit of the input not its price but that *plus* the effect on the price of all other units of the same factor. Sometimes this allowance will be trivial, sometimes vitally important. The elasticity of supply provides the key. Table 23–3 illustrates the point.

TABLE 23–3.   Firm in Monopsonistic Position

Number of Units of Input	Price of Input	Total Cost of Input	Marginal Cost of Input
9	$20	$180	
10	21	210	$30
11	22	242	32
12	23	276	34
13	24	312	36

IS THE MARGINAL PRODUCTIVITY PRINCIPLE USEFUL?[4]

Even though the principle may make sense, its usefulness has been questioned.

[3] A firm with monopsony power may sell in highly competitive markets and have no monopoly power.

[4] We consider here only criticism of the principle as a tool of analysis, not of the results to be expected if the forces work as predicted. Persons being paid according to the marginal productivity of their efforts may seem to get more or less than humane or other considerations warrant.

1. The elements are hard to measure. True. The significant fact, however, is that these *are* things that the manager should *try* to measure; his success depends upon how nearly he comes to correct measurement.

2. Most firms produce more than one product. Inputs ordinarily contribute to different outputs in varying proportions. What, then, is the marginal product (physical and revenue) of an input? Exact distinction is certainly difficult. Still, in most cases, there is a margin where any type of input (or output) can be varied, and this is the sensitive area to examine and measure. As inputs change by small amounts, what are the changes in the marginal revenue product? Rarely will things be so inextricably mixed that no separation of any significance can be made at any point.

3. Different kinds of input are not perfectly substitutable; discontinuities, the need to do things in fairly large units if they are to be done at all, make small changes impossible.[5] Yet resources can be combined with far more flexibility than a casual observer may suspect. Although there are cases of lumpiness, where changes from point to point are large rather than small, there are other cases of easy substitution in small amounts. As a general rule, the shorter the period involved, the more important the discontinuities.

TERMS AND CONCEPTS

derived demand	marginal revenue product
marginal productivity	principle of substitution
diminishing productivity	marginal physical product

QUESTIONS

1. We begin the study of the pricing of factors of production by looking at the business firm's planning of input use. What is the logic of this approach?

2. What part does actual or potential substitution of factors of production play in determining their prices?

3. "The business which arranges the production of an item acts as a middleman between the sellers of productive services and consumers of the product." Discuss.

4. Find examples of cases in which one input can be substituted for another in both the short run and the long run.

5. Why is the employer's best interest served by combining factors so that the marginal revenue product of each is equal to its price?

6. What would happen to the income of owners of a factor of production (including labor) whose productivity in physical terms dropped? What other conditions would influence the result?

---

[5] Building regulations create obvious discontinuities. In New York City, for example, if an apartment building rises above six stories, the construction must be different and far more costly from that for six stories or less. A seventh story would be impossibly expensive. Any building over 6 floors must be 10, 12, or more stories to justify the *extra* cost of not only the additional floors but of the first 6 as well.

7. Explain the relationship between the marginal physical product and the marginal revenue product.

8. "A whole economy cannot distribute more than it produces. For any single factor of production, however, the amount the factor produces sets less clear limits on what may be distributed to its owners." Discuss, distinguishing between the short run and the long run, assuming that businesses are seeking maximum profit.

9. "Our earnings depend fundamentally upon the worth of what we do for others, and that means for consumers rather than for the employer." Discuss.

10. If the prices of capital goods for an industry, such as auto manufacturing, rise less than the cost of labor, what results would you expect over a period of, say, 5 years?

11. Explain the "backward-sloping supply curve." Do you think it is realistic? May it help account for the decline in the average workweek since 1900?

APPENDIX: Supply of Productive Services: A Special Consideration

One point affecting the supply of productive services generally can be noted before we turn to the demand-supply elements of each major type. We treat it in an appendix because there is doubt about its practical significance.

The quantity of a factor of production supplied may, to some extent, be reduced by the offer of a higher rate of compensation. If so, the supply schedule has a feature not found in commodity supply schedules (Fig. 23-2).

FIGURE 23–2.   Supply of a Factor of Production with Backward-Sloping Section

As the demand rises, wage rates also rise. When demand first increases from D_1D_1 to D_2D_2, the quantity of the factor offered also rises from OA to OB. The next increase in demand, however, to D_3D_3 results in a decline in the amount offered to OC, even though the rate of pay is higher.

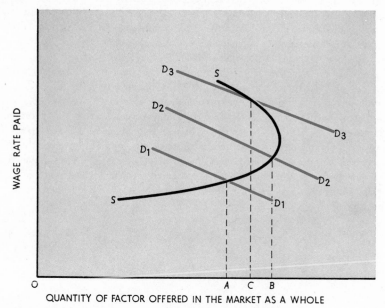

We can illustrate with labor. The higher the wage rate in a *particular* job, the more people will be willing to work at it; however, in the market as a whole, after some point, the amount of labor that will be offered may actually decline as wage rates rise. After a person has worked some amount, he will prefer leisure to more money income. He is tired, or he wants to play with

545

his children, or work his garden, or have some other recreation. But if he can get more pay for a few extra hours, he may be willing to work more; he can use the money, and he will sell an hour of leisure for $3 but not for $2. By paying a higher rate, the employer can get more hours of work from the same man.

However, the normal wage rate may go so high that the worker earns enough in his regular work period to buy what he generally wants; instead of more money, then, he chooses more leisure. The higher his rate of earnings, the more time he may take off—weekends and vacations. He gives up his off-hours second job. The great majority of "working wives" have jobs because the family needs the money. If the husband's earnings rise, the wife may stay at home, cutting the market supply of 'labor. The number of children seeking jobs depends partly on the earnings of parents. A farmer or a businessman may decide to take things easier if income is good; the more one earns and saves during the working years, the earlier one can retire.

Something similar may exist for the supply of nonlabor factors of production. We supply them, as we do labor, at a cost, the sacrifice of alternatives; other things the same, we can supply larger quantities only by giving up alternatives which require more and more sacrifice. The satisfactions given up may be much the same as those we seek in spending our money income. We offer our factors to get in return money to buy other things. The more money we have, the less urgent the wants satisfied by the expenditure of the marginal dollar. Demand for money income slopes downward while there is a rise in the costs of getting additional money income (the worth of alternatives sacrificed), in some cases at least.

Beyond a point, therefore, the higher the wage, interest, profit, or rental rate per unit of a factor of production, the less may be offered. If we can satisfy demand for money income more easily because of a higher rate of pay per unit of what we supply, we may reduce the quantity we offer. Forces making for "backward slope" in supply curves of factors of production certainly exist. Individual preferences differ. But there is no clear basis for measuring their net effect either in the short or the long run. Hence the slope of the total supply curve is uncertain. Clearly, as real incomes have risen, Americans have chosen more leisure, especially earlier retirement. In other respects, however, evidence of the "backward slope" phenomenon is not easily found.

24

WAGES

The progress of human society consists . . . in . . . the better and better apportioning of wages to work.

Thomas Carlyle

Most income is received, and distributed, as wages.[1] For most of us they seem inadequate. For employers, however, wages are generally much the biggest item of cost and often appear high.[2] Whether high or low, wages warrant careful study. We must understand the underlying principles, not only to get essential insight into the way the economic system functions but also because of the involvement of our personal affairs, as earners or as employers, as consumers and as investors.

Total Wage Income Most of the National Income. For the nation as a whole, labor income depends primarily upon what the people employed produce. (The dollar size of the income depends upon monetary factors which influence price levels.) If half of the approximately 20 percent that goes to suppliers of capital were shifted to wages—and making the utterly unrealistic assumption that such a large shift of property incomes to employees would not reduce the total national income—wages could be increased by not more than one ninth. Yet a rise of one tenth in national

---

[1] The single term "wages" will be used to represent all payments for labor services, including salaries, commissions, fees, tips, "fringes," etc. Look in the dictionary to find the origin of the term "salary."

[2] For business as a whole, wages far outweigh all other costs. For many companies, however, costs of materials and parts for assembly, or finished goods for resale (at wholesale or retail), exceed wage costs; the prices of such items, of course, must cover the wages which have been paid in earlier stages of production.

income would provide an increase of around 10 percent for labor income while permitting a growth of property incomes as well. For the nearly 80 million who at some time in 1967 received payment for their efforts, the amount of national income vastly overshadows in significance any possible change in the major distribution of the total. Real earnings depend upon production and productivity.[3]

Our study deals chiefly with (1) the way in which *relative* wage rates and earnings are determined (why do surgeons get $200 an hour and the assisting nurses, $3?); (2) how and why rates change (why have hourly earnings of unorganized domestic employees risen by a larger percentage than wages of railroad workers with their powerful unions?); and (3) the effect of wage rates on employment.

Difference between Wage Rates, Earnings, Income, and Take-Home Pay.

The *wage rate* is the payment per unit of time (or some other factor), such as $2 an hour, 10 percent of what we sell, or 25 cents for each unit produced. *Earnings* are the rate multiplied by the amount of time worked; $2 an hour for 2,000 hours a year leads to annual earnings of $4,000. By working more hours, a man with a lower wage rate can earn a larger total than a person who gets a higher rate. A high wage rate does not necessarily mean high earnings, or vice versa. *Income* is earnings plus such other receipts as interest, business earnings, and dividends. "Fringe" benefits, discussed later, and income tax withholding and other deductions separate earnings in the complete sense from *take-home pay* by amounts which are both large and often difficult to measure.

BASIC FORCES: DEMAND AND SUPPLY[4]

Although labor unions may seem to be "basic" forces in labor markets, we exclude them from discussion in this chapter.

Supply of Labor as a Whole.

The population total, of course, sets limits to the supply of labor. The rate of population growth influences supply. So does the age distribution. (A net increase of 18 million in the labor force from 1965 to 1975, almost twice that in the prior 10 years, most being under age 30, already shows effects in the labor market.)

Any population may vary substantially the amount of work it will do. When people are free to choose how much they will work, their choices

---

[3] The portion of national income going to labor rose from around 70 percent in 1899 to around 80 percent today.

[4] Some people feel that to analyze wages as we do the prices of commodities smacks of inhumanity. People are not commodities. The services they sell, however, are in essence like commodities because both have value to the extent that they satisfy human desires. They require the same type of economic analysis. The difficulties stemming from attempts to bring humane considerations into the economic analysis can be illustrated by the fact that poor people use most of their incomes to buy the services (or products of the services) of others.

vary. Whether one looks at the number of hours per week (or really minutes per hour if we allow for the "coffee break" and other interruptions) or years per life, the choices expressed more or less freely differ widely. The forces that make the differences are complex, partly subjective, partly arising outside the individual—from such trivialities as the attractiveness of the person at the next desk to rules about child labor and the age of retirement.

One example is the "working wife." In some cultures, married women, especially of the upper or middle classes, rarely work outside the home; employment indicates some "failure" by the husband. In this country, however, women commonly hold jobs until the first baby is on the way, partly because the shorter workweek and mechanical aids to housekeeping have increased the feasibility of work outside the home. Over 15 of the 27 million women in the 1967 labor force were living with their husbands and holding jobs outside the home. Women make up more than twice the 1870 percentage of the labor force.[5]

The more years we customarily spend in school, the smaller the fraction of the total population that will be holding full-time jobs. Another influence stems from government regulation. For example, laws generally impose burdens upon the employer if he offers work beyond certain hours, such as 40 per week. The condition of health, wage rates, the state of transportation, the number of holidays, and sports events are a few things that influence the amount of labor that will be supplied effectively from any given population. So, too, are opportunities for supplementary jobs, the "moonlighting" (a term derived from night work on a second job) that over 5 percent of all workers welcome, or accept, to help meet expenses. The willingness to work part time varies, but voluntary part-time workers make up nearly one eighth of the labor force.

In some parts of the world, income remains at about the level of subsistence. Any appreciable decline in real income would, in true Malthusian fashion, reduce both energy and total population—the supply of labor. Incomes in the Western world, however, are as a rule so much above the subsistence level that total labor supply has little relation to the needs of minimum existence. Yet a not dissimilar force does operate here and now. Families seeking a particular standard of living, one which may be far above subsistence, will sometimes offer the amount of work needed to achieve it. Many mothers, for example, get paying jobs, not to meet expenses of basic necessities but to help cover college costs or other outlays which the family consider part of the desirable standard of living. The supply of labor reflects this aspect of the concept of subsistence.

[5] A careful statistical analysis has concluded that the rise in the proportion of married women in the labor force represents in part the rise in money earnings obtainable, that is, a response to economic incentive. J. Mincer, "Labor Force Participation of Married Women," *Aspects of Labor Economics* . . . (National Bureau of Economic Research, 1962), pp. 63–97.

Demand for Labor as a Whole. National income, of course, depends not only upon the labor supply but also upon the total demand for goods and services. Employment theory, the subject of Part 3, dealt with the demand for labor as a whole; review is not necessary here.

Total Real Earnings. Output in *real* terms depends not only upon the amount of employment but also upon productivity—the intensity and skill of effort, the quality and quantity of capital equipment, the quality of techniques and management, natural resources, and other factors in relation to the total labor force. The general level of real earnings results from two related sets of broad forces: (1) those influencing the demand and supply of labor as a whole and (2) those influencing the effectiveness with which we work. Full employment and high man-hour productivity are the keys to high levels of real wages. Yet any level of real earnings involves issues of *specific* wage rates, and these also depend upon demand and supply.

Market Forces and the Determination of the Equilibrium Wage Rate for a Specific Type of Labor. By "specific type of labor" we mean people who do more or less distinct jobs, such as typing, riveting, practicing probate law, generally in a particular area. The 30,000 or so types of distinguishable jobs were grouped in 11 major categories in Table 3–2.

An employer's *demand* for labor, of course, derives from the demand for his product. As a rule, the demand for the output of his firm does not depend upon the wage rates he pays; whether a hat factory pays its bookkeepers $70 or $80 a week has an insignificant effect on the demand for its hats. The employer has some idea of the demand for his product. The best adjustment for his firm, we know, is the output where marginal revenue equals marginal cost. The manager should hire labor that will produce this output. His demand for workers will depend upon the marginal productivity of labor, i.e., the marginal revenue product—what he can get from the sale of additional (marginal) units of output attributable to the extra labor after deducting other variable costs. With workers of essentially uniform productivity and with a given demand for his product, the number he can afford to hire will depend upon the wage rate; the higher the wage rate, the smaller the amount of labor he will buy. His demand curve slopes downward.

Other employers of the same kind of labor will also have their downward-sloping demand schedules. All of these together make up the *total market demand* for such labor. This demand schedule, however, does not tell how much labor will be employed or the wage rate. To get such answers, we must also know supply conditions.

What determines the market *supply* of a particular kind of labor? Just as the supply of a commodity is determined by cost, the supply of labor for any type of work is determined by a cost—*opportunity cost* or the best alternative sacrificed. Generally this cost is the wage that might have been earned in another occupation. The cost of taking one job is the loss of the best thing (opportunity) sacrificed.[6] Some people have few alternatives, none of which is appealing; they will accept jobs at relatively low rates. Others have more attractive alternatives and so will not work on a specific job except at higher wages than the first group. A smaller number have much better opportunities and so need still higher inducements to accept any particular job. As we take account of all potentialities we arrive at a supply schedule that, when graphed, slopes upward. The higher the remuneration (wage rates plus other considerations), the more labor of that specific type that will be offered.

A demand curve sloping downward and a supply curve sloping upward create the conditions for an equilibrium (price-quantity adjustment) in the market—a balance of conditions such that if it is reached no one can benefit by a change so long as the underlying factors are unaltered. If the market is purely competitive, each firm will be able to hire as much of the labor of this type as it wants at the market price; and everyone who is qualified and who wants to work at the price will be able to get a job. The quantities demanded and supplied will come to balance as employers and workers seek their maximum advantage. Not everyone may be happy, but no one can do better. The equilibrium will change, of course, when underlying conditions of demand or supply change for any of the reasons we now examine.

Changes in Demand for a Type of Labor. Figure 24–1, which calls for careful study, shows the responses to a change in demand for a type of labor.

1. Any changes in the demand for the product will change the employer's demand for labor. An increase in demand for motorboats will increase the demand for labor in motorboat factories and for marina servicemen. A decline in the demand for movies with the rise of TV cuts the demand for Hollywood extras and, presumably, for popcorn.

2. A change in productivity will alter the demand for a type of labor (Fig. 24–2). Assume that workers produce more per hour. Then, for the same wage rate, the employer will find it profitable to hire more labor (assuming that the demand for the product does not change). Lower labor costs per unit of output (a) induce him to substitute labor for other factors and also (b) permit him to sell more units of his product at the lower price which competition will bring. If workers' productivity falls, however, the employer's most profitable output becomes one of smaller employment. He will wisely cut out the labor whose marginal revenue product is less than the wage rate.

---

[6] The sacrifice may include desired leisure, greater safety, more congenial working conditions, and other nonmonetary factors, both welcome and unwelcome.

FIGURE 24–1.   Responses to an Increase in the Demand for a Specific Type of Labor

Demand for the type of labor increases from *DD* to D_iD_i. The short-run supply, S_sS_s, is relatively inelastic. The wage rate rises to E_s and the quantity of man-hours hired increases from *OA* to *OB*. As time passes, however, the supply changes. Eventually the full adjustment of long-run supply, S_lS_l, is made. The wage rate drops to the level E_l, and the quantity of man-hours hired increases to *OC*.

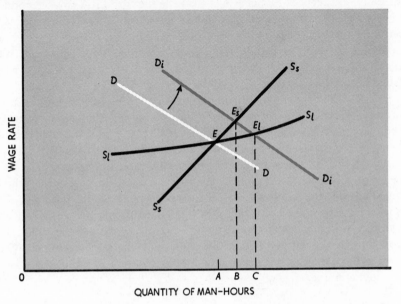

QUANTITY OF MAN-HOURS

3. Changes in the prices of other productive factors can alter the demand curve for a type of labor. Suppose that, with three pilots needed for each passenger plane, the price of planes falls considerably (or, as with the jets, performance improves relatively more than does cost); the airlines buy more planes because the lower cost makes expansion profitable. They must hire more pilots. But if the price of planes were to rise by more than performance, the opposite would be true; higher plane costs would reduce the demand for pilots. The demands for pilots and for planes are complementary.

Factors of production, to varying degree, can substitute for, or replace, one another. Thus, within economic and technological limits, demands for productive factors are *substitutive*. Suppose that by adding planes an airline can cut the number of meals it must serve. The demand for labor to provide airline meals drops. In deciding whether the purchase price of faster planes is justified, the airlines would consider the saving on food and on the serving of meals.

In short, the demand for labor of any particular type will depend upon the prices of the other factors of production which are used in the same

FIGURE 24–2.   Effects of Rising Productivity on Wage Rates and Employment

Rising output per man-hour of a type of labor lifts demand from DD to D_1D_1 to D_2D_2. The equilibrium wage rate rises to E_1 and then to E_2 and employment to OB and then to OC.

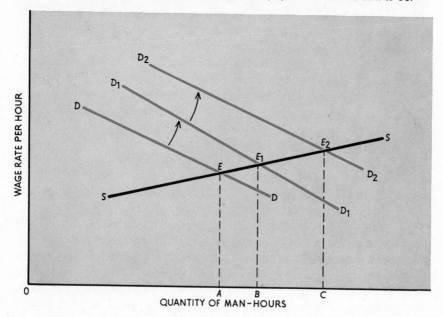

process. If factor *A* *substitutes* directly for man-hours, a rise in the price of *A* will tend to increase the demand for labor, and vice versa. If factor *A* is *complementary*, a rise in its price will reduce the demand for the labor. The same analysis applies to different types of labor which complement or substitute for each other.

Changes in the Supply of a Particular Type of Labor.   The supply of any particular type of labor depends largely upon the relative attractiveness of this and other kinds of work. As in the supply of commodities, long-run and short-run conditions can differ greatly. Supply may be relatively fixed in the short run, but highly elastic over the long run.[7]

Let us suppose that the pay for programmers for computers has risen substantially. The work, we assume, requires skills that many persons can acquire with 12 months of training. The higher income prospects will attract some people from other jobs and induce them to learn the skill. For 12 months there may be little change in the number of competent programmers, but thereafter more and more will qualify. As they seek

[7] The amount supplied in the short run may vary considerably, depending upon the wage rate (a movement along the supply curve), but at any given wage rate, the amount offered will change more slowly (the shift of the curve).

work, the earnings rate will gradually fall (assuming no upward shift in demand) until it no longer attracts more than a "normal" number of newcomers.[8]

Now let us look at the opposite situation: For a somewhat specialized type of work the wage rate has dropped to a low level; the best wage obtainable at the moment is unattractive for the long pull. Many workers will continue on the job because they have no better alternative, but newcomers will not involve themselves in such a fix. Repelled by the poor terms, they will seek jobs somewhere else. As time passes, some workers retire or die; gradually others find better jobs. Supply shrinks; as it does, wage rates will gradually rise, assuming no changes in other conditions.

When the demand for some types of labor rises substantially, the supply of labor for other jobs will tend to drop (or rise more slowly than otherwise in an expanding economy) as workers, after getting the necessary training, move to the jobs now relatively more attractive. Important changes may occur almost before they are recognized.

The supply of a type of labor requiring any special skills will only rarely change by a large amount in the short run, but demand may. Therefore, short-run changes in wage rates in any particular occupation (under purely competitive conditions) are more likely to result from changes in demand than from changes in supply. In the long run, however, changes in supply can exert a powerful influence. The time required will depend upon such things as the availability of training facilities and the knowledge of opportunities.

A Commentary on Wage Adjustment. Although an economy never adjusts perfectly, we should note the basic forces that operate: (1) Income is so important to the earner that most people will try to obtain more. They are hindered and helped by many things—from a wife's prodding to one's own bargaining ability compared with that of the employer; (2) Wages are a large enough element of cost that employers will generally resist requests for higher wage rates and try to obtain less, rather than more, expensive labor; (3) Yet employers will benefit from hiring workers up to the point where the wage rate paid equals marginal revenue product; the employer's own interest is to pay what is needed to get people to work—up to some point.

Fundamental elements of competition exist. People will seek out jobs which offer relatively high remuneration, while employers will search for ways to economize labor costs. The forces of supply and demand thus operate. Both sides gain more from employment than from unemployment. Both desire a settlement. At some wage rate, the amount of labor of a specific kind supplied will equal the amount demanded. No worker of

---

[8] The use of computers rises so rapidly that a large increase in the supply of programmers has not prevented upward movements of salaries.

the type can get a higher rate because employers cannot pay more and sell their products in competition with employers who pay the equilibrium rate. An employer cannot get the workers he wants while paying below the equilibrium rate. He would be foolish not to hire at this wage rate to obtain labor that would be profitable.[9]

The shifts needed to approximate equilibrium are, as a rule, relatively small. At the margin, a little bit more or less will often make the necessary adjustments. Even when the basic demand or supply forces change considerably, modest changes in price and quantity may bring a comfortable balance. Although elasticities of demand and supply differ widely from case to case, a modest percentage shift from one employer or area to another can reduce much of the discrepancy that will appear in normal change. Like a pebble in the shoe, a small change makes a big difference. Yet if monopoly or some other impediment prevents the adjustment, the discomfort may continue indefinitely.

Labor markets do seem so lacking in the conditions for purely competitive adjustment that the process we have described may appear unrealistic. Factual studies confirm such hunches by revealing wage-rate differentials large enough and persistent enough to prove that deficiencies in the adjustment process are more than minor. Parts of the market remain segmented. Many workers are unable or unwilling to wait long enough for the really best job—labor is highly perishable; a day not worked is a day lost.

Some economists believe we can obtain better insight into the determination of wage rates in particular jobs by thinking in terms of "bargaining" rather than marginal productivity. Concede, they say, that the latter sets limits. Still, in practice, there will exist a significant range within which the wage may settle. Employers' earnings, for example, may remain above or below equilibrium for a considerable period. Even more important in the "real world" (as distinguished from that of pure competition), the volume of employment in the job will adjust to offset wage-rate departures from equilibrium, with effects diffused through the economy. Since measurement of marginal productivity is difficult and since we cannot be certain of the exact equilibrium conditions, it is hard to predict what will in fact result (in terms of wage rates, employment, and profits) from any particular bargain.

EARNINGS IN SELECTED INDUSTRIES AND OCCUPATIONS

What are the earnings in different kinds of jobs? Two kinds of classifications are of interest—*occupational* and *industrial*. Table 24–1 shows

---

[9] The "human equation" makes labor different from wheat or cotton. People vary endlessly, and our performance differs from day to day. Consequently, two requirements for good competitive markets cannot be met fully: a uniform product and full or even extensive, knowledge. Letters of recommendation, for example, lack the accuracy and completeness of an SEC registration statement. Moreover, personal feelings inevitably influence hirings, firings, and promotions.

TABLE 24-1.   Median Earnings of Male Workers, Selected Occupations, 1965

All occupations	$5,339
Professional, technical, and kindred workers	7,668
Medical and other health workers, self-employed	$13,015
Engineers, salaried, technical	9,958
Teachers, salaried, elementary and secondary schools	6,732
Farmers and farm managers	2,630
Managers, officials, and proprietors, excluding farm	7,538
Managers, salaried	8,088
Managers, self-employed, retail	5,877
Clerical and kindred workers	5,511
Sales workers	5,552
Retail trade	4,467
Other salesworkers	6,326
Craftsmen, foremen, and kindred workers	6,270
Foremen	7,594
Craftsmen, construction	6,062
Other	6,135
Operatives and kindred workers	5,046
Manufacturing, durable goods	5,681
Manufacturing, nondurable goods	5,239
Other	4,291
Service workers	3,436
Waiters, cooks, and bartenders	3,715
Other	3,396
Farm laborers and foremen	734
Laborers, exc. farm and mine	2,410

Source: Statistical Abstract . . . 1967.

median earnings of men in selected occupations.[10,11] The earnings of women were markedly lower. The median for female workers in all occupations was $2,257, with the highest shown being for physicians, $5,517. Table 24-2 presents 1966 average earnings per full-time employee in several industries, all occupations being grouped together; the self-employed are not included.

In the summer of 1967 weekly earnings in auto manufacturing averaged $140; petroleum refining and contract construction showed somewhat

[10] Half of the cases lie above the median and half below.

[11] The figures give an impression of earnings lower than the benefits received and the costs to the employer. (1) Persons who worked less than a full year—for example, those entering or leaving the labor force during the year—did not have full-year earnings but received more per week working than the annual total indicates. (2) Fringes are not included. A survey of companies representing corporate employers found that, on the average, fringe payments were 26 percent of payroll. Payments for time not worked, holidays and vacations for the most part, equaled 8 percent of payroll. Pensions were another 8 percent, and social insurance taxes borne by the employer, 6 percent. Variations among companies were large. One third of employers paid more than 29 percent, averaging 81 cents per payroll hour. For a group of identical companies, fringe payments rose from 16 to 28 percent of payroll from 1947 to 1963. Chamber of Commerce of the United States, *Fringe Benefits, 1963* (Washington: The Chamber, 1964). For examples of one year's changes in various agreements, see R. Oswald, "Fringe Benefit Bargaining Gains," *The American Federationist* (February, 1966), pp. 16–20.

TABLE 24–2. Average Annual Earnings per Full-Time Employee, Selected Industries, 1966

All industries		$5,954
Farms		1,983
Mining		7,136
Contract construction		7,016
Manufacturing, total		6,647
Apparel	$ 4,022	
Food and kindred products	6,049	
Textile mill products	4,778	
Products of petroleum	8,647	
Automobiles	8,425	
Wholesale and retail trade		5,630
Finance, insurance, and real estate		6,336
Banking	5,780	
Security brokers, dealers, etc.	12,807	
Transportation		7,786
Railroads	7,653	
Pipeline	8,722	
Communications and public utilities		6,908
Services		4,481
Private households	2,781	
Medical and other health	3,821	
Miscellaneous repair	6,911	
Government and government enterprises		5,909
Federal, general government, civilian	7,838	
State-local, public education	6,009	
State-local, nonschool	5,684	

Source: Survey of Current Business, July, 1967.

higher averages, while banks were paying an average of $85 and laundries $64.

Clearly, differences are substantial. In fact, they are very much greater than suggested by figures of medians or of averages of large groups.

Professions also present wide variation. Physicians do much better on the average than do lawyers and dentists. Many physicians and not a few attorneys will net $30,000 a year (before taxes). So do some engineers, accountants, architects, and research scientists or civil servants. Occasionally, a dentist or professor gets near this range; rarely, a clergyman. Public school teachers, though paid on a lower scale, have gotten substantial percentage boosts; the $12,000 or more now paid experienced (nonadministrative) teachers in leading schools is more than all but a few women receive in other work. Occasionally artists, athletes, and entertainers gain very large incomes; the average, however, is anything but inspiring.

INEQUALITIES OF LABOR EARNINGS

The inequalities of incomes from labor are large and obvious. Are they difficult to explain in view of our belief in democracy, equality, a feeling that men's natural endowments may seem more equal than their earnings? Well, people are *not* the same. They differ in ability and willingness to do what others want. Such differences can account for much variation in earnings, even at equilibrium when the payment to any producer equals his marginal productivity. How much physical product (or service), we ask, does the marginal unit of any factor of production add to the firm's output? And what will the sale of this additional product add to the firm's receipts (over nonlabor costs)? To account for differences in labor earnings that would persist under equilibrium, the principle of marginal productivity suggests that we try to find what brings differences (1) in the *capacities* to do what others want and (2) in the *willingness* and (3) in the *opportunity* to use the capacities.

"Equalizing" Differences. 1. *Nonmonetary Considerations.* Differences in labor earnings persist to some degree because "Man does not live by bread alone." Employment means more than the pay. So much of life is spent on the job that the conditions of work influence the quality of life most significantly. Differences in wages tend to offset, or equalize, various nonmonetary considerations. The more attractive the work and all that goes with it, the greater the number of people who will prefer it. The larger the supply, the lower the equilibrium money wage rate (other things the same). Unattractive, repulsive work must offer higher earnings if the jobs are to be filled. Not everyone, of course, has the same preferences—fortunately so, because if all preferred one or a relatively few types of jobs, we would have to pay a great deal more than we do now for the other work we want done.

Some differences in work preferences are firmly rooted in rational calculation. Some may rest on fashion, tradition, or snobbishness that seem a bit foolish. Work that is dangerous, dull, demeaning, exhausting, nerve-wracking, or a threat to health will tend to require higher money wages to compensate for the nonmoney disadvantages. Night shifts, weekend and holiday work, and jobs in remote areas commonly bring premium pay. Greater leisure tends to offset lower money income.[12] An ambitious person may work for less now if he feels the opportunities are good. Some people are attracted by a sense of service. Positive interest in the work, even glamor, will have varying appeal; a chance to create or a sense of power and challenge will often play a part. Some people will sacrifice dollars to live in California, New York, or near their parents. Unfortunately, we have little reliable quantitative evidence about *how much* people will sacrifice money earnings for different kinds of nonmoney benefits.

Some nonmoney factors can be controlled by an employer. He should take into account how much he can wisely spend to make his jobs more attractive. Will air conditioning, better lighting, music with work, or

---

[12] Unions in recent years have at times deliberately sought longer vacations in lieu of some of a potential rise in hourly wage rates. In the steel industry, workers with long employment get 13 weeks of vacation once every 5 years.

better foremen pay? Such features become increasingly important for another reason—income taxes. Important nonmoney benefits are not considered part of the employee's taxable income, even though the employer deducts the expense in figuring the company's taxable income.

2. *Regularity of Work.* Some jobs are steadier and more secure than others. An intelligent worker will look not only at how much he gets per hour but also at the amount over a longer period, including his whole working life. One reason that construction workers have received relatively high hourly wage rates is that bad weather normally forces many days of unemployment each year. To offset the effect of time lost, a higher rate of hourly pay is needed.

3. *Training.* Some work requires more training than others. If preparation for a job is costly in time or money, people will be reluctant to make the necessary sacrifices unless earnings later promise to be high enough to compensate. Cost of developing a skill affects supply. Professional training costs far more than learning a simple manual job. Yet the amount by which earnings of highly trained engineers exceed those of machinists is greater than the cost of training alone would warrant. Why? Part of the explanation is that not everyone qualified can afford an investment in training which would eventually pay well. Others are unwilling to make the effort.

4. *Maintaining and Encouraging Differences in Capacities.* Earnings do more than reward and provide incentives. They do more than finance consumption as such. Earnings also help pay for what is essential to do the job. Different jobs require different living conditions. Some differences in pay are in fact differences in gross, not in true net, compensation. Work requiring intellectual, artistic, scientific, managerial, and manual skills calls for varying conditions of life. The supply will depend upon the extent to which compensation really pays for the conditions needed for the particular type of work. Capacities will not flower and flourish equally well under all conditions. Earnings help provide the differing essentials, from the lawyer's loose-leaf services reporting new events to the architect's travel and the boxer's training camp.

You are probably straining to ask an old, old question. "Why, then, does work with attractive activity, security, safety, prestige, good working conditions so often pay far more than dull, menial, uncertain jobs?" The company president has a position which seems more attractive than that of the typist and which certainly pays more. The professor seems to have a pleasanter job than the assistants who grade examinations, and he, too, gets higher pay. The store's purchasing manager faces a much greater variety of experiences, including travel, and is paid much more than the boy in the stock room. Competition seems not to have equalized. What is the explanation?

For one thing, competition is not perfect. More fundamental, however, is the fact that labor differs immensely in quality. Not everyone can do every kind of work equally well. Motivation and the inclination to press for better jobs also vary markedly. In short, there are fewer people who really (*a*) want to and (*b*) are able to compete for some jobs than for others. The typist cannot effectively compete for the corporation president's job and may not want to try for promotion to supervisor. Without such competition, the forces for eliminating inequalities are inevitably limited. The stock boy has less knowledge of markets than the purchasing officer with years of experience.

In a period of booming demand for labor, large numbers of workers have good chances of insisting upon pay that will offset differences in the attractiveness of jobs of essentially similar productivity. When demand is not so strong, the adjustments take more time to work out.

Differences in Ability.   One explanation of differences in wages stands out: abilities vary. The chief reason more people do not move to a job with higher pay is that they cannot do the work required. Why?

Nature gave men and women diverse physical, mental, and emotional characteristics. Some of these qualities, and especially the *right combinations of characteristics*, which are highly useful, are also, it seems, scarce. Truly superior capacities appear to be distressingly rare, yet exceedingly desirable. The possessors can, therefore, charge dearly for their services. Some of their incomes resemble a true "economic surplus"—a payment above the amount needed to bring the skills into existence. The high reward does not affect greatly the quantity of the capacity that nature produces. Yet the price does serve economically useful purposes. (1) It serves to "ration" and allocate the service to the uses most wanted by buyers who can pay. (2) It provides incentive for a person having the abilities to cultivate them and to make them available.

Much talent, unfortuantely, is not stimulated and matured to its highest capacity. Some goes unnoticed, and much receives only mediocre guidance and opportunity. One benefit from rising productivity of the economy is that higher income will permit fuller discovery and better training of human talents. The gains should be cumulative. The more fully we develop the human capacities which nature gives, the greater our income, the more we can spend on education; the more our real income will then rise, hopefully in an upward spiral.

World War II taught forcefully that untold millions could do much more than anyone dreamed when they had both incentive and opportunity (including leadership). Undoubtedly, enough more native ability exists so that, if trained, the added supply would reduce the scarcity element of high professional fees, executive salaries, and artists' earnings. Yet the process of income growth, which increases the supply of such productive capacity by facilitating its discovery and training, will also increase the demand, perhaps proportionately, perhaps even more. On the basis of aptitude-test findings, at least 6 percent of the population appear capable of earning Ph.D. or M.D. degrees, but less than 0.5 percent do so now. The proportion of the population over age 24 with college degrees is twice that of 1940 figure but still under 10 percent of the age group. Investment in college education still seems to yield as much—over 10 percent—as before World War II.

Experience suggests another conclusion, however—nature has been stingy in providing certain types of highly valuable talents. Large numbers of Americans do receive good opportunities. Yet superlative accomplishments are rare. The lack of A+'s on college exams is not chiefly the result of professorial blindness. Students with apparently equal opportunities make different records. Some personal qualities, and *combinations of qualities*, that are highly valuable seem to be inborn. Nature has limited the number of people who can hope to earn a living in professional sports or music. Fortunately, we can find substitutes for some rare qualities. The make-up staff is a partial substitute for beauty in actresses. Ever more highly developed machines help remove the limitations of human capacity; glasses reduce the handicap of bad eyesight. Specialization and cooperation permit us to develop and combine limited abilities to escape some of nature's limitations and thus multiply our achievements.

Differences in Effort. Earnings under pure competition would vary according to willingness to work. Some people are more energetic, ambitious, and anxious for money income (or good grades) than others. Even though some may produce no more per hour, they work (study) more hours a year—and get larger rewards. What else would one expect in a free society? People do have different preferences. Unfortunately, however, not all jobs offer equal opportunities for adjustment of individual effort to individual preference. A government employee on a fixed salary and prohibited by law from taking outside work is in a different situation from a salesman who can set his own working schedule. A person forced to retire at age 65 does not have the same opportunity to extend his lifetime earnings as does the lawyer or business owner, who is free to work as long as his health permits.

Geographical, Industrial, and Interfirm Differences. Earnings for apparently the same kind and amount of work vary from one part of the country to another. Though due partly to skill differences, hourly earnings in manufacturing average 50 percent more in the Far West than in some southern states and almost 25 percent more than in Massachusetts. Within areas, earnings vary from large cities to small towns. These differences are only partly explained by differences in living costs or the degree of skill required. There are also variations from one industry to another. Even within industries, earnings per worker differ from firm to firm (for about the same kind of work).

In the short run, such differences can be explained partially by variations in the amount and type of capital per employee, changing technology, managerial skill, consumer taste, and the availability of natural resources. Whatever influences the prosperity of the area, industry, or firm can for a time affect the demand for labor relative to the supply—and thereby wage rates and earnings—even in a highly competitive market. Yet wage differences continue more than temporarily. To account for the persistence, we must look at forces hindering movement toward equilibrium.

OBSTACLES TO EQUILIBRIUM ADJUSTMENT

The world we live in, of course, is not a world of pure competition. A host of forces modify demand-and-supply conditions from what they would be under pure competition. Naturally, wage rates and labor earnings are affected as a result.

"Pull," Chance, and Absence of Bargaining at Arm's Length. For an individual, favoritism, "pull," nepotism, and pure luck can affect earnings. Sons of successful parents have a better opportunity than the average boy to get a good education; sons of carpenters are admitted into the union more easily than others. Contacts and influence sometimes enable a person to receive more pay than he is worth. Business, however, cannot afford a large percentage of such waste, or risk the harm an incompetent person may do, especially in a position paying high compensation. Undoubtedly, chance plays a prominent role in deciding individual earnings. Knowledge of both job opportunity and worker capacity continues to be shockingly inadequate. Although chance is insignificant in determining the broad patterns of labor incomes, in specific cases it exerts a large and often wasteful influence.

In the market for top executives, despite some strongly competitive features, each case inevitably has unique elements. Each man and each job differ somewhat from all others. To find the right man for the spot—well, how can search be made efficiently? The height of tax rates has diverted attention from straight salary to pensions, stock options, and other rewards which involve less tax than salary in upper brackets—as well as expense accounts and such supplements as private use of the company plane. Even superficial investigation would probably disclose examples of wide degrees of both underpayment and overpayment of executives. A thorough study might lead to no clear conclusion about how well the total system attracts and allocates executive capacity.[13]

---

[13] The firm's whole pattern of executive compensation will be influenced by the highest salary. Any ill effects may appear slowly. Yet good men are scarce, and poor salaries at the senior and junior levels will not obtain high-quality executive services if most other firms pay more. Some of us get annoyed at the large amounts paid to someone higher. Human—but foolish. In production, we work together. Some deci-

Lack of Mobility. A more serious obstacle to reaching the best adjustment is lack of mobility—of workers and of business. *Ignorance* is a handicap. People often do not know where better jobs are open. Monetary features of different jobs are likely to be overemphasized because they are easily compared. Many aspects are difficult to evaluate: the prospects of advancement, the stability of employment, the personality of the immediate boss, the likelihood that earnings will rise if the price level goes up, the pension, and the future of the industry and the firm. Want ads dispel ignorance, but few workers will check the ads of papers in many communities. Employers do not, as a rule, aggressively advertise all

FIGURE 24–3. Weekly Earnings in Dollars of Constant Purchasing Power, 1950 and 1967* (In 1966 Prices)

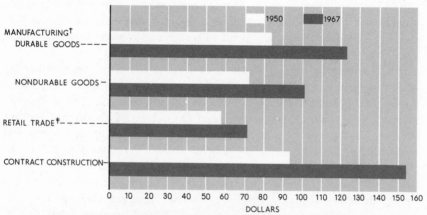

*Data for 1967 are as of September with rough estimate for seasonal adjustment. Total employer costs are higher because "fringes" are generally excluded.

†"Production" workers only, excluding, in general, supervisors above the foreman level, much office and managerial personnel, and research workers.

‡Excludes supervisors.

Source: Historical Statistics; Survey of Current Business, October, 1967.

the relevant information about job opportunities. Private (for a fee) and state employment agencies, unions, and schools and colleges give varying amounts of employment data. Government programs for providing more and better information about jobs and people were being stepped up in the mid-1960's.

---

sions are vastly important. The man down the line cannot make them, but he has a huge interest in having them made *well*. His future depends upon the decisions of those who work with him, especially those in the top spots. Except for a good wife, no one may help a man's future more than the person (or group) at the top of his company. A high salary schedule for key officers does not assure that they will be extremely competent, but low salaries will likely mean that the best talent will not come to the firm or stay long. Everyone down the line will suffer. A worker who has great talent on his team has the equivalent of a legion of slaves working for him. Advice to a person getting a job: Pick an employer who pays the top men fabulously.

The market for jobs differs inherently from the wheat or auto market. Considering the importance of what is involved, information is meager. Job decisions, even choices of careers, are frequently made with slight knowledge about alternatives. Ignorance of one's own capacities is greater than we recognize. No less important, perhaps, is employer ignorance of who is available. He may have a general idea of the number of "bodies" unemployed, but on the crucial problem of their capacities, especially variations in ability, he may be woefully ignorant. How can a company employment officer in Georgia know if Mr. X in Ohio is better than a man across town? How can an employer find out about the real qualities of an Indiana professor or a Chicago accountant? Employers seeking their own interest should perhaps be out "beating the bushes" for the best people (at the price) employed elsewhere: Yet even if they did, they would have extreme difficulty learning what people who are working for others can and will do. Another practice reduces mobility. Employers rely largely upon promotion to fill jobs above the lowest level. Outsiders have little chance.

The *expense of shifting* ties people to jobs that are inferior to those otherwise possible. A more than minor difference in wages is needed to justify pulling up stakes in one town and moving to another. Even shifting from a house near a plant on one side of the city to a location on the other is costly. If the employer pays moving costs, the expense makes him less willing to order transfers. The loss of seniority required in some job changes discourages movement. Moreover, many pension plans provide that a person who leaves before retirement loses some or all of the pension rights (those for which the employer has been assuming responsibility).

What about mobility of the company? Once a business is established, with buildings, equipment, and organization, the cost of moving to a better labor market may be prohibitive.

Specialization can reduce mobility. A person with highly developed skills for one type of work may be useless in some other. The natural reaction is to stay put. (Improvement of training and retraining facilities will reduce this obstacle to mobility, as many big employers know from experience.) The person moving up the ladder of specialization may find himself trapped by his own success; few, if any, other employers in the area may have similar jobs, to say nothing of vacancies.

Personal and family considerations keep some persons tied down—and impel others to move. Inertia, apprehension about the unknown, and reluctance to risk a change keep many people where they are. But restlessness, the visions of gold at the end of distant rainbows, easy transportation, annoyance at the way the mother-in-law influences the baby, hopes of better climate and fishing—all induce others to move.

Costs of Education and Training.   The cost of getting advanced education and training greatly exceeds what most families can or will finance.

Consequently, economic barriers are high enough to retard the growth of supply. Those fortunate and determined young men and women who eventually qualify can thus benefit from the scarcity element which results as others are excluded by the high costs of training. The public will pay more dearly for the services than if a larger number had gotten the education.

Even less highly developed skills are not easily acquired. And after a person has a specialty, he (or she) may have great difficulty gaining another. Who will teach and train? Who will pay the costs, especially of time away from work? The man who marries early, especially if he soon has children, can find himself trapped by inability to make the sacrifices needed to improve his skill or to develop a new one.

Some employers, including most large firms, devote effort to helping workers adapt themselves to the needs and opportunities of a changing world. The extent and variety of employer encouragement of training can hardly be imagined. IBM trains about 170,000 employees of other firms each year to enable them to use the more modern equipment. One of the many welcome results of high general demand for labor reappeared in the mid-1960's as employers stepped up their training programs.[14] Training under governmental plans also expanded greatly, especially as antipoverty experiments added new impetus.

Social Causes of Inequalities in Wages.   Social factors limit mobility. In some countries hereditary class lines keep some people out of certain jobs and force (or help) them into others. Religion may play a part in the job one can get. Such class and religious influences do not boom large in this country.[15] Yet prejudices are not unknown here, and some of us find our chances helped or hindered by factors that are essentially irrelevant to our ability to do the job. Employers who indulge their tastes in this way must pay a price. Some of the people they do not consider seriously may be better than some they hire. Any time a group is to be selected, whether for a football team or a business staff, the *arbitrary* exclusion of any potential candidates before the real selection begins will reduce the quality of the team finally chosen.

Two social interferences are of declining importance: discriminations against women and Negroes. These two groups make up a large fraction

[14] A special survey of manufacturers in New England showed that in 1965 they were training 18 percent more of their work force than in 1962. The average training program lasted 30 weeks, less than before as employers compressed apprenticeship into a little under 2 years. Offsetting high labor turnover and meeting the demands of new technology were chief reasons for the added training. Federal Reserve Bank of Boston, *New England Business Review* (September, 1966), pp. 11–14.

[15] A Catholic would probably not worry about the fact that his religion would bar him from a post as a Baptist minister. But he might resent the situation if religion prevented him from teaching in a public school, just as a Baptist might resent religious bars to his working in an office managed by someone of another creed.

of America's labor force. Yet they seldom appear in certain types of jobs, such as the top executive positions of banks and insurance companies. Marked contrast appears in sports and the arts, most notably music and acting, where women and Negroes get to the top. Earnings suffer from discrimination in different ways. (1) Some jobs that pay well are closed. (2) The excluded must then compete more aggressively for jobs remaining; a larger supply means lower earnings.

Why have employers barred these groups so arbitrarily? Explanations are mixed: pure prejudice, the fear that other employees would object, the assumption that women or Negroes could not do the job well. Some unions have made it impossible for employers to hire women or Negroes because the union will not admit them, and no one the union refuses to accept for membership can work for the company. Physical inabilities account for some of the exclusion of women. Educational facilities available to these two groups have been less adequate than for others.[16] Low earnings themselves make it difficult to obtain more specialized skills and to maintain health, personal appearance, and attitude that play a part in boosting productivity.

Over the years women have found more occupations open. Families can afford to give daughters better training. "Nothing succeeds like success." As women proved their ability, employers became more anxious to try them.

After 1940 the economic position of Negroes improved amazingly—or perhaps we should not be surprised. The demand for labor skyrocketed. Where could workers be found? A large source would be persons who had been unemployed or who were working only part-time. Many Negroes were in this group. Antagonism of other workers declined when jobs were plentiful. Higher incomes made it possible for Negroes to pay the expenses of moving from farms to cities and from the South to the North and West. A boom in the total demand for labor can work wonders. Movement of industry to the South boosted the demand for labor where Negroes were a large part of the population.

Although delicate social problems have persisted, the obstacles are gradually becoming less serious. State after state, and finally Congress, have legislated against job discrimination on the basis of sex or color. The Civil Rights Act of 1964 applies to almost all companies and unions with over 25 employees or members. Enforcement requires not only the overcoming of ancient prejudices but also finding out which aspects of which jobs actually do need to be done by women—not designing of dresses, but modeling of them, for example. Unfortunately, training cannot be

---

[16] Businesses have not put more effort into on-the-job training of women because so many young women do not expect to keep their jobs permanently. They have less real incentive than men to train for climbing the ladder. Women tend to be absent from work more than men (for example, when the children get sick); wives may quit jobs when the husband is transferred to another locality or receives a higher salary.

imparted by enacting a law; the past will slow the realization of the fundamental goal. In 1966 the Council of Economic Advisers estimated that if education and training put Negro productivity equal to that of whites, national output would expand $22 billion. If the rate of Negro unemployment fell to that of whites, output would rise another $5 billion.

Another discrimination looms as increasingly serious. People over 45 or 50 find that their age—age alone—impedes their getting new jobs. So far, legislation has done little, but a few experiments with voluntary plans have shown ways to prevent tragic human and economic waste. High demand for labor, in general, will work wonders, but bigger wonders, and faster, if training facilities and job information are more extensive than they have been and if nonrational discrimination is less.

Discrimination in Rates of Pay for Similar Work. "Equal pay for equal work." Critics charge that it is wrong for women to get paid less than men for the same work. But can such discrimination really be made effective? Perhaps. The difference between sexes is clear enough to make a basis for dividing the labor market. Moreover, women may not be as able as men to bargain aggressively. There is no doubt that wage rates for women are often lower than those for men. But is the work the same? If it is, you will ask: "Why does the employer hire men at all?" There must be some difference in what they do, year in and year out, to account for their higher pay. Otherwise it is foolish to hire men if women will do the same work more cheaply. The employer who used more of the less expensive labor exclusively would gain a competitive advantage.

States containing most of the country's population have had laws requiring equal pay for equal work, and Congress has made similar provision wherever interstate commerce is involved.[17] Administration, however, inevitably requires analysis of individual cases, a task which presents difficult problems.

Lack of Competition among Employers (Monopsony). When there is little or no rivalry among employers, the wage adjustment is certainly affected. If there is a single employer—one mine or factory, a group of employers (such as farmers) which operate as a unit in hiring labor in an area, or perhaps a Socialist government employing most of an economy's workers—the chances of reaching the competitive equilibrium are much reduced. Wage rates can be depressed and the wage structure somewhat distorted.

[17] From 1950 to 1966 the percentage of females over age 14 who were in the labor force rose from 31 to 38; for married women the increase was from 25 to 35 percent. This record suggests that the rates of pay offered are not unacceptable. The Women's Bureau of the U.S. Department of Labor publishes each year a bulletin, *Handbook on Women Workers*, which contains extensive information and helpful guidance about earnings and conditions in different jobs and laws affecting the employment of women.

Some firms have more or less clear policies against "pirating" (competing for) each other's employees. The college senior may find several employers competing for him; after he makes a selection, however, he will see that other firms keep a strictly hands-off attitude—no "raiding." Employers would nullify each other's efforts, and no one would benefit, except the employees. Dominant employers in a community may pursue a similar policy in the local labor market, perhaps without any explicit agreement.

The Process of Adjustment.   All of these obstacles make it difficult for workers to shift readily with changes in the demand for labor or for employers to hire and fire as their judgments of productivity would indicate as wise. Yet a small change of quantity and price at the margin may be all that is necessary to reach equilibrium. Not much weight is needed to upset a scale that is in balance and then not much to get it back in balance. So it may be that a little mobility will do the trick of adjusting the supply and demand for labor in a particular job.

In this country, there is no small amount of mobility.[18] Some consists of people actually quitting one job and going to another, while some comes as new workers seek the more attractive work. Each new crop of high school and college graduates contains a goodly number who, consciously or unconsciously, seek jobs with the better pay—and the industries, occupations, and regions with the most promise. The supply of labor in such places increases relative to that where things are less attractive.

In manufacturing, on the average, *over 1 percent of all employees quit voluntarily each month.* Total separations (turnover), including discharges and layoffs, average 3.5 to 4 percent a month. Clearly, there is much shifting around. Not all is welcome, but enough is constructive in one way or another to keep the adjustment process operating. Such shifting makes for unending adjustment and helps keep the parts of a complex and changing economy from becoming seriously out of balance.

Movement of employers also provides adjustment, the location of business depends upon many things, of course, but wage costs are vital. Any substantial geographical difference will impel some employers to move and, especially, guide the location of new plants. Gradually such adjustment makes a big impression on the relative demand for labor in different areas (Fig. 24–4). The pull of less expensive labor will tend to eliminate the cheapness, not, perhaps, in 5 years, but possibly in 15.

Firms that fail to meet competitive wage rates do not lose their labor at once. Some workers may, of course, quit promptly; more will drop out for one reason or another: marriage, retirement, a better job. Yet employ-

---

[18] In 113 labor market areas including nearly half of all workers, the work force rose 7.7 percent from 1957 to 1963. Yet in the 12 areas of "relatively substantial unemployment," the work force fell 6.2 percent. *Manpower Report of the President . . . 1964* (Washington: Superintendent of Documents, 1964), p. 33.

ees' reluctance to move when they have jobs, seniority, and homes will offset some income differentials. College faculties provide many examples. If you were an employer paying substandard wages, however, you would find it difficult to replace the people who leave with others of equal ability at the same wage. After the attrition of a few years or months, you would probably have lost enough employees to realize that you could not maintain your old wage standards and secure the *quality* of workers you need to meet competition.

Quality will probably be the really telling factor but so may numbers. Firms and industries that pay poorly will suffer from unsatisfactory quality of labor. They will lag behind; a poor productivity position may

FIGURE 24–4. Wage Rate Changes Resulting from Employer Movement in Two Labor Markets

As employers leave area A, demand for labor declines. In area B, where employers enter, demand for labor rises. The wage rates and quantity of employment move in opposite directions in the two areas until wage rates reach the same level, E_1. Note that we consider not absolute wage rates but rates per unit of output.

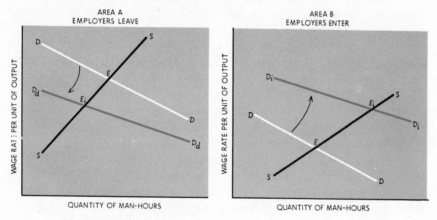

then prevent them from raising wage rates. The deterioration can be cumulative. Firms and industries that pay well, however, will find their prosperity accelerating on the basis of personnel continually recruited from the cream of the labor force.[19]

[19] More than one out of eight persons employed works for government. Generally, a legislative body fixes the rates of pay and the broad principles of employment. Administrators then define qualifications for various jobs: how much accounting experience a tax auditor should have, what will make a typist a stenographer, or how much Joe's nephew helped in the campaign. In attracting new workers, of course, governments must meet outside competition. The number of applicants meeting qualifications will suggest whether compensation for those jobs is below or above that in the private sector. In holding existing staff members, seniority, the pension, and inertia will keep people at salaries below what would be needed to attract them. Yet private employment will siphon off some. Teachers go to another school district. Lawyers and accountants enter private practice. Nurses go to private hospitals. Such

After World War II, the average annual earnings per full-time employee in the private economy was about $300 a year higher than for federal-state-local employees. By the early 1960's, however, the gap had been closed, and in 1966 the two averages were within a few dollars of each other (Table 24–2). There is no assurance that work requirements and skills required would call for equality in the governmental and private sectors at equilibrium. An especially serious complaint of presidents, governors, and mayors is that they cannot offer high enough salaries to obtain and retain men of top quality for key jobs.

METHODS OF WAGE PAYMENT: EFFECT ON EARNINGS

Employer Problems in Fixing Wage Rates. In a small plant, personal considerations and lack of full knowledge by both sides make it difficult to fix wage rates at the economic optimum—marginal revenue productivity. Huge "errors," 50 percent for example, will hardly persist long, but smaller ones may go on and on. The large firm has its problems, too. Big size impedes the small-stage adjustment of pure competition. If a plant is employing thousands, it must have rules, general policies. Fixing each person's rate of pay according to his (estimated) marginal productivity would be impracticable.[20] So pay rates are set for broad categories of work—$2 per hour for certain jobs. For some this is a bit high; for others, low. The practical test is whether the rate comes close to the equilibrium for the bulk of the group. Workers who are lax or sloppy, poorly trained, wasteful of materials, careless with machines, or impolite to customers can be shifted, disciplined, trained, or discharged. Those worth more are the natural candidates for promotion.

How much should a welder receive in relation to a bookkeeper or stock clerk, a draftsman in relation to a foreman? Although union pressure and increasing knowledge have brought some standardization of procedures, employers still use many criteria for fixing *relative wage rates* within the firm. (Always, however, supply and demand in the market operate, albeit slowly; stenographers in various firms will claim about the same pay.) "Job evaluation" or "job rating" has developed over the last generation.

If you were an employer anxious to bring order out of what you suspect is chaos in the company's wage structure, you might hire experts

---

trends, along with hiring experience, indicate somewhat the adequacy of pay and conditions of employment.

One serious difficulty, however, is judging the quality of people who remain in government jobs. The employer's ability to survive in competition cannot serve as a test of labor performance in relation to pay. "Adverse selection" may result as more of the better quality workers are drawn into private jobs, leaving public agencies with an undue proportion of less able persons.

[20] A big firm could not afford to make a separate bargain with each employee. We may hear of giant firms pitting their great power against weak individuals. Yet the giant must set its terms so it can obtain many individuals at about the same rate.

to make a special study. Each job would be examined and scored according to the skills and effort it requires, the hazards and responsibility; the scores provide a basis for helping decide how much more one job should pay than another. Such evaluation involves much judgment—"allowing and adjusting"—and difference of opinion; any system will gradually become out-of-date. Yet, this method provides opportunity for rational adjustment of relative wage rates and the economizing of personnel. Jobs requiring little skill can be filled by less expensive personnel. Another development helps both employer and worker—the improvement of methods of determining abilities so that employees can be steered into jobs for which they are best fitted.

Payment According to Output. There are two major bases on which people are paid: (1) the amount of time they put in, so much per hour or per year and (2) the amount of output they produce, commonly called "piece rates." Do earnings depend upon which method is used?

Many of us will certainly work harder if we can expect to gain from extra effort. We accomplish more when paid by the piece than by the hour. But will we earn more? The answer depends obviously upon the two rates of pay. A long-standing suspicion of employees has been that if they tried to boost their earnings by working harder under piece rates, the employer would reduce the rate. The worker's extra effort would have become useless or even worse. Having proved that he could produce more, he then had to maintain the higher rate of output to earn perhaps only a trifle more than he had gotten originally. There is also fear that extra effort will destroy some jobs.

When employees get a fixed amount per hour or per month, the public as a whole receives fewer goods and services than if workers have a more direct spur of incentive. Capital equipment is used less intensively. The employer incurs expense to keep workers from taking things "too easily." On the other hand, payment on a straight time basis eases record keeping and payroll preparation; waste of materials will be less if workers are not hurrying; maintenance of quality is easier if workers have no reason to try to get credit for items that are not quite up to standard.

Some firms and their employees have gotten splendid results from *incentive* plans. "Time and motion" study measures what a normal worker can accomplish; the work to be done is analyzed to determine the best methods (motions); then presumably normal employees trained to use these methods are timed with a stop watch, and their output is taken as the norm. Some unions help in setting norms and inspiring confidence in the fairness of an incentive plan. The AFL-CIO cooperates with the University of Wisconsin in running the Union Industrial Engineering Institutes to provide specialized training for union representatives who help in fixing the actual standards.

Experience has shown the desirability of special pressure on the employer to keep materials flowing smoothly and machines repaired. A worker on a piece-rate system sitting at a broken machine is not likely to be happy. A constant problem is keeping work norms up to date with the appearance of new production methods, new materials, new kinds of products, and improving skills. A good system must be dynamic, but change may be a repeated source of friction. The plans often show up large differentials in the ability and industry of workers, and big inequalities of earnings are not always popular.

Although payment according to output has intrinsic merit—because consumers want output, not input—many jobs are not suited to payment according to individual output. Where many men work on the same assembly line at a pace set by the line, individual incentive (except to avoid mistakes) has little scope. Yet payment may still be geared to accomplishment in some other way, such as group output.

Many types of "gain sharing" plans are in operation. Some are designed to "buy back" uneconomic work rules and get rid of featherbedding. The aim may be to aid transition to new techniques. The emphasis in some plans is on providing incentives for cost saving over a whole plant, perhaps to improve the company's competitive position while enabling employees to get more.

Tens of thousands of firms now provide *profit sharing*, which gives all employees, or key groups, an interest in total net profit. Plans may involve a definite contractual agreement promising employees a share of profits, often as an addition to the pension fund and not subject to income tax until retirement. Or the employer may give bonuses, related to the year's profit, more or less systematically but not according to a fixed contract. Some plans enable employees to buy the firm's stock, thus giving them a greater interest in its profitability. Although unions rarely press for profit sharing, this device does offer a partial solution to one problem of some unions—getting more from the most profitable firms without requiring a basic wage which will cut employment in other companies and drive marginal employers out of business.

TERMS AND CONCEPTS

wages	complementary factors	specialization
earnings	of production	labor mobility
income	substitutive factors	time and motion study
opportunity cost	of production	profit sharing

QUESTIONS

1. Why will an employer's desire to maximize profit lead him to hire labor until the marginal revenue product equals the wage rate? Would he lose by paying less?

2. What would make labor market adjustments more efficient?

3. What earnings differentials would exist in a purely competitive economy?

4. What are the advantages and disadvantages of payment according to output? Why do you suppose that Russia pays most of the labor force by piece rates?

5. "Labor turnover is essential for efficiency in production. Yet it can be a great waste." Discuss. What measures might help an employer get more nearly the ideal amount and kind of labor turnover?

6. What conditions restrict labor mobility?

7. If you were an employer, what qualities of (*a*) character, (*b*) personality, and (*c*) training would you seek?

8. How would you expect incentive methods of payment to affect the supply of effort?

9. Which jobs require most income to maintain the ability to perform the work effectively? Why?

10. An occupation which offers some extremely high rewards, it is said, will tend to have low average earnings. What factors would tend to bring such a result? Would they help explain the low earnings from acting? The high average earnings of doctors? Why?

11. A union economist has said, "There is nothing about a job that cannot be changed to suit the people." What are the implications of this statement?

12. What groups would benefit most (as earners) from restrictions on immigration? Why?

13. Distinguish between "wage rates" and "earnings." How does the decline in the workweek affect each? What is meant by "relative wage rates"?

14. Would you expect heavily progressive income taxes to influence the supply of highly skilled effort? Why?

25

LABOR UNIONS AND THEIR INFLUENCE ON WAGES AND EMPLOYMENT

Men and women of our American trade union movement, I feel that I have earned the right to talk plainly with you. . . . I want to urge devotion to the fundamentals of human liberty—the principles of voluntarism. No lasting gain has ever come from compulsion. If we seek to force, we but tear apart that which, united, is invincible.
Samuel Gompers in his final (1924) presidential address to the AFL

Labor unions are unincorporated voluntary associations. They differ greatly. They change—partly in response to changes in the world around, partly because of internal evolution. The problems they face differ and so do the results of their actions.

LABOR UNIONS TODAY: A SUMMARY[1]

During the 19th century the law ruled that people should not combine to injure others. Although the formation of employee groups was not prohibited, possibilities of success were slight because most of the things a labor organization would try to do would seem to hurt employers or consumers. The extreme rule, it is true, was relaxed gradually, but the law—and the prevailing economic philosophy of individualism—favored the view that individuals were to make their bargains with other individuals. The employer and the employee were assumed to be equally able to protect their interests. Then in some states, and nationally, laws came to support these groups and deliberately encouraged their growth.[2]

---

[1] The appendix to this chapter deals with the development of unions and the role of government.

[2] Discussions refer constantly to "rights": the "right to strike," the "rights of

Figure 25–1 shows the growth. Farmers, small businessmen, domestic servants, and many professional men make up four groups with almost as many persons as all unions but with virtually no unionization; some, however, have strong organizations bearing other names. In other sections of the economy almost every permanent employee belongs to a union—the manufacturing of aircraft, rubber products, agricultural equipment, electrical machinery, and autos; steelmaking; railway transport; brewing; meat packing; trucking; motion-picture production; professional entertainment.

FIGURE 25–1.   Labor Union Membership*

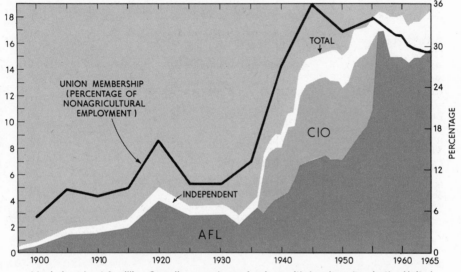

* Includes about 1 million Canadian members of unions with headquarters in the United States. The growth in the total of independents beginning in 1958 is the result primarily of the expulsion or suspension by the AFL-CIO of unions failing to meet its standards of ethical practice. Noninterstate independent and unaffiliated unions not included. Single-employer unions, though numerous, are generally small.
Source: *Historical Statistics of the United States, Colonial Times to 1957; Statistical Abstract.*

Government employees do not generally belong to unions, but printers and construction workers usually do. Less than half the employees in the manufacturing of cotton textiles, nonalcoholic beverages, and dairy products, and less than one fifth of employees in clerical jobs and retail trade,

---

property," "natural rights." Unfortunately, the word "right" has different meanings, both *legal* and *ethical*. They are not necessarily the same. Can a "right" be wrong? In Hitler's Germany, people had certain legal rights to abuse Jews—rights that were clearly wrong by our ethical standards. When Congress passes a law, it may create legal rights—things the courts will enforce. Yet, by other standards, they may be wrong. We should guard against the temptation to think that a thing to which we have a legal right is necessarily correct or that it is immutable. Legal "rights" can change overnight but not what is good or right ethically.

are union members. Most employers do not have to deal with unions, but most big employers do. Urban areas are much more generally unionized than town and rural areas, and the South less than the North and West. Unions tend to be weak in "white-collar" employment, including engineers, scientists, and others of the most highly trained.[3] In relation to total employment, union membership has been stable or declining. Figure 25–2 shows the membership of a few large unions.

FIGURE 25–2.   Largest Labor Unions: Approximate Membership

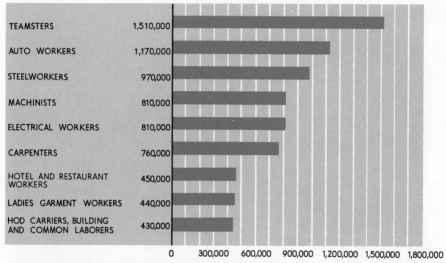

TEAMSTERS	1,510,000	
AUTO WORKERS	1,170,000	
STEELWORKERS	970,000	
MACHINISTS	810,000	
ELECTRICAL WORKERS	810,000	
CARPENTERS	760,000	
HOTEL AND RESTAURANT WORKERS	450,000	
LADIES GARMENT WORKERS	440,000	
HOD CARRIERS, BUILDING AND COMMON LABORERS	430,000	

0   300,000   600,000   900,000   1,200,000   1,500,000   1,800,000

Source: Bureau of Labor Statistics. Canadian members are included in some cases. Data approximate only.

No good way exists for measuring union influence. Some unions have power to halt industries on which our whole economy depends. Unions at times exert strong influence on government. Moreover, union agreements often apply directly to employees who are not members. You might, for example, work for a company without being a union member; yet your wages and working conditions might be governed by agreements made by the union. Where unions are prominent but not dominant, there may be hundreds of thousands of nonmembers who are largely union followers. Many firms grant nonunion employees "tandem" increases following a new agreement with the union.

Local and National Unions.   A union member ordinarily belongs to three levels of organization: (1) The *local* in the town or plant where he

---

[3] One study estimated that in 1960 about 13 percent of white-collar workers, "potentially union members," belonged to unions, compared with 56 percent of blue-collar workers.

works, one of about 77,000 in the whole country, belongs to (2) one of around 150 *national* unions, (3) which is probably one of the 130 affiliated with the AFL-CIO, a national *federation* of unions.[4]

The local may bargain with the employer and agree upon the details of the contract. A representative of the local—often called the "business agent" (a union employee) or "shop steward" (a fellow employee who is allowed by the employer to take time from the job for union affairs)— handles grievances and decides on the day-to-day problems.

The *national* unions vary widely in influence. Sometimes they conduct the negotiations with employers and settle on the major terms—in steel, railroads, and coal mining, for example. The national often sets general standards which local unions may, or must, try to observe. The national gives the local its charter and imposes conditions which locals must meet to join and to remain.[5]

The Federation. In 1955 two national federations combined into the AFL-CIO. It is a loose organization. It defines the jurisdiction of nationals. For example, where does the carpenters' province end and that of the electricians begin? Powerful national unions, however, do not necessarily accept the authority of the federation on such questions. The federation will try to intervene in the affairs of nationals and locals only in exceptional cases, such as the failure of member unions to deal with evidence of corruption. It conducts research and tries to influence lawmakers and the public, but it does not participate in bargaining.

Leadership within Unions. The change in the position of U.S. unions from underdogs fighting for life to strong, secure groups has altered the qualities needed in union leaders. An aggressive, fighting spirit; great energy and ruthlessness; missionary zeal and intense devotion; demagog-

---

[4] There are exceptions: locals without other affiliations, and national unions outside the federations. A union member may have another affiliation; several unions in the same city may form a council or city federation. In some cities, for example, the local federation has considerable influence in the day-to-day affairs of local construction and other unions. There are also state organizations cutting across the lines of national unions. Local and state groups may lobby for legislation or plan joint actions in labor disputes or participate in civic affairs.

[5] These conditions include such things as dues, memberhsip requirements, cooperation with other locals, representation in the affairs of the national, rules of work, and rights to benefits offered by the nationals (such as insurance, recreation or retirement facilities, and medical benefits). National officials may discipline locals; the national may even expel or take over a local, putting it into a form of "trusteeship" which can deprive members of almost all influence, year after year. The national must usually sanction a decision of a local to strike. Some nationals have welfare and other funds running into tens (and more than one with hundreds) of millions of dollars. The nationals give varying amounts of service to locals. Some nationals provide men to conduct the actual local bargaining; some pay the business agent; some help locals finance strikes; and some have research staffs which can give the locals useful aid in dealing with employers. A few, such as those in the garment trades, conduct research designed to help employers.

uery—such qualities may serve well in building a union. Quite another type of leader may be best when the union is firmly established. Patient negotiation, keen concern for the employer's problems, financial skill, the ability to plan constructively for the long run, and continued search for the favor of the public and government officials become keys to union success. The American labor movement has by no means made the transition in leadership.

Written constitutions lay down the framework, often in precise detail. Locals operate under charters from the national. Members vote on local matters and elect men to represent them at higher levels. Larger unions have staffs more or less like a civil service. Provisions are made for deciding controversies, with the executive officials ordinarily serving as judges. Elections are usually held every year or two, perhaps after campaigning to clarify issues. Some votes are farcical, and occasionally many years pass between elections. Leaders tend to stay in power—and build self-perpetuating oligarchies and sometimes dictatorships. When no one else's name gets on the ballot, a fairly common situation, the old standby can hardly lose.

Democracy within Unions.   Suppose you were an ordinary member of one of the giant unions. What would be your chances of influencing the leaders when they were bargaining with the *entire industry* and fixing *your* wage rate? Infinitesimal at any one time; you depend upon the few men representing you.

If the bargaining is being done by a member of your *local*, however, you may be more than a drop in the ocean. Even as an individual, you might be able to influence the men dealing for you. And if you will take the time, and have the persuasive ability, you may get others to join you. In unions, as in college politics, a determined minority may carry much more weight than a quiescent majority. Less vocal union members may have some influence, for a sensitive leader will become aware of wishes.

In the day-to-day affairs of a union, apathy is characteristic. The ordinary worker will spend his evenings in many ways that are more pleasant than going to a union meeting. In a local of a few hundred members, a turnout of 5 percent would be fairly normal, 10 percent high. The individual can be overwhelmed by the organization, sometimes losing important freedoms. Union officers have often had considerable power (now curbed by law) to expel members—a fast way to get rid of either the boss's spies or anyone seriously threatening the present union officers.

The freedom to quit the union is often the freedom to quit the job. Internal rivalries may result from matters of basic principle—or a desire to be boss. Rivalry for leadership may be constructive; it gives members a chance to learn about the issues and to express desires. It can, however, put the union statesmen at the mercy of the demagogues. If you were one of the majority of conscientious union leaders, you would have to expect the challenge of some upstart wanting your job who would say you were soft, not forcing the boss to pay enough, and easy on grievances. In self-defense, you might need to be more belligerent than you know to be in the union's interest—your rival would be worse. The union leader may become a sort of "captive." He has no place to go except higher in the union or back to the plant. His background and skills do not obviously qualify him for other positions; and since the work back at the bench seems drab, keeping the union job looms as exceptionally important.

A union leader can support a generous set of policies to be paid for by someone else. The employer must find customers willing to buy in the market. The union officer, however, is free from this responsibility. If he forces a bad policy, his own loss is small compared with that of the firm.

UNION OBJECTIVES

What needs have people sought to meet by forming unions? What goals do unions seek? In answering, we shall distinguish between members as such and the organization. While no clear distinction can be valid and some people might deny that any significant difference exists, the interests of members do differ in some ways from those of the union as an entity, as a "going concern."

Member-Oriented Objectives: More Income and Related Goals. One thing the member wants is more income. Employees, individually, have a sense of weakness in dealing with employers. Hope for more pay, then, seems to lie in dealing as a group with the employer—*collective bargaining*. A related objective is to get more income, not only this week but over a longer period, perhaps the whole working life and on into retirement—*job security* and independence and a pension. How desperately we want them, and how remote they can seem to the person dependent upon someone else for work. An employee's job may be controlled by a person with whom he has no personal ties. Again, he looks to joint action for a solution.

Members also see, in unions, *protection from the competition of other workers*. Suppose there are some persons who are unemployed (or earning less). They might be willing to work at lower wages than the union is getting. But the union's contract keeps the jobs for its members by preventing the employer from hiring at lower wage rates. A shortening of hours per week or per year (without lower income) remains an objective of collective action. Pressure for reducing the *workweek* has weakened, and when it does appear, the desire may not be fewer hours of work but the beginning of premium pay earlier in the week.[6] More paid holidays

---

[6] When electricians in New York got employers to agree on a 25-hour week, it was with the understanding that work in excess of 25 hours would be provided at overtime rates.

and longer vacations do appear high on the list of the goals of many bargaining sessions.

There are various nonfinancial needs which people seek through association in unions, things on and off the job. Friendship, unity, a sense of belonging to a group are sometimes important. More significant are (1) *protection against arbitrary or thoughtless treatment* by the boss, whether in day-to-day affairs or in bigger issues of discharge and layoffs, and (2) *provision of a means to correct grievances.*

Union-Oriented Objectives. Now we look at union-oriented objectives, those focusing on the organization as such.

Recognition. Recognition—in the past, this issue has been the center of much of the struggle. Today, as a rule, controversy over recognition is not a major issue in most negotiations. The employer has agreed to the principle of dealing with a union; the employees have decided which union shall represent them; and a contract reflects the agreement. Sometimes, however, it is not clear *which* union shall represent employees. A large minority may oppose any union. Perhaps there is a company union with strong support (including the employer's) or a competing national union. Different national unions sometimes appear as rivals, with the employer willing to recognize either but, obviously, not both. Nevertheless, controversies over recognition are a far cry from the battles of 30 years ago; when they appear, questions of union recognition are settled by voting under National Labor Relations Board auspices.

Union Security. Union leaders feel the need for protection against (1) potentially hostile management, (2) disinterest of workers, and (3) the inroads of rival unions. Leaders and many members want more security for the organization than is assured by recognition. They seek such security by requiring membership in the union for as many employees as possible. Employers (and some workers) may oppose the requirement of union membership as a condition of employment. Possible solutions to conflicts include:

1. The *closed shop:* only members of the union will be hired. Though the closed shop is now illegal, the musicians', building trades', printers', and some other unions, in effect, still enforce it. The employer may, in fact, be required to get employees through the union.[7] He can, therefore, hire only persons the union will admit to membership.

2. The *open shop:* the employer, while recognizing a union, is free to employ without regard to union membership. Hiring, firing, and promotion presumably take no account of union membership. By accident or design, however, the employer may eventually get a work force that is so largely nonunion that the union has little power. Union leaders fear such an outcome; employees with job seniority may have little need for a union; consequently,

---

[7] As central employment agencies, some unions provide useful services to employers. The National Maritime Union with its hiring halls is an example.

unless older workers are compelled to join and stay in the union, membership may tend to be concentrated among short-service workers.

3. The *union shop* leaves the employer free to hire anyone he wishes, but within a month or so of the hiring, the employee must join the union or lose his job.

4. Other arrangements include the *agency shop*, which came into the news during the 116-day steel strike of 1959–60. The employer must collect from workers who do not join the union an amount equal to dues and all other charges. The money goes to the union treasury.

Unions have had considerable success getting some form of union membership provision. Leaders feel that such provisions are necessary to preserve and build union strength. Since the union "carries the ball" in negotiations, they reason, everyone who benefits should help pay. The bigger the union, the stronger it can be and, presumably, the more it can hope to get for all workers. The employer, they argue, should not be tempted with the opportunity to staff the plant with nonunion members. Nor should the union be tempted to actions motivated merely to justify its existence to members. Moreover, union officers point out, correctly, that they cannot assume responsibility for enforcing discipline and contractual agreements unless they have control over members. Their officers can be more objective in handling grievances if all workers belong to the union. Finally, the life of the union leader will be easier if the employer must in fact do the job of holding the union together.

Compulsion to join a union to get or to retain a job deprives a worker of freedom: he may not like the union or its policies—autocratic and tyrannous union officials are not unknown—he may not want to pay dues; he might be able to do as well, or better, without the union—a complaint of some skilled workers. There is no basis for judging accurately the extent of involuntary membership today.[8] Employers often object to compulsory membership because of the added power the union gets; union leaders who may have little or no concern for the particular firm's welfare, or whose judgment is poor, gain large influence over the business.

Another union security device is the *check-off*. The employer deducts union dues from the members' pay and forwards the money directly to

[8] Where unionized employees have voted, they have been overwhelmingly in favor of the union shop. But in elections involving representation, the majority sometimes comes out for *no* union. Dues generally range from $25 to $30 a year for the national and about the same amount for the local, but lower and higher totals are common. In addition, one finds a wide variety of other charges—to build a strike fund, pay sickness expenses, or carry out a special organizing campaign. For the country as a whole, union dues, special assessments, and initiation fees probably exceed $600 million a year; total union income from property is not known. Dues may include a subscription to one of the 800 or more publications of labor unions. From puny newspapers to slick magazines, they not only tell members about union affairs but also convey the "labor point of view." The Bureau of Industrial Relations of the University of Michigan publishes, in abstract form, the essential contents of 50 leading union publications in the *Michigan Index to Labor Union Periodicals*.

the union. The check-off saves the union expense and trouble; union officials need not badger members for dues.

Grievance Procedure. The typical union wants an effective procedure for handling grievances. So do wise employers. Minor annoyances, as well as major conflicts or frustrations, reduce productivity and sometimes fester and grow into serious issues. There are likely to be many opportunities for improving human relations and raising productivity and satisfaction by discussion that airs and settles misunderstanding. An orderly system for employees, individually or in groups, to present grievances and get sympathetic, skilled, and authoritative hearing can be highly valuable to everyone. Most union-management agreements provide for a series of stages; ordinarily the last stage is a semijudicial hearing before an umpire or arbitrator.[9]

Grievance procedure often concerns issues of discipline and discharge. The contract states formal rules which limit the power of the foreman; it sets out general principles and perhaps specifies particulars. What warrants discipline, and how much? Poor workmanship, violation of safety rules, and waste of materials are only a few of the topics the contract may deal with specifically. But the most precise contract leaves room for doubt in individual situations. Did Joe disobey safety rules? Was Ruth careless in cutting a batch of valuable dress fabric? No general agreement can decide such questions, but it can spell out a procedure for settling them. Grievance procedure also deals with such problems as work loads, seniority, and allocation of overtime work.

Discipline, Discharge, and Seniority. Discharge and discipline provisions vary widely but generally offer the employee an important form of protection. The employer needs the control that is essential for efficient operation. What must it be in form and extent? Drunkenness in a bus driver calls for more serious discipline than in a crooner. Where work is intermittent or seasonal, the worker wants to be protected from being forced to "buy" a job from either a foreman or a union official. Union responsibility for helping enforce discipline differs greatly.

Agreements sometimes devote considerable attention to *seniority*, the relative rights of employees in particular jobs. A person's job is vital "property"; he wants to protect it but get a better one if he can. Here he may come in conflict with his fellow workers. Issues arise over layoffs and and promotions, with chance at overtime sometimes important. The union can try to get an agreement which will specify definitely what is to be done and thus reduce many disputes. Seniority may dominate—the longer a person has worked, the better his chances for good jobs and the greater his protection against layoffs. Seniority can provide an easy, objective rule

---

[9] In a recent year only a small fraction of 1 percent of grievances initiated in the vast General Motors Corporation were referred to the impartial umpire. Two out of three cases were settled in the first step of the four-step process.

that reduces dispute to a minimum; sometimes, however, it is complex, with one worker "bumping" the one below him on the list through many steps. Seniority can subordinate ability. It deprives employers of the chance to decide on the basis of efficiency; it does not necessarily adjust according to the "need" of workers; it reduces incentives of workers to excel to get promoted. Younger employees will hardly be enthusiastic about strict seniority. In general, the case for relying heavily on seniority in guiding layoffs is stronger than that for determining promotions, a fact reflected in most collective bargaining agreements.

Working Rules. Working rules are major objectives.[10] Just what is the specific job? What tools can one use? How much is a day's work? Rules may be specified in the contract, with provision made for deciding new questions. *Obstruction of technological change* has sometimes been a union objective. When a man has invested a lot in developing skill for a job, he may try to prevent some machine from taking it away. The group may do the same. Some unions have tried to prohibit the use of new tools or methods, though permanent success with such tactics is rare. Contracts may define the methods of adjusting to new technological changes—the speed with which new machines are introduced, the training of workers, the amount of specific types of labor to be used, dismissal or severance pay. *Attrition* may be relied upon; a major railroad settlement agreed, in general, that unneeded positions can be reduced by not over 6 percent a year by normal work-force reductions through retirement, death, and voluntary departure.

Other working conditions may be specified. What shall be the speed of an assembly line? How many looms shall a weaver in a textile plant tend? Who shall couple freight cars? Provisions must take account of technical needs for continuous operation; blast furnaces and oil refineries cannot be started and stopped daily. Some businesses must operate at odd hours—theaters and restaurants. The nature of the business may require special services—railroads, utilities, or ships at sea. Such unusual working schedules call for special provisions. Who is to get the better hours? What, if any, extra pay is to be given for Sunday or night work?

Featherbedding. Unions often try to obtain more jobs than employers would provide freely—make-work or "featherbedding" rules. In one way or another, the job is stretched out or magnified so that more union labor must be used. Bricklayers may limit the number of bricks to be laid in a day, railroad trainmen the number of miles traveled. Even a worker who is willing, as well as able, to accomplish more is not permitted by the

---

[10] The following is a working rule: "Spotting cars or switching at division terminals not in connection with crew's own train while yard engines are not on duty and which work was known to exist while yard engines were on duty and could have been performed by yard engines before going off duty or after coming on duty will be considered and treated as yard engine work."

union to do so. Restriction may take the form of limiting the speed of work, perhaps by formal rule, perhaps by custom.

Rules once reasonable are sometimes retained after new machinery and methods make them obsolete. Poor and wasteful methods may be required.[11]

Restrictions on Entry. Occasionally unions try deliberately to restrict membership, seeking the benefits that come from short supply—monopoly in a special form. An apprenticeship system may be used to limit the number of men who can get training. Yet, in recent years, the number of apprentices has often been less than permitted by the union. The employer may restrict employment of apprentices and helpers because the work they do is not worth their cost.

The membership rolls may be closed, or high initiation fees may keep membership down. Some unions have used licensing legislation to restrict entry to a trade. For reasons of health or safety, the public may well need the protection of licensing and inspection; the union may then get the city or state to restrict the number of licenses for taxis, barber shops, or plumbers.

"Fringe" Benefits and Other Goals. Increasingly, unions are demanding and getting "fringe" benefits. Pension rights and retirement provisions are now highly important. Holiday and vacation privileges, hospital and other medical benefits, may be provided. Life insurance, tools, lunches, travel time, and sick leave may be made available.

Unions have more objectives: getting a local playground, building a better ball team, helping with community affairs. As groups of human beings, their interests are richly varied, extending beyond dealings with employers. For some employees the union serves the similar social pur-

---

[11] Painters may refuse to use sprayers; extra "drivers" are required on trucks, standby orchestras when music is expected. The National Labor Relations Board upheld union-imposed fines on members who took advantage of incentive plans to earn more than a ceiling approved by the union. On the railroads, unions insist on the employment of firemen on diesel engines when there is nothing for them to do. Airline flight crews may count time traveling to and from flight duty as part of the month's work of 85 hours. When the Metropolitan Opera hires union ironworkers to repair metal on sets, it must pay an equal number of stagehands to look on; when a table and a lamp are to be moved on a stage, members of two different unions must be employed. Skilled workers may be required for work that could be done by less expensive labor. Electric equipment wired at the factory may have to be torn down and rewired by local electricians—or union members paid for such "work." Carpenters oppose prefabricated materials. Printers will not permit use of preset matter unless they get paid for redoing the job (when their work is thrown away). A Senate investigation of strikes at missile bases reported: "The most brazen featherbedding case concerned the so-called 'blessing' of manifolds at Vandenberg Air Force Base by union pipefitters. They refused to install prefabricated manifolds, claiming the right to assembly work on the site. The 'blessing' consisted of superfluously marking each manifold and then sitting around doing nothing for the time it would have taken to disassemble and reassemble the manifolds." *Senate . . . Report No. 1312,* 87th Cong., 2d sess. (1962), pp. 43–44. Examples of employer comments appear in Chamber of Commerce of the United States, *The Menace of Restrictive Work Practices* (Washington, D.C.: The Chamber, 1963).

poses of clubs, churches, and other organizations in developing a sense of "community." Yet member indifference to the union is widespread, and perhaps where a national union dictates to locals, the union sometimes destroys desirable ties between employer and employee.

Some leaders and members hope to use the union on the national scene. In addition to more laws and firmer administration to aid union activity directly, they work for policies which they believe will make for a better country. A few unions have been active in aiding the nation's foreign policies. Union representatives have been notably helpful in explaining this country to workers abroad.

Racketeering and Corruption. The racketeering scum in the labor world operates under a cover of concealment. The people involved, including the victims, are likely to keep quiet, and law enforcement officials themselves are sometimes involved or reluctant to antagonize union leaders.

The union boss may take advantage of the member—drawing union funds for personal uses, putting relatives on the payroll for little real work, charging a member for a job, or demanding kickbacks. A dockworker may have to turn over part of his pay to a union boss for assigning him a job that day; casual labor (a policeman off duty) may be able to get a temporary union card and a job by paying a union official. A union leader may make a "sweetheart" contract with the employer, depressing the wage rate in return for a generous payment. A union official may invest welfare funds where he can get a good commission.

A union may exploit employers. By threats of personal violence, destruction of property, and other methods of the gangster world, a union can sometimes force business to buy protection. The danger is especially great where giant unions, such as the Teamsters, deal with small employers. Exploitation of employers may not be so clear where a union leader goes into business on the side and solicits orders for fuel, insurance, or something else from employers, perhaps at standard prices, perhaps higher. Racketeering sometimes takes the form of unions and employers working together to exact higher prices from the public by methods which seem vicious.

LABOR-MANAGEMENT RELATIONS: COLLECTIVE BARGAINING

Although employer and employee have vastly more identity than conflict of interest, unions exist because some interests do conflict. Sometimes news-making strife develops. More often, settlement is peaceful. So we ask: *What are the techniques of industrial peace?*

Concession without Conflict. One party may give in completely. Surrender can prevent or end a struggle. Many employers—and unions—have done just this. Some make no issue over terms, preferring to follow a leader or "pattern."

Prevention. Another cause of industrial peace is the deliberate effort to build good relations and reduce the causes of conflict. Employers set up special staffs to deal with personnel problems: selection, placement, training, grievances, group relations, recreation. Research on these matters continues in businesses and universities. Specialists now know far more than in the past about how to prevent trouble and, positively, to make relations better. When lessons of modern psychology and social science are applied to employer-employee and employee-employee relations, the human problems can be solved more effectively. On the job and off, the worker gets more attractive treatment. Business tries to help fill some of the gaps of life that make for unhappiness, from loneliness to high golf scores. Some firms have made an impressive record of solid achievement. Some unions have gotten in stride, or taken the lead, in policies designed to improve conditions and prevent trouble.

Collective Bargaining. Even where relations are as harmonious as possible, disagreements seem inevitable—about wage rates if nothing else. The method of settlement, where there is a union, is ordinarily collective bargaining. To try to describe this process is a bit like trying to describe "basketball game"—no two are alike, but there are similarities. *Bargaining* is possible because both sides can help and hurt the other.

For the union, the vital element is the power to strike and effectively to prevent others from taking the jobs. Without the strike as an ultimate weapon, the union is fundamentally weak. Similarly, if there is to be true bargaining, an employer must be free to refuse to meet demands and to stop operations. The general trend of law has been to limit the power of employers. But in a major 1965 decision, the Supreme Court upheld the legality of a layoff or lockout calculated to get a union which is recognized as the bargaining agent to settle on terms favorable to the company.[12]

If you were starting negotiations, what would you do? Probably you would ask for more, or offer less, than you really expect. Many different issues may be involved. If you ask for a lot, who knows what you may be able to get—if not this time, then in later years, after the other side has become used to the idea? You look at other settlements, at the cost of living, the general state of business and the labor market, and the prospects

---

[12] ". . . [To argue that because] employees are locked out they are deprived of their right to call a strike . . . is wholly specious, for the work stoppage which would have been the object of the strike has in fact occurred." *American Ship Building Co. v. NLRB*, 380 U.S. 300 (1965). An employer may not lock out his employees to suppress union activities and collective bargaining itself; complete liquidation of a business to escape dealing with a union which has been certified as the bargaining agent is legal. *Textile Workers Union v. Darlington Mfg. Co.*, 380 U.S. 263 (1965).

of your firm. You prepare a case, naturally trying to pick and choose the facts that favor your side.

If you are to represent the union, you may raise the issue at a local meeting or get rank-and-file suggestions in other ways. Perhaps you made some promises when you were running for election—a bit embarrassing now. You talk with other officers, some of whom will sit with you through negotiations. Though you must ask for more than you will be able to get, you must keep hopes reasonable. You may have to figure what your rivals for union leadership will do. One of the toughest problems may be getting agreement among different groups of workers about their relative shares of any overall gain. Naturally, the deals other unions have been getting must be examined. The national headquarters can probably help. In fact, it may dominate you on at least some issues. Many unions will require you to submit your proposed demands to the members for approval.

If you are on the management side, you may wait for the union proposal or, better, plan in advance. The accountants must try to figure the costs, lawyers the legal position. You try to judge the demand for your product and what must be done to get and keep good workers. You ask your trade association for some pointers on what other firms are doing. You try to judge what the union *really* expects. Conceivably, you will prepare some requests of your own, although managements and unions are not accustomed to employer demands. You try to work out a strategy, taking account of such diverse things as your immediate and long-run market position, the reasonableness of the union, the relative importance of different issues, the rivalry within the union, public opinion, taxes, the humane merit of the issues, your patience, and next year's bargaining. If the plant is closed by a strike, will some competitor make a settlement and get the business? You prepare to prove that profits in relation to sales, wages, or the owners' investment are low. If man-hour production has gone up, you may try to show that the improvement is due to the better machines for which stockholders must be rewarded.

The actual bargaining may be friendly or a constant clash of wills. It may be sincere or a farce; one of the most exasperating things is to try to negotiate with someone who must refer everything to some boss in a distant corporation or union headquarters. *The right spirit is critically important.* Mutual agreement in full good faith to "live and let live" removes a dangerous source of conflict.

If the union believes that management is not out to break or weaken it and if the employer feels that the union does not want to wreck or weaken the company, then success in settling other issues is vastly easier. Prospects are better still if union leaders believe that management looks to them for constructive help and if management feels that the union wants to help the business. Spirit is important; feet under the same conference table may kick, but they need not.

When bargaining is on a national basis, many diverse issues may remain for local settlement, perhaps details about job standards or grievance procedures, perhaps parking space, eating facilities, rest periods, and so on. Recent auto and steel negotiations have shown that at one plant local negotiators for union and employer can reach agreement quickly; in other cases, much bargaining effort, and even strikes, precede settlement of the local issues. An agreement will usually be submitted to union members for ratification. Rejection is uncommon but not unknown.

Mediation and Other Outside Aid in Settling Disputes. The two sides may get into a deadlock, however. You become convinced that your opponent is pigheaded, grasping, even willing to ruin you. He reciprocates the feeling. Everyone gets tired, and as tempers become increasingly strained, more talk is likely to make things worse. Someone from the outside, fresh and impartial, may be able to help.

The federal and many state governments have mediation staffs.[13] In fact, they may offer their services, or the mayor or some prominent citizen may act. The mediator begins to sit in. He is not there to decide issues but to help you reach agreement. As you go over the points, he asks questions that may lead to clarification. He tells a joke when tempers are about to break. His tact and diplomatic skill create a better atmosphere. He keeps you talking—not always in the same room. As an old hand, he may suggest ingenious compromises, or his proposals may serve chiefly as face-saving measures.

The mediator may suggest *arbitration.* You and your opponent voluntarily agree to submit the issues still in dispute to an impartial third party and to abide by his decision. Each side presents its arguments somewhat as before judges. You no longer deal with your opponent as a rival but try to persuade third parties—a very different challenge. Arbitration is rarely used for making major settlements. But it is used widely for interpreting agreements and deciding questions that arise out of the contract while it is in force. The difference is profound. Agreeing in advance to accept someone else's decision *interpreting* a contract involves little risk, for the range of doubt is narrow.

Disputes in industries essential to the public's health or safety—or its ability to keep producing—prompt the query: "In view of the losses the general public may suffer from a strike, why not compel the sides to arbitrate if they cannot reach a decision voluntarily?" Could we not count upon competent, fair-minded arbitrators to reach a decision which, at its worst, would not be as serious as a strike? Perhaps so—yet compulsory arbitration has few supporters. It requires giving vast power to a few people; if there is enough goodwill on the part of the disputants to make a

---

[13] The Federal Mediation and Conciliation Service receives notice of over 81,000 disputes each year. Active help was given in 21,000 cases in 1966; work stoppages occurred in only a small percentage of the cases after mediation began.

compulsory system work, there ought to be enough to permit voluntary settlement. Unfortunately, our hatred of compulsion does not answer the question, "What *can* the public (including, of course, the great mass of workers) do to protect itself against the combined action of people controlling a key section of our economy when voluntary agreement seems impossible?" No good answer has yet been found. Governmental intervention is discussed later.

Employer and Union Concessions: How They Differ.   Is there a basic difference between what the employer and what the union give and receive at and after the bargaining table? In most cases the employer gives, and the employees receive from him, more money or things that have positive worth in the market. The employer can get the economic equivalent from his customers only by offering them things they want and for which they are able and willing to pay. What does the union give in return? More or better work? Perhaps, yet seldom does the union say: "Pay us more, and we shall produce more," something for which consumers will pay. If the employer raises his offer 10 cents an hour and the union lowers its demands 10 cents an hour, the amounts are equal. But is the exchange equal? The vital issue is whether employees are producing enough to "support" higher wages.

Defining the Area of Management Decision: "Management Security." The division of responsibility for management presents difficult conflicts. If you were a union leader, you would probably be a person with a drive for power, often, (though now less so than in the past,) one who had risen through struggles in which the employer was an antagonist. Almost everything the company does affects union members. They have an interest in things management wants to decide unilaterally, such as production methods or plant location. Would your efforts to participate in deciding such issues be usurping the functions of management? Some employers think so, and the resulting friction threatens good relations.

Some unions, however, actually ease the employer's job, especially in disciplining. Workers will accept things from the union that they will not "take" from the boss. On the other hand, agreements that eliminate problems of priority in hiring, firing, and promotion reduce the manager's opportunity to do what he thinks would most contribute to efficiency.

Two National Labor Relations Board decisions of the 1960's indicate why managements worry. One ruling penalized an employer heavily for failing to get union "approval" before shifting operations to a plant with lower costs; another ruled that a company must "bargain in good faith" about subcontracting work once done in the plant.

As unions have followed the old rule "More, always more," they have made some managements fear that the union, having made a beachhead, will press to conquer the continent if it can. But if the union has the welfare of the company at heart, if it favors greater efficiency, then management may benefit from union participation to a degree that would make the employer of the past shudder. Unions can help business achieve higher long-run efficiency by cooperating in reducing the human costs of production in making workers more satisfied and productive.[14] Examples exist. "Continuous negotiation" and "joint study committees," for example, represent attempts to deal with the multitude of issues which exist and develop after a contract has been signed.

In struggling for the best for its company, management today sometimes faces the weakening of its influence by another force, industry-wide—more accurately, multiemployer—bargaining. When a single agreement blankets an entire industry, the individual firm finds itself bound by provisions made by others. In coal mining, steel, oil refining, rail transport, or building construction in an area, the individual management is seriously restricted. Each firm may have a voice in the original preparation of the employers' case or in selecting negotiators; thereafter the firm (and local unions) may be at the mercy of the decisions of spokesmen who see things differently.

When Are Good Relations against the Public Interest?   Harmonious labor-management relations are not always good for everyone—when the two parties "gang up" on the public. The business may be in a position to pass higher costs on to the public. Management can then make concessions to employees which it can recover from consumers. So without apparently hurting owners much, it can be generous to employees, with the public suffering. Business and union leaders may work for monopolistic policies. What puts steel into the resistance of the individual employer is his fear of competition. If the industry acts as a unit, however, both sides can be good pals and work together—probably at the consumer's expense. (Another sufferer is the person who cannot get a job in the industry because the higher wage reduces employment.)

Maturity or Stagnation?   As unions mature, they often prefer existing arrangements. New working rules, though justified technologically, would disturb relations. Work classifications would be upset and with them seniority. Without deliberate intent to hamper progress, unions may

---

[14] Even if union leaders can prove that they have some legitimate interest in a problem, they may not be competent to solve it well. I have great interest in my eyeglasses, but the oculist, not I, has the skill to prescribe the lenses that will serve *me* best. Modern business decisions often require great skill and knowledge; the interest of the union members is that the decisions be made as well as possible. For most problems, the experience of the union leader does not give him the special training which management officials get. But union staffs sometimes include specialists who do have competence for judging a management proposal on the basis of its merits—and perhaps contributing to a constructive solution. Union officials, for example, have helped groups of relatively small firms cooperate in pension plans to save what would often be prohibitively high costs of administration.

contribute to stagnation; upsetting the status quo would disrupt a set of arrangements that, in fact, are functioning smoothly. Moreover, as unions take over more responsibility for dealing with the work force, they face inherently difficult problems. For example, deciding who is to be promoted can be hard. Fixed rules make decision easier but probably not better. Union-inspired rules reduce not only the freedom of management to decide on the basis of its estimate of qualifications but also the opportunity of workers to try to get ahead by working better.

Occasionally, from inside unions and from outside "friends of labor," as well as from others more likely to be critical, new complaints appear. Collective bargaining—"old before its time"—too often, it is said, fails to meet today's needs and those of day after tomorrow. The labor movement lacks the fire of ideology which some of its members and friends would admire. The development of unions was part of a surging movement, termed "the revolt of the masses," which swept over a turbulent world. The extension of political democracy gave new power to groups that had formerly been politically weak. In Europe more than in this country, the labor union was an instrument of social and political, as well as economic, change. Unions were a weapon in the class war, with a philosophy containing a strong element of antagonism and jealousy. There was much oversimplification of the economic issues. Goals tended to be either short run or visionary and vague. As short-run objectives were achieved, something of an ideological vacuum appeared.

Conditions have changed fundamentally in favor of unions. No longer does the old ideology fit. The preaching of class conflict is not prominent at top levels of the labor movement. Lower down, however, it continues, largely indirect and partly unconscious. To more and more members, such attitudes contrast with the reality of good wages, suburban life, and interest in a wide range of personal, community, and national issues. The old values of the union movement spark little enthusiasm.

When a union has become firmly entrenched, when the leaders have done the job of organizing, when getting wage increases that represent about all the fruits of rising productivity proves easy—then what become the goals? What is a union's moral justification for existence if its members gain primarily by preventing the whole public from enjoying the benefits of the higher productivity which society as a whole helps make possible? What are the implications of excluding younger people from the better jobs?

Unions, management, political leaders, and the community generally do not have well-formulated answers to such questions in a world where unions have "arrived" and possess much influence. As top-level union leaders participate in bargaining that forces them to consider the welfare of whole industries, regions, the country as a whole, even the entire free world; as they mix with leaders in civic, political, diplomatic, and other affairs; as they participate in academic seminars; as they work at union headquarters where "research staffs . . . damp down nonsense with sprays of hard fact"; as they accept new the responsibilities, many develop ideologies appropriate to the economic realities of the modern world.

UNION INFLUENCE ON WAGE RATES AND EMPLOYMENT

Unions and Productivity. *Real* income depends upon production. What we get for the years we work depends upon productivity—output per unit of input—and, of course, upon the hours and years we work. The things that decrease production depress income. So we ask: "Do unions have the power to affect productivity appreciably? If so, how do they use their power?"

Unions have power—economic and political. But the effect they might have on economic progress *over a period of years* remains a matter of speculation. Productivity has been determined largely by such things as the availability of natural resources, technical development, the accumulation of capital, management skill, industriousness, and education. Unions have generally not exerted strong influence on these underlying forces. Until the 1930's, unions were influential in only a few industries. As unions grew in power, they did not concentrate on things they could do constructively to increase productivity. So history tells little about what, and how much, unions might do positively and creatively over the long run to raise productivity.

Capital accumulation, a major source of improvement in productivity, has hardly been the job of unions. Today, however, their control of welfare and pension funds is increasing their potential influence in this respect. Research and the improvement of technology are rarely union activities. Union pressure for higher wages, however, may stimulate employers to look more aggressively for better methods.

Perhaps the main thing unions can do constructively is to make the job of management easier—to bring the knowledge of the man on the job to the aid of management, to create an atmosphere of welcome for improvement in methods, to aid in discipline, and sometimes to help one firm learn about operating methods that have proved successful elsewhere. Unhappily, the record to date includes not a few cases of union obstruction rather than support for technological improvements.

The labor movement, fortunately, contains leaders (and probably millions of members) who welcome increasing automation and other methods of raising productivity if jobs are safeguarded. Can the union movements be made a positive force for improving efficiency? One of many concrete examples of what is possible is a program sponsored by the plumbers' union jointly with employers. It is training members to meet the increasingly exacting requirements of modern technology, such as the microscopically fine tolerances of more and more industrial equipment.

Productivity is related to another union goal: shorter hours. Reduction of extreme workweeks probably brought no net drop in output because people worked more effectively per hour. However, after some point—one which is hard to spot—income in the form of goods and services must be less if the workyear gets shorter. Whether real income in the broadest sense has suffered depends upon the worth of the leisure obtained in relation to the goods and services not produced.

Whatever the effects of unions on *national* real income, there is no doubt that a union can have considerable effect on incomes in more *specific* cases. Unions try to influence both supply and demand.

Raising the Demand for Union Labor. Occasionally, in using methods already described, unions have tried to increase demands for union labor

FIGURE 25–3.   Increasing the Demand for Labor

This figure applies to (a) the effects of national policies raising the total demand for labor or (b) the efforts of a particular union to boost the demand for its services. Elasticities are hypothetical. The wage rate would rise from F to G and employment from A to B.

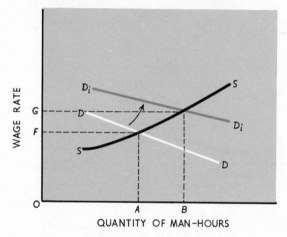

by make-work devices which force someone to buy more labor than he would freely or which boost demands for the employer's product (Fig. 25–3). Unions have tried to influence governmental policy to raise overall demands to stimulate employment. However, major efforts to raise wage rates have taken other forms.

Restricting the Supply of Union Labor. One way to get a higher price is to restrict supply (Fig. 25–4). Unions over the years have worked with considerable success to reduce the normal workweek, to increase vacations, to restrict child labor, and to lower the age of retirement. They have lobbied for laws to curtail immigration. Such actions reduce the *total supply* of labor. In addition, unions try to reduce the supply of *particular types* of labor. Some unions, for example, seek to prevent outsiders from acquiring certain skills. Or, after getting agreements with employers that require union labor, some unions restrict membership. Union members then will work only for a rate of pay above what they could get if a larger number of qualified workers were competing for the jobs. A higher price for the product will generally result from an increase in wage costs. If so, consumers will not buy so much; the employer(s) will need less labor. How much less depends upon the elasticity of demand. Unquestionably, a higher wage rate can be made effective if the labor supply is cut. The union members can benefit *but only if they can control the supply of labor.* If nonmembers can do the work, they will be attracted by the higher wage rate; it will then tend to fall.

FIGURE 25–4.   Restriction of Supply of Labor

Two demand curves are shown. $D_e D_e$ is relatively elastic, $D_i D_i$ relatively inelastic. When the supply of labor is reduced from SS to $S_r S_r$, the wage rate rises—to the level of E_e or E_i— and the amount of employment drops—to OB or OC. The changes in wage rates and employment depend, of course, upon the elasticities of both demand and supply.

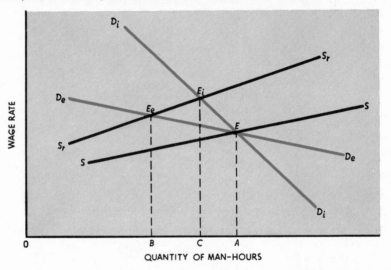

Professions with control over entry into training and qualifications to practice also have a way to control supply. An outsider can hardly be competent to judge the best dividing line between quantity and quality. By raising the skill requirements of physicians, doctors assure a better quality of medical service to those who will pay. Assuming relatively inelastic demand, doctors receive higher incomes. It is hard to imagine any occupational group with even a trace of gumption and self-respect that does not aspire to higher standards. Control of supply is one way to raise standards and earnings.

Setting a Minimum Rate: Exclusion of Potential Supply.   There is a less obvious but far more common method of getting the same result.

FIGURE 25–5.   Fixed Wage Rate Excludes Potential Supply

If the market were free, the wage rate would be *OE* and the amount of employment *OA*. The union agreement, however, puts the wage at *OW*. The amount of employment that laborers would be willing to supply would be *OC*, but the amount employers will hire is *OB*. Much as they might have preferred producing the output *OA*, employers have agreed with the union not to put the wage under *OW*. The quantity of man-hours excluded, compared with free-market equilibrium, is *BA*.

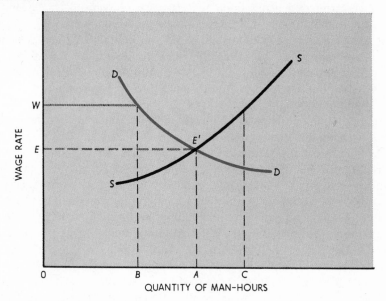

QUANTITY OF MAN-HOURS

Unions, or organizations with different names, can frequently raise their wage rates without *directly* controlling the supply of labor. They insist upon a minimum rate which exceeds significantly the equilibrium of pure competition; there will then be less business and, so, fewer jobs (Fig. 25–5). Newcomers, however, are not free to bid down the rate. *Price competition* (*on wages*) *is not permitted.* Union leaders may not even be conscious of the fact that fixing the wage rate is a form of exclusion of would-be competitors. When the basic wage rate for a group of jobs is set at, say, $3 an hour, anyone worth (appreciably) less is not really in the potential supply.

Earning Effects of Higher Wage Rates. If a union gets its members higher wage rates than would otherwise prevail, who pays? What are the other results? What is the effect of higher wage rates on earnings? When a union pushes up wage rates, we can generally expect two results: (1) consumers will pay more and (2) there will be less employment in the jobs this union controls. Except if the union were to help increase productivity as wage rates rose, one or the other of these results—more probably a combination—would come with rising wage rates, unless some other "squeeze" is possible. Sometimes, but probably not often on any appreciable scale, room for squeeze does exist. It will consist of some unused device at management's disposal to raise productivity or some surplus—profit or other distributive share—which can pay for a bit of higher labor cost without hurting consumers or cutting employment.

After raising wage rates, the effective power of a union to increase member earnings depends upon the elasticity of demand. If demand is inelastic, total earnings rise. If demand is elastic, earnings fall.

1. The time period is important. In any week, month, or year, demand for a *particular type* of labor may be inelastic, but over a longer period, it may be highly elastic. Consumption shifts to products with more attractive prices.[15] As time passes, adjustments of many kinds begin to whittle away the hours of work. Employers shift to other methods of production or to other localities, especially as new capacity is needed. Incentives for innovation are directed toward labor-saving devices.

2. The smaller the particular type of labor as a part of the total cost of a product, the less will the price of that labor affect the amount that will be hired. The total cost of plumbers is such a small part of the total cost of a building that plumbers' wages will not have an appreciable effect on the number of new houses purchased. Here the significant thing is to be insignificant. Yet straw upon straw may eventually break the camel's back. When unions are numerous, with each responsible for only a small part of the total cost, each may sensibly ignore the effect *it* has on the total cost. Why not do what it can to force up its own wage rates? When many unions act this way, however, the combined effect will be strikingly different from the effect of action by any one. Consumers may not be able to keep the price from rising, but they can cut the quantity purchased—a smaller house, a new auto less frequently, more "do it yourself."

3. If the demand for the final product is highly inelastic—the demand for missile launching bases or emergency surgery—the derived demand for labor needed to produce the final product will tend to be inelastic, depending, of course, upon the possibilities of substituting other factors of production. If the buyer is a government which agrees to pay any verified expense, the firm producing the item has rather slight reason for trying to keep wage rates down. Public utilities, which are required by law to keep on providing service, may not be able to adjust output when costs rise; even if a union forces wages up to a point where the employer loses money, he may be almost helpless to reduce the amount of labor he buys in the short run. Moreover, for some reason, a firm with near-monopoly powers may be reluctant to raise its price, even if marginal costs go up. A union may then feel that the price of the product to consumers will not

---

[15] Chicago newspaper printing may not be able to leave the city. Some kinds of printing, however, can move easily; others move at a cost which becomes a bargain at some wage differential. Construction is less easily shifted and so are services such as schooling, medicine, and law.

rise enough to make an appreciable difference in the quantity sold. Yet over time other factors will be substituted for labor.[16]

4. The size of the bargaining unit has a major bearing on the elasticity of demand for the services the union controls. If a union is dealing with only one of many firms producing coal, textiles, or transportation, it must recognize that a wage rise that forces the employer to boost his prices will shift business and employment to other firms. But if the bargaining can be made to cover the whole industry, the union and employers need have much less fear of competition. If the union can act as an industrywide monopolist, wage rates can go up farther and more easily than if each employer must consider the competition of others.

Sharing the Cost of Unemployment from Higher Wage Rates. When (other things the same) a union raises wage rates and the demand is not completely inelastic, the quantity of employment in the jobs affected will decline.[17] In an expanding economy, the result may be slower growth in jobs. How is the unemployment shared? There may be a short-run or transition period in which the members of the union absorb unemployment, perhaps by going on a short workweek. Earnings do not rise as much as expected, and a "surplus" of labor in the jobs affected appears. With men on short hours the employer will have no reason to hire replacements for workers who die, retire, or leave for any of the many reasons for labor turnover. If the union has power, it may restrict entrance to membership so that eventually a smaller number of members find full employment at the higher wage rate. Gradually, remaining union members will not suffer unemployment due to the rise in wage rates.

However, employment in the occupation will be less than if wages and prices were lower. If the firm is growing, expansion is slowed. What happens to persons who would have gotten jobs here? In the short run, they may experience unemployment. Over a longer period, however, they will probably get jobs elsewhere (Fig. 25–6). How? By competing, where they are free to do so, for jobs that are not so tightly restricted. Wage rates and average earnings in such jobs will be less than otherwise. The

[16] If demand is completely inelastic, those who pay the higher prices have less to spend on other things.

[17] One study measured the amount by which other factors of production were substituted for labor when wage rates rose, ignoring any effect from increases in the product prices. For manufacturing in Michigan the average decline in employment from a 1 percent increase in wage rates was 1.6 percent. In auto manufacturing, however, the employment loss was estimated at 2.8 percent for each 1 percent rise in wage rates. S. P. Sobotka, "Michigan's Employment Problem: The Substitution against Labor," *Journal of Business of the University of Chicago* (April, 1961), pp. 119–28. Critics of this analysis believe that factors other than wage rates accounted for more of the substitution of capital for labor than found by the author.

FIGURE 25–6.   Effect of Wage Rate in One Industry on Wage Rate and Employment in Another

The equilibrium wage rate would be the same in the two industries, M and N, that is, OE. In M, however, the union succeeds in maintaining the wage rate at OW. Employment is less than it would be by BA. The persons not employed seek jobs in industry N, so the supply schedule is S_iS_i. The wage rate settles at OZ and employment at OD. Note: AB and CD are not necessarily equal.

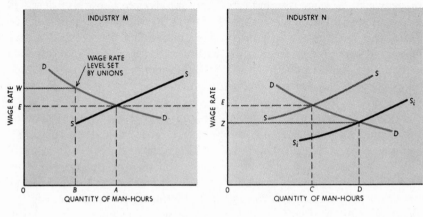

long-run results, therefore, include a different (*a*) wage structure and (*b*) distribution of the labor force from those that would have developed otherwise.

Legal Minimum Wages.   This analysis leads naturally into another topic, though one not involving unions specifically. Some workers earn little. Why not bypass the imperfect and apparently slow process of competition and unionization and pass a law raising wages at the low end of the scale? This is such an inviting prospect that many governments, including ours, have tried it. The results are disputed. No one questions that most employers will obey the law and pay what it requires—now generally $1.60 an hour. But this is only a beginning.

If the rate set is high enough to mean much, it will also force unemployment for persons whose productivity is below the minimum. This result is obvious if we take an extreme case. Let us assume a minimum wage for college teachers of $25,000 a year. Bliss indeed. Or would it be? Colleges could not hire as many teachers as they do now. Huge increases in tuition rates or government appropriations, of course, might help provide funds; but some students and taxpayers would refuse to pay, and enrollments would drop. There would be unemployment in college teaching for persons not worth $25,000 a year. Most of us presumably would have to look for jobs elsewhere. If the legal minimum salary were $3,000, however, it would scarcely affect employment. Why? It would be too low to be effective. Here we have extremes: one legal minimum vastly increasing wage rates and cutting employment, another too low to mean anything.[18]

Sometimes, of course, there will be room to raise wage rates at the expense of the employer, without cutting the amount of work. A higher wage may "shock" employers into greater efficiency or help improve productivity by creating better morale. Yet one should be highly skeptical of minimum wage legislation as a method of aiding the people at the bottom of the economic heap. A rate that is higher than marginal productivity will curtail employment. Persons with lowest productivity will tend to suffer by being forced into unemployment. We say "tend" because exceptions do appear. The basic forces will not work their full effects obviously and promptly. (When the lowest wage rate rises, formal or informal agreements may require that rates somewhat higher in the scale also rise to maintain earlier differentials.) The increase in unemployment cannot, however, be judged accurately. The wage-rate increase does not, of course, raise purchasing power; there may be a shift from employers or consumers, but hardly any overall rise.

BARGAINING AND THE EARNINGS OF UNION LABOR

How much attention do unions pay to elasticity of demand? Less, probably, than would be in the general public welfare. Should a union take serious interest in the people who do not receive jobs because the union gets a higher wage rate? The members who can count on keeping their jobs at the higher wage rates—normally the majority and especially those with seniority—may not worry much about the lack of jobs for the younger fellows, nor for those who will enter the labor market in later years when employment-reducing adjustments are exerting their full effects. Deliberate union concern for the effect on employment, especially of nonmembers, is unusual. Clearly, however, unions do not push wage rates as high as if the effects on employment were a matter of indifference.

---

[18] The Department of Labor has studied the effects of increases in federal minimum wage rates in particular industries. An economist who has specialized on wages and employment commented: ". . . [regarding] the Labor Department's studies of minimum wage. . . . There is a disparity between their conclusions and the conclusions I reach from examining the same statistics. . . .

"I recall one group of studies which claimed rather little fall in employment as a result of the rise in the minimum wage from 75 cents to $1. Actually, employment declined 4 percent in the first month or so and 8 percent within the next year; a total of 12 percent altogether. The Department of Labor didn't consider that much of a decline in employment, but I think it is quite a significant decline." C. D. Long in *Employment and Unemployment* . . . (Washington, D.C.: Chamber of Commerce of the United States, 1961), p. 46. The long-run effects on the growth of jobs in an expanding economy are more difficult to measure, but the general tendency may be indicated by nearly a decade of experience. Before 1956 the unemployment rate among both white and Negro boys was around 8 to 11 percent. After the minimum wage rose from 75 cents to $1 an hour, unemployment among white boys went up to 14 percent and for Negroes to 24 percent and stayed at this level year after year.

Have Unions Raised Labor Earnings?   Have unions had much effect on earnings of labor as a whole? Does this still seem like a stupid question with the answer obviously "yes"? (See Figure 25–7.)

FIGURE 25–7.   Wages, Man-Hour Output, and Unit Labor Costs, 1947–66

Since World War II, man-hour compensation has risen at a higher annual rate in manufacturing than has man-hour output. From 1960 to 1965 the relation was more favorable, and unit labor costs were relatively stable. Unit labor costs then turned up.

INDEX 1957–1959 = 100

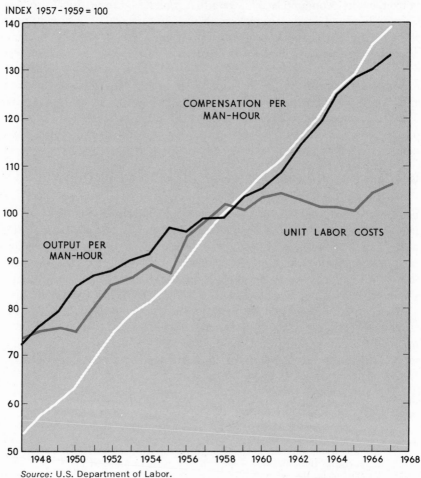

Source: U.S. Department of Labor.

Craft unions have undoubtedly raised *member* earnings. No one can measure the amount, for who knows what might have been—the effects on employment, for example? Memberships have been controlled and wage rates elevated so that earnings for members have certainly been higher than they would have been. Someone pays, however (unless the wage increase *itself* raises productivity). Consumers will pay more for the product affected, but part of the cost may be a reduction in the share of owners of property. To the extent that what one union gains is the result of restricting employment and thus increasing the pressure for jobs elsewhere, the weaker groups bear the brunt of lower wage rates.

In unionized plants, wage rates generally average more than those where there are no unions. Wage rates have often risen more where unions are strong than where they are weak. The explanation of both these conditions, however, may well be that these are the jobs requiring highest skills and using most capital equipment—where man-hour productivity is greatest. The difference between the earnings of a locomotive engineer and the unskilled track laborer can be explained, at least in part, by factors other than a union. What we cannot do is segregate the various possible effects and say for certain which ones result from unionization and which from other things.[19] A thorough analysis of the statistics indicates that, on the average, wage rates in recent years have been 10 to 15 percent higher in unionized industries than they would have been without union organization.[20]

Differences among industries, regions, and communities of various sizes are sufficiently important to obscure the effects of unionization alone. Where hourly wage rates are higher, it is generally impossible to judge how much, if any, employment has dropped—whether fewer workers on the payroll or fewer hours per year—so that *earnings* are lower even though more is paid per hour. The facts, however, are consistent with the conclusion that unions do exert an appreciable influence. Nevertheless, the subtle and indirect competition of nonunionized parts of the economy may limit, more than we realize, union success in raising real wages. This seems especially probable where union power does not rest on skill or government support of monopoly position.

Unions tend to claim (and to receive from their members) credit for increased earnings due not only to any union effort but also to the benefits resulting from more fundamental economic forces. In the two decades when union power multiplied, large percentage wage increases went to some nonunionized workers. Underlying economic forces—such as overall demand, the level of skill, increase in capital availability, and technical progress—are powerful indeed.

[19] One leading specialist writes: "All we know about collective bargaining suggests that the most important effects involve fundamental changes in an enterprise and its surrounding product and labor markets. It is really not possible to leave the enterprise and its markets alone, introduce a union, and then see what happens to the wage structure. The introduction of unionism typically involves a wholesale transformation. . . . It is unrealistic and improper to pose the problem in terms of comparing wages with or without a union, assuming all other wage-setting factors are unchanged. Collective bargaining changes most of the wage-setting variables." J. T. Dunlop in *Aspects of Labor Economics.* . . . (National Bureau of Economic Research, 1962), p. 343.

[20] H. Gregg Lewis, *Unionism and Relative Wages in the United States* (Chicago: University of Chicago Press, 1963).

Unions and the Structure of Wage Rates. Within organized labor, the lower paid members have generally fared better, percentagewise, than the more highly paid. The narrowing of differentials has resulted from wage settlements for general increases of a certain number of cents. If, when the "rounds" of wage rates began during World War II, you had been receiving $2 an hour while I was receiving $1, and each "round" was for 15 cents an hour, after six rounds you would be receiving $2.90, I $1.90, an hour; you are ahead 45 percent, while I am ahead 90 percent. Increases in percentage terms would have maintained the original relation.

Narrowing the gap between payment for high and low skills will affect their relative availability—to the disadvantage of an economy which has increasing need for more developed skills. The proportion of highly skilled labor in the total labor force may not be growing as much as our long-run interest requires. Unions, in some cases, have worked to reduce wage differentials among areas, to bring South and North, small town and large city, more nearly together. While this may seem to aid the worker with lower pay, the policy may also make it harder for his region to attract employers.

Unions have pressed to increase the relative importance of "fringes." Such "payments" are probably more common and larger in total than if union power had been materially less. Some recent contracts provide funds for earlier retirement, partly as a means of facilitating adjustment of labor force to new techniques of production.

Guaranteed Annual Wage: Supplementary Unemployment Benefits. A few unions have concluded agreements which go part of the way toward the "guaranteed annual wage." Labor, it is argued, must be considered more fully than in the past as a fixed cost. A regular employee must be provided pay (supplementing unemployment insurance benefits) for periods when he is not working. Possibilities vary tremendously. In effect, many employees receive such a guarantee because of the nature of the firm's business—life insurance office staffs—or because of seniority—older members of railroad brotherhoods. Obviously, however, the employer is limited by the market. Demand is often unstable.

The practical question is one of "how much." Some firms can certainly guarantee employment at standard rates to many employees, but not to all. Managements with strong incentives can devise policies that will reduce fluctuations in employment: coordinating hiring and firing, varying work schedules, adjusting vacations, diversifying skills of employees, producing for inventory in slack periods, subcontracting peak work or using more overtime, lowering prices in "off" seasons, varying products.[21] Yet change

---

[21] Some of these methods merely shift the fluctuations to other firms. In some countries, laws that compel an employer to keep workers on the payroll have discouraged expansion; the risks of adding to employment are excessive.

goes on constantly. Can any of us say what we will buy next year?

Agreements in the auto industry require the employer to build a reserve fund. When union members are out of work more than 1 week, they receive payments from the fund which when added to unemployment insurance benefits will equal 65 to 70 percent of the weekly wage up to 6 months or more.

GOVERNMENT AND UNIONS

Union growth has been influenced decisively by national, state, and local laws—once generally hostile, later giving decisive aid. The operations of unions today take place within a framework of law. The appendix which follows traces some of the history but cannot show adequately how the passing years have added to the complexity of labor law. The laws involve relations of employer and employees, of unions to their members, of unions to other unions, and of unions and employers to the public.

The public interest becomes most obviously apparent when strikes immobilize, or threaten to immobilize, railroads or other industries essential to the economy. Two "solutions" have been tried:

1. The President may appoint a fact-finding board. Its job is to collect and analyze the facts and to hear the arguments. It then reports the facts as it sees them and makes recommendations. Unlike arbitration, the parties concerned do not help select the board; nor do they promise in advance to accept the recommendations. The force of public opinion is supposed to get acceptance. The quality of the result rests upon many things, especially the competence, impartiality, and strength of the fact-finders. One obvious reality, however, is that they are not required to pay any increases in employment expense proposed. Boards must largely feel in the dark about the goals they should seek. Being temporary, they have no continuing responsibility.

2. *Government seizure* and operation of business vital to national welfare and safety was authorized during World War II. What about the practical powers? Obviously, neither bayonets nor court rulings will run trains or deliver fuel and food. However, property owners have no way to prevent the use of their property if government officials insist. The officials can seize the top management offices and issue orders which, coming through ordinary channels, subordinate management will likely observe. Will union members work? Generally they have. With appropriate legislation, the government might impose harsh penalties on individuals who refuse to obey, fine the union, weaken it financially, and withdraw its legal privileges. Seizure is a drastic method which hardly solves the troubles causing the dispute.

America does not have a way to deal with great concentrations of private power. Some unions can tie up the whole economy; many more can inflict huge losses on cities, regions, or large groups of bystanders. There are employers who can do the same, especially when they act in unison. How can we meet threats of pressures which in the short run can impose great loss? How can we deal with extortionate demands? These questions, still unsettled, raise issues of tremendous importance.[22] Perhaps an "arsenal" of possible actions could be provided. The President might be authorized to employ any of a half dozen or more devices. Action could then depend upon the conditions of the case. (But what President will not favor unions if he believes they have concentrated voting power?) Another approach would emphasize "certainty—specifically, more certainty that the government will not intervene except in rare emergencies."[23] The prospect of government intervention invites such reaction when one party believes that it will get more from establishing an "adversary" attitude and preparing a strong case for favorable decision from some governmental agency rather than trying for settlement. The extension of government influence into wage decisions (or those involving work rules) can affect the economy far more deeply and extensively than foreseen when the first steps are taken.

We need a clearer concept of the general public interest. Removal of some legal immunities of unions, such as broad freedom from injunctions and the practical exemption from local enforcement of the law of property and persons during labor strife, would make unions more nearly equal under the law to the rest of the public. Where legal privilege continues, corresponding responsibility might be established.

The complex rules which now apply to both the content and the method of collective bargaining need to be simplified and administration improved—both "easier said than done."

Reducing the size of giant unions deserves serious consideration. Giving the individual worker the opportunity of choosing between two or more unions to represent him might be feasible in some cases; labor specialists point out, however, that competition among unions is fraught with danger to the public. Few problems seem to arouse such controversy as those of revising labor law. In 1966 President Johnson, indicating his belief that the unsolved problems are serious, said that he would propose remedies for congressional consideration. After 2 years, however, he and his advisers remained unable to formulate proposals which he would recommend for addition to our body of labor law.

---

[22] Some economists may say, "Let's face it, unions are essentially monopolies. Therefore, we ought to apply the antitrust laws." Even recognizing the monopolistic nature of union power, other economists doubt that antitrust procedure is the appropriate device for dealing with this problem.

[23] Research and Policy Committee of the Committee for Economic Development, *Union Powers and Union Functions* . . . (New York: The Committee, 1964), p. 28, original in italics. A labor union official, summarizing arguments against compulsory arbitration, says that it does not end strikes; outsiders cannot know enough about the issues to decide wisely; innovation would be stifled if only because arbitration looks backward to precedents; preliminary stages of bargaining are inhibited. "But most fundamental of all, the case against compulsory arbitration is the case against compulsion itself." K. Fiester, "The Case against Compulsory Arbitration," *The American Federationist* (October, 1965), p. 18.

TERMS AND CONCEPTS

local union	union shop	arbitration
national union	agency shop	lockout
union federation	check-off	blacklist
collective bargaining	seniority	yellow-dog contract
closed shop	featherbedding	company union
open shop	fringe benefit	secondary boycott

QUESTIONS

1. In what respects does a wage rate fixed by collective bargaining restrict the effective supply of labor? Does it free the union from the need to impose explicit restrictions on entry to its membership?

2. "Basic economic forces are so powerful that unions can really do little to improve or hurt the well-being of the country." Discuss what forces you think the speaker had in mind.

3. Why do you suppose that unions have pressed for wage-rate increases during recessions as well as during periods of full employment?

4. Explain the difference between "member-oriented" and "union-oriented" objectives of labor unions. Give examples of each.

5. When, if ever, is it to the interest of a union to ignore the elasticity of demand for the employer's product? Why?

6. Rising legal minimum wages are sometimes defended as a way to enforce employers to become more efficient. What are the possibilities and the obstacles? Why do you suppose Congress raised minimum wage levels when unemployment was high in 1961?

7. What does a union produce? What can unions do to raise productivity?

8. "Unions can raise the wage rates of their members, but the possibilities are much narrower than often assumed." Discuss.

9. "If unions do actually succeed in aiding their members, the poorest groups in the economy are almost certain to suffer." Discuss, taking account of the effects on both living costs and employment.

10. Why do some unions and some employers favor industrywide bargaining?

11. Study arguments for and against the union shop and other types of compulsion on members.

12. Why do you suppose union growth has slowed?

13. "American labor leaders in the past came largely from immigrant groups and mining communities. Idealism and a strong sense of injustice were powerful motivating forces." What groups would you expect to provide union leaders in the future?

14. "An increase in wage rates will not raise purchasing power on balance [throughout the economy]. Those who pay lose as much as the recipients gain." Discuss.

15. "Neither the Taft-Hartley Act nor the Landrum-Griffin Act attacks the really serious problem of labor unions, their position as monopolists." Discuss. Do you believe there is such a problem? If so, what might be done in the public interest?

APPENDIX: Union Development and the Role of Government

ORGANIZATION

Building unions has been an uphill struggle, hard, often bitter, and even violent. Within our generation, however, conditions have changed profoundly. Labor-management controversy today involves only a tiny fraction of the disputes about *forming* a union and dealing with it that were once common.

Devices of Labor-Management Conflict. Many things made organization difficult; for example, the *legal system*, as enforced, usually sided with employers; police were willing to use force and courts to grant injunctions[1] to oppose unionization. The dominant public attitude favored "individual freedom" and the rights of property. Organizing difficulties also grew out of the continuing increase in the supply of labor due to immigration, depressions which intensified the competition for jobs, and lack of funds to support life during strikes. Potential leaders found better opportunities for themselves in jobs other than organizing, while the absence of entrenched class antagonism, the improvement in living conditions, and economic opportunity cut the appeal of unionization.

Employers refused to hire a union member. They used spies to locate union leaders and might close the plant (a *lockout*) to weaken the union before it was ready to strike. Employers used *black lists* (methods of indicating to each other those workers who might be disruptive in trying to form a union); *yellow dog* contracts (employment agreements in which an employee, as a condition of getting a job, agreed not to join a union); debt at a company store; and strikebreakers from outside to work during a strike. Later, by establishing *company unions* and improving conditions of work, employers sought to remove the appeal of outside unions.[2]

[1] An injunction is a court order; ordinarily it commands the persons enjoined to refrain from doing certain specified things. The purpose is to prevent irreparable harm, to preserve the status quo while ordinary procedures can operate. The injunction was developed long ago as a preventive device to serve where a later award of damages could not adequately compensate for injury done, such as cutting down beautiful old trees. A judge can issue an injunction without a hearing; and he can enforce it, without jury trial, with fines or imprisonment for contempt of court. In labor disputes, judges would issue injunctions forbidding picketing and other actions that were essential to union success.

[2] The employer likely paid the bills of a company union and might prevent the officers from vigorously representing the members. Yet some company unions became effective in settling grievances, fixing plant rules, defining seniority, and otherwise representing members. Spokesmen for organized labor have been antagonistic to company unions. Leaders of the large national unions are not impartial observers—the company union may be a serious rival.

What devices could (and can) workers employ? Group solidarity could be built around a craft until the cohesion needed for joint action was achieved. The *strike*, a joint refusal to work, might impose great hardship on the employer if he had a binding contract to deliver goods or was seriously pressed to get money to pay debts or had perishable material on hand or profits were good or the season at its peak. *Picketing* (men and women walking around the plant) was designed to persuade others not to work or customers not to buy; the picket line became a symbol, a sort of "mutual aid insurance"; union members would not cross each other's picket line. For workers opposing the union, "rough stuff" and less extreme intimidation were not unknown. The union's power was obviously greater if it had a *strike fund* for serious emergencies such as sickness, rent for strikers about to be evicted, perhaps food; national unions sometimes helped provide such funds. *Public sympathy* for the underdog was often an intangible aid. Sometimes a union enlisted the help of some other union, getting it to strike (a sympathetic strike) or to refuse to provide substitutes to do the work; though railroad firemen might be qualified to serve as engineers, they would not do so if the engineers struck. Stagehands may strike if musicians do, and unions in the building trades support each other. Sometimes employees stay on the job but *slow down*, perhaps under the guise of meticulous observance of obsolete and inconsistent rules. If workers, perhaps a small minority, get disgruntled, they may pull a *wildcat* or *flash strike* for a few hours or days, short-circuiting normal procedures, even defying union leaders. When a contract prohibits a strike, all may be "sick" the same day.

The *boycott*, refusal to buy the employer's product, by interfering with the marketing rather than the making of goods may induce him to come to terms; courts tolerate persuasion of buyers but hold illegal the use of coercion to hurt the employer by forcing others to boycott him. Sometimes the *secondary boycott* has proved effective; for example, if carpenters refuse to work with wood from nonunion plants, the latter are obviously under pressure to unionize.

Sabotage is the deliberate interference with production, ordinarily by malicious destruction or damage; the saboteur sets a machine control wrong so that material is wasted; scratches a product, reducing its salability; fails to oil parts; or deliberately antagonizes customers. Occasionally there are *acts of violence* against nonunion firms or loyal employees: a delivery truck is forced off the road, a stink bomb is thrown into a theater or acid into a dry-cleaning plant, or a man is "educated" by a small bomb at his home.

Efforts to Aid the Employer. Just as some employers have tried to meet pressure by improving conditions for employees, *some unions have tried to develop constructive ways of helping employers*. Some have sincerely tried to help raise efficiency. They may aid the employer in getting *publicity* for his product or *tariffs* that reduce foreign competition. Publicizing the *union label* is another device; the consumer is urged to buy things with a label that shows they were made with union labor. More important has been the use of *political pressure to expand markets* for union products or services.

For almost two generations the U.S. labor movement was dominated by the attitude of Samuel Gompers, founder of the AFL—unions should concentrate on dealings with employers and not try to change the underlying political system.[3] Yet during this period, unions made considerable use of political influence, chiefly at the local level. Construction unions presented an outstanding example; they worked, commonly with builders, to get favorable local legislation. Building codes were framed to give union members more work. Unions also helped to secure laws requiring that government purchases, such as printing, had to give preference to local union labor. At the state, and even the national, level, labor unions occasionally succeeded in getting legislation designed to help union members, such as laws setting the minimum crew on a railroad train.

Craft versus Industrial Unions.   The AFL, dating from 1886, developed around the principle of organization on *craft lines*—men doing the same kind of work should belong to the same union. Carpenters, teamsters, printers, and cigar makers would each have a separate union, even if they worked for the same employer. Generally, only groups with well-developed skills could organize on this basis and hold together. Another form of organization, however, competed for favor: *industrial* organization. Employees in the same industry—coal mining or clothing manufacturing—joined the same union, even though they performed different kinds of work. Yet, until the 1930's, the basis of the American labor movement was overwhelmingly the craft union based on skill. Unions consisted chiefly of the elite of labor.

The AFL thus offered little room or hope for the great mass of employees during the 1920's. In 1933, at the strategic moment when the New Deal began to give government encouragement to the extension of unionization, the AFL was not equipped to organize the mass-production industries. Steel and auto workers, for example, could not fit well into the older craft unions. Industrial unions provided the answer and much of the leadership; four large ones took the initiative. When expelled from the AFL, they established the forerunner of the CIO, which grew impressively. If Congress were considering a new labor law or the Treasury trying to sell war bonds, the AFL and CIO worked together. When their unions competed for the same workers as members, however, rivalry was keen and not always sportsmanlike. The AFL was traditionally more conservative on political and economic issues. Gradually differences narrowed, personal rivalries cooled; agreements to eliminate raiding and jurisdictional disputes were negotiated, paving the way for final merger.

GOVERNMENT AND UNIONS

The increase in union power that began in the 1930's relied heavily upon a change in laws of the national government. Congress made yellow-dog contracts unenforceable and greatly restricted the power of federal courts to issue injunctions in labor disputes. A 1933 law provided that industries, in working out their National Recovery Administration "codes" of production and prices, were to bargain collectively with employees. Unionization began to grow, penetrating areas and industries where before it had found the opposition impregnable.

---

[3] Until the 1930's, the AFL opposed government social insurance. The annual convention was set *after* election day to help keep politics out of union debates.

Wagner Act: An Aid to Union Organization. The stimulus supplied by the NRA vanished when the Supreme Court declared the law unconstitutional. Congress immediately filled the gap, and more. The Wagner (National Labor Relations) Act, 1935, applying where interstate commerce is involved, granted authority to organize and bargain collectively without employer interference. In addition, it made certain employer practices illegal: discrimination against an employee because of his union membership, threats, blacklisting, refusal to deal with a recognized union, and some others. Unions still had to get employees to join.

The National Labor Relations Board was created to interpret and help enforce the law. The NLRB is an administrative agency. It deals with two kinds of cases: (*a*) disputes about which, if any, union is to represent employees and (*b*) questions of the "fairness" of practices (of the employer) where unions are involved. It decides which of the cases brought to its attention it will investigate. It prosecutes where investigation indicates that prosecution is appropriate, decides, and reviews its own decisions. Although care has been taken to separate the prosecuting and adjudicating functions, no fully satisfactory division has yet been found.

Many difficulties arose in trying to decide what actions by labor and management were proper in preparing for elections to choose unions to represent employees. What if some workers in a plant might be claimed by craft unions while many wanted an industrial union and others a company union? What if workers came to dislike the leaders? Or if the union discriminated against some workers? Problems of unionization of foremen and supervisors proved difficult. In over 100,000 decisions in a 12-year period, the NLRB worked out an extensive body of rules. They decided which employer practices were unfair, the methods of choosing unions to represent employees, and the conditions for collective bargaining after a union had been certified to represent workers. When the NLRB has designated a union as bargaining agent, that union has exclusive rights.

The NLRB found employers using ingenious devices to get around the law, but union growth flourished. Union organizers, once they felt certain of a majority, could demand an election. If they won, the union was the sole bargaining agent for its members; the law said to the employer, even the most recalcitrant: "Deal with the union. Bargain collectively." Winning an election was much easier than winning recognition by a strike.[4]

At the outbreak of World War II, unions had grown to big, powerful, but in some cases, immature groups. Most union leaders pledged a "no-strike" policy. Labor peace prevailed generally. Wage rates, though presumably "frozen," crept up. Occasional strikes antagonized the public.

Taft-Hartley Act. Pressure for new legislation grew. Union leaders, however, refused to concede that the public interest might be served by change.

---

[4] The NLRB has 2,500 employees. About 6,000 cases get some staff attention each year. The vast majority are settled more or less informally, in the field, taking an average of around 50 days. Each year public hearings are held by a trial examiner in around 1,000 cases of alleged unfair labor practices. The Board itself reviews nearly 800. These take, on the average, around 500 days. Cases involving representation are ordinarily settled with less delay.

Standing firm as a giant tree, unions refused to cooperate in reform. The gale of public opinion was too strong, however, and although unions were not shattered like the big tree, they may have lost more than if they had been as flexible as the sapling.[5] Congress passed the Labor-Management Relations (Taft-Hartley) Act in 1947. Unfortunately, labor law has become so complex that no summary the layman can understand will accurately reflect the facts.

The key features of the previous legislation remain: legal support for organization, for collective bargaining with the freedom to strike, and for prohibition of unfair practices by employers. The law *prohibits the closed shop* but permits the union shop, unless state law forbids. A three-way grouping of other major provisions is helpful in spite of the fact that some features may properly fall in more than one group:

1. Protection of Members.   Excessive initiation fees are forbidden where the union shop prevails.

A union cannot force a man out of his job so long as he pays his dues.

A union member must agree before his dues are subject to check-off.

Exclusive union handling of grievances is eliminated.

Numerous provisions govern the use of health and welfare funds.

A union wishing to use the NLRB must file data about finances and the pay and election of officers.

Members have the right to learn about the union's finances, its constitution, and the way officers are elected.

Union members must get a chance to vote on accepting the employer's best offer before injunctions against "national emergency" strikes are removed.

2. Measures to Assure Fairer Treatment of Employers.   Certain union practices are defined as unfair and are prohibited: (*a*) Unions must not insist upon pay for work not done ("featherbed"), (*b*) refuse to bargain in good faith, (*c*) engage in sympathetic or (*d*) jurisdictional strikes, or (*e*) impose secondary boycotts. The employer may sue the union (not individual members) for damages arising out of strikes for illegal purposes or in violation of agreements. (No longer, as under the Wagner Act, are unfair labor practices limited to those of an employer.)

Employers may appeal to the NLRB to stop unfair union practices and to petition for an election to see if the union has the support of employees.

Supervisors, such as foremen, are not permitted to bargain collectively; the employer, however, may deal with them as a group.

When a collective bargaining agreement is expiring, unions must give 60 days' notice of any intent to strike.

More freedom of speech is granted employers to express their views about the desirability of union organization. (The employer, however, must not threaten or promise benefits to influence votes in union elections.)

---

[5] In 1946 Congress had given two warnings. The Lea Act prohibited the musicians' union from such "featherbedding" as requiring radio stations to hire local orchestras (to sit idly) while the station was broadcasting music received by wire from another city. The Hobbs Act was designed to prevent such things as the use of force by teamsters to add a local driver (as "protection" against violence) on trucks entering a city with a driver from outside.

A union may not deny responsibility for the acts of its agents.

The NLRB was reorganized and its powers changed, partly to make operations more efficient and partly to reduce prounion bias.

The federal conciliation agency was made independent of the Department of Labor.

3. Protection of the General Public. Strikes in essential industries may be banned by injunction for as long as 80 days upon request by the U.S. Attorney General.

Union officials must swear that they are not Communists if their union is to use the NLRB.

Union political activity is restricted. Unions, like business corporations, are forbidden to finance political activity from union treasuries.[6]

Unions have not been crippled appreciably.[7] The union shop flourishes. The essence of the closed shop continues in such industries as the building trades, printing, and shipping. Teamsters, construction, and some other unions even found loopholes which enabled them to continue using secondary boycotts. For example, teamsters refused to transport "hot cargo." They would not handle goods from (or to) a struck plant, thus putting pressure on other firms. Employers have not gone on union-busting campaigns, nor have they exhausted unions by pressing charges of unfair labor practices. Fear of such lawsuits, however, has provided impetus for unions to try to settle jurisdictional disputes among themselves, reducing what, from the public's point of view, has long been an inexcusable blot on the union record.

Unions have been strong enough to get large wage increases time and again since 1947. But hasn't union growth almost stopped? True, but chiefly for a reason not growing out of the law: the large, easily organized groups had already been unionized.

While an *employer* guilty of disobeying the law is required to compensate employees for losses they suffer as a result of his illegal actions, the NLRB does not require a *union* which is guilty of unlawful restraint or coercion of workers to "make employees whole" by adequate compensation. To do so would ordinarily require a back-pay order to cover earnings lost because of the unlawful union action. The NLRB has also declined to issue injunctions against unions to forbid intimidation and violence against workers. Publicity in congressional hearings was needed to alert union members to their rights under the law.

Landrum-Griffin Act. Ten years of experience brought widespread agreement that Taft-Hartley should be changed but no consensus on what would be best. Then a Senate subcommittee headed by Senator McClellan revealed shocking practices. In 1959 a majority of Congress agreed on the provisions of

---

[6] Energetic and extensive political activity of unions is financed by direct contributions of members. In addition, union funds are used on a wide scale for public "education" on campaign issues and candidates. COPE (Committee on Political Education) has been extremely active in political campaigns.

[7] Since World War II, several states have imposed stricter standards on intrastate union activity. Some states by "right to work" (anti-union-shop) laws and other devices have made conditions more difficult for unions. State rules, which vary widely, apply narrowly because of the supremacy of federal law.

a new law, the Labor-Management Reporting and Disclosure (Landrum-Griffin) Act. It is long, complex, and far from clear.

The law attempts to establish a "bill of rights" for union members. Unions must have constitutions and bylaws which spell out the procedures to be used in strike authorizations, collective bargaining, handling of funds, membership, and so on. Members have rights to participate in union affairs, to seek protection against improper disciplinary action, to sue officers, and if necessary, to go to federal courts. How much have these provisions really changed things? Most unions had been meeting the requirements, on paper and largely in fact. Those which had to change could meet technical requirements more easily than changing the spirit, the attitudes of human beings. Reform comes slowly.

The member's remedy of appeal to court is not only prohibitively expensive in the typical case. It also requires his open opposition to leaders who have great power in the ordinary affairs of the worker's life. (The worker is not given the right to refuse to join a union which is not of his choosing while keeping his job.)

The law requires extensive—and expensive—reporting of internal union finances to the Secretary of Labor (to be made available to the public) and the maintenance of detailed records. Employers are also required to report spending of certain types, in general any outlays for interfering with organization and bargaining. Local officers must be elected by secret ballot, at least every 3 years, national union officers every 5 years. Ex-criminals and Communists must not hold union office within 5 years of finishing the sentence or leaving the Party. Persons handling union funds must be bonded and meet standards of fiduciary responsibility. National unions may put a local under trusteeship only for "legitimate reasons," subject to written rules. A person out on strike may vote in an election to decide who is to represent the workers if the election is held within a year of the beginning of the strike.

The NLRB receives specific authorization to refuse jurisdiction in cases with minor interstate significance and to turn the cases over to the states. "Extortionate picketing" is made a federal offense; a union agent, for example, may no longer use picketing to "shake down" an employer for the benefit of the agent. Restrictions are placed on organizational, "stranger," picketing, that is, picketing by outsiders to compel an employer to force his workers to join the union. No such picketing is permitted if a union has been recognized or if there has been an election within a year. In other cases such picketing is limited to 30 days, but exceptions and loopholes apparently permit considerable extension of the period.

The act contains several provisions bearing on secondary boycotts. For example, it outlaws "hot cargo" clauses. Special provisions apply to construction and garment unions, for example, freeing them from the restrictions on picketing and secondary boycotts. Construction unions receive other special attention, such as the power to demand that a worker join the union 7 days after he begins work.

Does this law represent progress? One cannot answer without knowing which direction is "forward." Is it wise to enlarge rather than reduce governmental participation in labor-management relations? Strains are added to our political system. Mixing labor-management relations with politics is unlikely to improve either—and likely to harm both. But what are the alternatives? Can we move toward voluntarism? Little effort to do so is evident.

Other Government Aid for Labor. Aid in organizing is not the only benefit unions, and workers more generally, have gained through the use of political influence. Gradually, after the late 19th century, voters came to realize that largely unrestrained freedom had bad results for people too weak to use it. Legislatures and courts slowly approved government action to protect the worker.

Under what legal authority does government interfere with the freedom of employer and employee to bargain? Generally under the *police power* (or also, in case of the federal government, the power to regulate interstate commerce). The police power is a vague but mighty attribute of government. It is a power of voters to take measures to protect the community's morals, health, safety, and general welfare—a power whose scope has been expanding. What are its limits? No one knows, because the judges, who have the final word, differ and change their views. So do state legislatures. Consequently, variations in protective legislation have been wide.

Laws setting *standards of working conditions,* especially for women and children, were eventually approved; so were laws providing for *workmen's compensation* and minimum wages for women. *Standards of safety, lighting, and cleanliness* have come to be provided in federal, state, and local law; the use of dangerous materials is prohibited or the conditions of use restricted. The list of protective legislation is long. It represents the fruit of much controversy and devoted effort to help the weak. More and more employers find economic wisdom in doing voluntarily what seems desirable on humane grounds.

Entrance to dozens of occupations is restricted by state licensing systems, often administered in fact by the group already admitted. The Fair Labor Standards Act fixes a minimum wage of $1.60 in most cases.[8] For work over 40 hours a week, a person must generally receive one and one half times the regular rate; this rule grew out of a depression-bred desire to spread what seemed to be a limited quantity of available work. Several states have minimum wage laws applying to intrastate jobs; in some cases, an administrative board has power to set the figure. The law also bans child labor in interstate commerce. The Walsh-Healey Public Contracts Act (1936) gives the Secretary of Labor power to set minimum wages in firms having federal contracts over $10,000. On federal construction projects the Davis-Bacon Act requires payment of wage rates prevailing in the area as determined by the Secretary of Labor. With government buying so great today, the number of firms affected by such laws runs into the thousands, including, probably, most of those of any substantial size.

---

[8] Many types of employment were not covered—executives, agricultural and domestic workers, government employees, employees of small retailing establishments, and certain other categories. Amendments have brought more groups within the scope of the law, in some cases by providing a transition period.

26

RENT AND INTEREST

Landed proprietors are the only class, of any numbers or importance, who have a claim to a share in the distribution of the produce [of the economy], through their ownership of something which neither they nor any one else have produced.

J. S. Mill

Property income makes up about one fifth of the national income we receive and pay. Economists customarily distinguish three general types of property income—rent, interest, and profit.

DETERMINATION AND FUNCTION OF RENT

In economics the term *"rent"* has a meaning which differs enough from ordinary usage to require some background.[1]

Land Rent and the "Scarcity" of Space. Life and all economic activity require the use of space on the earth's surface. Our need for living space

---

[1] The theory of rent developed in Britain. At the time, leasing, rather than sale, of land was more nearly the rule than in the United States today. Payment of rent, therefore, was a natural subject for economic analysis. In this country, where sale (upon a mortgage) has been more common, we should perhaps focus on the price of land as a capital sum rather than on rent, an annual payment to the owner. The relation between annual net income (dollar yield) of land and price is simple, in principle:

$$\text{Price} = \frac{\text{Net income per year}}{\text{Prevailing market rate of interest}}.$$

If the prevailing rate of interest (after allowing for risk) is 5 percent, a piece of land expected to bring a net income of $1,000 a year would be worth $1,000/(5/100), or $20,000.

creates *demand* for land. Yet the overall supply is highly inelastic. How will its use be allocated among various possibilities? The amount of the earth's surface is fixed, and except for the oceans, it is owned by private individuals, groups, or governments. The owner generally has the right to use the land himself and to permit or to deny the use to others.

If you owned all the land in any part of the world that was isolated from the rest, how much could you charge for its use? No one else could exist without it, but if you tried to absorb the whole income of the others, they could not survive because they need food and other things in addition to space. The most you could charge would be the difference between the total output of the group and the amount required to keep it alive and to attract the labor and capital needed for whatever is produced. If you succeeded in wringing so much from the others, you might get a high annual rent indeed. And you would not need to fear the competition of new land. Unlike a manufacturer, you would not worry that your high price might attract competition from some new producer.

The price a landowner receives does not lead to an increase or decrease in the amount of space on the earth's surface. No matter how much demand increases, the total quantity offered in supply cannot vary (greatly) with price. As graphed, the supply schedule for land as a whole—space—is essentially vertical; changes in price have virtually no effect on the quantity supplied.

For land in its entirety, then, demand will determine the rent or price, supply being fixed. Rent depends upon the extent to which demand makes the limited quantity of land economically "scarce." Obviously, however, no one rents land as a whole, but particular plots.

Land Rent and Differences in the Desirability of Land. Land varies widely in desirability. Some is magnificently suited to our needs, and some is worthless. Between the best and the poorest are untold thousands of gradations. No two plots are identical; each is in a slightly different location from any other. The price anyone will freely pay for the use of a plot of ground will depend upon *its desirability*. Desirability, in turn, depends upon what a plot will produce.

Land will produce only with the cooperation of other factors of production. For use in any one place these factors can be obtained only if they earn as much as they can elsewhere. On some land, labor and machines would produce almost nothing. On less poor land, labor and machines might produce as much as they could in the best alternative use. Here, then, is "marginal" land—just good enough to make the other resources pay but not good enough to leave anything for the landowner. "No-rent land" we call it.[2] Such land *could* be made available without any

---

[2] The land we see in use does command a price or rent. Most of it would have value even if no expenditure had been made to develop and improve it. In many parts of the country, however, there is land which would bring no price if it were "on its own," having benefited from no outlays for development.

payment since, unlike a machine, it exists without costs of production.

Now let us assume that you own a piece of good farm land (without a house or building). What rent will it bring you? Your neighbor wants it to raise wheat. He knows what seed, labor, machinery, and a loan from the bank will cost. The maximum he can pay you is the *difference* between (1) what he receives from the sale of the total output and (2) the cost of the other factors of production (including the value of his own efforts). If you hold out for more, he will do better with his time and resources somewhere else. But you need not charge less, because he has no better opportunities (assuming other landowners to be as smart as you are). What you can get in rent, therefore, depends upon (1) forces

FIGURE 26–1.   Determination of Rent

The price of the product is determined by the forces of supply and demand in the market as a whole. The prices of productive resources other than land—and hence nonland costs—are also determined in the market as a whole. The two farms differ in productivity because of (1) fertility and (2) distance to the market. The owner of farm A can get a rent equal to the shaded area, the excess of the yield of his land over the total of other costs. The owner of farm B, however, cannot get any rent, because all the receipts from the sale of the product must be used to pay other costs.

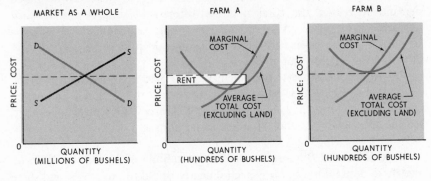

operating broadly in the market—costs and selling prices—and (2) the productivity of your land compared with that of other land.

The price of wheat and the nonland costs of production are determined independently of what happens on your farm. Your land must then compete with other land on the basis of relative productivity. You can charge only as much as your land contributes—the *net* difference between what is produced with and without your land. In Figure 26–1, costs of production, except for the use of the land, are shown on two farms, one with better quality land than the other.

On Farm *A* at the point where marginal cost equals marginal revenue (price), average cost is well below the price of the product, while on farm *B* average cost (at the point of best adjustment) just equals the price. The owner of the first farm can charge a rent for the use of his land, an amount equal to the shaded area, for this is the difference between (1) the costs excluding land and (2) the selling price. The owner of farm *B*, however, can charge no rent; if he were to say, "Pay me $1,000 or I will not let you use my land," he could expect no takers. If other costs were to fall, however, or if the price of the product were to rise, the owner of farm *B* could get a rent, and the owner of *A* could get more.

Fertility and Location as Influencing the Demand for Land. The demand for a plot of land will depend upon the attractiveness of that plot compared with others in (1) all natural features including fertility and (2) location. The more fertile (or the more richly endowed with oil or copper) your land, the greater the value of what it produces and the more it will be in demand. The greater the "original and indestructible" qualities of the land, the more the owner can charge for its use. The varieties of gradations are huge and so will be rents or *prices*. And location? Well, location influences the cost of transport—of the product to the buyer and of materials to the user of the land—and, consequently, the total amounts that can remain to the landowner.

The owner of "location" can charge for it. Land as space is immobile. A high rental (price) for land at Times Square will not bring land from the Western deserts to New York in the way that high wages will bring people. Yet there is always competition between *intensity* of use of land in a specific area and the spreading of labor and capital in more *extensive* use over a larger area. The demand for any specific location depends upon the availability of other locations. The lower the cost of transport, the more uniform will land values be.

Each plot of land can ordinarily be used for (any of) many purposes. Sometimes there will be doubt about which major type of use will be best. Should this space be used for a golf course or housing, stores or apartments, pasture or cultivation? The land lies on a "margin of transference" from one type of use to another. In other cases, choice involves different intensities of use in a general type.

Urban Land. The most striking cases of land rent arise in great cities. Choice plots no bigger than a village residential lot sell for tens of thousands of dollars. Clearly, location, not fertility, explains the difference. A person doing business on the best locations can appeal to many customers or users. The land can be used intensively and thus made to serve many thousands of people a day.[3] The labor and other nonland costs can be met; and yet, out of what the users will pay, there will remain a generous amount for the owner. Why?

1. The services of location may command prices above those prevailing

[3] In New York City, the single parcel of land with the highest value per square foot appears to be a small plot used almost exclusively for selling an orange beverage, nuts, frankfurters, and similar food and drink, and at low prices. The tenant pays an extremely high rent—and probably makes money. Why? This plot is at the corner of 34th Street and Sixth Avenue (Macy's), where a subway exit-entrance channels tired, thirsty, and hungry shoppers and others (perhaps feeling the need for cheap or hurried refreshment). Anyway, the "turnover is terrific."

generally. Users pay more for offices near the offices of others with whom the firm does business or where transportation is good, for accessibility to suppliers, for an apartment overlooking the park, or for an industrial location on the harbor.

2. To some extent, however, the high rent results not because the user can charge a higher price per unit but from his ability to do a *bigger volume* of business at a given price. The newspaper, the package of cigarets, or the things in Woolworth's cost no more at the highest rent spots in a huge city than in the suburbs where land is cheap. A variant of the same principle—doing a larger volume at no higher unit price—is indicated by the structure which is built tall to serve more people on a given land area.

Even the best locations, however, have only limited power to command income. Each must compete with a few others nearby and with many more a bit farther away in all directions. The limit on space at the crossroads of city traffic, the very factor that makes the four plots so valuable, also restricts the number of people that can be served. Congestion can grow until it eventually drives away business or adds other costs.

Beyond some point in height, additional floors of a building add more to cost than to revenue (diminishing returns); the landowner can receive nothing for the use of his land for a 50th floor if it would not bring the owner of the building enough additional revenue to cover the costs greater than required for a 49-floor structure.

Economist's Definition of Rent. *Pure economic rent is the payment for the use of land (or any factor of production) in excess of whatever is needed to keep that factor available for use in production.* For example, if a productive resource exists and will be available for use even if no payment is made, then anything paid for its use is economic rent. We say much the same thing in defining rent as the *payment for use of a factor of production which, for the time involved, is fixed in supply.* To the extent that the supply is fixed, the factor will be available for use in production; any payment to the owner is a rent because no such payment is needed to call the factor into existence for this use. Pure economic rent is a "surplus," a payment greater than is required to have the productive resources available.

Productive factors other than land are sometimes fixed in supply for a time. For months (or even years) the supply of steel mills, patent lawyers, or other specialized productive factors may be fixed about as definitely as land. *Temporarily,* the amount of such specialized capacity available for use in production depends only slightly upon whether we pay much or little. So by applying the principles which help analyze payment for land, one can learn more about the earnings and prices of other factors of production; we return to this point later.

In everyday usage, "rent" is a payment for the use of property: an apartment, a car, a plot of land, a machine, a library book, or bees to pollinize an orchard. The payment usually includes much more than pure economic rent, and sometimes it includes virtually no pure economic rent. For example, if you rent a furnished room, you receive the right to use space on the earth's suface, part of a building (for which you pay something for depreciation), the use of furniture, perhaps "cleaning" service, electricity, heat, the array of government services paid for by your landlord's real estate taxes.

Is Rent a Cost? High rents to landowners, Ricardo showed, were not the cause, but the result, of high food prices, during and after the Napoleonic wars. Rent was not a cost. What the owner of farm *A* (Fig. 26–1) can get is a *residual* of what is left over after paying other costs. The output will rise or fall if the price of the product, or if the price of any other input (factor of production), changes. For example, a rise in wage rates, machinery costs, taxes, or interest will reduce the share remaining to the owner unless offset by a rise in the price of the product.

The analysis to this point indicates that pure economic rent is determined by other prices and is not, itself, a price-determining force. In most cases, of course, the use of land for one purpose requires giving up opportunities for alternative uses. A decision to grow wheat keeps the land from being used for pasture or housing. An office building precludes the use of the same space for a department store or hotel. The devotion of land to any one purpose requires the sacrifice of alternatives. These sacrifices are costs. Anyone trying to get the use of land must outbid others. Ideally, the highest of the other bids will reflect the value of the best alternative sacrificed. For the renter, and for the community, the cost of whatever specific thing is produced on the land must include the value of the land in its next best use.

The businessman pays rent (or buys land, in effect paying the economic rent in advance); for him, of course, rent is a cost. For the economy as a whole, too, the use of land for one purpose is a cost—the sacrifice of alternatives.

Rent (Land Price) Guides the Use of Land. The public well-being requires that rent be charged (or that land have a price). The payment of rent helps allocate the fixed quantity of the productive capacity among various possible uses. The total real output depends upon the way that productive resources are allocated among the myriad possibilities. Would it not be wasteful to use for warehouses space highly desirable for stores or to build theaters where the public wants theaters less than office buildings or apartments?

The effort of owners to get the highest rent possible exerts a constructive influence for obtaining the most productive use of land, a scarce resource but one whose units are not equally scarce. The renter, having outbid others, is under pressure to use land better than would other potential businesses which could not pay quite so much. Our daily living, including our work, depends vitally on the efficiency with which land is used. Are our homes, stores, offices, and factories on the best possible spots, everything considered? As demands and costs change, do rents and land prices guide the use of land efficiently?

Refinements and Qualifications.   The broad principles need qualification. The supply of land in any economically meaningful sense is not absolutely fixed. The earth is always changing. By using labor and capital, man can control some of nature's changes, such as erosion. He can make changes of his own. The amount of usable surface on the earth is to some extent at our command. Men make deserts bloom by irrigation, marshlands thrive by drainage. Fertilizer and improved types of crops enhance the output from agricultural land. The economic attractiveness of city land can be altered by zoning, transportation revision, change of parks, demolition of firetraps, and so on.

The amount men do to preserve and to change the "economic quantity" of land will depend to some extent upon its rental rates (or price). Rent serves, therefore, not only to allocate the use of the existing quantity of land. Rent also guides changes in the economic quantity of land. The changes will in turn affect the price of competing land. In economic analysis, as in business practice, land becomes somewhat like capital—adjustable and changeable. Opening the wilderness or developing a new suburb can be exhausting, risky, and expensive far beyond the immediate gains. Some of the incentive is the hope of gain in land values—beyond the investment in sewers and other facilities and the worth of the developer's own efforts. Results of such efforts (often termed, accurately, "speculative") are by no means ideal, for development can be both "premature and immature."

Unearned Increment.   Nevertheless, much of what we pay for the use of land is for the work of nature. The land would be here whether or not men paid. Much of the dollar value has resulted from the growth of population and capital. Part of today's values must clearly be independent of anything the owners have contributed, even though a portion of the worth results from their investment of money and time. Nature creates the supply, society the demand. The owner receives the "gravy," or the roast itself.

If nature and society created the values, why should private owners reap them? This question has aroused dispute for centuries. It became a center of controversy in the late 19th century, when fortunes developed quickly as rapid growth of cities caused urban land values to boom. The family with a grandfather who had bought on the outskirts of town, and then held on, could revel in luxury on the Riviera and marry into

Europe's aristocracy. History had few examples of such sudden, large, and unmerited windfalls. Less dramatically than the Astors, tens of thousands of landowners reaped an increase in wealth from society's need for the use of land. Immigrants pouring into slums had to pay rent to rich landlords. Critics condemned. Why should a few get what nature and the public as a whole created? In city after city in all continents, land prices have zoomed since World War II. Hovels crowded around central cities occupy land which commands prices almost unbelievably high in view of the poverty of the occupants.

What of the future? Well, we know one fact: Population will grow tremendously. Tens of millions more humans competing for use of limited space will bid up the price. Some landowners are destined to reap unearned increments unless the public somehow takes that part of the increase in total value which is the result of general growth as distinguished from inputs by the owner.

Who Bears the Tax on Real Estate?[4]   The analysis of unearned increment leads to an important conclusion about the shifting of taxes on real estate. The part of the property tax which falls on the land reduces the net income. Since the price of land depends upon the net income expected, a tax which reduces the net income will reduce the capital value of the land. Assume a piece of land with a net annual income of $1,200 before property tax and $1,000 after tax; if the appropriate interest rate is 5 percent, the land will be worth $20,000. If the tax goes up by half, from $200 to $300, reducing the net yield to $900,[5] the new capital value will be $18,000. The process of adjusting the price of a capital asset to changes in taxes which affect net yield is known as "tax capitalization." The person owning the land when the tax is imposed suffers a loss of income (capital value). The person who buys later plans on the basis of the tax and does not suffer from the amount of tax. The tax cannot reduce the amount of land. Because no change in quantity (supply) follows as a result of the tax, there is no basis for shifting the tax to consumers (unless the rental contract so provides).[6]

---

[4] Study of this section may well be postponed and included with Chapter 31.

[5] The $100 additional revenue received by the taxing government may help provide services which make the locality more attractive and thereby increase the gross rental obtainable.

[6] In *Progress and Poverty* (1879) Henry George used this principle as the basis for a tax proposal which had wide appeal. Private ownership of land, he argued, permitted the owner to absorb the gains of progress in industry and commerce. He urged that (local and state) governments take all pure land rent in taxes. Rent would still serve its allocative functions. Owners of land would be under great pressure to put it to best use; otherwise they would not get enough income to pay their taxes. George thought there was enough such rent—on land alone—to pay all the costs of government; this "single tax" would permit the community to pay for schools, streets, and other expenses of government by taking only the values the community itself had created by its own development. Removal of taxes on buildings would encourage

The tax on buildings and other improvements, however, will be shifted to users. A tax increase causes the owner to suffer a loss of income. The supply of structures is highly inelastic in the short run. Therefore, prices of existing buildings will fall as the net income is reduced. The prices of new buildings will depend on construction costs. A person with new funds to invest will tend to put them into old buildings whose prices have gone down rather than into new ones, unless the costs of construction fall equally. New buildings will not be built until the expected net yield— after tax—equals what can be obtained in other, untaxed lines. The discouragement of new building reduces the quantity of housing, office, and other space available. Rents rise gradually (especially in a growing community) until the tax is shifted to users.[7]

Underground Resources—and the Sky Above. Not only the surface of the earth, but things under it are valuable. To "strike oil" or find a "gold mine" stand as symbols of good fortune. Individuals who did nothing to put things under the surface sometimes make fortunes because they happen to own land with highly valuable resources underneath. The lucky owner of something produced by nature can demand payment for the use of property he played no part in creating. As with land, the rent or price serves—not perfectly—two constructive functions: (1) the prospect of such gains provides an incentive for undertaking the risky and expensive job of trying to discover what exists; (2) the payment serves as an "allocating" device to induce efficient use of scarce resources.

Use of the skies requires economizing. As skyscrapers pushed up, "air rights" over land took on new significance. The way an owner used the space above his spot of ground affected the value of the land around. Air rights became property, subject to purchase and sale. In general, however, the price mechanism plays a decidedly incomplete role in guiding the use of space in the sky. And new problems have arisen with the development of air transport. Though the heavens seem limitless, congestion in the airways, already serious, will get worse despite large outlays for air traffic controls.

---

construction. The "single" aspect of George's proposal has been made obsolete by the large growth of government spending, but today there is substantial sentiment for altering the property tax to transfer more of the burden from buildings to land. The objective is to speed the allocation of land to its "highest and best use" and to encourage the replacement of junky buildings with new ones of higher quality.

[7] The burden on the renter may take the form of poorer quality as the owner reduces maintenance. The local spending of added tax funds may raise the demand for local real estate. Controlled rents or utility rates may be permitted to rise in order to pass the tax promptly to users.

Owner-occupied houses present a special consideration; the owner can deduct the property tax in computing income subject to federal tax; net burdens vary according to the owner's top income tax bracket. Companies using their own property (factory buildings, for example) will adjust to changes in real estate taxes, not through rental variations but other cost calculations.

Special Influences on Land Values: Linkage. Land values rise (and fall) not only because of a general increase in population or of a special effort of the owner. Many other developments can affect prices of plots of land in relation to each other. If government builds a new highway entrance to an urban area, if a city changes a zoning law or decides to clear a slum, or if a private business sets up a new plant, the value of land nearby may rise greatly. (A person who can get wind of a big decision before it becomes public may make a "killing.") Some actions reduce the value of neighboring land. Unfortunately, neither the market system nor government has yet developed ways of taking adequate account of these "third party" or "neighborhood" effects in making decisions or in financing the costs of whatever is, or might be, done.

The immobility of land makes land values subject to another special influence. The use being made of neighboring plots vitally affects the use that can be made of any one plot. A "linkage" of uses, and hence of land prices (rents), results. Each parcel's worth is linked to the use being made of other land around. The neighbors and what they do influence the value of land for any kind of business, residential, or recreational use. What can be done with a plot of land at any one time, and its worth, must reflect another linkage: the tie to past decisions. Buildings last a long time.[8] Structures built many years ago influence today's use of land. An obsolete building can depress the value, not only of the land on which it stands but also of real estate nearby; yet it may still be worth too much to justify demolition to permit construction of something more appropriate.[9]

QUASI-RENTS

Extending our horizon, we see economic "rents" other than those from land. We call them *quasi-rents*.

Some combinations of human capacities are much rarer than others, for example, those of big league athletes and movie stars. Not a large percentage of men have the handsome faces, powerful and lithe physiques, musical and dramatic talent, vibrant voices, stamina, and other native qualities needed to be excellent movie stars. Still fewer have these plus the inborn tendencies and the training that lead to brilliant personality and a willingness to work hard. The supply of persons with all these qualities, though by no means fixed, seems to be highly inelastic. If the public likes the performance of men with these abilities—and what is worse than the medicore entertainer—the favored few can earn vastly more than most of us. Some of the excess is an "economic rent." Perhaps the star's other alternatives might include $25,000 a year for nightclub appearances or $20,000 as an insurance salesman. What, then, is the economic rent? It is the excess over $25,000 (plus or minus the *net* other advantage of the

[8] Reductions in the standing stock are very slow; annual demolition rates from 1900 to 1940 averaged only 0.2 percent of the stock of nonfarm buildings.

[9] Further discussion of problems of land use appear in Chapter 39.

movies over night club singing). Why do movie firms pay more than $25,000? If they could avoid competition in hiring, they might not need to pay more. But if they paid only $25,000, how would the star's efforts be allocated among the various possibilities? An actual salary of $100,000 serves to direct him where he seems most valuable. It forces employers to economize more in using his time than in using that of the second-stringer who receives $25,000. The public benefits by obtaining more of the star's most appealing services. This gain results not because the high price produces more stars but because of pressure to economize that which is rare. This is the constructive service of "rent."

Elements of quasi-rent probably make up part of many large earned incomes: the exceptional doctor or lawyer, the topnotch business executive, the heavyweight prizefighter, and the lightweight jockey.

For "short" periods, the supply of capital equipment is also largely fixed. Existing facilities are durable and immobile. To increase greatly the total productive capacity of natural gas pipelines, specialized chemical plants, or other large and complex equipment takes years. At any one time, therefore, the owner has an asset whose supply is fixed, similar to land at a busy streetcorner. If the demand for the services of the equipment rises, he can temporarily get an income which is above the normal long-run equilibrium (Fig. 26–2), a quasi-rent even though usually called "profit" in business accounts.

FIGURE 26–2.   Quasi-Rent

Price rises from *OA* to *OB*. Quantity goes from *OM* to *ON*. At least one factor of production is fixed for the time being. Its owners can demand a higher return, a quasi-rent, equal to the difference between other costs and the price—the shaded area. If more of the fixed factor can be made available, the higher income being received will lead to an increase in the quantity. Price will then go down, and the quasi-rent will disappear.

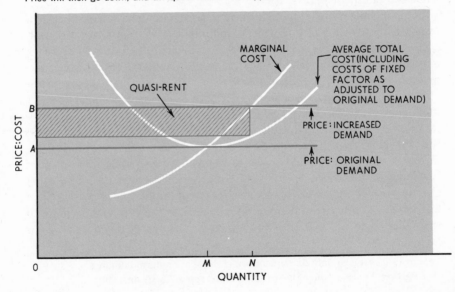

THE NATURE OF INTEREST: DISCOUNTING

Almost all adult Americans, and many children, receive interest. It may take the form of driblets we never recognize—the earnings of a pension fund or life insurance reserve. It may be obvious but still small—the growth in the savings account. For a relatively few people, however, interest is an important part of their income—some retired persons and individuals with invested fortunes. The total interest income one can get in a year will depend upon (1) the quantity of interest-bearing assets owned and (2) their percentage yield, a form of price. We also pay interest (1) indirectly in the prices of things we buy from business and in taxes to governments which owe debt and (2) directly when we buy on installments or when we borrow to get through college, start a business, or buy a house.

For most of us, however, interest is not a big item—either as a receipt or an expense. For the whole economy, personal interest income of nearly $50 billion (annual rate, early 1968) is over 7 percent of personal income. The apparent smallness of interest does not measure its significance any more than the amount of thread in a garment measures the importance. In a sense, interest is a thread that ties the economic present with the future. It plays a crucial role in investment decisions that affect the rate of economic growth and the level of employment. The prices of bonds, real estate, and other capital assets depend in part upon the rate of interest.

Productive power, we have already learned, is multiplied as a result of the use of capital equipment—machines, railroads, utilities. "Waiting," we also know, is necessary to release resources to build capital equipment. Earlier chapters showed why and how businesses may borrow, how our banking and monetary system operate, and how saving and investment affect employment and the price level. We now learn about the forces that make interest rates what they are.

Definition.   Interest is *payment for the use of money (loanable funds).* When we let someone else have our money with a promise to repay on specified terms, we do him a service for which he pays interest.

Interest is a price. It *allocates* something whose supply is limited. It also *induces* those who are able to supply something that is scarce to supply it.

Interest is ordinarily expressed as a rate per annum, not as so many dollars a year.[10] When you turn over money as a loan to someone else, you

[10] Ordinarily, one does not say each time "per annum" or "a year." In speaking of wages, we usually think of an amount of money and a period of time, $3 per hour per person. Interest computations, however, contain another dollar amount, a capital sum; instead of saying, somewhat clumsily, "$3 per $50 per year," we say "6 percent." The definition of interest as payment for the use of money on loan obviously leaves out of account any benefit a person receives directly from holding or using his own savings. If I put my own funds into any investment—a house, store, or set of tools—part of the benefit I get is the equivalent of interest and should be treated as *implicit interest,* the amount equaling what I could have gotten by lending the dollars to someone else.

get a financial asset: the borrower's note, a bond, a savings account passbook. The borrower agrees to return dollars under conditions stated definitely. As a rule, you will also get a certain number of dollars at regular intervals. If the amount is $6 a year for each $100 you provided, you receive an interest rate of 6 percent. The asset is property in financial, not real, terms. What it yields (brings in) each year—while the corpus, body, remains the same—is interest.

Time, Discount, and Valuation.   The amount a borrower will pay for an asset which is the source of the income—the value which the market puts on the asset—will equal

$$\frac{\text{Net dollar income per year}}{\text{Rate of interest prevailing in the market}}.$$

This is the principle indicated for land in footnote 1, but with allowance made for (1) the number of years the yield will come, (2) the amount payable at the end, and (3) the risk that some payments will not be made. Generally, something a long distance away is not worth as much to us as if it were at hand. Bringing it to us (or going to it) involves costs. The farther away, the greater such cost. The lower the transport costs, however, the smaller is the importance of distance. So it is with dollars due in the future.

Contracts involving interest call for payments of money in the future. The farther away, the greater the cost of getting to the "future dollars" and hence the less their value here (or now). We would pay more for a house we could occupy at once than for the same house which we could occupy only after 10 years. The difference would depend upon the net amount we would have to pay to rent comparable housing in the meantime. The allowance for such lower present value of things obtainable in the future we call *discount*. Discount is interest the other way around. If the interest rate is 6 percent, we say that a dollar due a year from now is worth, roughly, 94 cents today. One due in 5 years is worth about 82 cents now.

The present worth of a *series* of dollars coming (or which must be paid) in the future depends upon (1) the interest rate at which we discount them and (2) the years in which they are due (Fig. 26–3).[11] The higher the interest (discount) rate prevailing in the market, the less is today's value of a dollar due in the future. Moreover, the farther in the future the dollar is due, the less it is worth now. The present value of a bond, or other interest-bearing asset, is the sum of today's appraisal of all the future values.

---

[11] This discussion does *not* involve changes in the purchasing power of money except as *expectation* of such changes influences interest rates.

FIGURE 26–3.   Value Now of a Series of Payments of $100 a Year for 20 Years—3 and 6 Percent (Capitalizing an Asset)

The total value today of a series of payments of $100 a year for 20 years—the total of all 20 bars—is $1,488 if the interest (discount) rate is 3 percent and $1,147 if the rate is 6 percent.

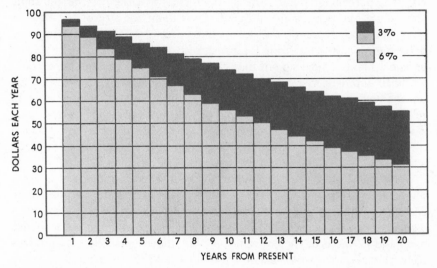

Although the number of dollars due does not change, their worth in terms of dollars today can rise or fall. Suppose that you have a $1,000 bond paying $40 a year and selling for $1,000, yielding you 4 percent. The interest yield on new bonds then rises to 5 percent. You cannot expect to find a buyer for your bond except at a price which will give him a 5 percent yield. He would be foolish to pay $1,000 for your bond which brings $40 a year when for $1,000 he can get a bond bringing $50 a year. The market price of your bond will fall below $1,000.

As interest rates change, from whatever cause, the *present* value of a series of dollars due in the future will also change. Let us now assume that the interest rate falls from 5 to 4 percent; this drop means that the market is discounting future dollars less. The dollar due in a year is now worth, not 95 but 96 cents. Today's capital values move in the opposite direction from the *interest rate*. If we have a bond that will pay $1,000 at the end of 10 years, its value rises when market rates of interest go down because we now discount those future dollars less. On the other hand, if the interest (discount) rate rises, dollars due in the future must be discounted more; the worth of the asset today falls. In other words there is a decline in the present capitalized (discounted) value of existing assets which yield an income fixed in terms of dollars.

To summarize: The value today of an asset promising dollars in the future depends upon the *number of dollars* it will bring, the *amount of time one must wait* for them, and the *prevailing scale of payment for the service of waiting (the interest rate)*.

Changes, Small or Large. The quoting of interest rates as percentages can deceive. If the interest rate (or any percentage) rises from 4 to 5, the increase is not 1 percent. It is one-fourth, or 25 percent. We may properly say "one percentage point." But as a percentage of the base, of the thing changing, "one percentage point" depends upon the size of the base. A "one percentage point" rise from 100 percent is 1 percent; but one percentage point" rise from 1 percent is a doubling, an increase of 100 percent. The practical significance can be important because interest rates are small numbers, as a rule such as 4, 5, 3. A change or difference of one or one-half percentage point may seem small, but it can be large in relation to the base. From 1947 to 1967, the rate paid on shortest term Treasury borrowing rose from roughly 0.4 to nearly 5 percent at times; this increase of 4.6 percentage points was 1,250 percent of the earlier rate.

Variety of Rates. Just as there is not *a* single wage rate, there is not a single interest rate. The bank that pays 4 percent on savings deposits may charge 6 percent for mortgage loans and 10 percent on loans to buy autos. The U.S. government pays 1.6 percent the first 6 months on a savings bond and 4.9 percent the last. On some new borrowing the U.S. government paid less than 4 percent in 1964 but over 5 percent in 1967, while small towns occasionally borrowed for 2 percent in the earlier year. Personal finance companies may charge 40 percent. Both the variety and the range of interest rates are large.

At any time there is a whole family of interest rates. All have some things in common, and for this reason they are tied together around some average or central tendency. Though the market for loanable funds is not perfectly competitive, the parts are related, thus linking different interest rates. Borrowers and lenders near the margins of different parts of the market can, and do, shift if terms in a part nearby seem relatively more favorable. "Interest rates do not move identically, but they do tend to move in the same general direction. Each rate goes with the pattern as any sheep goes with the flock. Thus some rates run ahead and some lag behind, but a central tendency of movement is normally apparent."[12] The pattern itself changes. While the short-term rate paid by the Treasury dropped by three fourths in the 1957–58 recession, the long-term rate sagged less than a sixth; during the economic expansion of 1961–64, the short-term rate rose by half while the long-term rate went up by less than one tenth. In the next two years, the short-term rate rose by around one half and the long-term rate by one fifth.

Cost of Servicing, Tax Exemption, and Risk. Things are not always what they are called, and interest is no exception. If you were selling a car

[12] E. S. Shaw, *Money, Income, and Monetary Policy* (Homewood, Ill.: Richard D. Irwin, Inc., 1950), p. 310.

to someone who did not have the cash, you might agree to let him pay in installments. If so, what would you find? You would encounter expense in the paper work involved in handling monthly payments. The buyer might sometimes be late and occasionally need prodding. The total gross interest you get would not be net. To collect, there are expenses you do not have if you sell for cash. Servicing costs on some loans are much higher than on others. Lenders may not quote a special service charge to cover this cost, but include it in the "interest"; this item accounts for some of the more extreme differences in rates, the 18 percent on financing of installment purchases and the 4½ percent or so paid by the U.S. Treasury on loans running about the same length of time. Some loan agreements include life insurance on the borrower so that if he dies the debt is wiped out by the insurance.

Some interest is exempt from taxes. For a person or a corporation subject to a 50 percent tax rate on income, $1 of tax-free interest is worth $2 of taxable interest. Borrowers (state and local governments) who can offer tax exemption need pay less interest, *ceteris paribus*, than others.

Risk is a fact of life. If the borrower's credit is not the very best—based on possession of assets and income plus evidence of determination to keep his promise—lenders will want some payment for the risk that contract terms will not be met fully. There are other risks (for both lender and borrower), such as changes in interest rates in the market, in the purchasing power of the dollar, and in the earnings obtainable if one's financial resources are put to alternative uses—the purchase of real estate, stocks, and other types of property. A *risk premium*, like costs of loan servicing, is concealed in the interest rate.

The "Pure" Rate of Interest.   *Gross* interest, therefore, differs from *net*, or *pure*, interest. When economists speak of "the" interest rate, they ordinarily have in mind a *net*, or *pure*, rate. It is the rate after allowance for risk and cost of loan servicing, and without tax exemption. It is perhaps typified by the yield on marketable U.S. government bonds of 5 or 10 years of maturity.

DETERMINATION OF THE RATE OF INTEREST: SUPPLY

Funds for lending are not unlimited. The use of a dollar of saving for one purpose requires the sacrifice of alternatives.

Supply of Money for Lending.   What is the source of supply of dollars to lend (or to use for buying such securities as bonds already outstanding)? (1) *Savings out of income* obviously provide much of the answer. Individuals, businesses, and private groups save. The saving consists of spending less on consumption than is received as income. The money accumulated can become available for lending to someone else. (2) Funds which businesses collect from consumers to offset *depreciation* may be money potentially available to lend to others. Presumably, if the prospects of lending are more attractive than buying equipment to replace what is wearing out, the company will lend. (3) The *banking system* and *government printing presses* can create new money. The dollars can be used to lend to someone, including the government. (4) Money for lending may also come from *funds accumulated in some past period* and held as deposits in checking accounts or private "hoards."

Liquidity Preference. "Supply" means more than the existence of something, in this case money not being used for consumption (or direct investment by the owner in a physical asset). The owner must also decide to make what he has—in this case funds for lending—available to others. Therefore, we must take account of the *willingness of owners of funds to make them available to others on loan.* Why do savers put their money at the disposal of others? Interest *is* paid. If I hold idle the dollars I have saved, I lose the interest they would earn. Clearly, I have an incentive to offer my funds on the best terms possible. Taking the long view, the smart thing is to keep my money "working." Unemployed savings are as fruitless as unemployed labor.

Taking the long view, however, may not be easy; mud puddles underfoot can distract us from enjoying magnificent mountain peaks in the distance. A person with funds for possible lending may focus on the short run. Changes within a year or so can be large enough to make it really worthwhile (or very expensive) to keep savings as cash rather than invested and earning interest. Bond prices may fall (or, as explained earlier, interest rates may rise). Within a few weeks in the summer of 1958, some U.S. government bonds fell in price by 3 year's interest. Figure 26–4 shows the fluctuations of one issue during a few years. If you

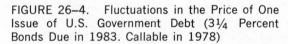

FIGURE 26–4.   Fluctuations in the Price of One Issue of U.S. Government Debt (3¼ Percent Bonds Due in 1983. Callable in 1978)

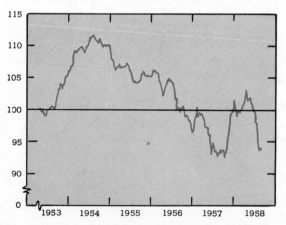

suspect a drop, a purchase now would seem unwise. But if you believe that interest rates will fall (bond prices rise), purchase now rather than delay will be to your interest.

Sacrificing liquidity involves risk. The risk is less for short-period loans than for long-term debt. Confidence in judgment will often be greater for the near than for the distant future; the longer the period, the greater the opportunity for change of fortune. The volume of funds that savers will offer depends partly, then, on estimates of changes in the future.

Money, we know, is a highly liquid asset, one which does not have to be "sold" to be used to get something else; its price in terms of dollars does not change. The freedom to act which liquidity gives is worth something. Since many savers are free to hold wealth in the form of cash if they wish, *the interest rate must be at least high enough to offset the worth of liquidity* at the margin. This feature was emphasized by Lord Keynes. Chapter 8 discussed reasons why people want to hold money and why their desires for cash may change. One influence is the expectation about what will happen to interest rates. Sometimes it has seemed that the yield needed to overcome the desire for liquidity can account for most of the determination of the *pure* rate of interest. "Liquidity preference" theories of interest emphasize this feature (sometimes treating it as part of the *demand* for money rather than as part of the supply of loanable funds).[13]

Interest and the Supply of Saving: Incentive Effect. Interest serves, as does any price, an incentive function—to induce supply. Does the volume of new *savings* depend much upon the rate of interest—the reward paid for lending? The supply of saving may be quite inelastic with respect to the rate of interest. Proportionately, a very large change in the rate of interest might be needed to alter the quantity of saving significantly. But what about sensitivity at the margin? Is there any appreciable response of saving–to–interest–rate changes? Let us try to answer by looking at *reasons for saving*.

1. People save freely to *transfer purchasing power through time*. We "abstain" from consumption now, "waiting" to consume later. Many of us

[13] An interest rate lower than about 2 percent, some economists have suggested, may not overcome the preference for liquidity. Below this level, the argument runs, the quantity of funds lenders will offer for loans extending beyond short periods (highly liquid short-term obligations) approaches zero because the interest inducement will not overcome liquidity preference. If such were the case, the monetary authorities, it has been said, would face a "liquidity trap"; any rise in bank lending capacity would not get interest rates any lower; this method of stimulating business would be ineffective. Testing the hypothesis would require experience which is not available because long-term interest rates have never fallen so low, except for brief periods when other forces were exerting powerful influences on investment. For a study of the record in many countries see S. Homer, *A History of Interest Rates* (New Brunswick, N.J.: Rutgers University Press, 1963). Another valuable analysis is J. W. Conard, *The Behavior of Interest Rates* . . . . (New York: Columbia University Press . . . , 1966).

want wealth to send children to college, for retirement, or to have a reserve for emergencies. The capital sum we seek is more important than differences in the price we can get for the use of our wealth. Some motives for saving are deeply personal, varying from one culture and one epoch to another. The belief that thrift is morally right may be a more potent motive than differences in the rewards obtainable.

2. Saving is done because of *commitments* which, though made freely, later acquire an element of compulsion. We buy a house, borrow much of the cost, and pledge to repay gradually. Each monthly installment includes some saving. Life insurance often involves periodic savings. Commitments like these are not irrevocable, but they may be so hard and expensive to change that we go along using them to save more (or possibly less) than we would like. What is the importance of the interest rate in such cases? The answer is difficult because interest operates on both sides of the transaction—one way when we go into debt and another as we repay. Heavier interest charges make it harder to retire debt (to save) but increase our desire to do so.

3. Some saving is *compulsory*. Your employer may require you to put some of your earnings into a fund to pay for a pension, or he may have promised to make such savings. The rate of interest as an incentive has little obvious effect.

4. *Earnings plowed back into businesses* account for considerable saving. Contracts may require repayment of debt. Earnings may be retained to finance expansion, to provide for contingencies, or to avoid personal income taxes for owners of corporations. The prevailing interest rate plays a part in making the decisions; yet many other considerations enter the picture. In a sense, businesses can short-circuit the rigor of the market as it works toward a balancing of demand and supply for loanable funds.

5. Every economy probably has people who save *automatically*. They have so much income that they can spend as much on living as they want and still have something left. Rate of interest as reward has no influence.

6. *Governments save* when they collect more in taxes than they spend on current expenses—a city paying a debt incurred to build water mains.

7. Some (nonbusiness) personal saving is certainly made because of the prospect of gain from lending funds. People, consciously or unconsciously, are attracted by the income they can get; the higher the rate of earnings on capital, the more they will save. They then have the choice of buying a physical asset, a security, or of lending money to others. If the best rate of interest on high quality bonds is 3 percent, the few cents a year from each dollar may mean little; if the rate is 6 (or 10) percent, however, many may say to themselves, "Here is a good way to earn money," and save more.

Interest as a Source of Funds for Saving.   Interest is not only an incentive but also a *source of income* from which savings are supplied. Here, again, the picture is blurred. The higher the yield, the greater the income of property owners and the easier for them to save. A high rate of interest thus tends to increase saving because of the *ability* aspect. Yet, as is true so often, there is a complication. If a person is aiming at accumulating a capital sum that will yield a given income—saving for retirement may be of this type—the higher the interest rate, the smaller the capital sum needed. For example, a man seeking $1,000 a year from bonds would need capital of $50,000 if the interest rate were 2 percent but only $20,000 if the rate were 5 percent. His supply schedule of saving may have a backward-sloping portion (Fig. 23–2).

Time Preference, Saving and Lending.   Another factor bearing upon the supply of saving is man's time preference, in a sense opposite that of point (1) above. To varying degree, men favor the present over the future and dislike waiting. The reason is partly an "Eat, drink, and be merry, for tomorrow we die" philosophy; it is partly that if we do not eat we shall die all the sooner. For most of us, however, not all income must go for immediate needs. But with such choice, we may be "impatient," "shortsighted." The fact that we shall certainly die gives a reason for failing to sacrifice today by saving for a future we may not live to enjoy.[14] Both *abstinence* from consumption and *waiting* do involve real costs, for at least some persons on whom society relies for new saving.

When we do save, there is a simple reason for not lending but instead acquiring nonconsumption property—*equipment is productive.* The sooner we get productive wealth—a better house, a tractor, an automatic machine—the earlier it can begin to work for us. Capital facilities create income. Hence, we prefer to get productive things sooner rather than later. Rather than lend savings to others, therefore, we may wisely prefer to buy assets (other than bonds). Consequently, anyone who wants to borrow the funds we have saved must pay interest to induce us to give up the possibility of buying real assets which will produce goods and services.

National Income and Saving.   The amount we save depends partly on income. Changes in national income may have more to do with the amount by which total saving changes in any short period than will any reasonably possible variations in interest rates. Part of our saving varies more with income than with price (interest). Of course, savings made because of prior contracts may be more stable than income; savings out of business earnings, however, depend closely upon income. Interest rates have little direct connection.

Negative Saving and the Rate of Interest.   Saving can be negative and often is for individuals. People who are retired use their prior savings to pay for current consumption—a normal, expected thing. Businesses use prior savings to finance operations when business is unprofitable. How does the rate of interest affect negative saving? One point is clear. The

---

[14] More accurately, even a rational person might save during part of his life and dissave later so that at his death his wealth would be zero, e.g., the purchase of an annuity for life. For society as a whole, capital would accumulate slowly under such circumstances.

higher the rate of interest, the less will be the need to consume capital to obtain a specific dollar amount in any year or other period. If I have $30,000 and need $2,000 a year to live, a 5 percent interest rate yielding $1,500 will permit me to get along the first year by drawing only $500 on my capital; a 4 percent interest rate will lead me to use up $800 of my capital.

DETERMINATION OF THE RATE OF INTEREST: DEMAND

Now let us look at the other blade of the scissors—demand.

Demand for Loans. Why do people want to borrow money? For many reasons—from the most reckless profligacy to the wisest foresight. The reasons will generally have this in common: a belief that with the funds the borrower can get assets, including intangibles such as education, which will bring benefits greater than the cost of the asset plus interest on the loan. Time preference, therefore, affects demand for borrowed funds as well as supply. Because a person (or a business) prefers things now rather than later, he is willing to pay for the use of funds to buy them. Such preference for the present may rest on immature impatience or mature calculation.

Demand for loans rests on the expectation of gain. The demand that counts, of course, is *effective* demand, a wish supported by something offered in return. Obviously, however, the payment, or "purchasing power," for borrowed funds is not dollars today. Dollars are what the borrower, the "demander," gets, not gives. He offers in return *promises* that dollars will be paid in the future.

By increasing its productive equipment, a business can enlarge its output. But the expansion will be worth carrying out only if the sales revenue from the added output will cover the added costs. What are these costs for a machine priced at $10,000? There is the expense of the machine itself and of its operation. The firm must be able to count upon receiving, during the life of the machine, enough more than the other operating expenses to pay for the machine itself. If the machine has a life of 5 years and if labor, materials, and other nonmachine costs of the new output will be $5,000 a year, the firm must be able to obtain $25,000 operating costs plus the $10,000. If it can count upon getting only this total, $35,000, it obviously cannot afford to pay interest in addition. If the prospective yield is greater, say $40,000, the firm will be able to pay interest. The *maximum* it can pay is the amount the asset will yield above its cost—in this case $5,000 over 5 years. If the interest were only $2,500 (5 percent a year for 5 years on $10,000), the firm would be foolish not to borrow the funds necessary to purchase the machine. If new equipment will reduce costs rather than add to output, the cost reduction will govern the amount of interest which can be paid.

The demand for borrowed funds rests largely upon the productivity of facilities to be used in production, including housing to create services to occupants. The higher this productivity, the more a wise person will pay to borrow. At any one time, there will be some few uses with very high productivity, others with somewhat less, and so on down in a descending scale. Productivity in the economic sense depends upon what one must pay for the equipment (as well as upon the output); the lower the cost of a machine, the greater its economic attraction. We know much less than

FIGURE 26–5.   Hypothetical Curves of the Net Yields (Productivity) of New Capital Equipment

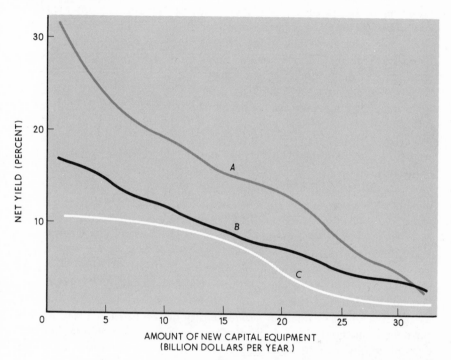

would be desirable about the productivity schedule of new capital assets, the productivity which is the basis for the demand for capital funds. Figure 26–5 shows three curves. One, *A*, starts at a high point and falls rapidly; *B* slopes downward but becomes flatter, indicating that investment opportunities are widespread at only slight differences in yield; *C* is lower than the others and falls rather rapidly to a point of low yield. Whatever the shape of the curve, it reflects the fact of diminishing returns. Assuming other things the same, the larger the amount invested at any time, the less attractive are the *additional* opportunities.

Uncertainty comes into calculations of demand as well as it did those of supply. A businessman, absolutely certain about what an asset would bring in the future (the marginal revenue product), would know how much he could afford to pay in interest. If no one would lend at that rate, then, obviously, "no deal." But at least the choice would be clear. However, when you cannot be certain about what an asset will produce, and such uncertainty is the rule, you must take chances. Your judgment will differ from that of some others. You may be willing to pay a higher rate of interest than others because of stronger conviction about the productivity of the asset; or you may be less optimistic. Certainty is impossible.[15] The demand of business enterprises for borrowed funds, therefore, rests upon *expected* productivity of capital. In practice, much can depend upon the expected intensity of competition; the more fully competitors seem to be adopting better methods, the more insistent the pressure on a firm to demand more money to finance improvements.

The demand for loans by consumers and governments must also be based on estimates of net benefit. Such estimates generally rest on less clear criteria of productivity than do business calculations; in fact, very poor judgments may influence decisions. This part of the demand for loans depends upon judgments and measurements different from those of businesses. Education and training are a form of investment. We may wisely save, or borrow, to invest in training. The addition to earnings that results can be considered in part as implicit interest even when no loan contract is involved.

There can be a rise or fall in the demand for "hoards" of cash by persons able to buy or sell bonds; the demand for debt securities relative to cash will change. Similarly, preferences for stocks in relation to bonds may change. At any time, too, the demand for borrowed funds will depend upon expectations about interest rates; if a rise in rates seems probable, for example, anyone planning to borrow will tend to increase immediate borrowing to cover future needs. Willingness to go into debt depends also upon expectations of changes in the price level, the availability of other forms of financing, the intensity of competition, taxes, distaste for debt as such, and legal and other factors. Finally, the amount any one firm or family can borrow will depend upon the amount of its debt already outstanding in relation to its equity capital.

Interest Rates and the Demands for Borrowed Funds. Does interest as the price for loanable funds have much effect on the amount used? Is the demand schedule elastic? In many cases, the answer is "No," sometimes "Yes." The uncertainty—one of great significance—is whether there is enough sensitivity to make the interest rate a tolerably smooth and effective "adjuster" of quantities supplied and demanded.

---

[15] Engineering studies of different equipment may lead to findings which leave no doubt about which is best, even when the wisdom of acting will itself be in doubt. A borrower must ordinarily get enough from the sale of whatever the asset produces to pay not only interest but also to repay the principal of the loan. Annual repayments of principal are often larger than the interest payments.

What should we expect? Interest is a price related to time. At any given *annual* rate—say 5 percent—the price for short periods, a day or a week, will involve relatively few dollars; for long periods, the amount becomes large. At any given railroad rate per mile, the charge will have less influence on a shipper's desire to use the railroad for a short haul than for one across the continent. Similarly, we should expect the greatest effect of the interest rate to be felt on long-range borrowing. This is just what we find. For some investments, interest is too small a part of the total cost for any conceivable changes to make a significant difference— investment in inventory, for example. The interest cost of financing an increase in inventory for 3 months is generally insignificant in relation to the other costs involved. If a business finds the bank charging 4 instead of 6 percent for loans to finance inventory (a decline of one third), this change means only 0.5 percent for a 3-month loan—trifling in comparison with other costs. The demand for loans to buy consumer goods also seems inelastic. The amounts consumers borrow do change with interest rates but, proportionately, rather little.

For some projects, however, interest costs loom large enough for changes to affect profitability significantly. Construction and other long-lived projects offer examples. An interest rate change of one fifth may alter the amount left for the owners by enough to swing a decision. Certainly, interest rates at some high level will cut borrowing for capital formation by making it too expensive.[16]

Will a fall in interest rates due to an increase in supply rather than to a drop in demand stimulate investment? In "normal" times it will. Parts of the market do not always vary by the same amount. A large decline in the short-term rate, for example, would hardly have much effect on long-term investment if the long-term rate came down only slightly. Funds do not remain idle for long. In a depression, forces other than the interest rate may be so much more powerful that a drop in interest rates due to a supply increase may have insignificant results.

The demand for loanable funds, like other demands, will hardly be stable. We can imagine businesses borrowing more and more, developing one after another investment opportunity down to the point where productivity just equals the equilibrium interest rate. Uncertainty, however, is a major obstacle to the systematic development of one layer after another of investment opportunities. Moreover, new ways of using capital appear constantly. A scientist develops a new process. A businessman finds a better method or gets a new idea. Consumers' tastes change. In a world where "the" interest rate is around 4 percent, there will suddenly develop a way to use capital to earn 50 percent a year (for a time). The demand for funds for investment gets boosts every day from innovation, new

---

[16] If inflation is rampant, there is clear advantage in borrowing to buy real things whose market price will rise. One can afford to pay even a very high interest rate.

development. Complex and ever-changing forces affect the demand for loans. A dribble or a flood of new opportunities will appear; some offer far greater net yields than do most investment opportunities being made —and very much above the interest rate.

Population growth increases the overall need for capital; just to stay where we are per person, we must have more total capital. Infants who have not saved will need housing and eventually the mass of productive facilities—and education—that make modern life possible. Moreover, rising income unquestionably leads us to expect more housing, highways, schools, as well as more industrial equipment per person.

FIGURE 26–6.   Determination of the Interest Rate: Simple Case

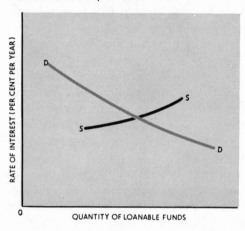

QUANTITY OF LOANABLE FUNDS

Demand and Supply and the Determination of the Interest Rate. When graphed, the demand schedule for funds to borrow slopes downward while the supply schedule slopes upward. The intersection of the curves indicates an equilibrium, the interest rate at which the quantity of funds being offered equals the quantity demanded (Figure 26–6). The forces of demand and supply—and so the interest rate—will probably be different for the long run than for the short run. They vary in different parts of the market and reflect a host of imperfections. Yet, as the sheep in the flock, they move as the dominant forces indicate. Figure 26–7 shows something of moves over the long run.

BANKS AND THE RATE OF INTEREST

One tempting delusion has misled men time and again—that capital can be made by creating money. In the 1930's, this idea got another lease on

FIGURE 26–7.   Interest Rate Trends

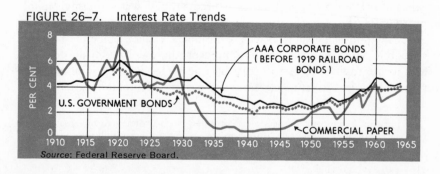

Source: Federal Reserve Board.

life. Money for lending can, we know, be created by banks or by the government's printing presses. This process is nearly costless. If funds can be "manufactured" so inexpensively, why not a very low rate of interest? Why not create new money to supply the demand for loanable funds until everyone can get what he wants for investment at a minuscule rate of interest? Capital goods are desirable and productive; we buy them with money. Will not cheap money make them plentiful and cheap?

The answers should be obvious. Real capital formation requires labor and materials—real things. When a business borrows money, it ordinarily does so to buy things. These will not come out of thin air, as deposits created by banks seem to do. Assume that the economy has idle productive capacity; then a business using funds which are newly created by banks may get what it wants by inducing others to produce what would not otherwise exist. This is a possibility but not a certainty. It explains why, in the 1930's, creating money could seem to be a way to create capital.

If the economy is cruising along at full employment, however, a business or government can obtain the things it wants only by bidding them away from someone else. Although the banking system can create money easily, the economy cannot create more physical things so easily. When the members of the economy save, however, they consume less than they produce. Then the money they lend is matched by something they created and for which they were paid—but did not consume. The borrower, in effect, can use the money to buy the things produced but not consumed.

In an economy operating at about full employment, new money may seem to provide more capital *in a money sense* but not in the sense of physical things—unless it leads to *forced saving.* By forcing up prices, more money in the economy can leave many of us with no choice; we must consume less—we are forced to "save," in the sense of consuming less of the national product. A given dollar income permits us to buy fewer resources; as higher prices make us cut consumption, saving in real terms results. Rising prices, therefore, may enlarge the gap between national product and total personal consumption. There may be capital creation, but it is not costless.

Can banks influence interest rates appreciably? For the short run, we answer "Yes." The banking system can offset small and temporary shifts in demand and supply of loanable funds.

Contraction of bank lending can reduce the supply of loanable funds and tend to raise the rate of interest. Injection of new money to increase the supply of loanable funds will reduce the interest rate, assuming demand to be unchanged. But without more injections of new funds will the lower rate persist? Not unless voluntary saving and the offering of funds for lending also increase by the same amount (or loan demand drops—highly unlikely, because the rise in the stock of money will ordinarily have stimulated business).

As borrowers spend their newly borrowed money, it moves around the income circuit. It has done its initial job of adding to the supply of loanable funds. If the people now receiving the money save *all* of it and then offer to lend it, the volume of loanable funds will continue to be larger (by the amount of the injection), and interest rates will continue to register the depressing effect. Far more likely, however, most of the increased funds will be spent. Using the approach of Chapter 8, M (money) has increased; V (velocity) we assume to remain about the same; PT (prices multiplied by the quantities of goods and services transacted) will rise.[17]

Unless there is a decline in the demand for loanable funds, then, or something new on the supply side, the initial reduction in the interest rate will prove temporary. To keep the rate down, additions to bank lending will be required—monetary policy which will tend to be inflationary. Yet inflation discourages lending, because lenders fear that the dollar will lose purchasing power during the loan contract. Inflation, however, increases the demand for loans. Borrowers need more money to handle the same volume of business at the higher price level, and they want to "beat" the price rise.

THE MARKET FOR LOANABLE FUNDS

Earlier chapters discussed financial institutions. We now look at a few more points, those bearing chiefly upon the effectiveness with which interest can perform the function of allocating a scarce resource.

Competition for Loanable Funds.   The discussions of wages and rent concluded that market imperfections are more than minor and that failure to make the best possible adjustments (by the standards of long-run competition) will be common. The market for loanable funds is also far from perfectly competitive. But does not money seem more mobile than land and labor? Our financial institutions provide many excellent facilities for transferring funds. The market contains astute and powerful borrowers—businesses and governments—determined to get the most favorable rate possible. The market also contains astute lenders—banks, insurance companies, and other institutions—who are anxious and able to take advantage of small differentials. There is a fluidity and prompt adjustment to small changes that will hardly be found in labor markets. Moreover, information about conditions is often good, and enough buyers and sellers operate to assure reasonably effective bargaining in broad areas.

Nevertheless, the markets for loanable funds are far from perfect. Imagine a small business trying to sell bonds in the big money markets. Or we may look at a man of modest income trying to borrow for personal reasons. Both cases illustrate an inescapable limitation: Most borrowers

[17] See Phillip Cagan, *Determinants and Effects of Changes in the Stock of Money, 1875–1960* (New York: Columbia University Press . . . , 1965).

ordinarily have few places to "shop around"; their personal situation creates a uniqueness similar to that of real estate. The lender will place heavy weight on the character of the borrower; as a rule, few lenders will be in a position to make the necessary judgment about an applicant for a loan. The lack of knowledge about borrowers can be a serious handicap. Once a loan has been made, the chance to "take it back" is gone, unless some property has been pledged as security.

In thousands of communities, there will not be over two or three possible lenders; borrowers may find no serious competition, especially price (interest rate) competition. In a large city, of course, there are more lenders, but many a borrower will be limited, in fact, to a few and find their interest charges fixed with little or no choice offered. Families or businesses in urgent need may face exorbitant rates; yet more often the terms are below what many borrowers would have been willing to pay.

"Rationing" of Loans.   The market for loanable funds fails to meet the conditions of perfect competition in other respects. (1) Some persons and businesses have an aversion to going into debt even at low interest rates. Perhaps nonrationally, they rule themselves out of the market. (2) Lenders are not always willing (and able) to loan any volume of funds that may be demanded at the price they fix. You have just secured a better job and a wife. You see ads for easy loans. You go to the bank, find it willing to lend at the equivalent of, say, 6 percent, and think of all the wonderful things you could do with the money: new clothes, a house, furniture, or purchase a stock which you believe will rise in price. So you might say: "Fine, I'll borrow $10,000," Your banker would hardly take you seriously, but instead of raising his price (interest rate) to reduce your request, he would say: "No, I can let you have only $500 now." He will not say: "You can have $500 at 6 percent, $600 at 9 percent, or $900 at 10 percent." Businesses run into the same thing. The lender's price may be inflexible, but he more or less arbitrarily adjusts the amount he will lend.

Personal Lending and Borrowing.   One way to get ahead financially is to save money and have it earn interest. Interest compounded adds up more than one may expect—at 4 percent doubling in less than 18 years. It is wonderful, indeed, to have money working for you. Savings banks and savings deposits in commercial banks offer safe, stable places to put funds to earn interest. Somewhat higher rates can be obtained from savings and loan associations at the potential cost of some delay in getting cash in an emergency. Government savings bonds offer a lower yield but with utmost certainty. Careful scrutiny of opportunities can reveal significant differences in yields.[18]

Borrowing and paying interest may also bring net gain. The significant

[18] G. H. Moore and P. A. Klein, *The Quality of Instalment Credit. . . .* (New York: Columbia University Press, 1967).

question is: "Will the use of borrowed funds give me as much advantage as they will cost?" Benefits are ordinarily more difficult to measure than are costs. If I borrow at 6 percent to buy an asset yielding 8 percent, the case may seem clear. Yet the comparison is still difficult because the asset may not in fact yield 8 percent while the debt is fixed. Most consumer borrowing, especially if we exclude buying houses, is for things whose services are difficult to value: an auto, washing machine, or education. The only advice of general validity is "Proceed cautiously." Waiting to buy will enable you to accumulate funds so that a bigger down payment will cut total interest cost.

If you are seriously considering borrowing, the question of terms arises. Perhaps the best starting point is this: *Shop around!* Feel no shame or stigma (unless you plan a disreputable use of the money). Remember—the must successful businesses go into debt. The lender may seem to be doing you a favor, but lending is *his* source of income. You will be charged, but a little effort to get the best terms possible may pay handsomely. Good advice is to check with one or two banks of highest repute.

In buying an auto, furniture, or house repair, do not borrow on the terms offered so easily by the seller, at least not until you compare them in detail with those of a bank. Sellers, by calling the excess over the purchase price a service charge or something of the sort instead of interest, may and sometimes do exact exorbitant amounts without violating laws against usury. Often you can save by pledging good securities or life insurance. Personal loan company rates tend to be extremely high; even credit unions and other forms of personal credit charges run around 10 percent or more. Except perhaps for mortgages, the cheapest terms will usually be those offered by a bank. Perhaps Congress will soon pass a long-debated "truth in lending" law; it would require stores selling on credit and other lenders to express interest in terms of a simple annual rate.

CRITICISMS OF INTEREST

Suspicion and hatred of the moneylender have ancient, and often well-justified, origins. Lenders have sometimes taken unconscionable advantage of the needs of borrowers. Where the loan was for consumption, the borrower may have had little to show for his debt (though he might have starved without it). His productive capacity did not increase; the fact that his ability to work did not fall offers little help in making him able to support a heavier burden (the interest). Loans for consumption have different significance from loans for production. Debt at high interest rates may snare a person who borrows for consumption into something like servitude. Yet lenders, too, have suffered. Many a borrower has defaulted.

Another basis for attacking interest has been to ridicule the argument that abstaining from consumption requires a real, subjective cost, something unpleasant, like work; that people must be rewarded if they are to put themselves to such discomfort; that interest is the payment which induces us to make the sacrifice. Obviously some rich people save without any personal hardship. Examples do not prove the whole case, however; and more than a germ of truth remains in the argument that we must pay to get anything like as much abstinence as is needed for the investment of the modern world. In order to obtain the saving that will meet our "needs," we offer an inducement to overcome aversion, at the margin, to sacrificing current consumption. If we want *lending*, we must pay enough to compensate for the opportunity the saver has of using funds (1) to buy and use capital equipment productively or (2) assure himself liquidity. We may, then, pay for some saving that would be done anyway.

A third basis of criticism stems from the fact that interest goes on and on while, it may seem, the personal sacrifice (whether of not consuming or of parting with liquidity) was made in the past. In fact, however, the lender's decision not to consume must in a sense be made continuously. He has the choice of holding on to a bond (or other debt of the borrower) or selling it for cash. By not selling, he sacrifices other alternatives: (1) the chance to buy productive property or hold cash and (2) consumption.[19] The service of "waiting" or "abstaining" is continuous. An economy needs saving which is never consumed. Sustained economic growth on a large scale requires that owners of bonds and other assets continue to abstain from consuming at least some of their earlier savings.

Finally, we note that managers of Communist economies have found that interest as an allocating device is useful—even necessary. Out of deference to Marx they may call it by other names. But they are learning to use essentially the "capitalist" interest concept to decide where limited resources for investment are to be allocated.[20]

TERMS AND CONCEPTS

property income	tax capitalization	present value
rent	linkage	"pure" interest rate
interest	quasi-rent	liquidity preference
time preference	discount	liquidity trap

QUESTIONS

1. "Pure economic rent is an unearned increment, and yet the charging of rent is essential for efficient allocation of productive capacity." Discuss.

---

[19] For an explanation of the doctrines of the Catholic Church by an economist familiar with modern tools of economic analysis, see B. W. Dempsey, S.J., *The Functional Economy* (Englewood Cliffs, N.J.: Prentice-Hall, Inc., 1958).

[20] A difference between Marx and "bourgeois" economists needs mention. Marx assumes that waiting, or the failure to consume, is not a useful activity which is scarce. He builds his system around the conclusion that capital equipment consists of labor and raw materials only. The payment of interest (and profit) for the waiting element seems to him robbery. His law of movement of capitalist society, his prophecies, including the dire forebodings of increasing misery for the masses, rest partly on the assumption that the waiting element in capital formation is not creative.

2. Wage rates and land rents are much higher than a century ago but not interest rates. Why?

3. In what sense is rent determined by price rather than itself being an element determining price?

4. How would you account for the range of interest rates in this country today?

5. What is the relation between market interest rates and the price of land? Of long-term bonds?

6. "The interest rate cannot be explained by the marginal productivity of capital since a great deal of borrowing is used for consumption rather than production." Discuss.

7. What would be the effects of a large increase in taxes on land?

8. Select three factors affecting the supply of, and three affecting the demand for, loanable funds and show why each might change.

9. What is quasi-rent?

10. What is time preference?

11. "The variation in the productivity of capital reflects the outcome of the race between capital accumulation and invention." What is the "productivity of capital"? What does "invention" mean here? In what sense is "invention" in a race with "capital accumulation"?

12. When, if ever, is interest a price paid to induce people not to consume?

13. What factors affect the demand for money to hold? What is the relation to the rate of interest? What is the risk in holding money?

14. How can the banking system influence interest rates?

15. What effect would the expectation of inflation have on interest rates?

16. Discuss the criticisms of interest.

27

PROFIT AND LOSS

It is only for the sake of profit that any man employs a capital in the support of industry; and he will always, therefore, endeavor to employ it in the support of that industry of which the produce is likely to be of the greatest value. . . . By directing that industry in such manner as its produce may be of the greatest value, he intends only his own gain, and he is in this, as in many other cases, led by an invisible hand to promote an end which was not part of his intention.

Adam Smith

One type of income remains, profit—or loss, for this distributive share can be, and often is, negative. Though not large in the national totals, profit and loss have mighty influence.

"Profit" as described by economists differs from the profit shown in the accounts of businesses and reported in the newspapers, or as interpreted by the tax collector. The economist's conception also differs strikingly from that of the "radical" who attacks the "profit" system, or the labor union which sees in profit "fair game" for higher wages, or sometimes of the politican who says that higher taxes can be paid out of profits without adverse effects.

Ours is often called a "profit system," not because profits are a large portion of income but because they act as the "sparking" element, an energizing force. The hope for profit and the fear of loss play a dominating role in the decision making of business. A misconception of "profit" (or "loss") can, itself, lead to bad decisions. If doctors mean different things when they say "disease X" and discuss remedies, someone will suffer.

645

Profit: A Preliminary Definition. Economic profit is what remains of gross income after payment of wages, rent, and interest. Speaking loosely, we can say that it is the residual. Having already discussed the ways these other shares are determined, do we not know what governs the one which remains? Not adequately, for complexities remain. Some center around this question: "For what do we pay (or not pay) over and above wages, interest, and rent when we buy services that yield profit (or loss)?"

Profit: Business Concepts. The appendix to Chapter 5 showed how accountants compile profit figures. The dollars the firm has received from different sources are totaled; then the payments for labor, materials, interest, and other such items are deducted along with estimates of depreciation. After other adjustments and the deduction of income tax, the accountant has the figure of net profit or loss.

The data generally available have two major defects (in addition to those arising from difficulties in estimating depreciation, depletion, and changes in inventory): (1) Not all businesses are covered, because, for practical reasons, data on millions of unincorporated firms combine payments for both owner services and their capital. (2) Business accounts, by ignoring *implicit costs*, understate true economic cost. Therefore, the profit figures appearing in business accounts include some implicit wages, interest, and rent. The economist calls the thing he seeks *pure* profit as a reminder that implicit costs should be—but are not—included as expenses in business accounts.

When we look at the corporate sector as a whole, we find that the equity put in by the owners—their original contributions of equity funds plus reinvested profit—totaled over $550 billion in 1966. If a figure of 4½ percent measures with reasonable accuracy the value of the alternatives to earn *pure* interest which are being sacrificed in making equity available, an implicit cost of $25 billion should be deducted in computing the net profit of corporations in 1966. This amount, in other words, is not economic profit at all but implicit interest. Moreover, some of the $23 billion or so remaining was implicit salary and rent—no one knows how much. The pure profit appears to have been around 4 percent; but this average does not, of course, give any sense of the few "big killings" because our system *does* reward some entrepreneurship magnificently.

THE SOURCES AND DETERMINATION OF PROFIT

Pure profits result when a firm can sell what it produces for more than the full costs of production (including *all implicit costs*). What conditions will make this possible?

Management Efficiency. *The hope of profit and the fear of loss provide incentives for economizing.* Such hope and fear help force, and guide, management to be economical. They provide drive for getting efficient allocation of resources, for preventing waste. Such human service operates at the heart of the economizing process, or mechanism, of a world not settled at stable equilibrium. As consumers we pay profit, in part, to get efficient direction of the use of productive capacity.

Innovation: Entrepreneurship. Successful innovation can bring large gains. The company which "gets there first" with something new that appeals to the public or something that reduces costs for itself or another business can benefit as a result. Buyers willingly pay a price that more than covers costs. Profit is at least partly the price we pay for innovation—for originality applied in practice.

Much change results from conscious human action motivated by a desire for gain. New things do not just get done; people do them. Some innovations are "busts." Some catch on like a spark in a dry haystack. Perhaps it burns out quickly. But for a time, at least, it glows brilliantly. The period of brilliance corresponds to the period when a firm makes pure economic profit. The individual (or the group) that successfully introduces the new thing is an innovator. The innovation itself may be a new product or service—Minnesota Mining's "Scotch tape," Diners' Club charging, or Cook's tours—or a new method of manufacturing—Carnegie's repeated successes in lowering costs of steel production, Ford's assembly line, or IBM's punch cards—or an original type of selling—Woolworth's stores. The innovator may, or may not, be the inventor, discoverer, or intellectual parent of the idea. Invention in the laboratory or the tinkerer's basement differs from introducing a new thing successfully in the hurly-burly of business. Getting acceptance of something new requires *entrepreneurship*.

Every venture with a new product or process differs at least a little from any other. The qualities of the successful entrepreneur, promoter, or innovator—whatever we call him—vary widely. He must generally have vision and daring combined with judgment and knowledge. He may be the supersalesman with vast personal attraction or hard, driving, even obnoxious. He may be most scrupulous, a man whose integrity and fine reputation are a key to success, or a "robber baron."

Some successes and failures are small, some huge. Some come quickly, others only after many years. Inevitably, however, innovation as a source of profit is temporary (unless coupled with monopoly). When other businessmen see that a new venture meets with success, they will follow the example. If the innovation is a new product, additions to output will lower selling price. (Ball-point pens sold originally for $12 each.) The handsome profits of the innovator will melt away—perhaps overnight if entry into production is easy, perhaps only over many years if entry is difficult.

Some changes are better than others. Profits are what society pays those who succeed in making the changes it likes, in anticipating desires and satisfying them. Today, much innovating is done by groups, not individuals. For proof, one need only list the new things that corporations have developed. Big decisions have been, to varying extent, the result of the efforts of many people: the director of research who selected the lines of inquiry to pursue, the head of marketing who guessed which of the things (technically possible) would most appeal to the public, the plant organizer who fit the new product in economically with the rest of the operations, the treasurer who scrounged for the money, the director of sales who built public acceptance.

Most of the work of most of the people who run businesses is not innovation. Much is *management* of a more or less customary type, just as most of our personal lives has a big element of routine. Management keeps things going, not in the routine of a rut but without much change from month to month. An organization must have the stability of established methods. Yet routine is not all of the business. Most officials have elbow room for trying the new; a few have considerable opportunity for guiding innovations. There is no hard and fast line between management—whose compensation, whatever called, is economically a wage or salary—and entrepreneurship—for which the community pays profits or losses.

Uncertainty as a General Source of Profit.   Another source of profits is uncertainty. Some uncertainties result from the possibility of innovation, but uncertainty has other sources. No one knows the future. Individuals and businesses adjust differently to the changing world. And as they adjust, they produce new change. Some are more successful, or lucky, in foreseeing the future than others. Gains result in some cases, losses in others. Uncertainty inevitably produces this result: A business can never be sure of the ideal adjustment to conditions as they develop. Even where competition is vigorous, many months or years are necessary to work out the long-run equilibrium; meanwhile, conditions continue to change. Most business activities are undertaken for the future and involve some commitment for years ahead. Decisions must be guided by forecasts of the future. Even a firm that is not attempting significant innovation must make all sorts of decisions about the unknown. Earnings reflect the quality of the judgments. Good decisions yield profit, bad decisions loss.

Some things in the future are highly certain (our commitments under a contract); others are highly uncertain (women's fashions in 1975); most lie between. In many respects at least, the more distant the future for which a decision is made, the greater the uncertainty. If we know what creates uncertainty, we know something about the source of *opportunities* for profit and loss.

Business Fluctuations: Changing Price Levels.   Ups and downs in the general level of business activity create uncertainties. Such broad movements can overwhelm the individual company. They upset plans. When the economy is swinging upward, businesses will generally benefit, some more than others. During contraction and depression, firms suffer. Businessmen are not blind to the fact of cycles; there is no uncertainty about that. But there is always doubt about the timing, the magnitude, and the detailed nature of the changes that will come in the future. By accident alone, some decisions will turn out gloriously successful, others the opposite.

Rising and falling prices of its *own* inputs or outputs can change a firm's income. Similarly, changes in the *general level* of prices create opportunities for a business to benefit or suffer. As a rule, a rising price level will create profits, a falling price level losses. During inflation, businesses using borrowed funds and having other fixed costs tend to find that expenses (as shown in the accounts) rise more slowly than the prices of outputs (regulated utilities being a major exception). When the price level goes down, the opposite will tend to occur. Some of the dollar profit (or loss) is in a sense fictitious because it is measured in money of different purchasing power.

Changes in Special Conditions as a Source of Uncertainty. In addition to fluctuations which affect all business, there are changes which will affect a firm, area, or industry more or less individually. *Nature* smiles or frowns; a few rainy weekends put an amusement park in the red; a dry spell destroys crops; a heat wave boosts the sale of air conditioners. A firm cannot be sure about future *production costs* or those of its competitors. Yet it must commit itself to production methods and buy machinery, borrow money, fix wage rates, and settle on its location. It cannot change quickly later. If costs turn out lower than expected, the firm will gain. Or in the time necessary for a company and its competitors to adjust to a new situation, there will be profits or losses that diverge from the equilibrium rate (*quasi-rents*). The builder who bet on automatic elevators did better after wage rates of elevator operators doubled than the one who had installed manual elevators. The corporation that obtained capital by debt or leasing rather than by equity financing benefited when tax rates tripled in a decade.

Similarly, with any given level of general business, most firms must be uncertain about the *demand* for their particular product. Consumer tastes change; sales of tuxedos sag while buying of tools for home repairs rises when millions of families move to suburbs. New patterns of work and play change demand; wide-scale elimination of Saturday as a workday cut demand for local transit (without reducing fixed costs) and raised purchases of athletic equipment. One company gets a jump on others by more appealing advertising or a better product. Such hazards plague the businessman—and keep him on his toes. If managers knew the demand ahead, they would come nearer the adjustment which gives a normal return on investment.

Many forces make for uncertainty. We discuss *government* later. Pure, unadulterated *luck* plays a part. Profits are to some extent "windfalls." Giant firms and the marginal farmer are at the mercy of the "fortuitous combination of circumstances." Yet much depends upon the skill with which the business manager prepares for uncertainty and adjusts to change as it develops. Witness the fact that every year firms in the same industry (or city) make very different records. The more that an economy can develop flexibility and adaptability—whether in machine tools, office floor layouts, inventory or price or wage policies, or mental attitude—the less will it need to pay for judgment in forecasting change or suffer from errors while they are being "corrected."

Profit and the Willingness and Ability to Risk Loss. A company's total profit depends not only upon the wisdom of the entrepreneur's decisions but also upon the size of the business, or of the transactions involved. With the same skill and effort, the profits can be small or large, depending upon the amount of resources. Pure profit includes something more than compensation for the nonroutine services of the businessman. Such an element makes up another aspect of profit: the payment to owners for submitting to the chances of losing equity capital.

In large corporations, the people who make the decisions—even the big decisions—seldom own more than a small fraction of the equity capital. Someone other than the decision maker stands to benefit or suffer as a result of the decisions. Sensible people, not liking to lose money, will not freely and knowingly assume the risk of loss unless they receive something in return. Our economy offers the hope of profit as compensation for the chance of loss. *Profit provides the incentive to induce people to take chances that may result in loss.* Profit is our payment to induce not only innovation but also more "normal" investment in an uncertain economy. Even to get business financing by debt, consumers must offer chances of profit. The person who lends money at interest acquires fixed claims, defined specifically and enforceable against others and their property. The others who promise to pay the debt *risk* their wealth—hoping for profit. Investment financed in debt form is possible only because someone furnishes risk capital.[1]

Who does the "chance taking" in our economy? People who provide not their personal effort but only property (chiefly owners of common stock) assume much of the risk. In a big corporation, one group bears the risk of loss of property, another makes the decisions.[2] A man with a

---

[1] Is there an exception when government issues debt to finance a highway, water, electric, or housing project? Not really. Taxpayers who guarantee the debt assume the risk.

[2] Though the responsible officers may own little of the corporation, they will have a big interest in its success; their sense of accomplishment, prestige, salary, and security are involved. Employees also take chances. If they are aware of the risks of

brilliant idea may be helpless without someone else's money; on the other hand, a person with funds to risk may have no unusual ideas. Together, the two may serve themselves and the economy fruitfully.

Some investments involve greater chances of loss than others. The cautious man may refuse chances that promise less than the mathematical odds. Others may enjoy the excitement of risk, and some seem willing to "pay" by taking "long shots." There is little measurable knowledge of underlying psychological attitudes about taking chances. People do gamble when they know the odds are strongly against them—but only if they believe there is a chance of gain. Odds induce some of us to risk $2 for a chance whose mathematical value is less than $1; for example, 1,000 may pay $2 each for a chance at a "prize" of $900. Though there must be some *incentive* to induce people to assume risks, no one knows how much or what the marginal inducement must be to get the risk taking we "need." But there *must* be *some* prizes.

Our *ability* to sustain losses is limited, even if the willingness were not. Savers certainly cannot pour endless sums down a rathole, even if they were somehow foolish enough to want to do so. If every venture turned out badly, society would grow less able to finance new ones. This fact faces a socialist economy just as it does one relying chiefly upon private enterprise. The more undertakings that are successful, however, the greater the ability to go ahead with other ventures. The capacity of an economy to finance new projects depends upon the results of past ventures. *The supply of risk taking is limited.*

"Price" of Risk Taking.   And demand for risk taking? Economic realities force us to take or "consume" some risks. Chance taking also yields handsome gains on some occasions; as a public, Americans want such gains and will undertake risk to get them. The economy, therefore, has a "demand" for risk taking. Forces of supply and demand work to adjust quantities offered and demanded and to create a "price"—for risk taking cannot become a free good. The greater the risk, the greater the reward that must be offered. But how much? Is there any clear proportion that (1) the inducement-to-undergo-uncertainty must bear to the (2) yield we can count upon. Risks of 3 to 1 may require a premium of only 2 to 1, or perhaps 5 to 1.

Crucial is *expectation* (at the margin). Conceivably, there might be continuing supply, even if no corporation were earning profit. The evidence would be the continued provision of funds to purchase new common stock or other forms of new risk assets. If you believe that there will be profits in the *future*, you may ignore a past in which losses exceeded

---

the firm failing or doing badly, they will expect pay advantages to offset the adverse features of joining up with a company whose future may be shaky. Thousands of corporations now have plans for sharing profit with employees or helping them buy the firm's stock.

gains. Moods, whims, "animal spirits," stock market fluctuations, and other factors not necessarily related to current profits affect expectations.

If profit is a price for a service, one asks: "Does it serve the price function of limiting the use of the scarce resource and allocating it to best advantage?" The answer is "Yes—with many reservations." In bidding for new risk capital, a firm must meet the competition of others. But unlike the competition for labor, money payment as the reward for the service of risk taking need not be made at once. Hopes and dreams can be the "currency" used to entice someone to take risks. "Gyp operators" can sell securities of slight value because the glib salesman can create hopes easily and without realized profits.

Where there is uncertainty, no one can know just which risk alternatives should be financed first. Bidding among possible "demanders" must be in essentially noncomparable and even irresponsible "currency"—hopes. Markets work imperfectly in allocating the flow of new funds for risk taking, including corporation earnings not paid out in dividends. Yet no one can know what would be best. Losses play their part, also imperfectly. They discourage new investment and force firms which do not cover costs to curtail operations.

Profits in Competitive Industries Tend to Disappear. Pure profit or loss in a highly competitive industry will not continue except as new conditions appear. In fact, however, competitive industries operate in a world of change which does constantly create opportunities for temporary profit or loss.

Monopoly. Some profit results from monopoly rather than serving as payment for the services we have discussed. Unfortunately, monopoly returns and pure economic profit tend to be impossibly difficult to disentangle. Chapter 19 discussed why a business, or a group of firms, that can reduce competition can get more income by doing so.[3] How large are monopoly profits? No one can say. Regulation trims the possibilities in some industries—utilities. The same firm may receive profit from both use of monopoly power and constructive innovation and risk taking; the highly profitable Aluminum Company of America was an innovator of improved production methods when its monopoly position was firm. No human being analyzing a profit and loss statement can prove that "this profit results from monopoly, that part from other sources."

Deceit, Dishonesty, and Exploitation. The sources of profit that we have described, monopoly excepted, are desirable, or inevitable, elements of a nonstatic economy. Some people, however, have seen profit as resulting from disreputable actions.

---

[3] Monopoly gain resembles the "extra" earnings which members of a labor union or professional group receive when they restrict entry.

Skulduggery, deception, corruption, shady or illegal practices, and other such actions can sometimes bring gain. No one has systematic information about the amount of such activity. Perpetrators will seldom advertise their actions. Eventually, some records become public, revealing examples of despicable actions. It is not always clear where tough competition or arrogant monopoly shades into sharp practice and then into dishonesty. The cases which occasionally appear in the news offer no sound basis for judgment. In total business income, such examples are probably trifling. The shyster businessman is a thorn in the social flesh, but his disreputable dealings are not characteristic of profitable business.[4]

Large profits have sometimes resulted from the *"exploitation"* of *natural resources*. (The economist would call some such returns "rents.") The firm may gain more from luck in securing a natural resource than from necessary and useful effort. Yet exploration is often highly uncertain; development requires "gambling." By no means do all efforts to find natural resources "pay off." Where profits include a big element of payment for extraction of natural resources, one must ask, "Are such gains economically unnecessary?" They may be the carrot that keeps the donkey going. "How big and juicy, then, must the carrot be to keep the critter moving ahead?" It is clearly misleading to conclude that because an oil company's earnings are derived in part from the sale of a gift of nature, the same is true of all its profit or of business in general. Relatively few companies engage in any appreciable amount of extraction of natural resources.

A more influential "exploitation" argument has been that of Karl Marx. The employer, Marx said, pays laborers less than the full value of what they produce; the difference, profit, is exploitation, *surplus value*. Marx's erroneous assumption is that nonlabor services—entrepreneurship and the provision of capital, waiting, and risk taking—are not productive.[5]

Government. Business success or failure sometimes depends upon the decisions of politicians, civil servants, and the military. To varying degree, the terms of such decisions are beyond the check of government auditors or competitive bargaining. The "entrepreneurship" that pays best may be

[4] Can deceit and other noxious actions help explain losses? Yes. The business that follows sharp practices may lose public confidence and in the longer run suffer terribly. Laborers will be reluctant to work for an employer with a history of bad treatment of employees. Can businesses be exploited? Of course, especially in the short run. A "squeeze" by unions may force a business into the red. Government seizure without adequate compensation—expropriation—is also a form of exploitation that our legal system seeks to prohibit. Yet some businesses forced to move for urban renewal or other governmental programs have not been rewarded adequately for the disruption of the business, the loss of customer relations, and other valuable intangibles.

[5] Payment of laborers appreciably less than the value of their marginal product may continue for even a substantial period if competition among employers is weak and mobility low.

that at City Hall, the state capitol, and Washington. The granting of tariff favors, or import quotas; the disposition of the public domain; the non-competitive awarding of a good military order; an exception in the tax law (as administered); a subsidy; the location of a new government project; a franchise or license may be the key to business profit. Other actions of government can lead to business losses—utility rates kept below costs, regulations and restrictions, heavy property or payroll taxes. Skillful "manipulation" of government officials, well within both the law and accepted standards of correct behavior, can occasionally do more to increase profits or prevent losses than many brilliant business decisions.

Capacity Utilization Rate.   In any short period, such as from one quarter of a year to another, the rate of profit will rise or fall with the extent of utilization of capacity. A small percentage drop in utilization can lead to a much larger relative fall in profit, and vice versa. The chief reason, of course, is the existence of fixed costs. Figure 27–3 gives indirect evidence of the relationship of changes in volume of production to profit.

PROFIT SEEKING AND RESOURCE ALLOCATION

The desire to make a profit, or avoid a loss, has a decisive influence on the allocation of resources. The profits actually realized indicate the industries and areas where additional resources and economic growth are most likely needed. Losses show where contraction is desirable. Profits and losses also reveal which firms, which departments within firms, and, to some extent, which methods are serving best, and worst, in economizing in the use of resources. Profits and losses, however, do more than indicate. They also reward and penalize. Thus they tend to ease the way of those who have done well and hinder those who have done poorly.

Every functioning economy contains forces which create the residuals we call profit and loss. Either by accident or design, these residuals may be clearly revealed or partially concealed. But neither manipulation of accounts nor fussing with names can alter realities—the fact that economic life has uncertainties, or the fact that final outcomes will sometimes differ from expectations. Since risks are inevitable, one practical problem is to find ways to make them serve constructively. Private ownership of residuals has proved to be one way to accomplish this objective.

Do businesses, in fact, seek maximum profit or minimum loss? Business-men, with every evidence of sincerity, say that the total results they seek include more than dollars, that money gains will be sacrificed knowingly for other objectives. Sometimes the sacrifice may be of a short run for long-run financial gain. To some extent, however, the total combination of results businessmen seek to maximize will include elements—prestige, respect, generosity, community welfare—on which the market does not put a price. No one knows how well businessmen make the necessary choices or how well the profit-loss system allocates resources to achieve such nonfinancial objectives. Except when a firm has some monopoly, however, it cannot sacrifice financial results to any great extent for long and survive, certainly not expand. The tens of thousands of firms incurring losses have even smaller opportunity of sacrificing financial gain. Unless they economize the resources and seek the rewards, on which the market sets a price, they will not survive. Narrow indeed is the freedom to ignore market direction of resource allocation, to ignore the pressure to minimize loss.

HOW LARGE ARE PROFITS?

Have Profits Exceeded Losses over the Years?   Are there any profits in the economy as a whole? Does this seem like a foolish question? Wages, rent, and interest obviously exist. Conceivably, however, losses may be greater than profits. It is by no means certain that profits in the economic sense (always, we recall, after deduction of implicit costs) are positive on balance. So we ask again: "What have been the net economic results for entrepreneurs, risk takers, profit seekers, loss shunners—whatever we call them? Have they earned net profits over the years?" Data are poor, especially for the countless firms that fell by the wayside. The successful firms survive, and as they grow, we learn about them and how much they earn. Yet for the many who fail no figures appear in the record. The data are thus biased toward understating losses.[6]

Income tax figures for corporations cover the 38 years through 1964 on a roughly comparable basis. This span includes the prosperity of the 1920's, the depression of the 1930's, the War, and the prosperous postwar years. During this period, nearly 15 million corporate tax returns showed net profit, and over 9 million net loss. Even in recent years of good business nearly two out of five corporations show losses. In 1964, for example, 515,000 corporations had aggregate losses of $7.2 billion, while 859,000 had after-tax profit of $24 billion. In the 5 years through 1966, after-tax profits averaged $39 billion. Figure 27-1 shows the record of profit in relation to owners' investment (i.e., net worth, the equity capital, the amounts put into the business in return for original issue of capital stock and as undistributed profit).[7] The average profit in most years has been more than implicit interest—but not a great deal more, perhaps 2 or 3 percent since the mid-1950's. But some companies have had spectacular results, proving that *really big successes* are possible.

Data on profits and losses of the nearly 10 million unincorporated businesses are most incomplete. The amounts reported for income tax

[6] Data have other weaknesses and apparent inconsistencies. Many profit figures include double counting; when one corporation receives dividends from stock in another, the same underlying profit may be counted twice in national or industry totals. Treatment of foreign earnings differs from one corporation to another. The accounting methods used for tax purposes are not always the same as those for reports to stockholders.

[7] Owners' investment as used here has no necessary relation to what present stockholders have paid for their shares.

FIGURE 27–1.   Corporate Profits as a Percentage of Owners' Investment and of Sales, 1922–64

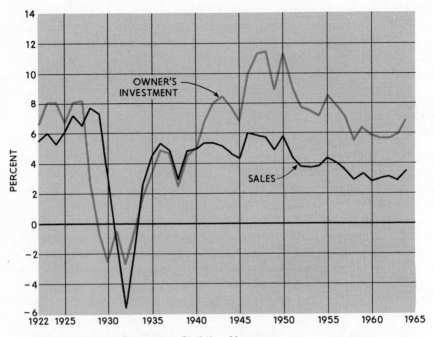

Source: U.S. Treasury Department, *Statistics of Income.*

purposes are known to understate income.[8] They are mixed with figures on professional earnings and income from other nonbusiness sources; the pure business element, therefore, cannot be separated. Nor is there any way to relate the business profit to the amount of the owner's investment or to allow for the worth of his own efforts. From the amount of tax paid, however, it is safe to say that some unincorporated businesses yield good profits on the risk capital invested. Most sole proprietorships and partnerships, however, probably yield little, and many nothing at all, above implicit interest and compensation for the owner.

The payments for entrepreneurship and risk taking have been only modestly above losses. Spectacular successes overshadow the "break-even" survivals and the painful deaths. On balance, consumers have paid little for risk taking and for the stimulating force of the hope of profits.

The depressing fact that so much has been lost suggests an opportunity

[8] For discussion of the problems of measuring income of unincorporated businesses, see C. Harry Kahn, *Business and Professional Income under the Personal Income Tax.* . . . (Princeton: Princeton University Press for National Bureau of Economic Research, 1964). Two of many factors influencing the figures may be noted. A million or so tax returns cover farms with little or no net income. Success tends to induce unincorporated firms to incorporate, for tax and other reasons.

for improving the general welfare—to reduce losses. We may feel as we look at examples of huge profits: "Here is something society should try to reduce." More important, however, is the reduction of losses, which represent waste.[9] But how?

Why Do Businesses Fail?   One approach is to look at the causes of business failures, a topic for which we have data with at least suggestive value (Table 27–1). Losses probably result from about the same causes as business failures.

TABLE 27–1.   Causes of U.S. Business Failures, 1966*

Underlying Causes	Percentage of Total Failures
Neglect (bad habits, poor health, marital difficulties, other)	3.1
Fraud	1.4
Lack of experience in the line	11.3
Lack of managerial experience	17.4
Unbalanced experience	18.4
Incompetence	46.3
Disaster and unknown	2.1

* Based on 13,061 failures. The average failure involved liabilities of $106,000. Nearly half of the firms were retailers; manufacturing accounted for 14 percent and construction for 19 percent. One third of the companies had been in business 3 years or less, 21 percent over 10 years.
   Source: Dun and Bradstreet, *The Failure Record through 1966* . . . (New York: Dun and Bradstreet, Inc., 1967).

Recent Profit Results.   Are profits high enough? Or too high? How can one judge? With what will a student compare a firm's profit figures? A single amount tells rather little. Nor does it enlighten us much to know that General Motors' 1966 profit was $1.8 billion, while Gillette earned $50 million. These companies are of rather different size. The thing to do is to compare profits with what interests us.

One person wants to know how much of what the consumer pays ends up as profit. He would compare profits with sales. Amerada Petroleum netted 39 percent on sales in 1966, Swift 0.2 percent. The degree of integration of the firm and other factors influence profit-to-sales ratios, limiting their usefulness for analysis of companies and industries. For corporations as a whole, as shown in Figure 27–1, profits as a percentage of sales have reversed a downward drift but remain below the levels of even the 1930's.

A more significant measure is the relation of profit to the amount the

[9] Losses are not entirely a social waste. They tell the community "Get resources out of this use." Losses provide a service which is like the pain of an infected appendix.

owners have invested. To find this figure, we compare profit with the total which owners have put into the company (net worth).[10] Thus, Avon Products' $55 million of profit in 1966 was 37 percent of its net worth, while U.S. Steel's $249 million was 7.8 percent of net worth. Perhaps we have a little money to invest and so are interested in profits per share of stock; then we divide profits by the number of shares. We can then compare the profit per share with the price of the shares on the stock market. The ratios vary tremendously. In the summer of 1967, when the stock market was generally buoyant, Xerox Corporation's earnings per share were around 1.4 percent of the market price of the stock (dividends were even less). Safeway, however, was earning 9 percent of the price of its shares.

Figure 27-2 shows, for leading corporations in a variety of industries, profits after taxes in 1966 as a percentage (1) of net worth and (2) of sales. In general, earnings were higher than interest rates, in some cases very much higher. Yet profits of some were too low to attract new equity capital, unless long-run prospects were far more promising. The variety among industries is, itself, striking. (Compare auto manufacturing and meat packing.) Finally, we should note that the giant corporation is something of a profit-loss "offsetter." Published figures represent totals which may include some operations that brought handsome profits and others with losses just as heavy as any to be found in firms heading for bankruptcy.

These *average* figures do not show *marginal productivity* of risk investment. Clearly, however, marginal productivity in some lines is high. As a rough but revealing indicator of marginal productivity, we have some data on the profitability of new equipment. Studies of business practice on installing machines reveal that manufacturing businesses commonly expect to get their investment back within 5 years or less.[11] Using rough calculations, we find that marginal productivity in the economist's meaning must frequently be 50 percent or even more, and often much above 10 percent. Even when there is no need for investment to expand, new outlays for cost reduction may pay handsomely.

Is There a Profit "Squeeze"?   Profit rates in the early 1960's were below those of the early and mid-1950's. Corporations were doing a much bigger volume of business. In the 10 years through 1966 owners put nearly $190 billion of new equity capital—reinvested profit and payment for

[10] Gillette outdid General Motors in profit as a percent of sales—12.6 to 8.9—and as a percent of net worth—32.6 compared with GM's 20.6.

[11] In planning investment, business managers sometimes think in terms of the number of years it will take for the equipment to "pay off" or "pay for itself." This method of calculation cannot give as good guidance as more refined measures; an obvious defect is that it ignores yields in the years after the cost has been returned. Economically, the best goal is to maximize the present net worth of the resources over which the company has command.

FIGURE 27–2.   Profits after Tax as Percentage of Net Worth and Sales, Leading Corporations in Selected Industries, 1966

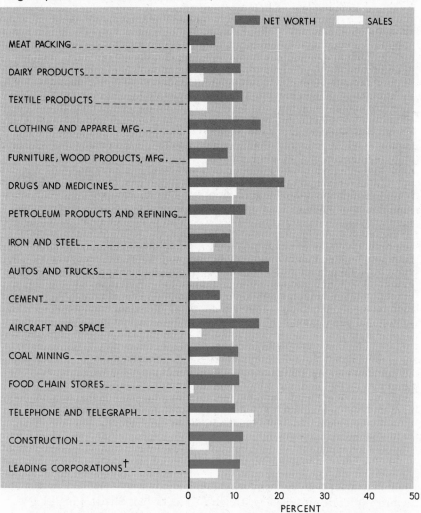

* These 3,850 corporations accounted for almost 90 percent of all corporation profits. Because these are the most successful corporations the figures are not representative of all the business world; 1966 was a year of high prosperity.
Source: First National City Bank of New York.

new stock—into corporations. Total 1966 profit was higher by about $13 billion, a yield of around 7 percent on the increased capital. (Payments to employees were up by $110 billion.) Unquestionably, 1966, a year of high prosperity, was also one of good profit. As it ended, however, profit margins were under pressure; costs were rising. Businessmen were talking again as they had in the early 1960's about a "squeeze" on profit. Some companies were having difficulty, and six of the 500 largest had losses; but experience left no doubt that excellent profits could be earned in the American economy.

WHO BEARS THE TAX ON PROFIT?[12]

The immediate result of a business tax increase is a cut in income left for owners. But can owners then shift the burden? Dispute arises because business income consists of different distributive shares. Business earnings may be made up of a "normal" return on investment, or a payment for risks, or some earnings of managers, or rent of natural resources plus a surplus in the sense of "pure" economic profit. The taxes on the pure surplus (and on the pure rent element) would rest on the owners, who would have no way to shift the burden.

The other elements of business income, however, are returns for services of resources that are both essential and limited in supply. To get these resources, the business and ultimately its consumers must offer a net payment equal to what will be offered elsewhere. Owners of resources have other choices. They may consume instead of saving, or having saved, they may invest where there is no tax on what the property earns (tax-exempt bonds) or only one tax on the earnings (mortgages or corporation debt). To get capital, the business whose earnings are taxed must offer returns *high enough after tax* to equal other net yields. Of course, money that is already invested is largely "stuck" so that the stockholders bear the brunt.[13]

As time passes, however, new capital will become available only if the net return is adequate. Management, in deciding on new products to be financed out of reinvested earnings, will plan on those that will pay a profit after tax. Total investment and eventual output, therefore, will tend to be smaller than otherwise. Hence prices will be higher. Some of the tax on business income is a cost passed on to consumers. The process can be slow and will be far from smooth and uniform; it may not be obvious. For example, what is really a tax on the payment for the use of capital (including risk) will not be labeled as a tax, any more than the freight in the price of coffee is billed as "freight." The tax appears as a higher gross yield which firms must pay for equity funds.[14] There is another effect.

---

[12] This section may be left for study of the income tax, Chapter 30.

[13] If the rate of tax on corporation income goes up, the value of common stock will fall about as the value of real estate falls when the tax rises. Some of the business tax, therefore, is "capitalized," falling on owners of the stock at the time of the tax increase. *New* buyers of stock, then, do not receive a lower net yield per dollar which they invest; the tax does not cut their income except as it tends to force down the net return on all investment.

[14] Government agencies regulating public utilities are supposed to set charges that provide a reasonable return after taxes. So if the corporation income tax rises, electric, telephone, railroad, and other utility rates also rise, after a lag which can be years rather than merely months. Perhaps, however, demand does not have the inelasticity that will permit shifting in full; owners must then shoulder the tax, although those consumers who continue to use the service pay a higher price as well.

The tax tends to make purchase of stock less attractive than otherwise. Consequently, more savings are directed to the purchase of bonds and other wealth not subject to the tax. The net yields of these assets tend to drop. *Property owners in general,* therefore, suffer.

IS THERE A PROFIT-MAKING CLASS?

Can we pick out any particular group and say: "These are the people who get the country's profits and suffer the losses"? If we could, it would certainly not be a group that had anything else in common: age, income, occupation, sex, political affiliation. We could be certain that virtually all farmers and owners of unincorporated businesses would fall in the group, but no statistician is likely to come up with even reasonably good figures about the profit and loss element in their earnings. If we jump the intellectual hurdle of necessity and think of profits and losses as only the returns of corporations, can we get better answers?

Over 20 million individuals own stock in publicly owned corporations, and perhaps 1 million more have stock in privately owned corporations. Slightly more women than men own stock. Breadth of ownership is growing—with more than three times as many owners in 1965 as in 1952. Each year more thousands of corporations adopt profit sharing plans for employees.

Around 60 percent of the country's families with incomes of $15,000 and over owned stock, but only 11 percent of those with income from $3,000 to $5,000; over one million families with incomes under $3,000 were direct owners of stocks. One of every three business administrative executives, 23 percent of clerical and sales workers, and 11 percent of craftsmen and foremen owned stock; 43 percent of the wealth of families headed by a person aged 65 or more was stock.[15]

Big corporations are large in number of owners as well as in the respects shown in Tables 4–1 and 4–2. General Motors, for example, has around 1,500,000 owners; Standard Oil (N.J.), 742,000; General Electric, 545,000; Ford, 433,000; Sears, IBM, U.S. Steel, and others, substantially more than 300,000; Bank of America, Du Pont, Mobil, and Consolidated Edison were among those with more than 200,000 owners each.

Various institutions had title to large amounts of stock for pension, personal trust, and insurance reserves. Over 100 million Americans may share, albeit minutely in most cases, in the ultimate ownership of the shares involved. Colleges and other nonprofit institutions own nearly 5 percent of all common stock listed on the New York Stock Exchange.

Although there is substantial concentration of ownership in a minority

[15] Of families and individuals with incomes below the poverty line, 16 percent owned publicly traded stock at the end of 1962—and one third of the unrelated individuals over age 65. D. S. Projector and G. S. Weiss, *Survey of Financial Characteristics of Consumers* (Washington, D.C.: Board of Governors of the Federal Reserve, 1966), p. 160.

of families, direct and indirect owners of corporations are a numerous and varied group. Certainly, they are not a "class" in the usual sense.

THE ATTACK ON PROFIT AND THE DEFENSE

Profit is the payment for services of immense value to our economy. Loss is the penalty for poor service. Perhaps it seems incredible that the *principle* of profit should be condemned. What can seem more sensible than building an "energizer" into the economy, than offering rewards for economizing, penalties for waste, and incentives to do things that are uncertain but that may be better? One might criticize the amount paid (too little or too much) but not the principle. Yet even the principle is sometimes questioned. Profits, and the economic system they typify, have long been a target of attack, though less so now than before World War II.

Why the criticism? Four practices make profit seem larger than in fact it is: (1) Accounting methods, by treating as profit the implicit return on equity investment and sometimes the compensation of managers, exaggerate the totals; (2) a frequent failure to offset losses against gains exaggerates the impression of the size of profits; (3) so, too, a recent tendency, notable in labor union literature, to speak of "cash flow" (profit plus depreciation) will mislead the unwary into conceiving profit as more than twice its actual size; (4) global figures of profits in billions fail to relate them to a relevant base, the equity capital.

Criticism of profit has other origins. (5) After the collapse of 1929–32, business found itself in the "doghouse," a common target of criticism. So profit, as the guiding force of business, was somewhat discredited. (6) Some people and groups (occasionally a religious group) feel that the search for personal gain is unworthy, and more unworthy, apparently, when called "profit" than "wages." (7) Profits and losses are condemned because they account for some of the big inequalities in income and wealth.

(8) Economic theory has contributed to misunderstanding. Economists have shown that individual firms sometimes have earnings properly termed a "surplus." By this we mean a receipt over and above what was necessary to get the firm to produce what it did. Such surpluses will become part of profit. Not a few economists have endorsed the view that a true surplus is "fair game" for anyone who can shoot for it, especially the tax collector. The great misconception is that since *some* profit is surplus, *all* must be. Some hot water in the tank may be surplus for the bath, but not all.

(9) Concern over economic instabilities has made some economists uneasy about the place of profit. From year to year the amount of profit often varies widely. Since business decisions depend partly upon profit incentives, the guidance of our system may be affected strategically by a most unstable element. Selection of a husband—a long-run commitment—on the basis of 1 week's impression might not always lead to best results. One period's profits or loss may provide no better basis for

long-run investment commitments. Psychological reactions are notoriously complex, but if businessmen *do* guide investment by changes in profit, fluctuations in real investment will be enhanced by the tie to the profit outlook. A moderate instability in profit will create more instability, perhaps, in business generally. The facts are by no means clear enough for a balanced judgment.[16]

(10) Some business leaders emphasize that profits are needed not only to provide incentives for equity capital but also to provide the capital itself. Corporation managements often find the reinvestment of profit prompter, surer, and cheaper than getting dollars by the sale of new securities. If the same money had gone to stockholders, personal income taxes would have taken a large fraction, and stockholders would undoubtedly have spent much of the remainder or found other uses for it than

FIGURE 27–3. Corporate Profits after Tax Related to Corporate Gross Product*

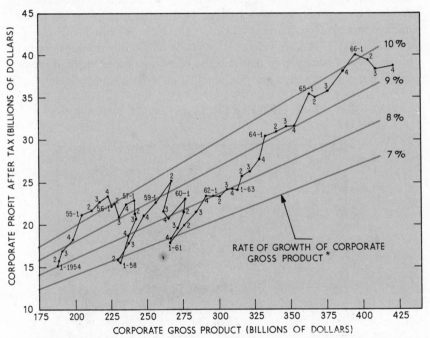

*—Data are seasonally adjusted at annual rates and exclude profits originating in the rest of the world. The labels of the plotted points indicate the year and the quarter; thus 64–1 means the first quarter of 1964. The "2" that follows stands for the second quarter.
† The four lines showing rates of growth of corporate gross product are statistical estimates based on four groups of quarterly data.
Source: *Survey of Current Business* (March, 1967).

[16] Large profits in "leading" corporations (or industries) have been criticized as inviting wage-rate demands which the particular companies may be able to pay without price increases and, in the short run, without substitution of capital for labor. To match the wage settlements, other firms will need to raise prices, leading to a drop in employment.

purchase of new corporation securities. (The forced saving deprives the stockholder of freedom to dispose of the earnings of his property and evades market tests for the allocation of capital funds.) However, if the earnings had gone to consumers in the form of lower prices or to employees in higher wages, corporations could have received relatively little of the money to finance expansion that was extremely productive. Consequently, the argument runs, large profits are useful, or essential, as a source of funds to pay for economic growth. The small and new firm tends to be especially dependent upon profit to finance growth—the building of net worth and the support which it in turn gives for increased borrowing.

Figure 27–3 shows that relatively high profits have been associated with high rates of growth of output. The periods, (quarters of the years from 1954 to 1966) of relatively low profit were those on the low growth line. Although cause and effect are interrelated—one cannot say with certainty that it was high profit which induced high output or high output which produced large profit, for both are true, but neither exclusively—a society which wants growth of output will be wise to look with favor on good profits. Figure 27–4 shows that dividends in relation to stock prices have for some years been lower than interest rates obtainable on high quality bonds. Rates of earnings are not much higher than interest rates.

FIGURE 27–4.   Yields on Stocks and Bonds (Annual Averages)

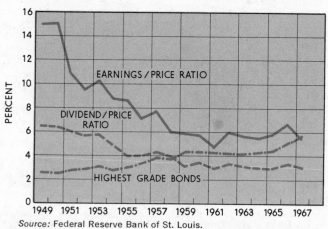

Source: Federal Reserve Bank of St. Louis.

TERMS AND CONCEPTS

pure profit	innovation	surplus value
implicit cost	risk capital	cash flow
entrepreneurship	expectations	economic profit

QUESTIONS

1. When you freely pay a price that provides a generous profit to the selling firm, for what services are you paying in the profit portion of price? Why do you do so?

2. How does competition tend to eliminate pure profit and loss? If a firm earns a high rate of profit year after year, does it necessarily have monopoly power? Why?

3. How does the function of the entrepreneur differ from that of the inventor? The risk taker?

4. Why can firms in the same industry have widely different rates of profit?

5. Account for the fact that losses are so frequent even when our economy is highly prosperous.

6. Occasionally, the term "unearned income" is applied to some payments to owners of property. In what sense, if any, is profit (loss) unearned? Why?

7. If you were asked to devise a tax on "excess profits," how would you define "excess"? (Assume no element of "war" profit.)

8. How is the amount of profit shown in the firm's accounts affected by the proportion of debt in the financial structure? By year-to-year fluctuations in the economy?

9. "Profit is more than the driving force for economic progress. It is also a device to help get efficient use of productive capacity already in existence." Comment.

10. Does the obvious fact that many people like to gamble prove that payment for risk taking throughout the economy in unnecessary? Why?

11. "If you make a profit selling to me, then I must be losing; you must be exploiting me in one way or another." Is this necessarily true? Why? If you are buying from someone who is selling at a loss, are you "exploiting" him? Why?

12. "Every economy will have residuals. Whether we call them profit and loss or another name, some will be good, some bad. The important thing is to use them constructively to get efficiency and to speed growth." Discuss.

13. How would you explain the changes in corporation earnings as a percentage of owners' investment during the years since 1950?

14. "It is mistaken to regard profits as an incentive for innovations. New inventions and discoveries depend little on economic matters." Discuss.

28

EFFECTIVE USE OF PERSONAL INCOME

Annual income twenty pounds, annual expenditure nineteen nineteen six, result happiness. Annual income twenty pounds, annual expenditure twenty pounds ought and six, result misery.

Charles Dickens

Good buying practices, a systematic saving and investment program, careful use of consumer credit, insurance against certain risks—all of these and more are required if the consumer is to attain the highest possible level of living on a given income.

National Commission on Economics and the Consumer, Economics and the Consumer, Joint Council on Economic Education

The income that counts is real income—goods and services. And it is not so much this year's real income as that of a lifetime, including what one can pass on to those one loves. This chapter deals, briefly, with how to use money income to get as much as possible of the goods and services we want most. We then discuss measures government has taken to influence lifetime income through social insurance.

SOME ASSUMPTIONS OF INDIVIDUALISM

A basic principle of an individualistic society, one of liberty and freedom, is that (mature) individuals are generally better judges of their own wants than of the wants of others. Tastes are personal. Freedom for consuming units to make their own spending decisions will give better results than a system in which one person decides for another. Exceptions there will be, but beyond the collective spending by government, they will be relatively limited. One exists when a father says that his children must "consume" education; he decides for someone else. Another occurs when I decide that I want something—health, a good biography, or national defense—but ask an expert—doctor, librarian, or general—to decide specifically what I should buy to achieve the end.

Even mature adults, however, often encounter difficulty in making choices. As never before in the world, Western man has a challenging opportunity. He has the chance to develop tastes whose satisfaction will yield a richer life than any possible before, except perhaps for a privileged few. What role does the economic system play in developing, as well as in satisfying, tastes? How well does the economy help us improve our ability to choose the best—in ends as well as in means? Questions of such profundity may be largely unanswerable, but not the query, "How can we use our income more efficiently?"

BUYING TO BEST ADVANTAGE

How can an economy produce more real satisfactions? One method is to increase the output of goods and services. Another is for us to learn to select and to use output more intelligently. If we devoted more serious effort to spending our money, even at some cost in getting it, many of us could expand our real income appreciably.

In thinking about avoiding waste in our spending, the adage "a penny saved is a penny earned" became obsolete with the income tax. A penny saved by care in spending is now worth more than a penny earned because government imposes no income tax on the penny saved.

Waste in spending robs us of good things. Getting income costs us too much of our life, or Dad's, to use it carelessly. Good management of spending can be guided by experience. *Personal budgeting* will help, careful planning, not worrying about minor things but knowing where we stand and are going. Figure 28–1 shows how, on the average, 2 groups of urban families with substantially different incomes allocated their consumption spending, the average for all families, and something about relative changes in a 10-year period for all families.

Each spending unit, of course, should plan its budget, not by what others do but in the light of its own income and preferences—and the future it faces. Realistic planning must include guides for making the plan work. Good budgeting must include provision for change, rational, rather than impulsive.

The Need for Information. Efficiency in decisions about the use of income depends upon knowledge. Consumers need to try seriously to get facts about what they want and the alternatives available. Most families have incomes which allow many opportunities for choice. Family members must decide among alternatives, about many of which they can know little. Buyers are often amateurs—more so than we like to admit. Which

FIGURE 28–1.   Expenditures of Urban Consumer Units by Major Types—
Average for Two Income Groups and All Consumer Units*

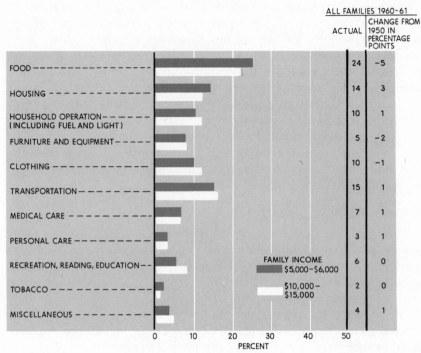

| | ALL FAMILIES 1960-61 ||
	ACTUAL	CHANGE FROM 1950 IN PERCENTAGE POINTS
FOOD	24	−5
HOUSING	14	3
HOUSEHOLD OPERATION (INCLUDING FUEL AND LIGHT)	10	1
FURNITURE AND EQUIPMENT	5	−2
CLOTHING	10	−1
TRANSPORTATION	15	1
MEDICAL CARE	7	1
PERSONAL CARE	3	1
RECREATION, READING, EDUCATION	6	0
TOBACCO	2	0
MISCELLANEOUS	4	1

FAMILY INCOME
$5,000–$6,000
$10,000–$15,000

0   10   20   30   40   50
PERCENT

* A person living alone or in a household with others but who was financially independent,
i.e., whose income and expenditures were not pooled with those of others, is treated as a consumer unit. Data apply to 1960–61.
Source: Bureau of Labor Statistics.

used car or brand of canned fruit will give best value? Which coat will be
least out of style year after next? Which washing machine will cost most
in repairs?[1] If one is planning to buy on installments, what are the full
carrying charges? And is it *really* wise to earmark future income by going
into debt. "Impulse" buying may be fun; but one ought to confine it to
minor items, not those which will commit any appreciable portion of
future discretionary income.

For that highly important purchase, housing, one cannot really compare alternatives to best advantage without facts, many involving intangibles, about schools, commuting, recreational facilities, and neighbors. And
what is the probable maintenance expense, the adaptability of the house or
apartment to needs of changing family size, the possibility of resale, the

[1] Growing use of mechanical equipment in the home creates need for more
"do-it-yourself" skills. With repair service so expensive, getting the training needed
for routine, and not-so-routine, jobs will enable one to save large amounts, a form of
tax exempt earning.

opportunity to put one's own effort into enhancing its value, or the trend of the neighborhood? Getting facts to answer such questions takes effort, but effort which can repay itself a hundred fold.

Consumer ignorance can be costly. But worse—the seller gets a chance to gain from the buyer's lack of perception. If the seller can make buyers think they are receiving more than he really gives them, or more than someone else is offering, he stands to benefit. The more complex the thing purchased (a surgeon's services or a TV set), or the greater its uniqueness (a particular concert or a woman's hat), the greater the possibilities that the seller can profit by misrepresentation and overpricing. In contrast, products which the consumer buys time and time again, especially those which are relatively simple to compare with others (boxed cookies or a brand of nylon hose), do not require much consumer effort in deciding which alternatives are most attractive. We stay away from the restaurant with discourteous waitresses or distasteful food. However, between the extremes—intricate things purchased rarely, and simple things purchased frequently—lies a big range. The consumer can have some knowledge of alternatives. He will have some independent check on the seller. But without making special effort to get information the typical person will not always have evidence enough to prevent costly mistakes.

The richness of the consumer's opportunity proves also to be a handicap. With so much choice we often cannot distinguish to make an optimum selection. Each person's experience will be limited to a few of the many things available. How can we get the facts needed to compare the many alternatives which a huge and changing productive system makes available?

Advertising.[2]   One answer is found in the advertising on which American businesses will spend around $18 billion in 1968. Presumably it helps the consumer and pays the advertiser. Critics tell us, however, (1) that prices must be higher to pay these costs, (2) that we may be deceived into buying less than the best value, and (3) that we are made to want things of trivial usefulness, our tastes changed—debased more often than elevated.

Advertising speeds obsolescence. Critics charge that there is waste when advertising makes us dislike last year's model which can still yield much good service?

Some social waste unquestionably results from the "competitive armament" aspect of advertising. To the contestant, the individual firm, what counts may not be the absolute amount it spends, but the amount in relation to the spending of its competitors; if soap company A spends

---

[2] What is said here about advertising applies in varying degrees to other types of selling expense. Prof. Jules Backman of New York University in *Advertising and Competition* (New York: New York University Press, 1967) analyzes evidence on advertising and its economic effects.

more, then soap company B must step up its outlay merely to offset A's increase. As each tries to get, and to stay, ahead, the spending rises. Although much advertising may nullify other advertising, the dollars support popular and scientific magazines, college papers, radio, TV, and newspapers.

Advertising has many elements. Some provide true information—this week's meat "special," the qualities of a new machine or drug, the places where labor is needed. Like other forms of communication and education, the information given in advertising can help consumers (and businesses) to allocate resources more efficiently. In fact, a great deal of the huge mass of trade-journal advertising directed to businesses, not households, is largely informative.

Yet advertising, in trying to add appeal, to persuade as well as to inform, uses expensive talent and other resources to "dress up" the facts. There is delusion, even downright deception, in some advertising, as well as not a little irrelevancy. More is spent than the essential function of providing information requires. Some results of the use of talent may be appealing—good art or a good laugh—other effects are repulsive.

More important for the consumer, perhaps, are the effects of advertising in creating new wants. Advertising makes us seek new things. As these new wants are satisfied, people presumably acquire new happiness; life can become richer, giving values which compare with those of simpler civilizations as the enjoyment of a great symphony by a man of cultivated taste compares with a child's enjoyment of a simple folk melody. There is no assurance, however, that the spending we are induced to make is really for richer living.

The deliberate use of resources to create wants may doom man to perpetual discontent. Advertisers, by using scientific knowledge of human personality (drawn from skillful research into our motivations), can play upon emotions to make us constantly less satisfied than we could be. Though we may receive ever more goods and services, our happiness may not increase. Advertising may thus deprive mankind of much of the true pleasure we expect from expanded production. Is it not disturbing to recognize that resources are used on a large scale to create, rather than to satisfy, wants?

All of us sense that advertising claims must be "cut down to size," but we seldom know just how.[3] Fortunately, the consumer is by no means helpless.

Business Aid to Buyers.   Intelligent business purchasing offers one effective method of keeping prices right for the consumer while offering

[3] Who believes the claims made for movies? Yet few of us doubt the accuracy of a product description in a Montgomery Ward catalog. How should one rate the advertising of candidates for political office?

him the qualities he wishes. Retail organizations not only maintain show-rooms with assortments from which to select. Some also test quality and tell the public that a product has met the firm's standards. A consumer may, understandably, be skeptical of such claims. If you were a manufac-turer, however, you would get a different impression of the seriousness with which leading stores or other buyers insist upon standards.[4] A few magazines also maintain testing laboratories and refuse to advertise prod-ucts which do not meet standards. (Even when the approval rests upon meeting the highest technical standards, it does not help the consumer much on the question of "value." A product may be pure, effective, beautiful, and meritorious, but also overpriced.) Trade associations have, in some cases, set and enforced standards of grading—lumber products, for example—which help protect the buyer; simpler and more uniform standards reduce waste. Standard clothing sizes contribute "no end" to our convenience, except when one company's size 38 is like another's 36.

Introducing a new product is hazardous. Businesses have great interest in trying to find what will most appeal to the consumer before they make final commitments on production. The *sample survey* is one device for determining buyer preferences, not only "in general" but in different locations, occupations, or age groups.

Branding and similar product differentiation give the consumer protec-tion. Businesses go to great expense to distinguish their outputs. The reputation established in this way can become a valuable possession. The owner would be foolish not to protect it. If he depreciates quality, the result may become identified with his brand and lower the product's salability. The business also has an incentive to maintain a consistent standard, a consistency which helps the buyer. X's bread today will probably be like yesterday's, whether excellent or mediocre. Branding, then, helps us to learn by experience, to accumulate knowledge. Similarly, stores prize a good reputation. A firm's concern for its future as a going concern (rather than being a "fly by night" output) is a valuable ally of the consumer.

Business aid to the consumer also comes from Better Business Bureaus. In over 100 cities, these nonprofit organizations keep watch on business practices, especially to detect frauds, cheating, and deception.

A shopper occasionally finds canned goods and fresh meat that are *graded*. Such grading is exceptional, even though some students of con-sumer problems have long urged its extension, somewhat as follows: Certain physical characteristics would be set as standards for meat, tires, paints, sheets or shirts, canned goods, and so on. There might, for exam-ple, be 3 grades of canned peas. Without looking inside the cans, the

---

[4] A big buyer, such as Sears Roebuck, may insist upon scrutinizing your opera-tions and fixing its payment partially upon how efficiently you seem to function. It may provide expert guidance to help you operate more economically. Its buyers are likely to know costs and to insist upon prices based upon efficency potentialities.

shopper could learn something about the quality from the grade. Not all grade B peas would be identical, but the range of variation would be small. The difference between grades A, B, and C would depend upon objective criteria. Along with more informative labeling, grading offers a method of giving the consumer a better chance at efficient choice.

Buyer Efforts to Get Better Values. Late in the 1920's appeared an exciting and disillusioning best seller, *Your Money's Worth.* Its message was: The consumer is a shockingly poor judge of many things he buys. The saying, "We get about what we pay for," is simply not true. We pay good money for things of little or no value and far too much for others. Deception to the point of economic (though not legal) fraud appeared common. More significant, if less striking, was sheer ignorance of values.

The book raised the question: "Why do not consumers work together to protect themselves?" The depression of the 1930's increased the urgency of stretching the family dollar. One and then two private organizations, Consumers' Research and Consumers Union, developed. They perform a unique function: providing the consumer with impartial knowledge. They test a wide variety of articles. Their conclusions are published in monthly report-magazines, citing brand names. Moreover, they give recommendations about what is the best and poorest "buy," reports on physical characteristics, and guidance about the relative importance of different features of products, such as ease of maintenance, operating cost, durability, and appearance. These organizations also provide information on such qualitative matters as the merits of different movies or musical recordings, developments in medicine, and a wide variety of other topics.[5]

Government Aid for Consumers. Everyone is a consumer. Is it not logical to use our chief agency for joint action, government, to help ourselves as consumers? Although the obvious answer would seem to be "Yes," the accomplishments have been more modest than extensive. Business and other pressure groups have often opposed rather than encouraged unbiased government measures to protect consumers. The individual has too little at stake to make it worth his while to go to Washington or the state capitol or even city hall to press his views. Producers, however, have a bigger pocketbook and a larger specific interest. They properly fear bureaucratic, rigid controls.

Good intentions and goals which are broadly of great merit are not enough. Sustained, adequate carry-through year in and year out will be necessary for success. Government is by no means inactive. The 5,300 employees of the Food and Drug Administration watch over the quality

---

[5] The two organizations reach directly persons who do over 5 per cent of consumer buying. Some businesses take serious account of the test methods, design suggestions, and ratings of these agencies. Governmental inquiries have used the information and arranged for special studies.

and purity of drugs, some foods, and cosmetics. No new drug may be placed on the market until the FDA has checked it for safety; every batch of certain medicines must pass its tests. It inspects over 43,000 producing establishments each year and makes over 103,000 laboratory analyses. The FDA does extensive research, especially on new medications. It sets some standards, such as defining "peach jam," inspects fruits and vegetables that may have traces of poisonous sprays, and supervises the wording on food containers reporting the ingredients. It checks canned goods to prevent sale of any that are dirty and impure, and tries to keep an eye on "cure-all" medical devices. Although its authority is limited to things passing in interstate commerce or advertised across state lines, such scope includes a great deal.

The Federal Trade Commission, in addition to its antimonopoly activity, also helps inform and protect the consumer by requiring informative labeling and trying to prevent "deceptive pricing," the practice of labeling an article with some extravagantly high price—"maker's list price," "made to sell for," or "nationally advertised at"—and then offering to sell for much less, though quite possibly at more than the thing is worth. FTC jurisdiction also extends to the accuracy of radio and TV advertising and much labeling. Many states have laws applying to intrastate commerce; but state enforcement is spotty.

Compared with the past, the present situation of government protection for the consumer is encouraging. Yet it leaves much to be desired. For example, though you can generally depend on a label to tell the truth—not advertising extravaganza—you do not necessarily get the whole truth. Occasionally, by focusing the spotlight of publicity, Congress may help. For example, investigation of deceptive packaging (the "great open spaces") induced some voluntary change. Stricter legal controls on labeling and packaging ("truth in packaging") are going into effect (1967) after extensive Congressional inquiries.[6] Proposed "truth-in-lending" legislation would aid the buyer by requiring sellers to quote interest charges on time payments in terms of simple interest—not "6 per cent" when in fact the charge is in the form of discount, not interest, and in fact very much higher; not $1 a week for 6 months but x dollars for the item and interest at, say, 20 per cent on the declining balance. The business world generally opposed the proposals as originally made in the 1950's. One reason was reluctance to reveal the height of charges in many cases. Other reasons were practical difficulties of computing, the dislike of more regulation, and the difficulty of convincing customers that an appar-

---

[6] When "regular" packages of detergents of different brands contain 19, 24½, 20½, and 20 ounces, or when the package sizes of one brand line hold 20, 49¼, 83¾, and 257 ounces, accurate price comparison by the housewife gets a bit difficult. Yet businesses point out that standardization of packaging machines and package dimensions reduces cost. It is economical to use packages of the same size for several products of differing weight.

ently high interest charge includes allowance for risk and collection expense. Years of discussion led to reformulation so that opposition weakened.

A Presidential Consumer Advisory Council in studying the problem of the consumer travelled around the country and got the views of consumers and businessmen. Its report, *Consumer Issues, '66,* deals with problems of the modern consumer, education for consumer buying, more effective use of standards, consumer credit, and methods of representing the consumer interest in government at all levels. Special sections discuss four subjects of particular importance—home maintenance and repair, autos, health services, and textiles. To say the least, the Council believes that much more can and ought to be done to improve our dealing with these and other of the more complex portions of consumer buying.

In addition to what governments do to prevent the consumer from being fleeced, they do much to help him make better decisions *if* he or she will take the initiative. Testing and experimentation are extensive. Some results are made public. The federal government offers thousands of inexpensive publications with information to help the consumer in one way or another. State universities and federal agencies are able to help us, for a slight charge, on a host of things: how to plant a lawn, prevent moth damage, or stretch the food dollar. For their own purposes, governments buy many things according to specifications. The National Bureau of Standards tests and helps fix standards, but, these are not generally available to the public.

Professional Associations. Perhaps nothing is more difficult to buy intelligently than are professional services.[7] Usually, a person does not know what he wants or should have, except in broad terms. Desiring health or a good legal document, we seek service because we do not know what we need precisely. How, then, can we select a supplier wisely? Professional associations assist by enforcing standards. If I can be certain that anyone permitted to practice medicine or law meets certain qualifications, I can act with some confidence. Professional associations also aid the consumer in other ways. Bar Associations, for example, offer legislative bodies drafts of laws designed to serve the public interest. The American Medical Association evaluates new medications and works to sustain and improve the quality of medical care.

Purchasing Securities: Financial Investment. Ordinarily, the wise household will not use all its income for consumption. It will also save. Then, however, it faces another "consumer" problem: what to do with

---

[7] If medical or legal services are involved, we may be in such extreme trouble that rational calculation is impossible. Seldom, if ever, can we know the fees that different doctors or lawyers charge, an ignorance that results partly because of professional ethics which prohibit advertising.

the money.[8] A few economic principles can help. First ask: "What do I seek most?" Usually, of course, we want to preserve our capital. Yet we also hope to get a good income from it. Some of us want the principal itself to grow, if possible. The emphasis will depend in part upon the specific reasons for which each person saves.

If the immediate objective is to get enough to marry and start house-keeping, the need is probably for an asset which can be converted into cash without loss within a few years, earning as much as possible in the meantime—a savings account in a bank or savings and loan association. Taking a longer-run view, the problem is more difficult. Some assets offer much greater chances than others of rising or falling in price. What should one do about uncertainty over the dollars' future purchasing power? Of the investments fixed in dollar amounts, U.S. Treasury Savings Bonds have desirable features. If one holds them for only a few years, however, they do not yield as much as a savings account and may be less convenient. Some good corporation bonds bring much more interest.

A person who desires still higher yields, who does not want to lose purchasing power in inflation, and who is willing to take risks for a capital gain, will seek something else. Real estate has often met these conditions. Yet few of us are trained to manage real estate. Equities in businesses may then be the answer—common and preferred stock. But which securities will best serve our needs? Most of us must turn to others for facts and recommendations. Perhaps the best general advice is to seek the guidance of a well-established financial organization.

What do you really want to emphasize—income now or capital gains over the long run? After deciding, you can start the search for the *best value*. Whether a thing is a good investment will depend upon what one gets for what one pays and in relation to alternatives. Stock in the country's best-run corporation with the best of prospects will be a poor selection if the price is "too" high. On the other hand, at some low price, stock in a poorly run business with dim prospects may be a good buy. Decisions should always hinge upon the price paid for what one obtains.

What are the prospects of various industries? Look at earnings per share; the higher the earnings per dollar of price per share, the more attractive the stock. Look also at earnings as a percentage of net worth (book value, the owners' investment). If the earnings rate is very high, expect competition to reduce it. Examine the trend, preferring a business whose net income trends upward. Do any special factors affect the firm? the industry? Look at dividends.

You may select stock on the basis of current cash payments, but if so look to see what additional earnings support the dividend. If you seek capital gains in the longer run, the preference will be for stocks of

---

[8] Usually, but not always, one does best by first repaying any debts owed. A pension plan may offer attractive terms for longer-run investment, especially if the employer matches extra contributions.

corporations whose earnings are being plowed back and used to good advantage—and where the prospects of higher profits seem better than yet reflected in the stock's price. The larger the fixed costs, including debt, the greater the risks. If business improves, can the firm handle an increased volume without heavy outlays for new plant capacity or overtime? Check on what securities the "big money" investors are buying, selling, and holding.

Gradually you weed out possibilities that are clearly not so good, *valuewise*, as others. With the group narrowed, you can study more intensively. If you follow such a procedure, you can do better over the years than the stock market as a whole. Why? Because most buyers and sellers will not take the time to study. Too many act on the basis of "tips" and hunches. They do not focus on the best-value principle.

Timing purchases and sales is a different matter from picking longrun values. Stock prices fluctuate too much for any but a handful of specialists to make rational judgments about just the best time to act. "Playing the market" differs from buying for the long pull. If the whole prospect seems too difficult, mutual funds will serve you. Some have made much better records than have others. Here again, the "pay off" from careful study can justify the effort.

Insurance.   Uncertainty is a fundamental "fact of life." From uncertainty spring hope and opportunity—and the risks of minor and major loss. We must live with risk. How can we do so best—how can we protect against losses when uncertainties turn out badly for us? Prevention and care provide part of the answer. Yet there is something more: insurance.

The principle of insurance is to spread the cost of risk—not the risk of missing a bus or being too late in asking for a "date," but big things. We are liable to certain costly tragedies. But no one knows whether, or when, they will strike any particular person or business. For the individual, there is a chance, but not a certainty. For a large group, however, some of the tragedies are certain. When we can learn about how often they will occur in a large group, and how much they cost, we can average the cost over the group. If everyone then pays a little, the few whom disaster strikes can be compensated. For the individual, then, the economic gamble has been eliminated. Individuals and businesses can now insure against a tremendous variety of risks.

The price—premium—is calculated on the basis of experience: frame houses with a certain kind of roof in a certain part of town; death rates of males of each age; explosions of boilers of specific types for specific uses. Because the future may be worse than the past, a safety factor is added, and also "loading" for costs, including taxes and the salesman's commission. The insurance company will allow for any income which premium funds paid in advance are likely to earn.

Often the premium is higher than the company really believes necessary, but the excess is refunded at the end of the year as a "dividend." Most mutual companies (owned co-operatively by the persons insured) pay dividends on all types of insurance; stock companies (owned by stockholders) sometimes pay dividends to policyholders, chiefly on life insurance. The major terms of policies covering similar risks are generally standardized. Details vary greatly, however, and nonprice competition appears.

How can a business or an individual make rational use of the extensive services of insurance? The most important step is to consult a skilled insurance counselor, for competent guidance can help tremendously. What would be the results if each risk turned into fact? How great would the loss be? One needs to distinguish between what is possible and what is probable. The major concern ought to be for the eventuality which is

FIGURE 28–2.   Comparison of Basic Life Insurance Policies

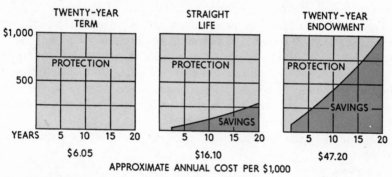

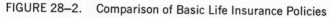

APPROXIMATE ANNUAL COST PER $1,000

Source: J. D. Cohen, *Decade of Decision* (New York: Institute of Life Insurance, 1958), p. 16.

possible even though not probable. The next step is to decide whether the results could be financially embarrassing; as a rule it is unwise to assume the cost of insurance of risks which could not cause serious inconvenience. Then one asks, "How much insurance?" Within the limits of a personal budget we should insure up to the *real* loss we would suffer; to spend more is a waste.

The biggest insurance expenditure of individuals is for *life insurance*. The loss against which we insure is the loss of earning power. Ordinarily, however, some of our life insurance premium goes for savings. Figure 28–2 illustrates. When we buy shoes, autos, or fire insurance, we buy these and the services they provide. In buying life insurance, however, one often buys more: a savings plan. Not every house burns down, but every person dies. Death is complete; only part of a house may be destroyed. A person can die only once; a house may burn several times. Only a small fraction of the public dies each year, just as only a small fraction of all houses catch fire each year. The principle of large numbers operates in both cases. A life insurance company can say to 1,000 people, for example: "We have no way of knowing which of you will die this year, but we are reasonably sure that not more than 15 will die. If each of you will pay us $15 now, we promise to pay $1,000 to the heirs of any who die this year."[9]

Life insurance policies have widely varying features. Some provide little or no saving. *Term* insurance (which got its name when most such policies ran for a rather short term of years) has an insignificant saving feature. The premium pays the cost of insurance, as on a fire insurance policy. At the end of the term, you get back no savings. The kind of insurance an employer takes out for his employees, group insurance, commonly has no saving feature; incidentally, it tends to be a good buy because administrative costs are kept at a minimum (and the employer often bears part of the expense). At the other extreme, endowment insurance has a relatively big saving feature. It provides that, after a period of perhaps 30 years, or upon reaching a certain age, the insured, if still living, will receive the face amount of the policy.

The choice of a type that is best for a particular person depends upon his needs. A big savings feature tends to discipline one into saving. Endowment policies can be timed to mature when one expects to need money. But a large saving element has a disadvantage—the commitment to an inflexible saving program. There may be years when a family simply cannot, or should not, save (in this particular way).[10] Readjustment of a life insurance program can be expensive.

For families with relatively low incomes, this savings element has a

---

[9] As people get older, death claims, in the group, will rise; those insured must pay more for each dollar of insurance. At age 55, for example, the death rate is about 6 times that at age 25. Yet life insurance is often sold at a *level premium* rate for long periods. The cost to the company rises as any group gets older. Still, at the age of 25 you can buy a policy insuring you for, say, 50 years at an annual premium that does not rise. A miracle? No. The explanation is the "savings" feature. We illustrate simply. You pay a premium of $20 a year per $1,000 of life insurance. Selling and other costs of $5 are charged, and death claims of $5. The company then sets aside $10, savings on your policy. If you die at the end of the first year, your heirs get $1,000 of which $10 is your savings and $990 from the insurance pool. If you live, during the second year another $10 is saved out of your premium, cutting the insurance to $980, as savings come to $20. So it goes, year after year. The amount the company can lose declines; more and more of the $1,000 your heirs stand to get is your own savings. The decline in the amount of the company's risk offsets, partly or entirely, the increase in the likelihood of your dying as you get older. Though your premium remains the same, you get less and less insurance. Moreover, you help pay in another way. The savings fund yields the company an income. As the savings build up, the interest becomes a considerable item. For example, assume that after several years your savings are $300; they earn the company over $12 a year; this income is available along with your premium to meet the cost of providing the $700 insurance which remains at risk.

[10] If you want to collect some of the savings in your policy, the company will loan the amount to you and use the cash value as security. It will charge a higher interest rate than it pays you but often less than the rate at banks and other lending institutions.

second disadvantage—an addition to the annual premium. For each dollar of premium there is less insurance—and insurance protection for the years before children can become independent is critically important. Insurance becomes less necessary as children become self-supporting. As one gets older, however, saving is needed for support after retirement. If a young father starts out with $200 a year for life insurance, he is probably much better off to buy term insurance, with no saving feature. Moreover, some insurance on both parents is probably better than all on the father. Never underestimate the value of the mother's services.

Companies offer a much greater choice of types of contracts, and options within contracts, than when our fathers were young. The variety of policy types leads to one difficulty; accurate comparison of net cost, but some companies offer lower net charges than do others.

In deciding on insurance other than life, one wisely follows the rule of insuring against losses which, even if unlikely, would be serious. *Disability* insurance to provide funds if the income producer becomes unable to work will generally be even more important than life insurance. He and the family must be supported and, probably, medical expenses paid.

We should insure our house against *fire* loss for the amount needed if it burned down. Fire insurance on furniture and clothing will cost a few packages of cigarets a year. The protection against financial loss from other hazards, such as hail and wind and other elements of "extended coverage," will cost only a little extra.

Bigger than fire insurance as a cost for most of us is *auto* insurance. We can insure against theft or damage to our car. More important, however, is insurance against damage that one's car may do to the body or property of others. Having a car wrecked is not financially pleasant, but much worse is to hurt someone who not only suffers but also gets a jury award of $100,000.

Most Americans now have insurance to cover *hospital* bills and often some of the doctors' charges. One difficulty in providing this type of insurance has been the control of costs. Few of us will commit suicide, or burn down our house, for the insurance. But if we have medical insurance, we may go to the hospital oftener, stay longer, and call the doctor more than if we were not protected. Moreover, the doctor may charge a little more if he knows an insurance company will pay. A much needed development is "medical disaster" insurance for the operations, accidents, and other cases whose costs can run into thousands of dollars; policies cover 80 per cent (or even more) of the costs above other insurance and $100 or so.

Increasingly, families insure against *personal liability:* your dog bites the neighbor, the handyman slips from your ladder, or your golf ball hits the duffer ahead and keeps him from work for a month. The loss may be large enough to bring great financial hardship unless covered by insurance.

In addition to the types of insurance mentioned so far, most families are also protected by "social insurance," a group of programs discussed in the next chapter.

TERMS AND CONCEPTS		
real income	FDA	term insurance
sample survey	National Bureau of	endowment policy
branding	Standards	deceptive pricing
Consumer's Union	truth-in-lending	grading

QUESTIONS

1. In what sense does our real income depend upon skill in purchasing? Compared with, say, 1900, how has the consumer's problem of intelligent choice become more difficult? Easier?

2. What would you consider appropriate local, state, and federal government aid to consumers in getting good value?

3. Must the cost of life insurance rise as one gets older? Why?

4. "By and large the consumer gets what he pays for." Discuss. What evidence would be needed to prove or disprove this assertion?

5. Analyze the appeal of 5 different advertisements. How useful is such advertising? Why do leading professional associations prohibit their members from advertising?

6. Get from a brokerage firm a sample of the information made available to buyers of stock.

7. "The consumer's best ally in the battle for good value is the buyer of the big merchandising organizations." In what sense do you think this statement is true?

8. Why do you suppose that our national government spends less each year in direct aids to consumer buying than many businesses spend on advertising? Investigate the work of the Food and Drug Administration and the Federal Trade Commission in aiding consumers.

9. "Our rising standard of living complicates our problems of buying to best advantage." Explain.

10. Insurance companies devote considerable effort to preventing losses. Find examples.

PART 6

GOVERNMENT FINANCE

The people of the United States now spend through government as much as they spend for food, clothing, and shelter. If one looks for a "growth industry," government certainly qualifies. Per capita government spending in 1968 will be over $1,200. For a family of five the average would then be over $6,000. Is this not big money?

The many problems blend economics and politics, and the aspects which are the more purely economic touch upon many different branches of economics. The biggest buyer, employer, borrower, lender, and giver in the country is the federal government. State and local governments, however, employ many more people and have been increasing their buying of non-defense goods and services more rapidly in recent years than has Uncle Sam.

29

SOCIAL INSURANCE: DEALING WITH POVERTY

In arriving at a concept of poverty and in prescribing solutions, it should be recognized that poverty in the United States involves specific people, families, and groups and is not a mass phenomenon.

A clear distinction should be made between those poor who are outside the productive life of the economy and those who are poor despite their ability to participate in the labor force.

All programs to alleviate poverty, except those whose success has been tested by trial and experience, should be designed and carried out in ways that make them adaptable to change as society improves its understanding of the problem.

Task Force on Economic Growth and Opportunity, Chamber of Commerce of the United States. (Three of the thirteen recommendations
of its first report, 1965.)

This chapter deals first with social insurance, then examines various private and governmental programs for meeting problems of human need, and concludes with discussion of the more recently instituted antipoverty programs.

SOCIAL INSURANCE

In the freest and best of markets some human beings would be unable to provide for themselves. Our humanitarian urges lead us to try to reduce the evils of poverty. Moreover, the market is subject to constant changes, bringing good fortune to some and distress to others, quite without individual desert. Some personal insecurity is a cost of life in a progressive, interdependent economy. The risks are part of the price of freedom with its personal and economic values. The economy as a whole can appropriately be charged with at least some of the losses falling on individuals.

683

The figures on income distribution in Chapter 22 include some of the result of nonmarket forces, notably *transfer payments* made through government. They bolster income at the poverty end of the income scale, while costing the taxpayer no small amount—$45 billion or so a year, depending on the precise programs included. Accomplishments we now take for granted seemed impossible a generation ago. But pressures to do more continue.

Workmen's Compensation. Accidents on the job may crush not only a man's leg or chest but also his family's finances. Medical expenses pile up just when income disappears. Years of savings melt away in a few weeks.

As industrialism developed, there was wide dispute about how much of the cost of on-the-job accidents should be charged to business and how much should be the employee's own burden. The common-law principle grew out of conditions of a simple society. An employer who met certain elastic standards of "reasonable care" was held to be without fault. In any case, the injured workman, to collect damages, had to bring suit against the employer, who could fall back upon three defenses: the contributory negligence of the employee, the negligence of another employee, and the fact that the employee, in taking the job, assumed its risks. To sue was time-consuming and expensive. Injured workers seldom got more than a small fraction of the equivalent of what they lost.

Spectacular changes came when states, beginning in 1911, compelled employers to pay compensation on a new basis, which generally required insurance. Costs became part of the normal expense of doing business; benefits were made definite. An employer must now generally insure with a private company or a state fund, or satisfy the state of his financial responsibility, giving a bond or other security. Total costs were about $2.5 billion in 1967.[1] Most benefit scales are set by law—so much for loss of an eye or a cut that keeps a person out of work a month. The benefit is usually related to the employee's wage—around half the average take-home pay—with a maximum period (10 years or so) or total amount; at least partial medical expense is now customary and, occasionally, some aid for rehabilitation and death benefits to survivors. Disease resulting from the occupation is often covered. Payments come as a matter of right upon proof that the injury (or disease) resulted from a hazard of employment and, usually, while on the job. Some malingering, unfortunately, escapes the administrators; employees are not always so badly hurt as they pre-

---

[1] During 1962 and 1963 benefit scales were increased in 25 states, while 14 more extended coverage or liberalized benefits in other ways. Generally, workers not covered work in agriculture, domestic service, and for firms with only two or three employees. For the country as a whole, costs are around 1 percent of the payroll of employees covered. The insurance rate commonly depends upon the employer's loss payments, or those of his industry, or both. For a compact summary, see Chamber of Commerce of the United States, *Analysis of Workmen's Compensation Laws* (Washington, D.C.: The Chamber, 1964).

tend, and doctors may make an extra call or two for an easy (though low) fee.

Prevention is better than cure plus dollar compensation. Steps for prevention have gone along with insurance. Governments at all levels have passed (and to a varying degree have enforced) laws designed to prevent accidents and disease. Insurance companies, employers, labor unions, and other groups have aided the study of how to prevent accidents and occupational disease, and press for use of the best methods.

The costs of accidents are still greater than inherently necessary. Some of the blame lies with ignorance and carelessness on the part of employees (goggles must be over the eyes rather than over the forehead to provide effective protection) and supervisors. Another reason is that employers, inventors, and designers of equipment have not exhausted the reasonable possibilities of developing and installing injury-prevention devices.

Old Age, Survivors, and Disability Insurance. For most of us, happily, old age is almost a certainty. The ability and the desire to earn a living in old age, however, are less certain. And who does not find repugnant the thought of being destitute or dependent financially upon one's children (just when their own financial needs are likely to be pressing)?

Coverage and Tax. Most people, of course, do save something for retirement, and business pension plans have grown rapidly.[2] For millions, however, a compulsory system, the Old Age, Survivors, and Disability Insurance program (OASDI), is a mainstay of hopes for retirement income. Almost everyone who works for someone else is now *covered*.[3] People who work for themselves are also covered.

When a person receives his first job in covered employment, he gets a social security number. The federal government maintains a separate account for each of more than 115 millions persons.

The 1968 tax was 8.8 percent of wages up to $7,800 a year (a maximum of $686), half from the worker and half imposed on the employer. Economic analysis indicates that, in general, the portion billed to the employer will in effect reduce the wage he would otherwise pay the employee, but to the extent that the employer's tax is a cost of doing business not reflected in lower wages, it is an expense which over the long

[2] Private pension plans do not generally vest claims to benefits except after several years of service and on a gradual basis over, perhaps, the last half of the working life. In other words, the employee does not have firm assurance that he will receive a pension. If he changes jobs or gets discharged, or if the employer goes out of business entirely or closes down a plant, the worker may lose all his pension rights. What he had been led to believe would be, say, $200 a month during retirement may be nothing at all. Or he may receive much less than he had expected.

[3] Railroad employees have a special system for retirement, disability, and unemployment. Federal, state, and local governments generally have pension systems, but many state-local plans have been modified to fit in with OASDI.

run consumers must bear. With either incidence of the tax, but more so in the first, the total cost will be upon the working population roughly in proportion to earnings up to $7,800. The self-employed pay all of their own tax, but their tax is only three fourths of what an employer and they as an employee would pay. Tax rates are scheduled to rise over 10 percent (plus 1.8 percent for Medicare), and Congress will probably raise the amount of annual earnings taxed (continuing the trend upward from $3,000 in 1950). The maximum tax in 1965 was $348. By 1968 the figure had almost doubled and will reach $881 in 1973, to go still higher under present law.

Benefits.   The **benefit structure** has become increasingly complex. No brief summary can be complete. A person who retires at age 65 or later whose earnings after 1950 averaged $400 a month gets $154 a month or $230 if his wife is over 65. If retirement is at age 62, 63, or 64, the monthly benefit is reduced. If earnings had averaged $200 a month before retirement at age 65, the couple receive $152; if earnings had been 3 times as much, $600 a month or more, their benefit is only double, $306 a month. The benefit is increased if there is a child under 18. The monthly minimum for a retired person or a dependent became $55 in 1968. There is no compulsion to retire, but a person loses the benefit each month that he is not retired. A person under 72 can earn up to $1,680 a year and continue to receive full benefits. Additional earnings reduce the benefit, 50 cents per dollar on $1,200, then dollar for dollar. After age 72, however, a person may earn any amount without sacrificing his monthly income.

The system also provides highly valuable benefits for survivors if a covered worker dies. Widows and dependent children and parents also get monthly benefits. (A widow with two dependent children whose husband had had average earnings of $500 a month would get $375 a month.) Buying equivalent private insurance would drain many dollars from the family budget. Furthermore, a worker suffering certain physical or mental disabilities gets benefits. A lump-sum death payment of $255 presumably allows for burial expenses. Benefit payments are exempt from income tax. Early in 1968, almost 22 million were receiving OASDI checks for retirement and 2.2 million for disability. Most checks were between $85 and $110, but will go up as the retired group includes more workers who have had more years of earnings at the higher levels of the last decade.

Equity (Insurance) Compared with Welfare Principle.   Benefits depart from what is called the "individual equity," or insurance, principle. Under it, as in private insurance and pension systems, the benefits would be about what each person (or group of persons in similar earnings, age, and perhaps other circumstances) had paid for. The trend of recent laws has been to give relatively bigger benefit increases to pensioners with low earnings histories. Benefits, therefore, are adjusted somewhat according to a sense of what people "ought" to have rather than in proportion to what each wage group has contributed. Moves toward "social adequacy" thus replace the *quid pro quo* or equity principle of a close relation between what a person pays and what he gets. Income redistribution—in a sense even a "public welfare" element—enters. Yet benefit scales are not tied closely to need; since other retirement income is not taken into account, rich as well as poor can get the same amounts.

The basic benefit (without allowance for marital status) is about 65 percent of the first $100 a month of earnings, 45 percent of the next $100 and 31 percent of the last $100 of taxable wage. But everyone now (1968) drawing benefits gets a lot more than the total of the taxes he paid plus those paid by his employer on his earnings plus allowance for compound interest. As the law stood in 1967, persons who had been covered from the beginning of the program in 1937 and retiring in the late 1960's would get benefits frequently four to seven times higher than the full payment made on their account (including the employer portion of the tax). Many millions who were brought into the system later, for example in the 1950's, and who have qualified for retirement benefits after relatively few quarters of work requiring payment of tax, get benefits which are very much bigger multiples of the tax than what they have paid.[4]

One who does not believe in Santa Claus will ask: "Who pays?" Most people who have been paying payroll tax have not begun to draw their benefits. The rights that have accrued are very much greater than the taxes that have been paid. Suppose you agreed to accept $1 a week for a year from a friend and then to pay him $100 at the end of the year. For 51 weeks, you would have more and more dollars, then——! In a sense, this is what OASDI does, except that the dollars being collected for more than 80 million workers in a year are being used to pay benefits to 22 million—a ratio of about 4 to 1.

Total annual benefits almost equal tax collections plus interest on a trust fund of $21 billion built up in the past. Payroll taxes are now much heavier than in the past. They must go still higher to keep the system on its "pay as we go" basis. But there are questions about how much taxes must go up. No one can be sure just how extensively people will seek retirement as early as they can qualify for benefits—or how long they will live.

To qualify for the present levels of benefits, young people now entering the labor force will pay many times as much in taxes as did their

---

[4] Tax Foundation, Inc., *Economic Aspects of the Social Security Tax* (New York: The Foundation, 1967), chap. V. For any person or group, the estimates of benefits in relation to tax must rest on several assumptions. The combination of assumptions chosen can lead to significant differences in conclusions. For a worker retiring in 1967 who had paid taxes on three fourths of the maximum earnings base for 30 years, his and his employer's tax paid (plus interest) would have been $3,947. He and his wife would be eligible for a pension of $2,023 a year; the present actuarial value for their remaining lives would be $22,000. The benefits were raised further in 1968.

fathers on similar earnings. On the basis of reasonable assumptions about interest rates and the worth of the disability and other benefits not strictly for the retirement pension, many of today's young workers will, it is said, be shortchanged. Some unquestionably stand to get less under present law than they could obtain from putting the same amounts as they will pay in tax (including the employer's tax) into plans offered by private insurance companies. A young person starting to work in 1967 after graduating from college at age 22 and earning $6,600 for 43 years would (with his employer) pay OASDI taxes of about $28,000; compound interest at 4 percent would be around $42,000. Assume that 20 percent of total cost was for disability insurance protection. Then he pays $56,000 for retirement alone. The pension of $3,420 a year for himself and wife would be worth $37,000.[5] Private insurance companies would offer a better deal for him because he would not be required, in effect, to pay part of the cost of benefits to persons with lower earnings. Perhaps, however, Congress will continue to raise the benefit scale so that today's younger people as they get older, will in effect, gain at the expense of those who are then the younger generation.

Portability of Benefits. Benefits are received without any "strings" if one meets the conditions specified. Unlike many pension systems of private and government employers, the benefits are "portable," independent of the employer. A worker may move from firm to firm without any effect on his OASDI benefits. Moreover, a person is free to save privately for retirement without endangering his benefit as he might under a system based on need.

As one looks at living costs, the benefits are hardly munificent. Yet if one looks at what used to be—nothing—and what today's recipients of pensions have paid toward the cost, the benefits are impressive. Congress seems almost to have formed a habit of voting increased benefits just before each congressional election. One reason is to offset the effects of inflation. Total costs get higher, of course.

Issues of Public Policy. Large issues of public policy arise over such questions as "How much reliance can be placed on compulsion in financing retirement?" "Should the redistributive (welfare) elements be enlarged at the sacrifice of the equity (insurance) element?" "Are younger workers really being discriminated against?" "Can we wisely use any bigger fraction of our ability to pay taxes for the finance of transfer expenditures, payments for which no productive services are provided?"

As time passes, more people will receive benefits and thus have economic power to consume without producing. Would accumulating a

---

[5] The estimates make rough allowance for changes enacted in 1968. Medicare taxes and benefits are not included.

reserve help prepare the economy for this certainty? Building up such a fund, in effect, would be compulsory saving. Fundamentally, the reserve's usefulness in the long run would depend largely upon whether it leads to more capital formation. If it does, society can then produce more easily and thus be better able to bear the real cost—provide the output needed to support people not working.

Private pension plans do accumulate capital, but a governmental system can rely upon the power to tax. Our system no longer pretends, as it did for some years, to operate on the implied assumption that a worker is setting aside funds to pay for *his* own benefit. His dollars go to pay benefits for persons retired now; eventually, he will get a claim on taxpaying workers in the future, not on a fund of productive wealth.

Medicare. Medical care for the aged presents a huge problem. More and more older people are living longer and longer. They need considerably more medical and nursing care than does the typical person under age 60 or so, often very much more. Age tends to reduce the body's ability to recover quickly; among older groups, chronic illness occurs more often, tragically serious illness strikes more frequently. The cost of reasonably adequate treatment tends to be large, too often staggeringly so, in relation to the individual's income from all sources, including savings built up in the past, contributions from the family, and receipts from private health and hospital insurance.

After years of debate about extending social insurance to medical care for the aged, *Medicare* went into effect in 1966. The benefit system has too many features to detail here. The major element, however, is the right of a person aged 65 or over to the cost of 60 days in a hospital plus much of the cost of hospital or nursing home care afterward. The patient must pay $40 of the cost for 60 days and then $10 a day after 60 days. Total costs in 1968 were at an annual rate of around $3 billion. Who bears the expense? For all workers covered by OASDI there is a tax of 1 percent of earnings up to $7,800 (half on the employer). For example, for each person getting paid $6,000 a year, $60 becomes available to pay the costs of hospital benefits for the aged.

In addition, persons over 65 who agree, as most have, to pay $3 a month get additional insurance; the U.S. Treasury, the general body of taxpayers, bears an equal amount of cost. (The $1.3 billion budgeted for 1968 will not be adequate for later years.) The insurance will supplement the compulsory benefits of hospital service by paying for 80 percent of fees of physicians and surgeons (over $50) plus a large fraction of the cost of health services in the home and for some dressings and equipment.

As had been expected, when more older persons became financially able to seek more hospital and other medical services, the pressures on facilities became intense. How many years will be needed to add the doctors, nurses, and other personnel—as well as nursing homes and hospitals—for reasonable adequacy? No one yet knows. But one thing *is* clear. The money cost will be higher than can be paid for by present taxes plus insurance premiums.

Unemployment Benefits.   In the 1930's, it was glaringly obvious that unemployment was not solely the result of individual shiftlessness. In fact, most unemployment was clearly due to broad economic forces. New Deal leadership insisted that society as a whole should provide at least a partial remedy.

Actually, there is a separate system for each state. Congress, in effect, forced the states to set up unemployment benefit systems and prescribed general conditions that had to be met; yet it left each state considerable freedom to adjust details. Compulsion worked as follows: Congress imposed a tax of 3 percent upon broad groups of employers, giving nothing in return. However, if states would establish unemployment insurance plans which met certain terms, nine tenths of the tax would be paid directly to a state fund for unemployment benefits. A state's employers would gain absolutely no benefit if the state did not have a plan, and its employees would lose the chance to receive benefits.

The tax falls on the employer alone (except in Alabama, Alaska, and New Jersey). The state tax rates average somewhat over 2 percent of the covered payroll—$3,000 to $4,000 or so a year per employee. The federal government collects 0.4 percent to pay costs of administration. Coverage is not so broad as for OASDI; several states exempt firms with fewer than four employees and some other groups.

After a few weeks of employment, a person is eligible for benefits 1 week, ordinarily, after being laid off. He must register with the official employment agency, which will refer him to "suitable" jobs if it knows of any. In fact, he will have considerable freedom to reject job offers without disqualifying himself. The weekly check cannot pay for much riotous living, but it does help prevent destitution. The one million or so people a month receiving benefits during the prosperous period of mid-1967 got on the average around $40 a week, with a range generally from about $35 to $45, varying from state to state and adjusted somewhat for the amount the person had been earning. The person gets checks from 5 to 6 months, or until the person gets work. There is considerable diversity in state rules about paying benefits to people out on strike or to those who refuse jobs. The effectiveness of administration also varies, especially in putting the unemployed in touch with employers who have unfilled jobs.

There is abuse. Where earnings from work are low or leisure attractive, the benefits ("rocking chair" or "fishing" money) may seem better than work. Seasonal workers and family employees in small businesses may abuse the system. Women who work 20 weeks a year in New York's canning industry, for example, can receive 26 weeks of benefits. A disproportionate amount of the total aid seems to go to seasonal workers who never expect jobs around the year. Administration has suffered from lack of funds. Moreover, the employment services have not been adequately financed to help get the right person in contact with one of the many job openings often available.

Conflict of objectives is obvious. If benefits are high enough to provide what seems desirable on humane grounds, they are likely to increase the temptation to abuse. If they are large enough to support purchasing power on a fairly high level, to combat recession, they will be not only costly but perhaps high enough to discourage initiative. If we have an automatic system, cheap to administer and not based on need, we must expert maddening crudities.

"Experience" or "merit" rating exists in all states. The principle is illustrated by one of several forms: Each employer's record is kept separate; the tax he pays is compared with benefits given his workers when they are unemployed. If his taxes build up a certain amount over the benefits, he is deemed to have a reserve; his tax rate then drops greatly as long as the favorable balance is maintained. Consequently, firms with stable employment pay much lower taxes over the years than those with fluctuating employment. The employer has an incentive to stabilize, and like other insurance, the good risks have the low rates. (But do they do their proper share in helping meet a broad social cost?) Moreover, the employer has an incentive to help prevent unjustified claims; Michigan once credited employers with discovering 85 percent of potential fraud cases. In some states, all employers must occasionally pay additional taxes to build a general state reserve.

As with so many programs, change has been slower than desired by some influential groups. States have liberalized benefit scales. But have they done enough? President Johnson has advocated substantial modifications to raise benefits and relax standards. Congress, however, reacting to opposition of employers who object to higher taxes, and who point to examples of abuse under existing rules, had not by early 1968 voted for large change.

SYSTEMATIC PROVISION FOR THE NEEDY: PHILANTHROPY

Private charity has played a valuable role in alleviating want throughout history. Local and state governments, too, have long assumed some responsibility for helping the very poor. In the 1930's, however, state-local efforts, together with those of private charity, were grossly inadequate. Washington stepped in and established a permanent system of aid for some groups of the needy. States and localities, however, still have heavy responsibility.

Income Maintenance Programs. The best-known government programs are designed to maintain, or at least provide, income. Washington, in effect, says to the states: "For every dollar you will put up to help four groups—your aged, children in poor families without a father or where the father is unemployed (ADC, Aid for Dependent Children), poor blind, and the totally and permanently disabled—Uncle Sam will give you a dollar or more, within limits." The average payment for the aged in 1968 was about $70 a month per person. Washington pays some of the costs of administration, and members of the staff of the Department of Health, Education, and Welfare see that federal grant funds are used as intended. States retain a large measure of freedom, however, and few take full advantage of the federal offers—tax money is too hard to get.

This aid is relief or welfare, for recipients must meet a "means test," i.e., prove need to receive the benefit. They do not work for the funds, and what they receive depends upon the judgment of officials. Aid may be adjusted to the needs of particular cases; it can be given in addition to other income.

When voting for medicare, Congress with rather little debate also provided for *Medicaid*, a program with unexpectedly great potentials. The federal government agrees to shoulder much of the cost of existing and expanded state-local programs of medical aid to lower income groups, including those somewhat above the income levels qualifying for relief aid (public assistance). Each state has considerable freedom in setting up a program. In most cases getting anything approaching the full financing offered by Uncle Sam will require state-local governments to increase their own funds for the "medically indigent." The total governmental financing for medical services will therefore rise markedly in the next few years—adding pressures on the health professions, hospitals, nursing homes, and all parts of the supply of health services.

Recently there has been evidence of public concern over apparent abuse of benefits. Cannot more recipients be provided with some work? Why does the number of dependent children rise when income per person moves up? In 1967, while liberalizing benefits, Congress decided on several changes. Some are highly controversial even though designed to answer the growing complaints about the apparently endless increase in the number of claimants for benefits. One change would require states to set up better work-training facilities and make greater effort to see that recipients of aid over age 16 who are able to do so make a serious effort to become more nearly self-supporting. More day-care facilities are to become available to help mothers who seek jobs. Aid for dependent children can be provided when a parent is present in the home but unemployed (reducing the incentive of fathers to desert). Another group of changes was designed to reduce the growth of illegitimacy by, among other things, making birth control information more accessible. One change was in response to an old criticism of the system: Persons on relief would be permitted to earn some income ($30 a month in general) without having their welfare payments reduced dollar for dollar (abolishing what had been called the "100 percent tax" on a poor person who made an effort on his own behalf). More funds were also made available for training social workers.

State and local governments, from their own funds, provide varying amounts of assistance to the poor. The federal government gives no cash aid for welfare that does not fall in one of the four categories. Millions also receive foodstuffs at a discount.

Compared with the early 1930's, relief is now fairly orderly and well developed. In 1967, 1.2 million families with 3.7 million children were getting about $147 a month each. Nearly 675,000 other families or individuals on relief got a monthly average of $38, plus some financing of medical care.

Some elements of the story are familiar: not enough funds for first-class administration, benefit that often fails to pay for a humane minimum standard of health and decency, and wide variation from place to place. Professionally trained social workers with moderate case loads are essential, not only to prevent cheating but, far more important, to help make aid constructive. Good social work requires trained staffs. Ahead lie immense opportunities for better, more creative, accomplishment by extensive use of the best of modern social work methods.

Maternal and Child Health and Child Welfare. Special services for mothers and children are encouraged by federal grants to states which have plans meeting certain requirements. Emphasis is on health services, such as prenatal clinics, immunization, and dental examinations; but many other services are also aided: foster-home placement, mental hygiene clinics, prevention of juvenile delinquency, help for crippled children, and special aid for mentally retarded children. These programs are in the process of expansion, in some cases being coordinated more closely with one or more of the many other governmental programs serving related objectives.

Private Philanthropy. The growth of government aid for the needy, with its welcome accomplishments, must not blind us to the vital role of private philanthropy. In providing even basic economic relief, private agencies still do much. The unique function of private agencies, however, lies more in the provision for unusual needs. Individuals or families, poor and not so poor, run into a host of problems for which neither government relief agencies nor the market provide a decent answer. The exceptional case likely requires special funds and human guidance which governments rarely provide; private agencies do help.

The college student paying less than the cost of his education, the bewildered child at the Travelers' Aid booth, the retired man getting inexpensive help from Legal Aid, the victim of a flood disaster helped by

Red Cross, the millions whose lives are enriched by churches—such examples hardly begin to suggest the extent to which we benefit from services paid for more or less by others.

These cases have another characteristic. The beneficiaries are not necessarily poor. Our civilization rests more than we may appreciate upon the voluntary provision of funds, time, and effort for a huge variety of services. All of us, rich and poor, benefit. Whether or not we pull our own weight, we should recognize an obligation. Perhaps there is truth in the steel company president's statement that no technical achievement can match the Community Chest as a contributor to our society.

A NEW ATTACK ON POVERTY: ECONOMIC OPPORTUNITY PROGRAMS

As shown by the two quotations which opened Chapter 22, presidents from both parties in times of high prosperity have urged measures to accelerate the process of reducing poverty. Because the problems are so complex, the aspirations of men of good will cannot be met by any simple action. Nor can good will suffice. Success also requires knowledge of the effectiveness of possible measures—then the action to carry them out.

Programs which get their original popular support as means of reducing poverty can, before long, get diverted. Farm aid, for example, costs billions each year but provides very little for truly poor farmers. Area redevelopment was advocated as a means of concentrating federal help in a few dozen areas of chronic economic distress, but to gain votes in Congress, the criteria for receiving such aid were made so generous that over 1,000 areas qualified at one time, largely destroying the original concept. Large amounts are paid each year in unemployment benefits, but the aid is spread so broadly that it cannot meet what might be held the humanitarian objectives—helping most those whose needs are greatest.

The biggest single aid to raising low incomes has been an increase in job opportunities. Many of the poor, however, have been helped only a little, or not at all—for example, those too old to work. Others are not able to support their families above the povery level even when the demand for labor booms. Immobility, especially of the rural poor, prevents some from taking advantage of distant job openings, at least for a time. Moreover, deficiencies in education, training, and health—and attitude—keep productive capabilities low, accounting for part of the "hard core" of poverty.

Efforts to remedy the many defects have been made throughout the economy, year after year, by business, government, and philanthropy. A new determination appeared early in the 1960's, and federal action increased on several fronts. Then in 1964, Congress enacted provisions for a program popularly called the "war on poverty," formally termed The Economic Opportunity Act (EOA). With later amendments, it consists of several elements. They focus not on amelioration or alleviation of need but on prevention over the longer run.

The EOA provided for some new programs and brought together a number which had previously been considered as separate entities. Thus, a proposal to create an away-from-home education and job-training center for disadvantaged youths was enacted as the Job Corps program. Plans for a domestic version of the overseas Peace Corps were brought to fruition in the portion of the EOA establishing the Volunteers in Service to America (VISTA) program. In addition, the EOA provided an essentially new approach to the problem of helping the poor to help themselves by authorizing the setting up—with funds largely from federal sources—of local community action agencies in which representatives of the poor themselves participate. Some 1,100 of these local groups were functioning in 1967. Figure 29-1 shows the relations among the many parts.

FIGURE 29-1.   Antipoverty Programs

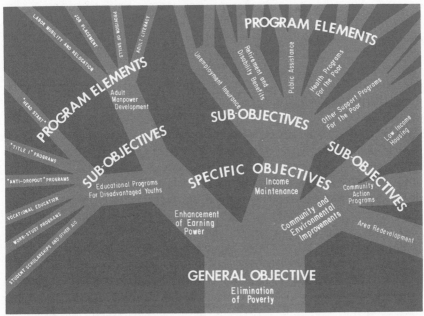

Source: National Industrial Conference Board, The Federal Budget: Its Impact on the Economy (New York, 1967), p. 27. Used with permission.

In the short time during which the various programs—several admittedly experimental—have been in operation, they have been the object of widespread popular attention. It is obviously too soon to judge the full effectiveness of the many parts. We certainly cannot yet determine the value of the total program in removing the root causes of poverty.

Headstart, operated by local community action agencies, seeks to offset the educational and cultural disadvantages of adverse home conditions for preschool age children. The goal is to increase the chances for benefiting from formal education later. Around 550,000 children participated in the summer of 1967. Though years will be required to test results adequately, Headstart seems to have met with considerable approval.

The same appears to be the case in regard to the Neighborhood Youth Corps (NYC). The Corps works with disadvantaged youths—around 300,000 in 1967—who continue to live at home. Stated objectives are to help young persons remain in school by providing part-time employment or by means of a full-time work program to assist dropouts and others. As the program developed, a third component—provision of summer jobs—was added.

The Jobs Corps, on the other hand, has come in for much adverse criticism. Each year it seeks to provide basic education and job training for about 40,000 "hard-core" poor youths in training centers away from home. Unfavorable publicity has resulted from alleged shortcomings in program content, delinquent actions by some Job Corpsmen, and high average costs. Inherently, the task is exceptionally difficult. The basis of selection of the young men and women—the very purpose of the program—assures that the job to be done is quite unlike that of typical educational or job-training programs. The groups consist largely of persons with very poor job experience (or none at all), bad educational records, attitudes not generally those associated with success in this country, and so on. At least some of the early difficulties appear to have been largely overcome as the program has "shaken down" with experience. Business firms operate several of the more successful training centers.

Community action groups have taken several forms and have devoted themselves to a broad range of goals; the groups differ, as was intended, according to local conditions. Some have succeeded in enlisting support from a variety of sources for dealing with local problems. By trying to "involve" the poor in new kinds of actions, some local groups have been severely criticized for arousing expectations which are unrealistically high, for ignoring established procedures and thus hampering existing private and governmental activities, for injecting forces of discontent and disruption into community life, and even for encouraging disorders in some urban centers. Other local groups, however, have been praised for heading off disturbances and for dampening social unrest and dissatisfaction among urban poor. Admittedly experimental, many of the individual projects undertaken in the new attack on poverty will not be successful. Careful examination will be required to eliminate features which accomplish little (in relation to cost). As time passes, we should gain greater knowledge about where the best opportunities lie.

The various EOA programs come under intense congressional scrutiny almost every year when they are seeking funds. Pressures for improvement certainly result. Hopes were originally too ambitious. Use of the term "war on poverty" gave an exaggerated notion of the dollars—and the real resources—which would and could be made available. The funds provided have been far less than the many billions going for other income maintenance, training, and social insurance programs. The amounts fall much below what the sponsors believe necessary for effective operation on a scale appropriate to the needs.

Administrative problems have been great. Leadership needs have exceeded the supply of qualified personnel. What would one expect in trying to implement "innovative" programs which attempt to experiment, to do many new things in meeting problems which had long resisted rapid and substantial improvement? Costs have often been high in relation to constructive accomplishment, or so it seems. But identifiable benefits are now often cited. The Office of Economic Opportunity makes sustained efforts to evaluate its own accomplishments. Yet some of the most significant results (good but in some cases also unwelcome) may be intangible—work attitudes, ability to read, wider awareness of realities in slum areas.

Economic analysis leaves no doubt that the difficulties to be overcome will depend in part upon the height of minimum wage rates. The number of jobs for persons of low skills in the private economy will be affected by the level of, and changes in, costs to the employer. The unhappy results of recent experience are suggested by Figure 29–2.

FIGURE 29–2. Unemployment Rates, Teenagers (White and Nonwhite), Men (White and Nonwhite), and Women

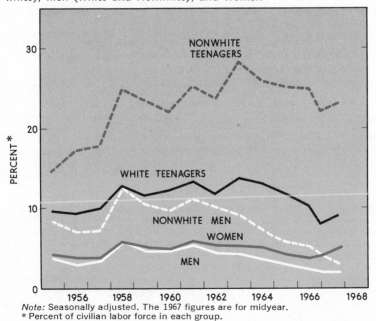

Note: Seasonally adjusted. The 1967 figures are for midyear.
* Percent of civilian labor force in each group.
Source: Department of Labor.

GUARANTEED MINIMUM INCOME: NEGATIVE INCOME TAX

If people are poor, is not the logical answer more funds? This country now spends tens of billions a year on programs whose purpose seems to be largely, or entirely, to aid persons with low incomes. Rearrangement of the payments on a more systematic basis might permit more humane and efficient accomplishment. One suggestion has been a "negative income tax," or some form of guaranteed minimum income. Proposals differ tremendously, however. Some would greatly increase total amounts while others would emphasize rational allocation.

The negative income tax approach is advanced, with good reason, as a promising method of utilizing an existing administrative system and concepts for new purposes—paying out money on a progressive basis according to need, the reversal of the basis for figuring tax. A person or family with income as measured for income tax purposes below some level, say $700 a person, would *receive* dollars. The lower the income, the greater the amount received. According to some proposals, such aid would replace much of the existing types. Social workers, it is believed, would be freed of much of their present more routine and "policing" responsibilities and thus have more time for helping solve the special problems of particular individuals. To prevent bad effects on work incentives, the scale of aid would be adjusted so that when a person worked he would not lose a dollar of aid for a dollar of earnings. In principle, a plan which would replace much of the existing and highly complex arrangements would seem to make good sense. The practical problems, however, would not be small.

How Much Government Provision?   The accomplishments of public and private programs are substantial. So are the costs. One's answer to the question "Should government programs be enlarged and new ones added?" will likely depend upon whether one focuses on benefits or on costs. The social worker and the tax economist may have rather different attitudes. Seldom can we expect to be able to measure cost against gain. There are gaps in the present system, and there are many places where larger payments would accomplish good things, things our sense of humanity impels us to want. As national income rises, the need for compulsory plans presumably falls.[6]

[6] A British economist, writing as a Liberal, after pointing out that redistribution is not the primary function of the social insurance system, concludes, ". . . the justification of the Welfare State is based on one of two main grounds: the necessity for paternalism because people in the main cannot look after themselves, or the necessity for nationalized social services because nationalization is the most efficient way of providing the services. . . . Must it be assumed, for example, that because a relatively small proportion of the community may suffer because of personal misfortune or fecklessness, we must have a gigantic pensions scheme for all so that we can avoid operating a means test for a few? . . . *The true object of the Welfare State, for the Liberal, is to teach people how to do without it.*" Alan Peacock, *The Welfare Society* (London: The Liberal Publication Department, 1960), p. 11.

The inevitable growth in the number of old persons, for example, may present a very difficult economic problem. Yet it may not, because improving levels of health combined with an opportunity to work may permit many more of those over 65 to keep producing. Benefits from private plans will grow substantially.

Generally, social insurance programs transfer resources from persons who are working to others who are not. Most of us approve of this principle but often disagree about how much is best. Needs for welfare remain substantial. If we raise taxes, even as much as present plans require, those who work must carry a heavy burden. Fortunately, rising production may reduce the load while rising productivity will enable us to carry it more easily. Research may reveal ways to reduce needs—how to cut the terrible drain of mental illness or how to use the family income with maximum effectiveness. New awareness of needs and opportunities will help in dealing with old and new problems. But Utopia does not lie just around the corner of this decade or the next.

TERMS AND CONCEPTS

OASDI	equity principle	Aid for Dependent Children
Medicare	contributory negligence	dren
workmen's compensation	payroll tax	War on Poverty
tion	social adequacy	OEO
merit rating	portability	Neighborhood Youth Corps
means test	Medicaid	Corps
VISTA	income maintenance	Job Corps
social worker	programs	negative income tax
Headstart		

QUESTIONS

1. In what respects does OASDI redistribute income?
2. What is the difference between the insurance and the welfare element in OASDI benefits?
3. How is unemployment insurance financed? What is the purpose and result of experience rating?
4. What are the major objectives of the new attack on poverty? The basic strategy?
5. What are the services in your community provided by privately financed philanthropic agencies?
6. How can OASDI benefits be changed to adjust for inflation? Who pays?
7. What will probably be the effects of extending the system of social insurance to cover medical costs?
8. Make a study of income maintenance programs in your community.
9. You are asked by your state legislature to report on unemployment benefits and taxes. What facts would you seek? What principles would guide your recommendations? Do the same for workmen's compensation.

30

GOVERNMENTAL FUNCTIONS AND SPENDING

In general, our national objectives would be best served by maximizing the area of individual choice. . . . Yet . . . certain government programs may contribute more to the general well-being than the private expenditures that have to be foregone—in this sense they are worth what they cost in taxes.

"Rockefeller Report" on the U.S. Economy

From birth (or before—the prenatal clinic) to death, from morning to night, things done by national, state, and local governments impinge upon us. And not only Americans are affected by our governmental policies because for years the future of mankind has hinged upon the defense spending of this country.

Disagreement about Scope of Government. The amount and purposes of government spending depend upon the answer to the question "What should we do through government?" Yet no free group of any great size can reach complete agreement on this subject. Only in part are the issues *economic*. Government finance inevitably involves the nature and function of government, questions of *political theory*. The latter go beyond the scope of economics; sincere and informed men differ widely. Some of us favor, others fear, big government. Such differences influence conclusions about issues which are more clearly economic, such as means of paying for college education.

A Reminder: Government Is People, Not Supermen. Government consists of people. When we speak of a "government" acting, we really

700

mean that certain people act. Government is not some superman, not an entity with knowledge and wisdom far surpassing that of individuals. We may personify government and unconsciously assume that it is some superhuman, monolithic, thinking, and acting being—perhaps a god, perhaps a devil. In essence, however, government is one way, one agency, by which human beings associate to work together. The people who act as government employees may or may not differ a little from the rest of us. The *organization* is unlike that of a business, a church, or a family.

How does the form of human association we call "government" differ from other forms? One distinction is that government is a legitimate agency for *coercing* people. Most associations for group action are voluntary: corporations, unions, clubs, churches. "Membership" in government, however, is compulsory. It enables some, presumably a majority of adult citizens who vote, to force everyone to do, or not to do, certain things. In every aspect of life, of course, forces we cannot control do hem us in. Who could conceive of unlimited freedom—in the family, on the job, as a consumer, in the classroom, on the playing field? Yet the compulsion forced on us by associations to which we belong more or less freely hardly matches the coercion which governments employ—military service, taxes, laws regulating our conduct—most of which we accept as a matter of course.

If our demand for something is great enough to make us willing to pay taxes to get it, why will it not be supplied in free markets? Why does the profit system seem inadequate as compared with one to be financed by taxes? We now try to answer these and related questions. Economists use somewhat different words and approaches in dealing with the same basic problem.

MAJOR FUNCTIONS OF GOVERNMENT: ECONOMIC ASPECTS OF SPENDING

Government can serve collective or social wants. There are some things which we desire as members of a group or can obtain only by concerted action. Some things cannot be divided into units for sale to (purchase by) individuals in the way that food and clothing are sold; the amount one person consumes does not reduce the amount available to others. Economists may speak of "public goods" in such cases or in referring to services needed to satisfy a few broad wants, notably security (national defense). There are not many really clear examples of pure public goods nor of a broader group termed "quasi-public goods"—except those in the first two categories below. Almost everything else which governments spend money to provide have counterparts and close substitutes in goods and services supplied in the private sector, perhaps by profit-motivated business, perhaps by philanthropy and nonprofit organizations. Clear lines can rarely be drawn.

Justice, Internal Order, and Regulation. We rely upon local, state, and the national government to provide a system of law, courts, and internal order. Obviously, the market system cannot provide such things well on the basis of free choice and sale at a price. "Justice" for sale is not justice. Moreover, everyone must "consume" a certain minimum of the fruits of a legal system and police protection if the group is to live happily, or even to survive. Such compulsion makes individual freedom possible; when government holds such power, individuals cannot use it privately. Only then do personal freedom and free markets become possible. Although they are vital, the provision of justice and internal order is not a major cost of government, except for localities; federal courts cost 45 cents a year per capita, the FBI 90 cents.

Sanitary, health, and much other regulation will also tend to fail unless compulsory and comprehensive. Even though cost per person may not be high, sale in the market with freedom not to accept would make no sense.[1] People cannot be left free to *exclude* themselves from either benefits or costs. Society has no effective means of getting the service—such as elimination of a source of infectious disease—while excluding from the benefits persons who would not choose to pay freely.

National Defense and Foreign Affairs. Only governments can adequately conduct diplomacy and organize the defense against outside enemies. The market system could not do the job on the basis of voluntary sale. People who decided not to buy would endanger and burden others. Most of us could not afford an atomic submarine, let alone a crew to use it. Individually, or as small groups, we could not conceivably decide what is best. Broad, collective interest is overwhelming. Large elements of coercion are essential, not only for fair distribution of cost but also for mobilizing all potential strength.

Education. Until recently, education was the most costly peacetime function of American governments. Why education? Is it more vital than food, clothing, or shelter? If it is so important, why do people resort to compulsion? Would they not voluntarily recognize the value and freely buy what they judge is worth the cost?

---

[1] *Fire protection* illustrates related considerations. Fire insurance companies once provided equipment to put out fires in the property of their policyholders. The inefficiency was obvious. Companies duplicated facilities. Buildings not insured got no protection, although, if they burned, neighbors as well as the owners would suffer. The community as a whole had an interest in fire protection everywhere, and the freedom of one man not to buy protection increased the cost to others. Moreover, charging for fire engines only when they are needed would hardly serve a useful economic purpose in the form of discouraging consumption; if there is a fire, it should be extinguished. A free market for fire protection, meaning freedom not to buy, actively endangers others. A unified system of both providing the service and forcing payment through taxes is logical.

Education differs from most things bought in the market. The potential consumer—the uneducated child—is incompetent to judge the value of the product (service) to him before he gets it. Judgment and experience are indispensable for good decisions, and force rather than persuasion is necessary when the consumer cannot decide wisely. Each human being, we feel, should have an opportunity for education, even if the parent may disagree. The lack of education does not create the kind of craving that induces even young children to demand food.

Although we get much education outside of schools, some kinds of education require systematic training (schooling). It produces results that are valuable for increasing the enjoyment of life, for enlarging a person's ability to do things which others want (his productivity), and for understanding society and the needs of citizenship. In the best sense, education is a liberating force which adds to chances for freedom; the use of compulsion to assure schooling enlarges freedom.

Formal education has exceptional value: The benefits of the use of resources in this way exceed the cost throughout a wide range. Some benefits, such as providing a basis for citizenship, are intangible and of a kind which the price system would not value highly enough. And does not everyone benefit from living in a community of educated people? A feeling that there is such benefit provides one reason why we require not only that a child attend school but also that the whole public help pay the cost. As members of the community, families without children of school age benefit from the education of the coming generation. The tax method of payment also provides a way to spread schooling costs over a lifetime rather than concentrating them in the years when children are in school.

Each of the arguments just made may be applied to uses of resources for purposes other than education. Yet the latter has characteristics which distinguish it from such other things as the provision of food, shelter, or medical care. At least a moderately good system of education can be provided without the use of a large fraction of total income; the necessary taxes do not need to be crushing. Moreover, we are free from a complication that often arises if the price system is not used to charge for a service: Consumption can be controlled by a simple form of "rationing"—limiting school hours and years. The absence of price as a factor restricting use is not critical.

Transportation.[2] Providing facilities for transportation presents considerations which differ somewhat from those cited for schooling. As our country was settled, the natural way to get roads was for farmers (and prisoners) to work on them because they had time, and to require every-

---

[2] The arguments in this section apply to some extent to communication. Our postal system, of course, is operated by government; unlike most countries, however, we rely upon privately owned but governmentally regulated facilities for telephone service.

one to do a part because of the obvious common interest. In towns the general interest in streets was so clear that government was a logical instrument for making everyone share the cost.

Productivity, we know, leans heavily upon the division of labor. Specialization requires exchange, and much specialization needs much exchange. Transportation is a cost of exchange; the lower the cost of transportation, the cheaper the exchange and the greater the possibilities of specialization. Within limits, then, developing transportation is a strategic way to improve the general welfare. The possibilities of effective monopoly are reduced. Opportunities for mobility increase. The benefits to the public as a whole are greater than the sum of what individuals would demand if they were required to pay a price for each use. Well beyond the "free market" margin, each dollar spent may bring the public more than a dollar's worth of benefit. Moreover, compulsion is necessary to build through other peoples' properties at a reasonable price and to develop an integrated system.[3] Defense needs also argue for good transport.

Other reasons support government financing of part of the expense of transportation. Some costs are largely fixed (overhead) and do not depend upon the amount of use. If a price or charge for each specific use was set to include an estimated amount for full cost, the charge would deter some users. The facilities would be used less fully, but little saving in real resources (costs) would result from the induced idleness (partial) of fixed facilities. Consequently, there would be a true net loss to the economy from the failure to use existing capacity more fully. By providing free use of the highways, etc., which will be in existence, the public can give itself more benefit than if a price were charged and use restricted.[4] Moreover, the actual process of charging for the use of streets and highways would itself be costly, and regulating a private owner would be at least a nuisance.

Relief and Social Insurance.   Government outlays for relief of the poor and for social insurance have grown tremendously—from $450 million in 1932 to perhaps $45 billion in 1968. Humanitarian feelings persuade, or compel, us to try to help people in need. We also desire to help preserve and raise productive capacity, to prevent the spread of disease, and to allay social discontent. Family help and voluntary philanthropy cannot always meet worthy human needs adequately. During certain periods of life—childhood and old age—persons are peculiarly handicapped in pro-

[3] The power of eminent domain can be given to private businesses, such as railroads, to compel private owners to sell property for use in the public interest.

[4] The conclusion applies only to the extent that (a) the fixed overhead would exist regardless of charge and (b) failure to impose a charge does not lead to traffic congestion which imposes social costs. These two requirements both involve aspects of the time period. For a week or month the proportion of total cost which is fixed is huge. When thinking of plans for the long run, however, all costs are variable, none are fixed. Similarly, patterns of travel change much less in response to charges in a week or so than over a period of years.

viding for themselves, so the absence of family support becomes especially unfortunate, even in a community with plenty of jobs. Illness and economic depression put self-dependence beyond the capacity of large numbers. And always there are human beings with low productivity. Finally, because some people cannot, and others will not, voluntarily provide for periods when they may be unemployed or retired (or without income for other reasons), compulsory systems of social insurance have been established.

Aid for Special Groups. Increasingly, the accepted scope of government spending seems to require one group to give something to another. If a group is not satisfied with the workings of the market—and who would not like more income?—then others seem "fair game." The problem is to muster enough votes. More than tiny amounts of government spending are explained by special-interest persuasion of the majority, or a more or less crude and even callous abuse of political power. Some of the policies, of course, may serve the general well-being in ways worth as much as they cost.

Control of the Level and Stability of Employment. National government, as we saw earlier, has responsibility for helping maintain a high level of employment; spending and taxation are directly involved.

How Much? Knowing that we should eat is a useful guide to action. Yet it does not tell us how much to eat. So, even though the public may agree to use political, rather than market, processes to do something, each case raises the question "How much?" Ordinarily, there will be little basis for determining whether a spending program should get a bit more or a bit less money. The benefit to be expected from carrying expenditure a little further cannot, in practice, be compared with the deprivation from the additional taxes needed. A new highway would give benefits; the new taxes to pay for it would be unpalatable. But which is greater? We can rarely be certain.

As government functions expand in number and in cost, new problems may be created, though not always recognized. The taxes needed to put a man on the moon or to build new river channels for barges, reduce our ability as consumers to provide for family needs or pay for schools; higher social security taxes to enlarge retirement benefits make it harder for families to save for emergencies. In other words, the fundamental problem of economic scarcity appears in new forms. Government's tool, *compulsion*, is not sharp enough to overcome limits growing out of basic economic forces. In looking at an attractive expenditure program, we have distressingly little ability to learn when the added costs become greater than added benefits.[5]

[5] Recognizing this problem, President Johnson in 1965 insisted that all federal agencies start to apply the Program, Planning, and Budgeting System. PPBS calls for

Other Criteria. If we shift from "kind of function" as a criterion for reliance on the governmental rather than the political process to either the "nature of political organization" or the "quality of personnel," we may find guidance for expenditure, but probably not much. For example, government is perpetual, but it is not the only form of perpetual organization—witness religious bodies and profitable corporations. Governments employ competent and incompetent people, but so do other employers. Governments are large and small. So are businesses. Comparative efficiency? Whatever the facts, there is seldom a serious claim that unusually high operating efficiency of governments makes government performance of a function desirable. Occasionally it is said that some projects are too big for private business. This argument must be used with caution. The Tennessee Valley Authority is a vast federal undertaking. Yet General Motors' tax bill alone has been more in *each* of several years than the whole capital investment in TVA through the first 18 years of its life. Business can operate on a big scale.

One feature of certain projects distinguishes them from most others. Some activities have more than small "neighborhood effects" (sometimes called "external effects" or "externalities"), good and bad. The result extend through much of the local community, the area, or the whole country. Flood control and recreation by-products of hydroelectric power projects offer examples. The effects, desirable and undesirable, are significant for people who are not parties to the transaction. If we leave to private business the performance of activities with desirable results of this type—good "third-party" consequences—then we cannot expect that enough will be done to serve either individual or collective wants adequately. A private firm cannot charge for the *full* value of all that it creates; our property law, therefore, does not permit a producer to possess all that results from his activities. However, the public acting as a whole, through government, may be able to take advantage of such opportunities if it knows the facts and acts on them—an "if" anything but small. The facts needed, of course, include those about the *full* effects of taxes or other revenues used to pay for the activity.

GROWTH OF GOVERNMENT SPENDING

Figure 30–1 summarizes the growth of government spending. The percentages of net national product are shown at the left; the dollar amounts appear above the bars.

The 1968 federal budget called for funds for 97 nondefense programs which had been *added* since 1960. Nondefense programs (other than

---

deliberate efforts to define precisely the purposes to be sought. Moreover, it asks that thinking be in terms of quantities, of the more and the less, so that priorities can be set in a rational way—and so that probable benefits can be compared with money costs. PPBS demands new skills and evidence. It can produce accomplishments only gradually.

FIGURE 30–1. Government Expenditures: Total and as a Percentage of Net National Product, 1902–67 (Money Amounts in Billions)

Expenditures include social insurance benefits and outlays of borrowed funds. Intergovernmental payments are counted only once, and utility and liquor store spending are excluded.

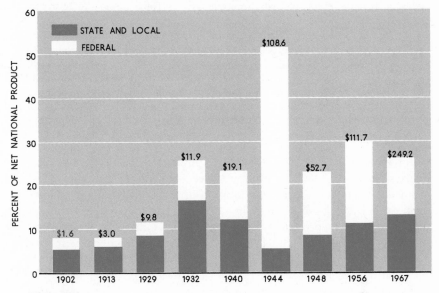

* Estimated.
Source: Tax Foundation, *Facts and Figures on Government Finance,* 14th ed., 1967 (New York: The Foundation, 1967).

space) which had been instituted within 15 years were budgeted for over $21 billion in 1968. Such facts send some blood pressures soaring. But we want to be rational, to see the underlying reasons. Why the rise?

1. *Past wars* left public debt and obligations to veterans. The "cold war" and Vietnam do even more to account for today's defense spending—and also outlays for *international aid* and the costly *conquest of space.*

2. *Rising prices* require more dollars just to keep doing the same things.

3. *Increasing population* and, over longer periods, growth of the area of the country raise total expense of government.

4. *Urbanization* has played a part. In cities people turn to collective action for some things that persons in smaller communities and on farms provide for themselves, perhaps less fully, or go without: police and fire protection, water, parks, and sewers. *Suburbanization* requires new school buildings, streets, and other facilities of government without any fully offsetting reduction in outlays in central cities.

5. "Rising expectations," a *rising standard* of what we want—better schools, streets, flood control—will appear in collective as well as in individual demand.

6. The *auto*, the truck, then the airplane, stimulated government spending.

7. *Humanitarianism* offers part of the answer. We will not tolerate the misery that earlier levels of relief for the poor and hospital standards implied.

8. *Pressure groups* and a willingness of the public to use government to help one group at others' expense seem to grow more influential.

9. The fact that we *pay in taxes, not prices,* may lead us to vote for more spending because of belief that the other fellow (today or in the future) can be made to bear the cost.

10. *Increased interdependence* has added to the demands for government activity. As economic and social life become more complex, the general interest extends more broadly and into more things. Common interests, it is argued, will be served adequately only by bigger government, one which spends more. (Some of us will question the validity of this argument as it is used in many specific cases.)

11. *Federal grant-in-aid programs* put compelling pressure on states and localities to undertake new programs.

Intertwined with these causes are three others.[6] (1) One was the depression of the 1930's. Society was deeply disrupted and took to government as a major agency for solution of more problems. (2) Government organizations—and programs—grow; unlike individuals, they do not die; nature cannot provide a "corrective." And unlike businesses, government agencies do not die because of failure to compete effectively. (3) We often lack reliable guides to "economizing"; so market restraints on expansion do not serve.

Has a decline in operating efficiency accounted for some of the growth? Though measurement is impossible, recent decades have probably brought not less but greater man-hour productivity of government personnel with the extension of the merit system, the use of new equipment and methods, and in many areas determined and informed action by citizen groups opposing waste.

Even if military outlays were cut greatly and if we were to allow for growth of population and price level increases, the remaining expansion would be formidable. Figure 30–2, in a sense, does adjust for (*a*) the influence of war (only state and local spending is included), (*b*) price rises (by adjusting for changes in the purchasing power of the dollar), and (*c*) population growth (by using per capita data). The adjusted figures show a tripling in the last quarter of a century. State-local spending has been rising relatively more rapidly than net national product and exceeds 13 percent. But a best seller of 1958 got considerable support for the argument that, compared with the affluence of the private sector of

[6] One reason that does not appear prominent is the extension of government activity in producing goods and services once provided by businesses. Growing use of highways, airports, and waterways which have tended to displace railroads and municipal operation of transportation facilities provide exceptions. Provision of electric power in some areas offers another case of governmental displacement of business. Yet the examples of government crowding out business are few.

FIGURE 30–2. Per Capita State and Local Government Spending, in Dollars of Constant Purchasing Power, 1902–66

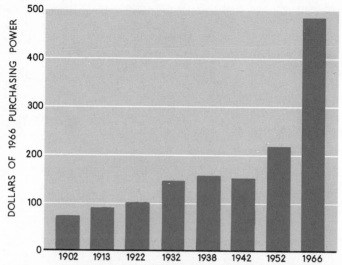

Sources: U.S. Bureau of the Census, *Historical Statistics on State and Local Government Finances, 1902-1953* and *Summary of Governmental Finances in the United States* series. Figures include capital outlays—nearly $95 per capita in 1966—and expenditure of funds received from the federal government—around $57 per capita in 1966. The adjustment for price level change rests on the consumer price index and is approximate only.

the economy, the government sector has been slighted. Such *"social imbalance,"* it is said, can be corrected only as voters allocate a bigger fraction of growing income to raising the quality and increasing the quantity of government services.

MAJOR ELEMENTS OF GOVERNMENT SPENDING

Until the 1930's (except during war) localities spent more than states or the national government. Today, of course, the blue ribbon for size goes to Washington. Most government spending is for the services of employees—teachers, mail carriers, judges, administrators—but relief, social insurance, and other transfer expenditures (for which no service is received) account for more than $1 out of $5 (excluding interest on public debt). To get tangible things—buildings, schoolbooks, weapons—governments generally buy from private business.

Federal Spending. Figure 30–3 shows major elements of federal spending for the 1968 fiscal year and 10 years earlier. Table 30–1 presents some details, a sampling only.

State Spending. Data on the spending of all states together, when combined as in Figure 30–4, give a general impression which hides much

FIGURE 30–3. Federal Government Expenditure, 1958 and 1968* (Fiscal Years)

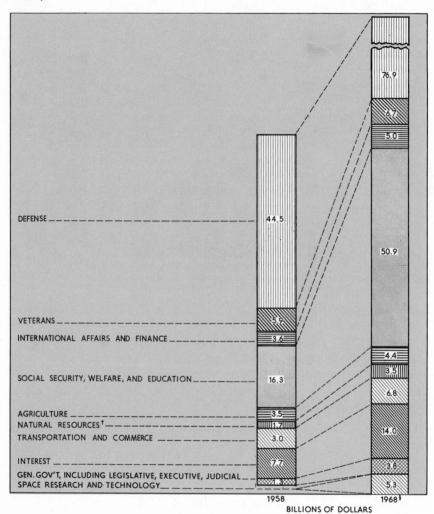

1958 1968‡
BILLINGS OF DOLLARS

* Includes spending from trust funds in most cases.
† Housing aid and area redevelopment included under general government.
‡ Estimated.
Source: President's Budget Message.

diversity. Your own state may spend in significantly different proportions, but it probably spends on most of the things in Table 30–1. Per capita state spending in 1966 varied from around $135 in New Jersey to over $300 in 11 states.

Local Spending. Some 81,000 local governments spend money. One third are school districts with small operations. But the nearly $5 billion of

TABLE 30–1.   Selected Items of Federal Government Expenditures, 1968 Fiscal Year*

	Millions		Millions
Military personnel	$21,800	Highways	$ 3,700
Military procurement	21,600	Space research and technology	5,300
Veterans' compensation and		Promotion of aviation, including	
pensions	6,100	airports	900
Conduct of foreign affairs	300	Postal deficit	540
Loans and grants for economic		Legislative functions	270
assistance abroad (nonmilitary)	2,400	Judicial functions	100
Public assistance (welfare)	3,000	Executive direction, including	
Promotion of public health	4,800†	budget	28
Stabilization of farm prices and		Tax collection	900
other farm aid	3,200	Federal Bureau of Investigation	190
Agricultural research	600		
Conservation and development		District of Columbia	130
of land and water resources		Research and development,	
(nonfarm)	2,400	all agencies	17,056‡

* July 1, 1967 to June 30, 1968. Figures rounded in most cases. Includes grants to state and local governments. Actual amounts will differ somewhat from these estimates.
    † Includes medical care for the aged.
    ‡ Department of Defense accounts for $7,300 million, atomic energy $2,500 million.
    Source: President's Budget Message and Review.

New York City puts it next to the federal government.[7] Figure 30–5 shows the major items of local spending per capita in 1966. This is the "government" that means so much in our daily lives.

Education stands out, with transportation second. The $36 or more billion to be spent on education in 1967 is nearly five times the 1950 figure, a substantial increase indeed. The amount per pupil, at over $600, was almost half again as high as a decade earlier.

The postwar "crop" of babies found physical facilities and staffs inadequate for the needs of over one million more pupils each year; enrollments in public schools in 1968 will be almost double the prewar peak and certain to rise higher; however, the drop in the birth rate promises substantial relief in the pressure to add classrooms and staff. The desire to raise standards will continue. Over the years, this country has sought to provide better education. It certainly provides more schooling for the average child—more days in the school year, more years in school, and more variety of subjects. Such increases are costly. So are other elements associated with quality—improvement which Sputnik in 1957 shocked many Americans into agreeing should be sought. Teachers' salaries have risen to a countrywide average around $7,000 but with one fifth under $5,500 and a rapidly growing number over $12,000.

[7] Some tabulations show the states of California and New York as spending more than New York City. If one excludes the grants which these states make to localities and which the localities spend, New York City unquestionably ranks as second to the national government.

FIGURE 30–4.   Expenditures of State Governments, Totals and Per Capita, 1966*

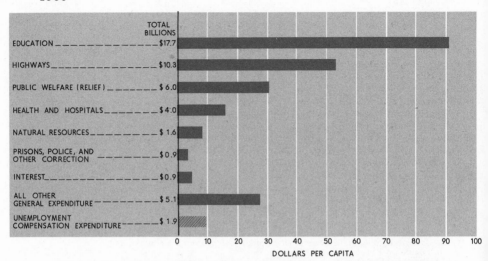

* The amounts for the specific functions include capital outlay, $10.2 billion; grants to local governments, $16.8 billion (including $1.8 billion for highways); and spending of funds received from the federal government, $11.7 billion (chiefly for highways and public welfare).
Source: Bureau of the Census.

College and university costs, until recently of rather slight weight, now raise serious issues in many state, and some local, budgets. Through most of our history, private institutions with no taxpayer support have provided most college education. Since World War II, however, governmentally supported colleges and universities have been growing more rapidly than private. Increasing demand for places in college has led state-local governments to step up their outlays for higher education—from $1.6 billion in 1955 to $7.2 billion in 1967. The total will probably double before 1975. The net addition to pressures on state-local tax revenues will depend in part upon the extent to which state-local colleges make use of tuition and other charges and partly on the growth of federal aid.

In spite of the huge federal highway program, local governments and states as well also face heavy pressure for more spending on streets and other transportation facilities. In cities, one need only try to take a drive or find a parking spot to see again the need for improvement. Many streets and highways were built for an era of fewer cars (or none at all). Today, the loss of life, the cost of accidents, the wear and tear on nerves, the waste of time, the added expense of congestion to business, the move to suburbs, the destruction of our cars by bad surfaces—all lead to the conclusion that heavy outlays on highways and streets will continue.[8] Moreover, both the

[8] The price system with taxes (or direct controls) could be used to ease some of the problem and save expense. We could induce some shift to railroads, buses, and other types of mass and bulk tranport where existing facilities are not used to capacity

FIGURE 30–5.   Local Expenditure per Capita for Selected Functions, 1966*

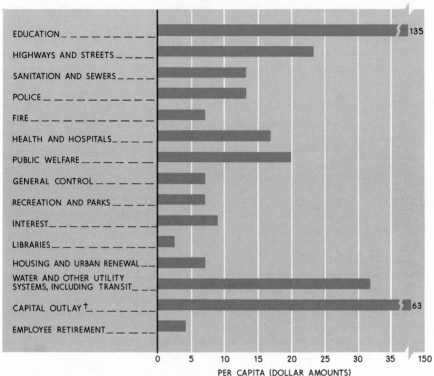

PER CAPITA (DOLLAR AMOUNTS)
* Includes spending of funds received from state and federal government.
† Included above in spending by function.
Source: Bureau of the Census.

shift and growth of population create many and diverse pressures for more local government spending: hospitals, police, parks, recreational facilities, sewers, airports, and so on. Dealing with air and water pollution, new attacks on poverty, the desire for pleasing architecture or good music, the replacing of slums, and the rebuilding of central cities—many such things will add to local government spending.

Economic Effects of Government Spending.   Chapter 13 showed how government spending (and taxes) affects the general level of national income. The spending also influences the allocation of productive capacity. People teaching school are not available for other jobs. Steel used in a new city hospital cannot be used for apartments. Food purchases for the

or could be expanded at relatively low cost; in cities, especially, the private auto is often a glaringly inefficient user of that scarce resource, street space. One set of rails and one lane reserved for high-speed buses will accommodate several times as many people as will the autos on streets that could be provided from an equal outlay of funds.

Army affect market prices to civilians. Time of skilled scientists devoted to space research cannot also be used for college classroom teaching, and so on.

Although the justification for an expenditure by government is the belief that the *general* public will benefit, individuals as such also gain—and not all equally. But how unequally? And what causes lead to

FIGURE 30–6.   Government Spending as Percentage of Total Income, 1965*

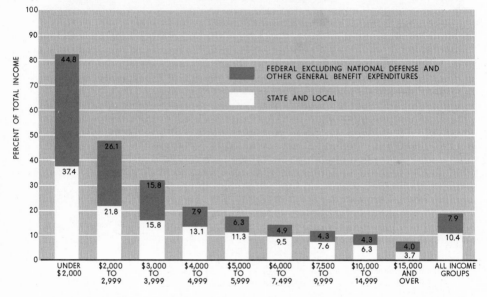

* Estimated.

Source: Tax Foundation, Inc., *Estimated Tax Burdens and Benefits of Government Expenditures by Family Income Class—1961 and 1965* (New York: The Foundation, 1966), p. 8. The results shown above indicate possible orders of magnitude. The full study presents estimates resting on several different assumptions and concepts, including some that allocate the benefits of defense spending. The broad patterns of the various estimates are generally the same, but the details differ. In all cases, the benefits of government spending are very much greater in relation to income for lower income groups. For the $15,000-and-over group, benefits as a percentage of income are relatively higher under some assumptions than shown above. Rarely, however, are they much above half as great in relation to income as that for the under-$10,000 groups.

the differences? Most government spending, of course, is not the kind which we can divide up (in the figures) to "distribute" in different amounts among different people—for example, the benefits of national defense or public schools. Some types, however, seem to present less difficult problems. Some veterans, for example, get dollar benefits we can measure. Yet if we wanted to say how much of these benefits went to city people or to men with low incomes or to bright students, we would find a shortage of facts. Figure 30–6 shows the results of a carefully made study of one big question: How do the benefits of government spending compare with income at different income levels? Including only nondefense spending, we find that total benefits are very great in relation to total income at lower income levels, but benefits are only a small fraction as large for the $15,000 group. Clearly, spending has a powerful redistributive effect. Taxation, as we shall see in the next chapter, accentuates this general tendency.

Americans—our ancestors, our fathers, some of us—have accomplished magnificent things through government. We now properly look ahead and focus on problems and opportunities for improvement. In doing so, it would be foolish to ignore great achievements, things that are a source of justified pride: schools, relief aid, highways, and the mammoth mobilization of military resources.

BUDGETING: ECONOMY IN GOVERNMENT

The growth of government spending has multiplied the importance of seeking efficiency in expenditure. Devices for boosting efficiency, though still inadequate, have been improving. Much of the progress involves the budgetary process.

What Is a Budget?   A budget may be a device to double our worry by troubling us about the same thing twice—before, as well as after, we spend. Unfortunately, advance concern may be the only way to avoid near catastrophe. A budget is a device to make our worry constructive. It is a statement of a financial plan of receipts and expenditures. Government budgets plan for the direction of around 30 percent of the country's economic activity. Therefore, the way in which they are made, from start to finish, and the way they are carried out combine into an economic factor of considerable importance. The budgetary process offers an opportunity for looking at the whole range of a government's financial problems. The possible alternatives can be compared, at least more deliberately and systematically than on other occasions. Budgets vary from simple documents of small school districts to the 1,200-page, 5-pound appendix to the federal budget, with its small type and masses of figures. Ordinarily, proposed expenditures are compared with the estimated actual spending of the current year.

Policy Issues.   On spending, two kinds of problems arise: (1) deciding on *policies,* or *programs,* and (2) finding ways to *carry out* established policies to best advantage. Policy problems include such things as whether to build a new school, to increase the pensions promised government employees, or to rely more heavily on guided missiles. They raise economic issues. On problems of collective demand, however, economics can give only incomplete guidance for selecting the *policy* alternatives. Prospective benefits can seldom be measured and compared with costs.

National defense, like food, is good; so are schools and better mail service. How can we maximize the benefit we get? This is a harder job in government than in business. *The businessman can use the same measuring rod, the dollar, in figuring both costs and what the public will pay for the output.* The amount the consumer will pay for a product in the market is his estimate of its value; the decisions of businessmen are constantly tested in the market. Most government services, in contrast, are not freely purchased at a price; for them, we lack what is ordinarily the chief measure of the value of output. Policy choice in government is hampered by difficulties of measurement, especially on the benefit side. PPBS (mentioned earlier) represents a determined effort to measure nontangible results of programs to help judge the desirability of continuation, expansion, reduction, or modification.

Major policy decisions affecting expenditures are often made outside the budgetary process. Congress establishes a farm program; the state legislature, a mental hospital system; the city, a new pay scale for policemen. The adoption of such programs can restrict greatly the later freedom of decision in voting appropriations during consideration of the budget.

Budgeting to Carry Out Policy. The second type of problem, finding how a program can be carried out most efficiently, also presents difficulties. Good budgetary procedures can help overcome them. The budget process provides a forum and should, in fact, force study of the problems, many of which can be solved in part by common-sense examination. Should we build a veterans' hospital in a congressman's home town or near the city where veterans live? What location would be best for a giant atom smasher or space research center? The use of methods developed in business will help answer many questions. (How often should postal or garbage trucks be replaced rather than repaired?) Other problems are more intricate. Some are peculiar to government—national defense. Always, however, intensive and expert study will at least improve our chances that the answers will be as good as possible. What do we really want to accomplish? What alternative methods might be used? Which of them offers the best value?

Initial Stages of Budget Making. Making the typical budget begins with a request to each unit of government to indicate the amount it needs to do what existing law requires, what it would like for new programs, and why. At this stage, there may be formal or informal directions. "Things are tight; keep to the very minimum" or "In the coming budget period, some elbow room for increases can be expected." Requests are examined, ordinarily higher up in the same department and then in the budget office.

The Federal Bureau of the Budget is an agency responsible directly to the President. Its staff consults with departments as they prepare requests; it interprets administration policy and tries to give constructive help. Of course, in any one year most expenditure proposals present few issues of choice; decisions have been settled by contract—such as interest on government debt—or, as noted earlier, by commitments on programs. Yet at the margin, there are problems about how best to carry out a program that has been agreed upon, about its size, and at least a few issues of policy about adopting or abandoning a program.

Over weeks or months the individual proposals are studied. There is bargaining, pushing and pulling, some careful analysis. Eventually, the tentative decisions are put together. Top officials, seeing how things "stack up," can fit the parts into overall policy. "Approved" requests often add up to more than the responsible officials think desirable, and cuts begin.

Problems of Competence and Objectivity. By this stage a crucial problem will have appeared. Who is *competent* to decide? Technical issues can sometimes be decided well by men who know the technical facts—the best type of construction for a particular bridge. Other cases, however, involve judgment of such things as the effect of changes in the salary level or in the size of school classes or the benefits of extending the sewer system; competence is not easily identified.

With few exceptions, crucial decisions must be made by people who cannot claim technical qualifications. The chief executive must say the final word; for most issues he is an amateur, the captive of his advisers. Some of the hope that government assumption of an activity will permit both objectivity and scientific skill in guiding the allocation of resources is an illusion. Except possibly for small localities, responsibility rests finally with people who must act upon far more problems than any single person can ever hope to master. It is not only in a large federal agency that the sheer magnitude of the job forces superficial judgment. Mayors and governors must act on sketchy information or on recommendations of subordinates who can know only part of the whole story of the government's activities and finances. American governments have not yet done what is reasonably feasible to make the best of an inherently difficult, but essential, job. Why not greater use of staffs trained more specifically in analyzing the chief branches of governmental activities?

Three problems, often noted, remind us of the old saying about the weather—we talk a lot but do little to change things. (1) The civil servant and the military official are no exception to the general rule that a person becomes "sold" on the things he is doing.[9] How can he be reasonably impartial? (2) "Entrepreneurship" in government often takes the form of pushing the growth of the agency. A man's salary and influence depend partly upon the size of his staff and the scope of its operations. Promotion

---

[9] Most of us who have worked in various government agencies recall that opportunities for improving our work always seemed obvious and huge if only more funds were available.

chances are better if the organization grows; subordinates get behind the push. The incentives are for expansion, the taxpayer to bear the cost. An agency that does not spend its appropriation shows that it can get along without the money; the budget-cutting ax will likely fall. (3) Budget requests made freely will tend to be padded. If you were an agency head you would know that the emphasis of people reviewing requests is to cut. You would probably want to press for more than you really need. Your agency will probably get cuts anyway; and to do its job, funds must not go below some level.

Top-Level Review.   Major problems will be reviewed by the President, governor, or mayor, and his top advisers. Less important issues must be decided at lower levels. Reviewing officials within agencies or in the Budget Bureau exercise great power; any request they reject can seldom get a sympathetic hearing later. Although the federal budget is nominally the President's, he cannot have studied more than major outlines and a few of the thousands of specific items. Experts do not always have opportunity to give the executive (and the legislature or the public) their best advice. The nonexperts who must decide cannot devote enough time to study all that the experts feel is necessary for a decision. The chief executive may read only a 2-page précis of the 100-page digest of the summary volume, of the selected evidence and conclusions, of years of work of a large staff. Moreover, experts may not always speak freely; policy decisions of superiors can control the whole administration. The public cannot be sure it gets the impartial judgments of civil servants. Legislators have no systematic way of learning the recommendations of experts which have been overruled by superiors in the executive branch.

The Budget before the Legislature.   The federal budget goes to Congress in January. The traditional method has been to show expenditure proposals by *agency* and *object*—the amount a Treasury agency will spend on typists of a certain grade or supplies or travel. This method provides a poor basis for analyzing the *purposes* for which the money is spent. Consequently, some budgets now present the data according to the *function* for which the money is to be spent—the program to be carried out, what is to be accomplished—and even, occasionally, cost per unit of output. Nevertheless, more effort should be devoted to answering the question "How will the public benefit from this spending?" Budgets can conceal as many buried secrets as a cemetery.

The legislative review of appropriation and revenue requests lasts for months. After World War II, Congress tried to say in essence: "Before we look at details, let's settle on the *broad* outlines. Then we can make the parts add up to the whole." These efforts failed, and piecemeal consideration remains the rule. Various subcommittees hold hearings on most appropriation proposals during the crowded spring and summer months.

Departmental officials appear to justify their requests; perhaps outsiders get a few minutes to present a case. Other members of Congress press for projects that have been treated too "harshly" by the executive. Special interests continue to push and pull for what they want.

The task has grown so large that in the opinion of some experts Congress has "lost control." There is not enough time. Consideration of major policy is mixed with minor operating problems. Decisions involving huge sums and profound issues often rest on incomplete analyses. In other cases, however, minor details receive extensive attention.[10] Most governors have the power to veto individual appropriation items, but the President must accept or reject the entire bill.

Weaknesses and Areas for Improvement. How might the budget process be improved? More broadly, what can help us get more efficiency in government spending? The following points suggest opportunities.

1. The present system mixes two essentially different problems: judging broad policies (formation of general programs) and the most efficient way to execute them. Clearer separation would permit more effective solution of both.

2. The bases for judging *capital transactions* are inadequate. American governments do not ordinarily treat depreciation as a cost, but spending on a capital project that will give services over many years is often budgeted as a current expense when made. Accounting for *accruing* assets and such liabilities as pension rights is incomplete. The use of unduly low interest rates to value (discount) future services from long-lived projects, such as dams, overstates their apparent worth.

3. The major emphasis is on cutting expenditure. Yet sometimes "economizing" requires an *increase* in spending. The present bias is doubtless right, but too sweeping.

4. Budgets are often excessively detailed; as a result the head of an agency has little freedom to use his judgment to improve operations. Some of the most important opportunities for management in the real sense are removed when appropriations specify almost to the last dollar how much is to be spent for what. Within limits, we would get better service by specifying the function to be performed, assigning funds and responsibility, and then giving the official on the job considerable discretion about how best to use the resources at his disposal.

5. *The effects of decisions in this year's budget on future spending are confused*—usually not shown at all. The proposals commonly involve sums (obligational authority) which, though committed this year, may not be paid out until later. More significant, a decision to make a modest expenditure this year may commit the government to large future outlays.[11] The

---

[10] A show of economizing can be made by slicing appropriations without requiring a cut in the rate of actual spending. Later *a deficiency appropriation* can be voted, offsetting the apparent saving made earlier.

[11] The President's budget for 1965 called for spending $10 million in the year to start a new program for urban mass transit but requested a 3-year authorization of

decision may be guided by the relatively small sum this year. Cost estimates of things to be done in the future often prove far below reality.

6. Continuation of existing expenditures tends to be approved, if not automatically at least much more readily than new programs, regardless of relative merits.

7. Much tax revenue—in several states, 50 percent or more—is *earmarked* for specific expenditure purposes. Large amounts are not subject to current control, no matter what the relative importance of alternative possible types of spending.

8. "Spending" may, in fact, be made as a *tax concession*—for plants to build defense items, for airports, for subsidized housing. When this method of "payment" is used, both the common citizen and the sophisticated official will have great difficulty finding out what a service really costs.

9. The accounts of more or less *independent agencies*, chiefly those engaged in business-type activity, may be omitted from the totals, except for net surpluses or deficits. As a result, the budget fails to reveal the extent of government activity and the resources used. Thus about $30 billion a year of federal outlays do not appear in even the broadest budget concepts.

10. Spending proposals are not considered along with taxing proposals, especially at the federal level.[12]

11. *Defense spending* presents exceptional problems: issues of the most intricate technical complexity; secrecy that may be used to conceal inefficiency; the lack of good measures of accomplishment (especially in the absence of conflict); the need for idle capacity to permit emergency expansion; traditional attitudes of the services; the pricing of new, complex, and secret equipment where competitive bidding is not really possible; the difficulties of attracting and holding top-quality personnel.

12. The concept of "economy" which applies properly to such transfer spending as welfare and farm aid has hardly been defined.

13. The security of many civil service jobs and the red tape and inflexibility of bureaucracy hinder the adoption of best management methods.

These and other problems are widely recognized. Earnest men, inside and outside government, are trying sincerely to find better ways to solve them.[13] Success is real but still inadequate. What methods offer promise?

$375 million. The 1968 budget asked for authorization to continue spending on the development of supersonic aircraft but gave no figures on what amounts would be involved. The 1967 authorization had been $280 million.

[12] "The present Chairman of the Committee on Ways and Means, Rep. Wilbur D. Mills, has attributed the continual increase in expenditure levels to the fact that there is no satisfactory method for weighing alternative courses concerning both expenditure requests and tax proposals. . . . 'At no place in the budgetary process is there a real opportunity to consider the fact that a given expenditure may require a tax increase and that as an alternative to that expenditure there not only is the possibility of making other expenditures but also the possibility of making no additional expenditures are all, and instead decreasing taxes, or at least not increasing them.' " Tax Foundation, *Controlling Federal Expenditures* (New York: The Foundation, 1963), p. 38. See also Tax Foundation, *State Expenditure Controls: An Evaluation* (New York: The Foundation, 1965).

[13] Herbert Hoover headed two postwar commissions which studied ways of getting more economy in the national government. Several states and cities have been

More mechanization, better personnel policies, centralized purchasing and more effective competitive bidding, standardization of purchases to permit large-scale buying, replanning of office layout and routing of work, scientific testing, elimination of avoidable overlapping, the installation of competent efficiency experts on government staffs, accounting designed to reveal costs of specific parts of each job, pricing of government services where price may induce economy in use and prevent true waste, consolidation of small units of government, planning (especially for capital

FIGURE 30–7. Marginal Benefits and Costs of a Program of Governmental Spending

The "first" dollars bring benefits which may be very high, no one can be sure. Up to total spending of OX, each dollar spent brings benefits worth more than the cost. When more dollars are spent on this function, however, the added (incremental, marginal) benefits are of less value than they cost.

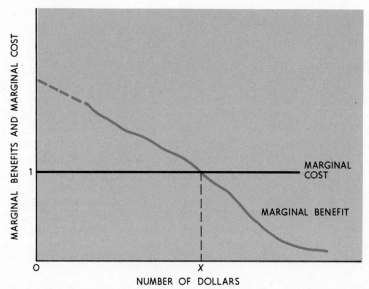

projects) that looks well into the future, more extensive and careful post-audit of spending, and greater reliance on private suppliers, builders, and engineers rather than government staffing and operation on its own—these are some of the methods of increasing efficiency in government spending.

The "big money," however, lies in choices about policies, not operating methods. The significant control of spending and especially of growth, requires control of the scope and quality of functions. Sometimes a sharper definition of the objective would help, for it might induce clearer

served by somewhat comparable groups. More or less permanent taxpayer or public expenditure organizations exist in most states and many localities. They have widely varied success.

thinking about alternative methods. Is farm aid to help poor farmers? If so, what is the most efficient way to achieve this objective? What are we seeking when we increase outlays to put a man on the moon, build more highways, or enlarge river navigation? What, then, will enable us best to achieve the objective? For things that are clearly desirable up to some point but not beyond, can we get guidance about where the point will be found (Fig. 30–7)?

Better answers to such queries will save sums that can be impressive. Yet if education, foreign aid, public health, policing, or some other function is to be expanded or improved on any substantial scale, the money must come from greater revenue. No foreseeable improvements in efficiency will release the necessary funds.

NOTE ON BUDGET CONCEPTS

Much doubt about what belongs in "the" federal budget has grown as federal finances have become more complex. For reasons which have some merit, the "administrative" budget excludes trust funds. Yet the amounts received and spent by such funds have become so very great that to ignore them is to ignore large totals, $48 billion of receipts in 1968 (more than one third as much as the total administrative budget receipts). Therefore, the "cash consolidated" budget which does include the trust funds seems better for many purposes. It fails, however, to meet the needs for the most refined guides to the flows of federal finances as related to national income. So another treatment of receipts and expenditures was developed, the "national income accounts" presentation. With three different concepts in use by 1967, the situation had become confusing, to say the least. The President appointed a study commission to recommend modifications. Its proposals may be reflected in the document which the President sends to Congress in 1968.

TERMS AND CONCEPTS		
public goods	PPBS	earmarked expenditures
neighborhood effects	obligational authority	
external effects	appropriations	program
social imbalance	public good	externality
	budget	

QUESTIONS

1. How does a decision on policy differ from one about carrying out policy?
2. What are the reasons for—and perhaps against—paying for schools and highways through government?
3. Why have state and local government expenditures grown since 1940? Federal?
4. What benefit does the general public receive from government spending on relief for the poor? From the postal deficit?

5. When may true economy in government require an increase in spending?

6. In what ways can business principles be used to get economy in government? What other principles and methods are available?

7. "We should think of spending on education as an investment, not a form of current consumption." Comment. How would your answer differ if the item involved were food? streets? police? relief? armaments? interest on debt?

8. Assume that you are the economic adviser to your governor. Write a memorandum explaining the kind of information he should have to decide whether to approve large outlays on new highways. On hospitals.

9. "The marginal dollar of government spending brings more value than the marginal pay-envelope dollar." What evidence would be needed to prove or disprove this conclusion?

10. How much do families on relief in you community receive? Prepare what you would consider an appropriate budget and discuss it with a social worker familiar with the problem of families receiving public assistance.

11. Attend a budget hearing before your town or city council and, if possible, the appropriate state agency.

31

TAXATION: PRINCIPLES AND PRACTICE

When I pay taxes, I buy civilization.

Oliver Wendell Holmes, Jr.

Taxes certainly do pay for some of the essentials of civilization. They are important in another respect. The way we raise this tax money has tremendous influence on our life.

HOW SHOULD TAX BURDENS BE SHARED? CRITERIA OF A GOOD TAX SYSTEM

Tax Bills Must Be Unequal. One fact is clear: *Tax bills must be unequal.* If America's total taxes were averaged equally over everyone—over $1,000 a person in 1967—the taxes for some families would exceed their income. For many more families the taxes would be so heavy that absolutely essential items of living could not be bought. There is no choice: Americans must decide, consciously or unconsciously, how to impose different tax loads on different people. Debate will be not only heated but at times even acrimonious. Although economic issues are involved, so also are problems of ethics, politics, and social living. This diversity of considerations rules out hope of finding any clear or "scientific" basis for decision.

Progression, Proportionality, Regression. Unequal burdens may be imposed by taxes and tax systems that are progressive, proportional, or regressive, in relation to income, wealth, spending, or some other base. (The *tax base* is the thing or object on which a tax is imposed, such as the dollar amount of income, sales, inheritance, or real estate value. The *tax* *rate* is the figure, usually a percentage, applied to the base to determine the amount of tax payable.) (1) A tax is *progressive* in relation to income if the tax, as a percentage of income, increases as income increases. The bigger the income, the larger the fraction or percentage that must be paid in tax. (2) A tax is *proportional* if it imposes the same percentage on all incomes. The man with high income pays more dollars than the man with low income, but each pays the same percentage. (3) A tax is *regressive* if the tax as a percentage of income goes down as income rises; the person with large income will probably pay many more dollars than the one with smaller income, but they will be a lower percentage of the larger income.

Taxes Are Borne by People, Not by Things.   Misconceptions about taxes often result from a simple error. *Things* do not bear taxes; *people* do.

FIGURE 31–1.   Progressive, Proportional, and Regressive Taxes

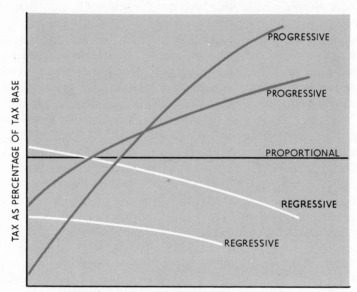

AMOUNT OF TAX BASE (INCOME, WEALTH, SALES)

The taxes may appear as high prices for what we buy or as lower incomes from our efforts and our investment. The tax may also appear as a direct charge on our income and wealth after we get them. Whatever the form, however, any tax is paid by people. We say, for convenience, that taxes fall on business, real estate, or sales. The important fact, however, is that whatever the first impact, the tax affects people: owners, consumers, or employees. Though a corporation is, in one sense, a thing with its own existence, taxes on it reduce the income of its owners or raise the price of its products or cut the payments to labor and suppliers. Voters cannot escape the problem of taxing human beings by pretending to tax things, such as corporations or real estate or radios. Taxes are a restriction on our freedom. We ought to be careful, indeed, in the way we impose them.

Some taxes are imposed *directly* on people—the personal income tax. The law puts other taxes on the sale of a thing or on the value of property; consequently, the taxes reach individuals *indirectly*—as a higher price for gasoline or rent—but must be paid out of income.

What principles can be followed in deciding how to apportion tax burdens? Realizing that people pay taxes, economists have focused on the question of equality and differences in the distribution of taxes on people. A "new look," however, considers also the effects of taxes on national income and its growth.

Fairness and Justice. "Justice," one of the chief goals of government, is a key requirement for good taxation. Taxpayer morale, the working of the tax system—the quality of government itself—depend in part upon the extent of public belief that taxes are fair, equitable, just. But what is equitable?

For one thing, to be equitable the law must be enforced equally, not more strictly toward one man than another.[1] Furthermore, the law to be enforced must itself be fair; in taxation this aspect of justice requires treating people differently, not equally. Men disagree about the unequal treatment of taxpayers which will be fair in any specific, real-life situation.[2] We ask, "What *kind of difference* between two taxpayers will justify how much difference in taxes?"[3] *B* and *A* each have $12,000 incomes and two children; *B* is a widower who pays a housekeeper $3,000 a year, while *A* is happily married to an industrious woman. Is it fair that *B*, in spite of his greater expense, must also pay higher tax than *A? C* smokes and *D* does not; otherwise they are the same as far as we can see. How much more tax should *C* pay because of this one difference? *E* and *F* are corporations with identical records, except that *E* has issued preferred stock and *F* the same amount of bonds. Should their taxes vary? Why? How much? *G* has four children, $8,000 money income, and lives on his own farm; *H* has two children, $7,000 money income, and lives in a city apartment. What, if any, difference in tax is fair? Some guidance for answering such question may be found in the points to be discussed now.

One general guide may be that relatively small differences in economic reality ought not to lead to relatively large differences in tax. Two other

---

[1] Injustice in enforcement may result from laws that are too complex to be administered, from failure to provide enough staff and equipment to do a job that can be done, or from corruption of officials combined with resistance of taxpayers.

[2] Other objectives—"mercy" is not the only one—may conflict with "justice." Appeals to fairness, equity, or justice for settling disputes will not help unless the disputants agree generally on their concepts of these terms.

[3] The approach implied by this question seeks taxes that are *neutral* except as burdens differ because of significant variations, factors that are relevant to the differences in results.

concepts are helpful. Horizontal equity requires that people in essentially similar circumstances be taxed equally. Vertical equity calls for taxing persons with different income, wealth, or consumption in some rational relation to the differences which are relevant for sharing the costs of government. But how, exactly?

Benefit. Some taxes can be imposed more or less according to the benefits received from spending the money. The greater the value of the services a person gets, the more his taxes—somewhat like market prices. One difference, however, can grow out of the element of compulsion that forces us to "buy" things through government which we would not purchase otherwise. For example, the tax on workers to pay for part of social security is levied partly (but now rather little) according to eventual benefit; but we have almost no freedom to reject social insurance. Taxes on gasoline and motor vehicles to help pay for highways, and some fees, such as those for inspecting elevators, have benefit elements. Most government services, however, do not lend themselves to charging on a benefit basis: schooling, welfare, police, national defense. The fruits they yield are *general* and cannot realistically be allocated among people. Some beneficiaries would not be able to pay the cost of the benefits they receive, even if coercion were attempted. No practical method of collecting charges may be appropriate.[4]

Ability to Pay. Economists and "the man in the street" usually endorse "ability to pay" as a guide. (It means more than merely seeking taxes from those who have the money.) Economic circumstances differ from one family to another. If the same amount of tax were taken from each, the real sacrifice for some would be much greater than for others. To reduce the human burden of taxes, therefore, we should collect most from families to whom the marginal income provides least in satisfaction. Assume that we wish to impose taxes so that they reduce welfare as little as possible. Then, the smaller the income, the more each marginal dollar will give in satisfactions, and the less that should be taken in taxes.

The principle seems sensible when stated in such general terms.[5] Yet acceptance of the principle is not enough; application is also required. In trying to do so, we find hard practical problems.

No one can really compare the psychologies of different families to measure the sacrifice due to tax-induced deprivation of different amounts of income. The want-satisfying power of income may fall, not in propor-

[4] Government enterprise operations are commonly financed by charges based on use—postal rates, water charges, etc. Much of the cost may thus be apportioned roughly according to benefit.

[5] Nevertheless, rational defense of the principle proves surprisingly difficult. See W. J. Shultz and C. Lowell Harriss, *American Public Finance*, 8th ed. (Englewood Cliffs, N.J.: Prentice-Hall, Inc., 1965), chap. ix.

tion to the amount of income, but more so, or less. People feel differently. Comparisons of satisfactions from person to person are far from scientific. We have no good basis for deciding that every family of the same size with an income of $8,000 would suffer equally from a tax of $1,000. Moreover, there is no way to learn how "typical" families at the $8,000 level compare psychologically with those at the $7,000 level. Applying the ability-to-pay principle to minimize the human burden would require us to know by how much the taxpaying "ability" varies with income. All of us may agree that the family with $8,000 is "able" to pay more than the family with $7,999 or the one with $7,500. But how much more? What if the families are of different size or differ in other ways? *What* variations, then, make *how much* difference in "ability"? Until the answers to such questions are known, "ability to pay" is not the reliable guide often assumed.

Common sense seems to support the conclusion that progressive taxes impose less human deprivation than levies that are regressive, or even proportional. Unfortunately, neither common sense nor any principle that is generally accepted gives clear guidance for using the ability-to-pay principle or tell us what its limits may be. Conceivably, progression may be so steep as to violate the principle of ability to pay. In any case, however, we shall likely agree that the poor ought not to have their distress aggravated seriously. Taxes that oppress the truly needy are in this respect bad.[6]

Reducing Inequality. Progressive taxes reduce economic inequalities and especially the tendency for inequality to feed upon itself. If greater economic equality is a goal of public policy, taxes can serve to achieve it. One test of a tax, then, can be whether it tends to reduce economic inequality. Measurement, and even definition, of "economic inequality" present difficulties. How does a regressive tax which takes 4 percent from an income of $4,000 ($160) and 3 percent from an income of $20,000 ($600) affect inequality?

Effects on Saving and Consumption. Taxes reduce the income available for consumption and saving. Per dollar of revenue, however, some taxes affect consumption (and saving) relatively more than others. Because consumption spending and saving have different effects on employment and prices and economic growth, the way we raise a given total of

---

[6] Pressure for very high progressive tax rates may result more from malice against a few—"soak the rich"—than from charity for those who need it. The top rates yield too little revenue to permit any appreciable relief of burden on the lowest income groups. A tax may be generally progressive and still impose burdens on the poor which seem excessive by humanitarian standards; a regressive tax, on the other hand, may burden low income groups very little. Obviously, much depends upon the amount of revenue raised by the tax.

taxes will influence national income. In general, each tax dollar collected from a very-low-income family will cut consumption and have little effect on saving. Higher in the income scale, however, each dollar of tax will reduce saving relatively more; at the very top, a dollar of tax may have no effect on consumption, coming entirely out of saving.

Some taxes affect the pattern of personal consumption more than do others. Taxes on particular commodities or services reduce the consumption of such things more than of untaxed items. Not everyone, of course, has the same preferences. Some people who shift consumption from highly taxed items to other things may have about the same eventual satisfaction. Other consumers, however, may sacrifice considerable personal welfare. In general, economists believe that this type of welfare loss will be least if tax is on income rather than specific commodities. When tax is on income, each person is free to cut his consumption in the form of those things which are least useful to him. But if an income tax affects the choice between leisure and money, the income tax must be treated, in this respect, as "distorting" choice in the same way as does a commodity tax.

High Tax Rates and Incentives. How do very high tax rates affect incentives? If government demands a large fraction of what one gets for developing skills, working long and hard, or assuming risks, why not take more time for play rather than study or work, refuse overtime, retire earlier, or put savings into secure rather than venturesome assets? If taxes reduce take-home pay, some people will work less; others will not exert themselves to raise their productive capacity. Some, on the other hand, may try to work more to attain the living standard they seek.[7]

Of course, the tax rates applicable must certainly affect the result—10 percent is rather different from 40 percent. The sensitive point is the tax rate on the top, or marginal, dollar of a person's income, the *marginal rate*. The highest marginal tax rates fall on people who have high earnings and who, presumably, have scarce and valuable capacities.[8] Perhaps it is hazardous for society to risk depriving itself of the full use of such abilities. As an increasingly complex society requires ever more hard-earned excellence to realize its expanding potentials, the curtailment of stimulating rewards does seem a bit foolish.

One point *is* clear. Businesses and individuals modify their economic

[7] What taxes do to dull incentives to work economists call the "incentive effect"; what a tax does to make us try to work more is the "income effect."

[8] One effort to measure reductions in labor effort attributable to the federal income tax led to an estimate of a decline of 2.5 percent from persons whose top bracket rate was 20 percent and a 11.4 percent reduction for those subject to a 91 percent rate. The author recognizes that such estimates rest upon evidence which leaves much to be desired. A. C. Harberger, "Taxation, Resource Allocation, and Welfare," *The Role of Direct and Indirect Taxes in the Federal Revenue System, A Conference Report* . . . (National Bureau of Economic Research and the Brookings Institution, 1964), p. 49.

decisions to take advantage of legal ways to escape tax (*avoidance*), especially when rates are high. At times no activity can bring benefits as large as those from steps to cut tax. High skills are utilized in socially unconstructive, but privately rewarding, efforts to reduce tax. Waste of talent results. Economic life is distorted, at least shifted to somewhat different channels from those of a low-tax world. Even policies otherwise inefficient may become sensible. High tax rates also encourage *illegal* activity, *evasion*. They tempt the corruption of the public and the civil service. High rates increase the pressures to make tax laws increasingly complex; special provisions get established. In the words of President Kennedy when advocating tax reduction in 1963:

> . . . rates ranging up to 91 percent not only check consumption but discourage investment, and encourage the diversion of funds and effort into activities aimed more at the avoidance of taxes than the efficient production of goods. The oppressive impact of those high rates gave rise to many of the undue preferences in the present law—and both the high rates and the preferences should be ended. . . . the highest rate should not exceed 65 percent . . . accompanied by appropriate reductions in the middle income ranges. This will restore an idea that has helped make our country great—that a person who devotes his efforts to increasing his income, thereby adding to the nation's income and wealth, should be able to retain a reasonable share of the results.

Taxes and Economic Growth.   High progressive taxes strike at a point which is strategic for economic growth: the reinvestment of business earnings. In the early life of a business, such reinvestment is especially important for providing equity capital. When taxes are high, the successful firm must give government a big fraction of its earnings. Is this not eating the seed corn? A tax which is "progressive" in apportioning the burden may retard progress in the sense of economic growth. On the other hand, a tendency of the tax system to discourage economic progress can be offset in part by well-designed exceptions or special provisions; most economists would probably judge the 7 percent investment tax credit (provided in the 1962 law) as generally effective in aiding growth by easing the tax burden on companies which install new equipment.

Economic growth will consist predominantly of what we do through business. Most jobs are created by businesses. Success in progressing economically will depend primarily upon the effectiveness and efficiency with which businesses operate. Society does not increase its chances of producing more effectively by imposing taxes on corporations. A corporation has every incentive to keep taxes as well as other costs as low as possible. The economizing, the efficiency-stimulating pressure to cut costs, is a major force for economic progress. In saving on taxes, however, a company does not economize on the use of those things which taxes buy—government services—in the same way that cutting wage or material costs will ordinarily result from economizing on the use of labor and materials.

A decision which from the point of view of the inherent economics is inferior may become best when taxes are taken into account. To the extent that taxes enter into the making of business decisions, the results are likely to be less good for the economy than if taxes had no influence on the choice of *what* to produce or *how*. Distorted allocation of productive capacity and frictions generated by taxes lead to waste even though we cannot see it. The higher the tax rate, the greater the inducement to sacrifice something desirable to save tax.

Economic growth requires capital accumulation. Capital accumulation requires saving. And dollar for dollar, the tax on corporation earnings probably falls with relatively heavy weight on potential savings.

The profit motive has worked powerfully. It will serve us in the future—the more fully we give it scope. Profits actually obtained influence the expectation of profit in the future. They also help finance more profit-seeking investment. Taxes on business firms reduce the prospective profit from new investment. As shown in Chapter 4, a 50 percent tax rate reduces a 14 percent yield from capital to 7 percent for the owner; if he insists on the prospect of such a yield, then projects which he expects will produce somewhat less than 14 percent before tax will not be financed. High tax rates "cut out" otherwise attractive undertakings.

Personal Distribution of Taxes: Concluding Comment. In planning a distribution of taxes, considerations other than income or wealth are pertinent. We might discriminate in favor of "senior citizens," or farmers, or veterans, or the blind, or owners of oil wells. Tendencies in this direction have already developed. A discrimination on one basis, however, may conflict with another objective or turn out to be worthless for achieving the apparent goal. For example, hoping to aid the needy aged, Congress made social security benefits tax exempt. The exemption means nothing to the poor pensioner, however, for he or she would pay no income tax even if the benefit were not specifically exempt. The retired executive who would otherwise be subject to a high tax on the benefit gets a relatively large tax saving. Foolish errors will probably be minimized if efforts to help specific groups are concentrated on the side of expenditures rather than tax concessions. Although real estate, sales and commodity, and business taxes are bound to burden the poor—and thus conflict with worthy objectives of public policy—some of the worst effects are at least mitigated by welfare and other government spending.

Adequacy and Stability. A good tax system will yield adequate revenue. But what is adequacy? At this point, modern analysis breaks with that of the past. The older test of adequacy was revenue equal to spending. For local and state governments this is still a good general principle.

For national governments, however, the most nearly adequate revenue will be that which in relation to spending will best aid in achieving national income goals. A good national tax system will have taxes whose yields fluctuate to help prevent inflation and depression. State-local governments need revenue stability in the sense that money keeps flowing in, even though business activity slackens. They also want revenue sources which bring more from year to year so that rising expenditures can be paid for without going to voters for higher tax rates or new taxes.

Regulation. The principle of selecting taxes for their regulatory effect is old; so is the practice, as evidenced by tariffs to reduce imports. Other examples are taxes to discourage nonmedicinal sale of opium or currency issue by state banks. Some taxes have a regulatory as well as a revenue goal—taxes on gambling and liquor. Congress has also imposed taxes to discourage the consumption of specific items which at the time competed with defense needs, such as manufacture of radios and use of long-distance telephone during the war.

Is the use of taxes to modify economic or social life a perversion of the taxing power? Some people say it is. Perhaps they mean little more than that some specific regulation is distasteful. The taxing power is one of government's strongest. Why not use it for objectives the public wants? If it is easier to use, or more effective, than the police power, property law, or some other means, then regulation through taxation seems logical. Unfortunately, dreams do not always become reality, and results may diverge sadly from untested initial hopes. The objectives of regulation easily get confused with those of revenue, and then neither will be served to best advantage.[9] The taxing method will sometimes be less refined than more direct methods of influencing the economy. It fails to control anyone who is willing and able to pay enough to escape; high liquor taxes, for example, do little to regulate liquor consumption of the wealthy.

Purely revenue measures will have large indirect effects. The structure of the economy will depend upon the architects of our tax laws; regardless of any deliberate intent, relatively favorable tax treatment will encourage growth in one part of the economy, unfavorable treatment will stunt another. We cannot ignore "regulatory" considerations except at our peril. Getting revenue equal to nearly one third of all national income will inevitably affect almost any conceivable aspect of the economy. As the rates of one tax rise, their "distorting" effects increase.

Search for Special Benefit. When tax legislation is being considered, much effort is devoted to special-interest pleas. The public interest can

[9] During World War II a tax was imposed on passenger travel to discourage use of facilities which were overcrowded. Yet after the war when the railroads had more and more unused passenger capacity, when it was economic folly to try to discourage fuller use, when government was unable to finance street and highway expansion to meet all the demand, and when some airlines were getting subsidies to compensate for inadequate travel, the tax was retained—because it brought revenue.

easily get squeezed out by effective "entrepreneurship" in promoting special interest. Seldom will a request be so narrowly selfish that it cannot claim support from at least one good principle. Nevertheless, if when dealing with tax issues we focus on the avoidance of unfairness as well as we can detect it, special-benefit features can be shown for what they are. Inevitably, however, if the public is to accomplish the many fine things it seeks to do through government, paying the costs will make the accomplishment of other fine things more difficult. Spending builds highways to progress, but taxes will erect roadblocks. Government expenditure makes possible public facilities for a better community, but taxes reduce our ability to build houses and produce other things also needed for a good community. How natural, then, for someone to point out that he can do his part of the total job better if not burdened by taxes. In seeking relief, however, is he not proposing heavier burdens for someone else?

Administration and Related Considerations. Legal and constitutional questions sometimes limit choice of taxes, more so for localities than for states and the federal government. And, there is always the question "Can this provision be *administered* reasonably well and inexpensively?" In general, the greater the effort to refine a tax and to adjust it with sensitive discretion to differences in business and personal conditions, the more difficult becomes good administration. For example, if a sales tax exempts medicines, sales to churches and to local governments, and articles returned to the store, troublesome problems of administration are inevitable.

The desire to prevent avoidance also gives rise to complexities which make administration and taxpayer compliance harder.[10] The income tax has become loaded with provisions to keep taxpayers from wiggling through loopholes (and other provisions which open loopholes); as a result, the whole system is harder to administer. Taxes which can be related closely to market transactions (the receipt of wages, for example) have administrative advantages over those which lean heavily upon judgments by an administrator (such as the valuation of real estate). Taxes that can be collected at a few points (the federal tax on cigarets, which are made in a few factories) are easier to administer than those collected at thousands of retail stores (such as the pre-1965 tax on cosmetics).

---

[10] To illustrate from the federal law:

   (*c*) *Allocation of Distributions.*—For purposes of subsections (*a*) and (*b*), section 315(*a*) shall be applied by applying paragraph (2) thereof, and then paragraph (1) thereof—

      (1) first to earnings and profits attributable to amounts included in gross income under section 951 (*a*)(1)(*B*) (or which would have been included except for subsection (*a*)(2) of this section).

      (2) then to earnings and profits attributable to amounts included in gross income under section 951(*a*)(1)(*A*) (but reduced by amounts not included under section 951 (*a*)(1)(*B*) because of the exclusion in subsection (*a*)(2) of this section), and

      (3) then to other earnings and profits.

The section referred to in (1) above in turn refers to two other sections, one of which refers to two other sections.

Certainty and the absence of arbitrariness are highly prized ingredients of a good tax.[11] The customs and traditions of the country, and the general quality of its civil service, make a big difference. Taxpayer *convenience* is important. Generally the most convenient tax is one collected when the taxpayer is best supplied with funds or when payment is part of one's ordinary affairs. A tax collected in a series of trifling sums, such as a gasoline tax, will be more convenient than one collected only once or twice a year, such as property tax. Income tax withholding is a great convenience to taxpayers (though a nuisance to employers).

In selecting taxes, we deal in a total situation which limits our freedom for change. What is best for a small town may not be best for the whole country. And we have a big heritage from the past. Having made adaptations to past decisions, we have an "overhead," a set of commitments, as a result. There is both truth and error in the saying "An old tax is a good tax." Upsetting an applecart spills apples, and changing a firmly established tax will bring disturbances of conditions to which people have become fully adjusted. The lesson? Not "No change," but "Look deeply at the adjustments to be upset."

Per dollar of revenue, some taxes are more expensive than others to operate well. Where there is choice, we should seek to reduce the costs of both taxpayer compliance and government administration.

Promotion of Efficiency in Government. A tax we never see and have no reason to worry about may be most convenient and minimize our emotional hardship. Yet it will violate another principle, that taxes should be open and direct so the public sees the cost of government. Otherwise, we have no way of judging whether expenditures are worth their cost. At best, it is hard to balance benefit and expense in government finance. If costs are hidden, we are less likely to choose to best advantage.

TAX COLLECTIONS AND TRENDS: AN OVERALL VIEW[12]

Until the 1930's, local taxes were largest, but now federal collections are nearly twice state-local levies combined. State taxes are slightly larger than county, city, township, school district, and special district taxes combined. Figure 31–2 presents data on tax collections in four selected years. Somewhat more meaningful data are graphed in Figure 31–3; taxes are expressed in per capita terms, adjusted for the growth of

[11] Like every point, this is most important where tax rates are high. If an individual or business cannot know the tax effects of some possible action and the tax rate is 50 to 70 percent, the tax-created obstacles to good decision making are greater than if the tax rate is 10 percent; the risk of loss from error in the first case may, in fact, often be prohibitive.

[12] Payroll taxes on employers and employees for social security are considered taxes in this book. Government practice, however, rarely includes these amounts (about $33 billion in 1968) as taxes but treats them as "insurance trust revenue."

population, and as dollars of the same purchasing power. In 64 years, taxes per capita increased more than 10-fold in terms of purchasing power.

From just before World War I to 1967, taxes rose from about 7 percent to about 28 percent of national income. Figure 31–4 compares the growth of tax receipts and national output since 1929. From 1950 to 1966 gross national product rose about 139 percent, tax collections 220 percent.

Figure 31–5 gives a general view of the relative importance of major types of taxes for all levels of government combined.

FIGURE 31–2. Tax Collections for Selected Fiscal Years, 1936–66*

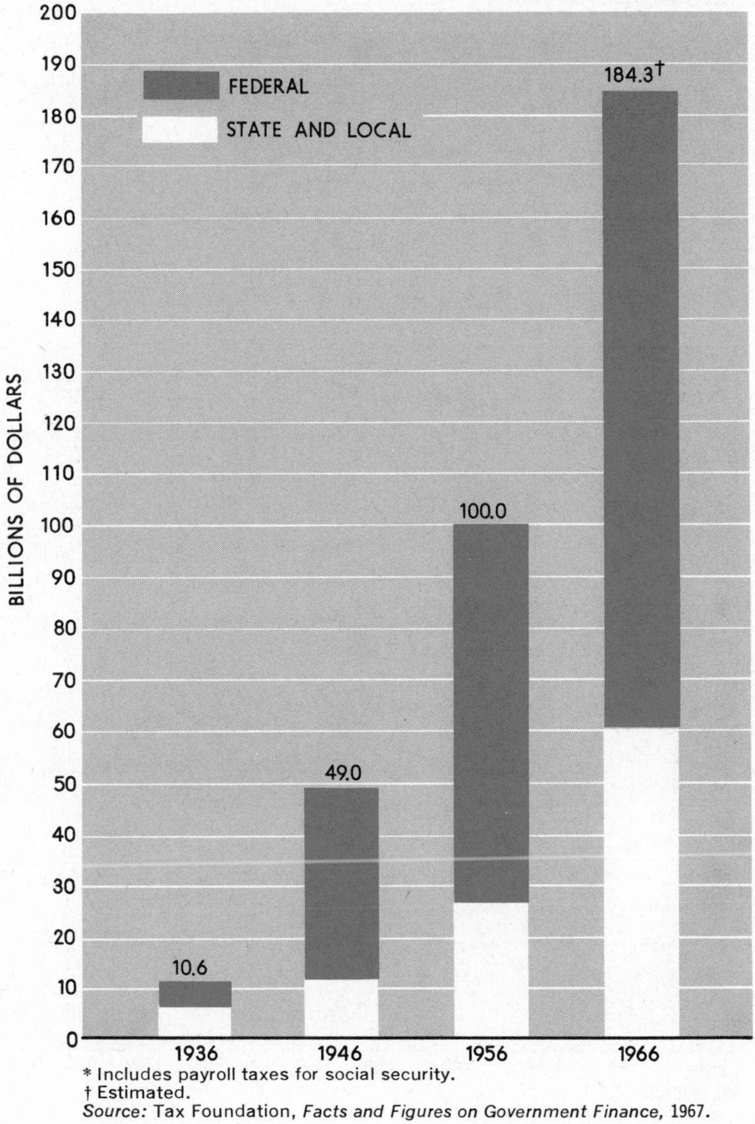

* Includes payroll taxes for social security.
† Estimated.
Source: Tax Foundation, *Facts and Figures on Government Finance,* 1967.

FIGURE 31–3.   Total Taxes per Capita in Dollars of Constant Purchasing Power, Selected Fiscal Years, 1902–66 (1966 Dollars)

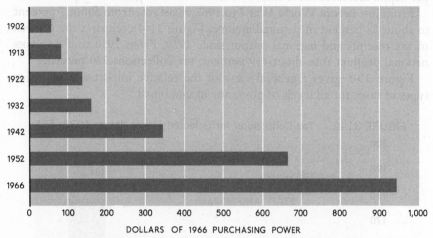

DOLLARS OF 1966 PURCHASING POWER

Source: See Figure 31-2. The adjustment for price change is only approximate.

FIGURE 31–4.   Taxes and Gross National Product, 1929–67*

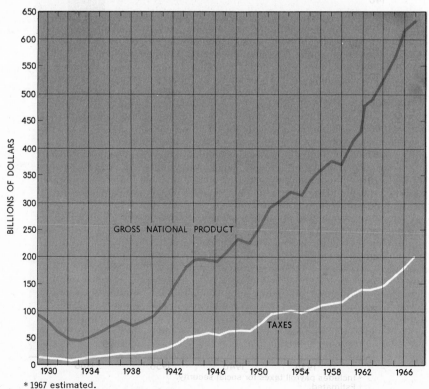

* 1967 estimated.
Source: Survey of Current Business.

TAXES IMPOSED BY THE FEDERAL GOVERNMENT

Table 31–1 shows the major sources of federal tax revenue.

Personal Income Tax. The country's biggest tax—$73 billion in 1968 —is the federal tax on personal income. In a sense, it is also a tax on some businesses, since the income of unincorporated firms is treated for tax purposes as the income of the owners.

In broad outlines, the *concept of income* used conforms moderately well with a reasonable economic definition, although many defects remain. Not everything that "comes in" is what we want to tax as income. Some is transfer (the money I get when I sell my car); some is merely on its way through my pocket to pay the cost of getting income (to restock my shelves if I am a grocer). Congress says that *taxable income* (the tax base) is gross income —wages, salaries, interest, rent, profit—minus (1) business costs and some personal costs of earning the income, (2) interest paid on borrowed funds, (3) many taxes, (4) contributions to most religious, educational, and

FIGURE 31–5.   Major Sources of Tax Revenue—Federal, State, and Local, 1966*

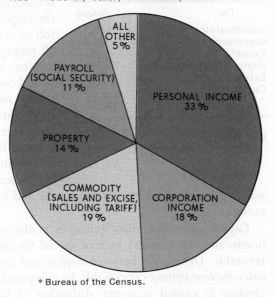

* Bureau of the Census.

other nonprofit philanthropic organizations, (5) some business and personal losses, (6) miscellaneous items, including some medical expenses, (7) the first $100 of corporation dividends, and (8) deductions of $600 for each family member or dependent (twice as much if over age 65).

The last, the personal exemption, assures that the income tax will not force living below some minimum nor burden the very poor. Some of the other deductions, such as business expenses, are essential when the tax falls on business (unincorporated). Yet we immediately face the problem of drawing lines between what is an *expense* of getting income and what is a *use* of income. Law and practice are arbitrary. The farmer may deduct the cost of seed for his vegetable garden, the city man may not; if a lawyer goes out of town on business, he may deduct the cost of his meals only if he stays overnight; union dues are deductible, but not the expense of getting to work. The exclusion of $100 of dividends recognizes that the corporation has already paid tax on this income.

The deduction of contributions encourages desirable actions. The other provisions all have some good rational support, but there is also good reason for criticizing each. Many problems of theory arise, especially in distinguishing between *gross* and *net* income. Large, too, are the practical problems of keeping records of deduction items and then of the government checking. Most taxpayers, however, need not list deductions; arbitrary amounts, roughly one tenth of gross income (but a minimum of $300 plus $100 per dependent), may be deducted in lieu of the specific items. Consequently, administration is much simplified. The Treasury and the employer do virtually the entire job of compliance for nearly half of all taxpayers.

TABLE 31–1. Federal Tax Collections, 1968 Fiscal Year

Tax	Billions
Individual income	$ 73.2
Corporation income	33.9
Excise*	13.7
Payroll (social security)	28.4
Estate and gift	3.1
Customs	2.1
Total	$154.4

* Includes taxes paid into highway trust fund.
Source: Budget . . . 1968.

Not everything an economist would consider income is included in taxable income. One item excluded is the annual use value, the saving in rent, received by one who occupies a house he owns. There are others: income in kind and "fringes," including expense account money. Social security benefits and interest from state and local government bonds are exempt.

Capital gains and losses (changes in the value of real estate, stocks, bonds, and other assets) receive special treatment which is often highly favorable. Distinction between capital and income is not easy. In many cases, income cannot conceivably be computed without taking account of changes in capital accounts; deduction of depreciation is an example. Changes in the amount of capital owned affect a person's economic position. And are not such changes those which should be the basis for personal taxation? (Views differ.) Let us assume that three men have the same capital at the beginning of the year and $10,000 in salary and dividends and save nothing during the year. One ends the year with his capital worth $10,000 more, the second with his capital worth $10,000 less, than at the beginning; the third's capital has not changed. Have their absolute and relative positions changed? Of course. But is such change significant for tax purposes? Most of us would probably agree that it must have some relevance.[13]

---

[13] Avoiding inequities among taxpayers is not the only reason for taking account of changes in capital values. The functioning of the economy is also involved. If losses are not treated as negative income, the risks of investment increase tremendously. People with much income simply could not afford to venture money if they got no

The 1968 rule generally favors anyone with capital gains as compared with those who have equal salary or dividends.

1. Only gains and losses that are "realized" are taxed. As a rule there is no tax until the owner of property sells it, and the owner (not Uncle Sam) has power to decide *when* to sell. I buy two kinds of stock; one goes up $1,000, the other down $1,000. I hold the one that has gone up (realizing no gain and paying no tax) and sell the one that has gone down (realizing the loss and getting some tax advantage). Gains not realized before death are *never* subject to income tax.

2. If an asset has been held over 6 months, only *half* of a gain is included for tax purposes.

3. The maximum rate on half the gain is 50 percent (25 percent of the full gain).

4. Losses can be offset against gains, $1,000 a year against other income, and carried forward indefinitely.

The dominating facts are (*a*) that only half of most capital gains are taxed, (*b*) that, regardless of a person's income, the maximum tax rate on a capital gain from an asset held more than 6 months is 25 percent, and (*c*) that permanent avoidance is possible by holding wealth until death. Here is a "bargain." Logic would lead us to expect just what is happening—the development of ways within the law to convert salaries, interest, rent, and profit into capital gain. Corporations, reinvesting profits, help convert what would be dividends into capital gains.

Exemption of the interest from state and local government bonds offers persons with large incomes a relatively inexpensive way to escape tax. They get tax saving that is greater than the advantage in lower interest to state and local governments. Why? The reason is that not all the bonds can be bought by people with the highest incomes. Some bonds must be sold to others to whom the tax advantage is less. A single person with an annual income around $40,000 can buy tax-exempt bonds that will give yields which benefit him as much as an 8 percent taxable yield. For really rich people, an annual taxable yield of 15 percent, or even more, would be needed to match what can be obtained from some tax-exempt bonds.

Tax *rates* were reduced in 1964 and now begin at 14, and rise to 70, percent. The *marginal rate* (the rate on the highest dollar of income) is 42 percent at $16,000, and 50 percent at $22,000 for a single person. The steepness of the progression is reduced for married couples because they are permitted to split their total income in figuring the tax. If their income is $10,000 above all deductions, they figure the tax not as one amount on $10,000 (about $2,200) but as two taxes on $5,000 (to total $1,800). The highest rates yield insignificant revenue. In fact, that part of the rate

---

tax concession for projects that turned out poorly while giving up in taxes most of the benefits of good ventures. Yet if gains are fully taxed, the successful venturer may find the results of many years' risks taxed all at once and be pushed into brackets where tax rates are high. Some special treatment is essential.

schedule over 22 percent yields scarcely one sixth of all personal income tax revenue.[14]

Rate progression creates a problem of timing. The tax on a given dollar amount of income depends partly upon *when* it is received. If income (net) comes in regularly over the years, the tax is less than if the same total net amount appears in a few big lumps with lean (or loss) years in between. Fluctuating incomes (except when they are always small) will pay more tax than steady ones adding to the same total amount unless special provisions allow averaging, as our law does—but in rather few cases.

If you run a business (incorporated or not) which loses money this year, you pay no tax. If you paid tax last year, the year before, or the third year earlier, you can refigure your taxable income, deducting this year's loss and getting a tax refund. Moreover, any part of the loss not "carried back" can be "carried forward" to offset against income in the next 5 years. This *carryback-carryforward* gives the risky business a better chance to survive.

Most of the tax on wages and salaries is collected by *withholding*. The remainder, as well as the tax on business and farm income, interest, dividends, rents, payments from trusts, royalties, and other forms, is payable in quarterly installments during the year, with a final balancing after the end of the year. Taxpayers file tax returns on which they disclose their income and deductions. Underreporting of income from interest, dividends, small business, farming, and professional practice has been extensive. But administration has been tightened. Almost everyone getting any income now has a number, and the company making the payment reports the amount and the number to the Internal Revenue Service. The figures go into computers and are to be compared with the taxpayer's own report. Success in concealing income will be rarer than in the past.

The great promise of the personal income tax, but one which we have realized only partially, is that it permits (1) equal taxation of people in essentially similar circumstances and (2) differentiation of burdens according to relevant considerations: income, size of family, costs of getting income, use of income. The structure of the federal income tax has weaknesses, although what to me may seem a weakness may seem a tower of strength to you. Certainly those who are favored will fight for the retention of the features they like. Nevertheless, some progress has been made in tax reform, not only in improving the structure of the tax but also in reducing rates. Yield will go up as the economy grows so that if the rise of federal spending is restrained, more rate cuts or other forms of tax relief will be possible.

---

[14] Approximately 90 percent of taxable income falls in brackets taxable at 22 percent or less (under $6,000 for a single person, twice that for married couples).

Corporation Income Tax. The next largest source of revenue is the tax on corporation earning. The bulk of corporation earnings are taxed at 48 percent. The rate on income under $25,000 is 22 percent.[15] The tax base is generally net income, receipts minus expenses (including interest on debt). Both the personal and corporation income taxes have a feature which offers one of the few ways to hold on to most of a big income. "Percentage depletion" is the key, though the system is more complex. The rule is this: In computing his tax, the owner of a natural resource can deduct a percentage of the gross proceeds (not over 50 percent of net income) each year, regardless of his investment. A manufacturer or other businessman can deduct as depreciation only as much as he has invested. But the owner of an oil well, coal mine, gravel pit, or most other types of natural resources can deduct a percentage of his gross income each year as depletion even after he has deducted all of his investment. You put $100,000 into an oil well. Over the years you can count as a cost (return of capital) not only your $100,000 but perhaps a million or more.[16] The annual percentage for oil and natural gas is 27½ percent. For most other minerals the rate is less.

Largely by actions presumably temporary, the tax rate on corporations rose from around 15 percent in the 1930's to more than three times that rate today. Why burden the organizations on which the country relies for economizing—organizations that allocate resources efficiently and undertake economic growth? Like throwing sand in the gears of machines, loading business with taxes seems a way to shackle ourselves—sufficiently ridiculous to ask why we got where we are.[17] Our answer might be that we eased into the situation by the slow easy stages of the drug addict, although this comparison is extreme. Getting out of the habit of taxing (ourselves through our) businesses, however, is likely to be as hard as curing the dope habit. In 1954, Congress, hoping to stimulate investment, granted permission for businesses to deduct as current expense much more depreciation in the years just after new plant and equipment are acquired. President Kennedy persuaded Congress to grant an "investment tax credit" to businesses; this permits them to deduct from their tax bills up to 7 percent of amounts spent on new capital equipment (subject to many

[15] The rate differential between "small" and "large" corporations is nearly 120 percent. Why such a gap? Large corporations are important as employers, as producers, as innovators, and as places for investment by persons of all income groups.

[16] For a person in a high tax bracket the opportunities are attractive. In figuring income tax, he deducts as a business expense much that he pays to a prospector who explores for oil. If these deductions come from a 70 percent tax bracket, the money he spends deprives him of 30 cents of the dollar and Uncle Sam 70 cents. Obviously, his maximum potential loss is cut greatly. Then if his men strike oil, the percentage depletion rule gives him a nice chunk of *tax-exempt* income.

[17] A tax rate of 50 percent, we recall, will lead to the rejection of investment projects to be financed by equity capital unless the pretax return is twice the amount needed to attract capital.

restrictions). This credit, along with a 1962 relaxation of rules governing depreciation deductions, will offset some of the force of high tax rates in discouraging modernization and expansion.[18]

One reason that business has done well (though not up to its potential) in spite of high corporation tax rates is that many corporations undoubtedly shift much of the tax to the consumer—making it to some extent a crude form of hidden sales tax.

Large reduction of corporation tax *revenues* seems improbable in view of the growth of spending. But substantial reduction in the tax *rate* could be made gradually—perhaps 2 percentage points a year. Economic growth would maintain the dollar yield or even permit some rise.

Commodity and Service Taxes.   The federal government imposes no general tax on sales, manufacture, turnover, or gross receipts. Until 1965, however, it taxed nearly three dozen items. Then a sweeping change eliminated the tax on almost all these items, except those with big yields.

Some were mass taxes designed to get large revenues from families at all levels of income—taxes on beer and cigarets, for example. Some fell ostensibly on "luxuries," things not essential for survival, such as jewelry, furs, sporting goods, and cosmetics. Some fell on necessities that were not large revenue producers—the tax on electric light bulbs. Others were introduced to discourage consumption of products which competed with armaments for labor and materials. A few added to costs of production by business. One set—taxes on gasoline, trucks, tires, and autos—related to benefit; most of their yield was to pay for highways.

Some were imposed as a percentage of price: 10 percent on the manufacturer's price of an auto; others were a flat amount per unit: $10.50 per gallon of distilled spirits. For a few there was no apparent justification, except revenue; others of no yield significance serve regulatory purposes (machine guns, opium, state bank notes, gambling).

Alcoholic beverage, tobacco, and motor fuel taxes were retained as big revenue producers. Gradual reductions in the rates of two other big revenue sources—auto manufacture and telephone usage—were begun; Vietnam costs, however, led to the reimposition of earlier rates on a temporary basis.

Presidents Eisenhower, Kennedy, and Johnson have urged Congress to make greater use of excise taxes of a "user charge" nature (chiefly on motor fuels used by airplanes and barges) to help pay for aids to navigation. Congress has not met the requests.

[18] On the other hand, a move to reduce the attractiveness of equity investment has also been made—elimination of the credit against tax of 4 percent of dividends received. This credit was designed to offset some of the twofold taxation of dividend income—to both the corporation and the shareholder. The issues are complex. Critics argued that much of the corporation tax was shifted to consumers, that 4 percent was too little to do much good in any case, and that relatively too much relief went to persons with large incomes.

Death and Gift Taxes. Property passing at death is taxed under the federal estate tax when the net amounts exceed $60,000 if the decedent is unmarried, or twice that amount if married. Rates range from 3 to 77 percent. The number and relationship of heirs has no bearing, except that half the wealth may be left to a surviving spouse tax free. Amounts to pay debts and charitable bequests are not taxed.

Noncharitable gifts above varying exemptions made during life are subject to gift taxes at rates related to, but well below those of, the estate tax. The gift tax makes up for some of the estate tax revenue that the government ordinarily loses when property is distributed before death. In spite of loopholes and crudities, these taxes impose heavy burdens on the transmission of large private fortunes. In relation to the revenue from the

TABLE 31–2.   Selected Federal Commodity and Service Taxes, Yields and Rates, 1968

Commodity or Service	Yield (Millions)	Rate
Liquor	$4,203	$10.50*
Tobacco	2,261	.08†
Motor fuel	3,645	.04‡
Autos, trucks, parts, tires, and tubes	3,051	7%
Telephone and telegraph service	1,200	10%
Sugar	111	.015§
Wagering	7	10%

* Per gallon of distilled spirits.
† Per package of 20 cigarets.
‡ Per gallon of gasoline.
§ Per pound.
Source: President's budget document for the 1968 fiscal year with later adjustments.

progressive portion of the personal income tax rate schedule, death tax yields are large.

For generations many economists have urged greater reliance upon inheritance and estate taxes. Here there seem to be opportunities for imposing progressive taxes that would bring revenue with less depressive effect, per dollar of revenue, on business than high-bracket income tax rates. Death taxes do not hit a man as he builds a business, affecting his incentive or ability to accumulate capital in the company.[19] Today's estate and gift taxes are unbelievably complicated. They offer opportunities for

[19] This generalization, like most others, is not entirely valid. The desirability of advance accumulation of liquid assets to pay death tax, and the use of methods permitted by law to escape some of the tax, lead owners of family businesses to arrange affairs in ways that impair somewhat the company's growth. See Carl S. Shoup, *Federal Estate and Gift Taxes* (Washington: The Brookings Institution, 1966).

arranging affairs to avoid much potential burden. They fall unequally on persons in largely similar circumstances because not everyone takes advantage of avoidance possibilities. Modernization of the laws would be desirable, but attempts have been put aside because of the greater urgency of other tax issues and lack of consensus about what would be best.

STATE TAXES

Tax collections for all states combined are shown in Table 31–3.

TABLE 31–3.   State Tax Collections by Type of Tax, 1967*

Tax Source	Millions	Per Capita
Total collections	$35,510	$180
Sales and gross receipts	18,551	94
General sales or gross receipts	8,924	45
Motor fuels	4,839	49
Alcoholic beverages	1,041	5
Tobacco products	1,602	8
Insurance	866	4
Public utilities	600	3
Other	679	3
License	3,632	18
Motor vehicles and operators	2,316	12
Corporations in general	615	3
Alcoholic beverage	138	1
Other	562	3
Income	7,136	36
Individual income	4,909	25
Corporation net income	2,227	11
Payroll for unemployment	3,600†	18
Property	862	4
Death and gift	795	4
Severance	577	3
Other	357	2

* Because of rounding details will not necessarily add to totals.
† Estimated.
Source: Bureau of the Census.

Revenues in 1966 were two and a half times those of 1956. Yet most states face nagging pressures for more. Except for a few prohibitions in the federal Constitution (states may not, for example, tax imports, exports, or interstate commerce, or create certain serious discriminations), states are sovereign and can impose whatever taxes they wish and can make them effective. Some state constitutions, however, restrict taxing power severely.

Commodity Taxes.   General sales taxes and levies on specific commodities provide most state tax revenues. Most state tax *retail sales*, exempting, however, rents, many services, and some other expenditures; a few exempt food.[20] Rates range from 2 to 5 percent.

Americans like their autos, and things people like a lot are good targets for legislatures seeking to separate us from our money. Taxes on gasoline and diesel fuel are imposed by all states, ordinarily 6 cents or more a gallon. Most states "earmark" motor fuel tax revenues for highways but tend to "shortchange" cities for local streets, traffic control, and other costs attributable to motorists and truckers. Closely related are annual license charges on owners of trucks and autos. Revenue from imbibers of alcoholic beverages are substantial. Some states run their own liquor stores and get revenue in the form of monopoly profit. More impose taxes, though rates are well below the federal tax. Only one state (North Carolina) fails to tax cigarets; the per-package rate is usually 6 to 11 cents.

With exceptions, such as the tax on gasoline (with its justification on the basis of benefit) and taxes on liquor (for regulatory purposes), economists have generally considered sales taxes less desirable than personal income taxes. Most economists probably still hold this view, but not so strongly. What alternatives are more attractive? Compared with *increases* in the personal income tax to make up revenue lost from repeal of sales taxes, the latter seem less obnoxious now than in the past. The major defect of sales taxes has seemed to be the burden they impose on the lower income groups. Yet to get anything like the tax revenue needed in most states, we *must* dip deeply into the income structure. Sales taxes that exempt rent, food (but few state sales taxes do), and medical services are only a little worse, from the point of view of their impact on the poor, than the best alternative we have to get the same revenue. It is the large family with low income that is burdened much more by sales taxes than by a broader income tax. Indiana and Hawaii provide end-of-the-year refunds to low-income taxpayers on $300 or more of purchases.

Income Taxes. Two out of every three states tax personal and corporation income. Despite variation in details, these taxes are broadly similar to the federal tax, except that rates are much lower. Exemptions are often higher, but husband-wife income splitting is rare. The net burden of these taxes to the taxpayer is less than may appear because they are deductible in computing the income on which the federal tax rates are imposed. Most states now collect personal income tax by withholding and cooperate with the Internal Revenue Service in administration.

---

[20] To prevent escape of sales tax by purchasing in another state, *use taxes* are on the statute books of all states having retail sales taxes. A resident of the state who buys outside must pay tax equal to the amount due if he made the purchase at home. Effective enforcement is confined largely to purchases (*a*) of autos, which must be registered to get a license, and (*b*) from mail-order and other relatively large sellers who can be required to collect the tax.

Property, Business, Death, and Other Taxes. At one time, states got most of their revenue from annual taxes on real estate and some other forms of property. Today, states generally leave this revenue source to local governments. Numerous state taxes fall on special types of business: amusements (especially horse racing), banks, insurance companies, railroads, and electric and gas utilities. It is rare, however, for any one of these taxes to be of more than nominal importance in a state's budget.

All states but one tax transfers of property at death; a dozen tax noncharitable gifts made during life. Although detailed provisions differ greatly, most states use the *inheritance* form, basing the tax on the amount received by each heir and his relationship to the decedent. Many states exempt most life insurance and some property in trusts. Some states once competed with others for wealthy residents by offering low death tax rates or none at all. To prevent one or a few states from destroying the power of others to impose death taxes, Congress tells property owners, in effect, "You need not pay all the federal estate tax in cash. Instead, we will accept, within varying limits, receipts for state death tax as payment of federal tax. If the state tax falls below the credit, the federal tax will not be any lower." The credit, therefore, removed much of the advantage one state could offer over another in death tax burdens.

There are also a host of minor taxes, some of which are occasionally important. Various license and franchise taxes, severance taxes (levies on natural resources extracted from the earth), and stock transfer taxes are used in one state or another. Finally, state payroll taxes finance unemployment insurance.

TABLE 31–4.   Local Government Revenue, 1966

Type	Total (Billions)
Taxes, total	$27.4
Property	23.8
Sales and gross receipts	2.0
Licenses, permits, and other	1.0
Individual income	0.5
Charges and miscellaneous	8.0
Intergovernmental revenue	17.8
Utility revenue*	5.3
Insurance and trust fund revenue†	0.8
Total revenue	59.3

* Because of rounding, details may not add to total. Gross revenues of water, electric, transit, and other systems; operating costs have *not* been deducted.
† Chiefly payments of employees into retirement funds.
Source: Bureau of the Census.

LOCAL REVENUE SOURCES

Most of us live subject to several local governments: counties, cities, towns or villages; school, sewer, water, and paving districts. Until recently, almost all local tax revenue came from the same general source, the property tax. It is still much the most important, but others are playing a growing role. Table 31–4 shows 1966 revenues of local governments, including nontax receipts, which play a large part in local finance. The per capita amounts shown in Figure 31–6 conceal wide diversity.

Property Tax. The property tax, until 1940 the biggest source of tax revenue in the country, is almost exclusively a local levy. Where there are overlapping local governments, each, as a rule, fixes its part of the total and shares in the result. Each parcel of real estate—land and buildings—is valued (assessed) about every 3 to 6 years. Typically, the law appears to require that property must be valued at what it would sell for under normal conditions of sale at about the time of the assessment. The general practice is to value at a considerably lower figure; a nationwide survey found 1961 assessments more often under than over 30 percent, sometimes under 10 percent, of actual market prices. Since, with rare exceptions, no deduction is allowed for mortgages or other debts, the property tax is by no means a tax on net wealth. Valuation is often done poorly so that there

FIGURE 31–6. Per Capita Amounts of Local Revenue, by Source, Fiscal Year 1966

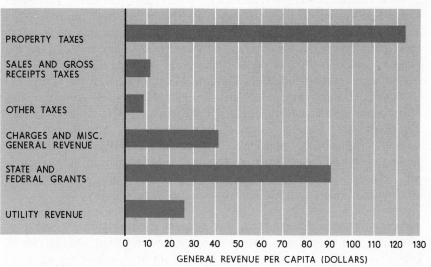

GENERAL REVENUE PER CAPITA (DOLLARS)

Source: Statistical Abstract.

is not only underassessment but wide *inequality* in the amount of underassessment. Some localities, however, often with state help, have made substantial improvement in the quality of assessment.

The annual tax usually amounts to nearly 2 percent of market value but sometimes much more. It affects some forms of investment more than others; anyone considering construction of a new building must be able to count on getting enough from users to cover some costs of government (the real estate tax), while an investment in securities rarely carries a comparable requirement. The tax is a fixed cost which, as a rule, declines only slowly when income from the property falls. In most localities tangible personal property—autos, machinery, business inventory, and furniture—and, less generally, intangible property (bank accounts, stocks and bonds, mortgages) are nominally subject to the tax. On such items, however, the tax is applied haphazardly and unequally; although revenue from the non–real-estate portion of the property tax is not large on the average, it is sometimes heavy, especially for businesses.

Property tax revenues have risen tremendously—on a per capita basis, tripling in the last 20 years, but they have not expanded as rapidly as local government spending. In some cases, there are legal limits to the rates that may be applied. Most important, perhaps, officials have been reluctant to raise assessments as market prices of land and buildings go up. (Owners *do* have many votes.) Local governments, hard-pressed for revenue, have found two major alternatives, state and federal grants (discussed in Chapter 33) and new taxes.

New Taxes.   Local governments have turned to new taxes. Hundreds of localities have their own taxes on sales, usually as a small addition to the state rate. Some have "income" taxes, although in fact most of these fall on little more than wages, salaries, and business income—at a rate of around 1 percent—with no personal deductions or exemptions; in Detroit and New York City, however, full-fledged net income taxes are in force. There are taxes on such things as cigarets, amusements, hotel rooms, autos, gasoline, utility services, extraction of natural resources, and scores of fees. Localities continue to search for more revenue sources. The problems are serious. In addition to opposition of voters, local officials find their taxing power restricted *legally* by state law and *economically* by intercommunity competition, i.e., the prospect that higher taxes will drive away more residents and businesses than higher spending will attract.

Fees, Licenses, Fines, Tolls, and Special Assessments.   Local governments, and federal and state as well, get revenue from charges which have something of a *price* (payment for a service), something of a *tax* (compulsory charge without special regard for benefit), and something of a *penalty* element. Fees (those for parking are now familiar), license charges, tolls, fines, stamp taxes, and special assessments are not always easy to distinguish.

Generally, a *fee* is a government charge more or less related to the cost of providing a service—recording a document in an official record or inspecting an elevator. The charge may not only bring some revenue but also serve somewhat as a price to limit consumption. *Licenses,* in addition to producing income, aid in control; auto registration and driver licenses make policing easier. *Fines* are imposed to deter law violation but also yield some revenue. Sometimes fees, licenses, and fines are little more than a lucrative source of private revenue because a local official is permitted to keep some or all of the money collected.

Many of today's college students will encounter personally the *special assessment.* If you buy a house in a new development, you are likely to find yourself paying assessments for streets, sewers, and perhaps other facilities. At least some of the benefit from these capital improvements will accrue to you as an owner of the property rather than to the community in general. It seems logical, therefore, to require that owners pay the cost. The special assessment is the device for charging such costs to those who benefit, ordinarily over a period of several years. Good as the principle appears, results suffer from the practical difficulties of deciding how much of a project's cost should be allocated to each property.

Tolls were common in America over a century ago and then nearly disappeared. After World War II they became familiar—motorists willingly pay extra for good facilities—but the interstate highway program makes no use of tolls. The federal government places no charges on the vast system of inland waterways built at taxpayer expense.[21]

SHIFTING AND INCIDENCE OF TAXES

Anyone on whom a tax is imposed may try to pass the burden to someone else. Certainly, when a cigaret or beer tax is collected from a business, we expect that the firm's managers will try to recover it as they do other costs. The process of passing a tax along to someone else is *shifting.* The place where it finally rests we call its *incidence.* Shifting may be *forward,* as from gasoline wholesaler to consumer, or *backward,* as from manufacturer to the supplier of a raw material or employee.

No one will freely shoulder another's tax. But we will if we must. The other fellow can get us to pay when he has power to withhold something we want badly enough for us to bear the tax to get the product or service. As a general rule, *only in business dealings can one person shift taxes to another.* Taxes, like wages and the cost of raw materials, get involved in the economic process and are passed along. Our study of pricing in Part 4 will help in understanding why economists conclude that the more generally a tax falls on all suppliers, the more easily they can shift it.

Taxes on *personal income* will generally rest on the family that pays them. If you have a job and taxes rise, you might go to the boss and try to get a raise; by bargaining hard, you might succeed. Generally, however, you will already have bargained as forcefully as you are able to do. The boss may say, "Things are tough, I know, but the tax will not make your services any more attractive to me or my customers. I cannot sell my product for any more because of the tax. So I just cannot afford to raise your pay." Unless the income tax raises productivity—or increases demand—there is little chance for the taxpayer to shift it to someone else.[22]

[21] Tolls are charged on the St. Lawrence Waterway and the Panama Canal.

[22] Yet, there are exceptions. (1) Labor unions may force employers to raise the wage scale over what it would be otherwise, a possibility. (2) The tax may discourage work. If, as a result of the tax increase, the supply of labor goes down more than the demand, some of the tax may be shifted to employers and consumers. The higher the

If income tax rates go down, can one expect employees to acquiesce in wage cuts?

Taxes on *commodities and services* are generally shifted to the consumer, whether the tax is imposed early (a state tax on electricity) or late (on a sale at retail) in the process of getting the product to the buyer. Exceptions may be numerous, however, for reasons which our analyses of the pricing process will enable us to understand—short-run and long-run differences, closeness of substitution, differences in demand and supply elasticities. The shifting of taxes on real estate and on business income are examined elsewhere.

THE DISTRIBUTION OF AMERICA'S TAXES

On the score of raising revenue—taking resources away from the private economy for use collectively—our system does an effective job. This huge "tax take" represents great social discipline. The system has many faults, but it accomplishes a major purpose of taxation: getting revenue.

FIGURE 31–7.   Federal, State, and Local Taxes as a Percentage of Total Income for All Families by Income Class—1965

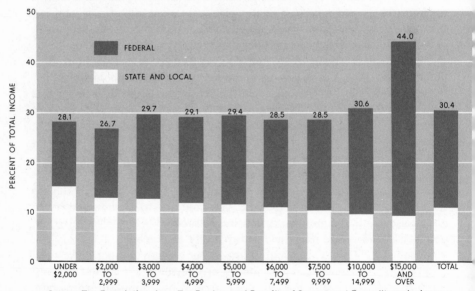

Source: Tax Foundation, Inc., *Tax Burdens and Benefits of Government Expenditures by Income Class, 1961 and 1965.*

tax rate, the greater the probability that some people will prefer more leisure (avoiding overtime or retiring at a younger age). To get their labor in the market, the community must then pay enough to absorb some of the tax. (3) Part of the personal income tax falling on unincorporated business may be shiftable as a business cost.

The country's total tax bill is known. Can we learn how much persons with incomes of different sizes pay in taxes? The picture is fairly clear (Fig. 31–7). At the bottom of the income distribution, the tax system is regressive; above $20,000, it is progressive, sometimes steeply so. In the range that includes most of the public, burdens are roughly proportional at around 29 percent of income. All such conclusions, however, are somewhat unsatisfactory; for one reason, no one knows for certain how some important taxes are shifted.

The poor pay taxes that are heavy in relation to their income. Those below the income tax exemption level must still pay (1) sales taxes, (2) taxes which have been business costs that become part of prices, including (3) real estate taxes reflected in rent or on property owned, and (4) social security taxes. Something depends upon *what* these people consume. At the upper end of the income distribution, over $15,000 or so, the income tax dominates. Of course, there are exceptions. Some families with large incomes pay rather little income tax. At all income levels, there will be a divergence from family to family, depending upon patterns of consumption, age, place of residence, occupation, wealth, and many other factors. Moreover, some tax bills are relatively high because those who pay them want better-than-average schools and other public services—and are freely willing to shoulder the costs.

TERMS AND CONCEPTS

progressive tax	marginal rate	corporation income tax
proportional tax	avoidance	percentage depletion
regressive tax	evasion	death taxes
tax base	personal income tax	gift tax
tax rate	transfer payment	excise tax
ability to pay	capital gains (loses)	shifting
incentive effect	withholding	incidence
income effect	carryback-carryforward	use tax
horizontal equity	tax equity	vertical equity

QUESTIONS

1. Why must tax burdens fall on individuals unequally? What principles can best guide legislative bodies in imposing unequal burdens?
2. What considerations should guide Congress and your state legislature in (*a*) reducing and (*b*) increasing taxes? Give your reasons.
3. In what sense are all taxes, including the tax on corporation income, burdens on *people?*
4. What are the reasons for and against trying to make greater use of the benefit principle in deciding how tax burdens are to be allocated?
5. Outline a schedule of personal income tax rates that seem to you to reflect fairly ability to pay. Explain your reasons.

6. Discuss three problems of defining "income" for purposes of personal taxation.
7. "One may advocate progression in a tax system while opposing tax rates of 50 percent or more." Discuss.
8. What changes would make the tax system of your state more nearly meet your standards of a good tax system? Why?
9. How does the property tax actually operate in your community? How might it be improved to help pay for more services of local government?
10. What are the features of a good tax system?

32

INTERGOVERNMENTAL FINANCIAL RELATIONS; GOVERNMENT DEBT

The American federal system was founded on the general principle that the National Government should act only where the States would be incompetent to act, or where action by individual States might be injurious to the harmony of the United States.
The Commission on Intergovernmental Relations

This chapter first discusses federal-state-local financial relations. We then turn to government borrowing and debt management.

FEDERAL-STATE-LOCAL RELATIONS[1]

Three levels of government fish in the same income stream. All want a bigger catch; yet the more one gets, the harder others find the fishing. This rivalry is not new. Congress has woven a revenue net which now stretches across the income stream and catches most of the big fish. State and local governments must take what is left, even though their appetites, too, have grown. The resources which the federal government uses—whether labor and materials or the money to buy them—are not available to other levels of government. The more Uncle Sam takes, the greater do taxpayers resist further burdens.

Many of the public-sector functions to be performed, however, are

[1] The material in this section draws heavily upon two more specialized studies by the author and published by the Tax Foundation, Inc., *Handbook of State and Local Government Finance* and *Federal Revenue Sharing with the States*, 1966 and 1967, respectively. Used by permission. International financial relations present such dissimilar issues as the sharing of costs of joint defense against Communism and the taxation of individuals and corporations residing or doing business abroad. U.S. law generally permits an individual or corporation to credit income tax paid to a foreign government against tax due here on income from abroad.

local and state rather than national. "Fiscal imbalance" results: The level of government which ought to be doing the job is not the one best able to raise the money. Some of the most lively debates in Washington, state capitols, and in most city halls deal with one or another aspect of this problem.

Issues Bearing on the Study of Intergovernmental Relations. Financial relations among the three levels of government have aroused concern for generations. The following summary points draw upon a large literature.

1. The American public believes that some functions can be performed best at the local level rather than the state, or by the state in preference to the national government. The placing of responsibilities for performing governmental functions, however, has not always been matched by the effective ability to raise revenue. For decades localities have faced increasing pressure to spend more, but their power to raise the necessary revenue has lagged. They have depended heavily upon the property tax. Though its yield has grown rapidly, especially since World War II, objections to the increasingly intensive use have been strong. Earlier, during the Great Depression, property owners often found themselves unable to pay the tax due; but welfare costs rose, and school and other functions had to go on. More recently, one objection to the heavier use of this tax is a conviction that to do so would lead some taxpayers to flee from, not enter, or not expand in, the community. When businesses are discouraged in this way, it is argued, the source of jobs and income will suffer.

2. Such mobility also concerns states, though to smaller extent. The taxes which one government can impose will depend upon what others do. A state, therefore, has more effective taxing power than the sum of its localities acting individually. Each local unit faces competition from close neighbors. But if the state government imposes a tax to raise equal revenue, mobility is less of a threat. Similarly, if the national government does the job, the tax in question cannot be modified by one state to entice either businesses or high income taxpayers away from other states.

3. The vast majority of local governments cannot possibly administer nonproperty taxes as effectively and efficiently as a state. Similarly, the federal government has some advantage over states in administering taxes. In short, the larger units of government are better able than smaller units to collect income, sales, death, and other nonproperty taxes. These are needed to provide some of the money for schools, public assistance, highways, and other functions.

4. States prescribe the obligations of localities to perform functions. States also grant the legal authority of local governments to tax and in other ways influence their power to raise revenue. State governments, therefore, exert commanding influence on local finances.

5. The spending in one community, and in one state, has "spillover"

effects outside. The amount spent for functions and the quality of performance in one state, or locality, will have significance elsewhere.

6. Overlapping (sometimes called double or multiple) taxation increases as more and more units at different levels of government utilize consumption, business, and income taxes. One burden piled on others may produce a total result significantly different from anything desirable. The revenue which one government can raise will be affected by the use which others are making of the same tax base. Moreover, costs of administration and compliance of such multiple taxes lead to waste and apparently needless use of resources.

7. The use of government to redistribute income by providing some groups with relatively more than others, perhaps in government service or perhaps in transfer payments of money, creates special problems of intergovernmental relations.

8. The exemption of governments from one another's taxes creates conflicts. For example, when the federal or a state government acquires real estate, the locality loses part of its property tax base. When a town or city engages in business-type activity, such as the provision of utility services, the state government cannot collect income tax as it could if a private, profit-making business supplied the service. Deductibility, such as local taxes in computing state or federal income tax, will relate the finances of different governments in ways which can be complex.

Coordination and Cooperation. In some respects states and localities have competing interests. Yet these governments also need to cooperate if they are to deal efficiently with problems of mutual concern—water, traffic, or policing in a metropolitan area; preventing evasion of state sales taxes; deciding on the relative state and local use to be made of the same tax base. Arrangements for getting such cooperation, though far from adequate, have developed and continue to do so.

Interstate compacts, e.g., those regarding license fees and motor fuel taxes paid by truckers or the development of river areas, are negotiated and approved by Congress. Less formal agreements among states deal with a variety of problems. Governors meet together to discuss their common concerns; so do mayors. Procedures to serve mutual interest are developing in urban areas. Dozens of separate governments in the same area claim independence, but in fact they depend on each other. In some cases, state governments provide authority or compulsion for neighboring localities to work together. Frequently, localities contract for services to be provided by one government in return for payment. The growth of professionalism among civil servants enlarges informal cooperation; influential results, even though largely unnoticed by the public, are modifying local performance and even policymaking. Local personnel discover many aspects of common interest in the solution of problems of policing, public health, education, and other activities.

In 1959 President Eisenhower signed a law setting up the Advisory Commission on Intergovernmental Relations. Its 25 members include congressmen, cabinet members, governors, mayors, members of state legislatures, county officers, and private citizens. A professional staff aided by expert consultants has produced excellent analyses of problems, some broad and some pinpointed to narrowly specific problems. The Commission has seen some of its recommendations adopted widely. For example, in their 1964–65 sessions 39 state legislatures enacted one or more proposals of the Commission. In 1965 Congress adopted a dozen recommendations. Although the list of unfinished business is long and growing, continuing progress can be expected—but not miracles or sweeping changes in such fundamentals as the reallocation of responsibility for a big function or of a major revenue source.

TABLE 32–1.   Intergovernmental Expenditure by Selected Function and Level of Government, 1960 and 1966 (Millions)

Source of Funds*	Edu-cation	High-ways	Public Welfare	Health & Hos-pitals	Natural Re-sources	Social In-surance Adminis-tration	Housing and Urban Renewal
1960:							
Federal	950	2,905	2,070	135	127	325	—
State	5,300	1,247	1,483	176	20	—	—
Local	†	41	31	72	†	—	—
1966:							
Federal	3,014	3,953	3,579	323	218	486	607
State	10,177	1,725	2,882	275	36	—	60
Local	35	32	43	86	3	—	—

* Local figures represent payments to state governments only; interlocal transactions excluded.

† Minor amounts not included.

Source: Department of Commerce, Bureau of the Census.

Intergovernmental Payments: Grants-in-Aid. Payments from governments at one level to those at another, especially state to local, began long ago. Their rapid growth in recent years, however, has altered their role beyond measure. Complex and widely diverse systems have been developed.

States frequently *share* with localities the revenue from one or more taxes. For example, Michigan gives cities and townships one eighth of sales tax proceeds on the basis of population; Wisconsin shares one third of personal income tax revenue with counties, cities, and towns. However, a large portion of state payments to local government, and almost all federal distributions, take the form of *grants-in-aid*.

Although federal grants to aid a few state-local activities go back many decades, the dollar amounts were small before the Great Depression. They then increased to meet serious emergencies. New programs were added and, with a few exceptions, they continued after prosperity returned. Since World War II federal grants have multiplied, not only in dollar amounts but also in the number of different programs. In 1955 around 90 federal *grant-in-aid* programs were in effect. A 1966 count found 399— health services had 86; education, 82; housing and community development, 32; public assistance plus "antipoverty" and other welfare services, 58; and so on.

Localities were getting about 30 percent of their revenues from states, and states were getting one fourth of theirs from the national government.

Functions Financed by Intergovernmental Payments.   Table 32–1 shows the major functions which are financed by intergovernmental payments. Education gets much the largest total, with highways and public welfare next and approximately equal.

Reasons for Grants.[2]   Why have intergovernmental grants grown so much? Some of the reasons are implied in the points made earlier. Local governments have felt pressures to enlarge expenditures more rapidly than the public wished to increase utilization of the property tax; states, after largely abandoning their own use of the property tax,[3] developed new revenue sources which could help finance payments to localities. Somewhat similarly, the federal government has been able to raise funds—by borrowing during the 1930's and more recently from a rapidly growing income tax base and progressive rates—with less difficulty than states or localities would have in getting such amounts. Some supporters of federal aids emphasize the argument that the federal revenue system utilizes taxes which come nearer to meeting the criteria of a good revenue system than do the taxes of states and localities.[4]

[2] For the sake of simplicity, the term "grant" will be used here to include tax sharing. Although this usage is now customary, the two have somewhat different economic and political significance. Grants carry with them more control over spending of the funds than does tax sharing. When the state and its localities share in the revenue from a tax, each feels the effect of fluctuations in yield; some grants, however, are for fixed amounts in the short run so that one level, usually the state, must absorb all of the results of yield variations.

[3] This action illustrates "separation of tax sources." One level of government gives up using one source of revenue so governments at another level can use it more fully. Other devices of intergovernmental financial cooperation are (1) the tax credit, as in the federal estate tax; (2) unified collection of a tax levied by more than one jurisdiction, a method now widely used in California and Illinois for state collection of local sales tax. Such practice is sometimes called "piggybacking" when the locality puts its tax on top of the state tax or even when a state income tax consists of little more than additions to the federal. (3) Tax deductions, such as federal allowance of state taxes as a deduction in computing taxable income; (4) tax sharing, e.g., one third of a state gasoline tax turned over to localities; and (5) cooperation in administration.

[4] The argument seems plausible. No one can be sure, however, what *changes* in the two revenue systems would result from the heavier use of one to relieve the other.

Another reason for the growth of "payments" from higher to lower levels of government has been a desire by various groups to influence both the total and the pattern of government expenditure. For example, how could the counties of a state—or the states of the nation—be induced to develop a unified highway system? Would it not be desirable to get all school districts to offer standards of education above the level some would provide? How could all states be induced to offer more medical aid to the aged poor?

The justification advanced for the extension of influence may be a belief that the quality of performance of a function in one community has significance outside. It is argued, for example, that the common responsibility for defense, the constant movement of population, the interdependence of all parts of the economy, and the needs of citizenship—all combine to make health, education, reduction of poverty, urban transit, and so forth more nationwide, and less completely local, matters than Americans once believed. When some areas fail to provide good quality government service, people far removed may suffer at least a little. Some spillover effects unquestionably develop. But to what extent? The benefit to people in one area of better performance by localities at the other side of the state or nation may be trifling. Nevertheless, the possibility of even a little potential benefit has been cited to support action to compel one group to help pay for services elsewhere without any evidence that on balance there is likely to be net benefit.

Support for the use of grants to influence expenditures also comes from a belief that the larger jurisdiction (state vis-à-vis localities or nation vis-à-vis states or localities) both can and will direct performance to achieve better results than would the smaller ones acting on their own. Examples of the correctness of the belief can be cited; but the depth and the extent cannot be measured, and criticism of actual results also rests on convincing evidence.

The growth of federal-to-state and state-to-local grants for assistance to the poor rests in part upon a belief that the provision of relief aid is more properly the responsibility of the larger, than of the smaller, units of government. Otherwise some localities (or states) would have much greater burdens per capita than would others. And the sources of distress and causes of poverty, it is argued, lie in forces operating on a broader scale than any locality (or state) can control. And will not the ability to finance relief aid be least just where the need is largest?

The growth of grants also results from the greater practical capacity of larger units to raise revenue. Localities contain all the taxpayers from whom states and the federal government can collect revenue. Why, then, is the ability of localities to raise taxes less than that of states? Inadequate facilities for administering some taxes, fear of suffering in the competition for business, and the greater force of opposition to tax increases when exerted close to home—all these limit the actual ability of many localities to pay their own way. States are somewhat freer than localities from interarea competition for business, but they cannot ignore it.

Taxes which apply to the whole state offer less room for competition among communities than when local taxes must raise the same revenue. National taxes eliminate both interlocality and interstate competition. Federal financing, therefore, seems a way around one obstacle to either local or state financing. And is it not human for local officials to prefer to have states (or Congress) levy taxes for local benefits?

Families and businesses which are free to decide where to locate will presumably take account of governmental services, tending to favor locations where services are relatively attractive. Some of the persons attracted, however, may be unable, or unwilling, to pay the taxes needed to cover the cost of such services. High standards of welfare aid, for example, or housing subsidy or superior public schools may draw into an area some families whose presence may add more to governmental costs than to revenue. Relatively high-quality government service which is supplied without a charge on the specific users will to some extent create its own demand for the service. The necessary taxes, however, will be higher than those elsewhere. The extra burdens may tend to drive away some individuals and businesses, perhaps those with relatively high taxpaying capacity but not attracted by the particular services (especially benefits for low-income groups).

Some people believe that government finances should be used to redistribute income from the more to the less prosperous. What would happen if some local governments were to attempt to do much more in this direction than at present? Imagine a local tax system designed to finance far more redistribution than in other communities, e.g., provide relatively extensive services for the poor to be paid for by taxes on those at the top of the income scale. In time, many businesses and individuals most burdened would tend to move to areas where they would not be compelled to pay for services bringing them little or no benefit. No single locality, nor even the largest state, on its own can do much through taxes and spending to alter greatly the distribution of income. The smaller the jurisdiction—school district, village, city, or state—the narrower the limits on its power to tax without providing benefits which the major taxpayers believe will be worth the approximate cost to them.[5] Consequently, Americans who hope to use government to force one group to pay for benefits to others can be expected to prefer federal taxes over reliance on state taxes—or state taxes rather than local—often press for the grant method of finance by pointing out the merits of the *function;* they describe the desirable things that can be accomplished, giving little or no attention to the effects of the taxes. Finally, Government officials who are

---

[5] Zoning can serve to exclude low income families by requiring high quality housing; the residents, though prosperous, may then pay less than the average of the area for public services.

closely associated with particular programs, seeing opportunities for better performance, are likely to urge expansions.

Bases for Distributing Grants.

Proposals for grants (or for tax sharing) must consider the question "On what basis shall the money be distributed?" Sometimes the goal is to return the dollars to the places from which they come—the *point of origin* determined accurately or asserted arbitrarily. Often, however, plans utilize one of two other systems:

1) Grant distribution may try for an element of *equalization,* perhaps by providing more for relatively poor areas than for the more prosperous.[6] For example, more funds for schools or for relief of the needy may be given to poorer communities than to the more prosperous, that is, more relative to some measure of income or need. Presumably, then, some of the spending in poorer localities is paid for by taxes from higher income areas. Allowance may be made, at least roughly, for the effort a community has exerted in utilizing its own revenue sources. Frequently, the objective is to assure at least a minimum standard of performance everywhere.

2) Grant funds may be used to offer incentives, *to stimulate* local (or state) governments to make efforts of certain kinds, to do more of something (or in a different way) than otherwise. A state, for example, may "say" to local governments, "For each dollar of your own money that you spend on function A, you can spend a dollar of state money." The prospect of getting $2 worth of a service by spending only $1 of money raised locally can induce localities to spend more than they ordinarily would on the designated activity. They will do so, not only because more dollars become available but also because of the incentive stemming from the nature of the grant. Sometimes, however, such a grant may do relatively less to increase the total outlay on the function than to change the emphasis and manner to comply with directions from the government which gives the funds.

Both equalization and stimulation have merits and weaknesses in theory and in practice. Stimulating grants, for example, can certainly be effective. In such cases, however, they are sometimes properly criticized for inducing "overspending" on the aided functions relative to others. Such a grant also tends to favor the more prosperous communities because they can afford to put up the money needed to take full advantage of the grant offer.[7] Equalization in grant distribution gets support from persons who believe that aiding the poorer localities (or states) also serves the broader public by making possible more and better government services of types

---

[6] The grant-in-aid literature uses the term "equalization" with many different shades of meaning. Rarely if ever does it imply getting all persons or areas on exactly the same basis as regards the program being considered.

[7] The state or federal tax system, of course, will take more tax dollars from people in such areas.

which have significance beyond local (or state) boundaries. But who can be sure? The recipient area may keep its own effort to pay for the function below what it would otherwise exert.[8]

The actual distribution of grants will depend upon the balance of political power in state legislatures, in Congress, and in the executive branch of government. Groups of voters who are overrepresented (in relation to population) in legislative bodies may succeed in getting for themselves relatively generous benefits. Recent reapportionment of both state legislatures and congressional districts has altered the balance of political power. Rural areas have generally lost power to urban areas, and there have been shifts in voting power which will affect city-suburb and intersuburb relations. The effects on distribution of grant funds will develop gradually.

As more federal grants are made directly to local governments, new problems of state-local relations must be faced. Governors, state legislatures, and state agencies are bypassed. How, then, can effective statewide programs be planned and administered? Yet in the view of some observers, society will benefit from freeing urban areas from the restrictions of state governments, which are, or are said to be, less than adequately concerned with the problems of cities.

Some Features of Grant Programs.   Grant programs are profoundly influencing American society. But in the absence of knowledge about what would have developed otherwise, judgment of the results must be tentative.

The programs have become increasingly complicated. Only experts may be able to understand some. The few persons who are qualified to evaluate the results are likely to be too specialized (and possibly biased) to have good judgments about the merits compared with those of other public programs or private alternatives.

Details of grants can get out of date, but modernization may be put off year after year because of disagreement about what would be preferable. In one state, for example, grants to induce school consolidation continued for many years after the objective had been essentially achieved.

When one level of government pays part of the cost of programs carried out by others, officials at the level which hands out the money have responsibility for seeing that the funds are used as intended. Frequently, however, the resulting supervision arouses criticism. A weakening of local independence may be alleged, perhaps with good reason. Such control can reduce the opportunity to adapt to differences in circumstances among localities (or states). Red tape can be worse than a nui-

[8] Grants which are relatively generous to areas of below-average income may delay movement of population to localities where the fundamental economic outlook offers greater promise. Grants may also discourage other adjustments which in the longer run would prove beneficial. Evidence as to what extent these possibilities become actualities is incomplete.

sance. It can obstruct innovation and tie the hands of persons who would like to try something that seems better. For a single program, the cost in time and money of filling out seemingly endless questionnaires (and maintaining the records required) and of handling the data submitted may not seem unreasonable. But for dozens of grant programs the total burden can weigh heavily.

"Direction from above," however, finds support as a source of positive advantage. Officials who administer grants (or lawmakers who establish programs) may set better standards than would otherwise prevail in some areas. Administrators who are able to draw upon broad experience can use it to induce—or force—improvement in performance. In many communities, for example, little or nothing may be known about the best of developments; some officials, if free to do so, will resist constructive change. The central agency distributing grants occasionally helps to arrange cooperation among localities or states.

Federal influence has grown rapidly, along with federal dollars. State and local lawmakers and administrators feel compelled to accept federal money when it is offered; their residents would save nothing in federal taxes by rejecting a grant. To get the money, however, even when the federal dollars are a small fraction of the total to be spent on the program, the receiving government may need to modify its operations to meet federal requirements. Some of the newer programs give federal officials considerable discretion in allocating funds. Governors, mayors, and other state-local officials are experiencing new problems in trying to get federal funds when the decision hinges upon the judgments of a few men in Washington rather than upon fixed rules known clearly in advance.

People close to various programs differ in their evaluations of the results of the controls (as distinguished from the money). There is wide agreement, however, that efforts for improvement of controls and coordination devices are increasingly necessary as grants exert wider influence and become more complex.

Proposals for Federal Revenue Sharing or General Purpose Grants. Despite the large growth of federal grants, proposals for still greater expansion find support. A few states and more localities, the argument runs, are not expanding and improving services rapidly enough within the limits of what appears potentially possible for the economy as a whole. Expansion of federal aid seems to offer a way toward improvement.[9] The

[9] Compared with the necessary federal taxes they would pay, the people of some states would get more, others less, from almost any expansion of federal grants. Federal taxes paid by the residents of each state can be estimated and compared with grants-in-aid now received by each state. For 1966 the people of Illinois, Indiana, and New Jersey, for example, paid about $1.70 or more in federal taxes for each dollar of nonhighway aid while for Arkansas and Mississippi the figure was around 30 cents, and in 8 other states 50 cents or less. Tax Foundation, *Allocation of the Federal Tax Burden by State* (New York: The Foundation, 1967), Table 3.

dollars alone will make a difference, and in addition, the control exerted might increase the effectiveness.

Proposals for a new form of federal aid to state-local treasuries attract impressive support, both in and out of Congress. The broad outlines are identified with Professor Walter Heller, who, while chairman of the Council of Economic Advisers, advocated such a new departure in federal-state-local relations. The features of the proposals vary in many details. Advocates seek combinations of objectives by combinations of methods, and rather differing combinations of each.

Two major elements can be identified:

1) A portion of federal personal income tax (or of income reported for tax) would be turned over to state-local governments (2) for spending with little or no federal guidance. The general setting envisaged by advocates of the plan naturally goes far to explain its features and the support behind it.

Growth of the economy will raise federal revenues (not counting trust fund receipts) by perhaps $6 to $8 billion a year without any increase in tax rates.[10] Economic growth, of course, will raise state-local revenues, but the growth from existing taxes at present rates will be less than federal, perhaps $4 to $4.5 billion a year.

Expenditures, it is argued, seem likely to present a contrasting picture. On the one hand, at the state-local level, pressures for large increases will appear year after year. However, the argument runs, the probable rise in federal spending, excluding the uncertainties of national defense, will lag behind the increase in revenue.[11] A federal budget surplus may appear within a few years after the end of Vietnam fighting.

A portion of personal income tax receipts would be turned over to the states. The money would go in the form of *general purpose* or *uncondi-*

---

[10] The personal income tax applies at *progressive* rates to the *additions* to taxable income, and most income growth falls above the personal exemption (and deductions) and thus in the range of taxable income. The potency of this relation as a "revenue raiser" is greater than seems to be widely recognized. Moreover, almost half of any change in corporation earnings is offset by an opposite change in taxes, and corporation profits rise over time as national income grows.

[11] An essentially side issue calls for mention—that revenue sharing would help prevent "fiscal drag" on the economy resulting from a budget surplus. Such a surplus means that the federal government is taking more dollars from the income stream than are being replaced by federal expenditure. The surplus is a form of saving. Holders of some federal debt will be repaid. The effects of such debt retirement will depend upon other conditions prevailing at the time in the economy. If capital markets are functioning well, the funds will go to pay for capital projects which would not otherwise be possible. Thus, total demand for goods and services will not decline but will consist more of investment and less of consumption than if there were no budget surplus. The notion that a budget surplus will make funds idle and thereby depress the economy can be valid under some circumstances and yet wrong more often than not. Tax rate reduction, of course, is always a possibility. It can serve as effectively as revenue sharing or expenditure increase to eliminate any budget surplus which seems likely to accumulate funds for which there is no demand to finance private capital formation.

tional grants rather than being earmarked for one or another function and spent under federal direction as is the case with present grants.

In effect, then, the federal tax system would substitute to greater extent than at present for state-local taxes, while leaving states and localities as much discretion in deciding on how to *use* the money as if they themselves had raised it. Deciding on actual details of the distribution would present many problems. The formula for distribution might—or might not—be relatively generous for low-income states. Many of the potentially significant differences in plans referred to earlier involve methods of distributing funds. Many supporters of sharing, however, prefer to tie funds to specific functions, such as education, but without the detailed controls that would be associated with an expansion of present grants.

State and local treasuries would benefit automatically from growth of the economy. But unless the business cycle is a thing of the past, state-local revenue instability would increase.

Another less obvious problem could prove more than troublesome. If the distribution of funds (sharing) were to be a fraction of either federal tax receipts or of the federal income tax base, state-local governments would gain a sort of vested interest in the federal income tax provisions at the time the plan was initiated. Governors and mayors would have an interest which would not necessarily be in harmony with that of the taxpayer.

Most students of grants-in-aid probably have mixed feelings about the general *principle* of earmarking or tying grant funds. The *control* will appeal to the sense of responsibility for assuring that money is used effectively, if only to avoid waste. Another reason is the desire of each group supporting a function—health research, elementary education, reduction of pollution—to advance a specific objective. Yet, there is also appeal in the prospect of freedom, flexibility, and opportunity to adapt to diversity of local and state needs. This is a country of tremendous variety. How can we expect good results without taking account of diversity of many kinds—stage of development (old or new city), age distribution of population, prior outlays and nature of established programs, size of community, state-local relations, topography, climate, and many others?

Some governmental problems are clearly national and must be dealt with by a centralized organization. Beyond national defense, there will be debate about the degree of *national* interest involved in a function. If income is to be *redistributed* on a substantial scale by government (e.g., by welfare aid financed by sharply progressive taxes), national government must be used. Would not state-local officials even argue that part of the normal growth of the tax base "belongs" to them? Such officials in their efforts to prevent change in the income tax exemption of municipal bond interest have given a foretaste of what to expect. Might they not oppose such possible desirable changes as increasing the personal exemption, redefining "income," altering deductions, or lowering rates?

Use of one or another plan for altering the income tax for short-run anticyclical (or other) needs would probably present even more difficulties than up to the present. Adding such a complication would be unfortunate. The case for relatively speedy tax change has enough merit to call for efforts to remove, rather than to add, obstacles.

The total amount to be distributed might be determined, not more or less automatically on the basis of a fixed formula—as now envisaged—but by votes of Congress, perhaps every year or so. Would not governors and mayors, state legislators and city councilmen, have reason to press Washington for bigger totals than the prevailing formula would provide? Thus a new problem would be added to our political system.

The division of new grant funds between states on the one hand and their local governments on the other will create controversy and new divisive conflicts—yet also open opportunities which have appeal to some advocates. Perhaps great things could be achieved by a new grant program with funds distributed on some new basis. Otherwise, however, the national interest in what happens in each particular community can rarely be even a tiny fraction of the interest of the people on the spot.[12]

Tied grants involve varying degrees of centralization. And centralization tends to locate authority far from the site of problems. As a result, difficulties of communication, to say nothing of other obstacles when the processes are those of government, preclude the persons who make major and even minor decisions from having any real understanding of the true situation. Standardized solutions are applied without adequate regard for variations which prevail over a huge economy.

Congress, for its part, can hardly formulate statutory rules which will deal efficiently with large differences over the country.[13] The United States is so large, conditions so diverse, that on grounds of efficiency alone there must be a strong presumption against programs of nationwide scope. Those in Congress and the executive branch who decide upon major policies and the most important of specific actions do not live where they can observe more than a tiny fraction of the results. Consequently, evaluation of program results can be far from realistic. If someone else is paying most of the bill, the person on the spot may have a biased impression of the worth of a program. Economy and efficiency are likely to suffer if performance is separated from the bearing of cost.

[12] Control is inevitable. The debates over federal aid to education contained many statements—even pledges?—by supporters of such aid that "control" would not accompany dollars. Yet was there any basis in logic or experience to accept such assertions? No—unless, as may have been the case, advocates of aid were thinking of "control" as the exercise of sweeping, nearly full, authority when "only" (extensive and increasingly detailed) "influence" was to be exercised.

[13] A possible alternative, congressional grant of much discretion for centralized but flexible administration of a program, also proves difficult. Top-level authorities cannot be familiar with the details of actual situations. Discretion leads to uncertainties. Moreover, communication failures diminish lower level incentives to criticize central actions and to propose solutions.

Unquestionably, there is good reason to provide that at least part of the big total of federal grant funds be given without strings. Then the people on the spot would have freedom and opportunity to do what they believe is best, aided by technical advice from various sources, including, but not limited to, national government.

The proliferation of grant programs, the increasing detail and specification of particular features, and a growing awareness that administration presents formidable difficulties which are not within sight of solution, all these and other considerations reenforce older criticisms of tying grants, especially when many programs are narrowly detailed. Frustrations over compliance and administration are growing. Problems have overwhelmed staffs; long delays in getting decisions seem inevitable, and then when the decisions are made, their quality is by no means up to the standards hoped for. Not enough qualified personnel are available to direct well. Procedures cannot be free from the problems of bureaucracy.

Costly planning and staffing are required for meeting the details inevitably associated with detailed programs. Special—and expensive—skills and staffs are needed to maneuver in Washington (and sometimes in regional centers having authority over the distribution of funds) to find what is potentially available and then to get the "just due."[14] No one can know how much inequity results from the failure of state and local governments to satisfy federal requirements. Members of Congress must use time to help governments in their districts through the mazes of officialdom.

To eliminate the most serious objections to tied grants, however, general purpose grants or general revenue sharing are not needed. The job could be done by consolidating grants into a few broad groups, not so broad probably as education, health, transportation, but into a number much smaller than at present. Here is a possible means of achieving one objective of some advocates of "the plan" without necessarily adopting other features.

Outlook.   Subject to uncertainties of defense spending, it seems clear that federal revenues should be enough higher by, say, 1970 to permit tax rate reduction, more expenditure than now scheduled, debt reduction, or some combination of these three. State-local revenue systems, plus federal grants-in-aid as greatly enlarged in recent years, will enable states and localities as a group to finance spending programs to provide for population increase and other foreseeable changes, with additional funds for

[14] A Midwest official of the Office of Economic Opportunity is quoted as saying: "It's almost impossible for anyone to get money from us—at least without a great deal of delay and frustration—if they don't have technical help." Another OEO official said, "The little indigenous committees in poor areas just don't understand the forms." *Wall Street Journal* Nov. 22, 1966).

quality improvement. Some communities will unquestionably face strain. The general outlook, however, by no means presents the crisis elements which helped give rise to proposals for federal revenue sharing. The other arguments for, and against, income tax sharing as compared with the alternatives do not lead to a clear conclusion.

Alternatives.   Three major alternatives exist.

1) Conditional, categorical, tied grants could be expanded but the categories broadened to reduce the details of control and permit recipient governments much greater freedom.

2) *Federal tax rates* could be reduced, perhaps each year or two. Because of rising GNP, total federal revenues could continue to rise as appropriate for spending and other needs. Reduction in tax rates, however, would enable the public to retain a larger fraction of its income than otherwise. Such a policy would enlarge personal freedom—to increase consumption, saving, and investment. The "tax bite" on the lowest income groups now taxed could be removed. The distorting and other adverse effects of high tax rates could be reduced. The relative importance of the federal government, and of the coercion involved in its taxation, would decline.

Taxpayers, being less heavily burdened by the federal government, would be better able to pay more state-local taxes. State legislatures and city councils, however, would encounter more difficulty in raising their own taxes than in cashing checks from Washington. State-local governments would probably not add to their revenues as much as the federal reduction. A majority of the public, it seems right to assume, would prefer some increase in private consumption and investment.

3) A third possibility has the support of at least two groups whose views deserve respect, the Committee for Economic Development and the Advisory Commission on Intergovernmental Relations. Every person paying federal income tax would get a *credit against his tax* for some of his state-local tax payments, or perhaps only for state income taxes. Such a credit could provide a powerful inducement for the few states without income taxes to adopt them, action which some people believe desirable. The tax credit would in any case ease the problems of all states in utilizing personal income taxation more extensively.

The tax credit would give greater relative advantage to the higher income states, but the federal grant system could be altered to get the distributive (equalizing) balance desired. The tax credit would put the actual revenue-raising responsibility at the state or local level. Spending decisions would be free from federal direction.

Finally, however, it may be well to look again at the outlook for state-local finances. A detailed study of each type of spending and each revenue source has shown that state-local governments will be in much better financial position in the years to 1975 than has been assumed.[15] Federal grants already on the books will also yield more and more funds. With taxes already voted, state-local governments will be able to pay for the services called for by rising population and to continue to improve quantity (per capita) and quality of service at least as rapidly as in the last decade. Figures for national aggregates, however, do not reveal the special problems of individual cases. And for some urban areas the outlook remains cloudy, or worse.

INTRODUCTION TO GOVERNMENT DEBT

Taxes are not the only source of government funds. Borrowing is another, one which raises a range of issues. Personal debt is a source of worry. How much better we feel to be free of obligations which are troublesome in the best of conditions and perhaps crushing burdens when our finances deteriorate. Because debts can be bad for individuals, some of us, perhaps unconsciously, transfer the same feelings to debts of government. Other voters, however, seem willing to vote for public borrowing with little thought about the ultimate effects.

STATE AND LOCAL GOVERNMENT BORROWING[16]

Until World War II, state and local debts were a large, or the largest, part of total American government debt. Since the war, they have grown rapidly. In the sense of what they buy, these debts are closer to most of us than federal debt. They have different economic significance.

Why State and Local Governments Borrow. Most state and local debt is incurred to finance capital construction: schools, highways, water systems. Such projects often require a large outlay at one time. Since the benefits will appear over many years, future users, rather than merely the users of today, can appropriately be expected to share the cost. Residents move in and out of a town; some who are around when a sewer or school is built may leave next year.

For the people of the community, as for a business, it is wise to borrow if the net benefits exceed the full costs. If an improvement in the hospital system or a new school would give a net yield of 6 percent and the full cost of borrowing were 4 percent, there is a clear economic case for borrowing. Yet, a stumbling block is obvious. We seldom know how much a project will yield in community advantages, especially since some benefits will be intangible. Sometimes, it is true, measurements may give a reasonably clear answer. A new heating plant for city buildings may

---

[15] Tax Foundation, *Fiscal Outlook for State and Local Government to 1975* (New York: The Foundation, 1966).

[16] Both kinds of debt are termed "municipal." They are bought and sold "over the counter," not on the stock exchanges.

promise to save enough labor and fuel to leave no doubt of the desirability of installing it. Often, however, the answer must hinge on things that cannot be measured. What would be the gain from a better mental hospital or prison?

The following generalization is likely true: A growing community can borrow (perhaps from savers in more settled areas) at costs below the benefits from many capital assets. Streets, school buildings, and other projects can be of large advantage, but local residents may not be able to pay for them fully at once. The tax system would not stand the strain. Borrowing provides a logical solution. As a community ages, however, more and more new construction comes to be for the replacement of older facilities. Therefore, the argument for net *increase* in borrowing becomes weaker. Still, in a progressive society, the demand for more and better government capital equipment grows.

Do state-local governments tend to overborrow? The benefits of pending, although hard to measure, are certainly more welcome than taxes. Consequently, debt may be incurred when the underlying justification is indeed weak. Officials may think: "Dance and get reelected today and let someone else pay the piper later." The voters join in the sentiments. Those who vote to borrow do not thereby incur a personal obligation, as they do when they go into debt as individuals.

Judgment of how much debt is "not too much" must often be unsatisfactory when the benefits of a capital project do not appear in a form available for paying debt charges—interest and amortization. The fruits may be valuable but intangible—better education or health. Debt servicing, however, requires money that can and will be voted in taxes; conceivably, large benefits from a project will not appear as appreciably higher capacity to pay taxes. Moreover, nearly a generation may pass before some gains appear in significantly improved money income.

State and local borrowing has played a constructive role in our growth. The history includes follies and scandals the like of which we wish to avoid. The greatest problem is not stupidity and corrpution. Rather, it is to avoid borrowing too much for projects which have some merit but whose cost would add to debt already high.

Limits on Borrowing. Because of fear that voters, perhaps out of unwarranted optimism, will borrow rather than tax, and thus commit future taxpayers unwisely, state constitutions or laws, or city charters, generally limit borrowing. (Some limits are essentially those fixed after defaults following excess borrowing a century ago.) These limits do not necessarily represent considered judgment based on modern reality. Yet they do restrain the growth of debt. They also induce states and localities to resort to one or another type of borrowing which, for technical reasons, falls outside the debt limits. Such debt requires payment of a higher interest rate than on "full faith and credit" debt. The limits are often expressed as percentages of the assessed value of real estate, reflecting the fact that local government revenues come largely from property taxes.

Methods of Borrowing. Today, as a rule, state and local bonds are sold to the highest competitive bidder; taxpayers can be reasonably sure of obtaining the best terms available. Generally, the terms call for systematic debt retirement through either *sinking funds* or *serial bonds.* The planning about whether or not to incur debt must thereby take account not only of the annual interest cost but also of a rough equivalent of depreciation. A government may pledge certain sources of revenue to pay interest and amortization. A highway or bridge "revenue" bond may thus get outside the debt limit. About $41 billion out of total state and local debts of $108 billion in 1966 were payable from pledged earnings or other special sources, with "full faith and credit" supporting the rest.

Interest Cost and Amount of State and Local Government Debt. In 1967, state and local governments could borrow on long term (15 years or so) for 4 to 5 percent, depending upon credit standing. Such rates are less than paid by the U.S. Treasury because interest from state-local debt is exempt from federal income tax.

The state debt outstanding in 1966 was over $29 billion. On a per capita basis, the state debt varied from $21 in Idaho to $563 in Delaware. Cities owed nearly half the local government debt; school districts owed $18 billion, special districts $17 billion. The annual interest cost for state-local debt averages $17 per capita the country over. State and local governments, however, in 1967 had over $20 billion of assets to offset debt.

FEDERAL GOVERNMENT BORROWING

Borrowing to Help Pay for War. When war must be fought, the government is like any of us as consumers: it needs things and services. It is like us in another respect: It gets what it needs by purchasing with money. It organizes war procurement in a money economy; so it must have money—and lots of it. Where can the dollars come from? There are three possibilities: taxes, borrowing, and the presses that print currency. In past wars, although the public shouldered heavy tax increases, it still needed to borrow large amounts.

Two significantly different sources of borrowed funds are possible: (1) savings from current income or (2) deposits newly created by banks. If the government borrows funds being saved, in effect the public turns over its control of a part of the current output of goods and services. Individuals and businesses spend less on consumption than they receive for what they produce. They let government have the remaining dollars to buy the rest of the national output. In one respect, such borrowing is like taxes: It produces no change in the total quantity of money flowing through the economy. Instead of getting tax receipts, however, the public gets bonds.

Borrowing raises the question "Can we pass the costs to future generations?" The answer depends partly upon the answer to another question: "Which costs, money or real costs?" *The real costs must be paid during the war.* The hours of combat, of boredom on watch, or of work in factories or on farms or in offices—all these are spent during the war. They cannot conceivably be brought up from future peacetime years. Similarly, the materials used to fight an enemy are consumed during the war, not 20 years later, when the bonds may fall due. Whether the public pays the dollars as taxes or loans, it must turn over the real resources during the fighting. Such costs cannot be shifted to future generations. The economy of the future, of course, will be poorer from any destruction of resources used to fight a war.

Money costs presents a more complicated problem. The people who fight, work, and sell their products during the war get dollars. Such money costs, like real costs, must be paid during the war. But the "we" who pay do have some choice. I may pay dollars in taxes and get tax receipts—the end of that transaction. Or I may turn over the same number of dollars and get bonds in return. If so, the transaction is not at an end, for later I can sell the bonds or wait until they fall due and the government pays me. I then have dollars to get real things, but someone must give me those dollars.

The money costs are, in a sense, shifted to later years. As a taxpayer in the future, I may be required to provide some of the dollars to repay my own bonds. But others will pay most of the cost (in taxes or out of savings to buy my bond). I am better off because I owned the bonds. To the extent that a country pays for war by borrowing, the generation buying bonds (on the whole but not always in individual cases) gets more in the future than if the war were paid for by taxes. Therefore, the men who decide how a war is to be financed can choose whether the money costs shall be borne at the time or in the future.

The incentives to finance by borrowing, rather than by taxing, are powerful. Receipts for past taxes will not be of much use when I must send my children to college, but bonds for which I can then get dollars may be veritable lifesavers. I, or my children, then get real resources. Someone else will not get them, for he did not buy bonds during the war.[17]

Other Reasons for Federal Government Borrowing. A national government may borrow to finance a capital project—the Panama Canal or new housing, for example. Such borrowing may be wise economically. If

---

[17] Must I eventually pay taxes to help repay my own bonds? Not necessarily, as we shall see in a moment.

the prospective advantage of a project seems greater than the value of the alternatives that must be sacrificed to build it, then, on the basis of pure economic principle, the country is better off to borrow and build than to go without the project. But would it not be better to get the money by taxing? Not necessarily.

People will generally resist paying taxes more than they oppose buying bonds of the same amount. If payment for a capital project requires taxes, people may refuse to pay taxes to build something that would yield the country benefits worth 10 percent a year when they would be willing to save enough to pay for it if, through their government, they could receive 4 percent on borrowed money. The best use of funds in private investment might yield less than 10 percent.

TABLE 32–2.   Ownership of U.S. Government Debt on Selected Dates*
(In Billions)

Type of Owner	1940	1946	1967
Commercial banks	$16	$ 75	$ 56
Federal reserve banks	3	23	46
Individuals, including personal trusts	10	64	74
Insurance companies	7	25	9
Mutual savings banks	3	12	4
Corporations	2	15	13
State and local governments	†	6	23
Miscellaneous‡	1	8	31
U.S. government	7	31	75
Total	$49	$259	$331

* Data for 1940 are for June, just before the sharp rise in defense spending; the 1946 figures are for the end of the year, long enough after the end of fighting to reflect most of the direct postwar readjustment; the 1967 figures are estimated for May.
† Under $500 million.
‡ Includes savings and loan institutions, pension funds, nonprofit institutions, brokers and dealers, foreign owners, and others. In 1967 foreign holdings were nearly $16 billion.
Source: Treasury Bulletin.

How often do such cases exist? The facts of politics make us leery of such reasoning as justification for borrowing to pay for national government spending on capital projects. Equally real is the possibility that we shall pay 5 percent for money to build a project where Senator X needs votes but where the benefits, especially those to the general public, will be 2 percent or less. Usually, of course, accurate measurement of benefit is impossible, even if experts are free to do their best.

There are other arguments against federal borrowing to pay for capital projects (except when stimulation of the economy is also an objective). A country as large as ours will seldom face the great lumpiness of an occasional big expenditure as do smaller governments. More or less regular additions to the federal government's stock of long-lived assets can appropriately come out of taxes. Some worthy projects would not get done if Congress were to stick to the "straight and narrow" and build only what the public would pay for out of taxes, but unworthy projects might then be avoided. Budgeting with balance as the goal will serve to curb waste in spending.

Size and Ownership of the Federal Debt. Table 32–2 shows the size and ownership of the federal debt in 1940, when we began to step up armament spending; at the end of 1946, when demobilization and the

FIGURE 32–1. Total per Capita Debt of Federal, State, and Local Governments in Dollars of Constant Purchasing Power, 1913–67 (Dollars of 1967 Purchasing Power)

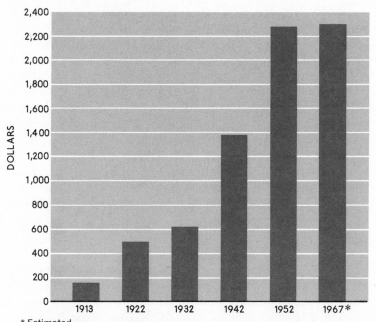

* Estimated.
Source: Debt data from *Statistical Abstract* and Bureau of the Census. Adjustment for price-level change, approximate only, is based on the Consumer Price Index.

immediate postwar debt adjustments were reasonably complete; and in 1967. Most of the debt was incurred during World War II, but some has been added in 15 of the 22 years since. Figure 32–1 gives perhaps better perspective by showing the increase of total government debt since just before World War I, with adjustment for (1) the growth in population and (2) the changing value of the dollar.

Debt Limit. Newspapers tell us once or twice a year that the federal debt is almost at the legal limit. Once it is reached, no more borrowing will be permitted. But this limit is fixed by law and may be changed by law. In fact, Congress *must* sometimes raise the limit *if* the Treasury is to get cash to spend as Congress *directs;* the debt grows because spending exceeds revenues.[18] The fundamental decisions are those on spending and revenue.

A legal limit can be far removed from any economic limit. Does it help prevent wasteful spending? Not directly. Does it, then, have any significant merit? Yes, say its defenders. Debates on raising the legal limit offer the *only* occasion on which Congress looks at the federal financial situation and prospects *as a whole.* Lifting the debt ceiling could, if some members of Congress wished, *force* an examination of fiscal policy in the broad sense. Neither tax nor appropriations debates require any look at the picture as a whole.

Interest Rate Ceiling.   Another ceiling (a holdover from World War I) set a limit of 4¼ percent payable on bonds with a maturity of 5 years or more. If market rates are above this level, what happens? Can the treasury find generous citizens willing to lend "below the market" as a favor? *No.* It must borrow on short term, paying the rates the market demands. Although it may legally sell 4¼ percent bonds at a discount so that the effective rate will be higher, Treasury officials insist upon respecting the spirit of the law. The ceiling complicates borrowing and cannot reduce market rates of interest. By 1967 it had forced such great reliance upon under–5-year debt that the Treasury asked for more freedom. Congress granted authority to borrow small amounts at market rates on notes with up to 7-year maturities. But this slight relaxation does nothing to help in getting debt structure to reflect the reality that most of the debt will exist for decades or indefinitely.

"We Owe It to Ourselves."   Most local government debts are like a private debt in that they are not owned by the same general group which owes them. Most national government debts, however, are owned within the nation. In one sense, they are assets of the same group for which they are liabilities. Taxes to pay the annual interest of around $70 per capita burden us. The interest, however, is income to the recipient.

Most bondholders, of course, do not benefit greatly from owning this particular debt rather than some alternative type of asset they could have purchased with the same dollars. Except for banks in some cases, owners of government debt got it only by giving up the opportunity to acquire other forms of wealth. Thus, other things the same, the interest received by each bondholder and his wealth are little, if any, larger than if the

---

[18] For the decade to 1967 there was a "permanent" ceiling of $285 billion supplemented by "temporary" authorization of higher amounts. After 1960 debt approached $300 billion and then exceeded it. Thus, even when the debt was not growing, the President had to come to Congress once or twice a year for an extension of the temporary authorization.

government debt did not exist. The obligation of taxpayers, however, is every bit as great as the debt. In this respect, the positions of the two groups are not offsetting, unless what has been obtained from the spending of the borrowed money brings taxpayers benefits as great as the burdens of the debt.

Economists do not agree on how much burden a national debt owned internally imposes.[19] Who knows what conditions would prevail if the debt had not come into existence? Although most economists would agree that a national debt is not such a burden as it appears to the man in the street, they also know that there are problems we cannot dispose of by pointing out that "we owe the debt to ourselves."

1. Even though the annual interest payments are *transfers* within the country, their benefits do not cancel the harm done by the taxes needed to raise the money. With total taxes at present levels, the additional (incremental) rates needed to get money to pay interest can distort economic decisions. By requiring higher marginal income tax rates (or adding to prices of goods), interest costs will indirectly increase tax-motivated rather than truly economizing business decisions, alter incentives, and cut purchases in the market. Some of the taxes which are higher because of the annual interest charge come from low-income families. Such transfer from taxpayers to bondholders can be criticized as burdening the poor to pay others who are more prosperous. But the federal tax system is so generally progressive and the debt is so widely held, e.g., by thrift institutions, social security, and other pension funds, that the criticism carries no appreciable weight. The mere administrative costs of collection of tax and the payment of interest involve amounts which, on a debt the size of ours, would pay the expenses of many first-rate colleges or hospitals.

2. The *mass* of a debt almost half as large as the value of 1 year's production of the whole economy in itself has significance. For the families and businesses who own the debt, it is wealth, mostly in a liquid form. This wealth is not matched, in the owner's thinking, with his liability for future taxes to service it. He has a *specific claim* but a *vague obligation*. Owners have assets which they do not match with what is their part of the community's liability. Why should they? Net personal wealth seems to be enlarged by this unusual type of accounting. Economic results probably include an increased willingness (*a*) to spend for consumption and (*b*) to invest additional savings in less liquid, more venturesome, forms.

The massiveness of the debt might be a cause of concern. If the debt

---

[19] A debt held outside the country presents more complicated issues. Interest paid gives foreigners a claim on the output of the debtor economy. Did the expenditure of the borrowed funds improve productive capacity in the borrowing economy enough, compared with what would exist if the debt had not been incurred, to finance the carrying charges in the form required?

were to begin to "move" *en masse* as more owners try to sell than to buy, the movement, like an avalanche or a herd of stampeding buffalo, could work harm which would never result from a smaller mass. Conceivably, falling prices could lead owners to try to sell before prices go still lower; a downward spiral might weaken financial institutions and the monetary system. Such a prospect is highly improbable. The debt is widely held and consists of many types, most of which will never be far out of line with others in the market. Moreover, the government itself could prevent a decline in bond prices by support through the Federal Reserve (open-market purchases—having what effects?).

Even without dramatic developments, the mass of the debt can create persistent, chronic problems. Total refundings of $80 to $90 billion a year cause, at the very least, churning and disturbance in the financial world and sometimes create more complications for monetary management. The Treasury's interest bill is so large that officials may yield to temptation to use the monetary system in ways described in Part 3 to lower interest rates—at risk of inflation.

3. A large government debt can reduce resistance to inflationary policies, or perhaps invite them. The debt is fixed in money terms. If the value of money falls, the real burden of the debt falls; less labor and physical output are needed to get the dollars required to pay the interest. Government may be tempted to choose policies which reduce the value of money. By doing so, officials may for a time ease one problem, that of getting dollars. Our officials are dead set against yielding to such temptations, but such has not always been the case in this country or in others.

Our economy has adjusted to public debts which would once have seemed insupportable. The adjustment has apparently been easy. Why? (*a*) Inflation since the war has cut the real burden of each dollar of debt—or shifted it as a partly hidden capital levy on the owners. (*b*) Productivity has increased so that each hour of work will pay the costs of more debt. (*c*) The economy has grown; the larger the national income, the more easily we can carry any given amount of debt.

Must Our Federal Debt Be Retired?   Personal debts must be paid or repudiated (through bankruptcy). Government debts are different; governments do not die. Like corporations, they may stay in debt perpetually. As individuals die, they pass on their part of the government debt obligation to the surviving group. Just because it lives in the nation the new generation *must* shoulder the obligation. Rather than paying off our debt, therefore, we can make someone else assume it. The new generation, in turn, can plan to bequeath the responsibility to its children—on and on.

One thing is essential: A government must observe faithfully the terms of its debt. The interest must be paid—every dollar on the day set in the contract. When the bond falls due, the owner must be repaid. If the government repays with money from taxes, debt is retired. The dollars for repayment can also be obtained from the sale of new securities. If so, the debt is "turned over," refinanced; the terms of the contract are honored meticulously, but there is no net reduction. The old bondholder, in effect, gets his cash from some new bondholder.

To be able to sell to new bondholders, especially on attractive terms in free markets, the government must keep its credit good. If it succeeds, it can refund decade after decade—unlike an individual, who can hardly expect to borrow after he dies. Society faces no inescapable compulsion to reduce the federal debt. At times, debt reduction might be worth the taxes needed to make it possible. Many of us, however, pay higher interest rates on personal debt than the federal debt costs. Tax reduction might serve us better.

Selling and Managing Federal Debt. The federal government, in borrowing, has problems and opportunities that differ somewhat from those of state and local governments. It deals in vastly greater amounts. National government can use its control of the money and banking system, and within some limits it can use compulsion or appeal to patriotism. Ours does not, as it might, favor its own debt with significant tax favors. The market for federal debt has become several markets. To get the best of each market, the Treasury "tailors" its debt offerings to fit varying needs.[20]

The Treasury, in planning the issue of debt and in managing it later, must offer high enough interest yields to reduce the dangers that would come if bondholders sought to sell on a large scale. Yet the Treasury also wants to keep interest costs down and perhaps to further such objectives as helping prevent cyclical fluctuations and aiding long-run economic growth. During World War II, Treasury officials probably reasoned like this: "We want to borrow at low rates to save taxpayer cost. How can we get people to lend to us cheaply? If they turn over their money for long periods, say 10 years, they cannot count on getting back all their dollars until the end of that time. They will want to be paid for tying up their money this way. But if they can get dollars easily on demand, they will lend us more and at lower interest rates. Therefore, let us promise to give bondholders their dollars on short notice if they wish." And that is what government did. But it made itself vulnerable to a sudden demand for cash to repay bondholders.

When the short-term debt is large, the government can never be far from the need to meet big maturities. In the summer of 1967, the average maturity of publicly held debt was only 4½ years. Such a condition is uncomfortable for the Treasury and a source of uncertainty to financial markets. It would be good to "stretch out" the debt—to lengthen the

---

[20] Four major debt forms are used: bills (usually 26 weeks or less), certificates (not over 1 year), notes (1 to 5, occasionally more, years), and bonds (running as long as 40 years).

average maturity by issuing more long-term bonds to pay off short-term issues. Such a shift, however, would draw upon sources of loans funds for housing and other long-term investment while putting funds chiefly into the short-term market.

TERMS AND CONCEPTS

fiscal imbalance	shared revenue	general purpose grant
multiple taxation	"piggybacking"	earmarking
overlapping taxation	matching grant	sinking fund
grant-in-aid	equalizing grant	serial bond
tied grant	Treasury bill	debt ceiling

QUESTIONS

1. What economic reasons can be cited for, and against, spending by one level of government of revenue raised by another?

2. What factors explain the growth of federal grants-in-aid?

3. "Grants-in-aid reduce the freedom of the recipient government." Discuss, distinguishing between general purpose and tied grants.

4. Assume two localities, one growing rapidly and the other stable. What, if any, differences would there be in the economic reasons for enlarging the debt of each locality? Why?

5. Must federal debt be reduced?

6. Who owns our federal debt? Whose obligation is it?

7. Can a state have more taxing power (economic) than all its localities combined? (Ignore legal restrictions.) What are the reasons for state grants to localities?

8. What is the difference between debt retirement and debt management?

9. "One way for Congress to help finance schools is to reduce federal taxes. Then states and localities could pay their own way. The ability to pay taxes does not increase by routing money through Washington." Discuss.

10. How does your state distribute funds to local governments? If you were the mayor of the largest city in the state, what would be your case for more funds from the state?

PART 7

INTERNATIONAL

ECONOMICS

Between the time we wake up and the time we arrive at class or work, most of us have probably used, directly and indirectly, dozens of things that came across a national boundary. How often do we think about their national origins? The economist and the citizen, however, must face this fact: National boundaries create economic problems. Engineering and medical truths are not fixed by legislatures. Neither are economic truths. But many economic problems arise out of what governments do. Few, perhaps, have as old and as distressing histories as the problems which governments have created for those who wish to deal across national frontiers. Though the lines dividing the world's political units have innumerable economic results, these boundaries have not been drawn to help mankind make the best possible economic decisions. Far from it. Some results are needlessly bad, as economists for generations have tried to convince the world. They have given this area intensive and extensive study. And they have been in *virtually unanimous agreement* on major issues of policy.

33

THE ROLE OF

INTERNATIONAL TRADE

Any nation's standard of living is a reflection of the productivity of its economy. . . . Foreign trade raises productivity—and hence the standard of living—because it enables a nation to concentrate its efforts on the particular types of activity in which it is most proficient.
National Association of Manufacturers (1960)

Prosperity, progress, and national security, perhaps even the future of mankind, depend upon international economic relations. Positive good, and avoidable evil, can result from governmental, as well as private, actions in the areas of economics we shall now study.

THE GAINS FROM INTERNATIONAL TRADE

Specialization and Mutual Benefit from International Trade. One fact overshadows all others. Trade benefits both sides, third parties, and often others even far removed—even though national boundaries may separate buyer and seller. The potential gains from specialization, from the division of labor, we recall, depend upon "the extent of the market." Interregional trade within a nation expands the market. International trade enlarges it even more, promoting greater efficiency in the productive use of resources and in stimulating progress.

People with essentially similar natural resources, inborn human capacities, and accumulated wealth can benefit by specializing and serving each other—those within a single city, for example. When material or human conditions differ, the chances of gain from specializing become still richer. International trade permits exchange over an area with far greater variations than found in any single country. Natural resources (including

781

climate), human abilities, and capital equipment are distributed differently over the world, and by no means in the same pattern as human desires. Moreover, nations vary in ways that New York and California do not: in language, custom, law, religion, political organization, and other characteristics that affect productivity. International trade offers a way to overcome the unfavorable effects of differences in resource availabilities. It does more. It enables groups to gain from each other's differences in abilities to produce.

Yet whether from ignorance, cussedness, or individual selfishness, men throughout the world fail chronically to recognize the benefits of trading with people of other lands. As we stir sugar from the Philippines in Brazilian coffee, some of us argue against dealing freely with foreigners.

Mass production requires a mass market. The absence of national boundaries within what is the United States has been one factor distinguishing the United States from Europe. There, more people live within an area containing substantial natural resources and capital. Yet political frontiers have cut the total European market into many parts. This fractioning of the whole—now being corrected—deprived everyone of some potential gains from mass production.

A point to be emphasized: *What one receives is the benefit from exchange.*[1] The good part of an exchange is what one gets, the bad is what one must give up.[2]

Exports use up our time and resources; imports are the work of others. Whether one is dealing with a foreigner or the next-door neighbor, the reason one gives up, sells, is to get something, usually money. The selling is a means to an end, the goal of buying. With the exception of charity, we export so that we can import. Even "relieving" a "surplus" at home is no gain unless the things obtained as a result are worth more. For trade to be beneficial, the total we receive must be worth more to us than what we provide to others. In turn, however, what we give up must be worth more to the recipient than what he sacrifices. Here is the essential: *mutual benefit from exchange.*

Sources of Gain from International Trade.   Several kinds of conditions contribute to making international trade beneficial. (1) The exchange of natural resources distributed unequally over the earth—tin, copper, electricity from high dams, use of sunny beaches, for example—will clearly bring benefits. (2) Almost as obvious is the gain

---

[1] Nevertheless, a country is said to have a *favorable* balance when exports of goods and services exceed imports. This peculiar terminology originated in the days of mercantilism when acquisition of gold and silver seemed an important goal of government policy. If commodity and service exports were greater than imports, precious metals could be obtained.

[2] Once an economy has developed export industries, the measurement of benefit is more complex. If exports permit more efficient domestic production, the import is no longer the only benefit. Items for consumption at home can be produced at somewhat less cost.

from the exchange of things whose production is suited to different climates and natural conditions—bananas and wheat, or tobacco and wood pulp. Sources are immobile, but the products can move. Or consumers can come to the unusual source—the German vacationing in Rome, the American learning British banking practices in London.

In addition, (3) the number of people, their native capacities and developed skills, and their tastes and (4) the stock of accumulated capital, vary widely. When the proportions of these factors (as well as those of natural resources) differ, the opportunities for use—that is, marginal productivities—will also differ. In one country, labor may be plentiful in relation to natural resources and capital. In another land, labor may be relatively short and capital more abundant. The economic activities most appropriate to the two economies will then be different. By exchanging products, however, the people of each economy can benefit from the relatively more favorable distribution of production possibilities in the other economy.

(5) A broadening of the market which permits larger-scale operations of a decreasing-cost industry will reduce unit costs. (6) The greater the freedom for international trade, the greater the competitive pressure on domestic producers to do the best possible; the general public will benefit from a weakening (often unseen) of actual or potential monopolistic restrictive agreements.

International trade offers a way around two barriers of considerable practical importance. (7) Many lands are too small and too poor to produce complex products—machines and medicines, for example. (8) New products and services appear in one country long before other economies can develop the specialized facilities needed to produce them. This "technological gap" will account for a considerable amount of international trade.

Within nations, people move. They take with them knowledge and capital. Such movements reduce inequalities among areas. From one nation to another, however, people and capital face greater obstacles in shifting. The restrictions of governments, language problems, expense, personal preference, tradition, and other elements hamper mobility. The existence of national boundaries, traditions, and distance itself must cut down the opportunity to reduce the differences in factor productivities. Trade, however, substitutes for the movement of productive resources as the things they create go from one region to another. Each area can use the productive factors which for it are relatively plentiful to get the output of resources which to it are "scarce" but which are relatively more plentiful elsewhere. But how can sources of potential mutual benefit be discovered?

Differences in Money Costs and Prices. An obvious way to locate benefits is to look at relative costs of possible alternatives. Using prices as a measure, one selects what is best. Businessmen will seek the best opportunities. As they place orders for shoes, oil, or steel, they try to buy where prices are lowest (allowing for transport costs), whether at home or abroad. More generally, they hunt for the largest differences between money costs of inputs and selling prices of outputs. The firms with lowest costs (and selling prices) of specific products will get the orders. Some such firms will be in other lands. Buyers in the importing country receive the benefit of a price lower than if there were no foreign trade.

Such dealings will set up forces which in turn change the earlier conditions. The movement of goods will tend to change their prices—raise them in the exporting country where quantities for consumption decline, while reducing prices in the importing country. How much will the original price differentials be narrowed? That depends upon the elasticities of demand and supply in the two countries.

If an economy is to export, it must have the productive capacity. A rise in export demand will call for more productive resources. Ordinarily, the industry can get these resources only by bidding them away from other, less productive, activities. Imports can aid such shifting. In some cases, they will displace domestic production—but only when the import price is lower. If the resources needed to produce the item domestically cost more, they presumably have better alternative uses—to produce something else. Imports, therefore, permit the economy to use its productive capacity more effectively.

The money measure guides the allocation of productive effort among the countries of the world. But because of differences in national currencies, as well as lack of knowledge and government restrictions, the guidance will be less clear and efficient than within the nation. Yet it produces much benefit. How much? No one can know. When once the trade has become established, the measurement of gain over what would have been is utterly impossible. What would otherwise exist is hardly even "guessable."

Differences in Cost Relationships: Comparative Advantage.   Some economies have an *absolute advantage* in the production of one or many products—their cost is lower. They can do the job with fewer inputs per unit of output. Would the economy, then, be wise to rely on its own production for all such outputs? Not necessarily, for economizing involves the choice of alternatives. Such choice cannot be efficient if it rests on absolutes. *Comparisons*, rather, are what count.

The principle of *comparative advantage* offers the most efficient guide. It tells us this: *Exchange is beneficial even when the advantage of one party is comparative or relative but not necessarily absolute.* For example, if the best lawyer in town is the best typist, it is not wise for him to do his own typing. He will do better to use his time practicing law and to hire someone less skillful to do his typing. The same thing goes for a whole country. For example, one economy, *A*, may be able to produce two products more cheaply than economy B; A has an absolute advantage over B in production of both. Yet it may pay A to import one product from B and pay with the other.

"Why buy from foreigners if we can produce something for less money or real inputs?" The answer: "We benefit most by using our resources in the *best* way possible, by choosing not a good, but the best, alternative." It may pay to import an item even if the price is greater than the price of the resources needed to produce it at home. We benefit from importing when by doing so we can use resources to better advantage—if we can, as it were, practice law rather than type. Our goal is the *best* use of our productive capacity.

Assume two countries, A and B, in which labor is the only important scarce factor of production; assume also that labor productivity for producing corn and cloth are as follows:

	A	B
Yards of cloth per man-day	8	2
Bushels of corn per man-day	2	1

In A, a day's labor will produce 8 yards of cloth, while in B a day's labor will yield only 2 yards. Labor in A is also more productive than in B in raising corn. The advantage is clearly with A in both products. A's greater advantage, however, is in producing cloth. Here, its labor is four times as productive as in B, compared with being only two times as productive in growing corn.

Assume that initially each country turns out both products. Each, however, can gain by a change—by specializing. If A shifts a man from producing corn, the loss per day is 2 bushels, but the gain in cloth is 8 yards. If B shifts a man the other way, from cloth to corn, there is a loss per man-day of 2 yards of cloth and a gain of 1 bushel of corn. By shifting still another man to producing corn, B will lose 2 more yards of cloth and gain a second bushel of corn. Together, from the labor of these three men (one in A and two in B), the countries have the same amount of corn but 4 more yards of cloth if they specialize and trade. In effect, A hires B to produce those things which, if A produced them, would leave it with smaller net output from its efforts during the day. As a result, A may concentrate its effort on the product in which its net gain is greater.

Using the same proportions—a cloth-corn ratio of 4 to 1 in A and 2 to 1 in B—it appears that any ratio of exchange between 4 to 1 and 2 to 1 will benefit both. Assume that trade develops and bargaining results in a ratio of 3 to 1. Then residents of A obtain a bushel of corn by giving up 3 yards of cloth instead of 4 as required when they produced corn for themselves. Residents of B gets 3 yards of cloth instead of 2 for a bushel of corn. Both gain.

This principle underscores the benefits of specialization and trade. Offhand, one might not expect that trade could be mutually beneficial if one of the two countries could produce everything traded for fewer real or monetary inputs than the other. Yet, even though one country has an absolute advantage over another in producing everything (most improbable), trade benefits both countries if the *relative* advantages differ. Sheep and cattle graze on almost barren mountains a thousand miles from the consumer, not because such land provides the best of grazing but because the better land, nearer markets, will produce more valuable output.

The comparative advantage of an economy will exist in those industries in which resources, in terms of productivity, are most plentiful (least expensive). In practice, prices show the most profitable things to do if the price system works efficiently. When they use prices, the businessman, worker, and investor will find the best advantage. Why, then, bother to state the principle? Because discussions of national policy often fail to use the proper criterion of cost—the value of sacrificed alternatives. The cost of the lawyer's doing his own typing is not what he would pay a stenographer but what he could earn practicing law in the time he would be typing. To find the best possibility, look at relationships, comparatives.[3]

The most profitable specializations depend not only upon the technical conditions of production and the prices of factors of production—unit costs—but also upon tastes and other factors affecting demands for different products. A change in the world demand for silk, for example, alters the advantage of Japan in devoting its resources to silk production rather than to, say, rayon or cameras. Both shifting demands and changes in production costs upset any established equilibrium. Production costs per unit also depend upon the volume of output and vary according to the time of the year and perhaps from one part of a country to another.

Terms of Trade.　How can we compare the basis on which products exchange so that we can get some idea of how much the people of one country give for the products of other lands? In some cases we can use a measure called the terms of trade. It relates the quantity of exports needed to obtain a unit of imports. The ratio of export prices to import prices for given "bundles" of goods for different times are expressed as index numbers. An auto might in one year buy 3,000 pounds of butter and the next year only 2,800. In such a case, the auto-butter terms of trade have turned against the auto-maker in favor of the butter producer. An index number that comprehends all (major) imports and exports will be much more difficult to compute, but more significant.

Clearly, the specialization that is best depends upon the terms of trade. In a stable world, the terms of trade change relatively slowly. Since

[3] Sometimes, possibly, the best approach may be a search to avoid the worst. Sift out the poorest. It is no small advantage to be able to discard the worst even if one is not certain which of the remaining possibilities is the best. An economy may have a comparative advantage in producing some parts of the output of a product and a comparative disadvantage for other parts.

World War II, however, some large and sudden shifts have occurred in the terms of trade. Shortly after fighting started in Korea, prices of raw materials and food rose much more than prices of manufactured products. Nearly 40 minutes of an American textile machine operator's time were needed to buy a pound of coffee in the early 1950's where before the war and again in 1961 only 15 to 20 minutes sufficed. With 1957–59 as 100, the 1965 index of the value of a "composite unit" of our exports was about 106, while for all imports it was 99. The index of the terms of trade, therefore, was 107. For 1951–55 the figure was 91. The terms of trade had turned in our favor between these two dates. For 1946–50, however, the index was 106.[4]

Varied Interests of a Complex Economy.   In an economy as varied as ours, national totals conceal tremendous differences. International dealings that are excellent for one group would be foolish for another. Atlantic coast builders sometimes import European cement when the transport cost would make such a purchase foolish for Iowans. We are a large wheat exporter; yet we also import wheat of varieties grown better in Canada. New Jersey is a big tomato producer, but during part of the year her residents will enjoy tomatoes from the West Indies. California, a large oil-producing state, regularly uses oil brought from far across the Pacific.

METHODS OF BUYING AND SELLING ABROAD

If you were a businessman, how would you go about finding what you might buy abroad and then actually making a purchase?

Much international trade has been in staples: cotton, grain, rubber, metals, coffee, oil. Organized markets would permit anyone to buy, with the utmost ease, by placing an order with a broker. Quality standards are carefully defined, and the mechanics of shipment and storage are well developed. If you have the money and know what you want, the process of buying is easier than that of getting an extra ticket for the big football game. The same applies to selling. The farmer may have no idea to whom his cotton goes eventually. The organization of middlemen functions smoothly.

For a company not dealing in such staples, however, the problem becomes more difficult, and much more varied.[5] Large firms maintain staffs in key foreign centers to keep a constant search for new items and better values, and to arrange with foreign producers to work to specifications. If you managed a firm not large enough to maintain a permanent

---

[4] Sometimes large changes take place in a short time. During 1957 the terms of trade of four countries exporting primarily metals and ores fell by 21 percent. At the same time four countries whose exports consisted primarily of sugar enjoyed a 13 percent rise in terms of trade.

[5] Arranging for services, such as shipping and insurance, can be done through brokers and agents.

staff abroad, you might send buyers to the chief fairs and other showings, or go yourself (and get a "tax deductible" trip to foreign lands). You could deal through businesses, either in this country or on the other side, which specialize in foreign trade.[6] Acting as agents, they bring buyers and sellers together, charging commissions. Sometimes they, themselves, buy for resale, taking the risks involved. These trading firms often specialize—steel, sausage casings, or Near Eastern products. They may help in checking on quality, packaging, shipment, clearance through authorities, financing, and investigating credit. Consulates and other government agencies provide valuable information. Trade magazines will help put you in touch with what is available. Banks here and abroad provide aids extending beyond the more traditional range of banking.

If you had something to sell abroad, you could use methods opposite those available to a buyer. Selling in foreign markets, however, often requires special effort. Sale of some things, such as autos or machinery, requires a dealer organization to service equipment and handle spare parts. Establishing such an organization abroad is likely to be expensive and time-consuming—easier in Canada, however, than in Japan or India. Not a few products and services must be adapted to the particular wishes of a variety of foreign customers. Some buyers require special financing. American industry has been criticized, less now than 15 years ago, for failing to make the special efforts needed to expand sales abroad. The potential of foreign markets grows, but competition becomes more intense. Methods of marketing, credit and servicing facilities, and advertising must be suited to particular conditions of each economy. Legal requirements and custom must be observed. The U.S. Department of Commerce is now actively trying to help American business expand exports. Small companies have exceptional need for such assistance because individually they cannot afford specialized staffs in many countries.

What if a dispute arises over some feature of a transaction? If friendly settlement is not possible, what could you do? Your adversary is in another country with its own courts. Still, your prospects are far from hopeless. Over centuries, detailed codes have been worked out with painstaking care; they have set up procedures for adjudication on a routine basis. On disputes arising over commercial matters you could take the initiative in foreign courts as if you were a citizen. Though far from perfect or inexpensive, reasonably good settlement arrangements exist in much of the world.

Buyers and sellers in different lands thus have many ways to deal with each other. Numerous obstacles remain, however. Such barriers as language, distance, custom, law, and government combine to create a substantial quantity of ignorance. Risks are numerous, sometimes large.

---

[6] The New York City classified telephone directory, Manhattan Section, contains 20 four-column pages of firms listed under "Exporters" and 15 such pages of "Importers."

Where both ignorance in this broad sense and also risk exist, there will be opportunities for large gain. Throughout history, the international trader has sometimes made apparently fabulous profits from apparently simple exchange. Why? A big gap separated the buyer in one country from the seller in another. The scope for the trader to profit by narrowing this gap was correspondingly large. Opportunities of this general nature undoubtedly remain, and new ones are generated while older ones are wiped out.

SOME GENERAL FEATURES OF INTERNATIONAL TRANSACTIONS

Method of Payment. Barter can be found in international trade, but as an exception. Most buying and selling uses money. Deals are in terms of money, not x tons of wood pulp for y electric toasters. Of course, the basic importance lies in the *real* goods and services, not the money. Money, however, is the common denominator which serves in most dealings. It serves in measuring (the terms of exchange) and also as payment. Fundamentally, *things exchange for things, but in the practical workings of trade, things exchange for money.*

Because different countries have different money units—dollars, pesos, lira—an international transaction involves two currencies. Their relationship, the number of francs to a dollar, will influence each potential purchase and sale in a way that does not appear in domestic business. Defects in the mechanism for making money payments in different currencies create difficulties in exchanging products and services.

Conduct of International Trade Predominantly Nongovernmental. International trade outside the Communist world is not ordinarily that of governments or of nations as political units. Negotiations and operations in foreign trade, buying and selling across national boundaries, consist, for the most part, of the dealings of businesses and individuals—private transactions. The dominant objective is benefit for private parties, not national glory or profit for the government treasury. True, governments, especially during and after World War II, have bought and sold goods to each other and to private foreign firms. Motives have varied from desire for gain in the normal economic sense to almost everything else that governments seek: geographic expansion, political domination, disposal of agricultural surpluses, military benefit, charity, economy and efficiency, preservation of balance in imports and exports, and furthering socialism at home. Yet outside Communist lands any shift of the *conduct* of foreign trade from business to government was incomplete and largely temporary. For the United States, actual buying and selling are still done overwhelmingly by businesses.

Government Controls on Foreign Trade. Governments, however, influence and even control international trade in many ways. Although the national political authorities may not be out trying to drum up trade and to negotiate bargains, with the treasury getting profits (and paying losses), the actions of governments still exercise a powerful influence. Control varies widely in method and purpose. It operates directly and indirectly. Some governmental policies help business; others create exasperating obstacles to efficiency.

What government influences might one find in trying to do business with a foreigner? A *tariff* is likely; the importer must pay a tax (tariff or customs duty), perhaps negligible, perhaps several times as great as the cost of the article. His government may use *quotas*. The legislature or some administrator may say that only a certain number of units of a product, tons of oil, for example, may be imported during the year. The businessman must apply for permission to bring in a part of the total. Perhaps the rules are clear and the answer prompt; but, in some countries, the administration may be corrupt, arbitrary, and tedious beyond words. Even where standards of political morality are high, frustrating delay, chance, and skill in dealing with bureaucracy can play a part in getting a share of the quota. A position established in the past may be so crucial that an aspiring newcomer would be about as well off using his time to play tiddlywinks as to try to get permission to import.

Some countries have *currency controls*. To buy from foreigners, one must pay them. Government rules, however, can make payment to foreigners impossible without official permission. Getting consent may be much like getting a quota, easy or difficult, formalized or arbitrary. Restrictions on the flow of capital funds inevitably (but perhaps indirectly) serve as restrictions on the export and import of goods and services which are paid for out of capital.

Requirements for *inspection, marking, packing*, and *sanitary standards* may plague one. Overburdened staffs may not give rulings on doubtful points for months and may then reverse themselves. Trade by an American firm with Iron Curtain countries requires specific permits which will not be given for items on a special (unpublished) list. Licenses to land aircraft and ships, or to establish banks or sell insurance, are limited and granted only upon conditions which the recipient would not agree to freely. *Reporting and clearances* take time and often require hiring an expert. *Special freight rates* may help or hurt. *Tourists* may be attracted by special government actions—frequently advertising and occasionally favorable rates for governmentally owned hotels or transport. *Subsidies* or *tax reductions* are sometimes given for exports or imports of particular products. Special rules may require that processing, or some fraction of final assembly, be done within the country; 40 percent, or an amount stepped up year by year, of the auto or household appliance may have to consist of parts made locally.

Government restrictions on the movement of peoples are numerous, with laws limiting or prohibiting immigration and emigration. Some governments, however, aid such movements; Israel has used government agencies to help absorb immigration on a relatively large scale, while the Netherlands has subsidized emigration. Governments also place restrictions on the movement of capital and of specific property, such as art objects.

Impossibility of Measuring Importance. How valuable is foreign trade? This is like asking "How important are the jacks in a deck of cards—or the imported nickel in a jet plane?" They are vital, but not a big part of the whole. About 4.5 million American workers—more than are employed in auto, steel, chemical, and textile manufacturing combined—are directly dependent upon exports. It would be hard to find an industry which could get along without some materials from abroad, except at significantly greater cost. And it would be well-nigh impossible to find a consumer with even the slightest comprehension of the number of imports woven into the fabric of his, or her, daily existence.

TABLE 33–1.   Combined Exports and Imports as a Percentage of National Income, Selected Countries

Country	Percent	Country	Percent
Belgium	75	Ireland	62
Brazil	20	Israel	40
Canada	46	Italy	28
Denmark	77	Switzerland	53
France	25	United Kingdom	43
India	15	United States	9

Source: United Nations. Data are for 1957. For each country, total exports and imports are combined and related to national income. In some countries, there is much import for reexport, swelling the totals.

Yet trade with other nations is relatively smaller for us than for most other lands (Table 33–1). Their life may depend upon being able to buy abroad—and to buy they must export. Events outside the country may upset, favorably or adversely, either buying or selling with mild or drastic repercussions inside.

Multilateral Nature of International Trade. International trade, like domestic, is highly complex, crisscross; economists call it "multilateral." In studying American history, we learn of "triangular trade" in colonial times. Britain shipped cloth and other manufactures to the British West Indies; they shipped molasses to New England, which then sent rum to England. In 1966 U.S. residents bought around $743 million of goods from Italy, while Italians bought $914 million from us.[7] Yet we bought $416 million from Hong Kong and sold $228 million there. Between

[7] These figures are rounded and do not include "invisibles," discussed later.

residents of two countries, trade may be very one-sided but continue indefinitely. Why? The imbalance can be offset by opposite imbalances. In our own country, for example, I may buy day after day from the Coca Cola Company and never sell it anything—a one-sided trade but one that does not worry me because I can somehow offset it by other exchanges. The same applies when we deal with foreigners. Even when all the transactions of people in a country are lumped together, there is no need for purchases or sales to balance with those of any one other nation.

Businessmen who do the buying and selling may have no idea about the total balances between nations. Does the Bostonian who buys a California orange worry about what of equal value he can sell to an orange grower in California or the railroader who helped bring it? If the businessman had to worry about finding such exact equalities, trade would wither. When nations as a whole try to trade bilaterally, balancing purchases and sales with those of each other, exchange drops. A system for multilateral clearing of payments serves with infinitely greater effectiveness.

THE BALANCE OF PAYMENTS: FOREIGN TRADE IN THE UNITED STATES ECONOMY

Nature of Basic Accounts: Use of Money Amounts. Discussions of international trade require a knowledge of the amounts involved, stated systematically. For this we use a set of accounts called the "balance of payments."

The accounting is based on the principles of double-entry bookkeeping. Typically, a product or a service exchanges for money. Each transaction, therefore, has a two-sided nature (for each party), a "things" or *real* side and a *money* side—a bale of cotton and $150. If there are several exchanges, we can think of adding the two sides to get the two totals—one of things and one of money. (Rather, there are four totals, two for buyers and two for sellers.)

The totals of things (tons of wheat and ton-miles of transport) on the buyer's and the seller's accounts are identical because, obviously, the things are identical; only ownership has changed. The money totals will also be identical because the money which the seller receives is that which the buyer gives up. When all the people in a nation are treated as an economic unit—a sort of huge family—their transactions with other groups can be thought of as a comprehensive total. Obviously, the goods and services which this economic family, the nation, receives will differ in physical terms from those it provides others. The purpose of trade is to gain by exchanging different things. As a result, one cannot make significant comparisons in physical terms of the "bundles" of things exchanged. The money aspects, however, can be compared because money provides a common measure of what we give up and what we receive. So in looking at the accounts of everyone in a country with everyone outside, we utilize money totals—the values of goods and services given up and of those received in return.

The Main Elements.   Many ways of arranging the facts are possible. Always, of course, the figures relate to a particular time period. The following groupings apply to both imports and exports.

1. Current goods and services.
    Merchandise—oil, machines, coffee, watches, autos, cotton, and so on.
        These are physical things—some, raw materials in crude form; others, highly processed manufactured items.
    Invisibles (services).
        Transportation, such as on oil tankers and passenger airlines.
        Tourist and travel spending for other purposes.
        Miscellaneous services, such as insurance and professional.
        Payments for the use of property—dividends, interest, and rent.
        Government, charitable, immigrant, and other unilateral transfer payments.
2. Gold movements.
3. Capital transactions—investments of all kinds, whether government or private, equity or debt, being made or repaid. (Money amounts; the values of physical things purchased and shipped will appear among goods and services.)
    Long-term.
    Current and short-term (or cash).

How does one decide where a figure belongs? We ask, "Does this transaction give us a *claim* on people in other countries or does it *obligate* us to make payments to foreigners?" All amounts paid or payable by us to others go on one side of the accounts. Amounts received or receivable by us go on the opposite side. In some cases, values in money terms must be estimated.

One fact must be emphasized: The claims upon, and the obligations to, others must be equal. So we speak of the *balance of payments.*[8]

The "Balance" Involved.   "Go slow," you may say. "A family can pay out more than it takes in, or vice versa." Right, but the principle of "balance" still holds. A family can pay more than it takes in by going into debt or by using up its assets, both being processes that change its net position. By accumulating cash, a family can make its outgo less than the inflow. For some purposes, then, "balance" not "payments" will be the key term. We give something—perhaps only an I O U—for everything we get, and vice versa (except for uses of charity). The fact of balance in the sense used here does not necessarily mean either good or bad alloca-

---

[8] A more limited concept, the difference between exports and imports of merchandise (perhaps including services), is called the "balance of trade."

tion of resources. If one or more countries have a balance-of-payments deficit on "normal" transactions, one or more others have a surplus.

When an economy has a *deficit* on account of goods and services and long-term capital flows year after year, as has the United States, the amounts it is obligated to "pay" are greater than the amounts it has a right to receive. How can such a deficit be met? Foreigners may take gold. Or they may accumulate dollars in this country. In the 10 years from 1957 to 1967, for example, foreigners increased their bank balances and short-term assets here by about $18 billion. They also acquired over $8 billion of gold.

Changes in bank balances and other highly liquid, short-term capital assets may be thought of as "balancing" or "equilibrating" items. They play an important part in balancing international trade. Perhaps the growth of debt to a creditor yapping at one's heels seems hardly a balancing item, but it can be part of the process. In international, as in domestic, business affairs, not every payment due is made; consequently, losses appear on one side of the accounts, matched with cancellation of debts payable on the other side. "Balance" remains, but it may seem hardly healthy and will certainly not represent a sustainable equilibrium. Nevertheless, the two-sided nature of every transaction, with the possible exception of charity, is a fact of life.

U.S. balance-of-payments figures do more than show the principles involved in the accounting. They also reveal important features of our economy.

U.S. Balance of Payments.   Table 33–2 shows the U.S. figures. Exports of merchandise were substantially larger than imports. This country, in other words, shipped out things of greater value than it received; this particular lack of balance has continued since the 1870's, but the amounts, of course, have varied widely. Figure 33–1 shows the variations from 1920 to 1966.

Looking at services and other invisible items, we find that this country's ships, airlines, and other transportation agencies provided foreigners with less transportation than we received from foreign firms. U.S. tourists bought substantially more goods and services outside the country— whether skiing in Canada, seeing a Shakespearean play at Stratford-on-Avon, or motoring in Mexico—than foreign visitors spent here. Miscellaneous services—insurance, professional, banking, educational, etc.—were received on balance. Property owned abroad, largely the branches and subsidiaries of American corporations, brought far more interest and dividends than we paid to foreigners for use of property they own here. This country and its troops abroad bought military goods and services of substantial amounts, and private gifts (including remittances by immigrants to families "back home" and services of missionaries) made to foreigners were greater than those we received. Former employers, including our government, paid pensions to foreigners.

TABLE 33–2. Balance of Payments of the United States with the Rest of the World, 1966 (In Billions)

Item	Credits: Exports and Other Items for Which Americans Receive Payments from Abroad	Debits: Imports and Other Items for Which Americans Make Payments Abroad	Net Credits (+) or Debits (−)
Merchandise (excl. military)	$29.2	$25.5	+3.7
Services	7.5	6.6	+0.9
Transportation	(2.6)	(2.9)	
Travel	(1.4)	(2.6)	
Other	(3.5)	(1.1)	
Military	1.6	3.6	−2.0
Income on investments	6.2	1.9	+4.3
Direct private	(4.0)	(0.6)	
Other private	(1.6)	(0.4)	
Government	(0.6)	(0.9)	
Remittances and pensions		1.0	−1.0
Government grants (excl. military) net		1.9	−1.9
Capital (net)	3.4*	6.6	−3.2
Private	(2.2)	(3.9)	
Government loans (chiefly foreign aid)	(1.2)	(2.7)	
Total	$46.3	$47.1	−0.8
Balancing items†			
Gold exports and official monetary adjustments	1.4		
Unrecorded	−0.6		

* Other than liquid funds such as increases in bank deposits in this country.
† An important portion of the "balancing" consists of capital transactions which take the form of increases in foreign holdings of bank balances and short-term securities in this country. Obligations of U.S. banks to foreigners increased by more than $1 billion in the period. The amounts are shown in the table under Debits, Capital.
Source: Survey of Current Business.

Net "outpayments" for military supplies and services, other than spending abroad, have been running around $2 billion, largely military aid to allies, but not including Vietnam fighting. Foreign aid grants and loans by our government exceeded the repayments of earlier loans by nearly $2 billion in total. These grants and loans helped pay for some of the exports of merchandise and services shown earlier.

On balance, American businesses and individuals exported capital in the form of loans, payments for shares of stock in foreign corporations, and

FIGURE 33–1.   Exports and Imports of Merchandise, 1920–66*

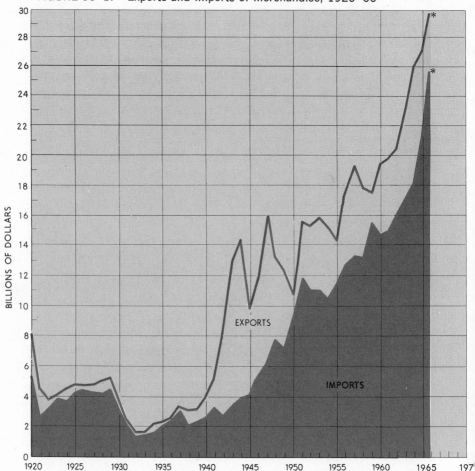

* Partly estimated.
Source: Department of Commerce.

the purchase by U.S. firms of property abroad or the export of capital goods for use in foreign plants.[9] The amounts were much greater than foreigners added to their investments in this country.

Some gold was exported, and our government borrowed abroad and from international financial institutions. When to the amounts tabulated so far we add estimates for unrecorded transactions, the totals result.

Major U.S. Imports and Exports.   More facts about broad groupings, specific items of trade, and directions of trade flows appear in Figures

[9] U.S. capital export figures do not include profits of U.S. corporations which have been earned and reinvested abroad. Nor are such profits included in any other item in the U.S. balance-of-payments accounts. This omission constitutes one source of understatement of the "desirable" element in the position of Americans in the world economy.

FIGURE 33–2. Merchandise Exports and Imports of the
United States, 1966

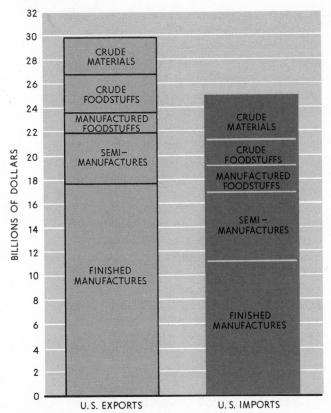

Source: Economic Almanac, 1967–68.

33–2, 33–3, and 33–4. If you let your imagination roam and your brain work, you will find that each item can make a fascinating story and help you sense a little of the role of international trade in our lives.

What of the future? For geographical reasons of climate and natural distribution we shall continue to rely on foreign sources for some raw materials and food stuffs: coffee, cocoa, bananas, wood pulp and newsprint, iron ore, tin, petroleum, and natural rubber. These combine into a large physical bulk and a substantial financial amount. There are others which, though perhaps highly important, do not loom large in the totals—industrial diamonds, chromium, cobalt, to name three. What manufactured goods are we likely to import? Well, what do we buy now? Some are items not produced in this country—special machines, for example. Others we can get abroad more cheaply—sewing machines and fine lenses—or in variety and quality—small cars and modern furniture—that appeal. Invisible nonmerchandise imports, especially tourist services, will likely grow—assuming peace, more and longer vacations, comfortable facilities for travel, attractive prices.

FIGURE 33–3.   Area Distribution of Foreign Trade: Exports and Imports of
Goods and Services* (Billions of Dollars)

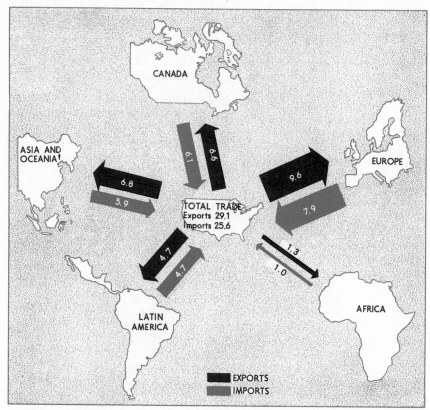

*Partly estimated. Excludes military aid but includes exports financed by other foreign aid.
Totals include amounts not allocable by area. Data are for 1966.
† Includes Australia and Near Eastern countries in Asia.
Source: Department of Commerce.

As we turn to exports, the things we give up to make purchases
possible, what do we see? Agricultural products, chiefly cotton, wheat,
and feed grains, continue to be important, partly because of special
government aids (subsidies) to exports. Manufactured goods, however,
make up a very much larger total. The future totals of foreign trade will
rest heavily upon the ability of American manufacturers to sell abroad, a
topic to which we shall return in Chapter 35.

DOMESTIC EMPLOYMENT AND INTERNATIONAL TRADE AND FINANCE

The study of international trade involves more than such questions as
"What trade will make available, for our consumption, the products of

FIGURE 33–4.   Merchandise Imports and Exports; Selected Items*

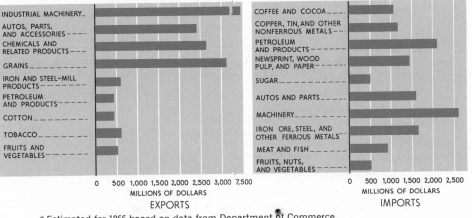

EXPORTS

IMPORTS

* Estimated for 1966 based on data from Department of Commerce.

foreign lands at the lowest cost possible?" The 1930's brought another question to the front: "How do flows of foreign trade affect employment?"

As total spending rises in one country, its imports rise, spreading the expansion to other lands. Prices and employment there tend to go up. Assume, however, that income in the United States falls; our demand for imported goods drops. Countries supplying us lose sales, and their employment falls. As a result, they will tend to cut down their imports from us and other countries, reinforcing a little the initial decline in income here. And everywhere some "multiplier effects" are to be expected, much as a change in investment as described in Chapter 10. A rise (or fall) in the level of national income in one country tends to produce increases (or declines) in other lands. Part of the "foreign" effects will be felt in prices, part in employment.

Some forces will work toward a new equilibrium. Changes in demand lead to *price* increases (or declines) in the various countries. These "price effects" alter *quantities* offered and demanded and thus move toward a new equilibrium. The "income effect" will also play a part. In early 1958, for example, when U.S. national income was suffering from a recession, we were importing 10 percent less from Canada than at the same time in 1957. As a result, money income and employment in Canada declined—there was less work to do in supplying us. Canadians, having less income, reduced their imports; from 1957 to 1958 their buying in the United States fell almost 20 percent. Thus, Canada's drop in exports (resulting from the reduction in our purchases from her) induced a decline in her imports. What followed from this latter response? The rate of contraction of income in Canada slowed down as imports became less of a "leakage."

But the lands which exported to Canada suffered a little. There was a chain effect. The income decline in Canada which resulted from the drop in her sales to the United States led to numerous but small declines in income in other countries as Canadians with lower incomes curtailed imports.

Changes in national income in different economies are linked together. They tend to move in the same direction but not in the same amounts, and usually with differences in timing. The offsets produced by domestic developments vary widely.

Ordinarily, imports are welcome as useful goods and services. But rules have their exceptions, and in a depression a rise in imports can lead to a loss of real income (but need not). The funds that flow out for payment may not come back as demand for exports. Oversimplifying somewhat and assuming no special offset in domestic policy, we can—using the terminology of Chapter 8—think of the payment to foreigners as reducing M and leading to a greater decline in buying (MV) over a year or so; if P does not decline to make up all of the adjustment, T will fall. Since some prices are bound to be too "sticky" to decline, some (or much) of the total adjustment will come in T, involving a drop in employment. The loss in output can be greater than the worth of the original import. Using different terms, if there is an outflow of funds of $10 (that would otherwise have been spent at home) of which only $5 comes back as increased demand for exports, there is a net loss of $5 (matched, of course, by the goods and services); if the multiplier is 2, however, the eventual income decline will be $10.

On the other hand, if foreigners buy more here as their own national income goes up, the rise in our exports will tend to increase our income. We may lose $5 of goods and services through an increase of exports. Yet the $5 received from foreigners may eventually total $10 of money demand. If it leads to utilization of labor and resources which would otherwise be idle, the output available for domestic consumption will actually be higher because of a net increase in production.

This connection between the income levels of different countries leads governments with policies for full employment and price-level stability to try to insulate their economies from some of the full force of international trade movements. A spurt in export demand may add forces of domestic inflation—a drop will create unemployment. Attempts to set up buffers, however, will involve restrictions and restraints which have indirect costs (distortions of production, investment, and consumption) that can outweigh benefits. Inevitably, any economy closely tied to others can expect some difficulties in stabilizing its own national income if the others fluctuate greatly. Fortunately, actual fluctuations have not as a rule been great. They have by no means piled on each other at the same time but have often been somewhat offsetting.

QUESTIONS

1. Why is the "good part" of international trade the import while the export is a sort of "necessary evil"? Are there exceptions? Explain.

2. What are the major elements in the "balance of payments"? How can there be a deficit?

3. Why do foreigners buy so much here if our wage rates are far above theirs?

4. What forces would tend to change the terms of trade for an economy in the short run? In the long run?

5. What is the difference between absolute and comparative advantage?

6. "The immobility of some resources can be overcome in an economic sense by international trade." discuss.

7. "The constructive role of specialized middlemen is even greater in international than in domestic trade." Discuss.

8. Assume that foreign purchases of U.S. cotton were cut off entirely. Trace the results in this country.

9. Explain how changes in national income can spread from one country to another. How might a drop of 5 percent in U.S. national income affect the economies of other countries?

10. "Exports provide a good way to get rid of our surpluses." Discuss.

11. Why is this country both a large importer and a large exporter of autos? Chemicals? Tourist services?

12. "Without imports, industry after industry would grind to a halt." Discuss.

13. "Depressions and inflations will not stay at home. In fact, they may sometimes be a country's most important export." Discuss.

34

INTERNATIONAL CURRENCY,
FINANCE, AND INVESTMENT

*Hence the stabilization of the rate of exchange depends in the first place
entirely upon the stabilization of the relative value of money; in other words,
upon the factors which regulate the value of money in both countries.*

Gustav Cassel

When I buy a cup of coffee, how does my money get to the Brazilians
who supplied the coffee beans? How does the European smoker pay the
American farmer for tobacco? We now answer these questions and then
proceed to problems arising from the financial relations of different
countries.

PAYMENT MECHANISM IN INTERNATIONAL TRADE

The mechanics of making payments across national boundaries are
more complex than those for domestic trade; but as with many of life's
intricate mechanisms, most of us use this one without ever realizing that
problems exist. Nevertheless, financial arrangements can in themselves
affect trade in real things—cotton, watches, oil—and hence influence jobs
and living standards. The importance of the mechanism becomes obvious
when it breaks down. Then for a time the payment mechanism seems to
overshadow the more basic, real economic factors. Money troubles choke
off exchange that would be mutually beneficial.

Payment in Different Money Units. In paying a foreign supplier, we
must give him money he wants. The Brazilian laborer will want cruzeiros.
Few American coffee drinkers ever heard of cruzeiros, fewer still ever
owned any. Yet somehow our dollars are transformed, and the Brazilian is
paid in his own currency. The process of payment involves an element
not found when the Californian pays for a Detroit auto.

Banks as Clearing Agents.   The New York coffee importer, let us assume, gets dollars from all over the country through the clearing arrangements of the domestic banking system. He then has (1) dollars and (2) an obligation to pay cruzeiros. U.S. exporters will have gotten (3) cruzeiros from the sale of, say, machinery in Brazil. (4) They want dollars to pay U.S. workers. Importers have what exporters want, and vice versa.

The obvious advantage is for the two groups of offsetting desires to be matched. But how will they find each other? Some will be in St. Louis, others in Seattle, South Bend, and hundreds of other places. A market is needed. Banks provide it, with the center in New York.

The importer who needs cruzeiros orders his bank to buy them and to charge his account in dollars, and that's that. What if the bank does not have a customer who wants to sell cruzeiros? The logical move is to try to buy them from some other bank. But how can the right one be found? A few banks in New York and other large cities each have a "foreign department" (not the branches abroad, but a division of the home office) which acts as a clearing agency—middleman—in foreign currencies. As correspondents, these banks serve the rest of the banking system, helping buyers and sellers of foreign funds to offset claims.

In the simplest form, U.S. exporters receive the dollars which importers collect as they sell imports to U.S. purchasers.[1] Importers in this country, on the other hand, buy the foreign money which U.S. exporters collect from the sale of products abroad. In fact, of course, both the demand and supply of foreign funds are influenced by tourist expenditures and all the invisibles, as well as capital movements. The total of all such monies is called "foreign exchange." The traveler's check that the U.S. tourist cashes in London for pounds to pay for his meals provides dollars for a Britisher to use to buy U.S. fruit, Arabian oil, or Italian silk.

The market in foreign exchange is multilateral. Americans may get dollars in exchange for Dutch guilders; the guilders pay for Argentine pesos; the pesos buy British pounds; the pounds in turn can meet the needs of Germans who have guilders; and so on. Banks, in effect, transfer claims so that excesses in one place can offset deficiencies in another. (Banks over the world keep dollar deposits in New York and pound deposits in London. Much clearing among different countries is accomplished by transfers of deposits in these accounts.) What "moves" is not paper currency—nor gold—but legal claims and knowledge. The bank's experts, sitting at their telephones, make these apparently complex exchanges. The

---

[1] Drafts, bills of exchange, and letters of credit are "instruments" often used in foreign transactions. Because of lack of personal acquaintance, differences in laws, and other factors, it is common in international trade to relate the financing to the actual shipments of physical things. The importer cannot get possession until he meets payment terms. In payment for goods moving in international trade, credit (a loan) is often involved. To illustrate, an importer gives something like a check but dates it 90 days in the future. The seller cannot cash the "check" at once; but he may turn it over to a bank, at a discount, to get cash immediately.

bank's customers will not know what has gone on, any more than a dancer could explain technically what a hip does.

Cost of Clearing.   This whole complex of banking arrangements costs something to run, and it involves risks. Who pays? The users, including all of us, pay. How? The price of one money in terms of another includes the cost of the transfer process. So far, we have said nothing about how many cruzeiros one receives for a dollar; but just as the grocer charges more for potatoes than he pays, the bank charges more for a foreign currency than it will pay. A New York bank, for example, may pay $2.39 for a British pound but charge $2.42. Out of the difference it hopes to cover its costs and make a profit. The amount of this "spread" depends largely upon competition, which in major world centers is active, even intense.

Big importers and exporters have enough at stake to shop around for the best offers and keep the cost down. Moreover, there are brokers who make a business of ferreting our apparent discrepancies and profit by *arbitrage*. This activity consists of buying and selling in different markets. If the same things are handled in several markets, their prices may not always move together precisely. The forces of demand and supply will not be identical in different markets; price discrepancies result and offer a chance for profit. If you were a broker in foreign exchange watching currency price quotations as they came over the cable, you might see the French franc, British pound, and U.S. dollar moving in slightly different ways. Perhaps you at once buy francs with dollars in New York, wire Paris to sell francs and buy pounds, and wire London to sell pounds and buy dollars—a process taking perhaps 5 minutes. You end with a few more dollars than you began. As you bought the currency that was "weak," or a bit cheap, and as you sold the one that was "strong," you helped narrow the gap.[2]

Lack of Equilibrium: Short Run.   What if imports and exports (in the broadest sense) are not in equilibrium? The quantity of foreign currencies demanded will not equal the quantity supplied. A temporary imbalance may be taken in stride. Individual exporters may accumulate foreign deposits or securities to use for payments later; or importers may for a time let debts due abroad grow or may borrow at foreign banks. Similarly, if international accounts for a whole country are temporarily out of equilibrium, perhaps because of a seasonal crop movement, there are devices for tiding over. Short-term loans often meet the need. Monetary policy, by inducing higher interest rates, can help attract international short-term loans. Gold flows, sales of outstanding securities, and

[2] Arbitrage can involve two or more currencies. It can involve currencies for future delivery as well as "spot" (immediate) delivery. One or more of the transactions may involve securities rather than currencies.

movements of prices of goods and services can also facilitate short-run adjustment.

Lack of Equilibrium: Long Run.   What if the imbalance is not offset within a few months? If an economy, year after year, imports more than it exports, or vice versa, what is the mechanism of payment? Even then relatively smooth adjustment is possible through changes in capital account. Over a long period, for example, the British exported more than they imported in goods and services. How did people in the rest of the world pay? In essence, the British accepted payment for the balance in the form of promises to pay (I O U's) or in the ownership of railroad and other property built with the money. Still, there are limits to the adjustments possible on capital account. When these limits are reached, trade (including invisible items) must adjust. But how? There are different methods. (1) The relative prices of goods and services entering into trade may change (perhaps by changes in the prices of foreign currencies, as we shall see in a moment). People in the country which has been importing more than it exports then respond to price increases by reducing purchases of imports. (2) Changes in incomes in different countries alter the quantities of goods bought and sold, as described in Chapter 33. (3) Government rules may limit the amounts to be bought or sold.

THE PRICE OF FOREIGN CURRENCY (EXCHANGE)

What determines the price of one currency in relation to another? How many francs can we buy with a dollar? The answers are rather more difficult than answers to such questions as what determines the price of cabbage, but the same underlying economic forces operate. Demand and supply rule. If the demand for dollars in London rises, their price in terms of pounds will tend to rise unless supply increases equally. The prices of foreign currency affect the quantity of goods and services imported and exported; when Mexico cut the price of its peso from 12 to 8 U.S. cents, our dollars would purchase much more in Mexico. As a result we bought more goods and services south of the border. Mexicans, however, had to cut their buying here; 1,000 pesos would buy only $80, no longer $120, and the dollar prices of U.S. machinery and other products did not fall. Commodity trade responds to changes in the prices of different currencies.

Exchange Rates of Currencies on the Gold Standard.   As a starter toward understanding the process, we assume that the values of different national monetary units—dollar, franc, or pound—are defined in terms of the same thing, gold. And we first examine the process as it worked in the past.

Legal claims to money were easily convertible into a certain physical amount of gold. Therefore, *the national money units were automatically related to each other.* An Englishman with pounds (or his banker) could use them to buy gold at a fixed price. Then he could use the gold to buy, say, dollars at a fixed price. To do so, however, he had to ship the gold to America—at some cost for packing and transportation, insurance, loss of interest during shipment, unpacking, and final delivery. He could not afford to convert pounds to gold and then gold to dollars at the same price equivalent. There had to be a margin to cover costs. But if currency prices moved beyond the points marking the upper and lower range of this margin, shipment would be better. The legal price of gold plus, or minus, the cost of shipment set the "gold points."

If British importers began to demand more dollars than were available in London, sellers of dollar claims could charge more. British importers, however, had another alternative, for they were not compelled to pay the sellers' prices for dollars. The importers (in fact, their banks) could buy gold in London and ship it to the United States to buy dollars. This would be profitable if the legal fixed price of dollars in the United States plus the cost of shipping gold were less than the price of dollar claims in London. For every currency, there was a high and a low gold point for every other currency on the gold standard. The difference between these limits was ordinarily not much more than about 1 percent, hardly enough for most businessmen to worry about but enough to keep lynx-eyed specialists alert to take advantage of temporary dislocations—and make a trifle from correcting them. The price of one money unit in terms of another could vary only slightly. Such stability was an aid to anyone planning and conducting foreign trade and investment. Gold (and capital for short-term lending) moved back and forth, like lubricating oil in a motor, eliminating the frictions of temporary imbalances.

This system could work, of course, only if there was someone with gold to sell at one end and someone to buy it at the other end. These conditions did exist. Demand and supply operated, with gold moving to "redress the balance."

The Gold Standard Adjustment (Old-Style).   Assume that American exports are greater than imports. Foreigners pay the difference in gold. What happens next? Incoming gold serves to increase bank reserves; and the quantity of U.S. money will increase, perhaps quickly, and perhaps to a multiple of the amount of gold. If the velocity of circulation of money, V, is unchanged and T, the quantity of goods and services being bought and sold, is approximately stable, the price level, P, rises. Foreigners will then buy a little less of our products and tend to ship us more of theirs to sell at our somewhat increased *price level.* The opposite results, of course, will be felt in the economy which is losing gold. And the fall in its price level makes it a less attractive place in which to sell. Money *costs of production* in the two economies move in opposite directions, accentuating the changes in product prices. Flows of goods and services change.

In this classic adjustment the "price effect" is the key element. Prices and relations between prices induce equilibrating changes. Economic historians are not in full agreement about how completely this set of processes worked out the adjustments in the past. Today, however, there are few if any economies in which price changes of this type can be counted upon to do much of the job. Monetary systems do not permit the responses which in the past were assumed to follow gold movements. Moreover, domestic prices (especially prices of labor) do not have the flexibility assumed, especially downward flexibility. Nor can we accept the implicit assumption that resources will be employed at virtually full capacity all the time the changes are in progress.

The United States lost over $10 billion of gold in the decade to 1968; France built up its holdings by $4 billion in the same period. Yet neither country's authorities permitted these gold flows to determine monetary policy in the "classical" manner.

Freely Fluctuating Exchanges. If the prices of currencies are not fixed in terms of gold (or in some other way), what determines the price of one in terms of another? The answer, "Demand and supply without the balancing effect of gold moving at fixed prices."

Let us assume that nation G has a currency—marks—completely free with no ties to gold and that all its foreign dealings are with a country which uses dollars. If importers in G bring in fewer goods and services than exporters send out, importers will be demanding fewer dollars than exporters are supplying. The price of dollars will fall in terms of marks. Importers in G will find that they need pay fewer marks for the same number of dollars. For example, imported shoes might have cost $10, equal to 42 marks; then as dollars cost less, the importer need pay only 40 marks to get $10. He will find it easier to sell shoes to residents of G at 40 marks (plus other costs) than at 42 marks. Imports are encouraged. As a result, the demand of importers for dollars will now rise.

Exporters, however, have the opposite experience. If they are selling aspirin abroad, for example, at $10 a case, they at first get 42 marks for a case; then, because importers in G will not pay as many marks for a dollar, the exporters can get only 40 marks for the sale abroad of the same quantity of aspirin. Exporting will become less profitable. To get 42 marks, the price in dollars must be $10.50. At the higher price, selling is more difficult, and the quantities sold abroad will drop. A drop in the supply of dollars which exporters offer for sale will raise the price of dollars in relation to marks.

Trade (including invisible items) may adjust readily to offset changes in the prices of currencies and to keep them narrow. Or there may be a trend—downward or upward—in the currency price, not indefinitely but until a new adjustment (equilibrium) is reached.[3] But there is a big difference between this system and that of the gold standard: *Prices of free currencies can fluctuate more widely than the prices of currencies on the gold standard.* People dealing in foreign markets cannot count upon the stability of their currency in terms of others. Demand and supply operate without the stabilizing influence of gold movements. The speculator, however, may help provide stability, buying and selling against the temporary movement and thus reducing fluctuations. (His actions may also accentuate fluctuations.) He may even be willing to guarantee a future price of, say, the mark in relation to the dollar. Since he cannot be certain about the future, his risks are greater than under the gold standard; he must charge accordingly. Business must then pay more to hedge against loss from fluctuation in the price of one currency in relation to another.

Exchange Control: Price Fixed but Quantity Controlled.

An intermediate situation developed and exists in some form in many countries. The price of gold in terms of currency is fixed by law, as under the gold standard. However, the quantity of gold—or a currency convertible into gold, such as the U.S. dollar—which is available for purchase or sale at that price is limited by a government agency. A businessman can be sure of the price he must pay in his currency for gold or for dollars or other foreign currencies whose prices are fixed in terms of gold. He cannot, however, be certain of *how much* foreign currency he can buy at that price. His dealings, therefore, are restricted by the rationing of the quantity of foreign exchange as well as by its price. Demand and supply operate, but neither price nor quantity can move freely.

Another "instrument" was developed during the 1930's and has been used deliberately by many governments—discriminatory pricing of currency. The price that the government sets on a particular foreign currency depends somewhat upon the product or service to be bought or sold. The intent is to make the best of each of several markets. If the elasticities of demand are guessed correctly and if the separate parts of the market are kept insulated from each other, there is a possibility of benefiting (though other countries may reciprocate). The variety of rates and conditions has sometimes been large, the uses of price discrimination, ingenious. In leading countries today, except for a range of 1 percent or

---

[3] The adjustment will be reached when the fundamental economic forces of the countries are in line. But when will such a condition exist? One suggested answer—see the quotation which opens this chapter—runs as follows: The economies are in balance when the currencies exchange so that a given amount of either currency will purchase the same quantity of things used for ordinary living in either country, allowing for tariffs and costs of transport. This explanation, the "purchasing power parity" theory, is by no means fully satisfactory. Consumption patterns vary so widely from country to country, and from time to time, that comparison of internal purchasing powers of different currencies is, at best, crude.

so, there is ordinarily only one official price for each currency. Exporters are compelled to sell foreign funds at that price; importers are able to buy at that price but sometimes in limited amounts only, and perhaps only for purposes approved by government officials. By controlling quantity, then, these officials can fix, and hold, a price which is away from the long-run equilibrium level. Or they may change the price arbitrarily.

A few countries have sometimes used a modification. Imports have been divided into classes and a certain amount of foreign currency allocated for each. Free bidding for these limited quantities led to widely divergent prices of the one currency in terms of the dollar or gold.

CURRENCY DEVALUATION

Power to Change Exchange Rates. One power of government is to define the price of the country's monetary unit in relation to the price of some other currency or gold. For example, the British government in September, 1949, said that a British pound (£) was worth not $4 (as it had been) but $2.80. In November, 1967, Britain again reduced the dollar price of the pound, to $2.40. We call such action *currency devaluation*.

As far as the law is concerned—which is a lot—these actions changed the terms of almost all international dealings of the British. Englishmen, for example, in 1949 had to pay about £3 for an imported item that formerly cost £2. Does this seem a bit rough?

If the Englishman worked in an export business, a day's labor that formerly brought the equivalent of, say, $12 (£3) now brought only $8.40 (£3)—British workers (and owners of capital) were, in fact, forced by devaluation to sell to foreigners more cheaply in terms of foreign money, even though the Englishmen received the same number of pounds. Overnight, a whole nation found its economic life changed by the stroke of a pen.

Reasons for Devaluation. Why would a government devalue its currency? It would do so for much the same reason that any price is reduced—to boost sales (exports). And there is another reason—to cut imports. Devaluation helps reduce the consumption of imports by requiring more units of the home currency to be given to get a foreign currency. In fact, devaluation has usually been an open recognition of an economic "fact of life" and a way to adjust to it. Let us see.

If imports are higher than exports for months and years, something must "give." The *rate of exchange* will certainly move if it is "free." This is what was happening when the Canadian dollar fell from $1.01 (United States) to $0.93 in 1961—currency devaluation brought about by demand and supply in the market. But what if the rate, a *price*, is controlled? Then any imbalance between imports and exports will be evident in the lack of balance between the *quantities* of foreign currency demanded and supplied at the official price. If imports exceed exports, gold will leave a country which is on the gold standard. As gold leaves, domestic monetary contraction may set in, probably bringing unemployment, distress, a drop in national income, and some price reductions. These will be unpleasant. But they can force "correction," encouraging exports and reducing imports. When such changes are required—fewer imports, more exports—devaluation will often seem better than domestic monetary contraction to reduce income and prices, for with such contraction (MV) will also come unemployment.

Quotas and other *direct controls* can also reduce imports. For example, officials may reduce the amount of wheat, machinery, or perfume imported; they may restrict invisible imports, such as spending abroad by their citizens as tourists. Direct controls work crudely and not in accordance with the widely varied preferences of the public. They rarely operate to correct the basic maladjustments. And the limited quantities which are imported must be allocated somehow among those who want larger amounts than are available. Black markets appear, with heavy costs of inefficiency and dishonesty. If the fundamental difficulties are not detected and remedied, more dislocations develop.

An economy which has been consistently importing more than it exports usually wants, not so much a reduction in imports as an increase in exports. How can foreigners be induced to buy more? One answer is to give them better value, selling at a lower price. The biggest element of what an economy sells is labor, or products of its labor. The basic problem, then, seems to be to offer better value in terms of labor services. Reducing wage rates is not easy; neither is raising productivity greatly. So, instead of trying to reduce the number of money units paid per day (perhaps from £3 to £2), governments find it easier to reduce the legal price of the money unit in relation to other currencies. Foreigners are automatically permitted to get the products of the economy more cheaply. Exports will be stimulated. The amount of the stimulus will depend, among other things, upon the availability of goods for export and the elasticity of foreign demand. Devaluation may permit more expansionary domestic fiscal and monetary policies to raise national income because pressure on the balance of international payments has been relieved; buying of imports will go down (because of devaluation) even though national income goes up.

As a permanent solution, devaluation has some weaknesses. Other countries may follow the example, largely nullifying each other's actions. Costs of production (in terms of the domestic currency) will tend to rise after devaluation. Why? Devaluation, we recall, makes imports, including raw materials, cost more in the depreciated currency; these higher prices become embodied in the domestic cost of living and create pressures for higher wages. Moreover, export industries seeking to meet the increase in foreign demand will tend to offer higher wage rates and perhaps higher prices for other factors of production. (Import industries, however, are likely to find that they cannot in fact cut wage rates.)

As a "shot in the arm," currency devaluation by stimulating exports (and permitting a more expansionary monetary policy at home) can give an economy a stimulus that may lead to increasing vigor on a permanent basis, certainly a reprieve during which to attempt more fundamental adjustments. It may be no more than a palliative, however. It will not assure a long-run solution, if only because the actions of other countries cannot be controlled.[4]

Devaluation and Currency Stabilization.   A change in the price of foreign exchange (currencies) affects anyone engaged in foreign trade or investment. Such change will in itself be at least somewhat upsetting. People wonder whether more devaluations are to be expected. A country might try to forestall them by going on a full free gold standard. It might also leave the exchange rate free to fluctuate.

Yet more than nominal fluctuations, or even the possibility of such fluctuations, add an uncertainty to business. At best, they are a nuisance; at the worst, they can stifle some trade and investment. To the other requirements of business success, fluctuations in the price of currency add what is a peculiarly difficult job—forecasting trends in international trade and investment, as well as government actions. A businessman trying to decide whether to build a factory or a ship to serve the foreign market would have to guess not only future costs in his country and selling prices in other lands but also what other currencies would be worth to him in his own currency. This added uncertainty is an obstacle, a cost. Hence there may be a real economy in removing the uncertainty.[5]

Dominant opinion has come to disapprove of more than small fluctua-

---

[4] If a country's price level is low relative to that of the outside world, exports may consistently exceed imports of goods and services. Germany and the Netherlands were in this situation in 1961. A rise in the domestic price level may seem to be a poor cure, if only because inflation itself has disruptive and inequitable effects. An easier solution is an upward revaluation of the price of the currency, making it more valuable in relation to gold and foreign currencies. Germany and the Netherlands raised the dollar prices of the mark and the guilder about 5 percent.

[5] Some economists question this conclusion. They suggest that a well-developed (speculative) market in foreign exchange will provide facilities for trading in "futures" of major currencies. Thus businesses would be able to hedge and thus eliminate uncertainty for the near future. For the longer run, the argument continues, fixed rates offer no real protection unless fixed at the "correct" point. If adjustment is inevitable, the results may be better if it occurs frequently in small amounts rather than as infrequent, but large, jumps. One argument for a fixed rate is that it will aid in the resistance to domestic forces for inflation. If prices at home rise when the exchange rate is fixed, pressures on the balance of payments will develop. If the public disapproves of the loss of gold (and foreign exchange), voters may support policies to check inflation. If the exchange rate is flexible, however, no strain or sense of crisis need develop, even though inflation creeps on.

tions in exchange rates. Yet to assure stability, governments that devalued their currencies during and after the 1930's were often unwilling to try the traditional gold standard; so they established special agencies to control the prices of their currencies. These agencies bought and sold foreign currencies or gold for international payment at fixed prices (or sometimes at a variety of prices). In this country, there was a minimum of interference with private businessmen. If the rate fixed proved to be about at the equilibrium level, reflecting balance between total forces of supply and demand, short-term variations would offset each other.

A relatively mild form of control was exercised by the U.S. Stabilization Fund during the 1930's. The Fund would buy or sell either dollars or gold to offset market forces which tended to make changes the Treasury felt were undesirable. Some fluctuations were tolerated, but only small ones. Some months the Fund would find the quantity of foreign currency demanded greater than the quantity supplied; the Fund would accept dollars in return for gold, which could then be used to buy foreign currency. Other months, the opposite.

To work such a system, what does a fund need? It must have dollars (the domestic currency) and gold (foreign currencies). Then it is able either to buy or sell at the fixed price. In doing so, it can provide stability as under the gold standard. But what if *two* countries try to operate currency stabilization funds? Obviously, they must cooperate—any real conflict will doom one to failure; Britain cannot succeed in keeping the pound-franc rate at one level while France keeps it at another. International cooperation is essential; the United States, Britain, France, and other countries cooperated extensively in the late 1930's.

Much tighter controls have been exercised in many countries. In a strict system, anyone wanting to make a payment in foreign currency must apply to an official agency for the funds. Anyone receiving foreign currency must sell it to the official agency at a fixed rate. Such controls, if they can be enforced, can keep a currency stable at a rate different from the equilibrium—by controlling quantity.

Exchange controls have come to be known perhaps less for their good results in removing instabilities than for bad effects. We in this country have little comprehension of what such controls can mean—where one may go for a vacation, the books one may buy, whether the controllers allocate foreign currency to purchase oranges here or beef there. The fate of a man's job or business may depend upon the decision of the official controlling foreign currencies. One firm suffers because it cannot get money to buy raw materials abroad while another loses or gains because currency controls determine the countries in which it must sell. Businesses cannot respond most efficiently to changing conditions either at home or abroad. Domestic business is protected from competition of imports, reducing pressures for greater efficiency and technical progress. In a country which is heavily dependent upon foreign trade, exchange control is a powerful tool for government direction of the internal economy. The control is likely to seem necessary or desirable when inflationary forces exist internally. It may be sweeping, pervasive, and evident; or it may be unobtrusive and limited to a few types of transactions, such as those involving large amounts of capital.

Controls on foreign exchange curtail freedom. Why, then, has the public put up with them? For the most part, ordinary people have had no alternative. Even in countries with a large measure of democracy, popular control of a matter as complex as this is impossible. Moreover, after controls have been established for a while, removal may seem dangerous. For one thing, parts of the domestic economy may have become distorted in relation to foreign economies. Some businesses (and their employees) bask in the shelter of protection from foreign competition. Removal would be upsetting and would be opposed.

Another reason against removing controls after they have been in effect can have persuasive influence. In the absence of controls people are free to export capital for political as well as economic reasons. Relatively small movements of capital may be large enough in relation to trade to endanger a country's entire supply of gold and foreign currency. In "normal" economic and political circumstances, it is improbable that trade movements for an entire nation would shift by enough to bring big changes in the price of its currency (if free to fluctuate) or in the stock of gold. Exceptional situations sometimes arise, however. In free markets they can bring capital movements which are large, sudden, and erratic. Currency systems may be subjected to strains that are disturbing to the point of being intolerable. "Insurance may seem to justify exchange controls."

POSTWAR CURRENCY DEVELOPMENTS

The International Monetary Fund. During World War II, worldwide postwar return to the old gold standard seemed out of the question. The world's stock of gold had become so concentrated in the United States that the remainder would hardly "go around." To some extent, moreover, a country on the gold standard must feel dependent on what happens in other lands. As a result, its measures for internal stability and full employment may be defeated if conflicting policies abroad are transmitted by the gold standard. There was also agreement that the replacement should be something better than the currency confusion and instability of the 1930's.

Representatives of many nations met at Bretton Woods in 1944. They decided to try to build a system which would have stable exchange rates, which would provide a free multilateral payments system without exchange controls, and which could permit adjustment to changing conditions. The International Monetary Fund is the result. Each member country has turned over to the Fund some of its own currency and some gold on a quota basis. These quotas have been increased, and in 1967, the Fund had about $2.7 billion in gold and the equivalent of $6.5 billion in securities and various currencies, with more on call. What is the job? It is to help members stabilize the prices of their currencies without imposing restrictions that hamper trade and investment.

Each member country sets the price of its currency in terms of gold; *all currencies, then, are related to each other in fixed proportions.* Each country agrees to keep its currency from fluctuating more than 1 percent. What if economic forces make such stabilization temporarily impossible? The Fund will help, if requested. Suppose that there has been a temporary source of disequilibrium, such as the 1956 closing of Suez which forced Britain to buy oil in areas where it had to pay dollars. Its dollar and gold holdings seemed inadequate. Rather than let the price of the pound drop as Britain supplied pounds to get dollars to buy oil, Britain went to the Fund and borrowed ("purchased") dollars. Later, after time for adjustments to be made, not on a crisis basis but in line with her long-run economic outlook, she repaid the borrowing. Ordinarily, a member may in one year borrow only one fourth of its Fund quota and may not, unless for an exceptional reason, be in debt for more than twice its quota. It pays an interest rate fee for whatever it has borrowed.

What if pressures on a currency persist? A member, after consulting with the Fund, may change the par of its exchange by not more than 10 percent. Any larger change must have the Fund's permission if the country is to continue to use the Fund. These larger changes are reserved for correcting "fundamental disequilibria" (not defined). The Fund also permits a member to impose import restrictions such as quotas on imports from countries whose currencies are "scarce," thus tolerating special discriminatory restrictions on trade.

The Fund as an operating organization has provided useful technical services and "loans" to a total of $13.2 billion by 1967, of which $8 billion had been repaid. Its influence has grown. The United States drew almost $700 in 1966.

Care was taken to keep from the Fund any authority over domestic economic policies of member countries. Inevitably, however, the forces giving rise to disequilibria in the market for foreign exchange include domestic economic conditons, such as inflation that stimulates the consumption of imports. Can the Fund really look forward to reconciling a multitude of independent domestic policies to get international stability? Not if there is much basic inconsistency. The Fund's resources are too small to meet really great pressures affecting many economies. Yet it has helped prevent some mistakes and correct others. It has given support for constructive domestic policies that may be politically unattractive. Influence may be behind the scenes. Or the government officials may be aided by being able to say, "To get the IMF help we must have, our country is required to do so and so."

Several countries are still unwilling to abolish exchange controls, permit free convertibility of the currency, and thus work toward the broad freeing of international economic relations.[6] One fear is loss of capital. Some national leaders, including those of several newly independent lands, welcome the ability to use exchange controls to try to mold domestic economic development. A common fear is that relaxation of controls on foreign exchange would require tightening of domestic monetary policy —causing some unemployment.

Inconvertibility as an Obstacle to Efficient Development. There remain controls to maintain currency exchange rates at nonequilibrium levels. Such restrictions on the conversion of currency have bad effects. What are they? Currency restrictions distort and misdirect day-to-day and month-to-month affairs. Men cannot seek out the most truly advantageous exchanges. Trade and investment cannot flow where the real opportunities are greatest. Two examples of distortion: (1) The government imposing controls will not permit the conversion of money into the currencies of those lands offering the greatest benefits from trade and investment. (2) Owners of wealth in countries that do permit free movement of funds are often unwilling to invest capital abroad where opportunities in a real sense are high; they fear, rightly, that exchange controls will prevent withdrawal later of profit or capital in currencies they want.

Trade is forced into bilateral, rather than multilateral, channels—or throttled entirely. Specialization and the division of labor are impeded. Preparations for the long run are warped and obstructed. One reason why controls persist is the lack of ability to compete effectively because efficiency in the use of real resources does not match that in other countries. The controls themselves, however, hinder improvements in productivity: They make some developments impossible; they add uncertainties which discourage other adjustments and capital import; and they shelter some firms and labor from pressure to do their very best.

The leading industrial nations have abandoned or greatly relaxed the network of currency restrictions. These reforms accompanied the removal of a "thorn in the flesh" that pained postwar life: a "dollar shortage."

Postwar "Dollar Shortage." Immediately after the war, there were huge foreign needs for food, fuel, machinery, and other things for lifesaving relief and imperative reconstruction. U.S. prices were then already high. What remained to foreign countries of generations of accumulations

[6] Any attempt to estimate the total significance on the world of economy of remaining exchange controls runs into difficulty if only because many of the 121 members of the Fund are very small. The significance of their controls, individually and even in total, may not be substantial for the rest of the world. And the restrictions of the larger countries are now mild. Communist lands, however, continue to impose tight restrictions on dealings with foreign economies.

of gold and foreign investments melted away like most families' savings during a serious illness. War-exhausted economies could not produce much for export. Population increases, added to years of shortages and war damage, created insistent domestic demands, which were generally aggravated by inflation. People had their own currency to buy domestic products, keeping them from export. In some cases domestic production costs were swollen by inflation, making exports harder. India and other lands in the "sterling bloc" were able to buy in Britain and pay with the I O U's Britain had given for things supplied during the war, draining the postwar British economy. War weariness, high taxes, and such things as housing shortages cut labor productivity. Continuing military spending burdened some economies. Trade relations built up over centuries between Eastern and Western Europe disintegrated.

U.S. Emergency Aid. The United States (and Canada) made large efforts to provide not only relief food and clothing but also dollars for Europe. The Marshall Plan alone gave Europe about $12 billion for reconstruction. Methods of raising the productivity of agriculture enabled Europe to become less dependent upon import of food. Productive capacity, from giant hydroelectric systems to small machines and raw materials to fill production pipelines, was added.[7] Within 5 years Western Europe raised food production and industrial output *above prewar levels*.

As the end of the problem seemed near, Korean fighting brought pressures for rearmament. U.S. leaders believed that it was to our interest to have friendly nations spend more on armament than they could and would pay for themselves. So we supplied funds and equipment for joint defense. Other programs have also developed, as we shall see later, to give aid largely outside Europe.

Dollar Surplus. The supply of dollars to other economies grew rapidly in the 1950's. The increasing presence of European autos on American streets was only one evidence of our rising purchase of imports. More and more foreign suppliers produced things which in style, price, and quality appealed to American consumers. American tourists crowded into Europe. Our military personnel and their families stationed abroad spent millions of dollars every day. Capital exports from the United States

---

[7] We provided Europe with dollars which were used to buy goods both here and abroad. Some were used directly to raise productive capacity, machine tools from America, for example. Other dollars served indirectly—they freed resources in Europe for investment there. For example, the labor and most of the materials for building a factory in Italy would be Italian. Yet the Marshall Plan paid. How? By providing food, fuel, and other things which the Italian economy then did not need to produce. Italian labor could devote more time to building the factory. A European receiving a Marshall Plan tractor, food, or machine had to pay for it in his own currency; to individual and business recipients the aid was not a gift. The money they paid went into special "counterpart fund" accounts which European governments with U.S. permission could use, e.g., for Fulbright grants to U.S. students. Many of the dollars went to other parts of the world as Europeans bought food and raw materials.

continued year after year. All these, along with various aid programs and other sources of dollars, totaled more than foreign demand for dollars to pay for American products and services.

Until 1958 foreigners were generally not only willing but even anxious to build up their holdings of dollars in American banks. These funds were useful in financing a growing volume of world trade. The dollar, beyond question, was freely convertible—a currency which could be used without restriction and one which would not change in terms of gold. Deficits in the U.S. balance of payments supplied other lands with liquid assets for making international payments. But when foreigners began to exercise their right to demand gold for dollars and when they began to prefer German, Dutch, or British bank balances or short-term securities to those in America which paid lower interest rates, then it was clear that "dollar shortage" had been replaced by "dollar surplus."

One of President Eisenhower's last major actions in the White House was designed to help deal with the problem; it was the subject of one of President Kennedy's first major messages to Congress. He did not promise early solution for what was one of the most difficult tasks facing the economy. Seven years later (early 1968) his successor faced much the same situation even though actions building on each other had been taken in the hope that some cumulative combination would be adequate.

One possible solution is not available to the U.S. under present conditions. If the price of a currency is free to fluctuate in relation to others, "shortages" and "surpluses" will not appear. The dollar, however, is widely used in international transactions. Our own trade and investment, and those of other lands, would be disrupted—no one knows how much—if the dollar were free to fluctuate. The resulting confusion would involve greater risks than leaders here and abroad wish to assume. So other approaches are necessary. They must take account of still more aspects of the broad problem.

In the short run, it is true, monetary policy which tends to raise interest rates here helps a little—attracting funds from abroad or holding funds which might otherwise leave for foreign markets offering higher interest yields. "Tight money," however, arouses criticism. Will it not discourage investment and reduce employment? Why, it is argued, let the tail wag the dog? Why let the relatively small amount involved in the balance-of-payments deficit determine monetary policy affecting the whole economy? The choice can be difficult when the balance-of-payments deficit exists along with need to fight unemployment. The Federal Reserve could not use monetary policy with its optimum effectiveness (reducing interest rates) because of the desire to hold foreign short-term capital in this country.

Not Enough Liquidity.   From small farmers to the heads of giant international enterprises, businessmen know that efficient operations require financial liquidity. How much? The amounts which are optimum in relation to the volume of transactions will vary but are greater in international than in domestic trade. By the mid-1960's, it seemed clear that before many years the world would have too little gold and too few internationally owned dollars and other fully convertible currencies to finance smoothly a greatly expanded and growing volume of world trade. Central banks need reserves to meet temporary stresses, and the greater the volume of business, the larger the money amounts. What remedies are possible? Experts disagree on both the seriousness of the problem and the best solutions.

After years of discussion, leading nations in 1967 agreed to proceed with trying to set up a new means of payment or medium of exchange for settling international payments obligations. Major countries would turn over gold to a new agency associated with the IMF. The agency would then issue a new type of credit. It would be accepted by central banks in payment of the obligations of other central banks. A net addition to the liquidity of the world's financial system thus comes into existence—or will, if the proposals do finally get the broad acceptance needed to make them operational, that is, actually in working order. One obstacle is the fact that countries whose central banks accept this new type of credit are in fact lending to the countries with balance-of-payments deficits which lead to the use of this new form of payment. The new international "paper money" will be called "Special Drawing Rights"—SDR's.

INTERNATIONAL INVESTMENT

Dealings across national boundaries include movements of capital. Sometimes the results have been tremendously fruitful, sometimes heartbreakingly disappointing.

Reasons for Foreign Investment.   Capital equipment or funds will be moved from one area to another for the same general reason that commodities move: the usefulness in one place promises to be greater than in the other. Investors, seeking to put their savings into projects with greater promise, will at times select some in other lands. The benefits may be overwhelming—investors receive a higher return, laborers and owners of natural resources in the underdeveloped area are helped to earn larger incomes, and consumers get new and better products or old ones more cheaply. A developed economy can often progress better with resources from outside; yet areas with natural resources may not have the capital, management, and skilled labor for development. In such cases, capital from abroad may enter to develop sources of supply; the guiding force is not declining investment prospects in the older economy but rather the supplementation of development there.

Capital transactions play another constructive role. As already indicated, they aid in short-run adjustments, like a lubricant. Buyers and sellers, instead of settling in cash at once, can often benefit by the use of loans (credit) for a few months. Sometimes shifts of short-term funds, "hot money," seeking a favorable interest rate or some speculative gain, are stabilizing, sometimes a source of disturbance.

Mechanics of Foreign Investment. We think of investment in two senses: money and real things. Let us look at these two parts as they operated in that "classic" era, the decades before World War I.

Suppose there were a promising project, such as building a railroad in America. British or U.S. promoters decide to go ahead, though knowing that they could not get enough savings in the United States to finance the project. The promoters have a solution, however; they offer bonds or stocks of the railroad company for sale in England. British purchasers pay in pounds which are credited to the account of the railroad company in London. The pounds may be spent in Britain to buy rails and other railroad equipment. The British economy, then, obviously provides *both* the funds and the real resources.

The U.S. railroad promoters, however, may want dollars to pay U.S. laborers. Then they will use their pounds in London to buy dollars (or gold) in the foreign exchange market. What happens, other than that laborers in America get paid in dollars? The price of the pound falls relative to the dollar. Imports into Britain are discouraged slightly, exports encouraged; in the United States the opposite conditions result. A little bit here, a little bit there, and the British economy (receiving the securities of the U.S. railroad) finds itself with fewer real resources, the United States with more. The real things which move (textiles, shipping services, or machine tools) may be far removed from any direct connection with the project. The railroad spends dollars on labor to build a roadbed—a real resource.

If this international capital movement is to be successful, there must eventually be a turn around. Not that the capital itself must come back; permanent investment is possible. The investors who put up the money, however, will expect to receive interest or dividends—money that must go in the opposite direction from the original capital movement. Let us assume that the British investors had bought bonds. The U.S. railroad must pay interest. So each year it takes some of the dollars it gets from shippers and deposits them in New York. Perhaps the British bondholders use the dollar currency to buy American output. More likely they want pounds. How would the railroad get the dollars converted into pounds to satisfy the British?

The problem is identical with that of a U.S. importer with payments to make to Britain. The railroad may buy pounds in the financial market; the price of the pound relative to the dollar will go up. This rise tends to encourage imports into Britain because each pound will buy more in America. British exports, however, will be discouraged. The results in the United States will be just the opposite. Consequently, there will tend to be a shift of real resources from the United States to Britain. Perhaps the British buy a little more wheat or cotton here, while we buy fewer manufactured products in Britain. The result is the reverse of that which took place when the capital came to America.

The purpose of the original transaction was to make a productive investment. The new equipment increases the railroad's earning capacity, it is hoped by more than enough to pay the foreign investors. Time after time, the investment has been sufficiently productive to yield everyone concerned an attractive gain. The increased productivity, however, is realized in one currency (dollars in our illustration), while some of the payment must be made in another (British pounds). But what happens if it is difficult to convert currency of the debtor country into that of the supplier? For example, if the British would not accept goods and services, we might find ourselves unable to get pounds to meet our legal obligations to British bondholders. However, in the decades when the British were great foreign investors, they were also willing to import *without restriction*.[8] Foreigners with goods could sell them in British markets without having to jump any tariff wall. Though prices were sometimes not attractive, there was always a market in Britain. The United States, however, was less wise. During the 1920's, for example, when we became a large lender, we even raised tariffs. This action made it harder for those who owed us money to send goods to get dollars to pay American bondholders.

Before 1914 and in the 1920's, the process of international capital transfer worked fairly smoothly, often free from government participation. Of course, governments were sometimes large borrowers in foreign countries. Yet they dealt directly with private institutions and not, as a rule, through other governments. Nor did public officials do much about the transfer of resources. The whole process was essentially one of private markets—not perfect or completely exempt from political influence, but generally free. The freedom was twofold: in getting money and in using it to buy real resources on the best terms offered.

Creditor and Debtor Nations. If the residents of a country *B* owe more to nonresidents all over the world than they are owed, *B* is a *debtor nation*. The same term can be used if foreigners own more real estate, factories, etc., in *B* than *B*'s residents own abroad. A *creditor nation* is one whose residents have net claims against outsiders. (Governments may not be involved at all.) The shift from debtor to creditor status requires changes in trade balances, somewhat in four stages:

1. *Borrowing.* At first, as a country borrows (or receives equity

_____

[8] Residents of the British Isles for many years before World War I freely made investments abroad at a rate in relation to national income which for us today would exceed $30 billion a year. The absence of restrictions on imports was, of course, consistent with, and even necessary for the success of, such massive capital export.

investment from) abroad, it can import more goods and services than it exports, paying in obligations to others, its own I O U's.

2. *Mature Debtor.* When it stops borrowing appreciably, the country must make payments on interest and principal. It can meet its obligations by a change in its trade balance if it exports enough more goods and services than it imports.

3. *Investing.* The third stage arrives when the excess of exports is large enough not only to meet all obligations but also to finance foreign investments—loans or acquisitions of property.

4. *Mature Creditor.* Gradually, if the investments are made wisely, an economy gets rights to *net* income from abroad. It can indefinitely import more goods and services than it exports and thereby enjoy a higher standard of living and enrichment—higher, one hopes, than if the wealth had been invested domestically.

Through these stages, international investment and trade balances are tied together intimately. In a world without serious restrictions, the change in trade balances would evolve gradually and to the mutual advantage of the economies involved. Tariffs and other restrictions, however, affect the adjustment, generally to the long-run disadvantage of all concerned (Chapter 35).

Conditions Needed for Foreign Investment. What conditions favor international investment? One is *confidence.* The investor must believe that a venture will yield enough more than its cost to justify sacrificing other possibilities. Yet investment abroad often involves more uncertainties than investment at home; economic hazards may seem greater where one deals in less familiar markets. The investor must also believe that he will be able to preserve his wealth and actually get possession of economic benefits from what it produces. Such a belief requires confidence in political stability and respect for ownership. Property as a right depends upon what government—the law, the courts, and the police—will recognize (as well as upon economic productivity). Governments have many ways to deprive owners of the fruit of their investment—taxation, exchange controls, many forms of regulation (forcing costs up or keeping prices down), outright confiscations, and "nationalization" with unsatisfactory compensation. Investment in long-lived physical assets (such as basic transport facilities, factories, refineries, hydroelectric projects, and housing) cannot be recovered on short notice; the same applies to the intangibles involved in building a business as a going concern.

If the political situation sours—and examples of souring politics have been all too numerous—investment may become worthless to the owner, even though it is productive economically. The owner of property, and especially the foreigner, has come to seem "fair game" for plucking—not everywhere, not for certain, and not always out of maliciousness. But the attitude exists. The net effect for a U.S. investor may be about the same when the Communists confiscate his property and a politically friendly nation uses exchange control or taxes to keep him from receiving the income. Countries that offer favorable political conditions (in the broadest terms) have a decided advantage in attracting foreign capital. Unfortunately, some countries with greatest per capita need are underdeveloped not only economically but also politically.[9]

Direct Investment. Foreign investment may be made directly by individuals—a New Yorker buying a ranch in Canada. Far more important is the investment by businesses. Ford, Anaconda, Woolworth, Standard Oil, and hundreds of other U.S. firms have plants abroad; so do businesses with British, Dutch, and other home bases. Such companies use their own money to make the investment; they build factories or refineries, develop mines and oil wells, and establish utilities, stores, and distributing organizations. The foreign units, often organized as corporations in the countries in which they operate, may be tied closely to the parent or have great independence. (See Figure 34–1.)

FIGURE 34–1. Direct Foreign Investment

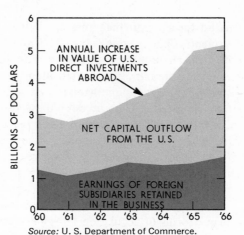

Source: U. S. Department of Commerce.

Why do businesses make direct investments abroad? (1) It may be cheaper to produce abroad and sell there than to produce here and export. Taxes, land, construction costs, and labor may be less expensive; transport costs will be lower. (2) Sometimes it is easier to sell abroad if things are

[9] The world needs a "code of international investment." Clear understanding of the rules that will be observed would reduce uncertainties. The Organization for Economic Co-operation and Development has prepared a draft treaty for setting up the "rules of the game," but ratification has not proceeded far. The World Bank is trying to establish a system of arbitration of disputes.

made in the country rather than imported. If nationalism affects sales, a U.S. firm may wisely decide to build a foreign plant instead of expanding at home. Moreover, a plant on the spot can adapt to the specific needs and tastes of foreign markets more easily than a factory here.

(3) Plants abroad may give a bargaining advantage in dealing with competitors in the offense-defense of international economic rivalry—for example, in getting an allocation for a share of the market when a cartel is effective. (4) Certain kinds of activity can be done only on the spot— running a railroad or extracting a natural resource. This form of direct investment has been the largest, with raw material (oil) development in the lead. The chief purpose is to serve parts of the world other than the area of the investment, although the latter may benefit hugely. (5) The economic troubles, and also the progress, of recent decades have created strong forces for direct investment abroad. One is to jump tariff walls. Rather than trying to produce in the United States, ship to another country, pay a tariff, and then sell, it may be better to set up productive capacity there, behind the tariff wall. The development in Europe of two groups of nations with low internal tariffs has stimulated U.S. manufacturers to produce in Europe. Products of a plant in Canada can qualify for the tariff preferences of the British Commonwealth. Countries which are seeking capital may deliberately use a tariff, quota, or other control to attract foreign firms to set up plants within their frontiers. Several countries, for example, restrict the import of many products in assembled form to stimulate local manufacture and assembly. (6) Controls on foreign currency discourage imports and thus encourage investment to produce in the area. Yet a business which cannot count upon getting earnings out of a country may have little incentive to send in more funds or machinery to modernize and expand. If it already has a plant, however, no use of earnings may be better than to plow them back, increasing its investment.[10] (7) Broader diversification can help stabilize profit. Several U.S. corporations found that foreign earnings held up better in recent recessions than did profits at home. Exports from this country to foreign affiliates of U.S. firms run to about $4 billion a year.

Direct investment may be *politically inspired*. Governments sometimes encourage businesses to get established in foreign lands. Why? (1) In the past, one reason has been to pave the way for later military or political action, such as intervention to protect actual or alleged violation of rights. (2) Governments have pushed private and semiprivate firms into overseas

---

[10] There are ways of exporting earnings despite exchange restrictions. Manufactured products may be exported when money may not. Many countries after the war forbade U.S. movie companies to take out earnings from showing U.S. films. Companies could use the local earnings, however, to make a movie on the spot and then export it; the showings in the United States earned dollars. (Lower income taxes and labor conditions which were more favorable provided additional incentives for filming abroad instead of in Hollywood.)

developments to assure supplies, notably oil, in case of war. (3) To save "dollar exchange," Britain and other lands have encouraged businesses to develop in foreign areas from which future supplies can be obtained without payment in dollars, e.g., areas which will be anxious to get imports from the economy whose companies export the capital. (4) The U.S. government has encouraged businesses to invest and operate abroad, primarily to help poorer countries develop their economies. In addition to some tax concessions, loans on favorable terms, the supply of information on a wide scale, and representation with foreign governments, Uncle Sam offers three types of insurance. Each costs 0.5 percent a year. (*a*) Convertibility insurance protects against loss from the inability to withdraw earnings because of exchange controls. (*b*) Expropriation insurance protects against loss from a foreign government's taking of property without adequate compensation. (*c*) The third protects against loss from war damages. Investments in any of about 60 lands with which agreements have been made (by 1967) can qualify. By 1967, nearly $3 billion insurance had been granted, and applications were rising.

Operating a business in a foreign country can be exasperating. In Canada or Holland, affairs may move smoothly. But often the headaches are painful. Restrictions on what a business may import or export are often serious. A quota (administered perhaps by a civil servant ignorant of production problems) may keep a plant from bringing in a machine (or merely spare parts) that would add greatly to efficiency. More than one country makes it almost impossible to discharge an employee. Patent and trademark protection are sometimes poor. Governmental or locally owned businesses may have preference in raising capital in the domestic market. Requirements that over half the voting stock be owned by citizens of the country may create embarrassments in control and management.[11]

Yet prospects for excellent profits exist, no doubt about that. Annual earnings (including undistributed foreign profits) on direct investments abroad have been averaging over 12 percent on invested capital. U.S. firms have been adding to their foreign properties by more than $3 billion annually. For many years petroleum attracted the lion's share. Increasingly, however, U.S. manufacturers are setting up plants abroad. A typical overseas foreign factory will rely upon the parent in the United States for some parts and subassemblies, especially the newer and more complicated types, and also for use of patents and management.

Oil companies operating abroad have for years followed broadly con-

[11] A U.S. firm dealing abroad must conform to both U.S. and foreign laws. Sometimes they conflict. Traditions and practices differ and may require actions that are distasteful as well as expensive. In a land where normal procedure is what would be considered corrupt in this country, what should a business do? If a government intervenes oppressively, how can a firm protect itself—its employees, customers, and owners—without running serious risk of being condemned for interfering in local politics? How much should it let U.S. diplomacy influence its business decisions?

structive policies for helping the local economies to develop. Practices which build the foreign economy can be illustrated by the Sears, Roebuck operations. Sears works to develop local sources of supply, studies the country's production possibilities, and helps to set up shops and small factories to make goods for sale. Finding raw materials, training managers and workers, adapting styles, financing, and other things needed to develop local production for a big retail chain have taken time and been expensive. The efforts have proved profitable not only to Sears but also to scores of local firms and tens of thousands of workers. Almost all of its sales in its Latin American stores come from local suppliers. United Fruit built and maintains an agricultural college, 15 major hospitals, 120 dispensaries, and other institutions for the general public in Central America.

More and more training programs for foreign workers are financed by U.S. firms—from simple local schools to advanced study in the best universities here and abroad. The difficulties of acting constructively in foreign cultures are often baffling, quite unlike those arising here. Fortunately, leading companies are exchanging information about practices which succeed and those which fail, in this area and that. Official agencies also provide facts and judgments about foreign economic conditions and business practices to help U.S. firms develop profitably and as "good citizens," abroad.

Opportunities for Borrowing and Investment by Governments. Important types of investment are not attractive to business, whether located in the borrowing or lending area. Schools, roads, hospitals, and other public works—"infrastructure"—may be highly useful and yet not attractive for investment by business. Government is the natural agency. Its borrowing to finance such projects may, in fact, be a necessary prelude to the development of some types of private business. Governments have borrowed abroad to finance utilities and public works; more than a century of experience has produced a record of many successes but also a deplorable number of examples of waste.

U.S. Foreign Investment. Table 34–1 summarizes the direct investments abroad of the people, and especially the businesses, of this country. In addition, private investors own bonds of foreign borrowers and shares of stock in foreign corporations totaling nearly $22 billion in 1967, plus around $10 billion of short-term banking and commercial claims against foreigners.

Special Problems of Foreign Investment. International investment cannot bring mankind its potential benefits until more countries and businesses find better solutions to certain problems we have not yet discussed. Both suppliers of capital and recipients have complaints. Most arise from other than more or less purely economic conditions. *Lenders* complain that borrowers have failed to respect obligations and that governments have not given foreign capitalists full protection.[12] Or, after the risks of oil discovery have been paid for and capital equipment installed, the government may insist upon a bigger share of the total income. Exchange restrictions and taxes (like Indonesia's 67 percent levy on funds sent to foreign owners of property, until remittances were prohibited) hinder outsiders in collecting earnings. Some poor lands object to paying, or allowing, rates of interest or profit consistent with the risks involved and the earnings obtainable in developed economies. Red tape, govern-

TABLE 34–1.   Direct Investments of U.S. Firms in Foreign Countries, at the Beginning of 1966

Country or Area	Amount (Billions)
Canada	$15.2
Latin America and Caribbean	10.8
Europe	13.9
Africa	1.9
Middle East	1.6
Asia	2.3
Australia and other	3.7
Total	$49.2

Industry	
Mining and smelting	$ 3.8
Petroleum	15.3
Manufacturing	19.3
Transportation, communication, and public utilities	2.1
Trade	4.2
Finance, insurance, agriculture, and miscellaneous	4.5
Total	$49.2

Source: *Survey of Current Business.* Because of rounding details may not add to totals.

mentally created uncertainties and delay, corruption, favoritism for local firms, cost-increasing discriminations, and failure to respect patents, trademarks, and copyrights remain all too common.

What are *borrowers'* complaints? (1) One is that lending economies will not accept payment in what the borrowers can offer. In a world of multilateral trade, it is not necessary that lenders accept just what borrowers can produce, but lenders must accept some goods and services on reasonable terms. (2) Foreign suppliers of capital, it is said, expect too much—prevailing interest rates plus a risk element, unduly high profits,

[12] In Latin America, we might note, U.S. firms pay more in taxes where they operate than in dividends to stockholders.

and an excessive fraction of ownership if a venture proves successful. (3) Fixed requirements for paying interest and principal may prove extremely burdensome when business is poor or when there is a shortage of foreign exchange. (4) Flows of capital may vary considerably from year to year, upsetting the balance of payments and causing erratic changes in employment. (5) The investment, though economically productive, may not be the best possible for the economy. Some kinds of activity may be relatively overdeveloped, others slighted. (6) Owners may take unfair advantage of the power that control of capital gives. (7) Foreign investment has sometimes been associated with monopolies which have been unprogressive, on occasion outrageously exploitative, and at times an opening wedge for political intervention.

Clearly, conditions have not been those of a free competitive market with bidding among rivals that assures the best terms possible. But how ought a total of earnings be shared? Some investors have received fabulous gains which might more properly have gone to the people of the area where the investment was made. (Why? Did the residents put the copper or oil in the ground below?) Others have lost heavily as ventures have failed. No one knows whether the world was paying more than the risks required when military and political disruption after 1914 made normal economic calculation impossible. Inevitably, some risks are great; overcoming them, costly.

"World Bank": International Bank for Reconstruction and Development.

During World War II, leaders began to ask: "Can't we find better ways to make decisions about investing (and managing) capital in foreign countries?" Direct investment probably followed rational calculation fairly well, but the interests of the firms involved did not necessarily lead to best advance of general welfare.

One need was obvious: to reduce economic and political risks. How? Careful advance preparation and skillful continuing direction will cut some economic risks. Others can be covered by insurance. The International Bank for Reconstruction and Redevelopment (World Bank) was established to help meet the needs for both guidance and insurance. It is a combination government-private institution. Governments supplied the original capital, using their own currencies;[13] most money for lending, however, has been obtained from the sale of bonds to private investors, at first chiefly in the United States but more recently in Europe. These bonds are secured, if all else fails, by a U.S. Treasury guarantee. The Bank's directors are appointed by governments. The staff, also interna-

---

[13] The authorized capital is $22 billion. Some 106 nations on a quota basis paid in $2.3 billion. Through mid-1967, the Bank had made over 500 loan commitments in 78 countries, totaling over $10.4 billion. Over half had gone for electric power and transportation. Income has been greater than expenses, plus allowance for possible future losses.

tional, is not, however, responsible to any government. Loans are made only after careful study of specific projects. The borrower may be a government or a private institution whose government will guarantee repayment. The Bank may also guarantee private loans, but there has been little demand for such aid. Private interests, however, have bought over one fifth of the I O U's the Bank has received from its borrowers.

Loans are limited to projects that cannot borrow privately; the Bank thus supplements, rather than supplants, private investment. Since it will finance such things as irrigation and utility projects, and health and training programs, it provides some "infrastructure" and "social foundation" which form part of the basis that helps to attract private investment in other projects. The charges—6 percent as a rule in 1967—are moderate by earlier standards. The funds provided are "hard currencies." The local economy must supply the funds needed in its own currency. The terms rquire systematic repayment of the principal. The Bank charges an insurance premium to build a fund to cover losses. Loan terms can be relaxed later so that in times of economic distress a borrower need not default but, with the Bank's consent, may adjust the terms.

There exist, then, the basic elements that will permit rational economic investment, assuming competence in the staff. The Bank's technical help, available at times to private firms, has turned out to be highly valuable. Loans now go chiefly for development in relatively backward areas. One disappointment has resulted from the difficulties which some poorer economies have in absorbing investment funds. Only gradually can a country without trained personnel and other elements of a developed economy use additional capital to good advantage. By 1967, however, the Bank's staff judged that the "absorptive" capacity of less developed lands was outrunning the Bank's ability to provide loan funds.

The Bank helped establish the International Finance Corporation to which the member countries have provided $100 million capital. It is designed to provide funds for private firms on a flexible basis. Together with new lending arrangements created by banks in several lands, the IFC is aiding highly constructive investment by private business. It acts as a catalytic agent to spur private funds into productive enterprise.[14]

The Bank has another offspring—the International Development Agency. It will make "softer" loans than the Bank to aid poor lands; two of its first loans were for 50 years at initial interest rates of less than 2 percent, payable in part in local currency. By 1967 credits committed came to $1.7 billion.

[14] Funds are advanced not on the customary fixed-interest basis but with interest plus a share in profits and a right to acquire stock to participate in the growth of the business. Most commitments have been for less than $3 million. Only a fraction of the applications have been promising enough to justify aid; by 1967 commitments had been made for over 125 projects in 36 countries.

TERMS AND CONCEPTS

bill of exchange	free exchange rate	International Mone-
foreign exchange	fixed exchange rate	tary Fund
arbitrage	currency devaluation	Marshall Plan
gold standard	direct exchange con-	infrastructure
"gold points"	trols	World Bank
purchasing power par-	dollar shortage	direct investment
ity	liquidity	

QUESTIONS

1. Ask your friends how payments for coffee get to the Brazilian farmer. Are their answers correct?

2. "Exports pay for imports." How does this statement help us understand the process of payment? Are there exceptions?

3. Explain why a country would devalue its currency. Can the benefit be more than temporary? Who in a country is likely to benefit and who to suffer? Why?

4. What forces make investment in poorer areas attractive in the world as it exists? Unattractive? Does the same apply to developed countries abroad?

5. How can a shortage of foreign currencies and gold result from domestic inflation?

6. In what respect can control on buying and selling of foreign currencies be a powerful tool of dictatorship?

7. How does the role of the World Bank differ from that of the International Monetary Fund?

8. How do restrictions on the convertibility of currency hamper trade?

9. When exchange rates are free to fluctuate, what determines their prices? Why may the Canadian dollar sell for less than the U.S. dollar when a few years ago the relation was the reverse?

10. Explain how a "creditor nation" gets repaid for funds it has loaned.

11. What would have been the economic development of America if Britons and other Europeans had not invested here? Describe the process by which the investment was made. How did we pay?

12. "Exchange fluctuation hinders the conduct of foreign trade and investment. Stability in exchange rates lowers the cost of doing business abroad." Discuss.

13. "An underdeveloped area cannot rely upon the judgment of foreign investors to select the types of investment which would best serve the inhabitants of the area." Comment. Why does capital from the United States go to areas with oil, minerals, and other natural resources?

14. "Whatever the prestige value, colonies bring no economic gain." Discuss.

APPENDIX
Colonies

The Communist Thesis: Imperialism. Communists consider international economic dealings one of the chief devils of capitalism. Marx assumed that profits at home are doomed to fall as capitalist growth continues. Then, he argued, businessmen will seek foreign lands to exploit natural resources, helpless labor, and hungry markets. Lenin added a point, predicting that the competition for foreign markets and sources of supply would lead to war. Businessmen, he argued, would force their governments into armed conflict to gain empire for economic exploitation. Although today both the danger to world peace and aggressive imperialism come, not from capitalist but from Communist lands, Communists continue to yelp the Lenin thesis. And they still use "colonialism" as a potent symbol of the evils of Western civilization.

Colonialism: Economic Aspects. What are—or were, for all but a few former colonies are now independent—the economic features of colonialism? The world has had such a large variety of colonial policies that generalization is most dangerous. When we say "The United States owns the Virgin Islands," what do we mean? Do "we" own the land and houses? Most likely they are the property of the people in the islands. The actual ownership of wealth is not necessarily affected by a change of national sovereignty. So our query should be spelled out: "What were the economic effects of political and military dominance of an area? Did colonies pay? What did political control add to what could be obtained in other ways?"

The Russians and Nazis proved this: Political and military control can be used to loot an area. Short-run gains may be large; food, machinery, and luxuries can be taken from a conquered area without payment. The Russians, at least for many years, used their domination of Eastern Europe to get more than normal competitive benefit from trade.

Fortunately, such policy does not typify colonialism of recent generations. The general tendency was for the ruling power to enforce a system of law and to encourage investment and economic development.[1] Sometimes its own nationals were given decided preference. After the American Revolution, however, the great colonizer, Britain, developed a system of freedom for investors and businessmen regardless of nationality, a system that is hard to

---

[1] Are colonies places to dispose of "surplus" production or saving? Whether or not there is "surplus" depends upon price. A high price can create a "surplus," a low price, a "shortage." It is unrealistic to think of an economy producing more than it can and will consume at some set of prices. It is easy, however, to think of prices high enough to keep some output from being sold. The main element of truth in statements that colonies served as outlets for "surpluses" was that higher prices than otherwise could be obtained.

imagine now for its absence of governmental regulation. (Today, Britain and France make large gifts each year to former and the few remaining colonies.) Political control did bring one clear advantage: It facilitated the enforcement of contracts and the creation of legal conditions favorable to commerce and investment. In this way, risk was reduced—the risk of loss because of government failure to enforce contracts. In some cases, the reduction of tribal and regional fighting also helped economic development. By the standards of our civilization, the natives gained, though population growth absorbed much of the benefit. Private investment capital put into railroads, plantation development, and mining aided both investors and local inhabitants.

Not all gains were mutual. Natives were sometimes exploited cruelly, but this deplorable result was not always a product of colonialism; native employers were at times just as bad. The dominant power (not true of Britain) might give its businesses a favored position as suppliers to people in the colonies, erecting barriers against outsiders. Presumably, then, its businesses charged more than the international competitive price.

Political control sometimes led to "distortion" of investment to suit the interests of the people at home or companies already in the colony. Native businesses were sometimes prevented from developing in competition with the mother country. Political power could also be used to buttress monopoly, such as control of production of a raw material, and to prevent wages from rising to the point which productivity would justify. The gainers might be businesses in the colony, those at home, or consumers. Natural resources might be sold to outsiders at unduly low prices. All these and other conditions appeared at one place or another. Did the general public of the mother country gain? Probably little, if at all.

Governing, especially military protection, was sometimes expensive. It was a rare colony that made net tax contributions to the home country. Colonial rivalry, too, incited governments to try for more armaments. No one can be sure how much less the British, French, Italians, or the people of the United States would have spent on defense if they had not had colonial responsibilities. Hidden costs also resulted, notably the distortion of economic activity as businesses or governments sought to alter the pattern of development to advance colonial prospects.

Were colonies valuable as a source of raw materials? Colonial status ordinarily gave the buyer in the mother country no benefit. The British firm buying tin or tea or jute from a British colony paid the same price as the German, U.S., or Belgian firm. A seller in the Singapore rubber market quoting a price did not ask the nationality of the buyer. Colonial status sometimes helped develop sources of supply, but in general there was no discrimination among buyers on the basis of nationality.

Probably, on balance, net gains from "owning" colonies have been small, if they have been positive.[2] Trade, of course, may have been vastly beneficial, but we find little basis for judging how much different it would have been without the colonial status. In a broad system of economic freedom (and world peace), the economic advantages of colonies would be slight at best. In

---

[2] Some prosperous countries have never (in modern times) been in a position to benefit from "owning" colonies—Switzerland, Sweden, Canada.

a world of trade restriction, however, the possession of colonies might enlarge somewhat the trading area and hence the benefits of the division of labor for the "possessing" country.

The many lands that have passed from colonial to independent status since World War II have generally found no easing of their economic problems as a result. Freedom, however, has created new opportunities for economic development along lines chosen by leaders of the new nations.

The picture of rich and powerful lands exploiting poor and weak ones seems a grotesque distortion today. Our own foreign aid is just the opposite, as we shall see later.

35

TARIFFS, INTERNATIONAL TRADE
POLICY, AND PROSPECTS

*The free trader holds that the people will employ their labor and capital
to the best advantage when each man employs his own in his own way,
according to the maxim that "A fool is wiser in his own house than a sage
in another man's house"—how much more, then, shall he be wiser than a
politician?*

William Graham Sumner

Trade and investment across national boundaries are the result of political,
as well as economic, decisions. In fact, governmental policies often exert a
dominating force. We have already examined exchange controls. Now we
look at the problem more broadly. Controls take several forms. To
simplify, we shall generally refer to the tariff. The analysis, for the most
part, also applies to quotas and other controls except that the latter tend to
be even more restrictive. The chapter concludes with a look at our
balance-of-payments problem.

THE TARIFF

Faith in the intuitive wisdom of mankind receives a shock when one
analyzes tariff history. Both the mighty magnates of business and the
humble man in the street seem easily misled by nonsense that economists
for generations have shown for just what it is—foolishness with just a few
minute grains of truth. "Economists" once agreed with the common
fallacies—in the days when bleeding was the cure-all for disease. Adam
Smith, attacking the arguments of the mercantilists, made such a convincing case for freedom that for two centuries most professional economists
have condemned trade restrictions. We now examine the arguments,

arguments about "protection," that is, import taxes or other barriers erected by government to shelter *some* domestic producers (*not* consumers) against competition from abroad.

The Case for Freedom.   Freedom is a condition to be prized in itself. Part of our basic philosophy is the belief that people should be subject to no more arbitrary restraint by others—in work, play, or consumption—than is clearly necessary for the *general* good. The presumption is that freedom is best—as means as well as end. Tariffs reduce the freedom of the majority to make the best use of (1) their efforts and property in production and (2) their income in consumption. Figure 35–1 illustrates

FIGURE 35–1.   Effect of a Tariff on Price and Output

If the United States were to rely upon its own output, price and quantity would adjust at the equilibrium indicated by E. Foreign producers, however, are willing to supply whatever quantities are desired at price OF. Assume that the United States imposes no obstacles on imports. The price in this country will then be OF with OM of quantity coming from domestic sources and the rest, MN, from abroad. If the United States had a tariff of FT, price would be higher here, OT, and total quantity demanded would then be OW. Output from domestic sources would be higher by MR. Imports would be less by WN plus MR.

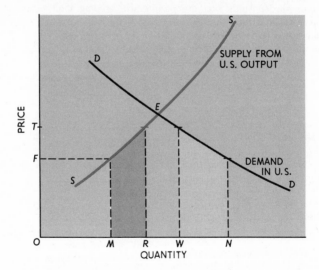

some effects of a tariff in one kind of case. Any attempt to justify barriers as furthering the public interest broadly must be highly persuasive to outweigh the conflict with freedom.

The case for freedom in international exchange has other support. Specialization increases the effectiveness of our efforts, but it depends upon exchange. If each nation, state, or family drastically reduced trade with outsiders, incomes would fall—to a primitive level in the last case. Impediments to exchange will lower productivity by cutting the extent to which we can specialize; they make us poorer. Tariffs not only reduce imports; they also hurt export possibilities. Barriers to international exchange reduce the freedom of producers to compete. Moreover, obstacles to trade deprive the public of benefits from competition, the competition that will reduce costs, raise quality, and generally spur advance by making the best anywhere available everywhere. Limits on the freedom of outsiders to compete will reinforce monopoly and backwardness of any sort. Freedom aids both plenty and progress. Yet tariffs flourish in a world struggling against poverty. Why?

Revenue.   Governments must have revenue. Taxes on commodities are one method of getting it. Goods that must cross a frontier, where governments are likely in any case to keep some watch, may be easy to tax—especially if the products, for example, coffee or wood pulp, are bulky enough to make smuggling impractical. If the item is both imported and produced at home, such as autos here, the tariff would need to be matched by an equivalent internal tax. Otherwise, buyers could escape the tax on the imported item by buying the domestic product, thus defeating the revenue purpose.

The merits and demerits of a tariff as a source of revenue must be judged by general criteria of public finance.[1] Although U.S. tariff making has been dominated by nonrevenue considerations, for much of the 19th century the tariff was a major source of revenue. Of course, the more that a tariff "protects" by reducing imports, the less revenue it brings.

Keep Our Money at Home.   Let's look at a little gem of a fallacy: A tariff can help keep money in the economy, build home markets. This is like a family keeping money at home, away from the grocer, and eating what will grow in the backyard—slow, sure starvation but with the dollars held firmly in possession. What is truly important? Not money but real income—what the money will buy. With a great deal of money at home, we can pay each other handsomely as we work our backyard potato bed before freezing from lack of fuel. Tariffs reduce the international division of labor so that money has less real purchasing power. Productivity, and hence our real income, must suffer; we may spend the same number of dollars, or even more, but get less for them.

Preventing the Competition of Cheap Foreign Labor.   The argument which probably influences voters the most is that the tariff will protect American workers from the competition of cheap foreign labor. How can

---

[1] The country imposing a tariff may not bear all of the burden because some of it in fact is shifted to residents of exporting economies. Assume that the price of bananas is about as much as we can and will pay; then we impose an import tax; foreign sellers, not being in a position to curtail production, must cut the pretariff price. Short-run and long-run effects will differ, of course; the tariff-imposing country's demand relative to that of the world as a whole has a significant influence on the shifting of its tariff to producers in the export economy.

the Cleveland factory employee receiving $4 an hour compete with a foreigner receiving $2? Let's turn the argument around. Why would the foreigner work for us so cheaply and send us his products? Unless he is trying to be charitable, we conclude: *Foreigners want things we produce.* In effect, persons working for low wages want to exchange their output for ours, produced by labor paid at far higher rates. We shall both benefit by such exchange as each specializes according to the principle of comparative advantage.

Because someone will work for us "cheaply," we can concentrate our effort where we can be *most* productive. Of course, if Americans try to do *exactly* the same thing the foreigner is doing, we cannot meet his competition and pay American wage rates. Suppose that precisely this result comes about. U.S. producers cannot match the price at which foreigners will make some specific product. The foreigners begin to sell more of it to us. Having more dollars, they then buy more from us, but not the same things they sell. The demand for labor in our export industries will rise, thus offsetting the decline where imports increase. Such a shift of labor might be temporarily painful in specific cases, not because we dislike better jobs but because some of them may be hard to find or costly to reach. The end result, however, is higher *real* income. Why? Because more of our total needs are being provided by people who work more effectively; some workers get jobs where productivity is better—in export industries.

The significant issue, of course, is not the comparison of wage rates per hour here and abroad but *wage and total costs per unit of output*. The highest hourly wages may be the least expensive, depending upon productivity. In low–wage-rate countries, one argument for tariffs is that protection is needed from the efficiency and low cost of U.S. industry, despite its high wages. American labor, with the relative abundance of capital provided it, *can* compete and win over much of the world's low–wage-rate labor. Should we not seek to use time and capital where they have the *greatest* comparative advantage? If foreign producers will do some things more cheaply, then we have a better chance to raise our living standards by shifting our efforts to what is better. Incidentally, two things in which the United States competes most effectively as an exporter are business machines and electronic equipment produced by firms noted for high wage rates.

Why, then, the appeal of this protariff argument? Men accept it because they fail to understand the basic economics, especially failing to see that foreigners want to sell so that they can buy. There is more, of course—a concern for the short run, recognition that adjustment may be unpleasant, even though in the long run it can yield excellent benefits. Not everyone realizes that *high real earnings* depend upon high productivity, which depends partly upon finding *what* is best to produce with the limited resources available.

Americans do face tough competition abroad. Other things the same, the higher our wage rates, the more difficult that competition. But American tariffs and other import barriers are not the means of dealing constructively with this problem. In fact, they aggravate it by delaying domestic adjustment to what is really best for us.

Helping Infant Industry.   Many countries today employ an argument that has been important in American history: Tariffs are useful as a form of economic planning to encourage *infant industries.* Starting a business is an uphill fight; a competitor who is well entrenched on higher ground can use his position to impede the new firm's rise.[2] If an industry once becomes established, it may not only survive but thrive—like an infant grown to manhood. A tariff, by putting foreign suppliers at a disadvantage, can permit the infant industry to charge domestic buyers more. Domestic consumers, like parents, pay to help the growth.

The infant grown to maturity may then help support its parents by (1) giving the public lower prices than would prevail otherwise and (2) using productive resources better than they would be used elsewhere. The human and the industrial infant differ, however. It is not always clear which new industries can grow to become self-supporting. After they are developed, which will have low *comparative* costs? Congress is not an ideal agency for making impartial analysis of long-run problems for the country as a whole; the chief interest of many members will be in the *next election,* not technology in 20 years. To grow, the infant must use resources, presumably diverting them from some other use. As consumers are forced by the tariff to pay higher prices to help one industry, they have less to spend on the products of others which may have equally great promise. What we want is not to preserve every industrial infant (as we do children) but only the sturdiest, as we do when we weed seedlings, so that many do not stunt all.

As an industry grows with special help, it probably becomes accustomed to standards which it can maintain only with continued assistance. A spoiled child is difficult to wean. The baby does not want to give up its nursing bottle. Industries which have grown with tariff protection seldom seem willing to relinquish it; the public is stuck.

Still more serious, perhaps, is the fact that by curtailing imports, the tariff makes it harder for foreigners to buy from us so that infant industries in the *export* fields have less chance to develop. And they may be the most promising. Moreover, any shift of productive resources to the protected industry takes them away from other firms and thus in another, but indirect and unrecognized, way adds to the difficulties of export.

---

[2] More serious as a competitor than foreign makers of the same thing may be domestic firms in other lines seeking the productive resources and the consumer's dollar.

The infant industry argument, like a little knowledge, can be a danger-ous thing. Sometimes it has merit. Yet, in practice, it is very hard to apply well. Not everyone who wants consideration as a baby is really an infant. And many industries may believe that it is pleasant to have someone else's care—not a subsidy collected in taxes raised by the government but a higher price collected from consumers. Countries trying to encourage manufacture are likely to be attracted by this argument but deluded and self-punishing in trying to use it. More than a tariff crutch is necessary to get the capital and skill needed to develop an efficient manufacturing industry. Looking beyond current burdens on consumers and export industries, one sees the danger that labor and other resources will settle where they cannot have a good future.

Tariffs for Defense. "Defense, however, is of much more importance than opulence." In these words, Adam Smith, that great champion of free trade, stated a point for protection: military considerations (but may it not be limited to the pre-hydrogen-bomb-in-guided-missile type of war?) At first glance one might say: "Since military preparedness is so crush-ingly expensive, if we are threatened we should exert even stronger efforts toward maximum efficiency. Economic analysis shows that tariffs force resources into less than their best use and reduce the full pressure of competition for utmost efficiency. Therefore, if we are cursed with a danger of war, we cannot afford the folly of self-impoverishment *via* the tariff." The latter argument has great, but not decisive, force.

Some things badly needed may not be obtainable from abroad during hostilities. In time of peace, therefore, it may be wise to modify the economy with war needs in mind. Peacetime military buying can help alter the structure of the economy to meet war production needs; stock-piling can insure supplies of storable materials. Yet some restrictions on imports can also help, if other conditions are favorable. The United States, for example, by burdening imports of Swiss watches may encourage a domestic watch industry that would be able to make timing devices in time of war.[3] On the other hand, Switzerland, even with a sky-high tariff on petroleum, could not develop a domestic oil extractive industry if oil is now below the Alps; a high price due to the tariff, however, would curtail consumption with the possible military advantage of reducing the econ-omy's dependence upon oil whose source might be cut off. For us, the potential shortage in a nonholocaust war seems likely to be not manufac-tured goods and skills but a few raw materials which no tariff can put underground any more than it can put oil under the Alps. Barriers to

[3] Since the Swiss (or other suppliers) would presumably reduce their purchases from us as we reduced our purchases of watches, would the export industries suffering also be those with potential military benefit? And might not an American watch industry, or any other sheltered from competition, fail to do all that is really possible to raise its efficiency?

imports such as those we put on oil along the Atlantic Coast, by encouraging peacetime use of domestic raw materials, may actually reduce resources which could be available during war. Moreover, any "defense" tariff might alienate and weaken our potential allies.

Although the military argument deserves respect, the principle is extremely difficult to apply. Scores of industries, all having some military significance, may seek help, but if more than a few requests are met, the cumulative loss of efficiency can be so large as to more than offset any gains. How can we forecast military needs, especially the needs that are likely to be most urgent, when the technologies of weapon systems change so rapidly? How much of a tariff will divert how much productive capacity? Finally, what are likely to be the conditions of a future conflict?

Diversification. In small economies it is argued that specialization, like putting all one's eggs in the same basket, is dangerous. What if the bottom drops out of the basket, or the foreign market for your product? On the other hand, if foreign sources of supply become tight, an economy may suffer a tight "squeeze." Diversification can provide some insurance, and barriers to imports can stimulate diversification. But they operate indirectly; often they are so concealed that the public cannot find how much it is paying or what it is really getting. Economies with the clearest need for diversification—predominantly one-product areas, such as Bolivia or Egypt—are likely to be not only unbalanced in their economic development but also too poor to justify much temporary sacrifice for diversification.

Economic Stability. A modern twist to the diversification argument is that a tariff may reduce foreign trade and, by diminishing an economy's dependence on others as buyer and seller, provide insulation against business fluctuations which originate elsewhere. The insulated economy, it is argued, is more master of its own fate so far as business cycles are concerned. Advocates of the policy are likely to assume that they have some reasonably good control over inflation and depression at home. (What nature can do to the food supply is another matter.) Even if the advocates could make domestic policy work as assumed, one must ask, "Is the benefit worth the cost?" Sacrifice of the advantages of specialization can be a staggering cost. One thing about poverty is that there is not much room to fluctuate on the down side. For the United States, certainly, the greater-stability argument has no significant merit.

Raising Employment. What if there is unemployment? Is it not better then to cut off some imports and employ Americans who are idle? Will not new barriers to imports create jobs at home? Can we thereby export that highly undesirable "product," unemployment? In the short run such possibilities exist. "Beggar-my-neighbor" policies, however, are almost certain to lead others to retaliate, perhaps even more vigorously. And except for only a brief period, the potential achievements are reduced by fundamental economic forces.

Aggregate employment depends upon forces which differ from those that determine the *allocation* or distribution of a given amount of employment among different kinds of work. A tariff can change the allocation of employment but not the total amount over any substantial period; an apparent gain from reducing imports will be offset by loss of exports, not necessarily next month but as time passes.[4]

During recession, however, one special consideration does deserve attention. If the government is putting more money into the hands of the public to stimulate business, some will be spent on things from abroad. A portion may not come back as demand for exports, at least for a long time. An expansionary fiscal and monetary policy may call for some way to "keep the money at home," reduce "leakages," especially if gold is scarce and devaluation of the currency seems undesirable. A tariff to reduce imports may do the job. The reasoning which takes account of support for expansionary domestic financial policies has more merit than the simple let-us-export-our-unemployment-by-cutting-imports argument. In any case, however, the practical difficulties of skillfully using a tariff for this purpose, to say nothing of raising employment over any long period, are about as great as those of breaking a world record in sports.

Equalize the Cost of Production: The "Scientific" Tariff. Defenders of tariff protection have argued seriously that a legitimate function of a tariff would be to equalize the cost of production here and abroad. This principle is magnificently misnamed the "scientific" tariff. If it cost, say, $400 to deliver a U.S. color TV set in France and $500 to make the equivalent set there, the French "scientific" tariff would be $100.

The "logic" is essentially that specialization and trade are bad, that exchange should be prohibited by burdens just equal to the benefit that could be gained from exchange. If it is cheaper to produce tea in Ceylon than in Wisconsin, the argument implies, a special tariff should be imposed high enough to assure that people in Wisconsin pay as much for tea as if they grew it themselves. Ridiculous, but widely endorsed! High tariffs would be imposed where we are relatively inefficient to force us as

---

[4] In the 1930's some economists concluded that this line of reasoning needed reexamination and that possible effects on domestic employment should come to the front in making tariff policy. Short-run factors might deserve more serious consideration. Exports and imports do not always move together in harmony. A tariff (or quota or currency restriction) reducing imports, therefore, could stimulate domestic production. It might do so, not only directly but also indirectly, by encouraging investment in new facilities. Exports might suffer less. Since in a depression export industries would probably not be investing much, any reduction by them in new investment would perhaps be less than the expansion by the others. However, the net increase in outlays on new investment could be only short-lived.

workers into jobs of low productivity and as consumers to pay more than if our supply were not so inefficient.

Since this argument does have friends, we must note a practical problem. How can one figure "cost of production"? Under which of widely varying conditions: size of firm, season, weather, efficiency, location, and, by no means least important, the extent to which a plant is utilized? Do we seek fixed, total, or marginal cost? Some cost figures will be much above others; setting a tariff on the basis of the highest will not only penalize consumers unmercifully but will also lead to gross distortion in the use of productive resources. Efficient firms would have a rare chance to profit at the expense of the consumer. One minor difficulty—or is it minor?—will be to discover foreign production costs.

Protection against Dumping. Sometimes producers have a "surplus" which they do not want to sell in the domestic market. They may *dump* abroad, selling for less (allowing for costs of transport) than at home. Two arguments for tariffs may result. A home tariff can prevent the goods from coming back. As regards the importing countries (where consumers benefit from the low price), producers may present the following argument: The long-run national interest requires that domestic sources of supply be not seriously damaged by price concessions from abroad which will be only temporary. A special tariff may then serve usefully. At times, however, the plea for protection against dumping is another form of the request for insulation against competition—permanently.

Retaining a Tariff to Prevent Injury from Removing It. After a tariff has been established, defenders argue that it must be kept because removal would hurt those who are being protected—a conflict with the infant industry argument. This reasoning has merit—not for holding to the tariff forever but for making elimination gradual or granting some aid for the adjustment of capital and labor. Transition problems, as one looks to the future, may seem great enough to discourage reform continuously, unless measures are provided for absorbing the worst shocks.

Miscellaneous Arguments. Other arguments, or variations of these, need brief reference. If a country imports something on which it imposes a domestic tax, a tariff to equal the domestic tax (but, of course, not in addition) is logical. By fostering new industries, a tariff may give workers a large variety of employments—an argument that appeals during the years of early growth. Social developments (such as helping either rural or urban life) may seem desirable enough to warrant some economic cost in the form of restrictions on imports. Sometimes it is argued that a tariff can serve usefully as a weapon for retaliating against other countries—like playing with fire, dangerous but conceivably defensible.

Finally, trade barriers may be used to reduce a balance-of-payments deficit. They may help, at least temporarily. As a rule, however, they will not strike at the sources of the trouble and may make them worse; some countries may retaliate, reducing export markets; costs of living and of production will tend to be higher than otherwise so that exporting becomes more difficult.

Lessons of Tariff History.   Economists believe that they are experts on the basic issues involved in tariff policy. And economists have long been in virtually complete agreement that protective tariffs are undesirable. Yet the American public—and that of the rest of the world—has generally ignored such advice. The explanation is as complex as politics, and for over a century the tariff was a dominant issue of national politics. We can learn important lessons from this history, lessons which in some cases apply to other aspects of public policy.

1. The interest of the *public as consumers* has always been, and still is, represented weakly. The tariff imposes costs in the form of higher prices, but the costs are diffused, concealed, and probably small for the individual family; it has always been difficult, no matter what the issue, to get enough sustained and concentrated interest among consumers to develop an effective organization. Against the consumer, however, range mighty interests with much at stake in tariff decisions. These groups press and prod, and "the squeaking axle gets the grease." The men camping on the doorsteps of Congress can exert influence entirely disproportionate to the numbers they represent or the merits of their case.

2. The power of relatively small pressure groups is increased by a willingness to trade support, to roll each other's logs. Logrolling, cooperative effort of neighbors helping each other, was fine on the frontier; in politics, however, it often consists of a few people cooperating to hurt many others. Congressman *A*, pressed by a manufacturer (or labor or farm group) to burden one type of import to help his district, needs many votes in Congress, most of which must come from congressmen who have no interest in the same product. What can *A* do? One step is to find other congressmen interested in the same industry. They can then get together to bargain with other groups. *A*'s group agrees to support barriers on, say, 23 other products—tariff increases most of which can only harm *A*'s constituents. As consumers they must all pay more, while only a few are likely to benefit as producers.[5]

3. A depressing feature of our tariff history has been the disregard for

[5] When individuals employ personal strength to force others to "hand over" (for no equivalent), we use strong terms to describe what is done and strong action to punish and prevent it. Yet many of us are willing to use voting power to do the same thing—to employ the force of government to take from others' pockets. Probably most congressmen dread these pressures to act against the general interest. Partly to increase the quality of its information and judgment on tariff issues, Congress established the U.S. Tariff Commission in 1916. It studies problems related to tariffs and removes some disputes from the legislative arena.

the interests of exporters. Part of the reason was the post-1861 political weakness of the South, a big exporting area. Moreover, for years our major exports were agricultural products for which there was a large world market. The world demand for wheat or cotton could not be affected in any observable way by differences in the volume of U.S. imports of, say, steel or woolen cloth. Our situation today, however, differs materially. A large reduction in our imports of watches, cheese, or petroleum may directly hurt the export demand for autos, fruit, or movies. More and more American exporters now realize that their sales abroad depend upon the success of foreigners in obtaining dollars by selling to Americans.[6]

REDUCTION OF TRADE BARRIERS

Reciprocal Trade Agreements Program. A major break in the U.S. tradition of protection came in 1913 when tariff rates were reduced substantially. In the 1920's, however, this country boosted rates. Another tariff jump came in 1930. Americans had loaned billions to people abroad, and now we were making it harder for them to send us goods that would (get them dollars to) pay the interest and the principal due. Although this blow to international trade hardly sent the world over the economic precipice, it did give another kick to industry and agriculture (and finance and politics) in other lands—and to ours—as the world economy spiraled downward.

The New Deal began in 1933 with contradictory policies. By reducing the gold value of the dollar, it added disruption to world trade and made it harder for us to buy foreign products while accentuating the intensity of our competition as sellers in foreign markets. Yet the New Deal also initiated the Reciprocal Trade Agreements, a long-range program of systematic tariff reduction. Secretary of State Hull, having had long experience in Congress, believed that a new approach was essential, one which could be freer from the logrolling methods of Congress, which would provide orderly change, and which would permit us to use the fact that we were willing to reduce tariffs to persuade other countries to reduce theirs. Congress authorized (1) the transfer of the *setting of tariff rates* to the executive branch of the government and (2) the use of the *treaty-making power* to change the tariff law but, in effect, with Senate ratification guaranteed in advance. In later renewals of the authorization, however, Congress reduced the scope of the executive action.

The State Department has been both the quarterback directing the plays and the ball carrier. But it has been assisted by a team of representatives of other government agencies and private business. The original

---

[6] Careful studies find that on the average the employment gain from a million dollar increase in exports fully offsets any loss of employment resulting from an equal growth of imports.

procedure was to begin negotiations by sounding out another government. Was it interested in reducing tariffs on items we send it while we would reduce our tariffs on things we buy from it? When there was serious interest, more study followed. Various of our government agencies studied the economic features of each product; the export and import industries involved all presented their views. Then followed diplomatic negotiations. Although tedious, they could rest upon a sound basis of industrial, financial, and general economic fact and analysis *of both economies*, as Congressional determination does not. The end result was a treaty. We agreed to reduce tariff rates on some items, and the foreign country cut its rates on others.

The treaties contained the "most-favored-nation clause." Each signer granted the treaty terms to all nations in the most-favored-nation group. (The Soviet bloc is excluded.) The reductions granted by the United States, therefore, apply to *all* imports of an item, not merely those from the country making the treaty. We thus struck blows at barriers to trade in general.

Who gains? U.S. consumers receive imports at less cost. U.S. exporters have a better chance to sell abroad. Our economy can use productive capacity more efficiently. Foreigners also benefit in the same two ways, as consumers and producers.

General Agreement on Tariffs and Trade.   The Hull treaty program suffered because negotiations were bilateral—between the United States and one other country at a time. This procedure was both slow and piecemeal. Moreover, it did not strike at other restrictions which had cursed the 1930's. Bilateral agreements, quotas, discriminatory tariffs, cartel restrictions, controls on foreign exchange, and other actions added cumulatively to the stifling of trade. Once they began to grow, they spread like a cancer. The men who during World War II began to plan for a world of peace hoped to break the vicious circle and prepare for freer multilateral trade. The U.S. trade treaties had made a good beginning, but something more general was needed.

With the United States taking the lead, 23 nations in 1947 negotiated the General Agreement on Tariffs and Trade—GATT. This agreement made substantial reductions in tariffs and other barriers to world trade. It also discouraged the erection of other impediments, such as internal taxes or domestic regulations discriminating against imports. GATT has worked for the elimination of quantitative restrictions on imports. Conferences are held periodically. They have worked to reduce barriers and to forestall the erection of new ones. A single conference negotiated 8,700 tariff concessions. The 70 or so members (not all participating fully) do about four fifths of all foreign trade. Each gives all others, and then receives from them, all concessions granted (with not a few exceptions). Agricultural products present the greatest difficulties. Many lands, the United States included, insist on restricting the import of farm products by the use of quotas and use subsidies to stimulate agricultural exports.

Results of U.S. Actions. This country has reduced its own tariffs more than anyone would have dreamed possible 30 years ago, while also assisting the general reduction of trade barriers in much of the world. Measuring the height of a tariff is extremely difficult and always inaccurate.[7] Yet rough figures are helpful. The U.S. tariff of the mid-1960's averages about 12 percent of the value of imports subject to tariff and about 6 percent of the value of all imports; in the early 1930's, the corresponding figures were over 50 percent and 18 percent. Tariff reductions help account for a multiplication of our international trade. Imports per capita were around $13 in the early 1930's—today $130; the comparable export figures are $16 and nearly $155. Figure 35–2 compares actual tariffs in the mid-1960's with those in 1935 for eight groups of commodities which include two thirds of all imports subject to tariff. Obviously, the rate reductions have been substantial. For all dutiable commodities the dollar value of 1966 imports was over 25 times the average early in the 1930's; free-list imports also rose, but relatively less—about ninefold. Special arrangements with Canada largely eliminate tariffs on autos and auto parts, thus permitting more efficient division of labor in an industry which spreads over both countries.

On many manufactured articles, however, our tariff remains high enough to be burdensome. Moreover, since reductions already granted may expire if Congress refuses to renew the program, foreign firms are naturally hesitant in making expensive commitments—such as establishing a selling organization here—to take full long-run advantage of existing concessions. Uncertainty thus adds an obstacle of some force.

Congressional opponents of tariff reduction have succeeded in adding

---

[7] To illustrate, we might have tariffs of 50 percent on two items—say, bulldozers and canned beef. The first might be meaningless because no country, even if our tariff were zero, could send bulldozers meeting U.S. competition. The second might be high enough to cut out all imports of canned beef. Then there would be no import of either of the two items. How could one measure the statistical significance of the two rates? Or, we might have a 50 percent rate on a certain kind of felt glove and 5 percent on steel girders and collect exactly the same revenue under each. How do we measure "height" of the two rates? There is another difficulty. Tariffs are often put in two forms, *ad valorem* and *specific*. An *ad valorem* rate is a certain percentage of value; if the rate on gloves is 50 percent, the tariff is 50 cents on a $1 pair of gloves and 55 cents if the price rises to $1.10. A *specific* duty is a certain dollar amount per physical quantity regardless of price; if the rate were 50 cents a pair of gloves, it would be 50 percent of the price when gloves were $1 and only 45 percent when the gloves were $1.10. A specific rate then varies as a percentage of value as the price changes. One purpose of specific rates is to conceal a very high percentage rate. The former duty of 72 cents a dozen combined with 40 percent *ad valorem* on balls for ballpoint pens was estimated to equal around 2,400 percent of the value. Rising price levels, however, reduce the effective weight of specific tariff rates.

FIGURE 35–2.   Tariffs in 1935 and 1962, Average Rates (in Percentage) on Imports of Selected Groups of Dutiable Commodities

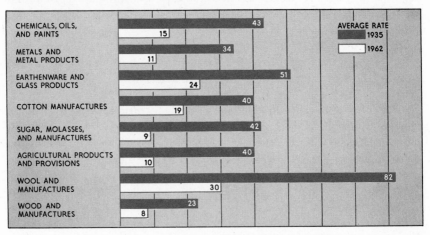

Source: Statistical Abstract. The 1962 rates applied generally into 1967.

more and more restrictions. For many years the law prohibited reductions below a "peril point" determined by the Tariff Commission as a rate below which domestic producers would be injured seriously. An "escape clause" in our agreements in effect requires reexamination of any reductions if U.S. producers are threatened with serious injury. If a U.S. industry complains, the Tariff Commission studies and makes recommendations, which the President then has the power to accept or refuse. The mere existence of escape clauses can have serious adverse effects on the whole program, because foreign suppliers cannot depend upon U.S. action. A firm abroad that succeeds in developing a good market here runs a serious risk that its own success will touch off restrictive U.S. action. Congress has also given the President power to impose quotas in certain case in which domestic producers are seriously threatened by imports.

Regional Trading Groups.   Four groups of nations have organized on a regional basis to reduce tariffs among themselves. Two, one in Central America and one in South America, are proceeding slowly; their trade among themselves does not loom large in the world or even, in many cases, for their economies. Two in Europe, however, have become highly significant in the world's economy.

The EEC, European Economic Community (the Common Market) includes Belgium, France, Italy, Luxemburg, the Netherlands, and Western Germany, the "Six." These countries by 1968 will have eliminated tariffs and quota restrictions among themselves (with some exceptions). (Greece has "partial membership," and a dozen new African countries have special status as the former French colonies.) The Common Market has become, for the most part, a free trade area with almost as many people as in the United States and a large fraction of the productive capacity. The group will have a common tariff against the outside world at rates averaging those of the six countries originally. These rates seem generally higher than ours; in some cases they are high enough to discourage imports materially. Member countries are also harmonizing domestic tax systems and relaxing or removing barriers to the movement of capital and labor. Original plans also called for considerable political unification, but France's opposition has checked movement toward this goal.

The "Outer Seven," the European Free Trade Association, EFTA, consists of the United Kingdom, Austria, Denmark, Norway, Sweden, Switzerland, and Portugal. This group has reduced tariffs among themselves to create a free trade area. They do not, however, contemplate a uniform tariff against the rest of the world; nor do they envision the growth of political unity.

Efforts to merge these two groups have not been successful. After long delay Britain indicated a desire to join the EEC. But negotiations moved slowly. Trouble arose from wide divergence between British and French and German policies for aiding farmers, plus difficulties in adjusting the special preferences in the British Commonwealth. De Gaulle used the French veto to end negotiations for a time. In 1966 Britain again sought to align itself with the Six; five members of EEC favor Britain's entry, but French opposition continued (into 1968) to block the move.

The reduction of tariffs within Europe helps account for the rapid and sustained growth of the economies affected. Our leaders who encouraged the formation of the two groups were correct in arguing that tariff cuts would benefit the nations doing so. In one respect, however, American predictions were wrong. EEC orientation has not become "outward" to get greater gain from more tariff reduction with more of the world but "inward"; reluctance to reduce tariffs against other countries reflects continuation of restrictionist attitudes. We can suffer, for one sixth of our total exports go to EEC lands. One result is reinforcement of other incentives of American firms to expand their production inside Europe.

Trade Expansion Act of 1962: The Kennedy Round. When the law governing our tariff agreements was about to expire in 1962, President Kennedy (with support from former President Eisenhower) proposed, and Congress passed, the Trade Expansion Act (TEA). Negotiations began in 1964. They were difficult but ended in 1967 with results which pleased, without completely satisfying, optimistic supporters. Average reduction of U.S. tariffs will be about 35 percent (see Table 35–1). Other leading countries will make cuts on the same order of magnitude. The significance of such sweeping tariff reductions extends beyond the cuts themselves. A new climate will favor investment in new productive

TABLE 35–1.   Tariff Reductions Granted at Kennedy Round Negotiations, 1967, Selected Items (Ad Valorem Rates, Percent)

	Prior Rate	New Rate (Final)
By the United States		
Motor vehicles	6.5	3.0
Motorcycles	10.0	5.0
Airplanes	10.0	5.0
Motors	12.5	6.0
Sewing machines	10.0	5.0
Computers	11.5	5.5
Movie projectors	11.5	5.5
Binoculars	30.0	20.0
Alloy iron or steel	8.5	6.0
Plywood	10.0	5.0
Synthetic drugs	10.5	5.0
Cheese	22.5	11.0

	Prior Rate	New Rate (Final)
By European Economic Community		
Motor vehicles	22.0	11.0
Airplanes	10.0	5.0
Electronic tubes	15.0	7.5
Steel structures	11.0	5.5
Synthetic fabrics	17.0	13.0
Chemicals (misc.)	18.0	14.4
By United Kingdom		
Motor vehicles	22.0	11.0
Cameras	40.0	20.0
Air conditioners	12.0	7.5
Aluminum alloys	10.0	5.0
Paperboard	13.3	10.0
Chemicals (misc.)	33.3	23.0

	Prior Rate	New Rate (Final)
By Canada		
Motor vehicles	17.5	15.0
Diesel engines	20.0	15.0
Cotton fabrics	22.5	20.0
Paper (misc.)	22.5	15.0
Chemicals	20.0	15.0
By Japan		
Motor vehicles	35.0	17.5
Aluminum	13.0	9.0
Synthetic fabrics	25.0	12.5
Paperboard	20.0	10.0
Chemicals (misc.)	20.0	15.0

Source: Department of State.

capacity where the economic potential is greatest. Nontariff barriers were lowered but continue to challenge efforts. Agricultural products, some chemicals, cotton, and steel all present problems.[8]

New Nations. The number of separate countries in the world has doubled since World War II. What effects will the acquisition of independence by these lands have on international trade and investment? It is too early to forecast with confidence, but several kinds of policies are already evident.

Some old barriers to trade, such as colonial preferences, are falling. New barriers are rising, however. Currency restrictions appear. So do quotas, tariffs, and other impediments to imports. Some countries make special effort to stimulate certain exports. There is strong pressure to arrange international groups to restrict marketings and thereby raise the prices of key exports such as oil, cocoa, and coffee. Many lands are trying to attract foreign capital. One thing, at least, is now clear: The increase in the number of politically independent countries will enlarge the number and extent of governmental intervention in foreign trade and finance, affecting not only the countries themselves but others as well.

OTHER BARRIERS TO TRADE AND INVESTMENT

Tariff Administration. A major complaint of businesses engaged in foreign trade is the red tape involved in meeting tariff and other requirements. Uncertainty and trouble can be a burden which, unlike a tariff rate, a business can never allow for accurately in advance. The regulations can be incredibly complex. Sometimes no one knows what they mean, and one official may rule differently from another. Compliance with labeling and inspection requirements is costly, a nuisance, and sometimes impossible. Methods of valuation are complicated and at times uncertain.

You might think it tough to get to the frontier with a load of perishable products and find the rules different enough from the last time to assure that your things spoil while you meet a new formality; or Christmas may pass before you can get a ruling on an order of toys. Commonly, an import might fall under any one of several possible classifications (products being defined to minute specifications—about 25,000—but not precisely). Months after goods are sold, you may learn that a reviewing official has decided that another of the 8,000 rates applies and that you owe more. There may not be enough officials to give reasonably prompt service. Fortunately for U.S. importers, the Bureau of Customs has made great progress in simplifying administration.[9]

[8] The steel industry in early 1968 pressed strongly for quotas to limit imports. They were over $1 billion a year. U.S. wage rates were so much higher than those of Europe and Japan that American producers saw no way of avoiding further loss of markets here unless imports were kept from rising.

[9] In 1968, the Bureau of Customs expects to deal with 64 million ships, autos, and planes with 210 million people arriving from foreign countries. It will examine 5.2

Cartels and Intergovernmental Commodity Agreements. Selling agreements of one sort or another restrict foreign trade—cartels, for example. Government aid is usually involved in making the agreements effective. In a few cases, U.S. exporters may combine to deal in international trade without fear of prosecution under the antitrust laws, but few such combinations exist. Governments themselves have gone into the "business" of combining to restrict trade, chiefly in agricultural products and certain raw materials. The United States participates in sugar, wheat, coffee, and some fishing agreements. The objective is to produce greater stability, most clearly for the benefit of producers, including those with high costs; prices are "supported" at high levels and by methods which tend to perpetuate the difficulties.

Quotas and Licensing. Man's search for methods of reducing foreign trade flourished in the 1930's. One result was the extensive development of quotas designed largely to check imports and their drains on holdings of gold and foreign currency. Quotas differ in their nature, but the general characteristics are common. The limiting device is a direct control on quantity, not, like a tariff, a boost of price to consumers which reduces quantity. Quotas are usually operated by the executive, with little or no legislative action except general authorization. At their best they can be flexible and adjusted easily to changing conditions. They may prove to be useful in bargaining with other countries.

In practice, quotas tend to be devilishly difficult to administer. Which importers are to get the business? Will the manufacturer who supported the other party in the election get the raw material he wants? Which foreign suppliers will be favored? What, precisely, is *the* product? How will quotas be fixed and changed? How will domestic prices be fixed? The uncertainty hurts business, but the reduction in imports enables domestic producers of the items involved to get higher prices, at the consumer's expense.

Closely related to quotas, and one method of enforcing them, are licenses. Countries may prohibit imports except where a specific license has been granted. Airtight control (except for evasion) is then possible. A government trying to manage an economy, especially in detail, will likely find quotas and related controls irresistibly tempting. The quantity of lumber imported can be geared to the planned construction program, for example. Some individual parts of a "system" may in fact be made to fit. A whole system, however, even in a strait-jacket economy and with the best of human management, cannot escape costly errors and disruptions—the job is too big.

---

million packages, process 3.7 million invoices, test 143,000 samples, and investigate 25,000 cases of suspected violation. This is no small work load for 9,000 employees receiving average salaries of about $10,000.

"Buy American." With the U.S. government the country's largest purchaser, sellers here feeling competition from foreigners might say: "Why not force the government to buy from us rather than from outsiders who offer lower prices?" Congress has provided that government orders must generally be given to U.S. producers unless their price exceeds that of a foreign supplier by 25 percent or so; an absolute prohibition of imports applies to purchases financed with federal funds for urban mass transit. Half of foreign aid cargoes must go in ships operated by American companies. Moreover, most foreign aid funds are now "tied" to expenditure in this country. Some states require that state-local purchases give substantial preference to U.S. suppliers.

Private Restrictions. Individuals may choose not to buy certain foreign products for any of many reasons. Larger groups may impose restrictions. Many Americans, for example, tried not to buy German products during the Hitler era. More recently, a few labor unions have proposed to use their influence to restrict certain imports.

In some cases—textiles and beef, for example—producers abroad have sometimes agreed "voluntarily" to limit sales to the United States; they hope to discourage the erection of restrictions by this country.[10]

BALANCE-OF-PAYMENTS PROSPECTS FOR THE UNITED STATES

Our balance-of-payments problem calls for action—but what kind? Why does the problem continue?

Absence of Self-Correcting Mechanism. When exchange rates are fixed (when the price of the dollar is fixed in terms of gold and other currencies), an increase in the quantity of dollars supplied to foreigners does not change the price. If the dollar were free to fluctuate, an adverse balance of payments would create forces leading to its own correction. Assume that Americans offered more dollars for foreign currencies than foreigners wanted at the price. The dollar would fall in relation to other currencies. Imports to the United States would then become more expensive and exports easier. The equilibrating mechanism would operate. But with exchange rates fixed, no such automatic adjustment takes place. Nor do gold movements now lead to domestic monetary changes which can be counted upon to do much equilibrating.

How Big Is Our Problem? The "hard core" of the problem seems to be an annual deficit of around $2 billion. For an economy the size of ours, $2 billion a year seems hardly large. It is tiny in relation to GNP and small in relation to each year's normal economic growth. It is not big in relation to America's combined exports and imports (invisibles included) of

---

[10] An industry which believes that foreign suppliers are dumping products in this country can start procedures which can take many months and hold up trade.

nearly $90 billion a year. But the cumulative total of only a few years could exceed the gold available for meeting it. Small percentage changes in the totals of imports and exports could increase or reduce the deficit by an amount which over only a few years would be very large in relation to America's resources for dealing with the imbalance.

Let us, therefore, examine some aspects for the export-import outlook. Unfortunately, many "unknowns" blur the picture.

The Outlook for Imports.   What factors will influence the demands of Americans for nondollar currencies? There are some near-certainties and more points about which the range of doubt is significant.

Imports of raw materials are certain to rise. Economic growth will increase our demand for iron ore, copper, petroleum, and other minerals, and for forest products, rubber, and other such items. Population growth will raise imports of tropical and semitropical foodstuffs.

American imports of manufactured and semimanufactured items will certainly increase. Rising income and growing population will boost total demand. What cannot be determined with anything even approaching accuracy is the proportion of the total which will be supplied domestically and the proportion from abroad. America is a big and profitable market. Our tariff level is not high on the average. Foreign producers often have distinctly lower costs than ours. Foreign suppliers have proved their ability to design products to appeal to Americans; and as incomes rise, design takes on more importance. Foreign productive capacity and productivity have soared and will continue to rise. From 1956 to 1966 U.S. imports of nonfood consumer goods more than doubled.

American demands for services from foreigners will also rise. Tourism shows every sign of continuing to grow. Travel to Europe and other parts of the world becomes easier and facilities more comfortable. However, on New Years Day, 1968, President Johnson urged Americans to make big cuts in plans for travel outside this hemisphere. He said that he would ask Congress to put some kind of tax or other restriction on foreign travel.

What will be American demand for banking, insurance, educational, and other services abroad? Large increase seems improbable. One "invisible import," the earnings of foreign investments in the United States, will certainly grow.

The Outlook for Exports.   America has always been a big exporter of agricultural products. It still is, although a large portion of total sales are subsidized directly or indirectly. We cannot count upon great agricultural increases of types which will help meet our balance-of-payments problem. Nor is the future likely to see much growth in exports of the products of U.S. mines and forests. The foreign demand for coal and relatively high-priced petroleum from this country shows no sign of rising significantly.

The crucial category is that of manufactures. This group includes a tremendous range of items, with consumer goods accounting for considerably less than producer goods. What of the future? We have the capacity to produce more for export. Can we sell more?

Most U.S. manufacturers make no appreciable effort to sell abroad, not even in Canada. If they were really to begin to try, how much might they sell to foreigners? The amounts might be considerable. There is no obvious reason to expect businesses to make an effort just to help the country's balance of payments. They would be wise to make the effort, however, if there is a good chance for profit. Rapidly rising incomes abroad and increasingly intense competition within this country seem likely to increase the incentives of American businessmen to export. With improved arrangements for helping American businesses sell abroad and with provision for longer term credits to buyers, there is room for optimism.

Earlier we noted that in the greatest market, Europe, the two trading groups favor their own producers. Moreover, trading blocs in Latin America will have somewhat the same kind of result but on a small scale. The vital, and the unknown, element is the *marginal* effect. It may be minor. It may be significant. Americans cannot plan on the assumption that the tariff differentials against us will be unimportant.

American manufacturers face a continuing problem. Can they retain "enough" comparative advantage? Will costs and prices in America remain sufficiently competitive? The United States has not "priced itself out" of the world market for manufacturers. But has it priced itself out of part of the market? It has. Will it do more of the same? Yes. The real question, however, is this: Can the United States keep ahead in major types of production?

Wage rates per hour in the United States are much above those elsewhere. Social insurance costs and related "fringes" are not easily compared; in money terms American manufacturers pay at least as much per man-hour on this score as most producers elsewhere. In the past, of course, productivity—output per man-hour—has been enough higher in America than abroad in enough industries to make U.S. manufactured products salable on a huge scale. Will this relative position continue?

Many things combine to influence productivity. The average American factory worker has had more capital equipment to work with than the average worker in Europe, Japan, and Latin America. The amount of mechanical and electrical energy per worker is large here. The average of education and training, though hard to measure, has been relatively high. The quality of management and the intensity of domestic competition have done much to keep productivity high. The size of the domestic market and the rate of technical progress have contributed immensely to America's ability to compete abroad in spite of our high wage rates. In some cases raw materials have been cheaper here. (See Fig. 35–3.)

FIGURE 35–3.   Manufacturing Costs of U.S. Firms at Home and Abroad

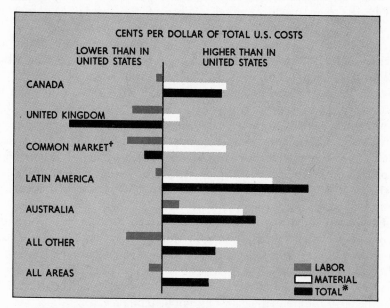

* Includes labor, materials, overhead, sales, and other.
† Belgium, France, Germany, Italy, Luxembourg, and Netherlands.
Source: National Industrial Conference Board, *Costs and Competition* (New York, 1961).

In Europe, Japan, and parts of Latin America and Asia, some manufacturers can now match the United States, not merely in one or two but in most of the respects that have favored America. There is compelling reason to believe that progress abroad will continue. Since wage rates abroad are much lower than here, total costs will also tend to be lower.

Rising productivity abroad is not the only change. Foreign productive capacity is greater every day. More of foreign demand can be satisfied without products from the United States. Some of the differences that have given this country a strong competitive advantage are disappearing. The export of American capital and the extension of "know-how" and management methods in foreign factories speed the whole process. Factories abroad controlled by U.S. companies sold perhaps $40 billion of output a year in the mid-1960's and were rising at a faster rate than exports of manufactured goods from this country. A new type of product or a new method of production can be matched in many countries without much of a lag. In the past, in contrast, years may have been required.

Forces favorable to the United States are also operating. In percentage terms wage rates in some countries may rise more rapidly than here. Rising incomes over the world create rising demand. Potential markets will grow as a result of the forces that also intensify the competition from which American producers will suffer.

Moreover, the rate of progress of American technology is rapid. No matter how good anything is, it will not stay in front long in the future unless it is improved. The possibilities of continuing improvement in American products and methods are promising. Competition is intense enough to keep American producers from resting on their past achievements.

Foreign Demand for Services. Tourism in the United States will grow. As incomes in Europe rise, for example, and as the costs of air travel drop, visitors to the United States will become more numerous. Will we have the command of foreign languages, the welcoming attitudes, and other things needed to build tourism here?

The demands by foreigners for transportation, banking, insurance, and many other types of services will depend partly upon the cost. The factors affecting American costs of services are rather like those already discussed as applying to manufacturers. Can U.S. producers keep productivity high enough to justify American wage scales?

One source of foreign exchange will certainly grow: income from investments by U.S. individuals and businesses abroad. Nongovernmental assets abroad will soon be yielding $7 billion a year.

Capital Exports and Imports. The future of capital transactions is exceedingly difficult to predict. What will be the comparative attractiveness of investment within and outside the United States? Will relatively low interest rate levels in the United States and the size and good organization of our capital markets continue to appeal to foreigners? Will profit prospects in this country become better, relative to those abroad, so that more equity capital will remain here?

To reduce the outflow of capital, Congress, at the Treasury's urging, passed the Interest Equalization Tax to last 3 years from July, 1963; it was renewed and increased in 1967. This complex law adds one to two percentage points to the cost of some foreign borrowing and sale of new equity securities in this country—but with many exceptions, e.g., for Canadians and people in a long list of underdeveloped lands, some bank loans, and direct investment abroad by U.S. corporations and individuals. Much tighter restrictions, some compulsory as authorized by earlier legislation and some "voluntary," were announced in January, 1968.

American businesses are now investing abroad an amount equal to about 4 percent of their total gross investment. Even a small change in the percentage sent, or kept, abroad can be large in relation to the deficit or surplus in our balance of payments. Foreigners invest considerable amounts here. The amounts may grow, but no one can be certain.

Military Spending and Foreign Aid. For reasons of broad strategy, it seems desirable to maintain United States troops in Europe, Japan, and other places outside the dollar area. The costs are borne primarily by America. Dollars are required to purchase food, housing, and other goods and services abroad. Three methods of reducing this dollar drain are being pursued. The number of troops kept outside America, Vietnam excepted, has been cut. More supplies are being purchased in this country and shipped to troops overseas, reducing the dollar drain but requiring larger total expense. Foreign governments are being urged—with only slight success—to assume more of the local costs. One of the haunting difficulties is the impossibility of weighing balance-of-payments advantages against national security disadvantages from contraction of overseas defense spending.

What about foreign aid? Over 80 percent of the dollars are used to buy goods and services in the United States. Foreign aid, therefore, does not contribute much to the balance-of-payments deficit. The logic of requiring aid dollars to be spent in the United States seems convincing. Admittedly, such a requirement conflicts with one fundamental American policy—the broadening rather than the reduction of the scope of freedom in foreign economic transactions. Yet the alternatives are less attractive.

The United States has been providing the lion's share of assistance to less developed nations. Although some others do a great deal, our government wants all of the more developed lands to increase their assistance efforts. Nevertheless, unless the Communists permit the world to reduce the waste of armament spending substantially, no conceivable amount of aid will be large enough to meet the "need." American leaders of both parties want to continue U.S. aid at no less than the present level. As of the moment, therefore, reductions in foreign aid are not likely to have significant effect upon the balance of payments.

Restraint on monetary expansion can help in the short run, i.e., to keep interest rates high enough to hold foreign short-term funds. But the Federal Reserve in keeping money "tighter" than otherwise may also hamper employment growth. As long as our balance of payments is in serious deficit, we are not masters of our own fate as regards domestic monetary policy. Avoidable unemployment may seem to be a high price to pay to hold foreign funds. But (with fixed exchange rates) more basic remedies are required to liberate domestic monetary policy.

Policies for the Longer Run. What, then, is the outlook, taking all considerations into account? Though clouded with uncertainties, the outlook offers little reason to hope that the deficit will disappear as a result of forces now foreseeable.

Two suggestions have been ruled out by the top officials of our government—freedom of the dollar to fluctuate and a change in the dollar price of gold (devaluation) to a new fixed level. Nevertheless, one or the other may eventually—but not soon—appear desirable to get money costs in the United States more nearly on a level with money costs elsewhere.

The one really good solution would be a rise in exports. America has productive capacity adequate in total for any conceivable addition needed to fill a gap in the balance of payments. We can "pay our own way." But how can we arrange the necessary changes? Some governmental action is required. Private business and financial markets as organized in the modern world will not do the job alone. What considerations must we bear in mind?

1. Domestic inflation would aggravate the problem.

2. Further expansion of government efforts to assist exporters might be fruitful. (a) Government can play a uniquely valuable role in collecting and distributing information. The individual business cannot possibly gather and analyze all the facts which will assist in selling abroad; extensive studies have already become available. More and more manufacturers are being introduced to the services of export organizations. (b) Governmental agencies can also help in publicizing American products, e.g., by sponsoring exhibits at trade fairs and displaying products at many events which most U.S. producers cannot afford to attend. A Commerce Department "mobile trade fair" (a ship) with 42 exhibits visited several Latin American port cities in 1964. Perhaps there is scope for additional assistance in the financing of exports through the Export-Import Bank without accepting undue risks. (c) More subsidies for exports of some farm products may be desirable for the very short run but not as permanent policy. (d) Encouragement for schools of business administration and other university groups to expand courses in international commerce will emphasize export opportunities and develop skills needed in dealing in foreign markets.

3. Officials will undoubtedly continue to press for relaxation of foreign restrictions on imports (especially discriminations against our products).

4. Programs to stimulate tourism are bearing fruit, with the number of foreign visitors in 1966 one half above the 1960 figure. The promotion outlays are relatively small. Over time they may yield good results if they are coordinated well with the efforts of transportation, hotel, and other private businesses interested in attracting tourists.

5. The United States will keep on trying to get other nations (a) to pay more of the costs of mutual defense and (b) to do more to finance economic development in poor countries. The most optimistic view of prospects, however, will include little help for the U.S. balance of payments in actions others will take in these two realms.

6. The tax law of 1962 makes special tax reductions for companies which install new machinery and equipment. American producers are spending more on modernization. As a result their competitive position in

world markets should improve. The 1964 tax law reduced by one tenth or more the tax on corporations, making capital investment here at least slightly more attractive.

Danger of Restrictions. We are not poised on a precipice with disaster a possibility. But we do face dangers. One is that imports will be cut down by various restrictive controls. Increases in tariff rates and the erection of trade barriers, especially quotas, will receive support. In most cases, perhaps, the fundamental support will come from the desire of Americans for shelter from foreign competition. But balance-of-payments arguments can be used to strengthen the forces seeking trade restrictions—even when the particular products may come from countries which promptly use dollars in buying here.

Outright rationing of capital exports once seemed highly improbable. How might controls on the export of capital work? The traditions and institutional arrangements in this country do not lend themselves to arbitrary direction of capital flows. The "banker" for much of the free world should preserve freedom. Nevertheless, some opponents of the Interest Equalization Tax came out for a "capital issues" committee to allocate capital funds available for export.

Uncertainty will continue. Fortunately, American leadership and that of many other nations includes many who will struggle for enlightened solutions so that we can "float the problem off on a rising volume of trade and capital movement."

TERMS AND CONCEPTS

tariff	most-favored-nation	quotas
comparative advantage	clause	exchange rate
infant industry	*ad valorem* tariff	balance of payments
"beggar-my-neighbor"	specific tariff	Interest Equalization
policy	GATT	Tax
"scientific" tariff	European Economic	capital flows
"dumping"	Community	foreign aid
reciprocal tariff agree-	cartel	Buy American
ments	logrolling	intergovernmental
Kennedy Round	licensing	commodity agree-
		ments

QUESTIONS

1. "The term 'protective tariff' is slick deception, for the tariff, rather than protecting the public, puts it more at the mercy of relatively inefficient producers." Discuss.
2. Is the tariff a form of government interference with business? How are export businesses affected?
3. Can trade restrictions effectively "export unemployment" in the short run? in the long run? Why?

4. Why were consumer and exporter interests so generally neglected in debates on tariff legislation?

5. "One of Europe's chief benefits from the Common Market reduction of tariffs may pass unnoticed. I refer to the stimulation of competition." Discuss.

6. Why does Japan, with wage rates far lower than those in this country, import much more from us than we buy from it? Does your answer support the argument that a tariff is needed to protect American workers from cheap foreign labor? Why?

7. Will not the natural forces of economic life automatically solve our balance-of-payments problem? Why?

8. "The chief cause for concern about our competitive position in world markets is not so much the height of hourly wage rates here as the rise in productivity in other lands." Discuss.

9. Why may nontariff trade barriers be more restrictive than a tariff?

10. Would large price-level increases in Europe help solve the U.S. balance-of-payments problem? Why?

11. Would reduction in foreign aid do much to reduce the deficit in our balance of payments? Why?

PART 8

ECONOMIC GROWTH

AND DEVELOPMENT

Our traditions emphasize progress, "getting ahead," as a desirable objective. Bettering man's economic position is one element of progress. The study of economic development, growth, and expansion has for a decade or more been the liveliest aspect of economics. Yet this analysis remains unsettled and itself growing. Each chapter that follows will reflect the developing nature of the subject. Two deal explicitly with growth. Another concerns socialism and communism more broadly; advocates of these ideologies now rest much of their case on the argument that these "systems" offer better means of speeding growth than does capitalism. Results anywhere depend not only upon "the system" in the sense of a great "ism"—capitalism, socialism, or communism—but also upon the specific things to be done. The concluding chapter, therefore, examines a few of the problems which will challenge this country in the years ahead.

ECONOMIC DEVELOPMENT

OF LOW-INCOME LANDS[1]

> . . . The real dangers [in dealing with the problems of underdeveloped countries] are complacency, lack of imagination, and the dull sense of hopelessness that settles upon those of little faith. World economic and social interdependence involves a new dimension in the task of creating a responsible society, which men will have to face realizing that statistics are only inadequate indications of desperate human need.
>
> World Council of Churches

Hope has become, or is becoming, a new factor in the economies of poor lands—hope for a rising standard of living. Leaders and untold millions of the masses no longer believe that abysmal poverty is their inevitable fate for generations ahead. Yet how can they make their hopes come true? How can poor lands develop economically, develop with speed and efficiency?[2] Such questions are vital to the masses of the world who live in age-old poverty—and to those of us who live in more developed lands. For Americans, too, are involved.

Our concern arises in part from humanitarian or moral considerations.

---

[1] No single term is fully satisfactory for designating these countries, or economies. "Backward" has connotations which sometimes offend. In this chapter, "poor" stands, albeit crudely, as a synonym for "underdeveloped" or the more recently favored term "developing."

[2] The term "development" carries the connotation of change in the structure and character of an economy toward those of lands with high incomes. "Development" is often almost a synonym of "modernization," becoming more like "economically advanced" countries. The term "growth" is more limited and is used to mean a rise in real income and product, the output consisting, more or less, of about the same things as in the recent past. This chapter, however, does not utilize the more refined distinctions.

Some of us feel them more strongly than do others. But who can be at peace with his own soul unless he feels that in some way he is helping to relieve the economic misery of other human beings?

A second reason for active U.S. concern has grown out of rivalry with Communism. Poor lands may be weak, but some can be important in the balance of world affairs. Others will become more significant as they grow stronger, or perhaps as increasing frustration leads them, probably in irrational desperation, to action endangering others and the peace of the world. Our failure to help, it is argued, can itself create resentment and enemies as others, in this world of easy movement and communication, compare our plenty with their hopeless misery. The way these countries develop economically, and the role we play in the process, may mean the difference between their being pro-Soviet, pro-China or pro–Free World. Is it not to our interest to have those siding with us stronger rather than weaker? Unfortunately, experience has shown that the poor lands we help cannot be counted upon to side with us in the world's political (and economic) rivalries.

A third reason is economic. The more prosperous other economies, the greater the potential opportunities for mutually beneficial economic exchange.

Students of economics have a fourth interest: the challenge. Here are problems of the greatest practical importance to mankind, problems which cannot be solved well without guidance the economist can give.

WHAT IS A POOR LAND?

Every country has poor people—and some of the world's richest families live in underdeveloped countries. Both "povery" and "development" are to some extent relative. Is a sparsely settled area with primitive living standards whose government receives large oil royalties poor? Certainly there is no clear line dividing poor from "not poor" lands. Even more certainly, however, most of the world is poor by standards Americans would set as acceptable for human life. Over half of mankind, we read, has per capita income of no more than about $10 a month. Whether or not such an estimate gives a reasonably accurate impression, there can be no doubt that by *any* criteria hundreds of millions are poor beyond our comprehension.

Most of the 80 to 100 independent countries—in Asia, Africa, the Middle East, Europe, Central and South America, and the islands of all oceans—which we might class as poor, have some things in common other than low per capita incomes. The working force is heavily concentrated in subsistence-level agriculture, using primitive equipment and methods and with only a few good acres per family. The monotonous, protein-short diet will not support sustained, vigorous activity. Families crowd together in one or two miserable, unheated rooms with no artificial light. Water comes from the village well. Rates of saving and capital formation are low. Markets are narrow, manufacturing comparatively unimportant. Most adults can neither read nor write, and rarely does educational attainment exceed the elementary level. Schools, roads, utilities, and other forms of "social overhead" are sparse. Birth and death rates are both high, the general level of health low. Little use is made of modern scientific and technological knowledge.

Despite the similarities, however, these lands differ tremendously. Some are plagued with overpopulation while others are sparsely settled; some are hot, some cold, some old, some new; some cover large areas, many are tiny; some have long been in touch with Western civilization, others not. Population may be homogeneous or mixed and divided; tribal customs little if any above the primitive level sometimes govern much behavior; religion plays a dominant role in some lands but is much less important in others; the relations between religious beliefs and economic matters vary widely. Natural resources, in relation to population, range from high to low; many countries have been colonies—a few underdeveloped areas still are—with today's attitudes affected for better or worse by what happened in the past. Attitudes toward acceptance of "what is" or the desire to change will range widely. So does ambition and apparent willingness to work and save.

The problems and the opportunities for economic development and growth differ. Basic, underlying economic principles apply the world over. Yet the conditions under which people seek to solve their economic problems diverge so widely that policies which are well suited in one area will be inappropriate for others. Thus, though every poor country needs more capital, the best methods of getting it in Liberia may not suit Free China (Taiwan); so, too, the opportunities for using capital vary.

While a "broad-brush" survey of the economics of development of poor lands must generalize, and can do so usefully, the actual problems call for careful adaptation to specific conditions. Two related aspects must be distinguished. To start, we need to know what forces produce development. Then arise "policy" questions which involve choices that someone, perhaps a government, may make among alternatives to help development (or to avoid impeding it). A person hoping to influence policy constructively must have knowledge of the underlying forces, and they are not always revealed by what appears on the surface.

The development *process*, according to some economists, can best be thought of as one of successive stages. Certain "preconditions" must evolve or be established. Then, it is said, comes a "takeoff" and relatively rapid improvement toward "maturity" and eventually high mass consumption. The analysis of the process as one of stages, while useful for highlighting aspects of the problem, tends to be somewhat artificial. The student, businessman, or government official charged with making policy can be misled into viewing as a series of separate parts a process which is more truly continuous but uneven, one of complex interrelations.

The initial impulse of anyone trying to recommend policies is to say, "Follow the example of those who have succeeded, such as the United States, Sweden, or Japan. Do what they did in the period of their great development." Wise advice, but the typical spokesman for an underdeveloped area wants more—something to accelerate the growth process, to do in two generations or less what took others three or four. Such desire is commendable. It can be satisfied in part—but not easily. Obstacles lie not only in the difficulties of the problems but also in the power of emotions which confuse judgment.

WHAT DO PEOPLE WANT?

Economic development is by and for people. It consists of creating conditions in which human beings will be able to serve themselves better. Is not the logical place for starting analysis and action to find what people want—or more truly significant, what they desire *most?* Nothing will be gained if people are forced or deceived into doing what they do not want, even though figures of national output may rise. To the extent that growing production consists of goods and services which are desired less than other things that might have been produced, there is loss (probably hidden) of sacrificed opportunity.

Efficient economic development requires an indication of the relative intensities of wants. Otherwise the productive resources which become available cannot be used where they will serve best. Moreover, the efforts and sacrifices men and women will make—the labor and other productive capacity which does become available—will be greater if the results which people expect have high, rather than low, appeal. The speed of development will depend to some extent upon the effectiveness of the means by which people can express their wants.

In a poor land, however, the discovery of the relative importance of wants will in itself prove difficult. For many people, of course, more food and better medical service must be clearly evident as a need. But as a wider range of choice becomes possible, a problem of discontinuity arises—opportunities in either consumption or work may involve big departures from what is familiar. Some alternatives may be completely unknown to the person affected. People can then make little or no use of experience to appraise alternatives. A professor of economics in a country largely underdeveloped sent native students into villages to conduct a sort of consumer survey. The peasants, when asked to indicate preferences among such things as bicycles, washing machines, coal stoves, and mattresses, frequently refused to answer, except, in effect, "They will never be for me."

Always when there are many truly important wants, choice is tantalizing. If some desires are for intangibles—the prevention of any infringement on national sovereignty, the retention of religious reluctance to kill animals, or either the preservation or change of a social structure—economic calculation becomes confused.

Important choices in poor lands today are often made by a few for the many. Whether the few are self-selected or chosen in free elections, the basis of selection is often largely irrelevant to questions of competence for making good economic decisions. The politician, general, lawyer, or engineer who gets to the top, perhaps by popular vote, may have no qualifications for using well the economic power that centers in his government—using the power to do what people want.

Leaders in underdeveloped lands often lack market guidance as we know it for revealing public preferences. Always, however, there is some market and room for improving it as an indicator of what human beings prefer as consumers and producers. Yet the markets cannot reflect social costs and benefits fully. Who can judge social ends wisely? The few making decisions for the many may feel that policies which apparently neglect public wishes will actually serve social or collective needs. The bias is probably to sacrifice the individual to the ruler's concept of group interest.

One basic choice highlights the problem: How should either a family or the central authorities decide about sacrificing the present for the future? How much of a poverty income shall be used for consumption today and how much for investment to permit tomorrow's income to be higher? Central authorities may firmly believe that they are better able than ignorant parents to decide for today's children and tomorrow's.

CAPITAL ACCUMULATION

Economic growth depends upon the acquisition of capital. Economists are by no means certain about the number of dollars of (wisely invested) capital needed in a typical poor land to increase the net income stream by $1 a year, the *capital-output ratio*. Figures of $3 of capital for $1 of added annual income are commonly cited, but variation must be wide. If this is about right as an average, a family with an annual income of $900 a year needs $300 more capital to work with (not necessarily to own) to raise its income to $1,000. The capital may come from within the economy or from outside.

Internal Sources. Poverty is itself a major obstacle to capital accumulation. When incomes are at subsistence levels, any increase will probably be used for consumption. Even a considerable percentage rise in income—a bountiful harvest—may lead to little saving. If free, families will choose to raise their miserable levels of current consumption rather than to save for the future. But until they have more capital equipment, they cannot raise their incomes much. To break out of the vicious circle seems impossible.

For untold millions it *is*. For populations as a whole, however, capital accumulation from internal sources is not impossible. A poor economy is not necessarily doomed to stagnation. Every land contains some families and businesses able to make voluntary private savings. A few people have good incomes. Some families will stint themselves unmercifully to improve their lot or to permit one member to go to school, buy an old truck, accumulate a little inventory for trading, or do something else to get ahead. Considerable capital formation, in fact, can take the form of dispersed and unrecorded improvement of farms.

But capital accumulation by such means will be slow. Can it be speeded? What can be done to encourage voluntary savings? Possibilities include freedom from the fears of inflation or confiscation, better banks and saving institutions, higher interest rates, close ties between saving and some specific thing desired (such as a house or land purchase), tax favors, reorientation of family responsibilities so that thrift does not increase obligations to support relatives, and propaganda. To some extent, the existence, or absence, of investment opportunities affects significantly the volume of saving; a really promising project will stimulate saving. Naturally, a method which is effective in one situation may fail in another.

Capital formation may occur with little or no saving in financial form as people work and create more than they consume. Often an outside impulse is needed—ideas, direction, and perhaps some material. Then hours that would otherwise have been idle can build houses, roads, dams, school buildings, and other things that will make for a better life. A relatively small amount of organizing effort and capital (materials from outside the community) can sometimes produce impressive results with little, perhaps no, (local) sacrifice of desired alternatives.[3]

The distribution of income will influence voluntary saving. Often, certainly, businesses will have higher propensity to save than will employees, peasants, or upper income groups having no tradition of saving and without active participation in business. A relatively high level of profit for business may be very conducive to capital accumulation and may be self-reinforcing. Suppose, for example, that the supply of labor is very elastic, then retention of profit can lead to a considerable increase in employment over time without a rise in wage rates. Then, assuming that productivity rises as more capital is used, profits will tend to grow, and so will employment. When other conditions are favorable, such business profits can finance more rapid growth of investment than if a bigger portion of the results of rising productivity were made available for consumption.

Forced saving is a possibility. Force may take different forms. Government may impose taxes, "profiteer" on government-owned businesses, or compel workers to buy (and hold) some form of saving certificates. The money obtained can be used to finance investment. The government may

---

[3] In some areas, living standards have been improved markedly as local labor has used time that would have been idle to build modest dwellings. Small amounts of outside capital and continuing leadership have enabled people to accomplish much. India's Community Development Program, for example, relies predominantly upon local resources to improve villages.

itself build—factories or utilities—or it may make funds available to private business. The Russian record shows that government can force saving on a scale large in relation to national income. While this method is not necessarily the most effective, certainly not if one allows for the human cost, dictatorships will claim an advantage over freer systems in this respect. Less extreme methods are available. A majority in a locality, for example, may vote taxes to pay for a capital project. Everyone is then forced to sacrifice to help pay for capital formation.[4]

Inflation offers another possible way to force saving, at least for a time. If the income of a large portion of the public can be kept from rising as rapidly as prices, consumption will probably be less than otherwise. Resources may then be freed for capital formation, at least temporarily. Inflation in itself, however, has bad effects on economic development— investment is misdirected (to inventory, projects with short "payoff" periods, and luxury housing); balance-of-payments problems are aggravated; voluntary saving and the import of capital are discouraged; direct controls to meet problems growing out of inflation create dislocations and distortions; uncertainty obstructs decision making; and so on.[5]

Capital from Abroad. No economy, however, need rely solely upon itself to finance investment. In other parts of the world there are accumulations of savings whose owners will make them available for use in poor countries—if conditions are favorable. The amount of such capital, of course, is limited and the competition sometimes keen, including demands in developed lands with good profit opportunities.

What can the people of poor lands do to attract foreign capital? The business firm can try to discover opportunities for profitable uses of foreign funds, to establish and improve relations with foreign banks and suppliers who may be willing to finance trade more extensively, to invite foreign companies with capital to enter into joint ventures. Scrupulous respect for agreements makes a big difference over the years.

Government may itself borrow. It can also do some things positively to attract investment, and it can avoid policies that discourage foreigners. A secure system of law and order and respect for property and

[4] Social insurance systems may be arranged to force saving by putting taxes above benefit payments. Just the opposite may result; taxes to pay for social insurance can reduce private saving while paying for consumption.

[5] Economists disagree about the net effects of inflation over the long run on economic development. A comparison of the experience of many countries since World War II led to the conclusion that the evidence available, admittedly imperfect, supports the argument that inflation does misdirect investment, curtail capital accumulation, aggravate seriously balance-of-payments difficulties, and hurt development in other ways. Yet some price-level increase seems to be an inevitable part of the process of economic growth in poor lands; in some countries high rates of inflation have, at least for a time, gone along with relatively rapid economic development. G. S. Dorrance, "The Effect of Inflation on Economic Development," *International Monetary Fund Staff Papers*, March, 1963, pp. 1–44.

contract—which only government can assure—will not themselves bring in foreign capital. Their absence, however, will keep it away. Specific positive actions may include tax advantages, such special concessions as a utility franchise or right to extract oil, assurance that currency and other restrictions will not prevent the repatriation of earnings and capital, and guarantees to protect patents and other intangibles. Things to avoid include corruption, red tape, cost-raising requirements, and high taxes.

Direct investment by foreign business firms will often offer great promise. The economy can get not only capital but also management. Know-how and capital in combination can be strikingly more valuable than the capital alone. Puerto Rico has shown that deliberate policies to attract foreign business firms can produce not miracles but substantial results.

INVESTMENT: THE DIRECTIONS OF DEVELOPMENT

Savings do not enlarge productive capacity until they are invested—within the country and wisely. Several issues arise. One is to get savings into some more creative form than jewelry, precious metals, or other hoards. In some societies changing age-old traditions proves difficult and slow. Another question is that of investing at home or abroad. A South American may not be a fool in preferring real estate or securities in Europe or the United States to local investment. Political instability and meager profit opportunities in poor lands can make the export of locally generated savings seem wiser than local commitment. If so, might not government somehow prevent capital export for purposes which, from the point of view of economy, are a relatively unproductive use of a really scarce resource? Government action might do so—but again it might not.

Large administrative effort is required for effective regulation of capital flow. Even more important, the compulsion endangers the very policies it seeks to further. It will discourage saving at home and reduce the willingness of foreigners to make their savings available.

Choosing among investment opportunities within the country presents difficult and continuing problems. How can best projects be selected? Let us look at some of the issues.

Agriculture versus Industry: Land Reform. If a deliberate choice is to be made, perhaps by an official agency, what should be the relative emphasis on industry—manufacturing or perhaps mining—compared with agriculture? A common but erroneous view identifies development with industrialization. People often associate high incomes with manufacturing. Yet the economic fate of most people in poor lands for a long time to come will be bound up with agriculture. Some of the best opportunities for investing creatively may be in connection with improved use of land—irrigation, tools, fertilizer, seed, marketing facilities, financing, fencing, housing. The gains could include better diets for those on the farms, more food to support an increase in nonfarm population, perhaps more agricultural output for export, and release of labor to provide workers for manufacturing, construction, trade, and services.

The predominant importance of agriculture makes land utilization crucial, and land use will be related to ownership. Plots in some places are too small and too dispersed for efficiency. In other countries, huge holdings are not managed well. Often rental terms do not encourage efficient use. Neither tenant nor landlord has incentive to exert himself to take advantage of opportunities. Change in ownership or owner-tenant relations can be very fruitful. Yet the social, economic, political, and technological ramifications of change in land ownership will be wide and complex. Not all actions called "land reform" will produce good results, and some patterns of change will be better than others. Success requires careful preparation, tied in with the financing of both new facilities and the compensation for change of ownership.

One record of outstanding success is that of the Free Chinese in Taiwan. They applied plans and lessons from experiments begun on the mainland in the 1930's but frustrated by the Japanese invasion and civil war. Tillers have become owners of virtually all farmland. Productivity per worker on the farm doubled in the 15 years to 1967 due in part to better incentives—the farmer no longer shared the fruits of his extra work with a landlord. As he got more income, he used more fertilizer and added simple equipment. Land reform included combination of parcels into more efficient sizes. Landlords got generally satisfactory compensation which the farmers paid relatively easily in a decade of large growth of output.

What Industries? The industries which can develop most successfully, whether new or the expansion of a going activity, will depend upon the facts of each particular land—the natural and human resources, the markets, and actual and potential competition. The search for prestige—steel mills—or the emulation of some other country can lead to costly errors. Labor-intensive activities will presumably be preferable to those requiring relatively large amounts of capital—but not always. Investigations of the type made by the World Bank can help private as well as governmental investors select rationally. The economist is likely to argue that the best of long-run development grows out of building on *comparative advantage*. Where the decision rests on other than the direction of free market forces, is it not wise to seek those things with the best chance of prospering in competition?

Today's comparative advantage, however, may not be permanent. So for this and other reasons, "balanced growth" may yield better long-run results; i.e., within carefully considered limits efforts to diversify may be preferable to intense specialization. To try many lines of development for variety alone may be foolish. But if some planning agency is choosing, perhaps it should encourage several lines which have promise even though not all match the best. As a result, the argument runs, internal specialization and trade can grow in more lines and bring benefits somewhat independently of ability to trade with the outside world. Domestic demand is needed to stimulate some kinds of useful and valuable activity which will itself create demand that in turn will make more kinds of business profitable. Workers in shoe factories will not consume much of their own output, but workers in shoe and furniture and food processing and other plants will consume each other's production if the opportunity exists. Factories to produce finished goods may be needed before sources of raw materials and component parts develop. Extending the scope of the domestic market can yield benefits—economies which are external to the particular industries expanding, "third-party" benefits—which are great enough to justify special effort and sacrifice.

Yet there are hazards in a program to channel limited resources for investment to achieve balance. Some projects will not be able to survive in competition—and poor economies cannot afford much waste in investment. The fact that people are poor accentuates the desirability of getting consumer goods as cheaply as possible and creating the jobs in which workers will be most productive.

A Few Big or Many Small?   In recent years there has been argument for directing development investment more or less arbitrarily, not for "balance" but for something really big which might not be justified by normal economic calculation. The large dam or highway or electrification project, it is said, may provide a base on which many other new activities can get established. Its "shock" or dramatic effect may be valuable. The peasant sees that something is really being done. "Spectaculars" may fire the imagination, set an inspiring example. Still, the risk is heavy. Inevitably, the unknowns are great where change is big. Although resource use in the project may turn out to be technically successful (but even this is not always true), the project may be a failure economically, obviously or less clearly because no one points out that the alternatives sacrificed would have been more productive.

Role of Planning.   In view of what has been said so far, who will not have asked, "Is a plan really needed"? When changes are being made, they should be integrated with each other—or at least not inconsistent and self-defeating. One reason is that each single choice will affect the outcome of others. Priorities will not all be equal.

Today's high-income lands, of course, developed without planning on a national scale. But might they not have done better with more coordination? Cannot poor lands accomplish more by assuring that changes fit into a consistent pattern? Answers to such questions will be debated.

Certainly, much can be gained from careful study. Where is the economy now? Where shall it try to go? Why? By what means? And so on. The forward look should start with as good a projection as possible of what will happen "automatically," i.e., if no changes are made in policies of government. Then can begin analysis of those alternatives about which choices are to be made. Some will be confined to this year's budget; others will have a much longer time perspective.

Examination of individual projects and examination of progress covering much of the economy can both be fruitful. The insistence that magnitudes be estimated and compared can in itself improve the quality of decisions. Even crude projections of capital productivity in different industries, or merely an outline of the total implications of various alternatives, can help in getting more realistic answers to questions which inevitably involve many uncertainties. In this sense, planning is a requirement for success. It will take two forms—"planning from above," dealing with aggregates for the whole economy, and "planning from below," which involves particular projects.

Planning of the government sector will be a waste of effort unless it takes account of what will go on in the private sector. Allowing for such interaction is so difficult it tends to be neglected, and this neglect helps explain the failure of many plans. One requirement for reasonable success is the continuing exchange of information between governmental planners and representatives of the private sector—"indicative planning," with information moving on a two-way street. Priorities must be established, with some parts of a program "hard" and some "soft," the latter allowing for the interplay of uncertainty and the effects of private, dispersed decision making. A rigid plan can be the source of great waste, and the tendency to try to blueprint and control more than can be administered well has characterized all too many plans.[6]

Housing.   What portion of resources for investment can wisely go into housing? The answer, "What the people want," is not likely to be accepted by all who are responsible for making decisions even if the indication of public preference were reliable. Housing, of course, creates services that are likely to be much needed and essential as population

---

[6] Experience has led one close student to observe that disappointment will at times be ". . . the result of the failure to distinguish between what the government can do and what 'ought to' be done by the private sector. This failure leads planners to conclude that government must *make sure* that the projections for the private sector come true, and that the 'targets' are reached—presumably by direct government action if the private sector does not live up to the planners' expectations. These anxieties about making sure that the plans are fulfilled are likely to lead to an extension of direct government action beyond the original intentions of any planner, particularly where government actions can be readily extended—for instance, in industry. Such an extension of government activity in fields where the private sector can perform as efficiently as government can, or better, is likely to be at the expense of the government's attention to tasks which only government can undertake. The result is that the efficiency of the economy goes down." J. H. Adler, "Plans, Projects, and Priorities," *The Fund and Bank Review*, September, 1964, pp. 74–80.

grows. Yet there is perhaps some truth in the crude view that factories, machinery, utilities, and schools are more creative than housing (above low standards). Possibly in the long run, the people will be better off to stint housing and build industry[7] to greater extent than would result from free choice.

Public Facilities. Social overhead capital, "infrastructure"—streets, highways, schools, hospitals, government offices, and other such facilities—will be needed. They are not likely to be provided privately. Also needed are electric, gas, water, transport, and communication facilities. They might be supplied largely by private capital, but there is a strong trend for government to undertake even these nongovernmental tasks.

In providing social overhead capital, the World Bank and other lending agencies can help supply both funds and leadership. Although it would be nice to get all sorts of public facilities quickly and to build fine structures in the process, there is a difference between the really necessary and the desirable. Unfortunately, there is rarely any real test of the productivity of such facilities. To the outsider, at least, the magnificence of new public buildings does sometimes seem to exceed what is appropriate for poor economies.

Despite their need for capital, poor nations on their own have only limited capacity to "absorb"—get reasonably high yields—from more than moderate additions of capital. Among other things, human factors are limiting.

THE HUMAN ELEMENT

Entrepreneurship. One of the scarcest resources of many poor countries is entrepreneurship. Perhaps this is the reason why some economies have progressed so slowly over the centuries. Entrepreneurship is a quality whose sources are elusive. How can it be found, developed, and given freedom and encouragement? Answers will vary from culture to culture. In some societies, for example, there may be considerable talent for trading and commerce, rather little for agricultural or industrial development. The best promotional abilities may be directed into politics or military service. In some cultures caste systems and religious beliefs discourage and restrict entrepreneurship. Yet barriers can be surmounted by the more venturesome individuals.

The development task calls for leaders to make bold moves, sometimes on a large scale. Even more, perhaps, it calls for many kinds of moves,

---

[7] Flying into many a city in underdeveloped countries, one will probably feel that investors (private or governmental) have put more than is wise for the economy into apartment houses relative to other forms of real investment. Part of the explanation is that managing an apartment building seems a good deal simpler than running a factory. Housing also seems to some people to offer protection against loss due to inflation.

each on a scale that is small relative to the economy but possibly large in the locality. The progress of the masses will depend in part upon how widely the qualities of drive and leadership are diffused. Things that are successful in one place can provide examples for many others.

Some entrepreneurial capacity can be imported, perhaps enough to make a decisive difference. Latent talent appears when conditions begin to be favorable. A little development may start the cumulative spiral upward—slowly, for long years are needed to develop many kinds of competence. At best, poor lands will continue to be held back by a shortage of skilled and enterprising leadership.

One moral ought to be obvious: Avoidable restrictions on entrepreneurial effort should be kept at a minimum. A government, for example, may not be able to do much positively to create entrepreneurship. It can, however, do a lot negatively to hamper activities which are essential for growth. Almost in the nature of things, many innovative efforts will be unconventional, often distasteful to someone. The entrepreneurial spirit may be combined with personal characteristics which many people would like to see curbed. Unfortunately, the desire of officials to "control"—business practices, prices, wages, investment, imports and exports—can exceed the capacity to regulate constructively.

Resistance of Privileged Groups to Change. The people already "on top" may drag their heels or actively oppose change. They do not want to pay higher taxes or sell their land cheaply. Who wants to give up privileges in business, society, the religious establishment, the army, or the bureaucracy? In some countries the opposition of a small, powerful, privileged, and unprogressive group is a major obstacle to change.

Incentives. What an economy develops into will hinge upon the incentives offered. This point seems almost too obvious to mention. Yet some countries seeking to speed development have tried to restrict narrowly a most powerful incentive: the chance of a large income, large relative to the wage, price of farm output, interest, or profit generally obtained and expected. The force of different incentives will vary from one culture to another. Money, priority on housing, a chance to get the children into school, honor—many such things can be used in ways to reward accomplishment. Effective too, though odious, can be the terrible personal penalties which a police state like Russia can impose for failure.

When managerial or technical personnel are to be attracted from outside, compensation may have to be at levels that seem exorbitant by local standards. Yet the results may amply justify such pay. A handful of really competent foreigners can enable thousands or tens of thousands in the country to work with distinctly greater efficiency.

Taxes in poor lands tend to be high relative to income above subsistence—and to trend upward to pay for higher government spending. Not only the amount of tax but also the structure of the tax system affects incentives. Traditional tax systems are likely to be regressive, but the imposition of steeply progressive rates may impair entrepreneurial incentive (and capital formation). Caution is called for—in total load and in particular rates. Quality of administration is also significant, for taxes as administered may be arbitrary, corrupt, and discouraging to effort and to creative investment beyond anything needed to get the dollars going to the government. A flat tax, perhaps payable in labor, might have a positive incentive effect, compelling men to work (e.g., on roads) and yet not imposing high marginal rates.

Social Legislation.   The masses or leaders trying to help the common man may press for social legislation patterned after that in developed countries. The opportunities vary considerably. Social legislation can help in the growth (as contrasted with the transfer) of real income—conceived most broadly to include intangibles of human treatment of other humans. Each case, however, must be examined carefully on its own merits and weaknesses and must take account of costs.

The leveling, redistributive programs of high income lands may seem tempting. Unfortunately, there is danger of trying too much and of creating taxes and restrictions which not only reduce capital formation but obstruct development in other ways. For example, job security laws which prevent discharge of poor or redundant workers impair efficiency. Minimum wage laws may price some labor out of the market. Within a country it may be possible to force one group to pay for goods and services at a higher rate than they would freely choose—building public works perhaps. Foreigners, however, cannot be readily compelled to buy a country's products at prices reflecting "socially just" wage rates not "validated" or warranted by productivity.

Population.   Most of humanity lives where their own children and grandchildren, by their mere existence, will create difficult obstacles to raising real per capita income. With stable population, the rise in living standards might be slow, but progress would be within the capacity of the economy.

When numbers increase as rapidly as in so much of the world, however, the future is undeniably grim. To raise per capita income in India to $15 or so a month by the year 2000, for example, will require annual growth of national real income at the very high rate of $3\frac{1}{2}$ percent, if population continues to expand at recent rates. Even if poor lands can get food for hundreds of millions of new mouths each decade, the difficulties of housing, clothing, and educating such numbers must stagger the imagination.

The development of science has already opened ways by which the masses can prevent unwanted births. Financing, education, and skilled assistance will be required on a very large scale indeed. But to what extent will people utilize the new methods? In some areas deeply held religious beliefs will discourage the use of some methods. In other places ignorance and the social mores, such as the desire to have many sons, will hold families to older ways. Can leadership from government or other sources be effective? It is too early to judge the long-run results from the starts made in India and a few other lands.

Even if birth rates were soon to drop substantially, huge population growth must be provided for. The number of people already alive with their youth and prime ahead assures at least a half century (probably much more) of tremendous population increase. This fact adds to the sense of urgency. Inevitably, tomorrow's needs will surpass those which are met so poorly today. In some countries classed as underdeveloped, the population increase will be nearly threefold within the working life of today's American college student.

Education, Training, and Health. More than 700 million persons over age 15, according to a UNESCO study, are unable to read and write. Ignorance keeps productivity low. Lack of skill prevents men and women from taking advantage of opportunities. Effort to educate and train can pay generously. Yet when the richest nation in the world finds that financing education persists as a really difficult problem, do not the poor lands, especially those with growing populations, face staggering difficulties? In view of the lack of schools, equipment, and teachers, how can people break out of the vicious circle and start the slow but cumulative process of improving mass education?

Fortunately, much can be accomplished with only a small fraction of what Americans spend per child. One need is for continued improvement in, and expanded use of, devices and methods which will help speed the process of learning. Radio, movies, improved books, and all sorts of audiovisual aids can serve far more effectively and cheaply than the methods used in richer lands when they were at comparable stages of development. But what should be taught first?—to whom? Here is a hard problem of "economizing."

On-the-job training is often required to extend traditional skills and to develop new ones. If, for example, new types of construction are introduced, workers must have guidance. One widespread need is for "middle management" and foremen. A part of the necessary training may be to overcome a reluctance of the educated to soil their hands in work—on the farm, in the factory, at the construction site.

For economic as well as humanitarian reasons, efforts to raise health standards deserve high priority. Again, conditions vary so greatly that each area's opportunities require special analysis.

RESEARCH: THE STATE OF THE ARTS

For a country like the United States, the advance of knowledge is one of the major means of aiding growth. What about poor economies? For them the same will be true, but in somewhat different ways. What types and directions offer most promise?

. The clearest need and the best opportunity will generally be for study of how best to apply to local conditions what has been learned elsewhere. Nigeria's agricultural, manufacturing, commercial, and governmental opportunities in some directions are not identical with those of Ceylon or Britain, even when they may seem similar. What is the best method of utilizing what has been discovered and perhaps applied elsewhere? The answer will require special study of a sort which others cannot be expected to make—the fertilizer most efficient for the crops that can be grown in local soil under the prevailing climate or the price differentials for product qualities which will induce the most profitable effort.

Poor economies have a wealth of world progress on which to draw in speeding their growth. In a sense they can start at the top. To do so, however, requires careful and competent analysis of the alternatives *they* face in using the fruits of research done all over the world.

One type of important research which outsiders are not likely to do is that pertaining to the economy—and to the society—itself. Businessmen, government officials, and ordinary people can do better if they have evidence of and analysis about their own affairs.

RELATIONS WITH THE REST OF THE WORLD

Any country, rich or poor, faces a variety of problems involving other economies. The costs of national defense, of course, can have great economic significance. Clearly, no country is the master of its own fate in this respect. What portion of its limited resources it will devote to defense must depend largely upon what others do—or what it judges others are doing. Military outlays almost everywhere are tragically high. The birth of new countries, unfortunately, has created new points of friction and magnified the wastes of defense spending—India-Pakistan, Israel-Egypt, Indonesia-Malaysia. Perhaps a country's first responsibility to its own people and their children (and the rest of mankind) is to settle all the potential disputes possible, even at what may appear a sacrifice of prestige or of aspirations for extending its power. When two huge lands, Russia and Communist China, and several smaller ones, have avowed policies of disruption and the foment of dissent and revolution elsewhere, poor and weak lands face external threats and internal subversion. Protection may be difficult and costly and never certain of success.

Relations with the outside world which are more specifically economic will have a determining influence on development. Typically, the desire for imports, both consumer and capital goods, exceeds by many times the ability to pay for them. Every country will look to its balance of payments and its terms of trade. How much can it sell abroad and at what price? What will it buy abroad, and how much must it pay? As a rule, the balance of payments tends to be adverse.

Even a modest investment program for development may call for imports which are large in relation to margins in the normal payments balance. Borrowing and other forms of capital import can help, but trade plays an indispensable role. It would be nice if foreigners would pay "more" and charge "less," improving the poor economy's terms of trade. Realism, however, dictates that every individual, family, and nation should face up to the problem of offering good values and living within the values others offer. More often than not, the only way to keep unit costs down is to have low wage rates. When this is the case, the short-run hope for even a slowly rising income must be long hours of work.[8]

Many poor countries face what, with justification, seems a cruel problem. Their only exports are such products as staples which other lands also produce and which can fluctuate widely in price. One result is difficulty in financing a reasonably steady investment program. Price stabilization agreements with other producing and consuming countries may bring benefits. Both experience and theory, however, suggest that in the not-very-long run the total results are likely to prove disappointing and even harmful. Raising prices tends to become more the objective than stabilization. Price boosting requires control of output, at best the source of innumerable difficulties and almost certainly impossible when many countries are involved.

The data underlying Figure 36–1 are often cited as proof of another point—that the terms of trade are moving against the producers of primary commodities—foodstuffs, minerals, and natural fibers—and in favor of producers of manufactured goods in developed lands. Therefore, it is argued, exporters of manufactured goods have some obligation to provide special aid to economies dependent upon raw materials.[9]

The use of tariffs, quotas, and other devices to restrict imports is one of the more tempting, and yet dangerous, government policies designed to influence development. An economist, of course, can think of conditions in which skillfully designed restrictions on imports might be constructive. But it is easier to show how the restrictions so often imposed will obstruct and increase the cost of development.

AVOIDING THE MISTAKES OF OTHERS

A significant portion of a medical doctor's counsel may consist of what not to do—valuable advice. Sometimes the economist finds himself in a comparable position, able to warn "against" even when he has little to offer as a remedy. The positive actions that can be taken to speed growth may seem limited, and they are—about like the job of the ordinary

[8] The economic development and growth of Western Europe, Canada, and the United States began and continued when a typical work year contained many more hours than most of us would now tolerate.

[9] A leading exponent of this argument is the Executive Secretary of the United Nations Economic Commission for Latin America, Raul Prebisch.

American in doubling his productivity in 5 years. Yet to avoid mistakes will in fact raise average accomplishment, perhaps considerably. Much of what anyone—farmer, teacher, businessman, or government official—does is very like what others have done countless times, with successes and failures. To copy the best is always possible. To repeat failures is also possible but a sad waste.

FIGURE 36–1.   Export Prices, 1950–67 (1958 = 100)

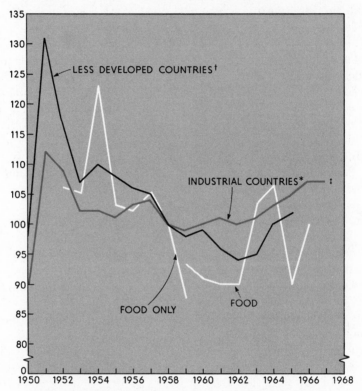

* United States, United Kingdom, 10 countries of Western Europe, Canada, and Japan.
† Approximately 40 countries of Africa, Asia, and Latin America.
‡ First quarter.
Source: International Monetary Fund, *International Financial Statistics,* September, 1967; *Economic Report of the President, 1967.*

What lessons may be learned from Soviet experience with central economic planning? What has long inflation done in Brazil? Why did France modify its traditional protectionism? Has a reluctance of "ruling classes" to try to guide reform blocked moderation and indirectly encouraged extremism? Or let us look at rather simple "mistakes" of our own past—building cities with unduly narrow streets, imposing a tax system unfavorable to investment, or neglecting the growth of tensions in labor-management relations. Developing economies ought to be able to avoid the worst of such errors.

ROLE OF GOVERNMENT

The role of government raises a delicate, but crucial, issue. It is delicate in the sense that outsiders may offend by trying to help. Most spokesmen for poor lands are government officials. They tend to think in terms of government action. To question the wisdom of government direction of development may seem a personal affront, an indignity to the nation, and evidence that one is a "capitalist reactionary." On the other hand, of course, the fact that an official proposes that some action in his country be governmental rather than business does not by any means indicate that he is necessarily a disciple of Russia.

With few exceptions government plays a prominent part in the economic life of poor lands, far bigger than governments played in the richer lands when they were beginning their development.[10] The arguments for some planning, we saw, are persuasive. Nevertheless, the large role of government in itself leads to *economic* problems. A few developing economies have a reasonably competent civil service and administrative organization. More often, however, the personnel and the system are qualified to handle only a narrow range of functions. In all too many cases, officials and staff have rather little education; nepotism, bribery, and corruption are common; concern for the next election or possible revolution overshadows long-run interests; snarls of red tape create wasteful confusion; mistakes are not corrected; narrow-interest groups—rich landowners or determined communists—may dominate without representing the public interest; the military demand a big slice of total revenues; tax collection is inadequate and unfair.

The inevitable limitations of the capacity of government officials and of the political process under the best of conditions, and the more common and more serious disabilities in poor lands, must make one skeptical of the economic wisdom of throwing much development responsibility on government. Unsatisfactory as private business may seem, riddled with defects as the market structure is likely to be, substitution of the political process will hardly lead to improvement. In vital areas—a framework of law, courts, monetary control, mass education, and basic infrastructure—only government can do what is needed. Such essentials will probably call for all the statesmanship and capacity to govern well that a poor land can muster. Not likely, as a rule, is the possibility that government *in addition* can handle business matters as well as people operating in markets.

What *is* likely is the chance that red tape will retard, that the use of compulsion will lead to wasteful resource allocation on a scale far larger

[10] R. L. Garner upon retiring as president of the International Finance Corporation said, "Over the past 14 years I have visited some 50 countries, most of them in earlier stages of development. The most substantial progress I have observed has come from the private sector, where it has been provided with basic facilities and a political and administrative climate in which it could exercise its talents. . . . In most instances of public ownership and operation of industry which I have observed, the results have been uneconomic." From address to Board of Governors, September, 1961.

than would a system in which private decision makers had their own resources at stake (one in which losses curtailed inefficient operations and profits financed growth of the successful). Where government of a developing land makes the major decisions (or exercises a veto), experience in case after case indicates that it is more likely to curb than to stimulate economic creativity. Specialists on economic growth will differ in their judgment of the optimum scope of governmental action in any particular case. They will agree that heavy reliance upon government (as it exists) can impede development. They will also agree that the provision of the essentials of good government can help immensely by enabling private activity to operate more productively than when government does a poor job of providing the framework within which men must live and work.

U.S. TECHNICAL ASSISTANCE, GIFTS, AND DEVELOPMENT LOANS

Technical Assistance. In 1949 President Truman, listing things he thought this country should do, proposed as the fourth a "bold new program" which became U.S. policy: Technical Assistance has grown as a program for helping underdeveloped areas. The conception is in the best tradition of enlightened, humane society.

Here is the idea: Knowledge, know-how of technically advanced nations, can be of inestimable benefit elsewhere. Hunger, disease, and economic stagnation are greater curses for much of the world than is essential in view of the progress of science and the resources available. If poverty-stricken masses and their leaders knew more about how to use available resources, they could improve their lot greatly, even without much capital. They might be able to break the vicious circle that keeps them sick, poor, and ignorant. Then they could begin the real journey up the road of economic progress.

Some results have been impressive. U.S. policy is to give *technical assistance*, coupled at times with gifts and loans. The U.S. government also provides some funds for equipment and supplies and agricultural products from our surpluses. However, much of the financing of individual projects (as well as the request for help) comes from the local countries. Several thousand U.S. technicians, "shirt-sleeve diplomats," work with many times as many foreigners in dozens of countries. Thousands of technicians have been brought to this country for training.

Projects have been widely diverse but generally technical. The record shows realism in the goal of "setting it up, showing them how to run it, and then going home." Close contact with humble people is common. There have been notable successes; throughout much of the world, the marginal productivity of some technical knowledge surpasses belief. When accompanied by a small quantity of miracle drugs, machines, or better seed, the results can be stupendous.[11]

---

[11] New fertilizer more than doubled rice yields in Liberia. Farmers in Iran were shown how to use sugar-beet pulp as cattle feed instead of throwing it away as waste. Hundreds of instructors for trade schools have been trained in Brazil. A school of

Yet there are obstacles. We have found it difficult sometimes to supply technicians. Happily, the cooperation of leading universities is helping provide skilled personnel. The poor and illiterate have only limited ability to absorb knowledge usefully. Trained staffs are small, the population not informed and not always sympathetic, and capital and other facilities limited. The speed of change may seem aggravatingly slow.

The United States also pays 40 percent of the assistance programs of the United Nations. The Peace Corps in 1968 will offer an estimated 19,000 American volunteers an opportunity to serve directly in helping others to learn how to help themselves. One third are in Latin America, almost as many in Africa.

Gifts and Loans for Development. Ignorance, of course, is not the only limiting factor. Capital shortages are undeniable, and our government is trying to help meet them. Policies have been in such flux that the details are confusing, but not the broad outlines. The U.S. government makes outright gifts (grants) and loans—programs generally administered by AID (Agency for International Development). Figure 36–2.

Gifts and loans for economic development have been averaging somewhat over $2.5 billion a year. Some is food, for which we receive local currency. Increasingly, development aid takes the form of loans, but "soft" loans, which have an element of gift in them because the terms are much more favorable to the borrower than those available in competitive markets, are numerous.

FIGURE 36–2. Priorities in Foreign Economic Assistance, 1968

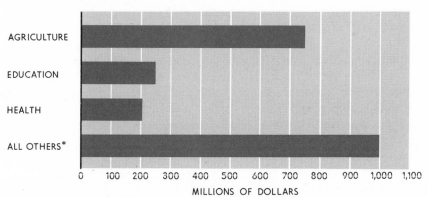

MILLIONS OF DOLLARS

* Includes general program (supporting) assistance, chiefly for the Alliance for Progress and Vietnam, which may indirectly also aid the three categories listed. Military assistance and Food for Freedom not included.
Source: Agency for International Development.

public administration has been set up in Manila. A network of 17,000 miles of highways in Turkey, which U.S. technicians helped plan and build, has cut important transport costs by 90 percent. Men from the U.S. Internal Revenue Service have helped improve tax administration in most of Latin America.

The dollars for grants and loans are used for a large variety of *specified projects*—power, transportation, irrigation, manufacturing, and other such development purposes. The loans go to governmental or quasigovernmental organizations or sometimes to private enterprises. Funds may also be used for *program assistance*, providing resources for the economy in general without earmarking for specific projects; such aid obviously helps reduce pressures growing out of balance-of-payment difficulties. Nearly half the nations of the world have received loans. Interest charges are low (often around 3 percent), repayment schedules generous (averaging almost 30 years, often with a grace period of several years). Many loans made before 1962 permit the borrowing land to repay at least part in its own currency.

One fourth of the foreign currencies received from the sale of farm products may be loaned to private business in the recipient countries. To date, the amounts so used have not been large.

Gifts for "military and supporting assistance" have fallen from over $2 billion annually to around $1.2 billion. A few countries, notably Turkey, Vietnam, Korea, and China (Taiwan), maintain larger defense forces against the Communist world than their own resources would permit. In addition to military supplies, we have provided dollars to help pay for such things as food, raw materials, and machinery. The recipient governments sell the imports for local currency. The funds thus obtained are used to pay for the upkeep of military establishments.

Castro's victory and evidence by 1960 of rising unrest elsewhere dramatized the case for new economic efforts in Latin America despite the fact that economic growth had generally been at a good rate. (Population expansion is so high that per capita incomes have risen slowly, and misery remains widespread.) The original plans of the Alliance for Progress called for the United States to supply $20 billion (including private investment) over a 10-year period. The Latin Americans assumed a heavy responsibility for self-help and domestic reform, for leadership and local capital accumulation. The economic difficulties, and also the political, are formidable. The program has lagged. Although U.S. aid did not come up to hopes, the chief sources of disappointment were local, not so much big failures as combinations of many smaller ones.

The foreign aid programs include a Contingency Fund for "urgent and unforeseen requirements." A natural disaster or a political upheaval may call for prompt action. (See Figure 36–3.)

Problems of Financial Aid to Foreign Countries.   Foreign aid creates delicate problems. Our government must become concerned with the internal economic affairs of various other nations. Yet internal economic affairs are likely to concern politics, especially if anything big is involved. We get an interest in foreign domestic politics that turns out to be uncomfortable and difficult. Diplomacy becomes more complicated.

What if U.S. experts really believe that religious convictions provide a barrier to economic development? Or that a fundamental change in land policy, in conditions leading to corruption, or in restrictive business or union practices is desirable? How much should we channel through the United Nations? Should we give aid to neutralist lands or favor only those who are committed to the anti-Communist cause?

Giving advice, or even imposing conditions, may seem desirable, but either can touch delicate sensibilities. U.S. experts may make mistakes because of ignorance of local conditions. Deliberate distortion—Communist propaganda, for example—can exaggerate distrust and suspicion. Fortunately, the accumulation of experience has enabled AID administrators to evaluate projects with greater sophistication. Insistence upon self-help efforts has grown more effective.[12] Emphasis on long-range effects increases.

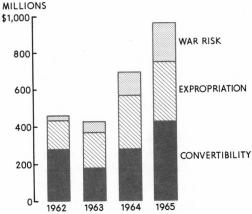

FIGURE 36–3.   Investment Guarantee: Insurance against Loss by War, Expropriation, and Lack of Convertibility; New Coverage by Year, 1962–66

Source: Agency for International Development.

Congress has been less enthusiastic about foreign aid than have presidents of both parties.[13] Uncertainty has ruled—and has created inefficien-

---

[12] AID gives the following examples of self-help:

"To the Philippines malaria control program, which has cut annual incidence from 2 million to 31,000 cases, and deaths from 12,000 to none, AID contributed $5.5 million for DDT, spray equipment, technicians, and training, and the Government of the Philippines contributed $13.8 million for staff, administration, and salaries for the spray teams and Philippine technicians.

"Taiwan's Shihmen Dam project, which now provides clean water for 100,000 persons, flood control and irrigation for 140,000 acres of rice land, and an electric generating capacity of 90,000 kilowatts, was financed by $37 million from AID for U.S. equipment, engineering, and construction services, and $35 million from the Republic of China for labor, materials, and other local costs.

"In Latin America's self-help housing projects, AID carries 30 percent of the cost (concrete mixers, wheelbarrows, other tools, and technical assistance); the local government carries 30 percent (land, site development, utilities, building materials, administration); and the eventual owners carry 40 percent of the cost by providing the labor themselves." Agency for International Development, *Foreign Aid in Perspective* (Washington, D.C., 1964), p. 7.

[13] Examples of glaring waste, poor judgment, sloppy administration, and gross miscalculation—by our own and foreign officials—have been revealed. They provide

cies. Best results require planning and operation over periods far longer than those of customary congressional appropriations. President Kennedy tried to obtain substantial freedom from the need to get annual appropriations. Congress, however, insists upon keeping close control.

Another problem involves the relative roles of government and private business. Channeling aid through government will tend to subject foreign business to governmental regulations and restrictions which act as a drag on enterprise. Our policy tends to favor the government sector abroad. But does not experience show that the best prospects for long-run development lie in competitive business? U.S. insistence that the recipient country have a "development plan" involves a risk—overcentralization and rigidity; for reasons indicated earlier, poor planning and execution can hinder development.

Finally, evaluation of benefits to the American taxpayer will never be clear. When a recipient country sides with U.S. rivals in world controversies, the American public may question the whole program.

Communist Rivalry.   The rivalry of the Russian bloc and China with the West extends to foreign aid. Russian help, only a small fraction as great as ours, is in the form of loans, not gifts. It includes financing of large and spectacular projects in selected areas where the "public relations" effects may be great. Being governmental, Russian aid can seek political results which we can hardly expect from the greater totals of U.S. business investment in poor lands.

To the extent that Russia succeeds in her declaration of "war in the peaceful field of trade" she may weaken us economically—and diplomatically and militarily. As a totalitarian country, Russia can concentrate at times and places to get not only economic gain but also military and diplomatic advantage. Perhaps she can fit short-run action into a consistent long-run program. Increasingly she has things other lands want, from modern steel mills to weapons only a little obsolete. Once her equipment is installed, the control of replacement parts can give her government officials a kind of power which our government cannot in fact exert when equipment of U.S. producers is used abroad.

The dictators can buy and use more of virtually anything produced abroad—and they can buy for political effect. For some raw-material-producing countries, large Russian orders may at times be most welcome —the purchase of Egyptian cotton. At slight cost to the Russian economy, a price somewhat above that in free markets, the Soviets might gain a big political advantage. Furthermore, the promise of steady buying— say X percent of Iceland's fish at a stable price—a sort of promise that

---

support for opponents of the program as a whole. Determined efforts have been made to improve administration, but in the nature of the case some projects will be disappointing.

our government can rarely give, might make many friends for Russia, nations as a whole, or individual businesses and groups within a country. Russia, by a deliberate policy of skillful buying, perhaps even by a policy to her economic advantage, could win friends and draw economies away from the free world. After a time, perhaps, the Kremlin as a buyer can make others economically dependent. Such possibilities looked more ominous for us a few years ago than recently. The Soviet record includes some bad mistakes; poor quality and high prices do not win friends. A dictatorship will not be so diabolically clever as we may imagine.

A nondictatorial nation—and even more, a coalition of countries with different interests and estimates of the situation—can hardly hope to meet on Russia's terms the kind of economic rivalry that the Soviet bloc presents. For us, therefore, it becomes even more vital to identify our own strengths and to lead from them. This is not easy. For example, the flexibility of private enterprise in a free economy, its ability to offer good value because of the benefits of competition, will be one of our major economic strengths in the long run. When national defense is involved, however, the private interest is not always identical with the public. We cannot expect U.S. or British producers to sell generators to India below cost to meet Russian competition. We cannot expect our businesses to adopt inventory policies to suit the wishes of governments of lands which export raw materials. Nor can we really hope for private groups here to give up pressure for government-imposed restrictions on imports even though the restrictions would lose some friends and weaken others.

On two scores, the theoretical and analytical and the practical, both of which are of the greatest significance for hundreds of millions of people, the *economics of development* stands as immensely challenging. What can have an equal significance for human welfare? We may dream of miracles and hope for them. The more realistic objective is to find a set of policies which can speed matters a little, or more. For this we can hope.

TERMS AND CONCEPTS

social overhead capital	comparative advantage	technical assistance
capital-output ratio	balanced growth	grants
forced saving	infrastructure	development loans
land reform	entrepreneurship	military assistance

QUESTIONS

1. What are the obstacles to capital accumulation in poor economies? What effect would inflation have over the long run?

2. Why can finding what people want the most help accelerate development?

3. "One economic advantage of a free society over dictatorship is in discovering entrepreneurship." Would you judge this to be true in an underdeveloped land? Why?

4. What might poor countries do to try to attract foreign businesses? What policies might discourage such direct investment?

5. Why are policies for rapid development likely to lead to balance-of-payments difficulties?

6. What is the rivalry between agriculture and industrialization in economic development?

7. How can planning help and hinder development in poor lands?

8. What arguments do you see for and against larger U.S. aid for poor countries? Describe some of the problems of rendering such aid effectively.

9. In what sense is population growth an obstacle to economic development in much of the world?

37

SOCIALISM AND RUSSIAN COMMUNISM

"Know thine enemy."

The search for a better world keeps us on the lookout, at home and abroad, for improved methods of economic organization just as we seek improved technology. Other economies may have features which could wisely be copied, perhaps with modifications, even by an economy which in general seems to function better. The development of present economic systems has usually been gradual, largely unconscious, and seldom with thorough rational effort to develop the very best. Must there not be opportunities for improvement? Anyone concerned with a special aspect of economies—business organization, taxation, financing foreign trade—will be wise to see how comparable problems are met elsewhere. Novel ideas can spark new thinking; they can arouse the questioning and criticism that are essential elements in the chain of challenge-response which helps lead to improvement. Study of others' experiences can also help prevent mistakes.[1]

[1] Yet getting maximum benefit from such study is harder than men sometimes recognize. The simple fact that something is foreign can slant our views, more so in economics than in chemistry. National pride, self-satisfaction, and crude intolerance close minds and account for needless waste of opportunity. The mere fact that something is foreign, of course, does not prove it is good, even if it is part of an economy which functions well. It may be a weaker feature; or, even if it is a strong one, it may not be good for transplanting in foreign soil. Wants and resources differ. Important variations are national; others are regional, racial, religious, and deeply rooted in tradition. An economic arrangement may work differently in two countries because noneconomic factors are not the same. Cultural differences, of course, may create no crucial obstacles for one land's adopting economic methods of another. But to forecast the results of efforts to transplant economic institutions requires the fullest range of knowledge of social sciences and humanities.

The serious issues, however, involve more than exchange of ideas about ways of doing specific things. Ideas about organizing the whole of economic life also differ—"grand alternatives" rather than gradual adaptations. Great visions move men. The Kremlin, has used a "vision," an ideology, to win support at home and abroad. Before examining our great rival, however, let us look at another "ideology": socialism.[2]

SOCIALISM

The century before World War I saw many socialist proposals and several attempts to put theories into practice on a small scale. The experiments failed, but socialism as a doctrine grew. As an ideology it captured minds and emotions with a force we today can hardly sense, thriving especially on criticism of capitalism. Many different views claimed the name "socialist," but most had in common considerable reliance on the analysis of Karl Marx.

Marx and his disciples tended to be bitter, to focus on the misery and evil they saw around, alleged to be a result of capitalism. The misery would deepen, they predicted, and capitalism would inevitably break down. Then the proletariat would seize the property which had permitted the capitalists to exploit the workers. The vigorous agitation of the Marxists was essentially negative in emphasizing what was bad; it had little concern for what could be done constructively to improve welfare. Hatred for the prosperous was, and has remained, a powerful propaganda weapon. Some socialists, however, looked more at the Judeo-Christian tradition of humanity and the positive hope of improving human welfare. Far less well developed was any analysis of what in practice would benefit the masses.

Agitation spread antagonism. Poverty remained although total and average income rose. Then World War I and later the Depression added to the misery of uncounted millions. In the 1920's and 1930's, capitalism was on the defensive. Dissatisfaction extended beyond the masses of the unfortunate and those who sympathized on emotional grounds. Some professional economists concluded that broader government planning of an economy, or outright government ownership and operation, would do better than markets in getting efficiency, equality, and full employment.

Criticism of Capitalism. When they criticize capitalism, what do socialists emphasize? Almost everyone has his pet gripes—blame what

[2] Fascism, which might be considered another "grand," or at least "sweeping," alternative is not easily defined or described. Private ownership of property remains, but government exercises extensive control. A crude, but not wholly erroneous, cliché runs to the effect that fascist economics combines bureaucratic centralization and domination with restrictive monopoly. Mussolini's Italy and Hitler's Germany differed widely in economic policy, while other countries sometimes included in the fascist category (e.g., Peron's Argentina) have utilized still different types of economic organization.

seems wrong on "the system." Some complaints are little more than that nature is poor, that the number of mouths is too large for what we produce. Yet more serious criticisms deserve attention.

Inequality in the distribution of income has been an outstanding complaint—wealth 'midst poverty,[3] exploitation of workers, injustice. Marx argued that the inherent necessity of the capitalist's search for profit forces him not only to pay less than labor is worth, exacting "surplus value," but to drive down wages, forcing more and more misery on workers. Conditions under capitalism could get only worse for the poor.

Socialists also argued that capitalism develops so much monopoly that the benefits claimed for a progressive system of free enterprise will not in fact appear. A third criticism had much weight in the 1930's: Depressions come under capitalism—and, it was said, get more and more severe.

Other criticisms appeared—capitalism was charged with causing wars; with fostering imperialism; with being ugly; with creating, rather than satisfying, wants; with wasting natural resources; with controlling newspapers, radio, colleges, judges, and churches. Materialism and its apparent failure to give proper place to humane and social values were repugnant to some people.[4] The evils in human nature were alleged to be accentuated by competitive pressures. Take your pick of what is wrong, or seems to be wrong, and you can probably find that some socialists have blamed it on capitalism.

Criticism will often serve a useful purpose. *The serious issue, however, will be whether an improvement can be made, and how, and at what cost.* Rational criticism must compare alternatives. Much irrationality may appear, however, under the pretense of comparing alternatives, such as the world of fact with some dream world. Dreams as aspirations are essential for progress, but dreams as substitutes for the analysis of reality can be seriously misleading.

The Socialist Program. Socialists have never agreed upon a program. Individuals and groups calling themselves "socialist" have proposed many programs, ranging from the detailed to the vague. The following generalizations represent widely accepted elements:

---

[3] "Poverty in the midst of plenty" was once a popular indictment of capitalism. The slogan implies that there was enough "plenty" to offset the poverty. Unfortunately, however, plenty in the sense of excess over requirements for efficiency and comfort was tiny compared with poverty in the sense of income below the same level. The real problem was to raise total income.

[4] Marx was an outstanding materialist. He and his disciples, in fact, claim that human personality is formed by economic forces, that changing the institutions which bear upon man will change his personality. Material values rank high. Socialism is not idealistic in the sense that, compared with capitalism, nonmaterial considerations overshadow material; rather, proponents of socialism rest much of their case upon the argument that they and their system could do a better job of providing material wants, and that human beings would improve as economic tensions decline.

The (major) "means of production" would be owned by government. Their operation would be for "use rather than profit," a guide by no means clearly defined. The range of consumer freedom might be broad or narrow—views differ. General direction would be "guided" centrally, with ultimate responsibility in the hands of elected officials. In the theory the many problems of management and entrepreneurship are more often ignored than faced and solved satisfactorily.

Both the accumulation and the allocation of savings for new capital goods would be (predominantly) by government. Similarly, wage rates and prices would be determined rather more by the political process and less by market forces than in capitalistic economies. Money wages might be supplemented by goods and services provided by government and paid for out of what would have been rents, profit, and interest. (Former owners of property might, or might not, be compensated.) Real income would be more nearly equal than under capitalism—with more weight to "need"—but not necessarily equal. If any significant amount of private ownership of property remained, there would be little opportunity for transfer by inheritance. Workers' groups might play a role in management but would not necessarily do so.

Economists with modern professional training, whatever their views about the best kind of economic organization, will agree that the economic programs of socialist groups, especially the socialist parties, before 1930 were seriously deficient. The "economics" failed to deal with some of the tough, important, problems—the microeconomic problems of allocation of scarce resources to bring greatest benefits, maintaining individual freedom, incentives, the guidance of investment, the selection and control of leaders, agriculture, foreign trade, and so on. In the 1930's, however, the economic problems were tackled by highly trained economists. The outcome was a body of theory, summarized in the appendix to this chapter, which attempted to show how a centrally directed economy in which government owned the productive resources but in which individuals as consumers and workers would have freedom of choice could operate efficiently. The major tool turned out to be a price system operating in free, competitive markets. Of course, there was a great deal more. On the level of pure analysis the theory did not solve all the hard economic problems. Unquestionably, however, a significant theoretical advance had been made.

The result required a kind of economic organization—one based predominantly on free markets—which diverged in major respects from the programs of socialist political parties. The theory had little or no evident influence on the leaders of socialist movements.

BRITISH SOCIALISM

Britain chose a socialist government in voting the Labour Party to power in 1945 and giving it control for 6 years. What did Labour do?

It had never intended to socialize all the economy, and certainly not to follow an economic blueprint of the type economic theorists would fashion. Its leaders tended to distrust the price system and to prefer government direction not only of broad outlines but also of many details. The program called for extensive planning and control of private sectors of the economy; for this, conditions were favorable. During the war, effective organizations had been developed for monopolizing the purchase of key imports, rationing, allocations, control of investment and labor, and so on; the public was accustomed to controls. Yet the results of war destruction, heavy outlays for defense, and postwar disruption created weighty difficulties.

Government took over ownership and management of certain industries (nationalization). In addition, Labour undertook central planning or control of more of the nation's economic life including (*a*) the regulation of much private investment and (*b*) the extension of social insurance (welfare state). Full employment became a major goal to be achieved, largely, by maintaining an adequacy of aggregate demand and "easy" money.

Although controls extended to many detailed activities, such as the repairs and improvements a man could make on his own house, there was no broad, detailed, long-range plan. Short-range crises dominated the attention of top officials. Among less important measures were ambitious but vague (and largely ineffective) plans for control of land use and encouragement of "working parties" to study problems of specific industries such as cotton textiles, any resulting action to be taken by unions and business on their own. Suggestions for employee participation in management were rejected, even for nationalized industries, on the grounds that managers' loyalties should be to the whole nation. Civil liberties were preserved, but individual freedom was restricted in many ways, such as by high taxes, rationing, and controls on the use of materials and foreign exchange. "Consumer sovereignty" was limited by numerous direct controls on particular parts of the economy—of course, an exhausting war had just been fought. Looking backward, one sees in Labour policies a lack of *positive* programs for raising national real income as needed to relieve the poverty that was such a central concern.

Government ownership was extended to the Bank of England (but not to the commercial banking system), coal mining, rail and much truck transport, electricity and gas, airlines, steel, medicine, and less important industries. Private owners of the property nationalized were paid in government bonds; the terms were at least moderately satisfactory to former owners. The most serious disputes arose over medical services and steel nationalization. The latter was neither a sick industry (such as coal) nor one obviously a public utility (such as railroads). Generally, former managements were retained, except that, at the top, the government set up new directing boards.

Nonsocialized parts of the economy which were subjected to extensive controls were housing and real estate, agriculture, and foreign trade. A "cradle to the grave" system of social security was established. It departed widely, however, from the part of the old creed "to each according to his need," for only in extreme cases were tests of need required.

What were the results? The story of coal was disappointing, but the industry had long been sick. The quantity of output failed to rise, quality declined; efforts to raise efficiency by mechanization and closing down poor mines were impeded by unions; prices increased greatly; mine managements found central direction onerous; output failed to meet needs.

Railroads, in poor condition when socialized, showed no striking evidence of improvement. Rates to shippers rose, a tribute to inflation more than to nationalization. Steel nationalization had hardly taken effect when a Conservative Government pleged to sell the industry back to private investors came into power. The health scheme proved so popular that the Conservatives later made only minor changes; people liked freedom from any worry about doctor, dentist, or hospital bills, but the passing years brought much dissatisfaction with the inadequacy of new facilities (medical personnel and hospitals), red tape, and quality. Costs were covered largely by hidden taxes and turned out to be much greater than expected. The social insurance benefits raised minimum living standards. High-income groups bore extremely heavy tax burdens, but the Labour Government increased substantially the taxes on low-income groups, chiefly commodity taxes.

Unions were by no means gloriously happy in socialized industries. Workers as part of the public which owned an industry did not become more industrious because ownership changed; "government" would have gotten any increase in profits. The Labour Government was reluctant to push policies unpopular with unions and was not widely successful in raising productivity, such as in construction to meet desperate needs for homes. The problem of powerful groups was not solved by socialization. (Labour once used troops to break a strike.) Occasional efforts to reform monopolistic practices of industry had little influence. Direct government controls from the war period were relaxed, although not rapidly. The civil service, while meeting the major demands, including honesty, aroused well-documented criticisms of the sluggishness of bureaucracy. Popular endorsement of large investment allocations by Labour to housing and relatively little to transport and industrial modernization and expansion may prove to have been shortsighted. The number of jobs continually exceeded the number of workers, and unemployment became only a memory.

British experience showed that socialization will not assure improvements in efficiency. The maintenance of full employment and rising prosperity after the Conservatives came to power in 1951, along with preservation of "welfare state" policies, added to the serious questioning by socialists of what to propose as constructive for the future. Conservatives succeeded in largely denationalizing steel and trucking by sale back to private owners. Rationing and most other restrictions were removed or, as with rent controls, greatly relaxed. Decentralization of management of coal and railroads was intended to raise efficiency.

Prosperity continued. Unemployment remained minimal under the Conservatives. More than a decade of rising income, combined with recognition of how little benefit could be claimed for nationalization and how insignificant (if any) were the remaining practical opportunities for income equalization by redistribution, plus the greater need for increasing productivity, prompted new thinking about socialist goals. Wide disagreement about both means and ends led to sharply divergent views within the party.

"Ideology" had been split into many parts. Some differences were matters of emphasis. Others, however, went deep—more nationalization versus more competition, more incentive versus more equalization, wide extension of governmental controls versus reliance upon more general fiscal and monetary policy. Clearly, in the campaign of 1964, which brought Labour once again to power, economic argument was blunted. Labour pledged to renationalize most of the steel industry (and eventually did so). The major emphasis was the ability of Labour to use monetary and fiscal policy (following a generally Keynesian pattern) more wisely than the Conservatives to maintain high prosperity. Labour's criticism of the failure of the British economy to grow as rapidly as others in Europe was not matched by clear indication of what would be done to improve matters.

Upon taking office, the Labour Party inherited a balance-of-payments problem which had been developing and which seriously hampered its freedom to act. To prevent devaluation of the pound, Labour felt obliged to use tax and monetary policies which it had condemned.

Restraints on the growth of aggregate money demand brought unemployment to levels not seen in a quarter of a century. A sort of "freeze" on wage-rate increases was neither very effective nor popular. Inflation continued. Measures taken to strengthen Britain's competitive position in the world were far indeed from the plans and hopes of earlier socialism. Even after the 1967 devaluation to $2.40 the international position of the pound was so weak that domestic policy had to be set largely in terms of economic pressures from outside.

In several other European countries, socialist parties have had considerable influence, or been in control, in the postwar period. While generalization is risky, there is no doubt that socialism has lost its revolutionary fervor. There remains wide support for broad government action in redistributing income, in controlling many parts of economic life, and in operating some industries.[5] Yet policies are largely pragmatic and programs anything but systematically socialistic. There is little or no enthusiasm for nationalizing any significant portion of industries now privately owned.

COMMUNISM IN RUSSIA

Russia's Communist Party has stated as one of its goals: "Through peaceful competition and in a historically short period of time, to overtake and surpass the most highly developed capitalist countries in per capita output." Russia's leaders challenge us in economics, and economic strength provides much of the base for military and diplomatic power. Moreover, communism as an ideology, and the economic systems of China and other non-Soviet communist lands, are forces in world rivalry. We have good reason to look at the Russian economy. So do the Russians, for their 1967 celebrations of the 50th anniversary of the revolution prompted much questioning self-examination.

Can we, however, trust Russian figures? Yes and no. Deliberate official falsification of economic statistics is now apparently uncommon.[6] Gaps, however, are sometimes large; errors are frequent; the system itself creates incentives for reporting inaccurately.

Communists seized power in 1917 when Russia was disrupted by World War I. The old leadership of business and government was largely "liquidated." Government took over the ownership of property. Obligations to foreign investors, as well as to Russian owners of property, were repudiated. The early years under Lenin and Trotsky saw extreme disorganization, inflation, and terrible poverty. By about 1927, however, output had regained the 1913 level.

Planning. Then began the first Five-Year Plan, something new which came to symbolize much of Communist economic policy. One plan followed another. The planning job is incredibly complex. Change after change in planning methods shows that the Russians have come to reject arrangements once praised to the sky.

Planning of operations takes place each year. General economic objectives are determined by central authorities—the political leaders, generals, and heads of the industrial hierarchies. The major goals are then put into

---

[5] Even in Western Germany, where private business has more freedom from governmental direction than in Europe generally, governments (national, provincial, and local) operate a substantial range of businesses. Most are what we would call public utilities.

[6] Foreigners can get access to a vast mass of material published in Russia and used internally. Scholars in the West, therefore, have much of the data which provide the basis of official Russian planning and operations. The quality of this information varies. Falsification of data has appeared in efforts to mislead. Today, exaggerated statements by leaders can ordinarily be corrected by persons who are familiar with data from other sources. But the best statistics available to even the Kremlin leaders are incomplete and inadequate.

tentative plan form by the Gosplan (State Planning Commission)—so much iron ore, aircraft, electricity. As proposals, these then pass down the line through regional and industrial agencies for review and the filling in of details.

Each part of the plan eventually reaches the particular plant or farm involved—around 200,000 units as of mid-1960's. The inputs which will be required are calculated according to norms set at higher levels—so many man-hours per ton of steel, so much steel for an apartment building. During these stages, suggestions, criticisms, and bargaining are possible. The plant manager or anyone else responsible for actually "turning out the goods" has powerful incentive to seek *low* goals and also allocations of inputs *greater* than will be required so that he can get "enough"; his future depends chiefly upon the output accomplishment. His incentive to misrepresent is an impediment to good planning which Russian planners recognize and condemn but have not overcome.

The plan goes back up the tiers of levels for the enormously complicated job of balancing the parts and reconciling changes.[7] "Bargaining" goes on between men whose relations are not those of buyer and seller nor those of boss and subordinate, men who must move, as it were, in the dark without the guidance of price or other effective measurement of worth.

Gosplan works out final "balances" for approval by the Council of Ministers. The results then go back down the line for more detailed plans for plant operations.

Plans are expressed in terms of (1) real resources (material requirements), (2) money, and (3) labor. All three are presumably integrated, in total and in allocations for all subparts. To date, however, planners have "succeeded" in this massively complex task only by "short cuts" around some of the most difficult obstacles. The materials balances are computed for about 200 types of items. When the amount of tin, wool, or other material called for will exceed the quantity to be available—a common occurrence—various "solutions," many arbitrary and to some extent inconsistent, are used to get a balance (at least on paper). Plans always call for larger totals of inputs than will be available. Within the plan, therefore, priorities are assigned. Consequently, if technical conditions permit, parts with top priority will almost certainly be fulfilled. Others will lag, spreading dislocation in amounts and directions not foreseeable.

Russians in a position to know criticize the planning mechanism for overcentralization, poor coordination, lateness,[8] and lack of rational guid-

---

[7] If one plant persuades officials to reduce its output quota of small motors, revision is also required in the plans of plants (*a*) which will supply materials and parts and those (*b*) which will use the motors. An increase in one plant's quota, of course, will require reallocation of materials and labor and thus upset quotas of other plants, on and on.

[8] Use of electronic computers, input-output techniques, linear programming, and other devices of the modern age may enable the Communists to plan more rationally. "A centrally planned economy depends on the efficiency—or the inefficiency—of

ance. As inconsistencies appear with the passing months, new alternatives arise; the strictures of the plan, however, impede adjustment. For more than two years (to early 1968) no final decision on an overall plan had been made. ". . . scarce as capital may be in the Soviet economy, the decision-making ability of the central planners constitutes the most important single bottleneck factor."[9] With an estimated 20,000,000 types of output (intermediate and final products from the 200,000 or so "enterprises"), efficient coordination in one plan defies any mechanism yet devised.

Capricious, impetuous changes have produced costly losses and distortions. A sudden large expansion of chemical facilities, for example, was undertaken without provision for some of the essentials. As a result, bottlenecks choked off realization of potential benefits. Putting agriculture under one plan and industry under another led to such results as sausage factories built far beyond the provision of sausage ingredients. An inherent source of inefficiency results from rigidity and obstacles to small-stage, continuous adjustment to changing conditions.

When restrictions on criticism were relaxed in 1957, Russians from top to bottom responded with examples of major and minor folly, of shocking waste which neither central planning nor severe penalty had spared the public. Two separate government agencies, for example, operated steamers on the same river. One fleet sailed down empty, the other came up empty. Minor bottlenecks hold up major operations.

One result of criticism, added to years of complaint about bureaucracy and overcentralization, was a basic reorganization begun in 1958: decentralization. The country was divided into around 106 regions (rather than about 438 ministries and departments). Within each, considerable economic autonomy and responsibility were assigned to regional officials. Moscow's directing power was drastically reduced. The central offices were to concentrate on major policies and avoid detail. Such a massive shift of active authority was in itself disrupting. And soon there appeared pressure for recentralization of authority. Regional freedom could not be reconciled with the needs of a central plan. Once again, then, the role of

---

managerial decision to a much greater extent than does the free-market economy, which benefits from the economizing functions of competitive pricing. So, the advantage that the Russians will derive from any improvement in such decision-making procedures is bound to be particularly great." W. Leontief, "The Decline and Rise of Soviet Economic Science," *Foreign Affairs*, January, 1960, pp. 261–72. Yet until the guides of a price system work effectively—e.g., revealing changes in the relative availability of copper and aluminum or the relative desirability of housing in Kiev and trucks for Siberia—the planning will itself be a source of dislocation. Arbitrary decisions misdirect activity in a system without mechanisms for promptly indicating where better alternatives are available.

[9] A. Erlich, "Development Strategy and Planning: The Soviet Experience," in M. F. Millikan (ed.), *National Economic Planning* (New York: Columbia University Press, 1967), p. 260. The volume has papers on five functional issues in planning and on the practices and experience of Russia, France, India, and Jugoslavia.

the men heading industries with national operations grew at the expense of the organizations responsible for all activities in a region.

Another experiment is underway. A few big "enterprises"—over 200 by 1968—were operating with much greater autonomy. Decisions about almost every aspect of what to produce, by what methods, and pricing and investment are left somewhat more to local plant management. How much more? With what effects? As yet no generalizations can be obtained.

Ownership.   The government owns all property except clothing, furniture, private houses occasionally, and other such purely personal property and some kinds of financial assets. It has sold bonds to the public on a voluntary, and also on an essentially compulsory, basis. In 1957 the Kremlin abolished compulsory bond purchase while repudiating most of the value of existing bonds. The government permits private bank accounts and does not prohibit inheritance.

Industrial Organization and Management.   Each major industry ("trust") is organized as a sort of huge monopoly with elements of what we would call both vertical and horizontal organization. Each individual plant belongs to such an industry grouping which includes all other plants of the same and closely related type. Each plant, however, also falls to some extent under the jurisdiction of authorities for the region.

Plants must pay wages and prices for inputs. Each industry charges prices for what it sells. The plant management, however, plays almost no role in setting wage rates and prices; these are fixed by men having no responsibility for the operation of any specific center of production.

Management rests upon a hierarchy of officials, but with technical decisions resting largely upon the plant manager. He will generally have been trained as an engineer. He rises through the production phases and tends to have familiarity with, and chief interest in, technological aspects. One American observer after another has noted the technical competence of Russian managers. Although they will have had a strong political indoctrination, loyalty to the regime is not enough to get one to a top position or to keep him there.

The job is demanding. Only a tough, ingenious, and competent man can rise to the top and stay. The job is to produce. Sales and finance present relatively few problems, but procurement usually does require much attention. The manager has little freedom to choose his (legal) sources of supply or the buyers to whom he sells. He cannot control his own capital budget; both the plowing back of the plant's net earnings and the use of what corresponds to depreciation depend upon decisions of higher echelons—except that the new experiments will allow selected plants appreciable freedom over some depreciation funds and net earnings. The lack of flexibility reduces efficiency. By U.S. standards, for example, there is not much use of subcontracting. Managers, however, live under constant pressure to use "out of channel" (including illegal) methods to get what is necessary for meeting quotas. To help prevent evasion of the rules, the central authorities maintain "control" and even espionage staffs. The manager operates government property, subject to constant prying and the threat of denunciation, perhaps by a subordinate seeking the job.

The incentive system is impressive—for good as well as bad features. Basic salaries are supplemented by bonuses for meeting the monthly quota. Failure to meet the production target by only a tiny amount will cost the manager 30 to 50 percent of his compensation. Moreover, job security is unknown. Higher officials quickly replace a manager who is not delivering the goods. Although turnover at the managerial level is neither so high nor so capricious as under Stalin, it is a reality which adds to the heavy pressure on everyone in a managerial position. The men who succeed may get ulcers, but they also get incomes which by Russian standards permit a high standard of living. The incentive system also creates powerful inducements to supply false information (understate productive capacity and misrepresent output), to acquire capital equipment and inventory beyond opportunities for efficient use, to hold back on innovation, to "hoard" labor, to skimp on quality, and to sacrifice the longer run for the immediate future. Recently in Russia, and in other communist lands (except China), the "profit" guide under some name has been endorsed by men with influence. Its use for guidance and incentive has been introduced here and there.

New "success criteria" go along with the greater freedom allowed some managers. Sales and profits (the latter somewhat like return on capital) get relatively greater weighting and physical output less. Rewards can be given for innovation of products and methods.

Russia's governmentally controlled press repeatedly criticizes the output of industry, especially as regards quality. Quotas expressed as numbers of units create powerful temptations to sacrifice quality for quantity. Despite a variety of checks and extreme penalties, managers resort to subterfuges to cover up failures. In a "tight seller's market," the user, whether another factory or an ordinary household, cannot exercise the control which Americans take for granted. Quality standards for military goods and some machinery, however, are very high.

The dominance of short-run objectives—"storming" to meet this month's quota—appears expensive. It discourages both the introduction of new methods that have not proved themselves[10] and the preservation of

---

[10] The typical plant will have a bigger percentage of employees on the maintenance staff than would be the case in this country. The manager, knowing that he cannot count upon hiring outsiders to repair equipment when it breaks down, and uncertain about his ability to acquire new machines when they are needed, wants to be able to keep what he has running. Nevertheless, a system of incentives focused on short-run quotas, with insecurity and high turnover of managers, gives little reason to sacrifice output today to get more next year or 5 years hence. Consequently, maintenance in a fundamental sense suffers.

equipment. Also contributing to costly waste, such as crosshauling and inventory hoarding, is the failure to coordinate even within the plan.

None of the transfers of power over planning has apparently done much to provide the knowledge and skill required for efficiency. One reason for such failure lies at the heart of the whole system—the method of pricing.

Pricing. The price system has a different role from that in a market economy. Prices, with such exceptions as part of the output of agricultural produce, are set by government officials. ("Black markets" exist for many things, such as spare parts and items urgently needed by plants to meet quotas.) Arbitrary features in the price-fixing process make comparison of prices with costs difficult for even the experts. Judgment of efficiency cannot be tested as in an economy where market forces give objective tests of the relative worth of alternatives. Coal and steel have been priced below cost, apparently to disguise the "losses" of heavy-goods industries using them on a large scale. As of 1967 the prices of a huge fraction of the things sold at intermediate stages were essentially unchanged from 1955. Subsidies also keep prices of housing and local transport below cost.

After some price-setting authority was transferred from central to regional officials, inconsistencies and imbalances resulted. The effects reach beyond the area directly involved. Most prices are inflexible in the sense that once fixed they remain unchanged for considerable periods.

Some Russian economists have been urging that prices be influenced more by market forces and that costs allow more clearly for inputs other than labor. A few economists have been trying to shake free from the Marxian theory that value depends upon labor inputs only.[11] These men know that efficient resource allocation requires the guidance of prices which reflect all the alternatives. The official economic publication of the Communist Party urges that greater effort be made to run the economy rationally by, among other things, relying more upon prices set by demand and supply and by applying cost accounting.

Early in 1965 came a momentous announcement. Several hundred producers of consumer goods were to be required to supply retail stores goods of quality at prices consumers would freely accept. Two years of experience showed that consumers did fare better than before. Otherwise, U.S. experts say the results, still in flux, are too varied to permit broad generalization.

Emphasis on Capital Investment. The consumer is slighted but not the military, which gets about twice as big a percentage of GNP as in this

[11] One of the best known is Professor S. Liberman of Kharkov University. Samples of arguments by Russian economists appear in H. G. Shaffer, *The Soviet Economy: A Collection of Western and Soviet Views* (New York: Appleton-Century-Crofts, 1963).

country—perhaps more. Heavy industry is also a great favorite. Power facilities have been pushed rapidly. The railroads, however—the mainstay of transportation—seem to have been slighted.

Starting with little industrial equipment, the Communists concentrated on industrialization for dual reasons, military security and development of basic productive capacity which the leaders believed to be essential for raising national income significantly. Considering the low level of income and of margin for sacrifice, a *very high rate of saving has been forced* on the public by prices (inclusive of taxes) much above wages plus other outlays for cost. Current consumption is sacrificed—cruelly and ruthlessly by our standards—for capital accumulation. As shown in Figure 37–1, gross investment is a considerably larger percentage of GNP than in the United States. And note the difference in allocation with our relatively greater emphasis on housing.

FIGURE 37–1.   Investment as a Percentage of Gross National Product—Russia and the United States, (1950–60 Average Annual Rate)

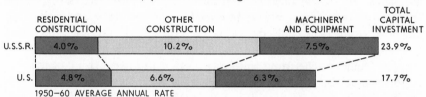

Source: S. H. Cohn, "Gross National Product in the Soviet Union: Comparative Growth Rates," *Dimensions of Soviet Economic Power* (Washington, D.C.: Joint Economic Committee, 1961), pp. 68–89.

The authorities, in making investment decisions, seek internal consistency among allocations for industries, regions, techniques, and other elements of the plan. But the hold of Marxist doctrine prevented, until recently, any forthright use of interest in allocating resources among investment projects. Crude methods have been applied to allow for differences in the time required for construction, in the timing of the fruits of investment, and in the relative "effectiveness" of different investment projects. Considerable debate in the 1950's reflected desire to improve "calculation for the time factor." One way or another, yield on invested capital, and even some allowance for the value of use of land and natural resources, are getting into calculations and the choice of alternatives.

Incentives.   The Soviet leaders seek to speed economic growth not only by imposing a high rate of forced saving and investment in heavy industry. They also emphasize incentives—positive and negative—hope and fear.

Penalties are severe. Poverty forces men and women, young and old, to work long and hard. Otherwise misery and want would be intolerable. The masses *must* exert themselves. But more than grinding poverty on the masses operates as a fear incentive. A manager's failure can bring loss of the few, or many, special privileges which distinguish his life from the bread-and-cabbage-soup slum existence of the workers in city and country. Failure may bring reassignment, or exile, to remote areas—occasionally even prison.

Positive incentives, however, are also strong. Earnings are highly unequal. Beyond the handsome bonuses for successful managers, large rewards are offered to others who accomplish much. Wage-rate differentials—rubles per hour or per unit of output—are large. The government deliberately seeks to stimulate the acquisition of skills by offering generous payments for skill differentials. Moreover, piece rates are the rule. In fact, the "speed up" is official policy. Incentive rates are at times highly progressive. Extra effort can bring large rewards, and they are not reduced appreciably by the income tax, which is only slightly progressive with a top rate of 13 percent.[12] Special receipts add significantly to real income in a few cases—vacations, prizes, perquisites (autos, housing, food, especially for top officials), and price discounts. The difference between the after-tax real earnings of managers and the mass of workers is relatively greater than in America.

Wives ordinarily work to supplement the husband's earnings. Unemployment is not admitted, but it exists; failure of details of plans to work out on schedule brings many idle hours. Much of the great farm population, of course, is largely inactive at certain seasons. The normal work-week in factory and office has been reduced to about 40 hours on 5 days. Rough estimates of man-hour productivity in factories put productivity at perhaps half that in this country—on the average—but some is excellent by any standards.

The masses have only limited power to choose jobs (housing shortages and lack of training, among other things, accentuate immobility) or to influence the conditions under which they work. Legally, however, the choice of jobs is free, and the shifting of industrial workers in search of better jobs has been a source of trouble because heavy turnover reduces efficiency. University graduates must work 2 to 4 years wherever they are assigned. Unions exist, but with little power; apparently, however, more effort is being made to get unions to help raise productivity. Rapid expansion in the nonagricultural sectors has created opportunities for rising in the scale of jobs, nevertheless, tendencies toward stratification exist with something of a self-perpetuating class system which favors the children of parents already well-established in the Party, industry, or

[12] The ordinary worker or salaried person is essentially free from progressive income tax as we know it. An official with income 40 times the average paid only about 13 percent of the total in income tax in the early 1960's. In the United States the tax on an income 40 times the average was around 64 percent, and in England 70 percent of income. However, the Russian writer, professional person in private practice, or "non-cooperative" artisan, shopkeeper, or priest is taxed at rates which go somewhat over 50 percent but by no means at rates as high as in "capitalist" lands.

bureaucracy. Although almost everyone is employed by government, some leeway for self-employment remains.

The Position of the Consumer.   The consumer, who is the ultimate "boss" in capitalist economies, is the forgotten, or at least the neglected, man or woman in Russia.

Average consumption, including health, education, and other free services, was apparently *lower* in 1952 than in 1928 but has risen markedly since then. The consumer has legal freedom of choice in spending his income, since formal rationing has been generally abolished. The average family, however, is so poor that it can enjoy little of the nominal freedom. Compared with a New York worker, a Moscow industrial worker in 1966 had to work 3 times as long for a pound of potatoes, 5 times for milk, 10 times for butter, 12 times for tea, 8 times for soap and eggs, and about 15 times as long for sugar. Clothing is very expensive. A man's shirt required the pay for 13 hours of work, a suit 183 hours. A rayon street dress cost the full earnings for a week and a day, women's shoes 38 hours. But the Russian does not pay out, as does the American, for insurance on his life, home, or auto.

Housing is especially short, averaging in square feet per capita about one seventh of ours—half the size of a 9 by 12 foot living room rug. Much of the new construction is needed to meet the needs of growing population. The quality of housing for all but the top 1 or 2 percent is poor; improvement has been very slow. American observers in 1967, however, were very favorably impressed with the technical and economic merits of new construction methods (including prefabrication much more advanced than used here) and some architectural and city-planning designs.

Retailing is done by government stores and by organizations a bit like cooperatives. After Stalin's death in 1953, policy shifted to give consumers more, but the promised easing of life for the consumer has been slow, partly because quality remains poor. Until recently, chronic shortages assured that everything offered for sale would find a buyer. But consumers have become reluctant to buy shoddy goods at high prices. In 1964 "surpluses" piled up to the point that price-cutting "discount" stores were established in a few cities.

Prices to consumers include a *high turnover (sales) tax*—hidden and designated "surplus product" to help conceal the burden of the cost of government. Accurate data on tax rates are not easily obtained, but the rates on all goods sold in state stores and cooperatives seem generally to range from 50 to 100 percent of price without tax—i.e., one third to one half of what the consumer pays is tax. Rates on some items.appear to be 900 percent or more. Even on such things as beef, butter, soap, and sugar the tax is twice or three times the amount paid for all expenses of production and distribution. The turnover tax is the chief source of government revenue. Rates on individual products can be altered to help balance quantities demanded and supplied, and, as more than once in recent years, the rate can be reduced to make life a little less difficult for the consumer.

By our standards, certainly, one of the great fundamental economic defects of the Soviet system is the failure to give people a reasonably good opportunity to use what they can produce in the way they want. Yet consumers are getting more, on the average. Plans announced for 1968 would allow growth of 8.6 percent for consumer goods compared with 7.9 percent for capital goods.

Agriculture.   Farming has been a weak link in Soviet growth because food production has increased at little more than a glacial pace. Nearly half of the total population live on farms. Their productivity is much below that in Western Europe or this country.

In the early 1930's, at the cost of great human suffering, huge farms were established. Most became collectives, nominally to be run by the peasants who had been forced to pool their land. Self-management soon became a fiction. Government officials directed operations. Members of the collectives shared the residual output remaining after the government had taken its portion.

Sweeping reorganization was begun in 1958, and experimentation with various methods has continued.[13] Compulsory deliveries were replaced by government purchase at prices set by government. Additional output can now be sold in the limited free market. Here is another example of deliberate Soviet effort to enlarge both incentive and freedom. The increase of opportunity for groups on the land to gain for themselves by producing more at lower cost came along with recognition of opportunity to introduce new technical methods.

Officials still believe in the efficiency of large-scale farming—giantism. Collectives are being merged into larger units. The relative importance of state farms is increasing. Khrushchev's "virgin-lands" campaign opened new areas in Siberia; they are run as state farms—and have not come close to the goals set. Moscow tries to prescribe programs without adequate allowance for differences of soil, climate, availability of machines, and the knowledge of the cultivator.

Partly, but only partly, because of bad weather, large imports of wheat have been required. To approach Western output per acre or per person,

---

[13] Among other changes the collectives purchased the tractors and machinery which had formerly been owned by Machine-Tractor Stations. These government agencies received payment in kind and exercised powerful influence over the farmers. The elimination of "two bosses on the land" was intended to make management more efficient. The farmer tends to devote what from the Kremlin's point of view is a disproportionate amount of effort on his allotment, where output per acre averages much above that on the collectives. The farmer can sell what he produces on his allotment. Such sales have accounted for no small percentage of some foods such as meat.

Russian agriculture needs huge amounts of capital: machinery, barns, livestock, roads, housing, spare parts, fertilizer, and so on. Plans for a big rise in capital allocation were cut back in 1967, but the level is above that of earlier Soviet years.

Foreign Trade and Banking.   Foreign trade is monopolized by government and conducted as part of the plan, to the extent that foreigners will buy and sell accordingly. A policy of building self-sufficiency within the Soviet bloc has been modified, partly because of desire for independence on the part of Romania and other satellites.

Imported machinery and other specialized equipment have played an important role in Russia's development. Recently, more goods have been available for export. Petroleum exports, for example, influence European markets substantially. Although, as noted in Chapter 36, Russia shows willingness to use economic power for political ends abroad, most foreign trade seems to be governed by economic considerations. In some cases, Russia grants favorable financing terms to encourage exports while also seeking loans to pay for its own imports.

The monetary unit, the ruble, is nominally tied to gold. The inflationary forces of war were offset by a drastic monetary reform—most of the old money was simply wiped out of existence. In 1960, however, to reduce and realign price quotations, Russia devalued the ruble for the third time since the war. In the reshuffle, as 11 old rubles were replaced by 1 new one, the "gold equivalent" of the new ruble was put above that of the dollar. The Russians do not permit a free market in foreign currencies.

The banking system serves as a central accounting agency. Each plant is credited with deposits for what it sells and debited for its withdrawals. The plant's bank accounts give a constant review of the firm's accomplishment. At any time, the bank ought to be able to report how any single economic unit conforms to the plan; in fact, the bank's accounting system does not provide the guidance information which might be expected. The bank will advance funds to a plant (or government agency) as called for by the plan.

Education and Research.   In the half century since the passing of Czarism, literacy and health standards have risen greatly. Efforts to improve education, especially in technical fields, find the Russians attempting new methods in the search for more effective results. Average levels of schooling are still low by Western standards, but the trend is upward. The best achievement is demonstrably excellent. Teaching seems to be attractive enough—partly because of the prestige of "intellectual" activity—to permit high selectivity. Professors rank high in the income scale.

Almost everyone gets at least 8 years in school. A select group then gets the rough equivalent of our high school instruction, mixed with some work on a job. Instruction emphasizes engineering and science, with heavy weight given to practical applications. On-the-job training is widespread. A small group gets a chance at the university. The competition here is severe, with children of the upper classes favored. A university degree is almost essential for rising out of the disdained "worker" class.

The bulk of scientific knowledge on which Russia has based its progress has been that of the West. Today, however, outlays for research are unquestionably large and results sometimes notable. Russians believe that their system permits better organization of research and eliminates wasteful duplication which is to be expected when, as in the West, hundreds of different and competing businesses and universities carry on research.

Growth of the Russian Economy.   The output and the productive capacity of the Russian economy grew rapidly after World War II. After allowing for special factors attributable to recovery from war, we must recognize that in some lines—but by no means all—growth was faster than when we were at comparable stages of development. Evaluation of *total* accomplishments is extremely difficult. In some lines, apparently, continuation of pre-World War I trends would have resulted in much higher output today. From 1950 to 1958 Soviet calculations showed growth of real national income at 10.9 percent a year; estimates by U.S. methods put the figure at 7 percent. For 1961 to 1966 the corresponding figures were 6.2 and 4.2 percent—respectable, certainly, but not outstanding.[14]

How should one allow for the things the Russians neglect: freedom, housing, or variety in consumer goods? How can one adjust for widely differing quality? What is the proper allowance for costs—the misery of farm collectivization in the 1930's, forced saving today?

The answers to such questions will depend in part upon the problems for which one seeks to study growth: military potential or the good life for the common man. One thing more than any other, of course, would speed economic growth for the masses of Russia: cooperation with this country and others in reducing the armaments race.

Russian Economy as a Rival.[15]   How does the Russian economy compare with ours in strength? Russia's population is about one seventh larger than ours—not a great disparity, especially since education and training in

[14] Abram Bergson, "A Hard Look at Russia's 'Creeping Capitalism,'" *Harvard Alumni Bulletin,* Oct. 28, 1967, p. 14. A more specialized treatment by the same economist is one of the essays in A. Balinky and others, *Planning and the Market in the USSR: The 1960's,* (New Brunswick: Rutgers University Press, 1967).

[15] Russia and the United States both have allies and other potential rivals. The economies of Western Europe, Canada, and others of our friends combine into a vastly greater total than those of Russia and her allies. As China has become more of a rival to Russia, the latter has lost some potential influence; ours, too, will suffer if China "forces" us to great expense in Asia or Africa.

Russia are, on the average, so much lower that productivity will be much below ours. Around 40 percent are non-Russian-speaking minorities. Heavy population losses and a drop in birth rates during World War II will for many years depress the size of the working force. Over the long run, however, improvements in agricultural techniques may release millions now tied to farms and thus add significantly to the industrial labor force.

The material means of production are substantially in our favor. Russia is generally well supplied with natural resources, but by no means bountifully compared with the non-Communist world. Her vast land area is mostly useless for agriculture with present techniques; eventually, of course, the mighty efforts to open new regions to food production will probably yield better results than to date. Yet almost all her area is north of Quebec. Nine tenths of her potential energy sources lie far removed from her labor supplies. Her great size and the dispersal of production require about twice as much transport per unit of product as in America; nevertheless, her railroads with about a third of our main-line mileage, have relatively little aid from trucks and pipelines.

Our industrial capacity is now much greater in absolute size, diversity, and flexibility. In important lines, however, Russia's growth must cause concern. Unquestionably, militarily oriented industry has enough power with modern techniques to work incredible destruction on the world.

As a way of life, the Russian system, though less repressive than under Stalin, repels us. As a basis for organizing the use of resources, it appears inefficient, at least by our ideas of what ought to be balanced as costs against gains. Yet it does produce powerful weapons controlled by dictators.

Communism as an ideology once appealed to some friends of the underdog, some men of good will who were dissatisfied with the poverty of the masses. Today, only an ignorant mind or a distorted soul could support the Soviet economic system on the grounds of what it does for the common man. On this score we, Western Europe, Canada, Japan, and other free economies can point to a vastly better record than can the Soviets. Yet the Russians still try to identify their system with "socialism" as a peace-loving, popularly controlled system in which the masses enjoy the fruits of their labors—and ours as one in which a few robber-baron capitalists ruthlessly exploit the masses, dominate government, and favor war for profit.

TERMS AND CONCEPTS

socialism	nationalization	surplus product
fascism	Gosplan	great value-price con-
surplus value	storming	troversy
means of production	materials balance	collectivization

QUESTIONS

1. What might be the "theoretical" benefits of central planning of an economy? The weaknesses?
2. Describe the planning process in Russia. Would problems be significantly different if consumers had more freedom? Why?
3. How do the Communists accumulate capital? Why do they tolerate substantial differences in individual earnings?
4. "Efficient planning is impossible without the guidance of a price system." Discuss.
5. How can planning errors in Russia lead to significant waste?
6. How does the Russian government raise revenue?
7. Discuss problems of plant management in a centrally directed economy.
8. "Central authorities who control investment control the economy." Comment.
9. "Russia's growth rates, though not the highest in the world, are a cause for concern to Americans." Discuss.
10. What features of capitalist economy have socialists hoped to change?
11. What aspects of Soviet economic policy encourage growth?
12. "British socialism succeeded in putting a floor below which income would not fall; it failed to improve productivity." Discuss.
13. What advantages and disadvantages would you expect from decentralization in an economy like Russia's?
14. Why do you suppose that relatively more new investment in Russia goes into industry and less into housing than in the United States, even though housing for the Russian masses has improved little in nearly half a century?
15. What would you estimate to be strengths and weaknesses of the Russian economy as a rival to the United States?
16. "An economy largely dependent on foreign trade cannot, then, plan the broad scope of its operations." Discuss.

APPENDIX
A Modern Economic Theory of Socialism

Is it possible to devise a "model" which might serve as a socialist's goal while meeting standards of economic efficiency? Until the 1930's, non-Marxist economists generally contended that a socialist economy could not function to provide both economic (and political) freedom and efficient utilization of resources. Newer theory, however, tries to show how a socialist economy might meet the tests of economic efficiency within a system having considerable freedom. The argument, in essence, is that socialism could do better than capitalism (free enterprise or private ownership) to achieve the economic and human values of laissez-faire or neoclassical economics. This highly refined theory is by no means the "socialism" of the man in the street, or of Stalin, Marx, Plato, British Labour Party leaders, or the reactionary.

General Outlines of Objectives and Conditions. 1. The economic objectives are (*a*) to give people as consumers and as producers the greatest possible freedom of choice (with some exceptions, such as forming businesses) and (*b*) to build the economic system to yield maximum net advantage to individuals as such. *Efficiency in the allocation of resources becomes a high goal.*

2. Productive equipment (nonhuman) would be owned by government. Private ownership would be limited to human productive capacities, consumer goods, possibly government bonds, and perhaps farms and small businesses.

3. The economy would be primarily *price-directed*, but *control* as well as ownership of major elements of the economy would be *highly centralized*. A planning agency would make directing decisions designed (*a*) to carry out the freely expressed wishes of the public as regards consumption and employment currently and (*b*) to determine the economy's growth.

4. The planning decisions and the factors affecting fundamental choices would be subject to popular criticism and control. Key political personnel and their decisions could be overruled by noneconomic processes (elections).

5. Consumption would be more equal than where nonhuman productive capacity as well as human energy and ability yields income to individuals. Yet, considerable inequality would remain—the amount and type that makes for productive efficiency.

6. Transition would be peaceful. Civil and political liberties would be preserved.

No such economy exists.

The problems remain those outlined in Chapter 1. There must be decisions about (1) what to produce, (2) how, (3) for whom. (4) Available supplies must be "rationed." Provision must be made for (5) economic progress and for (6) avoiding wastes of unemployment and inflation. A socialist economy faces these problems just as does capitalism. The fundamental principles of economizing are as generally applicable as the principles of medicine or engineering. The best adjustment to any given set of conditions has been reached when there is equality at the margins—then no change can bring improvement. The mathematically precise expressions of static economic equilibrium are independent of the type of system. The more difficult economic problems, however, are those associated with growth, not with static adjustment. For them, the form of the system *does* made a difference. Equally important are the relations of economics to politics, aesthetics, and human values.

Operating the System.   If you were a central planner in the model socialist economy, what would you do? Remember, your job is to *serve* the public—to help the people get what they want (including your job?) even though you think their choices are foolish. Public preferences fix the "what" to produce.

Equal distribution is not possible—not everyone can get a new auto and a new dishwasher this year, and only a few can live in new housing; nor is such equality desirable, if only because age and tastes differ. The billions of economic decisions made every day would be far beyond your scrutiny or that of any planning group that could act as a unit. Yet the cumulative effect of these myriad decisions would bear crucially upon the major policy decisions which make up the planning function. Your job is to help make the decisions of individual families more effective in getting what people want.

The major tool would be a *price system operating in free markets*. But why prices? Why not make everything free—steaks, fine houses, servants? The answers are easy—people want far more things than are produced. Some system of both *limiting* and *directing* consumption is essential. Some arrangement for getting things produced may also be helpful—the *incentive* problem. Payment for services can provide incentives.

Consumption would come from spending the income earned in production (plus welfare grants) minus taxes. The amounts paid as income would be costs of production to be recouped from sale of the product. At the outset, there would be a set of relative prices from the previous era. These would generally have balanced quantities demanded and supplied. Your best initial move would be to say, "Keep production running as it has. Try to maximize the difference between what you charge and your costs of production." And add, "You must compete. The best results of competing plants will guide us. No friendly agreements among managers."

Plant managers would pay only what is needed, after vigorously bargaining, to get labor and materials. They would sell at the highest price consumers would willingly pay. The efforts to maximize the difference between costs and prices make up the force for efficiency. If managers tried to sell for less or pay more for factors of production, then the balance of forces in the market (relative prices) would not indicate relative scarcity at the margin. The community would lose its tool for efficiency in allocating resources—"how" to produce.

"Trial and error" could lead to the equilibrium about as under capitalism. Everyone would watch prices and the signals they give for change. The guides would be the same as those of the traditional businessman—a rising demand for brown shoes, a slackening in demand for pork, a shift of taste from sedans to convertibles. Consumers would choose from the things available on the basis of tastes and relative prices. Prices should rise and fall, reflecting changes in demand and supply conditions. Rising or falling sales would show where prices and output should change. Wage rates would be adjusted to balance quantities supplied and demanded in each job, city, etc., to facilitate allocation according to (1) workers' desires and (2) what consumers will pay for the products.

So far you really have no job. The legal or military process of socialization, barring violence and protracted discussion with disturbing effects on investment, would not have made appreciable change in the physical system of production. The shift from private to government ownership would not have built more factories or houses, nor would it have made new inventions or unlocked secrets of science. The capacities of workers would not have increased much. Because productive capacity is still limited, it must be economized. The relative scarcities of productive capacity—factories, steel mills, apple orchards—will have been indicated (with exceptions like government property) by the prices before the "takeover." You are to see that this capacity is used to best advantage.

You tell plant managers that the costs which selling prices must cover will include the costs of capital equipment. How would these costs be figured if capital goods were owned by a single agency (government) and not traded in the market? At first, the values before the "takeover" would give a generally satisfactory guide. Thereafter, costs of production would determine. The charge must recover enough to replace the equipment as it wears out. A charge for capital is also needed to find out what types of capacity contribute most so that the use of old, and the guidance of new, investment can best serve the wishes of consumers. This control of investment is the real job and the real opportunity of the central planners. Profits and losses, taking account of all costs, show (1) where employment and output need to rise or fall and (2) which methods and products are best.

Investment.   At this point, the theory departs from the assumption of consumer sovereignty. It provides that the *amount* and the *rate* of new investment should be subject to central decision. In having given up private ownership of capital, society has abandoned (or freed itself from) the market mechanisms for adjusting consumption and investment. Families would have little reason to save or place to invest if they could not own property.[1] The financing of economic growth would need to rest on collective decision. Dictation of investment could facilitate general economic stabilization. If families are free to save or not, they are free to alter total buying and hence the level of employment.

The central authority, subject to basic economic limits and popular acceptance, must choose a rate of saving and investment for growth. The rate that is best is not clearly indicated by the principles which socialist econo-

---

[1] Private ownership of government bonds would modify this statement, but government control of investment would remain.

mists, or any others, have yet developed. Uncertainty and the need to rely upon judgment remain.

Once the total amounts have been fixed, what are the principles for *allocating* investment? Some plants would not be covering costs, while others would be yielding a generous return. Technical studies of the physical productivities of new methods would be possible about as under a system of private ownership. Conceivably, therefore, all possible investments could be listed in a scale. The most promising could be chosen within the limits of funds (resources) available. What about that symbol (to Marxists) of capitalist evil, an interest rate? It would be essential as an allocating device. Not all future benefits from investment would come on the same time schedule. An extra unit of output 15 years from now requires very different treatment in today's calculations from the same unit next year; the difference is what the unit under consideration could produce if invested for 14 years. The interest rate provides a measure or basis for discounting future units of output.

Forecasts of future investment results, of course, are much harder than finding what has been happening and what the physical returns may be. Assuming freedom of consumer choice and that technology will change, the risk involved can be nearly as large as under private direction. Future demands for finished products, the forces of competition, and costs of production all bear on today's investment decisions. These involve business issues. They apply to *specific* conditions (not to broad levels of national income). A *central planner* cannot expect to decide competently among the particular possibilities, each different from others—this resort hotel or that grain mill. He must rely heavily upon the judgment of the managers of the specific units involved, the person on the spot who alone can know some of the essential facts.

Management. The problem of management, a crucial one, involves more than guidance of investment. Most decisions would be made by salaried employees, as is often the case now—relatively routine problems a manager can deal with adequately in the light of given facts. Yet problems of judgment and responsibility—such as selecting subordinates, interpreting market developments, deciding on new methods—are strategic. They have great effect on what happens, both immediately for the specific unit and over the long run for the economy as a whole.

Private ownership has by no means found ideal methods of dealing with these problems, but socialism would abandon one important factor—when managers have their own wealth at stake, they benefit personally if they do well and suffer from mistakes. When owners do not themselves manage, they have a paramount reason to seek and reward good management. Moreover, the profit and loss system tends automatically to withdraw resources from the management that does poorly and to make them available to managements that succeed.

On the question of dynamic management, socialist blueprints are vague, tending to assume that the problems are routine. In fact, however, the critical decisions are anything but routine. Presumably, results would govern decisions about who is best. But how can results be determined and compared with what is reasonably possible? Do good financial results come from

monopoly prices to consumers, low wage rates, understatement of depreciation, a lucky swing of demand, or unusual efficiency? Perhaps taxes have
favored the plant. What if a manager has been overruled by the planning
agency and can blame bad results on its failure to allocate capital for some
improvement or on the pricing of capital equipment? What if he was refused
authorization for an "adequate" selling program or required to adjust inventory to meet an overall investment program rather than the needs of his plant?

The plans to get efficient resource utilization assume extensive competition. Choice of occupation would be as free as possible, and managers would
hire and pay on the basis of their estimate of the worth of the person for the
job. To get the best allocation of labor, competition should be free to direct
people and to determine their wage rates. In fact, however, large groups
(unions) would probably remain. Socialists may argue that the need for
unions ought to be smaller. If people are free, however, they will likely try to
combine and bargain collectively. The chances of gaining thereby are large
enough to be attractive. Moreover, if managers are judged by results, will
they not have incentives to "cooperate" for monopolistic reasons?

Differences in Income. Earnings would vary widely. With freedom of
choice, some people would work more hours a year than others. More
important, however, rates per hour would vary. Why? Consumers freely
value different kinds of productive services differently. The differences
would be needed to get the best balance among skills of varying worth, to
induce greatest economies in use of the scarcest types of labor, to induce
workers to move from work of less value to work of greater value, to pay for
differences in the costs of pursuing different occupations, and to provide
incentives for good performance. This inequality is far from the older
socialist goal of "from each according to his ability, to each according to his
needs." Yet it is essential for efficiency and progress as long as skills are not
equally plentiful at the margin.

Disposable income, however, would not be earnings; taxes would be imposed. Government, by its taxing and spending, might offset inequalities
more than today but would face the age-old problem of equality versus
incentive. Government would have whatever net income the capital and
natural resources earned. This yield might provide funds for new investment,
but it would not also, as socialists hoped before World War II, provide a
generous fund for subsidizing the poor.

What Benefits Are Claimed? The outline is so like that of a competitive
private enterprise economy that one asks, "Why would anyone advocate such
a system as contrasted with what we have?"

1. A major benefit claimed is that the private enterprise economy today
has so much monopoly that the benefits of competition are not, in fact,
obtained. Socialists hope that more centralization of direction can either (*a*)
force more competition or (*b*) by deliberate operation of big sectors as
monopolies get more efficient use.[2]

---

[2] In decreasing-cost industries, prices might be set at marginal cost, which is less
than total cost. Resources might then be used more fully than if prices must cover
total cost. Losses would be recouped from taxes.

2. Socialists place high value on the benefits to be expected from greater equalization of income. Progressive income taxes have not gone far enough to satisfy some observers, who feel (*a*) that property—gotten by inheritance, good business fortune, or luck such as owning land with oil—still provides unmerited income which in turn is too often spent on relatively unimportant consumption, and (*b*) that more equalization is an important way to reduce poverty.

3. A major "selling point" has been that socialism could reduce business cycle fluctuations and prevent great depressions. Socialists argue that central direction of investment could assure greater stability and, in fact, be more effective than the methods available to a private enterprise economy. Yet the problem is not simply one of investment but of the balance between savings and investment. If the public is free to use or not use its income, saving will be subject to fluctuation. If central direction remains in the hands of fallible humans, if the public is to have freedom in consumption, and if efficiency in investment is the criterion for judgment, how realistic a basis will there be for expecting great improvement?

4. If all major investment decisions were made centrally, they could be more nearly part of the same consistent scheme. Uncertainty as a cost might be reduced.

5. A free market fails to adjust adequately for some costs and benefits. Socialists believe that central direction and compulsion would raise real income by improving upon the results of certain free, uncoordinated, narrowly focused decisions. Typically, however, what is cited as a clear case is confused by the fact that (*a*) change would cost something, and we have no way of knowing how much gain on one score is worth how much sacrifice on another, or (*b*) we cannot really say when we should sacrifice freedom (for ourselves or others) for compulsion in altering decisions.

6. Incentives will improve, it is sometimes argued, when the boss is government. Workers will then be working for themselves. This argument does not rest on factual evidence of the productive superiority of government employees over those in private employment.

7. Less explicit claims are that better people could be put in positions of leadership and that centralization would provide more information for wise decision making. The appeal of the benevolent dictator has long tempted mankind. But how can society select and put in power central directors who are more competent, and men of better will, than those who make economic decisions today? The answer is not clear.

As an exercise in abstract economic analysis, this theory of socialism is more satisfactory than what used to be available. Yet it has more weaknesses than yet intimated. Just as the ideal of private enterprise must be modified when hard facts appear, so facts blur the vision of socialism.

Weaknesses of the Socialist Blueprint.   The following points apply mostly to comparisons of socialism with a mixed system such as ours, not the unreformed capitalism of a generation or a century ago. They might not apply to an economy without a substantial and fairly competent business community—for example, one with powerful remnants of feudalism.

1. Centralization creates familiar problems of bureaucracy—red tape, re-

moteness, slowness, inflexibility, expense, indifference along the line. The modern theory of socialism tries to meet this problem by assigning competition in markets the chief responsibility. While the mass of economic decisions would be left to the market, the vital investment decisions would be made at the higher levels. Since the choices are so important, the functioning of the economy would lean heavily upon bureaucracy.

2. When we need an operation, we turn to a surgeon, not a lawyer. *Competence* for the job is not a trivial matter. Are there things which politicians, civil servants, and the military are not most competent to handle (while, of course, doing other things very well)? Innovation, pioneering, and experimentation seem to be activities for which politicians and civil servants, and the organizations in which they must operate, are not clearly best qualified. On that major problem—how to find the best innovations and innovators—socialists have yet failed to indicate how their proposals would operate concretely to improve upon the present system, with all its imperfections. Certainly, the socialist blueprints fail to show how these dynamic phases of economic progress can, in fact, be done better by government officials under central authority than by businessmen with a great deal of freedom (including the chance to seek capital funds), incentive, and rivalry.

3. How can the planners be selected to assure competence and good will? Who would select them? The powers would be so great that the public would certainly need to keep some ultimate control through politics. Yet what if the voters select the wrong man, one who is incompetent, uninterested in some parts of the job, or evil? Positions controlling the planning would be "good jobs," among the society's greatest prizes, to be fought over—in political campaigns and inside the civil service. They might go to men with lack of scruples or with completely different qualifications—the "gift of gab."

Generous promises are not unknown in politics. The public might be duped. In a private enterprise system, of course, there are businessmen both stupid and detestable. But their power is only a fraction of that of the planners of a socialist state, and it is checked by bankruptcy and competition. Tremendous variety, constant change, great flexibility exist today. They give the public choice and lead to correction of error—not perfectly, of course, but extensively. Diffusion of economic power is an economic resource of tremendous value, one which centralization would sacrifice. A central planning agency could make errors that would be far more wasteful than those of any single private firm. It is hard to see great opportunities for better decisions than the private enterprise economy will reach, except the possibility of improvement in the integrating of major investment decisions to reduce wasteful inconsistencies. Without overwhelming assurance that the planners would be skillful and scrupulous of popular wishes, the risk of power centralization does not seem worth taking on purely economic grounds.

4. Centralization of economic power would endanger other freedoms, though tragic loss is not inevitable. Socialists may make the point, for example, that, in our system, poverty makes it impossible for many to establish newspapers or radio stations. But the socialist planners' control over investment could be equally restrictive and arbitrary. A variety of sources of economic power provides valuable insurance for the preservation and expansion of religious, political, civil, intellectual, and other freedoms. The substi-

tution of a single employer—government—for many, cuts a person's freedom to select and change his work. The monopoly of jobs (or investment) can threaten the critic with a loss of work or, more subtly, with a chance for promotion.

5. The greater mixing of politics and economics may well lead to poorer economic decisions. One possible way for groups to better their position is to induce government to give them more at someone else's expense rather than doing a more productive job in creating what others want. Groups build power when pressure by votes rather than by productivity, can bring results. The economic decisions that result are likely to be far from those of the competition which modern socialist economists recognize as generally necessary for the best allocation of resources. Would not selecting, rewarding, and disciplining managers be greatly influenced by political factors?

6. Large-scale central planning is bound to create inflexibilities. The inevitability of change requires constant adaptation. Detailed planning means that something unexpected happening one place will upset other parts of the plan. In a market-directed economy, adjustment takes place, more or less smoothly, freely, and as the persons close to the problem judge best. If you were working as part of a big plan, however, you would have to get some kind of permission and guidance for change—a time-consuming and probably a wasteful procedure. Planners, to keep the plan intact, may try to restrict freedoms of consumers and workers. The less that the individual is in a position to change his or her mind, the less the planners need fear that their plan with all its ramifications will be upset. The "good of the people" may take precedence over freedom.

7. Inflexibility can also obstruct innovation and technological progress. Planners might dislike the upsets which change requires, upsets which innovation will create. Established groups tend to prefer the status quo. It is possible, of course, that the planners would allocate bountifully for research and innovation.

8. International tensions would probably increase. Central planning would force governments to bargain over a large range of economic questions. The deals could not be separated nor always kept apart from the political, military, and other rivalries among governments. Questions of power, prestige, and honor would get involved in commercial dealings, reducing the chances of efficient economic bargaining. The normal job of diplomacy would be harder. Friendly relations could be disturbed by the deal on figs or watches when the bargains must be threshed out by ambassadors. The same transaction by businessmen would be taken as a matter of course.

9. One fact of economic life would hardly be altered by a change in the form of organization. Wants are partly for superiority; some of us want to be above our neighbors. Socialism could not put everyone ahead of everyone. If blue ribbons, dukedoms, generalships, or "Oscars" are given widely, much of their desirability disappears. The possibility of being ahead is, by its very nature, limited, and narrowly so. To the extent that these wants are important, the form of economic organization can make little overall difference.

38

ECONOMIC GROWTH IN THE UNITED STATES

[Growthmanship is a word] meant to describe an excessive preoccupation with economic growth, advocacy of unduly simple proposals for obtaining it, and the careful choice of statistics to prove that countries with a political and economic system you favor have made exceptionally good economic growth, and that the countries administered by your political opponents have made exceptionally poor economic growth.

Colin Clark

A discussion of economic growth in the United States, although drawing upon the underlying principles which apply to any economy, will differ in emphasis from that appropriate for underdeveloped lands.

PROBLEMS OF STUDYING ECONOMIC GROWTH

Definition. For present purposes let us think of economic growth as **a sustained rise in per capita real income.** A rise over a short period may be only cyclical, so we say *sustained.* We emphasize *real, not money,* income, partly because the dollar does change in value and partly because some of the things we prize are not exchanged for money. The choice of *per capita* income, less clearly justified, rests on the belief that concern is usually with the welfare of human beings as individuals or families.

Yet, we are sometimes interested in such national problems as military prowess. Then we might agree that there had been economic growth if national real income had risen even when, because of a population increase, per capita income had fallen. Many scholarly and public discussions of economic growth do in fact deal with national totals. In such cases, an increase in the labor force can produce what is considered to be economic growth.

Why the Concern about Economic Growth? Recent political campaigns and debates in Congress have said much about our economic growth (or our laggard rate of growth). Economists have been talking and writing and thinking about growth more than any other one topic. Why such interest?

No single reason accounts for the heavy emphasis. Yet one reason does embrace most of the group. Rising income—national as well as personal—helps in the solution of innumerable problems. The higher our rate of economic growth (assuming that "the price is right"), the easier we shall find the road toward other goals—reduction of poverty, 1.4 million more jobs a year for a growing labor force, the ability to finance adequate defense, and a higher living standard for all. Some economies have grown more rapidly than ours in recent years. Why?

The individual and the business firm will try in many ways to raise their incomes. As citizens, however, we influence the economy by what we have government do. Since government's role in the economy will inevitably be large, we need to know about forces which aid, and those which impede, growth. Only if we have such understanding can public policy on widely diverse matters take efficient account of the needs for long-run expansion.

In the two centuries or so before economists got to talking so much about economic growth, our economy obviously grew. The process shows no signs of ending. But that is not the point. Like so many other things, growth may be "more or less" and "better or worse."

For example, increase in total output since 1880 has been about 3 percent a year (measures vary). If this rate continues, gross national product per person will be about $500 greater in 1974 than 1964. But if the growth rate is 4 percent a year, GNP per capita would increase by more than $800. The difference is impressive. And if we project for a generation rather than for a decade, the difference between one rate of growth and another becomes still more striking.

Some of the recent concern of economists with growth arises from a belief that we can improve our performance. If Americans raise the annual rate by 1 percentage point (from 3 to 4 percent in total output), the cumulative effect over a lifetime will be tremendous. Some conditions will yield better growth results than others. But economists are perhaps more cautious than some years ago in believing that significant acceleration of our growth rate can be expected from policies not unduly difficult to put into effect.

Economic Growth a Complex Process. Thinking about economic growth is unsettled. We rely heavily on history, a complex web indeed. No simple analysis can account for the intricate past. Perhaps Americans did about as well as possible in opening the frontier and building the country's industry. Perhaps not. The result, of course, was produced by scores of different forces, some more important than others. The fact that a fine job was accomplished still leaves the question "How, if at all, could our fathers have done better?" Ample room exists for argument, from honest debate to partisan persuasion. Often there is no way to settle a dispute and thus get guidance for the future. Moreover, something that worked or failed in the past might turn out differently now.

TABLE 38–1.   Allocation of Growth Rate of Real National Income per Person Employed among the Sources of Growth

	Percentage Points in Growth Rate		
	1909–29	1929–57	1960–80
Total	1.22	1.60	1.62
Increase in total inputs	.66	.67	.48
Labor input, adjusted for quality	.42	.57	.37
Hours	.00	−.20	−.35
Effect of shorter hours on quality	.23	.33	.07
Education	.35	.67	.64
Increased experience and better use of women	.06	.11	.09
Land	−.11	−.05	−.04
Capital input	.35	.15	.15
Nonfarm residential structures	.07	.01	n.a.
Other structures and equipment	.17	.10	n.a.
Inventories	.08	.03	n.a.
U.S.-owned assets abroad	.02	.01	n.a.
Increase in output per unit of input	.56	.93	1.14
Restrictions against optimum use of resources	n.a.	−.07	.00
Reduced waste in agriculture	n.a.	.02	.02
Industry shift from agriculture	n.a.	.05	.01
Advance in Knowledge	n.a.	.58	.75
Change in lag in application of knowledge	n.a.	.01	.03
Economies of scale—independent growth of local markets	n.a.	.07	.05
Economies of scale—growth of national market	.28	.27	.28

n.a. = Not available.
Source: E. F. Denison, *The Source of Economic Growth in the United States . . .* (New York: Committee for Economic Development, 1962). See also by the same author *Why Growth Rates Differ, Postwar Experience in Nine Western Countries* (Washington, D.C.: The Brookings Institution, 1967).

Comparisons challenge. They also reflect a complex tangling of forces. Germany and Japan forged ahead more rapidly than France and Britain from the 1890's to 1914. What accounted for the differences? How does one explain differences between the growth in Japan and China or Spain and Belgium before 1914? Or between West Germany (high) and Denmark (low) since 1948? Conditions vary widely. What works well in Illinois today might be either excellent or terrible if applied in Maine or India.

Table 38–1 shows one economist's estimates of the factors accounting for the growth of real national income per employed worker from 1909 to 1957. Although marked changes are unlikely, the relative roles may differ in the future, as suggested by the last column in the table.

Costs and Content of Economic Growth. Growth has costs. To get an $x + 1$ percent rate of growth each year, people must sacrifice more than is needed for an x percent rate—quite a bit more. We may hope for something magic, or at least easy, something that will give lots of the "goodies" of growth for only trivial sacrifice. Some excellent "payoffs," developments which bring enormous yields for the sacrifices they require, are probable. To date, however, there is no basis for believing that such cases will become much more common. The search is on for ways to reduce the costs of growth, but no magic is in sight. And there is a danger: the tendency of advocates of this or that growth policy to underestimate the costs.

Another point. Some costs are never measured—today, the hours wasted because of congestion of city life; yesterday, the inability of pioneers to get doctors and the human suffering that would have been reduced if more of current production had gone to consumption and less to capital investment. Looking at what can be measured in the input-output accounts, we cannot see all costs (nor all benefits). Therefore, choices for the future must allow as well as possible for costs we cannot measure, including any which lie outside the bounds of economics.

Society consists of all sorts of people. Their preferences differ. What is a heavy cost to one may be unimportant to another. For example, an 80-year-old person with little income might consider unbearably heavy the sacrifices of saving for the next generation, while a young person would welcome the opportunity to reduce consumption now to have more 30 years later. If the old man is forced to save to finance growth, its human cost will be high indeed.

In speaking of either income or output, we mean *net* after the deduction of costs. In practice, however, can the figures allow adequately for costs? No. Man-hours and woman-hours of work today, for example, are free from some of the heavy drudgery of the past (indicating lower real cost). Getting to and from the job, on the other hand, may involve more strain (higher real cost). The majority of us probably find a dollar of saving less of a sacrifice than did the average man of a generation ago, a fall in cost that is impossible to measure. And how should we account for the using up of natural resources?

The output measure, real income (even when valued as accurately as possible and making some allowance for leisure) is also unsatisfactory. It does not cover everything men want. The most difficult problems appear in choices between values which we do not measure in monetary terms. Freedom, or freedoms, come first to mind. Most of us, certainly, think that freedom to choose what we want to consume is an important part of the good life. Yet business might be able to produce some things more cheaply if our range of choices were much narrower—if we demanded only one type of auto or style of dress. Restriction of freedom to vary the signaling systems of commercial airplanes is perhaps all to the good, because standardization brings economies without loss of significant liberty. But limitation on freedom to choose our doctors or diet—or, more fundamental, to have children—might seem a form of retrogression.

We want to be free to choose our work and the use of our property. Of course, we cannot have unlimited freedom, but we want more rather than less, even at the possible cost of some material output. If a dictator forced us to work 10 percent more, per capita output per year would probably increase. Growth at such a cost is hardly what we want. Compulsion on the use of property, however, strikes us as less obnoxious; special taxes on our property, zoning, eminent domain, and directors' decisions to reinvest profits are accepted as a matter of course. Still, we treasure the liberty to save or consume and to invest as we wish—and also the freedom not to progress. The person without ambition is not to be forced to do more than meet basic responsibilities. In using this freedom, however, he must give up claim to the fruits of progress.

A host of other freedoms—political, social, and religious—are important. Similarly, there are other values of life that do not get into our indexes of real income: security, justice, beauty, and humor, for example. Contrast the green valleys destroyed by strip mining and the beautiful resort areas developed around the "lakes" created by hydroelectric dams. The good life can be aided by rising economic productivity, but desirable values may also be sacrificed as we burn out our energies struggling to boost money income. One aspect of true economic *progress* is an increase in man's ability to make economic decisions serve a broadening area of life—and serve creatively.

A Target Rate of Growth?   Goals are sometimes helpful. When a goal has been accepted, its existence may be both stimulant and guide. Would Americans be wise, as some of our leaders suggest, to set an "economic growth" goal—so many percentage points a year in GNP or some other measure? Not now, certainly. Economists know too little about the past record, the causal forces, the retarding factors. We know too little about the existing potentialities. And no one knows, really, about the costs of different rates or kinds of growth. Consequently, the basis for informed public consensus does not yet exist. The public policies to achieve one growth rate or another cannot be laid out with the clarity that is necessary for wise public decision. In rejecting the notion of a target rate, we by no means reject the goal of faster growth or the deliberate effort to frame public policy to encourage growth.

The question "What will make an economy grow?" tempts one to dream of Utopias. The glamor and exciting challenge of magnificent dreams have their proper place. Yet journeys start with single steps. We shall try to take a few steps, focusing on five *strategic* factors: (1) expansion of knowledge, (2) fuller utilization of human capacity, (3) bettering of markets, (4) accumulation of capital, and (5) entrepreneurship. Stable money, the avoidance of wide economic fluctuations, and maintaining a high general level of employment are omitted because they have been discussed earlier.

EXPANSION OF KNOWLEDGE: INVENTION

More than six tenths of the increase in output per unit of input as estimated in Table 38–1 was attributed to the advance of knowledge. On this score the future seems highly promising. Productivity increases in part because research, invention, technological improvement in the broadest sense, enable us to use better methods to get more output per unit of input. In some cases, the benefits per dollar of cost are fabulous. One study estimates that we get $7 every year for each $1 spent in the past to develop hybrid corn. For the economy as a whole we have estimates of annual rates of return of 100 to 200 percent on amounts spent on research and development, allowing for failures as well as successes.

Expanding Volume of Research. The outlook is rosy. The beautiful glow comes from two sources: (1) The amount of research is large and growing. The expenditure in this country for expanding man's knowledge will reach nearly $22 billion in 1968, around three times that of a decade ago.[1] (2) Much research is done by businesses whose objective is to *use* it. They want to take advantage of new discoveries. Moreover, business, alert to the profits from invention, has incentive to try to use the successes of the independent researcher. Hence the waste of knowledge and discovery lying unused will be reduced. Figure 38–1 shows the rapid rise of spending. The absence of comparable growth in patent applications results in part from the rising dollar cost of research, in part from the fact that much research now goes for purposes, such as improving health, which do not lead to results which can or should be patented.

No human can know the optimum amount of a society's resources to use for the advancement of knowledge. The unknown, the region beyond the present frontier of knowledge, is just that—unknown. For the same reason, no one can know how best to allocate the resources an economy does devote to research—relative amounts for psychology, chemistry, economics, pedagogy, botany. Is it best that half of all outlays on research are concentrated in four or five industries—chemicals, electrical equipment, communications, and aircraft (space and missiles)?

---

[1] Half the total research outlays appear to be for military, space, and atomic energy projects. Government pays for nearly two thirds of all research, industry for almost one third, and universities for under 2 percent; industry, however, performs around 70 percent of the work and universities 10 percent.

FIGURE 38–1.   Patent Applications and Outlays for Research and Development

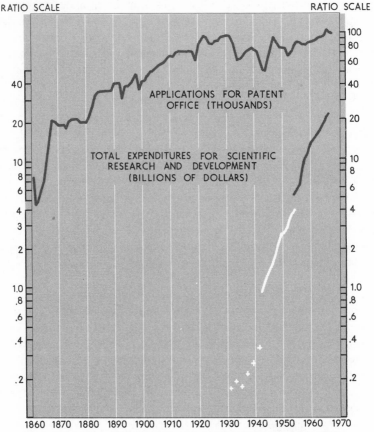

RATIO SCALE   RATIO SCALE

APPLICATIONS FOR PATENT OFFICE (THOUSANDS)

TOTAL EXPENDITURES FOR SCIENTIFIC RESEARCH AND DEVELOPMENT (BILLIONS OF DOLLARS)

1860 1870 1880 1890 1900 1910 1920 1930 1940 1950 1960 1970

+ Rough estimates not necessarily comparable with data for later years.
Source: U.S. Department of Commerce, *Long Term Economic Growth, 1860–1965;*
Statistical Abstract.

The complex interrelations of a modern economy lead us to emphasize the value of balance, of moving on a front broad enough to include all realms of knowledge.[2] For example, many economists, including those in businesses, believe that government at all levels has acted unwisely in failing to collect some basic statistics. Government (after 1945), while providing billions for research in physics, chemistry, and other natural sciences, refused for 6 years the $10 million needed for a Census of Manufactures to get primary data on the structure of our economy. Postwar recessions have found us lacking in facts about inventories, con-

---

[2] Research on polio vaccine, for example, would have been of slight value unless there had also been research on how to make the intricate equipment needed for production.

struction, costs, prices, job openings, and other economic magnitudes needed to guide public action.

Allocation of more resources to the advance of knowledge seems certain to bring rich fruits. To do so effectively, however, the demand for talent must compete with other demands, beginning at the very start of the educational process. The attractions must be adequate—total attractions: money, security, prestige, freedom, challenge, the opportunity to serve mankind, whatever it is that will get skilled people and their best efforts. Achievements will depend upon the adequacy (1) of training opportunities from early childhood through postdoctoral specialization and then (2) of assistants, laboratories, libraries, and other aids (including service in the home). Though "adequacy" is hard to define, it is harder to achieve. Funds and other conditions needed by investigators of promise are by no means assured, especially in government and universities.

Guidance of Inquiry. The decisions about how much to spend on research, and on what, are made by mortals. How can we get wise choices? The best answer is almost a tautology: have competent people decide. The decision makers may be businessmen, university officials, directors of private foundations, private individuals, or civilian and military officials of government. Pure luck will play a part, but the degree of competence also makes a big difference. More rapid success requires not only more well-trained young Ph.D.'s but also top men of long, proved experience built on first-rate academic training. Judging the judges by their accomplishment is a slow business when a single chemical development takes 10 years from "test tube to tank car." And we can never know "what might have been." In industrial research, however, success, by yielding profit, will tend to make other efforts possible. An initial failure or two, however, can kill a research life that might eventually make a great contribution.

Business Awareness of the Profitability of Research and Development (R.&D.). The strong human motive for gain can be enlisted in the struggle for intellectual progress (defined most broadly). The prospect of profit and the fear of loss impel business to search for ways to reduce costs and to appeal more effectively to the public. Competition helps—not necessarily the competition of thousands of small firms; the rivalry of giants may do.

Competition does more than intensify incentives. It diffuses economic power. More than one person or group will be able to make decisions and to finance them. The danger that the use of new and better methods will be prevented, either by chance or by deliberate scheming, is reduced if there are several potential users rather than one only. An undue proportion of talent may go for types of business and military research having fairly narrow, short-run focus; capacity is diverted not only from training younger men but also from more basic exploration. Only a few businesses promote fundamental, basic investigation—the kind which yields greatest benefit to civilization but which is rarely patentable. The economist can do little more than warn, "Maximizing profit today may not lead to greatest long-run profit. Heed the leaders who take a long view!" Colleges and universities, whose role in training and in research is central, find business both a rival and a partner—draining off talent and providing aid. When the aid goes for specific projects which corporations want, rather than for what university staffs would freely choose as most promising, results can hardly be best. Business also participates in research in social, political, economic, and humane problems; individual firms, trade associations, and special groups sponsor studies sometimes intended to be of public service in the best sense.

Using Our Discoveries.   Many an idea that would have helped the world has been wasted because no one knew about it or was able and willing to use it.[3] Perhaps there was not enough faith in the prospect of success, or perhaps the resources needed for development were not available. Someone who would have been hurt—a business fearing obsolescence of existing facilities—may have had power to obstruct. In choosing from among the possibilities, we are like a child with a dime in a candy store. The quality of judgment of the decision makers about the use of knowledge will have much to do with the results of research—how to make a better suit of clothes, close tax loopholes, or fly faster.

The amount that the work of scientists contributes to economic growth, then, depends partly upon the quality of entrepreneurship. The innovator may be a businessman, a government official, or a farmer. For good decisions he needs good answers to the question "Which policy will provide the most of what the public wants for the least cost?" Business considerations are involved widely but not exclusively. For example, on such matters as applying discoveries of better ways to teach reading, conduct diplomacy, or swim, economic guides are less adequate than for deciding which new factory process to install.

The firm that finances research usually has some concrete purposes in mind and will try to make capital available.[4] The long and wasteful

---

[3] The researcher's work may be partly lost because of his inability to explain clearly what he has done and its significance; good command of his language is an essential part of the professional equipment of the scientist in every field. Communication in the broad sense has been aided by a variety of improvements in indexing, digesting, and library facilities generally, and in the training of librarians.

[4] Yet the president of the country's second largest chemical company is reported as saying that his firm develops so many more good possibilities than it can finance that it selects only those where the reasons are overpowering. Research may be costly—laboratory facilities often costing $30,000 per scientist and operating expenses double or triple the salary—but the capital requirements for successful production will likely be many times the full costs of discovery. Broad research programs will turn up numerous promising possibilities which will not fit into the company's own opera-

process of getting scientist and businessman together tends to be cut but not always and not perfectly. College graduates entering industrial research may be amazed at the apparent inertia (added to red tape) in business. Compared with the cellar inventor, however, the scientist in an industrial laboratory probably has a better chance that his accomplishment will be used. "But, won't business try to keep the work of the laboratories secret?" Fortunately, the public has some protection. Our patent system requires extensive disclosure. Moreover, a scientific ethic, plus the scientist's concern for his own prestige and gain, press him to publish his results in scholarly journals. The news spreads.

Successful use of a new discovery depends, of course, upon the "state of the art." Some ideas cannot be used until many other discoveries have been made. Moreover, the capital equipment and the level of education of the working force bear decisively upon the gain that may come from discovery of knowledge. Progress tends to be cumulative.

Incentives and attitudes make a big difference. Do consumers want change? Will businessmen risk resources to make change possible? The economic forces of competition, including advertising, seem to assure that in our society the answers will be "Yes," especially if good profits and general prosperity enable American business and consumers to afford change. Success breeds success, and in ways more subtle than we may realize, our familiarity with change seems to make us receptive to more.[5]

Looking beyond the business world at problems of general economic, political, and social policy, however, we can be less certain that Americans will take reasonably full advantage of gains in knowledge. Somehow, rationality often seems to face greater obstacles in proving itself in nontechnical than in technical areas, partly because "proof" is seldom clear beyond dispute. (How impossible it seems to modernize a building code, civil service promotion system, or tax law!) Growth requires much basic stability in society but not *rigor mortis*. Opposition to change in institutions is both a source of strength and a drag. The closed mind is a massive but needless impediment. And mankind has a distressingly large number of minds closed on one or another issue.

Public Policies. What can the public, as such, do deliberately to expand knowledge and its use and thus push itself along the road of progress? Through government, we can certainly do things that help and others that hinder. Outright grants for research and the fostering of education come to mind at once. American governments might do more to finance inquiry, especially kinds of investigation which business and other agencies do not pursue on a reasonably adequate scale. More and

---

tions. The job then is to find users. Some firms now have whole departments engaged in the sale and licensing of the fruits of the research efforts.

[5] The employment effects of new methods—automation—are discussed in the next chapter.

more federal money is going into basic research. A possibility arises from the fact that the growth of productivity in services seems to lag behind that in fabrication. Perhaps government funds can be especially fruitful in aiding research directed toward services, as is now the case in the field of medical care. Each state and each locality has its own problems which require study.

Only a bit less obvious is the possibility of deliberately designing taxes with the needs of economic growth in view. Tax laws, for example, can encourage businesses to spend for research and to scrap old equipment to introduce new. Tax laws can dull or stimulate incentive to any kind of action. Government also has a role to play in preventing businesses, unions, and other groups from restricting the introduction of new and better things.

Profiting from Research in Other Countries. No economy is dependent solely upon its own research efforts, for investigation goes on the world over. Military considerations keep some findings secret, but many more become generally known. Russian scientific journals reach U.S. libraries. The speed of our own progress will depend partly upon our skill in using scientific accomplishments abroad.

FULLER UTILIZATION OF HUMAN CAPACITIES

With any *given* set of techniques, stock of capital equipment, and natural resources, a human population can vary its production significantly. Ask yourself, "What could I really do if I put in my very best efforts?" Though humans are sometimes abominable forecasters of even their own capacities, variation is possible in the accomplishments of most individuals.

Popular magazines continually point out many ways in which Americans could increase their productivity. Compared with the great problems of national policy, most of these opportunities may seem small. Yet they can add to an impressive total. Here again, progress can be cumulative. The more man accomplishes, the easier it is to achive more. When for several years there has been clearly more unemployment than is necessary, when the size of the labor force in general has not set limits to growth, it may seem a bit foolish to talk about anything but the achievement and maintenance of full employment. Our concern, however, is with longer run problems.

Health. Better *health* is a goal we prize for itself. In addition, as health improves, our productivity rises. A community, by raising health levels, can expand the average working life of its members, reducing time lost for sickness, postponing retirement, and improving work on the job.[6] Some

---

[6] Many advances in public health methods—vaccination and pasteurization are examples—have had to overcome public apathy and even active hostility.

things are relatively cheap—pasteurizing milk; others cost more—providing adequate diets. The provision of really enough medical personnel and hospital facilities for a growing population will be expensive; yet, in purely dollar terms, it can be highly rewarding.

Reduction of accidents, on and off the job, could increase average working lives, as well as reduce the resources absorbed in treatment.[7] Victory over the common cold would lead to a stupendous addition to man's productive capacity. Alcoholism and its bigheaded brother, the hangover, cut the effective lives of too many Americans. Mental health offers untold opportunities for improvement. Sympathetic understanding among close associates—parents-children, husband-wife, employer-employee, teacher-student—is a simple but powerful aid to better accomplishment.

Immobility and Discrimination. Part of the rise in average man-hour productivity has come from the transfer of workers from jobs of low productivity to jobs of higher productivity, from submarginal farms to modern factories. Perhaps the future will not offer such opportunities on as large a scale as the past, but it may. In any case, there will be extensive possibilities of improving income by changing jobs. The more easily that the changes can be made, the more easily the worker's income, and that of the economy, can grow. Things impeding the mobility of human resources slow growth. Discrimination, too, has deprived many Americans—the whole economy, in fact—of no small amount of real income.

Opportunities for the Disabled. Many people with physical and mental disabilities could work and produce something—and be better for it—if given opportunities. Peak demand for labor during the war led to successful employment of hundreds of thousands of formerly "submarginal" people. More recent efforts, some philanthropic, have disclosed both problems and possibilities of constructive employment of the partially disabled; on balance, the opportunities are large. Time and again rehabilitation has shown magnificent results in enhancing not only the quality of life but also the ability to produce for others.

Time on the Job. The length of the work year is a major consideration. How much *potential* increase in income shall we take in leisure and how much in other things? If we wish to increase output of goods and

---

[7] Let us illustrate what is possible. Long ago when Du Pont was primarily a maker of explosives, it began to emphasize safety on the job. Careful planning of methods, worker training, and special investment succeeded in reducing the rate of accidents involving loss of time to about 0.40 per million man-hours worked in 1956, a level which has been maintained since then. This is less than 1 percent of Du Pont's rate for 1912, the first year such safety records were kept. The rate in the chemical industry as a whole has been almost 9 times as high, that in all industry 15 times as great.

services, one obvious way is to work more—or at least not less. In most jobs the workweek which will give the greatest output is probably over, rather than under, the 35 to 40 hours that are now standard. When the workweek was 72 hours, the pressures to cut it were powerful. Today the human drives for reduction are less compelling than in the past. Is not leisure, like other items of consumption, subject to the principle of diminishing utility? We may choose, rationally and freely, to take more of a potential increase in well-being in the form of greater material output, less in leisure. If so, compared with the past, we can expect even larger gains in goods and services from the forces producing economic progress. But should not our policy be "each to his own taste"?

The length of the working life becomes an issue of growing importance. Compared with the past, Americans spend more years in youth getting ready to work; those who live retire earlier than their grandfathers. A big problem ahead is the age of retirement. The more years that people work, the more they produce. If laws, the shift from the farm, pension provisions, company rules, personal preference, and fashion cut our working lives, they reduce not only the individual's lifetime earnings, and hence his ability to finance comfortable retirement, but also the nation's production of goods and services (except leisure).[8] The greater the number of people who do not work, the lower is per capita real income, unless the value of their leisure is as great to them as what they would have produced would have been. Improvements in health are increasing the physical ability of older persons so that more are able to work in later life. The potential for economic growth on this score is rising. Our institutions, however, work in the other direction: toward compulsory retirement before people would choose freely to retire. The more we are prohibited from working, the lower the national real product and our own income.

Output would increase if all of us had greater opportunity to work (especially on our major job, not in "moonlighting") week-in, week-out. How many people would utilize such opportunity? No small number. The problem is one of economic and social organization. The obstacles are large, not insuperable. Some lie in the techniques of factory, store, and office routine. Fortunately, reduction in the sheer drudgery of work and improvement in working conditions create offsets. A few obstacles lie, perhaps, in our system of taxation. One man-made obstacle which discourages employers from offering such opportunities is the legal requirement for higher rates of pay for overtime. Occasionally, union restrictions create impediments to more work. Ignorance of work opportunities and

[8] For many older persons, comfort (often survival) requires considerable personal service. Increasingly, however, the cost of personal services rises, most notably services which, like nursing, require special training. The expense of even partial incapacity will be much higher than most retirement incomes will finance.

the inadequate development of labor market mechanisms are perhaps as important as any other factors.[9]

Morale. *Morale* certainly influences productivity. When we are enthusiastic, happy, and convinced of the worth of what we are doing, our accomplishment is greater than when we are discontented and frustrated. Not everyone will be at his best all the time. Man's knowledge of what causes morale to be high or low, though still inadequate, can often help appreciably to improve performance. Perhaps we can find keys to inexpensive but vastly productive ways of bettering human attitudes; the challenge to business, education, and labor is tremendous.

Education. The increasing store of knowledge must be acquired anew by each generation. What our libraries accumulate gets into our minds only if we make the effort. Demands for the more highly developed human skills will rise, probably to levels we now find difficult to conceive. See Figure 38-2. For truly high productivity an economy must have enormous quantities of advanced skills. How well are we meeting this challenge?

We progress, but all too slowly—at least many of us believe that more dollars spent on education would bring good returns in the next generation. The rapid growth of population forces so much effort on the quantity problem that quality improvement gets fewer resources than desirable. The "lead time" is long, and today the quality of future scientists, statesmen, engineers, and artists is being formed in elementary schools often crowded and poorly run. Teaching staffs will need substantial de-

FIGURE 38-2. Growing Demand for Skills (Estimated Percentage Change in Jobs, 1960-75)

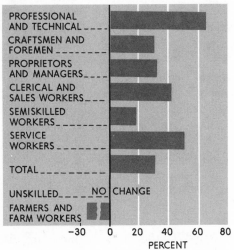

Source: Manpower Report of the President, 1964.

[9] Many young married women, eager to get money ahead to help furnish a house or finance a baby, would like to work, perhaps half time. Keeping house is more than a task for hours after work; before the first child comes, however, it may be far from a full-time job. Opportunities for part-time work exist today, of course, but probably more people of all ages and qualifications would gladly work if they could find part-time opportunities.

velopment, but as local school boards and state university officials know all too well, financial limits make the prospects discouraging.

Not only more money but also more of society's *most competent people* must go into teaching if the world is to get even moderately full advantage of the advances in knowledge which have already been made and which we expect to continue. And an ever bigger percentage of the public must study more. Perhaps the learning process can be accelerated. There *must* be ways to raise the productivity of schools and colleges. But the knowledge to be mastered grows rapidly and in all directions. How can society provide the facilities and the incentives for the long specialized training required? How can we combine the advantages of specialization in various fields of learning? For the integration of different kinds of learning is essential to make efficient use—perhaps any use at all—of the advances along many lines. Try to envision the types of training that can contribute to the success of a diplomat, judge, bank president, or head of an industrial research department.

A detailed analysis of the best, but far from satisfactory, data available concludes that the extra earnings yield a rate of return of around 13 percent a year from investment in college education. (This estimate does not include benefits to the general economy which are not part of the earnings of the college graduate.) But the payoff period is long; i.e., only 15 years after graduation does the yield reach 6 percent. ". . . the long payoff period increases the advantage of an education that is useful in many kinds of future environment. If 'liberal' education were identified with such flexible education, as well it may be, there would be an important economic argument for liberal education, as well as arguments based on intellectual and cultural considerations."[10]

Fortunately, our population contains considerable numbers with native ability to develop much higher skills than they do today. Perhaps we have not even begun to approach the limits of the potential development of capacities. Certainly, shortage of opportunity and poverty give only part of the explanation. Lack of *motivation*, explained partially by social and cultural factors, is also important. What conditions, what incentives would be needed to get larger numbers to take fuller advantage of opportunities—not only by attending institutions or training courses but also by making a serious effort to do as well as possible? Many a teacher yearns to know why so few students work with the industry of the best.

The development of some important skills can be improved and hastened by many methods of training on and off the job. Businesses are broadening the scope and expanding the effectiveness of on-the-job education. Companies accounting for more than half of all nonfarm private employment operate training programs. Since the results are profitable

---

[10] G. S. Becker, *Human Capital.* . . . (New York: Columbia University Press for National Bureau of Economic Research, 1964), pp. 122–23.

to those who pay the bill, this part of our educational system can be counted upon to contribute increasingly to human productive ability.

IMPROVING MARKETS

About one third of the increase in productivity (output in relation to input) was attributed in Table 38-1 to "economies of scale," local and national. Much of this progress results from what we call "improving markets"—more accurately, improving the entire *allocation mechanism*, including business, government, and private associations. Some betterment takes the form of enlarging the *size* of markets; some consists of enhancing the *efficiency with which markets function*. As markets broaden, the diverse factors producing external economies develop more easily. Specialization advances faster and farther. Alternatives can be appraised more accurately and choices made more intelligently. It is easier to adjust well to any given set of conditions, to move from the worse to the better. The reduction of waste aids growth.

Perhaps more important, however, *improving the quality of markets will facilitate the change needed for long-run growth.* If one thing is clear, it is that growth requires change, and uneven change. Output of air conditioners in 1963 was 26 times 1948 output, while purchases of outboard motors were below the 1948 level; output of women's suits fell 2.7 percent a year from 1948 to 1963, while the production of clothes driers rose over 20 percent a year. One Sunday in January 1968, when around 3 million Americans were unemployed, the *New York Times* had 81 pages of "help wanted" ads, several offering jobs at salaries of $50,000 or more.

Some growth is more of the same—more beef in the diet. Some growth, however, involves change in the structure of the economy— fewer farmers, more skilled factory workers, and still more people, proportionately, in service activities. Sensitive, efficient, extensive markets help make the changes easier. Flexibility and mobility aid both the painful and the pleasant adjustments that are part of the shifting of an expanding economy.

What, then, will enlarge markets and improve the way they function? Near the top of any list would be *better communication*, wider availability of knowledge. If we can tell each other what we have to offer and what we want, our chances of cooperating to better advantage are increased. The more people with whom we can exchange information, the better our chances of finding the best opportunities and hence of serving each other. Between buyer and seller, easier, cheaper, and fuller exchange of information, *accurate information*, will make markets function better. Advertising, grading, labeling, employment exchanges—the functioning of middlemen and traders—all serve, but not always as well as they might.

There is, unquestionably, sound basis for hope in an increase in the technical facilities for communication by lower costs that make facilities more readily available. The physical instruments of communication—

newspapers, telephone, radio, television—have improved to give us greater accuracy, speed, and scope. Electronic processing of masses of data brings to decision makers a wealth of usefully organized facts never before available.

The assembly, interpretation, and dissemination of facts are on a vast scale. Yet we are still far from a system in which all important, relevant facts become promptly available to those who, as producers or consumers, could benefit from knowing them. (Can we somehow improve our efficiency as buyers of consumer goods? Here there *must* be room for helping raise real income.) Communication is often poor in a market of the greatest importance—that for labor. Public and private employment exchanges, though better than in the past, are far from what we need. In fact, one of America's greatest wastes is probably the waste of human capacity that results because many of us learn so little about job opportunities and thus fail to make the best decisions reasonably possible. Only a minority of employers and employees yet have access to the guidance of personnel and placement experts.

Improvements in *transportation* make markets better. The cheaper we can move ourselves and things, the larger the area in which we can deal, the greater the specialization possible, the less the danger of monopoly. But this point has been made too often to need reemphasis. Except, perhaps, to note that, in an increasingly urban economy, traffic congestion becomes an ever-larger drag on both business and the enjoyment of life. Too many of the potential gains from working and living in cities are victims of our unwillingness to make the sacrifices, some of which would be difficult, needed to build more productive urban areas. Tariffs and other such impediments, of course, destroy benefits of trade, as would a rise in transport costs.

Competition is a powerful driving force for economic progress. Where competition is vigorous, individual gain depends overwhelmingly upon service to others. A person or a group will find that the surest way to get more from you is by serving you better. Good markets give to the vigor and drive of men in competition large scope and opportunity to force the new and the better toward the top. Here, of course, government plays an indispensable role; it fixes the conditions under which buyers and sellers operate. And it can stimulate competition and curb monopolistic tendencies.

The intangibles that support cooperation in markets contribute more to efficiency than we may realize. Honesty, for example, serves us more productively than billions of dollars worth of capital equipment. Other intangibles hurt—discrimination in the labor market. Each society has its own set of intangibles—respect for thrift, family loyalty, esteem for those who achieve the unusual, dislike for inequality, attitudes toward government; some serve economic welfare better than others. "Improving" them raises issues far beyond economics. Not least important is the willingness to give, accept, and act upon criticism. Self-satisfaction, politeness, concealment, whatever obstructs vigorous and intelligent criticism, tends to retard economic growth.

Several things we do through government do aid the functioning of markets—provision of good highways and intelligent regulation of business practices, for example. Others hurt: taxes, to mention one. Unfortunately, to get the huge funds governments need, taxes must be heavy. They not only impede like a brake but can also distort, shunting economic activity down side roads. Fortunately, we have made a good start toward revising the federal tax system. We want one which will not retard general progress any more than is essential and which will also not direct progress into specific lines that are less good than others. Or, if taxes are used deliberately to channel economic activity—stimulating the search for oil, for example—great care is required to be sure that this is an efficient method of achieving the objective and to prevent extra burdens on other types of good activity, such as building houses.

Financial arrangements also come high on the list of strategic features of markets. Growth requires financing while savings must be invested to avoid retrogression, issues which bring us to our fourth group of factors.

CAPITAL FORMATION

Capital formation lies at the heart of the growth process. At any time, few firms will be using the best equipment, and of course, better types are constantly developed as science advances. Purchase of new investment goods is essential, therefore, to make fuller use of technology already proved successful and, even more clearly, to exploit new discoveries.[11] Acquisition of better housing and more numerous consumer durables requires capital formation.

The United States seems assured of many billions of dollars of net new savings each year and more billions of depreciation funds available for buying better facilities. Yet merely providing living and working facilities for the *increase* in our population will require large amounts; $20,000 a worker means $28 billion a year when the work force increases 1.4 billion net; $20,000, however, will not buy a great deal of factory equipment, inventory, housing, utilities, and public facilities. Adding only $500 a year (a small part of the cost of a new room or a modest addition to the average factory worker's equipment) to the capital for production or living provided to each person employed in 1968 would require *more* each year than a year's total of personal saving. Savings for capital formation will not be abundant in relation to "need" unless our income and our propensity to save are higher than now appears likely. In the short run, of course, saving may tend to exceed the investment planned. Over the longer run,

[11] Maintaining the quality of the existing stock of capital is no small task. Much replacement is needed each year to prevent the average quality level from dropping.

however, the ability and willingness to save do limit capital formation. The sacrifices involved in doing without consumer goods today are among the major costs of economic growth.

Figure 38–3 shows estimates for the relation of population growth to needs for capital. Even an apparently small decline in the rate of increase in population will reduce the needs for capital to *maintain* per capita production and consumption. More of each year's savings can then go to raise the level of living.

FIGURE 38–3.   Capital Needs and Population Growth

Amount of capital needed to provide for one year of population growth at three rates of population increase on 1967 base.

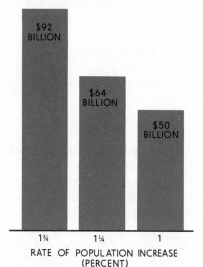

RATE OF POPULATION INCREASE
(PERCENT)

Source: Adapted from J. J. Spengler, "Now That the Birth Rate Has Slowed," *Challenge,* March–April, 1967, p. 11.

Not all new capital facilities, of course, are equally effective. Allocation inevitably makes a big difference. Some capital equipment appears to be much more productive than others. How can we direct new investment into the most fruitful lines? Business obviously has incentive to make the most effective choices possible within the range of opportunities open to each firm. The investment tax credit enacted in 1962 favors investment in machinery and equipment, the form presumably most likely to embody technological change.

Are we, as now often alleged, devoting too little to capital formation in the governmental sector? Will America suffer in the years ahead because of "social imbalance," poor balance between the private and the governmental portions of the economy? We certainly do need more schools and water systems and streets and prisons and the other things for which we rely upon government. But do we need to build at a faster rate than today? How can we decide such questions? No good method is evident. Taxes are high. So are governmental debts. But are they high in relation to the values governmental facilities would produce? To date, we have devised no satisfactory guides for allocating new resources for capital formation between the governmental and the private sectors.

Government has an indispensable role in capital formation which we must never overlook: the maintenance of the legal and political framework of internal peace and order. Since capital investment usually requires commitments that last over many years, confidence that government will enforce laws of property and contract gives a constructive sense of security.

ENTREPRENEURSHIP

Intangible human factors have decidedly tangible consequences for the economy. The sparks of a relatively few personalities—or dampness that extinguishes many a spark—will have far-reaching effects on the nature and the speed of economic change. Some people act as powerful, constructive catalysts in their economic environments, speeding development. Larger numbers contribute more than routinely, although not on the scale of the few. As a group, the people who make the real investment decisions, not only in business but also in government, have a determining influence upon national growth. The "vigor of enterprise" is the vigor of men and women.

Are the drives for growth and economic advance strong? *Incentive* in its broader sense is involved. Do economizing and the search for maximum profit come under some social ban as a selfish and unworthy activity? Or does the community bestow generous praise (as well as income *after taxes*) on the successful businessman? Is it the entrepreneur's ambition to become able to take things easy? To escape from the presumed grubbiness of making money? How are business leaders recruited and trained?

Does "the organization" stifle or enhance creativity? How free is entry? Can a civil service be developed to encourage progressive change? Is there confidence that neither serious depression nor inflation is likely? Will government create needless distress for risk takers by high taxes or other burdens on those who are successful?

The conditions these questions suggest differ. None is easily measured. Yet they bear closely on what makes an economy grow. Although the things esteemed today differ somewhat from those our grandfathers believed in, business and profit making are respected in the American scale of values.

It is not enough, however, that the public wants a rising standard of living and that businessmen want growth and have the vigor, resources, and social support to pursue it. *Competence* is equally necessary. Developing and selecting entrepreneurial skill must remain a major challenge for any society. But how? We still know little about the creation of truly great entrepreneurship. Present knowledge, however, enables us to do far more than was possible a generation ago to improve the competence of management. This is no small gain.

TERMS AND CONCEPTS		
R.&D.	economic growth	labor discrimination
entrepreneurship	immobility	social imbalance
cumulative progress	lead time	

QUESTIONS

1. What is the difference between the expansion and the diffusion of knowledge? How does each bear upon economic growth?

2. How does "social overhead" capital contribute to economic growth?

3. "Growth, like so many good things, has costs." Discuss.

4. "Social policy cannot create entrepreneurs; it can create conditions in which entrepreneurship can flourish—or wither." Discuss.

5. "Competition, mobility, ambition, thrift, and courage—and criticism, too—are prime essentials for economic progress." Discuss.

6. What do we mean by "improving the functioning of markets"? How can local, state, and federal governments help? Hinder?

7. Observe your own working habits and those of others. How, if at all, do you believe efficiency could be enhanced? Your accomplishment increased? Would the same conclusions apply to the economy as a whole?

8. "Economic progress results from invention of new social institutions as well as from technical discovery." Give examples.

9. What, if any, public policies might stimulate research?

10. "Every democracy must encourage high individual performance. If it does not, it closes itself off from the mainsprings of its dynamism. . . ." Discuss from the point of view of economic growth.

11. Estimate the capital needed for the job and for the type of dwelling you seek by age 35. If every person entering the labor force needed the same amount, what would be the total for the economy?

12. "Few things are so likely to raise our output today and that of our children in the future as happy home life. The welfare and happiness of the small group are not only ends but vital means to progress." Discuss.

13. How might an increase in overall economic stability speed growth over the long run?

14. Select one topic discussed in each of the prior parts of this book and show how it is related to economic growth. What governmental policies of recent years impede growth?

15. How might one argue that growth will be soundest and fastest in a "two-decker" economy, one with a firm base of welfare and economic justice and a "superstructure of the greatest possible freedom for enterprise and efficiency"?

39

AUTOMATION, URBANIZATION, AND OTHER ECONOMIC PROBLEMS AHEAD

[Government] is the most precious of human possessions; and no care can be too great to be spent on enabling it to do its work in the best way: a chief condition to that end is that it should not be set to work for which it is not specially qualified, under the conditions of time and place.
Alfred Marshall

College students will be more interested in the economic problems of the future than in those of the past or even the present. Every topic treated in this book does involve problems of the future. Some will take on new significance, while others we have scarcely mentioned will add challenges. So a few pages "dipping into the future" will give a forward look. We start with an old problem under a new name—and tackle it by reviewing points developed in earlier chapters.

AUTOMATION AND EMPLOYMENT

The term "automation" will be used here to mean much the same thing as technological change.[1] Frequently, a machine displaces human effort. Are we not dooming ourselves to heavy unemployment in the years ahead by the speed of technological advance? Who has not heard predictions of "ruin and despair," of millions of jobs wiped out each year? On the other hand, we hear that greater productivity is essential for raising our standard of living, that for a company to remain competitive in its industry, and for the United States to become more competitive in the world, productivity must rise. What are the problems and prospects?

---

[1] When the term "automation" came into use after the war, it had a specific and limited application: the substitution of electronic, hydraulic, mechanical, or other control devices for human organs of observation, decision, and control.

Why Automate? Some installation of machinery results from the development of products or methods which are essentially new and clearly desirable. These cases involve little or no substitution for something else. Much more typical, however, is the mechanization which represents an adaptation to changing prices of labor and capital equipment. Although in such cases some application of scientific advance may be present, very frequently the techniques have been available for some time. What is new is the fact that they have now become economically justified.

The employer uses more capital in relation to labor. He may be responding to a rise in wage rates, a decline in productivity of workers, a reduction in the price of the machine, or some combination. The speed with which businesses try to mechanize will depend heavily upon the trend of employment costs in relation to costs of capital—capital in the real sense of machinery and other tangible things and financing costs.

Employment Effects. The fact that employment outside government was 7 million higher in 1967 than in 1957 shows clearly that new jobs appeared during a decade of considerable technological progress. When a company orders new machines, one immediate effect is an increase in the demand for labor to make them. Thus mechanization creates demand for labor in capital goods industries. In the next stage, in the plants where the new equipment appears, what are the effects? Three kinds of results are likely to be mixed together.

1. Some workers will be displaced from certain jobs. Much of the adjustment (often the entire amount) takes the form of *attrition* through normal labor turnover rather than actual layoffs. Workers who might have been hired will not get such jobs. Any unemployment which results will rarely be identified with what has gone on in this plant.

2. Some decline in costs (perhaps combined with changes in the product, making it more attractive to consumers) will lead to price reductions or forestall increases. Consumers will buy more of the product. Total employment in the firm may then actually rise. This has been a frequent development.[2]

3. New types of labor are required—more maintenance workers, for example.

Another employment effect can be even more important. The improved processes may be essential if the company is to survive and offer any jobs. At the wage rates generally expected in our economy, workers' productivity must be "high." Otherwise the firm cannot continue to

---

[2] Automation in the central telephone exchanges began many years ago as dial systems were introduced. Yet telephone employment doubled in the 1940's while automation was being extended. In one chemical firm, skilled maintenance workers, once about half as numerous as operators, now outnumber them 3 to 1 in new plants. The last half century saw machines take over much office clerical work—yet the *proportion* of the labor force in clerical jobs rose from 3 to 14 percent.

operate. Workers themselves, of course, may accomplish more per hour from year to year; if so, their own actions justify higher wage rates. Often, however, rising productivity is bound up with the provision of more and better capital per worker. Jobs will not be available at the wage rates the worker expects unless he has more and better tools with which to work. To this extent, therefore, *more* rather than less automation becomes necessary to provide jobs.

Outlook.   Sharp differences of opinion are found among those who write and talk about the employment effects of automation in the years ahead. Many fears are grossly exaggerated. Complacency, however, represents another form of failure to recognize reality.

Has the speed of technological change become so much more rapid than that of the past that something new in *kind* results? Perhaps it has, but the evidence does not clearly point to any such result. Scientific progress is more rapid than in the past. It feeds upon itself. As a result, we may encounter accelerating rates of change that make it different in nature from that of our past. Nevertheless, the record of the last 10 years is not one of faster growth of output per man-hour than in many earlier periods. Figure 39–1 shows something of the time taken to make wide use

FIGURE 39–1.   Diffusion of Selected Technological Innovations (Percent of Firms Adopting Innovation*)

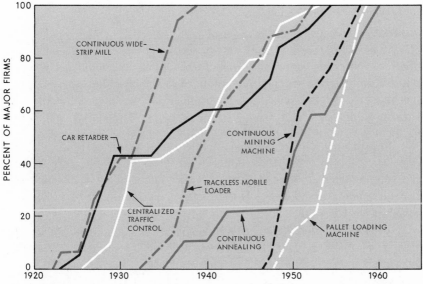

* Earliest date shown for each innovation is the year in which a firm first introduced the innovation, regardless of the scale on which it did so.
Source: Report of the National Commission on Technology, Automation, and Economic Progress (Washington, D.C.: U.S. Government Printing Office, 1966), Vol. I, p. 5. Data from Edwin Mansfield, "Diffusion of Technological Change," *Reviews of Data on Research and Development* (National Science Foundation, 1961).

in practice of seven technological innovations. These few cases illustrate that adoption—in the 1920's as in the 1950's—can be very rapid. But if for the whole economy technological change is accelerating, the speed is not great enough to constitute a difference in kind from that of the past.

One restraining element is the cost of using new methods and the inability of business to finance anything like "full" use of the best of technology.

To automate as completely as possible with present technology, only one major segment of the American economy, manufacturing, would require an expenditure of well over $2.5 trillion, assuming output is not increased. Even to modernize manufacturing to the levels of the new plants built in the 1950's would require over $500 billion. Since total spending on new plant and equipment in manufacturing amounts to about $15 billion per year, American manufacturing could not be modernized even to the level of the technology of the 1950's for over 30 years. And this is under the extreme assumption that all the expenditure is used for modernization and none for expansion. With the current division of capital outlays between modernization and expansion, modernization to the level of new plants of the variety built in the 1950's would require about 50 years.

To automate completely manufacturing industry with no increase in total output would require 2 centuries at current rates of modernization. If we expand output at the rate necessary to keep up with population growth, however, present rates of capital formation will never result in complete automation of manufacturing unless the cost of automation is reduced to less than one sixth of its present expense. That is unlikely to occur within the foreseeable future.[3]

How can we speed the process of automation on which our hope of rising real income rests so heavily? The working man—if his union's wage demands reflect his aspirations—wants what for the economy as a whole is possible only if we mechanize rapidly. Yet the machine, or the better machine, has often seemed an enemy of the working man. On rare occasions, outright destruction of new equipment by rioting has shown the intensity of the feeling. More persistent opposition has taken a steadier toll. Improvements in techniques—better machines or methods that reduce the labor needed to produce a given output—can throw some workers out of their jobs. Therefore, real conflict of interest may result from technological progress. What benefits the public receives can hurt the individual.

To repeat, technological progress and the use of more capital per worker lie at the heart of economic expansion. What can be done to ease the process of incorporating technological progress in our economy?

Policies for Facilitating Adjustment. The concern over labor displacement by automation has brought deliberate effort to facilitate adjust-

---

[3] Y. Brozen, *Automation: The Impact of Technological Change* (Washington, D.C.: American Enterprise Institute, 1963), pp. 4–5.

ment. High level of total demand for labor will probably do more than any other one thing. This conclusion of the economist was also central in the findings and recommendations of the 14-member Presidential Commission on Technology, Automation, and Economic Progress. Its 20 points of conclusions and recommendations, however, support many policies of a more specific nature.[4] The fact that the workers displaced directly or indirectly may not have the skills needed in jobs where demand for labor is rising adds to our needs for education. Private employers, in response, enlarge their training and retraining programs. So do governments.

Methods to cushion personal hardship, to improve mobility, to improve labor market information are all desirable, to meet unusual needs of particular regions, occupations, or industries. The Commission recommends use of "systems analysis," the very broad approach used in developing complex weapons and in space projects; the many, many aspects and features and elements of the entire, interconnected whole are studied in their relations to each other as well as in units important in themselves.

Not least important, and certainly not the easiest, is the subject of the next section.

FLEXIBILITY TO FORESTALL PROBLEMS

If an economy is flexible—if prices change easily with demand and supply, if human and material resources move at little real cost—most people adjust to change more or less gradually. "The genius of the private adjustment process is the flexibility with which it accommodates to individual circumstances."[5] People solve problems, or at least prepare to meet them, before anything like a crisis appears. Men and women adjust to new wants, new techniques, the many changes of life without great strain. Here is one explanation of the success this country has had over 3 centuries in taking advantage of economic opportunity. Flexibility is one of our outstanding economic superiorities to the Soviet and other centrally directed systems.

It is almost certain that, in a society as prosperous as ours, truly serious economic troubles would hardly develop if the economy were highly flexible. A hard core of poverty would remain, but the national income would be ample to deal with it tolerably well. Most people would probably be dissatisfied with their economic lot, and worries would nag everyone. But there would not likely be a sense of great pressure from big economic problems.

Yet why dream? No such flexibility has ever existed or ever will. The

---

[4] The Commission . . . , *Technology and the American Economy* (Washington, D.C.: U.S. Government Printing Office, 1966), Vol. I pp. 109–13. The Commission's report gives considerable attention to the *uses* to be made of the fruits of technological progress. Several specialized studies made for the Commission deal in detail with many aspects of the problems.

[5] *Ibid.*, p. 111.

dream, however, may help in formulating a realistic goal and in making policies. Of one thing we can be certain: Obstructions to adjustment can accentuate difficulties. Governmental and private restrictions which prevent or discourage small, gradual, voluntary, impersonal, dispersed adaptation to change will aggravate strains and discontinuities. Tensions build to a higher level before relief begins. Rigidity and inflexibility, in a sense, become *causes* (not, of course, the only causes) of the seriousness of economic difficulties.

Consequently, a basic objective should be to make the economy more, rather than less, flexible. The better we succeed, the fewer will be our serious economic difficulties. A greater number of small adaptations, many made with ease, prevent the development of bigger tensions and the need for difficult action to solve really tough problems. What, other than those varied elements of good markets already discussed, will make for flexibility? One thing is public desire for freedom and opportunity, for truly effective competition. But many of us prefer rigidities—in our own favor—and yield to temptation to support restriction, regulation, monopoly (under some other designation).

Another aid to flexibility is small, rather than big, economic units. But here the fact that large units often have production advantages complicates the problem. Giantism brings more than bargaining benefit, though that alone would create a formidable obstacle to success in protecting the public by restraining the growth of business and unions. There is real difficulty ahead in meeting what may be called, loosely, the monopoly problem. The less adequate our solution, the greater the danger of inflexibility.

A third complication arises from the size of the commitment of capital and training involved in much production today. Modern specialization requires such big material and human investments that simple, small-stage adjustment to change is sometimes out of the question and often onerous.

Difficulty also arises out of the extensive use of government. Economic adjustment made through the political process tends to involve a smaller amount of continuous change than goes on in markets. One thinks, for example, of modernizing the postal system or prison construction or reform of the judicial system or devising ways for state governments to cooperate efficiently with each other. Year after year we as the voting public let things lag—not always and by no means without some justification. Yet legislative and executive procrastination, plus the force of bureaucratic routine, add a type of inflexibility whose burden to the economy is greater the larger the role of government.

URBAN AREAS: HOUSING

All too slowly has the Western world come to recognize the problems which urbanization creates or accentuates. The problems are only partly economic; but to deal with the social, aesthetic, or political challenges, we must handle the economic. Present conditions are certainly not satisfactory—witness in city life juvenile waywardness, worry and frustration, dirt and ugliness. Mob violence in 1966 and 1967 seemed to confirm fears that the difficulties ahead are more formidable than society has recognized.

America is predominantly urban. For more and more of a rapidly growing population, life centers around cities, the great workshops and dormitories of the modern world. Both the efficiency of our working effort and the quality of life off the job depend upon how cities are built, especially the pattern of land use. For modern needs, however, our cities are sadly inadequate. Their basic layouts, streets, and most structures are relics of an entirely different past, one in which the auto was rare, or unknown, and population small by present standards.

The city possesses irresistible attractions for work and play. It offers certain types of economies of production that are utterly impossible in small communities; in the city, large numbers can specialize and exchange in close proximity. The city can reduce the costs of movement between people. Confrontation, which is central to much important economic activity, can as a rule be accomplished most efficiently when the various parties are in the same area. Yet today we see massive inefficiencies—getting in each other's way as we try to get around must already cost uncounted millions every working hour.

Urban blight curses every city as older areas deteriorate. Even though analysis of the evidence shows that on the whole conditions have been getting better rather than worse, blight does spread. Sometimes it feeds on itself, growing in cumulative fashion. No one escapes its costs though millions gain some relief by moving to suburbs. Yet new problems then arise, such as the costs of more complicated transport and peak-hour traffic snarls. Space "runs out," not literally but in the sense of availability at costs to which we are accustomed. Meanwhile, the life we seek is one of more space. Witness this fact: For individual houses instead of apartments, for wider streets, for one-floor factories with parking space instead of lofts and multistory plants to which workers come by foot or public transport, and for such other modern needs as recreation and beauty, the per capita land "requirements" for urban growth today are estimated at 10 to 20 times those of a century ago. Today we fail widely to meet desirable standards. How, then, are tens of millions more to be accommodated? Certainly not without serious difficulties for those who now live in urban areas.

Many of our finest buildings located on some of each city's most valuable land might be utilized to greater advantage. They stand largely or entirely idle 3 or 4 hours for each hour of actual use. Court houses and office buildings, banks and factories—and the streets and utilities which service them—are often largely dark and quiet most hours of the week, even when apparent needs for new construction seem to call upon limited supplies of new capital funds.

The problems are varied. The short-run problem is to make the best use of existing structures. We must preserve and improve the standing stock and economize in its use. But there must be new construction in old centers of cities if only because of the great inherent advantages of space at the center. To demolish and rebuild, however, is always costly. If land is used for housing or stores, it is not available for parks. As we commit limited urban space to this use and that, the amounts available for other purposes shrink in startling degree. City life makes one man's actions of concern to others but often in ways which markets do not "organize" efficiently.

Voluntary action can sometimes serve—congestion does lead to private parking garages in the city and also to the exodus of some families. For many things, however—traffic and noise control, sanitation, police and fire protection—the only effective method must utilize government.

The economic problem requires effective government. Our political institutions remain largely those of an era in which relatively small communities, acting independently, could serve the needs of local government. True, Supreme Court decisions have led to reapportionment in Congress and in state legislatures. Cities and suburbs now have more voice, and rural areas less, than a few years ago. Yet such change does not meet the political needs. Effective urban planning—of water supply, crime prevention, public recreation, air pollution, municipal colleges, traffic, relief for the needy—on a scale large enough to be reasonably efficient, requires cooperation of many distinct local governments. How can a large area get agreement on what to do and how to share costs? For easily understood reasons, some localities will be reluctant to join with others. And many local governments, especially large central cities, face financial strains of no small amount.

Success requires, among other things, a coherent, well–thought-out, realistic, but imaginative plan. It should take account of future needs for efficient production, pleasant living, varied recreation, and civilian defense. Individualism and the free market cannot deal with some crucial elements, if only because of the importance in urban areas of neighborhood effects. Success, then, depends upon the determination to put long-range public interest ahead of short-run individual interest (but always offering adequate compensation for damage done to present owners). Success calls for bold and extensive use of the power of eminent domain to permit development on a scale large enough to be truly efficient and effective. Unless government does use this power to coerce owners (for payment), a few can continually thwart the general need. Old linkages, unfortunately, will always retard progress, but being alert to their role, we can prepare to deal with them more effectively and humanely than in the past.

Initiative and the hard work of following through can come from civic leaders of all types. In several areas there has been progress. A few business, professional, and political leaders have accomplished great things in cities large and small. They have proved that obstacles can be overcome. The national government has begun to provide money and leadership for local planning, urban renewal, urban mass transit, and control of pollution.

Where building is a part of the program, cost will be of central concern.[6] Protection from monopolistic and unprogressive practices in construction will always be needed. Otherwise, public efforts can be turned into cost-raising policies of building unions (which are strong in most cities), contractors, and materials suppliers. Success in urban development requires courage—to evict occupants so that obsolete buildings can be demolished, to deal with motorists (and probably to curb the peak-hour use of autos in favor of mass-transport media) and arrange commuting facilities, and to prepare amenities and recreational facilities for a future population not yet able to vote. Another necessity in virtually every urban region is authority to act through and over areas that extend beyond present local, county, and even state political boundaries.

Government, chiefly local, has a big role to play, not only in planning, zoning, and assembling land in large units but also in building and financing public works, including open spaces and recreation areas. Costs will be huge, but since most of our wealth (human and nonhuman) is now in cities, investment to preserve and enhance it can yield handsome returns.

The years ahead will bring difficult housing problems. The millions of the poor are likely to find slums increasingly expensive as well as oppressive. Despite the concern which resulted from the riots of 1967, neither the dollars nor the skills, materials, and land required for quick "solution" will be available. The crude, quantitative needs for our population growth alone can be met. The economy will be able to build enough housing units, although rising land prices and construction costs will not be easily met.

Obtaining enough *good* housing, however, will constitute a harder problem. How can the old be upgraded? More and more families will want, and by traditional standards be able to afford, "larger" and "nicer" houses. The heads of these families will have responsible positions in business, the professions, science, and government. In many commu-

---

[6] Taxpayer subsidies have helped finance the construction of around 700,000 housing units (and demolition of somewhat more). It is difficult to judge the efficiency of the programs for dealing with either poverty or housing. The urban renewal program has resulted in many impressive changes in many cities. Yet the money and the human costs have been high. Hundreds of thousands of poor families, many Negro, have been forced to move, usually to less desirable and more expensive housing. Tens of thousands of businesses have been forced to relocate (receiving as moving expense an average below the $3,000 maximum permitted) or to cease operations. M. Anderson, *The Federal Bulldozer*. . . . (Cambridge: Massachusetts Institute of Technology Press, 1964). The inadequacy of compensation in thousands of cases must not be allowed in the future. For a well-rounded discussion, see B. J. Frieden, "Housing and National Urban Goals: Old policies and New Realities," Task Force on Economic Growth and Opportunity, *The Metropolitan Enigma* (Washington, D.C.: Chamber of Commerce of the United States, 1967), pp. 148–91.

nities their counterparts today rely heavily upon a stock of better houses made up largely of structures built before 1940. To multiply reasonably comparable housing will be very costly, not only because building costs far exceed those of the past but also because land and appropriate community facilities will be scarce.

GOVERNMENT AND ECONOMIC LIFE

Economists have tried to build tools which will help mankind. Many tools are to be used—or carefully not used—by people acting through government. Hence economics becomes especially significant when it touches politics—when it becomes *political economy*. After the 19th century—a period in which government, by pre-1815 and post-1914 standards, exerted only modest direct influence on economic life—we have seen large growth of government action. The dominant explanation (beyond war) was not that the public became convinced of the positive economic merits of the political process. The chief reason was that markets gave unsatisfactory results. Yet, impatient with man's irrationality and inhumanity in business, we may have been a bit naïve in assuming greater rationality and humanity in politics.

What Shall We Try To Do through Government? The issue today is only partly one between big and small government. Government will inevitably have great influence on economic life. More fundamental is the choice of *what* to do through government. Using government, for example, we can work to enlarge general freedom in the sense of the numbers and the richness of opportunities available. In doing so, we properly restrain those who would not participate if they were free to exclude themselves from this program or that—education, food and drug regulation, national defense, control of the monetary system.

Widely different, however, are policies which use government compulsion to help one group at the expense of another without enlarging general freedom—the tariff, tax exemption, obstruction of improvement in a building code. When government is "smaller," we are more free from the danger of error and the abuse of power by government and by those who would use government for narrow, rather than general, interest. In keeping government "small," however, we would give up some chances to use it constructively; there are things small government cannot do. Size of government and the specific things we do through the political process therefore, are related, but they are by no means identical. Henry Simons, one of the staunchest defenders of laissez-faire capitalism among professional economists, emphasized the desirability of strong and active government—but doing the "right" things. One of these is to hold power so that private groups do not use it in their narrow interests.

The time of key government officials, the funds we are willing to pay in taxes, and the attention we can give each issue during an election campaign are limited "resources." They will be spread dangerously thin when called upon to serve more and more demands. Many of us, for example, pay little attention to state government while trying sincerely to keep abreast of a few phases of national policy.

Piling up of functions enlarges the dangers of slowness and inflexibility, of inconsistency and self-defeating actions, and of lack of funds needed to do things well. Perhaps there is a form of diminishing returns so that beyond some point the more jobs we try to do through government, the less well we can do each. Why in so much of the country have Americans let the courts on which we rely for one of the two most vital functions of government, justice, get so overloaded and incompetent?

One looks long and hard for good evaluations of the results of governmental programs and of possible alternatives.

Today, government must be large. More than ever, therefore, the choice of what to try to do, or not to do, takes on added importance. First things come first, because second things, although desirable, may hinder accomplishment of things more important.

Balancing Objectives. What are "first things"? The answer involves issues broader than economics. To a large (but vaguely bounded) extent, economic activity is a means and not, itself, the end of life. A major element of our economic tradition has been the "liberalism" which envisaged the freeing of man from his fellow man who, acting through government, wanted to use coercion.[7] The freeing of individuals would permit both their own personal development and, with "the invisible hand" guiding, serve the public better than guidance by government officials.

Yet men acting through markets also coerced their fellow men. The freedom of individualism yielded abuses of man by man. The total results were mixed—the values of great economic growth and ugly cities are hard to compare in the light of the alternatives that might have been possible. Voters used their power to force changes. The decisions rested, of course, upon a range of considerations broader than economics.

We want many things: freedom, security, prosperity, justice, beauty, love, friendship, dignity, neighborliness, stability, progress, equality, democracy, peace, strength. Obviously, however, we cannot measure their relative desirability in any common terms. To some degree, one can be obtained only at the expense of others; there may, for example, be injustice in evicting a family to clear a slum for building a housing project others will enjoy. Fortunately, however, some policies cooperate to yield several desired objectives whose values exceed the costs.

One opportunity of economists is to search for, and distinguish be-

---

[7] Today the term "liberalism" has been preempted by those who would expand government to do what they believe is good for the public. Britain's attempt to regulate economic life was a prominent factor in sparking the American Revolution.

tween, possible areas of conflict and of cooperation, and especially to look at the long-run implications of policies. The economist's work is only a part of the job, but a useful part. The same applies to other disciplines. No one should be surprised that society has no ideal mechanism for balancing these objectives, but the impossibility of perfection is no reason for failure to do as well as we can. The rational approach can help. For example, our reason can warn us: Groups are often organized around one, or at most a few, of the interests that are important: national defense, public schools, job security. As groups use their power to press particular interests (admirable as they may be), other interests are likely to be sacrificed. Persuasive appeals, using the slickest publicity or getting the bulk of attention, may oversell us on something in itself good. The economist may "know the price of everything and the value of nothing." But as economists try to focus attention on costs, they will help others balance values.

One distinguished economist concludes a list of principles of a "democratic economy" with a point of penetrating significance: "Necessary governmental controls in the economy should be concentrated on *procedures* rather than on *substantive issues*. Instead of regulating prices, the government should seek to regulate mergers and the like; instead of regulating wages, the government should provide appropriate guidance to the process of collective bargaining."[8]

Level of Expectations.   Happiness may not be entirely the ratio of "satisfactions received" to "expectations," but there is no doubt that if we expect more than we get, unhappiness will be our fate. Perhaps one of America's gravest problems is to keep expectations realistic. Advertising on the one hand and political campaigns on the other *encourage* people to anticipate more than can possibly be provided from the productive resources at our disposal. The story is told of a ruler who undertook to learn economics. After a while he sighed to his teacher, "Why don't you just say 'There is no Santa Claus?' " While this perceptive insight does not encompass all of economics, it contains an important truth. What we can really expect to get every day, not just on Christmas, depends upon what we put in. Raising expectations is easier than doing what is necessary to satisfy them.

Defense and Other Spending.   Current defense spending is very much with us as an obvious and heavy drain on our economy—drain, that is, compared with what could be if nations were to settle their political difficulties. New types of weapons and equipment—and the skilled man-

---

[8] Clark Kerr, "An Effective and Democratic Organization of the Economy," in President's Commission on National Goals, *Goals for Americans* (Englewood Cliffs, N.J.: Prentice-Hall, Inc., 1961), p. 152. Italics supplied.

power to use them—will assuredly be costly. In overall "macro" terms, the cost, though heavy, need not really strain a growing economy.

"Micro" problems, however, can be serious as specific industries, areas, and groups are affected very differently. Big discontinuities can arise— sudden contract cancellations or increases in the demand for a particular skill or material. Space programs, and others, are also big enough to create problems almost unknown in our economy a generation ago. Changes may be too big for markets to handle smoothly. The public may need special preparation for meeting such cases efficiently. We want to avoid any nondefense "distortions" of defense spending, any temptations to continue buying to avoid unemployment or any reluctance of the best-qualified business to undertake defense work and devote skilled people to it. And unanswered questions remain. Will firms with large commitments to military production become more or less efficient as a result? How does the existence of a huge military-industrial complex affect the economy and the power of government? When Uncle Sam is such a big buyer, what influence do his officials gain as a result? For example, how much power do they gain to influence elections?

The Limits of Economics. A knowledge of economics will help in finding good answers to hard problems, as well as in avoiding error. The intuition of the man in the street, or the judgment of the person who has been successful in some other line, *may* give satisfactory answers to complicated economic problems. Without being immodest, however, economists feel certain that they can generally add to the quality of the analysis of the nonspecialist. The well-trained economist sees interrelations generally hidden from others. He looks beneath the surface of events and beyond the moment. He knows the operation of the broad forces of demand and supply, of money, of capital accumulation. He is alert to the role of cost; to distinguish between what is desirable—our dreams—and what is possible can contribute immensely to constructive results.

Yet economists will be the first to admit that their contribution is also partial. The economist does not know the future, for the responses of free people are not always certain. And how does the public value nonmaterial considerations? When the economist makes a recommendation, he must assume many things; some assumptions are probably less good than those which others, such as businessmen, bankers, ministers, or artists might make. A complex society requires cooperation.

Economists are in disagreement often enough to keep others aware that our discipline is not an engineering science. It does not offer precise, measurable, and accurate predictions. Theory is all too often inadequate when we seek to use it in specific problem situations. The gaps in knowledge of facts—statistical as well as the nonstatistical—are uncomfortably numerous and needlessly large. Yet today, the tools of economics, though they leave much to be desired, remain indispensable for making good public policy.[9]

Competent Use of Economic Analysis in Government.

What should men seek in appraising the use of economic knowledge in government? Let us distinguish two criteria: *competence* and the dominance of the *public interest*. On the first, there is no doubt about two points: (1) High-quality economic analysis and knowledge will be found in the federal government; by no means all civil service economists are topnotch. But government does have economists who know at least as much as any in the world. Elected and appointed officials, too, sometimes show high ability in understanding and using the tools of economics. (2) On the other hand, some officials who make policies of great importance are incompetent to deal with certain economic issues. Although perhaps highly skilled in dealing with some aspects of government, and excellent at judging other values, they are amateurs in economics.

Which group of officials is which? The public can hardly know. The common man faces uncommon requirements indeed. As decisions that affect his life, and the whole economy, hinge upon his choice of government officials, the voter must select men whose competence he cannot judge well. When he votes to assign a function to government, the voter does not thereby assure himself that he will get men who are really qualified to administer the program.

How can we test the competence of government officials? Public admission of error by politicians is rare. The competition of superior performance cannot always serve as a check. The rivalry that in business brings bankruptcy or profit cannot be relied upon in government. The competition for votes in the ballot box is different from the competition for votes in the cash register (or from the dollar freely given for philanthropy). Government officials have power to force us to do things we do not like (in addition to paying taxes). We hope that officials will do their job well. The test of experience will be far from adequate. How can we tell what would have developed under other policies? Among limitations,

[9] A leading sociologist, expressing a view which warrants a serious attempt to implement it, writes: "In effect, what we need is a System of Social Accounts which would broaden our concept of costs and benefits. The eventual purpose would be to create a 'balance sheet' that would be useful in clarifying policy choices." Although, he says, the word "accounts" suggests greater ability to measure than in fact is possible, the system he envisions would help move us toward four goals: (1) the measurement of social costs and net return, as proposed long ago by two great economists, A. C. Pigou and J. M. Clark; (2) the measurement of social ills, such as mental illness, juvenile delinquency, and their relationship to causes; (3) aid in developing performance budgets for such things as housing; (4) the indication of economic opportunity and social mobility, such as change in the condition of Negroes. "American society would be in a better position to appraise its achievements, its needs, and its shortcoming by being able to specify broad national goals and national priorities." Daniel Bell, "Notes on the Post-Industrial Society (II)," *The Public Interest*, Spring, 1967, pp. 116–18.

one is the fact that civil servants who disagree with policy set at the top, or officials who disapprove of the policy of another agency, are seldom at liberty to give the public the benefit of their views. And complexities seem to grow more rapidly than the ability of economists to recommend solutions.

Special Interest Groups and Their Search for Privilege.   A bigger problem is to get policies in the *public* interest. Perhaps unconsciously, many of us accept the view that seeking our own narrow aims through government is proper. You may ask: "Why worry? Is there any difference between self-seeking in business and markets and self-seeking through government?" One significant difference is this: In the business world, conditions can be established so that, by and large, to advance their own interests men must serve others. We believe that the search for personal gain is proper; few of us sense the connection between our selfishness and service to others. Ignoring this connection, then, we fall into the trap of seeking personal gain through government—that is, from others in the community from whom we could not obtain the result in free exchange: The real estate owner's fight for a zoning exception; the "senior citizen's" pressure for larger old-age benefits; the farmer's search for government price raising, the industrialist, for tariffs; the labor union's insistence on privilege before the law.

Individuals on their own will seldom be able to exert great pressure. When they band together, however, their combined influence may become decisive. Both economic and political power are involved. They grow in significance when joined. Banding together, a few can logroll their own schemes through the legislature. How can the community deal with large groups in the public interest? As they gain power, groups may become rivals of the government itself.

Interdependence forces, or permits, us to work together. Thereby we can enjoy the benefits of specialization. If we are to continue to do so, however, our system requires that we constantly make changes and adaptations, chiefly in small amounts, at a multitude of places, and not always pleasant. We need to be free to change, reacting to the wishes of others and inducing them to respond to our changing desires. **Freedom is a useful economic tool as well as a prized end in itself.**

This system is threatened when large minorities combine to improve their position, not by serving others more effectively but by demanding more without creating more. Perhaps like the highway robber, a group stops all movement until it gets more from us. Perhaps less dramatically, it obstructs change and exacts a little more, here and there, in small amounts. A small group could not make the demands stick; a large group can. The organization may consist of good people; it may function efficiently, with most persuasive publicity; its internal organization may be a model of democracy. Yet from the community's point of view, the broader issue is what the group, as such, does to outsiders (such as taxpayers or consumers).[10]

Meeting the Challenge of Groups.   One dilemma of freedom is that some persons will use their freedom to limit that of others. In seeking protection from the abuse of power by groups, the public almost inevitably looks to government. Big groups are too powerful to be dealt with by anything short of government.[11] Yet the public finds obstacles to using government partly because of the political power that groups have built.

Unions and farm groups, for example, are "in politics." Trade associations and other business groups, even without large numbers, may concentrate enough pressure on city, state, or national officials to get what they want. Group leaders, of course, are not likely to agree that the particular desires of their organization hurt the general public. (The appeal to the members, however, may be in terms of economic self-interest.) As self-serving groups gain political power, the difficulty of using government as a check to protect the public interest also grows.

Certain improvements do seem possible. Expansion of vigorous, rational criticism will help. The power of facts brought into the open will often win a battle. Finding the facts, analyzing them thoroughly, and getting them before the public will sometimes prevent an outrageous steal, obvious folly, or the continuation of really bad practices. Another possibility is more prohibition of specific practices which are against the public interest, even when done by groups whose actions are generally wholesome—trade association price fixing and union racketeering are examples. While desirable, however, such controls do not go to the central issue.

A more powerful policy would be to make groups (as acting agencies) smaller. The restriction on the size of units would fall within the scope of government as a general rule maker. This method would go to the heart of the serious problem: the centralization of economic and political power. For example, if giant firms were separated into smaller units and if, for bargaining purposes, a union's jurisdiction were limited to a single employer and no collusion were possible, the danger to the public would be substantially reduced. Unions would then be more nearly subject to the kind of competitive discipline that channels self-interest into public interest. Their opportunities for gain would appear to be tied more closely to improvements in productivity.

[10] Labor unions act as cohesive groups in their normal affairs, while businesses and farmers, no matter how much each may function as a group in the political sphere, do not generally combine in economic dealings (as they may in political). Farmers are too numerous, and businesses face antitrust laws.

[11] A different line of argument carried more weight when it was advanced some years ago than recently. Unions and business groups, it is said, exercise *countervailing power* and thus offset each other's influence. Experience has confirmed what some economists predicted: The ability of great power groups to "countervail" each other will tend to lead to unemployment or inflation or the denial of comparable gains to other groups.

No "pat" remedy is possible. Each interest group creates its own special challenges. Our judgments vary with changes in the news; we may get excited as a regional group trains its big guns on Congress for large spending on local projects at the expense of all the nation's taxpayers. Then we forget as the World Series nears. Rarely can we sustain attention on problems which are not of immediate personal interest. The few, relatively, with the big individual interest are likely to win over the many with a smaller interest each.

Groups Organized to Serve the Public Interest. Not all groups are self-serving in the distressing sense. One of the many admirable things about our society is the number of organizations with varied and public-spirited interests. Service clubs do often serve, in the best sense. The League of Women Voters and other women's organizations, for example, take an active, nonpartisan, and informed interest in public affairs. They provide a counterweight to more narrowly selfish groups. Positive results are achieved. Organizations such as the Committee for Economic Development (CED) make themselves felt. Though not always right, they help to keep a valuable balance and often to enlarge understanding of the issues. A focus on public interest is, itself, healthy. Groups of this type provide some of the eternal vigilance that is the price of liberty and progress.

Use of National or State-Local Government. The decision to use government to help achieve some end still leaves open the question, and opportunity, of selecting which of the three levels. A tendency to rely upon the national government gained force in the 1930's because of depression and in the 1940's because of war. The trend continues. One reason is that Uncle Sam seems better able to pay. Another is distrust in some circles of the quality and efficiency of state-local government.

Many problems, however, are not predominantly national. We might do better to lean more heavily on state and local government. Policy could be adapted to varying needs, and this *is* a land with great diversity. Costs could be identified more closely and balanced with gains. Inefficient policies could not be so easily foisted on the public by concealing costs or putting them (apparently) on outsiders.

Competition among states tends to protect freedom, to check the abuse of power by any one, and to limit what the minority can accomplish. If state and local government were used instead of national, the danger of mistakes with widespread consequences would decline. And, unfortunately, people, in using government, can make mistakes which, in the words of one experienced official, are "beauts." The defender of state-local responsibility insists that a good policy will win out in competition and that, over a rather short "long run," the state or local policy which free men prefer will prove its superior attractions.

Leadership and Citizenship. The better we master our jobs as citizens, the better we can achieve those goals which we seek through political action. Rising levels of general education and communication give reason to hope that voters will equal the responsibilities—or better, seize the opportunities. We require both effort and capability. Yet, the common man must delegate most of the job, choosing leaders (representatives) who act for him. The quality of leadership is crucial. We want statesmanship. To get it, we must try to let our leaders act as statesmen. Curbs on our own selfishness provide one essential. We must let leaders represent us at our best. Success requires both moral excellence and a high degree of competence.

TERMS AND CONCEPTS

automation	countervailing power	confrontation
economic flexibility	labor displacement	liberalism
laissez-faire capitalism	linkage	political economy

QUESTIONS

1. How do (*a*) availability of capital and (*b*) wage rates affect automation?
2. Why has employment expanded rapidly in years when mechanization has been increasing?
3. In what respects is urban blight a result of economic inflexibility? Why?
4. "One of the citizen's hardest jobs is to let his political leaders be statesmen." Discuss as regards economic issues.
5. How do flexibility and mobility aid economic adjustment?
6. "One danger is that we shall adopt by little moves more and more of Russia's methods of economic organization, sacrificing freedom and flexibility for governmental protection and control." Discuss.
7. Find examples of actions of organized groups that focus primarily upon public service rather than seeking gains for their members.
8. "The quality of land use and of housing will depend upon policies of government, especially local government." Discuss. If, as seems to be the case, federal government policies have destroyed more low-cost housing than they have built, how would you evaluate such results?
9. "If a person's economic interests and taxpaying obligations extend into many localities, he should have something to say about the governmental policies in each. Multiple voting might be one answer. Pressure-group activity might be another. Centralization in Washington might be a third." Discuss.
10. "The job future can be bright only if automation proceeds even more rapidly than so far in the 1960's." Discuss.
11. "Any project of social reconstruction which founds itself on reality must begin with the facts of social unity, not with those of class conflict." Discuss.

INDEX

INDEX

959

L

Label, union, 607

Labeling, 673, 933

Labor: *see also* Labor unions; Population; Wage and wages; demand for, 354, 548, 566, 593, 929 (*see also* Employment theory); Department of, 599; division of (*see* Division of labor); earnings, 376, 556; force, 64, 287, 548 ff; force participation rate, 66, 68; income, 211, 214; law, 603, 604; and location, 413; market, 548 ff, 934; mobility (*see* Mobility); in national income, 211 ff; press, 581; rigidity as cost, 449; Secretary of, 612, 613; supply, 68, 548 ff, 553; theory of value, 901

Labor-management relations, 585

Labor-Management Relations Act, 618

Labor-Management Reporting and Disclosure Act, 611

Labor-oriented activity, 414

Labor-saving equipment, 7

Labor Statistics, Bureau of, 206

Labor unions: 574 ff (*see also* Wage and wages); aid for employer, 586, 590, 604, 607; antitrust and, 455; bargaining, 586 ff; company, 606; corruption, 585; costs, 600; craft basis, 600, 608; democracy, 578, 611; discrimination, 566, 579, 584; earnings and, 207, 595, 599; employment and, 291, 297, 321, 593, 597; featherbedding, 583; formation, 606, 611; government and, 603, 604; grievance procedure, 582; guaranteed annual wage, 602; hiring halls, 434; ideology, 954; immigration, 68; industrial basis, 439, 608; inflation and (*see* Inflation); internal operation, 611; law and, 573, 606 ff; leadership, 577; major, U.S., 576; membership, 575; minimum rate, 595; as monopolies, 437, 453, 604, 947; objectives, 579, 947; political activity, 608, 611, 953, 954; politics within, 578; press, 581; pressure groups, 611, 954; productivity (*see* Featherbedding); racketeering, 585; relations with management, 433, 439, 585 ff, 611; restrictive practices, 584 (*see also* Featherbedding); Russia, 903; security, 580; settlement of disputes, 376, 439, 586 ff; socialism, 914; supply of labor and, 584; technological improvement and, 583, 940; unemployment and, 593, 597; as voluntary associations, 376, 574; wages (*see* Wage)

Laborers, 67, 556

Labour Party, British, 892

Ladies Garment Workers, 576

Lags, 281, 305

Laissez-faire, 910, 948; *see also* Invisible hand

Lamb, 493

Land: 614 ff (*see also* Natural resources; Rent); development, 920; differentials, 615 ff; ownership, 433, 530; population and, 59 ff, 621; prices, 506, 614; prices and farm aid, 506; productivity, 616; reclamation, 499, 506; reform, 870; retirement, 501, 507; supply of, 614, 617; tax, shifting of, 621; unearned increment, 620; urban, 617, 944; use, 619, 944; value, 57, 509, 614

Land-oriented activity, 413

Landowner, 530

Landrum-Griffin Act, 611

Lang, C. D., 599

Language, 68, 783

Large size, 98, 390, 482; *see also* Big business

Last-in, first-out, inventory valuation, 127

Latin America, 798, 825, 826, 853, 854, 857, 880, 883, 884

Laundries, 437, 557

Law: of demand, 344; economic, 12; and economic growth (*see* Legal system); enforcement, 37, 585, 936; of equal price, 368; and order, 936; rule of, 936; of supply, 360; of supply and demand, 359 ff

Lawyers, 70, 78, 80, 551, 561

Layoffs, 582, 586

"L.c.l.," 382

Lea Act, 610

Leaching, 47

Lead, 49

Leadership: business, 475, 560; inequality, 531; political, 531, 697, 956; price, 425, 437; quality of, 475, 531, 560, 697; underdeveloped areas, 874; within unions, 577, 591

Leading series, 281

League of Women Voters, 955

Leakage and multiplier, 246, 799, 840

Leases and leasing, 103, 107, 130, 185, 207, 296, 381, 432, 434; *see also* Rent

Least cost, 387, 538

Leather, 494

Legal Aid, 693

Legal minimum wages, 598

Legal monopolies, 432

Legal reserves, 151 ff, 166; *see also* Federal Reserve System

Legal services, 674

Legal system, 73, 81, 463, 606

Legal tender, 141

Legislative reapportionment, 761

Legislature, costs, 74

Leisure, 214, 292, 525, 529, 532, 545, 551, 558, 592, 930

*This book has been set in 10 and 9 point Jan-
son, leaded 2 points. Part and chapter numbers
are 48 point Helvetica Medium. Part titles are
18 point Helvetica Medium and chapter titles
are 16 point Helvetica Medium. The size of
the type page is 27 by 47 picas.*

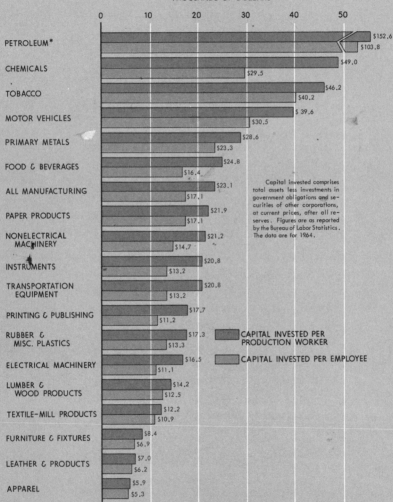

CAPITAL INVESTED PER EMPLOYEE IN U.S. MANUFACTURING

THOUSANDS OF DOLLARS

0	10	20	30	40	50

PETROLEUM* — $152.6 / $103.8

CHEMICALS — $49.0 / $29.5

TOBACCO — $46.2 / $40.2

MOTOR VEHICLES — $ 39.6 / $30.5

PRIMARY METALS — $28.6 / $23.3

FOOD & BEVERAGES — $24.8 / $16.4

ALL MANUFACTURING — $23.1 / $17.1

PAPER PRODUCTS — $21.9 / $17.1

NONELECTRICAL MACHINERY — $21.2 / $14.7

INSTRUMENTS — $20.8 / $13.2

TRANSPORTATION EQUIPMENT — $20.8 / $13.2

PRINTING & PUBLISHING — $17.7 / $11.2

RUBBER & MISC. PLASTICS — $17.3 / $13.3

ELECTRICAL MACHINERY — $16.5 / $11.1

LUMBER & WOOD PRODUCTS — $14.2 / $12.5

TEXTILE-MILL PRODUCTS — $12.2 / $10.9

FURNITURE & FIXTURES — $8.4 / $6.9

LEATHER & PRODUCTS — $7.0 / $6.2

APPAREL — $5.9 / $5.3

Capital invested comprises total assets less investments in government obligations and securities of other corporations, at current prices, after all reserves. Figures are as reported by the Bureau of Labor Statistics. The data are for 1964.

■ CAPITAL INVESTED PER PRODUCTION WORKER

□ CAPITAL INVESTED PER EMPLOYEE

* Consists of petroleum refining, extraction, and pipe-line transportation

Courtesy of the National Industrial Conference Board